Fundamentals of
Investment Management

Fundamentals of Investment Management

Fourth Edition

Geoffrey A. Hirt
Chairman of the Department of Finance
DePaul University

Stanley B. Block
Professor of Finance
Texas Christian University

IRWIN
Burr Ridge, Illinois
Boston, Massachusetts
Sydney, Australia

Executive editor:	Michael W. Junior
Marketing manager:	Ron Bloecher
Project editor:	Jean Lou Hess
Production manager:	Diane Palmer
Cover designer:	Matt Doherty
Art coordinator:	Mark Malloy
Compositor:	Carlisle Communications, Ltd.
Typeface:	10/12 Bembo
Printer:	R. R. Donnelley & Sons Company

Library of Congress Cataloging-in-Publication Data

Hirt, Geoffrey A.
    Fundamentals of investment management / Geoffrey A. Hirt, Stanley
B. Block. — 4th ed.
        p.   cm.
    Includes index.
    ISBN 0-256-09482-9
    1. Investments.   2. Investments—United States.   3. Investment
analysis.   I. Block, Stanley B.   II. Title.
HG4521.H579   1993   92–25193
332.6 — dc20

Printed in the United States of America

2 3 4 5 6 7 8 9 0 DOC 9 8 7 6 5 4 3

TO OUR WIVES, CHILDREN,
AND PARENTS

The Irwin Series in Finance

The Irwin Series in Finance
Consulting Editor Stephen A. Ross
Sterling Professor of Economics and Finance
Yale University

Financial Management

Block and Hirt
Foundations of Financial Management, *Sixth Edition*

Brooks
PC FinGame

Brooks
Fingame: The Financial Management Decision Game, *Third Edition*

Bruner
Case Studies in Finance: Managing for Corporate Value Creation

Fruhan, Kester, Mason, Piper, and Ruback
Case Problems in Finance, *Tenth Edition*

Harrington and Wilson
Corporate Financial Analysis, *Fourth Edition*

Helfert
Techniques of Financial Analysis, *Seventh Edition*

Higgins
Analysis for Financial Management, *Third Edition*

Jones
Introduction to Financial Management

Ross, Westerfield, and Jaffe
Corporate Finance, *Third Edition*

Ross, Westerfield, and Jordan
Fundamentals of Corporate Finance, *Second Edition*

Stonehill and Eiteman
Finance: An International Perspective

Investments

Bodie, Kane, and Marcus
Essentials of Investments

Bodie, Kane, and Marcus
Investments, *Second Edition*

Cohen, Zinbarg, Zeikel
Investment Analysis and Portfolio Management, *Fifth Edition*

Hirt and Block
Fundamentals of Investment Management, *Fourth Edition*

Lorie, Dodd, and Kimpton
The Stock Market: Theories & Evidence, *Second Edition*

Financial Institutions and Markets

Fraser and Rose
Readings on Financial Institutions and Markets, *Fourth Edition*

Rose
Money and Capital Markets: The Financial System in an Increasingly Global Economy, *Fourth Edition*

Rose
Commercial Bank Management: Producing and Selling Financial Services, *Second Edition*

Rose and Kolari
Financial Institutions: Understanding & Managing Financial Services, *Fourth Edition*

Real Estate

Berston
California Real Estate Practice, *Sixth Edition*

Berston
California Real Estate Principles, *Sixth Edition*

Brueggeman, Fisher, and Stone
Real Estate Finance, *Ninth Edition*

Smith and Corgel
Real Estate Perspectives: An Introduction to Real Estate, *Second Edition*

Shenkel
Real Estate Finance

Financial Planning and Insurance

Allen, Melone, Rosenbloom, and VanDerhei
Pension Planning: Pensions, Profit-Sharing, and Other Deferred Compensation Plans, *Seventh Edition*

Crawford and Beadles
Life Insurance Law, *Sixth Edition*

Hirsch and Donaldson
Casualty Claims Practice, *Fifth Edition*

Kapoor, Dlabay, and Hughes
Personal Finance, *Second Edition*

Kellison
Theory of Interest, *Second Edition*

Rokes
Human Relations in Handling Insurance Claims, *Revised Edition*

Preface

The first edition of *Fundamentals of Investment Management* was published in the early 1980s, and since then many changes have taken place in the financial markets. However, the one constant for this text has been a sincere commitment by the authors to present a book that captures the excitement and enthusiasm that we feel for the topic of investment management.

Throughout the book, we attempt to establish the appropriate theoretical base, while at the same time following through with real-world examples. Students ultimately should be able to translate what they have learned in the course to actual participation in the financial markets.

■ NEW FEATURES IN THE FOURTH EDITION

A number of features have been added to the Fourth Edition to make Hirt and Block an even more exciting and beneficial learning experience.

- We have added Chapter 6 on the Time Value of Money and Investment Applications as a review for those students who have grown rusty and lost their edge from their previous classes. Chapter 6 bridges the gap from economic and industry analysis to the dividend valuation models found in Chapter 7.

- The section on efficient markets has been reorganized into Section Three with Chapter 9 emphasizing technical analysis and the efficient market hypotheses. This is followed by Chapter 10 on Investments in Special Situations which focuses on many of the efficient market anomalies such as small stocks, low P/Es, and takeovers. We felt that this chapter was "lost" in its previous location.

- MarketBase^{SM}-E has been added as a special option for those wishing to use computer oriented data bases on the PC. MarketBase has packaged an educational version for Richard D. Irwin which includes data on over 4,700 stocks. Dr. Fred Shipley of DePaul University and Editor of *Computerized Investing* for the American Association of Individual Investors has put together a series of problems at the end of 10 chapters that will help educate the student in the art of data analysis, data searches, and portfolio construction.

- For many students, the world of video is "where the action is" and for them we have included a set of ten separate video programs from the award winning MacNeil/Lehrer report on PBS. These videos are real

world studies of financial situations over the last five years. Each segment covers between 6 and 12 minutes and can be used to highlight various topics in a chapter or as a means of creating discussion. They cover issues like the Salomon Brothers U.S. government bond scandal and people such as the Feshback Brothers, well known short sellers.

■ Critical thought cases have been added to the problem material in selected chapters. These cases were designed to create discussion about important issues in the investment industry. Their placement at the end of the problem section makes their use optional for the professor. However, topics such as insider trading, conflicts of interest in accounting audits, and creation of financial statements allow for good class interaction.

■ The CFA problems and solutions have been given expanded coverage. These problems and solutions are from previous Level I exams given annually by the AIMR. The exams cover topics related to stock valuation, financial analysis, bond valuation, duration, and so on. The CFA problem and solution sets give the student an appreciation for what they are learning in their investments class. They realize the knowledge gained is exactly what is expected of them if they were to pursue a career in the field of professional investments.

■ The chapter on international markets and investing has been entirely redone with much new data on the emerging markets of the less industrialized countries. This chapter is a good stand-alone chapter if you want to move it to a different part of the text such as after Chapter 3. It also has new correlation data and other material that allow this chapter to be tied into the diversification concepts found in the portfolio management section.

■ Finally we reorganized the book by grouping all the chapters in the area of options, futures, index futures and options, and commodities into one section called Derivative Products. Additionally we grouped international markets, mutual funds, and real assets into a separate section called Broadening the Investment Perspective. This reorganization along with the new Chapter 6 and the section on Issues in Efficient Markets makes the book more compartmentalized, more efficiently organized, and tighter in pedagogical approach.

■ PEDAGOGICAL FEATURES

The authors believe in establishing a very sound base for analysis. For example, in Chapter 7 the student is strongly encouraged to use appropriate valuation techniques to evaluate equities. These include present value techniques under different assumptions of growth rates. Similar approaches are used to evaluate bonds, options, and other forms of investments. At the same time, the authors consider it essential that real-world material be integrated into the

analysis. For example, in valuing equity securities, the common stock of J. M. Smucker is used rather than some hypothetical firm. Ratio and financial statement analyses are focused through the eyes of one reading the Coca-Cola annual report. The discussion of convertible bonds is based on securities issued by Home Depot. The same principle is followed in virtually every chapter of the book.

Approach in Teaching

The book is sufficiently flexible so that the instructor can use the text on a quarter or semester basis. Furthermore, there is a large enough range of topics to allow the instructor to use a traditional approach to investments or expand in a variety of new areas.

Traditional Approach

Part 1: Introduction to Investments
  The Investment Setting
  Security Markets
  Participating in the Market
  Sources of Investment Information

Part 2: Analysis and Valuation of Equity Securities
  Economic and Industry Analysis
  Time Value of Money and Investment Applications
  Valuation of the Individual Firm
  Financial Statement Analysis

Part 3: Issues in Efficient Markets
  Technical Analysis and Market Efficiency
  Investments in Special Situations

Part 4: Fixed-Income and Leveraged Securities
  Bonds and Fixed-Income Fundamentals
  Principles of Bond Valuation
  Duration and Reinvestment Concepts
  Convertible Securities and Warrants

Expanded Version Beyond Traditional Approach

All of the above plus sections 5 & 6

Part 5: Derivative Products
  Put and Call Options
  Commodities and Financial Futures
  Stock Index Futures and Options

Part 6: Broadening the Investment Perspective
  International Securities Markets
  Mutual Funds
  Investments in Real Assets

Adding in Portfolio Considerations

This section on portfolio consideration could be added to the traditional approach or used to complete the whole book.

Part 7: Introduction to Portfolio Management
  A Basic Look at Portfolio Management and Capital Market Theory
  Measuring Risks and Returns of Portfolio Managers

■ END-OF-CHAPTER MATERIAL

There are comprehensive questions and problems at the end of each chapter. The authors provide more problem material than any other introductory investment text. The problems are carefully annotated in the margin to indicate the topic covered (i.e., bond valuation, margin requirements, dividend valuation model, etc.). To further enforce the student's learning process, many of the analytical chapters also have questions and solutions from prior CFA Level I exams. The intent is to illustrate that much of what the students are learning is in line with what professional financial analysts are expected to know for certification. Also at the end of each chapter is a listing of the important words and concepts from the chapter. These items are fully defined in the glossary. Earlier in the Preface we discussed the addition of MarketBase-E and Critical Thought Cases in many chapters.

A number of the chapters have appendixes that cover such diverse topics as career opportunities in investments, individual retirement accounts, innovations in the debt markets, and the Black-Scholes Option Pricing model.

■ TEACHING SUPPORT PACKAGE

The teaching support package includes:

1. *Instructor's Manual and Test Bank.* ·The first element in the package contains detailed solutions for all the problems in the text. It also contains teaching strategies for the 22 chapters.

   Furthermore, there is a test bank of well over 1,000 questions. These include true-false, multiple-choice, matching quizzes, and many problems for those chapters that lend themselves to problem material.

2. *Transparency Masters.* New to this edition, there are approximately 200 transparencies to choose from in teaching from the fourth edition of *Fundamentals of Investment Management.* In addition to major illustrations from the text, a variety of supplemental transparencies are also available for enhancing classroom lectures.

3. *Ready Notes.* Also new to this edition, *Ready Notes* provides students with a ready format for taking notes during class lectures. This inexpensive supplement provides a duplicate of every transparency master so students spend less time scribbling notes—and more time listening to lectures.

4. *Investments Templates (Software).* There will be investment templates software to accompany the fourth edition of Hirt and Block. This software is based on LOTUS 1-2-3® templates and is based on the calculations and formulas found in the textbook. These templates are designed to test the sensitivity of the investment relationships found in the chapters of the textbook. The software will allow the student to solve most of the homework problems at the end of the chapters. For example, the templates and exercises include the stock valuation models found in Chapter 7, bond valuation, duration calculations, convertible bond analysis, option pricing models, and portfolio analysis models.

5. *MarketBase-E.* For those faculty who desire a computer interactive course, we are able to provide a serious package of over 4,700 securities including many foreign ADRs. MarketBase-E comes with its own users manual to walk students through the basic functions it can perform. The manual also supplies the user with over 60 problems and projects to work on using MarketBase-E. MarketBase-E is an excellent software data base available for PCs. Each company has a historical summary of its data, growth rates, earnings, dividends, income statement variables, and balance sheet variables as well as institutional holding and other data of interest to an investor. While Dr. Fred Shipley has provided a sampling of problems for MarketBase-E at the end of nine chapters, the students will enjoy simply "playing" with this data base package while the creative faculty will think up projects to work on that will challenge the student's curiosity. No more, "I can't find it in the library" from students. Now they will be able to find almost any company on their own data base.

6. *Investment Self-Study (Software).* This package will be available free for student use with the text. The diskette contains true-false questions and multiple-choice questions that are similar to those in the instructor's manual, but not the same. These questions may be studied a chapter at a time in a quiz format, and the student has the choice of taking either true-false, multiple-choice, or a combination quiz. The questions are randomly selected so that the student will be quizzed in a different order each time he or she requests a quiz from selected chapters. The student can also select a test from a combination of up to 10 chapters.

    Investment Self-Study also includes the complete glossary found at the back of the text plus some additional terms. From this glossary the student can select matching quizzes or look up definitions either by typing the word into the computer for a word search or by selecting a letter of the alphabet and scrolling through the words beginning with that letter. This glossary is also keyed into the true-false and multiple-choice questions so that when a student misses a question he or

she can look up key words directly after missing the question. A chapter outline and the summary for each chapter are also part of the tutorial.

7. *Videos*. Offered for the first time with this edition, the MacNeil/Lehrer NewsHour video series brings finance to life for students. Actual segments from these award-winning news reports offer a terrific opportunity for generating interesting classroom discussions.

■ ACKNOWLEDGMENTS

The authors wish to express special thanks to Carl Luft for his contribution of the Black-Scholes Option Pricing model material.

We are grateful to the following individuals for their thoughtful reviews and suggestions for the fourth edition: Paul Bolster, *Northeastern University*; Betty Driver, *Murray State University*; Adrian C. Edwards, *Western Michigan University*; Majed R. Muhtaseb, *California State Polytechnic University, Pomona;* Harold Mulherin, *Clemson University*; Richard Ponarul, *California State University*; and Dave Rand, *Northwest Technical College*; and Harry Klein, *MarketBase, Inc.*

For their prior reviews and helpful comments, we are grateful to Carol J. Billingham, *Central Michigan University*; Gerald A. Blum, *University of Nevada, Reno*; Keith E. Boles, *University of Colorado, Colorado Springs*; Jerry D. Boswell, *College of Financial Planning*; Joe B. Copeland, *University of North Alabama*; Marcia M. Cornett, *Southern Methodist University*; Jane H. Finley, *University of South Alabama*; Adam Gehr, *DePaul University*; Paul Grier, *SUNY-Binghamton*; David Heskel, *Bloomsburg University*; James Khule, *California State University–Sacramento*; Sheri Kole, *Copeland Companies*; Carl Luft, *DePaul University*; John D. Markese, *DePaul University*; Roger R. Palmer, *College of St. Thomas*; John W. Peavy III, *Southern Methodist University*; Linda L. Richardson, *University of Southern Maine*; Tom S. Sale, *Louisiana Tech University*; Art Schwartz, *University of South Florida*; Joseph F. Singer, *University of Missouri–Kansas City*; Ira Smolowitz, *Siena College*; Don Taylor, *University of Wisconsin, Platteville*; Frank N. Tiernan, *Drake University*; Allan J. Twark, *Kent State University*; Howard E. Van Auken, *Iowa State University*; and Bismarck Williams, *Roosevelt University*.

Finally we would like to recognize sponsoring editor Mike Junior, especially Ann Sass, our exceptional developmental editor, and an extremely effective group at Richard D. Irwin for their help in developing the fourth edition. Last, we would be remiss without recognizing the contributions of Carrie Nowakowski and Kristen Piotrowski, our capable and talented research assistants.

Geoffrey A. Hirt
Stanley B. Block

Contents in Brief

Contents

List of Real World Examples

Fundamentals of Investment Management

Part One

Introduction to Investments

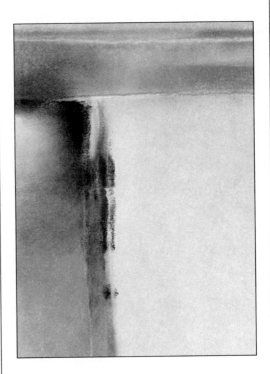

Outline

Insider trading became a big issue on Wall Street during the 1980s with the conviction of Michael Milken, Ivan Boesky, and Dennis Levine. But exactly what is insider trading and what is the fine line that separates insider information from other information?

One goal of investors has traditionally been to make money. Unfortunately, some investors want to get rich quick at any price and that price could be jail. During the last 10 years, the Securities Exchange Commission has beefed up its enforcement of insider trading rules. The collapse of investment banker Drexel Burnham Lambert was perhaps the peak of the insider trading scandal that sent Michael Milken, Dennis Levine, and Ivan Boesky to jail.

There are a multitude of events that can affect the stock and bond prices of publicly traded companies. For example, mergers, takeovers, corporate restructurings, leveraged buyouts, new products, changes in product sales, a new oil find, or the loss of a major customer can push prices up or down dramatically. If an investor were in a position to have this information and act on it before the general markets, there is no question that a handsome profit might occur. How an investor acquires information is at the heart of the insider trading laws.

Federal law states that you are in violation of the insider trading laws if you trade securities on information that you know or have reason to know is both nonpublic and likely to affect the stock price if the stock were publicly traded. In other words, you cannot trade on confidential stock tips from someone inside the company. Exactly how this law is interpreted by federal enforcement officials and the courts has become clearer in recent years but many gray areas remain.

When exactly are you in violation of insider trading rules? What if you see a known takeover artist landing in his private jet in a small town where a major company is headquartered and assume he is launching a bid for the company? Anyone could have this knowledge, so no violation occurs. What if you overhear a conversation between two investment bankers at a bar? This becomes touchy because it depends on whether you know who they are or just happen to believe that their conversation is accurate. If you don't know them, acting on their conversation is probably reckless on your part but certainly not a violation of the law. If, however, one of them is your uncle and you act on their conversation, then you are guilty of an insider violation.

In recent years, a reporter for *The Wall Street Journal* was indicted because he acted on information found in *The Wall Street Journal*'s "Heard on the Street" column before it was sold to the public. A truck driver for the publishing house that printed *Business Week* magazine was indicted because he passed on information to a relative before the magazine was put on sale. An employee of a printing house that put together prospectuses for new public offerings also violated insider trading laws.

Despite these and other recent examples, you don't have to work for a company to be classified as an insider. In many respects, the financial community has received a black eye because of these insider scandals. As a result, the discipline of finance needs to clean up its ethical behavior before the general public will view finance professionals with renewed respect. ∎

1

The Investment Setting

From early 1982 to October 19, 1987, the issues of the New York Stock Exchange increased in value 250 percent. On the Tokyo Stock Exchange, the advance over the same five and a half years was even greater, with a gain in excess of 400 percent. One Japanese stock alone, Nippon Telephone and Telegraph Company, carried a larger value than the entire West German stock market. This was one of the great bull markets of the post–World War II period.

Then came the great panic on Monday, October 19, 1987. In one day, the Dow Jones Industrial Average, the most-watched stock market indicator in the world, declined 22.6 percent. By contrast, the largest single day decline in the fabled stock market crash of 1929 was slightly over 12 percent. On Black Monday of 1987, IBM declined 31¼ points; Eastman Kodak, 26 points; Westinghouse Electric, 20½ points; and Du Pont, 18½ points. Over $500 billion in stock values was erased in one day on U.S. stock markets and over $1 trillion worldwide.

Common stocks are not the only volatile investment. In the past two decades, silver has gone from $5 an ounce to $50 and back again to less than $4. Gold has moved from $35 an ounce to $875 and back to $360 in 1991. The same can be said of investments in oil, real estate, and a number of other items. Since the 1987 crash, the stock market has gone on to reach new highs in the spring of 1992 while interest rates fell dramatically because of a lingering recession. Commercial real estate lost over 30 percent of its value during 1990–91. Other examples are constantly occurring both on the upside and downside as fortunes are made and lost.

How does one develop an investment strategy in such an environment? Suggestions come from all directions. The investor is told how to benefit from the coming monetary disaster as well as how to grow rich in a new era of prosperity. The intent of this text is to help the investor sort out the various investments that are available and to develop analytical skills that suggest what securities and assets might be most appropriate for a given **portfolio.**

We shall define an **investment** as the commitment of current funds in anticipation of receiving a larger future flow of funds. The investor hopes to be compensated for forgoing immediate consumption, for the effects of inflation, and for taking a risk.

Investing may be both exciting and challenging. First-time investors who pour over the financial statements of a firm and then make a dollar commitment to purchase a few shares of stock often have a feeling of euphoria as they charge out in the morning to secure the daily newspaper and read the market quotes. Even professional analysts may take pleasure in leaving their Wall Street offices to evaluate an emerging high-technology firm in Austin or Palo Alto. Likewise, the buyer of a rare painting, late 18th-century U.S. coin, or invaluable baseball card may find a sense of excitement in attempting to outsmart the market. Even the purchaser of a bond or money market instrument must do proper analysis to assure that anticipated objectives are being met. Let us examine the different types of investments.

■ FORMS OF INVESTMENT

In the text, we break down investment alternatives between financial and real assets. A **financial asset** represents a financial claim on an asset that is usually documented by some form of legal representation. An example would be a share of stock or a bond. A **real asset** represents an actual tangible asset that may be seen, felt, held, or collected. An example would be real estate or gold. Table 1–1 lists the various forms of financial and real assets.

As indicated in the left column of Table 1–1, financial assets may be broken down into five categories. **Direct equity claims** represent ownership interests and include common stock as well as other instruments that can be used to purchase common stock, such as warrants and options. Warrants and options allow the holder to buy a stipulated number of shares in the future at a given price. Warrants usually convert to one share and are long term, whereas options are generally based on 100 share units and are short term in nature.

Indirect equity can be acquired through placing funds in investment companies (such as a mutual fund). The investment company pools the resources of many investors and reinvests them in common stock (or other investments).

Table 1–1　　Overview of Investment Alternatives

Financial Assets	Real Assets
1. Equity claims—direct 　Common stock 　Warrants 　Options	1. Real estate 　Office buildings 　Apartments 　Shopping centers 　Personal residences
2. Equity claims—indirect 　Investment company shares (mutual funds) 　Pension funds 　Whole life insurance	2. Precious metals 　Gold 　Silver
3. Creditor claims 　Savings account 　Money market funds 　Commercial paper 　Treasury bills, notes, bonds 　Municipal notes, bonds 　Corporate bonds (straight and convertible to common stock)	3. Precious gems 　Diamonds 　Rubies 　Sapphires
4. Preferred stock (straight and convertible to common stock)	4. Collectibles 　Art 　Antiques 　Stamps 　Coins 　Rare books
5. Commodity futures	5. Other 　Cattle 　Oil 　Common metals

The individual enjoys the advantages of diversification and professional management (though not necessarily higher returns).

Financial assets may also take the form of **creditor claims** as represented by debt instruments offered by financial institutions, industrial corporations, or the government. The rate of return is often initially fixed, though the actual return may vary with changing market conditions. Other forms of financial assets are **preferred stock,** which is a hybrid form of security combining some of the elements of equity ownership and creditor claims, and **commodity futures,** which represent a contract to buy or sell a commodity in the future at a given price. Commodities may include wheat, corn, copper, or even such financial instruments as Treasury bonds or foreign exchange.

As shown in the right column of Table 1–1, there are also numerous categories of real assets. The most widely recognized investment in this category is *real estate,* either commercial property or one's own residence. For greater risk, *precious metals* or *precious gems* can be considered, and for those seeking psychic pleasure as well as monetary gain, *collectibles* are an investment outlet. Finally, the *other (all-inclusive)* category includes cattle, oil, and other items that stretch as far as the imagination will go.

Throughout the text, each form of financial and real asset is considered. What assets the investor ultimately selects will depend on investment objectives as well as the economic outlook. For example, the investor who believes inflation will be relatively strong may prefer real assets that have a replacement value reflecting increasing prices. In a more moderate inflationary environment, stocks and bonds may be preferred.

■ THE SETTING OF INVESTMENT OBJECTIVES

The setting of investment objectives may be as important as the selection of the investment. In actuality, they tend to go together. A number of key areas should be considered.

Risk and Safety of Principal

The first factor investors must consider is the amount of risk they are prepared to assume. In a relatively efficient and informed capital market environment, risk tends to be closely correlated with return. Most of the literature of finance would suggest that those who consistently demonstrate high returns of perhaps 20 percent or more are greater-than-normal risk takers. While some clever investors are able to prosper on their wits alone, most high returns may be perceived as compensation for risk.

And there is not only the risk of losing invested capital directly (a dry hole perhaps) but also the danger of a loss in purchasing power. At 8 percent inflation (compounded annually), a stock that is held for four years without a gain in value would represent a 36 percent loss in purchasing power.

Investors who wish to assume low risks will probably confine a large portion of their portfolio to short-term debt instruments in which the party responsible for payment is the government or a major bank or corporation. Some conservative investors may choose to invest in a money market fund in which the funds of numerous investors are pooled and reinvested in high-yielding, short-term instruments. More aggressive investors may look toward longer-term debt instruments and common stock. Real assets, such as gold, silver, or valued art, might also be included in an aggressive portfolio.

It is not only the inherent risk in an asset that must be considered but also the extent to which that risk is being diversified away in a portfolio. Though an investment in gold might be considered risky, such might not be fully the case if it is combined into a portfolio of common stocks. Gold thrives on bad news, while common stocks generally do well in a positive economic environment. An oil embargo or foreign war may drive down the value of stocks while gold is advancing, and vice versa.

The age and economic circumstances of an investor are important variables in determining an appropriate level of risk. Young, upwardly mobile people are generally in a better position to absorb risk than are elderly couples on a fixed income. Nevertheless, each of us, regardless of our plight in life, has different risk-taking desires. A surgeon earning $200,000 a year may be more averse to accepting a $2,000 loss on a stock than an aging taxicab driver.

One cruel lesson of investing is that conservative investments do not always end up being what you thought they were when you bought them. For example, "Old Blue," conservative IBM, failed to provide a competitive return for investors in 1990 and 1991 and actually lost value for many. The automobile industry suffered tremendous losses in 1991 after setting record profits in 1989, and stockholders lost value. Blue-chip real estate properties lost half their values in the Northeast in 1990–91 and 30 percent nationwide, and several major money market banks such as Citicorp lost over two thirds of their shareholder value and suffered declining credit ratings, which hurt bondholders. Even those short-term risk-averse investors in U.S. Treasury bills saw their income stream decline from 12 percent to 4 percent over several years as interest rates plummeted. This declining cash flow can be a shock to your system if you are living on the interest income.

Current Income versus Capital Appreciation

A second consideration in setting investment objectives is a decision on the desire for current income versus capital appreciation. Though this decision is closely tied to an evaluation of risk, it is separate.

In purchasing stocks, the investor with a need for current income may opt for high-yielding, mature firms in such industries as public utilities, machine tools, or apparel. Those searching for price gains may look toward smaller, emerging firms in high technology, energy, or electronics. The latter firms

may pay no cash dividend, but the investor hopes for an increase in value to provide the desired return.

The investor needs to understand there is generally a trade-off between growth and income. Finding both in one type of investment is unlikely. If you go for the high-yielding utilities, you can expect slow growth in earnings and stock price. If you opt for high growth such as a biotechnology firm, you can expect no cash flow from the dividend.

Liquidity Considerations

Liquidity is measured by the ability of the investor to convert an investment into cash within a relatively short time at its fair market value or with a minimum capital loss on the transaction.

Most financial assets provide a high degree of liquidity. Stocks and bonds can generally be sold within a matter of minutes at a price reasonably close to the last traded value. Such may not be the case for real estate. Almost everyone has seen a house or piece of commercial real estate sit on the market for weeks, months, or years.

Liquidity can also be measured indirectly by the transaction costs or commissions involved in the transfer of ownership. Financial assets generally trade on a relatively low commission basis (perhaps 1 or 2 percent), whereas many real assets have transaction costs that run from 5 percent to 25 percent or more.

In many cases, the lack of immediate liquidity can be justified if there are unusual opportunities for gain. An investment in real estate or precious gems may provide sufficient return to more than compensate for the added transaction costs. Of course, a bad investment will be all the more difficult to unload.

Investors must carefully assess their own situation to determine the need for liquidity. If you are investing funds to be used for the next house payment or the coming semester's tuition, then immediate liquidity will be essential, and financial assets will be preferred. If funds can be tied up for long periods, bargain-buying opportunities of an unusual nature can also be evaluated.

Short-Term versus Long-Term Orientation

In setting investment objectives, you must decide whether you will assume a short-term or long-term orientation in managing the funds and evaluating performance. You do not always have a choice. People who manage funds for others may be put under tremendous pressure to show a given level of performance in the short run. Those applying pressure may be a concerned relative or a large pension fund that has placed funds with a bank trust department. Even though you are convinced your latest stock purchase will double in the next three years, the fact that it is currently down 15 percent may provide some discomfort to those around you.

Market strategies may also be short term or long term in scope. Those who attempt to engage in short-term market tactics are termed *traders*. They may

buy a stock at 15 and hope to liquidate if it goes to 20. To help reach decisions, short-term traders often use technical analysis, which is based on evaluating market indicator series and charting. Those who take a longer-term perspective try to identify fundamentally sound companies for a buy-and-hold approach. A long-term investor does not necessarily anticipate being able to buy right at the bottom or sell at the exact peak.

Research has shown it is difficult to beat the market on a risk-adjusted basis. Given that the short-term trader encounters more commissions than the long-term investor because of more active trading, short-term trading as a rule is not a strategy endorsed by the authors.

Tax Factors

Investors in high tax brackets have different investment objectives than those in lower brackets or tax-exempt charities, foundations, or similar organizations. An investor in a high tax bracket may prefer municipal bonds (interest is not taxable), real estate (with its depreciation and interest write-off), or investments that provide tax credits or limited tax shelters, such as those in oil and gas or railroad cars.

In recent times, many investment advisers have cautioned investors not to be blinded by the beneficial tax aspects of an investment but to look at the economic factors as well. Furthermore, the Tax Reform Act of 1986 has greatly diminished the ability to use tax shams and tax shelters to protect income from taxation. One of the best tax-planning features is the individual retirement account (IRA), which is discussed in this chapter and later chapters.

Ease of Management

Another consideration in establishing an investment program is ease of management. The investor must determine the amount of time and effort that can be devoted to an investment portfolio and act accordingly. In the stock market, this may determine whether you want to be a daily trader or to assume a longer-term perspective. In real estate, it may mean the difference between personally owning and managing a handful of rental houses or going in with 10 other investors to form a limited partnership in which a general partner takes full management responsibility and the limited partners merely put up the capital.

Of course, a minimum amount of time must be committed to any investment program. Even when investment advisers or general partners are in charge, their activities must be monitored and evaluated.

In managing a personal portfolio, the investor should consider opportunity costs. If a lawyer can work for $150 per hour or manage his financial portfolio, a fair question would be, "How much extra return can I get from managing my portfolio, or can I add more value to my portfolio by working

and investing more money?" Unless the lawyer is an excellent investor, it is probable that more money can be made by working.

Assume an investor can add a 2 percent extra return to his portfolio but it takes 5 hours per week (260 hours per year) to do so. If his opportunity cost is $40 per hour, he would have to add more than $10,400 ($40 × 260 hours) to his portfolio to make personal management attractive. If we assume a 2 percent excess return can be gained over the professional manager, the investor would need a portfolio of $520,000 before personal management would make sense under these assumptions. This example may explain why many high-income individuals choose to have professionals manage their assets.

Decisions such as these may also depend on your trade-off between work and leisure. An investor may truly find it satisfying and intellectually stimulating to manage a portfolio and may receive psychic income from mastering the nuances of investing. However, if you would rather ski, play tennis, or enjoy some other leisure activity, the choice of professional management may make more sense than a do-it-yourself approach.

Retirement and Estate Planning Considerations

Even the relatively young must begin to consider the effect of their investment decisions on their retirement and the estates they will pass along to their "potential families" someday. Those who wish to remain single will still be called on to advise others as to the appropriateness of a given investment strategy for their family needs.

Most good retirement questions should not be asked at "retirement" but 40 or 45 years before because that's the period with the greatest impact. One of the first questions a person is often asked after taking a job on graduation is whether he or she wishes to set up an IRA. An IRA allows a qualifying taxpayer to deduct $2,000 from taxable income and invest the funds at a bank, savings and loan, brokerage house, mutual fund, or other financial institution. The funds are normally placed in interest-bearing instruments, such as a certificate of deposit, or perhaps in other securities, such as common stock. The income earned on the funds is allowed to grow tax-free until withdrawn at retirement. As an example, if a person places $2,000 a year in an IRA for 45 consecutive years and the funds earn 10 percent over that time, $1,437,810 will have been accumulated. Similar retirement and estate-planning issues will be mentioned later.

■ PROFILE ANALYSIS

The authors have developed an interesting risk profile to see which types of investments are appropriate for investors, based on their investment objectives. The questionnaire is presented in Appendix 1–A. After you have read this chapter, you may want to try it. You can apply the questions to your own or your family's financial goals.

Broker's New Cry: Asset Allocation

Eager to drum up new business, Wall Street is touting an investment technique to small investors that it has been pushing to institutional clients for years—asset allocation.

That's a fancy way of saying split up your money among stocks, bonds, cash equivalents, and other investments. Just how that split works depends on things like your age, investment objectives, and willingness to take risk.

Asset allocation can be done many ways, all building on the idea of diversification to spread risk. Some plans call for a never-changing portfolio makeup, such as the widely publicized "fixed mix" of equal investments in U.S. stocks, U.S. bonds, foreign stocks, real estate, and cash equivalents.

A look at Prudential Securities' plan shows how big brokerage firms are tailoring allocation programs in a bid to capture the largest number of investors. Prudential Securities' computer can spin out any one of 300 basic investment portfolios based on the investor's answers to its questionnaire.

Investors find that they often need to do fairly regular buying and selling to stay in line with their recommended asset mix. This is, in part, because the formulas themselves change along with an investor's age, family obligations, and general economic conditions.

Source: James A. White, *The Wall Street Journal*, October 6, 1988, p. C1. Reprinted by permission of *THE WALL STREET JOURNAL*, © 1988 by Dow Jones & Co., Inc. All Rights Reserved Worldwide.

Selling Asset Allocation
(Portfolios currently recommended under Prudential Securities' strategy)

Characteristic* Risk Level	25-Year-Old Moderate		45-Year-Old Aggressive		65-Year-Old Very Conservative	
Portfolio size	$160,000		$600,000		$1.2 million	
Excess cash flow	Low		High		Low	
Desired investments						
Income	60%		10%		100%	
Growth	40%		90%		0%	
Investments recommended						
Cash and equivalents	$ 64,000	(40%)	$ 30,000	(5%)	$ 120,000	(10%)
Fixed income	$ 40,000	(25%)	$ 60,000	(10%)	$ 780,000	(65%)
Moderate growth	$ 32,000	(20%)	$270,000	(45%)	$ 240,000	(20%)
Aggressive growth	$ 8,000	(5%)	$ 90,000	(15%)	0	—
Direct ownership	$ 8,000	(5%)	$120,000	(20%)	0	—
Tangible assets	$ 8,000	(5%)	$ 30,000	(5%)	$ 60,000	(5%)

*Data provided by investor.

■ MEASURES OF RISK AND RETURN

Now that you have some basic familiarity with the different forms of investments and the setting of investment goals, we are ready to look at concepts of
measuring the return from an investment and the associated risk. The return
you receive from any investment (stocks, bonds, real estate) has two primary
components: capital gains (or increase in value) and current income. The rate
of return from an investment can be measured as:

$$\text{Rate of return} = \frac{(\text{Ending value} - \text{Beginning value}) + \text{Income}}{\text{Beginning value}} \qquad (1\text{--}1)$$

Thus, if a share of stock goes from $20 to $22 in one year and also pays a
dollar in dividends during the year, the total return is 15 percent. Using Formula 1–1:

$$\frac{(\$22 - \$20) + \$1}{\$20} = \frac{\$2 + \$1}{\$20} = \frac{\$3}{\$20} = 15\%$$

Where the formula is being specifically applied to stocks, it is written as:

$$\text{Rate of return} = \frac{(P_1 - P_0) + D_1}{P_0} \qquad (1\text{--}2)$$

Where:

P_1 = Price at the end of the period
P_0 = Price at the beginning of the period
D_1 = Dividend income

Risk

The risk for an investment is related to the uncertainty associated with the
outcomes from an investment. For example, an investment that has an abso-
lutely certain return of 10 percent is said to be riskless. Another investment
that has a likely or expected return of 12 percent, but also has the possibility of
minus 10 percent in hard economic times and plus 30 percent under optimum
circumstances is said to be risky. An example of three investments with progressively greater risk is presented in Figure 1–1. Based on our definition of
risk, investment C is clearly the riskiest because of the large uncertainty (wide
dispersion) of possible outcomes.

In the study of investments, you will soon observe that the desired or
required rate of return for a given investment is generally related to the risk
associated with that investment. Because most investors do not like risk, they
will require a higher rate of return for a more risky investment. That is not to
say the investors are unwilling to take risks—they simply wish to be compen-

Figure 1–1   Examples of Risk

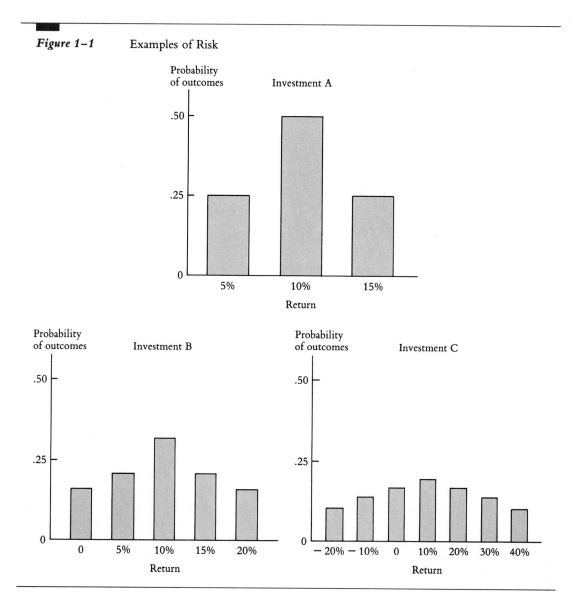

sated for taking the risk. For this reason, an investment in common stocks (which inevitably carries some amount of risk) may require an anticipated return 5 or 6 percent higher than a certificate of deposit in a commercial bank. This 5 or 6 percent represents a risk premium. You never know whether you will get the returns you anticipate, but at least your initial requirements will be higher to justify the risk you are taking.

■ ACTUAL CONSIDERATION OF REQUIRED RETURNS

Let's consider how return requirements are determined in the financial markets. Although the following discussion starts out on a theoretical "what if" basis, you will eventually see empirical evidence that different types of investments do provide different types of returns.

Basically, three components make up the required return from an investment:

1. The real rate of return.
2. The anticipated inflation factor.
3. The risk premium.

Real Rate of Return

The **real rate of return** is the return investors require for allowing others to use their money for a given time period. This is the return investors demand for passing up immediate consumption and allowing others to use their savings until the funds are returned. Because the term *real* is employed, this means it is a value determined before inflation is included in the calculation. The real rate of return is also determined before considering any specific risk for the investment.

Historically, the real rate of return in the U.S. economy has been from 2 to 3 percent. During much of the 1980s, it was somewhat higher (4 to 6 percent), but in the early 1990s, interest rates fell more than inflation, and the real rate of return came back to its normal level of 2 to 3 percent, which is probably a reasonable long-term expectation.

Because an investor is concerned with using a real rate of return as a component of a required rate of return, the past is not always a good predictor for any one year's real rate of return. The problem comes from being able to measure the real rate of return only after the fact by subtracting inflation from the nominal interest rate. Unfortunately, expectations and occurrence do not always match. The real rate of return is highly variable (for seven years in the 1970s and early 1980s, it was even negative). One of the problems investors face in determining required rates of return is the forecasting errors involving interest rates and inflation. These forecasting errors are more pronounced in short-run returns than in long-run returns. Let us continue with our example and bring inflation into the discussion.

Anticipated Inflation Factor

The anticipated inflation factor must be added to the real rate of return. For example, if there is a 2 percent real-rate-of-return requirement and the **anticipated rate of inflation** is 3 percent, we combine the two to arrive at an approximate 5 percent required return factor. Combining the real rate of return and inflationary considerations gives us the required return on an invest-

ment before explicitly considering risk. For this reason, it is called the risk-free required rate of return or, simply, **risk-free rate (R_F).**

We can define the risk-free rate as:

Risk-free rate = (1 + Real rate) (1 + Expected rate of inflation) − 1 (1–3)

Plugging in numerical values, we would show:

Risk-free rate = (1.02) (1.03) − 1 = 1.0506 − 1 = .0506 or 5.06%

The answer is approximately 5 percent. You can simply add the real rate of return (2 percent) to the anticipated inflation rate (3 percent) to get a 5 percent answer or go through the more theoretically correct process of Formula 1–3 to arrive at 5.06 percent. Either approach is frequently used.

The risk-free rate (R_F) of approximately 5 percent applies to any investment as the minimum required rate of return to provide a 2 percent *real return* after inflation. Of course, if the investor actually receives a lower return, the real rate of return may be quite low or negative. For example, if the investor receives a 2 percent return in a 4 percent inflationary environment, there is a negative real return of 2 percent. The investor will have 2 percent less purchasing power than before he started. He would have been better off to spend the money *now* rather than save at a 2 percent rate in a 4 percent inflationary economy. In effect, he is *paying* the borrower to use his money. Of course, real rates of return and inflationary expectations change from time to time, so the risk-free required rate (R_F) also changes.

We now have examined the two components that make up the minimum risk-free rate of return that apply to investments (stock, bonds, real estate, etc.). We now consider the third component, the risk premium. The relationship is depicted in Figure 1–2.

Risk Premium

The **risk premium** will be different for each investment. For example, for a federally insured certificate of deposit at a bank or for a U.S. Treasury bill, the risk premium approaches zero. All the return to the investor will be at the risk-free rate of return (the real rate of return plus inflationary expectations). For common stock, the investor's required return may carry a 6 or 7 percent risk premium in addition to the risk-free rate of return. If the risk-free rate were 5 percent, the investor might have an overall required return of 11 to 12 percent on common stock.

+ Real rate	2%
+ Anticipated inflation	3%
= Risk-free rate	5%
+ Risk premium	6% or 7%
= Required rate of return	11% to 12%

Figure 1–2   The Components of Required Rate of Return

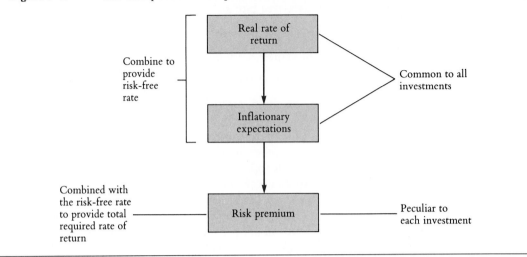

Corporate bonds fall somewhere between short-term government obligations (virtually no risk) and common stock in terms of risk. Thus, the risk premium may be 3 to 4 percent. Like the real rate of return and the inflation rate, the risk premium is not a constant but may change from time to time. If investors are very fearful about the economic outlook, the risk premium may be 8 to 10 percent as it was for junk bonds in 1990 and 1991.

The normal relationship between selected investments and their rates of return is depicted in Figure 1–3.

A number of empirical studies tend to support the risk-return relationships shown in Figure 1–3 over a long period. Perhaps the most widely cited is the Ibbotson study presented in Figure 1–4, which covers data from 1926 to 1990. Note the high-to-low return scale is in line with expectations based on risk. Of particular interest is the geometric mean column. This is simply the compound annual rate of return. The arithmetic mean is an average of yearly rates of return and has less meaning. Given that risk is measured by the standard deviation, the distribution of returns, which appears to the right of each security type, indicates which security has the biggest risk. Figure 1–4 shows in practice what we discussed in theory earlier in the chapter using Figure 1–1.

Because the study covered 64 years (including a decade of depression), the rates of return may be somewhat lower than those currently available. This is particularly true for the bonds and Treasury bills shown in Figure 1–4. Table 1–2, from *Stocks, Bonds, Bills and Inflation 1991 Yearbook,* shows returns for seven decades.

Table 1–3 illustrates a study by Salomon Brothers, an investment banking firm, that covers 13 investment categories and the consumer price index (CPI).

Figure 1–3   Risk–Return Characteristics

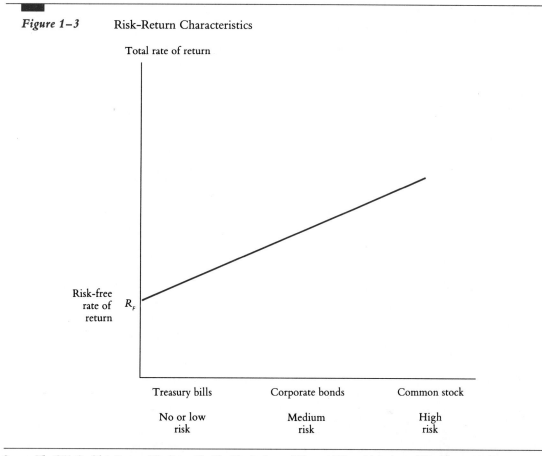

Source: *The CFA Candidate Program* (Charlottesville, Va.: The Institute of Chartered Financial Analysts, 1988–89), pp. 11–15.

The study is different from Figure 1–4 and Table 1–2 in that it covers real assets as well as financial assets. The information runs through June 1, 1991.

For the 20-year period, real assets tend to dominate the return rankings. This is primarily due to the high inflation rate during the 1970s and early 1980s. Real assets, because of increasing replacement value and scarcity, tend to perform best during periods of high inflation. However, the five-year column shows that many real assets, such as gold, silver, and stamps, performed poorly as inflationary expectations diminished. Financial assets fared better as interest rates came down during the five-year ranking. Stocks showed good performance for all periods because of their excellent performance in the bull market of the 1980s.

Because most of the material in the Salomon Brothers study was gathered during one of the most-inflationary time periods in U.S. history (aided by major oil price increases), you should not overly generalize from the results.

Figure 1–4   Basic Series: Summary Statistics of Annual Returns (1926–1990)

Series	Geometric Mean	Arithmetic Mean	Standard Deviation	Distribution
Common stocks	10.1%	12.1%	20.8%	
Small company stocks	11.6	17.1	35.4	
Long-term corporate bonds	5.2	5.5	8.4	
Long-term government bonds	4.5	4.9	8.5	
Intermediate-term government bonds	5.0	5.1	5.5	
U.S. Treasury bills	3.7	3.7	3.4	
Inflation	3.1	3.2	4.7	

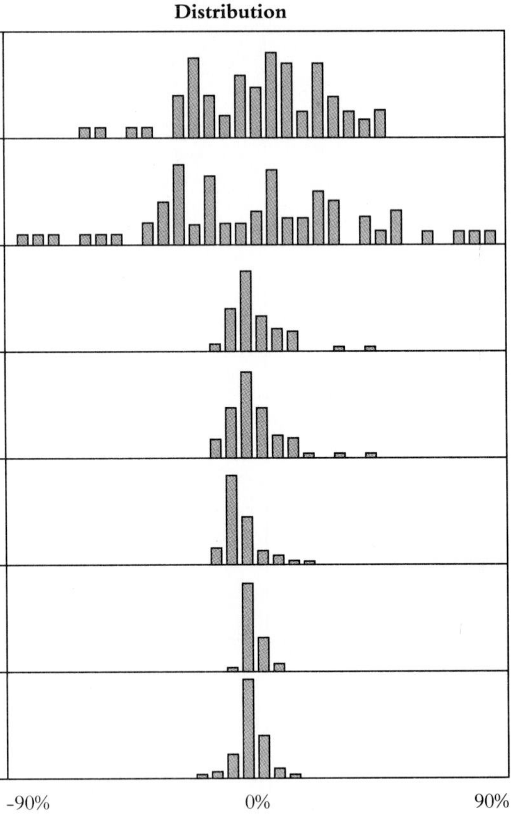

Source: *Stocks, Bond, Bills and Inflation 1991 Yearbook* (Chicago: R. G. Ibbotson & Associates, Inc., 1991).

Over longer periods, common stock tends to perform at approximately the same level as such real assets as real estate, coins, stamps, and so forth,[1] with each tending to show a different type of performance in a differing economic environment. More will be said about the impact of inflation and disinflation on investments later in the text.

[1]Examples of longer-term studies on comparative returns between real and financial assets are: Roger G. Ibbotson and Carol F. Fall, "The United States Wealth Portfolio," *The Journal of Portfolio Management,* Fall 1982, pp. 82–92; Roger G. Ibbotson and Lawrence B. Siegel, "The World Market Wealth Portfolio," *The Journal of Portfolio Management,* Winter 1983, pp. 5–17; and Alexander A. Robichek, Richard A. Cohn, and John J. Pringle, "Returns on Alternative Media and Implications for Portfolio Construction," *Journal of Business,* July 1972, pp. 427–43. (While Ibbotson and Siegel showed superior returns for metals between 1960 and 1980, metals have greatly underperformed other assets in the 1980s.)

Table 1-2	Compound Annual Rates of Return for Decades						
	1920s★	**1930s**	**1940s**	**1950s**	**1960s**	**1970s**	**1980s**
S&P 500 (large companies)	19.2%	0.0%	9.2%	19.4%	7.8%	5.9%	17.5%
Small company	−4.5	1.4	20.7	16.9	15.5	11.5	15.8
Long-term corporate	5.2	6.9	2.7	1.0	1.7	6.2	13.0
Long-term government	4.4	4.9	3.2	−0.1	1.4	5.5	12.6
Inter-term government	4.2	4.6	1.8	1.3	3.5	7.0	11.9
Treasury bills	3.7	0.6	0.4	1.9	3.9	6.3	8.9
Inflation	−1.1	−2.0	5.4	2.2	2.5	7.4	5.1

★Based on the period 1926–1929.
Source: *SBBI 1991 Yearbook.*

We have attempted to demonstrate the importance of risk in determining the required rate of return for an investment. As previously discussed, it is the third key component that is added to the risk-free rate (composed of the real rate of return and the inflation premium) to determine the total required rate of return. How does one *actually* determine the risk that is to be rewarded from a given instrument?

Systematic and Unsystematic Risk

You will recall that earlier we defined risk as related to the uncertainty of outcomes for a given investment. But it is not just the risk for an individual security that must be considered. Financial theory also requires that we consider the relationship between two or more investments to determine the combined risk level. Part of the risk of one investment may be **diversified** away with a second investment. For example, an investment in an oil company may be somewhat risky because oil prices may drop, but if you have a second investment in a petrochemical company that will benefit from lower oil prices, then you have diversified away part of the risk. Similarly, investments in foreign stocks often move in the opposite direction of investments in U.S. stocks. If you combine stocks from two or more countries, part of the risk is diversified away. Because diversification can *eliminate* part of the risk in an investment, not all risk is thought to be compensated for by proportionally higher returns.

Financial theory can be used to break down risk that is systematic and unsystematic in nature. **Unsystematic risk** is risk that can be diversified away in a well-constructed portfolio and thus is not assumed to be rewarded with higher returns in the financial markets. It represents the type of risk described in the preceding paragraph. **Systematic risk** is inherent in the investment and cannot be diversified away and is assumed to be rewarded in the marketplace. The relationship is indicated on page 22.

Table 1–3	Compounded Annual Rates of Return							
	20 Years	**Rank**	**10 Years**	**Rank**	**5 Years**	**Rank**	**1 Year**	**Rank**
Old Masters*	12.32%	1	15.84%	2	23.36%	1	6.53%	5
Stocks	11.65	2	16.03	1	13.33	3	11.77	3
Chinese ceramics*	11.59	3	8.07	5	15.12	2	3.64	8
Gold	11.50	4	−2.89	12	0.98	12	−0.73	12
Diamonds†	10.46	5	6.38	6	10.23	4	0.00	11
Stamps‡	10.03	6	−0.73	10	−2.43	13	−7.67	13
Bonds	9.35	7	15.15	3	9.66	5	13.20	2
Oil§	8.85	8	−5.92	13	8.50	6	20.66	1
3-month Treasury bills	8.62	9	8.79	4	7.02	7	7.13	4
Housing	7.27	10	4.37	7	4.55	9	4.70	7
CP‖	6.29	11	4.30	8	4.52	10	5.04	6
U.S. farmland	6.25	12	−1.81	11	1.28	11	2.10	9
Silver	4.99	13	−9.27	14	−4.80	14	−18.87	14
Foreign exchange	4.49	14	3.61	9	6.44	8	0.24	10

*Source: Sotheby's
†Source: The Diamond Registry
‡Source: Scott, Inc.
§Source: U.S. Department of Energy
‖Source: CPI—Consumer Price Index
Source: R. S. Salomon, Jr., "Annual Survey of Financial and Tangible Assets," Salomon Brothers, June 10, 1991.

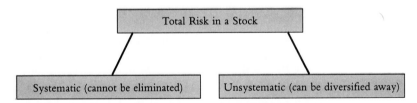

Systematic risk is measured by the related movement of a stock to the market. Even in a totally diversified portfolio, each stock will be vulnerable to changes in the *overall* market even if individual characteristics of the stocks have been largely diversified away. Based on systematic risk, if the market goes up or down by 10 percent, our stock may go up or down by 10 percent. The joint movement between a security and the market in general is defined as the **beta** coefficient. If a stock has equal volatility to the market (if the market changes by 10 percent, the stock changes by 10 percent), the beta coefficient is 1. If the stock is 50 percent more volatile than the market, the beta coefficient is 1.5 and so on. Systematic risk, as measured by the beta coefficient, is assumed to be compensated for by higher potential returns. That is, stocks that have high systematic risk or betas are assumed to provide higher returns to compensate for the additional risk. This same type of risk analysis can be applied to other types of investments as well.

In a later chapter, we will give a more thorough mathematical definition of how you separate out systematic and unsystematic risk. It is enough for now that you understand that the differences exist and the two forms of risk are not equally compensated. In the prior discussion of unsystematic risk, we mentioned the importance of diversifying away nonmarket-related risks. We discussed oil versus petrochemicals as presenting potential for diversifying oil price risks. Also foreign stocks versus U.S. stocks were given as an example. The auto parts replacement market may move in the opposite direction of new auto sales; the same can be said for the market for defense systems and public works projects. To establish an efficiently diversified portfolio, the investor must consider how projects correlate with each other. Generally, highly correlated projects provide little diversification benefits, while projects that have low correlations or are negatively correlated provide maximum diversification benefits.

Summary of Return Considerations

Based on our analysis to this point, we can say that each investment requires a total return that comprises a real rate of return, compensation for inflationary expectations, and a risk premium. The risk premium should be related to systematic risk (as opposed to unsystematic risk). In Chapter 7, "Valuation of the Individual Firm," you will become familiar with K_e, which is the total return on common stock. K_e represents a risk-free rate plus a risk premium and this risk premium is directly related to systematic risk. By glancing back to Figure 1–4, you can observe that over the very long term, the difference between a risk-free asset (such as a Treasury bill) and common stock is about 6 percent. This is the risk premium.

■ WHAT YOU WILL LEARN

The first part of the book covers the general framework for investing. You will look at an overview of the security markets (New York Stock Exchange, Chicago Board Options Exchange, and so on). Then you will examine the basics for participating in the market, such as opening an account, executing an order, investing individually or through a mutual fund, and so forth. Also in the first section of the book, you will become familiar with sources of important investment information so you can begin to make your university or public library a valuable asset.

You will then go through the classic process of analyzing and valuing a security. You will start with examining the economy, then move to the industry level, and finally move to the actual company. The authors go through the process of putting a value on a stock. There is also heavy emphasis on financial analysis. One chapter provides an in-depth analysis of the Coca-Cola Company to demonstrate procedures for identifying the strengths and weaknesses of a company. For enthusiasts of charting and other

forms of technical analysis, we examine the advantages and disadvantages of such approaches.

You will then move from stocks to bonds. Your level of interest should not diminish because bonds also offer an opportunity for income and, surprisingly, for large gains or losses. Because an emphasis of the book is to present the student with a wide investment horizon from which to choose, we then consider a variety of other investment alternatives. These include convertible securities and warrants, put and call options, commodities and financial futures, stock index futures and options, and real assets such as real estate and precious metals. We realize some of these terms may have little meaning to you now, but they soon will.

In the latter part of the book, we also consider the concepts of portfolio theory and how to put together the most desirable package of investments in terms of risk and return. We also consider the consequences of investing in a reasonably efficient stock market environment, one in which information is acted on very quickly. Can superior return be achieved in such a setting?

Many students taking an investments course are not sure of their ultimate career goals. We hope this course can be equally valuable to a future banker, CPA, insurance executive, marketing manager, or anyone else. However, for those specifically considering a career in investments, the authors present a brief summary of career opportunities in Appendix 1–B at the back of this chapter.

IMPORTANT WORDS AND CONCEPTS

portfolio 6

investment 6

financial asset 7

real asset 7

direct and indirect equity claims 7

creditor claims 8

preferred stock 8

commodity futures 8

liquidity 10

real rate of return 16

anticipated rate of inflation 16

risk-free rate (R_F) 17

risk premium 17

diversified 21

unsystematic risk 21

systematic risk 21

beta 22

DISCUSSION QUESTIONS

1. How is an investment defined?
2. What are the differences between financial and real assets?
3. List some key areas relating to investment objectives.
4. Explain the concepts of direct equity and indirect equity.

5. How are equity and creditor claims different?

6. Do those wishing to assume low risks tend to invest long term or short term? Why?

7. How might investing in something generally considered to be risky actually decrease an investor's risk?

8. What are some types of appropriate investments for investors in high tax brackets who wish to diminish their tax obligation? Comment on the effect of the Tax Reform Act of 1986 on tax shams and tax shelters.

9. How is liquidity measured?

10. Explain why conservative investors who tend to buy short-term assets differ from short-term traders.

11. Why is there a minimum amount of time that must be committed to any investment program?

12. In a highly inflationary environment, would an investor tend to favor real or financial assets? Why?

13. What is an individual retirement account (IRA)? What are the tax advantages it offers?

14. What two primary components are used to measure the rate of return achieved from an investment?

15. Many people think of risk as the danger of losing money. Is this the same way that risk is defined in finance?

16. What are the three elements that determine how much an investor should require in return from an investment?

17. Explain how an investor receiving a 4 or 5 percent quoted return in an inflationary environment may actually experience a negative real rate of return.

18. In Figure 1–4, what has been the highest return investment category over the 64-year period? What has been the lowest? Assuming risk is measured by the standard deviation, what can you say about the relationship of risk to return in Figure 1–4?

19. Why is *all* risk not thought to be compensated by proportionally higher return?

20. If stocks are combined into a portfolio, is it their systematic or unsystematic risk that is being reduced?

21. Explain the concept of a beta coefficient. Should large beta stocks have higher or lower required rates of return?

22. If required returns in the market turn out to be larger than initially anticipated, what is likely to happen to the market value of a previously purchased asset?

23. In considering Question 22, suggest some factors that might have caused the required rate of return to rise.

PROBLEMS

Rate of return

1. The stock of Dynamo Corporation went from $25 to $28 last year. The firm also paid 50 cents in dividends. Compute the rate of return.

Rate of return

2. In the following year, the dividend was raised to 70 cents. However, a bear market developed toward the end of the year, and the stock price declined from $28 to $22. Compute the rate of return (or loss) to stockholders.

Risk-free rate

3. Assume the real rate of return in the economy is 2.5 percent, the expected rate of inflation is 6 percent, and the risk premium is 5.5 percent. Compute the risk-free rate and required rate of return.

Required return

4. Assume the real return in the economy is 3.5 percent. It is anticipated that the consumer price index will go from 140 to 146.3. Shares of common stock are assumed to have a required return one third higher than the risk-free rate. Compute the required return on common stock.

Price change

5. A bond was originally purchased with a rate of return of 9 percent. The following year inflation caused the required rate of return to increase to 11 percent. Explain the effect of the required return change on the original bondholder.

MARKETBASE-E^{SM} EXERCISES

In the following exercise, please use your MarketBase-E Software and manual to screen for the required portfolios. You will have to figure out how to search through the data to pull out those companies meeting the requirements set down.

Using the MarketBase-E Software, please construct a portfolio of stocks that meet the following requirements:

1. a. You want to create a growth portfolio. For example, suppose growth rates of greater than 15%. How many companies have sales growth greater than 15%?

    b. Screen next on earnings per share growth greater than 15%. How many companies have earnings growth greater than 15%?

    c. Combine the results of the screens from parts (a) and (b) so that the companies in your portfolio have consistent growth in sales and earnings. How many companies have sales and earnings growth greater than 15%?

2. a. You want to create an income portfolio. For example, suppose you want stocks that have a dividend yield greater than 8 percent. How many companies have a dividend yield greater than 8%?

    b. Another criterion to use in selecting high dividend yield stocks is to look for those whose yield is greater than that of a market index like

the Standard & Poor's Index or the Dow Jones Industrial Average. The market has averaged a dividend yield of about 4.7%. How many companies yield more than this market average?

   c. We usually think of stocks with high dividend yields as "safe." Determine whether any of these companies are high risk by seeing if any of them have betas greater than the market beta (which is 1).

3. Are any of the companies you chose in question 1 selected in question 2 as well? What do you conclude from this?

Be prepared to discuss the decision process you went through in selecting your two portfolios.

SELECTED REFERENCES

Rates of Return

Fisher, Lawrence, and James H. Lorie. *A Half-Century of Returns on Stocks and Bonds.* Chicago: The University of Chicago School of Business, 1977.

———. "Rates of Return on Investment in Common Stock: The Year-by-Year Record 1926–1965." *Journal of Business,* July 1968, pp. 219–316.

Ibbotson, Roger G., and Carol F. Fall. "The United States Wealth Portfolio." *The Journal of Portfolio Management,* Fall 1982, pp. 82–92.

———, and Lawrence B. Siegel. "The World Market Wealth Portfolio." *The Journal of Portfolio Management,* Winter 1983, pp. 5–17.

———, and Rex A. Sinquefield. "Stocks, Bonds, Bills, and Inflation: Year-by-Year Historical Returns (1926–1974)." *Journal of Business,* January 1976, pp. 11–47.

Lorie, James H., and Lawrence Fisher. "Rates of Return on Investment in Common Stock." *Journal of Business,* January 1964, pp. 1–17.

"Ranking America's Biggest Brokers." *Institutional Investor,* April 1991, pp. 139–40.

Robichek, Alexander A.; Richard A. Cohn; and John J. Pringle. "Returns on Alternative Media and Implications for Portfolio Construction." *Journal of Business,* July 1972, pp. 427–43.

Rozeff, Micheal S. "Dividend Yields Are Equity Risk Premiums." *Journal of Portfolio Management,* Fall 1984, pp. 68–75.

Salomon Brothers. "Long-Term Returns and Asset Allocation Decisions," June 10, 1991.

Soldofsky, Robert M. "Risk and Return for Long-Term Securities." *Journal of Portfolio Management,* Fall 1984, pp. 57–67.

Stocks, Bonds, Bills and Inflation, 1991 Yearbook. Chicago: R. G. Ibbotson and Associates, Inc., 1991.

Setting Objectives

Blume, Marshall E., and Irwin Friend. "Risk, Investment Strategy and the Long-Run Rates of Return." *The Review of Economics and Statistics,* August 1974, pp. 259–69.

Editors of *Consumer Guide* with Peter A. Dickinson. *How to Make Money during Inflation Recession*. New York: Harper & Row, 1980.

Eilbott, Peter. "Trends in the Value of Individual Stockholdings." *Journal of Business,* July 1974, pp. 339–48.

Estep, Tony. "Manager Style and Sources of Equity Returns." *Journal of Portfolio Management,* Winter 1987, pp. 4–10.

Lease, Ronald C.; Wilbur G. Lewellen; and Gary S. Schlarbaum. "The Individual Investor: Attributes and Attitudes." *Journal of Finance,* May 1974, pp. 413–33.

Rosenberg, Barr. "Prediction of Common Stock Investment Risk." *Journal of Portfolio Management,* Fall 1984, pp. 44–53.

Updegrave, Walter L. "Choosing a Money Manager." *Money,* February 1992, pp. 80–87.

Yakov, Amihud, and Haim Mendelson. "Liquidity, Asset Prices and Financial Policy." *Financial Analysts Journal,* November–December 1991, pp. 56–66.

Career Information and Certification

The CFA Candidate Study and Examination Progress Review. Charlottesville, Va.: Institute for Investment Management and Research, 1992.

"College for Financial Planning Catalog." Denver, Colo.: College for Financial Planning, 1988.

Appendix 1–A: Investor Risk Profile

Investor Risk Profile

1. Liquidity: the ability to quickly realize cash from the sale at fair market value.
2. Safety of Principal: the principal is safe from bankruptcy or default.
3. Price Stability: the market value of the asset does not change in value.
4. Reinvestment Protection: protection against reinvesting cash flow at lower interest rates as interest rates decline.
5. Growth of Capital: the original investment increases over time to create capital gains.
6. Cash Income: the cash income relative to treasury bills.
7. Growth of Income: the ability of the cash income stream to increase over time.
8. Inflation Hedge: the ability of the total return (cash income plus capital gains) to keep pace with inflation over time.

Circle the appropriate response. If the following risk characteristic is very important to you, circle 7. If the risk is of little concern to you, circle 1. The choice of 4 would indicate that you are moderately concerned about this risk characteristic.

1 = not too important >>>>>> 7 = very important

1. Liquidity	1	2	3	4	5	6	7
2. Safety of Principal	1	2	3	4	5	6	7
3. Price Stability	1	2	3	4	5	6	7
4. Reinvestment Protection	1	2	3	4	5	6	7
5. Growth of Capital	1	2	3	4	5	6	7
6. Cash Income	1	2	3	4	5	6	7
7. Growth of Income	1	2	3	4	5	6	7
8. Inflation Hedge	1	2	3	4	5	6	7

A

Total your score: _____

If A totals 48 or more points you want it all. You want to be protected from all risks which is impossible. You can't have your cake and eat it too.

Your answers would be more consistent if you had high numbers in B and low numbers in C or low numbers in B and high numbers in C. Then you would be stating that you understand that several of these risks go together and several do not blend well.

B

Add Scores for items 1, 2, 3, 4, & 6: _____

If B totals between 30 and 35 you are risk averse and want liquid investments that have stable prices, safety of principal and generate an above average cash income. You would probably be comfortable buying: Treasury Bills, U.S. Notes, Utility Common Stocks, Certificates of Deposit, Money Market Funds, Income Oriented Mutual Funds, or small % of Blue Chip Stocks

Your ability to tolerate price instability will determine the length of the maturities you would be willing to buy in the bond market. The more stability you desire, the shorter the maturity you would desire.

C

Add scores for items 5, 7, and 8: _____

If C totals between 18 and 21 you are an aggressive investor seeking growth of income and principal and long-run protection against inflation.

You would probably be comfortable buying: Blue Chip Common Stocks, Growth Stocks, small NASDAQ Stocks, High Yield Bonds, Oil Drilling Partnerships, Gold and Silver, or International Stock Funds

If you have very low numbers in part B between 10 and 12, you are extremely aggressive. If you have moderate numbers in part B between 20 and 25 you would be moderately aggressive.

Appendix 1–B: Career Opportunities in Investments

Career opportunities in the field of investments include positions as a stockbroker, security analyst or portfolio manager, investment banker, or financial planner.

Stockbroker

A stockbroker generally works with the public in advising and executing orders for individual or institutional accounts. Although the broker may have a salary base to cushion against bad times, most of the compensation is in the form of commissions. Successful brokers do quite well financially.

Most brokerage houses look for people who have effective selling skills as well as an interest in finance. In hiring, some (though not all) brokerage houses require prior business experience and a mature appearance. Table 1B–1 lists the 30 largest brokerage houses. Further information on these firms (as well as others not included on the list) can be found in the Securities Industry Yearbook published by the Securities Industry Association, 10 Broad Street, New York, N.Y. 10005.

Security Analyst or Portfolio Manager

Security analysts study various industries and companies and provide research reports to their clientele. A security analyst might work for a brokerage house, a bank trust department, or any other type of institutional investor. Security analysts often specialize in certain industries, such as banking or the airlines. They are expected to have an in-depth knowledge of overall financial analysis as well as the variables that influence their industry.

The role of the financial analyst has been upgraded over the years through a certifying program in which you can become a Chartered Financial Analyst (CFA). There are approximately 15,000 CFAs in the United States and Canada. Achieving this designation calls for a three-year minimum appropriate-experience requirement and extensive testing over a three-year period. Each of the annual exams is six hours long and costs approximately $250 (the fee changes from year to year). There is also an initial, one-time registration fee (currently, $200). You can actually begin taking the exams while still in school (you can complete your experience requirement later).

Table 1B–1   30 Largest U.S. Brokerage Houses

1990 Rank	Name of Firm	Total Capital ($ millions)
1	Merrill Lynch & Co.	$9,567.0
2	Shearson Lehman Brothers	7,499.0
3	Salomon Brothers Holding Co.	7,162.0
4	Goldman, Sachs & Co.	4,700.0
5	Morgan Stanley Group	3,380.4
6	CS First Boston	1,612.0
7	Prudential Securities	1,585.0
8	Paine Webber Group	1,552.9
9	Dean Witter Reynolds	1,405.0
10	Bear, Stearns & Co.	1,387.7
11	Smith Barney, Harris Upham & Co.	1,012.0
12	Donaldson, Lufkin & Jenrette	919.0
13	Nomura Securities International	520.0
14	J. P. Morgan Securities	507.0
15	Kidder, Peabody & Co.	503.0
16	BT Securities Corp.	485.0
17	Citicorp Securities Markets	474.4
18	Shelby Cullom Davis & Co.	410.3
19	A. G. Edwards & Sons	332.0
20	Charles Schwab & Co.	280.0
21	Kemper Securities Group	279.0
22	Daiwa Securities America	270.0
23	UBS Securities	262.0
24	Deutsche Bank Capital Corp.	257.9
25	Oppenheimer & Co.	248.0
26	Aubrey G. Lanston & Co.	246.0
27	Dillon, Read & Co.	241.6
28	Van Kampen Merritt	239.0
29	Nikko Securities Co. International	223.0
30	Chemical Securities	203.0

Source: "Ranking America's Biggest Brokers," *Institutional Investor,* April 1991, pp. 139–40.

Each exam covers the topics shown in Table 1B–2, but the degree of difficulty increases as you progress from Exam I through Exam III. The bars show how much of the information is to be covered in Exams I, II, and III. An undergraduate degree in business with a major in finance or accounting or an economics degree is quite beneficial to the exam process (though other degrees are also acceptable). Of course, educational background must be

Table 1B–2   Areas of Study for CFA Exams

Candidate
Level

I   II   III

Ethical and Professional Standards, Securities Law and Regulations

Applicable Laws and Regulations
Nature and applicability of fiduciary standards
Pertinent laws and regulations
Organization and purpose of governing regulatory bodies

Professional Code and Standards
Code of Ethics
Standards of Professional Conduct
ICFA Bylaws, Article IX
AIMR Bylaws, Article X
AIMR Rules of Procedure

Ethical Standards and Professional Obligations
Relationships with:
(a) clients, customers, public;
(b) corporate managements;
(c) employers, associates, other analysts
Insider information
Supervisory responsibilites
Research reports and investment recommendations
Compensation
Conflicts of interest
Fiduciary duties
Professional misconduct
Investment suitabilty

Identification of Issues and Administration of Ethical Conduct
Fiduciary responsibility
Insider trading
Corporate governance and the institutional investor
The Prudent Man Rule
Competency and proper care
Conflicts of interest in setting and receiving compensation
General business ethical values and obligations
Ethical organization cultures

Candidate
Level

I   II   III

Financial Accounting

Role and Function of Basic Accounting Statements
Income statement
Balance sheet
Statement of cash flows

Using and Interpreting Accounting Statements
Revenue recognition
Inventory costing
Depreciation methods
Investments in marketable securities
Off-balance sheet financing
Troubled debt restructuring
Leases
Postemployment benefits
Income taxes
Prior period adjustments
Earnings per share
Analysis of liquidity cash flow
Foreign currency translation
Intercorporate investments
Business combinations

Special Topics
Goals of financial statement analysis
Implications of efficient market hypothesis
The setting of accounting standards
Adjustments to financial statements
International accounting
Price level adjustments
Current accounting issues

Quantitative Analysis

I   II   III

Introduction to quantitative methods
Mathematics of compound interst, present and future values
Basic statistics and regression analysis
Measures of risk
Introduction to derivative securities
Advanced regression analysis
Basic options and futures pricing
Advanced options and futures pricing

Table 1B–2   Areas of Study for CFA Exams *(continued)*

Candidate Level

Economics

I II III

Focus on Macroeconomics
Concept and measurement of GNP
Business fluctuations and economic forecasting
Inflationary process
Aggregate supply and demand
Macro schools of thought

International Economics
Comparative advantage
International payments
Foreign exchange

Focus on Microeconomics and Analysis
Consumer behavior and business decision making
Costs and supply of goods
Product life cycle
Business structure and regulation

Economic Forecasting
Forecasting tools
Relative success
Determinants of interest rates

Applications to Security Analysis and Portfolio Management
Economic factor returns
Currency hedging

Current Economic Issues
U.S.
Global

Techniques of Analysis—Fixed-Income Securities

I II III

Introduction
Features of fixed-income securities
International fixed-income market

Mathematical Properties
Price/yield relationship
Duration and convexity

Candidate Level

Techniques of Analysis—Fixed-Income Securities *(continued)*

I II III

Credit Evaluation
Bond ratings
Earnings and cash flow analysis
Asset protection
Contractural covenants

Market Analysis
Yield curves
Forecasting interest rates
International
Derivative securities

Portfolio Strategies
Active
Passive
Index
Immunization/dedication

Techniques of Analysis—Equity Securities

I II III

Introduction
Investment environment
Securities markets
Mechanics of securities transactions
History of stock market—rate of return comparisons
Global investing

Financial Analysis
Ratios
Decomposition of ROE
Analysis of financial statements
Capital structure

Valuation Approaches
Earnings
Dividend discount
Cash flow
Asset valuations
Technical analysis
Other
Anomalies

Table 1B–2   Areas of Study for CFA Exams *(concluded)*

Candidate Level

Techniques of Analysis—Equity Securities *(continued)*

I II III

Company Analysis and Evaluation
Fundamental analysis
Industry and economy context
Outline for analysis
Forecasting
Competitive environment
Corporate planning and strategy
Qualitative factors
Example of research report

Investment Strategies
Trends
Market inefficiencies
Psychological influences

Corporate Restructuring
Leveraged buyouts
Takeovers

Venture Capital and Closely Held Companies
Analysis
Valuation

Objective of Analysis—Portfolio Management

I II III

Principles of Financial Asset Management
Definition of portfolio management, basic concepts—return, risk, diversification, portfolio efficiency
Evolution of portfolio management—traditional and recent developments

Investor Objectives, Constraints, and Policies
Liquidity requirement
Return requirement
Risk tolerance
Time horizon
Tax considerations
Regulatory and legal considerations
Unique needs, circumstances, and preferences
Determination of portfolio policies

Asset Allocation
Expected return and risk
Estimation issues

Candidate Level

Objective of Analysis—Portfolio Management *(continued)*

I II III

Asset Allocation *(continued)*
The optimal portfolio
Dynamic strategies

Derivative Security Analysis
Boundaries and basic properties of option values
Arbitrage and option valuation
Option pricing models
Empirical analysis of options
Option pricing theory applied to other assets
Financial futures

Expectational Factors
Social, political, and economic
Capital markets
Individual financial assets

Integration of Portfolio Policies and Expectational Factors
Portfolio construction—asset allocation, active/passive strategies
Monitoring portfolio and responding to change—objectives, constraints and policies, expectational factors
Execution—timing, commission costs, price effects

Portfolio Performance Appraisal
Performance criteria—absolute performance, relative to portfolio objectives and risk level, relative to other portfolios with similar objectives
Measurement of performance—valuation of assets, accounting for income, rates of return and volatility
Evaluation of results—relationship to performance criteria, sources of results
Universe comparisons
Risk adjustment
Benchmark error
Ambiguity between skill and chance
Performance attribution
Normal portfolio
Nonparametric performance measurement
Incentive fees
Gaming performance measurement

Source: *The CFA Candidate Study and Examination Program Review* (Charlottesville, Va.: Institute for Investment Management and Research, 1992), pp. 4, 5.

supplemented with additional study prescribed by the Institute of Chartered Financial Analysts.

The address for more information is: Association for Investment Management and Research, P.O. Box 3668, Charlottesville, Virginia 22903 (phone 804-980-3668).

While many security analysts are not CFAs, those who carry this designation tend to enjoy higher salary and prestige. The number of openings for security analysts has shrunk because of the tight research budgets of many brokerage houses. This came about in the mid-1970s when commission charges went from fixed to freely competitive and fewer dollars were allocated to research.

Despite this situation, really top analysts are still in strong demand, and six-figure salaries for top analysts are common. The magazine *Institutional Investor* picks an all-American team of security analysts, the best in energy, banking, and so on. As we will see later in the text, some academic researchers question the legitimacy of such designations.

Portfolio managers are responsible for managing large pools of funds, and they are generally employed by insurance companies, mutual funds, bank trust departments, pension funds, and other institutional investors. They often rely on the help of security analysts and brokers in designing their portfolios. They not only must decide which stocks to buy or sell, but they also must determine the risk level with the optimum trade-off between the common stock and fixed-income components of a portfolio. Portfolio managers often rise through the ranks of stockbrokers and security analysts.

Investment Banker

Investment bankers are primarily involved in the distribution of securities from the issuing corporation to the public. Investment bankers also advise corporate clients on their financial strategy and may help to arrange mergers and acquisitions.

The investment banker is one of the most prestigious participants in the securities industry. Although the hiring of investment bankers was once closely confined to Ivy League graduates with the right family ties, such is no longer the case. Nevertheless, an MBA and top credentials are usually the first prerequisites.

Financial Planner

A new field of financial planning is emerging to help solve the investment and tax problems of the individual investor. Financial planners may include specially trained representatives of the insurance industry, accountants who have expertise in this area, and Certified Financial Planners (an individual may fall into more than one of these categories).

Certified Financial Planners (CFPs) are so designated by the College for Financial Planning in Denver. The CFP program includes the following parts.

CFP I   Introduction to financial planning.

CFP II   Risk management.

CFP III   Investments.

CFP IV   Tax planning and management.

CFP V   Retirement planning and employee benefits.

CFP VI   Estate planning.

The parts of the CFP program are further described in Table 1B–3. Each part is concluded with a comprehensive written exam. The program normally takes 24 months to complete, and program participants may study on their own or attend formal classes. Appropriate experience requirements are also needed for final certification. Information on the CFP program can be obtained by contacting the College for Financial Planning, 9725 East Hampden Avenue, Denver, Colorado 80231-4993 (phone 303-220-1200).

Table 1B–3   Areas of Study for the CFP (Certified Financial Planner) Program

Program Overview

CFP 1—Introduction to Financial Planning

The purpose of CFP I is threefold. First, it presents the six-stage financial planning process and an introduction to regulations affecting financial planners. Emphasis is placed on constructing financial statements and analyzing the client's current financial situation. Second, CFP I presents three critical areas applicable to financial planning: communication skills, the economic environment, and time value of money concepts. Third, it provides an introduction and overview of the content of CFP Program Parts II through VI.

CFP II—Risk Management

In CFP II, the candidate first studies principles of risk management and insurance to identify a client's risk exposures and select the appropriate risk management techniques. Because transferring risk through the use of insurance is the principal method of handling risk, the candidate is introduced to the basic insurance contract and practical insurance checklists. The study guide deals with property and liability insurance, including homeowners, personal auto, and umbrella policies. The candidate then analyzes life insurance, using a 13-step life insurance selection process that utilizes a 10-step needs determination approach. Finally, medical and disability insurance, social insurance, and compulsory compensation are covered.

CFP III—Investments

CFP III addresses the wide variety of investment vehicles that can be included in the client's personal investment portfolio. In this unit, the candidate learns the importance of the economic and business environment and studies the fundamentals of investing, including tools and mechanics of investing, security markets, tax considerations, sources of investment information, types of investment risk, and the analysis of corporate financial statements. In addition, the characteristics and valuation techniques of several investment vehicles are examined. The case analysis section introduces the portfolio construction and management process for the individual and also incorporates time value of money calculations. In the case section, the candidate is required to recommend asset categories and investment vehicles based on the client's needs, resources, and financial goals.

CFP IV—Tax Planning and Management

The first 11 assignments in CFP IV focus on the fundamentals of individual income taxation, tax

implications of various forms of business, planning for the acquisition and disposition of property, tax-advantaged investments, and tax planning for the family. More technical topics are discussed in the following three assignments: employee compensation issues and planning, special tax computations, and tax traps. Concepts are integrated in the final assignment, which prepares the candidate to evaluate client cases and make recommendations concerning tax planning techniques.

CFP V—Retirement Planning and Employee Benefits

The materials in CFP V begin with a discussion of personal tax-deferred retirement programs available to many working adults and include a framework for use in calculating annual savings needed to reach retirement income goals. Next, the candidate focuses on the key features of qualified retirement plan design, with emphasis on the advantages and disadvantages of specific types of qualified plans for the owners of small- to medium-sized businesses, including a flowchart of the retirement plan development and maintenance process with funding considerations. Government-sponsored plans, including social security, medicare, and federal and civil service and military programs, also are presented. In addition, CFP V examines life, health, and disability insurance; nonqualified deferred compensation; and other commonly provided employee benefits. The case study requires the candidate to select an appropriate qualified retirement plan for a small business owner and to analyze the tax implications of employee benefits.

CFP VI—Estate Planning

The final part of the CFP Program introduces the candidate to the process applied to the development of an estate plan. The fundamentals of federal estate and gift taxation are emphasized, as well as specific exclusion and valuation techniques that reduce the size of the gross estate. CFP VI highlights the characteristics of wills, intestacy, and the probate process. The use of trusts, property ownership forms, and will substitutes also is introduced. Specific assignments address life insurance, lifetime gifting, and coordination of the unified credit with the marital deduction as a part of estate planning, as well as charitable, intrafamily, and business transfers, and postmortem planning techniques that play an important part in estate planning. CFP VI concludes with a comprehensive case analysis that requires the candidate to select appropriate estate planning techniques based on a client's constraints and objectives.

Source: *College of Financial Planning Catalog* (Denver, Colo.: The College for Financial Planning, 1988), pp. 9, 11.

2

Security Markets: Present and Future

■ THE MARKET ENVIRONMENT

Changes in the financial markets that began in the 1980s have continued into the 1990s. Deregulation of financial institutions created new competitors for retail brokerage houses and allowed banks and savings and loan associations to offer discount brokerage services and money market deposit accounts. A series of mergers consolidated financial resources into well-capitalized financial-service-oriented companies. Insurance companies entered the financial services arena by offering mutual funds and annuity products to take advantage of retirement planning and the increased emphasis on individual asset management.

After rapid expansion in the 1980s, many financial service firms hit hard times or failed to live up to their promise in the early 1990s. Prudential never received the benefits expected from its merger with Bache, and in 1991, Prudential changed management and dropped Bache from the name. Drexel Burnham Lambert went bankrupt, and the "junk bond" market deteriorated with it. The recession of 1990–91 hurt commercial real estate in the Northeast, and real estate prices collapsed in other parts of the country as well.

The early 1990s continued to be a difficult time for financial institutions. Savings and loan associations and banks went out of business at a record pace, and the U.S. government insurance programs (Federal Savings and Loan Insurance Corporation and Federal Deposit Insurance Corporation) had to step in to cover depositors' losses. Unfortunately, these insurance funds did not have enough money to pay off depositors, and the U.S. government had to appropriate funds to make the guarantees good. Also, the U.S. government created the Resolution Trust Corporation to handle sales and liquidations of the assets acquired from the government takeover of failed banks and S&Ls. Insurance companies that had loaded up on risky junk bonds and commercial real estate suffered a serious erosion of capital when these two markets caved in. Several insurance companies, including Mutual Benefit Life and Executive Life of California, were taken over by state insurance commissions.

Despite all these retrenchments in the financial industry, investors probably have more alternative investments (securities) currently available to them than at any other time in history. They can buy traditional stocks and bonds, short-term money market instruments, real estate investments, and international securities as well as other riskier securities. One lesson learned is that it makes a difference what firm you use for your investment transactions.

The markets for stocks, bonds, options, and futures continue to become more international in scope as we approach the year 2000. The increased listing of foreign securities on international stock exchanges has led to around-the-world trading from one time zone to another and virtual 24-hour trading in stocks of large international corporations. Trading starts in Japan, is passed to London, then to New York, and back to Japan. The three markets encompass enough time zones to make continuous trading almost a reality. With all this trading, the New York Stock Exchange and Tokyo Stock

Exchange are in a continual battle to be the largest and most important market in the world for trading stock. International markets are covered separately in Chapter 18.

The Chicago Mercantile Exchange (MERC), the Chicago Board Options Exchange, and the Chicago Board of Trade are at the center of options and futures trading. The market for stock options and financial futures has become more integrated with the stock and bond markets through stock index options and futures contracts on stock indexes and bonds. The futures market led by the Chicago Mercantile Exchange is now operating 24 hours a day using a computerized trading system.

Even the traditional markets for common stocks have changed as the over-the-counter market through its NASDAQ automated quotation system has successfully increased its share of equity trades at the expense of the New York and American Stock Exchanges. Computer and communications technology are not only affecting the way securities are traded in the international market systems but are also affecting the way individuals and institutional investors trade. Much of the blame for the Crash of '87 on October 19, 1987, was focused on new trading methods made possible by computerized trading. The Dow Jones Industrial Average declined 508 points, or 22.6 percent, on that day, creating a record drop far in excess of the largest daily decline of October 1929 (slightly over 12 percent).

The impact of these changes as well as a complete discussion of securities available for investment will be presented in various chapters throughout the book. In this chapter, we examine how the market system operates, with an eye toward efficiency, liquidity, and allocation of capital. We then look at the role of the secondary or resale markets for stocks, bonds, and other securities. Finally, we examine some key protective legislation for the investor.

■ MARKET FUNCTIONS

Many times people will call their stockbroker and ask, "How's the market?" What they are referring to is usually the market for common stocks as measured by the Dow Jones Industrial Average, the New York Stock Exchange Index, or some other measure of common stock performance. The stock market is not the only market. There are markets for each different kind of investment that can be made.

A **market** is simply a way of exchanging assets, usually cash, for something of value. It could be a used car, a government bond, gold, or diamonds. There doesn't have to be a central place where this transaction is consummated. As long as there can be communication between buyers and sellers, the exchange can occur. The offering party does not have to own what he sells, but can be an agent acting for the owner in the transaction. For example, in the sale of real estate, the owner usually employs a real estate broker/agent who advertises and sells the property for a percentage commission. Not all markets have the same procedures, but certain trading characteristics are desirable for most markets.

Market Efficiency and Liquidity

In general, an **efficient market** occurs when prices respond quickly to new information, when each successive trade is made at a price close to the preceding price, and when the market can absorb large amounts of securities or assets without changing the price significantly. The more efficient the market, the faster prices react to new information; the closer in price is each successive trade; and the greater the amount of securities that can be sold without changing the price.

For markets to be efficient in this context, they must be liquid. **Liquidity** is a measure of the speed with which an asset can be converted into cash at its fair market value. Liquid markets exist when continuous trading occurs, and as the number of participants in the market becomes larger, price continuity increases along with liquidity. Transaction costs also affect liquidity. The lower the cost of buying and selling, the more likely it is that people will be able to enter the market.

Competition and Allocation of Capital

An investor must realize that all markets compete for funds: stocks against bonds, mutual funds against real estate, government securities against corporate securities, and so on. The competitive comparisons are almost endless. Because markets set prices on assets, investors are able to compare the prices against their perceived risk and expected return and thereby choose assets that enable them to achieve their desired risk-return trade-offs. If the markets are efficient, prices adjust rapidly to new information, and this adjustment changes the expected rate of return and allows the investor to alter investment strategy. Without efficient and liquid markets, the investor would be unable to do this. This allocation of capital occurs on both secondary and primary markets.

Secondary Markets

Secondary markets are markets for existing assets that are currently traded between investors. These markets create prices and allow for liquidity. If secondary markets did not exist, investors would have no place to sell their assets. Without liquidity, many people would not invest at all. Would you like to own $10,000 of Eastman Kodak common stock but be unable to convert it into cash if needed? If there were no secondary markets, investors would expect a higher return to compensate for the increased risk of illiquidity and the inability to adjust their portfolios to new information.

Primary Markets

Primary markets are distinguished by the flow of funds between the market participants. Instead of trading between investors as in the secondary markets, participants in the primary market buy their assets directly from the source of the asset. A common example would be a new issue of corporate bonds sold

by AT&T. You would buy the bonds through a brokerage firm acting as an agent for AT&T. Your dollars would flow to AT&T rather than to another investor. The same would be true of buying a piece of art directly from the artist rather than an art gallery.

Primary markets allow corporations, government units, and others to raise needed funds for expansion of their capital base. Once the assets or securities are sold in the primary market, they begin trading in the secondary market. Price competition in the secondary markets between different risk-return classes enables the primary markets to price new issues at fair prices to reflect existing risk-return relationships. So far, our discussion of markets has been quite general but applicable to most free markets. In the following sections, we will deal with the organization and structure of specific markets.

■ ORGANIZATION OF THE PRIMARY MARKETS: THE INVESTMENT BANKER

The most active participant in the primary market is the investment banker. Since corporations, states, and local governments do not sell new securities daily, monthly, or even annually, they usually rely on the expertise of the investment banker when selling securities.

Underwriting Function

The **investment banker** acts as a middleman in the process of raising funds and, in most cases, takes a risk by underwriting an issue of securities. **Underwriting** refers to the guarantee the investment banking firm gives the selling firm to purchase its securities at a fixed price, thereby eliminating the risk of not selling the whole issue of securities and having less cash than desired. The investment banker may also sell the issue on a **best-efforts** basis where the issuing firm assumes the risk and simply takes back any securities not sold after a fixed period.

Table 2–1 shows the method of distribution for new corporate securities. Unfortunately, the Securities and Exchange Commission stopped collecting and reporting these data, so the table, though dated, is still informative.

We can see by inspecting Table 2–1 that on average the best-efforts offerings in recent years only equal 10 to 15 percent of the total securities sold through public distribution, and the overwhelming majority of these issues were common stock. The more risk the investment banker takes, the higher the selling fee to the corporation. Some stock issues are so risky that the investment banker may charge too much of a fee for underwriting risk and distribution, so the firm chooses the best-efforts method as a cheaper alternative.

With underwriting, once the security is sold, the investment banker will usually make a market in the security, which means active buying and selling to ensure a continuously liquid market and wider distribution. In the case of best efforts and for direct offerings by the issuer, which are even smaller than

Table 2–1   Corporate Issues by Method of Distribution and by Type of Security: 1981–1987
(Primary issues registered under the Security Act of 1933) (in millions)

	Underwritten				Best Efforts			
Year	Total	Debt	Preferred	Common	Total	Debt	Preferred	Common
1987	$84,726	$45,871	$6,332	$32,523	$10,053	$2,031	$162	$ 7,860
1986	85,509	45,755	9,319	30,435	10,914	431	11	10,472
1985	54,377	32,288	4,959	17,130	9,833	504	5	9,324
1984	31,168	21,745	3,258	6,165	8,473	224	9	8,240
1983	40,826	16,049	4,918	19,859	8,454	152	16	8,286
1982	36,674	21,570	4,558	10,546	9,935	1,305	10	8,620
1981	46,678	32,499	1,678	12,451	10,139	1,206	4	8,929

	Direct by Issuer			
Year	Total	Debt	Preferred	Common
1987	$4,552	$ 320	$278	$3,954
1986	4,647	1,753	8	2,886
1985	2,683	308	49	2,326
1984	2,940	520	167	2,253
1983	2,543	339	28	2,176
1982	4,138	2,589	6	1,542
1981	6,689	3,091	10	3,589

Source: U.S. Securities and Exchange Commission.

best efforts, the firm assumes the risk of not raising enough capital and has no guarantees that a continuous market will be made in the company's securities. Table 2–1 shows that most long-term capital-raising efforts by corporations are through investment bankers and not directly by corporations.

Corporations may also choose to raise capital through private placements rather than through a public offering. With a private placement, the company may sell its own securities to a financial institution such as an insurance company, a pension fund, or a mutual fund, or it can engage an investment banker to find an institution willing to buy a large block of stock or bonds. Most private placements involve bonds (debt issues) instead of common stock.

Table 2–2 presents a historical picture of private and public bond offerings. Beginning with 1982, the economic recovery stimulated a huge increase in the volume of bonds issued. Between 1982 and 1984, new debt issues doubled, and between 1984 and 1986, new issues of debt almost tripled as corporations overdosed on their use of debt to finance mergers, acquisitions, leveraged buyouts, and stock repurchases. After 1986, new debt issues increased slightly until 1988 and then turned down as the recession of 1990 decreased the need for

Table 2–2 Gross Proceeds of Corporate Bonds Publicly Offered and Privately Placed (Dollars in millions)

	Total Issues	Publicly Offered		Privately Placed	
		Amount	Percent of Total	Amount	Percent of Total
1990	$276,259	$189,271	68.51%	$ 86,988	31.49%
1989	298,813	181,393	60.70	117,420	39.30
1988	329,919	202,215	61.29	127,704	38.71
1987	301,349	209,279	69.45	92,070	30.55
1986	312,697	231,936	74.17	80,761	25.83
1985	165,754	119,559	72.13	46,195	27.87
1984	109,683	73,357	66.88	36,326	33.12
1983	68,495	47,369	69.16	21,126	30.84
1982	54,066	44,278	81.90	9,788	18.10
1981	44,642	37,653	84.34	6,989	15.66
1980	53,206	41,587	78.16	11,619	21.84
1979	40,208	25,814	64.20	14,394	35.80
1978	36,872	19,815	53.74	17,057	46.26
1977	42,015	24,072	57.29	17,943	42.71
1976	42,380	26,453	62.42	15,927	37.58
1975	42,755	32,583	76.21	10,172	23.79
1970	30,315	25,384	83.73	4,931	16.27
1965	13,720	5,570	40.60	8,150	59.40
1960	8,081	4,806	59.47	3,275	40.53
1955	7,420	4,119	55.51	3,301	44.49
1950	4,920	2,360	47.97	2,560	52.03

Source: Selected issues of the *Federal Reserve Bulletin*.

new capital. As seen in Table 2–2, the basic percentages between publicly offered and privately placed bonds maintained their historical relationship, with publicly offered bonds issued through underwriters being by far the most popular method of raising debt capital.

Distribution

In a public offering, the distribution process is extremely important, and on some large issues, an investment banker does not undertake this alone. Investment banking firms will share the risk and the burden of distribution by forming a group called a *syndicate*. The larger the offering in dollar terms, the more participants there generally are in the syndicate. For example, the tombstone advertisement in Figure 2–1 for Duracell International Inc.'s issue of

common stock shows two groups of investment bankers. One group will sell 9.6 million shares in the United States, and the second group will sell 2.4 million shares in foreign countries. This split of the offering demonstrates the globalization of capital flows from country to country.

Merrill Lynch & Co. is a managing underwriter domestically, and Merrill Lynch International Limited is a managing underwriter internationally. Merrill Lynch was joined by Goldman, Sachs and Bear, Stearns as major partners in the underwriting syndicate. It is interesting to note that ABN AMRO, the largest bank in the Netherlands, is part of the international syndicate while no U.S. banks are part of the domestic syndicate. The international syndicate also includes a division of the French bank Credit Lyonnais; a German bank, Deutsche Bank; and a Belgian bank, Banque Bruxelles Lambert S.A. The Glass Stegal Act of the 1930s prevents U.S. banks from acting as investment bankers, and many major money center banks have complained they are at a competitive disadvantage in the international banking arena.

Firms are usually listed in the tombstone advertisement based on their clout in the investment banking community. The firms at the top of the advertisement usually have taken the biggest dollar position, and the firms at the bottom, a relatively small position. This is true in bond offerings as well as stock offerings. Each participant in the syndicate is responsible for selling the agreed-upon number of bonds or stock.

For most original offerings, the investment banker is extremely important as a link between the original issuer and the security markets. By taking much of the risk, the investment banker enables corporations and others to find needed capital and thus allows investors an opportunity to participate in the ownership of securities through purchase in the secondary markets. Notice that the common stock is priced at $28.75 per share in Figure 2–1. This is the price paid by the public. In the case of Duracell International, the investment bankers took some risk that the stock market would not fall much during the offering period. If the price should fall below $28.75 while the shares are still being sold to the public, the investment bankers in the syndicate will not make their original estimated profit on the issue. If the stock price drops too much below $28.75, the investment bankers could lose money on the offering.

Some significant changes are taking place in the investment banking industry. The number of firms in the syndicate is shrinking, but the size of the individual investment banking firms in the syndicate is increasing as investment bankers expand their capital base to compete in an international market for stocks and bonds. The financial strength of the investment bankers has increased to the point where they are able to assume more risk and thus absorb larger dollar positions in new offerings. Also, the rise of shelf registration under SEC Rule 415 (discussed in Chapter 11) increased the dominance of the large investment bankers. A shelf registration allows issuing firms to register their securities (mostly bonds and notes) with the Securities and Exchange Commission and then sell them at will as funds are needed. This allows investment bankers to buy portions of the shelf issue and immediately resell the

Figure 2-1

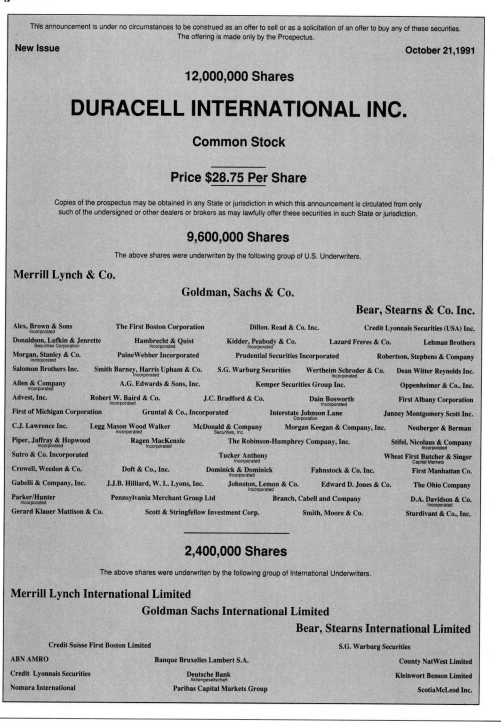

This announcement is under no circumstances to be construed as an offer to sell or as a solicitation of an offer to buy any of these securities. The offering is made only by the Prospectus.

New Issue   **October 21,1991**

12,000,000 Shares

DURACELL INTERNATIONAL INC.

Common Stock

Price $28.75 Per Share

Copies of the prospectus may be obtained in any State or jurisdiction in which this announcement is circulated from only such of the undersigned or other dealers or brokers as may lawfully offer these securities in such State or jurisdiction.

9,600,000 Shares

The above shares were underwriten by the following group of U.S. Underwriters.

Merrill Lynch & Co.

Goldman, Sachs & Co.

Bear, Stearns & Co. Inc.

Alex, Brown & Sons Incorporated	The First Boston Corporation	Dillon. Read & Co. Inc.	Credit Lyonnais Securities (USA) Inc.
Donaldson, Lufkin & Jenrette Securities Corporation	Hambrecht & Quist Incorporated	Kidder, Peabody & Co. Incorporated	Lazard Freres & Co.	Lehman Brothers
Morgan, Stanley & Co. Incorporated	PaineWebber Incorporated	Prudential Securities Incorporated	Robertson, Stephens & Company
Salomon Brothers Inc.	Smith Barney, Harris Upham & Co. Incorporated	S.G. Warburg Securities	Wertheim Schroder & Co. Incorporated	Dean Witter Reynolds Inc.
Allen & Company Incorporated	A.G. Edwards & Sons, Inc.	Kemper Securities Group Inc.	Oppenheimer & Co., Inc.
Advest, Inc.	Robert W. Baird & Co. Incorporated	J.C. Bradford & Co.	Dain Bosworth Incorporated	First Albany Corporation
First of Michigan Corporation	Gruntal & Co., Incorporated	Interstate Johnson Lane Corporation	Janney Montgomery Scott Inc.
C.J. Lawrence Inc.	Legg Mason Wood Walker Incorporated	McDonald & Company Securities, Inc.	Morgan Keegan & Company, Inc.	Neuberger & Berman
Piper, Jaffray & Hopwood Incorporated	Ragen MacKenzie Incorporated	The Robinson-Humphrey Company, Inc.	Stifel, Nicolaus & Company Incorporated
Sutro & Co. Incorporated		Tucker Anthony Incorporated		Wheat First Butcher & Singer Capital Markets
Crowell, Weedon & Co.	Doft & Co., Inc.	Dominick & Dominick Incorporated	Fahnstock & Co. Inc.	First Manhattan Co.
Gabelli & Company, Inc.	J.J.B. Hilliard, W. L. Lyons, Inc.	Johnston, Lemon & Co. Incorporated	Edward D. Jones & Co.	The Ohio Company
Parker/Hunter Incorporated	Pennsylvania Merchant Group Ltd	Branch, Cabell and Company	D.A. Davidson & Co. Incorporated
Gerard Klauer Mattison & Co.	Scott & Stringfellow Investment Corp.	Smith, Moore & Co.	Sturdivant & Co., Inc.

2,400,000 Shares

The above shares were underwriten by the following group of International Underwriters.

Merrill Lynch International Limited

Goldman Sachs International Limited

Bear, Stearns International Limited

Credit Suisse First Boston Limited		S.G. Warburg Securities
ABN AMRO	Banque Bruxelles Lambert S.A.	County NatWest Limited
Credit Lyonnais Securities	Deutsche Bank Aktiengesellschaft	Kleinwort Benson Limited
Nomura International	Paribas Capital Markets Group	ScotiaMcLeod Inc.

securities to institutional clients without forming the normal syndicates or tying up capital for several weeks. Shelf registration is popular with new bond offerings but less so with stock offerings where the traditional syndicated offering tends to exist.

Investment Banking Competition

Table 2–3 shows the top 10 lead underwriters of U.S. debt and equity for the first nine months of 1991 compared to the same period in 1990. It is interesting to note that the top 10 underwriters account for 86.6 percent of total underwriting volume. Volume for 1991 increased by more than 70 percent over 1990 as companies took advantage of falling interest rates and rising stock prices to refund debt and raise new low-cost capital. Merrill Lynch solidified its hold on first place, but Table 2–3 doesn't tell the whole competitive story.

Underwriters are more concerned with the fees from their activities than simply the amount of dollars underwritten. Table 2–4 shows a very different picture of the competition on a fee basis. While Merrill Lynch underwrote 422 issues compared to Goldman, Sachs' 229 issues, the difference in fees was not that different because Goldman Sachs made most of its money underwriting common stock, which carries a higher flotation fee than bonds. Alex Brown, which did not make the top 10 list in Table 2–3, was in third place in Table 2–4 on fees with only 41 issues. Alex Brown specializes in underwriting equity for companies going public for the first time. Bringing private

Table 2–3   Top Underwriters of U.S. Debt and Equity

Manager	Nine Months 1991 Amount (in millions)	Market Share	Nine Months 1990 Amount (in millions)	Rank	Market Share
Merrill Lynch	$ 73,423.9	18.0%	$ 37,726.7	1	15.8%
Goldman, Sachs	47,276.6	11.6	32,169.4	2	13.5
Lehman Brothers	42,830.5	10.5	16,589.1	6	7.0
First Boston	39,795.8	9.7	24,448.8	4	10.3
Salomon Brothers	38,614.7	9.5	25,105.7	3	10.5
Kidder Peabody	36,374.9	8.9	15,799.4	7	6.6
Morgan Stanley	32,127.6	7.9	23,095.7	5	9.7
Bear, Stearns	22,099.1	5.4	15,760.4	8	6.6
Prudential Securities	12,621.7	3.1	10,519.0	9	4.4
Donaldson Lufkin	8,573.5	2.1	4,789.3	11	2.0
Subtotals	$353,758.3	86.6%	$206,003.5		86.5%
Industry Totals	$408,310.9	100.0%	$238,189.5		100.0%

Table 2–4 Disclosed Fees from New Issue Underwriting

Manager	Nine Months 1991			Nine Months 1990			
	Amount (in millions)	Percent of Market	Number of Issues	Amount (in millions)	Rank	Percent of Market	Number of Issues
Merrill Lynch	$ 525.1	17.6	422	$ 237.6	1	15.3	269
Goldman, Sachs	485.8	16.2	229	210.3	2	13.5	159
Alex Brown	294.7	9.9	41	124.8	5	8.0	29
Salomon Brothers	247.8	8.3	160	164.7	3	10.6	108
Morgan Stanley	244.6	8.2	189	108.8	7	7.0	127
First Boston	225.7	7.5	198	129.0	4	8.3	118
Lehman Brothers	184.1	6.2	243	110.2	6	7.1	98
Paine Webber	94.0	3.1	54	83.3	8	5.4	32
Kidder Peabody	79.3	2.7	154	31.7	11	2.0	60
Smith Barney	58.6	2.0	48	58.4	9	3.8	38
Subtotals	$2,439.5	81.5%	1,738	$1,258.8		81.1%	1,038
Industry Totals	$2,991.7	100.0%	2,410	$1,552.7		100.0%	1,524

Source: *The Wall Street Journal,* October 1, 1991, p. C19. Reprinted by permission of *THE WALL STREET JOURNAL,* © 1991 Dow Jones & Company, Inc. All Rights Reserved Worldwide.

companies public for the first time is called an **initial public offering (IPO),** and the flotation costs to the selling company are much higher than offerings of new stock in public companies, called secondary offerings.

Underwriting competition is like a decathlon; there are many events for each contestant. Table 2–5 on page 50 presents the total size of each market and the leading investment banker for each market. This table defines the market niches and the specialized nature of the investment banking industry.

The worldwide market is becoming more important to all investment bankers. Table 2–6 on page 51 looks at the top 10 Euromarket underwriters. Four Japanese investment bankers are in the top 10, three U.S. firms, one Swiss, one German, and one French underwriter. While these Euromarkets are about half the size of U.S. markets, they will become increasingly important as the former Communist eastern block countries turn to private enterprise and capital markets for economic expansion.

■ ORGANIZATION OF THE SECONDARY MARKETS

Once the investment banker or the Federal Reserve (for U.S. government securities) has sold a new issue of securities, it begins trading in secondary markets that provide liquidity, efficiency, continuity, and competition. The **organized exchanges** fulfill this need in a central location where trading occurs between buyers and sellers. The **over-the-counter markets** also provide markets for exchange but not in a central location. We will first examine the organized exchanges and then the over-the-counter markets.

Table 2–5   Who's No. 1 in Each Market?

	Nine Months 1991		Nine Months 1990	
	Amount*	Top-Ranked Mgr.	Amount*	Top-Ranked Mgr.
U.S. domestic	$415.83[†]	Merrill Lynch	$238.24	Merrill Lynch
Straight debt	364.09	Merrill Lynch	214.46	Merrill Lynch
Convertible debt	6.03	Merrill Lynch	4.07	Merrill Lynch
Junk debt	3.41	Merrill Lynch	1.30	Bear, Stearns
Invest-grade debt	135.12	Merrill Lynch	72.75	Merrill Lynch
Mortgage debt	183.12	Kidder Peabody	112.24	Kidder Peabody
Asset-backed debt	39.83	First Boston	26.64	Merrill Lynch
Collateral securities	226.65	Kidder Peabody	145.22	Goldman, Sachs
Preferred stock	9.45	Merrill Lynch	3.56	Merrill Lynch
Common stock	36.26	Goldman, Sachs	16.14	Goldman, Sachs
IPOs	14.70	Alex Brown	8.51	Alex Brown
Closed-end funds	5.49	Alex Brown	4.12	Alex Brown
Taxable munis	2.71	Goldman, Sachs	1.76	Lehman
International debt	210.45	Nomura	139.35	Nomura
International equity	8.07	Goldman, Sachs	7.12	Nomura
Worldwide issues	634.36	Merrill Lynch	384.71	Merrill Lynch
U.S. issuers[‡]	416.69	Merrill Lynch	240.98	Merrill Lynch

*All managers   [†]Dollars in billions.   [‡]Worldwide.
Source: *The Wall Street Journal,* October 1, 1991, p. C19. Reprinted by permission of *THE WALL STREET JOURNAL,* © 1991 Dow Jones & Company, Inc. All Rights Reserved Worldwide.

Organized Exchanges

Organized exchanges are either national or regional, but both are organized in a similar fashion. Exchanges have a central trading location where securities are bought and sold in an auction market by brokers acting as agents for the buyer and seller. Stocks usually trade at various trading posts on the floor of the exchange. Brokers are registered members of the exchanges, and their number is fixed by each exchange. The national exchanges are the New York Stock Exchange (NYSE) and the American Stock Exchange (AMEX). Both these exchanges are governed by a board of directors consisting of one-half exchange members and one-half public members.

The regional exchanges began their existence trading securities of local firms. As the firms grew, they became listed on the national exchanges, but they also continued to trade on the regionals. Many cities, such as Chicago, Cincinnati, Baltimore, Detroit, and Boston, have regional exchanges. Today, most of the trading on these exchanges is done in nationally known companies. Trading in the same companies is common between the NYSE and such regionals as the Midwest Exchange in Chicago, the Pacific Coast Exchange in San Francisco and Los Angeles, and the smaller regionals. About 90 percent of

Table 2–6   Top Euromarket Underwriters (Non-U.S. debt and equity)

	Nine Months		
	1991		1990
Manager	**Amount ($ millions)**	**% of Market**	**% of Market**
Nomura Securities	$ 18,012.7	9.0	9.2
First Boston CS	14,403.0	7.2	5.7
Deutsche Bank	13,350.2	6.7	9.6
Daiwa Securities	11,279.7	5.7	3.7
Banque Paribas	10,825.4	5.4	3.5
Goldman, Sachs	10,503.2	5.3	2.9
Merrill Lynch	9,463.9	4.7	3.3
Morgan Stanley	8,231.8	4.6	1.8
Yamaichi Securities	8,542.0	4.3	2.3
Nikko Securities	7,443.4	3.7	2.9
Subtotals	$113,055.3	56.6%	44.8%
Industry Totals	$199,594.8	100%	100%

Source: *The Wall Street Journal,* October 1, 1991, p. C19. Reprinted by permission of *THE WALL STREET JOURNAL,* © 1991 Dow Jones & Company, Inc. All Rights Reserved Worldwide.

the companies traded on the Midwest and Pacific Coast Exchanges are also listed on the NYSE. This is referred to as dual trading.

October 20, 1987, the day after the crash of '87, was the busiest day in the history of the New York Stock Exchange. On October 19, 1987, the day of the crash, 604 million shares traded, and on the next day, 608 million shares traded. Table 2–7 shows this information as well as data on New York Stock Exchange listed firms that trade on other markets also. The all-time composite trade volume for NYSE firms trading *on all markets* was 661.8 million shares on October 19 (the day of the crash).

Consolidated Tape

Although dual listing and trading have existed for some time, it was not until June 16, 1975, that a consolidated ticker tape was instituted. This allows brokers on the floor of one exchange to see prices of transactions on other exchanges in the dually listed stocks. Any time a transaction is made on a regional exchange or over-the-counter in a security listed on the NYSE, this transaction and any made on the floor of the NYSE are displayed on the composite tape. The composite price data keep markets more efficient and prices more competitive between exchanges at all times.

The NYSE and AMEX are both national exchanges and for years did not allow dual listing of companies traded on their exchanges, but as of August 1976, securities were able to be dually listed between these exchanges. There doesn't

Table 2–7	Data on Trading Volume (Breakdown of trading in NYSE stocks)		
By Market	**Monday, October 19, 1987**	**Tuesday, October 20, 1987**	**1987 Daily Average**
New York	604,330,000	608,120,000	188,937,980
Midwest	21,666,900	24,326,200	12,529,086
Pacific	12,743,900	12,897,600	6,617,917
NASD	4,341,330	4,516,920	4,156,177
Philadelphia	6,602,100	6,294,600	3,072,138
Boston	4,788,100	4,223,900	2,825,407
Cincinnati	1,399,500	1,367,100	928,094
Instinet	261,900	128,100	193,498
Composite	661,874,420	656,133,730	219,260,296

Source: *New York Stock Exchange Fact Book,* 1988, p. 6. *The Wall Street Journal,* October 21, 1987, page 57. Reprinted by permission of *THE WALL STREET JOURNAL,* © 1987 by Dow Jones & Company, Inc. All Rights Reserved Worldwide.

seem to be any advantage to this since both are located in New York City, and traditionally, shares that trade on one exchange are not traded on the other.

Table 2–8 displays the number of trades (not number of shares) on all markets participating in the consolidated tape. Trading volume has been rather stable between 1980 and 1985 and reached a new plateau between 1986 and 1990, with 1987 being the peak year. While volume has steadily increased overall, the New York Stock Exchange is getting a smaller piece of the total trades in its own listed stock. The NYSE has seen its percentage of consolidated tape trades fall from 85.37 percent in 1980 to 66.17 percent in 1990 (bottom half of Table 2–8). The NYSE is seeing tough competition from other exchanges and the over-the-counter NASD system, which almost tripled its consolidated tape trades from 1988 (2.91 percent) to 1990 (8.53 percent). Competition in the 1990s is expected to become even more intense, and the NYSE faces a possible loss of prestige and profits if it can't reverse this long-term decline in market share.

Listing Requirements for Firms

Securities can be traded on an exchange only if they have met the listing requirements of the exchange and have been approved by the board of governors of that exchange. All exchanges have minimum requirements that must be met before trading can occur in a company's common stock. Since the NYSE is the biggest exchange and generates the most dollar volume in large, well-known companies, its listing requirements are the most restrictive.

Initial Listing Although each case is decided on its own merits, according to the *NYSE Fact Book,* the minimum requirements for a company to be listed on the New York Stock Exchange for the first time are as follows:

Table 2–8   Number of Trades Shown on the Consolidated Tape

Consolidated Tape Trades by Market, 1990

Year	NYSE*	AMEX	PSE	MSE	PHLX	BSE	CSE	NASD	INST	Total
1990	19,148,610	0	2,355,273	2,810,029	875,100	1,090,871	181,470	2,468,490	9,797	28,939,640
1989	19,727,062	0	2,378,200	2,970,627	965,448	900,529	125,215	1,419,914	7,794	28,494,789
1988	17,738,727	0	2,051,304	2,366,607	782,674	565,878	84,176	706,539	7,678	24,303,583
1987	22,634,989	0	2,863,513	2,749,171	1,074,834	712,071	81,236	630,559	6,412	30,752,785
1986	18,971,943	0	2,757,958	2,223,131	953,009	588,062	76,833	522,711	8,260	26,101,907
1985	14,648,648	0	1,876,326	1,609,287	752,781	428,112	62,307	334,837	19,163	19,731,461
1984	12,953,946	0	1,534,707	1,365,991	705,206	305,106	58,109	241,424	14,733	17,179,222
1983	15,050,791	43	1,661,907	1,318,868	751,002	241,520	94,171	248,820	7,250	19,374,372
1982	12,609,104	13	1,326,460	944,862	628,217	159,865	134,106	231,036	6,304	16,039,967
1981	11,701,098	673	910,634	644,176	547,219	129,593	123,911	136,519	3,329	14,197,152
1980	13,074,382	1,021	817,957	548,416	530,659	118,000	108,169	112,923	3,019	15,314,546

Distribution of Consolidated Tape Trades, 1980–1990

Year	NYSE*	AMEX	PSE	MSE	PHLX	BSE	CSE	NASD	INST	Total
1990	66.17%	0.00%	8.14%	9.71%	3.02%	3.77%	0.63%	8.53%	0.03%	100.00%
1989	69.23	0.00	8.35	10.43	3.39	3.16	0.44	4.98	0.03	100.00
1988	72.99	0.00	8.44	9.74	3.22	2.33	0.35	2.91	0.03	100.00
1987	73.60	0.00	9.31	8.94	3.50	2.32	0.26	2.05	0.02	100.00
1986	72.68	0.00	10.57	8.52	3.65	2.25	0.29	2.00	0.03	100.00
1985	74.24	0.00	9.51	8.16	3.82	2.17	0.32	1.70	0.10	100.00
1984	75.40	0.00	8.93	7.95	4.10	1.78	0.34	1.41	0.09	100.00
1983	77.68	0.00	8.58	6.81	3.88	1.25	0.49	1.28	0.04	100.00
1982	78.61	0.00	8.27	5.89	3.92	1.00	0.84	1.44	0.04	100.00
1981	82.42	0.00	6.41	4.54	3.85	0.91	0.87	0.96	0.02	100.00
1980	85.37	0.01	5.34	3.58	3.47	0.77	0.71	0.74	0.02	100.00

*Data after 1988 include rights and warrants.
Participating markets: NYSE, New York; AMEX, American; PSE, Pacific; MSE, Midwest; PHLX, Philadelphia; BSE, Boston; CSE, Cincinnati; NASD, National Association of Securities Dealers; INST, Instinet.
Source: *New York Stock Exchange Fact Book,* 1991, p. 23.

1. Demonstrated earning power under competitive conditions of: *either* $2.5 million before federal income taxes for the most recent year and $2 million pre-tax for each of the preceding two years *or* an aggregate for the last three fiscal years of $6.5 million *together with* a minimum in the most recent fiscal year of $4.5 million. (All three years must be profitable.)

2. Net tangible assets of $18 million, but greater emphasis is placed on the aggregate market value of the common stock.

3. Market value of publicly held shares currently equal to $18 million, but subject to adjustment within the following limits.

Maximum $18,000,000
Minimum   9,000,000
Present (12/1/91)   18,000,000

4. A total of 1.1 million common shares publicly held.
5. *Either* 2,000 holders of 100 shares or more *or* 2,200 total stockholders *together with* average monthly trading volume (for the most recent six months) of 100,000 shares.

The other exchanges have requirements covering the same areas, but the amounts are smaller.

Corporations desiring to be listed on exchanges have decided that public availability of the stock on an exchange will benefit their shareholders by providing liquidity to owners or by allowing the company a more viable means for raising external capital for growth and expansion. The company must pay annual listing fees to the exchange and some fees based on the number of shares traded each year.

Delisting   The New York Stock Exchange also has the authority to remove (delist) a security from trading when the security fails to meet certain criteria. There is much latitude in these decisions, but generally, a company's security may be considered for delisting if there are fewer than 1,200 round-lot (100 shares) owners, 600,000 shares or fewer in public hands, and a market value of the security of less than $5 million. A company that easily exceeded these standards on first being listed may fall below them during hard times.

Membership for Market Participants

We've talked about listing requirements for corporations on the exchange, but what about the investment houses or traders that service the listed firms or trade for their own account on the exchanges? These privileges are reserved for a select number of people. The NYSE has 1,366 members who own "seats," which may be leased or sold with the approval of the NYSE. Multiple seats are owned by many member firms such as Merrill Lynch, so the number of member organizations totaled 1,192. In recent years, the price of NYSE seats has ranged from a low of $35,000 in 1977 to a high of $1,150,000 in 1987. Prices fluctuate with market trends, going up in bull markets and down in bear markets. The members owning these seats can be divided into five distinct categories, each with a specific job.

Commission Brokers   The **commission brokers** represent commission houses, such as Merrill Lynch or Shearson Lehman Hutton, that execute

orders on the floor of the exchange for customers of that firm. Many of the larger retail brokerage houses have more than one commission broker on the floor of the exchange. If you call your account executive (stockbroker) and place an order to buy 100 shares of Exxon, the account executive will teletype your order to the NYSE where it will be transmitted to one of the firm's commission brokers who will go to the appropriate trading post and execute the order.

Floor Brokers   You can imagine that commission brokers could get very busy running from post to post on a heavy volume day. In times like these, they will rely on some help from **floor brokers,** who are registered to trade on the exchange but are not employees of a member firm. Instead, floor brokers own their own seat and charge a small fee for services (usually around $4 per 100 shares).

Registered Traders   The **registered traders** own their own seats and are not associated with a member firm (such as Merrill Lynch). They are registered to trade for their own accounts and do so with the objective of earning a profit. Because they are members, they don't have to pay commissions on these trades; but in so trading, they help to generate a continuous market and liquidity for the market in general. There is always the possibility that these traders could manipulate the market if they acted in mass, and for that reason, the exchanges have rules governing their behavior and limiting the number of registered traders at one specific trading post.

Odd-Lot Dealers   Odd lots (less than 100 shares) are not traded on the main floor of the exchange, so if a customer wants to buy or sell 20 shares of AT&T, the order will end up being processed by an **odd-lot dealer.** Dealers own their own inventory of the particular security and buy and sell for their own accounts. If they accumulate 100 shares, they can sell them in the market, or if they need 20 shares, they can buy 100 in the market and hold the other 80 shares in inventory. A few very large brokerage firms, such as Merrill Lynch, have begun making their own odd-lot market in actively traded securities, and it is expected that this trend will become common at other large commission houses. Odd-lot trading on other exchanges is usually handled by the specialist in the particular stock.

Specialists   The **specialists** are a very important segment of the exchange and make up about one fourth of total membership. Each stock traded has a specialist assigned to it, and most specialists are responsible for more than one stock. Specialists have two basic duties with regard to the stocks they supervise. First, they must handle any special orders that commission brokers or floor brokers might give. For example, a special order could limit the price

someone is willing to pay for General Telephone (GTE) stock to $30 per share for 100 shares. If the commission broker reaches the General Telephone trading post and GTE is selling at $31 per share, the broker will leave the order with the specialist to execute if and when the stock of GTE falls to $30 or less. The specialist puts these special limit orders in his "book" with the date and time entered so he can execute orders at the same price by the earliest time of receipt. A portion of the broker's commission is then paid to the specialist.

The second major function of specialists is to maintain continuous, liquid, and orderly markets in their assigned stocks. This is not a difficult function in the actively traded securities, such as General Motors, Du Pont, and AT&T, but it becomes more difficult in those stocks where there are no large, active markets. For example, suppose you placed an order to buy 100 shares of Ametek at the market price. If the commission broker reaches the Ametek trading post and no seller is present, the broker can't wait for one to appear since he has other orders to execute. Fortunately, the broker can buy the shares from the specialist who acts as a dealer—in this case buying for and selling from his own inventory. To ensure ability to maintain continuous markets, the exchange requires a specialist to have $500,000 or enough capital to own 5,000 shares of the assigned stock, whichever is greater. At times, specialists are under tremendous pressure to make a market for securities. A classic case occurred when President Eisenhower had a heart attack in the 1950s and specialists stabilized the market by absorbing wave after wave of sell orders.

The New York Stock Exchange keeps statistics on specialist performance and their ability to maintain price continuity, quotation spreads, market depth, and price stabilization. These data are given in Table 2–9. Price continuity is measured by the size of the price variation in successive trades. Column 1 is the percentage of transactions with no change in price or a minimum change of ⅛ of a dollar. Column 2 presents the percentage of the quotes where the bid and asked price was equal to or less than ¼ of a point. Market depth (Column 3) is displayed as a percentage of the time that 1,000 to 3,000 shares of volume failed to move the price of the stock more than ⅛ of a point. Finally, the NYSE expects specialists to stabilize the market by buying and selling from their own accounts against the prevailing trend. This is measured in Column 4 as the percentage of shares purchased below the last different price and the percentage of shares sold above the last different price.

While these statistics are not 100 percent, it would be quite unreasonable for us to expect specialists to maintain that kind of a record in all types of markets. However, some critics of the specialist system on the NYSE think these performance measures could be improved by having more than one specialist for each stock. Many market watchers believe competing dealers on the over-the-counter market provide more price stability and fluid markets than the NYSE specialist system.

Somewhat in response to these criticisms, the New York Stock Exchange created computer systems that help the specialists manage order inflows more efficiently. **Super Dot** (designated order transfer system) allows NYSE

Table 2–9 Market Quality and Specialists' Stabilization: 1981–1990

	Price Continuity	Quotation Spreads	Market Depth*	Stabilization Rate
1990	95.8%	84.5%	84.4%	83.1%
1989	95.9	81.5	87.1	86.0
1988	94.1	78.7	92.1	88.1
1987	89.0	67.5	87.2	90.7
1986	90.2	69.8	89.2	90.2
1985	92.3	70.6	89.8	89.2
1984	91.1	64.7	88.0	88.8
1983	88.7	60.7	86.2	90.0
1982	89.5	65.1	85.2	88.9
1981	87.2	60.4	81.6	90.2

*After 1988 based on 3,000 shares of volume—all other years in 1,000 shares of volume.
Source: *New York Stock Exchange Fact Book,* 1991, p. 20.

member firms to electronically transmit all market and limit orders directly to the specialist at the trading post or the member trading booth. This order routing system takes orders and communicates executions of the orders directly back to the member firm on the same electronic circuit.

As a part of Super Dot, specialists are informed through OARS (Opening Automated Report Service) of market orders received before the opening bell. This pre-opening knowledge allows specialists to know whether the supply and demand for a stock is in balance because OARS pairs the buy and sell orders. If a sell imbalance exists, the specialist knows before opening that the price will open lower than yesterday's closing price.

The NYSE reports that 98.5 percent of all market orders on Super Dot were received, processed, and reported back to the originator within two minutes. Another feature of Super Dot that greatly aids the specialist is the **Electronic Book.** This data base covers stocks listed on the NYSE and keeps track of limit orders and market orders for the specialist. You can imagine the great improvement in recording, reporting, and error elimination over the old manual entry in the "specialist's book."

■ OTHER ORGANIZED EXCHANGES

The American Stock Exchange

The American Stock Exchange trades in smaller companies than the NYSE, and except for one dually listed company on the NYSE in 1983, the stocks traded on the AMEX are different from those on any other exchange. Because

many of the small companies on the AMEX do not meet the liquidity needs of large institutional investors, the AMEX has been primarily a market for individual investors.

In an attempt to differentiate itself from the NYSE, the AMEX traded warrants in companies for many years before the NYSE allowed them. Even now, the AMEX has warrants listed for stocks trading on the NYSE. The AMEX also trades put and call options on approximately 200 stocks, with most of the underlying common stocks being listed on the NYSE. This market has been a stabilizing force for the AMEX.

To become more innovative and to attract more business, the American Stock Exchange announced plans in 1991 to trade warrants in foreign stock indexes. As a first step to this plan, the AMEX began providing up-to-the-minute information on:

Euro Top 100: 100 actively traded stocks in nine European countries.

Eurotrack 100: 100 stocks in 10 countries excluding England.

FT-SE 100: 100 large British stocks traded in London.

Eurotrack: Eurotrack 100 and FT-SE 100 combined.

FT-Actuaries: 835 of largest companies in 14 European countries.

CAC 40: 40 selected foreign stocks traded on the Paris Bourse.

Additionally, in an attempt to compete more directly with the NASDAQ for the market in small stocks, the AMEX created a new market in March 1992 for *emerging companies.*

The Chicago Board Options Exchange

Trading in call options started on the Chicago Board Options Exchange (CBOE) in April 1973 and proved very successful. The number of call options listed grew from 16 in 1973 to over 500 in 1991. A **call option** gives the owner the right to buy 100 shares of the underlying common stock at a set price for a certain period. The CBOE standardized call options into three-month, six-month, and nine-month expiration periods on a rotating monthly series. Other sequences have since been developed. The CBOE and the AMEX currently have many options that are dually listed, and the competition between them is fierce. The two exchanges also trade put options (options to sell). A number of smaller regional exchanges also provide for option trading, and the New York Stock Exchange began trading options in 1985.

A new wrinkle in the options game has been options on stock market indexes or industry groupings (called subindexes). The CBOE offers puts and calls on the Standard & Poor's 100 Index; the NYSE has options on the NYSE Index; the AMEX has options on the AMEX Market Value Index, and so on. More about these markets will be presented in Chapter 17.

Futures Markets

Futures markets have traditionally been associated with commodities and, more recently, also with financial instruments. Purchasers of commodity futures own the right to buy a certain amount of the commodity at a set price for a specified period. When the time runs out (expires), the futures contract will be delivered unless sold before expiration. One major futures market is the Chicago Board of Trade, which trades corn, oats, soybeans, wheat, silver, plywood, and Treasury bond futures. There are also other important futures markets in Chicago, Kansas City, Minneapolis, New York, and other cities. These markets are very important as hedging markets and help set commodity prices. They are also known for their wide price swings and volatile speculative nature.

In recent years, trading volume has increased in foreign exchange futures such as the West German mark, Japanese yen, and British pound as well as in Treasury bill and Treasury bond futures. One recent product having a direct effect in the stock market is the development of futures contracts on stock market indexes. The Chicago Mercantile Exchange, Chicago Board of Trade, New York Futures Exchanges (a division of the NYSE), and the Kansas City Board of Trade have all developed contracts in separate market indexes such as the Standard & Poor's 500 and the Value Line Index. Market indexes will be presented in the following chapter, and we will spend more time discussing futures markets in Chapters 16 and 17.

■ OVER-THE-COUNTER MARKETS

Unlike the organized exchanges, the over-the-counter markets (OTC) have no central location where securities are traded. Being traded over-the-counter implies the trade takes place by telephone or electronic device and dealers stand ready to buy or sell specific securities for their own accounts. These dealers will buy at a bid price and sell at an asked price that reflects the competitive market conditions. By contrast, brokers on the organized exchanges merely act as agents who process orders. The National Association of Securities Dealers (NASD), a self-policing organization of dealers, requires at least two market makers (dealers) for each security, but often there are 5 or 10 or even 20 for government securities. As previously mentioned, the multiple-dealer function in the over-the-counter market is an attractive feature for many companies in comparison to the single specialist arrangement on the NYSE and other organized exchanges.

OTC markets exist for stocks, corporate bonds, mutual funds, federal government securities, state and local bonds, commercial paper, negotiable certificates of deposits, and various other securities. These securities make the OTC the largest of all markets in the United States in dollar terms.

In the OTC market, the difference between the bid and asked price is the spread; it represents the profit the dealer earns by making a market. For example,

if XYZ common stock is bid 10 and asked 10½, this simply means the dealer will buy at least 100 shares at $10 per share or will sell 100 shares at $10.50 per share. If prices are too low, more buyers than sellers will appear, and the dealer will run out of inventory unless he raises prices to attract more sellers and balances the supply and demand. If his price is at equilibrium, he will match an equal number of shares bought and sold, and for his market-making activities, he will earn 50 cents per share traded. Although in the future many OTC stocks will no longer be reported on the basis of bid and asked prices but simply at a closing price, the concept of dealer spreads will remain.

Actually, the over-the-counter stock market has several segments and the National Association of Securities Dealers divides the more than 6,000 companies into the National Market System, the national list, and regional and local companies. Stocks in the National Market System receive the quickest and best reporting of their trading activity.

Stocks of companies such as Apple Computer, Coors Brewing, Intel, and MCI Communications can be found on the National Market System. These companies all have a diversified geographical shareholder base, while the national list and regional or local companies are usually smaller or closely held by management or the founding family. The small local stocks may not appear in *The Wall Street Journal* but will be found on the financial pages of large city newspapers in Dallas, Cleveland, Chicago, Minneapolis, Los Angeles, and other major cities under the heading "Local Over-the-Counter Markets." Many are also listed on special pink sheets put out by investment houses. OTC markets have always been very popular for smaller bank and insurance stocks because these stocks do not generate enough trading volume or have enough stockholders to merit their listing on the organized exchanges. Another reason is that many have only local interest.

NASDAQ

NASDAQ stands for the National Association of Securities Dealers Automated Quotations system. This system is linked by a computer network and provides up-to-the-minute quotations on approximately 5,000 of the OTC stocks traded on the NASDAQ system.

Table 2–10 presents the qualification standards for initial and continued listing on the NASDAQ National Market System. The big difference between the OTC standards and the NYSE listing requirements is that the OTC requires fewer shareholders of record, smaller assets, and less net income. While these qualifications allow many small companies to be included in the trading system, they do not preclude many large companies such as Apple Computer or MCI from trading. In fact, the National Association of Securities Dealers estimates that over 600 companies on the National Market System would be eligible for listing on the New York Stock Exchange, and many more would be eligible for the American Stock Exchange.

Table 2–10 NASDAQ National Market System Quantitative Standards

Standard	Initial Nasdaq/NMS Inclusion		Continued Nasdaq/ NMS Inclusion
	Alternative 1	Alternative 2	
Registration under Section 12(g) of the Securities Exchange Act of 1934 or equivalent	Yes	Yes	Yes
Net tangible assets★	$4 million	$12 million	$2 million or $4 million†
Net income (in last fiscal year or two of last three fiscal years)	$400,000	—	—
Pretax income (in last fiscal year or two of last three fiscal years)	$750,000	—	—
Public float (shares)‡	500,000	1 million	200,000
Operating history	—	3 years	—
Market value of float	$3 million	$15 million	$1 million
Minimum bid	$5	—	—
Shareholders	—	400	400§
If between 0.5 and 1 million shares publicly held	800	—	—
If more than 1 million shares publicly held	400	—	—
If more than 0.5 million shares publicly held and average daily volume in excess of 2,000 shares	400	—	—
Number of market makers	2	2	2

NASDAQ National Market System Qualitative Standards

To qualify for admission to NASDAQ/NMS, a company must adhere to corporate governance standards that require it to:

1. Have a minimum of two independent directors on its board.
2. Maintain an Audit Committee composed of a majority of independent directors.
3. Provide shareholders with annual reports and make quarterly as well as other reports available to them.
4. Examine all related-party trades for potential conflicts of interest.
5. Hold an annual meeting of shareholders and provide notice of such meeting to the NASD.
6. Specify in its bylaws a quorum of not less than 33⅓% of the outstanding shares of the company's common stock.
7. Solicit proxies and provide statements for all meetings of shareholders, as well as file such proxy solicitations with the NASD.
8. Secure shareholder approval for certain transactions and increases in the amount of stock outstanding.
9. Execute a NASDAQ/NMS listing agreement

★"Net tangible assets" means total assets (excluding goodwill) minus total liabilities.
†Continued NASDAQ/NMS inclusion requires net tangible assets of at least $2 million if the issuer has sustained losses from continuing operations and/or net losses in two of its three most recent fiscal years or $4 million if the issuer has sustained losses from the continuing operations and/or net losses in three of its four most recent fiscal years.
‡Public float is defined as shares that are not "held directly or indirectly by any officer or director of the issuer and by any person who is the beneficial owner of more than 10 percent of the total shares outstanding. . . ."
§Or 300 shareholders of round lots.
Note: Foreign issuers may be exempted if compliance would be in contravention of law or business practice in the issuers' country of domicile.
Source: *NASDAQ 1991 Fact Book.*

During the mid-1980s, many articles appeared comparing the New York Stock Exchange and the American Stock Exchange to the over-the-counter market and reporting on the inroads the National Association of Securities Dealers had made in retaining companies on the automated quotation system. Traditionally, companies that would reach listing qualifications for the exchanges would jump to the AMEX and then eventually to NYSE. This cannot be assumed to happen anymore.

NASDAQ has taken its place in world equity markets. Figure 2–2 shows the relative size of worldwide markets for 1990 based on total dollar trading volume. The NYSE and Tokyo exchange are almost even, followed by London and Germany's exchanges. In fifth place is the NASDAQ market at more than 10 times the AMEX volume. The multiple-dealer system, efficient computerized quotation systems, and enhanced reporting capability are several reasons for the increased competitive nature of the OTC markets.

Debt Securities Traded Over-the-Counter

Debt securities also trade over-the-counter. Actually, government securities of the U.S. Treasury provide the largest dollar volume of transactions on the OTC and account for billions of dollars in trades each week. These securities are traded by government securities dealers who are often associated with a division of a large financial institution, such as a New York, Chicago, or West Coast money market bank or a large brokerage house like Merrill Lynch. These dealers make markets in government securities, such as Treasury bills and Treasury bonds, or federal agency securities like Federal National Mortgage Association issues.

Municipal bonds of state and local governments are traded by specialized municipal bond dealers who, in most cases, work for large commercial banks. Commercial paper, representing unsecured, short-term corporate debt, is traded directly by *finance* companies, but a large portion of commercial paper sold by *industrial* companies is handled by OTC dealers specializing in this market. Every security has its own set of dealers and its own distribution system. On markets where large dollar trades occur, the spread between the bid and asked price could be as little as $1/16$ or $1/32$ of \$1 per \$1,000 of securities.

The Third and Fourth Markets: Part of Over-the-Counter Trading

Before the mid-1970s, commissions on the NYSE were fixed. This meant the same commission schedule applied to all transactions of a given size, and one broker could not undercut the other on the New York Stock Exchange. Several OTC dealers, most notably Weeden & Co., decided to make a market in about 200 of the most actively traded NYSE issues and to do this at a much smaller cost than the NYSE commission structure would allow. This trading

Figure 2–2

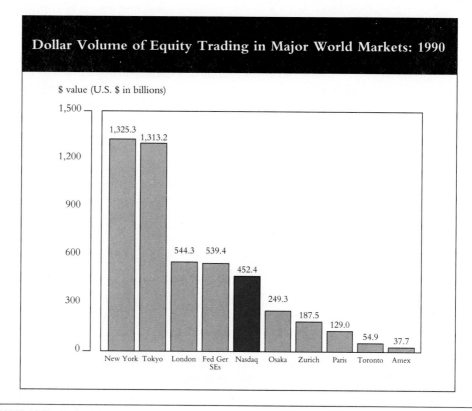

Source: *NASDAQ Fact Book, 1991*, p. 13.

in NYSE-listed securities in over-the-counter markets became known as the **third market.**

The third market diminished in importance for a while as the NYSE became more price competitive. However, in the 1980s and early 1990s, this market made a comeback. One advantage of the OTC market is that more than one specialist trades a security and trading flexibility is greater. During July 1984, ITT Corporation reported a significant dividend cut and lower earnings after the NYSE was closed, but Jefferies Corporation, an over-the-counter trading firm, traded 3 million shares by the time the NYSE opened the next morning. Another example occurred when the Justice Department announced the breakup of AT&T on a Friday. MCI, a competitor in communications, traded OTC, while AT&T traded on the NYSE. AT&T trading was halted until Monday because the specialist was unable to stabilize the market, whereas the 29 market makers in MCI stock in the OTC market transacted

over $75 million of securities before AT&T opened on Monday morning. At the time of this writing, much discussion is being held at the New York Stock Exchange about trading hours, revising rules, and generally competing more effectively with the third market and the OTC.

The **fourth market** is that market in which institutions trade between themselves, bypassing the middleman broker (replacing the broker with a computer). Much of the trading in this market is done through Instinet, Institutional Networks Inc. Instinet provides a low-cost automated stock trading system, with transactions available on over 3,500 securities, both listed and over-the-counter. The system allows banks, insurance companies, and mutual and pension funds to enter an order over a computer terminal for up to 1,000 shares. The computer searches a nationwide trading network until it finds the trader with the best price, then the computer holds the order 30 seconds so that another trader may offer a better price. While Instinet is only a small trading system, Merrill Lynch bought 8 percent of the company and has plans to tie the trading system into the quote-terminal desktop computer it is developing with IBM.

■ THE FUTURE OF THE CAPITAL MARKETS

Financial institutions, such as banks, pension funds, insurance companies, and investment companies (mutual funds), have always invested and traded in securities. However, the growth of these institutions and their participation in the capital markets have increased dramatically in recent years. Part of the increased share activity can be found in the accelerated growth of pension plans during this period. Also, the rapid rise in stock prices during the post-World War II period attracted a lot of individual investors into mutual funds.

Table 2–11 on institutional activity shows that significant changes have occurred during the past two decades as institutional trading has accounted for a relatively larger percentage of total trading on the New York Stock Exchange. A block trade is a transaction of 10,000 shares or more and is almost always carried out by institutions rather than individuals. In 1965, block trades accounted for only 3.1 percent of the reported volume on the NYSE, but by 1990, block trades represented approximately 50 percent (last column). This increased institutional activity is also evident by an examination of the third column of Table 2–11 which shows that between 1965 and 1990 the average number of block trades per day increased from 9 to 3,333.

Proof of the decreased importance of small investors and the increased importance of the institutional trader also is seen in Table 2–12 on page 66. The average size of a trade on the NYSE in 1965 was 224 shares (last column) while in 1990, it was almost 10 times as great, averaging 2,082 shares per trade.

These statistics do not mean individuals are getting out of the stock market entirely, but that many are investing indirectly in stocks through mutual funds, IRAs, and private pension plans. The market crash of 1987 and the high volatility of stock price movements subsequent to that event have scared off

Table 2–11   Institutional Activity on the New York Stock Exchange

Year	Total Number of Large Block Transactions per Year	Average Number of Large Block Transactions per Day	Block Shares (Thousands)	Block Trades as a Percent of Reported NYSE Volume
1965	2,171	9	49,262	3.1%
1967	6,685	27	N.A.	6.7
1969	15,132	61	N.A.	14.1
1970	17,217	68	450,908	15.4
1971	26,941	106	692,536	17.8
1973	29,223	116	721,356	17.8
1975	34,420	136	778,540	16.6
1977	54,275	215	1,183,924	22.4
1979	97,509	385	2,164,726	26.5
1981	145,564	575	3,771,442	31.8
1982	254,707	1,007	6,742,481	41.0
1983	363,415	1,436	9,842,080	45.6
1984	433,427	1,713	11,492,091	49.8
1985	539,039	2,139	14,222,272	51.7
1986	665,587	2,631	17,811,335	49.9
1987	920,679	3,639	24,497,241	51.2
1988	768,419	3,037	22,270,680	54.5
1989	872,811	3,464	21,316,132	51.1
1990	843,365	3,333	19,681,849	49.6

N.A. = Not available.
Source: *New York Stock Exchange Fact Book,* 1990.

many small investors. However, as markets eventually settle down and new regulations are enacted, the individual investor will continue to have a meaningful role in the market.

The National Market System

A national market system was mandated by Congress in the Securities Amendments Act of 1975. This is envisioned as a coordinated national system of security trading with no barriers between the various exchanges or the OTC market. There is sometimes confusion between the concept of a national market system and the National Market System listing segment of the OTC market. The former system is the subject of the present discussion. The latter has already been discussed.

Despite some delay in implementing a national market system due to industry foot-dragging and political changes in Washington, it is still a goal for the future. The system is strongly supported by the SEC. No one knows

Table 2–12   Reported Volume, Turnover Rate, Reported Trades (Millions of shares)

Year	Reported Share Volume	Average of Shares Listed	Percent Turnover	Reported Trades (Thousands)	Average Size of Trade
1965	1,556.3	9,643.6	16%	—	224
1967	2,530.0	11,280.5	22	9,822	257
1969	2,850.8	14,139.1	20	8,004	356
1970	2,937.4	15,573.6	19	7,566	388
1971	3,891.3	16,782.6	23	9,094	428
1973	4,053.2	20,062.6	20	9,025	449
1975	4,693.4	22,107.5	21	9,481	495
1977	5,273.8	25,296.5	21	8,222	641
1979	8,155.9	28,803.0	28	10,369	787
1981	11,853.7	36,003.5	33	11,696	1,013
1982	16,458.0	38,907.0	42	12,609	1,305
1983	21,589.6	42,316.9	51	15,051	1,434
1984	23,071.0	47,104.8	49	12,954	1,781
1985	27,510.7	50,759.4	54	14,649	1,878
1986	35,680.0	56,023.8	64	18,972	1,881
1987	47,801.3	65,711.4	73	22,635	2,112
1988	40,849.5	73,988.5	55	17,739	2,303
1989	41,698.5	79,573.5	52	19,639	2,123
1990	39,664.5	86,851.8	46	19,050	2,082

Source: *New York Stock Exchange Fact Book,* 1990.

exactly what form this national market might take, but several things will be required. Some are easily achieved, while others are not. The first is already in place—the composite tape that reflects trades on all exchanges for listed NYSE companies. There will also have to be competition between specialists and market makers. This is already occurring between the regional exchanges and the NYSE in dually listed securities. The prices seem to be more stable and the spreads between the bid and asked prices are closer for securities with competing market makers. A third occurrence is that the NYSE will most likely have to abolish Rule 390, which prohibits members of the NYSE from trading off the exchange in NYSE-listed securities. This has yet to occur.

Possibly the biggest dilemma in creating a national market system is fully developing a computerized system to execute limit orders. Currently, NYSE specialists execute most limit orders, which specify that a security must be bought or sold at a limited price or better. The national market system will need a computerized system to handle limit orders from all markets. Progress along these lines was being required by the SEC, and by the early 1990s, the

NYSE had created several computer systems to aid in trading. In 1984, the AMEX announced it had installed Autoper, an electronic order execution system that processes specialists' trades in a few seconds. This system uses a touch-screen that virtually eliminates clerical errors and allows market price trades of 300 shares or limit orders of up to 500 shares.

The national market system mandated by Congress could eventually take the form of NASDAQ, where several competing dealers make markets electronically. Clearly, the National Association of Securities Dealers hopes the national market system will follow its trading practices rather than the auction markets of the exchanges. The exchanges have complained to the SEC that the NASD's use of the term *National Market System* for its largest OTC companies should not be allowed because it gives the appearance that the OTC is *the* national market.

The NYSE will not capitulate easily to an over-the-counter system of trading. The traditional exchange auction markets have been able to absorb block trades without difficulty and serve the needs of institutional customers and individuals. The NYSE does not want to give up its dominant market position, but it had better stop to look at who is catching up.

Any truly national market system will rely on computers more than ever. Some systems in existence today even allow individual investors to use their personal computers to place stock market orders.

Any national market system will also have to interface with international markets whose continuous around-the-clock, around-the-world trading was mentioned earlier in the chapter.

■ REGULATION OF THE SECURITY MARKETS

Organized securities markets are regulated by the **Securities and Exchange Commission (SEC)** and by the self-regulation of the exchanges. The OTC market is controlled by the National Association of Securities Dealers. Three major laws govern the sale and subsequent trading of securities. The **Securities Act of 1933** pertains to new issues of securities, while the **Securities Exchange Act of 1934** deals with trading in the securities markets. The **Securities Acts Amendments of 1975** are the latest legislation, and their main emphasis is on a national securities market. The primary purpose of these laws was to protect unwary investors from fraud and manipulation and to make the markets more competitive and efficient.

Securities Act of 1933

The Securities Act of 1933 was enacted after congressional investigations of the abuses present in the securities markets during the 1929 crash and again in 1931. The act's primary purpose was to provide full disclosure of all pertinent investment information whenever a corporation sold a new issue of securities.

It is sometimes referred to as the "truth in securities" act. The Securities Act has several important features:

1. All offerings except government bonds and bank stocks that are to be sold in more than one state must be registered with the SEC.[1]

2. The registration statement must be filed 20 days in advance of the date of sale and include detailed corporate information. If the SEC finds the information misleading, incomplete, or inaccurate, it will delay the offering until the registration statement is corrected. The SEC in no way certifies that the security is fairly priced but only that the information seems to be factual and accurate. Under certain circumstances, the previously mentioned shelf registration is being used to modify the 20-day waiting period concept.

3. All new issues of securities must be accompanied by a *prospectus,* a detailed summary of the registration statement. Included in the prospectus is usually a list of directors and officers; their salaries, stock options, and shareholdings; financial reports certified by a CPA; a list of the underwriters; the purpose and use for the funds to be provided from the sale of securities; and any other reasonable information that investors may need to know before they can wisely invest their money. A preliminary prospectus may be distributed to potential buyers before the offering date, but it will not contain the offering price or underwriting fees. It is called a red herring because stamped on the front in red letters are the words *Preliminary Prospectus.*

4. Officers of the company and other experts preparing the prospectus or registration statement can be sued for penalties and recovery of realized losses if any information presented was fraudulent or factually wrong or if relevant information was omitted.

Securities Exchange Act of 1934

This act created the Securities and Exchange Commission to enforce the securities laws. It was empowered to regulate the securities markets and those companies listed on the exchanges. Specifically, the major points of the 1934 Act are as follows:

1. Guidelines for insider trading were established. Insiders must hold securities for at least six months before they can sell them. This is to prevent them from taking quick advantage of information that could result in a short-term profit. All short-term profits were payable to the corporation. Insiders were generally thought to be officers, directors,

---

[1] Actually, the SEC did not come into existence until 1934. The Federal Trade Commission had many of these responsibilities before the formation of the SEC.

major stockholders, employees, or relatives of key employees. In the last two decades, the SEC widened its interpretation to include anyone having information that was not public knowledge. This could include security analysts, loan officers, large institutional holders, and many others who had business dealings with the firm.

2. The Federal Reserve Board of Governors became responsible for setting margin requirements to determine how much credit one had available to buy securities.

3. Manipulation of securities by conspiracies between investors was prohibited.

4. The SEC was given control over the proxy procedures of corporations (a proxy is an absent stockholder vote).

5. In its regulation of companies traded on the markets, it required certain reports to be filed periodically. Corporations must file quarterly financial statements with the SEC, send annual reports to the stockholders, and file 10–K Reports with the SEC annually. The 10–K Report has more financial data than the annual report and can be very useful to an investor or loan officer. Most companies will now send 10–K Reports to stockholders on request.

6. The act required all securities exchanges to register with the SEC. In this capacity, the SEC supervises and regulates many pertinent organizational aspects of exchanges such as listing and trading mechanics.

The Securities Acts Amendments of 1975

The major focus of the Securities Acts Amendments of 1975 was to direct the SEC to supervise the development of a national securities market. No exact structure was put forth, but the law did assume that any national market would make extensive use of computers and electronic communication devices. Additionally, the law prohibited fixed commissions on public transactions and also prohibited banks, insurance companies, and other financial institutions from buying stock exchange memberships to save commission costs for their own institutional transactions. This is a worthwhile addition to the securities laws since it fosters greater competition and more efficient prices.

Other Legislation

In addition to these three major pieces of legislation, a number of other acts deal directly with investor protection. For example, the Investment Advisor Act of 1940 is set up to protect the public from unethical investment advisers. Any adviser with over 15 public clients (excluding tax accountants and lawyers) must register with the SEC and file semiannual reports. The Investment Company Act of 1940 provides similar oversight for mutual funds and investment

companies dealing with small investors. The act was amended in 1970 and currently gives the NASD authority to supervise and limit commissions and investment advisory fees on certain types of mutual funds.

Another piece of legislation dealing directly with investor protection is the Securities Investor Protection Act of 1970. The **Securities Investor Protection Corporation (SIPC)** was established to oversee liquidation of brokerage firms and to insure investors' accounts to a maximum value of $500,000 in case of bankruptcy of a brokerage firm. It functions much the same as the Federal Deposit Insurance Corporation. SIPC resulted from the problems encountered on Wall Street from 1967 to 1970 when share volume surged to then all-time highs, and many firms were unable to process orders fast enough. A back-office paper crunch caused Wall Street to shorten the hours the exchanges were formally open for new business, but even this didn't help. Investors lost large sums, and for many months, they were unable to use or get possession of securities held in their names. Even though SIPC insures these accounts, it still does not cover market value losses suffered while waiting to get securities from a bankrupt brokerage firm.

Insider Trading

The Securities Exchange Act of 1934 established the initial restrictions on insider trading. However, over the years, these restrictions have often proved to be inadequate. As previously indicated, the definition of *insider* may go beyond officers, directors, and major stockholders to include anyone with special insider knowledge. Both the Congress and the SEC are attempting to grapple with the issue of making punitive measures severe enough to discourage the illegal use of nonpublic information for profits.[2] Current and future legislation is likely to include tougher civil penalties and stiffer criminal prosecution. Also, the penalties for improper action will expand beyond simple recovery of profits to a penalty three or more times the profits involved.

The 1980s saw a rash of insider trading scandals involving major investment banking houses, traders, analysts, and investors. Ivan Boesky and Dennis Levine were the first of the well-known investors to end up in jail, and in June 1988, Steven Wang, Jr., an analyst at Morgan Stanley, was charged by the SEC of insider trading activities evolving from confidential information passed on to a wealthy Taiwanese businessman, Fred Lee. These insider trading scandals have plagued Wall Street and tarnished its image as a place where investors can get a fair deal.

On balance, all the legislation we have discussed has tended to increase the confidence of the investing public. In an industry where public trust is so critical, some form of supervision, whether public or private, is necessary and generally accepted.

---

[2]Insiders, of course, may make proper long-term investments in a corporation.

Program Trading and Market Price Limits

Program trading is identified by some market analysts as the primary culprit behind the 508-point market crash on October 19, 1987. **Program trading** simply means computer-based trigger points are established in which large volume trades are initiated by institutional investors. For example, if the Dow Jones Industrial Average (or some other market measure) hits a certain point, a large sale or purchase may automatically occur. When many institutional investors are using program trading simultaneously, this process can have a major cumulative effect on the market. This was thought to be the case not only on the October 19th crash but also for many other highly volatile days in the market.

Some have suggested that program trading be made illegal by a congressional act or, as a minimum, be voluntarily restricted in scope by the security exchanges and their member firms. The latter seems to be the more likely path now. Not all market participants envision program trading to be necessarily bad. One can argue that program trading simply accelerates the inevitable and gets it over with more quickly. Instead of the market going down by 500 points over six months because of a series of negative factors, it perhaps can happen in one day.[3] One thing is certain: program trading will get continued attention in the future.

Another topic that received much publicity after the market crash was the possibility of establishing price limits on daily market movements so that the market would not be allowed to go up or down by more than 50, 100, or perhaps 200 points in a given day without a temporary halt in trading. The prestigious Brady Commission that was appointed by the president to investigate the causes and cures for the crash actually made such a recommendation. Price limits have been instituted on the New York Stock Exchange and other exchanges and have generally proved beneficial during times of extreme market volatility.

■ SUMMARY

A smoothly functioning market is one that is efficient and provides liquidity to the investor. The success of a primary market, in which new issues are generally underwritten by investment bankers, is highly dependent on the presence of an active resale (secondary) market.

Secondary markets may be established in the form of an organized exchange or as an over-the-counter market. The predominant organized market is the New York Stock Exchange, but increasing attention is being directed to various

---

[3]Program trading is also used to arbitrage price differentials between the futures market and the cash market for securities. This is not only a potentially profitable transaction for market participants but also may increase market efficiency by ensuring that price discrepancies are quickly eliminated.

other markets. The possibility of a true national market system looms as a consideration for the future, with the completed first step being the development of a consolidated tape among different markets. NASDAQ (National Association of Securities Dealers Automated Quotations system) has done much to improve the communications network in the over-the-counter market and bring competition to the organized exchanges. The first full year of trading under NASDAQ's National Market System began in 1983, and more companies are remaining on the OTC market rather than being listed on the AMEX or NYSE.

The dominant role of the institutional investor has had an enormous impact on the markets with higher stock turnover and increasing market volatility. An enormous consolidation of market participants has also occurred on Wall Street, and the creation of financial service companies such as American Express and Sears seems to be a wave of the future.

The term *market* is broadening with different types of new investment outlets as witnessed by the expansion of options, futures contracts on stock indexes, options on futures, and many other commodity trading mechanisms. Of equal importance, the term *market* must be viewed from a global viewpoint with securities trading throughout the world on a 24-hour basis.

Finally, problems or imperfections in the marketplace during critical time periods have led to a wide array of securities legislation. The legislation in the 1930s regulated the securities markets and created the SEC. Subsequent laws have dealt with restructuring the market and investor protection. The market crash of 1987 has also called into question the adequacy of our current securities laws.

■ IMPORTANT WORDS AND CONCEPTS

market 41
efficient market 42
liquidity 42
secondary markets 42
primary markets 42
investment banker 43
underwriting 43
best efforts 43
initial public offering (IPO) 49
organized exchanges 49
over-the-counter markets 49
commission brokers 54
floor broker 55
registered traders 55
odd-lot dealer 55

specialists 55
Super Dot 56
Electronic Book 57
call option 58
NASDAQ 60
third market 63
fourth market 64
Securities and Exchange Commission (SEC) 67
Securities Act of 1933 67
Securities Exchange Act of 1934 67
Securities Acts Amendments of 1975 67
Securities Investor Protection Corporation (SIPC) 70
program trading 71

DISCUSSION QUESTIONS

1. What is a market?
2. What is an efficient market?
3. What is the difference between primary and secondary markets?
4. What is the difference between an investment banker providing an underwriting function and a "best-efforts" offering?
5. What is a private placement?
6. What generally determines how firms are listed in a tombstone advertisement?
7. Briefly describe the participants on an exchange.
8. How do critics think the specialist system on the NYSE might be improved?
9. How is the over-the-counter market different from the organized exchanges?
10. What is the highest priority segment of the OTC market in terms of reporting trading activity?
11. What is the NASDAQ and what service does it perform?
12. What are some differences between OTC standards for inclusion and NYSE listing requirements? (Suggest general categories of differences rather than actual numbers.)
13. Define a block trade. What does the increase in block trades since 1965 tend to indicate about the nature of investors in the market?
14. List some factors that are required for the implementation of a national market system.
15. Indicate the primary purpose of the Securities Act of 1933. Why was it enacted? Does the SEC certify that a security is fairly priced?
16. How has the definition of an insider (inside trader) expanded over the past two decades?
17. Explain the purpose of the Securities Investor Protection Corporation (SIPC).
18. What is program trading? Why does it have the potential to add to market volatility?
19. The concept of 24-hour market trading is mentioned a number of times in the chapter. What development has led to such a possibility?

CRITICAL THOUGHT CASE

The Securities and Exchange Commission is a federal agency created by Congress through the Securities Exchange Acts of 1933 and 1934 to protect investors. The stock market crash of 1929 and the Great Depression led the U.S. Senate to investigate the regulations of the securities industry. The existing laws were found to be inadequate, thus the formation of the securities industry watchdog, the SEC.

One of the main provisions of the 1933 act was to ensure full disclosure of facts by companies offering securities for sale to the public. Companies must submit a registration statement to the SEC for approval before securities could be sold. These statements contain financial information essential to a complete analysis of the investment at hand. A company prospectus disclosing this information is made available to the public.

Recently, disclosure of this information has posed many problems. As the world markets become increasingly competitive, foreign companies have access to important financial information about U.S. companies. In many cases, this same financial information on foreign companies is not available to U.S. companies. But, if foreign companies want to sell stock in the United States, the SEC requires them to submit the same financial information as U.S. companies. Many foreign companies are reluctant to do this because they believe it would give away their competitive advantage.

With the globalization of the world's securities markets, the New York Stock Exchange feels very strongly that to remain the leader in the industry, foreign securities must be traded in the United States. The NYSE has been attempting to attract major foreign companies for listing on the exchange, but many of these companies do not want to comply with the stringent financial disclosure requirements. If action is not taken quickly to rectify the situation, the NYSE believes it may lose its competitive position as the world's largest stock exchange.

The NYSE has been trying for some time to persuade the SEC to reduce corporate financial disclosure requirements for foreign companies. Although the SEC agrees in principle that it would be advantageous to investors to have foreign stocks listed on the exchange, it is not willing to lessen the disclosure standards for foreign companies. Investors would be at risk if this were allowed.

Questions

1. Should the SEC, for the sake of maintaining U.S. competitiveness in the world markets, lessen requirements for foreign companies?
2. If so, is this fair to U.S. companies and investors?
3. What are the consequences to the NYSE and New York City if the exchange is no longer the world leader it once was?

■ MARKETBASE-E EXERCISES

In the following exercise, please use your MarketBase-E Software and manual to screen for the required portfolios. You will have to figure out how to search through the data to pull out those companies meeting the requirements set down.

Institutional investors account for a large part of the daily trading in the stock markets. Use MarketBase-E to screen on institutional holdings.

1. *a.* Find how many companies have at least 70% of their stock held by institutions. Can you determine the general size of these companies in terms of revenues?

   b. Find how many companies have at least 60% of their stock held by institutions. Is there a big increase in the number of companies from the number in part *a*? Can you determine the general size of these companies in terms of market value?

2. *a.* Find how many companies have no more than 20% of their stock held by institutions. Can you determine the general size of these companies in terms of revenues?

   b. Find how many companies have no more than 10% of their stock held by institutions. Is there a big decrease in the number of companies from the number in part *a*? Can you determine the general size of these companies in terms of market value?

■ SELECTED REFERENCES

Security Exchanges

Cabanilla, Nathaniel B. "Directly Placed Bonds: A Test of Market Efficiency." *Journal of Portfolio Management,* Winter 1984, pp. 72–74.

Eubank, Arthur E., Jr. "Risk/Return Contrast: NYSE, Amex, and OTC." *Journal of Portfolio Management,* Summer 1977, pp. 25–30.

Farrar, Donald E. "Toward a Central Market System: Wall Street's Slow Retreat into the Future." *Journal of Financial and Quantitative Analysis,* November 1974, pp. 815–27.

New York Stock Exchange Fact Book. New York: New York Stock Exchange, 1988, 1990, 1991.

Sanger, Gary C., and John J. McConnell. "Stock Exchange Listings, Firm Value, and Security Market Efficiency: The Impact of NASDAQ." *Journal of Financial and Qualitative Analysis,* March 1986, pp. 1–25.

Stoll, Hans R. "The Pricing of Security Dealer Service: An Empirical Study of NASDAQ Stocks." *Journal of Finance,* September 1978, pp. 1153–72.

Tinic, S. M., and R. R. West. "Competition and the Pricing of Dealer Service in the OTC Market," *Journal of Financial and Quantitative Analysis,* June 1972, pp. 1707–28.

Trading Patterns by Investors

Dann, Larry Y.; David Myers; and Robert J. Raab. "Trading Rules, Large Blocks, and the Speed of Price Adjustment." *Journal of Financial Economics,* January 1977, pp. 3–22.

Roll, Richard. "A Simple Implicit Measure of the Effective Bid–Ask Spread in an Efficient Market." *Journal of Finance,* September 1984, pp. 1127–39.

The Market Crash of 1987

Edwards, Franklin R. "Does Futures Trading Increase Stock Market Volatility." *Financial Analysts Journal,* January–February 1988, pp. 63–69.

Friedland, Jonathan. "Rebuilding the Faith." *Institutional Investor,* February 1988, pp. 51–53.

Reich, Gary. "After the Fall." *Institutional Investor,* January 1988, pp. 33–37.

Regulation

Gastineau, Gary L., and Robert A. Jarrow. "Larger-Trader Impact and Market Regulation." *Financial Analysts Journal,* July–August 1991, pp. 40–51.

Gillis, John G. "SEC Major Issues Conference—1984." *Financial Analysts Journal,* September–October 1984, pp. 10–12.

3

Participating in the Market

Many different kinds of investors participate in the market, from the individual to the professional, and each participant needs to know about the structure and mechanics of the market in which he or she might invest. In this chapter, we examine the use of indexes to gauge market performance, the rules and mechanics of opening and trading in an account, and basic tax considerations for the investor.

■ MEASURES OF PRICE PERFORMANCE: MARKET INDEXES

We first look at tracking market performance for stocks and bonds. Each market has several market indexes published by Moody's, Standard & Poor's, Dow Jones, and other financial services. These indexes allow investors to measure the performance of their portfolios against an index that approximates their portfolio composition; thus, different investors prefer different indexes. While a professional pension fund manager might use the Standard & Poor's 500 Stock Index, a mutual fund specializing in small, over-the-counter stocks might prefer the NASDAQ (National Association of Securities Dealers Automated Quotations) Index, and a small investor might use the Value Line Average as the best approximation of a portfolio's performance.

■ INDEXES AND AVERAGES

Dow Jones Averages

Since there are many stock market indexes and averages, we will cover the most widely used ones. Dow Jones, publisher of *The Wall Street Journal* and *Barron's,* publishes several market averages of which the **Dow Jones Industrial Average (DJIA)** is the most popular. This average consists of 30 large industrial companies and is considered a "blue-chip" index (stocks of very high quality). Many people criticize the DJIA for being too selective and representing too few stocks.[1] Nevertheless, the Dow Industrials do follow the general trend of the market, and these 30 common stocks comprise over 25 percent of the market value of the 1,550 firms listed on the New York Stock Exchange.

Dow Jones also publishes an index of 20 transportation stocks and 15 utility stocks. Figure 3–1 shows a listing of the stocks in the Dow Jones Industrial, Transportation, and Utility averages as well as the daily price movements for the averages over a six-month period. In Table 3–1, you also see a listing of the daily movement of the three Dow Jones averages for July 11, 1991. It also

---

[1]On October 3, 1988, Dow Jones & Company began quoting a comparison index to the Dow Jones Industrial Average called the Dow Jones Equity Index. It is composed of 693 stocks but is not widely followed.

Figure 3–1   The Dow Jones Averages

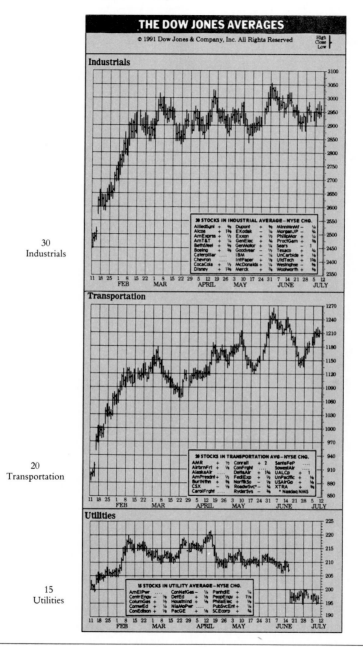

Table 3–1   Indexes and Averages Found in *The Wall Street Journal*

STOCK MARKET DATA BANK   7/11/91

MAJOR INDEXES

HIGH	LOW	(12 MOS)	CLOSE	NET CHG	% CHG	12 MO CHG	% CHG	FROM 12/31	% CHG
DOW JONES AVERAGES									
3035.33	2365.10	30 Industrials	2959.75	+ 14.98	+ 0.51	− 10.05	− 0.34	+ 326.09	+ 12.38
1251.76	821.93	20 Transportation	1213.50	+ 8.46	+ 0.70	+ 48.54	+ 4.17	+ 303.27	+ 33.32
220.89	190.96	15 Utilities	196.87	+ 1.70	+ 0.87	− 9.62	− 4.66	− 12.83	− 6.12
1091.26	839.00	65 Composite	1057.20	+ 6.45	+ 0.61	+ 5.45	+ 0.52	+ 136.59	+ 14.84
364.73	272.91	Equity Mkt. Index	351.89	+ 1.21	+ 0.35	+ 12.27	+ 3.61	+ 46.30	+ 15.15
NEW YORK STOCK EXCHANGE									
213.21	162.20	Composite	206.54	+ 0.67	+ 0.33	+ 7.22	+ 3.62	+ 26.05	+ 14.43
268.54	200.80	Industrials	260.17	+ 0.86	+ 0.33	+ 10.26	+ 4.11	+ 36.57	+ 16.36
94.27	80.96	Utilities	89.62	+ 0.37	+ 0.41	− 0.69	− 0.76	− 1.68	− 1.84
183.38	127.25	Transportation	176.69	+ 0.90	+ 0.51	+ 0.78	+ 0.44	+ 35.20	+ 24.88
158.19	103.26	Finance	149.93	+ 0.25	+ 0.17	+ 5.70	+ 3.95	+ 27.86	+ 22.82
STANDARD & POOR'S INDEXES									
390.45	295.46	500 Index	376.97	+ 1.23	+ 0.33	+ 11.53	+ 3.16	+ 46.75	+ 14.16
464.98	346.86	Industrials	449.55	+ 1.47	+ 0.33	+ 16.18	+ 3.73	+ 62.13	+ 16.04
307.74	208.77	Transportation	293.71	+ 1.22	+ 0.42	+ 13.03	+ 4.64	+ 59.04	+ 25.16
146.60	124.60	Utilities	137.04	+ 0.69	+ 0.51	− 0.78	− 0.57	− 6.55	− 4.56
31.69	18.80	Financials	29.41	+ 0.02	+ 0.07	+ 0.69	+ 2.40	+ 5.98	+ 25.52
NASDAQ									
511.31	325.44	Composite	488.37	+ 1.20	+ 0.25	+ 21.20	+ 4.54	+ 114.53	+ 30.64
575.67	344.11	Industrials	544.92	+ 0.92	+ 0.17	+ 37.45	+ 7.38	+ 138.87	+ 34.20
585.08	379.36	Insurance	539.63	+ 0.46	+ 0.09	+ 28.34	+ 5.54	+ 87.79	+ 19.43
337.41	235.25	Banks	321.54	+ 2.22	+ 0.70	− 13.18	− 3.94	+ 66.63	+ 26.14
225.92	142.41	Nat. Mkt. Comp.	215.44	+ 0.55	+ 0.26	+ 10.42	+ 5.08	+ 50.27	+ 30.44
229.93	135.93	Nat. Mkt. Indus.	217.04	+ 0.35	+ 0.16	+ 16.05	+ 7.99	+ 54.70	+ 33.69
OTHERS									
373.40	287.79	Amex	361.84	− 0.10	− 0.03	− 0.39	− 0.11	+ 53.73	+ 17.44
249.03	179.55	Value-Line (geom.)	236.82	+ 0.37	+ 0.16	− 10.80	− 4.36	+ 40.83	+ 20.83
178.70	118.82	Russell 2000	169.04	unch		− 0.39	− 0.23	+ 36.85	+ 27.88
3731.48	2772.31	Wilshire 5000	3605.36	+ 11.54	+ 0.32	+ 117.15	+ 3.36	+ 504.00	+ 16.25

Source: *The Wall Street Journal*, July 12, 1991, p. C2. Reprinted by permission of *THE WALL STREET JOURNAL*, © 1991 by Dow Jones & Company, Inc. All Rights Reserved Worldwide.

shows a Dow Jones 65-stock composite average that summarizes the performance of the Dow Jones industrial, transportation, and utility issues. Many other market averages are presented in the table, which we shall discuss later.

For now, let's return to the Dow Jones Industrial Average of 30 stocks. The Dow Jones Industrial Average used to be a simple average of 30 stocks, but when a company splits its stock price, the average has to be adjusted. For the Dow Jones Industrials, the divisor in the formula has been adjusted downward from the original 30 to below 1. Each time a company splits its shares of stock (or provides a stock dividend), the divisor is reduced to maintain the average

at the same level as before the stock split. If this were not done, the lower-priced stock after the split would reduce the average, giving the appearance that investors were worse off.

The Dow Jones Industrial Average is a **price-weighted average** which means each stock in the average is weighted by its price. To simplify the meaning of price weighted: If you had three stocks in a price-weighted average that had values of 10, 40, and 100, you would add the prices and divide by three. In this case, you would get an average of 50 (150 divided by 3). A price-weighted average is similar to what you normally use in computing averages. Price-weighted averages tend to give a higher weighting bias to high-price stocks than to low-price stocks. For example, in the above analysis, if the $100 stock goes up by 10 percent, with all else the same, the average will go up over three points from 50 to 53.3. However, if the $10 stock goes up by 10 percent, with all else the same, the average will only go from 50 to 50.3.

In mid-1991, IBM was trading at 93¼ while Bethlehem Steel was at 18½. Clearly, a 10 percent price movement up or down in IBM would have a greater impact on the Dow Jones Industrial Average than a 10 percent movement in Bethlehem Steel. Thus, we see the bias toward high-priced stocks in the Dow Jones Industrial Average.

Barron's, a weekly Dow Jones publication, carries *Barron's* 50 Stock Average as well as an index of low-priced securities that meets the needs of many small investors. *Barron's* also publishes other major averages and indexes that we shall discuss throughout the text.

For another view of industry performance, the analyst may also wish to observe the Dow Jones Industry Groups data found daily in *The Wall Street Journal.* Here you can also view the leading and lagging group for a given day, as shown in Table 3–2. You can see at the top of Table 3–2 on page 82 that financial services had an excellent day while precious metals did not fare so well.

Standard & Poor's Indexes

Standard & Poor's Corporation publishes a number of indexes. The best known is the **Standard & Poor's 500 Stock Index.** This index is widely followed by professional money managers and security market researchers as a measure of broad stock market activity. The S&P 500 Stock Index includes 400 industrial firms, plus 20 transportation firms, 40 utilities, and 40 financial firms. A listing of Standard & Poor's 500 Index and its component parts can be seen in Table 3–1. The stocks in the S&P 500 Stock Index are equivalent to approximately 75 percent of the total value of the 1,550 firms listed on the New York Stock Exchange.[2]

---

[2]Actually, some large, over-the-counter firms are also in the S&P indexes, though the indexes are predominantly made up of New York Stock Exchange firms.

Table 3–2 Dow Jones Industry Groups

July 11, 1991, 4:30 p.m. Eastern Time

GROUPS LEADING (and strongest stocks in group)

GROUP	CLOSE	CHG	%CHG
Financial services	315.23	+ 5.09	+ 1.64
Fed Natl Mtg	53⅜	+ 1½	+ 2.89
Amer Express	22⅞	+ ½	+ 2.23
Beneficial	56¼	+ ⅜	+ 0.67
Oilfield equip/svcs	144.09	+ 2.06	+ 1.45
Halliburton Co	37	+ 1	+ 2.78
Baker Hughes	23½	+ ½	+ 2.17
McDermott Int	18	+ ⅜	+ 2.13
Ins-Life	460.57	+ 6.25	+ 1.38
UNUM Corp	67⅞	+ 2½	+ 3.82
Prov Life.cl B	17¾	+ ⅜	+ 2.16
Capital Holding	50¼	+ 1	+ 2.03
Consumer services	413.57	+ 5.54	+ 1.36
Rollins Inc	23	+ ⅝	+ 2.79
Block (H & R)	58⅝	+ ¾	+ 1.30
Service Intl	23½	+ ¼	+ 1.08
Commu-wo/AT&T	235.32	+ 3.08	+ 1.33
Scientific-Atl	14⅝	+ ⅜	+ 2.63
Motorola Inc	64⅜	+ 1	+ 1.58
Comm Satell	28⅞	unch	unch

GROUPS LAGGING (and weakest stocks in group)

GROUP	CLOSE	CHG	%CHG
Precious metals	248.72	− 7.10	− 2.78
Homestake Mng	17¼	− ⅝	− 3.50
Newmnt Mng	40½	− 1⅛	− 2.70
ASA Ltd	53½	− 1⅜	− 2.51
Oil drilling	90.42	− 1.72	− 1.87
Global Marine	3½	− ½	− 12.50
Energy Svc	2¾	unch	unch
Parker Drilling	6⅜	unch	unch
Banks,money center	182.37	− 3.46	− 1.86
Citicorp	13⅜	− 1⅛	− 7.76
Mfrs Hanover	22	− ½	− 2.22
Morgan (J P)	52⅛	− ¾	− 1.42
Comptrs-wo/IBM	236.45	− 4.33	− 1.80
Tandem Cmptrs	13⅜	− ⅝	− 4.46
Sun Microsys	27¾	− 1	− 3.48
Hewlett-Pkrd	53½	− 1¼	− 2.28
Semiconductor	269.24	− 3.98	− 1.46
Intel Corp	45½	− 1¼	− 2.67
Appld Materls	30	− ¼	− 0.83
Avnet Inc	26¾	unch	unch

INDUSTRY GROUP PERFORMANCE (June 30, 1982=100)

GROUP	CLOSE	CHG	% CHG
Basic Materials	367.52	+ 1.68	+ 0.46
Aluminum	321.49	+ 2.48	+ 0.78
Other non-ferrous	220.04	+ 1.52	+ 0.70
Chemicals	433.29	+ 2.74	+ 0.64
Forest products	266.36	+ 2.87	+ 1.09
Mining,diversified	302.44	+ 1.08	+ 0.36
Paper products	467.67	+ 0.44	+ 0.09
Precious metals	248.72	− 7.10	− 2.78
Steel	118.01	+ 0.38	+ 0.32
Conglomerate	456.28	+ 4.65	+ 1.03
Consumer,Cyclical	420.77	+ 2.66	+ 0.64
Advertising	476.99	− 1.64	− 0.34
Airlines	341.61	+ 3.56	+ 1.05
Auto manufacturers	288.52	+ 0.77	+ 0.27
Auto parts & equip	250.54	− 0.07	− 0.03
Casinos	578.14	+ 1.92	+ 0.33
Home construction	339.06	− 0.69	− 0.20
Home furnishings	221.06	− 1.04	− 0.47
Lodging	285.67	+ 0.44	+ 0.15
Media	468.31	+ 4.79	+ 1.03
Recreation products	264.69	+ 1.09	+ 0.41
Restaurants	482.49	+ 2.45	+ 0.51
Retailers,apparel	1037.83	+ 4.46	+ 0.43
Retailers,broadline	609.29	+ 6.40	+ 1.06
Retailers,drug-based	443.89	+ 1.33	+ 0.30
Retailers,specialty	495.75	+ 2.13	+ 0.43
Textiles and apparel	664.52	+ 4.90	+ 0.74
Consumer,Non-Cycl	639.09	+ 1.38	+ 0.22
Beverages	709.45	+ 5.12	+ 0.73
Consumer services	413.57	+ 5.54	+ 1.36
Cosmetics	491.13	− 2.62	− 0.53
Food	798.28	− 1.99	− 0.25
Food retailers	689.47	+ 0.01	+ 0.00
Health care	383.75	+ 3.23	+ 0.85
Household products	659.86	+ 3.02	+ 0.46
Medical supplies	471.33	− 0.65	− 0.14
Pharmaceuticals	595.94	+ 1.15	+ 0.19
Energy	266.74	+ 1.51	+ 0.57
Coal	220.05	+ 1.64	+ 0.75
Oil drilling	90.42	− 1.72	− 1.87
Oil-majors	330.43	+ 1.76	+ 0.54
Oil-secondary	196.39	+ 1.39	+ 0.71
Oilfield equip/svcs	144.09	+ 2.06	+ 1.45
Pipelines	180.36	− 0.63	− 0.35
Financial	292.26	+ 0.54	+ 0.19
Banks,money center	182.37	− 3.46	− 1.86

GROUP	CLOSE	CHG	% CHG
Banks,regional	292.73	+ 0.84	+ 0.29
Banks-Central	476.29	+ 3.67	+ 0.78
Banks-East	224.93	+ 0.35	+ 0.16
Banks-South	250.71	+ 0.26	+ 0.10
Banks-West	285.43	− 0.74	− 0.26
Financial services	315.23	+ 5.09	+ 1.64
Insurance,all	337.72	+ 0.72	+ 0.21
Ins-Full line	198.85	+ 0.82	+ 0.41
Ins-Life	460.57	+ 6.25	+ 1.38
Property/Casualty	444.89	− 0.60	− 0.13
Real estate	417.44	− 0.49	− 0.12
Savings & loans	411.89	− 3.78	− 0.91
Securities brokers	360.21	+ 2.73	+ 0.76
Industrial	343.15	− 0.39	− 0.11
Air freight	197.95	+ 1.68	+ 0.86
Building materials	403.16	+ 1.76	+ 0.44
Containers/pkging	632.11	+ 4.16	+ 0.66
Elec comp/equip	355.46	− 0.83	− 0.23
Factory equipment	280.63	− 0.42	− 0.15
Heavy construction	313.30	− 2.84	− 0.90
Heavy machinery	155.27	+ 0.07	+ 0.05
Industrial services	346.42	− 1.33	− 0.38
Industrial,divers	309.46	+ 1.04	+ 0.34
Marine transport	428.36	− 0.74	− 0.17
Pollution control	836.18	− 12.26	− 1.45
Railroads	368.27	+ 1.27	+ 0.35
Transportation equip	231.87	+ 2.46	+ 1.07
Trucking	257.39	− 2.97	− 1.14
Technology	276.25	+ 0.24	+ 0.09
Aerospace/Defense	381.20	+ 3.32	+ 0.88
Commu-w/AT&T	366.62	+ 2.83	+ 0.78
Commu-wo/AT&T	235.32	+ 3.08	+ 1.33
Comptrs-w/IBM	187.21	− 1.68	− 0.89
Comptrs-wo/IBM	236.45	− 4.33	− 1.80
Diversified tech	266.46	+ 0.92	+ 0.35
Industrial tech	300.25	− 1.66	− 0.55
Medical/Bio tech	649.76	+ 3.20	+ 0.49
Office equipment	261.53	+ 1.02	+ 0.39
Semiconductor	269.24	− 3.98	− 1.46
Software	1540.56	+ 18.24	+ 1.20
Utilities	245.31	+ 1.27	+ 0.52
Telephone	324.94	+ 2.04	+ 0.63
Electric	202.78	+ 0.82	+ 0.41
Gas	148.36	+ 0.84	+ 0.57
Water	389.89	− 0.60	− 0.15
DJ Equity Market	351.89	+ 1.21	+ 0.35

History compiled by Dow Jones and Shearson Lehman Brothers

Source: *The Wall Street Journal,* July 12, 1991, p. C6. Reprinted by permission of *THE WALL STREET JOURNAL,*

Standard & Poor's also has other special purpose indexes. For example, the **Standard & Poor's 100 Index** is composed of 100 blue-chip stocks on which the Chicago Board Options Exchange has individual option contracts. (This terminology will become clearer when we study options later in the text.) The S&P 100 Index closely mirrors the performance of the S&P 500 Stock Index.

In the summer of 1991, Standard & Poor's Corp. introduced its MidCap Index. The **Standard & Poor's MidCap Index** is composed of 400 middle-size firms that have total market values between $300 million and $3 billion. The index was intended to answer the complaint that the S&P 500 Stock Index shows only the performance of larger firms. For example, IBM, which is part of the S&P 500 Index, had a total market value of over $50 billion in mid-1991. By creating an index of middle-size firms, portfolio managers with comparable-size holdings could more accurately track their performance against an appropriate measure. A comparison of the attributes of the S&P MidCap Index and the S&P 500 Stock Index can be seen in Table 3–3 for mid-1991.

All the S&P measures are true indexes in that they are linked to a base value. For the S&P 500 Stock Index, the base period is 1941–1943. The base period price in 1941–1943 was 10, so the S&P 500 Stock Index price of 376.97 on July 11, 1991, as previously shown in Table 3–1, represents an increase of 3,669.7 percent over this 50-year period. For the newer indexes, the base period does not go back so far.

The Standard & Poor's Indexes are **value-weighted,** which means each company is weighted in the index by its own total market value as a percentage of the total market value for all firms. For example, in a value-weighted index comprising the following three firms, the weighting would be:

Stock	Shares	Price	Total Market Value	Weighting
A	150	$10	$ 1,500	12.0%
B	200	20	4,000	32.0
C	500	14	7,000	56.0
			$12,500	100.0%

In each case, the weighting is determined by dividing the total market value of the stock by the total market value for all firms. In the case of stock A, that would be $1,500 divided by $12,500, or 12 percent. The same procedure is followed for stocks B and C.

Even though stock C has only the second highest price, it makes up 56 percent of the average because of its high total market value based on 500 shares outstanding. This same basic effect carries through in the Standard & Poor's 500 Index, with large companies such as IBM, AT&T, and Exxon having a greater impact on the index than smaller companies. Value-weighted

Table 3–3	Comparative Data on S&P MidCap Index and S&P 500 Index	
	S&P MidCap Index	**S&P 500 Index**
Total index market value	$350 billion	$2.4 trillion
Median company market value	$610 million	$2.2 billion
Median price per share	$27.63	$34.38
Median price-earnings ratio	17	15.9

indexes do not require special adjustments for stock splits because the increase in the number of shares automatically compensates for the decline in the stock value caused by the split.

Standard & Poor's also compiles value-weighted indexes for 90 different industries, and they are reported in the *Outlook,* a weekly Standard & Poor's publication.

Value Line Average

The **Value Line Average** represents 1,700 companies from the New York and American Stock Exchanges and the over-the-counter market. Some individual investors use the Value Line Average because it more closely corresponds to the variety of stocks small investors may have in their portfolios.

Unlike the previously discussed price-weighted average (the Dow Jones Industrial Average) and value-weighted indexes (S&P 400 and 500), the Value Line Average is **equal-weighted.** This means each of the 1,700 stocks, regardless of market price or total market value, is weighted equally. It is as if there were $100 to be invested in each and every stock. In this case, IBM or Exxon is weighted no more heavily than Wendy's International or Mattel Inc. This equal-weighting characteristic also more closely conforms to the portfolio of individual investors.

Other Market Indexes

Indexes are also computed and published by the New York Stock Exchange, American Stock Exchange, and the National Association of Securities Dealers. Each index is intended to represent the performance of stocks traded in a particular exchange or market. As is seen in Table 3–1, the NYSE publishes a composite index as well as an industrial, utility, transportation, and financial index. Each index represents the stocks of a broad group or type of company.

The National Association of Securities Dealers, which is the self-governing body of the over-the-counter markets, also constructs several indexes to represent the companies in its market. It publishes the NASDAQ com-

Table 3–4   World Stock Market Averages

Exchange	7/11/91 Close	Net Change	Percent Change
Tokyo Nikkei Average	22937.92	− 183.38	−0.79
Tokyo Topix Index	1798.87	+ 0.82	+0.05
London FT 30-share	1928.4	+ 10.3	+0.54
London 100-share	2510.5	+ 2.1	+0.08
London Gold Mines	222.8	+ 0.1	+0.04
Frankfurt DAX	1637.85	+ 3.11	+0.19
Zurich Credit Suisse	na		
Paris CAC 40	1752.13	− 5.25	−0.30
Milan Stock Index	1105	− 3.0	−0.27
Amsterdam ANP-CBS General	198.2	+ 0.3	+0.15
Stockholm Affarsvarlden	1149.8	+ 10.0	+0.88
Brussels Bel-20 Index	148.92	+ 1.55	+0.14
Australia All Ordinaries	1534.1	− 8.7	−0.56
Hong Kong Hang Seng	3892.12	− 9.11	−0.23
Singapore Straits Times	1471.46	− 4.71	−0.32
Johannesburg J'burg Gold	1391	− 54.0	−3.74
Madrid General Index	264.08	− 3.46	−1.29
Toronto 300 Composite	3507.89	− 3.72	−0.11
Euro, Aust, Far East MSCI-p	793.3	− 0.7	−0.09

p-Preliminary
na-Not available

posite, industrial, insurance, and banking indexes. The NASDAQ also publishes subindexes for stocks listed in the National Market System (see Table 3–1).

The American Exchange Market Value Index (AMEX) is composed of all stocks trading on the American Stock Exchange. This index is also shown in Table 3–1.

The indexes of the New York Stock Exchange, NASDAQ, and the American Stock Exchange are all value-weighted indexes.[3]

A relatively new index is the **Wilshire 5000 Equity Index.** It represents the *total dollar value* of 5,000 stocks, including all New York Stock Exchange and American Stock Exchange issues and the most active over-the-counter issues. By the very fact of including total dollar value, it is *value-weighted.* On

---

[3]Until October 1973, the American Stock Exchange Index was price-weighted.

Table 3–5   Bond Indexes

BOND MARKET DATA BANK							7/11/91

MAJOR INDEXES

HIGH	LOW (12 MOS)		CLOSE	NET CHG	% CHG	12-MO CHG	% CHG	FROM 12/31	% CHG

U.S. TREASURY SECURITIES (Lehman Brothers indexes)

3238.87	2933.95	Intermediate	3238.87 +	5.35 +	0.17 +	304.92 +	10.39 +	124.40 +	3.99
3815.81	3277.64	Long-term	3755.56 +	18.90 +	0.51 +	322.76 +	9.40 +	86.54 +	2.36
1356.57	1218.60	Long-term (price)	1293.94 +	6.20 +	0.48 +	4.31 +	0.33 −	28.38 −	2.15
3364.08	3009.10	Composite	3354.01 +	8.66 +	0.26 +	308.06 +	10.11 +	114.69 +	3.54

U.S. CORPORATE DEBT ISSUES (Merrill Lynch)

510.57	451.77	Corporate Master	509.63 +	1.06 +	0.21 +	50.36 +	10.97 +	28.63 +	5.95
386.00	347.58	1-10 Yr Maturities	386.00 +	0.41 +	0.11 +	37.53 +	10.77 +	22.29 +	6.13
377.35	326.63	10+ Yr Maturities	375.35 +	1.21 +	0.32 +	37.59 +	11.13 +	20.80 +	5.87
211.94	169.08	High Yield	211.94 +	0.08 +	0.04 +	24.87 +	13.29 +	37.56 +	21.54
368.28	325.40	Yankee Bonds	367.15 +	0.97 +	0.26 +	37.02 +	11.21 +	19.13 +	5.50

TAX-EXEMPT SECURITIES (Bond Buyer; Merrill Lynch: Dec. 31, 1986 = 100)

93-11	87-21	Bond Buyer Municipal	92-13 +	-4 +	0.14 +	-8 +	0.27 +	1-4 +	1.23
131.09	110.82	New 10-yr G.O. (AA)	129.71 +	0.97 +	0.75 +	11.32 +	9.56 +	6.71 +	5.46
134.84	117.43	New 20-yr G.O. (AA)	129.86 −	0.80 −	0.61 +	7.78 +	6.37 +	2.60 +	2.04
151.53	129.65	New 30-yr revenue (A)	150.70 +	0.76 +	0.51 +	14.75 +	10.85 +	9.44 +	6.68

MORTGAGE-BACKED SECURITIES (current coupon; Merrill Lynch: Dec. 31, 1986 = 100)

151.02	132.62	Ginnie Mae (GNMA)	150.72 −	0.20 −	0.13 +	17.22 +	12.90 +	7.28 +	5.08
151.15	133.75	Fannie Mae (FNMA)	150.72 −	0.05 −	0.03 +	16.68 +	12.44 +	7.24 +	5.05
150.82	133.53	Freddie Mac (FHLMC)	150.66 −	0.06 −	0.04 +	16.98 +	12.70 +	7.54 +	5.27

CONVERTIBLE BONDS (Merrill Lynch: Dec. 31, 1986 = 100)

140.49	115.06	Investment Grade	137.62 +	0.24 +	0.17 +	6.37 +	4.85 +	14.37 +	11.66
125.91	93.43	High Yield	123.60 +	0.12 +	0.10 +	8.04 +	6.96 +	22.40 +	22.13

Source: *The Wall Street Journal,* July 12, 1991, p. C8. Reprinted by permission of *THE WALL STREET JOURNAL,* © 1991 by Dow Jones & Company, Inc. All Rights Reserved Worldwide.

July 11, 1991, the Wilshire Index had a value of $3,605.36 billion. The index tells you the total value of virtually all important equities daily.

The direction of the indexes are all closely related, but they do not necessarily move together. If a pension fund manager is trying to "outperform the market," then the choice of index may be as crucial as to whether the fund manager maintains his or her accounts. The important thing for you, as well as for a professional, when measuring success or failure of performance, is to use an index that represents the risk characteristics of the portfolio being compared to the index. If you want only a general idea as to whether the market is going up or down over time, the choice of the average or index is not that critical since they all move fairly closely together.

International Stock Averages On a daily basis, *The Wall Street Journal* provides information on stock market averages across the globe. Table 3–4 on page 85 shows 19 market indicators for price changes in foreign markets. The most-watched foreign equity market is Japan, with many sophisticated investors and analysts following the Tokyo Nikkei Average as closely as the Dow Jones Industrial Average.

Bond Market Indicators Performance in the bond market is not widely followed by an index or average but is usually gauged by interest-rate movements. Since rising interest rates mean falling bond prices and falling rates signal rising prices, investors can usually judge the bond market performance

Table 3–6   Lipper Mutual Fund Performance Averages

LIPPER MUTUAL FUND PERFORMANCE AVERAGES

Weekly Summary Report
July 10, 1991

General Equity Funds — Dividends Reinvested Cumulative Performances

NAV Mil. $ Funds	No. Funds		10/11/90-07/11/91	07/12/90-07/11/91	07/12/90-07/11/91	12/31/90-07/11/91	07/03/91-07/11/91
20,201.1	141	Capital Appreciation	+ 33.87%	+ 4.57%	+ 4.57%	+ 20.30%	+ 2.04%
84,150.6	277	Growth Funds	+ 33.42%	+ 4.96%	+ 4.96%	+ 18.93%	+ 1.80%
13,035.6	91	Small Company Growth	+ 46.52%	+ 6.23%	+ 6.23%	+ 27.55%	+ 2.74%
87,164.6	222	Growth and Income	+ 27.99%	+ 5.82%	+ 5.82%	+ 15.57%	+ 1.15%
24,549.2	71	Equity Income	+ 23.51%	+ 5.99%	+ 5.99%	+ 13.29%	+ 0.88%
229,101.1	802	Gen. Equity Funds Avg	+ 32.69%	+ 5.35%	+ 5.35%	+ 18.76%	+ 1.69%
Other Equity Funds							
2,814.8	9	Health/Biotechnology	+ 56.92%	+ 32.04%	+ 32.04%	+ 32.03%	+ 3.32%
1,985.3	19	Natural Resources	+ 2.09%	- 5.89%	- 5.89%	+ 3.74%	+ 0.54%
293.5	7	Environmental	+ 22.63%	+ 11.74%	- 11.74%	+ 9.56%	+ 1.55%
2,040.9	21	Science & Technol.	+ 46.84%	+ 2.03%	+ 2.03%	+ 21.56%	+ 3.98%
1,600.3	31	Specialty/Misc.	+ 33.45%	+ 3.15%	+ 3.15%	+ 19.61%	+ 1.22%
7,356.7	23	Utility Funds	+ 13.89%	+ 8.22%	+ 8.22%	+ 4.97%	+ 0.29%
309.1	10	Financial Services	+ 53.58%	+ 14.66%	+ 14.66%	+ 31.80%	+ 2.10%
152.4	5	Real Estate	+ 26.23%	+ 1.51%	+ 1.51%	+ 20.80%	+ 0.26%
1,782.0	9	Option Income	+ 24.14%	+ 5.19%	+ 5.19%	+ 11.79%	+ 0.64%
15,061.6	52	Global Funds	+ 12.31%	+ 6.57%	+ 6.57%	+ 9.23%	+ 1.38%
10,644.5	71	International Funds	+ 4.17%	- 11.45%	- 11.45%	+ 4.87%	+ 1.03%
3,917.6	23	European Region Fds	- 5.20%	- 18.32%	- 18.32%	+ 4.09%	+ 0.90%
1,563.9	18	Pacific Region Funds	+ 8.32%	- 9.29%	- 9.29%	+ 11.53%	- 0.04%
2,953.9	37	Gold Oriented Funds	+ 1.58%	- 4.04%	- 4.04%	+ 3.26%	- 1.62%
281,284.1	1130	All Equity Funds Avg	+ 27.75%	+ 2.93%	+ 2.93%	+ 16.13%	+ 1.46%
Other Funds							
4,456.1	55	Flexible Portfolio	+ 19.88%	+ 5.85%	+ 5.85%	+ 10.64%	+ 0.75%
1,453.9	13	Global Flex Port.	+ 9.49%	- 0.43%	- 0.43%	+ 5.32%	+ 0.59%
15,031.9	62	Balanced Funds	+ 21.16%	+ 7.85%	+ 7.85%	+ 11.51%	+ 0.88%
581.9	6	Balanced Target	+ 21.02%	+ 8.20%	+ 8.20%	+ 9.48%	+ 0.73%
2,215.1	31	Conv. Securities	+ 23.24%	+ 4.61%	+ 4.61%	+ 16.29%	+ 0.87%
4,194.5	13	Income Funds	+ 17.03%	+ 8.29%	+ 8.29%	+ 10.07%	+ 0.48%
17,600.8	75	World Income Funds	+ 0.91%	+ 6.97%	+ 6.97%	+ 0.11%	+ 0.05%
164,289.6	567	Fixed Income Funds	+ 11.37%	+ 9.38%	+ 9.38%	+ 7.15%	+ 0.10%
491,401.4	1959	Total Long-Term Funds					
		Long-Term Average	+ 21.46%	+ 5.19%	+ 5.19%	+ 12.53%	+ 0.95%
		Long-Term Median	+ 19.40%	+ 7.30%	+ 7.30%	+ 11.70%	+ 0.70%
		Funds with % Change	1818	1768	1768	1866	1940
Lipper Indexes							
303.18	30	Capital Apprec Index	+ 33.61%	+ 6.02%	+ 6.02%	+ 21.13%	+ 2.71%
545.60	30	Growth Fund Index	+ 33.17%	+ 5.00%	+ 5.00%	+ 18.19%	+ 1.92%
275.09	30	Small Co Growth Index	+ 41.34%	+ 5.36%	+ 5.36%	+ 20.50%	+ 2.71%
825.61	30	Growth & Income Index	+ 27.04%	+ 5.77%	+ 5.77%	+ 15.24%	+ 1.11%
531.60	30	Equity Income Index	+ 23.26%	+ 7.32%	+ 7.32%	+ 13.78%	+ 0.85%
199.12	10	Sci & Tech Index	+ 44.71%	+ 0.64%	+ 0.64%	+ 20.92%	+ 3.73%
272.42	30	Global Fund Index	+ 8.03%	- 10.06%	- 10.06%	+ 2.01%	+ 1.40%
324.22	10	International Index	+ 2.58%	- 12.27%	- 12.27%	+ 4.15%	+ 1.04%
151.70	10	Gold Fund Index	+ 7.05%	+ 0.61%	+ 0.61%	+ 8.81%	- 0.38%
643.37	10	Balanced Fund Index	+ 22.78%	+ 8.28%	+ 8.28%	+ 12.72%	+ 0.98%
136.07	10	Conv. Secur. Index	+ 20.57%	+ 4.52%	+ 4.52%	+ 13.21%	+ 0.76%

Value 06/30/91		06/30/81-06/30/91	06/30/86-06/30/91	06/30/90-06/30/91	12/31/90-06/30/91	03/31/91-06/30/91
371.16	S&P 500 Reinvested	+ 324.60%	+ 75.55%	+ 7.38%	+ 14.24%	- 0.23%
2,906.75	Dow Jones Reinvested	+ 362.24%	+ 84.70%	+ 4.64%	+ 12.23%	+ 0.55%

Source: *Barron's*, July 15, 1991, p. 110. Reprinted by permission of *Barron's*, © 1991 by Dow Jones & Company, Inc. All Rights Reserved Worldwide.

by yield-curve changes or interest-rate graphs. Nevertheless, there is still a wide menu to choose from in *The Wall Street Journal* when tracking the performance of bond prices as indicated in Table 3–5. The indexes are broken down by different types of bonds: Treasury securities, corporate debt, tax-exempt issues, mortgage-backed securities, and convertibles. (All of these securities are discussed in Part 4.)

Mutual Fund Averages Lipper Analytical Services publishes the Lipper Mutual and Investment Performance Averages shown in Table 3–6. While mutual funds will be considered in depth in Chapter 19, for now it is interesting to observe the various categories that the funds are broken into to compute measures of performance. Also, observe in the next few columns of Table 3–6 that the starting point of the measurement period is very important in relation to the presence or absence of pluses (or minuses) in performance.

■ BUYING AND SELLING IN THE MARKET

Once you are generally familiar with the market and perhaps decide to invest directly in common stocks or other assets, you will need to set up an account with a retail brokerage house. Some of the largest and better-known retail brokers are Merrill Lynch, Shearson Lehman Brothers, and Prudential Securities, but there are many other good houses, both regional and national. When you set up your account, the account executive (often called stockbroker) will ask you to fill out a card listing your investment objectives, such as conservative, preservation of capital, income oriented, growth plus income, or growth. The account executive will also ask for your social security number for tax reporting, the level of your income, net worth, employer, and other information. Basically, the account executive needs to know your desire and ability to take risk in order to give good advice and proper management of your assets. Later in this section, we will also talk about discount brokers; that is, brokers who charge very low commissions but give stripped-down service.

Cash or Margin Account

The account executive will need to know if you want a cash account or margin account. Either account allows you five business days to pay for any purchase. A cash account requires full payment, while a **margin account** allows the investor to borrow a percentage of the purchase price from the brokerage firm. The percentage of the total cost the investor must pay is called the margin and is set by the Federal Reserve Board. During the great crash in the 1920s, margin on stock was only 10 percent, but it was as high as 80 percent in 1968. It has been at 50 percent since January 1974. The margin percentage is used to control speculation. When the Board of Governors of the Federal Reserve System thinks markets are being pushed too high by speculative fervor, it raises the margin requirement, which means more cash must be put up. The Fed has been hesitant to take action in this area in recent times.

Margin accounts are used mostly by traders and speculators or by investors who think their long-run return will be greater than the cost of borrowing. Most brokerage houses require a $2,000 minimum in an account before lending money, although many brokerage houses have higher limits. Here is how a margin account works. Assume you purchased 100 shares of Alcoa at $60 per share on margin and that margin is 50 percent.

Purchase: 100 shares at $60 per share	$ 6,000
Borrow: Cost (1 − margin percentage)	−3,000
Equity contributed—cash or securities	$ 3,000

You can borrow $3,000 or the total cost times (1 − margin percentage). The percentage cost of borrowing is generally 1 to 2 percent above the prime rate,

depending on the size of the account. Rather than putting up $3,000 in cash, a customer could put $3,000 of other approved financial assets into the account to satisfy the margin. Not all stocks may be used for margin purchases. The Securities and Exchange Commission publishes a list of approved securities that may be borrowed against.

One reason people buy on margin is to leverage their returns. Assume Alcoa stock rises to $80 per share. The account would now have $8,000 in stock and an increase in equity from $3,000 to $5,000.

100 shares at $80	$ 8,000
Loan	−3,000
Equity	$ 5,000

This $2,000 increase in equity creates a 67 percent return on the initial $3,000 of equity. The 67 percent return was accomplished on the basis of only a 33 percent increase in the price of stock ($60 to $80). With the increased equity in the account, the customer could now purchase additional securities on margin.

Margin is a two-edged sword, however, and what works to your advantage in up markets works to your disadvantage in down markets. If Alcoa stock had gone to $40, your equity would decrease to $1,000.

100 shares at $40	$ 4,000
Borrowed	−3,000
Equity	$ 1,000

Minimum requirements for equity in a margin account are called *minimum maintenance standards* (usually 25 percent). Your equity would now be at minimum maintenance standards where the equity of $1,000 equals 25 percent of the current market value of $4,000. A fall below $1,000 would bring a margin call for more cash or equity. Many brokerage firms have maintenance requirements above 25 percent, and when margin calls are made, the equity often needs to be increased to 35 percent or more of the portfolio value. Normally, you must maintain a $2,000 minimum in your account, so you would have been called for more equity when the stock was at $50 even though the minimum maintenance requirement had not yet been reached.

One feature of a margin account is that margined securities may not be delivered to the customer. In this case, the Alcoa stock would be kept registered in the street name of your retail brokerage house (e.g., Shearson Lehman Brothers), and your account would show a claim on 100 shares held as collateral for the loan. It is much like an automobile loan; you don't hold title to the car until you have made the last payment. In the use of margin, however,

there is no due date on the loan. The use of margin increases risk and is not recommended for anyone who cannot afford large losses or who has no substantial experience in the market.

Long or Short? — That Is the Question

Once you have opened the account of your choice, you are ready to buy or sell. When investors establish a position in a security, they are said to have a **long position** if they purchase the security for their account. It is assumed the reason they purchased the security was to profit on an increase in price over time and/or to receive dividend income. Investors who are long may take delivery of the securities (keep them in physical possession) if they have a cash account. Investors with a cash account may also choose to keep them on deposit in their brokerage account to facilitate bookkeeping, dividends, safe-keeping, and ease of sale. A margin account user has no choice but to keep them with the broker in street name.

Sometimes investors anticipate that the price of a security may drop in value. If they are long in the stock, some may sell out their position. Those who have no position at all may wish to take a **short position** to profit from the expected decline. When you short a security, you are borrowing the security from the broker and selling it with the obligation to replace the security in the future. How you can sell something you don't own is an obvious question. Your broker will simply lend you the security from the brokerage house inventory. If your brokerage house doesn't have an inventory of the particular stock you want to short, the firm will borrow the stock from another broker.

Once you go short, you begin hoping and praying that the price of the security will go down so that you can buy it back and replace the security at a lower price. In a perverse way, bad news starts to become good news. When you read the morning paper, you look for signs of unemployment, high inflation, and high interest rates in hopes of a stock market decline.

A short sale can only be made on a trade where the price of the stock advances (an uptick), or if there is no change in price, the prior trade must have been positive. These rules are intended to stop a snowballing decline in stock values caused by short sellers.

A margin requirement is associated with short selling, and it is currently equal to 50 percent of the securities sold short. Thus, if you were to sell 100 shares of General Electric (GE) short at $70 per share, you would be required to put up $3,500 in margin (50 percent of $7,000). In a short sale, the margin is considered to be good-faith money and obviously is not a down payment toward purchase. The margin protects the brokerage house in case you start losing money on your account.

You would lose money on a short sales position if the stock you sold short starts going up. Assume GE goes from $70 to $80. Since you initially sold 100 shares short at $70 per share, you have suffered a $1,000 paper loss. Your initial margin or equity position has been reduced from $3,500 to $2,500.

Initial margin (equity)	$ 3,500
Loss	− 1,000
Current margin (equity)	$ 2,500

We previously specified that there is a minimum 25 percent margin maintenance requirement in buying stock. A similar requirement exists in selling short. The equity position must equal at least 30 percent of the *current* value of the stock that has been sold short. In the present example, the equity position is equal to $2,500, and the current market value of GE is $8,000 ($80 × 100). Your margin percentage is 31.25 percent ($2,500 ÷ $8,000) or slightly above the minimum requirement. However, if the stock goes up another point or two and your losses increase, you will be asked to put up more margin to increase your equity position.

Of course, if the value of GE stock goes down from its initial base of $70, you would be making profits off the bad news. A 20-point drop in GE would mean a $2,000 profit on your 100 shares. Most market observers agree that it requires a "special breed of cat" to be an effective short seller. You often need nerves of steel and a contrarian outlook that can not be easily shaken by good news.

Aside from risk takers, some investors sell short to establish beneficial tax positions. For example, if you had bought Merck at $60 and five months later it was $100, you would have a $40 per share profit on paper. If you want to preserve the profit but wait until next year to pay the tax, you can **sell short against the box.** This means you can short shares against those you already hold. Since you own the stock and also have a short position, you can neither gain nor lose by price movements in the stock. In the following tax year, you can deliver the shares you hold to cover your short position. At that point, you will incur the tax obligations associated with the transactions. The total net profit will still be $40.

One final point on selling short. In the last 10 or 15 years, some investors have chosen to use other ways to take a negative position in a security. These normally involve put and call options, which are discussed in Chapter 15. Both selling short and option transactions can be effectively utilized for strategic purposes.

■ TYPES OF ORDERS

When an investor places an order to establish a position, he or she has many different kinds of orders from which to choose. When the order is placed with the account executive on a NYSE-listed stock, it is teletyped to the exchange where it is executed by the company's floor broker in an auction market. Each stock is traded at a specific trading post on the floor of the exchange, so the floor broker knows exactly where to go to find other brokers buying and selling the same company's shares.

Most orders placed will be straightforward market orders to buy or sell. The market order will be carried by the floor broker to the correct trading post and will usually trade close to the last price or within ¼ of a point. For example, if you want to sell 100 shares of AT&T at market, you would probably have no trouble finding a ready buyer, since AT&T may be trading a few million shares per day. But if you wanted to sell 100 shares of Bemis, as few as 1,000 shares might be traded in a day, and no other broker would be waiting at the Bemis post to make a transaction with the floor broker. If the broker finds no one else wishing to buy the shares, he will transact the sale with the specialist who is always at the post ready to buy and sell 100-share round lots. If the broker wants to sell, the specialist will either buy the shares for his or her own account at ⅛ to ¼ less than the last trade or will buy out of his or her book in which special orders of others are kept.

Two basic special orders are the limit order and the stop order. A **limit order** limits the price at which you are willing to buy or sell and assures you will pay no more than the limit price on a buy or receive no less than the limit price on a sell. Assume you are trying to buy a thinly traded stock that fluctuates in value and you are afraid that with a market order you might risk paying more than you want. So you would place a limit order to buy 100 shares of Bell Industries, as an example, at 16½ or a better price. The order will go to the floor broker who goes to the post to check the price. The broker finds Bell Industries trading at its high for the day of 16⅞, and so he leaves the limit order with the specialist who records it in his book. The entry will record the price, date, time, and brokerage firm. There may be other orders in front of yours at 16½, but once these are cleared, and assuming the stock stays in this range, your order will be executed at 16½ or less. Limit orders are used by investors to buy or sell thinly traded stocks or to buy securities at prices thought to be at the low end of a price range and to sell securities at the high end of the price range. Investors who calculate fundamental values have a basic idea of what they think a stock is worth and will often set a limit to take advantage of what they view to be discrepancies in values.

Many traders are certain they want their order to be executed if a certain price is reached. A limit order does not guarantee execution if orders are ahead of you on the specialist's book. In cases where you want a guaranteed "fill" of the order, a stop order is placed. A **stop order** is a two-part mechanism. It is placed at a specific price like a limit order, but when the price is reached, the stop turns into a market order that will be executed at close to the stop price but not necessarily at the exact price specified. Often, many short-term traders will view a common price with optimism for a certain trading strategy. When the stock hits the price, it may pop up on an abundance of buy orders or decline sharply on a large volume of sell orders, and your "fill" could be several dollars away from the top price. Assume AXE Corporation stock has been trading between $25 and $40 per share over the last six months, reaching both these prices three times. A trader may

follow several strategies. One strategy would be to buy at $25 and sell at $40 using a stop buy and a stop sell order. Some traders may put in a stop buy at $41 thinking that if the stock breaks through its peak trading range it will go on to new highs, and finally some may put in a stop sell at $23 to either eliminate a long position or establish a short position with the assumption the stock has broken its support and will trend lower. When used to eliminate a long position, a stop order is often called a *stop-loss order.*

Limit orders and stop orders can be "day orders" that expire at the end of the day if not executed, or they can be GTC (good till canceled) orders. GTC orders will remain on the specialist's books until taken off by the brokerage house or executed. If the order remains unfilled for several months, most brokerage houses will send reminders that the order is still pending so that the client does not get caught buying stock for which he or she is unable to pay. Orders have been known to stay on the specialist's books for years.

■ COST OF TRADING

Since May 1, 1975, commissions have been negotiated between the broker and customer, with larger orders getting smaller percentage charges. Before "May Day," commissions were fixed, and all brokers charged the same fee out of a published table for a given size order. Now there are individual variations, so check with several brokers. If commissions are of concern, you may want to do business with a "discount" broker who charges a discount of 25 to 75 percent from the old fixed-commission schedule.

Discount brokers are bare-bones operators providing only transactions and no research. They have found a niche with those investors who make up their own minds and do not need advice or personal service. The largest national discount broker is Charles Schwab & Co. To get a quote on the commission for a trade, you can call from anywhere in the country with a toll-free number (listed in your phone book). Many banks in local communities may also have subsidiaries that offer discount brokerage services, so you may wish to check with your local financial institution.

Regular brokerage houses still offer more personal service and more variety of services and are often part of a financial corporation involved in underwriting and investment banking, managing mutual funds and pension funds, economic advising, government bond dealings, and more. Unfortunately, you pay extra when dealing with a full-service broker. Table 3–7 lists the fees for a sampling of full-service brokers and discount brokers (the data are from mid-1991).

■ TAXES

In making many types of investments, an important consideration will be the tax consequences of your investment (taxes may be more significant than the brokerage commissions just discussed).

Table 3–7   Example of Round-Lot Commissions

	Full-Service Brokers Shares/Price				
	200 @ $25	300 @ $20	500 @ $15	500 @ $18	1,000 @ $14
Merrill Lynch	129.50	164.85	205.54	225.23	308.28
Shearson	139.61	166.39	212.15	235.26	351.51
Prudential	146.35	173.35	218.35	240.35	359.35
Dean Witter	130.59	155.15	197.15	218.50	341.31
	Discount Brokers				
Charles Schwab	89.00	95.60	101.50	106.60	123.60
Fidelity Brokerage	84.75	90.75	97.25	101.75	116.75
Quick & Reilly	60.50	65.00	77.75	81.50	94.00
Olde Discount	60.00	60.00	80.00	80.00	105.00

This section is intended only as a brief overview of tax consequences. For more information, consult a tax guide. Consultation with a CPA, CFP (Certified Financial Planner), or similar sources may also be advisable.

Before we specifically talk about the tax consequences of investment gains and losses, let's briefly look at the new tax rates under the 1990 Tax Act. The rates are presented in Table 3–8.

Refer to Table 3–8 and assume you have appropriately computed your taxable income after all deductions as $25,200. Further assume you are single so that you fall into the first category of the table. How much is your tax obligation? The answer is shown below.

Amount		Rate	Tax
1st	$20,350	15%	$3,053
Next	4,850	28%	1,358
	$25,200		$4,411

The total tax is $4,411. The rates of 15 percent and 28 percent are referred to as marginal tax rates. They apply to income within a given tax bracket. The average tax paid is a slightly different concept. It is simply the amount of taxes paid divided by taxable income, or 17.50 percent in this case.

$$\frac{\text{Taxes paid}}{\text{Taxable income}} = \frac{\$4,411}{\$25,200} = 17.50\%$$

Table 3–8   Tax Rates under the 1990 Tax Act (Rates apply to taxable income for 1991★)

Single	
Taxable Income	**Rate**
0–$20,350	15% of the amount
$20,350–$49,300	28% of the amount over $20,350
Over $49,300	31%[†]
Married (joint return)	
Taxable Income	**Rate**
0–$34,000	15% of the amount
$34,000–$82,150	28% of the amount over $34,000
Over $82,150	31%[†]

★The tax brackets will be adjusted slightly in future years to adjust for inflation.
[†]The rate in the third bracket will increase by .5% to 1.5% for those with incomes between $100,000 and $275,000 because of limitations on itemized deductions and the phase-out of personal exemptions. These factors are beyond the scope of our discussion.

Capital Gains and Loss Treatment

A **capital gain or loss** occurs when an asset held for investment purposes is sold. Under the 1990 Tax Act, there is no requirement for how long an asset must be held. Also under the 1990 act, the maximum rate on capital gains is 28 percent (approximately 3 percent less than the maximum rate applied to other forms of income as described in Table 3–8).

In computing capital gains for the year, the investor subtracts losses from gains. Some timing considerations are significant. The most important is that you can deduct up to $3,000 in security transaction losses in a given year against other forms of income. Thus, if you have a salary of $25,000 and you incur $3,000 in stock trading losses, your taxable income will only be $22,000 for that year.

Investors have some incentive to take losses (that is, translate dollar losses on paper to actual losses by selling the security or securities) before year-end. Perhaps an investor has sold $5,000 worth of stock at a profit during the year. When December comes, the investor may attempt to identify up to $8,000 of stocks to sell at a loss to cancel out the profit and create the maximum net loss of $3,000 for the year.

While investors should not let tax considerations override sound investment decisions (don't sell a potential long-term winner just for tax considerations), they have many ways to take losses and still maintain their basic position. For example, an investor might take a loss in one oil stock and buy another similar

Who Cheats on Their Income Taxes?

Each year the government loses 17 cents out of every dollar due on income taxes because of cheating by taxpayers. The cheating may take the form of not reporting income or taking non-existent or unjustified deductions. The total loss to the government is over $100 billion a year. This represents the unpaid taxes of otherwise honest Americans, not the additional tens of billions hidden by drug czars and other hardened criminals. If all taxes were properly collected, a large portion of our federal deficit could be wiped out.

The most frequent offenders are the self-employed. A 1990 Government Accounting Office (GAO) study revealed that auto dealers, restaurateurs, and clothing store operators underreport their taxable income by nearly 40 percent. Doctors, lawyers, barbers, and *accountants* underpay (cheat?) on 20 percent of their revenues. The most proficient of the nonreporters are in the food-service industry. Collectively, waiters and waitresses fail to report 84 percent of their tips, according to the GAO.

Claiming deductions for dependent children that do not exist is another favorite approach. In 1987, the IRS began requiring taxpayers to report and verify the social security numbers of all dependents over five years of age. The following year 7 million fewer dependents were claimed as deductions. It seems that many people had been listing the same child two or three times and even claiming dogs, cats, and birds as tax-deductible dependents.

Of course, not all feel guilty about not paying their full share of taxes. A shipyard manager who did not report income from yacht repairs on the weekend told *Money* magazine, "The government squanders the money I already pay. Why give more?"

Source: Marguerite T. Smith, "Who Cheats on Their Income Taxes?" *Money*, April 1991, pp. 101–8.

oil company at the same time (sell Exxon and buy Mobil, or vice versa). Furthermore, even a stock that has been sold for tax purposes can be repurchased after 30 days, and the loss is still deductible. Also, investors have many sophisticated ways to use options, convertibles, and other securities to maintain the potential for an upside move in a security they just sold.

One final point in dealing with the timing of losses. Although the maximum net loss (losses minus gains) deduction is $3,000 per year, a person can carry over larger losses to subsequent years and take up to a maximum of $3,000 in each ensuing year. Table 3–9 examines loss carryover potential for an investor.

We see the investor had net losses of $8,000 in 1992 of which $3,000 was written off against other income, leaving $5,000 to be carried forward. In 1993, another $3,000 was written off, so that $2,000 in losses was carried forward to 1994. In 1994, the investor had net losses of $1,800 during the year so that only $1,200 of the remaining $2,000 was utilized to accumulate the maximum $3,000 deduction. This left $800 to be carried over in subsequent years. Although not explicitly shown in the table, if the investor had net gains of $800 in 1995, the loss carryforward of $800 would simply mean no taxes would be owed on the gains.

Table 3–9   Tax Loss Carryover Analysis

1992		
$6,000 Gains	$14,000 Losses	$ 8,000 Net losses
		−3,000 Tax write-off
		$ 5,000 Tax loss carryover

1993		
$7,000 Gains	$ 7,000 Losses	0 Net loss
		$3,000 Tax write-off
		(carried over from 1992)
		$2,000 Remaining tax loss
		carryover ($5,000 − $3,000)

1994		
$4,200 Gains	$6,000 Losses	$1,800 Net loss
		1,200 Tax loss carryover
		$3,000 Tax write-off
		$ 800 Remaining tax loss
		carryover ($2,000 − $1,200)

IRAs and Taxes

Another important tax consideration for the investor is the use of individual retirement accounts (IRAs) to reduce current tax burdens and accumulate long-term wealth. The process through which a person may deduct $2,000 a year from current income and invest it tax-free until a future withdrawal is covered in detail in Appendix 3–A.

■ SUMMARY

The investor should have a basic understanding of measures of market performance, the rules and mechanics of opening and trading in an account, and tax considerations.

In gauging the movements in the market, the investor may view the Dow Jones Industrial Average, the Standard & Poor's 500 Stock Index, the Standard & Poor's MidCap Index, the Value Line Average of 1,700 companies, or the NASDAQ Averages (to name a few). To evaluate various industry data, the investor may turn to the Dow Jones Industry Group data, and for mutual funds, to the Lipper Mutual Fund Investment Performance Averages. There

also are a number of bond indexes and averages for foreign trading. The investor will try to evaluate performance in light of an index that closely parallels the makeup of the investor's portfolio.

In further considering the advisability of using an index to measure comparative performance, the investor may wish to determine whether it is price-weighted, value-weighted, or equal-weighted. The weighting measure determines how large an effect the movement of an individual security has on the index.

With some understanding of the various markets and the related means of measurements for those markets (such as the DJIA), the potential investor is now in a position to consider opening an account. The investor may establish either a cash or margin account and use the account to buy securities or to sell short (in which case a margin account is necessary). The investor can also execute a number of different types of orders such as a market order, a limit order, and a stop order. The latter two specify prices where the investor wishes to initiate transactions.

The investor must also consider the tax consequences of his or her actions. Although no one likes to sustain losses from investment activity, when they do occur, they should be properly utilized to shelter other income. The IRS allows a maximum deduction of $3,000 per year, and large losses can be carried forward. Finally, the investor may wish to route a portion of investments through an individual retirement account (IRA) because the initial contribution is tax deductible and subsequent funds grow tax-free until withdrawn at retirement. This topic is discussed in Appendix 3–A.

IMPORTANT WORDS AND CONCEPTS

Dow Jones Industrial Average (DJIA) 78
price-weighted average 81
Standard & Poor's 500 Stock Index 81
Standard & Poor's 100 Index 83
Standard & Poor's MidCap Index 83
value-weighted 83
Value Line Average 84
equal-weighted 84

Wilshire 5000 Equity Index 85
margin account 88
long position 90
short position 90
sell short against the box 91
limit order 92
stop order 92
capital gain or loss 95

DISCUSSION QUESTIONS

1. Why is the Dow Jones Industrial Average considered a "blue-chip" measure of value?
2. How is the Dow Jones Industrial Average adjusted for stock splits?
3. What are the criticisms and a defense of the Dow Jones Industrial Average?

4. Explain the price-weighted average concept as applied to the Dow Jones Industrial Average.

5. What categories of stocks make up the Standard & Poor's 500 Stock Index?

6. Why was the Standard & Poor's MidCap Index created? What is the size range for firms in the index?

7. What is a value-weighted index? Explain the impact that large firms have on value-weighted indexes such as the S&P 500.

8. What is an equal-weighted average? Which average has this characteristic?

9. Why might one say that the Wilshire 5000 Equity Index is the most comprehensive market measure?

10. Fill in the table below for the type of weighting system for the various indexes. Put an (x) under the appropriate weighting system.

	Price-Weighted	Value-Weighted	Equal-Weighted
NYSE Composite Index	_____	_____	_____
Value Line Average	_____	_____	_____
S&P 500 Index	_____	_____	_____
Dow Jones Industrial Average	_____	_____	_____
NASDAQ Composite	_____	_____	_____

11. If you did not wish a high-priced or heavily capitalized firm (one with high total market value) to overly influence your index, which of the weighting systems described in this chapter would you be likely to use?

12. Explain the difference between a cash and a margin account.

13. What is meant by the concept of minimum maintenance standards (or requirements) for margin?

14. Why is bad news "good news" to the short seller?

15. Explain how selling short against the box allows one to defer taxes until the following year.

16. Explain what is meant by a limit order. How does a stop order differ from a limit order?

17. What is the difference between day orders and GTC orders?

18. What do you give up and what do you gain when you use a discount broker in preference to a regular broker?

19. What is the difference between the meaning of the marginal tax rate and the average tax rate for a taxpayer?

20. What is the maximum amount of investment losses that can be deducted against other forms of income in any given year? What happens if the losses exceed this amount?

PROBLEMS

Computing an
index

1. Assume the following five companies are used in computing an index.

Company	Shares Outstanding	Base Period Jan. 1, 1969, Market Price	Current Period Dec. 31, 1992, Market Price
A	1,000	$ 4	$10
B	5,000	5	20
C	10,000	10	40
D	3,000	12	45
E	2,000	15	8

a. If the index is price-weighted, what will be the value of the index on December 31, 1992? (Take the average price on December 31, 1992, and divide by the average price on January 1, 1969, and multiply by 100.)

b. If the index is value-weighted, what will be the value of the index on December 31, 1992? (Take the total market value on December 31, 1992, and divide by the total market value on January 1, 1969, and multiply by 100.)

c. Explain why the answer in *b* is different from the answer in *a.*

Changing index
value

2. Assume the following stocks make up a *value-weighted* index.

Corporation	Shares Outstanding	Market Price
Maris	6,000	$30
Mantle	14,000	5
Howard	4,000	8
Richardson	30,000	20

a. Compute the total market value and the weights assigned to each stock.

b. Assume the shares of the Howard Corporation go up by 50 percent, while those of the Richardson Corporation go down by a mere 10 percent. The other two stocks remain constant. What will be the newly established value for the index?

c. Explain why the index followed the pattern it did in part *b.*

Margin purchase

3. Assume you buy 100 shares of stock at $50 per share on margin (50 percent). If the price rises to $60 per share, what is your percentage gain in equity?

Margin purchase
4. In Problem 3, what would the percentage loss be if the price had decreased to $35?

Minimum margin
5. Assume you have a 25 percent minimum margin standard in Problems 3 and 4. With a price decline to $35, will you be called on to put up more margin to meet the 25 percent rule? Disregard the $2,000 minimum margin balance requirement.

Minimum margin
6. Recompute the answer to Problem 5 based on a stock decline to $32. Under this circumstance, will you be called on to put up more margin?

Selling short
7. You sell 100 shares of PIM Corporation short. The price of the stock is $80 per share. The margin requirement is 50 percent.

   a. How much is your initial margin?

   b. If the stock goes down to $60, what is your percentage gain or loss on the initial margin (equity)?

   c. If stock goes up to $90, what is your percentage gain or loss on the initial margin (equity)?

   d. In part c, if the minimum margin standard is 30 percent, will you be required to put up more margin? (Do the additional necessary calculations to answer this question.)

   e. At what stock price (use a whole number) will you be required to put up more margin?

Margin purchase and selling short
8. You are very optimistic about the biotechnology industry so you buy 200 shares of Scientific Resources at $65 per share. You are very pessimistic about the trucking industry, so you short-sell 300 shares of Ace Trucking Corporation at $75. Each transaction requires a 50 percent margin balance.

   a. What is the initial equity in your account?

   b. Assume the price of each stock is as follows for the next three months (month-end). Compute the equity balance in your account for each month.

Month	Scientific Resources	Ace Trucking
January	$68	$70
February	60	77
March	59	56

Computing commissions
9. Assume an investor is going to buy 1,000 shares of stock at $14 per share. Based on the data in Table 3–7:

   a. How much will the commission be if the shares are purchased through Prudential? What is the commission if the shares are purchased through Quick & Reilly?

   b. What percent is the discount broker's commission of the full-service broker's commission?

Computing tax
obligation

10. Compute the tax obligation for the following:

  a. An individual with taxable income of $37,200.

  b. A married couple with taxable income of $110,000. (Use 31 percent as the top bracket rate for over $82,150).

  c. What is the average tax rate in part *b?*

Tax loss
carryover

11. Carl Bolden had the following stock transactions in 1992:

Stock X	$8,000	Gain
Stock Y	15,000	Loss
Stock Z	4,000	Loss

  a. How much of the loss can he deduct against 1992 income from other sources?

  b. How much is his tax loss carryover?

Tax loss
carryover

12. Assume that in the next three years Carl Bolden (from Problem 11) has the following gains and losses:

	1993	1994	1995
Gains	$4,000	$7,000	$3,500
Losses	6,000	5,000	2,500

How much of the loss carryover computed in Problem 11*b* will he use in each of the three years. Recall the maximum net loss write-off in any one year is $3,000. Also, you must take your loss write-offs as quickly as allowed.

Tax loss
carryover

13. Sheila Franklin has the following completed security transactions in 1993.

Stock A	$12,000	Gain
Stock B	5,000	Loss
Stock C	7,000	Gain

She is holding three stocks in her current portfolio.

Gamma	$10,000	Unrealized loss
Beta	6,000	Unrealized gain
Delta	7,000	Unrealized loss

An unrealized gain or loss simply means the gain or loss is on paper, but the stock has not yet been sold.

   a. For Sheila to realize a maximum net $3,000 loss for tax purposes in 1993, what stocks in her portfolio should she sell?

   b. Would she always want to follow this action?

CRITICAL THOUGHT CASE

Tony Maxwell had been writing the business column for the past eight years at a local newspaper in a West Coast city with a population of 500,000. He often interviewed brokers and local investors who had accumulated fortunes as a result of successful investments in companies within the region. Tony felt a little jealous of their success as he continued to exist on a $25,000 annual salary. He knew with two teenagers entering college in the next few years he would have trouble managing his finances.

Although Tony made investments from time to time, they were for small amounts because of the constraints on his financial resources. Furthermore, he seemed to suffer losses as often as he made gains. Although he had never sold short before, he decided to take this action more on instinct than anything else. He had observed the activities of Owens Manufacturing Company, a supplier of component parts for personal computers, and thought the management team was particularly weak. Luther Owens, the founder of the company, had recently died, and the top management position passed on to his son, Alston Owens. Alston lacked many of the management and technical skills of his father and seemed more proficient at lowering his golf handicap than increasing corporate profits.

As indicated, Tony Maxwell's decision to sell short was initially motivated by an intuitive feel for the company rather than any hard evidence. However, two weeks after he took his short position, he was interviewing a representative from Apple Computer Company when it was revealed that Owens Manufacturing was about to lose a major contract with the firm. Tony was excited about the fact that his initial short sell position was about to become successful because of the likely drop in Owens Manufacturing Company stock. Nevertheless, he had a couple of important thoughts in the back of his mind.

Questions

1. Because of his investment position, should Tony be allowed to write this story?

2. Should he immediately increase his short position in Owens Manufacturing Company before doing anything else?

■ MARKETBASE-E EXERCISES

In the following exercise, please use your MarketBase-E Software and manual to screen for the required portfolios. You will have to figure out how to search through the data to pull out those companies meeting the requirements set down.

1. *a.* The Dow Jones Industrial Average consists of 30 companies. Look up the names of these companies in a current paper. (*Barron's* or *The Wall Street Journal* have a list. There is also a listing in Figure 3–1.) What basic industries are represented by this average?

   b. Determine the total sales of all companies in the representative industries. (**Hint:** Sort by SIC code to do this.) For example, add total sales of all the oil companies, all the auto companies etc. Then determine what the relative ranking would be for each industry. Rank from the highest to the lowest sales.

2. Look up the divisor for the Dow Jones Average in *Barron's* or *The Wall Street Journal.* Take the most recent price for each stock from MarketBase-E and compute the index value using this divisor. How does this value compare with the current level of the Dow Jones Industrial Average?

■ SELECTED REFERENCES

Market Indexes

Butler, Hartman, L., Jr., and J. Devon Allen. "The Dow Jones Industrial Average Reexamined." *Financial Analysts Journal,* November–December 1979, pp. 23–30.

Chakravarty, Subrata, and Dana Wechsler Liden. "Dow Jones: A Belt, Suspenders and Elastic Waistband." *Forbes,* February 3, 1992, pp. 69–74.

Peters, Edgar E. "A Chaotic Attractor: The S&P 500." *Financial Analysts Journal,* March–April 1991, pp. 55–62.

Schultz, John W. "Misleading Averages." *Barron's,* July 7, 1977, p. 5.

Stock Trading

Chan, K. C. "On the Contrarian Investment Strategy." *Journal of Business,* April 1988, pp. 147–64.

Grube, R. Corwin; O. Maurice Joy; and Don B. Panton. "Market Response to Federal Reserve Changes in the Initial Margin Requirement." *Journal of Finance,* June 1979, pp. 659–74.

Ippolito, Richard A., and John A. Turner. "Turnover, Fees, and Pension Plan Performance." *Financial Analysts Journal,* November–December 1987, pp. 16–26.

Shepard, Lawrence. "How Good Is Investment Advice for Individuals?" *Journal of Portfolio Management,* Winter 1977, pp. 32–36.

West, Richard R., and Seha M. Tinic. "Institutionalization: Its Impact on the Provision of Marketability Services and the Individual Investor." *Journal of Contemporary Business,* Winter 1974, pp. 25–48.

Brokerage Services

"A Brokerage that Plays by Its Own Rules." *Business Week,* September 24, 1984, pp. 119–20.

Groth, John C.; Wilbur G. Lewellen; Gary G. Schlarbaum; and Ronald C. Lease. "An Analysis of Brokerage House Securities Recommendations." *Financial Analysts Journal,* January–February 1979, pp. 32–40.

Mahon, Gigi. "Sunny Side of the Street: Discount Brokers Increase Share of Trade." *Barron's,* June 11, 1979, p. 11.

Taxation

Ben-Horim, Moshe: Shalom Hochman; and Oded Palmon. "The Impact of the 1986 Tax Reform Act on Corporate Financial Policy." *Financial Management,* Autumn 1987, pp. 29–35.

The Tax Reform Act: Analysis and Planning Opportunities. New York: Arthur Young, 1986.

Understanding the 1986 Tax Changes: An Executive Summary. New York: Touche Ross, 1986.

Appendix 3–A: More Information on IRAs and Taxes

An individual retirement account (IRA) allows some taxpayers to deduct $2,000 from taxable income and invest the funds at a bank, savings and loan, brokerage house, or other financial institution. Not only is the $2,000 allowed to be deducted from earned income to reduce current taxes, but the income is allowed to grow tax-free until withdrawn at retirement. For the young investor who meets Internal Revenue Service restrictions, the use of IRAs may be particularly appropriate as an investment vehicle. Instead of investing $2,000 directly in the market, an investor may wish to set up an IRA with a brokerage house so that he or she can deduct the $2,000 from earned income before it is invested. While an individual may qualify for a $2,000 deduction, a couple filing a joint return may qualify for a $2,250 deduction if there is only one working spouse and $4,000 if there are two working spouses who aren't covered in employer pension plans. The money initially put into an IRA must be earned income and not gifts from others, inheritance funds, and so forth.

In Table 3A–1, we look at the potential accumulation in an IRA account based on annual contributions of $2,000 and various compound rates of growth on the funds. Note that the age at which contributions begin and the compounding rate are both significant. For example, a person who begins contributions at age 25 and earns a 10 percent return will accumulate $1,437,810 at age 70. If the same person had waited to age 45, the accumulation at age 70 (based on a 10 percent growth rate) would only be $196,694.

When you begin to withdraw funds from your IRA in later life, you do have to pay your normal tax rate on your annual withdrawals (but you have had the potential for tremendous tax-free accumulation up to that point). It should be pointed out that one can wait to begin withdrawing funds until anywhere from age 59½ up to age 70½ (it's up to you to choose). At that time, you must withdraw a specified minimum amount each year based on your life expectancy and the amount of funds in your IRA. One disadvantage of withdrawing funds before age 59½ is that you pay a 10 percent penalty on the early withdrawal as well as the normal tax rate on the funds withdrawn (this depends on your marginal tax bracket).

Because IRAs can be such an advantageous way to make stock market investments or draw interest on savings instruments, the IRS restricts the use of IRAs for those who *also* participate in work-related retirement plans. In

Table 3A–1   Value of IRA Fund at Age 70 ($2,000 Annual contribution)

Age Contributions Begin	Compound Annual Rate of Return			
	8 Percent	**10 Percent**	**12 Percent**	**14 Percent**
20	$1,147,540	$2,327,817	$4,800,036	$9,989,043
25	773,011	1,437,810	2,716,460	5,181,130
30	518,113	885,185	1,534,183	2,684,050
35	344,634	542,049	863,327	1,387,145
40	226,566	328,988	482,665	713,574
45	146,212	196,694	266,668	363,742
50	91,524	114,550	144,105	182,050
55	54,304	63,545	74,559	87,685
60	28,973	31,875	35,097	38,675

Table 3A–2   Phaseout of Allowable IRA Contributions for Taxpayers in a Work-Related Pension Plan

Individual		Joint Filing		
Income Level	**Maximum IRA Deduction**	**Income Level**	**Married, 1 Spouse Works**	**Married, 2 Spouses Work**
$25,000	$2,000	$40,000	$2,250	$4,000
26,000	1,900	41,000	2,138	3,800
27,000	1,700	42,000	1,913	3,400
28,000	1,500	43,000	1,688	3,000
29,000	1,300	44,000	1,463	2,600
30,000	1,100	45,000	1,238	2,200
31,000	900	46,000	1,013	1,800
32,000	700	47,000	788	1,400
33,000	500	48,000	563	1,000
34,000	300	49,000	338	600
35,000	100	50,000	113	200
Over $35,000	0	Over $50,000	0	0

Table 3A–2, we see the phaseout of allowable annual contributions to an IRA for those who participate in such work-related plans. For example, an individual who makes $30,000 and is in a work-related plan can contribute only $1,100 annually to an IRA as a tax-deductible item. If an individual is not in a work-related retirement plan, he or she can take the full $2,000 taxable deduction regardless of income level. Even those individuals who do not qualify for the $2,000 deduction can still put the funds in an IRA and allow them to grow tax-free until retirement. The taxpayer does not get the initial $2,000 deduction from income, but the subsequent return on the funds grows tax-free until retirement.

In summary, IRAs are generally a desirable way to shelter income from taxation initially (if you qualify) and allow it to grow tax-free until retirement. IRAs, however, are not a desirable investment if you are likely to have a liquidity problem one or two years after you make the contribution and end up having to pay a 10 percent withdrawal penalty[1] as well as your normal taxes on the funds withdrawn. Also, even if you make a contribution to an IRA in one year, you are not required to make a similar contribution in subsequent years (though the accumulations in Table 3A–1 are based on regular annual contributions).

DISCUSSION QUESTIONS

3A–1. Explain why IRAs offer the potential for large wealth accumulation if contributions are made on a regular basis.

3A–2. During what age "time frame" does one normally begin withdrawing funds from an IRA? What are the consequences if funds are withdrawn before this?

3A–3. If a person does not participate in a work-related pension plan, is there any restriction on income level as far as making tax deductible contributions to an IRA?

3A–4. Assuming a taxpayer(s) qualifies for an IRA, what is the maximum deduction for (*a*) an individual, (*b*) a couple filing a joint return if only one spouse works, and (*c*) a couple filing a joint return where both spouses work?

---

[1]Generally, the break-even point for using an IRA is about five years. That is, it takes about that long for the tax advantages to overcome the withdrawal penalty.

■ APPENDIX 3A PROBLEM

IRA contribution
and accumulation

3A–1. *a.* Andrew Lewis, a bachelor, has an income level of $29,000 and participates in a work–related pension plan. What is the maximum tax deductible contribution he can make to an IRA?

b. His sister Lucille is self-employed as a lawyer and makes $50,000 a year. She also is unmarried. What is the maximum deductible contribution she can make to an IRA?

c. Assume Lucille makes her maximum contribution from age 35 to age 70 and receives a 14 percent return on her funds. How much will she accumulate by age 70?

4

Sources of Investment Information

111

We are continually exposed to much information in this world of expanding and rapid communications. As the scope of investments has grown to include more than stocks and bonds, investment information has expanded to cover items such as gold and silver, diamonds, original art, antiques, stamps and coins, real estate, farmland, oil and gas, commodities, mutual funds, and other specialized assets. The problem investors are faced with is not only which investments to choose from the many available, but also where to find relevant information on specific investments.

First, the investor needs a basic knowledge of the economic environment. After determining the economic climate, the investor will proceed to a more detailed analysis of industries and unique variables affecting a specific investment. It is often said that the sign of an educated person is whether he or she knows where to find information to make an intelligent decision. The rest of this chapter will attempt to provide a list and descriptions of the basic information sources for some of the more common forms of investments as well as sources for general economic data.

You may want to refer to this chapter as you go through the chapters that follow. This chapter is not intended to be a guide for analysis—only an overview of what information is available. You may have heard the phrase "a picture is worth a thousand words." You will find that is certainly true of the tables and figures in this chapter. It is virtually impossible to discuss each and every variable found in them. To acquaint yourself more fully with information sources, we suggest you visit your college and local library and browse through their collections of economic and financial services. Appendix 4–A at the end of the chapter contains the addresses of a number of the sources mentioned in the chapter.

■ AGGREGATE ECONOMIC DATA

Economic data are necessary for analyzing the past and predicting trends. The economic environment that exists today and the one expected in the future will bear heavily on the types of investments selected when creating or managing an investment portfolio. Information on inflation, wages, disposable income, economic growth rates, interest rates, money supply, demographic trends, and so on are important economic data that will influence investor decisions. This information is available in many publications from the government, commercial banks, and periodicals. What follows is a brief description of some of the major sources of economic data.

Federal Reserve Bulletin

The *Federal Reserve Bulletin* is published monthly by the Board of Governors of the Federal Reserve System, Washington, D.C. It contains an abundance of monetary data such as money supply figures, interest rates, bank reserves, and various statistics on commercial banks. Fiscal variables such as U.S. budget

receipts and outlays and federal debt figures are also found in the *Bulletin*. This publication also contains data on international exchange rates and U.S. dealings with foreigners and overseas banks.

A complete description of the *Federal Reserve Bulletin* is outside the scope of this chapter, but a partial listing of the table of contents will provide a better idea of what information it contains. Each heading may be divided into more detailed sections that provide information for the previous month, the current year on a monthly basis, and several years of historical annual data.

Domestic Financial Statistics
Federal Reserve Banks
Monetary and Credit Aggregates
Commercial Banks
Financial Markets
Federal Finance
Securities Markets and Corporate Finance
Real Estate
Consumer Installment Credit
Domestic Non Financial Statistics
International Statistics
Securities Holdings and Transactions
Interest and Exchange Rates

Federal Reserve Banks

The 12 Federal Reserve banks in the Federal Reserve System represent different geographical areas (districts) of the United States. Each bank publishes its own monthly letter or review that includes economic data about its region and sometimes commentary on national issues or monetary policy. The 12 banks by district are as follows: Boston (1), New York (2), Philadelphia (3), Cleveland (4), Richmond (5), Atlanta (6), Chicago (7), St. Louis (8), Minneapolis (9), Kansas City (10), Dallas (11), and San Francisco (12).

Federal Reserve Bank of St. Louis

One district bank, the Federal Reserve Bank of St. Louis, publishes some of the most-comprehensive economic statistics on a weekly and monthly basis. *U.S. Financial Data* is published weekly and includes data on the monetary base, bank reserves, money supply, a breakdown of time deposits and demand deposits, borrowing from the Federal Reserve banks, and business loans from the large commercial banks. The publication also includes yields and interest rates on a weekly basis on selected short-term and long-term securities. An example of these published interest rates appears in Figures 4–1 and 4–2.

Figure 4–1

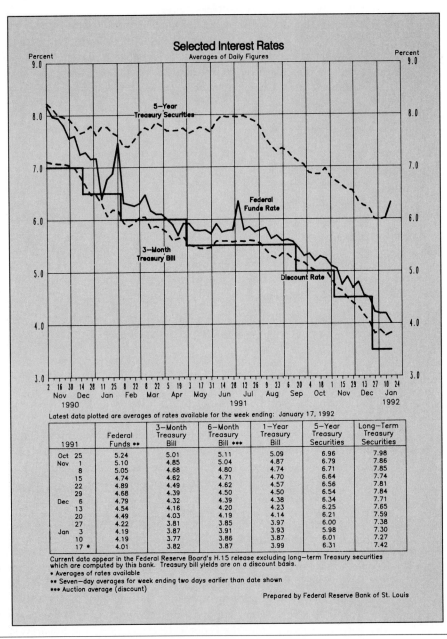

Source: *U.S. Financial Data,* January 16, 1992.

Figure 4–2

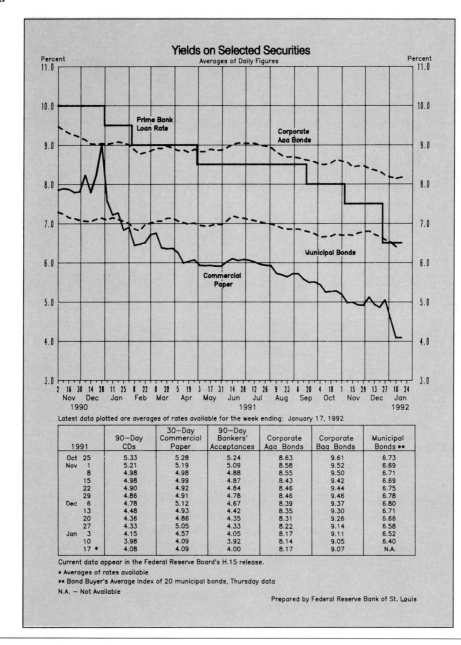

Yields on Selected Securities

Averages of Daily Figures

Latest data plotted are averages of rates available for the week ending: January 17, 1992

1991	90–Day CDs	30–Day Commercial Paper	90–Day Bankers' Acceptances	Corporate Aaa Bonds	Corporate Baa Bonds	Municipal Bonds **
Oct 25	5.33	5.28	5.24	8.63	9.61	6.73
Nov 1	5.21	5.19	5.09	8.58	9.52	6.69
8	4.98	4.98	4.88	8.55	9.50	6.71
15	4.98	4.99	4.87	8.43	9.42	6.69
22	4.90	4.92	4.84	8.46	9.44	6.75
29	4.86	4.91	4.78	8.46	9.46	6.78
Dec 6	4.78	5.12	4.67	8.39	9.37	6.80
13	4.48	4.93	4.42	8.35	9.30	6.71
20	4.36	4.86	4.35	8.31	9.26	6.66
27	4.33	5.05	4.33	8.22	9.14	6.58
Jan 3	4.15	4.57	4.05	8.17	9.11	6.52
10	3.98	4.09	3.92	8.14	9.05	6.40
17 *	4.08	4.09	4.00	8.17	9.07	N.A.

Current data appear in the Federal Reserve Board's H.15 release.

* Averages of rates available

** Bond Buyer's Average Index of 20 municipal bonds, Thursday data

N.A. — Not Available

Prepared by Federal Reserve Bank of St. Louis

Source: *U.S. Financial Data,* January 16, 1992.

Monetary Trends, published monthly, includes charts and tables of monthly data. The information is similar to that found in *U.S. Financial Data* but covers a longer time period. The tables provide compound annual rates of change, while the graphs include the raw data with trend changes over time. Additional data are available on the federal government debt and its composition by type of holder and on the receipts and expenditures of the government for both the National Income Account Budget and the High Employment Budget.

National Economic Trends is also published by the Federal Reserve Bank of St. Louis and presents monthly economic data on employment, unemployment rates, consumer and producer prices, industrial production, personal income, retail sales, productivity, compensation and labor costs, gross domestic product, the implicit price deflator for the GDP, personal consumption expenditures, gross private domestic investment, government purchases of goods and services, disposable personal income, corporate profit after taxes, and inventories. This information is presented in graphic form and in tables showing the compounded annual rate of change on a monthly basis. If raw data are needed, other economic publications are required.

Survey of Current Business

The *Survey of Current Business* is published monthly by the Bureau of Economic Analysis of the U.S. Department of Commerce. During 1991, the Commerce Department stopped publishing the *Business Conditions Digest,* and the *Survey of Current Business* now serves as the major outlet for economic time series data. It also contains a monthly update and evaluation of the business situation, analyzing such data as GNP, GDP, business inventories, personal consumption, fixed investment, exports, labor market statistics, financial data, and much more. For example, personal consumption expenditures are broken down into subcategories of durable goods, such as motor vehicles and parts and furniture and equipment; nondurables, such as food, energy, clothing, and shoes; and services.

The survey can be extremely helpful for industry analysis because it breaks data into basic industries. For example, data on inventory, new plant and equipment, production, and more can be found for such specific industries as coal, tobacco, chemicals, leather products, furniture, and paper. Even within industries such as lumber, production statistics can be found on hardwoods and softwoods right down to Douglas fir trees, southern pine, and western pine. To provide a more comprehensive view of what is available in the *Survey of Current Business,* a list of the major series updates follows:

GNP, GDP	Housing Starts and Permits
National Income	Retail Trade
Personal Income	Labor Force, Employment and
Industrial Production	Earnings

Manufacturers' Shipments, Inventories and Orders	Banking
Consumer Price Index	Consumer Installment Credit
Producer Price Index	Stock Prices
Construction Put in Place	Value of Exports and Imports
	Motor Vehicles

The *Survey of Current Business* includes many graphical presentations of economic time series data including the leading, lagging, and coincident indicators as shown in Figure 4–3. Overall, the *Survey* can be very helpful in understanding past economic behavior and in forecasting future economic activity with a higher degree of success.

Other Sources of Economic Data

So far, we have presented the basic sources of economic data. Many more sources are available. What is available to each investor may vary from library to library, so here are some brief notes on other sources of data.

Many universities have bureaus of business research that provide statistical data on a statewide or regional basis. Major banks, such as Citicorp, Morgan Guaranty Trust, Harris Trust, and Bank of America, publish monthly or weekly letters or economic reviews, including raw data and analysis. Several other government sources are available, such as *Economic Indicators* prepared by the Council of Economic Advisors and the *Annual Economic Report of the President*. Additionally, many periodicals, such as *Business Week, Fortune,* and *Barron's,* contain raw data as well as economic commentary. Moody's and Standard & Poor's investment services (introduced on the following pages) both publish economic data along with much other market-related information.

▪ INVESTMENT ADVISORY SERVICES

Investment information and advice is available from many sources—from large corporate financial services to individuals writing investment letters. A look through such financial magazines as *Barron's, Forbes,* and *Financial World* will turn up hundreds of investment services charging fees large and small for the information they sell. Most public libraries and universities subscribe from several of the major publishers, such as Moody's, Standard & Poor's, or Value Line.

Moody's

Moody's is owned by Dun & Bradstreet and publishes several data bases for bonds and stocks. *Moody's Manuals* are widely used and present historical financial data on the companies listed, their officers, and the companies' general corporate condition. The *Manuals* are divided into several categories

Figure 4-3   Cyclical Indicators (Composite indexes and their components)

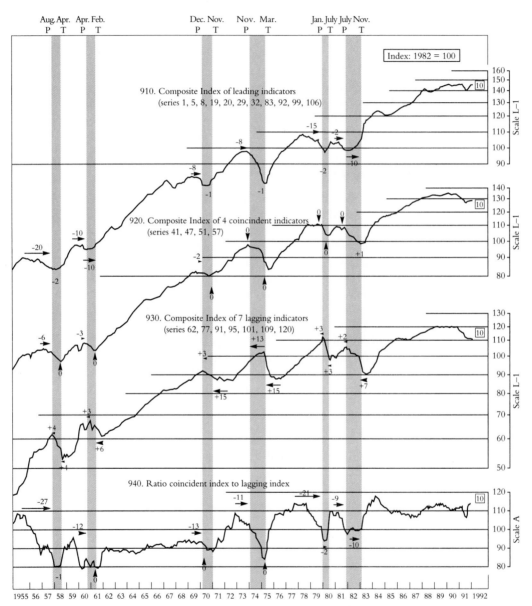

Note:— The numbers and arrows indicate length of leads (–) and lags (+) in months from business cycle turning dates.
Current data for these series are shown on page C-1.

Source: *Survey of Current Business* (Washington, D.C.: U.S. Department of Commerce Bureau of Economic Analysis, November, 1991), p. C–7.

(Banks and Finance, Industrial, Municipals and Government, OTC Industrial, Public Utility, and Transportation). Each manual has a biweekly news supplement that updates quarterly earnings, dividend announcements, mergers, and other news of interest. *Moody's Manuals* are comprehensive, with each category taking up one or two volumes and several thousand pages.

Moody's Bond Record, a monthly publication, contains data on corporates, convertibles, governments, municipals, and ratings on commercial paper and preferred stock. Corporate bond information includes the interest coupon, payment dates, call price, Moody's rating, and yield to maturity. The current price as well as the yearly and historical high-low prices are presented. The total amount of the bond issue outstanding is given with a designation for a sinking fund and the original issue date. Data on convertible bonds also include the conversion price, conversion value, and conversion period. Information on industrial revenue and municipal bonds is usually limited to the Moody's rating. *Moody's Bond Record* also contains historical yield graphs for various types of bonds over at least 30 years.

Moody's also publishes a weekly *Bond Survey* that reviews the week's activity in the bond market, rating changes, new issues, and bonds called for redemption. *Moody's Dividend Record* presents quarterly dividends and the date of declaration, date of record, date payable, and ex-dividend dates. This is an annual publication. *Moody's Handbook of Common Stock* is a quarterly reference guide that summarizes a company's 10-year historical financial data along with a discussion of corporate background, recent developments, and prospects. Approximately 1,000 companies are listed in the *Handbook.*

Only a brief description has been given for each Moody's publication, but enough has been presented for you to know whether a particular one may be worth looking at further.

Standard & Poor's

A second major source of information is the Standard & Poor's Corporation, a subsidiary of McGraw-Hill. Standard & Poor's has very comprehensive coverage of financial data. The following items will not all be discussed, but they provide a good look at what Standard & Poor's makes available to the investor.

> **Services for Business and Investment Decision Making:**
> **Fundamental Company Information:**
> Corporation Records
> Stock Guide
> Bond Guide
> Stock Reports
> Mutual Fund Profiles
> S&P Compustat

Broad Spectrum Industry Information:
Industry Surveys
Statistical Service
Analyst's Handbook
Industry Reports

Investment Advisory Services:
The Outlook
Emerging and Special Situations
Private Label Newsletters
S&P New Issues Institutional Research

Services Dealing with Indexes, Charting, and Stock Prices:
S&P Index Services
S&P 100 Information Bulletin
S&P 500 Information Bulletin
Daily Stock Price Record
Trendline Chart Services

Electronically Delivered Services:
S&P MarketScope
Corporations CD-ROM
S&P Corporate Descriptions Online
S&P Daily News Online
Standard & Poor's Register Online
S&P ComStock
Stock Guide/Bond Guide Database
Index Alert

Law Publications:
Review of Securities and Commodities Regulation
Review of Banking and Financial Services

Directory Services:
Standard & Poor's Register of Corporations, Directors and Executives
Compmark Data Services
Security Dealers of North America
Money Market Directory

Standard & Poor's Corporation Records are similar to *Moody's Manuals* except they are organized alphabetically rather than by trade categories. The *Corporation Records* are published monthly, and the six volumes are updated by daily supplements. Information found in the volumes includes historical company background, financial statements, news announcements, earnings updates, and other news of general interest. Companies found in the *Corporation Records* are listed, and their subsidiary companies are cross-listed.

Something that may be overlooked when examining the *Corporation Records* is the statistical section found in the T–Z volume. The statistical section includes a mutual fund summary, an address list of many no-load mutual funds,

and foreign bond statistics. Special tables contained in the T–Z volume list new stock and bond offerings on a monthly basis. This volume also presents a classified index of industrial companies listed by standard industrial classification code numbers (SIC). For example, if you want to find out about cereal breakfast food companies, you would first find the corresponding SIC number for cereal breakfast foods, which is listed in alphabetical order. The number, 2043, then leads you to the cross-listing of companies. These are the companies one would find listed under *2043 Cereal Breakfast Foods:*

Carnation Co.	Kellogg Company
The Clorox Company	Liggett Group Inc.
General Mills, Inc.	Nestlé S.A.
Gerber Products Co.	The Quaker Oats Co.
Iroquois Brands, Ltd.	Ralston Purina Co.

All of these companies make up an industry classification and may be found in the *Corporation Records*. This industry listing can be helpful when trying to compile a list of companies for an industry analysis.

Several other Standard & Poor's publications are quite useful and present concise, thumbnail sketches of companies, common stock variables, and corporate bonds. Table 4–1 on pages 122–123 depicts two pages from the *Stock Guide.* This is a monthly publication that enables investors to take a preliminary look at the common and preferred stock of several thousand companies and hundreds of mutual funds. The introduction to the *Stock Guide* presents name changes, new exchange listings, common stock rating changes, and a graph of Standard & Poor's Stock Price Indexes.

The *Bond Guide* has the same format as the *Stock Guide.* A monthly publication in booklet form, it presents data on corporate and convertible bonds. Table 4–2 on page 124 shows one page on corporate bonds with a long list of Connecticut Light and Power bonds at the top. The Standard & Poor's rating is presented along with other information. Table 4–3 on page 125 shows one page of convertible bonds from the *Bond Guide.* Looking at the table, we see convertible bonds having different coupons, interest payment dates, and maturities. Again, the Standard & Poor's rating is given. All the conversion data are presented with bond prices and common stock prices. Can you find how many shares of common stock an investor will receive for each $1,000 bond of Advest Group?[1]

One of the more popular of Standard & Poor's publications is the *Corporation Reports.* These reports are often mailed from brokerage houses to customers who want basic information on a company. In Table 4–4 on page 126, Hewlett-Packard provides a good example of what one would expect to find in such reports. This information can be compared to the entry in Table 4–1,

---

[1]The answer is 73.69 shares.

Table 4–1 Sample Pages, *Standard & Poor's Stock Guide*

100 HER-HOM

Standard & Poor's Corporation

¶ S&P 500 # MidCap 400 • Options Index	Ticker Symbol	Name of Issue (Call Price of Pfd. Stocks)	Market	Com. Rank. & Pfd. Rating	Par Val.	Inst. Hold Cos	Inst. Hold Shs. (000)	Principal Business	Price Range 1971-89 High	1971-89 Low	1990 High	1990 Low	1991 High	1991 Low	Nov. Sales in 100s	November, 1991 Last Sale Or Bid High	Low	Last	%Div Yield	P-E Ratio
1	HRLY	Herley Industries	OTC	B−	10¢	6	105	Mfrs microwave components	13⅝	1/16	1¾	1	10⅛	1⅛	2585	10⅛	7⅛	8⅛B	...	19
¶2•[1]	HSY	Hershey Foods	NY,B,M,P,Ph	A+	1	291	24479	Mfr chocolate,candy,pasta	37¾	1 7/16	39⅝	28¼	43⅞	35⅛	23597	41¾	36½	38	2.6	16
¶3•[2]	HWP	Hewlett-Packard	NY,B,C,M,P,Ph	A	1	710	129937	Electr data:measur/test instr	73⅝	3¾	50⅜	24⅞	56⅝	29⅞	108645	50⅞	44⅝	48⅛	1.0	16
4	HLU	Hewlett-Pack,Americus(Unit)	AS,M	NR	No	1	.7	Unit Tr for Hewlett-Packard	69	42¾	49½	28¼	50⅝	37	4	50½	48¼	48B	0.9	..
5	HLS	Score	AS,M	NR	No	9	1355	capital appreciation	30¾	5	6½	1	3⅝	¼	1317	¾	¼	¾	...	..
6	HLP	Prime	AS,M	NR	No	27	2091	divd income pay'g component	51¼	29½	46½	24	54⅝	29¼	390	49⅞	45¾	47½B	0.9	..
7	HXL	Hexcel Corp	NY,M,P,Ph	B+	1¢	45	3490	Honeycomb cores: plastics	43	1⅞	19¼	6¾	16⅝	9⅝	2724	12½	11¼	11¾	3.7	24
8	HLO	Hi-Lo Automotive	NY,M	NR	1¢	32	5856	Retail auto parts/accessories	....	....	....	....	15¼	9⅜	9199	12¾	9½	12½	...	16
9	HIB	Hibernia Corp Cl'A'	NY,M,Ph	B	No	41	3931	Commercial bkg,Louisiana	26	1 9/16	22⅞	5⅞	8¼	2⅜	13401	3⅛	2⅜	2¾	...	d
10	YLD	High Income Advantage	NY,M	NR	1¢	4	31	Closed-end investment co	10⅛	5¾	6⅞	3¼	5⅛	3½	12856	5⅛	4¾	4¾	11.4	..
11	YLT	High Income Advantage II	NY	NR	1¢	8	236	Closed-end diversified inv co	10	6¼	7⅜	3½	5⅝	3⅜	13526	5⅝	5	5¼	e11.4	..
12	YLH	High Income Advantage III	NY,M	NR	1¢	1	3	Closed-end diversified inv co	10	7⅞	8⅝	4⅛	6⅜	4	3877	6¼	5⅞	6	e12.0	..
13	HIPC	High Plains Corp	OTC	B−	10¢	6	290	Production/mktg of ethenol	7½	1/16	8⅝	1½	7⅛	3	3035	7⅛	5⅜	7⅛B	...	34
14	HYI	High Yield Income Fd	NY,M,Ph	NR	1¢	6	95	Closed-end investment co	10⅜	7	8	4⅜	7¼	4¾	3931	7¼	6¾	6¾	13.3	..
15	HYP	High Yield Plus Fund	NY,M,Ph	NR	1¢	3	140	Closed-end investment co	10⅛	7⅛	8	4⅝	7½	5¼	4121	7½	6¾	7	12.0	..
16	HIGHC	Highland Superstores	OTC	↓C	1¢	15	1600	Electronic/appliance stores	39¼	3¾	4⅝	1¼	2¾	11/16	3477	1¼	11/16	⅞B	...	d
17	HB	Hillenbrand Indus	NY,B,M,Ph	A+	No	135	14384	Burial caskets,hosp eq,lugg.	45⅛	1 7/16	48	30⅛	60⅝	37½	3907	60⅝	56¾	59½	1.0	25
18	HIL	Hillhaven Corp	AS,M	NR	15¢	95	32459	Operates nursing homes	....	....	2⅛	⅞	3⅜	1½	55252	2⅝	1¾	2⅜	...	..
19	HDS	Hills Dept. Stores	NY,Ph	D	1¢	19	1782	Regional discount retailer	12⅝	5	6	1	2⅜	⅝	6032	1⅛	¾	⅞	...	d
¶20•[3]	HLT	Hilton Hotels	NY,B,M,P,Ph	B+	2½	222	13677	Own/manage hotels & casinos	115½	1⅛	84⅜	26⅜	49⅞	34¼	15825	44¼	38½	39⅛	3.1	22
21	HIP	Hipotronics, Inc	AS,M	B+	10¢	31	1177	Hi volt test/pwr supply eq	18⅝	⅞	24¾	14½	24¾	17½	319	22⅜	20¾	20⅝B	1.7	12
22	HSI	Hi-Shear Indus	NY,M,Ph	B−	10¢	29	3422	Mfr aerospace technology sys	24⅛	2 1/16	16⅛	7⅜	14¼	8	1393	10	8	8⅝	...	d
23•[4]	HIT	Hitachi,Ltd ADR[55]	NY,B,M,P,Ph	NR	[55]..	34	4496	Elec eq, ind mchy: Japan	145	2⅜	108⅜	76¾	100¼	67½	2536	77¼	67½	68½	1.0	16
24	HTXA	Hitox Corp	OTC	NR	25¢	24	739	Mfr paint pigments/extenders	14⅜	8¼	9¾	4	12¼	3¾	2647	11¾	10¼	11½B	...	d
25	HMG	HMG/Courtland Prop	AS	NR	1	1	2	Real estate investment trust	25¼	2⅛	12⅝	4⅝	6¾	4⅛	81	4¼	4⅛	4⅛B	...	..
26	HMOA	HMO America	OTC	B−	1¢	35	3627	Health maintenance svcs	16¾	13/16	8⅛	4¼	17⅛	5⅜	52529	14⅝	12	12⅛B	...	13
27	HOEN	Hoenig Group	OTC	NR	1¢	..	...	Global securities broker, svcs	....	....	....	....	7¼	5	14970	7¼	5⅛	6⅛B	...	..
28	HOGN	Hogan Systems	OTC	B−	1¢	32	3703	Software prod for bank'g ind	26¼	3⅛	4¾	2	7	2 1/16	13665	5¾	4⅝	5B	3.0	12
29	HOL.A	Holco Mtge Accept I	AS	NR	1¢	1	.9	Invest in GNMA ctfs	6	3¼	3⅝	2⅝	7½	2⅞	495	6⅛	4	4B	e17.5	6
30	RVEE	Holiday RV Superstores	OTC	NR	1¢	6	127	Sale/svc recreat'n vehicles	4¾	2⅛	3¾	1⅛	3⅞	1	3341	1¾	1⅛	1⅜B	...	d
31	HOC	Holly Corp	AS,Ph	B	1¢	38	4647	Petroleum refin'g & mktg	41	½	29¾	19⅞	34⅝	22¼	423	28⅛	27½	27¾B	2.2	20
32	HTRFZ	Hollywood Pk Rlty (UNIT[58])	OTC	NR	10¢	14	83	REIT:horse racing track	30⅞	5	37¼	19¼	36½	21¼	533	31½	28	28B	1.4	d
33	HLN	Holnam Inc	NY	NR	1¢	19	2044	Mfr cement/constr'n products	....	....	7⅝	1⅞	6	3	688	4¼	4	4⅛	...	d
34	HOLX	Hologic Inc	OTC	NR	1¢	20	1368	Dvlp/mfr x-ray systems	....	....	31	7¼	12¼	4¾	11620	11	8	9B	...	53
35	HOLO	HoloPak Technologies	OTC	NR	1¢	7	170	Produce holographic foil	....	....	....	....	19½	16	1981	19¼	17¾	17¾B	...	27
36	HBENB	Home Beneficial Cl'B'	OTC	A	0.625	31	2775	Hldg:life,accident,health	46½	3⅛	38⅜	29½	45½	32	1015	44½	42¾	42¾B	3.3	9
37	HCEN	Home Centers	OTC	NR	No	3	250	Retail electr/appliance strs	21	¾	1⅜	⅝	1⅛	¼	601	¼	¼	¼B	...	d
¶38•[5]	HD	Home Depot	NY,B,M,P,Ph	B+	5¢	535	124126	Bldg mtls,home improv strs	17	5/16	29	15⅜	61½	23⅛	155817	61½	55½	60¼	0.2	53
39	HICI	Home Intensive Care	OTC	NR	1¢	16	617	Home infusion therapy svc	11	⅝	3⅛	1 7/16	9	1⅞	44819	9	7¼	7½B	...	38
40	HNSI	Home Nutritional Svcs	OTC	NR	1¢	43	2622	In-home medical care svcs	16⅞	13¾	23⅜	6	27	11	8632	27	22	22B	...	24
41	HORL	Home Office Ref Lab	OTC	NR	1¢	25	1557	Lab svcs to life insur indus	39¼	8¾	18⅛	8¾	15¾	9½	9920	15¾	11	13½B	5.3	14
42	HO	Home Oil Co	AS,M	NR	..	23	979	O&G explor,dev,prod'n Canada	....	....	....	....	15¾	12⅜	606	14½	13¾	13⅞B	...	66
#43	HSN	Home Shopping Network	NY,B,M,P,Ph	NR	1¢	68	18258	Retail mdse via own TV ntwk	47	3	9¼	2⅞	7⅝	3½	75011	7¼	5⅜	5⅜	...	d
44	HOME	Homedco Group	OTC	NR	1¢	47	4004	Provide home hlth care svcs	....	....	....	....	20¾	15	4949	20¾	17¾	18¼B	...	d
45	HFD	HomeFed Corp	NY,M,P	NR	1¢	38	4654	Savings & loan,San Diego,Cal	47½	11¾	33⅞	4½	7	⅛	18143	⅝	⅜	7/16	...	d
46	HOMG	Homeowners Group	OTC	NR	1¢	24	1490	Svcs/prod to R.E. brokers	12¼	5	12	4½	8½	4¼	3431	7¾	6⅝	7¼B	2.8	10

Uniform Footnote Explanations-See Page 1. Other: [1]ASE:Cycle 2. [2]CBOE:Cycle 2. [3]P:Cycle 1. [4]CBOE:Cycle 1. [5]Ph:Cycle 2. [51]Accum on pfd. [52]Incl $0.11119 non-taxable,'90. [53]4 Mo May'90. [54]Incl Chapter 11 liab. [55]ADR's represent'g 10 com par yen 50. [56]Approx. [57]100% non-taxable,'90. [58]Trades with 1 shr of Hollywood Park Operating. [59]Redemption of stk purch rt. [60]Incl redemption of sk purch rt. [61]89.3% owned by Holdernam Inc. [62]Fisc Jun'88 & prior,13 Mo Jan'89,earned$0.33. [63]Plan fiscal chge.to Dec. [64]10 Mo Sep'88.

Table 4–1 Sample Pages, *Standard & Poor's Stock Guide* (concluded)

HER-HOM 101

Common and Convertible Preferred Stocks

A full-page reproduction of a sample page from *Standard & Poor's Stock Guide* listing Common and Convertible Preferred Stocks (HER-HOM, indexes 1–46), with columns for Splits, Cash Dividends, Dividends (Latest Payment, Total $, Ind. Rate, Paid 1990, So Far 1991), Financial Position, Capitalization, Earnings $ Per Share, and Interim Earnings $ per Share.

♦Stock Splits & Divs By Line Reference Index ¹3-for-2, '88. ²10%, '87. ³Adj for 5%, '88. ⁵-for-4, '89. ⁶⁸5-for-1, '87. ⁷²-for-1, '87. ²²2-for-1, '88. ²³3-for-2, '88. ²⁴3-for-1, '88. ²⁵No adj for recap; '85.2-for-1, '88·Spl $ dstr; '89.
²³Adj for 3.5%, '87. ³²³3-for-2, '87; '89, '90, '91, '89, '90, '91. ²⁷2-for-1, '87. ⁴²2-for-1, '87. ⁴²2-for-1, '87.

123

Source: *Standard & Poor's Stock Guide*, December 1991.

■

Table 4–2 Page from *Standard & Poor's Bond Guide* (Corporate bonds)

Corporate Bonds

CON-CON 59

Title-Industry Code & Co. Finances (In Italics)	*I n d*	*Fixed Charge Coverage 1988*	*1989*	*1990*		*Year End*	*Million $ Cash & Equiv.*	*Curr. Assets*	*Curr. Liab.*	*Balance Sheet Date*	*L. Term Debt (Mil $)*		*Capital-ization (Mil $)*	*Total Debt % Capital*						
Exchange — Individual Issue Statistics	Interest Dates	S&P Debt Rating	Date of Last Rating Change	Prior Rating	Eligible	Bond Form	Redemption Provisions: Regular Price	Regular (Begins) Thru	Sinking Fund Price	Sinking Fund (Begins) Thru	Refund/Other Restriction Price	Refund/Other Restriction (Begins) Thru	Outst'g (Mil $)	Underwriting Firm	Underwriting Year	Price Range 1991 High	Price Range 1991 Low	Mo. End Price Sale(s) or Bid	Curr. Yield	Yield to Mat.
***Connecticut Lt & Pwr** (Cont.)*																				
1st & Ref U 6⅞s '98	aO	**BBB +**	6/84	BBB −	X	R	101.17	9-30-92	Z100.42	9-30-92	....	....	40.0	H1	'68	95⅛	87½	94¼	7.29	7.98
1st & Ref V 8¾s 2000	Jj	**BBB +**	6/84	BBB −	X	R	102.19	12-31-91	Z100.62	12-31-91	....	....	40.0	F2	'69	101⅞	95½	101¾	8.60	8.44
1st & Ref W 8⅞s 2000	aO	**BBB +**	6/84	BBB −	X	R	102.27	9-30-92	Z100.77	9-30-92	....	....	40.0	H1	'70	102⅛	95⅞	102	8.70	8.54
1st & Ref X 7⅜s 2001	jD	**BBB +**	6/84	BBB −	X	R	102.06	11-30-92	Z100.32	11-30-92	....	....	30.0	S1	'71	95⅛	86⅝	93	7.93	8.42
1st & Ref Y 7⅝s 2002	fA	**BBB +**	6/84	BBB −	X	R	102.53	7-31-92	Z100.56	7-31-92	....	....	50.0	F2	'72	96¼	87¾	94⅛	8.10	8.47
1st & Ref Z 7⅝s 2003	Ao	**BBB +**	6/84	BBB −	X	R	102.71	3-31-92	Z100.34	3-31-92	....	....	50.0	L4	'73	96	87	93¾	8.13	8.49
1st & Ref AA 8¾s 2004	Ms	**BBB +**	6/84	BBB −	X	R	103.25	2-29-92	Z100	....	....	....	65.0	F2	'74	101⅛	94	100¾	8.68	8.65
1st & Ref DD 8⅞s 2007	Mn	**BBB +**	6/84	BBB −	X	R	104.60	4-30-92	Z100	....	....	....	45.0	B9	'77	101¼	93¼	100	8.88	8.87
1st & Ref EE 9¼s 2008	Ms	**BBB +**	6/84	BBB −	X	R	105.52	2-29-92	Z100.62	2-29-92	....	....	40.0	F2	'78	103½	94⅞	103⅛	8.97	8.88
1st & Ref LL 8⅞s '96	mS	**BBB +**			X	R	102.54	8-31-92	[1]Z100	....	....	....	100	H8	'86	102½	97⅛	102¼	8.68	8.29
1st & Ref MM 9⅛s '97	Ao	**BBB +**			X	R	103.25	3-31-92	[2]Z100	....	®102.17	3-31-92	75.0	H8	'87	103	99⅛	103	8.86	8.41
1st & Ref NN 10s '95	aO	**BBB +**			X	R	101.98	9-30-92	[3]Z100	....	®100	9-30-92	80.0	G2	'87	103¾	101⅝	101⅝	9.84	9.48
1st & Ref OO 9¾s '94	mN	**BBB +**			X	R	101.93	10-31-92	[4]Z100	....	®100	10-31-92	95.0	H8	'87	103¾	98¾	101¾	9.58	9.05
1st & Ref PP 8½s '93	Ao	**BBB +**			X	R	101.86	3-31-92	Z100	....	®100	3-31-93	125	F2	'88	101⅞	99⅞	101¾	8.35	7.09
1st & Ref QQ 9¾s 2018	mN	**BBB +**			X	R	107.31	10-31-92	[5]Z100	....	®106.45	10-31-93	75.0	M6	'88	107¼	97⅝	105⅛	9.27	9.23
1st & Ref RR 9½s 2019	Jd	**BBB +**			X	R	107.43	5-31-92	[6]Z100	....	®106.19	5-31-94	75.0	F2	'89	102¾	94⅝	100⅛	9.49	9.49
1st & Ref SS 9⅜s 2019	mS	**BBB +**			X	R	107.23	8-31-92	[6]Z100	....	®106.02	8-31-94	75.0	S1	'89	103⅜	93½	101⅞	9.20	9.18
Connecticut Natural Gas	***73b***	***2.81***	***3.17***	***2.86***		***Dc***	***2.47***	***43.20***	***37.60***	***6-30-91***	***112.0***		***239.0***	***51.8***						
1st L 9s '96	Jj	**A −**	7/87	BBB +	X	R	101.50	12-31-91	100	....	Z100	....	12.0	S7	'71	101¼	100½	101¼	8.89	8.63
1st M 7.90s '97	Ms15	**A −**	7/87	BBB +	X	R	101.63	3-14-92	100	....	....	....	10.0	S7	'72	100⅛	93	99⅜	7.95	8.04
Conn.Yankee Atom.Pwr.	***72***	***2.06***	***1.66***	***1.78***		***Dc***	***0.02***	***46.30***	***104.0***	***12-31-90***	***202.0***		***310.0***	***66.5***						
Gen & Ref A[7] 12s 2000	Jd	**BBB −**	5/90	BB +	X	R	102.40	(6-1-97)	Z100	(6-1-94)	Z108.40	5-31-92	100	S1	'88	112½	106⅛	112⅜	10.68	9.82
Conoco, Inc[8]	***49a***	***Merged into duPont(El),see***																		
• SF Deb 9⅜s 2009	Ao	**AA**			X	R	102.17	3-31-92	100	....	....	....	190	M6	'79	102¾	99¼	101⅝	9.23	9.18
Conseco Inc	***35a***	***1.23***	***1.28***	***1.17***		***Dc***				***9-30-91***	***[9]260.0***		***575.0***	***45.2***						
• Sr Sub Nts 12½s '96	aO	**NR**				R	105.56	9-30-92	....	....	....	....	42.8	D3	'86	104½	84	104	12.02	11.39
• Sr Sub Nts 12¾s '97	jJ	**B**			Y	R	105.67	(7-1-92)	100	(7-1-95)	....	....	[10]209	D3	'87	105	84⅛	s104½	12.20	11.63
Consolidated Edison,N.Y.	***75***	***5.12***	***4.79***	***4.31***		***Dc***	***291.0***	***1212***	***968.0***	***6-30-91***	***3565***		***8817***	***42.4***						
• 1st & Ref V 4⅜s '92	Jd	**AA**	6/82	A +	X	CR	100	....	▲100	....	....	....	100	M6	'62	99⅛	96	99½	4.40	5.39
• 1st & Ref W 4⅜s '92	aO	**AA**	6/82	A +	X	CR	100	....	▲100	....	....	....	75.0	F2	'62	99	94	98¾	4.43	5.92
1st & Ref X 4⅜s '92	jD	**AA**	6/82	A +	X	CR	100	....	▲100	....	....	....	60.0	H1	'62	99¼	94⅜	99¼	4.41	5.15
• 1st & Ref AA 4⅝s '93	jD	**AA**	6/82	A +	X	R	100.25	11-30-92	▲100.24	11-30-92	....	....	75.0	H1	'63	97½	91⅛	97¾	4.73	5.83
1st & Ref CC 5s '96	Jj	**AA**	6/82	A +	X	R	100.80	12-31-91	▲100.22	12-31-91	....	....	100	M3	'65	93⅞	87½	93⅞	5.33	6.74
1st & Ref DD 5.90s '96	jD15	**AA**	6/82	A +	X	R	100.82	12-14-92	▲100	....	....	....	75.0	M6	'66	94½	86¾	94¼	6.26	7.28
1st & Ref EE 6¼s '97	fA	**AA**	6/82	A +	X	R	101.08	7-31-92	▲100	....	....	....	80.0	M6	'67	94⅞	87⅞	94⅞	6.59	7.37
1st & Ref FF 6.85s '98	aO	**AA**	6/82	A +	X	R	101.42	9-30-92	▲100	....	....	....	60.0	M6	'68	96	89⅛	96	7.14	7.61
1st & Ref GG 7.90s '99	Ao	**AA**	6/82	A +	X	R	101.91	3-31-92	▲100	....	....	....	80.0	M6	'69	100½	93½	100¼	7.88	7.85
1st & Ref HH 8.90s 2000	Jj15	**AA**	6/82	A +	X	R	102.46	1-14-92	▲100	....	....	....	125	M6	'70	102½	97½	102⅛	8.71	8.53
• 1st & Ref II 9⅜s 2000	mS15	**AA**	6/82	A +	X	R	102.59	9-14-92	▲100	....	....	....	150	M6	'70	105¼	100⅜	s103⅜	9.07	8.81
• 1st & Ref JJ 7.90s 2001	mS	**AA**	6/82	A +	X	R	102.46	8-31-92	▲100	....	....	....	150	M3	'71	100⅜	91½	98⅝	8.01	8.10
• 1st & Ref KK 7.90s 2002	Ao15	**AA**	6/82	A +	X	R	102.73	4-14-92	▲100	....	....	....	150	M3	'72	100	91¼	98⅜	8.03	8.13
• 1st & Ref MM 7¾s 2003	Fa15	**AA**	6/82	A +	X	R	103.17	2-14-92	▲100.39	2-14-92	....	....	150	M6	'73	98¾	89½	97⅜	7.96	8.11
• 1st & Ref NN 8.40s 2003	aO15	**AA**	6/82	A +	X	R	103.19	10-14-92	▲100	....	....	....	150	M3	'73	103	94½	101¼	8.30	8.23

Uniform Footnote Explanations-See Page 1. Other: [1] Limited to $1.0M yearly to 1991. [2] Limited to $0.75M yearly to 1992. [3] Limited to $0.8M yearly to 1992. [4] Limited to $0.95M yearly to 1992. [5] Limited to $0.75M yearly to 1993. [6] Limited to $0.75M yearly to 1994. [7] Red in whole for plant closure at prices,as def. [8] See Continental Oil. [9] Excl partnership debt. [10] Incl disc.

Source: *Standard and Poor's Bond Guide,* December 1991.

Table 4–3 Page from *Standard & Poor's Bond Guide* (Convertible bonds)

Convertible Bonds

Exchange / Issue, Rate, Interest Dates and Maturity			S&P Debt Rating	Bond Form	Outstdg. Mil-$	Conv. Ex-pires	Shares per $1,000 Bond	Price per Share	Div. Income per Bond	1991 Price Range High	1991 Price Range Low	Curr Bid Sale(s) Ask(A)	Curr. Yield	Yield to Mat	Stock Value of Bond	Conv Parity	Stock Data Month End	Stock Data P/E Ratio	Earnings Per Share Yr. End	1990	1991	Last 12 Mos
• Advest Group	9s Ms15	2008	NR	R	23.1	2008	73.69	13.57	....	80¾	52	s75	12.00	12.65	32¼	10¼	•4⅜	d	Sp	d0.87	Pd0.70	d0.70
Air & Water Tech[1]	8s Mn15	2015	B+	R	115	2015	[2]33.333	30.00	....	102	81	87½	9.14	9.32	61¾	26⅜	◆18½	d	Oc	□0.35	....	[7]d1.05
Air Wis Services[3]	7¾s Jd15	2010	B	R	33.0	2010	63.69	15.70	....	85⅞	66¾	80	9.69	10.17	55¾	12⅝	8¾	d	Dc	Δd0.22	....	[9]d2.93
• Airborne Freight[4]	6¾s fA15	2001	BBB	R	115	2001	28.169	35.50	8.45	102¾	95	86¼	7.83	8.89	59¼	30⅝	•21	15	Dc	1.76	....	[9]1.34
• A.L. Labs[5]	7¾s Jd15	2014	B+	R	60.0	2014	72.73	13.75	11.64	161	110	141⅞	5.46	4.71	141⅞	19⅝	•19½	21	Dc	0.84	....	[9]0.90
[6]Alabama Fed'l S&L[7]	7½s Jd	2011	NR	R	9.04	2011	97.83	10.22	....	85⅝	55	62	12.10	12.86	39¼	6⅜	4	2	Dc	Δd2.34	....	[9]1.65
Alaska Air Gr	7¾s Jd15	2010	BB+	R	14.6	2010	35.40	28.25	7.08	101⅞	79⅜	94	8.24	8.39	68¼	26⅝	•19¼	55	Dc	0.82	E0.35	[9]d0.38
• Alaska Air Gr[8]	6⅞s Jd15	2014	BB+	R	78.1	2014	29.76	33.60	5.95	94	72	82	8.38	8.71	57⅜	27⅝	•19¼	55	Dc	0.82	E0.35	[9]d0.38
• Alaska Air Gr[9](Zero)[10]	[11]	2006	BB+	R	[12]345	2006	12.396	....	2.48	34½	32	33⅛	....	7.83	23⅞	26¾	•19¼	55	Dc	0.82	E0.35	[9]d0.38
Alexander & Alex Sv	11s Ao15	2007	A−	R	66.9	2007	25.64	39.00	25.64	107⅜	100⅜	104¾	10.50	10.37	50	40⅞	•19½	17	Dc	±1.35	....	[9]1.10
• [13]Alleghany Corp	6½s Jd15	2014	BBB+	R	59.6	2014	[14]22.88	43.70	22.88	92½	72½	78½	8.28	8.69	43½	34⅜	•19	12	Dc	□0.69	E1.50	[9]2.20
Alliant Computer Sys	7¼s Mn15	2012	NR	R	39.2	2012	25.16	39.75	....	22	14½	15	....	....	⅞	6	5⁄16	d	Dc	d2.58	....	[6]d3.03
Allwaste Inc[8]	7¼s Jd	2014	B+	R	30.0	2014	83.75	11.94	....	78½	56	76½	9.48	9.87	44	9¼	5¼	58	Au	0.44	P0.09	0.09
◆ALZA Corp[15](Zero)[16]	[17]	2010	BB+	R	[12]863	2010	[2]4.326	....	....	37	23⅜	35	....	5.58	35	81	◆80⅞	77	Dc	±0.70	E1.05	[9]0.89
Ameribanc,Inc[18]	8s Ao	1995	NR	R	17.3	1995	53.33	18.75	10.67	127¼	86½	124	6.45	0.71	124	23⅜	23¼	75	Dc	d0.24	....	[9]0.31
America[19]West[20]Airlines[21]	11½s §Jj	2009	NR	R	35.3	2009	95.24	10.50	....	143⅜	13⅛	13⅛	....	Flat	13⅛	1½	1⅜	d	Dc	Δd4.26	....	[9]d11.40
America[22]West[20]Airlines[23]	7¾s §fA	2010	NR	R	33.6	2010	74.07	13.50	....	56½	10½	10½	....	Flat	10¼	1½	1⅜	d	Dc	Δd4.26	....	[9]d11.40
America West[20]Airlines[24]	7½s Ao	2011	D	R	35.3	2011	71.43	14.00	....	54½	10	10¼	....	Flat	9⅞	1½	1⅜	d	Dc	Δd4.26	....	[9]d11.40
Amer Bkrs Ins Gr([25]'91)	9¾s jD	2004	[26]. . .	R	[12]29.0	2004	73.26	13.65	43.96	138⅜	102½	124⅝	7.82	6.86	124⅝	17⅛	17	7	Dc	1.92	....	[9]2.44
• Amer Cap Bond Fund[27]	8½s Jj	1995	AAA	R	26.2	1995	52.08	19.20	87.49	No Sale		101⅝	8.36	....	101⅝	19⅝	•19½	..	Je	....		....
Amer Medical Int'l[28]	9½s mN15	2001	B−	R	3.05	2001	41.02	24.38	....	72½	39	65	14.62	16.87	34⅜	15⅞	◆8⅜	d	Au	d1.25	Pd0.38	d0.38
Amer Medical Int'l[28]	8¼s Ao	2008	B−	R	6.97	2008	25.00	40.00	....	65⅛	34	55	15.00	16.13	21	22	◆8⅜	d	Au	d1.25	Pd0.38	d0.38
• Amer Stores[29]	7¼s mS15	2001	BB+	R	175	2001	22.222	45.00	15.56	105½	90	s92½	7.84	8.39	65⅞	41¾	•29⅝	7	Ja	2.64	E3.85	[10]3.86
• Ames[29]Dept[20]Stores[30]	7½s §aO	2014	D	R	155	2014	46.51	21.50	....	15	4	s6½	....	Flat	5¼	1½	•1⅛	d	Ja	d21.47	....	[7]d8.45
• [31]Amoco Canada Petroleum 'A'	7⅜s $mS	2013	AA−	R	455	2013	[32]19.05	52.50	41.91	117	107	s108	6.83	6.67	90¼	56¾	•47⅜	16	Dc	3.77	E2.85	[9]3.11
• AMR Corp[33](Zero)[34]	[35]	2006	BBB	R	[12]1300	2006	5.769	....	....	43¾	39½	s41¼	....	6.29	34	71⅝	•58⅞	d	Dc	d0.64	Ed3.00	[9]d5.14
• Anacomp, Inc[36]	13⅞s Jj15	2002	NR	R	[12]23.2	2002	57.14	17.50	....	100¾	67½	s100	....	Flat	19⅜	17⅝	•3⅜	8	Sp	*0.04	P*0.38	0.38
• Anadarko Petroleum[37]	6¼s Mn15	2014	BBB+	R	100	2014	29.24	34.20	8.77	108½	92½	91½	6.83	7.01	74⅝	31⅜	•25½	85	Dc	1.04	E0.30	[9]0.76
◆Andal[38]Corp[39]	5½s mS15	1997	NR	R	1.83	1997	44.44	22.50	....	51	51	A51	10.78	20.23	2½	11½	◆9⁄16	d	Sp	d0.87	....	[6]d1.02
Andersen Group	10½s aO15	2002	NR	R	8.95	2002	61.84	16.17	3.09	84⅞	76½	83	12.65	13.52	48	13½	7¾	45	Fb	Δ0.27	....	[8]0.17
• Apache Corp[8]	7½s aO	2000	BB+	R	150	2000	52.14	19.18	14.60	121	89¾	105	7.14	6.74	86¾	20¼	•16⅝	23	Dc	0.90	....	[9]0.70
[40]Apache Cp[41]/Key Cp[42]	9s jJ15	2001	BB+	R	13.0	2001	Cv into Common[43]			85	80	85	10.59	11.63	....	....	•16⅝	23	Dc	0.90	....	[9]0.70
[44]Apollo Computer	7¼s Fa	2011	AA	R	105	2011	Conv into $729.17			85¾	77½	84½	8.58	8.95	....	....	....	..	Oc	....	....	....
◆Arrow Electronics	9s fA	2003	B−	R	30.0	2003	28.74	34.80	....	89¼	59¼	87½	10.29	10.92	38½	30½	•13⅜	d	Dc	0.44	Ed0.05	[9]d0.14
• Ashland Oil[45]	6¾s jJ	2014	BBB−	R	200	2014	19.48	51.34	19.48	89	77	84½	7.99	8.28	54⅝	43½	•28	10	Sp	3.27	P2.56	2.56
◆Atari Corp[46]	5¼s Apr29	2002	B−	R	46.1	2002	61.31	16.31	....	42	19½	39½	13.29	18.59	10	6½	◆1⅝	4	Dc	Δd0.11	....	[9]0.39
Atlantic Amer'n	8s Mn15	1997	CC	R	20.3	1997	91.41	10.94	....	65	60	60	13.33	20.51	4⅝	6⅝	½	d	Dc	Δd0.32	....	[9]d1.64
Autodie Corp[47]	7s §Mn	2011	NR	R	26.2	2011	28.88	34.63	....	92	5	6¼	....	Flat	6¼	2¼	2⅛	d	Au	d4.10	PΔd9.33	d9.33
• Avalon Corp[48]	7s Fa15	1992	NR	R	3.36	2-15-92	42.68	23.43	....	92	90	90	....	Flat	18¾	21⅛	•4⅜	d	Dc	d0.51	....	[9]d0.51

Uniform Footnote Explanations—See Page 224. Other: [1] (HRO)At 100 to 5-15-00 On Chge in Ctrl. [2] Into Cl A com. [3] UAL Corp plan acq 0.0606 com. [4] (HRO)At 100 for a Risk Event. [5] (HRO)At 100 for a Fundamental Chge,as defined. [6] Min denom $10,000. [7] Now Secor Bank, FSB. [8] (HRO)On Chge in Ctrl at 100. [9] (HRO)On 4-18-96('01) at $490.58($700.42). [10] (HRO)To 4-18-96,on Chge in Ctrl. [11] Due 4-18-06. [12] Incl disc. [13] Conv into & data of Amer Express. [14] Into Amer Express com. [15] (HRO)On 12-21-95('00&'05)prices as defined. [16] (HRO)To 12-21-95 on Chge in Ctrl. [17] Due 12-21-10. [18] To be exch for com when due. [19] (HRO)On Chge in Ctrl. [20] Filed bankruptcy Chapt 11. [21] Default 7-1-91 int. [22] (HRO)On Chge in Ctrl at curr red price. [23] Default 8-1-91 int. [24] Default 10-1-91 int. [25] (HRO)On 12-1-91 at 110. [26] Rating of BBB- has been suspended. [27] Int thru 12-31-94,adj aft as defined. [28] Now American Medical Hldgs. [29] (HRO)On Chge of Ctrl at 100. [30] Default 10-1-90 int. [31] Subsid & data of Amoco Corp. [32] Into Amoco Corp com. [33] (HRO)On 3-15-96('01)at $540.41($735.13). [34] (HRO)To 3-15-96,on Chge in Ctrl. [35] Due 3-15-06. [36] Int:1-15-84,pd 3-21-84:7-15-84,pd 8-15-84. [37] (HRO)To 5-15-94 at 100 on Chge of Ctrl. [38] Was Nat'l Kinney. [39] Int 5.25% to 3-9-82. [40] Data of Apache Corp. [41] Oblig jointly of Key Corp & Apache Corp. [42] Was Apache Petroleum L.P. [43] Into Apache at $32.50,Key at $13,any ratio. [44] Subsid of Hewlett-Packard. [45] (HRO)At 100 on Chge in Ctrl. [46] Offered outside U.S. [47] Default 5-1-91 int. [48] Was Tri-South(Mtg)Inv.

Source: *Standard & Poor's Bond Guide,* December 1991.

Table 4-4   Sample Pages, *Standard & Poor's Corporation Reports*

Read

Hewlett-Packard

1137

NYSE Symbol HWP Options on CBOE (Feb-May-Aug-Nov) In S&P 500

Price	Range	P–E Ratio	Dividend	Yield	S&P Ranking	Beta
Nov. 20'91	1991					
47³/₄	56⁵/₈–29⁷/₈	16	0.50	1.0%	A	1.45

Summary

Hewlett-Packard manufactures a broad array of electronic instruments and computer systems. Apollo Computer was acquired in May 1989 for about $470 million. In fiscal 1991, HWP introduced a line of workstations that more than doubled performance levels in the workstation market. Although gross margins will likely remain under pressure, earnings in fiscal 1992 should benefit from new products and operating cost controls.

Current Outlook

Earnings for the fiscal year ending October 31, 1992, are estimated at $4.05 a share, versus fiscal 1991's $3.02, which included a fourth quarter restructuring charge of $0.40.

Dividends should continue at $0.12½ quarterly.

Revenue growth for fiscal 1992 is projected at about 12%. A recently introduced line of RISC-based workstations, which more than doubles performance levels in the workstation market, should soon be available in greater volumes and provide a positive revenue impact in the first half of fiscal 1992. Order growth during the October quarter was particularly strong for the Peripherals and Network Product group, reflecting strong demand for HWP's new printers. Gross margins are likely to remain under pressure, reflecting competitive pricing and the product mix shift toward desktop computing products and peripherals. However, operating costs should be well controlled.

TRADING VOLUME
MILLION SHARES

1985	1986	1987	1988	1989	1990	1991	

Net Sales (Billion $)

Quarter:	1990-91	1989-90	1988-89	1987-88
Jan.	3.41	3.10	2.66	2.19
Apr.	3.73	3.31	2.86	2.50
Jul.	3.52	3.24	3.00	2.43
Oct.	3.83	3.58	3.38	2.71
	14.49	13.23	11.90	9.83

Revenues for the fiscal year ended October 31. 1991 (preliminary) advanced 9.5% from those of fiscal 1990, reflecting a 14% sales gain in peripherals and network products, a 4.2% advance in MDIM revenues, and a 15% increase in revenues from service for equipment, systems and peripherals. Gross margins narrowed sharply, but other expenses were well controlled. After a $150 million charge for voluntary severance programs and facility consolidations, pretax net gained 6.7%. Taxes were at 33.0%, versus 30.0%, and net income rose 2.2%. Share earnings were $3.02 on 3.3% more shares, against $3.06.

Common Share Earnings ($)

Quarter:	1990-91	1989-90	1988-89	1987-88
Jan.	0.83	0.72	0.83	0.71
Apr.	0.93	0.78	0.86	0.82
Jul.	0.76	0.73	0.79	0.80
Oct.	0.50	0.83	1.04	1.03
	3.02	3.06	3.52	3.36

Important Developments

Nov '91 — HWP reported that orders for the fourth quarter of fiscal 1991 totaled $3.7 billion, up 7.0% from the $3.5 billion in the year-earlier period. Orders outside the U.S. were flat, at $1.9 billion, and U.S. orders were up 14%, to $1.8 billion. During 1991, employment levels declined to 89,000 people from 92,000, primarily due to voluntary employee-reduction programs.

Next earnings report expected in mid-February.

Per Share Data ($)

Yr. End Oct. 31	¹1991	¹1990	¹1989	1988	1987	1986	1985	³1984	1983	1982
Book Value	NA	²26.07	21.15	19.35	19.52	17.08	15.50	13.82	11.33	9.37
Cash Flow	NA	5.40	5.37	4.81	3.83	3.27	3.07	3.52	2.44	2.16
Earnings	3.02	3.06	3.52	3.36	2.50	2.02	1.91	2.59	1.69	1.53
Dividends	0.48	0.420	0.360	0.280	0.230	0.220	0.220	0.190	0.158	0.120
Payout Ratio	16%	14%	10%	8%	9%	11%	12%	7%	9%	8%
Prices—High⁴	56⁵/₈	50³/₈	61¹/₂	65¹/₂	73⁵/₈	49⁵/₈	38⁷/₈	45¹/₂	48¹/₄	41³/₈
Low⁴	29⁷/₈	24⁷/₈	40¹/₄	43³/₄	35³/₄	35³/₄	28³/₄	31¹/₈	34¹/₄	18
P/E Ratio—	19–10	16–8	17–11	19–13	29–14	25–18	20–15	18–12	29–20	27–12

Data as orig. reptd. Adj. for stk. div(s). of 100% Aug. 1983, 100% Jul. 1981. 1. Reflects merger or acquisition. 2. Includes intangibles.
3. Reflects accounting change. 4. Cal. yr. NA-Not Available.

Standard NYSE Stock Reports
Vol. 58/No. 230/Sec. 12

December 2, 1991
Copyright © 1991 Standard & Poor's Corp. All Rights Reserved

Standard & Poor's Corp.
25 Broadway, NY, NY 10004

1137   Hewlett-Packard Company

Income Data (Million $)

Year Ended Oct. 31	Revs.	Oper. Inc.	% Oper. Inc. of Revs.	Cap. Exp.	Depr.	Int. Exp.	Net Bef. Taxes	Eff. Tax Rate	Net Inc.	% Net Inc. of Revs.	Cash Flow
1990	13,233	1,728	13.1	955	566	172	1,056	30.0%	739	5.6	1,305
[1]1989	11,899	1,657	13.9	857	462	126	1,151	28.0%	829	7.0	1,264
1988	9,831	1,592	16.2	648	353	77	[3]1,142	28.5%	816	8.3	1,169
1987	8,090	1,354	16.7	507	342	50	[3]962	33.1%	[2]644	8.0	986
1986	7,102	1,101	15.5	499	321	NA	[3]780	33.8%	[2]516	7.3	837
1985	6,505	1,057	16.2	632	299	NA	[3]758	35.5%	489	7.5	788
[2]1984	6,044	1,097	18.2	661	237	NA	[3]860	22.7%	665	11.0	902
1983	4,710	919	19.5	466	191	NA	728	40.7%	432	9.2	623
1982	4,254	834	19.6	362	158	NA	676	43.3%	383	9.0	541
1981	3,578	700	19.6	318	120	NA	580	46.2%	312	8.7	432

Balance Sheet Data (Million $)

Oct. 31	Cash	Assets	Curr. Liab.	Ratio	Total Assets	Ret. On Assets	Long Term Debt	Common Equity	Total Inv. Capital	% LT Debt of Cap.	% Ret. on Equity
1990	1,077	6,510	4,443	1.5	11,395	6.8%	139	6,363	6,763	2.1	12.4
1989	926	5,731	3,743	1.5	10,075	9.4%	474	5,446	6,168	7.7	16.5
1988	918	4,420	2,570	1.7	7,497	11.0%	61	4,533	4,770	1.3	17.9
1987	2,645	5,490	2,735	2.0	8,133	8.9%	88	5,022	5,264	1.7	13.7
1986	1,372	3,814	1,518	2.5	6,287	8.6%	110	4,374	4,635	2.4	12.4
1985	1,020	3,342	1,376	2.4	5,680	9.0%	102	3,982	4,212	2.4	13.0
1984	938	3,201	1,322	2.4	5,153	14.2%	81	3,545	3,738	2.2	20.6
1983	880	2,632	920	2.9	4,161	11.2%	71	2,887	3,195	2.2	16.4
1982	684	2,215	863	2.6	3,470	12.2%	39	2,349	2,565	1.5	17.8
1981	290	1,705	704	2.4	2,758	12.1%	26	1,920	2,054	1.3	17.9

Data as orig. reptd. 1. Reflects merger or acquisition. 2. Reflects accounting change. 3. Incl. equity in earns. of nonconsol. subs. NA-Not Available.

Business Summary

Hewlett-Packard produces a broad range of electronic instruments and systems for measurement, analysis and computation. Foreign operations provided 54% of revenues in fiscal 1990.

HWP's measurement, design, information and manufacturing (MDIM) equipment (37% of fiscal 1990 revenues) includes test and measurement instruments, small to medium-scale computers and handheld calculators. Computers include the HP 1000, designed for factory automation and real time data acquisition; the HP 3000, which runs the proprietary MPE operating system and is sold for business applications; and the 9000 line of UNIX-based technical computers, including workstations. Both the 3000 and 9000 families are based on HWP's Precision Architecture reduced instruction set computing (RISC) design. HWP also sells VECTRA IBM-compatible personal computers and a portable computer. In May 1989 HWP acquired Apollo Computer, a vendor of UNIX workstations, for $470 million. Apollo had revenues of $554 million in 1988.

Peripherals and network products (30%) include video displays; a variety of line, desktop and workstation printers, including the DeskJet and LaserJet; plotters; magnetic disc and tape drives and network products. HWP also services its equipment, systems, and peripherals (20%).

Medical electronic equipment and service (7%) products perform patient monitoring, diagnostic, therapeutic and data-management functions.

Analytical instrumentation and service (4%) includes gas and liquid chromatographs, mass spectrometers, and spectrophotometers.

Electronic components (2%) include microwave semiconductor and optoelectronic devices sold primarily to original equipment manufacturers.

Dividend Data

Dividends have been paid since 1965.

Amt of Div. $	Date Decl.	Ex-div. Date	Stock of Record	Payment Date
0.10½	Nov. 16	Dec. 19	Dec. 26	Jan. 16'91
0.12½	Jan. 18	Mar. 14	Mar. 20	Apr. 10'91
0.12½	May 17	Jun. 13	Jun. 19	Jul. 10'91
0.12½	Jul. 18	Sep. 19	Sep. 25	Oct. 16'91

Next dividend meeting: late Nov. '91.

Capitalization

Long Term Debt: $188,000,000.

Common Stock: 251,512,000 shs. ($1 par). Institutions hold about 50%; W.R. Hewlett & D. Packard families control some 26% (in part held by institutions).
Shareholders of record: 73,081.

Office—3000 Hanover St, Palo Alto, CA 94304. **Tel**—(415) 857-1501. **Chrmn**—D. Packard. **Pres & CEO**—J. A. Young. **Secy**—D. C. Nordlund. **Treas & Investor Contact**—G. F. Newman. **Dirs**—T. E. Everhart, J. B. Fery, R. J. Glaser, H. J. Haynes, W. B. Hewlett, S. M. Hufstedler, G. A. Keyworth II, P. F. Miller Jr., D. O. Morton, D. Packard, D. W. Packard, D. E. Petersen, W. E. Terry, H. P. Waldron, T. A. Wilson, J. A. Young. **Transfer Agent & Registrar**—Harris Trust & Savings Bank, Chicago. **Incorporated** in California in 1947. **Empl**—89,000.

Information has been obtained from sources believed to be reliable, but its accuracy and completeness are not guaranteed. Lawrence S. Freitag, CFA

line 3, for Hewlett-Packard to see the difference in the depth of coverage between the *Corporation Reports* and the *Stock Guide*. The *Corporation Reports* are contained in three separate multiple-volume sets, the New York Stock Exchange Stocks, American Stock Exchange Stocks, and Over-the-Counter and Regional Stocks. Each company is updated quarterly with new earnings, dividends, and recent developments. To develop an appreciation for the other Standard & Poor's services, peruse this material at your library.

Value Line

Value Line Investment Survey, a publication of Arnold Bernhard & Co., is one of the most widely used investment services by individuals, stockbrokers, and small bank trust departments. The *Value Line Investment Survey* follows 1,700 companies, and each common stock is covered in a one-page summary (see the one for Hewlett-Packard in Table 4–5. Value Line is noted for its comprehensive coverage, which can be seen by comparing Table 4–5 to Tables 4–1 and 4–4. Raw financial data are available as well as trendline growth rates, price history patterns in graphic form, quarterly sales, earnings and dividends, and a breakdown of sales and profit margins by line of business. Value Line contains 13 sections divided into several industries each. The first few pages beginning an industry classification are devoted to an overview of the industry, with the company summaries following. Each section is revised on a 13-week cycle.

Value Line has a unique evaluation system that is primarily dependent on historical relationships and regression analysis. From the valuation model, each company is rated 1 through 5, with 1 being the highest positive rating and 5 the lowest. Each company is rated on timeliness and safety. It should be noted that Value Line minimizes human judgment in making its evaluation.

Other Investment Services

Dun & Bradstreet publishes *Key Business Ratios* in bound form. This publication contains 14 significant ratios on 800 different lines of business listed by SIC code. Examples of ratios included are current assets to current debt, net profits on net sales, and total debt to tangible net worth. This publication has replaced the old Dun & Bradstreet 11-page pamphlet on key business ratios for 125 lines of business. Another good source of ratios is Robert Morris Associates, which provides ratios on over 150 industry classifications.

Dun's Marketing Services division of Dun & Bradstreet also publishes the *Million Dollar Directory.* Companies are listed in alphabetical order, by geographical location, and by product classification. The data provide names, addresses, phone numbers, and sales for each company. This could be helpful in identifying companies in the same industry or in writing to request such information as annual reports or product lists.

HEWLETT-PACKARD NYSE-HWP

| RECENT PRICE | 51 | P/E RATIO | 15.3 | (Trailing: 15.2) (Median: 17.0) | RELATIVE P/E RATIO | 1.03 | DIV'D YLD | 1.0% | VALUE LINE | 1096 |

| | High: | 24.3 | 26.9 | 41.3 | 48.3 | 45.5 | 38.9 | 49.6 | 73.6 | 65.5 | 61.5 | 50.4 | 56.6 |
| | Low: | 12.8 | 19.2 | 18.0 | 34.3 | 31.1 | 28.8 | 35.8 | 39.3 | 43.8 | 40.3 | 24.6 | 29.9 |

TIMELINESS 3 Average (Relative Price Performance Next 12 Mos.)

SAFETY 2 Above Average (Scale: 1 Highest to 5 Lowest)

BETA 1.30 (1.00 = Market)

1994-96 PROJECTIONS

	Price	Gain	Ann'l Total Return
High	95	(+85%)	18%
Low	70	(+35%)	10%

Insider Decisions

	D	J	F	M	A	M	J	J	A
to Buy	1	1	0	0	0	0	0	0	0
Options	0	1	1	0	0	0	1	5	0
to Sell	1	3	1	10	7	1	6	3	0

Institutional Decisions

	4Q'90	1Q'91	2Q'91
to Buy	140	192	179
to Sell	182	163	158
Hld's000	114549	119045	122212

Percent shares traded: 9.0 / 6.0 / 3.0

Target Price Range 1994 | 1995 | 1996

9.0 x "Cash Flow" p sh

2-for-1 split

Relative Price Strength

Shaded areas indicate recessions

Options: CBOE

1975	1976	1977	1978	1979	1980	1981	1982	1983	1984	1985	1986	1987	1988	1989	1990	1991	1992	© VALUE LINE PUB., INC.	94-96
4.44	4.96	5.97	7.45	9.98	12.87	14.59	16.97	18.48	23.57	25.32	27.73	31.45	41.97	50.07	54.21	58.85	66.25	Sales per sh A	90.15
.54	.58	.74	.90	1.16	1.50	1.76	2.16	2.44	3.05	3.07	3.27	3.83	5.08	5.43	5.35	5.50	6.65	"Cash Flow" per sh	9.65
.38	.41	.53	.66	.86	1.12	1.28	1.53	1.69	2.13	1.91	2.02	2.50	3.36	3.52	3.06	3.15	4.00	Earnings per sh B	6.00
.03	.04	.05	.06	.09	.10	.11	.12	.16	.20	.22	.22	.23	.28	.36	.42	.48	.55	Div'ds Decl'd per sh C	.85
.30	.46	.51	.69	.81	1.23	1.30	1.44	1.83	2.58	2.46	1.95	1.97	2.77	3.61	3.91	3.65	3.65	Cap'l Spending per sh	4.10
2.54	3.02	3.62	4.32	5.22	6.42	7.83	9.37	11.33	13.82	15.50	17.08	19.52	19.35	22.92	26.07	29.00	32.20	Book Value per sh	45.55
221.10	223.97	227.83	232.08	236.59	240.88	245.28	250.69	254.91	256.48	256.92	256.09	257.25	234.22	237.64	244.09	248.00	246.00	Common Shs Outst'g D	244.00
29.6	31.8	18.3	14.5	14.4	14.6	17.8	14.6	24.0	17.7	18.0	20.2	22.5	16.2	15.0	13.8	13.8		Avg Ann'l P/E Ratio	14.0
3.95	4.07	2.40	1.98	2.03	1.94	2.16	1.61	2.03	1.65	1.46	1.37	1.51	1.34	1.14	1.03	.93		Relative P/E Ratio	1.15
.3%	.3%	.5%	.7%	.7%	.6%	.5%	.5%	.4%	.5%	.6%	.5%	.4%	.5%	.7%	1.0%	1.1%		Avg Ann'l Div'd Yield	1.0%

CAPITAL STRUCTURE as of 7/31/91 E

Total Debt $1311 mill. Due in 5 Yrs $1121 mill.

LT Debt $190.0 mill.   LT Interest $16.0 mill.
(Total interest coverage: 10.4x)

(3% of Cap'l)

Pension Liability None

Pfd Stock None

Common Stock 249,900,000 shs.   (97% of Cap'l)
as of 4/30/91

	3578.0	4254.0	4710.0	6044.0	6505.0	7102.0	8090.0	9831.0	11899	13233	14600	16300	Sales ($mill) A E	22000
	20.8%	20.4%	20.1%	18.7%	16.9%	15.9%	16.9%	15.8%	14.1%	13.1%	13.0%	13.5%	Operating Margin	14.0%
	120.0	158.0	191.0	237.0	299.0	321.0	342.0	373.0	462.0	566.0	590	650	Depreciation ($mill)	965
	312.0	383.0	432.0	547.0	489.0	516.0	644.0	816.0	829.0	739.0	775	985	Net Profit ($mill)	1470
	46.2%	43.3%	40.7%	36.4%	35.5%	33.8%	33.1%	28.5%	28.0%	30.0%	33.0%	33.0%	Income Tax Rate	33.0%
	8.7%	9.0%	9.2%	9.1%	7.5%	7.3%	8.0%	8.3%	7.0%	5.6%	5.3%	6.0%	Net Profit Margin	6.7%
	1001.0	1352.0	1712.0	1879.0	1966.0	2296.0	2755.0	1850.0	1988.0	2067.0	2295	2445	Working Cap'l ($mill)	3690
	26.0	39.0	71.0	81.0	102.0	110.0	88.0	61.0	474.0	139.0	125	115	Long-Term Debt ($mill)	100
	1920.0	2349.0	2887.0	3545.0	3982.0	4374.0	5022.0	4533.0	5446.0	6363.0	7190	7925	Net Worth ($mill)	11120
	16.1%	16.1%	14.7%	15.2%	12.1%	11.6%	12.7%	17.8%	15.2%	11.6%	10.5%	12.5%	% Earned Total Cap'l	13.0%
	16.3%	16.3%	15.0%	15.4%	12.3%	11.8%	12.8%	18.0%	15.2%	11.6%	11.0%	12.5%	% Earned Net Worth	13.0%
	14.8%	15.0%	13.6%	14.0%	10.8%	10.5%	11.6%	16.5%	13.7%	10.0%	9.0%	10.5%	% Retained to Comm Eq	11.5%
	9%	8%	9%	9%	12%	11%	9%	8%	10%	14%	16%	14%	% All Div'ds to Net Prof	14%

CURRENT POSITION

	1989 E	1990	7/31/91
Cash Assets	926	1077	770
Receivables	2494	2883	2694
Inventory (FIFO)	1947	2092	2288
Other	364	458	701
Current Assets	5731	6510	6453
Accts Payable	642	660	653
Debt Due	1341	1896	1121
Other	1760	1887	1939
Current Liab.	3743	4443	3713

ANNUAL RATES of change (per sh)

	Past 10 Yrs.	Past 5 Yrs.	Est'd '88-'90 to '94-'96
Sales	17.0%	17.0%	11.0%
"Cash Flow"	16.0%	13.0%	10.5%
Earnings	14.0%	11.5%	10.5%
Dividends	15.5%	13.0%	16.0%
Book Value	15.5%	11.0%	12.5%

QUARTERLY SALES ($ mill.) A E

Fiscal Year Ends	Jan.31	Apr.30	Jul.31	Oct.31	Full Fiscal Year
1988	2192	2496	2434	2709	9831
1989	2657	2864	3001	3377	11899
1990	3103	3308	3242	3580	13233
1991	3408	3730	3524	3938	14600
1992	3750	4100	4000	4450	16300

EARNINGS PER SHARE A B

Fiscal Year Ends	Jan.31	Apr.30	Jul.31	Oct.31	Full Fiscal Year
1988	.71	.82	.80	1.03	3.36
1989	.83	.86	.79	1.04	3.52
1990	.72	.78	.73	.83	3.06
1991	.83	.93	.76	.63	3.15
1992	.95	1.00	.95	1.10	4.00

QUARTERLY DIVIDENDS PAID C

Calendar	Mar.31	Jun.30	Sep.30	Dec.31	Full Year
1987	.055	.055	.055	.065	.23
1988	.065	.065	.065	.085	.28
1989	.085	.085	.085	.105	.36
1990	.105	.105	.105	.105	.42
1991	.105	.125	.125	.125	

BUSINESS: Hewlett-Packard Company is a major designer and manufacturer of precision electronic products and systems for measurement and computation. Major product categories: measurement, design, information and manufacturing equipment; peripherals and network products, medical electronic equipment and instrumentation. Also manufactures solid-state components, primarily for in-house use. Service for equipment, systems and peripherals revenue, 23% in '90; foreign sales: 54%; R&D: 10.3%. '90 depreciation rate: 10.2%. Est. plant age: 4 years. Employs 92,000; has 73,080 shareholders. Insiders own 20% of stock. Chrmn.: David Packard. President & C.E.O.: John A. Young. Inc.: CA. Add.: P.O. Box 10301, Palo Alto, CA 94303. Tel.: 415-857-1501.

Increased shipments of its hot new workstations should be a plus for Hewlett-Packard. The computer manufacturer introduced its new *Model 700* line in March, and the extremely powerful, and very competitively priced, products were an immediate hit. Unfortunately, in the third fiscal period (ended July 31st), demand outstripped supply, due to the difficulty of getting a key chip, restraining revenue growth from that profitable line. Meanwhile, shipments of lower-margined peripheral products remained relatively strong, squeezing gross margins, and helping hold share-earnings growth in the period to just 3¢ over the year-ago level. The constraint on supplies of the *Model 700* started to ease in the just-ended October interim, and cost-cutting efforts likely led to renewed operating margin expansion, but those efforts probably generated about a 40¢-a-share charge in the final period. We think share earnings grew about 10¢ in fiscal 1991 and, assuming a stronger economy, we expect an advance of about 25% in the following 12 months. **Share net probably will reach $6.00 by mid-decade.** Continued rollouts of new products should keep the company's *Precision Architecture* family fresh, since the system was designed with an eye on future expansion. Meanwhile, Hewlett-Packard probably will also benefit from its commitment to "open systems" that let customers mix and match products from different vendors without losing their investments in existing application programs. That effort should be aided by H-P's *NewWave* product, which makes it relatively easy for customers to unite their computing resources to access data no matter where it resides on the system.

Still, Hewlett-Packard shares have only modest appeal. The equity is ranked 3, Average, for relative price performance over the next six to 12 months. The earnings gains we project for the 3 to 5 years ahead probably aren't sufficient to allow the issue to outleg the market over that span either. But earnings predictability is relatively high for a member of this group. Too, Hewlett-Packard's solid balance sheet puts it in a good position to withstand the adversities that periodically rock this industry.

George A. Niemond   *November 1, 1991*

(A) Fiscal year ends Oct. 31st. (B) Based on shares outstanding at end of each period until '88; then by method that approximates weighted average. Excludes nonrecurring gain. Factual material is obtained from sources believed to be reliable, but the publisher is not responsible for any errors or omissions contained herein. For the confidential use of subscribers. Reprinting, copying, and distribution by permission only. Copyright 1991 by Value Line Publishing, Inc. ● Reg. TM—Value Line, Inc.

from reversal of DISC taxes: '84, 46¢. Next earnings report due mid-Nov. (C) Next dividend meeting about Nov. 15. Next ex date about Dec 20. Approx. dividend payment dates: Jan. 15, April 15, July 15, Oct. 15. (D) In millions, adjusted for stock splits. (E) Finance subsidiary consolidated from 1989.

Company's Financial Strength	A++
Stock's Price Stability	45
Price Growth Persistence	35
Earnings Predictability	80

Another publication is the *Business One Irwin Business and Investment Almanac.* A section on finance and accounting covers key business ratios, financial statement ratios by industry, and corporate profits and margins. A section on the stock market covers over 100 pages and includes market averages, mutual funds, dividends, common stock prices and yields, and much more. Information on commodities, banks, financial institutions, economic data, and a great deal more is contained in this 700-page business almanac.

Wiesenberger Services, Inc., publishes one of the best-known sources of information on mutual funds. The annual issue covers a 10-year statistical history (a sample page appears in Chapter 19). Another publication that is like an investment service is the annual issue of *The Individual Investor's Guide to No-Load Mutual Funds* published by the American Association of Individual Investors.

Retail stockbrokers have long provided information to their clients. The more you can afford to pay and the bigger your account, the more research you may receive. Most large brokers, such as Merrill Lynch; Shearson Lehman; Prudential Securities; and Dean Witter, will provide investors information free or perhaps for a fee. You name what you want, and they have it—industry-company analysis, bond market analysis, futures and commodities, options advice, tax shelters in oil and gas and real estate, and so on. The brokerage industry provides much more sophisticated coverage of investments outside of stocks and bonds than they have in the past. This is partly because investors have become more sophisticated and partly because of the increasing numbers and complexity of alternative investments.

■ INDEXES, SEC FILINGS, PERIODICALS, AND JOURNALS

Indexes

One way to find relevant articles in periodicals and journals is to use indexes. Many will lead an analyst to useful information. The *Business Periodicals Index* references subjects in approximately 170 periodicals in the fields of accounting, advertising, banking, communications, economics, finance, insurance, investments, labor management, marketing, taxation, and other specific topics. The *Funk and Scott Index of Corporations and Industries* covers articles from over 750 publications in two volumes. Each article covered includes a brief description of its contents. The articles are taken from business, financial, and trade magazines, major newspapers, bank newsletters, and investment advisory services. One very popular index is *The Wall Street Journal Index,* which identifies the date, page, and column of articles appearing in *The Wall Street Journal.* The index is presented in two parts—corporate news and general news. Many libraries have several years of *The Wall Street Journal* on microfiche or microfilm. Among the many other indexes are *Who's Who in Finance and Industry,* Dun & Bradstreet's *Reference Book of Corporate Management,* and Standard & Poor's *Register of Corporations, Directors and Executives.* These last three focus on people and can provide important qualitative information about management.

Securities and Exchange Commission Filings *SEC*

As discussed in Chapter 2, the Securities and Exchange Commission was established by the Securities Exchange Act of 1934 and has the power to regulate trading on the exchanges and to require corporate disclosure of information relevant to the stockholders of publicly traded companies. The SEC even has the power to dictate accounting conventions.

Information available through the SEC consists primarily of corporate income statements, balance sheets, detailed support of accounting information, and internal data not always found in a company's annual report. Companies are required to file specific reports with the SEC. The annual 10-K Report is perhaps the most widely known and can usually be obtained free directly from the company rather than paying the SEC a copying charge. This report should be read in combination with the firm's annual report as it contains the same type of information but in greater detail. The 8-K Report must be filed when the corporation undergoes some important event that stockholders would be interested in knowing about, such as changes in control, bankruptcy, resignation of officers or directors, and other material events. 10-Q statements are filed quarterly no later than 45 days after the end of the quarter. This report includes quarterly financial statements, changes in stockholdings, legal proceedings, and other matters.

There are many other SEC reports. The most common are proxy statements that disclose information relevant to stockholders' votes; a prospectus, which must be issued whenever a new offering of securities is made to the public; and a registration trading statement, which is normally required for new issues by firms trading on an organized exchange or over-the-counter. Figure 4–4 presents a detailed listing of information available from SEC filings, including reports required for tender offers and acquisitions. This table is taken from Disclosure, Inc., a firm providing on-line computer access to SEC filings and other information sources to subscribers. These reports can be obtained from the Disclosure retrieval system with a one-business-day turnaround, or they can be ordered from the SEC with a seven-business-day turnaround. They can also be read at the SEC regional office, where the corporation is headquartered, or in the SEC's regional New York, Chicago, or Los Angeles offices. A list of SEC addresses is given in Appendix 4–B at the end of this chapter.

Periodicals and Newspapers

After using the *Business Periodical Index,* an investor will most likely be referred to several of the most-popular business periodicals such as *Fortune, Business Week, Forbes,* and *Financial World. Fortune* is published biweekly and is known for its coverage of industry problems and specific company analysis. *Fortune* has several regular features that make interesting reading. One, "Business Roundup," usually deals with a major business concern such as the federal budget, inflation, or productivity. Another feature, "Personal Investing," is

Figure 4–4 Securities and Exchange Commission Filings

REPORT CONTENTS	10-K	19-K 20-F	10-Q	8-K	10-C	6-K	Proxy Statement	Prospects	Registration Statements '34 Act F-10	Registration Statements '34 Act 8-A 8-B	Registration Statements '33 Act "S" Type	ARS	Listing Application	N-1R	N-1Q
Auditor															
Name	A	A						A	A		A	A		A	
Opinion	A	A							A			A		A	
Changes				A											
Compensation Plans															
Equity							F	F	A		F				
Monetary								F	A		F				
Company Information															
Nature of Business	A	A				F		A	A		A				
History	F	A						A			A				
Organization and Change	F	F		A		F		A		F	A				
Debt Structure	A					F		A	A		A	A		A	
Depreciation & Other Schedules	A	A				F		A	A		A				
Dilution Factors	A	A		F		F		A	A		A	A			
Directors, Officers, Insiders															
Identification	F	A				F	A	A	A		A	F			
Background		A				F	F	A			A				
Holdings		A					A	A	A		A				
Compensation		A					A	A	A		A				
Earnings Per Share	A	A	A			F			A			A		A	
Financial Information															
Annual Audited	A	A							A			A		A	
Interim Audited		A													
Interim Unaudited			A			F		F			F	F			
Foreign Operations	A							A	A		A		F		
Labor Contracts									F		F				
Legal Agreements	F								F		F				
Legal Counsel								A			A				
Loan Agreements	F		F						F		F				
Plants and Properties	A	F						F	A		F				
Portfolio Operations															
Content (Listing of Securities)															A
Management														A	
Product-Line Breakout	A							A			A				
Securities Structure	A	A						A	A		A				
Subsidiaries	A	A						A	A		A				
Underwriting								A	A		A				
Unregistered Securities								F			F				
Block Movements				F					A						

TENDER OFFER ACQUISITION REPORTS	13D	13G	14D-1	14D-9	13E-3	13E-4
Name of Issuer (Subject Company)	A	A	A	A	A	A
Filing Person (or Company)	A	A	A	A	A	A
Amount of Shares Owned	A	A				
Percent of Class Outstanding	A	A				
Financial Statements of Bidders			F		F	F
Purpose of Tender Offer			A	A	A	A
Source and Amount of Funds	A		A		A	
Identity and Background Information			A	A	A	
Persons Retained, Employed or to be Compensated			A	A	A	A
Exhibits	F		F	F	F	F

Legend A-always included-included-if occurred or significant F-frequently included -special circumstances only

Source: *A Guide to SEC Corporate Filings* (Bethesda, Md.: Disclosure, Inc., April 1983), pp. 12–13.

always a thought-provoking article presenting ideas and analysis for the average investor.

Forbes is also a biweekly publication featuring several company-management interviews. This management-oriented approach points out various management styles and provides a look into the qualitative factors of security analysis. Several regular columnists discuss investment topics from a diversified perspective. *Business Week* is somewhat more general than *Forbes*. It includes a weekly economic update on such economic variables as interest rates, electricity consumption, and market prices while also featuring articles on industries and companies. Many other periodicals, such as *Kiplinger's Personal Finance Magazine* and *Money,* are helpful to the financial manager or personal investor.

Newspapers in most major cities (Chicago, Dallas, and Cleveland, to name a few) have good financial sections. *The New York Times* has an exceptional financial page. However, the most widely circulated financial daily is *The Wall Street Journal,* published by Dow Jones & Company. It is read by millions of investors who want to keep up with the economy and business environment. Feature articles on labor, business, economics, personal investing, technology, and taxes appear regularly. Corporate announcements of all kinds are published. Table 4–6 on page 134, "Digest of Earnings Reports," is a daily feature that updates quarterly and annual earnings of firms.

New offerings of stocks and bonds are also advertised by investment bankers in the *Journal*. Prices of actively traded securities are presented by the market in which they trade. Common and preferred stock prices are organized by exchange and over-the-counter markets. Table 4–7 on page 135 is an example of common and preferred stock prices on the New York Stock Exchange.

Many other prices are printed in *The Wall Street Journal*. An investor will find prices of government Treasury bills, notes, and bonds, mutual funds, put and call prices from the option exchanges, government agency securities, foreign exchange prices, and commodities futures prices. Table 4–8 on page 136 is an example of the commodity futures prices from the *Journal*. The prices are listed by category and exchange. Because of the comprehensive price coverage on a daily basis and other features, it is hard to believe that an up-to-date intelligent investor would be able to function without *The Wall Street Journal*. Each fall, *The Wall Street Journal* publishes an educational edition that explains how to read *The Wall Street Journal* and interpret some of the data presented.

Barron's National Business and Financial Weekly, published by Dow Jones every Saturday, contains regular features on dividends, put and call options, international stock markets, commodities, a review of the stock market, and many pages of prices and financial statistics. *Barron's* takes a weekly perspective and summarizes the previous week's market behavior. It also has regular analyses of several companies in its section called "Investment News and Views." The common stock section of *Barron's* not only provides weekly high-low-close prices and volume, but also informs investors as to the latest earnings per share, dividends declared, and dividend record and payable dates. This can be seen in the bottom portion of Table 4–9 on page 137.

Table 4–6   The *Wall Street Journal* "Digest of Earnings Reports"

ACCLAIM ENTERTAINMENT (O)		
Quar Nov 30:	1991	1990
Revenues	$42,033,000	$37,593,000
Net income	2,468,000	319,000
Avg shares	21,415,000	18,820,000
Shr earns:		
Net income .	.12	.02

ADOBE SYSTEMS INC. (O)		
Year Nov 29:	1991	1990
Revenues	$229,653,000	$168,730,000
Net income	51,607,000	40,070,000
Avg shares	22,941,000	21,923,000
Shr earns:		
Net income .	2.25	1.83
13 weeks:		
Revenues	62,740,000	53,370,000
Net income	13,143,000	12,042,000
Avg shares	23,209,000	21,878,000
Shr earns:		
Net income .	.57	.55

ALAFIRST BANCSHARES INC. (A)		
Quar Dec. 31:	1991	1990
Net income	$814,000	$574,000
Avg shares	1,211,705	1,166,384
Shr earns (com		
Net inco		

...ANCORP (O)		
...ec 31:	1991	1990
Net income	$774,992	$754,836
Avg shares	1,331,580	1,381,752
Shr earns:		
Net income .	.58	.54

DREW INDUSTRIES INC. (O)		
Quar Nov 30:	1991	1990
Sales	$23,157,000	$20,532,000
Net income	333,000	(255,000)
Shr earns:		
Net income .	.07	(.05)
Figures in parentheses are losses.		

DYNAMIC CLASSICS LTD. (O)		
Quar Oct 31:	1991	1990
Sales	$10,679,496	$10,000,596
Net income	549,715	623,636
Shr earns:		
Net income .	.32	.36
6 months:		
Sales	17,162,231	14,427,312
Net income	606,970	536,371
Shr earns:		
Net income .	.35	.31

ABBREVIATIONS
A partial list of frequently used abbreviations: Acctg adj (Accounting adjustment); Extrd chg (Extraordinary charge); Extrd cred (Extraordinary credit); Inco cnt op (Income from continuing operations); Inco dis op (Income from discontinued operations).

HELEN OF TROY CORP. (O)		
Quar Nov 30:	1991	1990
Sales	$42,440,000	$40,029,000
Net income	3,278,000	1,691,000
Avg shares	4,685,249	4,672,602
Shr earns:		
Net income .	.70	.36
9 months:		
Sales	98,149,000	95,726,000
Net income	5,983,000	4,050,000
Avg shares	4,573,325	5,096,647
Shr earns:		
Net income .	1.31	.79

INT'L AIRLINE SUPPOR...		
Quar Nov 30:	19...	
...les		...3,046
		418,079
...609	3,825,000	
Net income .	.08	.11
6 months:		
Sales	14,013,073	8,845,979
	1,081,086	762,161
Avg shares	3,887,175	3,825,000
Shr earns:		
Net income .	.28	.20

MISSIMER & ASSOCIATES (O)		
Quar Nov 30:	1991	1990
Revenues	$3,371,000	$2,221,000
Net income	193,000	113,000
Shr earns:		
Net income .	.13	.08

(N) New York Stock Exchange
(A) American Exchange (O)
Over-the-Counter (Pa) Pacific
(M) Midwest (P) Philadelphia
(B) Boston (T) Toronto (Mo)
Montreal (F) Foreign.

KETEMA INC. (A)		
Quar Nov 30:	1991	1990
Sales	$41,908,000	$45,568,000
Net income	385,000	1,636,000
Avg shares	3,932,302	4,030,837
Shr earns (primary):		
Net income .	.10	.41
Shr earns (fully diluted):		
Net income .		.37
9 months:		
Sales	129,457,000	144,985,000
Net income	2,031,000	a(1,379,000)
Avg shares	3,932,302	4,168,641
Shr earns (primary):		
Net income .	.52	(.33)
a-Includes pre-tax charge of $5,841,-000 related to settlement of claims.		
Figures in parentheses are losses.		

RAG SHOPS INC. (O)		
Quar Nov 30:	1991	1990
Sales	$20,178,000	$16,585,000
Net income	1,513,000	1,064,000
Shr earns:		
Net income .	.34	.31

...Y BANCSHRS (O)		
Year ...	...01	1990
Net income ...		
Shr earns (prima...		
Net income .		
Quarter:		
Net income	3,313,000	2,760,000
Shr earns (primary):		
Net income .	.43	a.45
a-Adjusted to reflect a 5% stock dividend paid in May 1991.		

TSR INC. (O)		
Quar Nov 30:	1991	1990
Sales	$3,343,000	$3,397,000
Net income	91,000	(89,000)
Shr earns:		
Net income .	.06	(.05)
6 months:		
Revenues	$6,509,000	7,085,000
Net income	212,000	a108,000
Shr earns:		
Net income .	.13	.07
a-Includes a non–recurring gain of $558,000.		
Figures in parentheses are losses.		

One unique feature of *Barron's* is the "Market Laboratory" covering the last eight pages of each issue. Weekly data on major stock and bond markets are presented with the week's market statistics. Tables 4–10 and 4–11 on pages 138 and 139 show some of the tables from *Barron's* "Market Laboratory." Careful reading of this publication will turn up useful data in a compact summary form not found in other publications.

Other major papers are *Investor's Business Daily,* the *Wall Street Transcript* (weekly), and the *Commercial and Financial Chronicle* (weekly). Media General's *Industriscope* is an exceptional source of fundamental and technical indicators for the professional manager. Over 3,400 common stocks are divided into 60 industrial groups and analyzed based on relative strength (whether they are leading or lagging the market), trends, earnings, and other variables that may be useful to the analyst.

Table 4–7   New York Stock Exchange Composite Transactions (Common stock prices)

Quotations as of 5 p.m. Eastern Time
Wednesday, January 8, 1992

-A-A-A-

-B-B-B-

Source: *The Wall Street Journal*, January 9, 1992, p. C3. Reprinted by permission of *THE WALL STREET JOURNAL*, © 1992 by Dow Jones & Company, Inc. All Rights Reserved Worldwide.

Table 4–8   Commodity Futures Prices

Wednesday, January 8, 1992.
Open Interest Reflects Previous Trading Day.

-GRAINS AND OILSEEDS-

	Open	High	Low	Settle	Change	Lifetime High	Lifetime Low	Open Interest

CORN (CBT) 5,000 bu.; cents per bu.

Mar	250	253¼	249¾	253	+ 3	277¼	228½	109,760
May	256½	259¾	256¼	259½	+ 3¼	279½	234¾	52,362
July	261¼	264¼	261¼	264¼	+ 3	282	239½	41,561
Sept	261	262	260½	262¼	+ 2¼	265	236½	5,707
Dec	258½	262	258¼	261¾	+ 2¼	262½	236½	17,240
Mr93	265¼	268	265¼	268	+ 3	268	258	774

Est vol 53,000; vol Tues 27,316; open int 227,409, −660.

OATS (CBT) 5,000 bu.; cents per bu.

Mar	137	138¾	136¾	138	+ 1¼	157	126½	6,682
May	139¼	141	139	140¼	+ 1¼	159½	132	1,746
July	143	142½	143	+ 1¾	161½	138	412	

Est vol 1,200; vol Tues 309; open int 8,924, +1.

SOYBEANS (CBT) 5,000 bu.; cents per bu.

Jan	558½	565	557	564¾	+ 8	659	527½	6,895
Mar	559¼	566	558¾	565½	+ 7½	666	538	44,777
May	565½	572¼	565	572	+ 8	668	547	19,187
July	573	580½	573	580	+ 7½	668	554	21,648
Aug	577¼	584	577¼	584	+ 8½	660	565	2,404
Sept	579	586½	579	586¼	+10¼	628	557	1,404
Nov	582½	591½	582¼	591¼	+10	620¾	552	10,089
Ja93	593	593	593	598½	+ 8½	601	578½	669

Est vol 42,000; vol Tues 26,707; open int 107,161, −1,184.

SOYBEAN MEAL (CBT) 100 tons; $ per ton.

Jan	171.80	174.50	171.50	174.50	+ 2.10	197.00	161.30	6,723
Mar	171.40	174.40	171.10	174.20	+ 2.60	197.00	163.50	30,195
May	171.80	174.00	171.80	174.80	+ 2.90	194.00	164.50	13,185
July	173.50	177.00	173.50	176.70	+ 3.40	196.00	166.00	10,836
Aug	174.50	177.50	174.50	177.50	+ 3.40	188.50	170.90	2,307
Sept	175.50	178.50	175.50	178.50	+ 3.50	186.00	171.30	3,096
Oct	189.50	191.70	189.50	191.60	+ 2.60	194.00	182.30	1,477
Dec	191.00	193.50	191.00	193.00	+ 2.50	199.00	183.50	1,903

Est vol 25,000; vol Tues 12,455; open int 69,722, −421.

SOYBEAN OIL (CBT) 60,000 lbs.; cents per lb.

Jan	18.65	18.84	18.63	18.79	+ .11	24.15	18.35	3,543
Mar	18.93	19.10	18.87	19.02	+ .15	24.10	18.60	28,887
May	19.24	19.40	19.17	19.32	+ .17	24.00	18.95	19,379
July	19.53	19.68	19.48	19.60	+ .15	24.30	19.25	7,100
Aug	19.65	19.80	19.65	19.77	+ .16	22.35	19.47	2,520
Sept	19.80	19.80	19.80	19.85	+ .13	22.35	19.57	1,265
Oct	19.94	19.94	19.94	19.86	+ .06	22.30	19.66	1,107
Dec	20.15	20.25	20.15	20.25	+ .13	22.60	19.95	1,045

Est vol 17,000; vol Tues 16,180; open int 64,829, +154.

WHEAT (CBT) 5,000 bu.; cents per bu.

Mar	393¼	408	392½	403¼	+ 8¼	409¼	279	29,755
May	374½	392½	372½	381¼	+ 5½	384¼	280½	10,213
July	342¾	346	339	345½	+ 2¾	349	279	13,105
Sept	345¼	348	343	347¼	+ 2	352	292	1,156
Dec	354	357½	352	357½	+ 3	358½	329½	1,534

Est vol 18,500; vol Tues 11,209; open int 55,776, +499.

WHEAT (KC) 5,000 bu.; cents per bu.

Mar	392	400	389¼	398¼	+ 5½	404½	275½	21,215
May	372¼	381	370½	378¼	+ 2	382	273	7,137
July	344½	348	342½	346	+ ½	350	272	5,518
Sept	345½	350	344½	350	+ 2	352	314	834

Est vol 6,560; vol Tues 4,891; open int 34,725, −291.

WHEAT (MPLS) 5,000 bu.; cents per bu.

Mar	379¾	388	376	387	+ 6¾	393	279½	8,771
May	369	374	366¾	374	+ 4¼	379	284	3,661
July	356	354¾	353½	357	+ 1½	362	308	665
Sept	343	343	344½	+ ½	353	315	352	

Est vol 560; vol Tues 2,831; open int 13,436, −700.

BARLEY (WPG) 20 metric tons; Can. $ per ton.

Mar	88.50	89.50	88.50	89.30	+ .60	97.50	81.00	3,945
May	90.70	+ .50	96.00	85.70	1,087			
July	92.40	+ .40	96.90	91.00	226			
Oct	94.00	94.00	93.90	93.90	+ .50	94.80	74.70	228

Est vol 300; vol Tues 147; open int 5,546, +23.

FLAXSEED (WPG) 20 metric tons; Can. $ per ton.

Mar	193.50	194.90	193.50	194.50	+ 1.40	234.50	186.40	2,008
May	198.00	199.50	198.00	199.00	+ 1.30	232.00	190.70	1,333
July	202.30	203.00	202.50	203.00	+ 1.30	221.50	194.80	1,496
Oct	209.70	210.30	209.70	210.30	+ 1.30	216.50	202.20	301

Est vol 730; vol Tues 529; open int 5,160, +13.

CANOLA (WPG) 20 metric tons; Can. $ per ton.

Jan	262.40	264.70	262.40	264.70	+ 2.20	317.50	253.40	1,735
Mar	265.10	266.70	264.90	266.70	+ 1.60	320.50	261.60	9,748
June	270.10	271.80	270.10	271.60	+ 1.40	326.60	267.50	5,730
Sept	277.60	+ 1.40	309.00	275.50	99			
Nov	282.00	282.60	282.00	282.60	+ 1.70	286.50	278.20	450

Est vol 1,260; vol Tues 2,340; open int 17,762, −103.

WHEAT (WPG) 20 metric tons; Can. $ per ton.

Mar	101.10	102.00	101.10	102.00	+ .60	106.00	89.00	4,984
May	102.10	102.80	102.10	102.70	+ .60	106.50	90.00	3,306
July	104.00	104.00	104.00	104.00	+ .40	105.00	101.00	1,006
Oct	104.60	+ .50	106.50	102.30	272			

Est vol 390; vol Tues 330; open int 9,568, +2.

-LIVESTOCK & MEAT-

CATTLE-FEEDER (CME) 44,000 lbs.; cents per lb.

Jan	79.10	79.10	78.40	78.60	− .37	87.80	75.70	2,440
Mar	76.75	76.75	76.05	76.32	− .25	87.10	74.00	3,730
Apr	75.70	75.70	75.17	75.30	− .32	87.00	73.25	1,500
May	74.75	74.85	74.17	74.22	− .40	83.00	72.65	1,392
Aug	74.45	74.50	74.05	74.05	− .20	83.00	72.65	698
Sept	73.55	73.60	73.30	73.50	− .10	82.40	72.15	86
Oct	73.50	73.50	73.30	73.30	− .05	79.50	72.10	108

Est vol 2,272; vol Tues 2,709; open int 9,972, −20.

CATTLE-LIVE (CME) 40,000 lbs.; cents per lb.

Feb	73.85	74.10	73.30	73.37				20,221
Apr	74.50	74.90	74.05	74.20				
June	69.77	69.20						

-METALS & PETROLEUM-

	Open	High	Low	Settle	Change	Lifetime High	Lifetime Low	Open Interest

COPPER-HIGH (CMX) 25,000 lbs.; cents per lb.

Jan	94.00	94.50	93.80	93.90	− .55	106.60	93.80	1,128
Feb	94.35	94.65	94.20	94.20	− .45	105.70	94.20	1,003
Mar	94.20	95.25	94.20	94.35	− .60	106.80	93.90	28,047
May	94.70	94.90	94.70	94.75	− .55	103.00	93.50	668
July	95.50	95.65	95.50	95.15	− .45	102.00	94.30	3,561
Sept	95.25	95.25	95.25	95.15	− .40	101.00	95.70	265
Sept	95.30	95.85	95.30	95.15	− .40	103.45	95.20	2,115
Oct	95.05	− .40	98.40	96.00	227			
Nov	95.45	− .40	98.40	96.00	237			
Dec	95.90	96.10	95.80	95.50	− .40	101.10	91.60	2,526
Mr93	95.80	95.80	95.80	95.50	− .40	100.50	92.80	714
May	95.45	− .40	99.30	93.70	151			
July	95.85	95.85	95.85	95.45	− .40	96.65	95.00	100

Est vol 7,500; vol Tues 6,385; open int 47,216, +1,072.

GOLD (CMX) 100 troy oz.; $ per troy oz.

Jan	350.80	+ 1.10	363.20	351.00				
Feb	351.50	352.20	350.70	351.50	+ 1.00	456.50	348.50	52,591
Apr	353.50	454.10	352.80	353.50	+ .80	446.00	350.70	19,777
June	365.50	355.90	354.70	355.50	+ .70	467.00	353.80	16,080
Aug	357.40	357.40	357.10	357.40	+ .70	426.50	355.00	6,232
Oct	359.30	359.30	359.00	360.30	+ .70	410.80	358.50	1,857
Fb93	361.50	361.50	360.70	361.40	+ .60	431.00	390.40	3,681
Apr	363.40	+ .50	404.20	378.00	636			
Apr	365.30	+ .40	410.00	368.50	3,560			
Aug	367.30	+ .30	418.50	366.00	2,055			
Dec	374.50	374.50	374.50	374.50	− .40	402.80	374.50	629

Est vol 40,000; vol Tues 21,993; open int 111,741, −2,330.

PLATINUM (NYM) 50 troy oz.; $ per troy oz.

Jan	336.00	336.00	335.00	336.80	+ 3.70	451.50	330.00	532
Apr	335.50	338.00	335.00	337.50	+ 3.70	424.50	329.50	12,042
July	338.00	338.00	337.00	339.20	+ 3.70	427.50	332.00	1,576
Oct	344.00	344.00	344.00	344.50	+ 3.70	404.00	336.00	1,179
Ja93	345.70	+ 3.70	355.00	340.00	496			

Est vol 1,437; vol Tues 1,612; open int 15,845, +268.

PALLADIUM (NYM) 100 troy oz.; $ per troy oz.

Jan	79.75	81.00	79.75	80.80	+ 1.55	103.50	77.80	3,293
June	80.00	81.25	80.00	81.55	+ 1.55	101.75	78.65	285
Dec	83.60	+ 1.55	90.20	80.80	177			

Est vol 117; vol Tues 108; open int 3,761, −10.

SILVER (CMX) 5,000 troy oz.; cents per troy oz.

Jan	394.6	+ 2.9	596.0	381.5	72			
Mar	395.0	398.0	394.0	398.0	+ 2.8	613.0	381.0	51,954
May	398.5	401.5	398.5	401.5	+ 2.7	589.0	384.5	11

SILVER (CBT) 1,000 troy oz.; cents per troy oz.

Jan	395.0	+ 3.0	406.0	382.0	6			
Feb	394.0	395.8	394.0	395.8	+ 3.8	476.0	378.0	673
Apr	397.0	399.5	397.0	399.5	+ 3.5	485.0	383.0	554
June	400.0	403.0	399.0	403.0	+ 3.5	494.0	387.0	4,216
Dec	412.5	+ 3.5	460.0	399.0	404			
Fb93	415.0	416.0	415.0	416.0	+ 3.5	445	408.0	105

Est vol 350; vol Tues 37; open int 5,985, −2.

CRUDE OIL, Light Sweet (NYM) 1,000 bbls.; $ per bbl.

Feb	18.53	18.65	17.83	17.87	− .82	27.00	17.50	59,700
Mar	18.52	18.64	17.85	17.89	− .75	26.75	17.25	54,587
Apr	18.60	18.62	18.00	18.03	− .67	26.50	17.50	39,484
May	18.60	18.65	18.05	18.10	− .62	24.60	17.30	18,580
June	18.63	18.65	18.15	18.17	− .57	24.50	17.70	20,084
July	18.62	18.62	18.25	18.27	− .50	23.90	17.90	12,077
Aug	18.50	18.50	18.25	18.29	− .49	21.80	17.75	9,373
Sept	18.67	18.67	18.42	18.35	− .45	24.00	17.78	8,354
Oct	18.65	18.65	18.45	18.41	− .42	21.56	18.45	7,786
Nov	18.80	18.80	18.50	18.47	− .39	21.48	18.50	4,596
Dec	18.80	18.80	18.62	18.56	− .36	24.00	18.25	11,331
Ja93	18.80	18.80	18.62	18.56	− .35	21.36	18.62	4,467
Feb	18.75	18.75	18.75	18.67	− .34	21.79	18.67	3,382
Mar	18.78	18.78	18.73	18.62	− .33	21.26	18.51	3,793
May	18.68	− .31	21.10	19.18	1,460			
June	18.85	18.85	18.83	18.72	− .29	23.00	18.51	575
July	18.76	− .27	19.60	19.25	3,960			
Sept	18.84	− .25	21.13	19.30	3,226			
Dec	19.14	19.14	19.14	18.98	− .21	23.00	18.70	9,993
Ju94	19.20	− .19	21.35	19.52	10,469			
	19.42	− .17	21.08	19.70	3,520			

Est vol 133,812; vol Tues 108,648; open int 302,730, +9,773.

HEATING OIL NO. 2 (NYM) 42,000 gal.; $ per gal.

Feb	.5080	.5110	.4920	.4926	− .0152	.7070	.4910	45,631
Mar	.5180	.5200	.5020	.5037	− .0156	.6750	.5820	22,082
Apr	.5140	.5155	.5005	.5003	− .0125	.6365	.5000	8,936
May	.5100	.5100	.4980	.4980	− .0100	.6160	.4825	8,407
June	.5060	.5060	.4940	.4940	− .0085	.6020	.4800	2,532
July	.5085	.5085	.4950	.4966	− .0081	.5965	.4950	10,515
Aug	.5140	.5140	.5000	.5046	− .0081	.5975	.4725	4,766
Sept	.5255	.5255	.5220	.5171	− .0081	.6090	.5220	1,600
Oct	.5350	.5395	.5315	.5266	− .0081	.6170	.5315	1,376
Nov	.5430	.5430	.5340	.5331	− .0081	.6260	.5430	896
Dec	.5540	.5550	.5530	.5456	− .0081	.6350	.5530	1,508
Ja93	.5476	− .0081	.6375	.5640	305			

Est vol 35,801; vol Tues 41,947; open int 110,683, +1,817.

GASOLINE, Unleaded (NYM) 42,000 gal.; $ per gal.

Feb	.5240	.5260	.5220	.5206	− .0208	.6490	.5090	11,015
Mar	.5375	.5400	.5220	.5264	− .0200	.6565	.5090	16,763
Apr	.5840	.5840	.5660	.5674	− .0200	.6960	.5500	25,439
May	.5895	.5895	.5700	.5715	− .0246	.6900	.5525	22,802
July	.5820	.5820	.5700	.5710	− .0210	.6770	.5500	6,827
July	.5760	.5760	.5645	.5620	− .0190	.6630	.5270	8,815
Aug	.5560	.5600	.5560	.5515	− .0175	.6500	.5380	1,153
Sept	.5375	− .0170	.6300	.5580	2,740			
Oct	.5170	− .0165	.6020	.5430	1,367			

Est vol 30,900; vol Tues 29,849; open int 124,973, +1,453.

NATURAL GAS (NYM) 10,000 MMBtu.; $ per MMBtu's

Feb	1.310	1.338	1.290	1.290	− .014	2.040	1.265	2,302
Mar	1.280	1.300	1.270	1.290	− .000	1.820	1.675	3,061
Apr	1.250	1.250	1.225	1.235	− .005	1.500	1.210	1,997
May	1.250	1.255	1.240	1.240	+ .001	1.495	1.210	1,822
June	1.250	1.260	1.245	1.250	+ .011	1.510	1.210	1,903
July	1.315	1.315	1.300	1.304	− .016	1.550	1.265	1,205
Aug	1.305	− .016	1.550	1.260	925			
Oct	1.425	1.440	1.425	1.435	+ .024	1.640	1.420	1,055
Dec	1.835	1.855	1.835	1.840	+ .024	1.985	1.780	1,022
Ja93	1.935	1.960	1.935	1.960	+ .036	1.955	1.880	993

Est vol 3,773; vol Tues 2,403; open int 19,861, +262.

BRENT CRUDE (IPE) 1,000 net bbls.; per bbl.

Feb	17.80	17.82	16.85	16.79	− .77	22.03	16.85	30,541
Mar	17.58	17.65	16.85	16.84	− .72	21.69	16.85	18,149
Apr	17.55	17.55	16.84	16.84	− .64	21.36	16.84	7,221
May	17.50	17.58	16.85	16.85	− .60	21.15	16.85	4,177
June	17.46	17.47	16.85	16.84	− .60	20.92	16.85	7,257
Aug	17.00	17.00	16.85	16.95	− .50	20.76	16.85	2,510
Sept	17.19	17.19	17.19	17.03	− .51	21.07	17.19	1,950
Oct	17.15	17.25	17.13	17.13	− .45	19.90	17.19	1,402
Oct	17.29	17.29	17.19	18.14	− .46	17.29		620

Est vol 39,244; vol Tues 31,013; open int 13,627, +4,462.

GAS OIL (IPE) 100 metric tons; $ per ton

Jan	163.50	164.75	157.75	157.75	− 9.00	231.00	158.25	14,258
Feb	164.50	165.00	158.50	158.50	− 7.50	221.00	158.25	19,258
Mar	163.25	164.50	158.75	159.00	− 7.00	220.00	158.75	8,281
Apr	160.00	162.50	157.50	158.50	− 6.75	204.00	158.00	8,095
May	162.25	162.50	157.75	157.50	− 6.00	185.50	158.50	2,133
June	162.75	163.00	158.50	158.75	− 6.75	187.75	158.50	2,133
July	162.75	164.25	160.50	161.00	− 6.00	184.55	160.50	2,745
Aug	166.25	166.25	162.75	162.75	− 7.00	184.25	174.75	546

Est Vol 26,547; vol Tues 14,499; open int 59,224, +63.

OTHER COMMODITY FUTURES

Settlement prices of selected contracts. Volume and open interest of all contract months.

			Net	Lifetime		Open
Vol.	High	Low	Close	Change	High	Low	Interest

... (CME) 40,000 lbs.; ...

| | | | 49.55 | | | | |

Table 4–9 Market Transactions from *Barron's*

THE WEEK'S STATISTICS

THE MARKETS

THE INDICATORS

THE INDEXES

BARRON'S STATISTICS

NEW YORK STOCK EXCHANGE COMPOSITE LIST

These composite stock quotations include trades on the Midwest, Pacific, Philadelphia, Boston and Cincinnati stock exchanges, as reported by the National Association of Securities Dealers and Instinet, excluding only those that did not trade last week.

Mkt Sym	52-Weeks High	52-Weeks Low	Company Name	Tick Sym	Div Amt	Vol 100's	Div Yld	Earn P/E	Week's High	Week's Low	Week's Last	Net Chg.	EARNINGS Interim or Fiscal Year	EARNINGS Year ago	DIVIDENDS Latest divs.	DIVIDENDS Record date	DIVIDENDS Payment date
			A-B-C														
	16⅞	9¼	AAR	AIR	.48	3476	3.6	18	13½	12¾	13¼	+ ¼	Nov6m.39	X.43	q.12	10-28	12-4
x	11⅝	10⅜	ACM Gvt Fd	ACG	1.26	x7219	11.2	...	11⅝	11¼	11¼	− ⅛	....	....	.06	1-13	1-24
▲	10⅜	8¾	ACM OppFd	AOF	1.01e	2222	10.1	...	10⅜	9½	10	+ ½	....	....	.084	1-6	1-17
	11⅛	9⅜	ACM SecFd	GSF	1.26	9775	11.6	...	11⅛	10	10⅞	− ⅛	....	....	.10½	12-27	1-10
	9½	8¼	ACM SpctmFd	SI	1.01	3743	10.9	...	9⅜	9⅛	9¼	+ ⅛	....	....	.0145	1-6	1-17
nx	9⅛	7⅝	ACM MgdIncFd	AMF	1.01	x2061	11.4	...	9⅛	8⅞	8⅞	− ⅛	....	....	M.039	1-13	1-24
	12⅞	11½	ACM MgdMultFd	MMF	1.35	1479	10.6	...	12⅞	12⅝	12¾	− ⅛	....	....	.1125	12-31	1-24
	21½	5	ADT adr	ADTA	.32e	1432	4.7	2	7⅛	6½	6⅞	− ¼	ADR....	....	.32	4-29-91	7-9-91
n	9½	5	ADT	ADT		15299	...	...	7⅜	6	6⅞	− ⅜	....	....	....	....	....
▲	32⅞	18⅛	AFLAC	AFL	.40	11699	1.3	18	32⅞	30⅜	31⅜	+1½	Sep9m1.31	1.03	q.10	11-15	12-2
▲	26	14⅜	AL Labs A	BMD	.16	4958	.6	28	26	23	25⅛	+1⅞	Sep9mX.64	.58	q.04	12-26	1-9
	1⅞	¼	AM Int	AM		2255	...	...	1	⅞	15/16	...	Nov3mD.16	....	Y	....	10-30-84
	12	4⅛	AM Int pf	AMp	1.50j	172	...	...	5¼	4⅞	5	...	....	....	Y	....	8-15-91
	11¾	9⅛	AMEV Sec	AMV	1.05	436	9.0	...	11¾	11⅛	11⅝	+ ⅜	....	....	M.0875	12-26	1-15
▲	75½	44¼	AMR	AMR		50773	...	...	75½	69¼	69⅜	−2¼	Sep9mD1.70	2.80	Y	....	2-15-80
	27¼	25	ANR pf	ANPp	2.67	5	10.1	...	26½	26¼	26½	+ ¼	....	....	q.66⅞	11-15	12-1
	44¼	33⅛	ARCO Chm	RCM	2.50	842	6.5	20	39½	38⅜	38¾	− ½	Sep9m1.25	2.40	q.62½	11-8	12-6
	2⅜	1	ARX	ARX		1185	...	...	1¾	1⅜	1½	...	Sep3mD.04	.01	Y	....	5-25-88
	56	41½	ASA	ASA	3.00	5849	6.1	...	50½	46⅜	48⅞	+1¾	....	....	q.75	11-21	11-29
	6½	2⅛	ATT Cap yen wt	YDT.WS		253	...	...	4⅞	4¼	4⅞	+ ¼	....	....	....	....	....
x	69½	39¼	AbbotLab	ABT	1.00	x30093	1.5	27	68¼	64⅝	65⅞	−1⅜	Sep9m1.81	1.57	q.25	1-15	2-15
x	14⅝	9⅞	Abitibi g	ABY	.50	x168	...	...	12⅜	12⅛	12¼	− ⅜	Sep9mD.42	D.35	q.12½	1-15	1-31
	6	3⅜	AcmeElec	ACE		119	...	...	4⅞	4¾	4¾	− ⅛	Sep13w.11	D.04	Y	....	12-3-91
▲	8¾	4¾	AcmeCleve	AMT	.40	2527	5.2	...	8¾	7⅛	7¾	+ ½	91Sep.44	.44	q.10	11-1	11-15
	40	22¾	Acuson	ACN		14683	...	21	33	31	31¼	− ¼	Sep9m1.17	.97	....	....	....
	20¼	14¼	AdamsExp	ADX	1.63e	1118	8.6	...	19¼	18¾	19	... ✦	....	....	.12	2-18-92	3-1-92
	9⅛	3⅞	AdobeRes	ADB		3428	...	...	4¾	4⅜	4½	− ¼	Jun6mD.40	D.91	....	....	....
	20⅛	12⅞	AdobeRes pf	ADBpB		254	...	...	14¼	13	13	−1	....	....	Y	....	11-15-91
	18	10¾	AdobeRes pf	ADBpA		205	...	...	11¾	11⅛	11⅛	− ⅞	....	....	Y	....	11-15-91
▲	20½	4⅜	AdvMicro	AMD		154360	...	13	20½	18	19⅛	+ ⅞	➤91Dec1.53	D.78	....	....	....
▲	46½	19¼	AdvMicro pf	AMDp	3.00	3428	6.7	...	46½	43½	44⅞	+1⅛	....	....	q.75	12-1	12-15
▲	6⅞	2¼	Advest	ADV		2079	...	...	6⅞	5⅜	6⅜	+1	91SepD.70	D.87	Y	....	12-17-91
▲	71¾	54¾	Aegon	AEG	3.72r	345	5.3	7	71¾	70¼	70⅜	− ½	Jun6m5.13	4.50	1.1151	9-6-91	9-18-91
	49⅛	31⅞	AetnaLife	AET	2.76	17289	6.3	9	44½	42¾	43⅞	+ ⅞	Sep9m3.75	L4.23	q.69	1-31	2-15
	10⅜	6⅜	AffilPub	AFP	.24	7633	2.6	85	9½	9	9⅜	+ ⅜	Sep39w.02	.26	q.06	2-14	3-1
n	23¾	21½	AgriMinl	AMC		2869	...	...	23¾	22¼	23⅛	+ ¼	...	...	....	....	...
	20⅞	12	Ahmanson	AHM	.88	13283	5.4	10	17⅜	15⅞	16¼	− ⅞	Sep9m1.55	1.64	q.22	11-12	12-2
	26¼	24	Ahmanson pf	AHMpB	2.40	4894	9.3	...	26⅛	25½	25¾	...	....	....	.60	11-12-91	12-2-91
	20	2⅞	Aileen	AEE		1646	...	16	19⅝	18⅜	18½	+ ⅛	91Nov1.15	.47	....	....	....
▲	80¾	51¼	AirProduct	APD	1.56	11690	1.9	18	80¾	75⅜	80½	+3⅛	91SepX4.45	X4.15	q.39	1-3	2-10
	30	16⅝	AirbornFrght	ABF	.30	6549	1.2	18	26	23¼	24¾	+1⅛	Sep9m1.09	1.51	q.07½	11-20	12-4
	24½	12½	Airgas	ARG		1743	...	25	24⅜	22⅜	23¾	+ ⅝	Sep6m.50	.45	....	....	....
	15½	8⅛	Airlease	FLY	1.68	1287	16.2	6	11½	8⅞	10⅜	+1¾	Sep9m1.20	1.46	q.42	12-31	2-14
	26⅜	21¾	AlaPwr pf	ALPpG	2.06e	290	7.8	...	26¼	25⅝	26¼	+ ⅜	....	....	.48	12-3	1-1
	11	9⅜	AlaPwr pf	ALPpS	.87	271	8.1	...	10¾	10½	10¾	...	....	....	q.218	12-3	1-1
	104½	96	AlaPwr pf	ALPpF	9.00	z940	8.7	...	104	102½	103	...	....	....	q2.25	12-3	1-1
	107	100	AlaPwr pf	ALPpD	9.44	z300	8.9	...	106	105	106	+2	....	....	q2.36	12-3	1-1
▲	101¼	88¾	AlaPwr pf	ALPpC	8.16	z69500	8.1	...	101¼	100¼	100¾	+1⅜	....	....	q2.04	12-3	1-1
▲	103	87½	AlaPwr pf	ALPpB	8.28	z2490	8.2	...	103	100¼	101	−1	....	....	q2.07	12-3	1-1
x	25⅜	17¾	AlaskaAir	ALK	.20	x3056	.9	...	22½	21½	22⅛	+ ⅝	Sep9m.46	1.66	q.05	1-15	2-5
	20	10¼	AlbanyInt	AIN	.35	8080	2.0	63	17½	15⅜	17½	+ ¾	Sep9m.28	.30	q.08¾	12-10	1-2
	34¼	20½	AlbertoCl	ACV	.22	1570	.7	27	32	30	30¾	− ¼	91Sep1.06	1.30	q.05½	11-4	11-20
	25½	16¾	AlbertoCl A	ACVA	.22	2617	.9	20	24⅜	23¼	23¼	−1⅜	91Sep1.06	1.30	q.05½	11-4	11-20
	51⅜	32⅜	Albertsons	ABS	.56	14751	1.5	20	39⅛	37	37⅜	−1⅞	Oct39w1.33	1.20	q.14	2-7	2-25
	24	18	Alcan	AL	.60	15979	2.9	27	20½	19⅞	20⅜	− ¼	Sep9mD.07	1.50	q.15	11-20	12-20
	35⅞	29	AlcoStd	ASN	.92	3787	2.7	17	35	33⅛	34	−1	91Sep1.95	1.76	q.23	11-25	12-10
	27⅜	18	Alex&Alex	AAL	1.00	6934	4.9	19	20½	19¾	20⅜	+ ½	Sep9m.61	.86	q.25	12-2	12-31
	37½	19¾	Alexanders	ALX		151	...	...	25⅛	24	25⅛	+1⅛	Oct12wD.84	D.78	Y	....	9-9-80
▲	111⅜	78⅝	AlleghanyCp	Y	1.86t	89	1.7	13	111⅜	108½	109	+ ½	Sep9m5.53	7.80	S2%	4-1-91	4-26-91
▲	30	20¼	AllegLud	ALS	.88	5074	3.0	21	30	28	29¾	+1⅞	Sep39w.85	1.88	q.22	11-29	12-27
	46½	34⅞	AllegPwr	AYP	3.20	5150	7.2	12	45	44	44¼	− ⅜	Sep12m3.65	3.60	q.80	12-16	12-30
▲	22¼	8¾	AllenGp	ALN	.20b	3205	.9	16	22¼	19⅞	21⅞	+2⅛	Sep9m1.01	1.22	S10%	12-13-91	1-17-92
▲	25⅜	16⅝	AllenGp pf	ALNpA	1.75	399	7.0	...	25⅜	23	25	+2⅜	....	....	q.43¾	1-31	2-15
	25½	16¾	Allergan	AGN	.36	6941	1.5	19	24⅞	23¼	24	...	Sep9mD1.30	.83	q.09	11-18	12-9
▲	35⅞	15¼	AllncCapMgt	AC	2.02e	3360	5.8	18	35⅞	32¼	34⅞	+2⅜	Sep9m1.52	.81	.54	11-8-91	11-15-91
	13⅜	9⅞	AllncGlblEnv	AEF	.18e	1382	1.5	...	12	11½	11¾	− ⅛	....	....	.18	12-31-91	1-10-92
	29¼	13	AlliantTech	ATK		2023	...	5	23¼	21⅜	23¼	+1⅜	Sep6m2.03	....	....	....	....
▲x	25⅛	18¼	AlldIrishBk pf	AIBp	2.97	x2219	12.2	...	25⅛	23⅝	24⅜	+1½	....	....	.742	1-16-92	1-31-92
	22	17	AlldIrishBk	AIB	.99e	1	5.4	...	18½	18½	18½	+ ¼	....	....	.363	11-27-91	12-27-91
	6¾	2¼	AlliedPdts	ADP		866	...	4	3⅛	2⅞	3	...	Sep9mD2.55	D.21	Y	....	11-15-82
▲	46⅝	25⅞	AlliedSgnl	ALD	1.00	28500	2.2	...	46⅝	42½	44⅞	+2⅜	Sep9mD2.85	2.54	q.25	11-15	12-10
	10⅝	9⅝	AllmonTr	GSO	.66e	956	6.8	...	10	9¾	9¾	− ¼	....	....	.64½	12-6-91	12-27-91
x	10	8⅜	AllstMunOpp	AMO	.72	x1052	7.9	...	9¼	9⅛	9⅛	...	....	....	.06	1-10	1-24
x	9⅞	8⅝	AllstMunOppII	AOT	.78	x870	8.1	...	9¾	9⅝	9⅝	+ ⅛	....	....	.065	1-10	1-24
nx	9⅞	8¼	AllstMunOppIII	AIO	.72a	x615	7.5	...	9⅝	9⅜	9⅝	+ ⅛	....	....	.06	1-10	1-24
x	10⅞	9⅝	AllstMunIn	ALM	.72a	x1188	6.8	...	10¾	10½	10⅝	...	....	....	.06	1-10	1-24
▲x	10⅜	9⅛	AllstMunInII	ALT	.69a	x2917	6.8	...	10⅜	10	10⅛	...	....	....	.0575	1-10	1-24
▲x	9⅞	8⅝	AllstMunInIII	ALL	.66a	x353	6.7	...	9⅞	9½	9⅞	+ ¼	....	....	.055	1-10	1-24
nx	10⅛	8¾	AllstMunPrem	ALI	.72a	x2923	7.2	...	10⅛	9⅞	10	+ ⅛	....	....	.06	1-10	1-24
	43⅛	31¾	ALLTEL	AT	1.48	3677	3.8	16	39¾	39	39¼	− ⅛	Sep9mX1.74	1.66	q.37	12-6	1-3
	73⅛	53¾	Alcoa	AA	1.60a	13406	2.5	46	65⅝	62⅜	62¾	−1⅞	Sep9m2.97	5.01	q.40	11-1	11-25
	1⅜	¼	AmBase	ABC		3360	...	...	15/32	11/32	13/32	+1/32	Sep9mD4.86	D3.93	Y		4-1-90

Source: *Barron's*, January 13, 1992, p. 52. Reprinted by permission of *BARRON'S*,

Table 4–10 Market Laboratory—Stocks from *Barron's*

MARKET LABORATORY/STOCKS

World Stock Markets Indexes

	1/10/92 Close	Week's Change	– 1991 – High	Low
Australia All-Ord.	1668.00	+ 8.30	1713.70	1341.60
Belgium Cash	1107.00	+ 3.90	N.A.	N.A.
Canada Composite	3593.39	N.A.	3985.11	3047.94
France CAC	1837.44	+ 67.14	N.A.	N.A.
Hong Kong Hang Seng	4348.92	+ 41.79	4271.34	N.A.
Italy Milan	1048.00	N.A.	N.A.	N.A.
Japan Nikkei 225	22381.90	N.A.	38712.77	20983.50
Netherlands ANP-CBS	194.60	N.A.	206.30	167.69
Singapore Straits	1488.07	+ 7.18	1593.77	1030.69
Spain Madrid	253.09	+ 9.44	309.74	167.60
Sweden AffGen	954.09	+ 32.50	1329.90	828.00
Switzerland CrSuisse	465.70	+ 8.80	679.00	464.10
U.K./FinTimes 100 Stocks	2477.90	– 26.20	2645.70	1932.50
Germany DAX	1615.71	+ 12.09	1968.55	1334.89

Indexes are based on local currencies.

NYSE Half-Hourly Volume

Daily	Jan. 6	7	8	9	10
9:30-10:00	33,310	34,280	35,230	38,520	35,930
10:00-10:30	28,410	24,270	27,400	30,280	24,970
10:30-11:00	19,930	22,720	29,930	29,870	21,230
11:00-11:30	19,960	20,530	26,630	24,990	21,990
11:30-12:00	17,510	19,030	28,300	19,280	19,760
12:00-12:30	17,160	15,700	21,080	17,500	15,440
12:30- 1:00	11,610	13,050	15,310	22,410	10,670
1:00- 1:30	11,140	14,120	15,140	13,260	10,690
1:30- 2:00	11,140	13,240	15,240	15,230	12,520
2:00- 2:30	12,880	13,580	17,980	20,760	19,000
2:30- 3:00	16,390	15,450	13,500	18,520	12,080
3:00- 3:30	15,290	20,630	16,990	17,910	13,820
3:30- 4:00	27,250	24,680	26,960	23,250	17,960

Institutional Trading Monthly Statistics

NYSE	Oct. Average	Sept. Average	Yr.-to-Date Average
Inst Buy	72.2	65.9	70.6
Inst Sell	73.5	67.1	69.6
Net Buy (Sell)	(1.3)	(1.2)	1.1
Retail Buy	64.8	60.0	66.5
Retail Sell	61.6	55.9	66.0
Net Buy (Sell)	3.2	4.1	0.5
Member Buy	40.9	36.7	39.9
Member Sell	42.8	39.6	41.5
Net Buy (Sell)	(1.9)	(2.8)	(1.6)
AMEX			
Inst Buy	3.3	3.6	3.1
Inst Sell	3.7	3.9	3.2
Net Buy (Sell)	(0.4)	(0.3)	(0.1)
Retail Buy	7.9	7.6	7.4
Retail Sell	7.8	7.2	7.3
Net Buy (Sell)	0.2	0.4	0.1
Member Buy	2.4	2.2	2.3
Member Sell	2.3	2.3	2.3
Net Buy (Sell)	0.2	(0.1)	0.1
NASDAQ			
Inst Buy	39.7	39.1	37.7
Inst Sell	37.6	36.6	35.4
Net Buy (Sell)	2.1	2.5	2.3
CORP. BONDS			
Inst. Buy	13,176.0	13,666.9	12,391.2
Inst Sell	10,610.8	11,149.7	10,528.4
Net Buy (Sell)	2,565.2	2,517.2	1,862.8

All stock figures in million shares, all bond figures in million dollars of market value traded in secondary market. Average for each trading day for which reliable information is available. Compiled by Securities Industry Association, based on reports from brokers and institutions using the Institutional Delivery System.

Shearson Lehman Brothers Inc. Auction Rate Preferred Index

	Last Week	Prev. Week	Yr. Ago Week
Total Index	4.125	4.259	7.243
Banks	4.099	4.127	7.637
Industrial	4.469	4.617	7.041
Insurance	3.582	3.582	6.390
Financial	4.007	4.192	7.031
Thrift	3.949	4.109	7.783
Utility	4.097	4.285	6.939

Weighted average of last week's auctions: 3.606

The dividend rates on auction-preferred issues are set by auction each week, with each issue's dividend reset every seven weeks. The dividends in the index are the weighted average yield of all public issues rated A or better.

Trading Activity

All numbers in thousands save percentages

	Last Week	Prev. Week	Year Ago
NYSE	1,310,790	915,890	712,660
30 Dow Inds	136,176	r103,429	89,577
20 Dow Trans	29,536	18,355	23,655
15 Dow Utils	21,487	16,822	13,371
65 Dow Stks	187,199	r138,606	126,603
Amex	103,282	93,070	50,070
NASDAQ	1,392,673	877,160	584,943
NYSE 15 Most Active			
Average Price	33.61	40.60	39.61
% Tot Vol	12.00	11.55	10.72
Stock Offer ($000)z	131,000	None	3,000
Barron's Low Price			
Stock Index	338.03	320.20	288.31
Vol (000)	12,844.0	9,420.6	11,438.1
% DJI Vol	9.41	9.66	11.78

Daily	Jan. 6	7	8	9	10
NYSE 15 Most Active					
% Tot Vol	14.42	12.94	14.00	13.79	12.28
Avg. Price	34.71	37.92	36.96	33.97	35.72

z-Source: Securities Data Co.

Daily Stock Volume

NYSE (a)	241,980	251,280	289,690	291,780	236,060
30 Inds	27,637.8	25,742.7	29,410.4	29,944.0	23,441.1
20 Trans	4,877.9	5,699.4	7,058.6	6,923.4	4,976.4
15 Utils	4,329.8	3,424.2	4,178.3	3,820.0	5,734.5
65 Stks	36,845.5	34,866.3	40,647.3	40,687.4	34,152.0
Amex (a)	19,255	19,664	21,539	23,755	19,069
NMS (b)	208,547	219,212	274,952	282,679	216,888

(a)Compositetradesnotincluded.(b)NMS-National Market System.

Market Advance/Decline Volumes

NY Up	116,757	113,503	149,053	147,796	67,553
NY Down	101,211	106,872	114,622	113,752	140,165
% (QCHA)	+.77	+.44	+.86	+.76	–.30
Amex Up	7,300	11,105	11,325	13,297	8,143
Amex Down	6,034	6,184	6,161	6,630	8,265
% (QACH)	+1.06	+1.30	+1.32	+.98	+2.47
NASD Up	149,137	153,194	207,718	224,359	100,202
NASD Down	57,025	64,810	70,189	57,824	125,726

Supplied by Quotron, "QCHA" is the average percentage movement for all exchange listed stocks each day on an unweighted basis.

NYSE Odd-Lot Trading

Shares in thousands

Daily	Jan. 3	6	7	8	9
Purchases	1,321.6	1,423.3	1,240.5	1,418.2	1,406.6
Short Sales, z	72,528	49,219	43,433	9,797	155,297
Other sales	1,137.5	1,155.9	1,134.7	1,200.2	1,228.3
Total Sales	1,210.0	1,205.1	1,178.1	1,210.0	1,383.6

z-Actual sales.

Closing Tick

Daily	Jan. 6	Jan. 7	Jan. 8	Jan. 9	Jan. 10
NYSE	+235	+ 473	+ 319	– 10	+ 405
Amex	+135	+ 73	+ 75	+ 77	+ 32
DJIA	–2	+ 22	– 8	– 6	+ 28

The tick shows the number of stocks whose last change in price was an increase, less the number whose last change was a downtick. It is computed for the NYSE, the American Stock Exchange and for the stocks in the Dow Jones Industrial Average. High positive figures indicate a strong market near the close, while negative ones indicate a weak one.

Arms Index

Daily	Jan. 6	7	8	9	10
NYSE	1.16	.98	1.17	1.00	1.27
AMEX	1.10	.67	.74	.85	1.00
NASDAQ	.67	.56	.52	.53	1.09

The Arms index, also known as the short term trading index, is the average volume of declining issues divided by the average volume of advancing issues. It is computed separately for the NYSE, the American Stock Exchange and Nasdaq. A figure of less than 1.0 indicates more action in rising stocks.

Large Block Transaction Summary

These are single trades of 100,000 shares and over, and 50,000 to 99,999 shares made each day. An uptick is at a price higher than the last previous trade. A downtick is at a price lower than the last previous trade.

NYSE		Up Ticks	Down Ticks	No Chg.	Totals
100,000 Shares and Over	Jan 6	36	33	67	136
	Jan 7	26	42	42	110
	Jan 8	22	34	57	113
	Jan 9	43	41	79	163
	Jan 10	24	39	54	117

		Up Ticks	Down Ticks	No Chg.	Totals
50,000-99,999 Shares	Jan 6	78	69	138	285
	Jan 7	74	108	184	366
	Jan 8	84	99	193	376
	Jan 9	89	90	210	389
	Jan 10	51	94	161	306

Weekly Volume By Markets In NYSE-Listed Stocks

Shares in thousands

	Last Week	Prev. Week	Year Ago
NYSE	1,310,790	915,890	712,660
Midwest	74,480	58,206	43,166
Pacific	58,204	42,875	29,528
NASDAQ	111,775	74,826	44,057
Phila.	28,209	20,054	15,194
Boston	26,308	20,731	15,410
Cincinnati	12,379	9,648	7,177
Instinet	2,638	933	2,448
Total	1,624,783	1,143,163	869,640

Other Market Indexes

Daily	Jan. 6	7	8	9	10
NYSE Comp.	229.85	229.69	230.23	230.23	228.95
Ind.	286.43	286.24	286.99	287.31	286.04
Util.	101.77	101.39	101.39	100.76	99.77
Tran.	200.26	201.60	200.83	200.18	199.53
Fin.	173.91	174.16	174.94	174.99	173.59
Amex Index	399.27	401.71	403.48	407.57	405.64
S&P 500 Index	417.96	417.40	418.10	417.61	415.10
Ind.	494.06	493.46	494.37	494.52	492.20
Trans.	338.35	341.12	339.22	336.51	334.23
Utils.	154.36	153.58	153.52	152.18	150.36
Fins.	34.40	34.40	34.55	34.45	34.11
MidCap	147.63	148.08	149.12	150.69	149.70
NASDAQ Cmp	597.90	602.29	610.32	619.80	615.70
Ind.	683.80	690.39	702.22	714.77	709.63
Insur.	604.86	605.61	607.89	615.32	613.67
Banks	358.24	363.84	363.35	362.85	363.21
NMS Comp.	265.00	266.96	270.46	274.73	272.76
Ind.	273.91	276.61	281.30	286.46	284.19
Value Line(A)	339.47	340.43	342.77	344.50	343.00
Value Line(G)	252.11	252.70	254.34	255.51	254.31
Wilshire 5000	4055.92	4059.40	4074.93	4085.08	4062.29
Russell 1000	221.26	221.20	221.75	221.85	220.52
Russell 2000	194.37	195.77	198.11	200.58	199.31
Russell 3000	235.35	235.39	236.11	236.40	234.98

(A)-Arithmetic Index. (G)-Geometric Index.

Market and Volume Reports

All numbers in thousands save percentages and ratios

New York Stock Exchange

	Week Dec. 27	Prev. Week	Year-Ago Week
TOTAL VOLUME			
Weekly	696,976.4	1,079,451.9	351,192.7
Average Daily	174,244.1	215,890.4	87,798.2
MEMBER ACTIVITY			
Specialists Buys (#†)	73,839.1	100,101.3	37,042.0
Specialists Sales (#†)	76,036.3	97,138.7	35,149.3
Floor Traders Buys	51.7	28.4	9.1
Floor Traders Sales	16.0	21.8	0.0
Other Member Buys (#)	73,917.6	137,308.9	35,471.2
Other Member Sales (#)	82,557.8	136,306.9	35,225.0
Total Member Buys	147,808.4	237,438.7	72,522.3
Total Member Sales	158,610.1	233,467.4	70,374.3
Net Member Buy/Sell	–10,801.6	+3,971.2	+2,148.0
Member volume as % of total	21.98	21.81	20.34
SHORT SALES			
Total	70,149.3	77,970.5	27,771.4
Public	21,963.0	27,569.0	10,445.3
Members Total	48,186.3	50,401.5	14,326.1
Specialists	31,981.5	33,008.1	10,029.7
Floor Traders	0.0	1.0	0.0
Other Members	16,204.8	17,392.5	4,296.4
Specialists/Public Short Ratio	1.5	1.2	1.0
Members/Public Short Ratio	2.2	1.8	1.4

Customers Odd-Lot Activity

NYSE	Week Dec. 27	Prev. Week	Year-Ago Week
Purchases, shares	2,709.4	4,666.0	972.3
Purchases $	128,920.2	204,914.7	36,298.8
Sales, shares	3,252.6	4,519.0	1,967.6
Sales $	131,217.6	174,303.2	61,689.7
Short Sales, shares	385.5	209.0	15.3
Short Sales $	17,378.5	9,043.5	682.1

Source: New York Stock Exchange, 11 Wall Street, New York, N.Y. Phone (212) 656-3000.

American Stock Exchange

	Week Dec. 27	Prev. Week	Year-Ago Week
TOTAL VOLUME			
Weekly	62,520.1	93,315.8	34,262.2
Average Daily	15,630.0	18,663.2	8,565.5
MEMBER ACTIVITY			
Specialists Buys (#†)	6,299.4	8,296.1	4,053.7
Specialists Sales (#†)	6,880.9	8,054.4	3,400.8
Floor Traders Buys	146.9	171.4	41.3
Floor Traders Sales	131.5	111.3	52.6
Other Member Buys (#)	2,930.5	4,530.4	1,797.9
Other Member Sales (#)	6,032.3	5,936.2	2,295.8
Total Member Buys	9,376.8	12,997.9	5,892.9
Total Member Sales	13,044.7	14,101.9	5,749.2
Net Member Buy/Sell	–3,667.9	–1,104.0	+143.7
Member volume as % of total	17.93	14.52	16.99
SHORT SALES			
Total	1,144.6	1,809.8	705.9
Public	818.3	1,239.3	439.5
Member Total	326.3	570.5	266.4
Specialists	18.0	127.6	18.4
Floor Traders	19.7	23.9	13.4
Other Members	288.6	419.0	234.6
Specialists/Public Short Ratio	0.0	0.1	0.0
Members/Public Short Ratio	0.4	0.5	0.6

Customers Odd-Lot Activity

AMEX	Week Dec. 27	Prev. Week	Year-Ago Week
Purchases, shares	50.5	71.0	23.2
Sales, shares	112.1	154.1	108.7

#Includes transactions effected by members acting as Registered Competitive Market-Makers. †Including offsetting round-lot transactions arising from odd-lot dealer activity by specialists and other members. w-Shares and warrants. Source: American Stock Exchange, 86 Trinity Place, New York, N.Y. Phone (212) 306-1000.

Source: *Barron's,* January 13, 1992, p. 129. Reprinted by permission of *BARRON'S,* © 1992 by Dow Jones & Company, Inc. All Rights Reserved Worldwide.

Table 4–11   Market Laboratory—Bonds from *Barron's*

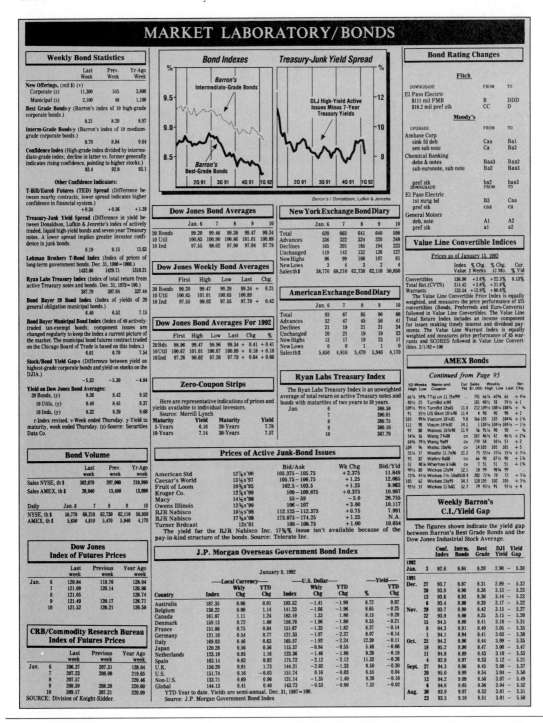

MARKET LABORATORY/BONDS

Weekly Bond Statistics

	Last Week	Prev. Week	Yr-Ago Week
New Offerings, (mil $) (v)			
Corporate (z)	11,300	545	3,600
Municipal (z)	2,100	48	1,100

Best Grade Bonds-y (Barron's index of 10 high-grade corporate bonds.)
8.21   8.20   8.97

Interm-Grade Bonds-y (Barron's index of 10 medium-grade corporate bonds.)
8.79   8.84   9.64

Confidence Index (High-grade index divided by interme- diate-grade index; decline in latter vs. former generally indicates rising confidence, pointing to higher stocks.)
93.4   92.8   93.1

Other Confidence Indicators:

T-Bill/Euro$ Futures (TED) Spread (Difference be- tween nearby contracts; lower spread indicates higher confidence in financial system.)
+0.34   +0.36   +1.39

Treasury-Junk Yield Spread (Difference in yield be- tween Donaldson, Lufkin & Jenrette's index of actively traded, liquid high-yield bonds and seven-year Treasury notes. A lower spread implies greater investor confi- dence in junk bonds.)
8.19   9.13   12.63

Lehman Brothers T-Bond Index (Index of prices of long-term government bonds. Dec. 31, 1980 = 1000.)
1432.60   1429.71   1310.21

Ryan Labs Treasury Index (Index of total return from active Treasury notes and bonds. Dec. 31, 1979 = 100.)
387.79   387.64   337.44

Bond Buyer 20 Bond Index (Index of yields of 20 general obligation municipal bonds.)
6.40   6.52   7.15

Bond Buyer Municipal Bond Index (Index of 40 actively- traded tax-exempt bonds; component issues are changed regularly to keep the index a current picture of the market. The municipal bond futures contract traded on the Chicago Board of Trade is based on this index.)
6.61   6.70   7.54

Stock/Bond Yield Gap-s (Difference between yield on highest-grade corporate bonds and yield on stocks on the DJIA.)
−5.32   −5.30   −4.84

Yield on Dow Jones Bond Averages:

20 Bonds, (y)	8.36	8.42	9.52
10 Utils, (y)	8.40	8.45	9.37
10 Inds, (y)	8.32	8.39	9.68

r-Index revised. v-Week ended Thursday. y-Yield to maturity, week ended Thursday. (z)-Source: Securities Data Co.

Bond Volume

	Last week	Prev. week	Yr-Ago week
Sales NYSE, th $	302,870	207,960	219,990
Sales AMEX, th $	26,040	13,490	13,090

Daily	Jan. 6	7	8	9	10
NYSE, th $	58,770	68,210	62,730	62,110	50,850
AMEX, th $	5,650	4,810	5,470	5,940	4,170

Dow Jones Index of Futures Prices

		Last week	Previous week	Year Ago week
Jan.	6	120.84	119.76	128.04
	7	121.09	120.14	126.86
	8	121.05		126.74
	9	121.49	120.17	126.71
	10	121.52	120.21	126.50

CRB/Commodity Research Bureau Index of Futures Prices

		Last week	Previous week	Year Ago week
Jan.	6	206.37	207.31	128.04
	7	207.23	208.08	219.85
	8	207.57		220.46
	9	208.59	208.20	220.60
	10	209.17	207.21	220.09

SOURCE: Division of Knight-Ridder.

Bond Indexes / Treasury-Junk Yield Spread

Barron's Intermediate-Grade Bonds
Barron's Best-Grade Bonds
DLJ High-Yield Active Issues Minus 7-Year Treasury Yields

Barron's / Donaldson, Lufkin & Jenrette

Dow Jones Bond Averages

	Jan. 6	7	8	9	10
20 Bonds	99.20	99.46	99.38	99.47	99.34
10 Util	100.85	100.90	100.86	101.01	100.89
10 Ind	97.55	98.02	97.90	97.94	97.79

Dow Jones Weekly Bond Averages

	First	High	Low	Last	Chg.
20 Bonds	99.20	99.47	99.20	99.34	+ 0.21
10 Util	100.85	101.01	100.85	100.89	
10 Ind	97.55	98.02	97.55	97.79	+ 0.42

Dow Jones Bond Averages For 1992

	First	High	Low	Last	Chg.	
20 Bds	98.96	99.47	98.96	99.34	+ 0.41	+ 0.41
10 Util	100.67	101.01	100.67	100.89	+ 0.18	+ 0.18
10 Ind	97.26	98.02	97.26	97.79	+ 0.64	+ 0.66

Zero-Coupon Strips

Here are representative indications of prices and yields available to individual investors.
Source: Merrill Lynch

Maturity	Yield	Maturity	Yield
5-Years	6.16	20-Years	7.78
10-Years	7.14	30-Years	7.57

Prices of Active Junk-Bond Issues

		Bid/Ask	Wk Chg	Bid/Yld
American Std	12⅞s'00	105.375 – 105.75	+ 2.375	11.849
Caesar's World	13½s'97	105.75 – 106.75	+ 1.25	12.065
Fruit of Loom	10⅜s'95	102.5 – 103.5	+ 1.25	9.863
Kroger Co.	12⅝s'99	109 – 109.875	+ 0.375	10.997
Macy	14⅛s'98	55 – 59	− 5.0	26.755
Owens Illinois	12⅜s'99	106 – 107	+ 3.00	10.117
RJR Nabisco	10⅛s'98	112.125 – 112.375	+ 0.75	7.991
RJR Nabisco	17⅝s'09	173.875 – 174.25	+ 1.25	N.A.
Turner Brdcast	12s'01	108 – 108.75	+ 1.00	10.654

The yield for the RJR Nabisco Inc. 17⅝% issue isn't available because of the pay-in-kind structure of the bonds. Source: Telerate Inc.

J.P. Morgan Overseas Government Bond Index

January 9, 1992

	Local Currency			U.S. Dollar			Yield	
Country	Index	Wkly Chg	YTD Chg	Index	Wkly Chg	YTD Chg	%	YTD Chg
Australia	187.35	0.08	0.01	193.52	−1.41	−1.90	8.72	0.07
Belgium	138.22	0.90	1.14	141.23	−1.66	−1.96	8.65	−0.25
Canada	161.87	1.11	1.24	183.10	1.33	1.80	8.15	−0.20
Denmark	159.13	0.72	1.00	158.76	−1.96	−1.88	8.55	−0.21
France	151.88	0.75	0.84	151.87	−1.35	−1.82	8.37	−0.14
Germany	121.10	0.54	0.77	121.33	−1.97	−2.37	8.07	−0.14
Italy	169.03	0.46	0.63	165.57	−1.92	−2.24	12.09	−0.11
Japan	120.28	0.56	0.56	115.37	−0.84	−0.55	5.48	−0.08
Netherlands	123.19	0.95	1.16	123.36	−1.46	−1.88	8.29	−0.18
Spain	163.14	0.82	0.92	175.72	−2.12	−2.12	11.32	−0.26
U.K.	150.20	0.91	1.73	144.21	−2.02	−1.33	9.50	−0.30
U.S.	151.74	0.16	−0.03	151.74	0.16	−0.03	6.55	0.04
Non-U.S.	133.71	0.69	0.90	131.14	−1.35	−1.40	8.20	−0.10
Global	144.13	0.41	0.40	143.73	−0.53	−0.66	7.32	−0.02

YTD-Year to date. Yields are semi-annual. Dec. 31, 1987 = 100.
Source: J.P. Morgan Government Bond Index

New York Exchange Bond Diary

	Jan. 6	7	8	9	10
Total	620	665	641	640	598
Advances	336	322	324	320	248
Declines	165	201	185	194	223
Unchanged	119	142	132	126	127
New Highs	96	99	108	107	81
New Lows	4	3	2	4	
Sales th$	58,770	68,210	62,730	62,110	50,850

American Exchange Bond Diary

	Jan. 6	7	8	9	10
Total	93	87	85	90	88
Advances	52	47	45	50	41
Declines	21	19	21	21	24
Unchanged	20	21	19	19	23
New Highs	13	17	19	23	17
New Lows	0	0	1	1	0
Sales th$	5,650	4,810	5,470	5,940	4,170

Ryan Labs Treasury Index

The Ryan Labs Treasury Index is an unweighted average of total return on active Treasury notes and bonds with maturities of two years to 30 years.

Jan.	
6	388.58
7	390.01
8	389.75
9	389.10
10	387.79

Bond Rating Changes

Fitch

DOWNGRADE — FROM — TO
El Paso Electric
$111 mil FMB — B — DDD
$10.2 mil pref stk — CC — D

Moody's

UPGRADE — FROM — TO
Ambase Corp
sink fd deb — Caa — Ba1
sen sub note — Ca — Ba3
Chemical Banking
debs & notes — Baa3 — Baa2
sub euronote, sub note — Ba2 — Baa3

pref stk — ba2 — baa3
DOWNGRADE — FROM — TO
El Paso Electric
1st mrtg bd — B3 — Caa
pref stk — caa — ca
General Motors
deb, note — A1 — A2
pref stk — a1 — a2

Value Line Convertible Indices

Prices as of January 13, 1992

	Index % Chg. 2 Weeks	% Chg. 12 Mo.	Cur. % Yld
Convertibles	136.96 +3.6%	+22.3%	8.13%
Total Ret.(CVTS)	314.42 +3.8%	+31.6%	
Warrants	133.54 +12.9%	+80.6%	

The Value Line Convertible Price Index is equally weighted, and measures the price performance of 575 convertibles (Bonds, Preferreds and Euro-Converts) followed in Value Line Convertibles. The Value Line Total Return Index includes an income component for issues making timely interest and dividend pay- ments. The Value Line Warrant Index is equally weighted and measures price performance of 85 war- rants and SCORES followed in Value Line Convert- ibles. 3/1/82 = 100

AMEX Bonds

Continued from Page 95

52-Weeks High Low	Name and Coupon	Cur Yld	Sales $1,000	Weekly High Low Last	Net Chg
66⅝ 54⅞	TTaj un 11.35s'99†		741	66⅝ 66¾ 66	+4¼
40½ 25	TurnBd zr64		161	40½ 38 39½	+1
109½ 95½	TurnBd 12s01	11.0	212	109½ 108¾ 108¾	+ ¾
91	55½ US Bknt 10¼s98	11.4	4	90 90 90	+2
105	99¾ Viacom 10¼s01	9.8	366	105 103 104¾	+1¼
111	98 Viacom 14¾s02	14.1	1	104½ 104½ 104½	−1½
97	88 Wainoc 10¾s98	11.9	1	34 91¼ 90 90	− ¾
54¾	36 Wang 7¾s08	cv	263	46½ 42 46½	+2¼
60¾	39½ Wang 9s09	cv	739	54 50½ 53	+2
109	⅜ Watsc 10s96	cv	14	105 105 105	+5
55¼	37 Westbr 11.76s96	21.2	75	55¼ 55¼ 55¼	+3¼
93	62 Wstinv 8s08	cv	66	90 87½ 90	+1¼
51	48⅛ Whernse 6¼s06	cv	5	51 51 51	+1¼
99½	80 Wickes 12s94	12.1	10	99 98¾ 99	
72¾	43¼ Wickos 7¼s–10s05	10.4	282	72¾ 70 72	+3¼
105	62 Wickes 15s95	14.3	118	105 102 105	+3½
93½	57 Wickes 11¼s01	12.7	79	93½ 91 93½	+4

Weekly Barron's C.I./Yield Gap

The figures shown indicate the yield gap between Barron's Best Grade Bonds and the Dow Jones Industrial Stock Average.

		Conf. Index	Intrm. Bonds	Best Grade	DJI Yield	Yield Gap
1992						
Jan.	3	92.8	8.84	8.20	2.90 −	5.30
1991						
Dec.	27	93.7	8.87	8.31	2.99 −	5.32
	20	93.9	8.90	8.36	3.13 −	5.23
	13	93.6	8.93	8.36	3.14 −	5.22
	6	93.4	8.96	8.39	3.17 −	5.22
Nov.	29	93.7	8.99	8.42	3.15 −	5.27
	22	93.9	8.88	8.35	3.15 −	5.20
	15	94.5	8.90	8.41	3.10 −	5.31
	8	94.3	8.91	8.40	3.05 −	5.35
	1	94.1	8.94	8.41	3.03 −	5.38
Oct.	25	94.2	8.96	8.44	3.09 −	5.35
	18	95.2	8.90	8.47	3.00 −	5.47
	11	94.8	8.89	8.43	3.10 −	5.33
	4	92.9	8.97	8.33	3.12 −	5.21
Sept.	27	94.3	8.96	8.45	3.08 −	5.37
	20	95.0	8.99	8.54	3.04 −	5.50
	13	94.2	9.09	8.56	3.07 −	5.49
	6	94.6	9.05	8.56	3.04 −	5.52
Aug.	30	93.9	9.07	8.52	3.01 −	5.51
	23	93.5	9.10	8.51	3.01 −	5.50

Journals

Most journals are academic and, because of this, are more theoretical than investor-oriented. However, there are exceptions, such as the *Financial Analysts Journal,* which is a publication of the Association for Investment Management and Research. This journal has both academic and practitioner articles that deal mainly with analytical tools, new laws and regulations, and financial analysis. *The Journal of Portfolio Management* and the *Institutional Investor* are also well read by the profession. The more scholarly, research-oriented academic journals would include the *Journal of Finance,* the *Journal of Financial Economics,* and the *Journal of Financial and Quantitative Analysis.* These journals include information on the development and testing of theories such as the random walk and efficient market hypothesis, the capital asset pricing model, and portfolio theories and much empirical research on a variety of financial topics. The *Journal of Financial Education* and *Financial Practice and Education* include articles on classroom topics and computer applications.

■ COMPUTER DATA BASES

More computer-accessible data bases have become available in the last several years as home computer usage has increased and data-based storage management has improved. Several major sources of data are available for use in large mainframe computers on magnetic tapes or are accessible on an interactive, time-sharing basis. Many of these data bases are now accessible from a personal computer.

The Use of Mainframe Computers

The following data bases are made to be used on large mainframe computers. Compustat is published by Investors Management Science Company, a subsidiary of Standard & Poor's Corporation. The *Compustat tapes* are very comprehensive, containing 20 years of annual financial data for over 3,000 companies. Each year's data for the industrial companies include over 300 balance sheet, income statement, and market-related items. Compustat has an industrial file that includes company data from the New York and American stock exchanges and the over-the-counter market. Also included is a file on utilities and banks. Besides the annual file, which is updated weekly, users can order tapes with quarterly data, also updated weekly.

A second data base created by Compustat is called the Price-Dividend-Earnings tape (PDE), which contains monthly data on per-share performance. These tapes are leased to financial institutions for a fairly large sum or to nonprofit educational institutions at a significant discount. The tapes may be paid for in cash or in soft dollars (commissions funneled through an S&P brokerage subsidiary).

These tapes are useful for analyzing large numbers of companies in a short time. Ratios can be created, analyzed, and compared. Trends and regression analysis can be performed. Searches can be implemented for specific kinds of companies. For example, one could read through the tapes and screen for companies meeting certain parameters, such as:

1. Dividend yield greater than 6 percent.
2. Earnings growth greater than 15 percent per year.
3. Price-earnings ratio less than the Standard & Poor's 500 Stock Index.
4. Market price less than book value.

Interactive Data Corporation also provides the same information as the Compustat tapes on a time-sharing basis.

The *CRSP tapes* are maintained by the University of Chicago in the Center for Research in Security Prices. The information provided is oriented to earnings, dividends, stock prices, and dates of mergers, stock splits, stock dividends, and so on. The tapes are extremely useful (data begin in 1926) for historical research on stock performance. They are widely used in academia for research on the efficient market hypothesis, the capital asset pricing model, and other investment questions.

Value Line also has made computer tapes of its 1,700 companies available. Again, these have market price data as well as financial statement items. The Federal Trade Commission has aggregate industry data, and the Federal Reserve Bank of St. Louis has made tapes of monetary data available for academic researchers.

The Use of Personal Computers

The past few years have brought a proliferation of data bases for the personal computer. Most programs have been written for IBM-compatible personal computers operating under DOS. The increased speed of computer chips and larger hard drives allow for large data bases and sophisticated programs to analyze the data. As individual investors' computing power increases, they are increasingly using many of these data bases.

The owner of a personal computer with communications ability and a modem (phone hookup) can now dial a family-oriented data base such as *Prodigy,* which allows the user to look up information on individual stocks, construct portfolios, and do other personal financial planning involving shopping for consumer goods and travel planning.

If you require more comprehensive data, the Dow Jones News Retrieval System might be better suited to your needs. This data base is oriented to the business user and includes financial data, current and historical information on stock quotes, commodity quotes, access to Disclosure's SEC reports mentioned previously, and much more. Other comprehensive information outlets,

such as *The Source* and *CompuServe,* also provide financial data, general information, government statistics, and electronic mail. Chase Econometrics and Nite-Line specialize in financial, business, and economic data, while Citishare Corporation offers U.S. economic statistics.

Moody's and Standard & Poor's offer comprehensive data bases to the institutional investor, libraries, and corporations. One Moody's service covers news stories on over 18,000 U.S. companies and 5,000 international companies. It also offers financial company profiles for all NYSE, AMEX, and 1,500 OTC companies. Standard & Poor's offers many on-line services covering data on 55,000 companies from S&P's *Register of Corporations, Directors and Executives.* It provides financial information on stock, bonds, options, futures, foreign exchange, and more from over 50 markets and exchanges through an on-line service called S&P ComStock. It also has MarketScope, which includes earnings and dividend forecasts on over 1,000 companies as well as a reference section and profiles for 5,000 U.S. companies. MarketScope also includes a buy-sell ranking system for 800 companies, technical indicators, economic data, daily commentary, and so on.

Many old-line financial companies such as Value Line and Standard & Poor's are offering their financial data on microcomputer floppy disks with monthly updates. Data bases either emphasize fundamental or technical analysis. MarketBase and Value Screen II are two of the leading PC data bases. They provide mostly fundamental data emphasizing income and balance sheet figures, monthly price, dividend, and earnings data; and calculated financial ratios. These programs allow investors to "screen"(specify characteristics desired and then have the computer look for companies fitting the description). If you subscribe to MarketBase, you would be able to search through over 5,000 companies as compared to 1,600 companies for Value Screen II.

In addition to the data bases available for the personal computer, new software to access and analyze the data is being created at an extremely rapid pace. The raw data can either be downloaded (quickly transferred) onto a floppy disk or into your computer memory to save time and be analyzed later, or it can be read directly into a software program designed to perform calculations.

Some programs analyze and create charts of the technical behavior of price movements, and others evaluate the financial data from income statements and balance sheets. Using the Dow Jones Investment Evaluator, you can access the Dow Jones News Retrieval System to obtain information for stocks, bonds, warrants, options, mutual funds, or Treasury issues. Information related to 10-K statements, ratios, earnings growth rates, earnings per share forecasts, and so forth are available on 2,400 companies. The Dow Jones Market Analyzer, the Dow Jones Microscope, and the Dow Jones Investor Workshop all allow access to the Dow Jones information network. Once the correct data are entered into these software programs, they then create standardized analysis from preprogrammed instructions. Also, new programs are now able to transfer data from a news retrieval service straight into a spreadsheet program such

as Lotus 1-2-3 or Excel. This saves time and money and allows the individual flexibility to create his or her own financial analysis.

Not all these programs are available for every personal computer. Most programs are for the IBM personal computer and compatible systems or for Apple's McIntosh computer. Before buying a PC, check to make sure which software programs run on your computer. The box on page 144 provides information on international databases available for the PC. Most of these are quite expensive and are designed for use by professionals rather than individual investors.

■ INFORMATION ON NONTRADITIONAL MARKETS ✕

For this section, we define nontraditional as being out of the realm of stocks, bonds, and government securities. A major area that received increased attention during the last decade has been commodities and financial futures. A key source of information on commodities is the *Commodity Yearbook*.

Commodity Yearbook

This is a yearly publication which can be supplemented by the *Commodity Yearbook Statistical Abstract* three times a year. The *Commodity Yearbook* runs several feature articles of educational interest, covering commodities or situations in the forefront of commodity trading.

In addition to the featured articles, the *Yearbook* covers each traded commodity from alcohol to zinc. For example, corn is covered in six pages. The first page is a description of the corn crop and occurrences for the current year. The next five pages cover much data in tabular form for the past 13 years. The tables show world production of corn, acreage, and supply of corn in the United States, corn production estimates and disposition by value in the United States, corn supply and disappearance, distribution of corn in the United States, corn price support data, average price received by farmers for corn in the United States, and the weekly high-low-close of the nearest month's futures price. Each commodity has a similarly detailed evaluation and statistical summary.

Other publications about commodities come from main-line brokerage houses and specialty commodity brokers. In addition, the commodities exchanges publish educational booklets and newsletters. The International Monetary Market publishes the *I.M.M. Weekly Report,* which discusses the interest-rate markets, the foreign exchange markets, and gold. It also presents weekly prices for all interest rate futures, foreign exchange markets, gold, and selected cash market information such as the federal funds rate and the prime rate. The Chicago Board of Trade publishes the *Interest Rate Futures Newsletter.* As investors continue to become active in these markets, an investor (speculator) can be sure to find more available data.

International Data Providers (PC Data Base Products) Current Company-Level Data

Name	Non-U.S. Coverage	Scope	Timeliness	Accessibility	History
MSCI PC	2,000 companies 19 markets	Fundamentals Prices	Monthly Daily via modem	Good	20 years available
I/B/E/S	5,400 companies 27 markets	Earnings estimates	Weekly Daily via modem	Depends on delivery platform	3 years
WorldScope via Lotus One-Source	5,000 companies 25 markets	Fundamentals Prices	Weekly	Good CD-ROM	10 years
CIFAR	4,500 companies 40-plus markets	Fundamentals Prices	Monthly	CD-ROM	7 years
Moody's	5,500 companies 100 markets	Background Fundamentals	Quarterly	Text only	3 year balance sheet
IDC (Datasheet)	11,000 prices 1,934 fundamentals 24 markets	Prices Some fundamentals	Daily	Dial up	1982+
Reuters	All companies 110 markets	Prices Some background	Real-time	Dedicated line Excel Link	No
Datastream	12,000 prices 4,200 fundamentals 24 markets	Prices Fundamentals	Daily Some real-time	Dial up Lotus Link	5–20 years depending on country
EuroEquities	1,200 companies 15 markets	Fundamentals Earnings estimates	Biweekly		8 years
Compustat International version	3,000 companies 24 markets	Fundamentals		CD-ROM	1982+
IFC Emerging Markets	600 companies 19 markets	Prices Ltd. fundamentals	Monthly	Lotus spreadsheet	1975+
MSCI Emerging Markets	700 companies 14 markets	Prices	Monthly	Flat file	No

Note: These PC data base products are expensive and are primarily used by institutional investors.
Source: Acadian Asset Management, Inc.; Association for Investment Management and Research; and International Society of Financial Analysis, Investing Worldwide II. AIMR, California, 1991, p. 52.

■ SUMMARY

Information is easy and yet difficult to find. The problem beginners have is knowing where to look and what to look for, and this chapter has attempted to provide some guidance and sample data. The problem advanced investors have is knowing what information is usable. This may also haunt beginners once they find the sources. To become proficient in finding data, spend a day in your library looking through the volumes. This will increase your awareness of the types of information available. Then do some of the exercises at the end of this chapter to see if you can find specific data. As for knowing what information is useful, the authors hope to shed some light on that as we proceed through the book.

■ DISCUSSION QUESTIONS

1. What type of information is part of aggregate economic data?
2. The Federal Reserve Bank of St. Louis has a number of comprehensive economic publications. What are they?
3. What is one of the major benefits provided by the *Survey of Current Business* in regard to industry data?
4. What are the three categories of economic time series indicators found in the *Survey of Current Business?*
5. Of the major advisory services for investors, which ones would likely be found in most libraries?
6. What is special about the T–Z volume of Standard & Poor's *Corporation Records?*
7. What is the Standard & Poor's *Stock Guide?* What is included in the introduction.
8. Briefly describe the Value Line evaluation system.
9. Assume one needs information about an industry or company. Suggest three types of indexes for periodicals or journals that can be used.
10. What type of information is contained in the following three filings with the SEC: 10–K, 8–K, 10–Q?
11. Under what category in *Barron's* would weekly data on stock and bond market statistics be found?
12. Who publishes *Compustat?* What type of information is available on *Compustat?*
13. What information is available through the Dow Jones News Retrieval System? Can you access this service with a personal computer?
14. Suggest some sources for information about commodities.
15. Choose a company and look it up in *Moody's, Standard & Poor's,* and *Value Line* to see the information provided and compare the data.

16. Select an industry and find the SIC code. Then look up all firms listed in this business. (Suggestion—the SIC code can be found in the T–Z volume of *Standard & Poor's Corporation Records,* which will also provide the list of firms by the SIC number.)

17. Look up the implicit price deflator for the GDP (one source is the St. Louis Federal Reserve Bank's *National Economic Trends*) and total corporate profits after taxes (same source). These data can be useful for current projects and will expose you to a good source for this type of information.

18. Select a company, go to *The Wall Street Journal Index* for the previous year, and identify the dates of all news stories about the company.

MARKETBASE-E EXERCISES

In the following exercise, please use your MarketBase-E Software and manual to screen for the required portfolios. You will have to figure out how to search through the data to pull out those companies meeting the requirements set down.

1. In Chapter 4, Hewlett Packard is used as an example to highlight the Standard and Poor's Corporate Reports and the Value Line Industry Survey. Please find Hewlett Packard on MarketBase-E and compare the data between MarketBase-E, S&P, and Value Line.
   a. Make a list of any data found in MarketBase-E that is not found on the other two sources of information.
   b. Select all the companies with the same industry code as Hewlett-Packard. Are all these companies listed in the Value Line Survey and the S&P Corporate Reports? If not, why do you suppose not?

2. Among other criteria, Value Line also lists securities with high dividend yields in their Summary and Index section Value Line ranks companies in yield from the highest down. Find the dividend yield of the last company in the high-yield category. Use MarketBase-E to select according to the same dividend yield criteria. How many companies do you have in common with Value Line?

Appendix 4–A: Names and Addresses of Important Data Sources

Federal Reserve Bank of:
Atlanta, Ga. 30301
Boston, Mass. 02106
Chicago, Ill. 60690
Cleveland, Ohio 44101
Dallas, Texas 75222
Kansas City, Kan. 64198
Minneapolis, Minn. 55480
New York, N.Y. 10045
Philadelphia, Pa. 19105
Richmond, Va. 23219
San Francisco, Calif. 94120
St. Louis, Mo. 63166

Federal Reserve Bulletin
Board of Governors of the
Federal Reserve System
Washington, D.C. 20551

Stock and commodity exchanges:
American Stock Exchange
86 Trinity Place
New York, N.Y. 10006

Chicago Board of Trade
LaSalle at Jackson
Chicago, Ill. 60604

Chicago Mercantile Exchange
30 South Wacker Dr.
Chicago, Ill. 60606

New York Stock Exchange
11 Wall Street
New York, N.Y. 10005

The following U.S. government
publications can be requested from the:
Superintendent of Documents
U.S. Government Printing Office
Washington, D.C. 20402

Survey of Current Business
Weekly Business Statistics
Economic Indicators
Economic Report of the President
Statistical Abstract of the United States
Statistical Bulletin

Periodicals:
The Wall Street Journal and *Barron's*
Dow Jones & Company
Subscriptions Office
200 Burnett Rd.
Chicopee, Mass. 01021

Changing Times
The Kiplinger Magazine
1729 H St., N.W.
Washington, D.C. 20006

Disclosure Journal
Disclosure, Inc.
1450 Broadway
New York, N.Y. 10018

Forbes
60 5th Avenue
New York, N.Y. 10011

Financial World
Macro Communications Inc.
150 East 58th Street
New York, N.Y. 10155

Business Week
1221 Avenue of the Americas
New York, N.Y. 10020

Money Magazine
Fortune
Time Inc.
3435 Wilshire Blvd.
Los Angeles, Calif. 90010

Investor's Daily Financial Services, Inc.
P.O. Box 26991
Richmond, Va, 23261

Financial Analysts Journal
1633 Broadway
New York, N.Y. 10019

Investment services:

Moody's Investors Service
99 Church Street
New York, N.Y. 10007

Standard & Poor's Corporation
345 Hudson Street
New York, N.Y. 10014

Value Line Services
Arnold Bernhard & Co.
5 East 44th Street
New York, N.Y. 10017

Dun & Bradstreet
99 Church Street
New York, N.Y. 10007

Dun's Marketing Division
3 Century Drive
Parsippany, N.J. 07054

Computer data bases:

Compustat
P.O. Box 239
Denver, Colo. 80201

CRSP Tapes
Center for Research in Security Prices
University of Chicago
Graduate School of Business
Chicago, Ill. 60637

Interactive Data Corporation
122 East 42nd Street
New York, N.Y. 10017

MarketBase
MarketBase, Inc.
P.O. Box 37
Needham Heights, Mass. 02194

Appendix 4–B: Regional and Branch Offices of the SEC

Where You Can Find the Reports: A Directory

Financial and other data included in registration statements, reports, applications, and similar documents filed with the commission are available for study in the public reference room in the main office in Washington, D.C. Copies of these documents may be obtained for 10 cents per page, with a $5 minimum. Cost estimates are available by writing to Public Reference Room, Securities and Exchange Commission, Washington, D.C. 20549.

Current annual reports and other periodic reports filed by companies whose securities are listed on the national exchanges are also available for study in the SEC's New York, Chicago, and Los Angeles regional offices.

Registration statements and subsequent reports filed by those companies whose securities are traded over-the-counter and that register under the Securities Exchange Act are also available at the New York, Chicago, and Los Angeles offices.

SEC filings can also be examined at the regional office serving the area in which the issuer's principal office is located. These regional offices are located in Atlanta, Boston, Denver, Fort Worth, and Seattle.

Prospectuses covering recent public offerings of securities registered under the Securities Act may be examined in all regional offices.

Broker-dealer and investment adviser registrations, as well as Regulation A notifications and offering circulars, may be examined in the particular regional office in which they were filed.

Regional and Branch Offices

Region 1:
New York Regional Office
26 Federal Plaza
New York, N.Y. 10278
(212) 264-1636
Region: New York and New Jersey.

Region 2:
Boston Regional Office
150 Causeway Street

Boston, Mass. 02114
(617) 223-2721
Region: Maine, New Hampshire, Vermont,
Massachusetts, Rhode Island,
and Connecticut.

Region 3:
Atlanta Regional Office
1375 Peachtree Street, N.E.
Suite 788
Atlanta, Ga. 30367
(404) 881-4768
Region: Tennessee, Virgin Islands, Puerto Rico,
North Carolina, South
Carolina, Georgia, Alabama,
Mississippi, Florida, and Louisiana
east of the Atchafalaya River.

Miami Branch Office

Dupont Plaza Center
300 Biscayne Blvd. Way, Suite 1114
Miami, Fla. 33131
(305) 350-5765

Region 4:
Chicago Regional Office
Northwestern Atrium
500 W. Madison, 14th Floor
Chicago, Ill. 60601-2511
(312) 353-7390
Region: Michigan, Ohio, Kentucky,
Wisconsin, Indiana, Iowa,
Minnesota, Missouri, Kansas City,
Kan., and Illinois.

Detroit Branch Office

1044 Federal Bldg.
Detroit, Mich. 48226
(313) 226-6070

Region 5:
Fort Worth Regional Office
411 W. Seventh St.
Fort Worth, Texas 76102
(817) 334-3821
Region: Oklahoma, Arkansas, Texas,
Louisiana west of the Atchafalaya
River, and Kansas (except Kansas City)

Houston Branch Office
Federal Office and Courts Bldg.
515 Rusk Avenue, Room 5615
Houston, Texas 77002
(713) 226-4986

Region 6:
Denver Regional Office
410 17th Street
Suite 700
Denver, Colo. 80202
(303) 837-2071
Region: North Dakota, South Dakota,
Wyoming, Nebraska, Colorado,
New Mexico, and Utah.

Salt Lake Branch Office

Boston Bldg., Suite 810
Nine Exchange Place
Salt Lake City, Utah 84111
(801) 524-5796

Region 7:
Los Angeles Regional Office
10960 Wilshire Blvd.
Suite 1710
Los Angeles, Calif. 90024
(213) 473-4511
Region: Nevada, Arizona, California, Hawaii, and Guam.

San Francisco Branch Office

450 Golden Gate Avenue, Box 36042
San Francisco, Calif. 94102
(415) 556-5264

Region 8:
Seattle Regional Office
3040 Federal Building
915 Second Avenue
Seattle, Wash. 98174
(206) 442-7900
Region: Montana, Idaho, Washington, Oregon, and Alaska.

Region 9:
Washington Regional Office
Ballston Center Tower 3
4015 Wilson Blvd.
Arlington, Va. 22203
(703) 557-8201

Region: Pennsylvania, Delaware, Maryland,
Virginia, West Virginia, and
District of Columbia.

Philadelphia Branch Office

William J. Green, Jr., Federal Bldg.
600 Arch Street, Room 2204
Philadelphia, Pa. 19106
(215) 597-2278.

U.S. Securities and Exchange Commission, Washington, D.C. 20549

General information:
Office of Public Affairs
(202) 272-2650

Investor complaints:
Office of Consumer Affairs
(202) 523-5516

Filings by registered companies:
Public Reference Room
1100 L Street, N.W.
(202) 523-5360

Forms and publications:
(202) 523-3761
For the Official Summary, $70 a year, $6.50 per issue, contact: Superintendent
of Documents, Government Printing Office, Washington, D.C. 20402. *Phone:*
(202) 783-3238.

Source: John Markese, "Culling Information from the SEC," *American Association of Individual Investors Journal,* January 1984, pp. 31–34.

Part Two

Analysis and Valuation of Equity Securities

Outline

Historically, the stock market and the economy have been intertwined. Most stock market analysts agree that the stock market usually leads economic activity by six to nine months but once in gear, the economy drives corporate earnings and dividends, which in turn impact stock values. Occasionally, there are external events that cause shocks to the economy. One recurring economic shock during the last twenty years has been the unpredictability of oil prices.

The Iranian revolution and the Persian Gulf War, started by the Iraqi invasion of Kuwait, are two events that caused wild gyrations in oil prices. Unfortunately, the United States as well as many other industrial economies import a majority of their oil and any increase in oil prices can have an inflationary impact that ripples through the whole economy. When inflationary expectations rise, so do interest rates and when that happens bond prices fall and eventually so do stock prices.

Oil has so many uses that a rising oil price affects the price of plastic, fertilizer, automobiles, and many other dependent products. Many industries are severely affected by rapidly increasing oil prices. For example, gasoline becomes more expensive, many people shift their demand from large cars to smaller, more fuel efficient cars. This has happened many times throughout the 1970s and 1980s. A steep oil price increase also can reduce the sale of automobiles, gasoline, and products dependent on plastic such as compact disks.

Perhaps one of the most affected industries is the airline industry. Aviation fuel is a major cost of air travel and even a small increase in the price of oil can affect the earnings of airlines such as Delta, United or American. In fact, several airlines, including Midway Airlines in Chicago, have been forced to file for bankruptcy due to the impact of the oil price rise caused by the Persian Gulf War.

If the airline industry raises ticket prices to compensate for the increased cost of operations, passenger traffic can shrink dramatically, sending ripple effects throughout the travel industry. Reduced air travel translates into lost income for hotels, resorts, and car rental firms, as well as other recreational expenditures such as food, golf, and theater. Specific companies such as Hilton, Marriott, Disney, and Hertz can feel the effects of an oil price rise.

A large oil shock, such as the one occurring in 1973–74, can cause a recession if all the negative effects mentioned above occur at the same time. Stock prices in 1973–74 decreased dramatically and many analysts would say the major blame was on the inflationary impact of the oil price shock. Many times since 1974, oil price increases (or decreases) have played a major role in the fortunes of many industries by influencing profits and consumer demand.

As you go through this section on the economy, industry analysis, and company stock analysis, think about the external shocks that may affect the industry or company being analyzed. Remember many of these events, both positive and negative, are not controllable by management. On the other hand, management must have a plan for dealing with them. Analysts must be able to quickly factor these economic shocks into their valuation models. ∎

5

Economic and Industry Analysis

To determine the value of the firm, fundamental analysis relies on long-run forecasts of the economy, the industry, and the company's financial prospects. Short-run changes in business conditions are also important in that they influence investors' required rates of return and expectations of corporate earnings and dividends. This chapter presents the basic information for analysis of the economy and industry, while other chapters in this section focus on the individual firm.

Figure 5–1 presents an overview of the valuation process as an inverted triangle. The process starts with a macroanalysis of the economy and then moves into industry variables. Next, common stocks are individually screened according to expected risk-return characteristics, and finally the surviving stocks are combined into portfolios of assets. This figure is not inclusive of all variables considered by an analyst, but is intended to indicate representative areas applicable to most industries and companies.

■ ECONOMIC ACTIVITY AND THE BUSINESS CYCLE

An investor begins the valuation process with an economic analysis. The hope is that an accurate forecast and examination of economic activity will provide the basis for accurate stock market predictions and indicate which industries may prosper. The analyst needs information on present and expected interest rates, monetary and fiscal policy, government and consumer spending patterns, and other economic data. To be successful, investors must understand business cycles and be able to forecast accurately. Unfortunately, these are not easy tasks, but the rewards can be significant if the timing is right.

Whether analysts use statistical methods, such as regression analysis and probability theory, or simply seat-of-the-pants judgment, they are still basing their forecast on expectations related to past data and experiences. Past information usually is not extrapolated into the future without being adjusted to conform with the subjective beliefs of the decision maker. Even when highly sophisticated statistical methods are used, subjectivity enters into the decision in some fashion.

Most likely, past knowledge will be helpful, but modifications for the present effects of worldwide currency fluctuations, international debt obligations, and other factors, which were not so important previously, need to be included in any forecast now. Since most companies are influenced to some degree by the general level of economic activity, a forecast will usually start with an analysis of the government's economic program.

Federal Government Economic Policy

Government economic policy is guided by the Employment Act of 1946 and subsequent position statements by the Federal Reserve Board, the President's Council of Economic Advisors, and other acts of Congress. The goals established by the Employment Act still hold and cover four broad areas. These

Figure 5–1   Overview of the Valuation Process

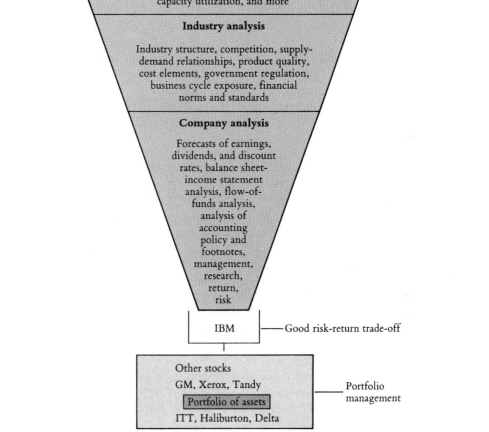

Economic analysis

Business cycles, monetary-fiscal policy, economic indicators, government policy, world events and foreign trade, public attitudes of optimism or pessimism, domestic legislation, inflation, GDP growth, unemployment, productivity, capacity utilization, and more

Industry analysis

Industry structure, competition, supply-demand relationships, product quality, cost elements, government regulation, business cycle exposure, financial norms and standards

Company analysis

Forecasts of earnings, dividends, and discount rates, balance sheet-income statement analysis, flow-of-funds analysis, analysis of accounting policy and footnotes, management, research, return, risk

IBM ——— Good risk-return trade-off

Other stocks
GM, Xerox, Tandy

Portfolio of assets

ITT, Haliburton, Delta

Portfolio management

goals, the focus of monetary and fiscal policy, are as follows with a second interpretation in parentheses:

1. Stable prices (a low inflation rate).
2. Business stability at high levels of production (low levels of unemployment).

3. Sustained economic growth (real growth in gross national product or gross domestic product).
4. A balance in international payments (primarily a balance of exports and imports but also including cash flows in and out of the United States).

These goals are often conflicting in that they do not all respond favorably to the same economic stimulus. Therefore, goal priorities and economic policies change to reflect current economic conditions. In the 1950s and early 1960s, the United States did not have an international trade problem or spiraling inflation, so economic policy focused on employment and economic growth. The economy grew rapidly between 1961 and 1969, and because of the Vietnam War, unemployment reached very low levels. The demand for goods and competition for funds were very high during the war, and eventually war expenditures, large budget deficits, full employment, and large increases in the money supply caused many problems. Inflation accelerated to high levels, interest rates reached record heights, and an imbalance of international payments finally resulted in two devaluations of the U.S. dollar in the early 1970s.

By the time Jimmy Carter took office in January 1977, the primary goals were once again to reduce unemployment, control inflation, and create a moderate level of economic growth that could be sustained without causing more inflation (a very difficult task!). The achievement of these goals was thrown into the hands of the Federal Reserve Board. The Fed's tight money policy caused a rapid increase in interest rates to control inflation, and these high rates depressed common stock prices as the required rate of return by investors reached record levels. Ronald Reagan inherited most of the same problems as Carter but tried new ways of reaching the goals. As the 1980s began, Reagan relied more on fiscal policy than previous administrations in his desire to control inflation and increase economic growth. He instituted a three-year tax cut to increase disposable income and stimulate consumption and thus economic growth, and at the same time, he negotiated reductions in government spending. These policies were successful in sharply reducing inflation and creating strong growth in the gross domestic product (GDP), but they were accomplished with record government deficits.

The economy continued to expand until July 1990, when most economists determined a recession started. These 90 months of expansion were the longest peacetime expansion in history. The expansion created record employment, reduced unemployment percentages, and lowered interest rates and inflation from the high levels of 1980 and 1981. The stock market began a major bull market in 1982 in response to these improved conditions but also sustained the biggest one day crash ever October 19, 1987.

Unfortunately, the recession that began in July 1990 was extremely painful. Major companies such as IBM, AT&T, TRW, and General Motors announced staff reductions totaling more than several hundred thousand employees. At this writing, the authors do not know the outcome of this recession, but the

stock market as a leading indicator of economic activity was setting record highs in the spring of 1992, which often bodes well for the economy.

Since the 3rd edition of this book was published, the world has changed dramatically from what we have known since the end of World War II. The Berlin Wall came down and East and West Germany became one country. The Communist bloc countries started fledgling capitalist economies. And on January 1, 1992, the Union of Soviet Socialist Republics ceased to exist as a country and was replaced by a commonwealth of republics whose dominant country is Russia.

As we enter this new era, we cannot always rely on the past for indications about the future. The changes in Europe will continue as these economies develop and new political alliances arise. The knowledge of economic theory and its applications will increase in importance to investors pursuing international strategies or U.S. companies pursuing foreign opportunities. The ability to interpret these events could have significant financial implications both to the U.S. economy and to those of the other industrial nations.

Fiscal Policy ✓

Fiscal policy can be described as the government's taxing and spending policies. These policies can have a great impact on economic activity. One must realize at the outset that fiscal policy is cumbersome. It has a long implementation lag and is often motivated by political rather than economic considerations since Congress must approve budgets and develop tax laws. Figure 5–2 presents a historical picture of government income and expenditures. When the government spends more than it receives, it runs a **deficit** that must be financed by the Treasury.

A forecaster must pay attention to the size of the deficit and how it is financed to measure its expected impact on the economy. If the deficit is financed by the Treasury selling securities to the Federal Reserve, it is very expansive. The money supply will increase without having any significant short-run effects on interest rates. If the deficit is financed by selling securities to individuals, there is not the same expansion in the money supply, and short-term interest rates will rise unless the Federal Reserve intervenes with open-market trading.

A look at Figure 5–2 shows that **surpluses,** in which revenues exceed expenditures, have been virtually nonexistent from 1961 to 1990 and the annual deficit increased dramatically during the 1980s. Surpluses tend to reduce economic growth as the government slows its demand for goods and services relative to its income. In an analysis of fiscal policy, the important consideration for the investor is the determination of the flow of funds. In a deficit economy, the government usually stimulates GDP by spending on socially productive programs or by increasing spending on defense, education, highways, or other government programs. The Reagan administration

Figure 5–2   Federal Budget Seasonally Adjusted Annual Rates

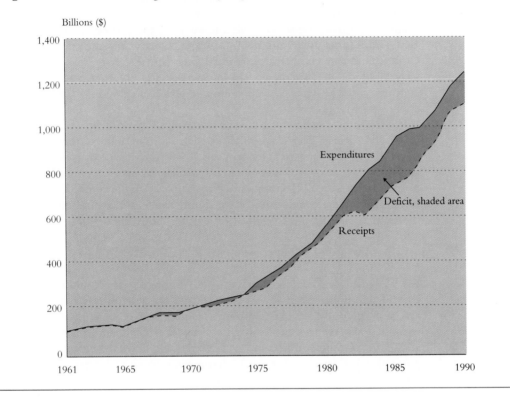

Billions ($)

instituted budget cuts in education and social programs at the same time it reduced tax revenues through tax cuts. This strategy was one that attempted to shift GDP growth from the government sector into the private sector. In the Bush administration, there has been an inconsistency in fiscal policy as the government has shifted back and forth between raising and lowering taxes to deal with the dual problems of the 1990s—high budget deficits and slow economic growth.

One other area of fiscal policy deals with the government's ability to levy import taxes or tariffs on foreign goods. As a free market economy, we have fought for years with our trading partners to open their countries' markets to U.S. goods. Figure 5–3 depicts the annual trade deficits that started piling up beginning in 1982. This deficit occurred because U.S. consumers purchased more foreign goods than U.S. companies sold to foreigners. As we entered the 1990s, this problem had not gone away. 1992 began with President Bush taking a group of 21 leading executives to Japan to discuss the 1991 $41 billion U.S. trade deficit with Japan. The purpose of this trip was to open Japanese

Figure 5–3   Imports and Exports in Current Dollars

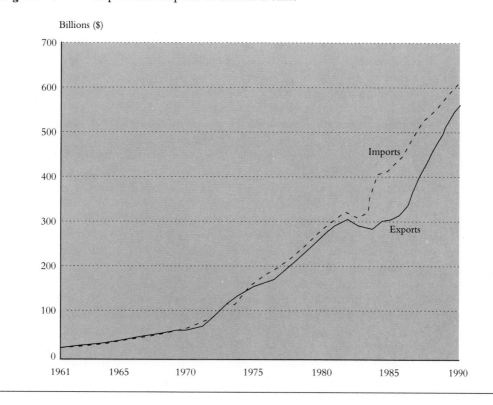

markets to U.S. goods or have the Japanese face the possibility of U.S. trade barriers, such as import tariffs or taxes. These taxes would raise the price of Japanese goods, thus making them less competitive with U.S. goods and eventually reducing this deficit. The conference with Japan produced little in the way of immediate results.

Monetary Policy ✓

Monetary policy is conducted by the Federal Reserve Board of Governors through several methods of controlling the money supply and interest rates. Monetary policy can be implemented very quickly to reinforce fiscal policy or, when necessary, to offset the effects of fiscal policy.

The Federal Reserve has several ways to influence economic activity. First, it can raise or lower the reserve requirements on commercial bank time deposits or demand deposits. **Reserve requirements** represent the percent of total deposits that a bank must hold as cash in its vault or as deposits in Federal

Reserve banks. An increase in reserve requirements would contract the money supply. The banking system would have to hold larger reserves for each dollar deposited and would not be able to lend as much money on the same deposit base. A reduction in reserve requirements would have the opposite effect. The Fed also changes the discount rate periodically to reflect its attitude toward the economy. This **discount rate** is the interest rate the Federal Reserve charges commercial banks on very short-term loans. The Fed does not make a practice of lending funds to a single commercial bank for more than two or three weeks, and so this charge can influence an individual bank's willingness to borrow money for expansionary loans to industry. The Fed can also influence bank behavior by issuing policy statements, or jawboning.

Beyond these monetary measures, the tool most widely used is **open-market operations** in which the Fed buys and sells securities for its own portfolio. When the Fed sells securities in the open market, purchasers write checks to pay for their securities, and demand deposits fall, causing a contraction in the money supply. At the same time, the increase in the supply of Treasury bills sold by the Fed will force prices down and interest rates up to entice buyers to part with their money. The Fed usually accomplishes its adjustments by selling securities to commercial banks, government securities dealers, or individuals.

If the Fed buys securities, the opposite occurs; the money supply increases, and interest rates go down. As you will see in Chapter 7, the interest rate is extremely important in determining the required rate of return, or discount rate for a stock.

Many economists believe Federal Reserve open-market activity and the resultant changes in the money supply and interest rates are good indicators of the policy position taken by the Fed. If the money supply increases and interest rates fall, the general consensus is that the Fed is encouraging economic expansion. As the money supply decreases or increases slowly and interest rates rise, the expectation is that the Fed is "tightening up" monetary policy to restrict economic growth and inflation. The Federal Reserve cannot totally control the money supply. Money market funds, the resultant monetary expansion created by banks lending money, and changing spending patterns by the population all contribute to the difficulty in controlling the money supply.

In its attempt to stimulate the economy out of the 1990–91 recession, the Federal Reserve Board drove interest rates down to their lowest levels in decades. At the beginning of 1992, the Fed discount rate was 3.5 percent, one-year Treasury bills were in the 4.0 percent range, and the prime rate was 6.5 percent.

Government Policy, Real Growth, and Inflation

In November 1991, the U.S. Commerce Department's Economic Bureau of Analysis shifted from gross national product to gross domestic product as the measure of economic activity for the U.S. economy. The **gross domestic product (GDP)** measurement makes us more compatible with the rest of the

world and measures only output from U.S. factories and consumption within the United States. Gross domestic product would not include products made by U.S. companies in foreign countries, but gross national product would. The actual difference between the two measurements is very slight but enough to give different economic signals.

Figure 5–4 on page 166 depicts 30 years of GDP in current dollars and in inflation-adjusted 1987 dollars. In the bottom of the figure, we see changes in the annual growth rate of real GDP. This information needs to be looked at in context with the annual percentage change in the consumer price index (CPI), which is used as a proxy for inflation. Notice the inverse relationship between real GDP and the CPI. Since real GDP is the "nominal" GDP adjusted for inflation, the change in real GDP is inversely related to the rate of inflation. As inflation rises, real GDP falls (as indicated in 1970, 1975, 1980–81, and 1989–90), and as inflation subsides, as in 1982–83, real GDP rises. Since real GDP is the measure of economic output in real physical terms, it does not do any good to stimulate the economy only to have all the gains eroded by inflation.

To understand the major sectors of the economy and the relative influence of each sector, we divide gross domestic product into its four basic areas: personal consumption expenditures, government purchases, gross private investment, and net exports. Figure 5–5 on page 167 shows the contribution of each one to the total GDP over the past three decades. It becomes clear from Figure 5–5 that personal consumption is growing faster than the other sectors and is the driving force behind economic growth. In the next section we look at the cyclical nature of GDP.

■ BUSINESS CYCLES AND CYCLICAL INDICATORS

The economy expands and contracts through a **business cycle** process. By measuring GDP and other economic data, we can develop a statistical picture of the economic growth pattern. The National Bureau of Economic Research (NBER) is the final authority in documenting cyclical turning points. The NBER defines recessions as two or more quarters of negative real GDP growth and documents the beginning and end of a recession. Table 5–1 on page 168 presents a historical picture of business cycle expansions and contractions in the United States. While the modern day data may be more relevant, it is interesting to see that economic cycles have existed and been defined for over 130 years.

Table 5–1 measures each contraction and expansion and then presents summary data at the bottom of the table for all business cycles and for cycles in peacetime only. A **trough** represents the end of a recession and the beginning of an expansion, and a **peak** represents the end of an expansion and the beginning of a recession. In general, we see at the bottom of Table 5–1 that during peacetime cycles between 1945 and 1982, contractions (recessions) have lasted an average of 11 months, while expansions have averaged 34 months. Thus, one *complete* business cycle during modern *peacetimes* lasts almost four years whether measured from trough to trough or peak to peak. This has led

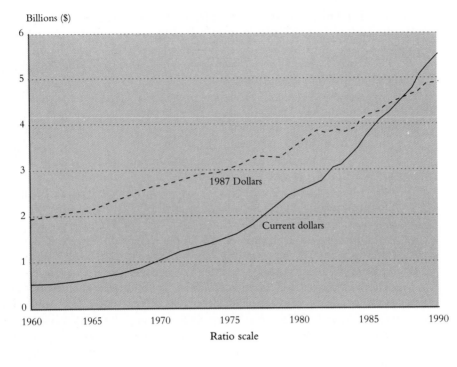

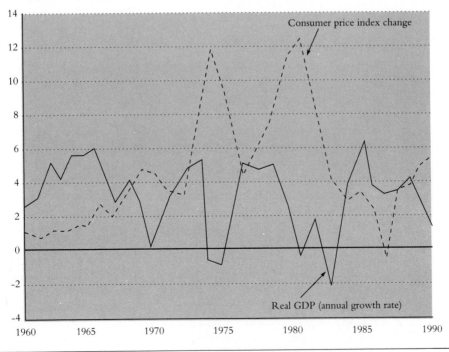

Figure 5–5   Breakdown of Gross Domestic Product in Current Dollars

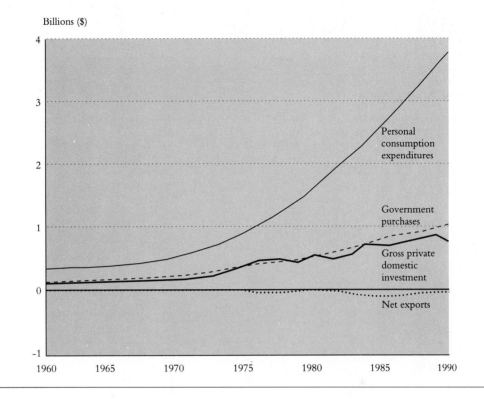

Billions ($)

Personal consumption expenditures

Government purchases

Gross private domestic investment

Net exports

many to call the cycle politically induced by the four-year presidential elections. While there may be some truth in this statement, there are many other theories about what causes the economy to cycle. However, if investors can make some forecast concerning the beginning and ending of the business cycle, they will be better able to choose what types of investments to hold over the various phases of the cycle.

As of this writing, the NBER has not yet officially classified the end of the expansion that began in 1982 (we think July 1990) or the end of the recession. By July 1990, the expansion had reached 90 months in duration and was by most accounts in a contraction. This rather unusual expansion when compared to the average shown in Table 5–1 is almost three times as long as normal.

So far, we have discussed the government's impact on the economy. Fiscal policy and monetary policy both provide important clues to the direction and magnitude of economic expansions and contractions. Other measures are used to evaluate the direction of the business cycle. These measures, called

Table 5–1 Business Cycle Expansions and Contractions in the United States

Business Cycle Reference Dates		Duration in Months			
				Cycle	
Trough	Peak	Contraction (Trough from previous peak)	Expansion (Trough to peak)	Trough from Previous Trough	Peak from Previous Peak
December 1854	June 1857	—	30	—	—
December 1858	October 1860	18	22	48	40
June 1861	April 1865	8	46	30	54
December 1867	June 1869	32	18	78	50
December 1870	October 1873	18	34	36	52
March 1879	March 1882	65	36	99	101
May 1885	March 1887	38	22	74	60
April 1888	July 1890	13	27	35	40
May 1891	January 1893	10	20	37	30
June 1894	December 1895	17	18	37	35
June 1897	June 1899	18	24	36	42
December 1900	September 1902	18	21	42	39
August 1904	May 1907	23	33	44	56
June 1908	January 1910	13	19	46	32
January 1912	January 1913	24	12	43	36
December 1914	August 1918	23	44	35	67
March 1919	January 1920	7	10	51	17
July 1921	May 1923	18	22	28	40
July 1924	October 1926	14	27	36	41
November 1927	August 1929	13	21	40	34
March 1933	May 1937	43	50	64	93
June 1938	February 1945	13	80	63	93
October 1945	November 1948	8	37	88	45
October 1949	July 1953	11	45	48	56
May 1954	August 1957	10	39	55	49
April 1958	April 1960	8	24	47	32
February 1961	December 1969	10	106	34	116
November 1970	November 1973	11	36	117	47
March 1975	January 1980	16	58	52	74
July 1980	July 1981	6	12	64	18
November 1982		16	—	28	—
Average, all cycles:					
1854–1982 (30 cycles)		18	33	51	51*
1854–1919 (16 cycles)		22	27	48	49†
1919–1945 (6 cycles)		18	35	53	53
1945–1982 (8 cycles)		11	45	56	55‡
Average, peacetime cycles:					
1854–1982 (25 cycles)		19	27	46	46‡
1854–1919 (14 cycles)		22	24	46	47§
1919–1945 (5 cycles)		20	26	46	45
1945–1982 (6 cycles)		**11**	**34**	**46**	**44**

Note: Underscored figures are the wartime expansions (Civil War, World Wars I and II, Korean War, and Vietnam War), the postwar contractions, and the full cycles that include the wartime expansions.
*29 cycles.   †15 cycles.   ‡24 cycles.   §13 cycles.
Source: *Business Conditions Digest* (U.S. Department of Commerce Bureau of Economic Analysis, July 1988).

economic indicators, are divided into leading, lagging, and coincident indicators. The National Bureau of Economic Research classifies indicators relative to their performance at economic peaks and troughs.

√ **Leading indicators** change direction in advance of general business conditions and are of prime importance to the investor who wants to anticipate rising corporate profits and possible price increases in the stock market. **Coincident indicators** move roughly with the general economy, and **lagging indicators** usually change directions after business conditions have turned around.

The National Bureau of Economic Research publishes its indicators in the monthly publication *Survey of Current Business*. This publication includes moving averages, turning dates for recessions and expansions, cyclical indicators, composite indexes and their components, diffusion indexes,[1] and information on rates of change. Many of the series are seasonally adjusted and are maintained on a monthly or quarterly basis.

Table 5–2 presents a summary of cyclical indicators by economic process and cyclical timing with Part A of the table presenting timing at business cycle peaks and Part B showing timing at business cycle troughs. Thus, in the first part, we see the leading, coincident, and lagging indicators for business cycle peaks, and in the second part, similar indicators for the bottoming out of business cycles (troughs). While we would not expect you to study or learn all the leading or lagging indicators for a cyclical peak or trough, it is important that you know they are heavily relied on by economists and financial analysts. Let's look more specifically at how they are used.

√ *Leading Indicators*

Of the 108 leading indicators shown in Parts A and B of Table 5–2, 61 lead at peaks and 47 lead at troughs. Of these, 11 basic indicators have been reasonably consistent in their relationship to the business cycle and are considered most important. These 11 leading indicators have been standardized and used to compute a composite index that is widely followed. It is a much smoother curve than each individual component since erratic changes in one indicator are offset by movements in other indicators. The same can be said for a similar index of four coincident indicators and six lagging indicators.

Figure 5–6 on page 172 shows the performance of the composite index of leading, lagging, and coincident indicators over several past business cycles. The shaded areas are recessions as defined by the NBER. The minus figures indicate how many months the index preceded the economy. (Lagging indicators have plus signs.)

---

[1]A diffusion index shows the pervasiveness of a given movement in a series. If 100 units are reported in a series, the diffusion index will indicate what percentage followed a given pattern.

Table 5–2 Cross Classification of Cyclical Indicators by Economic Process and Cyclical Timing

A. Timing at Business Cycle Peaks

Cyclical Timing \ Economic Process	I. Employment and Unemployment (15 series)	II. Production and Income (10 series)	III. Consumption, Trade, Orders, and Deliveries (13 series)	IV. Fixed Capital Investment (19 series)	V. Inventories and Inventory Investment (9 series)	VI. Price, Costs, and Profits (18 series)	VII. Money and Credit (28 series)
Leading (L) Indicators (61 series)	Marginal employment adjustments (3 series) Job vacancies (2 series) Comprehensive employment (1 series) Comprehensive unemployment (3 series)	Capacity utilization (2 series)	Orders and deliveries (6 series) Consumption and trade (2 series)	Formation of business enterprises (2 series) Business investment commitments (5 series) Residential construction (3 series)	Inventory investment (4 series) Inventories on hand and on order (1 series)	Stock prices (1 series) Sensitive commodity prices (2 series) Profits and profit margins (7 series) Cash flows (2 series)	Money (5 series) Credit flows (5 series) Credit difficulties (2 series) Bank reserves (2 series) Interest rates (1 series)
Roughly Coincident (C) Indicators (24 series)	Comprehensive employment (1 series)	Comprehensive output and income (4 series) Industrial production (4 series)	Consumption and trade (4 series)	Business investment commitments (1 series) Business investment expenditures (6 series)			Velocity of money (2 series) Interest rates (2 series)
Lagging (Lg) Indicators (19 series)	Comprehensive unemployment (2 series)			Business investment expenditures (1 series)	Inventories on hand and on order (4 series)	Unit labor costs and labor share (4 series)	Interest rates (4 series) Outstanding debt (4 series)
Timing Unclassified (U) (8 series)	Comprehensive employment (3 series)		Consumption and trade (1 series)	Business investment commitments (1 series)		Sensitive commodity prices (1 series) Profits and profit margins (1 series)	Interest rates (1 series)

Table 5-2   Cross Classification of Cyclical Indicators by Economic Process and Cyclical Timing (*concluded*)

B. Timing at Business Cycle Troughs

Economic Process / Cyclical Timing	I. Employment and Unemployment (15 series)	II. Production and Income (10 series)	III. Consumption, Trade, Orders, and Deliveries (13 series)	IV. Fixed Capital Investment (19 series)	V. Inventories and Inventory Investment (9 series)	VI. Price, Costs, and Profits (18 series)	VII. Money and Credit (28 series)
Leading (L) Indicators (47 series)	Marginal employment adjustments (1 series)	Industrial production (1 series)	Orders and deliveries (5 series) Consumption and trade (4 series)	Formation of business enterprises (2 series) Business investment commitments (4 series) Residential construction (3 series)	Inventory investment (4 series)	Stock prices (1 series) Sensitive commodity prices (3 series) Profits and profit margins (6 series) Cash flows (2 series)	Money (4 series) Credit flows (5 series) Credit difficulties (2 series)
Roughly Coincident (C) Indicators (23 series)	Marginal employment adjustments (2 series) Comprehensive employment (4 series)	Comprehensive output and income (4 series) Industrial production (3 series) Capacity utilization (2 series)	Consumption and trade (3 series)	Business investment commitments (1 series)		Profits and profit margins (2 series)	Money (1 series) Velocity of money (1 series)
Lagging (Lg) Indicators (41 series)	Job vacancies (2 series) Comprehensive employment (1 series) Comprehensive unemployment (5 series)		Orders and deliveries (1 series)	Business investment commitments (2 series) Business investment expenditures (7 series)	Inventories on hand and on order (5 series)	Unit labor costs and labor share (4 series)	Velocity of money (1 series) Bank reserves (1 series) Interest rates (8 series) Outstanding debt (4 series)
Timing Unclassified (U) (1 series)							Bank reserves (1 series)

171

Source: *Business Conditions Digest* (U.S. Department of Commerce Bureau of Economic Analysis, July 1988).

Figure 5–6   Composite Indexes (Leading, lagging, and coincident indexes)

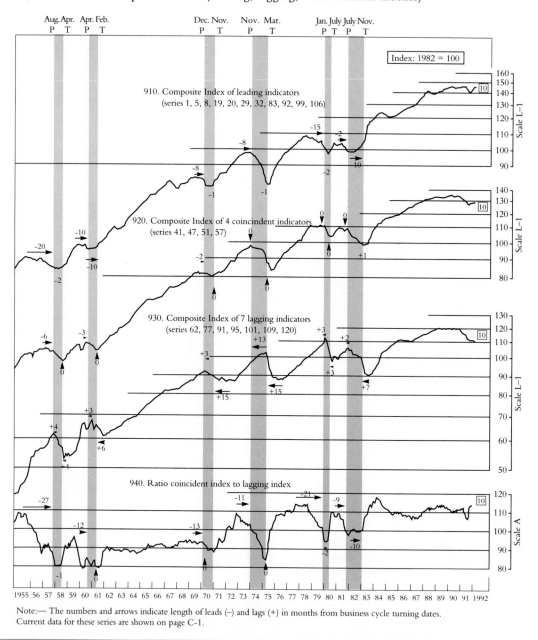

Note:— The numbers and arrows indicate length of leads (–) and lags (+) in months from business cycle turning dates. Current data for these series are shown on page C-1.

Source: *Survey of Current Business* (U.S. Department of Commerce Bureau of Economic Analysis, November 1991).

Table 5–3   Components of the Leading, Coincident, and Lagging Indicators (Series title and unit of measure)

Leading Indicators

1. Average weekly hours of production or nonsupervisory workers, manufacturing (hours).
5. Average weekly initial claims for unemployment insurance, state programs (thous.).
8. Mfrs. new orders in 1982 dollars, consumer goods and materials industries (bil. dol.).
32. Vendor performance, percent of companies receiving slower deliveries (percent).
20. Contracts and orders for plant and equipment in 1982 dollars (bil. dol.).
29. New private housing units authorized by local building permits (index: 1967 = 100).
36. Change in inventories on hand and on order in 1982 dollars, smoothed (ann. rate, bil. dol.).
99. Change in sensitive materials prices, smoothed (percent).
19. Stock prices, 500 common stocks (index: 1941–43 = 10).
106. Money supply M2 in 1982 dollars (bil. dol.).
111. Change in business and consumer credit outstanding (ann. rate, percent).

Roughly Coincident Indicators

41. Employees on nonagricultural payrolls (thous.)
51. Personal income less transfer payments in 1982 dollars (ann. rate, bil. dol.)
47. Industrial production (index: 1977 = 100).
57. Manufacturing and trade sales in 1982 dollars (mil. dol.)

Lagging Indicators

91. Average duration of unemployment (weeks)
77. Ratio, manufacturing and trade inventories to sales in 1982 dollars (ratio).
62. Labor cost per unit of output, manufacturing-actual data as a percent of trend (percent).
109. Average prime rate charged by banks (percent).
101. Commercial and industrial loans outstanding in 1982 dollars (mil. dol.).
95. Ratio, consumer installment credit outstanding to personal income (percent).

Note: The net contribution of an individual component is that component's share in the composite movement of the group. It is computed by dividing the standardized and weighted change for the component by the sum of the weights for the available components and dividing that result by the index standardization factor. See the February 1983 *Business Conditions Digest* (p. 108) or the 1984 *Handbook of Cyclical Indicators* (pp. 67–68) for the weights and standardization factors.
Source: *Business Conditions Digest* (U.S. Department of Commerce Bureau of Economic Analysis, July 1988).

While the composite index of leading indicators (top of Figure 5–6) has been a better predictor than any single indicator, it has varied widely at peaks and troughs. Table 5–3 presents the components for the 11 leading, 4 roughly coincident, and 6 lagging indicators.

Studies have found that the 11 leading indicators do not exhibit the same notice at peaks as they do at troughs. The notice before peaks is quite long, but the warning before troughs is very short, which means it is very easy to miss a turnaround to the upside, but on the downside, you can be more patient waiting for confirmation from other indicators. Indicators occasionally give false signals. Sometimes the indicators give no clear signal, and with the large variability of leads and lags versus the average lead time, an investor is lucky to get close to predicting economic activity within three or four months of peaks and troughs. Despite economic indicators and forecasting

methods, investors cannot escape uncertainty in an attempt to manage their portfolios.

One very important fact is that the stock market is the most reliable and accurate of the 11 leading indicators. This presents a very real problem for us because our initial objective is to forecast (as well as we are able) changes in common stock prices. To do this, we are constrained by the fact that the stock market is anticipatory and, in fact, has worked on a lead time of nine months at peaks and five months at troughs.

■ MONEY SUPPLY AND STOCK PRICES

One variable that has been historically popular as an indicator of the stock market is the money supply. The money supply is supposed to influence stock prices in several ways. Studies of economic growth and the money supply by Milton Friedman and Anna Schwartz found a long-term relationship between these two variables.[2]

Why does money matter? If you are a **monetarist,** money explains much of economic behavior. The quantity theory of money holds that as the supply of money increases relative to the demand for money, people will make adjustments in their portfolios of assets. If they have too much money, they will first buy bonds (a modification of the theory would now include Treasury bills or other short-term monetary assets), stocks, and finally, real assets. This is the direct effect of money on stock prices sometimes referred to as the *liquidity effect.*

The indirect effect of money on stock prices would flow through the GDP's impact on corporate profits. As money influences economic activity, it will eventually influence corporate earnings and dividends and thus returns to the investors. Many studies have found that a significant relationship exists between the money supply variable and stock prices. However, even here, there have been some conflicting patterns in the last decade as shown in Figure 5–7. Note that in the first half of 1982, the money supply (M2) was increasing slightly while stock prices were declining sharply. This goes against the historical norm of comparable movements that can be seen in the same figure.

There are many important predictors of economic patterns and stock market movements, but an investor must be flexible and consider as many variables as possible rather than simply relying on one or two factors. You may wish to acquaint yourself with many of the leading, coincident, and lagging indicators presented previously in Table 5–3 as you become active in the stock market.

---

[2]Milton J. Friedman and Anna J. Schwartz, "Money and Business Cycles," *Review of Economics and Statistics,* Supplement, February 1963.

Figure 5–7   Money Supply, Stock Prices, Corporate Profits, and Corporate Net Cash Flow
Cyclical Indicators (Leading indicators)

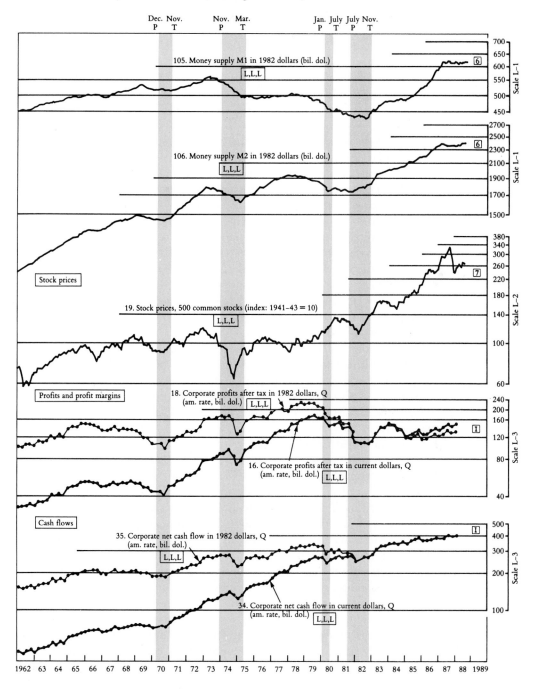

Source: *Business Conditions Digest* (U.S. Department of Commerce Bureau of Economic Analysis, July 1988).

■ BUSINESS CYCLES AND INDUSTRY ANALYSIS

Each industry may be affected by the business cycle differently. Industries where the underlying demand for the product is consumer-oriented will quite likely be sensitive to short-term swings in the business cycle. These industries would include durable goods such as washers and dryers, refrigerators, electric and gas ranges, and automobiles. Changes in the automobile industry will also be felt in the tire and rubber industry as well as by auto glass and other automobile component suppliers.

Table 5–4, which appeared in the *Chicago Tribune,* shows the impact of this ripple effect through many industries. The automobile industry purchases 77 percent of the output from the natural rubber industry (tires and bumpers), 67 percent of the output from the lead industry (batteries), and so on to 10 percent of the copper output (electrical and tubing). Additionally, the automobile industry accounts for more than 4 percent of the GNP. The U.S. automobile industry employs 800,000 people, and one in seven people (12.5 million) in America has a job in an industry somewhat dependent on the automobile industry. While the automobile industry has had a slightly diminished effect on the total U.S. economy beginning with the 1974 recession, it still has a major impact on our GDP. It is true that when the automobile industry is in a recession, so is the whole economy.

Figure 5–8 shows the automobile industry's sales from 1960 to 1990 relative to the real GDP's growth rate. Notice the similarity of the pattern. The peaks in economic activity (1965, 1973, 1976–78, 1985) all correspond with peaks in the auto industry. The recessions of 1970, 1974–75, 1981–82, and 1990–91 all correspond with troughs in automobile sales. This close relationship is why it is often said the United States lives in an automobile economy.

Not all industries are so closely related to the business cycle. Necessity-oriented industries, such as food and pharmaceuticals, are consistent performers since people have to eat, and illness is not dependent on the economy. Industries that have products with low price elasticities[3] that are habitual in nature, such as cigarettes and alcohol, do not seem to be much affected by business cycles, either. In fact, some industries do better during a recession. The movie industry prospers during a recession as more people substitute low-cost entertainment for more expensive forms. This is one pattern that may not remain the same, however. As cable television and VCRs come into their own, people may find it even more convenient to stay at home than to go to the movies when money is tight. This is one thing that makes investments exciting, the ever-changing environment.

Housing is another example of an industry that historically has done well in recessionary environments. As the economy comes to a standstill, interest

---

[3]Price elasticity represents the sensitivity of quantity purchased to price.

Table 5–4	Automobile Industry and Its Impact on Other Industries

The automotive industry purchases these percentages of the output of other U.S. Industries:*		**What's in a Car**
		A typical American car includes:†
Natural rubber	77%	1,774 lbs. of steel
Lead	67	460 lbs. of iron
Malleable iron	63	222 lbs. of plastic
Synthetic rubber	50	183 lbs. of fluids
Platinum	39	146 lbs. of aluminum
Zinc	23	135 lbs. of rubber
Aluminum	18	86 lbs. of glass
Steel	12	25 lbs. of copper
Copper	10	24 lbs. of lead
		18 lbs. of zinc

*Motor Vehicle Manufacturers Association.
†World Book Encyclopedia.

rates tend to come down, and prospective home purchasers are once again able to afford mortgage rates on a home. In the period of extremely high mortgage rates in the early 1980s, a precipitous drop in mortgage rates helped to stimulate growth in the housing market. The Federal Reserve followed such a policy again in 1991 by pushing interest rates down to their lowest level in decades. Sales of existing housing units picked up, and people refinanced their mortgages at lower rates, giving them more disposable income. As mortgage costs came down, housing became more affordable to more people. For example, if interest rates declined 3 percentage points on a $120,000 loan, the same priced house would now cost $300 per month less in interest expense.

Sensitivity to the business cycle may also be evident in industries that produce *capital* goods for other business firms (rather than consumer goods). Examples would be manufacturers of business plant and equipment, machine tools, or pollution-control equipment. A lag often exists between the recovery from a recession and the increased purchase of capital goods, so recoveries within these industries may be delayed.

Service industries have also become extremely important in our economy. While service-oriented business firms (doctors, lawyers, accountants) are generally less susceptible to the business cycle, there are exceptions. Examples of cyclically oriented service providers include architects, civil engineers, and auto repair shops.

We do not mean to imply that cyclical industries are bad investments or that they should be avoided. We merely point out the cyclical influence of the

Figure 5–8   New Auto Sales and Real GNP: 1961–1990

Millions of units

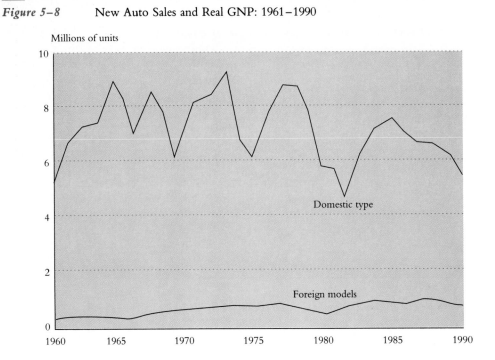

Arithmetic scale (%)

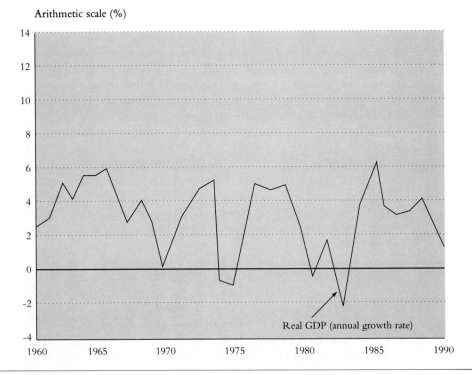

economy. Often cyclical industries are excellent buys in the stock market because the market does not look far enough ahead to see a recovery and its impact on cyclical profits.

■ INDUSTRY LIFE CYCLES

Industry life cycles are created because of economic growth, competition, availability of resources, and the resultant market saturation by the particular goods and services offered. Life cycle growth influences many variables considered in the valuation process. The particular phase in the life cycle of an industry or company determines the growth of earnings, dividends, capital expenditures, and market demand for products.

Figure 5–9 shows an industry life cycle (although it could very well be a company life cycle) and the corresponding dividend policy most likely to be found at each stage. A small firm in the initial stages of development (Stage I) pays no dividends because it needs all of its profits (if there are any) for reinvestment in new productive assets. If the firm is successful in the marketplace, the demand for its products will create growth in sales, earnings, and assets, and the industry will move into Stage II. At this stage, sales and returns on assets will be growing at an increasing rate, and earnings will still be reinvested. In the early part of Stage II, stock dividends (distributions of additional shares) may be instituted, and in the latter part of Stage II, *low* cash dividends may be started to inform investors that the firm is profitable.

Obviously, industries in Stage I or early Stage II are very risky, and the investor does not really know if growth objectives will be met or dividends will ever be paid. But if you want to have a chance to make an investment (after careful research) in a high-growth industry with large potential returns, then Stage I or II industries will provide you with opportunities for gains or losses. Since actual dividends are irrelevant in these stages, an investor will be purchasing shares for capital gains based on expected growth rather than current income. As the industry enters Stage III, the growth rate is still positive, but the rate of change starts declining. This is often the point where investors do not recognize that the growth rate has begun to decline, and they still pay large premiums over the regular market for stocks in these industries. However, when the market does realize the growth rate is diminishing, stock prices can take a sizable tumble.

In Stage III, sales expansion continues but at a decreasing rate, and returns on investment may decline as more competition enters the market and attempts to take away market share from existing firms. The industry has grown to the point where asset expansion slows in line with production needs, and the firms in the industry are more capable of paying cash dividends. Stock dividends and stock splits are still common in Stage III, and the dividend payout ratio usually increases from a low level of 5 to 15 percent of earnings to a moderate level of 25 to 40 percent of earnings. Finally, at Stage IV, maturity, the firm maintains a stable growth rate in sales similar to that of the economy

Figure 5–9   Industry Life Cycle

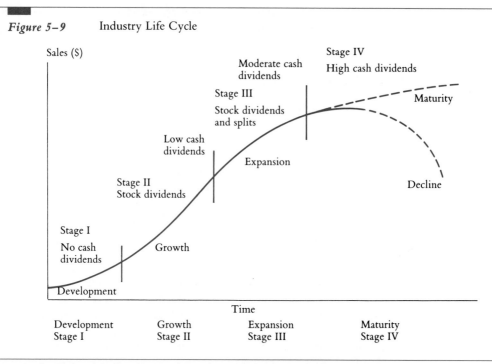

Source: Stanley Block and Geoffrey Hirt, *Foundations of Financial Management,* 6th ed. (Homewood, Ill.: Richard D. Irwin, 1992).

as a whole, and when risk premiums are considered, its returns on assets level out to those of the economy. Automobiles might be a good example of a mature industry.

In unfortunate cases, industries suffer declines in sales (for example, passenger railroads) if product innovation has not increased the product base over the years. In Stage IV, assuming maturity rather than decline, dividends might range from 40 to 60 percent of earnings. These percentages will be different from industry to industry depending on individual characteristics.

It is also important to realize that growth companies can exist in a mature industry and that not all companies within an industry experience the same growth path in sales, earnings, and dividends. Some companies are simply better managed, have better people, have more efficient assets, and have put more money into productive research and development that has created new products or improved products.

For example, electric utilities are generally considered mature, but utilities in states such as Florida and California that have undergone rapid population explosions over the last decade would still have higher growth rates than the industry in general. Computer companies such as IBM were fast approaching maturity until technical innovations created new markets. Now personal computers and local area networks not only have added vitality to older markets

but also have created new industries. You can trace the histories of many industries to see that this pattern repeats itself.

The warning to the investor is to not become too enamored with a company just because it is in a "growth industry." Its time of glory may have passed. Other investors improperly ignore companies that are in the process of revitalization because they no longer carry the growth-stock tag. More will be said about growth stocks in Chapter 7.

Other Industry Factors to Consider

A financial analyst may wish to evaluate other significant factors for a given industry. For example, is the industry structure monopolistic like a regulated utility, oligopolistic like the automobile or steel industry, partially competitive like the drug industry, or very competitive like the market for farm commodities? Questions of industry structure are very important in analyzing pricing structures and price elasticities that exist because of competition or lack of it.

Questions of supply and demand relationships are very important as they affect the price structure of the industry and its ability to produce quality products at a reasonable cost. The cost variable can be affected by many factors. For example, high relative hourly wages in basic industries such as steel, autos, and rubber are somewhat responsible for the inability of the United States to compete in the world markets of these products. Availability of raw material is also an important cost factor. Industries like aluminum and glass have to have an abundance of low-cost bauxite and silicon to produce their products. Unfortunately, the aluminum industry uses very large amounts of electricity in the production process, and so the low cost of bauxite may be offset by the high cost of energy. Energy costs are of concern to all industries, but the availability of reasonably priced energy sources is particularly important to the airline and trucking industries. The list could go on and on, but as analysts become familiar with a specific industry they learn the crucial variables.

Most industries are also affected by government regulation. This applies to the automobile industry where safety and exhaust emissions are regulated and to all industries where air, water, and noise pollution are of concern. Many industries engaged in interstate commerce, such as utilities, railroads, and telephone companies, are strongly regulated by the government. On the other hand, many industries, such as airlines, trucking, and natural gas production companies, are being deregulated, and these industries are facing a new climate where the old game plan may no longer prove successful. Most industries are affected by government expenditures; this is especially true for industries involved in defense, education, and transportation.

These are but a few examples to alert you to the importance of having a thorough understanding of your industry. This is why in many large investment firms, trust departments, and insurance companies, analysts are assigned to only one industry or to several related industries so they may concentrate their attention on a given set of significant factors.

■ SUMMARY

The primary purpose of this chapter is to provide you with a process of valuation and an appreciation of some of the variables that should be considered. The valuation process is based on fundamental analysis of the economy, industry, and company. This method assumes decisions are made based on economic concepts of value over the long-term trend of the stock market. The purpose of the process is to eliminate losers from consideration in your portfolio and to thereby provide you with a good opportunity to build a sound portfolio.

The first step in the valuation process is an analysis of the economy and long-term economic trends. The difficulties of attaining government policy goals are discussed as a trade-off between conflicting objectives (high growth versus low inflation). Fiscal and monetary policy are discussed as the primary tools used to stimulate economic activity. Interest rates are influenced by inflation, with the end result being a higher required rate of return for the investor.

Business cycles are short-term swings in economic activity; they affect stock prices because they change investor expectations of risk and return. To forecast economic activity, cyclical indicators are presented as leading, lagging, and coincident indexes. The one index potentially most valuable to an investor is the composite index of 11 leading indicators. Unfortunately, stock prices are one of the most accurate leading indicators, and we must try to find another indicator that leads stock prices. The most-popular and economically rational leading indicator is the money supply. The money supply influences economic activity by increasing or decreasing interest rates and corporate profits, which, in turn, eventually affect corporate dividends. Money also has a direct effect on stock prices by changing liquidity. An investor cannot escape risk, however, and the money supply is no sure way to forecast stock prices. The leads are too similar, and many factors have clouded the effect of changes in the money supply on the economy and stock prices. The best solution is to use a combination of economic variables that will tend to provide insights into future economic developments and the stock market.

The sensitivity of various types of industries to the business cycle is also examined. Firms in consumer durable goods as well as those in heavy capital goods manufacturing (plant and equipment) are perhaps most vulnerable to the business cycle. Industries are also examined from the standpoint of their life cycle growth path. This growth path affects earnings, dividends, and market valuation and provides a perspective on the valuation process that will be discussed further in the next chapter.

IMPORTANT WORDS AND CONCEPTS

fiscal policy 161	business cycle 165
deficit 161	trough 165
surpluses 161	peak 165
monetary policy 163	leading indicators 169
reserve requirements 163	coincident indicators 169
discount rate 164	lagging indicators 169
open-market operations 164	monetarist 174
gross domestic product (GDP) 164	industry life cycles 179

DISCUSSION QUESTIONS

1. As depicted in Figure 5–1, what are the three elements in the valuation process?

2. What are the four goals under the Employment Act of 1946?

3. What is fiscal policy? Does it tend to have a long and short implementation period?

4. What is monetary policy?

5. How specifically can the Fed influence economic activity?

6. In regard to Federal Reserve open-market activity, if the Fed buys securities, what is the likely impact on the money supply? Is this likely to encourage expansion or contraction of economic activity?

7. How does gross domestic product (GDP) differ from gross national product (GNP) as a measure of economic activity?

8. What is the historical relationship between real GDP and inflation? What lesson might be learned from observing this relationship?

9. What is the advantage of using a composite of indicators (such as the 11 leading indicators) over simply using an individual indicator?

10. Do leading indicators tend to give longer warning before peaks or before troughs? What is the implication for the investor?

11. Give some examples of how different types of industries would relate to the business cycle.

12. Why do industry life cycles exist? How does the dividend policy generally relate to the life cycle of the firm or industry?

13. Develop a list of industries in each phase of the life cycle and look up their dividend record to see if they correspond to the general view of the chapter.

14. Observe the performance of the 11 leading indicators for the next month. Compare this to changes in stock prices and interest rates.

MARKETBASE-E EXERCISES

In the following exercise, please use your MarketBase-E Software and manual to screen for the required portfolios. You will have to figure out how to search through the data to pull out those companies meeting the requirements set down.

1. Chapter five focused on economics and industry analysis. Using the SIC codes below (industry designations), select all the companies found under the industry listings for:

   a. Airlines - SIC 4510
   b. Brewing - SIC 2082
   c. Chemicals - SIC 2800
   d. Pharmaceuticals - SIC 2830
   e. Food - SIC 2080

2. *a.* The brewing and food industries are related, as are the chemical and pharmaceutical industries. You can see this because their SIC codes begin with the same first two digits. Use MarketBase-E to select all the companies that are related by having the same first two digits of their SIC codes 28 (chemicals and pharmaceuticals) and 20 (food and beverages).

   b. What common characteristics do you see in these companies?

SELECTED REFERENCES

Business-Cycle Analysis

Federal Reserve Historical Chart Book and *Federal Reserve Quarterly Chart Book.* Washington, D.C.: Federal Reserve Board of Governors, selected issues.

Friedman, Milton J., and Anna J. Schwartz. "Money and Business Cycles." *Review of Economics and Statistics,* Supplement, February 1963.

Hardouvelis, G. A. "Reserve's Announcements and Interest Rates: Does Monetary Policy Matter?" *Journal of Finance,* June 1987, pp. 407–22.

Herbst, Anthony F., and Craig W. Slinkman. "Political-Economic Cycles in the U.S. Stock Market." *Financial Analysts Journal,* March–April 1984, pp. 38–44.

Levin, Jay H. "On the International Transmission of Monetary Policy under Floating Exchange Rates." *Quarterly Review of Economics and Business,* Spring 1984, pp. 78–86.

Rogalski, Richard J., and Joseph D. Vinso. "Stock Returns, Money Supply and the Direction of Causality." *Journal of Finance,* September 1977, pp. 1017–30.

Spindt, P. A., and V. Tarham. "The Federal Reserve's New Operating Procedures: A Postmortem." *Journal of Monetary Economics,* January 1987, pp. 107–23.

Forecasting

Elliott, J. W. "A Direct Comparison of Short-Run GNP Forecasting Models." *Journal of Business,* January 1973, pp. 33–60.

Gray, William. "The Stock Market and the Economy in 1988." *The Journal of Portfolio Management,* September 1984, pp. 73–80.

Heathcotte, Bryan, and Vincent P. Apilado. "The Predictive Content of Some Leading Economic Indicators for Future Stock Prices." *Journal of Financial and Quantitative Analysis,* March 1974, pp. 247–58.

Nelson, Charles R. "Rational Expectations and the Predictive Efficiency of Economic Models." *Journal of Business,* July 1975, pp. 331–43.

Reichenstein, William. "Touters Trophies: Ranking Economists' Forecasts." *Financial Analysts Journal,* July–August 1991, pp. 20–21.

VanHoose, David D. "Discount Rate Policy and Alternative Federal Reserve Operating Procedures in a Rational Expectations Setting." *Journal of Economics and Business,* November 1988, pp. 285–93.

Industry Analysis

Fama, Eugene F., and Kenneth R. French. "Business Cycles and the Behavior of Metal Prices." *Journal of Finance,* December 1988, pp. 1075–93.

Latane, Henry A., and Donald L. Tuttle. "Profitability in Industry Analysis." *Financial Analysts Journal,* July–August 1968, pp. 51–61.

Livingston, Miles. "Industry Movements of Common Stocks." *Journal of Finance,* June 1977, pp. 861–74.

Reilly, Frank K., and Eugene Drzycimski. "Alternative Industry Performance and Risk." *Journal of Financial and Quantitative Analysis,* June 1974, pp. 423–46.

Appendix 5–A: Example of an Industry Analysis by the Standard & Poor's Corporation—The Processed Food Industry

STANDARD & POOR'S

industry surveys

© 1991 Standard & Poor's Corporation USPS No. 517-780.

PROCESSED FOODS

Slow growth continues

The U.S. food industry continued to register slow growth in 1990, as consumer outlays for food, both at-home and away-from-home, rose 5.1%, to an estimated $466 billion, according to the U.S. Department of Agriculture (USDA). However, food outlays as a percentage of disposable personal income (which was up 5.9% in 1990) continued to decline, to 11.8% from 11.9% in 1989, and from 13.8% as recently as 1980. The decline reflects the inelastic nature of the aggregate demand for food: as personal income rises, the proportion spent on food declines, since the demand for nonfood items outpaces the demand for additional food. Recent findings by the U.S. Department of Labor confirmed this theory, when the agency found that households with pre-tax incomes of $5,000 to $9,999 spent 30.7% of their after-tax income on food, while households with incomes of $15,000 to $19,999 spent 20.5%, and those with incomes of $30,000 to $39,999 spent 15.3% of after-tax income on food.

Wholesale food shipments for the nation's 21 food processing industries—which range from meat packers to candy producers—reached an estimated $226 billion in 1990, a 9.0% increase from 1989, according to the U.S. Census Bureau. The relatively modest growth was consistent with the long-term trend in the food processing indus-

try, as again, price increases, population growth, export growth, demographic changes, increased purchases of value-added products, and the introduction of new value-added products all contributed to the gain. Shipments varied widely by category, however, ranging from an estimated 19% increase for natural and processed cheese to a 4.5% decline for dried fruits, vegetables, and soups. Shipments of meat, the largest category, with $89 billion in sales, rose nearly 11%. However, the gain largely reflected red meat price increases (production declined 1.5% due to tight cattle and hog supplies) and strong production increases for poultry products (6.8% price-adjusted growth), which benefited from increased U.S. per-capita consumption and export growth.

Food prices outpace CPI

At year-end 1990, prices for ingredients from farmers (commodities) were up a modest 1.6% (versus 6.5% in 1989), year to year, compared with a 4.9% (5.2%) increase from manufacturers. These minor increases largely reflected

Kenneth Shea, Food & Tobacco Analyst

WHERE THE FOOD DOLLAR GOES

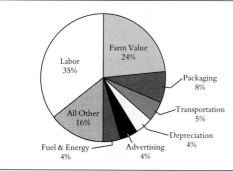

Source: The Food Institute

FOOD EXPENDATURES AS A PERCENTAGE OF DISPOSABLE INCOME

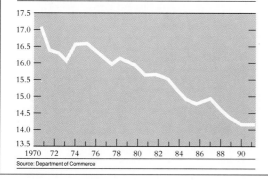

Source: Department of Commerce

FOOD PRICE INDEXES VS. THE CPI
(1982-84=100)

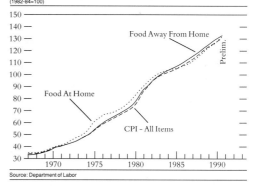

Source: Department of Labor

FOOD PRICE INDEXES
(1982=100)

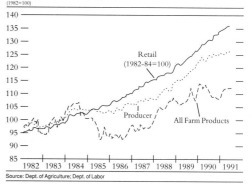

Source: Dept. of Agriculture; Dept. of Labor

Top 25 food companies

(Ranked by 1990 sales, in millions of dollars)

Company	1989	1990	% chg.
1. Philip Morris Cos.	[1]25,802	26,368	2.2
2. ConAgra Inc.	8,591	[2]17,253	100.8
3. Anheuser-Busch Cos.	9,364	1,011	(89.2)
4. PepsiCo	8,153	9,992	22.6
5. Coca-Cola	8,000	8,900	11.3
6. IBP	8,502	8,586	1.0
7. Archer Daniels Midland	7,200	7,130	(1.0)
8. Nestle Holdings	5,961	6,781	13.8
9. Campbell Soup	5,700	6,200	8.8
10. RJR Nabisco	9,888	[3]5,783	(41.5)
11. H.J. Heinz	5,492	5,761	4.9
12. Borden	5,386	5,661	5.1
13. Sara Lee	5,255	5,460	3.9
14. CPC International	4,701	5,103	8.6
15. Ralston Purina	4,555	5,086	11.7
16. Kellogg	4,349	4,652	7.0
17. General Mills	3,999	4,520	13.0
18. Tyson Foods	2,538	[4]3,850	51.7
19. Chiquita Brands	3,503	[5]3,823	9.1
20. Joseph E. Seagram & Sons	2,275	3,404	49.6
21. Procter & Gamble	3,029	3,318	9.5
22. Quaker Oats	2,756	3,270	18.6
23. Kroger	3,200	3,183	(0.5)
24. Whitman Corp.	2,500	3,000	20.0
25. Associated Milk Products	2,744	2,987	8.8

[1]Based on combined sales of Philip Morris and Kraft, which became a wholly owned subsidiary of Philip Morris on 12/7/88. [2]Includes Beatrice Company, acquired 8/90. [3]DelMonte Fresh Fruit sold 12/89, DelMonte Processed Food sold 1/90. [4]Acquired Holly Farms Corp. 7/18/89. [5]Does not include Dinner Bell Foods acquired 8/90.

Source: The Food Institute.

Major food category annual price changes

Food	Percent change		
	1988	1989	1990
All food	4.1	5.8	5.8
Food at home	4.2	6.5	6.5
Meat	2.4	4.0	10.1
Beef and veal	5.5	6.4	8.0
Pork	−3.0	0.6	14.7
Poultry	7.2	9.9	−0.2
Fish & seafood	5.8	4.5	2.2
Eggs	2.3	26.6	4.7
Dairy products	2.4	6.6	9.4
Fresh fruit	8.3	7.0	12.1
Fresh vegetables	6.3	10.7	5.6
Processed fruits & vegetables	7.9	6.3	6.2
Cereals & bakery products	6.4	8.4	5.7
Sugar & sweets	2.7	4.7	4.4
Fats & oils	4.6	7.2	4.2
Nonalcoholic beverages	0.0	3.5	2.0
Other prepared foods	3.7	6.4	4.5
Food away from home	4.1	4.6	4.7

Source: U.S. Department of Labor.

abundant grain supplies. For consumers, however, prices repeated their year-earlier increase of 5.8%, which was the largest jump since 1981. At both the manufacturing and consumer level, price increases were highest for meat and dairy goods (due mainly to tight market supplies) and frozen juices (primarily reflecting the December 1989 freeze in Florida and Texas).

For the fourth time in the past five years, food prices in 1990 rose by more than the 5.4% jump in the Consumer Price Index (CPI) for all consumer products and services. Consumer demand for food remained relatively strong through 1990's first half, contributing to the upward movement in prices. We believe a decline in personal real dispos-

able income in the second half cooled demand and held back further price increases.

Labor, packaging costs up modestly

The largest component of food production costs is labor. Wage increases in 1990 were comparatively modest for food processors, most of whom are not unionized. Hourly earnings in food manufacturing rose about 3.6%, according to the USDA, largely reflecting increases in the number of workers employed, and worker wages and benefits. Hourly earnings of workers in food processing, wholesaling, and retailing rose 3.7%, 3.0%, and 3.7%, respectively, in 1990. These moderate increases can also be explained by changes in the labor force, such as greater employment of part-time and entry-level workers who typically earn lower wages. Overall, higher labor costs accounted for about half the $19 billion increase in the nation's food bill last year.

Packaging constitutes the third-largest food manufacturing cost (behind commodities, which accounted for 24% of costs last year) and represents about 8% of total food outlays. In 1990, costs for food containers and packaging materials rose only 0.8%. Prices for metal containers and foil, which make up about a quarter of packaging materials, were down considerably in 1990, due to increased competitive conditions and greater capacity in the aluminum industry.

Energy prices, while comprising only 3.5% of the total manufacturing bill, rose a sharp 8.4%, due mainly to the Persian Gulf War. Diesel fuel prices rose about 20% and electric rates rose about 2%, boosting energy costs of food processing and distribution. Financing costs dipped 9.7%, benefiting from a decline in short-term interest rates and a slight reduction in debt burdens. Advertising costs, however, rose 5.8%, as competition for market share remained intense.

Profits rise, as costs moderate

Aftertax profits of the 15 food processors that comprise the *S&P Food Index* equaled approximately 5.6% of sales in 1990, up from 5.3% in 1989. The increase reflects a significantly larger rise in net income (16%) than in sales (10%). While the profit margin expansion is primarily due to an easing in manufacturing costs (as discussed above), it also reflects the favorable impact of recent restructuring efforts (Gerber, Campbell Soup), acquisition-related synergies (ConAgra, Hershey), and growth in overseas markets, in which processors also benefited from foreign currency translation gains against the U.S. dollar (CPC International, Wrigley, Heinz, Kellogg). While most of the major U.S.-based food processors benefited from these easing cost pressures, they also found it necessary to plow much of those profits into heavier marketing and promotional efforts in order to combat slowing unit volume growth weakened by the U.S. recession. While Quaker Oats, for example, enjoyed widening gross margins in 1990, its selling, general and administrative expenses increased sharply, due mainly to increased promotional spending to support its cereals and Gatorade business in the U.S. and Gatorade in Europe.

In 1990, the stock prices for those companies comprising the *S&P Food Index* advanced 5.1%, versus a 6.6% decrease for the *S&P 500*. In 1991's first quarter, the *S&P Food Index* climbed nearly 17%, versus a 13.6% gain for the *500*. This strong performance reflected the industry's ability to produce steady, dependable earnings and dividend increases even in the face of an economic slowdown. Consistent demand, high value-added content, and long-lived consumer franchises should continue to enable the mature,

albeit competitive, food processing industry to record steady, above-average earnings gains in both the near and long term.

Back to basics in the '90s

Following a proliferation of mergers and takeovers in the 1980s, U.S. food companies find themselves paying down debt and divesting non-food business lines in order to focus more on operating efficiency in an increasingly competitive and economically depressed U.S. market.

At a recent conference sponsored by the Consumer Analysts Group of New York, leading food company executives said that improving unit sales and operating efficiencies were top priorities, given the U.S. economic slowdown and an increasingly competitive playing field. In response to such conditions, we expect that many companies will focus more attention on growing overseas markets, continue divestiture of nonstrategic assets, and accelerate new product activity.

Further expansion into foreign markets will be particularly important to U.S. food companies in 1991, with the economic downturn in the U.S. and the increasing demand for consumer-branded products in many foreign markets, especially Western Europe and Asia. The removal of trade barriers in Europe beginning in 1992, together with Eastern European countries now experimenting with free market systems, present tremendous growth opportunities for maturing U.S. food companies. Tariffs, documentation, product labeling, and ingredient laws are among the regulations that are being revised to simplify commerce among the 12 member nations of the European Economic Community, a $4.3 trillion market with 325 million consumers.

While some U.S. companies (*e.g.,* Kellogg, CPC International, Quaker Oats) have long had a large presence in Europe, many others have only recently stepped up efforts to participate in this arena. Gerber Foods, for example, in April 1991 said it would take over the marketing of its *Gerber* baby food from licensee CPC International, and may also take over the marketing and advertising of its baby food in other overseas markets, in order to penetrate growing European markets more aggressively with its well-known franchise of baby foods. In August 1990, Philip Morris' Kraft General Foods unit, the U.S.'s largest food processor, acquired the European operations of Jacobs Suchard AG, the Swiss-based coffee and candy producer, in order to strengthen its competitive position there. Sara Lee, already the second-largest coffee roaster in Europe (with a 14% market share), expanded its European sales base with the February 1991 acquisition of a 51% interest in Compack Trading and Packing Company, Hungary's third-largest food company and that country's largest coffee roaster. Other similar moves by U.S. food companies are likely to follow.

Restructuring also will continue to be a predominant theme in 1991 and beyond. Most food companies are still reversing past "diworseification" efforts by shedding non-strategic businesses and ridding themselves of marginally profitable lines in order to focus on building unit sales of core businesses. Examples include Campbell Soup's ongoing restructuring efforts, which have included the divestiture of certain low-return businesses, as well as plant closings and personnel reductions; Borden's aggressive two-and-a-half-year, $650 million worldwide program of plant construction, modernization, and consolidation (estimated to be completed in 1992); and Quaker Oats' recent spinoff of its troubled Fisher-Price toy business.

Capital spending for the food group is likely to remain heavy in 1991, as companies make further strides toward

Wholesale food price indexes
(1982 = 100)

Food group	1985	1986	1987	1988	1989	1990
Meats	90.9	93.9	100.4	99.9	104.8	116.9
Poultry	110.4	116.7	103.4	111.4	120.8	113.6
Fish	114.6	124.9	140.0	151.7	144.3	148.6
Eggs	95.6	99.5	87.6	88.6	119.6	117.6
Dairy	100.2	99.9	101.6	102.2	110.6	117.2
Fats & oils	124.0	103.3	103.9	118.9	116.6	123.2
Proc. fruits & veg.	108.0	104.9	108.6	113.8	120.0	124.8
Sugar & sweets	107.9	109.6	112.6	114.6	120.1	123.1
Cereal & bakery prods.	110.3	111.0	112.6	122.9	131.1	134.1
Beverages	107.7	114.5	112.5	114.3	118.3	120.8
All food	103.9	105.5	107.8	111.5	117.7	123.2
Industrial commodities	103.7	99.9	102.5	106.3	111.6	115.8

Source: Department of Labor.

lowering production costs through plant and equipment upgrades (including expansion of plant capacities) and the development and installation of the latest technology. Promotional spending also is likely to remain high, as companies try to build unit sales of core, branded offerings through product enhancement and line extensions.

According to *Gorman's New Product News*, 10,301 new food products were introduced in 1990, up more than 12% from 1989 levels. Of the 15 food categories tracked, ranging from soups to pet foods, 11 registered increases in new products, while only four showed declines. Categories posting the greatest percentage gain in new products were baking ingredients and processed meat, while those showing the greatest decline in new product activity were baby foods and desserts. New product activity is expected to flourish again in 1991, as the food group, still burdened by substantial debt loads from the 1980s, will again emphasize internal growth over growth by acquisition.

Demographic changes bring opportunities

In keeping with changes in the modern American lifestyle—two-wage-earner families and minimal time devoted to food preparation at home—microwave oven penetration of U.S. households increased from about 35% in 1985 to more than 80% in 1990. The pervasiveness of the microwave oven has created an increasing demand for high-quality microwavable foods. In order to satisfy this demand, companies have introduced a variety of new food products specifically designed for preparation in microwave ovens, and sales

*U.S. population projections

Age group	1990 Number (thou.)	1990 % of total	1995 Number (thou.)	1995 % of total	2000 Number (thou.)	2000 % of total
Under 5 yrs.	18,408	7.4	17,799	6.9	16,898	6.3
5 to 14 yrs.	35,662	14.3	37,606	14.5	37,334	13.9
15 to 19 yrs.	17,381	7.0	17,529	6.8	19,074	7.1
20 to 24 yrs.	18,482	7.4	17,275	6.7	17,394	6.5
25 to 29 yrs.	21,386	8.6	18,841	7.3	17,611	6.6
30 to 34 yrs.	22,342	8.9	21,825	8.4	19,341	7.2
35 to 39 yrs.	20,172	8.1	22,196	8.6	21,772	8.1
40 to 44 yrs.	17,655	7.1	20,070	7.7	22,069	8.2
45 to 49 yrs.	13,941	5.6	17,482	6.7	19,879	7.4
50 to 54 yrs.	11,539	4.6	13,807	5.3	17,337	6.5
55 to 64 yrs.	21,363	8.5	21,324	8.2	24,158	9.0
65 Yrs. & over	31,560	12.6	33,764	13.0	34,882	13.0
All Ages	249,891	100.0	259,518	100.0	267,749	100.0

*Includes Armed Forces abroad.
Source: Department of Commerce, Population Series P-25.

Selected foods shipments

(In millions of dollars)

Title	1989 Mil. $	1989 % of total	1990 Mil. $	1990 % of total	% chg.
Meat products	80,099	38.6	88,628	39.2	10.6
Meat packing	45,739	22.0	49,831	22.0	8.9
Prepared meats	15,786	7.6	18,514	8.2	17.3
Poultry	18,574	9.0	20,284	9.0	9.2
Dairy products	43,370	20.9	48,471	21.4	11.8
Butter	1,766	0.9	1,455	0.6	(17.6)
Cheese	11,785	5.7	14,009	6.2	18.9
Ice cream & frozen desserts	4,602	2.2	4,984	2.2	8.3
Fluid milk	18,778	9.1	20,831	9.2	10.9
Fruits & vegetables	40,400	19.5	42,806	18.9	6.0
Canned specialties	4,967	2.4	5,276	2.3	6.2
Dried fruits & veg. & soups	2,607	1.3	2,490	1.1	(4.5)
Pickles, sauces & dressings	5,207	2.5	5,531	2.4	6.2
Frozen fruits & veg.	7,170	3.5	7,490	3.3	4.5
Frozen specialties	5,985	2.9	6,465	2.9	8.0
Cereals & breakfast foods	6,415	3.1	6,876	3.0	7.2
Bakery products	22,733	11.0	24,256	10.7	6.7
Breads & cakes	14,470	7.0	15,372	6.8	6.2
Cookies & crackers	6,820	3.3	7,431	3.3	9.0
Frozen bakery products	1,443	0.7	1,453	0.6	0.7
Candy products	7,825	3.8	8,240	3.6	5.3
Processed fish	6,645	3.2	6,800	3.0	2.3
TOTAL FOOD PRODUCTS	207,487	100.0	226,077	100.0	9.0

Source: U.S. Department of Commerce.

Per capita food consumption, by food group

(Index, 1982 = 100)

	1985	1986	1987	1988	1989
Meats	103.6	101.4	97.1	98.6	95.4
Fish	117.1	117.9	126.8	130.1	127.6
Poultry	109.8	113.6	122.9	126.9	134.4
Eggs	96.1	95.5	95.8	92.5	88.7
Dairy products	106.6	106.1	107.7	104.5	101.7
Fats & oils	110.1	110.1	106.7	105.6	103.8
Fresh fruits	102.6	108.4	113.3	112.7	110.3
Dried & frozen fruits & juices	110.0	117.3	110.2	110.4	104.0
Fresh vegetables	106.4	106.4	112.0	115.9	119.6
Potatoes	106.6	108.5	108.8	106.2	108.7
Wheat flour	106.5	107.3	110.8	110.8	105.1
Rice & pasta	92.3	105.0	114.9	119.9	129.0
Sugar & sweeteners	102.0	101.4	103.8	104.3	104.5

Source: Department of Agriculture.

of these products have skyrocketed. For example, the total U.S. microwave popcorn market, according to estimates from Golden Valley Microwave Foods, is now about $1 billion annually. According to data compiled by independent grocery research firms, sales in 1990 also rose in the market for other microwave foods—sales of frozen microwave breakfast foods exceeded $790 million; frozen microwave sandwiches, $250 million; and frozen microwave french fries, $40 million. The widespread increase in the number of microwave ovens in home kitchens is not exclusively a U.S. phenomenon. In 1990, microwave oven penetration in Canada and the U.K. was approximately 50%, while penetration in Japan was about 65%.

Another major recent demographic development is the growth in the number of people aged 25 to 40. These so-called baby boomers are demanding foods that taste good, are more nutritious, and are lower in calories, salt, and

cholesterol. It is not surprising that one of the most successful food products of recent times has been ConAgra's *Healthy Choice* line of "healthy" frozen entrees, which capitalized on both increased health consciousness and the use of microwave ovens. With the many products that are emulating *Healthy Choice*, the frozen entree category should continue to grow at least modestly, further propelled by the fact that the number of people 65 or older—who demand convenience and nutritionally-balanced meals—is projected to increase at more than twice the rate of the total population.

Aside from frozen foods, other food offerings touting health benefits continue to proliferate. Kraft General Foods, for example, achieved impressive success in 1990 with its no-fat salad dressings and no-fat versions of *Sealtest* ice cream and *Entenmann's* baked goods, among other things. Other new products launched in 1990 aimed at healthier eating include Hunt-Wesson's *Lite Shortening* and Smucker's *Light Fruit Spreads*, as well as numerous reduced-calorie salad dressings and low-sugar, low-salt peanut butter.

FDA cracking down on health claims

While the U.S. food industry keeps rolling out new, allegedly healthier products, the Food & Drug Administration (FDA)—the federal agency that, among other things, monitors advertising claims—is busy trying to keep the industry honest. After receiving numerous complaints from consumers and trade groups about the use of the term "fresh" on food products that are made with heat-treated ingredients or ingredients that have been concentrated and then reconstituted, the FDA asked the food industry to refrain from "any new or increased" use of the term "fresh" on the labeling of processed foods until it can devise a regulation defining the use of that term. Under its new Commissioner, David Kessler, the FDA has assumed a decidedly more aggressive stance. In one recent well-publicized victory, the FDA succeeded in forcing Procter & Gamble to remove the word "fresh" from its *Citrus Hill Fresh Choice* orange juice packaging, after U.S. marshals seized an allegedly mislabeled *Citrus Hill* shipment in a suburban Minneapolis warehouse. The FDA said P&G had misled consumers with its freshness claims because its juice is made from concentrate.

Shortly thereafter, Ragu Foods, bowing to intensified pressure from the FDA, agreed to stop using the term "fresh" or any other language suggesting that its sources are fresh. Other similar agreements are in the offing. The FDA is currently negotiating with several other companies over their freshness claims to ensure that "no company has any marketing advantage over another by promoting its product as something it is not." In 1963, the FDA published an order with definitions and standards of identity for orange juice and orange juice products. Recently, the agency said it expected to issue in the near future a proposed regulation on use of the term "fresh" on food labels. Until then, however, the agency said it would make case-by-case decisions as to whether the term is misleading.

According to marketing experts, the two most effective marketing pitches for foods are claims that it is "fresh" and has "no cholesterol." It is little wonder, then, that the next marketing puffery on the FDA's hit list was the "no cholesterol" claim made for certain kinds of high-fat products, including cooking oils. In mid-May, the FDA notified Procter & Gamble, CPC International, and Great Foods of America that the no-cholesterol boasts and depiction of a heart on their product labels were deceptive, as consumers could mistakenly believe that such products by themselves

benefit the heart and overall health. In fact, proponents say, such products are 100% fat, which is generally considered to contribute to an unhealthy diet. These actions may be just the tip of an iceberg, however, as consumers are increasingly demanding more honest health claims and more descriptive product labeling on the food products they purchase.

Snack foods gain popularity

Despite the trend toward greater demand for nutritious and low-calorie entrees, the demand for sweet snack products, notably cookies, crackers, and candy and other confectionery products, has risen consistently in recent years. This paradoxical development seems to indicate to market researchers that consumers, while increasingly concerned about the importance of a healthy diet, also enjoy rewarding themselves occasionally by indulging in foods that, although not especially good for them, nevertheless provide eating satisfaction.

The cookies and crackers segment, according to the Commerce Department, regularly records increased consumption. In 1990, estimated combined per-capita consumption rose a brisk 4.0%. One explanation for the phenomenon is the increase in the demographic group of 35 to 54 year-olds,

who, according to the Bureau of Labor Statistics, regularly spend more on bakery products than any other group. Also, cookie and cracker manufacturers are increasingly targeting new premium-brand cookies toward health-conscious consumers, by using honey and fruit juices as alternative sweeteners to sugar, and replacing tropical oils and white flour with soybean oil and whole wheat flour. Per-capita consumption of all types of candy was forecast by the Commerce Department to rise 1.5% in 1990. Per-capita growth for candy and other confectionery products, however, has slowed a bit from the 2.3% annual rates recorded in the 1980s, reflecting, in part, the gradual aging of the U.S. population.

Fiber still lures consumers

Adding confusion to the already numerous conflicting claims made by various groups on the potential benefits of oat bran, a new study conducted by a team of Chicago scientists offered further evidence that oat bran does, in fact, lower blood cholesterol. The study, published in April in the *Journal of the American Medical Association*, found that 2 ozs. to 3 ozs. of oat bran added daily for six weeks to the diets of subjects with high cholesterol could lower

---

What's in a name?

Branded product manufacturers have been in the forefront of acquisition activity in recent years for one important reason: recognizable quality sells products, and products that sell well generate predictable cash flows. Because the U.S. food market has reached maturity, real growth for any one company is primarily attained by increasing its share of the market, and strong brand franchises are an important means to that end.

A strong brand position and the consumer loyalty it generates have numerous benefits: pricing flexibility and leverage, improved chances of success for subsequent new products, and greater production efficiencies.

Pricing flexibility is perhaps the most important factor. If brand loyalty is substantial, prices can be raised without a serious decline in volume or market share. While strong market share does not necessarily confer brand loyalty, a correlation does exist. Brand loyalty also depends on how proprietary the product is. Certain food categories— ready-to-eat cereals, frozen foods, baked goods, and condiments, for example—have a high degree of product differentiation, while brands in such categories as canned goods, bread, and milk are more interchangeable.

A strong market position also can affect pricing leverage *vis-à-vis* the food retailer and wholesaler. A retailer does not have an advantage in bargaining on price for such products as CAMPBELL's soups, HEINZ ketchup, GERBER baby foods, or KELLOGG's cereals: failing to stock these products would alienate many customers.

A good market position for a particular branded product that sells well and offers good margins to the retailer can improve the chances of success for a product line extension or an entirely new product, both of which are important avenues of growth for manufacturers. Many new products fail not because of consumer resistance to the product, but rather because they are not adequately displayed in the grocery store. Recognition of the company's umbrella brand is a factor in consumer acceptance. New product introductions also benefit from an existing national distribution network, since new items can be introduced more cheaply and quickly. A major benefit of national distribution is the ability to efficiently use television network advertising, where volume-based discounts are generous.

At the same time, secondary brands have experienced a steady erosion of their franchise with retailers, who are striving to reduce inventories, and with consumers, who are offered private-label and generic products at prices that make it difficult for secondary brands to compete. Therefore, packaged food companies try to develop a strong consumer loyalty to their branded products through a high level of advertising and promotional support. This support is usually greater for new products than for established brands, but conditions sometimes dictate a reversal of these priorities. Support for established brands depends on competitive conditions in their individual markets, the opportunity to increase share or expand growth for the category, and the availability of funds. When earnings are strong, support tends to be increased.

Finally, well-known brand names can generate production efficiencies as market share and volume expand. Greater volume generally reduces the fixed overhead costs of unit production and distribution to the benefit of operating margins. In fact, growth can snowball as greater volume leads to lower prices, which in turn generate additional volume. The benefits of production efficiencies are not, however, as great for packaged food companies as food processors. Since processors limit their business to the initial stages of production—soybean crushing, flour milling, corn refining, or meat packaging—their fixed, or capital, costs as a percent of sales tend to be higher.

About 40% of all food manufacturers' shipments are branded packaged goods, 25% are sold to other food processors and manufacturers of diverse consumer products, and 33% are sold to foodservice operations. Secondary manufacturers and foodservice firms traditionally have competed on the basis of price and service, but as the number of food manufacturers contracts, more competitive markets have forced a higher level of ad spending and promotion spending for such traditionally undifferentiated products as red meats, poultry, fish, and dairy. ■

cholesterol levels by 7% to 10%. The study contradicted a much-publicized earlier study, conducted by researchers at Brigham and Women's Hospital in Boston and published in *The New England Journal of Medicine*, which concluded that "oat bran has little cholesterol-lowering effect" and that "high-fiber and low-fiber dietary grain supplements reduce serum cholesterol levels about equally, probably because they replace dietary fats." The Chicago study team, however, found that the reduction in serum cholesterol levels can be attributed to the independent effect of beta-glucan, found in oat bran, rather than fat calorie substitution.

Regardless of who is right, it is clear that, even in the midst of such conflicting health claims, oat bran and other fiber-based food products are still very popular among consumers. Whether found in breakfast cereals, breads, bake mixes, or even in pretzels, most consumers have acknowledged at least the digestive benefits of fiber foods, and find enough variety of texture and flavor to prevent appetite boredom. Although the cholesterol-reducing benefit will surely be debated for years to come, current findings have convinced millions of people that high-fiber products can reduce blood serum cholesterol. Food processors, therefore, will continue to roll out ever-increasing numbers of new fiber-based products. ■

COMMODITIES

Prices likely to ease further in '91

After easing considerably in 1989 and 1990, commodities prices are expected to fall somewhat moderately again in 1991, as the combined effect of stable consumption, increased production, and higher stock levels should push prices slightly lower. Exports, after rising 12% in 1989, leveled off in 1990, and may edge nominally lower in 1991, due mainly to lower prices from coarse grains and oilseeds, and a smaller volume of wheat shipments. The Soviet Union's ability to obtain credit to purchase U.S. commodities will significantly affect U.S. exports in 1991.

WHEAT

World wheat production is expected to be down about 6% in 1991, to 554.5 million metric tons, with U.S. curtailments accounting for almost 50% of the decrease. The U.S. Department of Agriculture (USDA) projects U.S. winter wheat production this year at 1.5 billion bushels, a drop of 26% from 1990 levels and potentially the second-smallest crop of the past decade. The projected decline reflects reduced plantings resulting from a worldwide slump in wheat prices, as well as anticipated drops in harvested acres and crop yields. U.S. wheat farmers are expected to harvest only 40.5 million acres this year, down 19% from 1990, due mainly to drought damage in parts of Texas and extensive winter kill in the Pacific Northwest.

Yields are expected to average 36.9 bushels an acre, down 3.8 bushels from last year. Assuming average yields for spring wheat, overall U.S. wheat production in 1991 will likely total approximately 2.1 billion bushels, down about 25% from 1990. Further, the USDA expects Soviet wheat output in 1991 to fall 16 million metric tons, to 92 million tons, and sees substantial production declines for Canada, Australia, and Eastern Europe. However, the agency expects these declines to be partially offset by larger wheat crops from the European Community and India.

Wheat prices continued their downward slide from about

WHEAT PRICES
(In Cents Per Bushel; Quarterly Averages)

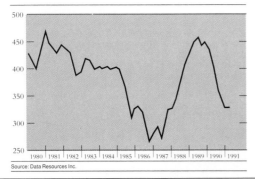

Source: Data Resources Inc.

SOYBEAN PRICES
(In Cents Per Bushel; Quarterly Averages)

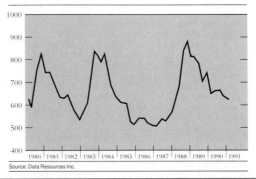

Source: Data Resources Inc.

CORN PRICES
(In Cents Per Bushel; Quarterly Averages)

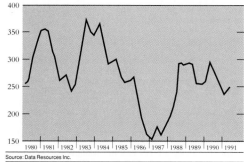

Source: Data Resources Inc.

WHOLESALE MEAT PRICES
(In Cents Per Pound; Quarterly Averages)

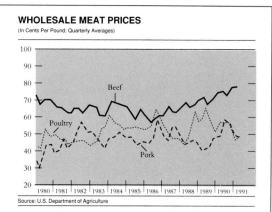

Source: U.S. Department of Agriculture

$3.50 a bushel a year ago, to $2.45 a bushel in February 1991. Prices have rebounded somewhat, to about $2.60 currently; this is probably due to the reduced U.S. plantings of spring wheat (down about 10%) and the assumption that the Soviets will receive credits to buy U.S. grain stocks. The USDA projects the average price per bushel of wheat will be $2.61 in 1991 and will range between $2.80 and $3.20 in 1992.

CORN

The 1990 U.S. corn harvest, estimated at 7.9 billion bushels, rose 5% from the high levels of 1989, and about 61% from the drought-reduced levels of 1988. With corn usage for 1990–91 expected to be off only slightly, carryover supplies should remain about unchanged at 1.4 billion bushels. Global corn output in 1991 is forecast to rise 2% to 471 million tons, with most of the gain coming from the U.S. and China. Drought will remove South Africa from the corn export market and could possibly make the country a net importer for the first time since 1985. U.S. corn exports and outstanding shipments are currently about 25% behind a year ago; sales are up to Eastern Europe, but are lagging to the USSR, Mexico, South Korea, and Japan.

Larger U.S. plantings this spring are expected to result in a crop of 8.3 billion bushels in 1991, up about 5% from last year. While both domestic usage and exports are projected to be above 1990–91 levels, overall usage will still be less than production, which will raise carryover into 1992 by 16%. With mid-1991 prices averaging about $2.30 per bushel, down slightly from about $2.35 a year ago, corn prices are expected to remain in the range of $2.25 to $2.35 per bushel in 1991, due largely to competition from low world wheat prices. (Livestock producers have been using wheat as a substitute for coarse grains in feed rations.)

SOYBEANS

Soybean prices as of mid-1991 were averaging $5.65 a bushel, about the same level as a year ago, but down substantially from $7.22 during the summer of 1989. Much of the price drop over the last two years followed more-normal yields and higher-than-expected ending stocks. The current USDA forecast places season-average soybean prices between $5.50 and $5.90 a bushel, as a number of conflicting factors help keep prices stable. For example, while U.S.

soybean ending-stock estimates have been revised upward to 360 million bushels, total global oilseed stocks remain near long-term norms. And although U.S. plantings in 1991 are below a year earlier and this spring's South American soybean crop is expected to be below last season's, world-wide supplies of alternative oilseeds remain plentiful.

U.S. soybean production in 1990 totaled 1.92 billion bushels, unchanged from a year ago, but 24% above the drought-stricken levels of 1988. According to the USDA's *Prospective Plantings* report, farmers plan to sow 57.1 million acres of soybeans in 1991, down from 1990's 57.8 million. Prices are projected to settle in the range of $4.75 to $6.25 in 1991.

MEAT

Beef production in 1991 is expected to increase about 1% from a year ago, reflecting expanding commercial cattle slaughter and heavier average dressed-carcass weights. However, since slaughter this year has remained below original industry expectations, prices in 1991 should range higher than year-earlier levels, reaching $77 to $82 per cwt (hundredweight), up from $56 to $78 per cwt last year. Average per-capita beef consumption, which fell about one pound in 1990 to 67.8 pounds, should continue its decline, although only slightly.

Reaping most of the benefits of the flight from beef are broiler producers, who should see per-capita consumption in 1991 reaching 74.2 pounds, up from 70.1 pounds in 1990 and 67.1 pounds in 1989. Consumer appetite for chicken continues to grow, as the public responds to relatively lower broiler prices, the convenience of various forms of chicken, and health concerns. Production of broilers advanced more than 7% in 1990, and is expected to rise another 5% to 6% in 1991. This increased production, combined with lower levels of exports and competition from other types of meats, should drive chicken prices still somewhat lower in 1991, to $0.49 to $0.55 per pound versus $0.55 in 1990 and $0.59 in 1989.

Pork prices will likely hover between $50 and $55 per cwt during 1991's second half, down slightly from about $55 in mid-May and $59 a year ago, reflecting farmers' estimates that this year's hog slaughter may be up as much as 4% from last year. As a result of higher beef prices, per-capita consumption of pork is forecast at 50.7 pounds in 1991, almost a pound higher than last year's levels, but down from 1989's average of 52.0 pounds.

MILK PRICES
(Dollars Per Hundred Weight; Quarterly Averages)

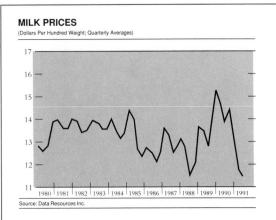

Source: Data Resources Inc.

DAIRY

After reaching a record of nearly $16 per cwt in early 1990 (due to the 1989 drought and the cheese sector's vigorous bidding for milk), prices have dropped dramatically, to about $11.30 currently, reflecting substantial increases in commercial production, large stocks, and weakened commercial use. (Commercial use has been constrained by the recession and continued high retail prices.) Milk prices are expected to average about $11.50 in 1991. Retail egg prices will likely average around 90 to 92 cents per dozen in 1991, significantly below the near record $1.01 a year ago. The projected price drop reflects a 1.6% increase in table-egg production in 1991's first quarter and an expected 1.0% increase in the second quarter.

Price/profit relationship complex

During 1988, when prices for corn and soybeans rose dramatically, the profits and stock prices of such big agricultural commodity users as Kellogg and General Mills were relatively unaffected. One explanation for this is that demand for food is relatively inelastic: when grain costs rise, food companies are usually able to pass the increases on to consumers. When grain prices fall back again, however, manufacturers do not necessarily lower prices, so gross profits expand.

Another reason for the lack of correlation between grain prices and company profits is that agricultural goods typically account for less than 25% of the total cost of bringing a product to market. Furthermore, today's complex products often contain a variety of fruits, vegetables, grains, and oils, the prices of which do not necessarily move in unison.

Food companies can also maintain profit margins by hedging their commodities purchases with futures contracts. This technique is not foolproof, however: futures contracts cannot hedge cost increases when commodities prices remain at high levels for the life of the contract (usually one year or less). As a result, price increases that last longer than one season will ultimately be absorbed by the company or passed on to the consumer. ■

6

Time Value of Money and Investment Applications

■ OVERVIEW

In the previous chapter, we discussed economic analysis and presented a short view of industry analysis along with a comprehensive example of an analysis of the food industry in Appendix 5–A. As Figure 5–1 illustrated, fundamental analysis starts with an analysis of the economy, moves to the industry, and finally to the company. An appropriate analysis also ends with a comparison of relative values between companies. One objective is to find undervalued companies and combine them into efficient portfolios.

The automobile industry is closely related to the economy, and several other industries such as rubber, steel, plastic, and lead are highly related to the automobile industry. To choose which automobile company is the most undervalued or "best purchase" or the most overvalued or "best sale," an analyst needs to know what the returns will be from each company and when these returns will occur.

Returns take the form of cash flows, and their timing is very important in determining both the rate of return and the current value of the returns. In Figure 1–4 and Table 1–2, we introduced various historical returns on a variety of investments such as Treasury bills, corporate bonds, common stock, oil, gold, and Chinese ceramics.

Before making an investment, the investor needs to calculate an expected rate of return on the investment, and to do this the investor needs to know the timing of the cash flows. For example, to determine the expected return from an investment in gold bullion, the investor needs to know the current cost of an ounce of gold; when it will be sold and at what expected price; the storage costs, insurance costs, and other costs of holding the gold; and any other expected cash inflows and outflows related to owning the gold.

In the case of a U.S. government bond, the investor needs to know the same type of data, but the forecasting of the cash flows is contractually known when the bond is bought. It will pay a guaranteed interest payment every six months, and at maturity it will repay the bondholder the $1,000 principal originally borrowed. The investor knows these cash flows in advance; therefore, calculating what the bond is worth is much easier than calculating the value of investments with unknown or highly risky cash flow streams.

In this chapter, we review the time value of money concept, which most of you were exposed to in financial management and accounting classes. Knowledge of money's time value is necessary to evaluate rates of return on investments and to determine the value of common stocks, bonds, and other assets presented in the following chapters. The concept that money's value is based on when the money will be received assumes that money can be invested to earn a rate of return greater than zero.

Many applications for the time value of money exist. Applications use either the compound sum (sometimes referred to as *future value*) or the present value. Additionally some cash flows are annuities. An **annuity** represents cash flows that are equally spaced in time and are constant dollar amounts. Car

payments, mortgage payments, and bond interest payments are examples of annuities. Annuities can either be present value annuities or compound sum annuities. In the next section, we present the concept of compound sum and develop common applications related to investments.

■ COMPOUND SUM

Compound Sum: Single Amount

In determining the **compound sum,** we measure the future value of an amount that is allowed to grow at a given rate over a period of time. Assume an investor buys an asset worth $1,000. This asset (gold, diamonds, art, real estate, etc.) is expected to increase in value by 10 percent per year, and the investor wants to know what it will be worth after the fourth year. At the end of the first year, the investor will have $1,000 × (1 + .10), or $1,100. By the end of year two, the $1,100 will have grown by another 10 percent to $1,210 ($1,100 × 1.10). The four-year pattern is indicated below.

1st year: $1,000 × 1.10 = $1,100
2nd year: $1,100 × 1.10 = $1,210
3rd year: $1,210 × 1.10 = $1,331
4th year: $1,331 × 1.10 = $1,464

After the fourth year, the investor has accumulated $1,464. Because compounding problems often cover a long time, a generalized formula is necessary to describe the compounding process. We shall let:

S = Compound sum
P = Principal or present value
i = Interest rate, growth rate, or rate of return
n = Number of periods compounded

The simple formula is:

$$S = P(1 + i)^n \qquad\qquad (6\text{--}1)$$

In the above example, the beginning amount, P, was equal to $1,000; the growth rate, i, equaled 10 percent; and the number of periods, n, equaled 4, so we get

$$S = \$1,000\ (1.10)^4,\ \text{or}\ \$1,000 \times 1.464 = \$1,464$$

The term $(1.10)^4$ is found to equal 1.464 by multiplying 1.10 four times itself. This mathematical calculation is called an exponential, where you take (1.10) to the fourth power. On your calculator, you would have an exponential key y^x where y represents (1.10) and x represents 4. For students with calculators, we have prepared Appendix E at the end of the book for both Hewlett-Packard and Texas Instruments calculators.

Table 6–1	Compound Sum of $1 ($S_{IF}$)						
Periods	**1%**	**2%**	**3%**	**4%**	**6%**	**8%**	**10%**
1	1.010	1.020	1.030	1.040	1.060	1.080	1.100
2	1.020	1.040	1.061	1.082	1.124	1.166	1.210
3	1.030	1.061	1.093	1.125	1.191	1.260	1.331
4	1.041	1.082	1.126	1.170	1.262	1.360	1.464
5	1.051	1.104	1.159	1.217	1.338	1.469	1.611
10	1.105	1.219	1.344	1.480	1.791	2.159	2.594
20	1.220	1.486	1.806	2.191	3.207	4.661	6.727
30	1.348	1.811	2.427	3.243	5.743	10.063	13.268

For those not proficient with calculators or who have calculators without financial functions, Table 6–1 is a shortened version of the compound sum table found in Appendix A. The table tells us the amount $1 would grow to if it were invested for any number of periods at a given rate of return. Using this table for our previous example, we find an interest factor for the compound sum in the row where $n = 4$ and the column where $i = 10$ percent. The factor is 1.464, the same as previously calculated. We multiply this factor times any beginning amount to determine the compound sum.

When using compound sum tables to calculate the compound sum, we shorten our formula from $S = P(1 + i)^n$ to:

$$S = P \times S_{IF} \qquad\qquad (6\text{–}2)$$

where S_{IF} equals the interest factor for the compound sum found in Table 6–1 or Appendix A. Using a new example, assume $5,000 is invested for 20 years at 6 percent. Using Table 6–1, the interest factor for the compound sum would be 3.207 and the total value would be:

$$S = P \times S_{IF} \ (n = 20, \ i = 6\%)$$
$$S = \$5,000 \times 3.207$$
$$S = \$16,035$$

Compound Sum: Annuity

Our previous example was a one-time single investment. Let us examine a **compound sum of an annuity** where constant payments are made at equally spaced periods and grow to a future value. The normal assumption for a compound sum of an annuity is that the payments are made at the end of each period, so the last payment does not compound or earn a rate of return.

Figure 6–1 demonstrates the timing and compounding process when $1,000 per year is contributed to a fund for four consecutive years. The $1,000 for each period is multiplied by the compound sum factors for the appropriate

Figure 6–1   Compounding Process for Annuity

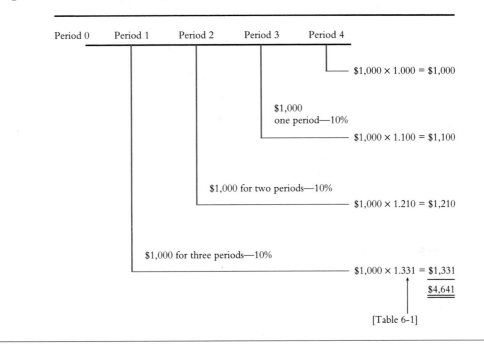

periods of compounding. The first $1,000 comes in at the end of the first period and has three periods to compound; the second $1,000 at the end of the second period, with two periods to compound; the third payment has one period to compound; and the last payment is multiplied by a factor of 1.00 showing no compounding at all.

Because compounding the individual values is tedious, compound sum of annuity tables can be used. These tables simply add up the interest factors from the compound sum tables for a single amount. Table 6–2 on page 200 is a shortened version of Appendix B, the compound sum of an annuity table showing the compound sum factors for each period and rate of return. Notice that all the way across the table, the factor in period one is 1.00. This reflects the fact that the last payment does not compound.

One example of the compound sum of an annuity applies to the individual retirement account (IRA) and Keogh retirement plans. The IRA allows workers to invest $2,000 per year in a tax-free account, and the Keogh allows a maximum of $30,000 per year to be invested in a retirement account for self-employed individuals. Assume Dr. Piotrowski shelters $30,000 per year from age 35 to 65. If she makes 30 payments of $30,000 and earns a rate of return of 8 percent, her Keogh account at retirement would be over $3 million.

Periods	1%	2%	3%	4%	6%	8%	10%
1	1.000	1.000	1.000	1.000	1.000	1.000	1.000
2	2.010	2.020	2.030	2.040	2.060	2.080	2.100
3	3.030	3.060	3.091	3.122	3.184	3.246	3.310
4	4.060	4.122	4.184	4.246	4.375	4.506	4.641
5	5.101	5.204	5.309	5.416	5.637	5.867	6.105
10	10.462	10.950	11.464	12.006	13.181	14.487	15.937
20	22.019	24.297	26.870	29.778	36.786	45.762	57.275
30	34.785	40.588	47.575	56.085	79.058	113.280	164.490

Table 6–2   Compound Sum of an Annuity of $1 (SA_{IF})

$$S = R \times SA_{IF} \ (n = 30, \ i = 8\% \ return) \qquad (6\text{--}3)$$
$$S = \$30,000 \times 113.280$$
$$S = \$3,398,400$$

While this seems like a lot of money in today's world, we need to measure what it will buy 30 years from now after inflation is considered. One way to examine this is to calculate what the $30,000 payments would have to be if they only kept up with inflation. Let's assume inflation of 3 percent over the next 30 years and recalculate the sum of the annuity.

$$S = R \times SA_{IF} \ (n = 30, \ i = 3\% \ inflation)$$
$$S = \$30,000 \times 47.575$$
$$S = \$1,427,250$$

To maintain the purchasing power of each $30,000 contribution, Dr. Piotrowski needs to accumulate $1,427,250 at the estimated 3 percent rate of inflation. Since her rate of return of 8 percent is 5 percentage points higher than the inflation rate, she is adding additional purchasing power to her portfolio.

■ PRESENT VALUE CONCEPT

Present Value: Single Amount

The **present value** is the exact opposite of the compound sum. A future value is discounted to the present. For example, earlier we determined the compound sum of $1,000 for four periods at 10 percent was $1,464. We could reverse the process to state that $1,464 received four years from today is worth only $1,000 today if one can earn a 10 percent return on money during the four years. This $1,000 value is called its present value. The relationship is depicted in Figure 6–2.

Figure 6–2   Relationship of Present Value and Compound Sum

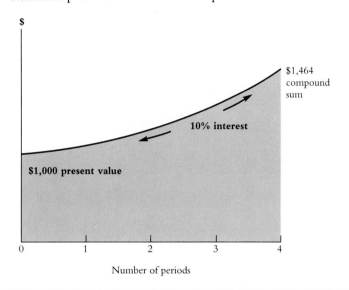

The formula for present value is derived from the original formula for the compound sum. As the following two formulas demonstrate, the present value is simply the inverse of the compound sum.

$$S = P(1 + i)^n \text{ Compound sum}$$
$$P = S \times 1/(1 + i)^n \text{ Present value} \tag{6-4}$$

The present value can be determined by solving for a mathematical solution to the above formula, or by using Table 6–3, the present value of $1. When we use Table 6–3, the present value interest factor $1/(1 + i)^n$ is found in the table and represented by PV_{IF}. We substitute it into the formula above.

$$P = S \times PV_{IF} \tag{6-5}$$

Let's demonstrate that the present value of $1,464, based on our assumptions, is worth $1,000 today.

$$P = S \times PV_{IF} \ (n = 4, \ i = 10\%) \text{ Table 6-3 or Appendix C}$$
$$P = \$1,464 \times 0.683$$
$$P = \$1,000$$

Present value becomes very important in determining the value of investments. Assume you think a certain piece of land will be worth $500,000 ten years from now. If you can earn a 10 percent rate of return on investments of similar risk, what would you be willing to pay for this land?

Periods	1%	2%	3%	4%	6%	8%	10%
Table 6–3	**Present Value of $1 (PV_{IF})**						
1	0.990	0.980	0.971	0.962	0.943	0.926	0.909
2	0.980	0.961	0.943	0.925	0.890	0.857	0.826
3	0.971	0.942	0.915	0.889	0.840	0.794	0.751
4	0.961	0.924	0.888	0.855	0.792	0.735	0.683
5	0.951	0.906	0.863	0.822	0.747	0.681	0.621
10	0.905	0.820	0.744	0.676	0.558	0.463	0.386
20	0.820	0.673	0.554	0.456	0.312	0.215	0.149
30	0.742	0.552	0.412	0.308	0.174	0.099	0.057

$$P = S \times PV_{IF} \ (n = 10, \ i = 10\%)$$
$$P = \$500{,}000 \times 0.386$$
$$P = \$193{,}000$$

This land's present value to you today would be $193,000. What would you have 10 years from today if you invested $193,000 at a 10 percent return. For this answer, we go to the compound sum factor from Table 6–1.

$$S = P \times IF_s \ (n = 10, \ i = 10\%)$$
$$S = \$193{,}000 \times 2.594$$
$$S = \$500{,}642$$

The compound sum would be $500,642. The two answers do not equal $500,000 because of the mathematical rounding used to construct tables with three decimal points. If we carry out the interest factors to four places, 0.386 becomes 0.3855 and 2.594 becomes 2.5937 and the two answers will be quite similar.

At the end of the compound sum of an annuity section, we showed that Dr. Piotrowski could accumulate $3,398,400 by the time she retired in 30 years. What would be the present value of this future sum if we brought it back to the present at the rate of inflation of 3 percent?

$$P = S \times PV_{IF} \ (n = 30, \ i = 3\%)$$
$$P = \$3{,}398{,}400 \times 0.412$$
$$P = \$1{,}400{,}141$$

The amount she will have accumulated will be worth $1,400,141 in today's dollars. If the rate of inflation averaged 6 percent over this time, the amount would fall to $591,322 ($3,398,400 × 0.174). Notice how sensitive the present value is to a 3 percentage point change in the inflation rate. Another concern

is being able to forecast inflation correctly. These examples are simply meant to heighten your awareness that money has a time value and financial decisions require this to be considered.

Present Value: Annuity

To find the **present value of an annuity,** we are simply finding the present value of an equal cash flow for several periods instead of one single cash payment. The analysis is the same as taking the present value of several cash flows and adding them. Since we are dealing with an annuity (equal dollar amounts), we can save time by creating tables that add up the interest factors for the present value of single amounts and make present value annuity factors. We do this in Table 6–4, a shortened version of Appendix D. Before using Table 6–4, let us compute the present value of $1,000 to be received each year for five years. We could use the present value of five single amounts and Table 6–3 as follows:

Period	Receipt	IF @ 6%	
1	$1,000 ×	0.943 =	$ 943
2	$1,000 ×	0.890 =	$ 890
3	$1,000 ×	0.840 =	$ 840
4	$1,000 ×	0.792 =	$ 792
5	$1,000 ×	0.747 =	$ 747
		4.212	$4,212 Present value

Another way to get the same value is to use Table 6–4. The present value annuity factor under 6 percent and 5 periods is equal to 4.212, or the same value we got from adding the individual present value factors for a single amount. We can simply calculate the answer as follows:

where:

A = the present value of an annuity,

R = the annuity amount, and

PV_{IFA} = represents the interest factor from Table 6–4.

$$A = R \times PV_{IFA} \ (n = 5, \ i = 6\%) \qquad (6\text{–}6)$$
$$A = \$1,000 \times 4.212$$
$$A = \$4,212$$

Present value of annuities applies to many financial products such as mortgages, car payments, and retirement benefits. Some financial products such as bonds are a combination of an annuity and a single payment. Interest payments from bonds are annuities, and the principal repayment at maturity is a single payment. Both cash flows determine the present value of a bond.

Table 6–4	Present Value of an Annuity of $1 (*PVA*$_{IF}$)						
Periods	**1%**	**2%**	**3%**	**4%**	**6%**	**8%**	**10%**
1	0.990	0.980	0.971	0.962	0.943	0.926	0.909
2	1.970	1.942	1.913	1.886	1.833	1.783	1.736
3	2.941	2.884	2.829	2.775	2.673	2.577	2.487
4	3.902	3.808	3.717	3.630	3.465	3.312	3.170
5	4.853	4.713	4.580	4.452	4.212	3.993	3.791
8	7.652	7.325	7.020	6.773	6.210	5.747	5.335
10	9.471	8.983	8.530	8.111	7.360	6.710	6.145
20	18.046	16.351	14.877	13.590	11.470	9.818	8.514
30	25.808	22.396	19.600	17.292	13.765	11.258	9.427

Present Value: Uneven Cash Flow

Many investments are a series of uneven cash flows. For example, buying common stock generally implies an uneven cash flow from future dividends and the sale price. We hope to buy common stock in companies that are growing and have increasing dividends. Assume you want to purchase Caravan Motors common stock on January 1, 1993. You expect to hold the stock for five years and then sell it at $60 in December 1997. You also expect to receive dividends of $1.60, $2.00, $2.00, $2.50, and $3.00 during those five years.

What would you be willing to pay for the common stock if your required return on a stock of this risk is 14 percent. Let's set up a present value analysis for an uneven cash flow using Appendix C, the present value of a single amount. Since this is not an annuity, each cash flow must be evaluated separately. For simplicity, we assume all cash flows come at the end of the year. Also, the cash flow in 1997 combines the dividend and expected $60 sale price.

Year	Cash Flow	*PV*$_{IF}$ 14%	Present Value
1993	$ 1.60	0.877	$ 1.40
1994	$ 2.00	0.769	$ 1.54
1995	$ 2.00	0.675	$ 1.35
1996	$ 2.50	0.592	$ 1.48
1997	$63.00	0.519	$32.70
Present value of Caravan Motors under these assumptions.			$38.47

If you were satisfied that your assumptions were reasonably accurate, you would be willing to buy Caravan at any price equal to or less than $38.47. This price will provide you with a 14 percent return if all your forecasts come true. But there are plenty of chances for errors. First, you can incorrectly forecast the dividends and/or more importantly the stock price, which is where most

of your estimated value comes from. Also, you could mistakenly estimate your required rate of return of 14 percent by not judging risk appropriately. The required rate of return is sometimes called the *discount rate;* that is, the rate used to determine the present value. Since the present value is always less than the future value, it is said that the future value is "discounted" or brought back to the present by using a discount rate.

■ REVIEW OF RISK AND REQUIRED RETURN CONCEPTS

Before moving to Chapter 7, it would be helpful to review and consolidate the concepts of risk and required return presented in Chapter 1. Calculation of the required rate of return is extremely important because it is the rate at which future cash flows are discounted to reach a valuation. An investor needs to know required rate of return on the various risk class of assets to reach intelligent decisions to buy or sell.

Chapter 1 examined rates of returns for various assets and returns based on Ibbotson and Associates data and explained how the risk-free rate on Treasury bills is a function of both the real rate of return and an inflation premium. The required return was a function of the risk-free rate plus a risk premium for a specific investment.

In this section, we develop a simple methodology based on the capital asset pricing model for determining a required rate of return when valuing common stocks in a diversified portfolio. First, we determine the risk-free rate. The **risk-free rate** (R_F) is a function of the real rate of return and the expected rate of inflation. Some analysts express the risk-free rate as simply the addition of the real rate of return and the expected rate of inflation, while a more accurate answer is found as follows:

$$(6–7)$$

$$R_F \text{ (risk-free rate)} = (1 + \text{Real rate})(1 + \text{Expected rate of inflation}) - 1$$

We now add a risk component to the risk-free rate to determine K_e, the total **required rate of return.** We show the following relationships.

$$K_e = R_F + b (K_M - R_F) \qquad (6–8)$$

where:

$$K_e = \text{Required rate of return}$$
$$R_F = \text{Risk-free rate}$$
$$b = \text{Beta coefficient}$$
$$K_M = \text{Expected return for common stocks in the market}$$
$$(K_M - R_F) = \text{Equity risk premium}$$

The risk-free rate, in practice, is normally assumed to be the return on U.S. Treasury bills. **Beta** measures individual company risk against the market risk (usually the S&P 500 Stock Index). Companies with betas greater than 1.00 have more risk than the market; companies with betas less than 1.00 have less

risk than the market; and companies with betas equal to 1.00 have the same risk as the market. It stands to reason then that high beta stocks ($b > 1.00$) would have higher required returns than the market.

The last term ($K_M - R_F$), the **equity risk premium,** is very difficult to observe because it represents the extra return or premium the stock market must provide compared to the rate of return an investor can earn on Treasury bills. If we observe the historical relationship between stocks and bills from Figure 1–4, we see that common stocks have returned an average of 10.1 percent over the 64-year period 1926 to 1990, and Treasury bills have returned an average of 3.7 percent over the same time.

This is a long period that included some extreme events such as the Depression of the 1930s and World War II. Nevertheless, it is a good starting point from which to begin our measurement. We will use an expected return on common stocks of 11 percent (slightly higher than the historical norm to reflect the strong market performance of the last decade). For the risk-free rate of return on Treasury bills, we shall use 5 percent. This also is a bit higher than the results from the Ibbotson data of the 64-year study, but keep in mind that data included interest rates of 1 to 2 percent during the Depression.

Let's compute a required rate of return for a sample company with a beta of 1.3. If the risk-free rate is 5 percent and the expected return in the market is 11 percent, we should have a required return as follows.

$$K_e = R_F + b\ (K_M - R_F)$$
$$K_e = 5\% + 1.3\ (11\% - 5\%)$$
$$K_e = 5\% + 1.3\ (6\%)$$
$$K_e = 5\% + 7.8\% = 12.8\%$$

K_e, the required rate of return, can now be used as a discount rate for future cash flows from an investment. This methodology will be helpful as you work through the dividend valuation models for common stock in Chapter 7.

The investor must understand that when investors are more risk averse (pessimistic), the equity risk premium ($K_M - R_F$) goes up, and when investors are less risk averse (optimistic), the premium is smaller. It should be clear that many variables affect required rates of return.

■ SUMMARY

This short chapter is intended to review the concepts of time value of money and risk-return considerations you may have encountered in previous courses. We relate the time value of money concepts to the analysis of cash flows found in the investment decisions. Examining the economy, industry, and company should lead to a valuation of the company's worth, and the present value of future cash flows is one of the most widely accepted methods of calculating value. This chapter links the evaluation of the economy and industry with the methodology involved with stock evaluation in Chapter 7.

Time value of money concepts are incomplete without an understanding of how the discount rate is developed. The capital asset pricing model (CAPM) is developed to show one way of calculating a required rate of return. The advantage of the CAPM is that it includes the major variables that influence required rates of return. These variables are the real rate of return, the expected inflation rate, the risk-free rate, the systematic risk (beta) of an individual company, and the equity risk premium. Using this model helps us understand the dynamic process involved in finding the appropriate rate of return for valuation purposes.

IMPORTANT WORDS AND CONCEPTS

annuity 196

compound sum 197

compound sum of an annuity 198

present value 200

present value of an annuity 203

risk-free rate 205

required rate of return 205

beta 205

equity risk premium 206

DISCUSSION QUESTIONS

1. How does the concept of a compound sum of an annuity differ from that of a compound sum of a single amount?
2. Why is it said that the concept of present value is the opposite of the concept of compound sum?
3. Why is the concept of present value important in determining the value of an investment?
4. Why does the valuation of stocks normally involve the present value of uneven cash flows?
5. How is the required rate of return (K_e) used in models to determine the valuation of future cash flows?
6. What can be said about the risk of firms that have betas greater than 1.0?
7. What is the equity risk premium? What happens to the equity risk premium when investors become pessimistic? What effect does this have on required rate of return and equity valuation?

PROBLEMS

Compound sum—single amount

1. Mike Donegan receives a bonus from his employer of $3,200. He will invest the money at a 12 percent rate of return for the next eight years. How much will he have after eight years?

Compound
sum—annuity

2. Sonny Outlook will invest $2,000 in an IRA at the end of each year for the next 40 years. With an anticipated rate of return of 11 percent, how much will the funds accumulate to after 40 years?

Present
value—single
amount

3. Barbara Samuels received a trust fund at birth that will be paid out to her at age 18. If the fund will accumulate to $400,000 by then and the discount rate is 9 percent, what is the present value of her future accumulation?

Present
value—annuity

4. Ross "The Hoss" Sullivan has just renewed his contract with the Chicago Bears for an annual payment of $3 million per year for the next eight years. The newspapers report the deal is worth $24 million. If the discount rate is 14 percent, what is the true present worth of the contract?

Present
value—uneven
cash flow

5. Joann Zinke buys stock in Collins Publishing Company. She will receive dividends of $2.00, $2.40, $2.88, and $3.12 for the next four years. She assumes she can sell the stock for $50 after the last dividend payment (at the end of four years). If the discount rate is 12 percent, what is the present value of the future cash flows? (Round all values to two places to the right of the decimal point.) The present value of future cash flows is assumed to equal the value of the stock.

Present
value—uneven
cash flow

6. Sherman Lollar wins a malpractice suit against his accounting professor and the judgment provides him with $3,000 a year for the next 40 years plus a single lump-sum payment of $10,000 after 50 years. With a discount rate of 10 percent, what is the present value of his future benefits?

Equity risk
premium

7. Assume $R_F = 6\%$, $K_M = 13\%$, $b = 1.2$. What is the value of K_e? What is the value of the equity risk premium?

Required rate of
return and value

8. If another stock had a $b = 0.8$, and the information was the same as that in Problem 7, what would K_e be? If both stocks had equal future cash flows, which would have a higher current value—the one with a beta of 1.2 or 0.8?

7

Valuation of the Individual Firm

Basic Valuation Concepts

Dividend Valuation Models
> General Dividend Model
>
> Constant Growth Model
>
> A Nonconstant Growth Model

Earnings Valuation Models
> The Combined Earnings and Dividend Model

The Price-Earnings Ratio
> The P/E Ratio for Individual Stocks
>
> The Pure, Short-Term Earnings Model
>
> Relating an Individual Stock's P/E Ratio to the Market

Other Valuation Models Using Average Price Ratios and 10-Year Averages

Forecasting Earnings per Share
> Least Squares Trendline
>
> The Income Statement Method

Growth Stocks and Growth Companies

Assets as a Source of Stock Value
> Natural Resources

Appendix 7–A: Sustainable Growth Model

We have been building the foundation for the valuation of the individual firm, which is depicted as the last major step of the valuation process in Figure 5–1. **Valuation** is based on economic factors, industry variables, and an analysis of the financial statements and the outlook for the individual firm. Valuation determines the long-run fundamental economic value of a specific company's common stock. In the process, we try to determine whether a common stock is undervalued, overvalued, or fairly valued relative to its market price. Furthermore, most of the orientation in this chapter is to long-run concepts of valuation rather than to determining short-term market pricing factors.

■ BASIC VALUATION CONCEPTS

The valuation of common stock can be approached in several ways. Some models rely solely on dividends expected to be received during the future, and these are usually referred to as **dividend valuation models.** A variation on the dividend model is the **earnings valuation model,** which substitutes earnings as the main income stream for valuation. Earnings valuation models may also call for the determination of a price-earnings ratio, or multiplier of earnings, to determine value. Some models rely on long-run historical relationships between market price and sales per share, or market price and book value per share. Other methods may include the market value of assets, such as cash and liquid assets, replacement value of plant and equipment, and other hidden assets, such as undervalued timber holdings. For the first part of our discussion, we develop the dividend valuation model and then move to earnings-related approaches. We conclude with a consideration of asset values.

■ DIVIDEND VALUATION MODELS

The value of a share of stock may be interpreted by the shareholder as the present value of an expected stream of future dividends. Although in the short run, stockholders may be influenced by a change in earnings or other variables, the ultimate value of any holding rests with the distribution of earnings in the form of dividend payments. Though the stockholder may benefit from the retention and reinvestment of earnings by the corporation, at some point, the earnings must generally be translated into cash flow for the stockholder.[1] While dividend valuation models are theoretical in nature and subject to many limitations, they are the most frequently used models in the literature of finance.

---

[1]Some exceptions to this principle are noted later in the chapter.

General Dividend Model

A generalized stock valuation model based on future expected dividends can be stated as follows:

$$P_0 = \frac{D_1}{(1 + K_e)^1} + \frac{D_2}{(1 + K_e)^2} + \frac{D_3}{(1 + K_e)^3} + \ldots + \frac{D_\infty}{(1 + K_e)^\infty} \quad (7\text{-}1)$$

where:

P_0 = Present value of the stock price

D_i = Dividend for each year, for example, 1, 2, 3 . . . ∞

K_e = Required rate of return (discount rate)

This model is very general and assumes the investor can determine the right dividend for each and every year as well as the annualized rate of return an investor requires.

Constant Growth Model

Rather than predict the actual dividend each year, a more widely used model includes an estimate of the growth rate in dividends. This model assumes a constant growth rate in dividends to infinity.

If a constant growth rate in dividends is assumed, Formula 7–1 can be expressed as:

$$P_0 = \frac{D_0(1 + g)^1}{(1 + K_e)^1} + \frac{D_0(1 + g)^2}{(1 + K_e)^2} + \frac{D_0(1 + g)^3}{(1 + K_e)^3} + \ldots + \frac{D_0(1 + g)^\infty}{(1 + K_e)^\infty} \quad (7\text{-}2)$$

where:

$D_0(1 + g)^1$ = Dividends in the initial year

$D_0(1 + g)^2$ = Dividends in year 2, and so on

g = Constant growth rate in the dividend

The current price of the stock should equal the present value of the expected stream of dividends. If we can correctly predict the growth of future dividends and determine the discount rate, we can ascertain the value of the stock.

For example, assume we wanted to determine the present value of ABC Corporation common stock based on this model. We shall assume ABC anticipates an 8 percent growth rate in dividends per share, and we use a 12 percent discount rate as the required rate of return. The required rate of return (discussed in Chapters 1 and 6) is intended to provide the investor with a minimum real rate of return, compensation for expected inflation, and a risk premium. Twelve percent is sufficient to fulfill that function in this example.

Rather than project the dividends for an extremely long period and then discount them back to the present, we can reduce previously presented Formula 7–2 to a more usable form:

$$P_0 = D_1/(K_e - g) \qquad\qquad (7\text{–}3)$$

This formula is appropriate as long as two conditions are met. The first is that the growth rate must be constant. For the ABC Corporation, we are assuming that to be the case. It is a constant 8 percent. Second, K_e (the required rate of return) must exceed g (the growth rate). Since K_e is 12 percent and g is 8 percent for the ABC Corporation, this condition is also met. Let's further assume D_1 (the dividend at the end of period 1) is $3.38.

Using Formula 7–3, we determine a stock value of:

$$
\begin{aligned}
P_0 &= D_1/(K_e - g) \\
&= \$3.38/(0.12 - 0.08) \\
&= \$3.38/0.04 \\
&= \$84.50
\end{aligned}
$$

This value, in theory, represents the present value of all future dividends. The meaning is further illustrated in Table 7–1, in which we take the present value of the first 20 years of dividends ($43.71) and then add in a figure of $40.79 to arrive at the present value of all future dividends of $84.50 as previously determined by Formula 7–3. The $40.79 value represents the present value of dividends occurring between 2013 and infinity (that is after the 20th year).

We must be aware that several things could be wrong with our analysis. First, our expectations of dividend growth may be too high for an infinite period. Perhaps 6 percent is a more realistic estimate of expected dividend growth. If we substitute our new estimate into Formula 7–3, we can measure the price effect as dividend growth changes from an 8 percent rate to a 6 percent rate.

$$
\begin{aligned}
P_0 &= \$3.38/(0.12 - .06) \\
&= \$3.38/0.06 \\
&= \$56.33
\end{aligned}
$$

A 6 percent growth rate (a 2 percent change) cuts the present value down substantially from the prior value of $84.50.

We could also misjudge our required rate of return, K_e, which could be higher or lower. A lower K_e would increase the present value of ABC Corporation, whereas a higher K_e would reduce its value. We have made these points to show how sensitive stock prices are to the basic assumptions of the model. Even though you may go through the calculations, the final value is only as accurate as your inputs. This is where a security analyst's judgment and expertise are important—in justifying the growth rate and required rate of return.

Table 7–1   Present Value Analysis of ABC Corporation

Year	Expected Dividends $g = 8\%$	Present Value Factor $K_e = 12\%\star$	Present Value of Dividends
1993	$ 3.38	.893	3.02
1994	3.65	.797	2.91
1995	3.94	.712	2.81
1996	4.26	.636	2.71
1997	4.60	.567	2.61
1998	4.97	.507	2.52
1999	5.37	.452	2.43
2000	5.80	.404	2.34
2001	6.26	.361	2.26
2002	6.76	.322	2.18
2003	7.30	.287	2.10
2004	7.88	.257	2.03
2005	8.51	.229	1.95
2006	9.19	.205	1.87
2007	9.93	.183	1.81
2008	10.72	.163	1.75
2009	11.58	.146	1.69
2010	12.51	.130	1.63
2011	13.51	.116	1.57
2012	14.59	.104	1.52
PV of dividends for years 1993–2012			43.71
PV of dividends for years 2013 to infinity			40.79
Total present value of ABC Common Stock			$84.50†

*Figures are taken from Appendix C at the end of this book.
†Notice that this value is the same as that found on the previous page using Formula 7–3.

A Nonconstant Growth Model

Many analysts do not accept the premise of a constant growth rate in dividends or earnings. As we examined in Chapter 5, industries go through a life cycle in which growth is nonlinear. Growth is usually highest in the infancy and early phases of the life cycle, and as expansion is reached, the growth rate slows until the industry reaches maturity. At maturity, a constant, long-run growth rate that approximates the long-run growth of the macro economy may be appropriate for a particular industry.

Some companies in an industry may not behave like the industry in general. Companies constantly try to avoid maturity or decline, and so they strive to develop new products and markets to maintain growth.

In situations where the analyst wants to value a company without the constant-growth assumption, a variation of the constant-growth model is possible. Growth is simply divided into several periods with each period having a present value. The present value of each period is summed to attain the total value of the firm's share price. An example of a two-period model may illustrate the concept. Assume that JAYCAR Corporation is expected to have the growth pattern shown in Figure 7–1.

It is assumed JAYCAR will have a dividend growth rate of 20 percent for the next 10 years and an 8 percent perpetual growth rate after that. JAYCAR's dividend is expected to be $1 next year, and the appropriate required rate of return (discount rate) is 12 percent. Taking the present value for the first 10 years of dividends and then applying the constant dividend growth model for years 11 through infinity, we can arrive at an answer. First, we find the present value of the initial 10 years of dividends.

Year	Dividends (20 Percent Growth)	PV Factor (12 Percent)*	Present Value of Dividends First 10 Years
1	$1.00	.893	$ .89
2	1.20	.797	.96
3	1.44	.712	1.03
4	1.73	.636	1.10
5	2.07	.567	1.17
6	2.48	.507	1.26
7	2.98	.452	1.35
8	3.58	.404	1.45
9	4.29	.361	1.55
10	5.15	.322	1.66
			$12.42

*Figures are taken from Appendix C at the end of this book.

We then determine the present value of dividends after the 10th year. The dividend in year 11 is expected to be $5.56, or $5.15 (for year 10) compounded at the new, lower 8 percent growth rate ($5.15 × 1.08). Since the rest of the dividend stream will be infinite, Formula 7–3 can provide the value of JAYCAR at the end of year 10, based on a discount rate of 12 percent and an expected growth rate of 8 percent.

$$P_{10} = D_{11}/(K_e - g)$$
$$= \$5.56/(.12 - .08)$$
$$= \$5.56/.04$$
$$= \$139$$

Figure 7–1   JAYCAR Growth Pattern

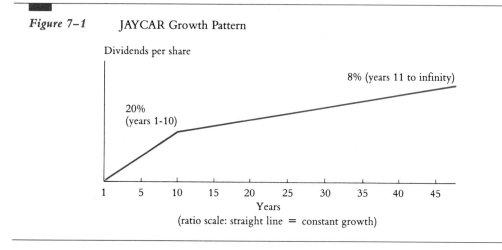

(ratio scale: straight line = constant growth)

An investor would pay $139 at the end of the 10th year for the future stream of dividends from year 11 to infinity. To get the present value of the 10th-year price, the $139 must be discounted back to the present by the 10-year PV factor for 12 percent from Appendix C (.322). This part of the answer is $139.00 × .322, or $44.76. The two parts of this analysis can be combined to get the current valuation per share of $57.18.

Present value of the dividends from years 1 to 10	$12.42
Present value of 10th year price ($139.00 × .322)	44.76
Total present value of JAYCAR common stock	$57.18

■ EARNINGS VALUATION MODELS

Dividend valuation models are best suited for companies in the expansion or maturity life cycle phase. Dividends of these companies are more predictable and usually make up a larger percentage of the total return than capital gains. Earnings-per-share models are also used for valuation. For example, the investor may take the present value of all future earnings to determine a value. This might be appropriate where the firm pays no cash dividend and has no immediate intention of paying one.

The Combined Earnings and Dividend Model

Another, more comprehensive valuation model relies on earnings per share (EPS) and a price-earnings ratio (earnings multiplier) combined with a finite

Table 7–2   Smucker Co. Corporation Present Value Analysis at Beginning of 1992

Part A: Present Value of Dividends for 5 Years

Year	(1) Estimated Earnings per Share (Growth=13%)	(2) Estimated Payout Ratio	=	(3) Estimated Dividends per Share	×	(4) Present Value Factor K_e (12%)	=	(5) Present Value of Dividends
1992	$1.36	.30		0.41		0.893		0.37
1993	1.54	.30		0.46		0.797		0.37
1994	1.74	.30		0.52		0.712		0.37
1995	1.97	.30		0.59		0.636		0.38
1996	2.23	.30		0.67		0.567		0.38
								$ 1.87

Part B: Present Value of Common Stock Price at End of 1993

Year	EPS	×	P/E =		Price	×	PV Factor	
1996	$2.23		18		$40.14		0.567	22.76
								$24.63

A + B = Total Present Value of Smucker Common Stock at Beginning of 1992

dividend model. The value of common stock can be viewed as a dividend stream plus a market price at the end of the dividend stream. Using J. M. Smucker Co. as an example, we develop a present value for the stock at the beginning of 1992. (The numbers are shown in Table 7–2.)

The total present value (stock price) for Smucker is shown at the bottom of Table 7–2 to be $24.63. Note that Part A of Table 7–2 describes the present value of the future dividends, while Part B is used to determine the present value of the future stock price. These are assumed to be the two variables that determine the current stock price under this model.

In Part A, earnings per share are first projected for the next five years. The earnings are then multiplied by the company's estimated payout ratio of 30 percent to determine anticipated dividends per share for those five years. In this example, we assume the required rate of return to be 12 percent. You need to recognize that this required rate will change continuously with market conditions. The present value of five years of dividends is shown in column (5) of Part A as $1.87.

In Part B, we multiply estimated 1996 earnings per share of $2.23 by the P/E ratio (earnings multiplier) of 18 to arrive at an anticipated price five years into the future. This price of $40.14 is then discounted for five years at 12 percent to arrive at a present value of $22.76. This present value of the stock is equal to the present value of the dividend stream for five years ($1.87) plus

the present value of the future stock price ($22.76) for a total current value of $24.63 at the beginning of 1992.

This model can be used with your choice of time periods. Five years is not a magic number. As the time period used increases, the estimate of earnings per share becomes more uncertain for cyclical companies, and the future stock price based on an earnings multiplier (P/E ratio) becomes a risky forecast. Some companies in industries such as utilities or pharmaceuticals have more predictable earnings streams than those in consumer-sensitive markets such as automobiles and durables, but they still may exhibit fluctuating P/E ratios. The next section develops the concept of the price–earnings ratio, which was used as the earnings multiplier in Table 7–2.

■ THE PRICE-EARNINGS RATIO

Mathematically, the **price-earnings ratio** (P/E) is simply the price per share divided by earnings per share, and it is ultimately set by investors in the market as they bid the price of a stock up or down in relation to its earnings. Price-earnings ratios are often expressed in the financial press as historical numbers using today's price divided by the latest 12-month earnings.

For companies with cyclical earnings, a P/E using the latest 12-month earnings might be misleading because these earnings could be high. If investors expect earnings to come back to a normal level, they will not bid the price up in relation to this short-term cyclical swing in earnings per share, and the P/E ratio will appear to be low. But if earnings are severely depressed, investors will expect a return to normal higher earnings, and the price will not fall an equal percentage with earnings, and the P/E will appear to be high. This was apparent in the automobile industry during 1991 and 1992. Prices of Ford and General Motors stock went up in early 1992 even as the companies announced losses because investors were anticipating an industry recovery during the summer of 1992.

In our Smucker example in Table 7–2, we used a P/E of 18 in 1996. This P/E ratio of 18 is determined by historical analysis and by other factors such as expected growth in earnings per share. The P/E of a company is also affected by the overall conditions in the stock market in general. At the time of this writing, Smucker had a P/E of 28, but its 5-year average P/E was 17.6× and its 10-year average high P/E was 18.7×. The 18 used in Table 7–2 is a judgment call.

Even though the current P/E ratio for a stock in the market is known, investors may not agree it is appropriate. Stock analysts and investors probably spend more time examining P/E ratios and assessing their appropriate level than any other variable. Although the use of P/E ratios in valuation approaches lacks the theoretical underpinning of the present value-based dividend and earnings valuation models previously discussed in the chapter, P/E ratios are equally important. The well-informed student of investments should have a basic understanding of both the theoretically based present value approach and the more pragmatic, frequently used P/E ratio approach.

What determines whether a stock should have a high or low P/E ratio? Let's first talk about the market for stocks in general, and then we will look at individual securities.

Stocks generally trade at a relatively high P/E ratio (perhaps 15 or greater) when there are strong growth prospects in the economy. However, inflation also plays a key role in determining P/E ratios for the overall market.

To illustrate the latter point, Figure 7–2 presents the relationship between the year-end Standard & Poor's 500 composite P/E ratio and the annual rate of inflation measured by the change in the consumer price index (CPI). The graphical relationship between these two variables shows they are inversely related. The price-earnings ratio goes down when the change in the CPI goes up, and the reverse is also true.

The dramatic drop in the P/E ratio in 1973–74 can be attributed in large measure to the rate of inflation increasing from 3.4 percent in 1972 to 12.2 percent in 1974, or a change of more than three times its former level. For a brief period in 1976, inflation decreased to an annual rate of less than 5 percent, only to soar to 13.3 percent by 1979. The average rate of inflation for 1982 was reduced to 3.8 percent, and the market responded by paying higher share prices for one dollar of earnings (that is, higher P/E ratios).

From 1983 through 1985, the consumer price index hovered around 3 to 4 percent, but in 1986, inflation subsided to 1.1 percent, and the S&P price-earnings ratio soared. In 1987, the S&P 500 P/E ratio remained high until the crash of October 1987 brought stock prices down to lower levels. During the sobering and risk-averse period after the crash, market prices were fairly stable.

As fears of higher inflation rose during 1989, the S&P 500 P/E ratio came back to the low-midrange of its 25-year history shown in Figure 7–2. As was pointed out in Chapter 1 and earlier in this chapter, required rates of return are directly influenced by the rate of inflation. As inflation increases, the required rate of return on common stocks, K_e, rises, and prices decline. This is the basic mechanism that causes inflation to influence P/E ratios. The higher price-earnings ratios in 1991 reflect both the impact of falling inflationary expectations and depressed earnings suffered by corporations during the recessionary period of 1990–91.

Other factors besides inflationary considerations and growth factors influence the P/E ratio for the market in general. Federal Reserve policy and interest rates, federal deficits, the government's leading indicators, the political climate, the mood and confidence of the population, international considerations, and many other factors affect the P/E ratio for the overall market. The astute analyst is constantly studying a multitude of variables in analyzing the future outlook for P/E ratios.

The P/E Ratio for Individual Stocks

Although the overall market P/E ratio is the collective average of individual P/Es, those factors that influence the market P/E do not necessarily affect P/E ratios of individual companies consistently from one industry to another. An

Figure 7–2   Inflation and Price-Earnings Ratios

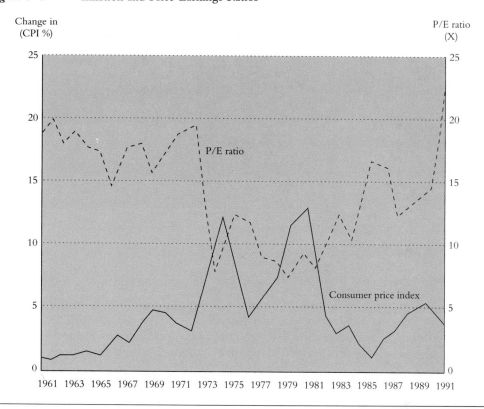

individual firm's P/E ratio is heavily influenced by its growth prospects and the risk associated with its future performance. Table 7–3 on page 220 shows examples of growth rates and P/E ratios for different industries and firms. Generally, a strong expected future growth rate for 1991–96 (column 4) is associated with a reasonably high P/E for late 1991 (column 6).

The relationship can be complicated by other considerations. For example, the publisher Dow Jones & Company shows a high P/E ratio of 31 in late 1991. This is associated with a modest 10 percent expected growth rate for EPS in 1991–96. This inconsistency is caused by Dow Jones's decline in EPS in both 1990 and 1991. Its slightly reduced price over an artificially low earnings base gives the appearance of a high P/E ratio. This high P/E ratio is phantom in nature and will work itself down to its more normal level of 20 as earnings improve.

In addition to the future growth of the firm and the risk associated with that growth, investors and analysts also consider a number of other factors that influence a firm's P/E ratio. These cannot be easily quantified, but they affect a broad range of stocks. Included in this category are the debt-to-equity ratio and the dividend policy of the firm. All things being equal, the less debt a firm has, the more likely it is to be highly valued in the marketplace.

Table 7–3   P/E and Growth in EPS

(1) Industry	(2) Company	(3) 5-Year EPS Growth, 1987–91	(4) Expected Growth in EPS, 1991–96	(5) Median P/E	(6) P/E Late 1991	(7) Expected Normal P/E
Appliances	Maytag	2.0%	7.0%	12.0×	15.4×	11.5×
Newspaper	Dow Jones	1.5	10.0	22.0×	31.4×	20.0×
Railroads	CSX	5.0	11.0	9.5×	12.2×	10.0×
Drugs	Bristol-Myers	11.5	16.0	15.0×	20.4×	20.0×
Fast foods	McDonald's	15.0	12.5	13.0×	13.7×	13.5×
Trucking	Roadway	2.0	10.5	13.0×	16.7×	14.0×
Tobacco	Philip Morris	23.0	22.0	9.5×	14.7×	12.0×
Brokerage	Merrill Lynch	−5.5	NMF	13.0×	8.5×	11.0×

NMF = Not meaningful data.
Source: Value Line Investment Survey, selected issues (Value Line Inc.).

The dividend policy is more elusive. For firms that show superior internal reinvestment opportunities, low cash dividends may be acceptable. But maturing companies may be expected to pay a high cash dividend. For the latter group, a reduction in cash dividends may be associated with a lower P/E ratio.

Certain industries also traditionally command higher P/E ratios than others. Investors seem to prefer industries that have a high technology and research emphasis. Thus, firms in computers, medical research and health care, and sophisticated telecommunications often have higher P/E ratios than the market in general. This does not mean firms in these industries represent superior investments, but merely that investors value their earnings more highly.[2] Also, fads and other factors can cause a shift in industry popularity. For example, because Ronald Reagan emphasized military strength, defense-oriented stocks were popular during his administration. Jimmy Carter stressed the need for environmental control, and stocks dealing in air and water pollution control traded at high P/E ratios during his tenure.

The quality of management as perceived by those in the marketplace also influences a firm's P/E ratio. If management is viewed as being highly capable, clever, or innovative, the firm may carry a higher P/E ratio. Investors may look to magazines such as *Forbes* or *Business Week,* which highlight management strategies by various companies, or to management-oriented books. Of course, it is possible that today's trendsetters may represent tomorrow's failures.

Not only is the quality of management important to investors in determining the firm's P/E ratio, but the quality of earnings is also. There are many

---

[2]William Kittrell, Geoffrey A. Hirt, and Roger Potter, "Price-Earnings Multiples, Investors' Expectations, and Rates of Return: Some Analytical and Empirical Findings" (Paper presented at the 1984 Financial Management Association meeting).

interpretations of a dollar's worth of earnings. Some companies choose to use very conservative accounting practices so their reported earnings can be interpreted as being very solid by investors (they may even be understated). Other companies use more liberal accounting interpretations to report maximum earnings to their shareholders, and they, at times, overstate their true performance. It is easy to see that a dollar's worth of conservatively reported earnings may be valued at a P/E ratio of 15 to 17 times, whereas a dollar's worth of liberally reported earnings should be valued at a much lower multiple.

All of these factors affect a firm's P/E ratio. Thus, investors will consider growth in sales and earnings, future risk, the debt position, the dividend policy, the quality of management and earnings, and a multitude of other factors in arriving at the P/E ratio. The P/E ratio, like the price of the stock, is set by the interaction of the forces of demand and supply. Those firms that are expected to provide returns greater than the overall economy, with equal or less risk, generally have superior P/E ratios.

The Pure, Short-Term Earnings Model

Often investors/speculators take a very short-run view of the market and ignore using present value analysis with its associated long-term forecasts of dividends and earnings per share. Instead, they only use earnings per share and apply an appropriate multiplier to compute the estimate value.

Applying this approach to Smucker's financial data initially presented in Table 7–2, we can arrive at a value of $24.48, based on a 1992 earnings estimate of $1.36 and a normal price-earnings ratio of 18.

$$P_0 = EPS_{1992} \times P/E_{normal}$$
$$= \$1.36 \times 18$$
$$P_{1992} = \$24.48^3$$

Every valuation method has its limitations. Although this method is simplified by ignoring dividends and present value calculations, earnings need to be correctly estimated, and the appropriate price-earnings (P/E) multiplier must be applied. Unfortunately, even if the estimated EPS is correct, you have no assurance that the market will agree with your P/E ratio. Since the normalized P/E used is 18 and the current P/E was 28, Smucker stock will appear overvalued.

Relating an Individual Stock's P/E Ratio to the Market

Smucker is the leading producer of jams, jellies, and preserves in the United States. The company also makes ice cream toppings, peanut butter, and syrups. While you may have tasted many of Smucker's products, you may not be familiar with the financial data presented in Table 7–4. This table provides a

---

[3]This value is not precisely the same as the price in Table 7–2, which was based on discounting future flows.

Table 7–4   Smucker Stock Valuation Data Table

Year	SPS	DPS	EPS	CFPS	BVPS	Stock Price High	Stock Price Low	P/E Ratio High	P/E Ratio Low	S & P 500 P/E Ratio High	S & P 500 P/E Ratio Low	Relative P/E Ratios High	Relative P/E Ratios Low
1982	$ 6.77	$0.09	$0.41	$0.52	$2.29	$ 4.70	$ 2.00	11.46	4.88	11.31	8.10	1.01	0.60
1983	$ 7.25	$0.11	$0.47	$0.59	$2.64	$ 5.80	$ 3.80	12.34	8.09	12.31	9.86	1.00	0.82
1984	$ 7.77	$0.13	$0.53	$0.69	$2.97	$ 7.00	$ 4.50	13.21	8.49	10.24	8.88	1.29	0.96
1985	$ 8.95	$0.15	$0.54	$0.74	$3.22	$12.90	$ 6.50	23.89	12.04	14.51	11.20	1.65	1.07
1986	$ 9.80	$0.16	$0.60	$0.83	$3.66	$12.50	$ 9.30	20.83	15.50	17.54	14.05	1.19	1.10
1987	$10.67	$0.19	$0.78	$1.05	$4.26	$15.00	$ 9.80	19.23	12.56	19.24	12.80	1.00	0.98
1988	$12.47	$0.23	$0.94	$1.27	$4.91	$15.70	$11.70	16.70	12.45	11.94	10.22	1.40	1.22
1989	$14.35	$0.28	$1.03	$1.38	$5.68	$19.50	$14.40	18.93	13.98	15.73	12.04	1.20	1.16
1990	$15.40	$0.35	$1.08	$1.47	$6.44	$23.20	$16.10	21.48	14.91	17.40	13.94	1.23	1.07
1991	$17.40	$0.38	$1.20	$1.60	$7.25	$35.00	$20.00	29.17	16.67	20.40	14.80	1.43	1.13
Average	$11.08	$0.21	$0.76	$1.01	$4.33	$15.13	$ 9.81	18.72	11.96	15.06	11.59	1.24	1.01

summary of sales per share (SPS), dividends per share (DPS), earnings per share (EPS), cash flow per share (CFPS), book values per share (BVPS), the high and low stock prices, and high and low P/E ratios for the company. Also shown are the high and low P/E ratios for the Standard & Poor's 500 Stock Index over the same period.

In the last two columns, the high and low P/E ratios for Smucker are compared to the high and low P/E ratios for the S&P 500. For example, in 1982, Smucker's high P/E ratio was 11.46, and the S&P 500 high P/E was 11.31. When Smucker's high P/E is divided by the Standard & Poor's 500 high P/E, a relative P/E of 1.01 is calculated in the high relative P/E column. This indicates Smucker's high P/E ratio was at 101 percent of the market, or selling at a 1 percent premium to the market.

For each year, a high and low relative P/E ratio was calculated for Smucker with the average of the high and low shown on the last line. Smucker's high P/E relative averages 1.24 and its low P/E relative averages 1.01 percent of the market P/E. When we add the high and low and divide by two, we get an average of 1.12, which indicates Smucker historically sells at 112 percent of the S&P 500 P/E ratio. One could further assume that when the market is high priced, Smucker is priced higher. The low P/E relative shows variability, but for the last seven years, Smucker's low P/E relative has been below 1.00 only once. This indicates that since 1985, investors have been willing to pay a premium for Smucker's common stock both at the peaks and troughs of the market. Actually, Smucker has a beta of 0.90, which also gives it lower risk than the market.

To apply this knowledge to a model, we must be able to forecast earnings per share, and we also have to know the current S&P P/E ratio at the time we calculate the value. Part A of Table 7–5 indicates earnings per share are ex-

Table 7–5   Projected Earnings and Valuation

Part A: Growth Rate—Annually Compounded 10-Year Trendline Growth Equals 13%
Forecast of EPS: $1.20 (1991) × 1.13 = $1.36 (1992)

Part B: Relative P/E Model

	Relative P/E		S&P 500 Current P/E		Smucker's Expected P/E		Smucker's Estimated 1992 EPS		Smucker's Estimated Value Based on Relative P/E
Average high P/E	1.24	×	23	=	28.52	×	1.36	=	$38.79
Average low P/E	1.01	×	23	=	23.23	×	1.36	=	$31.59
Average P/E	1.12	×	23	=	25.76	×	1.36	=	$35.03

pected to grow at 13 percent per year. Using this information, we forecast EPS of $1.36 for 1992.

At the time of the analysis, the S&P 500 Stock Index was selling at a P/E ratio of 23.0 times earnings. The relative P/E model shown in Part B of Table 7–5 uses the high, low, and average P/E relative times the S&P 500 P/E to find the appropriate price-earnings ratio for Smucker based on its relationship to the current market level. When applied to the $1.36 EPS estimate, we find that Smucker should be selling between $38.79 per share at its high price and $31.59 at its low price. This would indicate that at a market price of less than $31.59, Smucker would probably be a good buy. Since Smucker was selling at $32 per share at the time of this analysis, the relative P/E model indicates it is a hold.

One consideration when using this model is the analyst's opinion about the level of the market P/E. Since we have already discussed the artificially high P/E that existed in the market at the beginning of 1992, it might be prudent (more conservative) to use a more normal market P/E instead of the P/E that currently exists. Smucker is not a cyclical company, and when earnings for the Standard & Poor's 500 recover from their recessionary low, the market P/E is likely to fall in the range of 15 to 20 as long as inflation does not rise from its current level. Going back to Figure 7–2 on page 219 should help reinforce the point that the S&P price earnings ratio is at a 30-year historical high. Analysts eventually must exercise their judgment in determining the appropriate normal data to use in this and all other models.

▪ OTHER VALUATION MODELS USING AVERAGE PRICE RATIOS AND 10-YEAR AVERAGES

Table 7–4 also includes data for sales per share, dividends per share, book value per share, and cash flow per share for Smucker. Some people like to look at the relationship of these price variables when deciding to buy or sell a stock. These models use the average price to average per share data to determine whether a stock is selling for a price that is above or below its historical relationship.

| Table 7–6 | Other Valuation Models Using Average Price Ratios and 10-Year Averages |

A. Price to Sales Model

$$\frac{\text{Average price*}}{\text{Average sales per share}} = \frac{\$12.47}{\$11.08} = 1.125 \text{ Price-to-sales ratio}$$

Value = Price-to-sales ratio × Estimated 1992 SPS

$$1.125 \times \$19.31 = \$21.72$$

B. Price to Dividend Model

$$\frac{\text{Average price*}}{\text{Average dividends per share}} = \frac{\$12.47}{\$0.21} = 59.38 \text{ Price-to-dividend ratio}$$

Value = Price-to-dividend ratio × Estimated 1992 DPS

$$= 59.38 \times \$.44 = \$26.13$$

C. Price to Book Value Model

$$\frac{\text{Average price*}}{\text{Average book value per share}} = \frac{\$12.47}{\$4.33} = 2.88 \text{ Price-to-book value ratio}$$

Value = Price-to-book value ratio × Estimated 1992 BVPS

$$= 2.88 \times \$8.19 = \$23.59$$

D. Price to Cash Flow Model

$$\frac{\text{Average price*}}{\text{Average cash flow per share}} = \frac{\$12.47}{\$1.01} = 12.35 \text{ Cash flow per share ratio}$$

Value = Price-to-cash flow ratio × Estimated 1992 CFPS

$$= 12.35 \times \$1.81 = \$22.35$$

*This represents the average of the 10-year high and low stock prices in Table 7–4.

Using the data in Table 7–4, we develop these four models in Table 7–6. In each case in Table 7–6, we multiply the historical ratio times the estimated 1992 amount to compute the estimated value. For example, in Part A of Table 7–6, Smucker exhibits a price-to-sales ratio of 1.125 or 112.5 percent, which indicates that over the 10 years covered, Smucker stock has sold at 112.5 percent of its sales per share. Multiplying this ratio times estimated sales per share for 1992 of $19.31 produces a value of $21.72. The dividend-to-price ratio (in Part B) indicates Smucker has sold at over 59 times its annual dividend, which is not unusual for a growth stock. This dividend model indicates a value of $26.13 per share.

The book value model in Part C shows Smucker has sold at 2.88 times its book value per share and indicates a price of $23.59 per share. The cash flow model in Part D became popular during the leverage buyout days of the 1980s and produces a value of $22.35. These values are all lower than the market price of $32 per share at the time these calculations were done, which implies Smucker is selling higher than its fair value relative to these models. These models are sometimes used because these variables are more stable than earnings per share, and, thus, the models present more "normal" values.

■ FORECASTING EARNINGS PER SHARE

The other side of choosing an appropriate P/E ratio is forecasting the earnings per share of a company with the proper growth rate. Investors can get earnings forecasts in several ways. They can rely on professional brokerage house research, investment advisory firms such as Value Line or Standard & Poor's, or financial magazines such as *Forbes* or *Business Week,* or they can do it themselves.

Least Squares Trendline

One of the most-common ways of forecasting earnings per share is to use regression or **least squares trend analysis.** The technique involves a statistical method whereby a trendline is fitted to a time series of historical earnings. This trendline, by definition, is a straight line that minimizes the distance of the individual observations from the line. Figure 7–3 depicts a scattergram for the earnings per share of XYZ Corporation. The earnings of this company have been fairly consistent, and so we get a good trendline with a minimum of variation. The compounded growth rate for the whole 10-year period was 16.5 percent, with 9.8 percent for the first 5 years and 20.4 for the last 5 years. This shows up in Figure 7–3 as two distinct five-year trendlines. There are many statistical programs on PCs and mainframes that run regression analysis, and even hand-held calculators have the ability to compute a growth rate from raw data.

Figure 7–3   Least Squares Trendline for EPS of XYZ Corporation

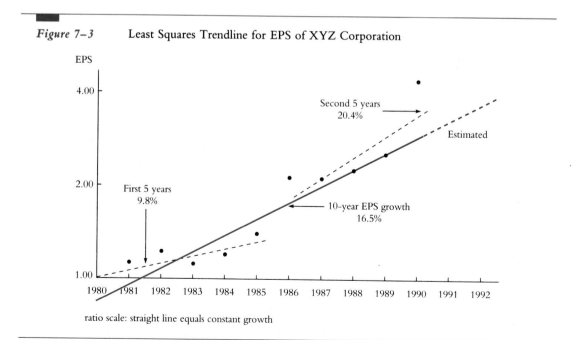

ratio scale: straight line equals constant growth

Table 7–7	Growth in Earnings per Share	
Years	Earnings per Share CSX Corporation (Past 10-Year EPS)	Earnings per Share International Paper (Past 10-Year EPS)
1981	2.97	5.04
1982	1.82	1.36
1983	2.07	1.87
1984	3.15	1.94
1985	2.92	0.81
1986	2.73	2.56
1987	2.78	3.60
1988	2.86	6.57
1989	3.45	7.72
1990	3.63	6.47

Whenever a mechanical forecast is made, subjectivity still enters the decision in choosing the data that will be considered in the regression plot.

Using CSX, a fairly stable railroad company, and International Paper, a cyclical forest products paper company, we compare earnings-per-share trends in Table 7–7. Both companies have achieved 6.5 percent growth over time, but International Paper has been much more subject to the ups and downs in the economy.

The values are plotted in Figure 7–4. From that figure, it is clear that CSX would provide the more reliable forecast based on past data. Its trendline is fairly consistent with a few minor ups and downs. To forecast International Paper, you would not start in 1985 and end in 1989 (trough to peak). Starting in 1981 and going to 1989 would probably also not provide a "true" trendline because the line would begin at a cyclical peak and end at another cyclical peak. Clearly, an International Paper forecast based on 10 or 12 years of data is more reliable than a 3- or 5-year forecast. With companies that follow economic cycles, the best forecasting period encompasses at least two peaks and two troughs or several business cycles.

The Income Statement Method

A more process-oriented method of forecasting earnings per share is to start with a sales forecast and create a standardized set of financial statements based on historical relationships. The sales forecast must be accurate if the earnings estimates are to have any significance. This method can be involved and

Figure 7–4   CSX Corp. and International Paper Trendlines

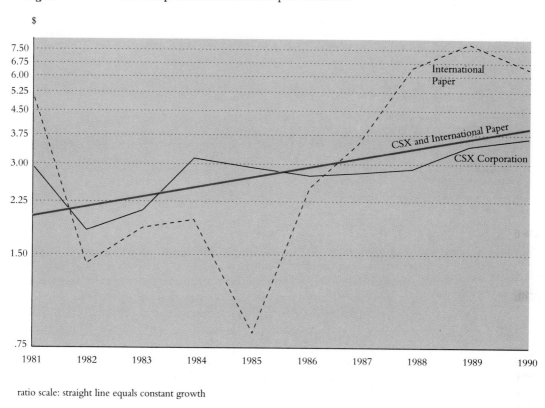

ratio scale: straight line equals constant growth

provides a student with a very integrated understanding of the relationships that go into the creation of earnings.

Several important factors are included in this method of forecasting. The analyst is forced to examine profitability and the resultant fluctuations in profit margins before and after taxes. The impact of short-term interest expense and any new bond financing can be factored into the analysis as well as any increase in shares of common stock from new equity financing.

Most analysts use an abbreviated method of forecasting earnings per share. They use a sales forecast combined with after-tax profit margins. For example, let us assume the Hutchins Corporation has a sales and profit margin history as set forth in Table 7–8. The sales have been growing at a 10 percent growth rate, and so the forecast is a simple extrapolation. However, the profit margin has fluctuated between 6.5 percent and 9.1 percent, with 8.2 percent being the average. Common stock outstanding has also grown by an average of 1.4

| | | | After-tax | | | | | | Earnings |
Year	Sales ($000s)	×	Profit Margin	=	Earnings ($000s)	÷	Shares (000s)	=	per Share
1986	$1,250,000		7.9%		$ 98,750		30,000		$3.29
1987	1,375,000		9.1		125,125		31,500		3.97
1988	1,512,500		8.5		128,562		33,200		3.87
1989	1,663,750		6.7		111,471		35,000		3.18
1990	1,830,125		8.3		151,900		35,200		4.31
1991	2,013,137		8.5		171,117		37,000		4.62
1992e	2,214,452		8.2		181,585		38,400		4.73
1993e	2,435,896		9.0		219,230		39,800		5.50

Table 7–8   Abbreviated Income Statement Method—Hutchins Corporation

e = Estimated.

million shares per year. Given the cyclical nature of the profit margin, 8.2 percent was used for 1992, which is expected to be an average year. Nine percent was used for 1993, a year expected to be economically more robust. Multiplying the profit margin times the estimated sales produced an estimate of earnings that was divided by the number of shares outstanding to find the earnings per share. Once the EPS is found, it still must be plugged into a valuation model to determine an appropriate value.

A third and somewhat more sophisticated method for forecasting earnings per share is termed the *sustainable growth model*. The model is presented in Appendix 7–A.

■ GROWTH STOCKS AND GROWTH COMPANIES

In assessing the worth of an investment, stockholders, analysts, and investors often make reference to such terms as growth stock and growth companies. As part of the process of improving your overall valuation skills, you should have some familiarity with these terms.

A **growth stock** may be defined as the common stock of a company generally growing faster than the economy or market norm. These companies are usually predictable in their earnings growth. Many of the more-popular growth stocks, such as 3M, Coca-Cola, and McDonald's, are really in the middle-to-late stages of the expansion phase. They tend to be fully valued and recognized in the marketplace.

Growth companies, on the other hand, are those companies that exhibit rising returns on assets each year and sales that are growing at an increasing rate (growth phase of the life cycle curve). Growth companies may not be as well known or recognized as growth stocks. Companies that may be considered to be growth companies might be in such industries as cable

television, cellular telephones, personal computers, medical electronics, and so on. These companies are growing very rapidly, and extrapolations of growth trends can be very dangerous if you guess incorrectly. Growth companies have many things in common. Usually, they have developed a proprietary product that is patented and protected from competition like the original Xerox process (now other companies can use the dry process). This market protection allows a high rate of return and generates cash for new-product development.

There are also other indicators of growth potential. Companies should have sales growth greater than the economy by a reasonable margin. Increasing sales should be translated into similar earnings growth, which means consistently stable and high profit margins. Additionally, the earnings growth should show up in earnings per share growth (no dilution of earnings through unproductive stock offers). The firm should have a low labor cost as a percentage of total cost, since wages are prone to be inflexible on the downside but difficult to control on the upside.

The biggest error made in searching for growth-oriented companies is that the price may already be too high. By the time you identify the company, so has everyone else, and the price is probably inflated. If the company has one quarter where earnings do not keep up with expectations, the stock price could tumble. The trick is to find growth companies before they are generally recognized in the market, and this requires taking more risk in small companies trading over-the-counter.

■ ASSETS AS A SOURCE OF STOCK VALUE

Until now, our emphasis has been primarily on earnings and dividends as the source of value. However, in certain industries, asset values may have considerable importance. These assets may take many forms—cash and marketable securities, buildings, land, timber, old movies, oil, and other natural resources. At times, any one of these assets may dominate a firm's value. Furthermore, companies with heavy cash positions are attractive merger and acquisition candidates because of the possibility that a firm with highly liquid assets could be taken over and its own cash used to pay back debt incurred in the takeover.

In the 1970s and 1980s, natural resources also had an important influence on value. Let's briefly examine this topic.

Natural Resources

Natural resources such as timber, copper, gold, and oil often give a company value even if the assets are not producing an income stream. This is because of the present value of the future income stream that is expected as these resources are used up. Companies such as International Paper, Weyerhaeuser, and other

forest product companies have timberlands with market values far in excess of their book values and, in some cases, in excess of their common stock prices.

Oil companies with large supplies of oil in the ground may have to wait 20 years before some of it is pumped, but there may be substantial value there. In the case of natural gas pipeline companies, increasing reserves have changed the way these companies are viewed by the market. They used to be considered similar to utilities because of their natural gas transmission system, but now they are also being valued based on their hidden assets (energy reserves). **Hidden assets** refer to assets that are not readily apparent to investors in a traditional sense, but add substantial value to the firm.

Investors should not overlook hidden assets because of naive extrapolation of past data or failure to understand an industry or company. Furthermore, assets do not always show up on the books of a company. They may be fully depreciated, like the movies *Sound of Music, Jaws,* or *Star Wars,* but still have substantial value in the television market.

SUMMARY

This chapter presents several common stock valuation models that rely on dividends and earnings per share. For the valuation to be accurate, the forecast of earnings and dividends needs to be correct.

Firms can be valued in many ways, and an analyst may use several methods to substantiate estimates. Valuation models based primarily on dividends look at future projections of dividends and the associated present values of the dividends. Assumptions must be made as to whether the dividend growth pattern is constant, accelerating, or decreasing.

Valuation using the earnings method requires that a price-earnings ratio be used as a multiplier of EPS. Price-earnings ratios are influenced by many variables, such as growth, risk, capital structure, dividend policy, level of the market in general, industry factors, and more. A careful study of each situation must be concluded before choosing the appropriate P/E. The price-earnings ratio is a function of two fluctuating variables—earnings and price. The two variables combine to form a ratio that is primarily future-oriented. High price-earnings ratios usually indicate positive expectations of the future, whereas low price-earnings ratios connote negative expectations.

To choose a P/E that is reasonable, the analyst must have some idea about the expected growth rate in earnings per share. Investors may find earnings estimates in investment advisory services, in statistical forecasts by brokerage houses, through their own time series statistical regression analysis, or by using the income statement method. Growth stocks were discussed more with the view of alerting the student of what to look for when trying to identify a growth stock or company than with the concept of valuation. The previously developed methods of valuation can be used on growth stocks as long as care is taken to evaluate the duration and level of growth.

We also presented some basic ideas about the value of companies based not on their earnings or dividend stream but on their assets such as cash or natural resources. Throughout the chapter, it was pointed out that every industry and company is unique. Management, products, organization structure, accounting systems, and philosophy are different for each. The role of an analyst is to understand the intricacies of several related industries and companies so as to enlighten the investing public.

■ IMPORTANT TERMS AND CONCEPTS

valuation 210	least squares trend analysis 225
dividend valuation models 210	growth stock 228
earnings valuation model 210	growth companies 228
price-earnings ratio 217	hidden assets 230

■ DISCUSSION QUESTIONS

1. How is value interpreted under the dividend valuation model?
2. The discount rate in the dividend model is referred to as the required rate of return. What three factors make up the required rate of return?
3. What two conditions are necessary to use Formula 7–3?
4. Is there any conflict between the assumption of constant growth (g) in Formula 7–3 and the industry life cycle?
5. How can companies with nonconstant growth be analyzed?
6. In considering P/E ratios for the overall market, what has been the relationship between price-earnings ratios and inflation?
7. What factors besides inflationary considerations and growth factors influence P/E ratios for the general market?
8. For cyclical companies, why might the current P/E ratio be misleading?
9. What two factors are probably most important in influencing the P/E ratio for an *individual stock?* Suggest a number of other factors as well.
10. What type of industries tend to carry the highest P/E ratios?
11. What is the essential characteristic of a least squares trendline?
12. What two elements go into an abbreviated income statement method of forecasting?
13. What is the difference between a growth company and a growth stock? What are some industries in which there are growth companies?
14. How should a firm with natural resources be valued?
15. What is an example of a valuable asset that might not show any "value" on a balance sheet?

■ PROBLEMS

1. Assume D_1 = $1.80, K_e = 13 percent, g = 9 percent. Using Formula 7–3 for the constant growth dividend valuation model, compute P_0.

2. Using the data from Problem 1:

   a. If D_1 and K_e remain the same, but g goes up to 10 percent, what will the new stock price be? Briefly explain the reason for the change.

   b. If D_1 and g retain their original value ($1.80 and 9 percent), but K_e goes up to 15 percent, what will the new stock price be? Briefly explain the reason for the change.

3. Using the original data from Problem 1, find P_0 by following the steps described below:

   a. Project dividends for years one through three (the first year is already given). Round all values that you compute to two places to the right of the decimal point.

   b. Find the present value of the dividends in part *a*.

   c. Project the dividend for the fourth year (D_4).

   d. Use Formula 7–3 to find the present value of all future dividends, beginning with the fourth year's dividend. The present value you find will be at the end of the third year (the equivalent of the beginning of the fourth year).

   e. Discount back the value found in part *d* for three years at 13 percent.

   f. Observe that in part *b* you determined the percent value of dividends for the first three years and, in part *e*, the present value of an infinite stream after the first three years. Now add these together to get the total present value of the stock.

   g. Compare your answers in part *f* to your answer to Problem 1. Comment on the relationship.

4. The Haltom Corporation anticipates a nonconstant growth pattern for dividends. Dividends at the end of year one are $2.40 per share and are expected to grow by 15 percent per year until the end of year five (that's four years of growth). After year five, dividends are expected to grow at 5 percent as far as the company can see into the future. All dividends are to be discounted back to the present at a 9 percent rate (K_e = 9 percent).

   a. Project dividends for years one through five (the first year is already given). Round all values that you compute to two places to the right of the decimal point.

   b. Find the present value of the dividends in part *a*.

   c. Project the dividend for the sixth year (D_6).

d. Use Formula 7–3 to find the present value of all future dividends, beginning with the sixth year's dividend. The present value you find will be at the end of the fifth year.

Use Formula 7–3 as follows: $P_5 = D_6/(K_e - g)$.

e. Discount back the value found in part *d* for five years at 9 percent.

f. Add together the values from part *b* and part *e* to determine the present value of the stock.

g. Explain how the two elements in part *f* go together to provide the present value of the stock.

Nonconstant growth dividend model

5. Rework Problem 4 with a new assumption, that dividends at the end of the first year are $1.60 and that they will grow at 18 percent per year until the end of the fifth year, at which point they will grow at 6 percent per year for the foreseeable future. Use a discount rate of 12 percent throughout your analysis. Round all values that you compute to two places to the right of the decimal point.

Combined earnings and dividend model

6. R. L. Lynch investment bankers will use a combined earnings and dividend model to determine the value of the Pierce Corporation. The approach they take is basically the same as that in Table 7–2. Estimated earnings per share for the next five years are:

1992	$4.00
1993	4.40
1994	4.84
1995	5.32
1996	5.85

a. If 35 percent of earnings are paid out in dividends, and the discount rate is 14 percent, determine the present value of dividends.

b. If it is anticipated that the stock will trade at a P/E of 17 times 1996 earnings, determine the stock's price at that point in time and discount back the stock price for five years at 14 percent.

c. Add together part *a* and part *b* to determine the stock price under this combined earnings and dividend model.

P/E ratio analysis

7. Mr. Brown of Northwest Investment Company is evaluating the P/E ratio of Alaska Consumer Electronics (ACE). The firm's P/E is currently 13. With earnings per share of $2, the stock price is $26.

The average P/E ratio in the consumer electronics industry is presently 12. However, ACE has an anticipated growth rate of 15 percent versus 10 percent for the industry norm, so 2 will be added to the industry P/E by Mr. Brown. Also, the operating risk associated with ACE is less than that for the industry because of its long-term contract with Sears. For this reason, Mr. Brown will add another factor of 1 to the industry P/E ratio.

The debt-to-total-asset ratio is not as encouraging. It is 50 percent, while the industry ratio is 40 percent. In doing his evaluation, Mr. Brown decides to subtract a factor of ½ from the industry P/E ratio. Other ratios, including dividend payout, appear to be in line with the industry, so Mr. Brown will make no further adjustments along these lines.

However, he is somewhat distressed by the fact that the firm only spent 3 percent of sales on R&D last year, when the industry norm is 5 percent. For this reason he will subtract a factor of 1 from the industry P/E ratio.

Despite the relatively low research budget, Mr. Brown observes that the firm has just hired two of the top executives from a competitor in the industry. He decided to add a factor of ½ to the industry P/E ratio because of this.

a. Determine the P/E ratio for ACE, based on Mr. Brown's analysis.

b. Multiply this times earnings per share and comment on whether you think the stock might possibly be under- or overvalued in the marketplace at its current P/E and price.

P/E ratio analysis

8. Refer to Table 7–4. Assume that because of unusually bright long-term prospects, analysts determine that Smucker's P/E ratio in 1992 should be 70 percent above the average high S&P 500 P/E ratio for the last 10 years. (Carry your calculation of the P/E ratio two places to the right of the decimal point in this problem.) What would the stock price be, based on projected earnings per share of $1.36 (for 1992)?

P/E ratio analysis

9. Refer to Problem 8 and assume new circumstances cause the analysts to reduce the anticipated P/E in 1992 to 10 percent below the average low S&P 500 P/E for the last 10 years. Furthermore, projected earnings per share are reduced to $1.18. What would the stock price be?

Income statement method of forecasting

10. Security analysts following Wolfson Corporation use a simplified income statement method of forecasting. Assume that 1992 sales are $20 million and are expected to grow by 12 percent in 1993 and 1994. The after-tax profit margin is projected at 6.1 percent in 1993 and 5.9 percent in 1994. The number of shares outstanding is anticipated to be 500,000 for 1993 and 510,000 for 1994. Project earnings per share for 1993 and 1994.

P/E ratio and price

11. The average price-earnings ratio for the industry that the Wolfson Corporation is in is 16X. If the company has a P/E ratio 20 percent higher than the industry ratio of 16 in 1993 and 25 percent higher than the industry ratio also of 16 in 1994:

a. Indicate the appropriate P/Es for the firm in 1993 and 1994.

b. Combine this with the earnings per share data in Problem 10 to determine the anticipated stock price for 1993 and 1994.

P/E ratio and price

12. Relating to Problems 10 and 11, assume you wish to determine the probable price range in 1994 if the P/E ratio is between 18 and 22. What is the price range?

CFA MATERIAL

The following material contains sample questions and solutions from a prior Level I CFA exam. While the terminology is slightly different from that in this text, you can still view the skills necessary for the CFA exam.

CFA Exam Question

3. As a firm operating in a mature industry, Arbot Industries is expected to maintain a constant dividend payout ratio and constant growth rate of earnings for the foreseeable future. Earnings were $4.50 per share in the recently completed fiscal year. The dividend payout ratio has been a constant 55 percent in recent years and is expected to remain so. Arbot's return on equity (ROE) is expected to remain at 10 percent in the future, and you require an 11 percent return on the stock.

   a. Using the constant growth dividend discount model, *calculate* the current value of Arbot common stock. *Show* your calculations.

   After an aggressive acquisition and marketing program, it now appears that Arbot's earnings per share and ROE will grow rapidly over the next two years. You are aware that the dividend discount model can be useful in estimating the value of common stock even when the assumption of constant growth does not apply.

   b. *Calculate* the current value of Arbot's common stock using the dividend discount model assuming Arbot's dividend will grow at a 15 percent rate for the next two years, returning in the third year to the historical growth rate and continuing to grow at the historical rate for the foreseeable future. *Show* your calculations.

Solution: Question 3 — Morning Session (I–91) (15 points)

a. Constant growth (single-stage) dividend discount model:

$$\text{Value}_0 = \frac{D_1}{K - g}$$

D_1 = Next year's dividend

K = Required rate of return

g = Constant growth rate

$D_1 = (\text{EPS}_0)(1 + g)(P/o) = (4.50)(1.045)(.55) = \$2.59$

K = given at 11% or .11

$g = (\text{ROE})(1 - P/o) = (.10)(1 - .55) = .045$

$\text{Value}_0 = \dfrac{\$2.59}{11 - .045} = \dfrac{\$2.59}{.065} = \$39.85$

b. Multistage dividend discount model (where $g_1 = .15$ and g_2 is .045):

$$\text{Value}_0 = \frac{D_1}{(1+K)} + \frac{D_2}{(1+K)^2} + \frac{D_3/(K-g_2)}{(1+K)^2}$$

$D_1 = (\text{EPS}_0)(1 + g_1)(\text{P/O}) = (4.50)(1.15)(0.55) = \$2.85$

$D_2 = (D_1)(1 + g_1) = (\$2.85/(1.15) = \$3.27$

$K = \text{given at 11\% or .11}$

$g_2 = .045$

$D_3 = (D_2)(1 + g_2) = (\$3.27)(1.045) = \$3.42$

$$\begin{aligned}
\text{Value}_0 &= \frac{\$2.85}{(1.11)} + \frac{\$3.27}{(1.11)^2} + \frac{\$3.42/(0.11-0.045)}{(1.11)^2} \\
&= \frac{\$2.85}{(1.11)} + \frac{\$3.27}{(1.11)^2} + \frac{\$52.62}{(1.11)^2} \\
&= \$2.56 + \$2.65 + \$42.71 \\
&= \$47.92
\end{aligned}$$

CFA Exam Question

7. The constant growth dividend discount model can be used both for the valuation of companies and for the estimation of the long-term total return of a stock.

Assume: $\$20$ = Price of a stock today

8% = Expected growth rate of dividends

$\$.60$ = Annual dividend one year forward

a. Using *only* the above data, *compute* the expected long-term total return on the stock using the constant growth dividend discount model. *Show* calculations.

b. *Briefly discuss three* disadvantages of the constant growth dividend discount model in its application to investment analysis.

c. *Identify three* alternative methods to the dividend discount model for the valuation of companies.

Solution: Question 7—Morning Session (I–90)(10 points)

(Reading reference: Cohen, Zinbarg & Ziekel, Chapter 10)

a. The dividend discount model is: $P = \dfrac{d}{k - g}$

Where: P = Value of the stock today

d = Annual dividend one year forward

k = Discount rate

g = Constant dividend growth rate

Solving for k: $(k - g) = \dfrac{d}{p}$; then $k = \dfrac{d}{p} + g$

So k becomes the estimate for the long-term return of the stock.

$$k = \frac{\$0.60}{\$20.00} + 8\% = 3\% + 8\% = 11\%$$

b. Many professional investors shy away from the dividend discount framework analysis due to its many inherent complexities.

(1) The model cannot be used where companies pay very small or no dividends and speculation on the level of future dividends could be futile. (Dividend policy may be arbitrary.)

(2) The model presumes one can accurately forecast long-term growth of earnings (dividends) of a company. Such forecasts become quite tenuous beyond two years out. (A short-term valuation may be more pertinent.)

(3) For the variable growth models, small differences in g for the first several years produce large differences in the valuations.

(4) The correct k or the discount rate is difficult to estimate for a specific company as an infinite number of factors affect it that are themselves difficult to forecast, e.g., inflation, riskless rate of return, risk premium on stocks, and other uncertainties.

(5) The model is not definable when $g > k$ as with growth companies, so it is not applicable to a large number of companies.

(6) Where a company has low or negative earnings per share or has a poor balance sheet, the ability to continue the dividend is questionable.

(7) The components of income can differ substantially, reducing comparability.

c. Three alternative methods of valuation would include: (1) price-earnings ratios; (2) price-asset value ratios (including market and book asset values); (3) price-sales ratios; (4) liquidation or breakup value; and (5) price-cash flow ratios.

■ MARKETBASE-E EXERCISES

In the following exercise, please use your MarketBase-E Software and manual to screen for the required portfolios. You must figure out how to search through the data to pull out those companies meeting the requirements set down.

1. Determine the companies with the following characteristics:

a. Companies with price-earnings ratios less than 8. How many are there? Value Line lists low PE companies in their Selection and Opinion section. What is the highest PE ratio in that list? How many companies in the MarketBase-E database have smaller PE ratios?

b. Companies with price-book value ratios less than 1. How many are there? Value Line lists companies with low price to book value ratios

in their Selection and Opinion section. What is the highest price to book value ratio in that list? How many companies in MarketBase-E have smaller price to book value ratios?

c. Companies with price-sales ratios less than .4. How many companies are there? Value Line lists companies with low price to sales ratios in their Selection and Opinion section. What is the highest price to sales ratio in that list? How many companies in the MarketBase-E database have smaller price to sales ratios?

d. Companies with free cash flow to price (FCP) ratios greater than 100%. How many are there? Value Line lists companies with low price to cash flow ratios in their Selection and Opinion section. What is the lowest free cash flow to price ratio in that list? How many companies in MarketBase-E have smaller free cash flow to price ratios?

2. Determine the number of companies with the following characteristics:

a. Companies with price-earnings ratios greater than 40. What happens if you increase the criterion to PEs greater than 80?

b. Companies with price-book value ratios greater than 4. How many companies are there?

c. Companies with price-sales ratios greater than 4.

d. Companies with free cash flow to price ratios greater than 300%.

3. Use MarketBase-E to find securities that might not be correctly valued according to the dividend valuation approach. You will have to program the valuation formula into MarketBase-E. Then use the value you determined to check against the database.

4. a. Benjamin Graham suggested a valuation model that says a company's P/E ratio should be:

$$(8.5 + 2G) \text{ times } [4.4\% / (\text{Current AAA Bond Yield})]$$

Find the current AAA bond yield. Use this model to determine if any companies are undervalued by this approach. Use the annually compounded earnings growth rate over five years for G.

b. Add a "fudge factor" so that companies must be undervalued by 20%. Are there any companies that satisfy this criterion?

c. Recompute the Graham valuation formula from part (a) using annually compounded earnings growth over the past three fiscal years. Does this change in periods result in a change in the number of companies that are undervalued?

d. Recompute the valuation from part (a) to find companies that are overvalued by the Graham formula.

5. a. Examine the relationship between P/E ratios and growth. Use MarketBase-E to find those companies with P/E ratios that are lower than their growth rates.

b. MarketBase-E has a statistic called the value of ROE—it is a company's ROE divided by the company's P/E. Screen the database to find those companies with a value of ROE greater than 1. How many companies fit this criterion?

     c. Add a further criterion to the previous part. Select from the previously chosen list those companies whose growth rate of earnings is greater than 25%. What effect did the growth criterion have?

SELECTED REFERENCES

Considerations in Valuing Securities

Black, Fischer. "The Dividend Puzzle." *Journal of Portfolio Management,* Winter 1976, pp. 5–8.

Loderer, Claudio F.; Dennis P. Sheehan; and Gregory P. Kadlec. "The Pricing of Equity Offerings." *Journal of Financial Economics,* March 1991, pp. 35–57.

Miller, Merton, and Franco Modigliani. "Dividend Policy, Growth, and the Valuation of Shares." *Journal of Business,* October 1961, pp. 411–33.

Morris, James R. "The Role of Cash Balances in Firm Valuation." *Journal of Financial and Quantitative Analysis,* December 1983, pp. 533–46.

Reinganum, Marc R. "The Anatomy of a Stock Market." *Financial Analysts Journal,* March–April 1988, pp. 16–28.

Tobin, James. "A Mean-Variance Approach to Fundamental Valuations." *Journal of Portfolio Management,* Fall 1984, pp. 26–33.

Price-Earnings Ratio Considerations

Basu, S. "Investment Performance of Common Stocks in Relation to Their Price-Earnings Ratios: A Test of the Efficient Market Hypothesis." *Journal of Finance,* June 1977, pp. 663–82.

Beaver, William, and Dale Morse. "What Determines Price-Earnings Ratios?" *Financial Analysts Journal,* July–August 1978, pp. 65–76.

Chung, Peter S. "An Investigation of the Firms Effect Influence in the Analysis of Earnings to Price Ratios of Industrial Common Stocks." *Journal of Financial and Quantitative Analysis,* December 1974, pp. 1009–29.

Good, Walter R. "When Are Price/Earnings Ratios Too High—or Too Low?" *Financial Analysts Journal,* July–August 1991, pp. 9–12.

Earnings Forecast

Kerrigan, Thomas J. "When Forecasting Earnings It Pays to Watch Forecasts." *Journal of Portfolio Management,* Summer 1984, pp. 19–26.

Klemkosky, Robert C., and William P. Miller. "When Forecasting Earnings, It Pays to Be Right!" *Journal of Portfolio Management,* Summer 1984, pp. 13–18.

Moses, O. Douglas. "Cash Flow Signals and Analysts' Earnings Forecast Revisions." *Journal of Business, Finance and Accounting,* November 1991, pp. 807–32.

Growth Stocks

Mao, James C. T. "The Valuation of Growth Stocks: The Investment Opportunities Approach." *Journal of Finance,* March 1966, pp. 95–102.

Statman, Meir. "Growth Opportunities vs. Growth Stocks." *Journal of Portfolio Management,* Spring 1984, pp. 70–74.

Appendix 7–A: Sustainable Growth Model

The **sustainable growth model** looks at how much growth a firm can generate by maintaining the same financial relationships as the year before. The process of generating earnings using the sustainable growth model provides many insights into the financial interactions that produce earnings. This method requires an understanding of several ratios—the first being the return on equity and the retention ratios.

The return on equity can take several forms. First, let's define equity to equal (1) assets − liabilities; (2) net worth; and (3) book value. These are all equal even though we call them by different names. We will use the term *book value* to equal the equity of the firm. The return on equity (ROE) is equal to:

$$\text{ROE} = \frac{\text{Net income or After-tax earnings}}{\text{Book value}} \qquad (7A-1)$$

We can also express earnings and book value on a per share basis and the formula becomes:

$$\text{ROE} = \frac{\text{Earnings per share (EPS)}}{\text{Book value per share (BVPS)}} \qquad (7A-2)$$

Because we are using the sustainable growth model, we want to know what the return on equity was, based on the book value at the beginning of the year. This makes sense because it is the book value at the beginning of the year that is in place to generate earnings. We return to Table 7–4 to examine Smucker's return on equity for 1991.

$$\text{ROE} = \frac{\$1.20_{1991} \text{ (full year)}}{\$6.44_{1990} \text{ (year end)}^{*}}$$

$$\text{ROE} = 18.63\%$$

Since we want to forecast earnings per share, we will look at the process of growth on a per share basis. We can rearrange formula 7A–2 by multiplying both sides by the book value per share (BVPS) and we end up with:

$$\text{EPS} = \text{ROE} \times \text{BVPS} \qquad (7A-3)$$

Using this information, we will examine how earnings per share can grow if the financial relationships stay the same from year to year. Let's take

---

*We use year end 1990 (beginning of 1991) BUPS to measure return on equity for 1991.

Smucker as our example and state that the BVPS was $6.44 in 1990 (year end) and return on equity was 18.63 percent, which we already computed. Substituting these numbers into Formula 7A-3 gives us:

$$\text{EPS} = \text{ROE} \times \text{BVPS}$$
$$\$1.20 = 18.63\% \times \$6.44$$

This is the value of earnings per share for 1991. Future growth in earnings comes from the firm reinvesting in new plant and equipment and thus being able to generate more income for next year. In the case of Smucker, the firm paid out a dividend of $.38 in 1991 and retained $.82 ($1.20 − $.38). The $.82 gets added to the beginning book value per share to get ending book value of $7.26 ($6.44 + $.82) for 1991.

If Smucker can continue to earn 18.63 percent on its equity, it will earn $1.35 per share for 1992. This can be computed as follows:

$$\text{EPS}_{1992} = \text{ROE} \times \text{BVPS}_{\text{year end 1991}}$$
$$\text{EPS}_{1992} = 18.63\% \times \$7.26$$
$$\text{EPS}_{1992} = \$1.353$$

The growth rate in earnings per share using this model can be calculated by taking the increased earnings of $.153 and dividing by beginning earnings of $1.20. This produces an earnings per share growth rate of 12.7 percent.

One of the conditions of growth is that the firms must retain some earnings. If Smucker paid out all its earnings in dividends, it would start 1992 with the same book value and would experience no growth. The more earnings retained, the higher the growth rate would be. In Smucker's case, it retained $.82 out of $1.20 in earnings. This is called the **retention ratio,** which is sometimes denoted by B to keep it from being confused with a rate of return symbol.

(7A-4)

$$\text{Retention ratio (B)} = \frac{\text{Earnings per share} - \text{Dividends per share}}{\text{Earnings per share}}$$

$$\text{Retention ratio (B)} = \frac{\$1.20 - \$.38}{\$1.20}$$

$$\text{Retention ratio (B)} = .6833 \text{ or } 68.33\%$$

The outcome of this analysis is that the growth in earnings per share is a function of the return on equity and the retention ratio. We can calculate growth in EPS as follows:

$$\text{Growth } (g) = \text{Return on equity} \times \text{Retention ratio} \qquad (7A-5)$$
$$g = \text{ROE} \times \text{B}$$

Using Smucker as an example, we have:

$$g_{\text{eps}} = 18.63\% \times 68.33\%$$
$$g_{\text{eps}} = 12.7\%$$

The sustainable growth model would predict a 12.7 percent growth rate for 1992 based on Smucker's dividend policy and return on equity. This rate will continue into the future as long as Smucker maintains its return on equity and its retention ratio.

■ IMPORTANT WORDS AND CONCEPTS

sustainable growth model 240   retention ratio 241

■ DISCUSSION QUESTIONS

1. Do you think the sustainable growth model would be appropriate for a highly cyclical firm?
2. Based on the sustainable growth model, if a firm increases the dividend payout ratio (1 − the retention ratio), will this increase or decrease the growth in earnings per share in the future?

■ PROBLEMS

Sustainable growth model

1. The Bolten Corporation had earnings per share of $2.60 in 1991 and book value per share at the end of 1990 (beginning of 1991) was $13.

   a. What was the firm's return on equity (book value) in 1991?

   b. If the firm pays out $0.78 in dividends per share, what is the retention ratio? How much will book value per share be at the end of 1991? Add retained earnings per share for 1991 to book value per share at the beginning of 1991.

   c. Assume the same rate of return on book value for 1992 as you computed in part *a* for 1991. What will earnings per share be for 1992? Multiply rate of return on book value (part *a*) by book value at the end of 1991 (second portion of part *b*).

   d. What is the growth rate in earnings per share between 1991 and 1992?

   e. If the firm continues to earn the same rate of return on book value and maintains the same earnings retention ratio, what will the sustainable growth rate be for the foreseeable future?

8

Financial Statement Analysis

Financial statements present a numerical picture of a company's financial and operating health. Since each company is different, an analyst needs to examine the financial statements for industry characteristics as well as for differences in accounting methods. The major financial statements are the balance sheet, the income statement, and the statement of cash flows. A very helpful long-term financial overview also is provided by a 5- or 10-year summary statement found in the corporate annual report. One must further remember that the footnotes to these statements are an integral part of the statements and provide a wealth of in-depth explanatory information. More depth can often be found in additional reports such as the 10-K filed with the Securities and Exchange Commission and obtainable on request (free) from most companies.

Fundamental analysis depends on variables internal to the company, and the corporate financial statements are one way of measuring fundamental value and risk. Financial-statement analysis should be combined with economic and industry analysis before a final judgment is made to purchase or sell a specific security. Chapter 7 presented methods of valuation that used forecasts of dividends and earnings per share. Earnings per share combined with an estimated price-earnings ratio was also used to get a future price. Careful study of financial statements provides the analyst with much of the necessary information to forecast earnings and dividends, to judge the quality of earnings, and to determine financial and operating risk.

■ THE MAJOR FINANCIAL STATEMENTS

In the first part of this chapter, we examine the three basic types of financial statements—the income statement, the balance sheet, and the statement of cash flows—with particular attention paid to the interrelationships among these three measurement devices. In the rest of the chapter, ratio analysis is presented in detail, and deficiencies of financial statements are discussed along with the role of the security analyst in interpreting financial statements.

Income Statement

The **income statement** is the major device for measuring the profitability of a firm over a period of time. An example of the income statement is presented in Table 8–1 for the Coca-Cola Company. Note that the income statement is for a defined period, whether it be one month, three months, or a year. The statement is presented in a stair-step fashion so that we may examine the profit or loss after each type of expense item is deducted.

For 1990, the Coca-Cola Company had net operating revenues (sales) of $10.2 billion. After subtracting the cost of goods sold, selling, administrative, and general expenses, the firm's operating income was $1.95 billion. Because of a high level of cash, cash equivalents, and marketable securities during 1990, Coca-Cola had interest income that was 73.6 percent of its interest expense.

Table 8–1   Coca-Cola Income Statement

THE COCA-COLA COMPANY AND SUBSIDIARIES
Consolidated Statements of Income
(Dollars in thousands except per share data)

Year Ended December 31,	1990	1989	1988
Net operating revenues	$10,236,350	$8,622,287	$8,065,424
Cost of goods sold	4,208,850	3,548,570	3,429,065
Gross profit	6,027,500	5,073,717	4,636,359
Selling, administrative, and general expenses	4,075,936	3,347,932	3,038,058
Operating income	1,951,564	1,725,785	1,598,301
Interest income	169,985	205,035	199,333
Interest expense	230,979	308,034	230,513
Equity income	110,139	75,490	92,542
Other income (deductions)—net	13,727	4,847	(33,243)
Gain on sale of Belmont Springs Water Co., Inc.	—	61,187	—
Income from continuing operations before income taxes	2,014,436	1,764,310	1,626,420
Income taxes	632,532	571,471	537,434
Income from continuing operations	1,381,904	1,192,839	1,088,986
Equity income (loss) from discontinued operation	—	21,537	(44,283)
Gain on sale of discontinued operation (net of income taxes of $421,021)	—	509,449	—
Net income	1,381,904	1,723,825	1,044,703
Preferred stock dividends	18,158	21,392	6,426
Net income available to common shareholders	$ 1,363,746	$1,702,433	$1,038,277
Income (Loss) per common share:			
Continuing operations	$ 2.04	$ 1.69	$ 1.48
Discontinued operation	—	.77	(.06)
Net income per common share	$ 2.04	$ 2.46	$ 1.42
Average common shares outstanding (in thousands)	668,570	691,962	729,225

Source: *The Coca-Cola Company Annual Report,* 1990, p. 46.

This is an uncommonly high ratio of interest income to interest expense, but this pattern occurred in all three years shown in the consolidated statements of income. An analyst might conclude Coca-Cola has a policy of keeping a high level of cash as a current asset. Coca-Cola also had income of $110 million from equity interests in other publicly held companies.

Altogether, Coca-Cola reported income from continuing operations before taxes of over $2.0 billion. After paying taxes of $632 million, income from continuing operations after taxes was $1.38 billion. Notice that Coca-Cola disposed of some assets in 1988 and 1989, and that income (loss) is listed separately as is the $509 million gain on the sale of discontinued operations in

1989. Since income from discontinued operations was material to the total results in 1989, the analyst needs this information. The income statement indicates earnings per share from continuing operations, discontinued operations, and a total for the two.

In 1989, the total net income per share was $2.46, which included $0.77 from discontinued operations. In comparing 1990 earnings per share, it would look like Coca-Cola had a bad year because EPS fell from $2.46 to $2.04. Since the analyst is primarily concerned with income from continuing operations as an indicator of future earnings, it would make more sense to compare the $2.04 in 1990 to the $1.69 from continuing operations in 1989, which gives us a positive earnings trend rather than a downward trend.

Coca-Cola has been repurchasing shares of common stock. Notice how shares outstanding in computing earnings per share (last row) have fallen from 729 million in 1988 to 668 million shares in 1990. Generally, shares outstanding can be calculated by taking issued shares on the balance sheet and subtracting treasury stock. Since shares outstanding for annual purposes are usually computed on an averaging basis, it is likely that fewer shares were outstanding at 1990 year end. In forecasting earnings, the analyst also needs to know how long this company strategy will continue.

Are these good income figures or bad? As we shall see later, the analyst's interpretation of the numbers will depend on historical figures, on industry data, and on the relationship of income to balance sheet items such as assets and net worth.

Balance Sheet

The **balance sheet** indicates what the firm owns and how these assets are financed in the form of liabilities or ownership interest. While the income statement purports to show the profitability of the firm, the balance sheet delineates the firm's holdings and obligations. Together, these statements are intended to answer two questions: How much did the firm make or lose, and what is a measure of its worth? A balance sheet for the Coca-Cola Company is presented in Table 8–2 on pages 248 and 249.

Note that the balance sheet is given at one point in time, in this case December 31, 1990. It does not represent the result of transactions for a specific month, quarter, or year, but rather is a cumulative chronicle of all transactions that have affected the corporation since its inception. This is in contrast to the income statement, which measures results only over a short, quantifiable period. Generally, balance sheet items are stated on an original cost basis rather than at market value.

The Coca-Cola Company was chosen for analysis because of its product diversification, its international scope, and its well-known soft drinks such as Coca-Cola, Tab, Sprite, and Diet Coke. Its food division's major product is Minute Maid orange juice. This division accounted for 15.7 percent of revenues but only 4.8 percent of operating income in 1990. Coca-Cola began a

major restructuring in 1985 by spinning off wholly owned subsidiaries but retaining minority interests in several of the newly owned public firms. In a major sale in 1989, Coca-Cola sold Columbia Pictures to Sony, the Japanese entertainment giant. This sale accounted for the $509 million gain on the income statement.

Companies where Coca-Cola still holds minority interests show up in the balance sheet under the section, "Investments and other assets." These companies are: Coca-Cola Enterprises Inc., Coca-Cola Amatil Limited, and other assets that are principally bottling companies. The Coca-Cola Company reports the earnings of these companies using the equity method of reporting, which means the ownership percentage from these equity interests of $110 million in 1990 is included in Coca-Cola's income statement.

Statement of Cash Flows

In November 1987, the accounting profession designated the **statement of cash flows** as the third required financial statement, along with the balance sheet and income statement. Referred to as Financial Accounting Standards Board (FASB), *Statement No. 95,* it replaced the old statement of changes in financial position (and the sources and uses of funds statement).

The purpose of the new statement of cash flows is to emphasize the critical nature of cash flow to the operations of the firm. Cash flow generally represents cash or cash-equivalent items that can easily be converted into cash within 90 days (such as a money market fund).

The income statement and balance sheet are normally based on the accrual method of accounting, in which revenues and expenses are recognized as they occur, rather than when cash actually changes hands. For example, a $100,000 credit sale may be made in December 1992 and shown as revenue for that year—despite the fact the cash payment would not be received until March 1993. When the actual payment is finally received under accrual accounting, no revenue is recognized (it has already been accounted for previously). The primary advantage of accrual accounting is that it allows us to match revenues and expenses in the period in which they occur to appropriately measure profit; but a disadvantage is that adequate attention is not directed to the actual cash flow position of the firm.

One can think of situations in which a firm made a $1 million profit on a transaction but will not receive the actual cash payment for two years. Or perhaps the $1 million profit is in cash, but the firm increased its asset purchases by $3 million (a new building). If you merely read the income statement, you might assume the firm is in a strong $1 million cash position; but if you go beyond the income statement to cash flow considerations, you would observe the firm is $2 million short of funds for the period.

As a last example, a firm might show a $100,000 loss on the income statement; but if it had a depreciation expense write-off of $150,000, the firm would actually have $50,000 in cash. Since depreciation is a noncash deduction,

Table 8–2   Coca-Cola Balance Sheet

THE COCA-COLA COMPANY AND SUBSIDIARIES
Consolidated Balance Sheets
For the Years Ended December 31, 1989 and 1990
(in thousands except per share data)

	1990	1989
Assets		
Current assets:		
Cash and cash equivalents	$1,429,555	$1,096,020
Marketable securities, at cost (approximates market)	62,569	85,671
	1,492,124	1,181,691
Trade accounts receivable, less allowances of $29,510 in 1990 and $14,347 in 1989	913,541	768,335
Finance subsidiary—receivables	38,199	52,093
Inventories	982,313	789,077
Prepaid expenses and other assets	716,601	812,304
Total current assets	4,142,778	3,603,500
Investments and other assets:		
Investments:		
Coca-Cola Enterprises Inc.	666,847	695,195
Coca-Cola Amatil Limited	569,057	524,931
Other, principally bottling companies	788,718	710,297
Finance subsidiary—receivables	128,119	140,520
Long-term receivables and other assets	321,977	354,881
	2,474,718	2,425,824
Property, plant, and equipment:		
Land	147,057	146,482
Buildings and improvements	1,059,969	950,251
Machinery and equipment	2,204,188	1,890,960
Containers	374,526	307,012
	3,785,740	3,294,705
Less allowances for depreciation	1,400,175	1,273,486
Total fixed assets	2,385,565	2,021,219
Goodwill and other intangible assets	275,126	231,993
Total assets	$9,278,187	$8,282,536

Table 8–2   Coca-Cola Balance Sheet (*concluded*)

	1990	1989
Liabilities and Shareholders' Equity		
Current liabilities:		
Accounts payable and accrued expenses	$1,576,426	$1,386,516
Loans and notes payable:		
Finance subsidiary	161,432	184,691
Other	1,742,179	1,234,617
Current maturities of long-term debt	97,272	12,858
Accrued taxes	719,182	839,248
Total current liabilities	4,296,491	3,657,930
Long-term debt	535,861	548,708
Other liabilities	332,060	294,358
Deferred income taxes	264,611	296,055
Total debt	$5,429,023	$4,797,051
Shareholders' equity:		
Preferred stock, $1 par value—		
Authorized: 100,000,000 shares; Issued: 3,000 shares of Cumulative Money		
Market Preferred Stock in 1990 and 1989; Outstanding: 750 shares in 1990;		
3,000 shares in 1989, stated at aggregate liquidation preference	75,000	300,000
Common stock, $0.50 par value—		
Authorized: 1,400,000,000 shares; Issued: 840,487,486 shares		
in 1990; 837,819,578 shares in 1989	420,244	418,910
Capital surplus	512,703	437,324
Reinvested earnings	6,447,576	5,618,312
Unearned compensation related to outstanding restricted stock	(67,760)	(45,892)
Foreign currency translation adjustment	4,031	(7,206)
	7,391,794	6,721,448
Less treasury stock, at cost (172,248,315 common shares in 1990;		
163,789,772 common shares in 1989)	3,542,630	3,235,963
Total shareholders' equity	3,849,164	3,485,485
Total shareholders' equity and liabilities	$9,278,187	$8,282,536

Source: *The Coca-Cola Company Annual Report,* 1990, pp. 44–45.

Figure 8–1   Illustration of Concepts Behind Statement of Cash Flows

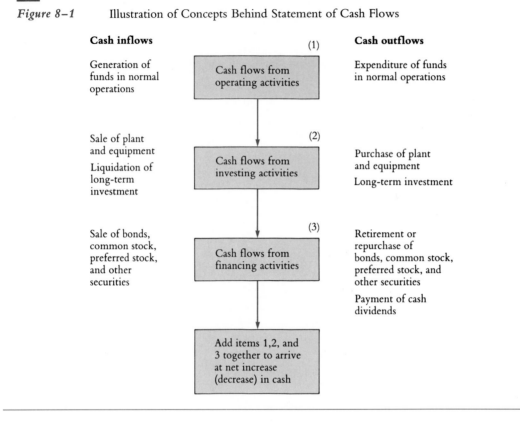

the $150,000 deduction in the income statement for depreciation can be added back to net income to determine cash flow.

The statement of cash flows addresses these issues by translating income statement and balance sheet data into cash flow information. A corporation that has $1 million in accrual-based accounting profits can determine whether it can actually afford to pay a cash dividend to stockholders, buy new equipment, or undertake new projects. In the low-profit and cash-tight era of today, cash flow analysis has taken on a very special meaning.

The three primary sections of the statement of cash flows are:

1. Cash flows from operating activities.
2. Cash flows from investing activities.
3. Cash flows from financing activities.

After each of these sections is completed, the results are added to compute the net increase or decrease in cash flow for the corporation. An example of this process is shown in Figure 8–1. This statement informs us about how the

Table 8–3   **THE COCA-COLA COMPANY AND SUBSIDIARIES**
Consolidated Statements of Changes in Financial Position (in thousands)

Year Ended December 31,	1990	1989	1988
Operating activities:			
Net income	$1,381,904	$ 1,723,825	$ 1,044,703
Depreciation and amortization	243,888	183,765	169,768
Deferred income taxes	(30,254)	37,036	43,915
Equity income, net of dividends	(93,816)	(76,088)	(35,758)
Foreign currency adjustments	(77,068) ·	(31,043)	27,945
Gain on sale of businesses and investments before income taxes	(60,277)	(1,006,664)	—
Other noncash items (primarily nonrecurring charges in 1990)	97,752	24,360	13,351
Net change in operating assets and liabilities			
(1990 reflects estimated tax payments of approximately			
$300,000 related to the 1989 gain on the sale of			
Columbia Pictures Entertainment, Inc., stock)	(178,202)	279,382	(83,736)
Net cash provided by operating activities	1,283,927	1,134,573	1,180,188
Investing activities:			
Additions to finance subsidiary receivables	(31,551)	(57,006)	(172,866)
Collections of finance subsidiary receivables	58,243	188,810	145,358
Purchases of investments and other assets	(186,631)	(858,510)	(128,526)
Proceeds from disposals of investments and other assets	149,807	126,850	77,049
Proceeds from sale of businesses	—	1,680,073	—
Decrease (increase) in marketable securities	16,733	(3,889)	19,702
Purchases of property, plant, and equipment	(592,971)	(462,466)	(386,757)
Proceeds from disposals of property, plant, and equipment	19,208	60,665	43,332
Purchases of temporary investments	(113,875)	(145,009)	(258,481)
Proceeds from disposals of temporary investments	241,373	—	452,851
Collection of notes receivable—Columbia Pictures			
Entertainment, Inc.	—	—	544,889
Net cash provided by (used in) investing activities	(439,664)	529,518	336,551
Net cash provided by operations after reinvestment	844,263	1,664,091	1,516,739
Financing activities:			
Issuances of debt	592,417	336,370	140,929
Payments of debt	(81,594)	(410,690)	(992,527)
Preferred stock issued (redeemed)	(225,000)	—	300,000
Common stock issued	29,904	41,395	29,035
Purchases of common stock for treasury	(306,667)	(1,166,941)	(759,661)
Dividends (common and preferred)	(552,640)	(490,655)	(443,186)
Net cash used in financing activities	(543,580)	(1,690,521)	(1,725,410)
Effect of exchange rate changes on cash and cash equivalents	32,852	(22,896)	(29,543)
Cash and cash equivalents:			
Net increase (decrease) during the year	333,535	(49,326)	(238,214)
Balance at beginning of year	1,096,020	1,145,346	1,383,560
Balance at end of year	$1,429,555	$ 1,096,020	$ 1,145,346

Source: *The Coca-Cola Company Annual Report,* 1990, p. 47.

cash was created (operations, investing, financing), where it was spent, and the net increase or decrease of cash for the entire year.

Let's look at Coca-Cola's statement of cash flows in Table 8–3. Cash provided from operating activities (top one third of the statement) was $1.283 billion in 1990. The major items were net income, depreciation and amortization, and taxes paid on the gain derived from the sale of Columbia Pictures Entertainment, Inc., stock. Investing activities used $439 million of cash; the major items were $592 million spent on property, plant, and equipment and the rest involving shuffling of temporary investments. In 1989, proceeds from the sale of businesses accounted for a cash inflow of $1.680 billion and created a net inflow from investing activities.

In 1990, financing activities used $543 million of cash. Coca-Cola issued new debt to raise $592 million but then paid off debt, retired preferred stock and common stock, and paid dividends of $552 million. The financing activities in the statement of cash flow indicate Coca-Cola retired an average of almost $750 million of common stock in 1988, 1989, and 1990. Despite the repurchase of preferred and common in 1990, Coca-Cola generated an increase in cash of $333 million, ending the year with a cash balance of $1.429 billion.

An analysis of this statement can pinpoint many strengths or weaknesses in a company's cash flow. We can see that Coca-Cola has made some major moves within the last three years, especially the disposition of Columbia Pictures Entertainment, Inc. The company has a strong positive cash flow even after repurchasing large amounts of its common stock. Many companies are not so fortunate. For example, a number of hard-pressed firms in the energy industry in the 1980s had insufficient earnings to pay dividends or maintain or expand long-term asset commitments. In such cases, short-term borrowing is required to meet long-term needs. This can lead to a reduction of short-term working capital and a dangerous operating position.

■ KEY FINANCIAL RATIOS FOR THE SECURITY ANALYST

We have just summarized the three major financial statements that will be the basis of your analysis in this section emphasizing financial ratios. Ratio analysis brings together balance sheet and income statement data to permit a better understanding of the firm's past and current health, which will aid you in forecasting the future outlook.

Ratio Analysis

Ratios are used in much of our daily life. We buy cars based on miles per gallon, we evaluate baseball players by their earned run averages and batting averages and basketball players by field-goal and foul-shooting percentages, and so on. These are all ratios constructed to judge comparative performance. Financial ratios serve a similar purpose, but you must know what is being measured to construct a ratio and to understand the significance of the resultant number.

Financial ratios are used to weigh and evaluate the operating performance and capital structure of the firm. While an absolute value such as earnings of $50,000 or accounts receivable of $100,000 may appear satisfactory, its acceptability can be measured only in relation to other values.

For example, are earnings of $50,000 actually good? If a company earned $50,000 on $500,000 of sales (10 percent profit-margin ratio), that might be quite satisfactory, whereas earnings of $50,000 on $5 million could be disappointing (a meager 1 percent return.) After we have computed the appropriate ratio, we must compare our firm's results to the achievement of similar firms in the industry as well as to our own firm's past performance. Even then, this "number-crunching" process is not always adequate because we are forced to supplement our financial findings with an evaluation of company management, physical facilities, and numerous other factors.

Ratio analysis will not uncover "gold mines" for the analyst. It is more like a physical exam at the doctor's office. You hope you are all right, but if not, you may be content to know what is wrong and what to do about it. Just as with medical illness where some diseases are easier to cure than others, the same is true of financial illness. The analyst is the doctor. He or she determines the illness and keeps track of management to see if they can administer the cure. Sometimes ailing companies can be very good values. Penn-Central went into bankruptcy, and its common stock could have been purchased at $2 per share for several years. In 1991, Penn-Central traded in the $17 to $27 range after a three-for-two stock split in 1982 and a two-for-one stock split in 1988. Chrysler and Lockheed were both on the brink of bankruptcy in the 1970s until the government made guaranteed loans available. Both Chrysler and Lockheed could have been bought at less than $3 per share. After recovering and generating higher stock prices, they both split their common stock. These were all sick companies that returned to health, and any investor willing to take such great risk would have been well rewarded.

Bankruptcy Studies

In a sense, ratio analysis protects an investor from picking continual losers more than it guarantees picking winners. Several studies have used ratios as predictors of financial failure. The most notable studies are by William Beaver and Edward Altman. Beaver found that ratios of failing firms signal failure as much as five years ahead of bankruptcy, and as bankruptcy approaches, the ratios deteriorate more rapidly, with the greatest deterioration in the last year. The Beaver studies also found (*a*) "Investors recognize and adjust to the new solvency positions of failing firms," and (*b*) "The price changes of the common stocks act as if investors rely upon ratios as a basis for their assessments, and impound the ratio information in the market prices."[1]

---

[1] William H. Beaver, "Market Prices, Financial Ratios, and the Prediction of Failure," *Journal of Accounting Research,* Autumn 1968, p. 192.

The first Altman research study indicated that five ratios combined were 95 percent accurate in predicting failure one year ahead of bankruptcy and were 72 percent accurate two years ahead of failure, with the average lead time for the ratio signal being 20 months.[2] Altman developed a Z score that was an index developed through multiple discriminate analysis that could predict failure. Altman modified and improved his model's accuracy even further by increasing the number of ratios to seven.[3] This service is currently sold to institutional investors by Zeta Services Inc. The Z (zeta) score relies on the following variables:

1. Retained earnings/total assets (cumulative profitability).
2. Standard deviation of operating income/total assets (measure of earnings stability during last 10 years).
3. Earnings before interest and taxes/total assets (productivity of operating assets).
4. Earnings before interest and taxes/interest (leverage ratio, interest coverage).
5. Current assets/current liabilities (liquidity ratio).
6. Market value of common stock/book value of equity (a leverage ratio).
7. Total assets (proxy for size of the firm).

The greater the firm's bankruptcy potential, the lower its Z score. The ratios were not equally significant, but together they separated the companies into a correct bankruptcy group and nonbankruptcy group a high percentage of the time. Retained earnings/total assets has the heaviest weight in the analysis, and leverage is also very important. In the next section, we present six classifications of ratios that are helpful to the analyst. Many more would be used, but these represent the most widely used measures.

Classification System

We divide 20 significant ratios into six primary groupings:

A. Profitability ratios:
    1. Operating margin.
    2. After-tax profit margin.
    3. Return on assets.
    4. Return on equity.

B. Asset–utilization ratios:
    5. Receivables turnover.
    6. Inventory turnover.

[2]Edward I. Altman, "Financial Ratios, Discriminant Analysis, and the Prediction of Corporate Bankruptcy," *Journal of Finance,* September 1968, pp. 589–609.

[3]Edward I. Altman, *Corporate Financial Distress* (New York: John Wiley & Sons, 1983).

    7. Fixed-asset turnover.

    8. Total asset turnover.

C. Liquidity ratios:

    9. Current ratio.

    10. Quick ratio.

    11. Net working capital to total assets.

D. Debt-utilization ratios:

    12. Long-term debt to equity.

    13. Total debt to total assets.

    14. Times interest earned.

    15. Fixed charge coverage.

E. Price ratios:

    16. Price to earnings.

    17. Price to book value.

    18. Dividends to price (dividend yield).

F. Other ratios:

    19. Average tax rate.

    20. Dividend payout.

The users of financial statements will attach different degrees of importance to the six categories of ratios. To the potential investor, the critical consideration is profitability and debt utilization. For the banker or trade creditor, the emphasis shifts to the firm's current ability to meet debt obligations. The bondholder, in turn, may be primarily influenced by debt to total assets—while also eyeing the profitability of the firm in terms of its ability to cover interest payments in the short term and principal payments in the long term. Of course, the shrewd analyst looks at all the ratios, with different degrees of attention.

A. Profitability Ratios The **profitability ratios** allow the analyst to measure the ability of the firm to earn an adequate return on sales, total assets, and invested capital. The profit-margin ratios (1, 2) relate to income statement items, while the two return ratios (3, 4) relate the income statement (numerator) to the balance sheet (denominator). Many of the problems related to profitability can be explained, in whole or in part, by the firm's ability to effectively employ its resources. We shall apply these ratios to Coca-Cola's income statement and balance sheet for 1990, which were previously presented in Tables 8–1 and 8–2. The values are rounded for ease of computation (dollars in millions).

Profitability ratios (Coca-Cola, 1990—in millions):

1. Operating margin $= \dfrac{\text{Operating income}}{\text{Sales (revenue)}} = \dfrac{\$\,1,952}{\$10,236} = 19.07\%$

2. After-tax profit margin $= \dfrac{\text{Net income}}{\text{Sales}} = \dfrac{\$\,1,382}{\$10,236} = 13.50\%$

3. Return on assets

(a) $\dfrac{\text{Net income}}{\text{Total assets}}$ $= \dfrac{\$1,382}{\$9,278}$ $= 14.89\%$

(b) $\dfrac{\text{Net income}}{\text{Sales}} \times \dfrac{\text{Sales}}{\text{Total assets}} = 13.50\% \times 1.1033$ $= 14.89\%$

4. Return on equity

(a) $\dfrac{\text{Net income}}{\text{Stockholders' equity}^4}$ $= \dfrac{\$1,382}{\$3,849}$ $= 35.90\%$

(b) $\dfrac{\text{Return on assets}}{(1 - \text{Debt/Assets})^5}$ $= \dfrac{14.89\%}{1 - 0.5852} = 35.90\%$

The profitability ratios indicate Coca-Cola is quite profitable, but the analysis of its return on equity using 4(b) indicates its high return on stockholders' equity is largely a result of heavy total debt to assets. The disparity between return on assets and return on equity is solely the result of financing 58.52 percent of assets with debt.

Du Pont Analysis Notice that the return on assets and return on equity have parts (a) and (b), or two ways to determine the ratio. The methods employed in (b), which arise from the Du Pont Company's financial system, help the analyst see the relationship between the income statement and the balance sheet. The return on assets is generated by multiplying the after-tax profit margin (income statement) by the asset-turnover ratio (combination income statement–balance sheet ratio).

The Du Pont Company was a forerunner in stressing that satisfactory return on assets may be achieved through high profit margins or rapid turnover of assets, or a combination of both. The Du Pont system causes the analyst to examine the sources of a company's profitability. Since the profit margin is an income statement ratio, a high profit margin indicates good cost control, whereas a high asset turnover ratio demonstrates efficient use of the assets on the balance sheet. Different industries have different operating and financial structures. For example, in the heavy capital goods industry (machinery and equipment), the emphasis is on a high profit margin with a low asset turnover, while in food processing, the profit margin is low, and the key to satisfactory returns on total assets is a rapid turnover of assets.

Du Pont analysis further stresses that the return on equity stems from the return on assets adjusted for the amount of financial leverage by using the total debt-to-asset ratio. About 58.5 percent of the Coca-Cola Company's assets are financed by debt, and the return on equity reflects a high level of debt financing

---

[4]A working definition of stockholders' equity is the preferred and common stock accounts plus retained earnings. Coca-Cola also has a few other adjustments. The total can be found on the second line from the bottom at the end of Table 8–2 on page 249.

[5]Debt/Assets $= \$5,429/\$9,278 = 0.5852$

Figure 8–2   Du Pont Analysis

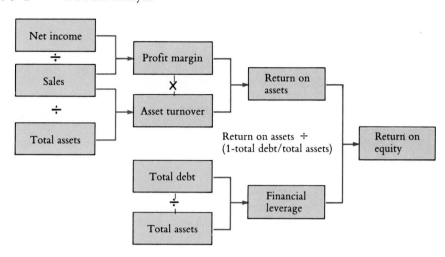

because the return on equity of 35.90 percent is 2.4 times as large as return on assets of 14.89 percent. As a detective, the financial analyst can judge how much debt a company employs by comparing these two measures of return. Of course, you will want to check this clue with the debt-utilization ratios. The total relationship between return on assets and return on equity under the Du Pont system is depicted in Figure 8–2.

In computing return on assets and equity, the analyst must also be sensitive to the age of the assets. Plant and equipment purchased 15 years ago may be carried on the books far below its replacement value in an inflationary economy. A 20 percent return on assets that were purchased in the late 60s or early 70s may be inferior to a 15 percent return on newly purchased assets.

B. Asset-Utilization Ratios With **asset-utilization ratios,** we measure the speed at which the firm is turning over accounts receivable, inventory, and longer-term assets. In other words, asset-utilization ratios measure how many times per year a company sells its inventory or collects its accounts receivable. For long-term assets, the utilization ratio tells us how productive the fixed assets are in terms of sales generation.

Asset-utilization ratios (Coca-Cola, 1990 — in millions):

5. Receivables turnover $= \dfrac{\text{Sales}}{\text{Receivables}} = \dfrac{\$10,236}{\$914} = 11.20 \times$

6. Inventory turnover $= \dfrac{\text{Sales}}{\text{Inventory}} = \dfrac{\$10,236}{\$982} = 10.42 \times$

$$7. \text{ Fixed-asset turnover } = \frac{\text{Sales}}{\text{Fixed assets}} = \frac{\$10,236}{\$2,386} = 4.29\times$$

$$8. \text{ Total asset turnover } = \frac{\text{Sales}}{\text{Total assets}} = \frac{\$10,236}{\$9,278} = 1.10\times$$

The asset-utilization ratios relate the income statement (numerator) to the various assets on the balance sheet. Given that Coca-Cola's primary products are soft drinks and food, the receivables-turnover and inventory-turnover ratios reflect high turnover. Since most of the company's consumable products are not perishable, these ratios seem satisfactory. However, the large amount of cash and marketable securities, as seen on the balance sheet, reduces the total asset turnover.

C. Liquidity Ratios

The primary emphasis of the **liquidity ratios** is a determination of the firm's ability to pay off short-term obligations as they come due. These ratios can be related to receivables and inventory turnover in that a faster turnover creates a more-rapid movement of cash through the company and improves liquidity. Again remember that each industry will be different. A jewelry store chain will have much different ratios than a grocery store chain.

Liquidity ratios (Coca-Cola, 1990 — in millions):

9. Current ratio

$$\frac{\text{Current assets}}{\text{Current liabilities}} = \frac{\$4,143}{\$4,296} = .96$$

10. Quick ratio

$$\frac{\text{Current assets } - \text{ Inventory}}{\text{Current liabilities}} = \frac{\$4,143 - \$982}{\$4,296} = .74$$

11. Net working capital to total assets

$$\frac{\text{Current assets } - \text{ Current liabilities}}{\text{Total assets}} = \frac{\$4,143 - \$4,296}{\$9,278} = -.016$$

The first two ratios (current and quick) indicate whether the firm can pay off its short-term debt in an emergency by liquidating its current assets. The quick ratio looks only at the most-liquid assets, which include cash, marketable securities, and receivables. Cash and securities are already liquid, but receivables usually will be turned into cash during the collection period. If there is concern about the firm's liquidity, the analyst will want to cross-check the liquidity ratios with receivable and inventory turnover to determine how fast the current assets are turned into cash during an ordinary cycle.

The last liquidity ratio is a measure of the percentage of current assets (after short-term debt has been paid) to total assets. This indicates the liquidity of the assets of the firm. The higher the ratio, the greater the short-term assets relative to fixed assets and the safer a creditor is. Net working capital to total

assets is nonexistent for Coca-Cola. In some firms, this would indicate serious trouble, but for Coca-Cola it is probably not a problem. The total borrowing power of the firm remains strong, but this ratio along with the low current ratio indicates a high reliance on short-term borrowing, which could be a disadvantage to the firm if interest rates increase. The quick ratio probably indicates most correctly in Coca-Cola's case that liquidity is probably not a problem. Since the company holds $1.4 billion in cash and marketable securities, the quick ratio is adequate. Also consider that the firm generated net cash flow of $333 million in 1990 after the repurchase of $530 million of preferred and common stock. Remember, ratios are pieces of the puzzle, and you cannot tell by looking at one piece whether the firm is healthy.

D. Debt-Utilization Ratios

The **debt-utilization ratios** provide an indication of the way the firm is financed between debt (lenders) and equity (owners) and therefore helps the analyst determine the amount of financial risk present in the firm. Too much debt can not only impair liquidity with heavy interest payments but can also damage profitability and the health of the firm during an economic recession or industry slowdown.

Debt-utilization ratios (Coca-Cola, 1990 — in millions):

12. Long-term debt to equity $= \dfrac{\text{Long-term debt}}{\text{Stockholders' equity}} = \dfrac{\$536}{\$3,849} = 13.93\%$

13. Total debt to total assets $= \dfrac{\text{Total debt}}{\text{Total assets}} = \dfrac{\$5,429}{\$9,278} = 58.52\%$

14. Times interest earned $= \dfrac{\text{Income before interest and taxes}[6]}{\text{Interest}} = \dfrac{\$1,952}{\$231} = 8.45 \times$

15. Fixed-charge coverage $= \dfrac{\text{Income before fixed charges and taxes}[7]}{\text{Fixed charges}[8]} = \dfrac{\$1,952}{\$231} = 8.45 \times$

We have already discussed the impact of financial leverage on return on equity, and the first two ratios in this category indicate to the analyst how much financial leverage is being used by the firm. The more debt, the greater the interest payments and the more volatile the impact on the firm's earnings. Companies with stable sales and earnings such as utilities can afford to employ more debt than those in cyclical industries such as automobiles or airlines. Ratio 12, long-term debt to equity, provides information concerning the long-term capital structure of the firm. In the case of Coca-Cola, long-term

---

[6]Income before fixed charges and taxes is the same as operating income as shown in Table 8–1.

[7]Since there are no other fixed charges besides interest, the numerators are the same in Formulas 14 and 15.

[8]The denominators are also the same in Formulas 14 and 15.

liabilities represent 13.9 percent of the stockholders' equity base provided by the owners of the firm. Ratio 13, total debt to total assets, looks at the total assets and the use of borrowed capital. Each firm must consider its optimum capital structure, and the analyst should be aware of industry fluctuations in assessing the firm's proper use of leverage. Coca-Cola seems safe, given that its business is not subject to large swings in sales.

The last two debt-utilization ratios indicate the firm's ability to meet its cash payments due on fixed obligations such as interest, leases, licensing fees, or sinking-fund charges. The higher these ratios, the more protected the creditor's position. Use of the fixed-charge coverage is more conservative than interest earned since it includes all fixed charges. Now that most leases are capitalized and show up on the balance sheet, it is easier to understand that lease payments are similar in importance to interest expense. Charges after taxes such as sinking-fund payments must be adjusted to before-tax income. For example, if a firm is in the 40 percent tax bracket and must make a $60,000 sinking-fund payment, the firm would have had to generate $100,000 in before-tax income to meet that obligation. The adjustment would be as follows:

$$\text{Before-tax income required} = \frac{\text{After-tax payment}}{1 - \text{Tax rate}}$$

$$= \frac{\$60,000}{1 - 0.40} = \$100,000$$

Coca Cola's fixed-charge coverage is the same as its interest-earned ratio because it has no fixed charges other than interest expense.

E. Price Ratios The **price ratios** relate the internal performance of the firm to the external judgment of the marketplace in terms of value. What is the firm's end result in market value? The price ratios indicate the expectations of the market relative to other companies. For example, a firm with a high price-to-earnings ratio has a higher market price relative to $1 of earnings than a company with a lower ratio.

Price ratios (Coca-Cola, December 31, 1990—in millions):

16. Price to earnings $= \dfrac{\text{Common stock price}}{\text{Earnings per share}} = \dfrac{\$46.50}{\$\ 2.04} = 22.79 \times$

17. Price to book value $= \dfrac{\text{Common stock price}}{\text{Book value per share}^9} = \dfrac{\$46.50}{\$\ 5.75} = 8.09 \times$

18. Dividends to price (Dividend yield) $= \dfrac{\text{Dividends per share}}{\text{Common stock price}} = \dfrac{\$\ 0.80}{\$46.50} = 1.72\%$

---

^{9}Book value per share $= \dfrac{\text{Stockholders' equity}}{\text{Number of shares}} = \dfrac{\$3,849}{669} = \$5.75.$

Coca-Cola's price-earnings ratio indicates the firm's stock price represents $22.79 for every $1 of earnings. This number can be compared to that of other companies in the soft drink industry and/or related industries. As indicated in Chapter 7, the price-earnings ratio (or P/E ratio) is influenced by the earnings and the sales growth of the firm and also by the risk (or volatility in performance), the debt-equity structure of the firm, the dividend-payment policy, the quality of management, and a number of other factors. The P/E ratio indicates expectations about the future of a company. Firms that are expected to provide greater returns than those for the market in general, with equal or less risk, often have P/E ratios higher than the overall market P/E ratio.

Expectations of returns and P/E ratios do change over time, as Table 8–4 illustrates. Price-earnings ratios for a selected list of U.S. firms in 1981, 1988, and 1991 show that during this 10-year period, price-earnings ratios rose between 1981 (the year before the bull market began) and 1988. By 1991, the economy was stuck in a recession, corporate earnings were down, but stock prices were high due to falling interest rates and expectations of a recovery. It was no surprise, given this scenario, that the market P/E measured by the Standard & Poor's 500 Stock Index was 50 percent higher than in 1988.

P/E ratios are more complicated than they may appear at first glance. The level of the market was higher in 1991, but not all companies exhibited higher P/E ratios. A high P/E ratio can result from many sets of assumptions. P/E ratios can be high because of high expected growth in earnings per share. For

Table 8–4   Price-Earnings Ratios for Selected U.S. Corporations

Corporation	Industry	P/E Ratio*		
		December 31, 1981	October 24, 1988	November 4, 1991
Exxon	International oil	5	12	13
Texas Utilities	Public utility	6	7	8
Union Carbide	Chemical	5	10	12
Bank America	Banking	7	9	9
CBS	Broadcasting	7	16	NMF
Halliburton	Oil service	11	26	21
Winn-Dixie	Retail	8	15	17
IBM	Computers	9	14	17
Upjohn	Ethical drugs	10	18	16
McDonald's	Restaurant franchises	10	15	15
Texas Instruments	Semiconductors	15	13	NMF
S&P 500	Market index	8	13	20

*P/E is calculated by taking the market price and dividing by the previous 12 months' earnings per share.
Source: *Barron's,* November 4, 1991. Reprinted by permission of *BARRON'S,* © 1991 Dow Jones & Company, Inc. All Rights Reserved Worldwide.

a company in a cyclical industry like semiconductors, the P/E can be high because of low earnings. CBS and Texas Instruments, in Table 8–4, had losses for 1991, so the P/E is not meaningful and can not be calculated.

Price-earnings ratios deserve significant analysis to determine the reason for their levels. The investor should not jump to conclusions based on one number. For example, IBM's high P/E ratio does not indicate a company with high expected growth in earnings but rather a company whose earnings are declining faster than the price because of poor competitive industry performance. The real question for IBM, in terms of what price per $1 of earnings is merited, is whether it will recover its lost position of market leader in computers. Every company has to be examined carefully before making careless use of P/E ratios when computing stock values.

The price-to-book-value ratio relates the market value of the company to the historical accounting value of the firm. In a company that has old assets, this ratio may be quite high, but in one with new, undepreciated fixed assets, the ratio might be lower. This information needs to be combined with a knowledge of the company's assets and of industry norms.

The **dividend yield** is part of the total return that an investor receives along with capital gains or losses. It is usually calculated by annualizing the current quarterly dividend, since that is the cash value a current investor would receive over the next year.

The price-to-earnings and price-to-book-value ratios are often used in computing stock values. The simple view of these ratios is that when they are relatively low compared to a market index or company history, the stock is a good buy. In the case of the dividend yield, the opposite is true. When dividend yields are relatively high compared to the company's historical data, the stock may be undervalued. Of course, the application of these simple models is much more complicated. The analyst has to determine if the company is performing the same as it was when the ratios were at what the analyst considers a normal level.

F. Other Ratios The other ratios presented in category F are to help the analyst spot special tax situations that affect the profitability of an industry or company and to determine what percentage of earnings are being paid to the stockholder and what is being reinvested for internal growth.

Other ratios (Coca-Cola, 1990 — in millions):

19. Average tax rate $= \dfrac{\text{Income tax}}{\text{Taxable income}} = \dfrac{\$633}{\$2,014} = 31.4\%$

20. Dividend payout $= \dfrac{\text{Dividends per share}}{\text{Earnings per share}} = \dfrac{\$0.80}{\$2.04} = 39.2\%$

These other ratios are calculated to provide the analyst with information that may indicate unusual tax treatment or reinvestment policies. For example,

Picking Stocks by the Book Is a Standby Some Swear By

Investment fads come and go, but many successful investors still swear by one of the oldest and easiest ways to buy stocks.

Year in and year out, in bull markets and bear markets, they say, the best way to find undervalued companies and possible takeover candidates is to buy stocks that are selling below their book value.

Book value is generally defined as a company's net worth, its assets minus its liabilities. Those who use the buy-below-book strategy typically focus on "tangible" book value. This excludes such intangibles as patents and goodwill, which is a monetary value commonly placed on things such as reputation when one company acquires another.

"A price below book value is a beginning tool in the hunt for bargain stocks, not an end in itself," says Mark Keller, vice president of securities research at A. G. Edwards. For example, he says, "If you buy a company that sells below book value yet has a high debt, it may never recover."

Some of the biggest proponents of buying below book are the followers of the late Benjamin Graham, generally considered the father of modern security analysis.

In Mr. Graham's view, investors should concentrate on buying stocks below or close to their book value, or no more than 30 percent above that figure. "The greater the premium above the book value, the less certain the basis for determining intrinsic value, and the more this value depends on the changing moods and measurements of the stock market," Mr. Graham wrote in his 1949 book, *The Intelligent Investor.*

For a simulated test, one portfolio manager took 500 of the largest companies and "bought" 100 of the lowest price-to-book-ratio stocks at the first of the year and sold them at the end of the year. From 1969 to July 1988, this approach resulted in an average annual total return of 14.4 percent, including dividends, [compared to the average stock return of 10.8 percent for the S&P 500 Stock Index].

Source: Earl C. Gottschalk, Jr., *The Wall Street Journal,* November 3, 1988, p. C1. Reprinted by permission of *THE WALL STREET JOURNAL,* © 1988 Dow Jones and Company, Inc. All Rights Reserved Worldwide.

the tax ratio for forest products companies will be low because of the special tax treatment given timber cuttings. A company's tax rate may also decline in a given year due to special tax credits. Thus, earnings per share may rise, but we need to know if it is from operations or favorable tax treatment. If it is from operations, we will be more sure of next year's forecast, but if it is from tax benefits, we cannot normally count on the benefits being continued into the future.

The **dividend-payout ratio** provides data concerning the firm's reinvestment strategies. It represents dividends per share divided by earnings per share. A high payout ratio tells the analyst the stockholder is receiving a large part of the earnings and the company is not retaining much income for investment in new plant and equipment. High payouts are usually found in industries that do not have great growth potential, while low payout ratios are associated with firms in growth industries.

■ USES OF RATIOS

The previous section presented 20 ratios that may be helpful to the analyst in evaluating a firm. How can we further use the data we have gathered to check the health of companies we are interested in analyzing?

One way is to compare the company to the industry. This is becoming more difficult as companies diversify into several industries. Twenty years ago, firms competed in one industry, and ratio comparisons were more reliable. Now companies have a wide range of products and markets.

Table 8–5 shows that while the food division dominates the asset-turnover ratio with a 2.11 turnover, its low operating profit margin of 5.86 percent drags down operating return on total assets. The biggest contributor to Coca-Cola's bottom line is the international division. The company has much less investment internationally than domestically, and this shows up in higher ratios. While the food division is not a major contributor to the Coca-Cola Company currently, improvements in its operating performance and profitability could enhance the stock price. Coca-Cola evidently thinks the food division is worth the investment since it continues to put capital expenditures into this area.

Coca-Cola is no exception. Table 8–6 presents the business segments in which Coca-Cola operates. Soft drinks and foods comprise the business segments with soft drinks divided into United States and International. This additional information adds a new dimension to our analysis. The soft drink segment is by far the largest segment, accounting for almost 84 percent of the operating revenues and all of the operating income in 1990. The interesting fact is that the international soft drink division accounts for 60 percent of consolidated-operating revenues and 92 percent of consolidated operating income. The foods division is not nearly as profitable as soft drinks. The corporate category is misleading since it holds the identifiable assets associated with the equity interest in other investments. It also includes overhead and staff but generates no income.

Companies in oligopolies such as Coca-Cola in the soft drink industry are hard to evaluate on a ratio basis because one or two firms (Pepsi and Coke) dominate the industry, and so industry ratios are not a helpful measure of performance. In the case of the food division of Coca-Cola, this would not be

Table 8–5	Selected Values by Segment for the Coca-Cola Company, 1990		
	USA Soft Drinks	**International Soft Drinks**	**Food**
Revenue/assets	1.46×	1.67×	2.11×
Operating income/assets	21.17%	49.05%	12.38%
Operating income/sales	14.55%	29.40%	5.86%

Table 8–6   The Coca-Cola Company and Subsidiaries: Lines of Business

The company operates in two major lines of business: soft drinks and foods (principally juice-basd beverages). Information concerning operations in these businesses at December 31, 1990, 1989, and 1988, and for the years then ended, is presented below (in millions):

1990	Soft Drinks United States	Soft Drinks International	Foods	Corporate	Consolidated
Net operating revenues	$2,461.3	$6,125.4	$1,604.9	$ 44.8	$10,236.4
Operating income	358.1★	1,801.4	93.5	(301.4)	1,951.6
Identifiable operating assets	1,691.0	3,672.2	759.2	1,131.2†	7,253.6
Equity income				110.1	110.1
Investments				2,024.6‡	2,024.6
Capital expenditures	138.4	321.4	68.2	65.0	593.0
Depreciation and amortization ...	88.5	94.4	28.3	32.7	243.9

1989	Soft Drinks United States	Soft Drinks International	Foods	Corporate	Consolidated
Net operating revenues	$2,222.2	$4,759.2	$1,583.3	$ 57.6	$ 8,622.3
Operating income	390.6	1,517.6	87.4	(269.8)	1,725.8
Identifiable operating assets	1,814.4	2,806.0	695.3	1,036.4†	6,352.1
Equity income				75.5	75.5
Investments				1,930.4‡	1,930.4
Capital expenditures	136.3	215.6	61.6	49.0	462.5
Depreciation and amortization ...	73.9	48.4	30.7	30.8	183.8

1988	Soft Drinks United States	Soft Drinks International	Foods	Corporate	Consolidated
Net operating revenues	$2,012.0	$4,503.8	$1,512.1	$ 37.5	$ 8,065.4
Operating income	351.9	1,338.8	89.3	(181.7)	1,598.3
Identifiable operating assets	1,711.9	2,097.1	694.1	1,035.5†	5,538.6
Equity income				92.5	92.5
Investments				1,912.0‡	1,912.0
Capital expenditures	80.2	159.2	82.0	65.4	386.8
Depreciation and amortization ...	66.9	42.8	32.0	28.1	169.8

Intercompany transfers between sectors are not material.
★Includes nonrecurring charges aggregating $49 million.
†General corporate identifiable operating assets are composed principally of marketable securities and fixed assets.
‡Investments include investments in soft drink bottling companies and joint ventures for all periods and CPE for 1988. The company's investment in CPE, which was sold in November 1989, approximated $598.1 million at December 31, 1988.
Source: *The Coca-Cola Company Annual Report,* 1990, p. 59.

Table 8–7   Selected Ratio Comparisons for the Coca-Cola Company, 1990

		Industries	
	Coca-Cola	Food	Beverage
Operating margin	19.1%	11.0%	18.5%
After-tax profit margin	13.5%	4.5%	7.8%
Return on equity	39.9%	20.3%	24.0%
Long-term debt to equity	13.9%	54.0%	77.7%
Price-to-earnings ratio	22.8×	15.4×	19.6×
Dividend yield	1.7%	2.3%	1.7%
Average tax rate	31.4%	37.9%	32.8%
Payout ratio	39.2%	37.0%	35.0%

the case since this industry consists of many firms, and industry comparison would be helpful. Table 8–7 looks at Coca-Cola compared to the food industry, and since Coca-Cola dominates the soft drink industry, we must compare its performance to another competitive industry, the beverage industry (beer).

Given the set of ratios in Table 8–7, Coca-Cola compares favorably with the ratios for both the food and beverage industries. The beverage industry is dominated by Budweiser, while the food industry is not dominated by any one company. Because Coca-Cola has low long-term debt, its interest expense may be lower than that of the food and beverage industries, allowing it to bring more of its operating profit down to the after-tax profit margin. The payout ratio for Coca-Cola is slightly higher than for the two industries, showing that these industries are reinvesting a larger percentage of their profits for growth.

Coca-Cola's return on equity is higher than that of the comparative industries and reflects a better level of profitability. The fact that the profitability ratios favor Coca-Cola has been translated into the market in terms of a higher P/E ratio for Coca-Cola. Additionally, the market thinks Coca-Cola will grow faster than the two industries.

In general, after reviewing all the financial statements and ratios, Coca-Cola looks to be in good financial shape. The food division needs to improve profitability, and Coca-Cola needs to use more long-term debt in its capital structure to replace short-term borrowings that have more volatile interest rates and therefore may carry more risk as a financing vehicle.

It is important to realize that Coca-Cola is an international company that may be affected by political and economic events abroad. Foreign revolts and a rising dollar can hurt Coca-Cola's earnings. Fortunately, its earnings during 1988–90 benefited from a falling dollar. This made the translation of foreign profits more valuable in dollars and aided Coca-Cola's earnings per share.

Table 8–8 on pages 268 and 269 shows the breakdown of the company's worldwide sales and profitability by region. Using the 1990 data, all U.S.

products account for about 38 percent of net operating revenues, but they account for only 23 percent of operating income. The European Community is the second largest market with 27 percent of revenues and the Pacific and Canadian market is third with 20 percent of revenues but provides the highest amount of operating income ($671.7 million) of all regions. The international markets all provide operating profit margins (operating income/net operating revenues) of 23 to 32 percent; the United States is in last place with a comparatively dismal 11.2 percent profit margin.

When international sales growth is analyzed, it becomes clear that Coca-Cola's revenue growth is occurring in its most profitable markets. An economist might credit this phenomenon to a lack of competition from alternative beverages in these regions compared to the competition from many alternatives in the United States. One concern has to be future competition in Europe, Latin America, the Pacific Rim, and Africa. If competitors such as Pepsi and Budweiser become more aggressive and successful competitors, Coca-Cola's profit margins and resulting earnings could grow more slowly, and the P/E and stock price could suffer declines.

■ COMPARING LONG-TERM TRENDS

Over the course of the business cycle, sales and profitability may expand and contract, and ratio analysis for any one year may not present an accurate picture of the firm. Therefore, we look at **trend analysis** of performance over a number of years to examine long-term performance.

Table 8–9 on pages 270 and 271 presents the 10-year summary of selected financial data for Coca-Cola. One can see the overall growth in net operating revenues since 1980. Net income has grown even more rapidly. Also, note under "Year-end position" the large accumulation in cash and marketable securities by Coca-Cola over the last decade. This 10-year summary statement provides other in-depth perspectives on the company and its relative performance.[10]

■ A GENERAL STUDY OF INDUSTRY TRENDS

In this section, we expand the horizon by shifting our attention to four very diverse industries and look at their comparative trends over time based on their rates of return on equity and long-term debt to equity. The specially picked industries are airlines, brewing, chemicals, and drugs. By studying these important industries, the analyst develops a feel for comparative performance in our economy.

The return on equity for the four industries shown in Table 8–10 indicates wide differences in profitability. Table 8–10 on page 272 is graphed in Figure 8–3 on page 273, and the trends are more visible. The drug industry has

---

[10]A few of the ratios are slightly different from those shown earlier in the chapter due to different time periods for calculation.

Table 8–8   Coca-Cola's Operations in Geographic Areas

Information about the company's operations in different geographic areas at December 31, 1990, 1989, and 1988, and for the years then ended, is presented below (in millions):

1990	United States	Latin America	European Community	Northeast Europe and Africa	Pacific and Canada	Corporate	Consolidated
Net operating revenues	$3,931.0	$813.0	$2,804.8	$562.8	$2,080.0	$ 44.8	$10,236.4
Operating income	440.4★	300.2	666.5	174.2	671.7	(301.4)	1,951.6
Identifiable operating assets	2,414.2	640.3	1,818.8	400.1	849.0	1,131.2†	7,253.6
Equity income						110.1	110.1
Investments						2,024.6‡	2,024.6
Capital expenditures	204.0	59.7	203.5	38.8	22.0	65.0	593.0
Depreciation and amortization	115.6	18.0	54.5	7.6	15.5	32.7	243.9

1989	United States	Latin America	European Community	Northeast Europe and Africa	Pacific and Canada	Corporate	Consolidated
Net operating revenues	$3,678.7	$646.2	$1,855.1	$425.2	$1,959.5	$ 57.6	$ 8,622.3
Operating income	468.2	226.7	540.6	147.3	612.8	(269.8)	1,725.8
Identifiable operating assets	2,476.0	515.4	1,342.8	328.8	652.7	1,036.4†	6,352.1
Equity income						75.5	75.5
Investments						1,930.4‡	1,930.4
Capital expenditures	196.4	30.7	133.9	24.6	27.9	49.0	462.5
Depreciation and amortization	103.5	11.8	18.0	4.9	14.8	30.8	183.8

the highest returns on equity, with very little variation due to industry or economic effects. A rising profitability trend is quite visible and is causing some political pressure on the pharmaceutical industry because of the exploding health-care costs in the United States.

The chemical industry has the next highest returns, but it is more volatile than drugs. This industry shows two distinct periods of profitability—one from 1981 to 1985 when profits were depressed, and the second five years when profits rose with the improving health of the economy. The chemical industry is greatly affected by the business cycle.

The brewing industry is third in profitability but perhaps the most stable over the 10-year cycle and relatively untouched by business cycle effects. The airline industry is by far the most cyclical and least profitable over time. The deregulation of this industry and the rapid expansion that followed hurt profitability.

Although it may be easy to generalize about industries and their relationship to economic cycles, individual companies within each industry seem to stand

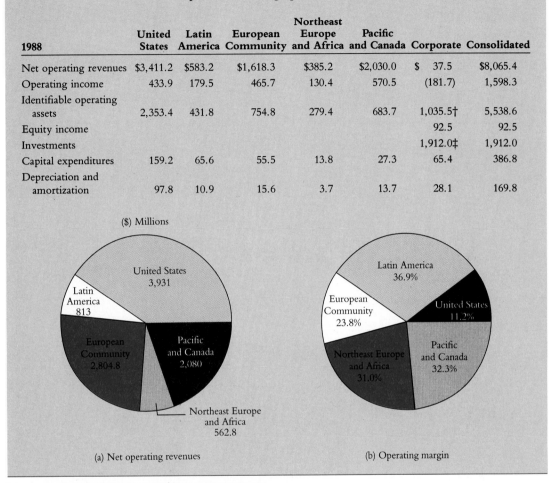

1988	United States	Latin America	European Community	Northeast Europe and Africa	Pacific and Canada	Corporate	Consolidated
Net operating revenues	$3,411.2	$583.2	$1,618.3	$385.2	$2,030.0	$ 37.5	$8,065.4
Operating income	433.9	179.5	465.7	130.4	570.5	(181.7)	1,598.3
Identifiable operating assets	2,353.4	431.8	754.8	279.4	683.7	1,035.5†	5,538.6
Equity income						92.5	92.5
Investments						1,912.0‡	1,912.0
Capital expenditures	159.2	65.6	55.5	13.8	27.3	65.4	386.8
Depreciation and amortization	97.8	10.9	15.6	3.7	13.7	28.1	169.8

Table 8–8　　Coca-Cola's Operations in Geographic Areas (*concluded*)

(a) Net operating revenues (b) Operating margin

Intercompany transfers between geographic areas are not material.
Identifiable liabilities of operations outside the United States amounted to approximately $1,498.3 million, $1,082.8 million, and $946.2 million at December 31, 1990, 1989, and 1988, respectively.
*Includes nonrecurring charges aggregating $49 million.
†General corporate identifiable operating assets are composed principally of marketable securities and fixed assets.
‡Investments include investments in soft drink bottling companies and joint ventures for all periods and CPE for 1988.
The company's investment in CPE, which was sold in November 1989, approximated $598.1 million at December 31, 1988.
Source: *The Coca-Cola Company Annual Report,* 1990, p. 60.

out. By looking at companies and the industry together over time, the best and worst become apparent to the trained analyst.

In the brewing industry, Anheuser-Busch stands out as slightly better than the Canadian brewer Labatt Ltd. While it appears that Coors has been struggling with low returns on equity, it should be noted it used no long-term debt in its capital structure until 1990. Use of debt at the same level as Anheuser-Busch would almost double Coors's return on equity but still leave it at the lowest level

Table 8–9 Selected Financial Data for Coca-Cola Company (Dollars in millions except per share data)

Year Ended December 31,	1980	1981	1982	1983	1984	1985	1986	1987	1988	1989	1990
Summary of operations[1]											
Net operating revenues	**$4,640**	**$4,836**	**$4,760**	**$5,056**	**$5,442**	**$5,879**	**$6,977**	**$7,658**	**$8,065**	**$ 8,622**	**$10,236**
Cost of goods sold	2,594	2,675	2,472	2,580	2,738	2,909	3,454	3,633	3,429	3,548	4,208
Gross profit	2,046	2,161	2,288	2,476	2,704	2,970	3,523	4,025	4,636	5,074	6,028
Selling, administrative, and general expenses	1,366	1,441	1,515	1,648	1,855	2,163	2,446	2,665	3,038	3,348	4,076
Provisions for restructured operations and disinvestment	—	—	—	—	—	—	180	36	—	—	—
Operating income	680	720	773	828	849	807	897	1,324	1,598	1,726	1,952
Interest income	56	85	119	90	133	151	154	232	199	205	170
Interest expense	30	34	76	77	128	196	208	297	230	308	231
Equity income	14	20	25	35	42	52	45	64	92	75	110
Other—net	(13)	(20)	11	2	13	69	410	40	(33)	66	13
Income from continuing operations before income taxes	707	771	852	878	909	883	1,298	1,363	1,626	1,764	2,014
Income taxes	313	339	379	374	360	314	471	496	537	571	632
Income from continuing operations	$ 394	$ 432	$ 473	$ 504	$ 549	$ 569	$ 827	$ 867	$1,089	$ 1,193	$ 1,382
Net income	**$ 422**	**$ 482**	**$ 512**	**$ 559**	**$ 629**	**$ 722**	**$ 934**	**$ 916**	**$1,045**	**$ 1,724**	**$ 1,382**
Preferred stock dividends	—	—	—	—	—	—	—	—	7	22	18
Net income available to common shareholders	$ 422	$ 482	$ 512	$ 559	$ 629	$ 722	$ 934	$ 916	$1,038	$1,702[2]	$ 1,364
Average common shares outstanding (in millions)[3]	741	742	779	817	793	787	774	755	729	692	669
Depreciation	$ 87	$ 94	$ 104	$ 111	$ 119	$ 130	$ 151	$ 152	$ 167	$ 181	$ 236
Capital expenditures	241	279	273	324	300	412	346	304	387	462	593

Table 8–9   Selected Financial Data for Coca-Cola Company (Dollars in millions except per share data) *(concluded)*

Year Ended December 31,	1990	1989	1988	1987	1986	1985	1984	1983	1982	1981	1980
Per common share data[3]											
Income from continuing operations	$ 2.04	$ 1.69	$ 1.48	$ 1.15	$ 1.07	$ .72	$ .69	$ .62	$ .61	$ .58	$ .53
Net income	2.04	2.46[2]	1.42	1.21	1.21	.92	.79	.68	.66	.65	.57
Cash dividends	.80	.68	.60	.56	.52	.49	.46	.45	.41	.39	.36
Market price at December 31	46.50	38.63	22.31	19.06	18.88	14.08	10.40	8.92	8.67	5.79	5.56
Year-end position											
Cash, cash equivalents, and marketable securities	$1,492	$1,182	$1,231	$1,489	$ 895	$ 843	$ 768	$ 559	$ 254	$ 344	$ 235
Property, plant, and equipment—net	2,386	2,021	1,759	1,602	1,538	1,483	1,284	1,247	1,233	1,160	1,045
Total assets	9,278	8,283	7,451	8,606	7,675	6,341	5,241	4,540	4,212	3,373	3,152
Long-term debt	536	549	761	909	996	801	631	428	423	132	121
Total debt	2,537	1,981	2,124	2,995	1,848	1,280	1,310	520	493	227	213
Shareholders' equity	3,849	3,485	3,345	3,187	3,479	2,948	2,751	2,912	2,779	2,271	2,075
Total capital[4]	6,386	5,466	5,469	6,182	5,327	4,228	4,061	3,432	3,272	2,498	2,288
Financial ratios											
Return on common equity[5]	39.2%	37.6%	34.7%	26.0%	25.7%	20.0%	19.4%	17.7%	18.7%	19.9%	19.7%
Return on capital[6]	26.0%	25.6%	21.3%	18.3%	20.1%	16.8%	16.7%	16.4%	17.9%	18.8%	18.9%
Total-debt-to-total-capital	39.7%	36.2%	38.8%	48.4%	34.7%	30.3%	32.3%	15.2%	15.1%	9.1%	9.3%
Net-debt-to-net-capital[7]	22.8%	14.0%	18.9%	15.4%	10.9%	15.6%	19.7%	5.6%	13.6%	2.9%	7.7%
Cash common stock dividend payout ratio	39.2%	27.6%[8]	42.1%	46.0%	43.1%	53.8%	57.9%	65.3%	62.8%	59.5%	63.2%

[1]In 1982, the company adopted SFAS No. 52, "Foreign Currency Translation."

[2]Net income available to common shareholders in 1989 includes after-tax gains of $545 million ($0.79 per common share) from the sale of the company's equity interest in CPE and the company's bottled water business.

[3]Adjusted for a two-for-one stock split in 1990 and a three-for-one stock split in 1986.

[4]Total capital equals shareholders' equity plus total debt.

[5]Return on common equity is calculated by dividing income from continuing operations less preferred stock dividends by average common shareholders' equity.

[6]Return on capital is calculated by dividing income from continuing operations before interest expense by average total capital.

[7]Net debt and net capital are net of temporary investments and cash, cash equivalents, and current marketable securities in excess of minimum operating requirements and exclude debt and excess cash of the company's finance subsidiary.

[8]The dividend payout ratio in 1989, excluding the after-tax gains from the sale of the company's equity interest in CPE and the company's bottled water business, was 41 percent.

Table 8–10   Return on Equity (selected companies—in percent)

	1981	1982	1983	1984	1985	1986	1987	1988	1989	1990
Airline industry	**NMF**	**0.0%**	**NMF**	**9.4%**	**4.1%**	**0.4%**	**6.6%**	**14.7%**	**11.7%**	**NMF**
AMR (American)	2.0%	NMF	14.9%	13.3	15.2	9.3	7.0	14.5	12.1	NMF
Delta	14.1	2.0	NMF	16.7	20.2	3.6	13.6	13.9	17.6	11.6%
Southwest Air	19.4	14.1	13.0	13.7	10.1	9.8	3.4	10.2	12.2	7.8
UAL (United)	NMF	1.0	8.9	13.8	6.8	1.9	0.1	30.6	20.7	5.6
US Air Group	14.5	12.9	13.1	16.5	12.3	9.3	10.3	8.0	NMF	NMF
Brewing industry	**11.6**	**11.9**	**15.6**	**16.4**	**16.3**	**17.2**	**14.7**	**14.9**	**15.8**	**15.8**
Anheuser-Busch	18.0	15.1	17.0	17.5	18.0	19.9	21.3	23.1	24.7	22.9
Coors (Adolph)	6.9	5.1	10.4	5.0	5.7	6.0	4.7	4.4	3.7	5.3
Labatt Ltd.	17.4	19.0	19.2	15.8	15.0	16.2	16.2	12.2	12.4	7.1
Molson Cos. Ltd.	16.2	18.0	18.1	11.3	9.5	9.8	13.3	13.7	14.7	14.8
Chemical industry	**11.9**	**7.1**	**8.5**	**10.9**	**8.1**	**11.9**	**15.1**	**23.6**	**23.1**	**16.0**
Dow	11.5	4.4	5.8	9.6	9.2	14.3	21.6	33.2	31.3	15.9
Du Pont	10.3	8.5	9.3	11.6	9.7	11.5	11.9	13.6	15.7	14.1
Monsanto	13.4	9.4	10.6	12.1	6.3	9.2	10.7	15.6	16.3	12.0
Olin	11.7	7.8	8.5	10.0	5.8	8.9	11.1	14.3	18.6	11.7
Union Carbide	12.3	6.0	4.3	7.4	1.9	12.9	22.9	37.8	26.1	13.2
Drug industry	**17.9**	**19.0**	**19.7**	**20.7**	**21.3**	**23.6**	**24.3**	**25.5**	**28.6**	**30.3**
Lilly, Eli	19.8	20.0	21.6	22.1	21.7	20.4	20.6	23.6	25.0	32.5
Merck	19.9	18.8	18.5	19.4	20.5	26.3	42.8	42.3	42.5	46.5
Pfizer	13.0	16.9	20.5	20.4	19.8	19.3	17.8	18.4	16.0	15.7
Upjohn	18.8	13.0	15.2	15.3	15.7	17.2	18.2	19.4	22.3	25.7
Warner-Lambert	0.7	11.8	14.1	15.6	26.6	28.9	33.8	34.1	36.5	34.6

NMF = Not meaningful data.

of the four firms. The comparative returns on this industry are missing Miller Brewing, which is owned by Philip Morris and not broken out separately.

The chemical industry had a difficult time dealing with the 1981–82 recession and did not recover until 1986. The industry as a whole is cyclical, but Du Pont and Monsanto exhibit the most consistency, with Dow and Union Carbide showing the most variation of return. Union Carbide had a disaster in Bhopal, India, in 1985 when a gas leak in a chemical plant killed hundreds of people. As the return-on-equity ratio shows, Union Carbide had barely recovered from a recession when this disaster lowered returns to 1.9 percent in 1985. By 1988, the company recovered to have the highest return in equity in the industry.

The airline industry is the most cyclical industry with NMF (not meaningful data) indicating losses. In addition to business cycle sensitivity, it, like the chemical industry, is very sensitive to the price of oil (airline fuel). Southwest Airlines has at least been able to keep from losing money during this period. This industry as a whole has a large percentage of debt, with Delta being the lowest.

Figure 8-3   Return on Equity—Airlines, Brewing, Chemicals, and Drugs

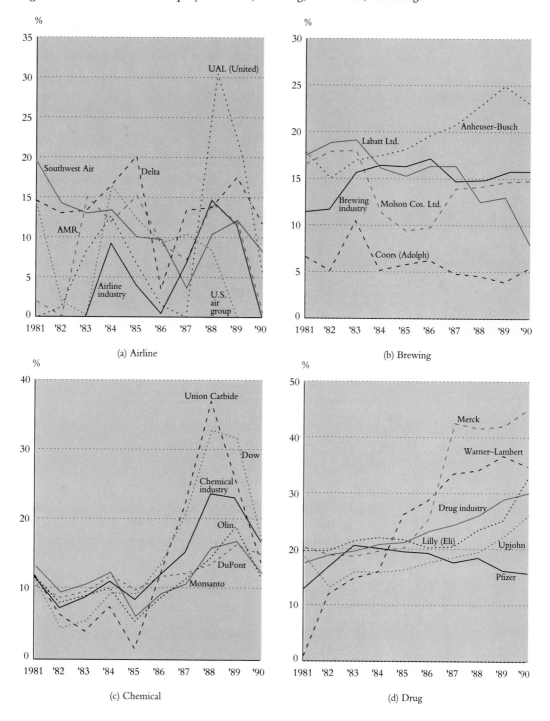

Table 8–11   Long-Term Debt to Equity (selected companies—in percent)

	1981	1982	1983	1984	1985	1986	1987	1988	1989	1990
Airline industry	150.8%	180.2%	139.2%	123.4%	128.3%	134.7%	72.3%	76.8%	57.9%	81.2%
AMR (American)	180.3	160.2	98.8	87.3	80.7	96.1	98.3	83.4	61.2	87.8
Delta	19.1	35.5	121.8	64.1	41.6	66.7	52.6	33.0	26.8	50.2
Southwest Air	33.3	44.2	50.4	13.7	81.8	66.2	48.8	65.1	60.3	54.1
UAL (United)	107.4	160.1	82.1	52.1	147.4	90.0	48.8	167.7	85.2	74.7
U.S. Air Group	79.4	68.8	53.9	56.3	47.2	40.2	94.9	64.4	65.2	126.3
Brewing industry	37.0	38.7	35.6	29.3	32.2	42.9	35.0	44.1	53.3	49.9
Anheuser-Busch	67.7	53.5	46.8	37.5	35.0	43.3	48.3	52.1	106.7	85.5
Coors (Adolph)	0.0	0.0	0.0	0.0	0.0	0.0	0.0	0.0	0.0	10.1
Labatt Ltd.	77.1	65.1	64.4	55.2	68.3	87.4	89.0	74.1	60.1	49.0
Molson Cos. Ltd.	66.8	69.5	62.2	59.4	58.9	33.1	31.2	25.0	60.1	49.0
Chemical industry	56.3	47.4	42.6	36.0	41.0	47.3	45.2	41.0	47.8	60.7
Dow	81.3	69.5	55.5	54.2	66.7	65.9	65.5	46.0	48.4	59.7
Du Pont	70.1	54.1	41.3	28.8	25.9	24.8	21.8	20.7	26.3	34.5
Monsanto	33.3	28.7	25.6	22.7	61.3	43.1	40.1	37.1	37.3	40.4
Olin	37.7	36.4	45.7	42.6	51.6	52.4	56.4	69.4	75.3	65.2
Union Carbide	39.9	47.1	48.4	48.0	43.5	304.2	229.6	125.0	87.3	98.6
Drug industry	18.3	17.1	15.7	11.5	11.0	19.8	13.8	11.6	18.7	17.2
Lilly, Eli	2.8	2.4	4.3	5.3	10.0	14.4	12.0	12.0	7.2	8.0
Merck	12.0	15.3	15.8	7.0	6.5	6.5	7.9	5.0	3.3	3.2
Pfizer	40.7	26.3	22.2	13.6	11.1	8.4	6.4	5.3	4.2	3.8
Upjohn	47.5	47.4	51.9	33.7	29.1	28.8	26.1	14.1	14.8	30.9
Warner-Lambert	37.5	49.2	42.4	35.6	40.2	37.7	33.6	31.9	26.9	21.8

The drug industry has the highest and most consistent performance, with Merck pulling away from the group beginning in 1986. Even Pfizer with the lowest returns is about equal to the industry averages for brewing and chemicals in 1990.

In Table 8–11 and Figure 8–4, the same four industries' long-term debt-to-equity ratios are given, which might explain the impact of financial leverage on the return on equity and possibly explain why some companies and industries are more volatile than others. In general, the airline industry had the most debt, followed by the chemical, brewing, and drug industries.

The basic business of airlines requires a large capital commitment in terms of airplanes. A large amount of debt is needed to finance them because profitability is not sufficient to provide enough internal funds. Delta traditionally has had a low level of long-term debt, but in 1983, the firm increased its borrowing dramatically to purchase new equipment. Since then, it has reduced its long-term debt-to-equity ratio to more reasonable levels. United Airlines

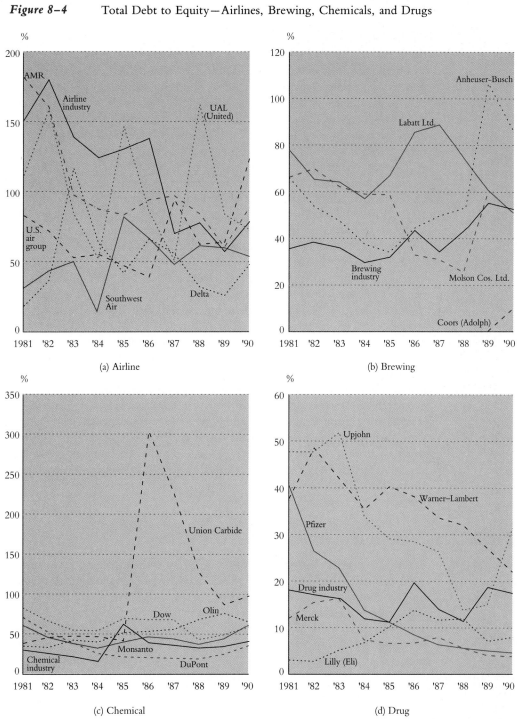

Figure 8-4   Total Debt to Equity—Airlines, Brewing, Chemicals, and Drugs

(a) Airline

(b) Brewing

(c) Chemical

(d) Drug

saw its debt soar in 1988 as several restructuring and leverage buyout proposals caused it to take on more debt to ward off unwanted suitors.

The airline industry is burdened with debt, and the cyclical nature of the industry compounds earnings swings. The Iraqi invasion of Kuwait in 1991 and the resultant increase in oil prices and reduced passenger traffic spelled the end for several airlines that could not withstand the shock to their fragile financial conditions. Pan American Airlines was divided into salable parts. Midway Airlines declared bankruptcy and was almost rescued by Northwest Airlines until that company backed out at the last minute.

All the other industries are in safe territory as far as long-term debt goes. Coors has little long-term debt, while Labatt has steadily reduced debt since 1987. Du Pont traditionally has had the lowest debt ratio in chemicals, but the purchase of Conoco Oil in 1981 caused long-term debt to rise significantly. The company has been reducing its debt burden, and since 1984 the company has been steadily at the low end of the industry. The Bhopal incident forced Union Carbide to increase its debt dramatically in 1986–87 to cover the expenses associated with this disaster, but it has since reduced long-term debt-to-equity drastically. The drug industry has traditionally had the lowest long-term debt-to-equity ratio of the four industries, mostly because consistently high returns allow internal generation of funds through retained earnings.

These tables only cover two ratios, but they should show that industry comparisons allow one to pick the quality companies and find the potential losers. These two ratios (return on equity and long-term debt to equity) can be extremely important when making risk-return choices between common stocks. By comparing the two tables, we can see a distinct relationship between the ratios. The drug industry is in the lowest risk, highest return position by having the highest return on equity and at the same time having the lowest debt-to-equity ratio. The airline industry shows extremely high risk by having the highest debt-to-equity ratios and at the same time exhibiting lower and more volatile returns on equity.

■ DEFICIENCIES OF FINANCIAL STATEMENTS

Several differences occur between companies and industries, and, at times, inflation has additionally clouded the clarity of accounting statements. Some of the more important difficulties occur in the area of inflation-adjusted accounting statements, inventory valuation, depreciation methods, pension funds liabilities, research and development, deferred taxes, and foreign exchange accounting. We do not have space to cover all of them, but we will touch on the most important ones.

Inflation Effects

Inflation causes phantom sources of profit that may mislead even the most alert analyst. Revenue is almost always stated in current dollars, whereas plant and equipment or inventory may have been purchased at lower price levels.

Table 8–12   Comparison of Replacement-Cost Accounting to Historical-Cost Accounting

	10 Chemical Companies		8 Drug Companies	
	Replacement Cost	Historical Cost	Replacement Cost	Historical Cost
Increase in assets	28.4%	—	15.4%	—
Decrease in net income before taxes	(45.8)	—	(19.3)	—
Return on assets	2.8	6.2%	8.3	11.4%
Return on equity	4.9	13.5	12.8	19.6
Debt-to-assets ratio	34.3	43.8	30.3	35.2
Interest-coverage ratio (times interest earned)	7.1×	8.4×	15.4×	16.7×

Note: Replacement cost is but one form of current cost. Nevertheless, it is widely used as a measure of current cost.
Source: jeff Garnett and Geoffrey A. Hirt, "Replacement Cost Data: A Study of the Chemical and Drug Industry for Years 1976 through 1978" (Working paper).

Thus, profit may be more a function of increasing prices than of satisfactory performance.

Inflation has decreased during the 1980s and early 1990s, but still can cause major distortions in the financial statements even if not as large as those experienced in the 1970s when inflation was in double digits for several years.

Much of the distortion of inflation shows up on the balance sheet since most of the values on the balance sheet are stated on a historical or original-cost basis. This may be particularly troublesome in the case of plant and equipment and inventory, which may now be worth two or three times the original cost or—from a negative viewpoint—may require many times the original cost for replacement.

The accounting profession has been groping with this problem for decades, and the discussion becomes particularly intense each time inflation rears its ugly head. In October 1979, the Financial Accounting Standards Board (FASB) issued a ruling that required about 1,300 large companies to disclose **inflation-adjusted accounting** data in their annual reports. This information shows the effects of inflation on the financial statements of the firm. The ruling on inflation adjustment was extended for five more years in 1984 but was later made optional. As inflation temporarily slowed, many companies chose not to disclose inflation-adjusted statements in addition to the historical cost statements.

Nevertheless, the impact of inflation cannot be ignored. From a study of 10 chemical firms and 8 drug companies using current-cost (replacement-cost) data found in the financial 10-K statements these companies filed with the SEC, it was found that the changes shown in Table 8–12 occurred in their assets, income, and other selected ratios. The impact of these changes is still important as an example of the changes that take place on ratio analysis during periods of high inflation.

The comparison of replacement-cost and historical-cost accounting methods in Table 8–12 shows that replacement cost increases assets but at the same time reduces income. This increase in assets lowers the debt-to-assets ratio

since debt is a monetary asset that is not revalued because it is paid back in nominal dollars.

The decreased debt-to-assets ratio would indicate the financial leverage of the firm is decreased, but a look at the interest-coverage ratio tells a different story. Because the interest-coverage ratio measures the operating income available to cover interest expense, the declining income penalizes the ratio, and the firm shows a decreased ability to cover its interest cost.

As long as prices continue to rise in an inflationary environment, profits appear to feed on themselves. The main objection is that when prices do level off, management and unsuspecting stockholders have a rude awakening as expensive inventory is charged against softening retail prices. A 15 to 20 percent growth rate in earnings may be little more than an "inflationary illusion." Industries most sensitive to inflation-induced profits are those with cyclical products, such as lumber, copper, rubber, and food products, as well as those in which inventory is a significant percentage of sales and profits. Reported profits for the lumber industry have been influenced as much as 50 percent by inventory pricing, and profits of a number of other industries have been influenced by 15 to 20 percent.

Inventory Valuation

The income statement can show considerable differences in earnings, depending on the method of inventory valuation. The two basic methods are FIFO (first-in, first-out) and LIFO (last-in, first-out). In an inflationary economy, a firm could be reporting increased profits even though no actual increase in physical output occurred. The example of the Rhoades Company will illustrate this point. We first observe its income statement for 1992 in Table 8–13. It sold 1,000 units for $20,000 and shows earnings after taxes of $4,200 and an operating margin and after-tax margin of 35 percent and 21 percent, respectively.

Assume that in 1993 the number of units sold remains constant at 1,000 units. However, inflation causes a 10 percent increase in price, from $20 to $22 per unit. Total sales will go up to $22,000, but with no actual increase in physical volume. Further assume the firm uses FIFO inventory pricing, so that inventory first purchased will be written off against current sales. We will assume that 1,000 units of 1992 inventory at a cost of $10 per unit are written off against 1993 sales revenue. If Rhoades used LIFO inventory, and the cost of goods sold went up 10 percent also, to $11 per unit, income will be less than under FIFO. Table 8–14 shows the 1993 income statement of Rhoades under both inventory methods.

Table 8–14 demonstrates the difference between FIFO and LIFO inventory methods. Under FIFO, Rhoades Corporation shows higher profit margins and more income even though no physical increase in sales occurs. This is because FIFO costing lags behind current prices, and the company generates "phantom profits" due to capital gains on inventory. Unfortunately, this inventory will need to be replaced next period at higher costs. When and if prices turn lower

Table 8–13   Rhoades Corporation Income Statement

RHOADES CORPORATION
First-Year Income Statement
Net Income for 1992

Sales	$20,000 (1,000 units at $20)
Cost of goods sold	10,000 (1,000 units at $10)
Gross profit	10,000
Selling and administrative expense	2,000
Depreciation	1,000
Operating profit	7,000
Taxes (40 percent)	2,800
Earnings after taxes	$ 4,200
Operating margin	$ 7,000/$20,000 = 35%
After-tax margin	$ 4,200/$20,000 = 21%

Table 8–14   Rhoades Corporation Income Statement

RHOADES CORPORATION
Second-Year Income Statement Using FIFO and LIFO
Net income for 1993

	FIFO	LIFO
Sales	$22,000 (1,000 at $22)	$22,000 (1,000 at $22)
Cost of goods sold	10,000 (1,000 at $10)	11,000 (1,000 at $11)
Gross profit	12,000	11,000
Selling and administrative expense	2,200 (10% of sales)	2,200 (10% of sales)
Depreciation	1,000	1,000
Operating profit	8,800	7,800
Taxes (40 percent)	3,520	3,120
Earnings after taxes	$5,280	$ 4,680
Operating margin	$ 8,800/$22,000 = 40%	$ 7,800/$22,000 = 35.4%
After-tax margin	$ 5,280/$22,000 = 24%	$ 4,680/$22,000 = 21.2%

in a recessionary environment, FIFO will have the opposite effect and drag down earnings. LIFO inventory costing, on the other hand, relates current costs to current prices, and although profits rise in dollar terms from 1992, the margins stay basically the same. The only problem with LIFO inventory accounting is that low-cost layers of inventory build up on the balance sheet of the company and understate inventory. This will cause inventory turnover to appear higher than under FIFO.

While many companies shifted to LIFO accounting in the 1980s, FIFO inventory valuation still exists in some industries, and the analyst must be alert to the consequences of both methods.

Extraordinary Gains and Losses

Extraordinary gains and losses may occur from the sale of corporate fixed assets, lawsuits, or similar events that would not be expected to occur often, if ever again. Some analysts argue that such extraordinary events should be included in computing the current income of the firm, while others would leave them off in assessing operating performance. The choice can have a big impact on ratios that rely on earnings or earnings per share. Extraordinary gains can inflate returns and lower payout ratios if they are included in earnings. The analyst concerned about forecasting should include only those earnings from continuing operations; otherwise, the forecast will be seriously off its mark. Unfortunately, there is some inconsistency in the manner in which nonrecurring losses are treated despite determined attempts by the accounting profession to ensure uniformity.

Pension Fund Liabilities

One area of increasing concern among financial analysts is the unfunded liabilities of corporate pension funds. These funds eventually will have to pay workers their retirement income from the pension fund earnings and assets. If the money is not available from the pension fund, the company is liable to make the payments. These unfunded pensions may have to come out of earnings in future years, which would penalize shareholders and limit the corporation's ability to reinvest in new assets.

Foreign Exchange Transactions

During the 1980s, current values shifted dramatically as the dollar rose in the early part of the decade, fell in the middle part, and rose during the later part of the 1980s. Foreign currency fluctuations have a major impact on the earnings of those companies heavily involved in international trade. The drug industry is significantly affected. Coca-Cola, with over 70 percent of operating income coming from foreign operations in 1990, is a prime example of a company greatly affected by swings in the currency markets. For example, when the dollar declines relative to foreign currencies, earnings from foreign subsidiaries get translated into more U.S. dollars and help the earnings of U.S. companies like Coca-Cola. Coca-Cola's foreign exchange currency transactions and translations were a positive adjustment of $20 million in 1989 and a negative adjustment of $13 million in 1988. Since Coca-Cola is available in 155 countries, the firm has a diversification effect with some currencies rising and others falling. However, a major change in a given part of the world could cause this diversification effect to lose its impact.

Other Distortions

Other problems exist in accounting statements and methods of reporting earnings. A mention of some of them might provide you with areas that require further investigation. Additional areas for detective work are in accounting methods for the following: research and development expenditures, deferred taxes, tax credits, merger accounting, intangible drilling and development costs, and percentage depletion allowances. As you can see, many issues cause analysts to dig further and to be cautious about accepting bottom-line earnings per share.

■ SUMMARY

Chapter 8 presents the basics of accounting statements and ratio analysis. After going through an income statement, a balance sheet, and the statement of cash flows, ratios are presented that help tie together these statements.

Ratio analysis is used to evaluate the operating performance and capital structure of a firm. Ratios will not help to find a gold mine, but they can help to avoid buying sick companies. Using ratio analysis, a brief description of two bankruptcy studies was given that emphasized the ability of ratios to spot troubled firms with a potential for failure.

Twenty ratios were classified into six categories that measured profitability, asset utilization, liquidity, debt utilization, relative prices, and taxes and dividend policy. The Coca-Cola Company was used as an example as we computed each ratio. The Du Pont method was presented to demonstrate the relationship between assets, sales, income, and debt for creating returns on assets and equity.

Ratios are best used when compared to industry norms, company trends, and economic and industry cycles. It is becoming more difficult to use ratio analysis on an industry basis as firms become more integrated and diversified into several industries. Four industries were used—airlines, brewing, chemicals, and drugs—to examine industry trends and differences. Each company was compared to industry norms, and the difference between companies and industries was easily seen.

Finally, the deficiencies of financial statements were discussed. The effect on ratios was examined for replacement cost versus historical cost data. Other distortions were discussed such as extraordinary gains and losses and pension fund liabilities.

Financial analysis is a science as well as an art, and experience certainly sharpens the skills. It would be unrealistic for someone to pick up all the complex relationships involved in ratio analysis immediately. This is why analysts are assigned industries they learn inside and out. After much practice, the analytical work is easier, and the true picture of financial performance becomes focused.

IMPORTANT WORDS AND CONCEPTS

income statement 244

balance sheet 246

statement of cash flows 247

profitability ratios 255

asset-utilization ratios 257

liquidity ratios 257

debt-utilization ratios 259

price ratios 260

dividend yield 261

dividend-payout ratio 263

trend analysis 267

inflation-adjusted accounting 277

extraordinary gains and losses 280

DISCUSSION QUESTIONS

1. Does a balance sheet that is dated year-end 1992 reflect only transactions for that year?

2. Explain why the statement of cash flows is particularly relevant in light of the fact that the accrual method of accounting is used in the income statement and balance sheet.

3. Can we automatically assume a firm that has an operating loss on the income statement has reduced the cash flows for the firm during the period?

4. What ratios are likely to be of greatest interest to the banker or trade creditor? To the bondholder?

5. If a firm's operating margin and after-tax margin are almost the same (an unusual case), what can we say about the firm?

6. If a firm has a high return on assets and a low net-income-to-sales margin, what can the analyst infer about the firm?

7. Comment on the heavy capital goods industry and the food-processing industry in terms of performance under the Du Pont system of analysis.

8. In computing return on assets and return on equity, how does the age of the assets influence the interpretation of the values?

9. If a firm's return on equity is substantially higher than the firm's return on assets, what can the analyst infer about the firm?

10. How do the asset-utilization ratios relate to the liquidity ratios?

11. Can public utility firms better justify the use of high debt than firms in the automobile or airline industry? Comment.

12. Why will the fixed-charge-coverage ratio always be equal to or *less* than times interest earned?

13. What might a high dividend-payout ratio suggest to an analyst about a company's growth prospects?

14. Comment on the relative profitability of Coca-Cola's international soft drinks and food divisions using data from Table 8–6. Is the difference due to a better turnover of assets?

15. Using data from Table 8–7, compare Coca-Cola's profitability to those of the beverage and food industries. Do the price-to-earnings ratios in the table reflect relative profitability?

16. Why is the airline industry so much more subject to the effects of a recession than the drug industry?

17. Select the industry in Table 8–10 with the highest return on equity. Was this high return accomplished as a result of high profitability, high debt utilization, or both?

18. Explain the probable impact of replacement-cost accounting on the ratios of return on assets, debt to total assets, and times interest earned for a firm that has substantial old fixed assets.

19. In examining Table 8–13 and the first column of Table 8–14, explain why earnings after taxes and the ratios have improved despite a constant unit sales volume.

■ PROBLEMS

Du Pont analysis
1. Given the following financial data: net income/sales = 5 percent; sales/total assets = 2.5; debt/total assets = 60 percent; compute:

   a. Return on assets.

   b. Return on equity.

Du Pont analysis
2. Explain in Problem 1 why return on equity was so much higher than return on assets.

Du Pont analysis
3. A firm has a return on assets of 10 percent and a return on equity of 15 percent. What is the debt-to-total-assets ratio?

General ratio analysis
4. A firm has the following financial data:

Current assets	$900,000
Fixed assets	500,000
Current liabilities	400,000
Inventory	150,000

If inventory increases by $200,000, what will be the impact on the current ratio, the quick ratio, and the net working capital to total assets ratio. Show the ratios before and after the changes.

5. Given the following financial data:

Assets:	
Cash	$ 1,000
Accounts receivable	3,500
Inventory	1,500
Fixed assets	4,000
Total Assets	$10,000
Liabilities and stockholders' equity:	
Short-term debt	$ 2,000
Long-term debt	1,000
Stockholders' equity	7,000
Total liabilities and stockholders' equity	$10,000
Income before fixed charges and taxes	$ 3,000
Interest payments	500
Lease payment	700
Taxes (34 percent tax rate)	612
Net income (after taxes)	1,188

Compute:
a. Return on equity.
b. Quick ratio.
c. Long–term debt to equity.
d. Fixed charge coverage.

6. Assume in part *d* of Problem 5 that the firm had a sinking fund payment obligation of $100. How much before-tax income is required to cover the sinking fund obligation? Would higher tax rates increase or decrease the before-tax income required to cover the sinking fund?

7. In Problem 5, if total debt were increased to 50 percent of assets and interests payments went up by $200, what would be the new value for return on equity?

8. Assume the following financial data:

Short-term assets	$200,000
Long-term assets	300,000
Total assets	$500,000
Short-term debt	$100,000
Long-term debt	50,000
Total liabilities	150,000

Common stock	150,000
Retained earnings	250,000
Total liabilities and stockholders' equity	$550,000
Total earnings (after-tax)	$ 48,000
Dividends per share	$ 1.40
Stock price	$ 42
Shares outstanding	16,000

a. Compute the P/E ratio (stock price to earnings per share).

b. Compute the ratio of stock price to book value per share (note that book value equals stockholders' equity).

c. Compute the dividend yield.

d. Compute the payout ratio.

Tax considerations and financial analysis

9. Referring to Problem 8:

a. If the tax rate were 40 percent, what could you infer the value of before-tax income was?

b. Compute after-tax return on equity.

c. Now assume the same before-tax income computed in part *a,* but a tax rate of 25 percent; recompute after-tax return on equity (using the simplifying assumption that equity remains constant).

d. Assume the taxes in part *c* were reduced largely as a result of one-time, nonrecurring tax credits. Would you expect the stock value to go up substantially as a result of the higher return on equity?

Divisional analysis

10. The Diversified Corporation has three different operating divisions. Financial information for each is as follows:

	Bowling	**Machine Tools**	**Toys**
Sales	$2,000,000	$10,000,000	$16,000,000
Operating income	220,000	800,000	2,000,000
Net income (A/T)	100,000	600,000	900,000
Assets	1,000,000	8,000,000	6,000,000

a. Which division provides the highest operating margin?

b. Which division provides the lowest after-tax profit margin?

c. Which division has the lowest after-tax return on assets?

d. Compute net income (after-tax) to sales for the entire corporation.

 e. Compute net income (after-tax) to assets for the entire corporation.

 f. The vice president of finance suggests the assets in the Machine Tool division be sold off for $8,000,000 and redeployed in Toys. The new $8,000,000 in Toys will produce the same after-tax return on assets as the current $6,000,000 in that division. Recompute net income to total assets for the entire corporation assuming the above suggested change.

 g. Explain why Toys, which has a lower return on sales than Machine Tools, has such a positive effect on return on assets. Try to use numbers to support your answer.

Approaches to security evaluation

11. Security Analyst A thinks the Oliver Corporation is worth 12 times current earnings. Security Analyst B has a different approach. He assumes 40 percent of earnings (per share) will be paid out in dividends and the stock should provide a 4 percent current dividend yield. Assume total earnings are $10,000,000 and that there are 5,000,000 shares outstanding.

 a. Compute the value of the stock based on Security Analyst A's approach.

 b. Compute the value of the stock based on Security Analyst B's approach.

 c. Security Analyst C uses the constant-dividend-valuation model approach presented in Chapter 7 as Formula 7–3. She uses Security Analyst B's assumption about dividends (per share), and assigns a growth rate (g) of 9 percent and a required rate of return (K_e) of 12 percent. Is her value higher or lower than that of the other security analysts?

■ CRITICAL THOUGHT CASE

Barry Minkow founded ZZZZ Best Co., a carpet-cleaning firm, when he was 15 years old. He ran the business from his family's garage in Reseda, California. The company became one of the biggest carpet-cleaning firms in California, and Minkow was a millionaire by age 18. Minkow took his company public by selling its stock when he was 21, and his personal worth was estimated at close to $10 million. At that time, ZZZZ Best ("Zee Best") had 1,300 employees and 1986 sales of $4.8 million. Minkow boldly predicted that 1987 revenues would exceed $50 million.

 In July 1987, ZZZZ Best management filed for bankruptcy protection and sued Minkow for misappropriating $21 million in company funds. In addition, several customers accused ZZZZ Best of overcharging them in a credit-card scam. Minkow publicly admitted the overcharges but blamed them on sub-

contractors and employees. He also said he had fired those responsible and had personally repaid the charges.

The Securities and Exchange Commission and other law enforcement agencies began investigating Minkow and his company. It became apparent that ZZZZ Best was built on a foundation of lies, dishonesty, and inconsistent accounting practices. The company had submitted phony credit-card charges and had issued press releases claiming millions of dollars in bogus contracts, sending the price of the company's stock even higher. The SEC investigated other charges, including the possibility of phony receivables, bogus financial accounting statements, organized crime connections, and securities law violations by Minkow and other executives. The SEC placed an independent trustee in charge of the company until its accounting records could be sorted out.

The Los Angeles Police Department investigated charges that ZZZZ Best was a money-laundering operation for organized crime. The investigation linked Minkow and ZZZZ Best with drug dealings and organized crime members.

These allegations ultimately led Minkow to resign from ZZZZ Best for "health reasons." But his resignation was not the end of his troubles. ZZZZ Best's new management sued Minkow for embezzling $3 million of the company's funds for his personal use and misappropriating $18 million to perform fictitious insurance restoration work. The suit charged that Minkow actually diverted this money to an associate's refurbishing business, which was part of an elaborate scheme designed to allow Minkow to take corporate funds for his own and others' personal use. According to the suit, these discrepancies in the company's accounting practices are the reasons behind the bankruptcy filing. As a result, ZZZZ Best's accounting firm quit.

Questions

1. Given the extent of fraud in this case, should ZZZZ Best's accounting firm be held responsible for not discovering the fraudulent activities?

2. What is the responsibility of the broker and financial analyst in recommending the company to investors? To what extent are they responsible for their investment recommendations?

CFA MATERIAL

The following material contains sample questions and solutions from a prior Level I CFA exam. While the terminology is slightly different from that in this text, you can still view the skills necessary for the CFA exam.

CFA Exam Question

Table 1   Tennant Company

**Selected Historic Operating and Balance Sheet Data
As of December 31, 1975, 1981, and 1987
(in thousands)**

	1975	1981	1987
Net sales	$47,909	$109,333	$166,924
Cost of goods sold	27,395	62,373	95,015
Gross profits	20,514	46,960	71,909
Selling, general, and administrative expenses	11,895	29,649	54,151
Earnings before interest and taxes	8,619	17,311	17,758
Interest on long-term debt	0	53	248
Pretax income	8,619	17,258	17,510
Income taxes	4,190	7,655	7,692
After-tax income	$ 4,429	$ 9,603	$ 9,818
Total assets	$33,848	$ 63,555	$106,098
Total common stockholders' equity	25,722	46,593	69,516
Long-term debt	6	532	2,480
Total common shares outstanding	5,654	5,402	5,320
Earnings per share	$ 0.78	$ 1.78	$ 1.85
Dividends per share	0.28	0.72	0.96
Book value per share	4.55	8.63	13.07

Question 1 is composed of two parts, for a total of 15 minutes.

1. As shown in Table 1 above, Tennant's operating results have been less favorable during the 1980s than the 1970s based on three representative years, 1975, 1981, and 1987. To develop an explanation, you decide to examine Tennant's operating history employing the industrial life cycle model, which recognizes four stages as follows:

   I. Early development.
   II. Rapid expansion.
   III. Mature growth.
   IV. Stabilization or decline.

   a. Describe the behavior of revenues, profit margins, and total profits as a company passes through *each* of the *four* stages of the industrial life cycle.

   b. Using 1975, 1981, and 1987 results as representative, discuss Tennant's operating record from 1975 through 1987 in terms of the industrial life cycle record.

(*15 minutes*)

Solution: Question 1 — Morning Section (I–88) (15 points)

a. During the early development stage, revenue growth is rapid. However, profit margins are negative until revenues reach a critical mass. From that point forward, rapidly improving margins combine with continued strong revenue growth to create extremely rapid earnings progress.

Profit margins continue to expand during the rapid-expansion phase but level out during the mature-growth phase. Despite gradual tapering of profit margins, earnings continue to rise during the mature-growth phase due to continuing revenue growth. However, earnings progress is significantly slower than during the rapid-expansion phase.

The final stage of earnings stabilization or decline is characterized by a continuing moderation in the rate of sales growth and deteriorating profit margins. In the extreme, declining revenues in combination with decreasing profit margins lead to significant earnings declines.

b. Tennant appeared to be in the rapid-expansion to the mature-growth stage between 1975 and 1981. Although pretax margins weakened, the company was able to double pretax earnings while sales revenues increased even more rapidly. However, a sharp change occurred after 1981. Sales growth moderated and profit margins declined sharply. On this basis, Tennant clearly entered the mature-growth stage between 1981 and 1987. Based on profit trends, it could be argued that the company had progressed to stage IV, stabilization and decline. However, a continuation of reasonably strong revenue growth suggests this is not the case.

(Good answers to this question will recognize that the life cycle of a corporation is identified primarily by trends in revenue growth and profit margins. An ideal answer might include simple calculations along the line shown below.)

	1975	1981	1987
Sales	$47,909	$109,333	$166,924
Percent change during prior 6 years	N.A.	128.2%	52.7%
Pretax earnings	$ 8,619	$ 17,311	$ 17,758
Percent change during prior 6 years	N.A.	100.8%	2.6%
Pretax margins	18.0%	15.8%	10.6%

Question 2 is composed of two parts, for a total of 25 minutes.

2. The director of research suggests that you use the Du Pont model to analyze the components of Tennant's return on equity during 1981 and 1987 to explain the change that has occurred in the company's return on equity. She asked you to work with the five factors listed below.

   I. EBIT margin.

   II. Asset turnover.

  III. Interest burden.

  IV. Financial leverage.

  V. Tax retention rate.

  a. Compute 1981 and 1987 values of *each* of these *five* factors.
(*15 minutes*)

  b. Identify the individual component that had the greatest influence on the change in return on equity from 1981 and 1987 and briefly explain the possible reasons for the changes in the value of this component between the two years.
(*10 minutes*)

Solution: Question 2—Morning Section (I–88) (25 points)

a.

	Value	
Tennant equity return components	**1981**	**1987**
I. EBIT margins	15.8%	10.6%
II. Asset turnover	1.72×	1.57×
III. Financial leverage	1.36×	1.53×
IV. Interest burden	0.1%	0.2%
V. Tax retention rate	55.6%	56.1%

b. Increases in financial leverage and the tax retention rate acted to increase return on equity between 1981 and 1987. Declining EBIT margins, a decline in asset turnover, and an increase in interest burden tended to reduce profitability.

  The dominant factor was the 33 percent decline in EBIT margins. This was due to the increase in SG&A and Tennant's entering mature growth. Interest burden was a relatively trivial factor, and the tax-retention rate changed only nominally. The decrease in asset turnover and increase in financial leverage were more meaningful but tended to cancel each other.

■ MARKETBASE-E PROBLEMS

In the following exercise, please use your MarketBase-E Software and manual to determine the following ratios. You will have to figure out how to search through the data to pull out those companies meeting the requirements set down.

1. *a.* MarketBase-E provides a number of financial ratios, including the current ratio and the ratio of long-term debt to capital (long-term

debt + equity). Use MarketBase-E to select companies whose current ratio is greater than 2 and whose long-term debt to capital ratio is less than .333. How many companies satisfy these criteria?

b. Use MarketBase-E to sort these companies by their ROE in descending order. Make a list of the first 10 companies in this sort and their current ratios, long-term debt to capital ratios, and return on equity.

c. Compare these 10 companies to the MarketBase-E averages. Is there any pattern observable in this list? (For example, are these companies better or worse than the averages in each category?)

2. *a.* Select companies that have an ROE of at least 25%.

 b. Use MarketBase-E to sort these companies by their price-book value ratio in ascending order. Make a list of the first 10 companies in this sort and their long-term debt to capital ratios and return on equity.

 c. How do these companies compare to the MarketBase-E averages?

3. *a.* Select companies with a dividend yield of greater than 6%. How many companies are there?

 b. Now select from these high dividend yield companies, those companies whose ROE is greater than 25%. How has this profitability criterion reduced the number of companies?

 c. From parts (*a*) and (*b*) you see that high return on equity and a high dividend yield do not always go together. Can you offer an explanation for this observation?

4. *a.* Sort the MarketBase-E companies by current ratio in descending order. Make a list of the first 10.

 b. Sort the MarketBase-E companies by debt ratio in ascending order. Make a list of the first 10.

 c. Sort the MarketBase-E companies by ROE in descending order. Make a list of the first 10.

 d. Is there any overlap among the lists you made for parts (*a*), (*b*) and (*c*)? What does this tell you about these ratios? In particular, would you normally expect to find companies with both low debt (low risk) and high profitability?

5. *a.* MarketBase-E does not give you total asset turnover. You can calculate this, however, using the DuPont formulas. Since ROI is profit margin times total asset turnover, divide the profit margin into the return on investment to determine total asset turnover.

 b. Sort the MarketBase-E companies by return on investment in descending order. Make a list of the first 10.

 c. Now sort the MarketBase-E companies by profit margin in descending order. Make a list of the first 10.

 d. Now sort the MarketBase-E companies by the user value you created for total asset turnover in descending order. Make a list of the first 10.

    e. Is there any overlap among the lists you made for parts (*b*), (*c*) and (*d*)? What does this tell you about these ratios? In particular, is high return on investment associated with high turnover, high profit margin, both or is there no apparent relationship?

SELECTED REFERENCES

Financial Reporting

Briloff, Abraham J. "Cannibalizing the Transcendent Margin: Reflections on Conglomeration, LBOs, Recapitalizations and Other Manifestations of Corporate Mania." *Financial Analysts Journal,* May–June 1988, pp. 74–82.

Hunter, John E., and T. Daniel Coggin. "Measuring Stability and Growth in Annual EPS." *Journal of Portfolio Management,* Winter 1983, pp. 75–78.

Jansson, Solveig. "Research: Back to the Drawing Board." *Institutional Investor,* January 1988, pp. 63–64.

Joy, O. Maurice; Robert H. Litzenberger; and Richard W. McEnally. "The Adjustment of Stock Prices to Announcements of Unanticipated Changes in Quarterly Earnings." *Journal of Accounting Research,* Autumn 1977, pp. 207–25.

Reinganum, Marc R. "The Anatomy of a Stock Market Winner." *Financial Analysts Journal,* March–April 1988, pp. 16–28.

Safian, Kenneth. "Corporate Profits and Valuation: A Different Approach." *Financial Analysts Journal,* January–February 1988, pp. 8–13.

Sondhi, Ashwinpaul, C.; George H. Sorter; and Gerald I. White. "Transactional Analysis," *Financial Analysts Journal,* September–October 1987, pp. 57–65.

Swales, George S., Jr. "Another Look at the President's Letter to Stockholders." *Financial Analysts Journal,* March–April 1988, pp. 71–72.

Walker, Ernest W., and J. William Petty II. "Financial Differences between Large and Small Firms," *Financial Management,* Winter 1978, pp. 61–68.

The Use of Ratios

Backer, Morton, and Martin L. Gosman. "The Use of Financial Ratios in Credit Downgrade Decisions." *Financial Management,* Spring 1980, pp. 53–56.

Chen, Kung H., and Thomas A. Shimerda. "An Empirical Analysis of Useful Financial Ratios." *Financial Management,* Spring 1981, pp. 51–60.

Distortions in Reported Data

Choi, Frederick D. S., and Richard M. Levich. "International Accounting Diversity: Does It Affect Market Participants?" *Financial Analysts Journal,* July–August 1991, pp. 73–82.

Fabozzi, Frank J., and Robert Fonfeder. "Have You Seen Any Good Quarterly Statements Lately?" *Journal of Portfolio Management,* Winter 1983, pp. 71–74.

"Pension Liabilities: Improvement Is Illusory." *Business Week,* September 14, 1981, pp. 114–18.

Part Three

Issues in Efficient Markets

Outline

A few thousand highly paid portfolio managers have basically replaced individual investors as the key players in the marketplace. Has the age of sophisticated stock analysis replaced the "hot tip" days of yesteryear?

The Great Market Crash of 1929 was caused, in part, by a *herd* instinct. The market was dominated by individual investors rather than professional money managers, and the mood of the day went from blind optimism to panic as the market crashed. Investors followed each other like sheep to slaughter.

In the following decades, the nature of market participants changed. Although 60 percent of the stocks in the United States are still owned by individuals, professional money managers do most of the daily trading. These money managers are supposedly brilliant and dispassionate professionals armed with their MBA degrees and computers. One would assume they could pick stocks scientifically. Hire them, and the return on your investment would likely be much greater than if you invested on your own.

Not so, says Bob Glauber, a Harvard Business School professor. Glauber headed the Brady Commission that investigated and reported on the market crash of October 1987. He says it is easy to forget that professional investors are also human beings subject to the same emotions as the rest of us. They tend to look at what everybody else is doing and follow the herd. Thus, seven decades after the crash of the 1920s, there is still a herd instinct on Wall Street, only it is carried out by a more sophisticated, trained group of analysts and money managers.

Of course, there are exceptions to the "follow the leader" mentality. Some would suggest that unusually insightful analysis can produce high returns that set one apart from the pack. This may well be true, but for how long? A new insight or technique that produces superior returns is likely to be quickly copied in the great electronic markets in the United States, London, or Japan.

The herd instinct may eventually turn a good idea into a disaster. For example, one may use short-selling or options to protect against a fall in stock values in a portfolio. This is basically a conservative strategy, but it turns into an ill-fated one if everyone does it at the same time.

The creative individual investor may have a better chance to outperform the market than a hard-driven, computer-inspired MBA who is constantly watching the market tape. ■

9

A Basic View of Technical Analysis and Market Efficiency

In the preceding three chapters, we followed a fundamental approach to security analysis. That is, we examined the fundamental factors that influence the business cycle, the performance of various industries, and the operations of the individual firms. We have further examined the financial statements and tools of measurement that are available to the security analyst. In following a fundamental approach, one attempts to evaluate the appropriate worth of a security and perhaps ascertain whether it is under- or overpriced.

In this chapter, we shall examine a technical approach to investment timing. In this approach, analysts and market technicians examine prior price and volume data, as well as other market-related indicators, to determine past trends in the belief that they will help forecast future ones. Technical analysts place much more emphasis on charts and graphs of *internal market data* than on such fundamental factors as earnings reports, management capabilities, or new-product development. They believe that even when important fundamental information is uncovered, it may not lead to profitable trading because of timing considerations and market imperfections.

We shall also devote much time and attention in this chapter to the concept of market efficiency; that is, the ability of the market to adjust very rapidly to the supply of new information in valuing a security. This area of study has led to the efficient market hypothesis, which states that all securities are correctly priced at any point.

At the outset, be aware there are many disagreements and contradictions in the various areas we will examine. As previously implied, advocates of technical analysis do not place much emphasis on fundamental analysis, and vice versa. Even more significant, proponents of the efficient market hypothesis would suggest that neither technical nor fundamental analysis is of any great value in producing superior returns.

In light of the various disagreements that exist, we believe it is important that the student be exposed to many schools of thought. For example, we devote the first part of the chapter to technical analysis and then later offer research findings that relate to the value of the technical approach as well as the fundamental approach. Our philosophy throughout the chapter is to recognize that there is a gap between practices utilized by brokerage houses (and on Wall Street) and beliefs held in the academic community, yet the student should be exposed to both.

■ TECHNICAL ANALYSIS

Technical analysis is based on a number of basic assumptions:

1. Market value is determined solely by the interaction of demand and supply.
2. It is assumed that though there are minor fluctuations in the market, stock prices tend to move in trends that persist for long periods.
3. Reversals of trends are caused by shifts in demand and supply.

4. Shifts in demand and supply can be detected sooner or later in charts.

5. Many chart patterns tend to repeat themselves.[1]

For our purposes, the most significant items to note are the assumptions that stock prices tend to move in trends that persist for long periods and these trends can be detected in charts. The basic premise is that past trends in market movements can be used to forecast or understand the future. The market technician generally assumes there is a lag between the time he perceives a change in the value of a security and when the investing public ultimately assesses this change.

In developing the tools of technical analysis, we shall divide our discussion between *(a)* the use of charting and *(b)* the key indicator series to project future market movements.

■ THE USE OF CHARTING

Charting is often linked to the development of the Dow theory in the late 1890s by Charles Dow.[2] Mr. Dow was the founder of the Dow Jones Company and editor of *The Wall Street Journal*. Many of his early precepts were further refined by other market technicians, and it is generally believed the Dow theory was successful in signaling the market crash of 1929.

Essential Elements of the Dow Theory

The **Dow theory** maintains there are three major movements in the market: daily fluctuations, secondary movements, and primary trends. According to the theory, daily fluctuations and secondary movements (covering two weeks to a month) are only important to the extent they reflect on the long-term primary trend in the market. Primary trends may be characterized as either bullish or bearish in nature.

In Figure 9–1, we look at the use of the Dow theory to analyze a market trend. Note that the primary movement in the market is positive despite two secondary movements that are downward. The important facet of the secondary movements is that each low is higher than the previous low and each high is higher than the previous high. This tends to confirm the primary trend, which is bullish.

Under the Dow theory, it is assumed that this pattern will continue for a long period, and the analyst should not be confused by secondary movements. However, the upward pattern must ultimately end. This is indicated by a new pattern in which a recovery fails to exceed the previous high (abortive recovery) and a new low penetrates a previous low as indicated in the top part of

---

[1]R. D. Edwards and John Magee, Jr., *Technical Analysis of Stock Trends* (Springfield, Mass: John Magee, 1958).
[2]*The Wall Street Journal*, December 19, 1900.

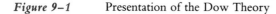

Figure 9–1   Presentation of the Dow Theory

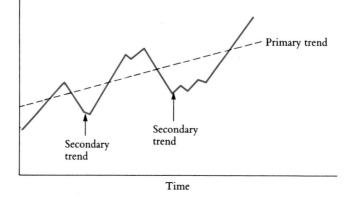

Figure 9–2. For a true turn in the market to occur, the new pattern of movement in the Dow Jones Industrial Average must also be confirmed by a subsequent movement in the Dow Jones Transportation Average as indicated on the bottom part of Figure 9–2.

A subsequent change from a bear to a bull market would require similar patterns of confirmation. While the Dow theory has proved helpful to market technicians, there is always the problem of false signals. For example, not every abortive recovery is certain to signal the end of a bull market. Furthermore, the investor may have to wait a long time to get full confirmation of a change in a primary trend. By the time the transportation average confirms the pattern in the industrial average, important market movements may have already occurred.

Support and Resistance Levels

Chartists attempt to define trading levels for individual securities (or the market) where there is a likelihood that price movements will be challenged. Thus, in the daily financial press or on television, the statement is often made that the next barrier to the current market move is at 3400 (or some other level). This assumes the existence of support and resistance levels. As indicated in Figure 9–3, a support level is associated with the lower end of a trading range and a resistance level with the upper end.

Support may develop each time a stock goes down to a lower level of trading because investors who previously passed up a purchase opportunity may now choose to act. It is a signal that new demand is coming into the market. When a stock reaches the high side of the normal trading range,

Figure 9-2   Market Reversal and Confirmation

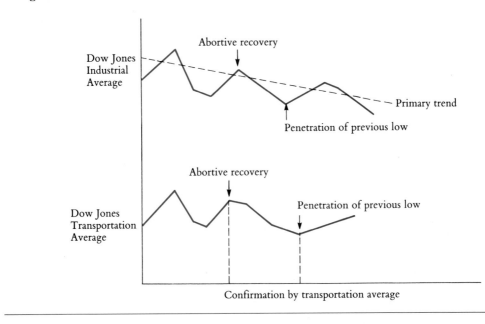

Dow Jones
Industrial
Average

Abortive recovery

Primary trend

Penetration of previous low

Dow Jones
Transportation
Average

Abortive recovery

Penetration of previous low

Confirmation by transportation average

Figure 9-3   Support and Resistance

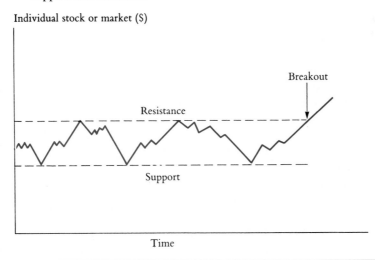

Individual stock or market ($)

Breakout

Resistance

Support

Time

resistance may develop because some investors who bought in on a previous wave of enthusiasm (on an earlier high) may now view this as a chance to get even. Others may simply see this as an opportunity to take a profit.

A breakout above a resistance point (as indicated in Figure 9–3) or below a support level is considered significant. The stock is assumed to be trading in a new range, and higher (lower) trading values may now be expected.

Volume

The amount of volume supporting a given market movement is also considered significant. For example, if a stock (or the market in general) makes a new high on heavy trading volume, this is considered to be bullish. Conversely, a new high on light volume may indicate a temporary move that is likely to be reversed.

A new low on light volume is considered somewhat positive because of the lack of investor participation. When a new low is established on the basis of heavy trading volume, this is considered to be quite bearish.

In the early 1990s, the New York Stock Exchange averaged a volume of 150 to 170 million shares daily. When the volume jumped to 200 to 250 million shares, analysts took a very strong interest in the trading pattern of the market.

Types of Charts

Until now, we have been using typical line charts to indicate market patterns. Technicians also use bar charts and point and figure charts. We shall examine each.

Bar Chart   A bar chart shows the high and low price for a stock with a horizontal dash along the line to indicate the closing price. An example is shown in Figure 9–4.

We see on November 12 the stock traded between a high of 41 and a low of 38 and closed at 40. Daily information on the Dow Jones Industrial Average is usually presented in the form of a bar chart, with daily volume shown at the bottom as indicated in Figure 9–5.

Trendline, published through a division of Standard & Poor's, provides excellent charting information on a variety of securities traded on the major exchanges and is available at many libraries and brokerage houses. Market technicians carefully evaluate the charts, looking for what they perceive to be significant patterns of movement. For example, the pattern in Figure 9–4 might be interpreted as a head-and-shoulder pattern (note the head in the middle) with a lower penetration of the neckline to the right indicating a sell signal. In Figure 9–6 on page 305, we show a series of the price-movement patterns presumably indicating market bottoms and tops.

Figure 9–4   Bar Chart

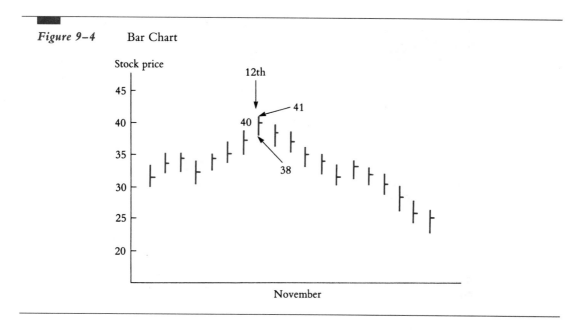

Though it is beyond the scope of this book to go into interpretation of chart formations in great detail, special books on the subject are suggested at the end of our discussion of charting.

Point and Figure Chart A point and figure chart (PFC) emphasizes significant price changes and the reversal of significant price changes. Unlike a line or bar chart, it has no time dimension. An example of a point and figure chart is presented in Figure 9–7 on page 306.

The assumption is that the stock starts at 30. Only moves of two points or greater are plotted on the graph (some may prefer to use one point). Advances are indicated by Xs, and declines are shown by Os. A reversal from an advance to a decline or vice versa calls for a shift in columns. Thus, the stock initially goes from 30 to 42 and then shifts columns in its subsequent decline to 36 before moving up again in column 3. A similar pattern persists throughout the chart.

Chartists carefully read point and figure charts to observe market patterns (where there is support, resistance, breakouts, congestion, and so on). Students with a strong interest in charting may consult such books as Colby and Meyers, *The Encyclopedia of Technical Market Indicators,*[3] and Zweig,

[3]Robert W. Colby and Thomas A. Meyers, *The Encyclopedia of Technical Market Indicators* (Homewood, Ill.: Business One Irwin, 1988).

Figure 9–5   Bar Chart of Market Average

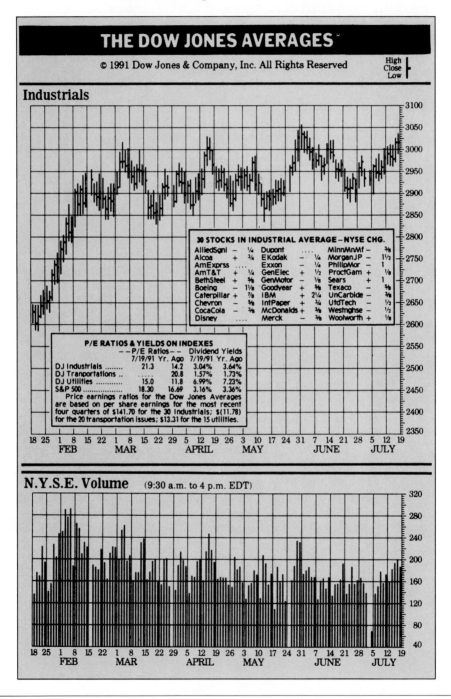

THE DOW JONES AVERAGES

© 1991 Dow Jones & Company, Inc. All Rights Reserved

High
Close
Low

Industrials

30 STOCKS IN INDUSTRIAL AVERAGE — NYSE CHG.

AlliedSgnl	− ¼	Dupont	....	MinnMnMf	− ⅜
Alcoa	+ ¾	EKodak	− ¼	MorganJP	− 1½
AmExprss	....	Exxon	− ¼	PhilipMor	− 1
AmT&T	+ ¼	GenElec	+ ½	ProctGam	+ ⅛
BethSteel	+ ⅜	GenMotor	− ⅛	Sears	+ 1
Boeing	− 1⅛	Goodyear	+ ⅜	Texaco	− ⅝
Caterpillar	+ ⅞	IBM	+ 2¼	UnCarbide	− ⅜
Chevron	− ⅜	IntPaper	+ ¾	UtdTech	− ½
CocaCola	− ⅜	McDonalds	+ ⅜	Westnghse	− ½
Disney	....	Merck	− ⅜	Woolworth	+ ⅛

P/E RATIOS & YIELDS ON INDEXES

	− − P/E Ratios − −		Dividend Yields	
	7/19/91	Yr. Ago	7/19/91	Yr. Ago
DJ Industrials	21.3	14.2	3.04%	3.64%
DJ Tranportations ..	.....	20.8	1.57%	1.73%
DJ Utilities	15.0	11.8	6.99%	7.23%
S&P 500	18.30	16.69	3.16%	3.36%

Price earnings ratios for the Dow Jones Averages
are based on per share earnings for the most recent
four quarters of $141.70 for the 30 Industrials; $(11.78)
for the 20 transportation issues; $13.31 for the 15 utilities.

18 25 | 1 8 15 22 | 1 8 15 22 29 | 5 12 19 26 | 3 10 17 24 31 | 7 14 21 28 | 5 12 19
FEB   MAR   APRIL   MAY   JUNE   JULY

N.Y.S.E. Volume   (9:30 a.m. to 4 p.m. EDT)

18 25 | 1 8 15 22 | 1 8 15 22 29 | 5 12 19 26 | 3 10 17 24 31 | 7 14 21 28 | 5 12 19
FEB   MAR   APRIL   MAY   JUNE   JULY

Figure 9–6   Chart Representation of Market Bottoms and Tops

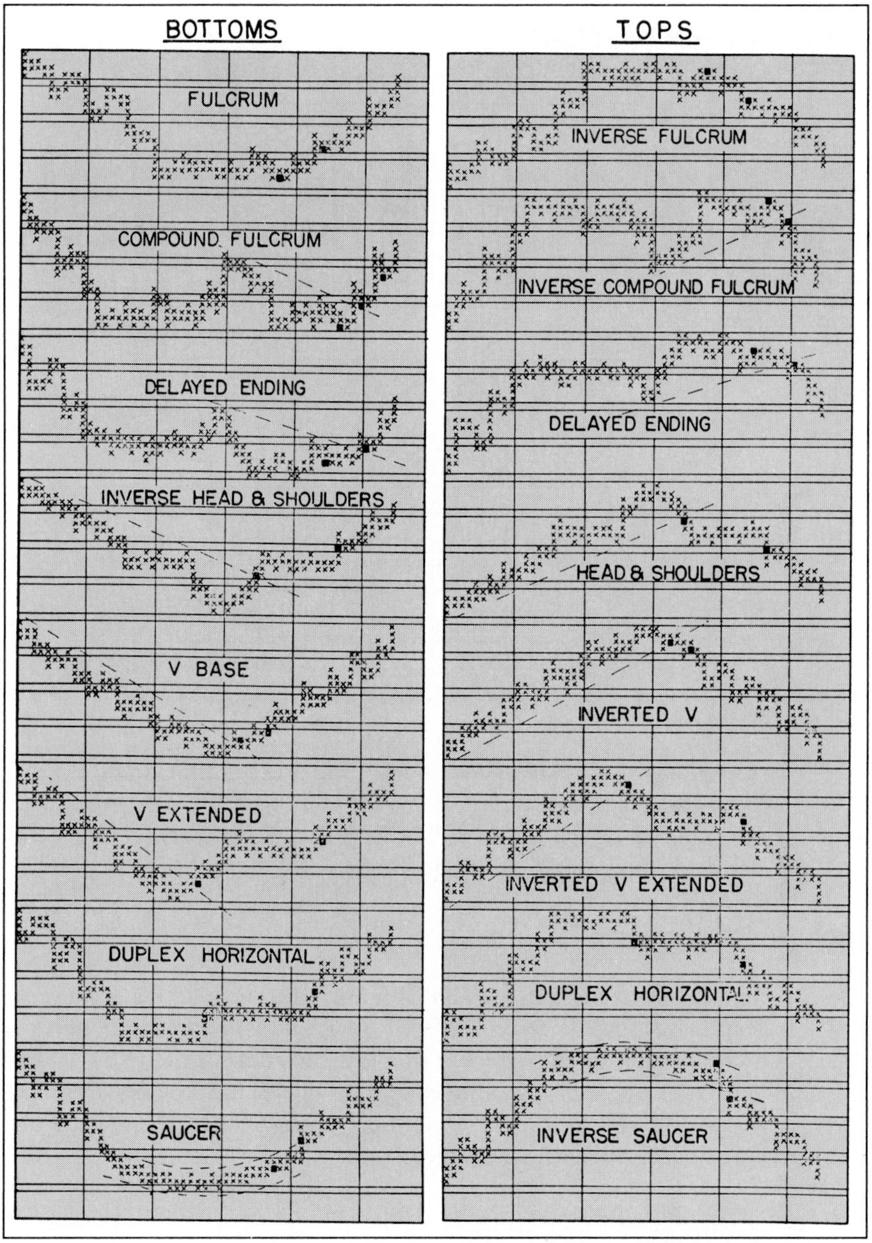

Source: Irwin Shishko, "Techniques of Forecasting Commodity Prices," *Commodity Yearbook* (New York: Commodity Research Bureau, 1965), p. 4.

Figure 9–7   Point and Figure Chart

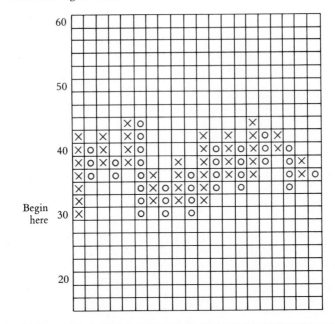

Understanding Technical Forecastings.[4] The problem in reading charts has always been to analyze patterns in such a fashion that they truly predict stock market movements before they unfold. To justify the effort, one must assume there are discernible trends over the long term.

■ KEY INDICATOR SERIES

In the television series "Wall Street Week," host Louis Rukeyser watches a number of indicators on a weekly basis and compares the bullish and bearish indicators to determine what the next direction of the market might be.

In this section, we will examine bullish and bearish technical indicator series. We will first look at contrary opinion rules, then smart money rules, and finally, overall market indicators.

Contrary Opinion Rules

The essence of a **contrary opinion rule** is that it is easier to figure out who is wrong than who is right. If you know your neighbor has a terrible sense of

---

[4]Martin E. Zweig, *Understanding Technical Forecasting* (Princeton, N.J.: Dow Jones, 1978).

direction and you spot him taking a left at the intersection, you automatically take a right. In the stock market there are similar guidelines.

Odd-Lot Theory   An odd-lot trade is one of less than 100 shares, and only small investors tend to engage in odd-lot transactions. The odd-lot theory suggests you watch very closely what the small investor is doing and then do the opposite. *The Wall Street Journal* reports odd-lot trading on a daily basis, and *Barron's* reports similar information on a weekly basis. It is a simple matter to construct a ratio of odd-lot purchases to odd-lot sales. For example, on July 17, 1991, 649,199 odd-lot shares were purchased, and 798,147 shares were sold, indicating a ratio of 0.813. The ratio has historically fluctuated between 0.50 and 1.35.

The odd-lot theory actually suggests the small trader does all right most of the time but badly misses on key market turns. As indicated in Figure 9–8, the odd-lot trader is on the correct path as the market is going up; that is, selling off part of the portfolio in an up market (the name of the game is to buy low and sell high). This net selling posture is reflected by a declining odd-lot index (purchase/sales ratio). However, as the market continues upward, the odd-lot trader suddenly thinks he or she sees an opportunity for a killing in the market and becomes a very strong net buyer. This precedes a fall in the market.

The odd-lot trader is also assumed to be a strong seller right before the bottom of a bear market. Presumably, when the small trader finally gets grandfather's 50 shares of AT&T out of the lockbox and sells them in disgust, it is time for the market to turn upward.

As if to add injury to insult, a corollary to the odd-lot theory says one should be particularly sensitive to what odd-lot traders do on Monday because

Figure 9–8   Comparing Standard & Poor's 500 Index and the Odd-Lot Index

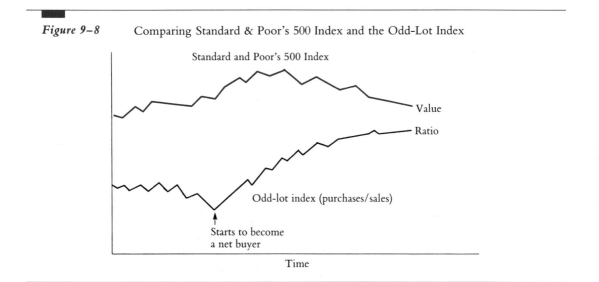

odd-lotters tend to visit each other over the weekend, confirm each other's opinions or exchange hot tips, and then call their brokers on Monday morning. The assumption is that their chatter over the barbeque pit or in the bowling alley is even more suspect than their own individual opinions.

While the odd-lot theory appeared to have some validity in the 1950s and 1960s, it was not a particularly valuable tool in the last two decades. For one thing, the odd-lotters outguessed many of the professional money managers in selling off before the stock market debacle of the mid-1970s and late 1980s, and they began buying in advance of a recovery.

Short Sales Position A second contrary opinion rule is based on the volume of short sales in the market. As you recall from Chapter 3, a short sale represents the selling of a security you do not own with the anticipation of purchasing the security in the future to cover your short position. Investors would only engage in a short sale transaction if they believed the security would, in fact, be going down in price in the near future so they could buy back the security at a lower price to cover the short sale. When the aggregate number of short sellers is large (that is, they are bearish), this is thought to be a bullish signal.

The contrary opinion stems from two sources: first, short sellers are sometimes emotional and may overreact to the market; second and more important, there now is a built-in demand for stocks that have been sold short by investors who will have to repurchase the shares to cover their short positions.

Daily short sale totals for the New York Stock Exchange are recorded in *The Wall Street Journal*. Also once a month (around the 20th), *The Wall Street Journal* reports on total short sale figures for the two major exchanges as well as securities traded on those exchanges (based on midmonth data). This feature usually contains comments about current trends in the market.

Technical analysts compute a ratio of the total short sales positions on an exchange to average daily exchange volume for the month. The normal ratio is between 2.0 and 3.5. A ratio of 2.0 would indicate the current short sales position is equal to twice the day's average trading volume.

As the short sales ratio (frequently called the short interest ratio) approaches the higher end of the normal trading range, this would be considered bullish (remember this is a contrary opinion trading rule). As is true with many other technical trading rules, its use in predicting future performance has produced mixed results.[5]

Investment Advisory Recommendations A further contrary opinion rule states you should watch the predictions of the investment advisory services and do the opposite. This has been formalized by Investors Intelligence

---

[5]Randall Smith, "Short Interest and Stock Market Prices," *Financial Analysts Journal*, November–December 1968, pp. 151–54; and Barton M. Briggs, "The Short Interest—A False Proverb," *Financial Analysts Journal*, July–August 1966, pp. 111–16.

Stop Studying and Turn on The TV—"The Super Bowl Effect"

Twenty-five Super Bowl games have been played between 1967 and 1991. Stock market analysts found an amazing pattern in evaluating the results of those games. In years in which the game is won by a team from the National Football Conference (or teams that were once part of the National Football League such as Baltimore or Pittsburgh), the stock market went up 16 out of 18 years. In years in which the game is won by a team from the American Football Conference, the stock market went down six out of seven years.

This means an investor could have used the results of the Super Bowl, which is played in January, to correctly predict the performance of the stock market for the year in 22 out of the 25 years. A market technician that could come up with a better predictive device than the Super Bowl would no doubt be considered one of the great market gurus of all time. The so-called Super Bowl Effect was even analyzed in an article in the highly prestigious *Journal of Finance* by Professors Krueger and Kennedy. They found the predictive power of the Super Bowl to be significant at almost any conceivable level of testing.[*]

[*]Thomas M. Krueger and William F. Kennedy, "An Examination of the Super Bowl Stock Market Predictor," *Journal of Finance,* June 1990, pp. 691–97.

(an investment advisory service itself) into the Index of Bearish Sentiment. When 60 percent or more of the advisory services are bearish, you should expect a market upturn. Conversely, when only 15 percent or fewer are bearish, you should expect a decline.[6]

Lest one take investment advisory services too lightly, however, observe the market impact of a recommendation by Joseph Granville, publisher of the *Granville Market Letter.* On Tuesday, January 6, 1981, Mr. Granville issued a late-evening warning to his subscribers to "sell everything." He helped cause a $40 billion decline in market values the next day. Although subsequent events proved Mr. Granville wrong in his prediction of an impending bear market, the fact that one man could trigger such a reaction is an indication of the number of people who are influenced by the suggestions of advisory services. Mr. Granville has been followed by many other so-called gurus in the 1980s, and early 1990s, most of whom have their day in the sun and then eventually fall into disrepute as they fail to call a major turn in the market or begin reversing their positions so often that investors lose confidence. No doubt a new series of such stars will appear in the mid-1990s.

Put-Call Ratio A final contrary opinion rule applies to the put-call ratio. Puts and calls represent options to sell or buy stock over a specified time period

---

[6]John R. Dortman, "The Stock Market Sign Often Points the Wrong Way," *The Wall Street Journal,* January 26, 1989, p. C1.

at a given price. A put is an option to sell, and a call is an option to buy. Options have become very popular since they began trading actively on organized exchanges in 1973. As you will see in Chapter 15, there are many sophisticated uses for options to implement portfolio strategies (particularly to protect against losses). However, there is also a great deal of speculation by individual investors in the options market. Because some of this speculation is ill conceived, ratios based on options may tell you to do the opposite of what option traders are doing.

The ratio of put (sell) options to call (buy) options is normally about 0.60. There are generally fewer traders of put options than call options. However, when the ratio gets up to 0.70 or higher, this indicates increasing pessimism by option traders. Under a contrary opinion rule, this indicates a buy signal (he turned left so you turn right). If the put-call ratio goes down to 0.40, the decreasing pessimism (increasing optimism) of the option trader may indicate it is time to sell if you are a contrarian. The put-call ratio has a better than average record for calling market turns.[7] Put-call ratio data can be found in the "Market Laboratory" section of *Barron's*.

Smart Money Rules

Market technicians have long attempted to track the pattern of sophisticated traders in the hope that they might provide unusual insight into the future. We shall briefly observe theories related to bond market traders and stock exchange specialists.

Barron's Confidence Index   The *Barron's* **Confidence Index** is used to observe the trading pattern of investors in the bond market. The theory is based on the premise that bond traders are more sophisticated than stock traders and will pick up trends more quickly. The theory would suggest that a person who can figure out what bond traders are doing today may be able to determine what stock market investors will be doing in the near future.

Barron's Confidence Index is actually computed by taking the yield on 10 top-grade corporate bonds, dividing by the yield on 10 intermediate-grade bonds, and multiplying by 100.

$$(9-1)$$

$$Barron's\ Confidence\ Index = \frac{Yield\ on\ 10\ top\text{-}grade\ corporate\ bonds}{Yield\ on\ 10\ intermediate\text{-}grade\ bonds} \times 100$$

The bonds in this index are presented in Table 9–1.

The index is published weekly in the "Market Laboratory" section of *Barron's* magazine. What does it actually tell us? First, we can assume that the top-grade bonds in the numerator will always have a smaller yield than the

---

[7]Earl C. Gottschalk, Jr., "Using Dumb Money as a Market Guide," *The Wall Street Journal*, January 17, 1989, p. C1.

Table 9–1 Issues in *Barron's* Confidence Index

Best Grade Bonds

Name	Coupon	Maturity
AT&T	8¾%	2000
Anheuser-Busch	8⅝%	2016
Balt G&E	8⅜%	2006
DuPont	8½%	2006
Exxon Pipeline	8¼%	2001
Gen. Elec.	8½%	2004
GMAC	8¼%	2006
IBM	9⅜%	2004
Ill. Bell T	7⅝%	2006
Proc. & G.	8¼%	2005

Intermediate Grade Bonds

Name	Coupon	Maturity
Ala Power	9¾%	2004
Beneficial	9%	2005
Cater Trac	8%	2001
Comwlth Ed	9⅛%	2008
Firestone	9¼%	2004
GTE	9⅜%	1999
Honeywell	9⅜%	2009
Union Carbide	8½%	2005
USX Corp	7¾%	2001
Woolworth	9%	1999

Source: *Barron's*, July 15, 1991, p. 135. Reprinted by permission of *BARRON'S*, © 1991 by Dow Jones & Company, Inc. All Rights Reserved Worldwide.

intermediate-grade bonds in the denominator. The reason is that the higher-quality issues can satisfy investors with smaller returns. The bond market is very representative of a risk-return trade-off environment in which less risk requires less return and higher risk necessitates a higher return.

With top-grade bonds providing smaller yields than intermediate-grade bonds, the Confidence Index will always be less than 100 (percent). The normal trading range is between 80 and 95, and it is within this range that technicians look for signals on the economy. If bond investors are bullish about future economic prosperity, they will be rather indifferent between holding top-grade bonds and holding intermediate-grade bonds, and the yield differences between these two categories will be relatively small. This would indicate the Confidence Index may be close to 95. An example is presented below

in which top-grade bonds are providing 9.4 percent and intermediate-grade bonds are yielding 10.1 percent.

$$\textit{Barron's Confidence Index} = \frac{\text{Yield on 10 top-grade corporate bonds}}{\text{Yield on 10 intermediate-grade bonds}} \times 100$$

$$= \frac{9.4\%}{10.1\%} \times 100 = 93(\%)$$

Now let us assume investors become quite concerned about the outlook for the future health of the economy. If events go poorly, some weaker corporations may not be able to make their interest payments, and thus, bond market investors will have a strong preference for top-quality issues. Some investors will continue to invest in intermediate- or lower-quality issues but only at a sufficiently high yield differential to justify the risk. We might assume that the *Barron's* Confidence Index will drop to 84 because of the increasing spread between the two yields in the formula.

$$\textit{Barron's Confidence Index} = \frac{\text{Yield on 10 top-grade corporate bonds}}{\text{Yield on 10 intermediate-grade bonds}} \times 100$$

$$= \frac{9.9\%}{11.8\%} \times 100 = 84(\%)$$

The yield on the intermediate-grade bonds is now 1.9 percentage points higher than that on the 10 top-grade bonds, and this is reflected in the lower Confidence Index reading. As confidence in the economy is once again regained, the yield spread differential will narrow, and the Confidence Index will go up.

Market technicians assume there are a few months of lead time between what happens to the Confidence Index and what happens to the economy and stock market. As is true with other such indicators, it has a mixed record of predicting future events. One problem is that the Confidence Index is only assumed to consider the impact of investors' attitudes on yields (their demand pattern). We have seen in the 1980s and early 1990s that the supply of new bond issues can also influence yields. Thus, a very large bond issue by AT&T or Exxon may drive up high-grade bond yields even though investor attitudes indicate they should be going down.

Short Sales by Specialists   Another smart money index is based on the short sales positions of specialists. Recall from Chapter 2 that specialists make markets in various securities listed on the organized exchanges. Because of the uniquely close position of specialists to the action on Wall Street, market technicians ascribe unusual importance to their decisions. One measure of their activity that is frequently monitored is the ratio of specialists' short sales to the total amount of short sales on an exchange.

When we previously mentioned short sales in this chapter, we suggested that a high incidence of short selling might be considered bullish because short sellers often overreact to the market and provide future demand potential to

cover their short position. In the case of market specialists, this is not necessarily true. These sophisticated traders keep a book of limit orders on their securities so that they have a close feel for market activity at any given time, and their decisions are considered important.

The normal ratio of specialist short sales to short sales on an exchange is about 45 percent. When the ratio goes up to 50 percent or more, market technicians interpret this as a bearish signal. A ratio under 40 percent is considered bullish.

Overall Market Rules

Our discussion of key indicator series has centered on both contrary opinion rules and smart money rules. We now briefly examine two overall market indicators: the breadth of the market indicator series and the cash position of mutual funds.

Breadth of the Market A breadth of the market indicator attempts to measure what a broad range of securities is doing as opposed to merely examining a market average. The theory is that market averages, such as the Dow Jones Industrial Average of 30 stocks or the Standard & Poor's 500 Stock Average, are weighted toward large firms and may not be representative of the entire market. To get a broader perspective of the market, an analyst may examine all stocks on an exchange.

The technician often compares the advance-declines with the movement of a popular market average to determine if there is a divergence between the two. Advances and declines usually move in concert with the popular market averages but may move in the opposite direction at a market peak or bottom. One of the possible signals for the end of a bull market is when the Dow Jones Industrial Average is moving up but the number of daily declines consistently exceeds the number of daily advances. This indicates conservative investors are investing in blue-chip stocks, but there is a lack of broad-based confidence in the market. In Table 9–2, we look at an example of divergence between the advance-decline indicators and the Dow Jones Industrial Average (DJIA).

In column 4, we see the daily differences in advances and declines. In column 5, we look at the cumulative pattern by adding or subtracting each new day's value from the previous total. We then compare the information in column 4 and column 5 to the Dow Jones Industrial Average (DJIA) in column 6. Clearly, the strength in the Dow Jones Industrial Average is not reflected in the advance-decline data, and this may be interpreted as signaling future weakness in the market.

Breadth of the market data can also be used to analyze upturns in the market. When the Dow Jones Industrial Average is going down but advances consistently lead declines, the market may be positioned for a recovery. Some market technicians develop sophisticated weighted averages of the daily advance-declines to go along with the data in Table 9–2.

Table 9–2   Comparing Advance-Decline Data and the Dow Jones Industrial Average

Day	(1) Advances	(2) Declines	(3) Unchanged	(4) Net Advances or Declines	(5) Cumulative Advances or Declines	(6) DJIA
1	850	750	350	+ 100	+ 100	+ 7.09
2	800	810	340	− 10	+ 90	+ 4.52
3	792	821	337	− 29	+ 61	+ 3.08
4	780	828	342	− 48	+ 13	+ 5.21
5	719	890	341	− 171	− 158	− 2.02
6	802	812	336	− 10	− 168	+ 5.43
7	783	824	343	− 41	− 209	+ 3.01
8	692	912	340	− 226	− 435	+ .52

While a comparison of advance-decline data to market averages can provide important insights, there is also the danger of false signals. Not every divergence between the two signals a turn in the market, so analysts must be careful in their interpretation. The technical analyst generally looks at a wide range of variables.

Mutual Fund Cash Position   Another overall market indicator is the cash position of mutual funds. This measure indicates the buying potential of mutual funds and is generally representative of the purchasing potential of other large institutional investors. The cash position of mutual funds, as a percentage of their total assets, generally varies between 5 percent and 20 to 25 percent.[8]

At the lower end of the boundary, it would appear that mutual funds are fully invested and can provide little in the way of additional purchasing power. As their cash position goes to 15 percent or higher, market technicians assess this as representing significant purchasing power that may help to trigger a market upturn. While the overall premise is valid, there are problems in identifying just what is a significant cash position for mutual funds in a given market cycle. It may change in extreme market environments.

■ EFFICIENT MARKET HYPOTHESIS

We shift our attention from technical analysis to that of examining market efficiency. As indicated at the beginning of the chapter, we shall now view any

---

[8]The cash dollars are usually placed in short-term credit instruments, as opposed to stocks and bonds.

contradictions between the assumptions of fundamental or technical analysis and findings of the **efficient market hypothesis (EMH).**

We previously said an efficient market is one in which new information is very rapidly processed so that securities are properly priced at any given time.[9] An important premise of an efficient market is that a large number of profit-maximizing participants are concerned with the analysis and valuation of securities. This would seem to describe the security market environment in the United States. Any news on IBM, AT&T, an oil embargo, or tax legislation is likely to be absorbed and acted on very rapidly by profit-maximizing individuals. For this reason, the efficient market hypothesis assumes that no stock price can be in disequilibrium or improperly priced for long. There is almost instantaneous adjustment to new information. The EMH applies most directly to large firms trading on the major security exchanges.

The efficient market hypothesis further assumes information travels in a random, independent fashion and prices are an unbiased reflection of all currently available information.

More generally, the efficient market hypothesis is stated and tested in three different forms: the weak form, the semistrong form, and the strong form. We shall examine each of these and the related implications for technical and fundamental analysis.

■ WEAK FORM OF THE EFFICIENT MARKET HYPOTHESIS

The **weak form of the efficient market hypothesis** suggests there is no relationship between past and future prices of securities. They are presumed to be independent over time. Because the efficient market hypothesis maintains that current prices reflect all available information and information travels in a random fashion, it is assumed there is little or nothing to be gained from studying past stock prices.

The weak form of the efficient market hypothesis has been tested in two different ways—tests of independence and trading rule tests.

Tests of Independence

Tests of independence have examined the degree of correlation between stock prices over time and have found the correlation to be consistently small (between + .10 and − .10) and not statistically significant. This would indicate

---

[9]A slightly more precise definition is that securities are priced in an unbiased fashion at any given time. Because information is assumed to travel in a random, independent fashion, there is no consistent upside or downside pricing bias mechanism. Although the price adjustment is not always perfect, it is unbiased and cannot be anticipated in advance.

stock price changes are independent.[10] A further test is based on the frequency and extent of runs in stock price data. A run occurs when there is no difference in direction between two or more price changes. An example of a series of data and some runs is presented below.

Runs can be expected in any series of data through chance factors, but an independent data series should not produce an unusual amount of runs. Statistical tests have indicated security prices generally do not produce any more runs than would be expected through the process of random number generation.[11] This would also tend to indicate that stock price movements are independent over time.

Trading Rule Tests

A second method of testing the weak form of the efficient market hypothesis (that past trends in stock prices are not helpful in predicting the future) is through trading rule tests. Because practicing market technicians maintain that tests of independence (correlation studies and runs) are too rigid to test the assumptions of the weak form of the efficient market hypothesis, additional tests by academic researchers have been developed. These are known as trading rule or filter tests. These tests determine whether a given trading rule based on past price data, volume figures, and so forth can be used to beat a naive buy-and-hold approach. The intent is to simulate the conditions under which a given trading rule is used and then determine if superior returns were produced after considering transaction costs and the risks involved.

As an example of a trading rule, if a stock moves up 5 percent or more, the rule might be to purchase it. The assumption is that this represents a breakout and should be considered bullish. Similarly, a 5 percent downward movement would be considered bearish and call for a sell strategy (rather than a buy-low/sell-high strategy, this is a follow-the-market-trend strategy). Other trading rule tests might be based on advance-decline patterns, short sales figures, and similar technical patterns. Research results have indicated that in a limited number of cases, trading rules may produce slightly positive returns,

[10]Sidney S. Alexander, "Price Movements in Speculative Markets: Trends or Random Walks," *Industrial Management Review,* May 1961, pp. 7–26; and Eugene F. Fama, "The Behavior of Stock Market Prices," *Journal of Business,* January 1965, pp. 34–105.

[11]Ibid.

but after commission costs are considered, the results are neutral and some-times negative in comparison to a naive buy-and-hold approach.[12]

Implications for Technical Analysis

The results of the *tests of independence* and *trading rules* would seem to uphold the weak form of the efficient market hypothesis. Security prices do appear to be independent over time or, more specifically, move in the pattern of a random walk.

Some challenge the research on the basis that academic research in this area does not capture the personal judgment an experienced technician brings forward in reading charts. There is also the fact that there are an infinite number of trading rules, and not all of them can or have been tested. Nevertheless, research on the weak form of EMH would seem to suggest prices move independently over time, past trends cannot be used to predict the future, and charting and technical analysis may have limited value.

■ SEMISTRONG FORM OF THE EFFICIENT MARKET HYPOTHESIS

The **semistrong form of the efficient market hypothesis** maintains that all public information is already impounded into the value of a security, and therefore, one cannot use fundamental analysis to determine whether a stock is undervalued or overvalued.

Basically, the semistrong form of the efficient market hypothesis would support the notion that there is no learning lag in the distribution of public information. When a company makes an announcement, investors across the country assess the information with equal speed. Also, a major firm listed on the New York Stock Exchange could hardly hope to utilize some questionable accounting practice that deceptively leads to higher reported profits and not expect sophisticated analysts to pick it up. (This may not be equally true for a lesser known firm that trades over-the-counter and enjoys little investor attention.)

Researchers have tested the semistrong form of EMH by determining whether investors who have acted on the basis of newly released public information have been able to enjoy superior returns. If the market is efficient in a semistrong sense, this information is almost immediately impounded in the value of the security, and little or no trading profits would be available. The implications would be that one could not garner superior returns by trading on public information about stock splits, earnings reports, or other similar items.

---

[12]Eugene F. Fama and Marshall Blume, "Filter Rules and Stock Market Trading Profits," *Journal of Business,* supplement, January 1966, pp. 226–41; and George Pinches, "The Random Walk Hypothesis and Technical Analysis," *Financial Analysts Journal,* March–April 1970, pp. 104–10.

Tests on the semistrong form of the efficient market hypothesis have generally been on the basis of risk-adjusted returns. Thus, the return from a given investment strategy must be compared to the performance of popular market indicators with appropriate risk adjustments. As will be described in Chapter 21, the risk measurement variable is usually the beta. After such adjustments are made, the question becomes: Are there abnormal returns that go beyond explanations associated with risk? If the answer is yes and can be shown to be statistically significant, then the investment strategy may be thought to refute the semistrong form of the efficient market hypothesis. The investor must also cover transaction costs in determining that a given strategy is superior.

For example, assume a stock goes up 15 percent. The security is 20 percent riskier than the market. Further assume the overall market goes up by 10 percent. On a risk-adjusted basis, the security would need to go up in excess of 12 percent (the 10 percent market return $\times$ 1.2 risk factor) to beat the market.

The risk adjustment measure may be viewed as:

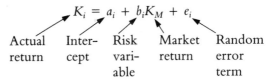

$$K_i = a_i + b_i K_M + e_i$$

| Actual return | Inter-cept | Risk variable | Market return | Random error term |

Each of these items will receive further attention in Chapter 21. For now, our concern is whether an investment strategy can produce consistently superior, abnormal returns.

Tests examining the impact of such events as stock splits and stock dividends, corporate announcements, and changes in accounting policy have indicated the market is generally efficient in a semistrong sense. For example, a study by Fama, Fisher, Jensen, and Roll indicated that almost all of the market impact of a stock split occurs before a public announcement.[13] There is little to be gained from acting on the announcement.

According to the semistrong form of the efficient market hypothesis, investors not only digest information very quickly, but they also are able to see through mere changes in accounting information that do not have economic consequences. For example, the switching from accelerated depreciation to straight-line depreciation for financial reporting purposes (but not tax purposes) would tend to make earnings per share look higher but would provide no economic benefit for the firm. Research studies indicate this would have no positive impact on valuation.[14]

---

[13]Eugene F. Fama, Lawrence Fisher, Michael G. Jensen, and Richard Roll, "The Adjustment of Stock Prices to New Information," *International Economic Review,* February 1969, pp. 2–21.

[14]T. Ross Archibald, "Stock Market Reaction to Depreciation Switch-Back," *Accounting Review,* January 1972, pp. 22–30; and Robert S. Kaplan and Richard Roll, "Investor Evaluation of Accounting Information: Some Empirical Evidence," *Journal of Business,* April 1972, pp. 225–57.

Similarly, investors are not deceived by mere accounting changes related to inventory policy, reserve accounts, exchange translations, or other items that appear to have no economic benefits. The corporate treasurer who switches from LIFO to FIFO accounting to make earnings look better in an inflationary economy will probably not see the firm's stock price rise as investors look at the economic consequences of higher taxes associated with the action and disregard the mere financial accounting consequences of higher reported profits.[15] Under this circumstance, the effect on stock may be neutral or negative.

Implications for Fundamental Analysis

If stock values are already based on the analysis of all available public information, it may be assumed that little is to be gained from additional fundamental analysis. Under the semistrong form of the efficient market hypothesis, if General Motors is trading at $40, the assumption is that every shred of public information about GM has been collected and evaluated by thousands of investors, and they have determined an equilibrium price of $40. The assumption is that anything you read in *The Wall Street Journal* or Standard & Poor's publications has already been considered many times over by others and is currently impounded in the value of the stock. If you were to say you think GM is really worth $42 because of some great new product, proponents of the semistrong form of the efficient market hypothesis would suggest that your judgment cannot be better than the collective wisdom of the marketplace in which everyone is trying desperately to come out ahead.

Ironically, although many would suggest that fundamental analysis may not lead to superior profits in an efficient market environment, it is fundamental analysis itself that makes the market efficient. Because everyone is doing fundamental analysis, there is little in the way of unabsorbed or undigested information. Therefore, one extra person doing fundamental analysis is unlikely to achieve superior insight.

Although the semistrong form of the efficient market hypothesis has research support, there are exceptions. These are referred to as **anomalies** or deviations from the basic proposition that the market is efficient. For example, Basu has found that stocks with low P/E ratios consistently provide better returns than stocks with high P/E ratios on both a nonrisk-adjusted and risk-adjusted basis.[16] Since a P/E ratio is publicly available information that may be used to generate superior returns, this flies in the face of the more-common conclusions on the semistrong form of the efficient market hypothesis. Banz[17]

---

[15]Shyam Sunder, "Stock Price and Risk Related to Accounting Changes in Inventory Valuation," *Accounting Review,* April 1975, pp. 305–15.

[16]S. Basu, "Investment Performance of Common Stocks in Relation to Their Price-Earnings Ratios: A Test of the Efficient Market Hypothesis," *Journal of Finance,* June 1977, pp. 663–82. Also, S. Basu, "The Information Content of Price-Earnings Ratios," *Financial Management,* Summer 1975, pp. 53–64.

[17]Rolf W. Banz, "The Relationship between Returns and Market Value of Common Stocks," *Journal of Financial Economics,* March 1981, pp. 3–18.

and Reinganum's[18] research indicates that small firms tend to provide higher returns than larger firms even after considering risk. Perhaps fewer institutional investors in smaller firms make for a less-efficient market and superior potential opportunities. Oppenheimer and Schlarbaum have also shown that investors can generate superior risk-adjusted returns by following widely disseminated rules by Graham and Dodd on such factors as dividends, capitalization, firm size, and P/E ratios and by using only public information.[19] Additional evidence of this nature continues to accumulate, and in Chapter 10, covering special situations, we present an extended discussion of some of the above items and other possible contradictions to the acceptance of the semistrong version of the efficient market hypothesis. We also comment on measurement problems in that chapter.

Thus, even if the semistrong form of the efficient market hypothesis appears to be generally valid, exceptions can be noted. Also, it is possible that while most analysts may not be able to add additional insight through fundamental analysis, there are exceptions to every rule. It can be assumed that some analysts have such *extraordinary* insight and capability in analyzing publicly available information that they can perceive what others cannot. Also, if you take a very long-term perspective, the fact that a stock's value is in short-term equilibrium may not discourage you from taking a long-term position or attempting to find long-term value.

■ STRONG FORM OF THE EFFICIENT MARKET HYPOTHESIS

The **strong form of the efficient market hypothesis** goes beyond the semistrong form to state that stock prices reflect not only all public information but *all* information. Thus, it is hypothesized that insider information is also immediately impounded into the value of a security. In a sense, we go beyond the concept of a market that is highly efficient to one that is perfect.

The assumption is that no group of market participants or investors has monopolistic access to information. If this is the case, then no group of investors can be expected to show superior risk-adjusted returns under any circumstances.

Unlike the weak and semistrong forms of the efficient market hypothesis, major test results are not supportive of the strong form of the hypothesis. For example, specialists on security exchanges have been able to earn superior rates of return on invested capital.[20] The book they keep on unfilled limit orders would appear to provide monopolistic access to information. An SEC study

---

[18]Marc R. Reinganum, "Misspecification of Capital Asset Pricing—Empirical Anomalies Based on Earnings Yield and Market Values," *Journal of Financial Economics,* March 1981, pp. 19–46.

[19]Henry R. Oppenheimer and Gary C. Schlarbaum, "Investing with Ben Graham: An Ex Ante Test of the Efficient Markets Hypothesis," *Journal of Financial and Quantitative Analysis,* September 1981, pp. 341–60.

[20]Victor Niederhoffer and M. F. M. Osborne, "Market-Making and Reversal on the Stock Exchange," *Journal of the American Statistical Association,* December 1966, pp. 897–916.

actually found that specialists typically sell above their latest purchase 83 percent of the time and buy below their latest sell 81 percent of the time.[21] This implies wisdom that greatly exceeds that available in a perfect capital market environment. Likewise, an institutional investor study, also sponsored by the SEC, indicated specialists' average return on capital was over 100 percent.[22]

Another group that appears to use nonpublic information to garner superior returns is corporate insiders. As previously described, an insider is considered to be a corporate officer, member of the board of directors, or substantial stockholder. The SEC requires that insiders report their transactions to that regulatory body. A few weeks after reporting to the SEC, the information becomes public. Researchers can then go back and determine whether investment decisions made by investors appeared, on balance, to be wise. Did heavy purchases by insiders precede strong upward price movements, and did sell-offs precede poor market performance? The answer appears to be yes. Research studies indicate insiders consistently achieve higher returns than would be expected in a perfect capital market.[23] Although insiders are not allowed to engage in short-term trades (of six months or less) or illegal transactions to generate trading profits, they are allowed to take longer-term positions, which may prove to be profitable. It has even been demonstrated that investors who follow the direction of inside traders after information on their activity becomes public may enjoy superior returns.[24] (This, of course, represents contrary evidence to the semistrong form of the efficient market hypothesis as well.)

Even though there is evidence on the activity of specialists and insiders that would cause one to reject the strong form of the efficient market hypothesis (or at least not to accept it), the range of participants with access to superior information is not large. For example, tests on the performance of mutual fund managers have consistently indicated they are not able to beat the market averages over the long term.[25] Although mutual fund managers may get the first call when news is breaking, that is not fast enough to generate superior returns.

---

[21]Securities and Exchange Commission, *Report of the Special Study of the Security Markets,* part 2 (Washington, D.C.: U.S. Government Printing Office, 1965).

[22]Securities and Exchange Commission, *Institutional Investor Study Report* (Washington, D.C.: U.S. Government Printing Office, 1971).

[23]James H. Lorie and Victor Niederhoffer, "Predictive Statistical Properties of Insider Trading," *Journal of Law and Economics,* April 1966, pp. 35–53; Joseph E. Finnerty, "Insiders and Market Efficiency," *Journal of Finance,* September 1976, pp. 1141–48; and Jeffrey Jaffe, "Special Information and Insider Trading," *Journal of Business,* July 1974, pp. 410–28; and Shannon P. Pratt and Charles W. DeVere, "Relationship between Insider Trading and Rates of Return for NYSE Common Stocks, 1960–1966," in *Modern Developments in Investment Management,* ed. James H. Lorie and Richard Beasley (New York: Praeger Publishers, 1972), pp. 268–79.

[24]Pratt and DeVere, "Relationship," pp. 268–79.

[25]Michael Jensen, "The Performance of Mutual Funds in the Period 1945–1964," *Journal of Finance,* May 1968, pp. 389–416.

While the strong form of the efficient market hypothesis suggests more opportunity for superior returns than the weak or semistrong forms, the premium is related to monopolistic access to information rather than other factors.

It should also be pointed out that those who act *illegally* with insider information may initially achieve superior returns from their special access to information, but the price of their actions may be high. For example, Ivan Boesky and Michael Milken, convicted users of illegal insider information in the late 1980s, were forced to give up their gains, pay heavy fines, and serve jail sentences. In their particular cases, they traded on insider information about mergers well before the public was informed. Although they were not officers of the companies or on the boards, they had special fiduciary responsibilities as money managers that they violated.

■ SUMMARY

Following the discussion of fundamental analysis in Chapters 5 through 8, we examined technical analysis in this chapter and, more significantly, the impact of the efficient market hypothesis (EMH) on both fundamental and technical analysis.

While fundamental analysis deals with financial analysis and determinants of valuation, technical analysis is based on the study of past price and volume data as well as associated market trends to predict future price movements. Technical analysis relies heavily on charting and the use of key market indicators to make forecasts.

Charting came into prominence with the development of the Dow theory in the late 1800s by Charles Dow. The theory stresses the importance of primary trends that may be temporarily obscured by daily and secondary movements. For a long-term, bullish trend to be reversed, there must be an abortive recovery followed by penetrations of previous lows, and patterns in the Dow Jones Industrial Average must be ultimately confirmed by the Dow Jones Transportation Average. Similar patterns of movement in the opposite direction would signal the end of a bear market.

Technical analysts also observe support and resistance levels in the market as well as data on volume. Line, bar, and point and figure charts are used to determine turns in the market.

Market technicians also follow a number of key indicator series to predict the market—contrary opinion indicators, smart money indicators, and general market indicators.

Although there have been traditional arguments about whether fundamental or technical analysis is more important, a great deal of current attention is directed to the efficient market hypothesis and its implications for all types of analysis.

The efficient market hypothesis maintains that the market adjusts very rapidly to the supply of new information, and because of this, securities tend to

be correctly priced at any given time (or very rapidly approaching this equilibrium value). The EMH further assumes information travels in a random, independent fashion and prices are an unbiased reflection of all currently available information. Furthermore, past trends in prices mean little or nothing.

The efficient market hypothesis has been stated and tested in three different forms.

a. The weak form states there is no relationship between past and future prices (they are independent over time).

b. The semistrong form suggests all public information is currently impounded in the price of a stock and there is no concept of under- or overvaluation based on publicly available information.

c. The strong form suggests *all* information, public or otherwise, is included in the value of a security. The implication of the strong form is that security prices are not only highly efficient, they are perfect.

Substantial research tends to support the weak form of the efficient market hypothesis, which causes many researchers to seriously question the overall value of technical analysis. However, many on Wall Street would vigorously debate this position. The semistrong form of the efficient market hypothesis is also reasonably supported by research, and this fact would tend to question the value of fundamental analysis by the individual investor. (It is, however, the collective wisdom of all fundamental analysis that leads to the efficient market hypothesis in the first place.) There are some contradictions to the semistrong form of the efficient market hypothesis, and much research is aimed at supplying additional contradictory data. The semistrong form probably does not apply with equal emphasis to smaller firms that are not in the institutional investor's limelight.

The strong form of the efficient market hypothesis is not generally accepted. Thus, the market does not perfectly adjust to all information (insider as well as public). Evidence suggests stock exchange specialists and corporate insiders may be able to achieve superior returns based on the monopolistic use of nonpublic data. However, very few groups demonstrate successful access or use of nonpublic information.

IMPORTANT WORDS AND CONCEPTS

technical analysis 298

Dow theory 299

support 300

resistance 302

contrary opinion rule 306

Barron's Confidence Index 310

efficient market hypothesis (EMH) 315

weak form of the efficient market hypothesis 315

semistrong form of the efficient market hypothesis 317

anomalies 319

strong form of the efficient market hypothesis 320

■ DISCUSSION QUESTIONS

1. What is technical analysis?
2. What are the views of technical analysts toward fundamental analysis?
3. Outline the basic assumptions of technical analysis.
4. Under the Dow theory, if a recovery fails to exceed the previous high and a new low penetrates a previous low, what does this tell us about the market?
5. Also under the Dow theory, what other average is used to confirm movements in the Dow Jones Industrial Average?
6. What is meant by a support level for a stock or a market average? When might a support level exist?
7. In examining Figure 9–7, if the next price movement is to 34, will a shift to a new column be indicated? (Assume the current price is 36.)
8. What is the logic behind the odd-lot theory? If the odd-lot index starts to move higher in an up market, what does the odd-lot theory indicate the next movement in the market will be?
9. How reliable has the odd-lot theory been in recent times?
10. What is the logic behind *Barron's* Confidence Index?
11. If the advance-decline movement in the market is weak (more declines than advances) while the DJIA is going up, what might this indicate to a technician about the market?
12. Categorize the following as either contrary opinion or smart money indicators (as viewed by technicians).
    a. Short sales by specialists.
    b. Odd-lot positions.
    c. Short sales positions.
    d. *Barron's* Confidence Index.
    e. Investment advisory recommendations.
    f. Put-call ratio.
13. Under the efficient market hypothesis, what is the assumption about the processing of new information, and what effect does this have on security pricing?
14. What does the weak form of the efficient market hypothesis suggest? What are the two major ways in which it has been tested?
15. Would low correlation coefficients over time between stock prices tend to prove or disprove the weak form of the efficient market hypothesis?
16. Under the semistrong form of the efficient market hypothesis, is there anything to be gained from a corporate treasurer changing accounting methods to increase earnings per share when there is no associated economic benefit or gain?
17. Why does fundamental analysis tend to make the market efficient?

18. Suggest some studies that would indicate the market is not completely efficient in the semistrong form.

19. What does the strong form of the efficient market hypothesis suggest? Are major test results generally supportive of the strong form?

20. How do specialists, insiders, and mutual fund managers fare in terms of having access to superior information to generate large returns? (Comment on each separately.)

21. Project: Follow a number of technical indicators over the next few weeks and compare actual market performance to suggested market performance (by the indicators).

■ SELECTED REFERENCES

Technical Analysis

Colby, Robert W., and Thomas A. Meyers. *The Encyclopedia of Technical Market Indicators.* Homewood, Ill.: Business One Irwin, 1988.

Dorfman, John R. "The Stock Market Sign Often Points the Wrong Way." *The Wall Street Journal,* January 26, 1989, p. C1.

Edwards, R. D., and John Magee, Jr. *Technical Analysis of Stock Trends,* 5th ed. Springfield, Mass.: Stock Trends Service, 1966.

Gottschalk, Earl C., Jr. "Using Dumb Money as a Market Guide." *The Wall Street Journal,* January 17, 1989, p. C1.

Krueger, Thomas M., and William F. Kennedy. "An Examination of the Super Bowl Stock Market Predictor." *The Journal of Finance,* June 1990, pp. 691–97.

Lee, Wayne Y., and Michael E. Solt. "Insider Trading a Poor Guide to Market Timing." *Journal of Portfolio Management,* Summer 1986, pp. 65–71.

Murphy, J. Austin. "Futures Fund Performance: A Test of the Effectiveness of Technical Analysis." *Journal of Futures Markets,* Summer 1986, pp. 175–86.

Pinches, George. "The Random Walk Hypothesis and Technical Analysis." *Financial Analysts Journal,* March–April 1970, pp. 104–10.

Sweeney, Richard J. "Some New Filter Rule Tests: Methods and Results." *Journal of Financial and Quantitative Analysis,* September 1988, pp. 285–300.

Zweig, Martin E. *Understanding Technical Forecasting.* Princeton, N.J.: Dow Jones & Company, Inc., 1978.

Fundamental Analysis

Ball, Roy, and Phillip Brown. "An Empirical Evaluation of Accounting Income Numbers," *Journal of Accounting Research,* Autumn 1968, pp. 159–78.

Banz, Rolf W. "The Relationship between Returns and Market Value of Common Stocks." *Journal of Financial Economics,* March 1981, pp. 3–18.

Basu, S. "Investment Performance of Common Stocks in Relation to Their Price-Earnings Ratios: A Test of the Efficient Market Hypothesis." *Journal of Finance,* June 1977, pp. 663–82.

_____. "The Information Content of Price-Earnings Ratios." *Financial Management,* Summer 1975, pp. 53–64.

Bernstein, Barbara, and Peter L. Bernstein. "Where the Postcrash Studies Went Wrong." *Institutional Investor,* April 1988, pp. 173–77.

Brennan, Michael J., and Patricia J. Hughes. "Stock Prices and the Supply of Information." *The Journal of Finance,* December 1991, pp. 1665–91.

Fama, Eugene F.; Lawrence Fisher; Michael G. Jensen; and Richard Roll. "The Adjustment of Stock Prices to New Information." *International Economic Review,* February 1969, pp. 1–21.

Jacobs, Bruce I., and Kenneth N. Levy. "On the Value of 'Value'." *Financial Analysts Journal,* July–August 1988, pp. 47–62.

Jensen, Michael. "The Performance of Mutual Funds in the Period 1945–1964." *Journal of Finance,* May 1968, pp. 389–416.

Reinganum, Marc R. "Misspecification of Capital Asset Pricing—Empirical Anomalies Based on Earnings Yield and Market Values." *Journal of Financial Economics,* March 1981, pp. 19–46.

Sunder, Shyam. "Stock Price and the Risk Related to Accounting Changes in Inventory Valuation. *Accounting Review,* April 1975, pp. 305–15.

Efficient Markets

Fama, Eugene F. "Efficient Capital Markets: II." *The Journal of Finance,* December 1991, pp. 1575–1617.

Finnerty, Joseph E. "Insiders and Market Efficiency." *Journal of Finance,* September 1976, pp. 1141–48.

Jaffe, Jeffrey. "Special Information and Insider Trading." *Journal of Business,* July 1974, pp. 410–28.

Oppenheimer, Henry R., and Gary G. Schlarbaum. "Investing with Ben Graham: An Ex Ante Test of the Efficient Market Hypothesis." *Journal of Financial and Quantitative Analysis,* September 1981, pp. 341–60.

Rozeff, Michael S., and Mir A. Zaman. "Market Efficiency and Insider Trading: New Evidence." *Journal of Business,* January 1988, pp. 25–44.

10

Investments in Special Situations

In a previous discussion of market efficiency in Chapter 9, we suggested that while the security markets were generally efficient in the valuing of securities, there were still opportunities for special returns in a number of circumstances. Just what these circumstances are is subject to debate.

In most instances, special or **abnormal returns** refer to gains beyond what the market would normally provide after adjustment for risk. Transactions costs must also be covered. In this chapter, we will explore such topics as market movements associated with mergers and acquisitions, the underpricing of new stock issues, the impact of an exchange listing on a stock's valuation, the stock market impact of a firm repurchasing its own shares, and the small-firm and low P/E effects.

■ MERGERS AND ACQUISITIONS

Many stocks that were leaders in daily volume and price movement in the late 1970s and 1980s represented firms that were merger candidates; that is, companies that were being acquired or anticipated being acquired by other firms. The stocks of these acquisition candidates often increased by 60 percent or more over a relatively short period. The list of acquired companies includes such well-known names as Conoco, Gulf Oil, Kraft, EDS, General Foods, and Anaconda Copper.

Premiums for Acquired Company

The primary reason for the upward market movement in the value of the acquisition candidate is the high premium that is offered over current market value in a merger or acquisition. The **merger price premium** represents the difference between the offering price per share and the market price per share for the candidate (before the impact of the offer). For example, a firm that is selling for $25 per share may attract a purchase price of $40 per share. Quite naturally, the stock will go up in response to the offer and the anticipated consummation of the merger.

As expected, researchers have consistently found that there are abnormal returns for acquisition candidates.[1] A study has indicated the average premium paid in a recent time period was approximately 60 percent, and there was an associated upward price movement of a similar magnitude.[2] This is a much larger average premium than in prior time periods and may be attributed to the recog-

---

[1]Gershon Mandelker, "Risk and Return: The Case of Merging Firms," *Journal of Financial Economics,* December 1974, pp. 303–35; Donald R. Kummer and J. Ronald Hoffmeister, "Valuation Consequences of Cash Tender Offers," *Journal of Finance,* May 1978, pp. 505–16; Peter Dodd, "Merger Proposals, Management Discretion and Stockholder Wealth," *Journal of Financial Economics,* December 1980, pp. 105–38; and Steven Kaplan, "The Effect of Management Buyouts on Operating Performance and Value," *Journal of Financial Economics,* October 1989, pp. 217–54.

[2]Henry Oppenheimer and Stanley Block, "An Examination of Premiums and Exchange Ratios Associated with Merger Activity during the 1975–78 Period" (Financial Management Association Meeting, 1980).

Table 10–1		Premiums Paid in Mergers and Acquisitions		
Acquiring Firm	**Acquired Firm**	**Price Paid in Cash for Acquired Company's Stock**	**Value of Acquired Firm Three Months before Announcement**	**Premium Paid (Percent)**
Chevron	Gulf Oil	$80.00	$38.00	110.53%
Beatrice Food Co.	Harmon Int'l. Ind.	35.25	20.00	76.25
Parker Pen Co.	Manpower, Inc.	15.20	11.50	32.18
Colt Industries	Menaso Man.	26.60	15.00	77.33
Pepsico, Inc.	Pizza Hut, Inc.	38.00	22.375	69.83
Walter Kidde & Co.	Victor Comptometer	11.75	7.375	59.32
Dana Corporation	Weatherford Co.	14.00	9.375	49.33
Allis Chalmers Corporation	American Air Filter	34.00	19.50	74.36
Time, Inc.	Inland Containers	35.00	20.75	68.67
Chemical Bank	Texas Commerce Bank	32.75	20.25	61.73

nition of high replacement value in relationship to current market value. The premium was based on the difference between the price paid and the value of the acquisition candidate's stock *three months* before announcement of the merger. Some examples of premiums paid during the 1980s are presented in Table 10–1.

The only problem from an investment viewpoint is that approximately two thirds of the price gain related to large premiums occurs before public announcement. It is clear that people close to the situation are trading on information leaks. In the early 1980s, the highly prestigious investment banking house of Morgan Stanley was embarrassed by charges brought by the U.S. Attorney's Office that two of its former merger and acquisition specialists were conspiring to use privileged information on takeovers to make profits on secret trading accounts.[3] Later in the 1980s, notorious insider traders Ivan Boesky, Michael Milken, and Dennis Levine served jail sentences for their misuse of information related to unannounced mergers.

Those who attempt to legitimately profit by investing in mergers and acquisitions can follow a number of routes. First, some investors try to identify merger candidates before public announcement to capture maximum profits. This is difficult. While researchers have attempted to identify financial and operating characteristics of acquisition candidates, the information is often

---

[3]"Two Former Morgan Stanley Executives Accused of Plot Involving Takeover Data," *The Wall Street Journal,* February 4, 1981, p. 2.

contradictory and may even change over time.[4] In prior time periods, acquisition candidates were often firms with sluggish records of performance, whereas many of the recent acquirees are high-quality companies that have unusually good records of performance (Alcon Labs, Coca-Cola Bottling of Los Angeles, Steak and Ale, and EDS).

Some alert analysts keep a close eye on such sources as *Industriscope's* "Stocks in the Spotlight," which pinpoints securities undergoing unusual volume or pricing patterns (this could be for any number of reasons). Other investors identify industries where companies are being quickly absorbed and attempt to guess which firm will be the next to be acquired. Prime examples of such industries in recent times were natural resource firms being acquired by multinational oil companies and food companies being absorbed by tobacco companies or other firms in the food or consumer product industry.

While trying to guess an acquisition candidate before public announcement can be potentially profitable, it requires that an investor tie up large blocks of capital in betting on an event that may never come to pass. Others prefer to invest at the time of announcement of a merger or acquisition. A gain of the magnitude of 20 percent or more may still be available (over a few months' time period). Perhaps a stock that was $25 before any consideration of merger is up to $34 on announcement. If the actual price is $40, there may still be a nice profit to be made. The only danger is that the announced merger may be called off, in which case the stock may sharply retreat in value, perhaps all the way back to $25 (that is, assuming another potential acquiring company does not enter the picture). Examples of price drops associated with merger cancellations are shown in Table 10–2.

The wise investor must carefully access the likelihood of cancellation. Special attention must be given to such factors as the possibility of antitrust action, the attitude of the target company's management toward the merger, the possibility of unhappy stockholder suits, and the likelihood of poor earnings reports or other negative events. In a reasonably efficient market environment, the potential price gain that exists at announcement may be well correlated with the likelihood of the merger being successfully consummated. That is to say, if it appears the merger is almost certain to go through, the stock may be up to $37.50 at announcement based on an anticipated purchase price of $40. If a serious question remains, the stock may only be at $33. When a merger becomes reasonably certain, arbitrageurs come in and attempt to lock in profits by buying the acquisition candidate at a small spread from the purchase price.

One of the most interesting features of the late 1980s merger movement was the heavy incidence of **unfriendly takeovers;** that is, the bidding of one company for another against its will. Such events often lead to the appearance of

---

[4]Robert J. Monroe and Michael A. Simkowitz, "Investment Characteristics of Conglomerate Targets: A Discriminant Analysis," *Southern Journal of Business,* November 1971, pp. 1–15; and Donald J. Stevens, "Financial Characteristics of Merger Firms: A Multivariate Analysis," *Journal of Financial and Quantitative Analysis,* March 1973, pp. 149-58.

Table 10-2	Stock Movement of Potential Acquirees in Canceled Mergers		
Acquirer—Potential Acquiree	**Preannouncement**	**One Day after Announcement**	**One Day after Cancellation**
Mead Corporation—Occidental Petroleum	20⅜	33¼	23¼
Olin Corp.—Celanese	16	23¾	16¾
Chicago Rivet—MITE	20¾	28⅛	20¾

a third company on the scene, referred to as a **"white knight,"** whose function is to save the target company by buying it out, thus thwarting the undesired suitor. The new suitor is generally deemed to be friendly to the interests of the target company and may be invited by it to partake in the process. Examples of white knights occurred when Gulf Oil thwarted an offer from Mesa Petroleum and went with Standard Oil of California (renamed Chevron) in 1984. Similarly, Marathon Oil rejected an offer from Mobil to merge with U.S. Steel in 1982.

As one might guess, these multiple-suitor bidding wars often lead to unusually attractive offers. A 40 to 60 percent premium may ultimately parlay into an 80 to 100 percent gain or more. For example, the bidding for Gulf Oil sent the stock from 38 to 80.

Acquiring Company Performance

What about the acquiring company's stock in the merger and acquisition process? Is this a special situation; that is, does this stock also show abnormal market gains associated with the event? A study by Mandelker indicated that it did not.[5] Long-term economic studies have indicated that many of the anticipated results from mergers may be difficult to achieve.[6] There is often an initial feeling of optimism that is not borne out in reality. The **synergy**, or "2 + 2 = 5," effect associated with broadening product lines or eliminating overlapping functions may be offset by the inability of management to mesh divergent philosophies. However, companies do appear to be more adept at the process than in prior periods; conservatively managed firms, such as General Motors, Du Pont, and Atlantic Richfield, are replacing the funny-money conglomerate gunslingers of another decade. Nevertheless, most investors would prefer to position themselves with the acquired firm, which is certain to receive a high premium, rather than with the acquiring firm, which has to pay it.

---

[5]Gershon Mandelker, "Risk and Return: The Case of Merging Firms," *Journal of Financial Economics,* December 1974, pp. 303–35. Also see Anup Agrawal, Jeffrey F. Jaffe, and Gershon Mandelker, "The Post-Merger Performance of Acquiring Firms," *Journal of Finance* (forthcoming).

[6]T. Hogarty, "The Profitability of Corporate Managers," *Journal of Business,* July 1970, pp. 317–27.

Form of Payment

Another consideration in a merger is the form of payment. Cash offers usually carry a slightly higher premium than stock offers because of the immediate tax consequences to the acquired firm's shareholders. When stock is offered, the tax obligation usually may be deferred by the acquired company's stockholders until the stock of the acquiring firm is actually sold. This may occur relatively soon or many years in the future.

The recent merger movement has seen a much heavier utilization of cash as a medium of payment than in prior time periods (in the 50 percent range as opposed to 25 percent earlier). Many of the old accounting advantages associated with stock or residual stock items (convertibles, warrants) in mergers have been diminished by accounting rule changes.

Leveraged Buyouts

Some corporations are also taken over through **leveraged buyouts** (LBOs). Here, either the management of the company or some other investor group borrows the needed cash to repurchase all the shares of the company. The balance sheet of the company serves as the collateral base to make the borrowing possible. After the leveraged buyout, the company may be taken private for a period, in which unprofitable assets are sold and debts reduced. The intent is then to bring the company to the public market once again (or resell it to another company) at a large profit over the initial purchase price. Successful leveraged buyouts, in which profits of 50 percent or more were made, include those of Blue Bell, Leslie Fay, Metromedia, SFN, and Uniroyal. The largest leveraged buyout (or financial transaction of any kind) involved RJR Nabisco in 1988. The price tag was in excess of $25 billion.

Not all leveraged buyouts are successful. Sometimes the debt burden associated with the transaction is so large that a company has difficulty recovering after an LBO. A classic case is the Southland Corporation (owners of 7-Eleven convenience stores), which found itself in bankruptcy court after putting an unmanageable amount of debt on its books.

■ NEW STOCK ISSUES

Another form of a special situation is the initial issuance of stock by a corporation. There is a belief in the investment community that securities may be underpriced when they are issued to the public for the first time. That is to say, when a company **goes public** by selling formerly privately held shares to new investors in an initial public offering, the price may not fully reflect the value of the security.

Why does this so-called underpricing occur, and what is the significance to the investor? The underpricing may be the result of the investment banker's firm commitment to buy the shares when distributing the issue. That is, the investment banker normally agrees to buy the stock from company A at a set price

and then resells it to the public (along with other investment bankers, dealers, and brokers). The investment banker must be certain the issue will be fully subscribed to at the initial public market price or the banker (and others) will absorb losses or build up unwanted inventory. To protect his position, the investment banker may underprice the issue by 5 to 10 percent to ensure adequate demand.

Studies by Miller and Reilly;[7] Ibbotson, Sindelar, and Ritter;[8] and Muscarella and Vetsuypens,[9] and others have indicated positive excess returns are related to the issue of the stock. Miller and Reilly, for example, observed positive excess returns of 9.9 percent one week after issue. However, the efficiency of the market comes into play after the stock is actively trading on a regular basis, and any excess returns begin to quickly disappear. The lesson to be learned is that, on average, the best time to buy a new, unseasoned issue is on initial distribution from the underwriting syndicate (investment bankers, dealers, brokers), and the best time to sell is shortly after.

The point has been strongly made by recent research by Barry and Jennings.[10] They calculated positive excess returns of 8.69 percent on the first date of trading for new issues, but discovered that 90 percent of that gain occurred on the opening transaction.

Participating in the distribution of a new issue is not always as easy as it sounds. A really hot new issue may be initially oversubscribed, and only good customers of a brokerage house may be allocated shares. Such was the case in the feverish atmosphere that surrounded the initial public trading of Apple Computer and Genentech. Genentech actually went from $35 to $89 in the first 20 minutes of trading (only to quickly come back down). For the most part, customers with a regular brokerage account and a desire to participate in the new-issues market can find adequate opportunities for investment, though perhaps in less spectacular opportunities than those described above.

Performance of Investment Bankers

Research studies indicate that large, prestigious investment banking houses do not generally provide the highest initial returns to investors in the new issues they underwrite.[11] The reason for this is that the upper-tier investment bankers

---

[7]Robert E. Miller and Frank K. Reilly, "An Examination of Mispricing Returns, and Uncertainty for Initial Public Offerings," *Financial Management,* Winter 1987, pp. 33–38.

[8]Roger G. Ibbotson, J. Sindelar, and Jay R. Ritter, "Initial Public Offerings," *Journal of Applied Corporate Finance,* Fall 1988, pp. 37–45.

[9]Chris Muscarella and Mike Vetsuypens, "A Simple Test of Barron's Model of IPO Underpricing," *Journal of Financial Economics,* September 1989, pp. 125–35.

[10]Christopher B. Barry and Robert H. Jennings, "The Opening Performance of Initial Offerings of Common Stock," *Financial Management* (forthcoming).

[11]Brian M. Neuberger and Carl T. Hammond, "A Study of Underwriters' Experience with Unseasoned New Issues," *Journal of Financial and Quantitative Analysis,* March 1974, pp. 165–74. Also, see Dennis E. Logue, "On the Pricing of Unseasoned New Issues, 1965–1969," *Journal of Financial and Quantitative Analysis,* January 1973, pp. 91–103; and Brian M. Neuberger and Chris A. La Chapelle, "Unseasoned New Issue Price Performance on Three Tiers: 1975–1980," *Financial Management,* Autumn 1983, pp. 23–28.

tend to underwrite the issues of the strongest firms coming into the market. Less risk is associated with these strong firms.[12] These firms generally shop around among the many investment bankers interested in their business and eventually negotiate terms that would allow for very little underpricing when they reach the market. (They want most of the benefits to go to the corporation, not to the initial stockholders.)

Factors to Consider in a New Issue

Although the best strategy in a new public offering is often to sell the stock soon after it becomes public, some investors may choose to take a longer-term position. In this case, the investor should consider the management of the firm and its performance record. In most cases, a firm that is going public will have past sales and profit figures that can be compared to others in the industry. In one study, the average sales volume for a firm approaching the new issues market was $22.9 million with $1.8 million in after-tax profits and $14.6 million in assets.[13]

The investor also should take a close look at the intended use of funds from the public distribution. There are many legitimate purposes, such as the construction of new plant and equipment, the expansion of product lines, or the reduction of debt. The investor should be less enthusiastic about circumstances in which funds are being used to buy out old stockholders or to acquire property from existing shareholders.

■ EXCHANGE LISTINGS

A special situation of some interest to investors is an **exchange listing,** in which a firm trading over-the-counter now lists its shares on an exchange (such as the American or New York Stock Exchange). Another version of a listing is for a firm to step up from an American Stock Exchange listing to a New York Stock Exchange listing.

An exchange listing may generate interest in a security (particularly when a company moves from the over-the-counter market to an organized exchange). The issue will now be assigned a specialist who has responsibility for maintaining a continuous and orderly market.[14] Furthermore, there may be greater

---

[12]Richard Carter and Steven Manaster, "Initial Public Offerings and Underwriter Reputation," *Journal of Finance,* September 1990, pp. 1045–67.

[13]Stanley Block and Marjorie Stanley, "The Financial Characteristics and Price Movement Patterns of Companies Approaching the Unseasoned Securities Market in the Late 1970's," *Financial Management,* Winter 1980, pp. 30–36.

[14]This is not always a superior arrangement to having multiple market makers in the over-the-counter market. It depends on how dedicated the specialist is to maintaining the market. Some banks and smaller industrial firms may choose the competitive dealer system in the over-the-counter market in preference to the assigned specialist.

Table 10–3	Minimum Requirements for NYSE Exchange Listing

1. Demonstrated earning power under competitive conditions of: *either* $2.5 million before federal income taxes for the most recent year and $2 million pre-tax for each of the preceding two years, *or* an aggregate for the last three fiscal years of $6.5 million *together with* a minimum in the most-recent fiscal year of $4.5 million. (All three years must be profitable.)
2. Net tangible assets of $18 million, but greater emphasis is placed on the aggregate market value of the common stock.
3. Market value of publicly held shares, at least equal to $18 million.
4. A total of 1,100,000 common shares publicly held.
5. *Either* 2,000 holders of 100 shares or more, *or* 2,200 total stockholders *together with* average monthly trading volume (for the most recent six months) of 100,000 shares.

marketability for the issue as well as more readily available price quotes. An exchange listing may also make the issue more acceptable for margin trading and short selling. Large institutional investors and foreign investors may also consider a listed security more appropriate for inclusion in their portfolios.

Listed firms must meet certain size and performance criteria provided in Table 10–3 (and previously mentioned in Chapter 2 for the NYSE). Although the criteria are not highly restrictive, meeting these standards may still signal a favorable message to investors.

A number of research studies have examined the stock market impact of exchange listings. As might be expected, a strong upward movement is associated with securities that are to be listed, but there is also a strong, sell-off after the event has occurred. Research by Van Horne,[15] Fabozzi,[16] and others[17] indicates that the total effect may be neutral. Research by Ying, Lewellen, Schlarbaum, and Lease (YLSL) would tend to indicate an overall gain.[18]

The really significant factor is that regardless of whether a stock has a higher net value a few months after listing as opposed to a few months before listing, there still may be profits to be made. This would be true if the investor simply bought the stock four to six weeks before listing and sold it on listing. Because

---

[15]James C. Van Horne, "New Listings and Their Price Behavior," *Journal of Finance,* September 1970, pp. 783–94.

[16]Frank J. Fabozzi, "Does Listing on the AMEX Increase the Value of Equity?" *Financial Management,* Spring 1981, pp. 43–50.

[17]Richard W. Furst, "Does Listing Increase the Market Value of Common Stock?" *Journal of Business,* April 1970, pp. 174–80; and Waldemar M. Goulet, "Price Changes, Managerial Accounting and Insider Trading at the Time of Listing," *Financial Management,* Spring 1974, pp. 303–6.

[18]Louis K. W. Ying, Wilbur G. Lewellen, Gary G. Schlarbaum, and Ronald C. Lease, "Stock Exchange Listing and Securities Returns," *Journal of Financial and Quantitative Analysis,* September 1977, pp. 415–32.

an application approval for listing is published in the weekly bulletin of the American Stock Exchange or the New York Stock Exchange well before the actual date of listing, a profit is often possible. The study by YLSL, cited above, indicates there may be an opportunity for abnormal returns on a risk-adjusted basis in the many weeks between announcement of listing and actual listing (between 4.40 percent and 16.26 percent over normal market returns, depending on the time period). In this case, YLSL actually reject the semi-strong form of the efficient market hypothesis by suggesting there are substantial profits to be made even after announcement of a new listing. The wise investor may wish to sell on the eventual date of listing because sometimes a loss in value may occur at that point.

The reader should also be aware of the potential impact of delisting on a security; that is, the formal removal from New York Stock Exchange or American Stock Exchange listing, and a resumption of trading over-the-counter. This may occur because the firm has fallen substantially below the requirements of the exchange.[19] As you would expect, this has a large negative effect on the security. Merjos found that 48 of the 50 firms in her study declined between the last day of trading on an exchange and the resumption of trading over-the-counter.[20] The average decline was 17 percent. While the value was not risk adjusted, it is large enough to indicate the clear significance of the event.

■ STOCK REPURCHASE

The **repurchase** by a firm of its own shares provides for an interesting special situation. The purchase price is generally over current market value and tends to increase the demand for the shares while decreasing the effective supply. Before we examine the stock market effects of a repurchase, we will briefly examine the reasons behind the corporate decision.

Reasons for Repurchase

In some cases, management believes the stock is undervalued in the market. Prior research studies have indicated that repurchased securities have generally underperformed the popular market averages before announcement of repurchase.[21] Thus, management or the board of directors may perceive this to be an excellent opportunity because of depressed prices. Others, however, might

---

[19]Firms may also be delisted because they have been acquired in a merger or acquisition, in which case the shares are no longer traded.

[20]Anna Merjos, "Stricken Securities," *Barron's,* March 4, 1963, p. 9.

[21]Richard Norgaard and Connie Norgaard, "A Critical Evaluation of Share Repurchase," *Financial Management,* Spring 1974, pp. 44–50; and Larry Y. Dann, "Common Stock Repurchases: An Analysis of Returns to Bondholders and Stockholders," *Journal of Financial Economics,* June 1981, pp. 113–38.

see the repurchase as a sign that management is not creative or that it lacks investment opportunities for the normal redeployment of capital.[22] Empirical study indicates firms that engage in repurchase transactions often have lower sales and earnings growth and lower return on net worth than other, comparable firms.[23] There also tends to be a concentration of these firms in the lower-growth areas, such as apparel, steel, food products, tobacco, and aerospace.

Another reason for the repurchase of shares is the acquisition of treasury stock to be used in future mergers and acquisitions or to fulfill obligations under an employee stock option plan. Shares may also be acquired to reduce the number of voting shares outstanding and thus diminish the vulnerability of the corporation to an unwanted or unsolicited takeover attempt by another corporation. Finally, the repurchase decision may be closely associated with a desire to reduce stockholder servicing cost; that is, to eliminate small stockholder accounts that are particularly unprofitable for the corporation to maintain.

Actual Market Effect

From the viewpoint of a special situation, the key question is, What is the stock market impact of the repurchase? Is there money to be made here or not? Much of the earlier research said no.[24] However, more recent research would tend to indicate there might be positive returns to investors in a repurchase situation.[25] Most of the higher returns are confined to formal tender offers to repurchase shares (perhaps 10 to 20 percent of the shares outstanding) rather than the use of informal, unannounced, open-market purchases. Under a formal tender offer, the corporation will specify the purchase price, the date of purchase, and the number of shares it wishes to acquire.

Of particular interest is the fact that most of the positive market movement comes *on* and *after* the announcement rather than before it. The implications are that there may be trading profits to be made here.

Dann determined that the average premium paid over the stock price (the day prior to announcement) was 22.46 percent as indicated on the top line of Table 10–4 found at the top of the next page.

---

[22]Charles D. Ellis and Allen E. Young, *The Repurchase of Common Stock* (New York: The Ronald Press, 1971), p. 61.

[23]Norgaard and Norgaard, "A Critical Evaluation."

[24]A good example is Ellis and Young, *The Repurchase of Common Stock*, p. 156.

[25]Terry E. Dielman, Timothy J. Nantell, and Roger L. Wright, "Price Effects of Stock Repurchasing: A Random Coefficient Regression Approach," *Journal of Financial and Quantitative Analysis,* March 1980, pp. 175–89; Larry Y. Dann, "Common Stock Repurchases: An Analysis of Returns to Bondholders and Stockholders," *Journal of Financial Economics,* June 1981, pp. 113–38; Theo Vermaelen, "Common Stock Repurchases and Market Signaling: An Empirical Study," *Journal of Financial Economics,* June 1981, pp. 139–83; R. W. Masulis, "Stock Repurchase by Tender Offer: An Analysis of the Causes of Common Stock Price Changes," *Journal of Finance,* May 1980, pp. 305–19; and Josef Lakonishok and Theo Vermaelen, "Anomalous Price Behavior around Repurchase Tender Offers," *Journal of Finance,* June 1990, pp. 455–77.

Table 10–4   Summary Statistics for the Tender Offer Sample, 1962–1976 (143 Observations)

Characteristic of Offers	Mean (Percent)	Median (Percent)
Tender offer premium relative to closing market price one *day* prior to announcement	22.46%	19.40%
Tender offer premium relative to closing market price one *month* prior to announcement	20.85	18.83
Percentage of outstanding shares sought	15.29	12.57
Percentage of outstanding shares acquired	14.64	11.93
Percentage of outstanding shares tendered	18.04	14.27
Number of shares tendered ÷ number of shares sought	142.30	115.63
Number of shares acquired ÷ number of shares sought	111.35	100.00
Value of proposed repurchase relative to pre-offer market value of equity	19.29	15.28
Value of actual repurchase relative to pre-offer market value of equity	18.63	13.90
Duration of offer	22 days	20 days

Source: Larry Y. Dann, "Common Stock Repurchases: An Analysis of Returns of Bondholders and Stockholders," *Journal of Financial Economics,* June 1981, p. 122.

This high premium helps to generate a return of 8.946 percent on the day of announcement and 6.832 percent one day after announcement as indicated in Table 10–5. This represents a two-day return of approximately 15.8 percent.[26]

The predominant argument for the beneficial effects of the repurchase is that management knows what it is doing when it purchases its *own* shares. In effect, management is acting as an insider for the benefit of the corporation, and we previously observed in Chapter 9 that insiders tend to be correct in their investment decisions. This factor, combined with the high premium, may provide positive investment results. Of course, these are merely average results over many transactions, and not all tender offers will prove to be beneficial events. The investor must carefully examine the premium offered, the number of shares to be repurchased, the reasons for repurchase, and the future impact on earnings and dividends per share.

One of the major developments of 1987 (the year of the crash) was the unusually large number of stock repurchases. More than 1,400 companies announced plans to buy back over $80 billion in stock. Many of these buybacks came after the Dow Jones Industrial Average declined 508 points on Black Monday, October 19, 1987. As one example, Citicorp sold $1.2 billion in new stock in September 1987 at $58.25 a share only to buy back almost $200 million on October 20 at a mere $37.50 a share. The largest announced stock buybacks for the historic year of 1987 are shown in Table 10–6.

---

[26]Professor Dann's observations are based on raw data rather than normalized returns. However, they are of sufficient magnitude to be important.

Table 10–5   Common Stock Rates of Return over a 121-Day Period around Announcement
of Common Stock Repurchase Tender Offer

Trading Day	Mean Rate of Return (Percent)	Trading Day	Mean Rate of Return (Percent)
−60	.217%	0	8.946%
−50	−.034	1	6.832
−40	.058	2	.908
−30	−.562	3	−.041
−25	−.125	4	.133
−20	−.071	5	.158
−19	.026	6	.230
−18	−.346	7	.129
−17	−.317	8	.051
−16	−.413	9	−.211
−15	.377	10	.213
−14	−.228	11	.172
−13	−.738	12	−.024
−12	.051	13	.181
−11	−.424	14	−.143
−10	−.578	15	.497
−9	.188	16	−.105
−8	−.391	17	−.236
−7	.107	18	.148
−6	.417	19	.141
−5	−.169	20	−.057
−4	.943	25	−.003
−3	.239	30	−.025
−2	.490	40	.133
−1	.959	50	−.069
		60	.161

Source: Larry Y. Dann, "Common Stock Repurchases: An Analysis of Returns to Bondholders and Stockholders," *Journal of Financial Economics,* June 1981, p. 124.

■ THE SMALL-FIRM AND LOW P/E RATIO EFFECT

Two University of Chicago doctoral studies in the early 1980s have contended
that the true key to superior risk-adjusted rates of return rests with investing
in firms with small **market capitalizations.** (Market capitalization refers to
shares outstanding times stock price.) In a study of New York Stock Exchange
firms, covering from 1936 to 1975, Banz indicates that the lowest quintile
(bottom 20 percent) firms in terms of market capitalization provide the highest
returns even after adjusting for risk. Banz suggests, "On average, small NYSE

Table 10–6   Biggest Announced Stock Buybacks of 1987

Company	Common Shares (in Millions)	Value	Company	Common Shares (in Millions)	Value
General Motors	64.0	$ 4.72 billion	Procter & Gamble	10.0	$810.0 million
Sante Fe Southern Pacific	60.0	3.38 billion	Salomon	21.3	808.7 million
Ford	27.9	2.00 billion	Hewlett-Packard	15.3	750.0 million
Coca-Cola	40.0	1.80 billion	Nynex	10.0	736.3 million
Henley Group	64.5	1.76 billion	Chrysler	27.0	729.0 million
Gencorp	12.5	1.63 billion	Burlington Industries	8.0	640.0 million
IBM	12.9	1.57 billion	Monsanto	8.0	627.0 million
American Express	40.0	1.35 billion	ITT	10.0	625.0 million
Allied-Signal	25.0	1.11 billion	Hospital Corp. of America	12.0	612.0 million
Owens-Illinois	20.0	1.11 billion	Atlantic Richfield	8.3	600.0 million
J. C. Penney	20.0	1.04 billion	Schlumberger	20.0	595.0 million
Hercules	15.0	1.02 billion	Tektronix	15.6	593.2 million
IC Industries	30.8	1.00 billion	Boeing	15.0	592.5 million
Merck	5.4	1.00 billion	Kimberly-Clark	9.0	547.5 million
Philip Morris	10.0	933.5 million	Kraft	10.0	547.5 million
Bristol-Myers	25.0	925.0 million	Eaton	8.5	500.0 million
NCR	14.0	825.3 million	K mart	17.9	500.0 million

Note: Figures represent announcements, not actual purchases, and may include more than one announcement. Values are actual dollar amounts when available or estimates based on closing prices before announcements.
Source: Merrill Lynch & Co.
Source: *The Wall Street Journal*, January 4, 1988, p. 8B. Reprinted by permission of *THE WALL STREET JOURNAL*, © 1988 by Dow Jones & Company, Inc. All Rights Reserved Worldwide.

firms have had significantly larger risk-adjusted returns than larger NYSE firms over a 40-year period."[27]

Some criticized Banz for using only NYSE firms in his analysis and for using a time period that included the effects of both a depression and a major war. Small firms had incredibly high returns following the Depression. A similar type study, produced by Reinganum[28] at about the same time, overcame these criticisms. Reinganum examined 2,000 firms that were traded on the New York Stock Exchange or the American Stock Exchange between 1963 and 1980. He annually divided the 2,000 firms into 10 groupings based on size,

---

[27]Rolf W. Banz, "The Relationship between Returns and Market Value of Common Stocks," *Journal of Financial Economics,* March 1981, pp. 3–18.

[28]Marc R. Reinganum, "Misspecification of Capital Asset Pricing—Empirical Anomalies Based on Earnings Yield and Market Values," *Journal of Financial Economics,* March 1981, pp. 19–46. Also, "A Direct Test of Roll's Conjecture on the Firm Size Effect," *Journal of Finance,* March 1982, pp. 27–35; and "Portfolio Strategies Based on Market Capitalization," *Journal of Portfolio Management,* Winter 1983, pp. 29–36.

Table 10–7	Synopsis of Results—Reinganum Study		
(1) Grouping*	(2) Median Market Value (Capitalization, in Millions)	(3) Median Share Price	(4) Average Annual Return
MV 1	$ 4.6	$ 5.24	32.77%
MV 2	10.8	9.52	23.51
MV 3	19.3	12.89	22.98
MV 4	30.7	16.19	20.24
MV 5	47.2	19.22	19.08
MV 6	74.2	22.59	18.30
MV 7	119.1	26.44	15.64
MV 8	209.1	30.83	14.24
MV 9	434.6	34.43	13.00
MV 10	1,102.6	44.94	9.47

*MV = Market value.
Source: Marc R. Reinganum, "Portfolio Strategies Based on Market Capitalization," *Journal of Portfolio Management*, Winter 1983, pp. 29–36.

with the smallest category representing less than $5 million in market capitalization and the largest grouping representing a billion dollars or more.

A synopsis of the results from the Reinganum study are presented in Table 10–7.

Column (2) indicates the median value of the market capitalization for the firms in each group. Column (3) is the median stock price for firms in each group, while column (4) indicates average annual return associated with that category.

As observed in column (4), the smallest capitalization group (MV 1) outperformed the largest capitalization group (MV 10) by over 23 percentage points per year. Although not included in the table, in 14 out of the 18 years under study, the MV 1 group showed superior returns to the MV 10 group. In another similar analysis, Reinganum found that $1 invested in the smallest capitalization group would have grown to $46 between 1963 and 1980, while the same dollar invested in the largest capitalization group would have only grown to $4. As did Banz, Reinganum adjusted his returns for risk and continued to show superior risk-adjusted returns.

Such superior return evidence drew criticisms from different quarters. Roll suggested that small-capitalization studies underestimate the risk measure (beta) by failing to account for the infrequent and irregular trading patterns of stocks of smaller firms.[29] Stoll and Whaley maintained that transaction costs

---

[29]Richard Roll, "A Possible Explanation of the Small Firm Effect," *Journal of Finance*, September 1981, pp. 879–88.

associated with dealing in smaller capitalization firms might severely cut into profit potential.[30] They indicated the average buy-sell spread on small-capitalized, low-priced stocks might be four or five times that of large-capitalization firms. Reinganum has maintained that even after accounting for these criticisms, small-capitalization firms continue to demonstrate superior risk-adjusted returns.[31]

Given that there might be advantages to investing in smaller firms, why haven't professional money managers picked up on the strategy. This, in part, is a catch-22. Part of the reason for the inefficiency in this segment of the market that allows for superior returns is the absence of institutional traders. This absence means less information is generated on the smaller firms, and the information that is generated is reacted to in a less-immediate fashion. Studies suggest an important linkage between the absence of organized information and superior return potential.[32]

Advocates of the small-firm effect argue that it is this phenomenon alone, rather than others, such as the low-P/E-ratio effect, that leads to superior risk-adjusted returns. Peavy and Goodman would argue that the low-P/E-ratio effect is also important.[33] In following up on the earlier work of Basu[34] on the importance of P/E ratios, they compensated for other factors that may have resulted in superior returns, such as the small size of the firm, the infrequent trading of stock, and the overall performance of an industry. They did this by using firms that had a market capitalization of at least $100 million, that had an active monthly trading volume of at least 250,000 shares, and were in the same industry. Thus, none of these factors was allowed to be an intervening variable in the relationship between returns and the level of P/E ratios.

After following these parameters, Peavy and Goodman showed a significant relationship between the firm's P/E ratios and risk-adjusted returns. Firms were broken down into quintiles based on the size of their P/E ratios. Quintile 1 contained firms with the lowest P/E ratios, quintile 2 had the next lowest P/E ratios, and so on up the scale. A portion of their results is presented in Table 10–8.

Note that lower P/E stocks have higher risk-adjusted returns. While Table 10–8 shows data only for the electronics industry, a similar pattern was found for other industries.

[30]H. A. Stoll and R. E. Whaley, "Transaction Costs and the Small Firm Effect," *Journal of Financial Economics,* March 1985, pp. 121–43.

[31]Marc R. Reinganum, "Misspecification of Capital Asset Pricing—Empirical Anomalies Based on Earnings Yield and Market Values," *Journal of Financial Economics,* March 1981, pp. 19–46.

[32]Avner Arbel and Paul Strebel, "Pay Attention to Neglected Firms," *Journal of Portfolio Management,* Winter 1983, pp. 37–42.

[33]John W. Peavy III and David A. Goodman, "The Significance of P/Es for Portfolio Returns," *Journal of Portfolio Management,* Winter 1983, pp. 43–47.

[34]S. Basu, "Investment Performance of Common Stocks in Relation to Their Price-Earnings Ratios: A Test of the Efficient Market Hypothesis," *Journal of Finance,* June 1977, pp. 663–82.

Table 10–8	P/E Ratios and Performance: The Electronics Industry (1970–1980)		
Quintile	Average P/E	Average Quarterly Return (Risk-Adjusted)	Average Beta
1	7.1	8.53	1.15
2	10.3	4.71	1.12
3	13.4	4.34	1.13
4	17.4	2.53	1.19
5	25.5	1.86	1.29

Source: John W. Peavy III and David A. Goodman, "The Significance of P/Es for Portfolio Returns," *Journal of Portfolio Management,* Winter 1983, pp. 43–47.

In summarizing this section, some researchers such as Banz and Reinganum argue that small size is the primary variable leading to superior returns, while others argue that it is the low-P/E-ratio effect. Perhaps it is a bit of both. Some would argue the existence of even a third or fourth variable that is even more important than small size or low P/E ratio (such as dividend yield or low volume).[35] What is important is that smaller firms with low P/E ratios that are often neglected by major investors seem to provide a superior risk-adjusted return.

◾ OTHER STOCK-RELATED SPECIAL SITUATIONS

Although the authors have attempted to highlight the major special situations related to stocks in the preceding pages, there are other opportunities as well. While only brief mention will be made in this section, the student may choose to follow up the footnoted references for additional information.

The January Effect Because stockholders may sell off their losers in late December to establish tax losses, these stocks are often depressed in value in early January and may represent bargains and an opportunity for high returns.[36] In fact, the January effect and the potential for high returns has attracted so much attention that it often is used as a variable to explain other phenomena as well as itself. For example, Keim has found that roughly half the small-firm effect for the year occurs in January. In other words, if you want to play the small-firm effect game, start early in the year.[37]

---

[35]Solveig Jansson, "The Big Debate over Little Stocks," *Institutional Investor,* June 1982, pp. 141–48.

[36]Ben Branch and J. Ryan, "Tax-Loss Trading: An Inefficiency Too Large to Ignore," *Financial Review,* Winter 1980, pp. 20–29.

[37]Donald B. Keim, "Size-Related Anomalies and Stock Return Seasonality," *Journal of Financial Economics,* March 1983, pp. 13–32. Also see Richard Roll, "Vas ist das? The Turn of the Year Effect and the Return Premium of Small Firms," *Journal of Portfolio Management,* Winter 1983, pp. 18–28.

It's the "January Effect," but Will It Occur in January?

Something mysterious happens every January in stock and bond markets around the world.

Small-company stocks rise sharply—overwhelming increases in large-company stocks for that month. High-yield, high-risk "junk" bonds also get a large hunk of their yearly appreciation in January.

Why it happens still isn't understood. One thing is known, however: A growing number of traders and speculators believe it's possible to make a short-term profit by playing the January effect.

The strategy is simple. Around mid-December, investors buy small-company stocks selling for depressed prices or a mutual fund that invests in small-company stocks. After prices surge in early January, these investors lock in their gains by selling the stocks or switching out of their mutual fund and into a money market fund. Some investors take a similar approach with mutual funds that invest in junk bonds.

Still, it is possible to lose money trying to play the January effect. In bear markets like the Januaries of 1978 and 1982, small stocks lost money.

"Even though they outperform large stocks, they can't fight the tape," says one trader.

One problem for investors trying to capitalize on the January effect is transaction costs. Brokers' commissions, poor prices from wide bid-and-asked spreads on thinly traded over-the-counter stocks, and taxes can all erode returns, points out Robert Haugen, co-author of *The Incredible January Effect.* "Still, historically, the force is with you," he says.

Since the effect first got wide notice in 1981, Goldman, Sachs & Co. says the performance difference between small stocks and large stocks in January has been narrowing. Since 1982, small stocks rose an average of 4.2 percent in January, compared with 3.8 percent for large stocks. That's not nearly as significant as the 7.4 percent versus 1.4 percent comparison for 1926 to 1981.

Earl C. Gottschalk, Jr., *The Wall Street Journal,* December 14, 1988, pp. C1, C16. Reprinted by permission of *THE WALL STREET JOURNAL,* © 1988 by Dow Jones & Co., Inc. All Rights Reserved Worldwide.

The Weekend Effect   Research evidence indicates stocks tend to peak in value on Friday and generally decline in value on Monday. Thus, the theory is that the time to buy is on late Monday and the time to sell is on late Friday. While over many decades this observation is valid,[38] generally the price movement is too small to profitably cover transaction costs. However, if you *know* you are going to sell a stock that you have held for a long time, you may prefer to do so later in the week rather than early in the week.

The Value Line Ranking Effect   *The Value Line Investment Survey* contains information on approximately 1,700 stocks (see Chapter 4). Using a valuation model, each company is rated from 1 through 5 for profitable market

[38]Frank Cross, "The Behavior of Stock Prices on Fridays and Mondays," *Financial Analysts Journal,* November–December 1973, pp. 67–69; Kenneth R. French, "Stock Returns and the Weekend Effect," *Journal of Financial Economics,* March 1980, pp. 55–69; and Lawrence Harris, "A Transaction Data Study of Weekly and Interdaily Patterns in Stock Returns," *Journal of Financial Economics,* May 1986, pp. 99–117.

performance over the next 12 months. One is the highest possible rating, and 5 is the lowest. One hundred stocks are always in category 1. Researchers have generally indicated that category 1 stocks provide superior risk-adjusted returns over the other four categories and the market in general.[39] Of course, frequent trading may rapidly cut into these profits. Note in Figure 10–1 on page 346 the incredible performance of Value Line group 1 category compared to the other four categories.

The Surprise-Earnings Effect As indicated in Chapter 9 in the discussion of efficient markets, accounting information tends to be quickly impounded in the value of a stock, and there appears to be little opportunity to garner superior returns from this data. Even if a firm reports a 20 percent increase in earnings, there is likely to be little market reaction to the announcement if the gain was generally anticipated. However, an exception to this rule may relate to truly *unexpected* earnings announcements.[40] If they are very positive, the stock may go up for a number of days after the announcement and thus provide a superior investment opportunity. The opposite would be true of a totally unexpected negative announcement.

■ TRULY SUPERIOR RETURNS OR MISMEASUREMENT

In our discussion in the previous chapter and in this chapter, we pointed out the possibility that high returns may be the result of a superior strategy in a less than efficient capital market or the result of mismeasurement. The latter would refer, for example, to assuming you got a superior risk-adjusted return when you did not. You simply misspecified the extent of the risk component or used the wrong model. If all risk-adjusted superior return studies were the result of misspecification, we could then once again assume the market is perfectly efficient.

The predominant view is that while there is some mismeasurement, many opportunities truly reflect market inefficiencies. There are "special situations" that if properly analyzed provide an opportunity for abnormally high risk-adjusted returns. The most literal and unbending interpretations of efficient markets no longer carry the weight they did two decades ago.[41]

[39]Fisher Black, "*Yes*, Virginia, There Is Hope: Test of the Value Line Ranking System," *Financial Analysts Journal*, September–October 1973, pp. 10–14; Clark Holloway, "A Note on Testing an Aggressive Strategy Using Value Line Ranks," *Journal of Finance*, June 1981, pp. 711–19; and Scott E. Stickel, "The Effect of *Value Line Investment Survey* Rank Changes on Common Stock Prices," *Journal of Financial Economics*, March 1985, pp. 121–43.

[40]Richard Rendleman, Charles Jones, and Henry A. Latane, "Empirical Anomalies Based on Unexpected Earnings and the Importance of Risk Adjustments," *Journal of Financial Economics*, November 1982, pp. 269–87.

[41]Eugene F. Fama, "Efficient Capital Markets: II," *Journal of Finance*, December 1991, pp. 1575–1617.

Figure 10–1   Performance of Value Line Groups

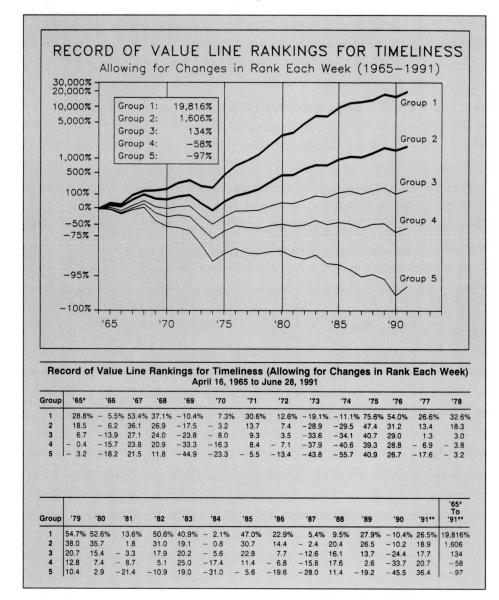

RECORD OF VALUE LINE RANKINGS FOR TIMELINESS
Allowing for Changes in Rank Each Week (1965–1991)

Group 1:	19,816%
Group 2:	1,606%
Group 3:	134%
Group 4:	−58%
Group 5:	−97%

Record of Value Line Rankings for Timeliness (Allowing for Changes in Rank Each Week)
April 16, 1965 to June 28, 1991

Group	'65*	'66	'67	'68	'69	'70	'71	'72	'73	'74	'75	'76	'77	'78
1	28.8%	− 5.5%	53.4%	37.1%	−10.4%	7.3%	30.6%	12.6%	−19.1%	−11.1%	75.6%	54.0%	26.6%	32.6%
2	18.5	− 6.2	36.1	26.9	−17.5	− 3.2	13.7	7.4	−28.9	−29.5	47.4	31.2	13.4	18.3
3	6.7	−13.9	27.1	24.0	−23.8	− 8.0	9.3	3.5	−33.6	−34.1	40.7	29.0	1.3	3.0
4	− 0.4	−15.7	23.8	20.9	−33.3	−16.3	8.4	− 7.1	−37.9	−40.6	39.3	28.8	− 6.9	− 3.8
5	− 3.2	−18.2	21.5	11.8	−44.9	−23.3	− 5.5	−13.4	−43.8	−55.7	40.9	26.7	−17.6	− 3.2

Group	'79	'80	'81	'82	'83	'84	'85	'86	'87	'88	'89	'90	'91**	'65* To '91**
1	54.7%	52.6%	13.6%	50.6%	40.9%	− 2.1%	47.0%	22.9%	5.4%	9.5%	27.9%	−10.4%	26.5%	19,816%
2	38.0	35.7	1.8	31.0	19.1	− 0.8	30.7	14.4	− 2.4	20.4	26.5	−10.2	18.9	1,606
3	20.7	15.4	− 3.3	17.9	20.2	− 5.6	22.8	7.7	−12.6	16.1	13.7	−24.4	17.7	134
4	12.8	7.4	− 8.7	5.1	25.0	−17.4	11.4	− 6.8	−15.8	17.6	2.6	−33.7	20.7	−58
5	10.4	2.9	−21.4	−10.9	19.0	−31.0	− 5.6	−19.6	−28.0	11.4	−19.2	−45.5	36.4	−97

Source: *Value Line Selection and Opinion*, July 19, 1991, p. 772.

■ SUMMARY

In this chapter, we examined various forms of special situations for the investor. Perhaps none has received more attention than the great wave of mergers and acquisitions of the last decade. Because of the premiums paid by the acquiring companies, there is substantial upward potential in the stocks of the acquired firms. However, two thirds of the gain comes before public announcement, and for that reason, some analysts attempt to identify potential target companies before announcements are made. One of the problems of investing in mergers and acquisitions is that announced plans may be called off, and there may be substantial retractions in value for the stock of the target company. A final point of observation is that stocks of acquiring firms generally do no better than the market in general.

Next, we observe the price patterns of firms going public (selling their stock to the general public for the first time). There appears to be abnormal returns after issue, and then the efficiency of the market comes strongly into play. The reason for the initial excess returns is the underpricing by investment bankers to ensure a good reception for the new issue. Stocks of firms underwritten by prestigious underwriters may show smaller returns because of the bargaining power of the issuing firm and the lower level of risk involved.

Exchange listings may or may not provide higher values for the securities involved; the research is somewhat contradictory in this regard. However, the interesting feature suggested by the Ying, Lewellen, Schlarbaum, and Lease research is that there may be excess returns between the point of announcement and listing (regardless of whether there is a sell-off after listing). This is at variance with the semistrong form of the efficient market hypothesis.

There is also conflicting evidence on the impact of a firm's repurchase of its own shares in the marketplace. Recent research, however, indicates the high premiums paid (22.46 percent) on cash tender offers may provide upward market movement at and immediately after the point of announcement.

Studies of the small-firm effect indicate there may be superior return potential in investing in smaller-capitalization firms. One justification for the effect is that there is less efficiency in this segment of the market due to minimal institutional participation. Others suggest it is the low P/E ratios of many of these neglected firms that eventually lead to superior returns.

Finally, researchers have indicated some special opportunities for profits related to seasonality, unexpected earnings reports, and the Value Line ranking system.

■ IMPORTANT WORDS AND CONCEPTS

abnormal return 328	white knight 331
merger price premium 328	synergy 331
unfriendly takeovers 330	leveraged buyouts 332

■ DISCUSSION QUESTIONS

1. Define special or abnormal returns.
2. What is the basis for upward movement in the stock of an acquisition candidate?
3. What is an unfriendly takeover?
4. What is the primary danger in investing in merger and acquisition candidates?
5. What factor(s) will determine the extent of upward price potential for an acquisition candidate at the time of a merger announcement?
6. Do the stocks of acquiring companies tend to show strong upward market movement as a result of the merger process? Comment on the reasoning behind your answer.
7. Why do cash tender offers frequently carry a higher premium than stock offers?
8. Why does abnormal return potential sometimes exist in the new-issues market?
9. What are some factors to consider before buying a new issue?
10. Why might firms that are underwritten by large, prestigious investment banking houses not necessarily provide the highest initial returns to investors in the new-issue market?
11. What are some reasons a firm may wish to have its security listed on an exchange?
12. What was the major finding of the Ying, Lewellen, Schlarbaum, and Lease study? How does this relate to the semistrong form of the efficient market hypothesis?
13. What are some reasons a firm may repurchase its own stock?
14. What are some negative connotations associated with a firm repurchasing its own shares?
15. Relate the existence of positive returns on stock repurchases to the type of offer (formal versus informal).
16. According to researchers such as Banz and Reinganum, what is the general performance of small firms relative to larger firms?
17. What does the term *market capitalization* mean?
18. What criticisms of the small-firm effect were offered by Roll and Stoll and Whaley? Were these considered valid by Reinganum?
19. What explanation might be offered for the possible market inefficiency in the small-firm segment of the market?
20. What problem does an institutional investor have when he or she tries to purchase shares of a small firm?

21. Advocates of the small-firm effect argue that it is this factor *alone* that leads to superior risk-adjusted returns. Does the Peavy and Goodman study support this position?

22. What does Table 10–8 indicate about the relationship between a firm's P/E ratio and its average quarterly return?

23. Why might the first week in January be a good time to purchase stocks that were losers in the prior year?

24. If a corporation has an anticipated large positive earnings report, is that a good time to buy? What if the positive report were unexpected?

25. Project: Identify a recently announced merger or acquisition. Determine the price of the acquisition candidate's stock three months before announcement. Compare this to the actual offer by the acquiring company in terms of cash or stock. Also, compare this to the acquisition candidate's stock price at the point of announcement. Determine the percentage premium over the acquisition candidate's stock value in each case. Do these premiums seem reasonable in light of the quality of the companies involved and the likelihood of the merger going through? (Note: You can use *The Wall Street Journal Index* to determine the first date of announcement and the stock prices.)

■ CRITICAL THOUGHT CASE

Jane Hailey, the vice president of finance for Global Retail Stores, Inc., was excited about the way preliminary negotiations had gone for Modern Woman Corp., a retail chain of 45 stores that specialized in professional wear for the working female. The Modern Woman Corp. traded on the NASDAQ at a price of 18 bid, 18½ ask. Jane's own analyses indicated a buyout price as high as $30 could be justified based on the firm's futures prospects. The initial secret discussions had touched on a price in the $26 to $28 range, but Jane thought the officers of the Modern Woman Corp. were probably eyeing at least 10 percent more for their stock. Otherwise, the negotiations were very amicable.

Jane's annual salary exceeded $200,000 a year, but like many successful people she would have liked even more. However, she knew it was illegal for her to trade on such privileged inside information. Fortunately, she thought, she had a younger brother who was a senior in medical school and could benefit from the potential upward movement in Modern Woman's stock once the news became public. Although she would tell him of the impending merger, she would be very careful not to lend or advance him any funds for fear of reprisal by the Securities and Exchange Commission. If he made any investment, it would be purely on his own.

Question

1. Comment on Jane Hailey's intended action.

MARKETBASE-E EXERCISES

1. *a.* This chapter discusses a number of anomalies, one of which is the small-firm effect. In an effort to capture this effect, use MarketBase-E to select companies with the following characteristics. (These are slightly modified criteria from the American Association of Individual Investors, which calls companies like this *Shadow Stocks*.)

   (1) Market value between $10 and $100 million.

   (2) Institutions own less than 15% of the outstanding stock.

   (3) The company is not a financial firm, such as a bank, savings and loan, or insurance company. (This is to eliminate firms whose financial statements are not comparable to the others.) **Hint:** Use wildcards with the SIC code to make this choice.

   b. Add the constraint that the firms must have positive earnings for each of the past two years. What effect does this have on the number of companies selected?

   c. It has been suggested that the American Stock Exchange and NASDAQ National Market System companies have different characteristics than the NYSE companies. Add the further requirement that the companies be listed on the NYSE. How many companies are now included?

   d. Redo the selection for NYSE companies and remove the requirement that the companies have positive earnings for the past two years. Does this have as great an effect on the companies selected as it did for all the companies as seen in part *b.*

SELECTED REFERENCES

Market Inefficiency

Beebower, G. L., and A. P. Varikooty. "Measuring Market Timing Strategies." *Financial Analysts Journal,* November–December 1991, pp. 78–84.

Fama, Eugene F. "Efficient Capital Markets: II." *Journal of Finance,* December 1991, pp. 1575–1617.

Rosenberg, Barr; Kenneth Reid; and Ronald Lanstein. "Persuasive Evidence of Market Inefficiency." *Journal of Portfolio Management,* Spring 1985, pp. 9–16.

Mergers and Acquisitions

Agrawal, Anup; Jeffrey F. Jaffe; and Gershon Mandelker. "The Post-Merger Performance of Acquiring Firms." *Journal of Finance* (forthcoming).

Dodd, Peter. "Merger Proposals, Management Discretion and Stockholder Wealth." *Journal of Financial Economics,* December 1980, pp. 105–38.

Kaplan, Steven. "The Effect of Management Buyouts on Operating Performance." *Journal of Financial Economics,* October 1989, pp. 217–54.

Mandelker, Gershon. "Risk and Return: The Case of Merging Firms." *Journal of Financial Economics,* December 1974, pp. 303–35.

Masulis, R. W. "Costly Propositions—Some Big Mergers Have Lately Fallen Through." *Barron's,* May 14, 1979, pp. 9–16.

Oppenheimer, Henry, and Stanley Block. "An Examination of Premiums and Exchange Ratios Associated with Merger Activity during the 1975–78 Period." Financial Management Association Meeting, 1980.

New Stock Issues (Initial Public Offerings)

Baron, D. P. "A Model for the Demand for Investment Bank Advising and Distribution Services for New Issues." *Journal of Finance,* September 1982, pp. 955–76.

Barry, Christopher B. and Robert H. Jennings. "The Opening Performance of Initial Offerings of Common Stock." *Financial Management* (forthcoming).

Barry, Christopher B.; Chris J. Muscarella; and Michael R. Vetsuypens. "Underwriter Warrants, Underwriter Compensation and Cost of Going Public." *Journal of Financial Economics,* March 1991, pp. 113–35.

Block, Stanley, and Marjorie Stanley. "The Financial Characteristics and Price Movement Patterns of Companies Approaching the Unseasoned Securities Market in the Late 1970s." *Financial Management,* Winter 1980, pp. 30–36.

Carter, Richard, and Steven Manaster. "Initial Public Offering and Underwriter Reputation." *Journal of Finance,* September 1990, pp. 1045–67.

Ibbotson, Roger G. "Price Performance of Common Stock New Issues." *Journal of Financial Economics,* September 1975, pp. 235–72.

———; J. Sindelar; and Jay R. Ritter. "Initial Public Offerings." *Journal of Applied Corporate Finance,* Fall 1988, pp. 37–43.

Logue, Dennis E. "On the Pricing of Seasoned New Issues, 1965–1969." *Journal of Financial and Quantitative Analysis,* January 1973, pp. 91–103.

Miller, Robert E., and Frank K. Reilly. "An Examination of Mispricing Returns, and Uncertainty for Initial Public Offerings." *Financial Management,* Winter 1987, pp. 33–38.

Muscarella, Chris, and Mike Vetsuypens. "A Simple Test of Barron's Model of IPO Underwriting." *Journal of Financial Economics,* September 1989, pp. 123–35.

Neuberger, Brian M., and Chris A. La Chapelle. "Unseasoned New Issues' Price Performance on Three Tiers: 1975–1980." *Financial Management,* Autumn 1983, pp. 23–28.

Reilly, Frank K. "New Issues Revisited." *Financial Management,* Winter 1977, pp. 28–42.

Rock, K. "Why New Issues Are Underpriced." *Journal of Financial Economics,* January–February 1986, pp. 187–212.

Exchange Listings Effect

Fabozzi, Frank J., and Richard W. Furst. "Does Listing Increase the Market Value of Common Stock?" *Journal of Business,* April 1970, pp. 174–80.

Goulet, Waldemar. "Price Changes, Managerial Accounting and Insider Trading at the Time of Listing." *Financial Management,* Spring 1974, pp. 303–6.

Ying, Louis K. W.; Wilbur G. Lewellen; Gary G. Schlarbaum; and Ronald C. Lease. "Stock Exchange Listing and Securities Returns." *Journal of Financial and Quantitative Analysis,* September 1977, pp. 415–32.

Stock Repurchases

Dann, Larry Y. "Common Stock Repurchases: An Analysis of Returns to Bondholders and Stockholders." *Journal of Financial Economics,* June 1981, pp. 113–38.

Dielman, Terry E.; Timothy J. Nantell; and Roger L. Wright. "Price Effects of Stock Repurchasing: A Random Coefficient Regression Approach." *Journal of Financial and Quantitative Analysis,* March 1980, pp. 175–89.

Lakonishok, Josef, and Theo Vermaelon. "Anomalous Price Behavior around Repurchase Tender Offers." *Journal of Finance,* June 1990, pp. 455–77.

Masulis, R. W. "Stock Repurchase by Tender Offer: An Analysis of the Causes of Common Stock Price Changes." *Journal of Finance,* May 1980, pp. 305–19.

Norgaard, Richard, and Connie Norgaard. "A Critical Evaluation of Share Repurchase." *Financial Management,* Spring 1974, pp. 44–50.

Vermaelen, Theo. "Common Stock Repurchases and Market Signaling: An Empirical Study." *Journal of Financial Economics,* June 1981, pp. 139–83.

The Small-Firm Effect

Arbel, Auner, and Paul Strebel. "Pay Attention to Neglected Firms." *Journal of Portfolio Management,* Winter 1983, pp. 37–42.

Banz, Rolf W. "The Relationship between Returns and Market Value of Common Stocks." *Journal of Financial Economics,* March 1981, pp. 3–18.

Barry, Christopher B., and Stephen J. Brown. "Differential Information and the Small-Firm Effect." *Journal of Financial Economics,* June 1984, pp. 283–94.

Jansson, Solveig. "The Big Debate over Little Stocks." *Institutional Investor,* June 1982, pp. 141–48.

Keim, Donald B. "Size Related Anomalies and Stock Return Seasonality." *Journal of Financial Economics,* March 1983, pp. 13–32.

Loeb, Thomas F. "Is There a Gift from Small-Stock Investing?" *Financial Analysts Journal,* January–February 1991, pp. 39–44.

Reinganum, Marc R. "Misspecification of Capital Asset Pricing—Empirical Anomalies Based on Earnings Yield and Market Values." *Journal of Financial Economics,* March 1981, pp. 19–46.

_____. "A Direct Test of Roll's Conjecture on the Firm Size Effect." *Journal of Finance,* March 1982, pp. 27–35.

_____. "Portfolio Strategies Based on Market Capitalization." *Journal of Portfolio Management,* Winter 1983, pp. 29–36.

Roll, Richard. "A Possible Explanation of the Small-Firm Effect." *Journal of Finance,* September 1981, pp. 879–88.

_____. "Vas ist das? The Turn of the Year Effect and the Return Premium of Small Firms." *Journal of Portfolio Management,* Winter 1988, pp. 18–28.

Stoll, H. R., and R. E. Whaley. "Transaction Costs and the Small-Firm Effect." *Journal of Financial Economics,* June 1983, pp. 57–80.

Low-P/E Effect

Basu, S. "Investment Performance of Common Stocks in Relation to Their Price-Earnings Ratios: A Test of the Efficient Market Hypothesis." *Journal of Finance,* June 1977, pp. 663–82.

Goodman, David A., and John W. Peavy III. "The Risk Universal Nature of the P/E Effect." *Journal of Portfolio Management,* Summer 1985, pp. 14–17.

Peavy, John W., III, and David A. Goodman. "The Significance of P/Es for Portfolio Returns." *Journal of Portfolio Management,* Winter 1983, pp. 43–47.

The January Effect

Branch, Ben, and J. Ryan. "Tax-Loss Trading: An Inefficiency Too Large to Ignore." *Financial Review,* Winter 1980, pp. 20–29.

Keim, Donald B. "Dividend Yields, Size, and the January Effect." *Journal of Portfolio Management,* Winter 1986, pp. 54–61.

The Daily and Weekend Effect

Cross, Frank. "The Behavior of Stock Prices on Fridays and Mondays." *Financial Analysts Journal,* November–December 1973, pp. 67–69.

French, Kenneth R. "Stock Returns and the Weekend Effect." *Journal of Financial Economics,* March 1980, pp. 55–69.

Harris, Lawrence. "A Transaction Data Study of Weekly and Interdaily Patterns in Stock Returns." *Journal of Financial Economics,* May 1986, pp. 99–117.

The Value Line Effect

Black, Fisher. "*Yes,* Virginia, There Is Hope: Test of the Value Line Ranking System." *Financial Analysts Journal,* September–October 1973, pp. 10–14.

Holloway, Clark. "A Note on Testing an Aggressive Strategy Using Value Line Ranks." *Journal of Finance,* June 1981, pp. 711–19.

Huberman, Gur, and Shmuel Kandel. "Value Line Rank and Firm Size." *Journal of Business,* October 1987, pp. 577–90.

Stickel, Scott E. "The Effect of *Value Line Investment Survey* Rank Changes on Common Stock Prices." *Journal of Financial Economics,* March 1985, pp. 121–43.

The Earnings Effect

Kormendi, Roger, and Robert Lipe. "Earnings Innovations, Earnings Persistence, and Stock Returns." *Journal of Business,* July 1987, pp. 323–46.

Rendleman, Richard; Charles Jones; and Henry A. Latane. "Empirical Anomalies Based on Unexpected Earnings and the Importance of Risk Adjustments." *Journal of Financial Economics,* November 1982, pp. 269–87.

Part Four

Fixed-Income and Leveraged Securities

Outline

The fixed income markets include many different types of securities from municipal bonds to convertible corporate bonds, but the dominant group of securities are the U.S. government's bills, notes, and bonds. U.S. government securities markets are the prime markets around the world. In time of political trouble, U.S. government securities provide a safe haven for investors from Japan to Germany. Billions of dollars trade every day in these markets where it is not unusual for the U.S. Treasury Department to offer $10 to $15 billion of new securities in one day. These markets dwarf the stock markets and it is estimated that they account for close to $65 trillion of trading volume per year. What would happen to the integrity of these markets if a trading scandal occurred in this low risk, high quality market?

In 1991, we found out when Salomon Brothers cornered the market on a new offering. According to Treasury Department regulations, any one security dealer can only bid and receive 35 percent of the total offering. Through misrepresentation and illegal bidding, Salomon Brothers was able to corner over 85 percent of a U.S. Treasury offering in two-year notes. The ability to corner the market caused major losses at other trading firms such as Yamaichi International where they were unable to fill orders for customers at the auction and had to buy bonds from Salomon at a premium. Salomon not only violated the "rules of the game," which caused an outrage on the street, but they broke the law.

The federal government acted quickly to bar Salomon Brothers from further trading in U.S. government securities and many legal claims were filed by Salomon's clients, customers of competitors who were deprived securities, and the other broker-dealers who were deprived profits or forced into losses. The Securities and Exchange Commission investigated trading practices at other bond trading firms and Congress started hearings.

Salomon's Board of Directors acted quickly to rectify the situation by hiring the acclaimed investor and Chairman of Berkshire Hathaway, Warren Buffett, as its new interim chairman. Warren Buffett was on the board of directors at Salomon and owned a large position in Salomon when the trading scandal occurred. He cleaned house of top management, brought in a different style of management, assured the government he would bring Salomon into compliance with all U.S. Treasury regulations concerning U.S. securities trading, and put his reputation on the line to clean up what many thought were unethical trading practices at Salomon Brothers. In the process, he earned accolades from many but lost many former premier Salomon traders as he implemented new payments and bonus practices.

When Buffett was finished dealing with the trading scandal, Salomon had admitted its illegal activities, paid a large fine, fired those responsible for the scandal, and was once again allowed by the U.S. Treasury Department to be a primary government bond dealer. It will probably take Salomon Brothers a long time to recover its lost prestige and many of its customer who left in disgust or who found other bond dealers because of Salomon's several month suspension as a primary dealer. ∎

11

Bond and Fixed-Income Fundamentals

As the reader will observe in various sections of this chapter, bonds actually represent a more substantial portion of new offerings in the capital markets than common stock. Some of the most financially rewarding jobs on Wall Street go to sophisticated analysts and dealers in the bond market.

In this chapter, we will examine the fundamentals of the bond instrument for both corporate and government issuers, with an emphasis on the debt contract and security provisions. We will also look at the overall structure of the bond market and the ways in which bonds are rated. The question of bond market efficiency is also considered. While most of the chapter deals with corporate and government bonds, other forms of fixed-income securities also receive attention. Thus, there is a brief discussion of short-term, fixed-income investments (such as certificates of deposit and commercial paper) as well as preferred stock.

In Chapter 12, we will shift the emphasis to actually evaluating fixed-income investments and devising strategies that attempt to capture profitable opportunities in the market. In Chapter 13, we will look at the interesting concept of *duration*. We begin our discussion by considering the key elements that go into a bond contract.

■ THE BOND CONTRACT

A bond normally represents a long-term contractual obligation of the firm to pay interest to the bondholder as well as the face value of the bond at maturity. The major provisions in a bond agreement are spelled out in the **bond indenture,** a complicated legal document often over 100 pages long, administered by an independent trustee (usually a commercial bank). We shall examine some important terms and concepts associated with a bond issue.

The **par value** represents the face value of a bond. Most corporate bonds are traded in $1,000 units, while many federal, state, and local issues trade in units of $5,000 or $10,000.

Coupon rate refers to the actual interest rate on the bond, usually payable in semiannual installments. To the extent that interest rates in the market go above or below the coupon rate after the bond is issued, the market price of the bond will change from the par value. A bond initially issued at a rate of 8 percent will sell at a substantial discount from par value when 12 percent is the currently demanded rate of return. We will eventually examine how the investor makes and loses substantial amounts of money in the bond market with the swings in interest rates. A few corporate bonds are termed **variable-rate notes** or **floating rate notes,** meaning the coupon rate is fixed for only a short period and then varies with a stipulated short-term rate such as the rate on U.S. Treasury bills. In this instance, the interest payment rather than the price of the bond varies up and down. In recent times, zero-coupon bonds have also been issued at values substantially below maturity value. With **zero-coupon bonds,** the investor receives return in the form of capital appreciation over the life of the bond since no semiannual cash interest payments are received.

The **maturity date** is the date on which final payment is due at the stipulated par value.

Methods of bond repayment can occur under many different arrangements. Some bonds are never paid off, such as selected **perpetual bonds** issued by the Canadian and British governments, which have no maturity dates. A more normal procedure would simply call for a single-sum lump payment at the end of the obligation. Thus, the issuer may make 40 semiannual interest payments over the next 20 years plus one lump-sum payment of the par value of the bond at maturity. There are also other significant means of repayment.

The first is the **serial payment** in which bonds are paid off in installments over the life of the issue. Each serial bond has its own predetermined date of maturity and receives interest only to that point. Although the total bond issue may span over 20 years, 15 to 20 maturity dates are assigned. Municipal bonds are often issued on this basis. Second, there may be a **sinking-fund provision** in which semiannual or annual contributions are made by a corporation into a fund administered by a trustee for purposes of debt retirement. The trustee takes the proceeds and goes into the market to purchase bonds from willing sellers. If no sellers are available, a lottery system may be used to repurchase the required number of bonds from among outstanding bondholders.

Third, debt may also be retired under a call provision. A **call provision** allows the corporation to call or force in all of the debt issue prior to maturity. The corporation usually pays a 5 percent to 10 percent premium over par value as part of the call provision arrangement. The ability to call is often *deferred* for the first five years of an issue (it can only occur after this time period).

The opposite side of the coin for a bond investor is a put provision. The **put provision** enables the bondholder to have an option to sell a long-term bond back to the corporation at par value after a relatively short period (such as three to five years). This privilege can be particularly valuable if interest rates have gone up since the initial issuance, and the bond is currently trading at 75 to 80 percent of par. A put bond generally carries a lower interest rate than conventional bonds (perhaps 1 to 2 percent lower) because of this protective put privilege. If one buys a put bond and interest rates go down and bond prices up (perhaps to $1,200), the privilege is unnecessary and is merely ignored.

■ SECURED AND UNSECURED BONDS

We have discussed some of the important features related to interest payments and retirement of outstanding issues. At least of equal importance is the nature of the security provision for the issue. Bond market participants have a long-standing practice of describing certain issues by the nature of asset claims in liquidation. In actuality, only infrequently are pledged assets sold and the proceeds distributed to bondholders. Typically, the defaulting corporation is reorganized, and existing claims are partially satisfied by issuing new securities to the participating parties. Of course, the stronger and *better secured* the initial claim, the higher the quality of the security to be received in a reorganization.

A number of terms are used to denote **secured debt**, that is, debt backed by collateral. Under a **mortgage** agreement, real property (plant and equipment) is pledged as security for a loan. A mortgage may be senior or junior in nature, with the former requiring satisfaction of claims before payment is given to the latter. Bondholders may also attach an **after-acquired property clause** requiring that any new property be placed under the original mortgage.

A very special form of a mortgage or collateralized debt instrument is the **equipment trust certificate** used by firms in the transportation industry (railroads, airlines, etc.). Proceeds from the sale of the certificate are used to purchase new equipment, and this new equipment serves as collateral for the trust certificate.

Not all bond issues are secured or collateralized by assets. Most federal, state, and local government issues are unsecured. A wide range of corporate issues also are unsecured. There is a set of terminology referring to these unsecured issues. A corporate debt issue that is unsecured is referred to as a **debenture.** Even though the debenture is not secured by a specific pledge of assets, there may be priorities of claims among debenture holders. Thus, there are senior debentures and junior or subordinated debentures.

If liquidation becomes necessary because all other avenues for survival have failed, secured creditors are paid off first out of the disposition of the secured assets. The proceeds from the sale of the balance of the assets are then distributed among unsecured creditors, with those holding a senior ranking being satisfied before those holding a subordinate position (subordinated debenture holders).[1]

Unsecured corporate debt may provide slightly higher yields because of the greater suggested risk. However, this is partially offset by the fact that many unsecured debt issuers have such strong financial statements that security pledges may not be necessary.

Companies with less favorable prospects may issue income bonds. **Income bonds** specify that interest is to be paid only to the extent that it is earned as current income. There is no legally binding requirement to pay interest on a regular basis, and failure to make interest payments cannot trigger bankruptcy proceedings. These issues appear to offer the corporation the unusual advantage of paying interest as a tax-deductible expense (as opposed to dividends) combined with freedom from the binding contractual obligation of most debt issues. But any initial enthusiasm for these issues is quickly reduced by recognizing they have very limited appeal to investors. The issuance of income bonds is usually restricted to circumstances where new corporate debt is issued to old bondholders or preferred stockholders to avoid bankruptcy or where a troubled corporation is being reorganized.

---

[1]Those secured creditors that are not fully satisfied by the disposition of secured assets may also participate with the unsecured creditors in the remaining assets.

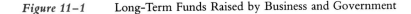

Figure 11–1　　Long-Term Funds Raised by Business and Government

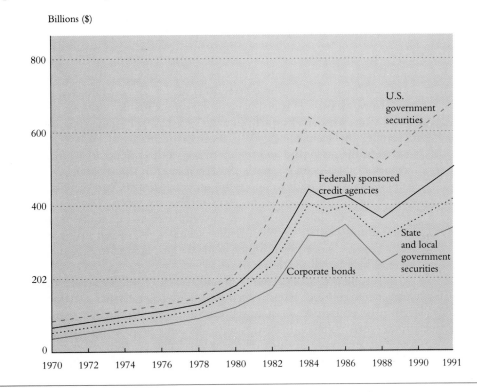

■ THE COMPOSITION OF THE BOND MARKET

Having established some of the basic terminology relating to the bond instrument, we are now in a position to take a more comprehensive look at the bond market. Corporate issues must vie with offerings from the U.S. Treasury, federally sponsored credit agencies, and state and local governments (municipal offerings). The relative importance of the four types of issues is indicated in Figure 11–1.

Over the 21-year period presented in Figure 11–1, the two fastest growing users of funds (borrowers) were the U.S. government and corporations. The former's needs can be attributed to persistent federal deficits that must be financed by increased borrowing. In the case of corporations, low profitability, combined with internal expansions and mergers, has led to tremendous borrowing needs. State and local governments have been active participants with municipal bond issues used to finance local growth and cover local deficits. Finally, federally sponsored credit agencies must call on the long-term funds

market. Please observe the explosive growth in long-term borrowing by all sectors of the economy since 1980.

U.S. Government Securities

U.S. government securities take the form of Treasury bills, Treasury notes, and Treasury bonds (only the latter two are considered in Figure 11–1). The distinction among the three categories relates to the life of the obligation.

Treasury bills (T-bills) have a maximum maturity of one year and common maturities of 91 and 182 days. Treasury bills trade on a discount basis, meaning the yield the investor receives occurs as a result of the difference between the price paid and the maturity value (and no actual interest is paid). A further discussion of this is presented later in the chapter.

Treasury bills trade in minimum units of $10,000, and there is an extremely active secondary, or resale, market for these securities. Thus, an investor buying a Treasury bill from the government with an initial life of approximately six months would have no difficulty selling it to another investor after two or three weeks. Since the T–bill now has a shorter time to run, its market value would be a bit closer to par.

A second type of U.S. government security is the **Treasury note,** which is considered to be of intermediate term and generally has a maturity of one to seven years. Finally, **Treasury bonds** are long term in nature and mature in 7 to 30 years. Unlike Treasury bills, Treasury notes and bonds provide direct interest and trade in units of $1,000 and higher. Because there is no risk of default (unless the government stops printing money or the ultimate bomb explodes), U.S. government securities provide lower returns than other forms of credit obligations. Interest on U.S. government issues is fully taxable for IRS purposes, but is exempt from state and local taxes.

Some Treasury notes and bonds have been repackaged into zero-coupon bonds by major brokerage firms and investment bankers such as Merrill Lynch and Goldman Sachs. These firms buy U.S. "governments" and put these securities in trust (usually a commercial bank acts as trustee). A security is divided into two parts—one generating a cash flow from the interest payments and the other providing principal at maturity. These two parts are then sold separately to investors with specific needs. The principal payment part is generically called a zero-coupon Treasury bond, but each investment bank labels its own product with names such as TIGRs (for Merrill Lynch's Treasury Investment Growth Receipts), and RATs, CATs, and GATORs for other firms. For example, Merrill Lynch's TIGRs are called Principal TIGRs (the zero-coupon part) and Serial TIGRs (which pay interest at six-month intervals for up to 40 payments). In the mid-1980s, the U.S. Treasury also began trading zero-coupon bonds on its own.

Since zero-coupon bonds pay no interest, all returns to the investor come in the form of increases in the value of the investment. For example, 15-year

zero-coupon bonds might initially sell for 18 percent of par value. You might buy a $1,000 instrument for $180.[2]

The Internal Revenue Service taxes zero-coupon bonds as if interest were paid annually even though no cash flow is received until maturity. The tax is based on amortizing the built-in gain over the life of the instrument. For tax reasons, zero-coupons are usually only appropriate for nontaxable accounts such as individual retirement accounts, Keogh plans, or other nontaxable pension funds.

Federally Sponsored Credit Agency Issues

Referring back to Figure 11–1, the second category represents securities issued by federal agencies. The issues represent obligations of various agencies of the government such as the Federal Home Loan Bank and the Federal Housing Administration (FHA). Although these issues are authorized by an act of Congress and are used to finance federal projects, they are not direct obligations of the Treasury but rather of the agency itself.

Though the issues are essentially free of risk (there is always the implicit standby power of the government behind the issues), they carry a slightly higher yield than U.S. government securities simply because they are not directly issued by the Treasury. Agency issues have been particularly active as a support mechanism for the housing industry. The issues generally trade in denominations of $5,000 and up and have varying maturities of from 1 to 40 years, with an average life of approximately 15 years. Examples of some agency issues are presented below.

	Minimum Denomination	Life of Issue
Federal Home Loan Bank	$10,000	12–25 years
Federal Intermediate Credit Banks	5,000	Up to 4 years
Federal Housing Administration	50,000	1–40 years
Export-Import Bank	5,000	Up to 7 years
U.S. Postal Service	10,000	25 years

---

[2]On zero-coupon bonds, the yield to maturity is a true rate over the life of the security since the price paid includes the assumption of continuous compounding at the yield to maturity. Zero-coupon securities are the most price sensitive to a change in interest rates of any bond having the same maturity. This is fine when interest rates decline but can be disastrous when rates rise. More will be said about zero-coupon bonds in Chapter 13.

Interest on agency issues is fully taxable for IRS purposes and is generally taxable for state and local purposes although there are exceptions. (For example, interest on obligations issued by the Federal Housing Administration are subject to state and local taxes, but those of the Federal Home Loan Bank are not.)

One agency issue that is of particular interest to the investor because of its unique features is the **GNMA (Ginnie Mae) pass-through certificate.** These certificates represent an undivided interest in a pool of federally insured mortgages. Actually, GNMA, the Government National Mortgage Association, buys a pool of mortgages from various lenders at a discount and then issues securities to the public against these mortgages. Security holders in GNMA certificates receive monthly payments that essentially represent a pass through of interest and principal payments on the mortgages. These securities come in minimum denominations of $25,000, are long term, and are fully taxable for federal, state, and local income tax purposes. A major consideration in this investment is that the investor has fully consumed his or her capital at the end of the investment. (Not only has interest been received monthly but also all principal has been returned over the life of the certificate, and therefore, there is no lump-sum payment at maturity.)

State and Local Government Securities

Debt securities issued by state and local governments are referred to as **municipal bonds.** Examples of issuing agencies include states, cities, school districts, toll roads, or any other type of political subdivision. The most important feature of a municipal bond is the tax-exempt nature of the interest payment. Dating back to the U.S. Supreme Court opinion of 1819 in *McCullough v. Maryland,* it was ruled that the federal government and state and local governments do not possess the power to tax each other. An eventual by-product of the judicial ruling was that income from municipal bonds cannot be taxed by the IRS. Furthermore, income from municipal bonds is also exempt from state and local taxes if bought within the locality in which one resides. Thus, a Californian buying municipal bonds in that state would pay no state income tax on the issue. However, the same Californian would have to pay state or local income taxes if the originating agency were in Texas or New York.

We cannot overemphasize the importance of the federal tax exemption that municipal bonds enjoy. The consequences are twofold. First, individuals in high tax brackets may find highly attractive investment opportunities in municipal bonds.[3] Some have referred to municipal bond investments as welfare

---

[3]It should be noted, however, that any capital gain on a municipal bond is taxable as would be the case with any investment.

Table 11–1	Marginal Tax Rates and Return Equivalents		
Yield on Municipal (Percent)	15 Percent Bracket	28 Percent Bracket	31 Percent Bracket
6%	7.1%	8.3%	8.7%
7	8.2	9.7	10.1
8	9.4	11.1	11.6
9	10.6	12.5	13.0
10	11.8	13.9	14.5
11	12.9	15.3	15.9
12	14.1	16.7	17.4

for the rich. The formula used to equate interest on municipal bonds to other taxable investments is:

$$Y = \frac{i}{(1 - t)} \tag{11-1}$$

where:

Y = Equivalent before-tax yield on a taxable investment

i = Yield on the municipal obligation

t = Marginal tax rate of the investor

If an investor has a marginal tax rate of 31 percent and is evaluating a municipal bond paying 7 percent interest, the equivalent before-tax yield on a taxable investment would be:

$$\frac{7\%}{(1 - .31)} = \frac{7\%}{.69} = 10.14\%$$

Thus, the investor could choose between a *non*-tax-exempt investment paying 10.14 percent and a tax-exempt municipal bond paying 7 percent and be indifferent between the two. Table 11–1 presents examples of trade-offs between tax-exempt and nontax-exempt (taxable) investments at various interest rates and marginal tax rates. Clearly, the higher the marginal tax rate, the greater the advantage of tax-exempt municipal bonds.

A second significant feature of municipal bonds is that the yield the issuing agency pays on municipal bonds is lower than the yield on taxable instruments. Of course, a municipal bond paying 7 percent may be quite competitive with taxable instruments paying more. Average differentials are presented in Table 11–2.

You should notice in Table 11–2 that the yield differences between municipal bonds and corporate bonds was normally 2 to 4 percentage points until

Table 11–2   Comparable Yields on Long-Term Municipals and Taxable Corporates (Yearly Averages)

Year	Municipals Aa	Corporates Aa	Yield Difference
1991	6.80%	9.09%	2.29
1990	7.15	9.56	2.41
1989	7.51	9.46	1.95
1988	8.38	9.66	1.28
1987	8.50	9.68	1.18
1986	7.35	9.47	2.12
1985	8.81	11.82	3.01
1984	9.95	12.25	2.30
1983	9.20	12.42	3.22
1982	11.39	14.41	3.02
1981	10.89	14.75	3.86
1980	8.06	12.50	4.44
1979	6.12	9.94	3.82
1978	5.68	8.92	3.24
1977	5.39	8.24	2.85
1976	6.12	8.75	2.63
1975	6.77	9.17	2.40
1974	6.04	8.84	2.80
1973	5.11	7.66	2.55
1972	5.19	7.48	2.29
1971	5.36	7.78	2.42

Source: *Moody's Municipal & Government Manual, Moody's Industrial Manual,* and *Moody's Bond Record* (published by Moody's Investors Service, Inc., New York, N.Y.), selected issues.

after the passage of the Tax Reform Act in 1986. Starting in 1987, the differential has moved closer to 1 to 2 points. This is because the marginal tax rates of investors are now lower, and thus, the relative tax advantages of municipal bonds have diminished. A major distinction that is also important to the bond issuer and investor is whether the bond is of a general obligation or revenue nature.

General Obligation versus Revenue Bonds   A **general obligation issue** is backed by the full faith, credit, and "taxing power" of the governmental unit. For a **revenue bond,** on the other hand, the repayment of the issue is fully dependent on the revenue-generating capability of a specific project or venture, such as a toll road, bridge, or municipal colosseum.

Because of the taxing power behind most general obligation (GO) issues, they tend to be of extremely high quality. Approximately three fourths of all

municipal bond issues are of the general obligation variety, and very few failures have occurred in the post–World War II era. Revenue bonds tend to be of more uneven quality, and the economic soundness of the underlying revenue-generating project must be carefully examined (though most projects are quite worthwhile).

Municipal Bond Guarantee A growing factor in the municipal bond market is the third-party guarantee. Whether dealing with a general obligation or revenue bond, a fee may be paid by the originating governmental body to a third-party insurer to guarantee that all interest and principal payments will be made. A number of states, including California and Michigan, now have provisions to guarantee payments on selected issues. There are also two large private insurers. The first is a consortium of four insurance companies that market their product under the name of the Municipal Bond Insurance Association (MBIA). The second is the American Municipal Bond Assurance Corporation (AMBAC). Both will insure general obligation or revenue bonds.

A bond that carries a guarantee will have a slightly lower yield and a better secondary, or resale, market. This may be important because municipal bonds, in general, do not provide as strong a secondary market as U.S. government issues. The market for a given municipal issue is often small and fragmented, and high indirect costs are associated with reselling the issue.

Corporate Securities

While corporate bonds represent only 35 to 40 percent of the total bond market (which also includes U.S. government securities, federally sponsored credit agencies, and municipal bonds as shown in Figure 11–1), they are the dominant source of new financing for the U.S. corporation. Corporate bonds have been the most significant form of new financing for U.S. corporations as shown in Figure 11–2.

Bonds normally supply 75 to 80 percent of firms' external financial needs. Even during the great bull stock market of 1982 to 1986, corporations looked as heavily as ever to the debt markets to provide financing (this was justified by the decreasing interest rates during this period).

The corporate market may be divided into a number of subunits, including *industrials, public utilities, rails* and *transportation,* and *financial issues* (banks, finance companies, etc.). The industrials are a catchall category that includes everything from high-technology companies to discount chain stores. Public utilities represent the largest segment of the market and have issues that run up to 40 years in maturity. Because public utilities are in constant need of funds to meet ever-expanding requirements for power generation, telephone services, and other essentials, they are always in the bond market to raise new funds. The needs associated with rails and transportation as well as financial issues

Figure 11–2   Long-Term Corporate Financing

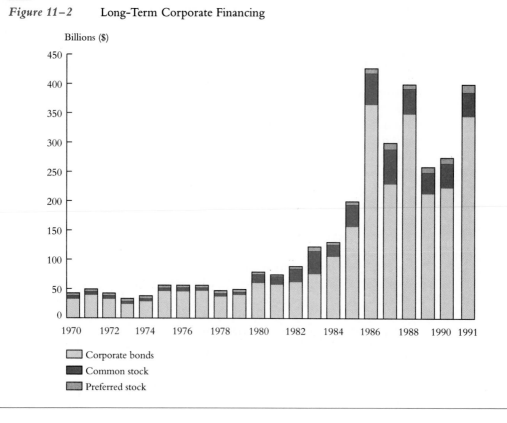

Billions ($)

Corporate bonds
Common stock
Preferred stock

tend to be less than those associated with public utilities or industrials. Table 11–3 shows comparative yields for the two main categories.[4]

The higher yields on public utility issues represent a supply-demand phenomenon more than anything else. A constant stream of new issues to the market can only be absorbed by a higher yield pattern. In other cases, the higher required return may also be associated with quality deterioration as measured by profitability and interest coverage. During 1983–84, the default of the Washington State Power Authority on bonds issued to construct power-generating facilities sent waves through the bond market. Again in 1984, when Public Service of Indiana canceled construction of a partially complete nuclear power plant, nuclear utility issues (both stocks and bonds) suffered severe price erosion, and the bond market demanded high risk premiums on bonds of almost all nuclear utilities.

---

[4]Financial and transportation issues are generally not broken out of the published data.

Table 11–3	Comparative Yields on Aa Bonds among Corporate Issuers	
	Industrial	**Public Utility**
1991	9.01%	9.25%
1990	9.41	9.65
1989	9.35	9.55
1988	9.41	10.20
1987	9.73	9.83
1986	9.49	9.44
1985	11.57	12.02
1984	12.39	13.02
1983	11.94	12.74
1982	15.01	16.48
1981	13.01	14.03
1980	11.16	11.95
1979	9.24	9.70
1978	8.42	8.76
1977	7.90	8.41
1976	8.87	9.39
1975	8.81	9.45
1974	7.85	8.15

Source: *Moody's Bond Record* (published by Moody's Investors Service, Inc., New York, N.Y.), selected issues.

Corporate bonds of all types generally trade in units of $1,000, and this is a particularly attractive feature to the smaller investor who does not wish to purchase in units of $5,000 to $10,000 (which is necessary for many Treasury, federally sponsored credit agency issues, and municipals). Because of higher risk relative to government issues, the investor will generally receive higher yields on corporates as well. All income from corporates is taxable for federal, state, and local purposes. Finally, corporate issues have the disadvantage of being subject to calls. When buying a bond during a period of high interest rates, the call provision must be considered a negative feature because the high-yielding bonds may be called in for early retirement as interest rates go down.

The list of innovative products in the corporate debt market is ever growing. Appendix 11–A provides an example of recent developments as presented by John D. Finnerty.

■ BOND MARKET INVESTORS

Having considered the issuer or supply side of the market, we now comment on the investor or demand side. The bond market is dominated by large institutional investors (insurance companies, banks, pension funds, mutual

funds) even more than the stock market. Institutional investors account for 90 to 95 percent of the trading in key segments of the bond market. However, the presence of the individual investor is partially felt in the corporate and municipal bond market where the incentives of low denomination ($1,000) corporate bonds or tax-free municipal bonds have some attraction.

Institutional investors' preferences for various sectors of the bond market are influenced by their tax status as well as the nature of their obligations or liabilities to depositors, investors, or clients. For example, banks traditionally have been strong participants in the municipal bond market because of their substantial tax obligations. Their investments tend to be in short- to intermediate-term assets because of the short-term nature of their deposit obligations (the funds supplied to the banks). One problem that banks find in their bond portfolios is that such investments are often preferred over loans to customers when the economy is weak and loan demand is sluggish. Not so coincidentally, this happens to be the time period when interest rates are low. When the economy improves, interest rates go up, and so does loan demand. To meet the loan demand of valued customers, banks liquidate portions of their bond portfolios. The problem with this recurring process is that banks are buying bonds when interest rates are *low* and selling them when interest rates are *high*. This can cause losses in the value of the bank portfolio.

The bond market investor must be prepared to deal in a relatively strong primary market (new issues market) and a relatively weak secondary market (resale market). While the secondary market is active for many types of Treasury and agency issues, such is not the case for corporate and municipal issues. Thus, the investor must look well beyond the yield, maturity, and rating to determine if a purchase is acceptable. The question that must be considered is: How close to the going market price can I dispose of the issue if that should be necessary? If a 5 or 10 percent discount is involved, that might be unacceptable. Unlike the stock market, the secondary market in bonds tends to be dominated by over-the-counter transactions (although listed bonds are traded as well).

A significant development in the late 1980s has been the heavy participation of foreign investors in U.S. bond markets. Foreign investors now bankroll between 10 to 15 percent of the U.S. government's debt. While these investors have helped to finance the U.S. government's deficits, if at any point they decided to withdraw a major portion of their funds, the effects on the U.S. financial markets would be disruptive. For this reason, our government is sensitive to the demands and desires of its foreign creditors.

■ DISTRIBUTION PROCEDURES

In February 1982, the Securities and Exchange Commission began allowing a process called shelf registration under SEC Rule 415. **Shelf registration** permits large companies to file one comprehensive registration statement that outlines the firm's plans for future long-term financing. Then, when market

conditions seem appropriate, the firm can issue the securities through an investment banker without further SEC approval. Future issues are said to be sitting on the shelf, waiting for the most advantageous time to appear. An issue may be on the shelf for up to two years. An example of bonds awaiting distribution on May 27, 1991, is presented from *Moody's Bond Survey* in Table 11–4 on the next page.

Approximately half of the new public bond issues are distributed through the shelf registration process. The balance is issued under more traditional procedures in which the bonds are issued shortly after registration by a large syndicate of investment bankers in a highly structured process.

Private Placement

A number of bond offerings are sold to investors as a **private placement;** that is, they are sold privately to investors rather than through the public markets. Private placements are most popular with investors such as insurance companies and pension funds, and they are primarily offered in the corporate sector by industrial firms rather than public utilities. The lender can generally expect to receive a slightly higher yield than on public issues to compensate for the extremely limited or nonexistent secondary market and the generally smaller size of the borrowing firm in a private placement.

■ BOND RATINGS

Bond investors tend to place much more emphasis on independent analysis of quality than do common stock investors. For this reason, both corporate financial management and institutional portfolio managers keep a close eye on bond rating procedures. The difference between an AA and an A rating may mean the corporation will have to pay ¼ point more interest on the bond issue (perhaps 9½ percent rather than 9¼ percent). On a $100 million, 20–year issue, this represents $250,000 per year (before tax), or a total of $5 million over the life of the bond.

The two major bond-rating agencies are Moody's Investors Service (a subsidiary of Dun & Bradstreet, Inc.) and Standard & Poor's (a subsidiary of McGraw-Hill, Inc.). They rank thousands of corporate and municipal issues as well as a limited number of private placements, commercial paper, preferred stock issues, and offerings of foreign companies and governments. U.S. government issues tend to be free of risk and therefore are given no attention by the bond-rating agencies. Moody's, founded in 1909, is the older of the two bond-rating agencies and covers twice as many securities as Standard & Poor's (particularly in the municipal bond area). Other less well known bond-rating agencies include Fitch Investors Service, Inc. (an old-line rating agency that specializes in bank securities) and Duff & Phelp, Inc.

The bond ratings, generally ranging from an AAA to a D category, are decided on a committee basis at both Moody's and Standard & Poor's. There

Table 11–4   Examples of Shelf Registration

Prospective Offerings—Shelf Registrations under SEC Rule 415

Date of Registration	Original Amount ($Million)	Unsold Amount ($Million)	Registrants	Lead Underwriter	Types of Securities Prospectively Rated	Page Nos.	Prospective Ratings
07/22/88	300.0	150.0	Bank of Boston Corp.	TBD	Sub. Debt Securities		(P)B3
06/23/89	750.0	750.0	Bank of Boston Corp.	TBD	Sr. Unsec. Debt Securities		(P)B1
09/01/89	250.0	250.0	Bank of New England Corp.	TBD	Various Debt Securities		—
05/01/87	125.0	125.0	Bank of New York Company, Inc.	TBD	Sub. Capital Notes		(P)Baa1
03/24/88	285.0	35.0	Bank of New York Company, Inc.	TBD	Cum. Preferred Stk.		(P)"a3"
					Non-Cum. Preferred Stk.		(P)"a3"
08/14/89	500.0	500.0	Bank of New York Company, Inc.	TBD	Sr. Debt Securities		(P)A3
					Sub. Debt Securities		(P)Baa1
02/28/85	500.0	47.3	Bankers Trust New York Corp.	TBD	Sr. Debentures		(P)A1
					Sub. Debentures		(P)A2
08/10/90	500.0	400.0	Bankers Trust New York Corp.	TBD	Sr. Debentures	4734	(P)A1
					Sub. Debentures	4734	(P)A2
04/25/91	500.0	500.0	Bankers Trust New York Corp.	TBD	Sr. Debt Securities		(P)A1
					Sub. Debt Securities		(P)A2
09/07/90	2795.0	1770.0	BankAmerica Corp.	TBD	Sr. Debt (w/warrants)		(P)A2
					Sub. Debt (w/warrants)		(P)A3
					Preferred Stock		(P)"a2"
09/21/89	500.0	67.9	Barclays Bank plc	TBD	Non-Cum. Dollar-Denom. Pref.		(P)"aa1"
04/03/91	250.0	250.0	Barclays Bank plc	TBD	Stock Index Warrants		—
11/29/82	100.0	100.0	Barnett Banks, Inc.	FBC	Various Debt Securities	216	(P)Baa1
08/10/90	100.0	45.0	Barnett Banks, Inc.	TBD	Sub. Debt Securities		(P)Baa2
03/21/91	300.0	200.0	Barnett Banks, Inc.	TBD	Sr. Debt Securities		(P)Baa1
					Sub. Debt Securities		(P)Baa2
09/18/90	550.0	450.0	Baxter International Inc.	TBD	Various Debt Securities	4233	(P)A3
12/24/90	100.0	100.0	Bear Stearns Companies Inc (The)	BS	Government Securities Warr.		(P)A2
08/31/90	900.0	200.0	Bell Atlantic Cptl Funding Corp.	TBD	Gtd. Debt Securities		(P)Aa3
05/03/88	300.0	125.0	Bell Tel Co of Pennsylvania	TBD	Various Debt Securities	6718	(P)Aa1
12/17/90	2000.0	1200.0	Beneficial Corp.	TBD	Various Debt Securities	7712	(P)A2
08/25/89	200.0	200.0	Berkley (W R) Corporation	TBD	Sr. Debt Securities	4031	(P)A3
08/17/89	400.0	400.0	Berkshire Hathaway Inc.	SB	Various Debt Securities		(P)Aa1
10/04/89	200.0	50.0	Boatmens Bancshares Inc.	TBD	Sub. Debt Securities		(P)A3
03/19/91	1000.0	1000.0	Boeing Co.	TBD	Various Debt Securities	6620	(P)Aa3
12/13/90	426.0	426.0	Boise Cascade Corp.	TBD	Various Debt Securities	7315	(P)Baa1
12/14/87	475.0	125.0	Borden, Inc.	TBD	Various Debt Securities	4273	(P)A1
06/30/89	165.0	65.0	Boston Edison Co.	GS	First Mtge. Bonds	5962	(P)Baa1
					Unsec. Notes	5962	(P)Baa2
03/01/91	2505.8	2305.8	BP America, Inc.	TBD	Gtd. Debt (w/warrants)	6814	(P)Aa3
06/17/83	500.0	500.0	BP North American Finance Corp.	TBD	Gtd. Debt Securities	2386	(P)Aa3
07/14/88	400.0	400.0	British Columbia, Province of	SL	Various Debt Securities	7932	(P)Aa1
10/21/88	1000.0	500.0	British Telecom Finance, Inc.	GS	Gtd. Debt Securities	4846	(P)Aaa
03/05/87	200.0	100.0	Brown-Forman Corporation	TBD	Various Debt Securities		(P)Aa3
03/14/91	300.0	200.0	Browning-Ferris Industries Inc.	TBD	Various Debt Securities	6813	(P)A2
03/19/87	300.0	100.0	Brunswick Corp.	TBD	Various Debt Securities		(P)Baa1
03/04/91	300.0	100.0	Campbell Soup Co.	TBD	Various Debt Securities	6620	(P)Aa2
06/25/85	1500.0	600.0	Canada (Government of)	SB	Bonds	3489	(P)Aaa
05/02/86	1400.0	1400.0	Canada (Government of)	TBD	Bonds		
04/25/83	300.0	300.0	Canadian National Railway	MYW	Various Debt Securities	2788	(P)Aa2
06/26/85	100.0	75.0	Canadian Pacific, Ltd.	TBD	Eq. Tr. Certificates	3230	★
03/29/91	750.0	750.0	Capital Cities/Abc, Inc.	TBD	Sr. Debt (w/warrants)	6407	(P)A1
					Sub. Debt (w/warrants)	6407	(P)A2
05/25/90	400.0	225.0	Capital Holding Corp.	GS	Various Debt Securities	6005	(P)A2
04/24/86	180.0	180.0	Carolina Power & Light Co.	TBD	Cum. Preferred Stk.	6776	(P)"a2"
12/18/90	325.0	100.0	Carolina Power & Light Co.	TBD	First Mtge. Bonds	7326	(P)A2
09/24/90	600.0	600.0	Caterpillar Financial Svcs Corp.	TBD	Various Debt Securities	4244	(P)A2
03/21/91	100.0	100.0	Caterpillar Financial Svcs Corp.	CIM	Var. Denom. Flt. Rt. Demand Notes	6738	(P)A2
05/09/91	700.0	700.0	Caterpillar Financial Svcs Corp.	TBD	Various Debt Securities		—
05/07/91	500.0	500.0	Caterpillar Inc.	TBD	Various Debt Securities		—
10/05/90	100.0	100.0	Centex Corp.	TBD	Sub. Debt Securities		(P)Baa3

Source: *Moody's Bond Survey* (published by Moody's Investor Service, Inc., New York, N.Y.), May 27, 1991, p. 5837.

are no fast and firm quantitative measures that specify the rating a new issue will receive. Nevertheless, measures pertaining to cash flow and earnings generation in relationship to debt obligations are given strong consideration. Of particular interest are coverage ratios that show the number of times interest payments, as well as all annual contractual obligations, are covered by earnings. A coverage of 2 or 3 may contribute to a low rating, while a ratio of 5 to 10 may indicate the possibility of a strong rating. Operating margins, return on invested capital, and returns on total assets are also evaluated along with debt-to-equity ratios.[5] Financial-ratio analysis makes up perhaps 50 percent of the evaluation. Other factors of importance are the nature of the industry in which the firm operates, the relative position of the firm within the industry, the pricing clout the firm has, and the quality of management. Decisions are not made in a sterile, isolated environment. Thus, it is not unusual for corporate management or the mayor to make a presentation to the rating agency, and on-sight visitations to plants or cities may occur.

The overall quality of the work done by the bond-rating agencies may be judged by the agencies' acceptance in the business and academic community. Their work is very well received. Although Paine Webber and some other investment houses have established their own analysts to shadow the activities of the bond-rating agencies and look for imprecisions in their classifications (and thus potential profits), the opportunities are not great. Academic researchers have generally found that accounting and financial data were well considered in the bond ratings and that rational evaluation appeared to exist.[6]

One item lending credibility to the bond-rating process is the frequency with which the two major rating agencies arrive at the same grade for a given issue (this occurs well over 50 percent of the time). When "split ratings" do occur (different ratings by different agencies), they are invariably of a small magnitude. A typical case might be AAA versus AA rather than AAA versus BBB. While one can question whether one agency is looking over the other's shoulder or "copying its homework," this is probably not the case in this skilled industry.

Nevertheless, there is room for criticism. While initial evaluations are quite thorough and rational, the monitoring process may not be wholly satisfactory. Subsequent changes in corporate or municipal government events may not trigger a rating change quickly enough. One sure way a corporation or municipal government will get a reevaluation is for them to come out with a new issue. This tends to generate a review of all existing issues.

---

[5]Similar appropriate measures can be applied to municipal bonds, such as debt per capita or income per capita within a governmental jurisdiction.

[6]James O. Horrigan, "The Determination of Long-Term Credit Standing with Financial Ratios," *Empirical Research in Accounting: Selected Studies,* supplement to *Journal of Accounting Research* 4 (1966), pp. 44–62; Thomas F. Pogue and Robert M. Soldofsky, "What's in a Bond Rating?" *Journal of Financial and Quantitative Analysis,* June 1969, pp. 201–8; and George E. Pinches and Kent A. Mingo, "A Multivariate Analysis of Industrial Bond Ratings," *Journal of Finance,* March 1973, pp. 1–18.

The Bond Rating Game: Who Really Runs the Corporation?

When Shell Canada, an integrated oil company with many U.S. investors, decided to sell its coal business, it called Moody's and Standard & Poor's first. Although its own financial analysis indicated the move was appropriate, it would not have made the decision without the blessings of the two major U.S. bond-rating agencies as well as similar rating agencies in Canada. The sell-off provided a $120 million write-off that could have caused a downgrading of Shell Canada's double-A rating, and the firm was not about to take a chance.

The firm's concern was well justified. Its action was taken in June 1991 (a recession year). During the first six months of 1991, 422 corporations suffered a downgrading in ratings while only 88 had an increase. In the prior decade, the big causes for downgradings were the aftereffects of acquisitions or attempts by corporations to defend themselves against takeovers. In the 1990s, these factors were less important, and the major concern was poor earnings performance in a debt-laden economy.

Three good rules for firms to follow in dealing with bond-rating agencies is never surprise the agencies, tell all, and show good intent. A number of years ago, Manville Corporation was severely downgraded not for poor performance, but because it took Chapter 11 bankruptcy protection because it faced asbestos damage litigation. The decision may have been right at the time, but the firm did not have the blessings of the bond-rating agencies.

Actual Rating System

Table 11–5 shows an actual listing of the designations used by Moody's and Standard & Poor's. Note that Moody's combines capital letters and small *a*'s, and Standard & Poor's uses all capital letters.

The first four categories are assumed to represent investment-grade quality (high or medium grades). Large institutional investors (insurance companies, banks, pension funds) generally confine their activities to these four categories. Moody's also modifies its basic ratings with numerical values for categories Aa through B. The highest in a category is 1, 2 is the midrange, and 3 is the lowest. An Aa2 rating means the bond is in the midrange of Aa. Standard & Poor's has a similar modification process with plusses and minuses applied. Thus, AA + would be on the high end of an AA rating, AA would be in the middle, and AA − would be on the low end.

It is also possible for a corporation to have issues outstanding in more than one category. For example, highly secured mortgage bonds of a corporation may be rated AA, while unsecured issues carry an A rating.

The level of interest payment on a bond is inverse to the quality rating. If a bond rated AAA by Standard & Poor's pays 9 percent, an A quality bond might pay 10.5 percent; a BB, 12 percent; and so on. The spread between these yields changes from time to time and is watched closely by the financial community as a barometer of future movements in the financial markets. A relatively small spread between two rating categories would indicate investors

		Standard	
Quality	**Moody's**	**& Poor's**	**Description**
High grade	Aaa	AAA	Bonds that are judged to be of the best quality. They carry the smallest degree of investment risk and are generally referred to as "gilt edge." Interest payments are protected by a large or exceptionally stable margin, and principal is secure.
	Aa	AA	Bonds that are judged to be of high quality by all standards. Together with the first group, they comprise what are generally known as high-grade bonds. They are rated lower than the best bonds because margins of protection may not be as large.
Medium grade	A	A	Bonds that possess many favorable investment attributes and are to be considered as upper-medium-grade obligations. Factors giving security to principal and interest are considered adequate.
	Baa	BBB	Bonds that are considered as medium-grade obligations—they are neither highly protected nor poorly secured.
Speculative	Ba	BB	Bonds that are judged to have speculative elements; their future cannot be considered as well assured. Often the protection of interest and principal payments may be very moderate.
	B	B	Bonds that generally lack characteristics of the desirable investment. Assurance of interest and principal payments or of maintenance of other terms of the contract over any long period may be small.
Default	Caa	CCC	Bonds that are of poor standing. Such issues may be in default, or there may be elements of danger present with respect to principal or interest.
	Ca	CC	Bonds that represent obligations that are speculative to a high degree. Such issues are often in default or have other marked shortcomings.
	C		The lowest-rated class in Moody's designation. These bonds can be regarded as having extremely poor prospects of attaining any real investment standing.
		C	Rating given to income bonds on which interest is not currently being paid.
		D	Issues in default with arrears in interest and/or principal payments.

Table 11–5 Description of Bond Ratings

Sources: *Moody's Bond Record* (published by Moody's Investors Service, Inc., New York, N.Y.) and *Bond Guide* (Standard & Poor's).

generally have confidence in the economy. As the yield spread widens between higher and lower rating categories, this may indicate loss of confidence. Investors are demanding increasingly higher yields for lower-rated bonds. Their loss of confidence indicates they will demand progressively higher returns for taking risks.

■ JUNK BONDS

Lower-quality bonds are sometimes referred to as **junk bonds.** Any bond that is not considered to be of investment quality by Wall Street analysts is put in the junk bond category. As previously indicated, investment quality means the bond falls into one of the four top investment grade categories established by Moody's and Standard & Poor's. This indicates investment grade bonds extend down to Baa in Moody's and BBB in Standard & Poor's (Table 11–5). A wide range of quality is associated with junk bonds. Some are very close to investment quality (such as the Ba and BB bonds) while others carry ratings in the C and D category.

Bonds tend to fall into the junk bond category for a number of reasons. First are the so-called fallen angel bonds issued by companies that once had high credit rankings but now face hard times. Second are emerging growth companies or small firms that have not yet established an adequate record to justify an investment-quality rating. Finally, the largest part of the junk bond market is made of companies undergoing a restructuring either as a result of a leveraged buyout or as part of fending off an unfriendly takeover offer. In both these cases, equity capital tends to be replaced with debt and a lower rating is assigned.

Many junk bonds behave more like common stock than bonds and rally on good news, actual interest payments, or improving business conditions. Several institutions such as Merrill Lynch and Fidelity Investments manage mutual funds with a junk bond emphasis.

The main appeal of junk bonds historically is that they provided yields 300 to 800 basis points higher than that for AAA corporate bonds or U.S. Treasury securities. Also, until the recession of 1990–91, there were relatively few defaults by junk bond issuers. Thus, the investor got a substantially higher yield with only a small increase in risk.

However, in the 1990–91 recession, junk bond prices tumbled by 20 to 30 percent, while other bond values stayed firm. Examples of junk bond issues that dropped sharply in value included those issued by Eastern Airlines, Gibraltar Financial, Rapid-American Corporation, Revco, Campeau Corporation, and Resorts International. Many of these declines were due to poor business conditions. However, the fall of Drexel Burnham Lambert, the leading underwriter of junk bond issues, also contributed to the difficulties in the market. That problem was further compounded when Michael Milken, the guru of junk bond dealers, was sentenced to 10 years in prison for illegal insider trading.

As the economy was coming out of the recession in early 1992, junk bonds once again began to gain in popularity. Many of these issues had their prices battered down so low that they appeared to be bargains. It was not unusual to see yields of 15 to 18 percent. Furthermore, with the likelihood of improving business conditions, junk bonds appeared to once again be a viable investment. These securities appear to have a place in the portfolio of investors with a reasonable risk tolerance. This is particularly true for bonds that are in the middle to lower B categories.

■ BOND QUOTES

The Wall Street Journal and a number of other sources publish bond values on a daily basis. Table 11–6 on the next page provides an excerpt from the daily quote sheet for corporate bonds.

In the first column, the company name is followed by the annual coupon rate and the maturity date. For example, the table shows American Brands with a coupon rate of 9⅛ percent maturing in 16 (the year 2116). The current yield (Cur Yld) represents the annual interest or coupon payment divided by the price and is 9.1 percent. The volume (Vol) is indicated to be 36 bonds traded, and the closing price is 100¼. The bond quote does not represent actual dollars but percent of par value. Since corporate bonds trade in units of $1,000 par value, 100.25 percent represents $1,002.50.

A student interested in further information on a bond could proceed to *Moody's Bond Record,* published by Moody's Investors Service, or the *Bond Guide,* published by Standard & Poor's. For example, using *Moody's Bond Record,* as shown in Table 11–7, the reader could determine information about a firm. Let's look at Aluminum Co. of America's 7s of 2011. The designation in the left margin indicates the industry classification of the firm. The issue has a Moody's bond rating of A2 and a current call price of 100 percent of par, or $1,000.00. *Moody's Bond Record* further indicates interest is payable on April and October 15 of each year (Interest Dates column). The current price of the bonds is 79⅜, or $793.75 ($1,000 × 79.375%).

Table 11–8 on page 380 features quotes on U.S. government securities. Treasury notes and bonds are traded as a percentage of par value, similar to corporate bonds. Historically, price changes in the market have been rather small, and bonds are quoted in ⅓₂nds of a percentage point. For example, the price for the 7½ Treasury note due January 1996 is quoted at 101.08 bid and 101.10 asked.[7] These prices translate into 101⅛₃₂ and 101¹⁰⁄₃₂ percent of $1,000. The bid price on a $1,000 bond would be $1,012.50 ($1,000 × 101.25%) and the asked price is $1,013.75 ($1,000 × 101.375%). The total spread between the bid and ask price is $1.25.

While Treasury notes and bonds are quoted on the basis of price, Treasury bills are quoted on the basis of yield. Look at the Treasury bills on the right side of Table 11–8. These yields represent the discount from the par value of $10,000. As a general example, a $10,000 Treasury bill quoted at 5 percent, with one year to maturity, would provide $500 in interest and would sell on a discount basis for $9,500. The effective yield would be 5.26 percent ($500/$9,500). The same 5 percent Treasury bill with six months to maturity would provide $250 in interest ($500/2) and sell for $9,750. The effective yield would be 5.12 percent ($250/$9,750 × 2).

---

[7]The bid price is the value at which the bond can be sold and the asked price is the value at which it can be bought.

Table 11–6 Daily Quotes on Corporate Bonds

CORPORATION BONDS
Volume, $36,910,000

Bonds	Cur Yld	Vol	Close	Net Chg
AMR zr06	...	2	40⅝	+ ⅛
Advst 9s08	cv	5	75	+ 1
AetnLf 8⅛07	8.6	21	94¼	− 1¼
AlaP 7¾s02	8.3	41	93⅞	+ ⅞
AlaP 8⅞s03	8.8	7	101	+ ¼
AlaP 9¾s04	9.4	20	104	− ½
AlaP 8¾07	8.9	4	98¾	− 1¼
AlaP 9½08	9.2	10	103	− ¾
AlskAr 6⅞14	cv	10	88	...
AlskAr zr06	...	4	33½	...
AlldC zr92	...	2	92½	...
AlldC zr96	...	20	70¾	− 2
AlldC zr2000	...	201	45⅜	+ ⅜
AlldC zr01	...	30	43¼	+ 1⅛
AlldC zr03	...	5	33¾	...
AlldC zr05	...	15	27¾	+ ¼
AlldC zr09	...	135	18½	− ¼
AAirl 4¼92	4.4	30	97	+ 11/16
AMAX 9.23s95	9.3	55	99½	...
ABrnd 9⅛16	9.1	36	100¼	+ ¼
ATT 5⅝95	6.0	28	94¼	− ⅛
ATT 5½97	6.1	37	90⅝	+ 1⅜
ATT 6s00	7.0	9	86	...
ATT 7s01	7.7	103	91¼	− ¼
ATT 7⅛03	7.9	27	90½	+ ⅛
ATT 8.80s05	8.6	57	101⅞	+ ⅛
ATT 8⅝s07	8.6	123	100⅝	− ⅛
ATT 8¾00	8.6	280	102¼	...
ATT 8⅝26	8.8	292	97½	− ⅜
vlAmes 7½14f	cv	38	11¾	− ½
Amoco 6s98	6.6	15	91⅜	+ 1⅛
Amoco 7⅞07	8.2	35	96⅝	+ ¼
Amoco 7⅞96	7.8	10	101	+ ½
Amoco 8⅝16	8.6	135	99¾	+ ⅛
AmocoCda 7⅜13	6.6	63	111¾	+ 1¾
Ancp 13⅞02f	cv	60	91	+ 1
Anhr 8⅝16	8.8	21	98⅛	+ ½
Apache 7½00	cv	290	106½	+ 2½
ArizP 7.45s02	8.3	6	89¼	− ¾
ArizP 10⅝00	10.3	21	103	− ½
Arml 9.2s00	10.9	5	84½	...
AshO 8.2s02	8.8	50	92⅞	...
ARch dc7s91	7.0	50	100	+ 1/16
ARch 10⅜95	9.6	10	108½	...
ARch 10½95	10.0	10	104⅝	− ⅜
ARch 9½96	9.1	5	104½	+ 1½
ARch 9¼93	8.9	15	104	+ 1
AubrnHl 15⅞20	19.8	289	80	...
AvcoF 8.35s	8.7	2	95¾	+ 2⅝
Avnet 8s13	cv	10	93½	+ ½
Avnet 6s12	cv	27	84	...
BPNA 9¼01	9.2	24	100⅜	+ ¼
BPNA 9¼16	9.3	70	100	+ ⅛
BRE 9½08	cv	10	102	+ ½
BakrHgh 9½06	cv	12	102¼	− ¾
Ballys 6s98f	cv	2	43¼	+ ¼
Bally 10s06f	cv	65	52	...
BalGE 8⅜06	8.6	15	97⅞	− ⅛
BalGE 9⅛16	9.0	40	101	− ¼
BncFla 9s03	cv	5	47½	+ 1½
Banka 7⅞03	8.6	10	91½	...
Banka 8⅞05	9.0	44	98⅞	+ ⅞
Banka 8¾01	8.8	235	99⅝	+ ⅞
Bkam zr92	...	77	92⅛	− ⅛
Bkam zr93	...	15	87⅝	...
Barnt 8½99	8.9	25	95⅞	− ⅛
BellPa 8⅝06	8.5	29	102	+ 1⅜
BellPa 7⅛12	8.3	53	85½	+ ⅛
BellPa 7½13	8.3	60	90	+ 1½
BellPa 9⅝14	9.2	20	104½	− ½
BellPa 8⅛17	8.7	1	93⅛	− 1⅝

Bonds	Cur Yld	Vol	Close	Net Chg
DetEd 9.15s00	9.0	23	102	...
DetEd 8.15s00	8.4	2	96½	...
DetEd 7½03	8.2	30	91½	+ ⅜
DetEd 11⅞00	11.1	1	107	− ½
Disney zr05	...	260	46	+ ¼
Dow 7.75s99	7.9	10	97⅝	+ 1¾
Dow 8⅞2000	8.8	1	101⅛	...
Dow 8½s05	8.7	5	98⅛	+ 1½
Dow 8½s06	8.7	147	97⅝	− ⅛
duPnt 8.45s04	8.5	205	99⅝	+ ⅛
duPnt 8½06	8.5	40	100	+ ¼
duPnt dc6s01	7.2	106	83¾	...
duPnt 8½16	8.8	583	96¼	+ ¼
duPnt 7½93	7.5	32	100½	− ½
duPnt zr10	cv	40	26	+ ⅛
DukeP 7⅜02	8.0	5	92	− 1⅝
DukeP 9¾04	9.3	25	105	...
DukeP 9½05	9.1	35	103⅞	− ½
DukeP 8⅜06	8.5	15	98	− ¾
DuqL 8¾00	8.7	5	100⅞	− ⅛
DuqL 9s06	9.0	2	99¾	+ ¼
DuqL 8⅜07	9.1	1	92⅛	− 2
DuqL 10⅛09	9.7	9	104	− ⅜
EKod 8⅝16	9.1	176	95¼	− ⅛
EmbSult 10½94	10.4	7	101	...
EmbSult 11s99	11.1	18	99½	− ½
Enron 10¾98	10.1	50	106⅝	+ ⅛
Ens 10s01	cv	5	102¼	+ ¼
Exxon 6s97	6.6	148	91⅛	+ ⅛
Exxon 6½98	7.0	20	92⅜	...
ExxP 8¼01	8.2	40	101	+ ½
vjFairfd 13¼92	...	428	47⅜	+ 3½
FedN zr19s	...	55	9	− ¼
Fldcst 6s12	cv	219	61½	+ 1½
FUnRE 10¼09	cv	14	90½	+ ½
FleetF 11¼93	10.7	1	105	...
FleetFn 8½10	cv	11	129	+ 2
Flemg 6½96	cv	26	98½	+ 2
FrdC 7½92	7.4	75	100¾	− ½
FrdC 8.7s99	8.8	35	99¼	− ½
FrdC 8⅜01	8.8	42	95⅝	− ⅞
FrdC 8⅜02	8.7	50	96½	+ ½
FrdC 8½02	8.8	5	96¾	+ ¾
FrpMCG zr11	...	20	25	...
FreptM 10⅞01	10.7	41	102	− 2
Frpt dc6.55s01	cv	10	87	+ 1
FreptM zr06	...	26	26¾	...
Fuqua 9½98	11.4	20	83½	+ 1
Fuqua 9⅞97	10.7	10	92¼	...
GMA 8s93M	8.0	5	100¼	...
GMA 7¾94	7.8	55	100	+ ⅛
GMA 7¼95	7.4	5	98	+ ½
GMA 7⅛92	7.1	20	100⅛	+ ⅜
GMA 7.85s98	8.1	22	96¾	+ ⅜
GMA 8⅞99	8.8	50	100⅜	...
GMA 8¾s00	8.8	106	99¾	...
GMA 8¾s01	8.8	89	99½	− ¼
GMA 8⅛96	8.1	15	100⅛	− ¼
GMA 8s02	8.4	10	94¾	+ ¼
GMA 8¼06	8.8	30	94⅛	− ⅛
GMA 8.65s08	9.0	5	96½	− 1
GMA dc6s11	8.5	233	71	+ ⅛
GMA zr12	...	44	141	− 2
GMA zr15	...	15	111¾	− ¼
GMA 10⅜95	10.0	7	103½	...
GMA 8⅞96	8.8	25	100⅝	− ⅞
GMA 8s96	8.0	35	99¾	...
GMA 8¼16	9.0	8	92	+ ½
GMA 8s93J	7.9	125	101¼	+ ⅛
GMA 7.80s93	7.7	10	101¾	...
GMA 8s94	8.0	14	100½	− ¾
GMA 7⅛92l	7.1	5	100 1/32	...
GMA 7⅞97	8.1	55	97⅝	...
GMA 7.45s94	7.6	10	98½	− ¾

Source: *The Wall Street Journal,* August 23, 1991, p. Cl4. Reprinted by permission of *THE WALL STREET JOURNAL,* © 1991 by Dow Jones & Company, Inc. All Rights Reserved Worldwide.

Table 11–7 Background Data on Bond Issues

8 Alli—Amer **MOODY'S BOND RECORD** August 1991

CUSIP	ISSUE	MOODY'S RATING	INTEREST DATES	CURRENT CALL PRICE	CALL DATE	SINK FUND PROV	CURRENT PRICE	YIELD TO MAT.	1991 HIGH	1991 LOW	AMT. OUTST. MIL. $	ISSUED	PRICE	YLD.
019512AD	•Allied Signal, Inc. deb. 9.875 2002	A3 r	J&D 1	N.C.	----	No	103 bid	9.43	101 5/8	101 5/8	250	5-20-87	99.10	12.25
019512AG	• nts. 9.20 2003	A3 r	F&A 15	N.C.	----	No	99 7/8 bid	9.20	----	----	100	2-6-91	99.85	9.22
019512AC	• deb. 9.50 2016	A3 r	J&D 1	N.C.	----	No	99 1/4 bid	9.57	----	----	100	6-4-86	100.00	9.50
019519AE	Allied Stores nts. 6.00 1992[1]	Caa r	†1-15-90	100.00	to 5-15-92	No	37 bid	flat	53 1/2	19	116.3	5-12-82	56.74	14.25
019520AA	sr.nts. 10.50 1992	Caa r	†1-15-90	N.C.	----	No	42 bid	flat	53 1/2	19	200	3-10-87	100.00	10.50
019520AB	sr.sub.deb. 11.50 1997	Ca r	†1-15-90	103.29	fr 3-15-92	Yes	12 1/2 bid	flat	16	02	700	3-10-87	100.00	11.50
020039AB	Alltel Corp. deb. 10.375 2009	A2 r	A&O 1	106.49	fr 4-1-94	No	107 3/8 bid	9.49	108 7/8	104 1/2	150	4-5-89	99.37	10.45
020039AC	deb. 9.50 2021	A2 r	M&S 1	107.12	fr 3-1-96	No	99 1/8 bid	9.58	101 1/8	98	200	3-5-91	100.00	9.50
020039AA	deb. 8.875 2022	A2 r	M&S 1	106.88	fr 3-1-92	No	93 1/2 bid	9.52	94 1/8	91	50.0	3-5-87	99.73	8.90
020825AA	♦Alpine Group Inc. sr.sub.deb. 13.50 1996	Caa r	A&O 1	106.00	fr 10-1-91	Yes	67 bid	flat	70	49 1/2	50.0	10-3-86	100.00	13.50
022249AE	•Alum. Co. of Amer. s.f.deb. 6.00 1992	A2 r	M&S15	100.00	to 9-15-92	Yes	99 sale	6.94	100	95 5/8	23.9	8-30-67	99.13	6.07
022249AG	• s.f.deb. 7.45 1996	A2 r	M&N15	100.38	to 11-14-91	Yes	96 1/2 bid	8.28	97 3/4	94	67.1	11-11-71	100.00	7.45
022249AL	deb. 7.00 1996	A2 r	M&N15	100.00	to 11-15-96	No	93 1/4 bid	8.61	93 7/8	92 1/4	182	11-10-81	53.86	14.70
022249AH	• s.f.deb. 9.45 2000	A2 r	M&N15	101.89	to 5-14-92	Yes	102 bid	9.11	104	102	119.8	5-13-75	100.00	9.45
022249AK	deb. 7.00 2011	A2 r	A&O15	100.00	to 4-15-11	No	79 3/8 bid	9.29	81 7/8	76 3/8	123.9	4-22-81	48.36	14.70
022771AC	Amalgamated Sugar sr.sub.nts. 15.25 1994	B3 r	M&N 15	102.50	to 5-15-94	Yes	91 1/2 bid	19.33	91 1/2	63	90.0	5-16-84	94.54	16.38
023127AJ	AMAX Inc. zero cpn.nts. 0.00 1992	Baa3 r	N.P.	100.00	to 3-15-92	No	93 bid	12.07	94 3/8	77 1/4	68.1	3-16-82	22.50	15.52
023127AL	• sub.nts. 9.23 1995[3]	Ba1 r	JAJ&O15	103.00	to 4-15-95	No	98 sale	9.88	99 1/2	91	100	4-2-85	98.00	14.89
023127AC	• s.f.deb. 8.50 1996	Baa3 r	M&S1	100.00	to 2-28-92	Yes	98 sale	9.04	98	90	21.63	3-9-71	100.00	8.50
023127AF	• s.f.deb. 9.375 2000	Baa3 r	J&J15	101.73	to 1-14-92	Yes	99 bid	9.55	101	93 1/2	31.43	1-14-75	99.25	
023127AG	• s.f.deb. 8.625 2001	Baa3 r	M&S 1	101.97	to 2-28-92	Yes	95 bid	9.42	96	85 5/8	31.37	2-25-76	99.25	
023127AN	• nts. 9.875 2001	Baa3 r	J&D 13	N.C.	----	No	98 7/8 bid	10.04	----	----	300	6-6-91	100.00	9.88
023164AA	•Ambase Corp. sr.sub.nts. 14.875 1998	Ca r	J&J 15	N.C.	----	No	90 1/2 bid	17.27	80	32	150	6-10-88	99.32	
023164AB	• s.f.deb. 11.75 2008[4]	Caa r	A&O 1	§104.73	to 4-14-92	Yes	53 bid	----	69	50	125	Ref. fr. 4-16-93 @ 103.938		
022904AA	Ambassador General nts. 12.00 1996[5]	Ba3 r	M&S 15	104.50	fr 9-15-91	Yes	93 1/2 bid	13.81	93 1/2	68	175	9-10-86	99.75	12.04
001669AA	♦AMC Entertainment sr.sub.deb. 13.60 2000	B1 r	J&D 1	106.80	to 11-30-91	Yes	90 1/8 bid	15.64	92	82	50.0	11-26-85	100.00	13.60
001669AB	♦ sr.sub.deb. 11.875 2001	B1 r	J&J 1	105.94	to 7-1-96	Yes	80 1/8 bid	15.92	85	78	50.0	7-2-86	100.00	11.88
023663AB	•Amer. & Fgn. Power sr.deb. 5.00 2030[6]	Baa2	M&S 1	107.50	to 2-28-10	No	50 5/8 sale	10.09	52	47	39.56	3-1-30	90.00	
023771AC	•Amer. Airlines sub.deb. 4.25 1992[7]	Baa1 r	J&J 1	100.00	to 6-30-92	Yes	96 sale	8.90	96 3/4	93	21.34	6-21-67		
023771AQ	• sub.deb. 6.25 1996	Baa1 r	M&S 1	100.00	to 3-1-96	No	86 3/4 bid	9.91	90 1/2	79	100	3-7-86	100.00	6.25
023771AG	• sub.deb. 5.25 1998[8]	Baa1 r	J&J1	100.00	to 7-1-98	Yes	77 1/8 bid	9.89	78	71 1/8	1.9	6-1-80	Exch.	
001765AF	nts. 9.75 2000	Baa1 r	M&S 15	N.C.	----	No	100 1/8 bid	9.72	101	96 5/8	200	3-7-90	100.00	9.75
001765AB	deb. 9.10 2016	Baa1 r	M&N1	N.C.	----	No	----	----	----	----	100	5-7-86	100.00	9.10
001765AC	• deb. 9.00 2016	Baa1 r	M&S 15	N.C.	----	No	94 7/8 sale	9.54	94 7/8	91	96.79	9-11-86	98.79	9.32
001765AD	s.f.deb. 8.625 2017	Baa1 r	M&S 1	§106.90	to 2-28-92	Yes	86 1/8 bid	10.14	87 3/8	78 1/2	100	Ref. fr. 3-1-97 @ 104.31		
001765AE	deb. 10.20 2020	Baa1 r	M&S 15	N.C.	----	No	98 7/8 bid	10.32	101 1/8	90 3/4	125	3-7-90	100.00	10.20
001765AG	deb. 9.88 2020	Baa1 r	J&D 15	N.C.	----	No	96 bid	10.30	98 3/8	88 1/4	100	6-15-90	100.00	9.88
023771AM	AMER. AIRLINES INC. sec.eq.ctf. 13.70 B 1995	A2 r	J&J6	N.C.	----	Yes	----	----	----	----	22.4	8-29-84	100.00	13.70
023771AN	sec.eq.ctf. 14.375 B 2005	A2 r	J&J6	105.92	fr 1-6-95	Yes	----	----	----	----	62.5	8-29-84	100.00	14.38
023778AA	certificates 9.71 A1 2007[9]	A2	J&J 7	N.C.	----	No	----	----	100	100	236.4	6-25-91	100.00	
023778AB	certificates 10.18 A2 2013[9]	A2	J&J 7	N.C.	----	No	----	----	100	100	133.9	6-25-91	100.00	
024703AM	•**AMER. BRANDS, INC.** nts. 8.75 1992	A3 r	M&N 1	N.C.	----	No	99 1/2 bid	9.18	----	----	150	10-25-90	99.82	8.84
024703AL	• nts. 9.00 1999	A3 r	J&D 15	N.C.	----	No	99 bid	9.18	100 1/8	98 3/8	100	6-12-89	99.80	9.05
024703AJ	• deb. 9.125 2016	A3 r	M&S 1	104.44	fr 3-1-96	Yes	97 5/8 bid	9.37	100	94 3/8	150	2-28-86	99.75	9.15
----	nts. 8.875 1992	A3 r	JUL 30	N.C.	----	No	98 7/8 bid	10.09	----	----	150	7-10-87	100.88	8.66
024812AA	♦Amer. Cablesystems sr.sub.nts. 11.75 1996	B2 r	M&N1	103.35	to 4-30-92	No	96 bid	12.90	97	71	100	5-7-86	100.00	11.75
025202AA	Amer. Comm. Ind. s.f.sub.deb. 12.375 1996	— r	F&A 1	100.00	----	Yes	----	----	----	----	20.0	2-10-81		
----	Amer. Cont. Ind. inc.deb. 4.50 1998	N.R. r	MAR 15	100.00	----	Yes	----	----	----	----	0.230	1-1-53		
----	Amer. Cont'l Corp. nts. [12]	Aa1		N.C.	----	No	----	----	----	----		11-20-85	00.00	
----	nts. [12]	Aa1		N.C.	----	No	----	----	----	----		11-20-85	00.00	
----	nts. [12]	Aa1		N.C.	----	No	----	----	----	----		11-20-85	00.00	
025242AP	sr.deb. 12.00 2001	N.R. r	MONTHLY	100.00	to 6-1-01	No	----	----	----	----	25.0	6-6-86	100.00	12.00
025242AM	sr.sub.nts. 14.75 1995	N.R. r	A&O15	100.00	to 4-14-92	Yes	----	----	----	----	50.0	4-18-85	98.70	15.00
025321AA	•Amer. Cyanamid s.f.deb. 7.375 2001	A1 r	A&O15	101.28	to 4-14-92	Yes	92 bid	8.60	96 1/4	89 1/4	63.7	4-22-71	99.00	7.46
025321AB	• s.f.deb. 8.375 2006	A1 r	M&S15	103.15	to 3-14-92	Yes	96 sale	8.86	96 1/2	93 1/2	87.8	3-10-76	99.50	
025807AK	Amer. Export Lines s.f. 7.75 1994[14]	Aaa r	M&S26	101.45	to 10-1-91	Yes	99 7/8 bid	7.76	99 7/8	98	4.070	9-2-77	100.00	7.75
025807AJ	s.f. 7.75 1994[15]	N.R. r	M&S26	101.45	to 10-1-91	Yes	----	----	----	----	4.150	9-2-77	100.00	7.75
025807AL	s.f. 7.95 I 2006[16]	Aaa r	J&D 1	102.82	to 10-1-91	Yes	92 bid	8.91	92 1/2	89 3/4	17.4	9-2-77	100.00	7.95
025807AM	s.f. 7.95 II 2006[17]	Aaa r	J&D1	102.82	to 10-1-91	Yes	92 bid	8.91	92 1/2	89 3/4	17.4	9-2-77	100.00	7.95
025816AB	Amer. Express Co. nts. 7.375 1991	Aa2 r	M&N 1	N.C.	----	No	100 1/8 bid	6.45	100 3/8	99 1/2	200	10-28-86	99.70	7.45

Source: *Moody's Bond Record* (published by Moody's Investor's Service, Inc., New York, N.Y.), August 1991, p. 8.

■ BOND MARKETS, CAPITAL MARKET THEORY, AND EFFICIENCY

In many respects, the bond market appears to demonstrate a high degree of rationality in recognition of risk and return. Corporate issues promise a higher yield than government issues to compensate for risk, and furthermore, federally sponsored credit agencies pay a higher return than Treasury issues for the same reason. Also, lower-rated bonds consistently trade at larger yields than higher-quality bonds to provide a risk premium.

Table 11–8 Daily Quotes on Government Issues—Treasury Bonds, Notes, and Bills

TREASURY BONDS, NOTES & BILLS

GOVT. BONDS & NOTES

Rate	Maturity Mo/Yr	Bid	Asked	Chg.	Ask Yld.
$8\frac{1}{4}$	Aug 91n	100:00	100:02	....	3.51
$8\frac{3}{8}$	Sep 91n	100:09	100:11	− 1	4.61
$9\frac{1}{8}$	Sep 91n	100:11	100:13	....	4.68
$12\frac{1}{4}$	Oct 91n	100:30	101:00	....	4.68
$7\frac{5}{8}$	Oct 91n	100:12	100:14	....	5.04
$6\frac{1}{2}$	Nov 91n	100:06	100:08	....	5.26
$8\frac{1}{2}$	Nov 91n	100:21	100:23	....	5.08
$14\frac{1}{4}$	Nov 91n	101:30	102:00	+ 1	4.87
$7\frac{3}{4}$	Nov 91n	100:18	100:20	....	5.24
$7\frac{5}{8}$	Dec 91n	100:23	100:25	....	5.26
$8\frac{1}{4}$	Dec 91n	100:29	100:31	− 1	5.32
$8\frac{1}{2}$	Mar 94n	104:19	104:21	....	6.52
7	Apr 94n	101:02	101:04	− 1	6.53
$4\frac{1}{8}$	May 89-94	94:04	95:04	+ 3	6.10
7	May 94n	101:00	101:02	....	6.57
$9\frac{1}{2}$	May 94n	107:01	107:03	....	6.61
$13\frac{1}{8}$	May 94n	116:08	116:10	....	6.49
$8\frac{1}{2}$	Jun 94n	104:23	104:25	....	6.63
8	Jul 94n	103:19	103:21	+ 1	6.59
$6\frac{7}{8}$	Aug 94n	100:20	100:22	....	6.62
$8\frac{5}{8}$	Aug 94n	105:03	105:05	− 1	6.68
$8\frac{3}{4}$	Aug 94	105:15	105:19	....	6.64
$12\frac{5}{8}$	Aug 94n	115:29	115:31	+ 1	6.62
$8\frac{1}{2}$	Sep 94n	104:27	104:29	+ 1	6.72
$9\frac{1}{2}$	Oct 94n	107:19	107:21	+ 2	6.75
$8\frac{1}{4}$	Nov 94n	104:06	104:08	....	6.76
$10\frac{1}{8}$	Nov 94	109:18	109:22	+ 2	6.73
$11\frac{5}{8}$	Nov 94n	113:28	113:30	+ 2	6.74
$7\frac{5}{8}$	Dec 94n	102:16	102:18	+ 1	6.76
$8\frac{5}{8}$	Jan 95n	105:08	105:10	+ 1	6.84
3	Feb 95	93:31	94:31	+ 3	4.58
$7\frac{3}{4}$	Feb 95n	102:23	102:25	+ 1	6.84
$10\frac{1}{2}$	Feb 95	110:30	111:02	+ 3	6.86
$11\frac{1}{4}$	Feb 95n	113:08	113:10	+ 1	6.87
$8\frac{3}{8}$	Apr 95n	104:17	104:19	+ 2	6.93
$8\frac{1}{2}$	May 95n	105:00	105:02	+ 4	6.93
$10\frac{3}{8}$	May 95	110:30	111:02	+ 2	6.95
$11\frac{1}{4}$	May 95n	113:25	113:27	....	6.96
$12\frac{5}{8}$	May 95	118:10	118:14	+ 3	6.92
$8\frac{7}{8}$	Jul 95n	106:07	106:09	+ 2	7.00
$8\frac{1}{2}$	Aug 95n	105:02	105:04	+ 3	7.00
$10\frac{1}{2}$	Aug 95n	111:24	111:26	+ 1	7.04
$8\frac{5}{8}$	Oct 95n	105:15	105:17	+ 3	7.06
$8\frac{1}{2}$	Nov 95n	105:00	105:02	+ 2	7.09
$9\frac{1}{2}$	Nov 95n	108:19	108:21	+ 2	7.09
$11\frac{1}{2}$	Nov 95	115:22	115:26	+ 1	7.10
$9\frac{1}{4}$	Jan 96n	107:24	107:26	+ 3	7.14
$7\frac{1}{2}$	Jan 96n	101:08	101:10	+ 3	7.15
$7\frac{7}{8}$	Feb 96n	102:20	102:22	+ 2	7.16
$8\frac{7}{8}$	Feb 96n	106:13	106:15	+ 2	7.16
$7\frac{1}{2}$	Feb 96n	101:08	101:10	+ 3	7.15
$7\frac{3}{4}$	Mar 96n	102:03	102:05	+ 1	7.19
$9\frac{3}{8}$	Apr 96n	108:11	108:13	+ 2	7.21
$7\frac{5}{8}$	Apr 96n	101:18	101:20	+ 2	7.21
$7\frac{3}{8}$	May 96n	100:18	100:20	+ 2	7.22
$7\frac{5}{8}$	May 96n	101:17	101:19	+ 1	7.22
$7\frac{7}{8}$	Jun 96n	102:16	102:18	+ 2	7.24
$7\frac{7}{8}$	Jul 96n	102:16	102:18	+ 2	7.24
$7\frac{7}{8}$	Jul 96n	102:20	102:22	+ 3	7.22
8	Oct 96n	102:31	103:01	+ 3	7.28
$7\frac{1}{4}$	Nov 96n	99:25	99:27	+ 3	7.29
8	Jan 97n	102:28	102:30	+ 3	7.33
$8\frac{1}{2}$	Apr 97n	104:31	105:01	+ 2	7.39
$8\frac{1}{2}$	May 97n	104:29	104:31	+ 4	7.42
$8\frac{1}{2}$	Jul 97n	104:28	104:30	+ 3	7.45

TREASURY BILLS

Maturity	Days to Mat.	Bid	Asked	Chg.	Ask Yld.
Aug 29 '91	3	4.95	4.85	−0.13	4.92
Sep 05 '91	10	5.03	4.93	−0.06	5.02
Sep 12 '91	17	5.08	4.98	−0.07	5.07
Sep 19 '91	24	4.97	4.87	−0.07	4.97
Sep 26 '91	31	5.10	5.06	−0.08	5.15
Oct 03 '91	38	5.20	5.16	+0.01	5.27
Oct 10 '91	45	5.20	5.16	....	5.28
Oct 17 '91	52	5.20	5.16	....	5.29
Oct 24 '91	59	5.26	5.22	+0.03	5.34
Oct 31 '91	66	5.25	5.23	....	5.37
Nov 07 '91	73	5.27	5.25	....	5.39
Nov 14 '91	80	5.28	5.26	+0.01	5.41
Nov 21 '91	87	5.31	5.29	+0.03	5.43
Nov 29 '91	95	5.29	5.27	+0.02	5.43
Dec 05 '91	101	5.28	5.26	+0.01	5.43
Dec 12 '91	108	5.28	5.26	+0.01	5.43
Dec 19 '91	115	5.27	5.25	+0.01	5.41
Dec 26 '91	122	5.27	5.25	+0.01	5.43
Jan 02 '92	129	5.28	5.26	+0.02	5.45
Jan 09 '92	136	5.29	5.27	+0.01	5.47
Jan 16 '92	143	5.32	5.30	+0.04	5.49
Jan 23 '92	150	5.31	5.29	+0.02	5.50
Jan 30 '92	157	5.31	5.29	+0.03	5.51
Feb 06 '92	164	5.32	5.30	+0.03	5.52
Feb 13 '92	171	5.32	5.30	+0.02	5.51
Feb 20 '92	178	5.32	5.30	+0.04	5.53
Mar 12 '92	199	5.28	5.26	+0.02	5.50
Apr 09 '92	227	5.35	5.33	+0.05	5.58
Apr 23 '92	241	5.37	5.35	+0.04	5.60
May 07 '92	255	5.37	5.35	+0.03	5.61
Jun 04 '92	283	5.33	5.31	+0.04	5.58
Jul 02 '92	311	5.35	5.33	+0.02	5.62
Jul 30 '92	339	5.34	5.32	+0.03	5.62

Source: *The Wall Street Journal,* August 23, 1991, p. C14. Reprinted by permission of *THE WALL STREET JOURNAL,* © 1991 by Dow Jones & Company, Inc. All Rights Reserved Worldwide.

Taking this logic one step further, bonds should generally pay a lower return than equity investments because the equity holder is in a riskier position because of the absence of a contractual obligation to receive payment. As was pointed out in Chapter 1, researchers have attributed superior returns to equity investments relative to debt over the long term.

A number of studies have also investigated the efficiency of the bond market. A primary item under investigation was the extent of a price change that was associated with a change in a bond rating. If the bond market is efficient, much of the information that led to the rating change was already known to the public and should have been impounded into the value of the bond before the rating change. Thus, the rating change should not have led to major price movements. Major research has generally been supportive of this hypothesis.[8] Nevertheless, there is evidence that the bond market may still be less efficient than the stock market (as viewed in terms of short-term trading profits.)[9] The reason behind this belief is that the stock market is heavily weighted toward being a secondary market in which *existing* issues are constantly traded between investors. The bond market is more of a primary market, with the emphasis on new issues. Thus, bond investors are not constantly changing their portfolios with each new action of the corporation. Many institutional investors, such as insurance companies, are not active bond traders in existing issues but, instead, buy and hold bonds to maturity.

■ OTHER FORMS OF FIXED-INCOME SECURITIES

Our interest so far in this chapter has been on fixed-income securities, primarily in the form of bonds issued by corporations and various sectors of the government. There are other significant forms of debt instruments from which the investor may choose, and they are primarily short term in nature.

Certificates of Deposit (CDs) The **certificates of deposit (CDs)** are provided by commercial banks and savings and loans (or other thrift institutions) and have traditionally been issued in small amounts such as $1,000 or $10,000, or large amounts such as $100,000. The investor provides the funds and receives an interest-bearing certificate in return. The smaller CDs usually have a maturity of anywhere from six months to eight years, and the large $100,000 CDs, 30 to 90 days.

The large CDs are usually sold to corporate investors, money market funds, pension funds, and so on, while the small CDs are sold to individual investors.

---

[8]Steven Katz, "The Price Adjustment Process of Bonds to Rating Classifications: A Test of Bond Market Efficiency," *Journal of Finance,* May 1974, pp. 551–59; and George W. Hettenhouse and William S. Sartoris, "An Analysis of the Informational Content of Bond Rating Changes," *Quarterly Review of Economics and Business,* Summer 1976, pp. 65–78.

[9]George E. Pinches and Clay Singleton, "The Adjustment of Stock Prices to Bond Rating Changes," *Journal of Finance,* March 1978, pp. 29–44.

One main difference between the two CDs, besides the dollar amount, is that there may be a secondary market for the large CDs, which allows these investors to maintain their liquidity without suffering an interest penalty. Investors in the small CDs have no such liquidity. Their only option is to redeem the certificate before maturity to the borrowing institution and suffer an interest loss penalty.

Small CDs have been traditionally regulated by the government, with federal regulatory agencies specifying the maximum interest rate that can be paid and the life of the CD. In 1986, all such interest-rate regulations and ceilings were phased out, and the free market now determines return. Any financial institution is able to offer whatever it desires. Almost all CDs are federally insured for up to $100,000 in the event of the collapse of the financial institution offering the instrument. This feature became particularly important in the late 1980s and early 1990s due to the problems in the savings and loan and banking industries.

Commercial Paper Another form of a short-term credit instrument is **commercial paper,** which is issued by large business corporations to the public. Commercial paper usually comes in minimum denominations of $25,000 and represents an unsecured promissory note. Commercial paper will carry a higher yield than small CDs or government Treasury bills and will be in line with the yield on large CDs. The maturity is usually 30, 60, or 90 days (though up to six months is possible).

Bankers' Acceptance This instrument often arises from foreign trade. A **bankers' acceptance** is a draft drawn on a bank for approval for future payment and is subsequently presented to the bank for payment. The investor buys the bankers' acceptance from an exporter (or other third party) at a discount with the intention of presenting it to the bank at face value at a future date. Bankers' acceptances provide yields comparable to commercial paper and large CDs and have an active secondary or resale market.

Money Market Funds The **money market funds** represent a vehicle to buy short-term fixed-income securities through a mutual fund arrangement.[10] An individual with a small amount to invest may pool funds with others to buy high-yielding large CDs and other similar instruments indirectly through the fund. There is a great deal of flexibility in withdrawing funds through check-writing privileges.

Money Market Accounts The **money market accounts** are similar to money market funds but are offered by financial institutions rather than mutual funds. Financial institutions introduced money market accounts in the

---

[10]Most brokerage houses also offer money market fund options.

early 1980s to compete with money market funds. These accounts pay rates generally competitive with money market funds and normally allow up to three withdrawals a month without penalty. One advantage of a money market account over a money market fund is that it is normally insured by the federal government for up to $100,000. However, due to the high quality of investments of money market funds, this advantage is not particularly important in most cases.

Both money market funds and money market accounts normally have minimum balance requirements of $500 to $1,000. Minimum withdrawal provisions of $250 to $500 may also exist. Each fund or account must be examined for its rules. In any event, both provide much more flexibility than a certificate of deposit in terms of access to funds with only a slightly lower yield.

■ PREFERRED STOCK AS AN ALTERNATIVE TO DEBT

Finally, we look at preferred stock as an alternative to debt because some investors may elect to purchase preferred stock to satisfy their fixed-income needs. **Preferred stock** pays a stipulated annual dividend, but does not include an ownership interest in the corporation. A $50 par value preferred stock issue paying $4.40 in annual dividends would provide an annual yield of 8.8 percent.

Preferred stock as an investment falls somewhere between bonds and common stock as far as protective provisions for the investor. In the case of debt, the bondholders have a contractual claim against the corporation and may force bankruptcy proceedings if interest payments are not forthcoming. Common stockholders have no such claim, but are the ultimate owners of the firm and may receive dividends and other distributions after all prior claims have been satisfied. Preferred stockholders, on the other hand, are entitled to receive a stipulated dividend and must receive the dividend before any payment to common stockholders. However, the payment of preferred stock dividends is not compelling to the corporation as is true in the case of debt. In bad times, preferred stock dividends may be omitted by the corporation.

While preferred stock dividends are not tax deductible to the corporation, as would be true with interest on bonds, they do offer certain investors unique tax advantages. The tax law provides that any corporation that receives preferred or common stock dividends from another corporation must add only 30 percent of such dividends to its taxable income. Thus, if a $5 dividend is received, only 30 percent of the $5, or $1.50, would be taxable to the corporate recipient.[11]

Because of this tax feature, preferred stock may carry a slightly lower yield than corporate bond issues of similar quality as indicated in Table 11–9.

---

[11]An individual investor does not enjoy the same tax benefit.

Table 11–9   Yields on Corporate Bonds and High-Grade Preferred Stock

Year	(1) High-Grade Bonds (Percent)	(2) High-Grade Preferred Stock (Percent)	(2) − (1) Spread
1991	8.97%	8.55%	−.42
1990	9.40	9.14	−.26
1989	9.33	9.08	−.25
1988	9.75	9.05	−.70
1987	9.68	8.37	−1.31
1986	9.47	8.76	−.71
1985	11.82	10.49	−1.33
1984	13.31	11.59	−1.72
1983	12.42	10.55	−1.87
1982	14.41	11.68	−2.73
1981	14.75	11.64	−3.11
1980	12.50	10.11	−2.39
1979	9.94	8.54	−1.40
1978	8.92	7.76	−1.16
1977	8.24	7.12	−1.12
1972	7.49	6.56	−.93
1967	5.66	5.13	−.53
1962	4.47	4.21	−.26
1957	4.03	4.36	.33
1952	3.04	3.75	.71
1947	2.70	3.51	.81

Source: *Moody's Industrial Manual* and *Moody's Bond Record* (published by Moody's Investor Service, Inc., New York, N.Y.), selected issues.

Features of Preferred Stock

Preferred stock may carry a number of features that are similar to a debt issue. For example, a preferred stock issue may be *convertible* into common stock. Also, preferred stock may be *callable* by the corporation at a stipulated price, generally slightly above par. The call feature of a preferred stock issue may be of particular interest in that preferred stock has no maturity date as such. If the corporation wishes to take preferred stock off the books, it must call in the issue or purchase the shares in the open market at the going market price.

An important feature of preferred stock is that the dividend payments are usually *cumulative* in nature. That is, if preferred stock dividends are not paid in any one year, they accumulate and must be paid before common stockholders can receive any cash dividends. If preferred stock carries an $8 dividend and

Table 11–10   Examples of Outstanding Preferred Stock Issues, May 1988

Issuer	Moody's Rating*	Par Value	Call Price	Market Price	Yield (Percent)
Duke Power Co. 8.70% cumulative preferred	aa2	$100	$101.00	$102.00	8.53%
Ohio Edison Co. 8.20% cumulative preferred	baa2	100	103.30	83.50	9.82
Interstate Power 9% cumulative preferred	a1	50	53.50	48.85	9.21

*Lowercase letters are used by Moody's to rate preferred stock.
Sources: *Moody's Bond Record* (published by Moody's Investor Service, Inc., New York, N.Y.) and *The Wall Street Journal.*

dividends are not paid for three years, the full $24 must be paid before any dividends go to common stockholders. This provides a strong incentive for the corporation to meet preferred stock dividend obligations on an annual basis even though preferred stock does not have a fixed, contractual obligation as do bonds. If the corporation gets behind in preferred stock dividends, it may create a situation that is difficult to get out of in the future. Being behind or in arrears on preferred stock dividends can make it almost impossible to sell new common stock because of the preclusion of common stock dividends until the preferred stockholders are satisfied.

Examples of existing preferred stock issues are presented in Table 11–10. The issues are listed in *Moody's Bond Record,* and the daily price quotes may be found in the NYSE Composite Stock Transactions section of *The Wall Street Journal* or other newspapers.

SUMMARY

Debt continues to play an important role in our economy from both the issuer's and investor's viewpoints. The primary fund-raisers in the bond market are the U.S. Treasury, federally sponsored credit agencies, state and local governments, and corporations. The corporate sector is made up of industrials, public utilities, rails and transportation, as well as financial issues. The amount of new, long-term debt financing in the United States greatly exceeds the volume of equity financing.

Bond instruments are evaluated on the basis of a number of factors, including yield, maturity, method of repayment, security provisions, and tax treatment. The greater the protection and privileges accorded the bondholder, the lower the yield. Thus, U.S. Treasury securities generally provide a lower yield than federally sponsored credit agency issues, and corporate securities provide a higher yield than governmental offerings. Because interest received on mu-

nicipal bonds is tax-exempt to the recipient, they provide the lowest promised yield. However, when one converts this figure to an equivalent before-tax return on a taxable instrument, the return may be attractive. Preferred stock also offers some unique tax advantages in the form of a 70 percent tax exemption on dividends paid to corporate purchasers.

A significant feature for a bond issue is the rating received by Moody's Investors Service or Standard & Poor's. The ratings generally range from AAA to D and determine the required yield to sell a security in the marketplace. Although there are no firm and fast rules to determine a rating, strong attention is given to such factors as cash flow and earnings generation in relation to interest and other obligations (coverage ratios) as well as to operating margins and return on invested capital and total assets. Financial-ratio analysis makes up perhaps 50 percent of the evaluation, with other factors of importance including the nature of the industry, the relative position of the firm within the industry, the pricing ability of the firm, and the overall quality of management (similar criteria have also been developed for municipal bonds).

The bond market appears to be reasonably efficient in terms of absorbing new information into the price of existing issues. Some researchers have suggested the bond market may be slightly less efficient than the stock market in pricing outstanding issues because of the lack of a highly active secondary, or resale, market for certain issues. Insurance companies, pension funds, and bank trust departments are not normally active traders in their bond portfolios.

Short-term investors with a need for fixed income may look to certificates of deposit, commercial paper, bankers' acceptances, money market funds, money market accounts, and the previously discussed government securities as sources of investment. Such factors as maturity, yield, and minimum amount must be considered.

Finally, preferred stock may also be thought of as an alternative form of a fixed-income security. Although dividends on preferred stock do not represent a contractual obligation to the firm as would be true of interest on debt, they must be paid before common stockholders can receive any payment. The preferred stock alternative may be important to the issuing firm because it provides some balance to the corporate capital structure.

■ IMPORTANT WORDS AND CONCEPTS

bond indenture 358	serial payment 359
par value 358	sinking-fund provision 359
coupon rate 358	call provision 359
variable-rate notes 358	put provision 359
floating-rate notes 358	secured debt 360
zero-coupon bonds 358	mortgage 360
maturity date 359	after-acquired property clause 360
perpetual bonds 359	equipment trust certificate 360

DISCUSSION QUESTIONS

1. What are some of the major provisions found in the bond indenture?
2. Does a serial bond normally have only one maturity date? What types of bonds are normally issued on this basis?
3. Explain how a sinking fund works.
4. Why do you think the right to call a bond is often deferred for a time?
5. What is the nature of a mortgage agreement?
6. What is a senior security?
7. Discuss the statement, "A debenture may not be more risky than a secured bond."
8. How do zero-coupon bonds provide returns to investors? How is the return taxed?
9. Explain the concept of a pass-through certificate.
10. What is an agency issue? Are they direct obligations of the U.S. Treasury?
11. What tax advantages are associated with municipal bonds?
12. Distinguish between general obligation and revenue bonds.
13. How might an investor reduce the credit risk in buying a municipal bond issue?
14. What is an industrial bond?
15. What is shelf registration?
16. What is meant by the private placement of a bond issue?
17. What is a split bond rating?
18. What does a bond quote of 72¼ represent in dollar terms?
19. Why might the bond market be considered less efficient than the stock market?
20. What is the advantage of a money market fund? How does it differ from a money market account?
21. Why would a corporate investor consider preferred stock over a bond? What is meant by the cumulative feature of preferred stock issues?

■ PROBLEMS

Municipal bond

1. If an investor is in a 31 percent marginal tax bracket and can purchase a municipal bond paying 6.35 percent, what would the equivalent before-tax return from a nonmunicipal bond have to be to equate the two?

Bond quotes

2. Using the data in Table 11–6, indicate the closing *dollar* value of the Bell Pacific (Bell Pa) bonds that pay 9⅝ interest and mature in 2014 (the year is shown as 14). State your answer in terms of dollars based on a $1,000 par value bond.

Bond quotes

3. Using the data in Table 11–8, indicate the asked price for the 10⅜ government bond maturing in May 1995. The asked price is the purchase price for the bond. State your answer based on a $1,000 bond value.

Treasury bill

4. Assume a $10,000 Treasury bill is quoted to pay 6 percent interest over a six-month period.

   a. How much interest would the investor receive?

   b. What will be the price of the Treasury bill?

   c. What will be the effective yield?

Treasury bill

5. In Problem 4, if the Treasury bill had only three months to maturity:

   a. How much interest would the investor receive?

   b. What will be the price of the Treasury bill?

   c. What will be the effective yield?

Comparative after-tax returns

6. A corporation buys $100 par value preferred stock of another corporation. The dividend payment is 8.2 percent of par. The corporation is in a 34 percent tax bracket.

   a. What will be the after-tax return on the dividend payment? (Show the answer in dollars and percent.) Fill in the table below.

Par value	_____
Dividend payment (%)	_____
Actual dividend	_____
Taxable income (30% of dividend)	_____
Taxes (34% of taxable income)	_____
After-tax return (Actual dividend − Taxes)	_____
Percent return = $\dfrac{\text{After-tax return}}{\text{Par value}}$	_____

   b. Assume a second investment in a $1,000 par value corporate bond pays 9.3 percent interest. What will be the after-tax return on the interest payment? (Show answers in dollars and percent.) Fill in the table on the next page.

Par value	_____
Interest payment (percent)	_____
Actual interest	_____
Taxes (34 percent of interest)	_____
After-tax return (Actual interest − Taxes)	_____
Percent return = $\dfrac{\text{After-tax return}}{\text{Par value}}$	_____

  c. Should the corporation choose the corporate bond over the preferred stock because it has a higher quoted yield (9.3 percent versus 8.2 percent)?

CRITICAL THOUGHT CASE

Gail Rosenberg still had her head in the clouds when she joined Salomon Brothers, Inc., in June 1990. While she was proud of her newly awarded MBA from the Wharton School of Business at the University of Pennsylvania, she was even prouder of joining the most prestigious investment banking house on Wall Street, the famous Salomon Brothers. She had received five job offers, but this is the one she wanted. Not only would she train with the best and brightest on Wall Street, but she also would be working for a firm in which 90 employees made over $1 million a year. How many Fortune 500 companies, law firms, or other employers could claim such a record? She was pleased with her own starting salary of $70,000 a year and could see matters only getting better in the future.

After some general training and appenticeship-type work, she was assigned to the government bond trading unit in February 1991. Here she would help in the bidding and distributing of U.S. Treasury bills and notes. Salomon Brothers was the largest participant among investment banking houses in this field, so she knew she would quickly learn the ropes.

Her first major participation would be in the Treasury bill auction for May 1991. Salomon Brothers would bid on behalf of many of its clients and probably have some influence on the ultimate price and yield at which the Treasury bills were sold. As Gail got on her PC to help process orders, she noticed Salomon Brothers submitted bids for clients that did not exist. It was no surprise to Gail that Salomon Brothers captured 85 percent of the bidding and virtually controlled the pricing of the securities.

In a state of shock, Gail went to her immediate supervisor and reported what she had observed on her computer screen. She was told to calm down, that she was no longer in school, and she was witnessing a common practice on "The Street." She was further informed that John Gutfreund, chairman of the board of Salomon Brothers, and President Thomas Strauss implicitly ap-

proved of such practices. She felt a little like Oliver North in the Iran-contra affair coverup. She had worked very hard to get to this tender point in her career and was now disillusioned.

Question

1. What strategy or advice can you offer to Gail Rosenberg?

■ CFA MATERIAL

The following material contains sample questions and solutions from a prior Level I CFA exam. While the terminology is slightly different from that in this text, you can still view the skills that are necessary for the CFA exam.

CFA Exam Question

The investment manager of a corporate pension fund has purchased a U.S. Treasury bill with 180 days to maturity at a price of $9,600 per $10,000 face value. He has computed the discount yield at 8 percent.

a. *Calculate* the bond equivalent yield for the Treasury bill. *Show* calculations. *(3 minutes)*

b. *Briefly state two* reasons why a Treasury bill's bond equivalent yield is always different from the discount yield. *(2 minutes)*

Solution: Morning Section (I–86) (5 points)

a.
$$BEY = \frac{(F - P)}{P} \times \frac{365}{N}$$

where:

    BEY = Bond equivalent yield

        F = Face value

        P = Price

        N = Days to maturity

$$BEY = \frac{(\$100 - \$96)}{\$96} \times \frac{365}{180} = 8.45\%$$

b. (1) The bond equivalent yield is computed using the actual purchase price of the instrument in the denominator, while the discount yield is calculated using the face value.

(2) The bond equivalent yield is based on a 365-day year, whereas the discount yield is computed using a 360-day year.

■ SELECTED REFERENCES

General Bond Information

Altman, Edward I. "Defaults and Returns on High-Yield Bonds through the First Half of 1991." *Financial Analysts Journal,* November–December 1991, pp. 67–77.

Bond Guide. Standard & Poor's Corporation.

Moody's Bond Record. Moody's Investors Service.

Nunn, Kenneth P., Jr.; Joanne Hill; and Thomas Schneeweis. "Corporate Bond Price Data Sources and Return/Risk Management." *Journal of Financial and Quantitative Analysis,* June 1986, pp. 197–208.

Municipal and U.S. Government Bonds

Van Hore, James C. "Call Risk and Municipal Bonds." *Journal of Portfolio Management,* Winter 1984, pp. 53–57.

Yawitz, Jess B.; George H. Hempel; and William J. Marshall. "A Risk-Return Approach to the Selection of Optimal Government Bond Portfolios." *Financial Management,* Autumn 1976, pp. 36–45.

Yawitz, Jess B., and William J. Marshall. "Risk and Return in the Government Bond Market." *Journal of Portfolio Management,* Summer 1977, pp. 48–52.

Bond Management Strategies

Chance, Don M.; Wayne Marr; and G. Rodney Thompson. "Hedging Shelf Registrations." *Journal of Futures Markets,* Spring 1986, pp. 11–27.

Johnson, James M. "When Are Zero-Coupon Bonds the Better Buy?" *Journal of Portfolio Management,* Spring 1984, pp. 36–41.

Trainer, Francis H., Jr.; David A. Levine; and Jonathan A. Reiss. "A Systematic Approach to Bond Management in Pension Funds." *Journal of Portfolio Management,* Spring 1984, pp. 30–35.

Research on Bond Ratings

Ang, James S., and K. A. Patel. "Bond Rating Methods: Comparison and Validation." *Journal of Finance,* May 1975, pp. 631–40.

Gentry, James A.; David T. Whitfold; and Paul Newbold. "Predicting Industrial Bond Ratings with a Probit Model and Funds Flow Components." *Financial Review,* August 1988, pp. 269–86.

Grier, Paul, and Steven Katz. "The Differential Effects of Bond Rating Changes among Industrial and Public Utility Bonds by Maturity." *Journal of Business,* April 1976, pp. 226–39.

Hettenhouse, George W., and William S. Sartoris. "An Analysis of the Informational Content of Bond Rating Changes." *Quarterly Review of Economics and Business,* Summer 1976, pp. 65–78.

Ogden, Joseph P. "Determinants of the Ratings and Yields on Corporate Bonds: Test of the Contingent Claims Model." *Journal of Financial Research,* Winter 1987, pp. 329–39.

Pinches, George E., and Kent A. Mingo. "A Multivariate Analysis of Industrial Bond Ratings." *Journal of Finance,* March 1973, pp. 1–18.

Reilly, Frank K., and Michael D. Joehnk. "The Association between Market-Determined Risk Measures for Bonds and Bond Ratings." *Journal of Finance,* December 1976, pp. 1387–1403.

Reiter, Sara A., and David A. Ziebart. "Bond Yields, Ratings and Financial Information: Evidence from Public Utility Issues." *Financial Review,* February 1991, pp. 45–73.

Appendix 11–A: Evaluation of Debt Innovations

Security	Distinguishing Characteristics	Yield Reduction or Risk Reallocation	Enhanced Liquidity	Reduction in Transaction Costs	Other Benefits
Zero-coupon bonds	Noninterest bearing. Payment in one lump sum at maturity.	Issuer assumes reinvestment risk. Issues sold in Japan carried below-market yields reflecting their tax advantage over conventional debt issues.			Straight-line amortization of original issue discount pre-TEFRA. Japanese investors realize significant tax savings.
Stripped Treasury securities	Coupons separated from corpus to create a series of zero-coupon bonds that can be sold separately.	Yield curve arbitrage; sum of the parts can exceed the whole.			
Adjustable-rate notes and floating-rate notes	Coupon rate floats with some index, such as the 91-day Treasury bill rate.	Issuer exposed to floating interest-rate risk, but initial rate is lower than for fixed-rate issue.	Price remains closer to par than the price of a fixed-rate note.		
Extendible notes	Interest rate adjusts every 2–3 years, at which time note holder has the option to put the notes back to the issuer if the new rate is unacceptable.	Coupon based on 2–3 year put date, not on final maturity.		Lower transaction costs than issuing 2- or 3-year notes and rolling them over.	
Putable bonds and adjustable tender securities	Issuer can periodically reset the terms, in effect rolling over debt without having to redeem it for cash until the final maturity.	Coupon based on the type of interest-rate period selected, not on final maturity.		Lower transaction costs than having to perform a series of refundings.	

Source: John D. Finnerty, *Financial Management Collection*, Financial Management Association, Winter 1988, p. 4.

Security	Distinguishing Characteristics	Yield Reduction or Risk Reallocation	Enhanced Liquidity	Reduction in Transaction Costs	Other Benefits
Medium-term notes	Notes are sold in varying amounts and in varying maturities on an agency basis.			Agents' commissions are lower than underwriting spreads.	
Negotiable certificates of deposit	Certificates of deposit are registered and sold to the public on an agency basis.		More liquid than nonnegotiable CDs.	Agents' commissions are lower than underwriting spreads.	
Mortgage pass-through certificates	Investor buys an undivided interest in a pool of mortgages.	Reduced yield due to the benefit to the investor of diversification and greater liquidity.	More liquid than individual mortgages.		
Collateralized mortgage obligations (CMOs)	Mortgage payment stream is divided into 3–5 classes, which are prioritized in terms of their right to receive principal payments.	Reduction in prepayment risk to classes with prepayment priority. Designed to appeal to different classes of investors; sum of the parts can exceed the whole.	More liquid than individual mortgages.		
Receivable backed securities	Investor buys an undivided interest in a pool of receivables.	Reduced yield due to the benefit to the investor of diversification and greater liquidity. Significantly cheaper than pledging receivables to a bank.	More liquid than individual receivables.		
Euro-notes and Euro-commercial paper	Euro-commercial paper is similar to U.S. commercial paper.	Elimination of intermediary brings savings that lender and borrower can share.		Corporations invest in each other's paper directly rather than through an intermediary.	

Security	Distinguishing Characteristics	Yield Reduction or Risk Reallocation	Enhanced Liquidity	Reduction in Transaction Costs	Other Benefits
Interest-rate swaps	Two entities agree to swap interest-rate-payment obligations, typically fixed rate for floating rate.	Weaker credits can borrow from banks and swap for fixed rate so as to achieve a lower fixed rate than they could by borrowing directly from traditional fixed-rate lenders.			
Credit-enhanced debt securities	Issuer's obligation to pay is backed by an irrevocable letter of credit or surety bond.	Stronger credit rating of the letter of credit or surety bond issuer leads to lower yield, which can more than offset letter of credit/surety bond fees.			Enables a privately held company to borrow publicly while preserving confidentiality.

12

Principles of Bond Valuation and Investment

The old notion that a bond represents an inherently conservative investment can be quickly dispelled. A $1,000, 10 percent coupon rate bond with 25 years to maturity could rise $214.80 or fall $157.60 in response to a 2 percent change in interest rates in the marketplace. Investors enjoyed a total return of 43.79 percent on long-term high-grade corporate bonds in 1982 and 25.37 percent in 1985. However, the same bond investors would have had a negative total return in 8 out of the 24 years between 1968 and 1991. Losses were as high as 10 percent.

In this chapter, we will examine the valuation process for bonds, the relationship of interest-rate changes to the business cycle, and various investment and speculative strategies related to bond maturity, quality, and pricing.

■ FUNDAMENTALS OF THE BOND VALUATION PROCESS

The price of a bond at any given time represents the present value of future interest payments plus the present value of the par value of the bond at maturity. We say that:

$$V = \sum_{t=1}^{n} \frac{C_t}{(1 + i)^t} + \frac{P_n}{(1 + i)^n} \qquad (12\text{--}1)$$

where:

V = Market value or price of the bond

n = Number of periods

t = Each period

C_t = Coupon or interest payment for each period, t

P_n = Par or maturity value

i = Interest rate in the market

We can use logarithms and various mathematical calculations to find the value of a bond or simply use Table 12–1 and Table 12–2 to determine the present value of C_t and P_n and add the two. (Expanded versions of these two tables are presented in appendixes at the end of the text.) Much of the material in this section draws on the earlier discussion of time value of money in Chapter 6.

Assume a bond pays 10 percent interest or $100 (C_t) for 20 years (n) and has a par (P_n) or maturity value of $1,000. The interest rate (i) in the marketplace is assumed to be 12 percent. The present value of the bond, using annual compounding, is shown to be $850.90 as follows:

Present Value of Coupon Payments (C_t) (from Table 12–1)	Present Value of Maturity Value (P_n) (from Table 12–2)
$n = 20$, $i = 12\%$	$n = 20$, $i = 12\%$
$100 × 7.469 = $746.90	$1,000 × .104 = $104.00
Present value of coupon payments	= $746.90
Present value of maturity value	= 104.00
Value of bond	= $850.90

Table 12–1	Present Value of an Annuity of $1 (Coupon Payments, C_t)					
Number of Periods	**Interest Rate (i)**					
(n)	**4 Percent**	**5 Percent**	**6 Percent**	**8 Percent**	**10 Percent**	**12 Percent**
1	0.962	0.952	0.943	0.926	0.909	0.893
2	1.886	1.859	1.833	1.783	1.736	1.690
3	2.775	2.723	2.673	2.577	2.487	2.402
4	3.630	3.546	3.465	3.312	3.170	3.037
5	4.452	4.329	4.212	3.993	3.791	3.605
10	8.111	7.722	7.360	6.710	6.145	5.650
20	13.590	12.462	11.470	9.818	8.514	7.469
30	17.292	15.373	13.765	11.258	9.427	8.055
40	19.793	17.160	15.046	11.925	9.779	8.244

Table 12–2	Present Value of a Single Amount of $1 (Par or Maturity, Value P_n)					
Number of Periods	**Interest Rate (i)**					
(n)	**4 Percent**	**5 Percent**	**6 Percent**	**8 Percent**	**10 Percent**	**12 Percent**
1	.962	.952	.943	.926	.909	.893
2	.925	.907	.890	.857	.826	.797
3	.889	.864	.840	.794	.751	.712
4	.855	.823	.792	.735	.683	.636
5	.822	.784	.747	.681	.621	.567
10	.676	.614	.558	.463	.386	.322
20	.456	.377	.312	.215	.149	.104
30	.308	.231	.174	.099	.057	.033
40	.208	.142	.097	.046	.022	.011

Because the bond pays 10 percent of the par value when the competitive market rate of interest is 12 percent, investors will pay only $850.90 for the issue. This bond is said to be selling at a discount of $149.10 from the $1,000 par value. The discount is determined by several factors, such as the years to maturity, spread between the coupon and market rates, and the level of the coupon payment. While the $850.90 price was calculated using annual compounding, coupon payments on most bonds are paid semiannually. To adjust for this, we *divide* the annual coupon payment and required interest rate in the market by two and *multiply* the number of periods by two. Using the same example as before but with the appropriate adjustments for semiannual compounding, we show a slightly lower price of $849.30 as follows:

Present Value of Coupon Payments (C_t) (from Table 12–1)	Present Value of Maturity Value (P_n) (from Table 12–2)
$n = 40$, $i = 6\%$	$n = 40$, $i = 6\%$
$\$50 \times 15.046 = \$752.30$	$\$1,000 \times .097 = \$97.00$
Present value of coupon payments	$= \$752.30$
Present value of maturity value	$=\ \ \ 97.00$
Value of bond	$= \$849.30$

We see a minor adjustment in price as a result of using the more exacting process. To check our answer, Table 12–3 presents an excerpt from a bond table indicating prices for 10 percent and 12 percent annual coupon rate bonds at various market rates of interest (yields to maturity) and time periods. Though the values are quoted on an annual basis, the assumption is that semiannual discounting, such as that shown in our second example, was utilized. Note that for a bond with a 10 percent coupon rate, a 12 percent market rate (yield to maturity), and 20 years to run, the value in the table is 84.93. This is assumed to represent 84.93 percent of par value. Since the par value of the bond in our example was $1,000, the answer would be $849.30 ($1,000 × 84.93%). This is the answer we got in our second example. A typical modern bond table may be 1,000 pages long and cover time periods up to 30 years and interest rates from ¼ to 30 percent. For professionals working with bonds on a continual basis, financial calculators and computers are replacing these tables, with quicker response time.

■ RATES OF RETURN

Bonds are evaluated on a number of different types of returns, including current yield, yield to maturity, yield to call, and anticipated realized yield.

Current Yield

The **current yield,** which is shown in *The Wall Street Journal* and many daily newspapers, is the annual interest payment divided by the price of the bond. An example might be a 10 percent coupon rate $1,000 par value bond selling for $950. The current yield would be:

$$\frac{\$100}{\$950} = 10.53\%$$

The 10.53 percent indicates the annual cash rate of return an investor would receive in interest payments on the $900 investment but does not include any adjustments for capital gains or losses as bond prices change in response to new market interest rates. Another problem with current yield is that it does not take into consideration the maturity date of a debt instrument. A bond

Yield to Maturity (Percent)	Coupon Rate (10 Percent)				Coupon Rate (12 Percent)				Yield to Maturity (Percent)
	1 Year	**5 Years**	**10 Years**	**20 Years**	**1 Year**	**5 Years**	**10 Years**	**20 Years**	
8%	101.89%	108.11%	113.50%	119.79%	103.77%	116.22%	127.18%	139.59%	8%
9	100.94	103.96	106.50	109.20	102.81	111.87	119.51	127.60	9
10	100.00	100.00	100.00	100.00	101.86	107.72	112.46	117.16	10
11	99.08	96.23	94.02	91.98	100.92	103.77	105.98	108.02	11
12	98.17	92.64	88.53	84.93	100.00	100.00	100.00	100.00	12
13	97.27	89.22	83.47	78.78	99.09	96.41	94.49	92.93	13
14	96.38	85.95	78.81	73.34	98.19	92.98	89.41	86.67	14

Table 12–3   Excerpts from Bond Value Table

Source: Reprinted by permission from the *Thorndike Encyclopedia of Banking and Financial Tables,* 1981, Copyright © 1981, Warren Gorham and Lamont Inc., 210 South Street, Boston, Mass. All rights reserved.

with 1 year to run and another with 20 years to run would have the same current yield quote if interest payments were $100 and the price were $950. Clearly, the one-year bond would be preferable under this circumstance because the investor would not only get $100 in interest but also a $50 gain in value ($1,000 − $950) within a *one-year* period, as the prices goes to its $1,000 maturity value.

Yield to Maturity

Yield to maturity is a measure of return that considers annual interest received, the difference between the current bond price and its maturity value, and the number of years to maturity. Returning to our earlier example, if a bond pays $100 in annual interest and sells for $849.30 with 20 years to maturity, the investor would be receiving $100 annually plus the $150.70 differential spread over 20 years, or $7.54 per year. This would indicate a total annual return of $107.54. We would also think of the investor's average investment as being approximately the midpoint between the initial investment of $849.30, and the ending value of $1,000. Actually, it is slightly different from this due to mathematical averaging procedures over time. The value for approximate yield to maturity can be found through using Formula 12–2.[1]

$$Y' = \frac{\text{Coupon payment } (C_t) + \dfrac{\text{Par value } (P_n) - \text{Market value } (V)}{\text{Number of periods } (n)}}{(0.6) \text{ Market value } (V) + (0.4) \text{ Par value } (P_n)} \quad (12\text{–}2)$$

[1]This formula is recommended by Gabriel A. Hawawini and Ashok Vora, "Yield Approximations: A Historical Perspective," *Journal of Finance,* March 1982, pp. 145–56. It tends to provide the best approximation.

On an annual basis, we indicate:

Y' = Approximate yield to maturity

Coupon payment = \$100

Par or maturity value = \$1,000

Market value = \$849.30

Number of periods = 20

$$Y' = \frac{\$100 + \dfrac{\$1,000 - \$849.30}{20}}{(0.6)\$849.30 + (0.4)\$1,000}$$

$$= \frac{\$100 + \dfrac{\$150.70}{20}}{\$509.58 + \$400}$$

$$= \frac{\$107.54}{\$909.58}$$

$$= 11.82\%$$

This answer is merely an approximation of the exact yield to maturity. The precise answer can only be found mathematically by returning to Formula 12–1 and determining the precise interest rate *(i)* that allows us to discount back all future coupon payments *(C_t)* and the par or maturity value *(P_n)* at the end of *n* periods to arrive at the current price. The yield to maturity may be thought of as the internal rate of return or yield on the bond. Since computing the exact yield to maturity is a very involved, trial-and-error process, bond tables are readily available to allow us to determine this value. All we have to do is return to Table 12–3, the bond value table, and use it in a slightly different fashion. We pick our coupon rate, read across the table for number of years, look into the table for price (stated as a percent of par value of \$1,000), and then read to the outside column to determine yield. A 10 percent coupon rate bond with 20 years to run, selling at \$849.30 (84.93 in the table), provides the investor with a yield to maturity of 12 percent.[2] Financially oriented calculators or computer software may also be used to find yield to maturity. In Appendix E, you have instructions for using hand-held calculators to determine yield to maturity and other values.

Note the exact answer in this case is 0.18 percent above the approximation (12 percent versus 11.82 percent). In the jargon of bond trading, each 1/100th of 1 percent is referred to as a **basis point,** so we say the difference is 18 basis points. The approximate-yield-to-maturity method tends to understate exact yield to maturity for issues trading at a discount (in this case, the bond is priced

---

[2]Interpolation may also be used to find intermediate values in the table.

at $849.30). The opposite effect occurs for bonds trading at a premium (above par value).[3]

The concept of yield to maturity is used interchangeably with the term **market rate of interest.** When we say the market rate of interest is 12 percent, it is the equivalent of saying the required yield to maturity is 12 percent.

Yield to Call

As discussed in the preceding chapter on bond fundamentals, not all fixed-income securities are held to maturity. To the extent a debt instrument may be called in before maturity, a separate calculation is necessary to determine yield to the call date. The answer is termed the **yield to call.** Assume a 20-year bond was initially issued at a 13.5 percent interest rate, and after two years, rates have dropped. Let us assume the bond is currently selling for $1,180, and the yield to maturity on the bond is 11.15 percent. However, the investor who purchases the bond for $1,180 may not be able to hold the bond for the remaining 18 years because the issue can be called. Under these circumstances, yield to maturity may not be the appropriate measure of return over the expected holding period.

In the present case, we shall assume the bond can be called at $1,090 in five years after issue. Thus, the investor who buys the bond two years after issue can have his bond called back after three more years at $1,090. To compute yield to call, we determine the approximate interest rate that will equate a $1,180 investment today with $135 (13.5 percent) per year for the next three years plus a payoff or call price value of $1,090 at the end of three years. We can adjust Formula 12–2 (approximate yield to maturity) to Formula 12–3 (approximate yield to call).

$$Y_c' = \frac{\text{Coupon payment } (C_t) + \dfrac{\text{Call price } (P_c) - \text{Market price } (V)}{\text{Number of periods to call } (n_c)}}{(0.6) \text{ Market value } (V) + (0.4) \text{ Call price } (P_c)} \quad (12\text{–}3)$$

On an annual basis, we show:

Y_c' = Approximate yield to call

Coupon payment = $135

Call price = $1,090

Market value = $1,180

Number of periods to call = 3

---

[3]In all our bond problems, we are assuming we are buying the bond at the beginning of an interest payment period. To the extent there is accrued interest, we would have to modify our calculations slightly.

$$Y'_c = \frac{\$135 + \dfrac{\$1,090 - \$1,180}{3}}{(0.6)\$1,180 + (0.4)\$1,090}$$

$$= \frac{\$135 + \dfrac{-\$90}{3}}{\$708 + \$436}$$

$$= \frac{\$135 - \$30}{\$1,144}$$

$$= \frac{\$105}{\$1,144}$$

$$= 9.18\%$$

The yield to call figure of 9.18 percent is 264 basis points less than the previously computed yield to maturity figure of 11.82 percent. Clearly, the investor needs to be aware of the differential, which represents the decrease in yield the investor would receive if the bond is called. Generally, any time the market price of a bond is equal to or greater than the call price, the investor should do a separate calculation for yield to call.[4]

In the case where market interest rates are much lower than the coupon, there is always the chance the company will call the bond. Because of this possibility, the call price often serves as an upper price limit, and further reductions in market interest rates will not cause this callable bond to increase in price. In other words, investors' capital gain potentials may be quite limited with bonds subject to a call.

Anticipated Realized Yield

Finally, we have the case where the investor purchases the bond with the intention of holding the bond for a period that is different from either the call date or the maturity date. Under this circumstance, we examine the **anticipated realized yield.** This represents the return over the holding period.

Assume an investor buys a 12.5 percent coupon bond for $900. Based on his forecasts of lower interest rates, he anticipates the bond will go to $1,050 in three years. The formula for the approximate realized yield is:

$$Y'_r = \frac{\text{Coupon payment } (C_t) + \dfrac{\text{Realized price } (P_r) - \text{Market price } (V)}{\text{Number of periods to realization } (n_r)}}{(0.6)\text{Market value } (V) + (0.4)\text{Realized price } (P_r)} \quad (12\text{--}4)$$

---

[4]Bond tables may also be used to find the exact value for yield to call. A source is *Thorndike Encyclopedia of Banking and Financial Tables* (Boston: Warren, Gorham & Lamont, 1981).

The terms are:

    Coupon payment = $125

    Realized price = $1,050

    Market price = $900

    Number of periods to realization = 3

$$Y'_r = \frac{\$125 + \dfrac{\$1,050 - \$900}{3}}{(0.6)\$900 + (0.4)\$1,050}$$

$$= \frac{\$125 + \dfrac{\$150}{3}}{\$540 + \$420}$$

$$= \frac{\$125 + \$50}{\$960}$$

$$= \frac{\$175}{\$960}$$

$$= 18.23\%$$

The anticipated return of 18.23 percent would not be unusual in periods of falling interest rates.

Reinvestment Assumption

Throughout our analysis, when we have talked about yield to maturity, yield to call, and anticipated realized yield, we have assumed the determined rate also represents an appropriate rate for reinvestment of funds. If yield to maturity is 11 percent or 12 percent, then it is assumed coupon payments, as they come in, can also be reinvested at that rate. To the extent that this is an unrealistic assumption, investors will wish to temper their thinking. For example, if it is anticipated that returns can be reinvested at a higher rate in the future, this increases true yield, and the opposite effect would be present for a decline in interest rates. The reinvestment topic is more fully developed in Chapter 13.

■ THE MOVEMENT OF INTEREST RATES

In developing our discussion of bond valuation and investments, we have observed that lower interest rates bring higher bond prices and profits. A glance back at Table 12–3 (right-hand portion) indicates a 12 percent coupon rate, 20-year bond will sell for $1,171.60 if yields to maturity on competitive bonds decline to 10 percent and for $1,276.00 when yields decline to 9 percent. The maturity of the bond is also important, with the impact on price being much greater for longer-term obligations.

The investor who wishes to make a substantial profit in the bond market must try to anticipate the turns and directions of interest rates. While much of the literature on efficient markets would indicate this is extremely difficult,[5] Wall Street economists, bank economists, and many others rely on interest-rate forecasts to formulate financial strategies. The fact that short-term and long-term rates do not necessarily move in the same direction or move with the same magnitude makes the task even more formidable. Nevertheless, some historical analysis and knowledge of interest-rate patterns over the business cycle are useful in making investment decisions.

Interest rates have long been viewed as a coincident indicator in our economy; that is to say, they are thought to move in concert with industrial production, gross domestic product, and similar measures of general economic health. This is generally true, although in the recessions of 1969–70, 1973–75, 1980–81, 1981–1982, and 1990–91, the change in interest rates actually lagged behind the decline in industrial production.

While inflationary expectations have the greatest influence on long-term rates, a number of other factors also influence overall interest rates. The demand for funds by individuals, business, and the government represents one side of the equation, with the desire for savings and Federal Reserve policy influencing the supply side. A classic study by Feldstein and Eckstein found that bond yields were inversely related to the money supply (the slower the growth, the higher the interest rates) and directly related to economic activity, the demand for loanable funds by the government, the level of inflation, and changes in short-term interest rate *expectations*.[6]

Term Structure of Interest Rates

Of general importance to understanding the level of interest rates is the development of an appreciation for the relationship between the level of interest rates and the maturity of the debt obligation. There is no one single interest rate but, rather, a whole series of interest rates associated with the given maturity of bonds.

The **term structure of interest rates** depicts the relationship between maturity and interest rates. It is sometimes called a yield curve because yields on existing securities having maturities from three months to 30 years are plotted on a graph to develop the curve. To eliminate any business risk consideration, the securities analyzed are usually U.S. Treasury issues. Examples of four different types of term structures are presented in Figure 12–1.

---

[5]Michael J. Prell, "How Well Do the Experts Forecast Interest Rates?" Federal Reserve Bank of Kansas City, *Monthly Review*, September–October 1973, pp. 3–13; Oswald D. Bowlin and John D. Martin, "Extrapolations of Yields over the Short Run: Forecast or Folly?" *Journal of Monetary Economics*, 1975, pp. 275–88; and Richard Roll, *The Behavior of Interest Rates* (New York: Basic Books, 1970).

[6]Martin Feldstein and Otto Eckstein, "The Fundamental Determinants of the Interest Rate," *The Review of Economics and Statistics*, November 1970, pp. 363–75.

Figure 12–1   Term Structure of Interest Rates

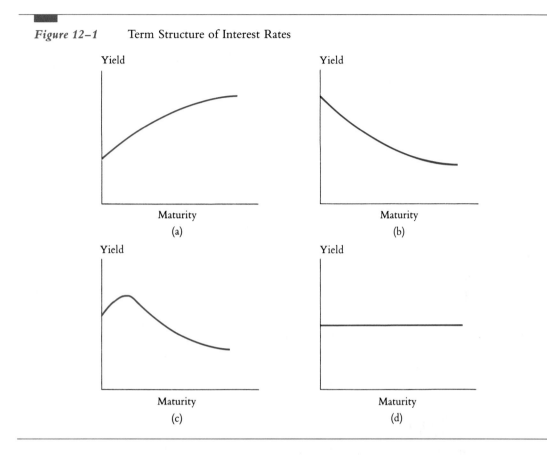

In panel (a), we see an ascending term structure pattern in which interest rates increase with the lengthening of the maturity dates. When the term structure is in this posture, it is a general signal that interest rates will rise in the future. In panel (b), we see a descending pattern of interest rates, with this pattern generally predictive of lower interest rates. Panel (c) is a variation of panel (b), with the hump representing intermediate-term interest rates. This particular configuration is an even stronger indicator that interest rates may be declining in the future. Finally, in panel (d), we see a flat-term structure indicating investor indifference between debt instrument maturity. This generally indicates there is no discernible pattern for the future of interest rates. Several theories of interest rates are used to explain the particular shape of the yield curve. We shall review three of these theories.

Expectations Hypothesis   The dominant rationale for the shape of the term structure of interest rates rests on a phenomenon called the **expectations**

hypothesis. The hypothesis is that any long-term rate is an average of the expectations of future short-term rates over the applicable time horizon. Thus, if lenders expect short-term rates to be continually increasing, they will demand higher long-term rates. Conversely, if they anticipate short-term rates to be declining, they will accept lower long-term rates. An example may be helpful. Suppose the interest rate on a one-year Treasury bill is 8 percent, and that after one year, it is assumed a new one-year Treasury bill may be bought to yield 10 percent. At the end of year 2, it is assumed that a third one-year Treasury bill may be bought to yield 12 percent. In other words, the investor can buy (this is sometimes called roll over) three one-year Treasury bills in yearly succession, each with an expected one-year return.

But what about investors who buy one-, two-, or three-year securities today? The yield they will require will be based on expectations about the future. For the one-year security, there is no problem. The 8 percent return will be acceptable. But investors who buy a two-year security now will want the average of the 8 percent they could expect in the first year and the 10 percent expected in the second year, or 9 percent.[7] An investor who buys a three-year security will demand an average of 8, 10, and 12 percent, or a 10 percent return. Higher expected interest rates in the future will mean that longer maturities will carry higher yields than will shorter maturities. The reverse would be true if interest rates were expected to go down.

The expectations hypothesis tends to be reinforced by lender/borrower strategies. If investors (lenders) expect interest rates to increase in the future, they will attempt to lend short-term and avoid long-term obligations so as to diminish losses on long maturity obligations when interest rates go up. Borrowers have exactly the opposite incentive. When interest rates are expected to go up, they will attempt to borrow long term now to lock in the lower rates. Thus, the desire of lenders to lend short term (and avoid long term) and the desire of borrowers to borrow long term (and avoid short term) accentuates the expected pattern of rising interest rates. The opposite motivations are in effect when interest rates are expected to decline.

Liquidity Preference Theory The second theory used to explain the term structure of interest rates is called the **liquidity preference theory,** which states that the shape of the term structure curve tends to be upward sloping more than any other pattern. This reflects a recognition of the fact that long maturity obligations are subject to greater price-change movements when interest rates change. Because of the increased risk of holding longer-term maturities, investors demand a higher return to hold long-term securities rel-

---

[7]The expectations hypothesis actually uses the geometric mean (compound growth rate) rather than the arithmetic mean (simple average) used in the example. For a short number of years, the two means would be quite similar.

ative to short-term securities. This is called the liquidity preference theory of interest rates. Since short-term securities are more easily turned into cash without the risk of large price changes, investors will pay a higher price for short-term securities and thus receive a lower yield.

Market Segmentation Theory The third theory related to the term structure of interest rates is called the **market segmentation theory** and focuses on the demand side of the market. The theory is that there are several large institutional participants in the bond market, each with its own maturity preference. Banks tend to prefer short-term liquid securities to match the nature of their deposits, whereas life insurance companies prefer long-term bonds to match their long-run obligations. The behavior of these two institutions, as well as that of savings and loans, often creates pressure on short-term or long-term rates but very little in the intermediate market of five-to-seven year maturities. This theory helps to focus on the accumulation or liquidation of securities by institutions during the different phases of the business cycle and the resultant impact on the yield curve.

As stated earlier, the expectations hypothesis is probably the most dominant theory, but all three theories have some part in the creation of the term structure of interest rates. Also, as we discussed, the curve takes on many different shapes over time. For example, as viewed in Figure 12–2, in May 1981, the yield curve had reached new high levels and was steeply downsloping in anticipation of lower interest rates. Lower rates came, and by May 1983, the curve had shifted down significantly for all maturities and was now presenting a more-normal upsloping yield curve. Over the two-year period from May 1981 to May 1983, three-month Treasury bills dropped from 16.99 percent to 8.48 percent, for a total decline of 851 basis points. Long-term Treasuries went from 13.26 percent to 10.75 percent over the same two-year period for a decline of only 251 basis points. One year later, by May 1984, interest rates had started to rise on fears that large government deficits would rekindle rampant inflation. Between May 1983 and May 1984, long-term rates rose to 14.21 percent, or a change of 346 basis points, more than wiping out the previous decrease.

Moving forward to January 1988, interest rates were down considerably from their former level. Part of this decline can be attributed to the stock market crash a few months earlier, which caused the Federal Reserve to sharply lower interest rates to avoid a financial panic. By September 1991, interest rates on all maturities were at their lowest level of the last decade. This was due to a recession-riddled, no-growth economy in which the Federal Reserve drove down interest rates in hopes of stimulating business activity. Also, the lack of a desire by businesses to borrow and expand contributed to lower interest rates. The question being asked at year-end 1991 was, what would be the next major movement in the term structure of interest rates? Would a strong economic recovery raise inflationary expectations and cause interest rates to go

Figure 12–2   Yield Curve Patterns

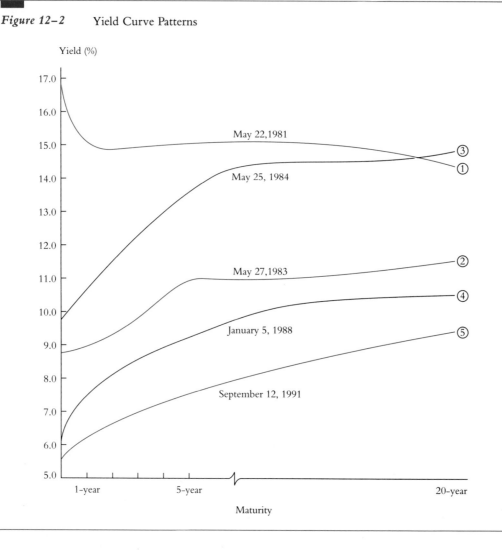

higher? Or would a slow recovery allow interest rates to remain at unusually low levels for a long period?

Before concluding our discussion of the term structure of interest rates and proceeding to the development of investment strategies, one final observation is significant. Short-term rates, which are most influenced by Federal Reserve policy in attempting to regulate the money supply and economy, are much more volatile than long-term rates. An examination of Figure 12–3 indicates that *short-term* prime commercial paper rates move much more widely than *long-term,* high-grade corporate bond rates.

Figure 12–3   Relative Volatility of Short-Term and Long-Term Interest Rates

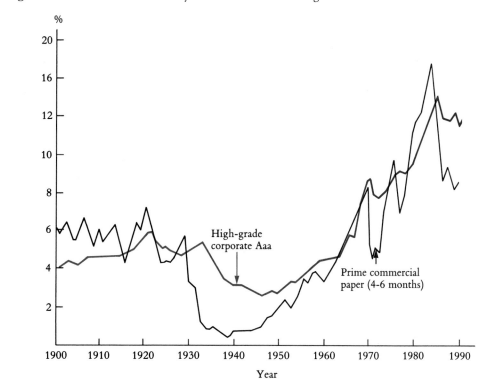

Source: *Federal Reserve Bulletins* (Washington, D.C.: Federal Reserve Board of Governors).

■ INVESTMENT STRATEGY: INTEREST-RATE CONSIDERATIONS

Thus far in this chapter, we have examined the different valuation procedures for determining the price or yield on a bond and the methods for evaluating the future course of interest rates. We now bring this knowledge together in the form of various investment strategies.

When the bond investor believes interest rates are going to fall, he will take a bullish position in the market by buying long-term bonds and try to maximize the price movement pattern associated with a change in interest rates. The investor can do this by considering the *maturity, coupon rate,* and *quality* of the issue.

Because the impact of an interest-rate change is much greater on long-term securities, the investor will generally look for extended maturities. The impact of various changes in yields on bond prices for a 12 and a 6 percent coupon rate bond can be examined in Table 12–4. For example, looking at the −2% line for the 12 percent coupon bond, we see a 2 percent drop in competitive yields would cause a 1.86 percent increase in value for a bond with 1 year to maturity

Table 12–4   Change in Market Prices of Bonds for Shifts in Yields to Maturity

12 percent coupon rate

Yield Change (Percent)	Maturity (Years)				
	1	**5**	**10**	**20**	**30**
+3%	−2.69%	−10.30%	−15.29%	−18.89%	−19.74%
+2	−1.81	−7.02	−10.59	−13.33	−14.04
+1	−0.91	−3.57	−5.01	−7.08	−7.52
−1	+0.92	+3.77	+5.98	+8.02	+8.72
−2	+1.86	+7.72	+12.46	+17.16	+18.93
−3	+2.81	+11.87	+19.51	+27.60	+30.96

6 percent coupon rate

Yield Change (Percent)	Maturity (Years)				
	1	**5**	**10**	**20**	**30**
+3%	−2.75%	−11.67%	−19.25%	−27.39%	−30.82%
+2	−1.85	−7.99	−13.42	−19.64	−22.52
+1	−0.94	−4.10	−7.02	−10.60	−12.41
−1	+0.95	+4.33	+7.72	+12.46	+15.37
−2	+1.92	+8.90	+16.22	+27.18	+34.59
−3	+2.91	+13.74	+25.59	+44.63	+58.80

but an 18.93 percent increase in value for a bond with 30 years to maturity. For the same 2 percent drop in rates, the 6 percent coupon bond would increase 1.92 percent (1 year to maturity) and 34.59 percent (30 years to maturity). The relationship between these two bonds further shows that the lower 6 percent coupon bond is more price sensitive than the higher 12 percent coupon bond.

We can also observe that the effect of interest-rate changes is not symmetrical. Drops in interest rates will cause proportionally greater gains than increases in interest rates will cause losses, particularly as we lenghten the maturity. An evaluation of the 30-year column in Table 12–4 confirms that both bonds are more price sensitive to a decline in yields than to a rise in yields.[8]

Though we have emphasized the need for long maturities in maximizing price movement, the alert student will recall that short-term interest rates generally move up and down more than long-term interest rates as was indi-

---

[8]A sophisticated investor would also consider the concept of *duration*. Duration is defined as the weighted average time to recover interest and principal. For a bond that pays interest (which includes most cases except zero-coupon bonds), duration will be shorter than maturity in that interest payments start almost immediately. Portfolio strategy may call for maximizing duration rather than maturity in order to achieve maximum movement. A complete discussion of this topic is presented in Chapter 13.

cated in Figure 12–3. What if short-term rates are more volatile—even though long-term rates have a greater price impact—which then do we choose? The answer is fairly direct. The mathematical impact of long maturities on price changes far outweighs the more volatile feature of short-term interest rates. A one-year, 12 percent debt instrument would need to have an interest-rate *change* of almost 9 *percent* to have the equivalent impact of a 1 percent change in a 30-year debt obligation.

Bond-Pricing Rules

The relationships we have presented in this section can be summarized in a set of bond-pricing rules. Prices of existing bonds have a relationship to maturities, coupons, and market yields for bonds of equal risk. These relationships are evident from an examination of previously presented Table 12–4. If you look at the change in bond prices in Table 12–4, you may be able to describe many of the relationships presented in the list below.

1. Bond prices and interest rates are inversely related.
2. Prices of long-term bonds are more sensitive to a change in yields to maturity than short-term bonds.
3. Bond price sensitivity increases at a decreasing rate as maturity increases.
4. Bond prices are more sensitive to a decline in market yields to maturity than to a rise in market yields to maturity.
5. Prices of low-coupon bonds are more sensitive to a change in yields to maturity than high-coupon bonds.
6. Bond prices are more sensitive when yields to maturity are low than when yields to maturity are high.

Understanding these six bond-pricing relationships is at the heart of creating bond trading and investment strategies. The next chapter on duration provides a more comprehensive analysis of price sensitivity, coupon rates, maturity, market rates, and their combined impact on bond prices.

Example of Interest-Rate Change

Assume we buy 20-year, $1,000 Aaa bonds at par providing a 12 percent coupon rate. Further assume interest rates on these bonds in the market fall to 10 percent. Based on Table 12–5, the new price on the bonds would be $1,171.60 ($1,000 × 117.16).

Though we could assume the gain in price from $1,000 to $1,171.60 occurred very quickly, even if the time horizon were one year, the gain is still 17.16 percent. This is only part of the picture. An integral part of many bond-interest-rate strategies is the use of margin or borrowed funds. For government securities, it is possible to use margin as low as 5 percent, and on high-quality utility or corporate bonds, the requirement is generally 30 per-

Table 12–5	Bond Value Table (Coupon Rate 12 Percent)		
Yield to Maturity (Percent)	**Number of Years**		
	10	**20**	**30**
8%	127.18%	139.59%	145.25%
10	112.46	117.16	118.93
12	100.00	100.00	100.00
14	89.41	86.55	85.96

Source: Reprinted by permission from the *Thorndike Encyclopedia of Banking and Financial Tables,* 1981, copyright © 1981, Warren, Gorham and Lamont Inc., 210 South Street, Boston, Mass. All rights reserved.

cent. In the above case, if we had put down 30 percent cash and borrowed the balance, the rate of return on invested capital would have been 57.2 percent.

$$\frac{\text{Return}}{\text{Investment}} = \frac{\$171.60}{\$300.00} = 57.2\%$$

Though we would have had to pay interest on the $700 we borrowed, the interest on the bonds (which belongs to the borrower/investor) would have partially or fully covered this expense. Also, if interest rates drop further to 8 percent, our leveraged return could be over 100 percent on our original investment.

Lest the overanxious student sell all his or her worldly possessions to participate in this impressive gain, there are many admonitions. Even though we think interest rates are going down, they may do the opposite. A 2 percent *increase* in interest rates would cause a $134.50 loss or a negative return on a leveraged investment of $300 (or 44.8 percent). At the very time it appears that interest rates should be falling due to an anticipated or actual recession, the Federal Reserve may generate the opposite effect by tightening the money supply as an anti-inflation weapon as it did in 1970, 1974, 1979, and 1981.

Deep Discount versus Par Bonds

Another feature in analyzing a bond is the current pricing of the bond in regard to its par value. Bonds that were previously issued at interest rates significantly lower than current market levels may trade at deep discounts from par. These are referred to as **deep discount bonds.** As an example, the Missouri Pacific 4¾ percent bonds due to mature in 2020 were selling at $540 in the fall of 1991. Their bond rating was A and the yield to maturity was 8.40 percent.

Deep discount bonds generally trade at a lower yield to maturity than bonds selling at close to par. There are two reasons for this. First, a deep discount bond has almost no chance to be called away. Even if prices go up because of falling interest rates, the price is still likely to be below par value. Because of this protection against a call, the investor in deep discount bonds accepts a lower yield. Also, investors in deep discount bonds have the potential for

Figure 12–4   Yield Spread Differentials on Long-Term Bonds

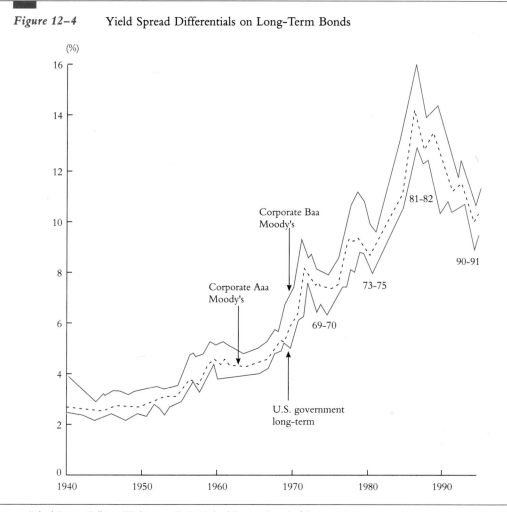

Source: *Federal Reserve Bulletins* (Washington, D.C.: Federal Reserve Board of Governors).

higher percentage price increases (because of the low price base at which the investment is made).

Yield Spread Considerations

As discussed in the previous chapter, different types or grades of bonds provide different yields. For example, the yield on Baa corporate bonds is always above that of corporate Aaa obligations to compensate for risk. Similarly, Aaa corporates pay a higher yield than long-term government obligations. In Figure 12–4, we observe the actual yield spread between Moody's corporate Baa's, Moody's corporate Aaa's, and long-term government securities.

Let's direct our attention to total spread between corporate Baa bonds and government securities (corporate Aaa's fall somewhere in between). Over the long term, the spread appears to be between 75 and 100 basis points.[9] Nevertheless, at certain phases of the business cycle, the yield spread changes. For example, in the early phases of a recession, confidence tends to be at a low ebb, and as a consequence, investors will attempt to shift out of lower grade securities into stronger instruments. The impact on the yield spreads can be observed in the recessions of 1969–70, 1973–75, 1981–82, and 1990–91. In all cases, the yield spread between corporate Baa's and government securities went over 150 basis points, only to narrow again during the recovery. Remember that in Chapter 9, on technical analysis, one of the market indicators was the *Barron's* Confidence Index, which measured the ratio of high-grade bonds to medium-grade bonds. The closer the confidence index is to 1.00, the smaller the spread between rates and the more optimistic investors are about the economy. The further the index is below 1.00, the greater the spread in yields and the less the confidence.

Investors must determine how the yield spread affects their strategy. If they do not need to increase the quality of the portfolio during the low-confidence periods of a recession, they can enjoy unusually high returns on lower-grade instruments relative to higher grades.

■ BOND SWAPS

The term **swap** refers to selling out of a given bond position and immediately buying into another one with similar attributes in an attempt to improve overall portfolio return or performance.

Often there are bonds that appear to be comparable in every respect with the exception of one characteristic. For example, *newly issued bonds* that are the equivalent in every sense to outstanding issues generally trade at a slightly higher yield.

Swaps may also be utilized for tax-adjustment purposes and are very popular at the end of the year. Assume you own a AAA rated AT&T bond that you bought five months ago and are currently sitting on a 20 percent capital loss because of rising interest rates. You can sell the bond and claim the loss (up to $3,000) against other income.[10] This will save you taxes equal to the loss times your marginal tax rate. You can then take the proceeds from the sale and reinvest in a bond of equal risk, and you will have increased your total cash returns because of tax benefits.

Another common swap is the **pure pickup yield swap** in which a bond owner thinks he can increase the yield to maturity by selling a bond and

---

[9]The concept of higher yields on Baa bonds should not be confused with that of junk bonds. In the latter case, the yield is substantially higher, but so is the risk of default.

[10]Losses above $3,000 can be carried forward to future years.

buying a different bond of equal risk. The key to this swap is that the bond price of one or both bonds has to be in disequilibrium. This assumes the market is less than totally efficient. By selling the bond that is overpriced and purchasing the bond that is underpriced, the investor is increasing the yield on the investment. If by chance the true quality and risk of the two bonds are different, the bond trader may have swapped for nothing or may even end up losing on the trade. Other types of swaps exist for arbitrages associated with interest-payment dates, call transactions, conversion privileges, or any quickly changing factor in the market.

SUMMARY

The price of a bond is based on the concept of the present value of future interest payments plus the present value of a single-sum payment at maturity. The true return on a bond investment may be measured by yield to maturity, yield to call, or anticipated realized yield. A study of interest rates in the business cycle indicates that while interest rates were at one time a coincident indicator, their movement has tended to lag behind the drop in business activity during recent recessions.

The term structure of interest rates depicts the relationship between maturity and interest rates over a long time horizon. The slope of the curve gives some indication as to future movements, with an ascending pattern generally followed by higher interest rates and a descending pattern associated with a possible decline in the future. While these movements hold true in the long run, it is somewhat difficult to project interest movements in the short run.

An investor who wishes to capture maximum gains from an anticipated interest-rate decline should maximize the length of the portfolio while investing in low-coupon, interest-sensitive securities. Deep discount bonds also offer some protection from call provisions.

A complete analysis of a bond portfolio will also include a consideration of the yield spreads between low- and high-quality issues. The spread between long-term U.S. government bonds and corporate Baa's has been as high as 150 basis points or more during certain periods in the 1970s, 1980s, and early 1990s. This factor can have a strong influence on bond portfolio construction.

IMPORTANT WORDS AND CONCEPTS

current yield 400

yield to maturity 401

basis point 402

market rate of interest 403

yield to call 403

anticipated realized yield 404

term structure of interest rates 406

expectations hypothesis 407

DISCUSSION QUESTIONS

1. Why are bonds not necessarily a conservative investment?
2. How can the market price of a bond be described in terms of present value?
3. Why does a bond price change when interest rates change?
4. Why is current yield not a good indicator of bond returns? (Relate your answer to maturity considerations.)
5. What is the significance of the yield-to-call calculation?
6. What is the bond reinvestment assumption? Is this necessarily correct?
7. What is the meaning of term structure of interest rates?
8. What does an ascending-term structure pattern tend to indicate?
9. Explain the general meaning of the expectations hypothesis as it relates to the term structure of interest rates.
10. Explain the liquidity preference theory as it relates to the term structure of interest rates.
11. How might the market segmentation theory help to explain why short-term rates on government securities increase when bank loan demand becomes high?
12. Under what circumstances would the yield spread on different classes of debt obligations tend to be largest?
13. List the six principles associated with bond-pricing relationships.
14. How do margin requirements affect investor strategy for bonds?
15. Explain the benefits derived from investing in deep discount bonds.
16. What is a bond swap investment strategy? Explain how it might relate to tax planning.

PROBLEMS

Bond price

1. Given a 15-year bond that originally sold for $1,000 with an 11 percent coupon rate, what would be the price of the bond if interest rates in the marketplace on similar bonds are now 12 percent? Interest is paid semiannually. (Do the two-step calculation.)

Bond price

2. Given the facts in Problem 1, what would be the price if interest rates go down to 8 percent? (Once again, do a semiannual analysis and use two steps.)

Current yield

3. What is the current yield of an 11 percent coupon rate bond priced at $880?

Approximate yield to maturity

4. *a.* What is the approximate yield to maturity of an 11 percent coupon rate, $1,000 par value bond priced at $880 if it has 12 years to maturity? Use Formula 12–2.

   b. Explain why the answer in Problem 4*a* is different from that in Problem 3.

Approximate yield to maturity

5. What is the approximate yield to maturity of a 13 percent coupon rate ($1,000) par value bond priced at $1,150 if it has 15 years to maturity? Use Formula 12–2.

Yield to call

6. *a.* Using the facts given in Problem 5, what would be the yield to call if the call can be made in four years at a price of $1,060? Use Formula 12–3.

   b. Explain why the answer is lower in Problem 6*a* then in Problem 5.

   c. Given a call value of $1,060 in four years, is it likely the bond price would actually get to $1,150?

Anticipated realized yield

7. *a.* Using the facts given in Problem 5, what would be the anticipated realized yield if the forecast is that the bond can be sold in three years for $1,240? Use Formula 12–4. That is, assume the bond has a 13 percent coupon rate ($130) and a current price of $1,150.

   b. Now break down the anticipated realized yield between current yield and capital appreciation. (Hint: Compute current yield and subtract this from anticipated realized yield to determine capital appreciation.)

Use of bond table

8. An investor places $900,000 in 20-year bonds (12 percent coupon rate), and interest rates decline by 3 percent. Use Table 12–4 to determine the current value of the portfolio.

Expectations hypothesis

9. The following pattern for one-year Treasury bills is expected over the next four years.

Year 1	6%
Year 2	7%
Year 3	9%
Year 4	11%

   a. What return would be necessary to induce an investor to buy a two-year security?

   b. What return would be necessary to induce an investor to buy a three-year security?

   c. What return would be necessary to induce an investor to buy a four-year security?

   d. Diagram the term structure of interest rates for years 1 through 4.

Margin purchase

10. *a.* Assume an investor purchases a 20-year, $1,000 bond with a coupon rate of 10 percent. The market rate falls to 8 percent. What would be the return on the investment if the buyer borrowed part of the funds

with a 25 percent margin requirement? Assume the interest payments on the bond cover the interest expense on the borrowed funds. (You can use Table 12–3 in this problem to determine the new value of the bond.)

b. Assume the same 20-year bond in part *a* is purchased with 25 percent margin, but market rates go up to 12 percent from 10 percent instead of going down to 8 percent. You can once again use Table 12–3 to determine the price of the bond. What is the percentage loss on the cash investment?

Deep discount bond

11. Assume an investor is trying to choose between purchasing a deep discount bond or a par value bond. The deep discount bond pays 5 percent interest, has 20 years to maturity, and is currently trading at $571 with a 10 percent yield to maturity. It is callable at $1,050.

The second bond is selling at its par value of $1,000. It pays 12 percent interest and has 20 years to maturity. Its yield to maturity is also 12 percent. The bond is callable at $1,080.

a. If the yield to maturity on the deep discount bond goes down by 2 percent to 8 percent, what will the new price of the bond be? Do semiannual analysis.

b. If the yield to maturity on the par value bond goes down by 2 percent to 10 percent, what will the new price of the bond be? Do semiannual analysis.

c. Based on the facts in the problem and your answers to parts *a* and *b*, which bond appears to be the better purchase? (Consider the call feature as well as capital appreciation.)

Tax swap

12. Mr. Williams bought $10,000 of bonds four months ago. The bonds were purchased at par with a 10 percent coupon rate. Now interest rates in the market are 14 percent for similar obligations with 10 years to maturity. The rapid rise in interest rates was caused by an unexpected increase in inflation.

a. Determine the current value of Mr. Williams's portfolio. Use Table 12–3 to help accomplish this.

b. How large a deduction from other income can Mr. Williams take if he sells the bonds?

c. If he is in a 31 percent tax bracket, what is the tax write-off worth to him in terms of tax shield benefits?

d. Assume he will replace the old 10 percent bonds with 11.2 percent bonds selling at $875. Based on your answer in part *a*, how many new bonds can be purchased? Round to the nearest whole number.

■ CFA MATERIAL

The following material contains sample questions and solutions from a prior Level I CFA Exam. While the terminology is slightly different from that in this text, you can still view the skills that are necessary for the CFA exam.

CFA Exam Question

4. *a.* *Briefly explain* why bonds of different maturities have different yields in terms of the (1) expectations, (2) liquidity, and (3) segmentation hypotheses.
   (5 minutes)

   b. Briefly describe the implications of each of the three hypotheses when the yield curve is (1) upward sloping, and (2) downward sloping.
   (5 minutes)

Solution: Question 4 — Morning Section (I–86) (10 points)

a. (1) The expectations hypothesis maintains that the current long-term rate should equal the average of current and expected future short-term rates. Unless the current and expected future rates are all equal, the averages will be different for different maturities.

   (2) The liquidity hypothesis maintains that since longer securities have greater risk, interest rates should increase with maturity as a compensation to investors.

   (3) The segmentation hypothesis maintains that individual borrowers are constrained to particular segments of the maturity spectrum. The interest rate for a given maturity will thus depend on the supply and demand for funds in each segment.

b. *Upward sloping yield curve:*

   (1) Expectations — short-term interest rates are expected to be higher in the future.

   (2) Liquidity — as predicted, longer-term securities have higher return to compensate for risk.

   (3) Segmentation — signifies relatively less demand for long-term bonds than short-term bonds.

   Downward sloping yield curve:

   (1) Expectations — short-term interest rates are expected to be lower in the future.

   (2) Liquidity — this is inconsistent with the liquidity hypothesis. When liquidity plus expectations is considered, a decrease in future short-term rates that is larger than the liquidity premium is indicated.

   (3) Segmentation — signifies relatively higher demand for long-term bonds than for short-term bonds.

CFA Exam Question

5. You are considering the purchase of a 10 percent, 10-year bond with a par value of $1,000.

   a. Using Tables I and II, *compute* the price you should pay for this bond assuming semiannual interest payments and 8 percent yield to maturity.
   (2 minutes)

Table I   Present Value of $1

Periods	3 Percent	4 Percent	5 Percent	6 Percent	7 Percent	8 Percent
4	.8885	.8548	.8227	.7921	.7629	.7350
6	.8375	.7903	.7462	.7050	.6663	.6302
8	.7874	.7307	.6768	.6274	.5820	.5403
10	.7441	.6756	.6139	.5584	.5083	.4632
12	.7014	.6246	.5568	.4970	.4440	.3971
14	.6611	.5775	.5051	.4423	.3878	.3405
16	.6232	.5339	.4581	.3936	.3387	.2919
18	.5874	.4936	.4155	.3503	.2959	.2502
19	.5703	.4746	.3957	.3305	.2765	.2317
20	.5537	.4564	.3769	.3118	.2584	.2145

Table II   Present Value of $1 Annuity

Periods	3 Percent	4 Percent	5 Percent	6 Percent	7 Percent	8 Percent
4	3.7171	3.6299	3.5460	3.4651	3.3872	3.3121
6	5.4172	5.2421	5.0757	4.9173	4.7665	4.6229
8	7.0197	6.7327	6.4632	6.2098	5.9713	5.7466
10	8.5302	8.1109	7.7217	7.3601	7.0236	6.7101
12	9.9540	9.3851	8.8633	8.3838	7.9427	7.5361
14	11.2961	10.5631	9.8986	9.2950	8.7455	8.2442
16	12.5611	11.6523	10.8378	10.1059	9.4466	8.8514
18	13.7535	12.6593	11.6896	10.8276	10.0591	9.3719
19	14.3238	13.1339	12.0853	11.1581	10.3356	9.6036
20	14.8775	13.5903	12.4622	11.4699	10.5940	9.8181

b. A year from now, you expect that the yield to maturity for this bond will be 6 percent. Using Tables I and II, *compute* the realized compound yield during the year, assuming a reinvestment rate of 5 percent and semiannual interest payments. *Identify* and *comment* on the significance of each of the components of the calculated realized compound yield.

(7 minutes)

Solution: Question 5 — Morning Section (I–87) (10 points)

a. $50 × 13.5903 (4% − 20 periods) $ 679.52

       $1,000 × 0.4564   456.40

       Value $1,135.92

b. $50 × 13.7535 (3% − 18 periods) $ 687.68
$1,000 × .5874   587.40
Value of bond 1 year from now $1,275.08
Realized compound yield:

Ending wealth value:

$1,275.08 — ending price of bond
   50.00 — interest at end of year
   50.00 — mid-year interest payment
    1.25 — 5% interest on interest for ½ year
$1,376.33

$$\text{Realized compound yield} = \frac{\$1,376.33}{\$1,135.92} - 1 = 1.2116 - 1$$

$$= 21.16\%$$

There are three components of the realized compound yield calculated above: price appreciation due to decline in rates from 8 percent to 6 percent; coupon interest; and interest on interest.

The total return in dollars for the year was $240.41. Of that total return, $139.16, or about 58 percent, was due to price appreciation; $100, or about 42 percent, was due to coupon interest; and about 0.5 percent was due to interest on interest.

Because the realized compound yield is calculated over only one year in which rates have fallen, the interest-on-interest component will be very small, and the appreciation component is the largest. Had the coupon been smaller than 10 percent, the appreciation component would have been even larger.

■ SELECTED REFERENCES

Investment Strategies with Bonds

Barnes, Tom; Keith Johnson; and Don Shannon. "A Test of Fixed-Income Strategies." *Journal of Portfolio Management,* Winter 1984, pp. 60–65.

Brick, Ivan E., and S. Abraham Ravid. "Interest Rate Uncertainty and the Optimal Debt Maturity Structure." *Journal of Financial and Quantitative Analysis,* March 1991, pp. 63–81.

Fong, H. Gifford, and Frank J. Fabozzi. "How to Enhance Bond Returns with Naive Strategies." *Journal of Portfolio Management,* Summer 1985, pp. 57–60.

Leibowitz, Martin L. "Goal Oriented Bond Portfolio Management." *Journal of Portfolio Management,* Summer 1979, pp. 13–18.

Ma, Christopher K., and Garry M. Weed. "Fact and Fancy of Takeover Junk Bonds." *Journal of Portfolio Management,* Fall 1986, pp. 34–37.

Rosenberg, Hilary. "The New Lure of Foreign Bonds." *Institutional Investor,* March 1988, pp. 143–47.

Smirlock, Michael. "Seasonality and Bond Market Returns." *Journal of Portfolio Management,* Spring 1984, pp. 42–44.

Bond Yields

Ferri, Michael G. "How Do Call Provisions Influence Bond Yields?" *Journal of Portfolio Management,* Winter 1979, pp. 55–57.

Homer, S., and M. L. Leibowitz. *Inside the Yield Book: New Tools for Bond Market Strategy.* Englewood Cliffs, N.J.: Prentice Hall, 1972.

Schaefer, Stephen M. "The Problem with Redemption Yields." *Financial Analysts Journal,* July–August 1977, pp. 29–35.

Empirical Studies

Dann, Larry Y., and Wayne H. Mikkelson. "Convertible Debt Issuance, Capital Structure Change and Financing—Related Information: Some New Evidence." *Journal of Financial Economics,* June 1984, pp. 155–86.

Joehnk, Michael D., and James F. Nielsen. "Return and Risk Characteristics of Speculative Grade Bonds." *Quarterly Review of Economics and Business,* Spring 1975, pp. 27–46.

Yawitz, Jess B.; Kevin J. Maloney; and Louis H. Ederington. "Taxes, Default Risk, and Yield Spreads." *Journal of Finance,* September 1985, pp. 1127–40.

13

Duration and Reinvestment Concepts

■ REVIEW OF BASIC BOND VALUATION CONCEPTS

In Chapter 12, we discussed the principles of bond valuation. The value of a bond was established in Formula 12–1 as follows:

$$V = \sum_{t=1}^{n} \frac{C_t}{(1 + i)^t} + \frac{P_n}{(1 + i)^n}$$

where:

V = Market value or price of the bond

n = Number of periods

t = Each period

C_t = Coupon or interest payment for each period, t

P_n = Par or maturity value

i = Interest rate in the market

Based on this equation, as interest rates in the market rise, the price of the bond will decline because the present value of the cash flows is worth less at a higher discount rate. The opposite is true if interest rates decline. We also demonstrated in Table 12–4 that bonds with long-term maturities were generally more sensitive to changes in interest rates than were short-term bonds. Reproduction of part of Table 12–4 below shows that a 30-year bond exhibits larger price changes in response to a change in yield than do shorter-term obligations. For example, a 2 percent drop in interest rates would cause a 1.86 percent increase in value for a bond with one year to maturity, but an 18.93 percent increase in value for a bond with 30 years to maturity. Given the relationship between the life of a bond and the price sensitivity just described, it is particularly important that we have an appropriate definition of the life or term of a bond.

(Reproduction of Table 12–4) Change in Market Prices of Bonds for Shifts in Yields to Maturity (12 Percent Coupon Rate)

Yield Change (Percent)	Maturity (Years)				
	1	5	10	20	30
+3%	−2.69%	−10.30%	−15.29%	−18.89%	−19.74%
+2	−1.81	−7.02	−10.59	−13.33	−14.04
+1	−.91	−3.57	−5.01	−7.08	−7.52
−1	+.92	+3.77	+5.98	+8.02	+8.72
−2	+1.86	+7.72	+12.46	+17.16	+18.93
−3	+2.81	+11.87	+19.51	+27.60	+30.96

The first inclination is to say the term of a bond is an easily determined matter. One supposedly merely needs to look up the maturity date (such as

1995 or 2004) in a bond book, and the matter is settled. However, the notion of effective life of a bond is more complicated than this. The situation is somewhat analogous to the quoted coupon rate on the bond, not really conveying the true yield on the obligation. Similarly, the maturity date on a bond may not convey all important information about the life of a bond.

In studying the true characteristics about the life of a bond, not only must the final date and amount of the maturity payment be considered but also the pattern of coupon payments that occurs in the interim. If you were to receive $1,000 after 20 years and no interest payments during the term of the obligation, clearly the effective life is 20 years. But suppose in addition to the $1,000, you were also to receive $100 per year for the next 20 years. Part of the payment is coming early and part of the payment is coming late, and the weighted average term of the payout is certainly less than 20 years. The higher the coupon payments relative to the maturity payment, the shorter the weighted average life of the payout. The **weighted average life** refers to the time period over which the coupon payments and maturity payment on a bond are recovered. In the next section, we shall go through the simple mathematics of computing the weighted average life of the payout; for now it is enough to know that such a concept exists.

The important consideration is that *bond price sensitivity* can be more appropriately related to *weighted average life* than to just the maturity date. While many bond analysts simply relate price sensitivity to maturity (and we did that also in Chapter 12), there is a more sophisticated approach related to weighted average life.

Before we move on to calculate weighted average life, there is an investment decision we wish you to consider. Assume you have to decide whether to invest in an 8 percent coupon rate bond with a 20-year maturity or a 12 percent coupon rate bond with a 25-year maturity. Which bond will have the larger increase in price if interest rates decline? You may choose the 25-year, 12 percent coupon rate bond because it has the longer maturity, but don't answer too quickly on this. Let's consider weighted average life and then eventually come back to this question of price sensitivity.

■ DURATION

The concept of weighted average life of a bond falls under the general topic of duration. We shall first of all do a simple example of weighted average life and then more formally look at duration. Assume we have a five-year bond that provides $80 per year for the next five years plus $1,000 at the end of five years. For ease of calculation, we are using annual coupon payments in our analysis. Semiannual analysis would change the answer only slightly. An approach to computing weighted average life is presented in Table 13–1.

First, we see the weighted average life of the bond, based on the annual cash flows, is 4.4290 years. Let's see how this is calculated. In column (1) is the year in which each cash flow falls, and in column (2) is the size of the cash flow for

Table 13–1   Simple Weighted Average Life

(1) Year, t	(2) Cash Flow	(3) Annual Cash Flow (2) ÷ by Total Cash Flow	(4) Year × Weight (1) × (3)
1	$ 80	.0571	.0571
2	80	.0571	.1142
3	80	.0571	.1713
4	80	.0571	.2284
5	80	.0571	.2855
5	1,000	.7145	3.5725
Total cash flow →	$1,400	1.0000	4.4290

each year plus the total cash flow. Column (3) calls for dividing the annual cash flow in column (2) by the total cash flow at the bottom of column (2) to determine what percentage of the total it represents. For example, the annual cash flow of $80 on the first line of column (2) represents .0571 of the total cash flow of $1,400. ($80 ÷ $1,400 = .0571.) The same basic procedure is followed for all subsequent years. In column (4), each year is multiplied by the weights (percentages) developed in column (3). For example, year 1 is multiplied by .0571 to arrive at .0571 in column (4). Year 2 is multiplied by .0571 to arrive at .1142 in column (4). This procedure is followed for each year and each weight. The final answer is 4.4290 for the weighted average life of the bond.

If you can understand the approach presented in Table 13–1, you should have no difficulty following a more formal and appropriate definition of weighted average life called duration. **Duration** represents the weighted average life of a bond where the weights are based on the *present value* of the individual cash flows relative to the *present value* of the total cash flows. An example of duration is presented in Table 13–2. Present value calculations are based on the market rate of interest (yield to maturity) for the bond, which in this case, we shall assume to be 12 percent.

The only difference between Table 13–1 and Table 13–2 is that in Table 13–2, the cash flows are present valued before the weights are determined. Thus the cash flows (2) are multiplied by the present value factors at 12 percent (3) to arrive at the present value of cash flows (4). The total present value of cash flows at the bottom of column (4) is also the same as the price of the bond. In column (5), weights for each year are determined by dividing the present value of each annual cash flow (4) by the total present value of cash flows (bottom of column 4). For example in year 1, the present value of the cash flow is $71.44, and this is divided by the total present value of cash flows of $855.40

Table 13–2   Duration Concept of Weighted Average Life

(1)	(2)	(3)	(4)	(5)	(6)
				PV of Annual Cash Flow (4)	
		PV **Factor**	*PV* **of Cash**	÷ **by Total** *PV*	**Year ×** **Weight**
Year, *t*	**Cash Flow** *(CF)*	**at 12 Percent**	**Flow** *(CF)*	**of Cash Flows**	**(1) × (5)**
1	$ 80	.893	$ 71.44	.0835	.0835
2	80	.797	63.76	.0745	.1490
3	80	.712	56.96	.0666	.1998
4	80	.636	50.88	.0595	.2380
5	80	.567	45.36	.0530	.2650
5	$1,000	.567	567.00	.6629	3.3145
		Total *PV* of → cash flows *(V)*	$855.40	1.000	4.2498 ↑ Duration

to arrive at .0835 in column (5). Similarly, the weight in year 2, as shown in column (5), is determined by dividing $63.76 by $855.40 to arrive at .0745. In column (6), each year is multiplied by the weights developed in column (5). For example, year 1 is multiplied by .0835 to arrive at .0835 in column (6). Year 2 is multiplied by .0745 to arrive at .1490. This procedure is followed for each year, and the values are then summed. The final answer for duration (the weighted average life based on present value) is 4.2498. Duration, once determined, is the most representative value for effective bond life and the measure against which bond price sensitivity should be evaluated.

The formula for duration can be formally stated as:

$$\text{Duration} = \underbrace{\frac{CF\ PV}{V}}_{\text{Weight}} \underbrace{(1)}_{\text{Year}} + \underbrace{\frac{CF\ PV}{V}}_{\text{Weight}} \underbrace{(2)}_{\text{Year}} + \underbrace{\frac{CF\ PV}{V}}_{\text{Weight}} \underbrace{(3)}_{\text{Year}}$$

$$+ \dots + \underbrace{\frac{CF\ PV}{V}}_{\text{Weight}} \underbrace{(n)}_{\text{Year}} \qquad (13\text{–}1)$$

where:

CF = Yearly cash flow for each time period

PV = Present value factor for each time period (from Appendix C at the end of the book)

V = Total present value or market price of the bond

n = Number of periods to maturity[1]

In Table 13–3, we observe durations for an 8 percent coupon rate bond with maturities of 1, 5, and 10 years. The discount rate is 12 percent. The procedure used to compute duration in Table 13–3 is the same as that employed in Table 13–2. Although many calculations are involved, you should primarily direct your attention to the last value presented in column (6) for each of the three bonds. This value represents the duration of the issue.

We see in Table 13–3 that the duration for a one-year bond is 1.0. Since all cash flows are paid at the end of year 1, duration equals the maturity.[2] As maturity increases (to 5 and 10 years), duration increases but less than the maturity of the bond. With a 5-year bond, duration is 4.2498, and with a 10-year bond, duration is 6.8381. Duration is increasing at a decreasing rate because the principal repayment in the last year becomes a smaller percentage of the total present value of cash flow, and the annual coupon payments become more important.[3]

■ DURATION AND PRICE SENSITIVITY

Once duration is computed, its most important use is in determining the price sensitivity of a bond. In Table 13–4, we consider the maturity, duration, and percentage price change for an 8 percent coupon rate bond based on a 2 percent decrease and on a 2 percent increase in interest rates. The *market* rate of interest for computing duration in Table 13–4 is 8 percent. Duration is related not only to maturity but also to coupon rate and market rate of interest. For example, in Table 13–3, the coupon rate of interest was 8 percent and the market rate of interest was 12 percent. In the calculations in Table 13–4, the coupon rate is 8 percent and the initial market rate of interest is assumed to be 8 percent. Because of the different market rates of interest in Tables 13–3 and 13–4, the duration for a given maturity (such as 5 or 10 years) will be different. The point just discussed will be further clarified later in the chapter, so even if you do not fully understand it, you should still continue to read on.

---

[1]Using the symbols from Formula 12–1, duration can also be stated as:

$$\text{Duration} = \sum_{t=1}^{n} \frac{C_t \dfrac{1}{(1+i)^t}}{V}(t) + \frac{P_n \dfrac{1}{(1+i)^n}}{V}(n)$$

If semiannual analysis is used throughout the calculation, the answer should be divided by two to convert the figure to annual terms.

[2]If semiannual analysis were used, the duration would be slightly less than the maturity in the first year.

[3]A sinking-fund provision can also have an effect on duration, causing the weighted average life of the bond to be shorter.

Table 13–3   Duration for an 8 Percent Coupon Rate Bond with Maturities of 1, 5, and 10 Years Discounted at 12 Percent

1-Year Bond

(1) Year, *t*	(2) Cash Flow *(CF)*	(3) *PV* Factor at 12 Percent	(4) *PV* of Cash Flow *(CF)*	(5) *PV* of Annual Cash Flow (4) ÷ by Total *PV* of Cash Flows	(6) Year × Weight (1) × (5)
1	$ 80	.893	$ 71.44	.0741	.0741
1	1,000	.893	893.00	.9259	.9259
		Total *PV* of → cash flows	$964.44	1.0000	1.0000 ↑ Duration

5-Year Bond

1	$ 80	.893	$ 71.44	.0835	.0835
2	80	.797	63.76	.0745	.1490
3	80	.712	56.96	.0666	.1998
4	80	.636	50.88	.0595	.2380
5	80	.567	45.36	.0530	.2650
5	1,000	.567	567.00	.6629	3.3145
		Total *PV* of → cash flows	$855.40	1.0000	4.2498 ↑ Duration

10-Year Bond

1	$ 80	.893	$ 71.44	.0923	.0923
2	80	.797	63.76	.0824	.1648
3	80	.712	56.96	.0736	.2208
4	80	.636	50.88	.0657	.2628
5	80	.567	45.36	.0586	.2930
6	80	.507	40.56	.0524	.3144
7	80	.452	36.16	.0467	.3269
8	80	.404	32.32	.0418	.3344
9	80	.361	28.88	.0373	.3357
10	80	.322	25.76	.0333	.3330
10	1,000	.322	322.00	.4160	4.1600
		Total *PV* of → cash flows	$774.08	1.0000	6.8381 ↑ Duration

Table 13–4   Duration and Price Sensitivity (8 Percent Coupon Rate Bond)

(1) Maturity	(2) Duration	(3) Impact of a 2 Percent Decline in Interest Rates on Price	(4) Impact of a 2 Percent Increase in Interest Rates on Price
1	1.0000	+ 1.89%	− 1.81%
5	4.3121	+ 8.42	− 7.58
10	7.2470	+14.72	−12.29
20	10.6038	+22.93	−17.03
25	11.5290	+25.57	−18.50
30	12.1585	+27.53	−18.85
40	12.8787	+30.09	−19.55
50	13.2123	+31.15	−19.83

We see in Table 13–4 that the longer the maturity or duration, the greater the impact of a 2 percent change in interest rates on price. However, we shall also observe how much more closely the percentage change in price parallels the change in duration as compared to maturity. For example, between 25 and 50 years, duration increases very slowly (column 2) and the same can be said for the increase in the percentage impact that a 2 percent decline in interest rates has on price (column 3). This is true despite the fact that the maturity period has increased by 100 percent, from 25 to 50 years.

As a rough measure of price sensitivity, one can multiply duration times the change in interest rates to determine the percentage change in the value of a bond.

$$\text{Percentage change in the value of a bond approximately equals} \rightarrow \text{Duration} \times \text{Change in interest rates}$$

The sign in the final answer is reversed because interest-rate changes and bond prices move in opposite directions. For example, if a bond has a duration of 7.2470 years, and interest rates go down by 2 percent, a rough measure of bond value appreciation is +14.494 percent (7.2470 × 2). Columns (2) and (3) in Table 13–4, across from 10 years maturity, indicate this is a good approximation. That is, when duration was 7.2470, a 2 percent drop in interest rates produced a 14.72 percent increase in bond prices (not too many basis points away from our formula value of +14.494 percent). The

approximation gets progressively less accurate as the term of the bond is extended.[4] It is also a less valid measure for interest-rate increases (and the associated price decline). Even with these qualifications, one can observe a more useful relationship between price changes and duration than between price changes and maturity.

It is for this reason that the analyst must have a reasonable feel for the factors that influence duration. The length of the bond affects duration, but as previously mentioned, it is not the only variable. Duration is also influenced by market rate of interest and the coupon rate on the bond. It is theoretically possible for these two factors to outweigh maturity in determining duration. That is to say, it is possible that a bond with a shorter maturity than another bond may actually have a longer duration and be more price sensitive to interest rate changes.

Duration and Market Rates

Market rates of interest (yield to maturity) and duration are inversely related. The higher the market rate of interest, the lower the duration. This is because of the present-value effect that is part of duration. Higher market rates of interest mean lower present values. For example, in Table 13–2, if the market rate of interest in column (3) had been 16 percent instead of 12 percent, the final answer for duration would have been 4.1859. The new value is computed in Table 13–5 on page 434. Clearly, it is less than the 4.2498 duration value in Table 13–2.

To expand our analysis, in Table 13–6 on page 434 we see the duration values for an 8 percent coupon rate bond at different market rates of interest. As market rates of interest increase, duration decreases. This can be easily seen in the 20-year row (reading across). At a 4 percent market rate of interest, duration for the 8 percent coupon rate bond is 12.3995. At 8 percent, it is 10.6038, and at 12 percent, 8.9390.

Also note in Table 13–6 that an equal change in market rates of interest will have a bigger impact on duration when rates move down than when they move up. For example, in the 50-year row, a 4 percentage point decrease in market rates of interest (say, from 8 percent to 4 percent) causes duration to increase by 7.0358 years, from 13.2123 to 20.2481 years. A similar increase from 8 percent to 12 percent would cause duration to decrease by only 3.8407 years, from 13.2123 to 9.3716 years.

---

[4]The approximation can be slightly improved by using modified duration instead of actual duration. Modified duration is defined as: Duration ÷ (1 + Market rate of interest/Number of coupon payments per period). For more information, see Michael H. Hopewell and George C. Kaufman, "Bond Price Volatility and Term to Maturity: A Generalized Respecification," *American Economic Review*, September 1973, pp. 749–53.

Table 13–5   Duration of an 8 Percent Coupon Rate Bond with a 16 Percent Market Rate of Interest

(1) Year, *t*	(2) Cash Flow *(CF)*	(3) PV Factor at 16 Percent	(4) PV of Cash Flow *(CF)*	(5) PV of Annual Cash Flow (4) ÷ by Total PV of Cash Flows	(6) Year × Weight (1) × (5)
1	$ 80	.862	$ 68.96	.0935	.0935
2	80	.743	59.44	.0806	.1612
3	80	.641	51.28	.0695	.2085
4	80	.552	44.16	.0598	.2392
5	80	.476	38.08	.0516	.2580
5	1,000	.476	476.00	.6451	3.2255
			Total PV of → $737.92 cash flows	1.0000	4.1859 ↑ Duration

Table 13–6   Duration Values at Varying Market Rates of Interest (Based on 8 Percent Coupon Rate Bond)

Maturity (Years)	Market Rates of Interest				
	4 Percent	6 Percent	8 Percent	10 Percent	12 Percent
1	1.0000	1.0000	1.0000	1.0000	1.0000
5	4.3717	4.3423	4.3121	4.2814	4.2498
10	7.6372	7.4450	7.2470	7.0439	6.8381
→ 20	12.3995	11.4950	10.6038	9.7460	8.9390
25	14.2265	12.8425	11.5290	10.3229	9.2475
30	15.7935	13.8893	12.1585	10.6472	9.3662
40	18.3274	15.3498	12.8787	10.9176	9.3972
50	20.2481	16.2494	13.2123	10.9896	9.3716

Duration and Coupon Rates

In the previous section, we learned that duration is inversely related to the market rate of interest. We now look at the relationship between duration and the coupon rate on a bond. As the coupon rate rises, duration decreases. Why? The answer is that high coupon rate bonds tend to produce higher annual cash

Table 13–7	Duration and Coupon Rates (25-Year Bonds)		
Market Rate of Interest	**Coupon Rates**		
	4 Percent	**8 Percent**	**12 Percent**
4%	16.2470	14.2265	13.3278
6	14.7455	12.8425	12.0407
8	13.2459	11.5290	10.8396
10	11.8112	10.3229	9.7501
12	10.4912	9.2475	8.7844

flows before maturity and thus tend to weight duration toward the earlier to middle years. On the other hand, low coupon rate bonds produce less annual cash flows before maturity and have less influence on duration. Duration is weighted more heavily toward the final payment at maturity, and duration tends to be somewhat closer to the actual maturity on the bond. At the extreme, a zero-coupon bond has the same maturity and duration.

The relationship between duration and coupon rates can be seen in Table 13–7. Here three different coupon rate bonds are presented. Each bond is assumed to have a maturity of 25 years. The best way to read the table is to pick a market rate of interest in the first column and then read across the table to determine the duration at various coupon rates. For example, at an 8 percent market rate of interest, duration is 13.2459 at a 4 percent coupon rate, 11.5290 at an 8 percent coupon rate, and 10.8396 at a 12 percent coupon rate. Clearly, the higher the coupon rate, the lower the duration (and vice versa).

The impact of coupon rates on duration is also demonstrated in Figure 13–1. Note that with a zero-coupon bond, the line is at a 45-degree angle; that is, duration and years to maturity are always the same value. There is only one payment, and it is at maturity.

You can also observe in Figure 13–1 that progressively higher coupon rates lead to a lower duration. As an example, go to point N on the horizontal axis and observe duration for 4 percent, 8 percent, and 12 percent interest. Clearly the higher the coupon rate, the lower the duration value.

Because the higher the duration, the greater the price sensitivity, it follows that an investor desiring maximum price movements will look toward lower coupon rate bonds. As previously demonstrated, low coupon rate and high duration go together, and high duration leads to maximum price sensitivity. The relationship of low coupon rates to price sensitivity was briefly discussed in Chapter 12 under investment strategy. We now see that the unnamed explanatory variable at that point was duration.

Figure 13–1   The Effect of Coupon Rates on Duration

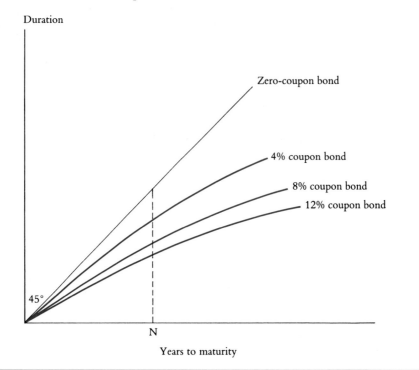

BRINGING TOGETHER THE INFLUENCES ON DURATION

The three factors that determine the value of duration are the maturity of the bond, the market rate of interest, and the coupon rate. Duration is positively correlated with maturity but moves in the opposite direction of market rates of interest and coupon rates; that is, the higher the market rate of interest or the coupon rate, the lower the duration. Earlier in this chapter, you were asked to consider whether you should invest in an 8 percent coupon rate, 20-year bond or a 12 percent coupon rate, 25-year bond. Since we were assuming interest rates were going to go down, you were looking for maximum price volatility. Had you not studied duration, you probably would have selected the bond with the longer maturity. This would generally be a valid assumption as indicated in Chapter 12. However, the primary emphasis to the sophisticated bond investor when assessing price volatility, or sensitivity, is duration.

Note that the bond with the longer maturity (25 years versus 20 years) also has a higher coupon rate (12 percent versus 8 percent). The first factor (longer maturity) would indicate higher duration, but the second factor (higher

coupon rate) would indicate a lower duration. What is the net effect? The answer can be found in earlier tables in this chapter. Let's assume that the *market rate of interest* is 12 percent for both bonds. Table 13–6 presented information on 8 percent coupon rate bonds for varying maturities and market rates of interest. To determine the duration on the 8 percent coupon rate, 20-year bond, assuming a 12 percent market rate of interest, we read across the 20-year row to the last column in the table and see the answer is 8.9390. (Note that all bonds in Table 13–6 have an 8 percent coupon rate, so we must identify the value associated with 20 years and a 12 percent market rate of interest.)

To determine the duration for the 12 percent coupon rate, 25-year bond with a 12 percent market rate of interest, we must go to Table 13–7. Note that all bonds in this table have a 25-year maturity, so read down to a market rate of interest of 12 percent and across to a coupon rate of 12 percent. The value for duration on this bond is 8.7844.

Based on the above analysis, the answer to the question posed earlier in the chapter is that the bond with the shorter maturity (8 percent coupon rate for 20 years) has a higher duration than the bond with the greater maturity (12 percent for 25 years) and thus is the most price sensitive.[5]

Bond	Duration
8%, 20 years	8.9390 ← greater price sensitivity
12%, 25 years	8.7844

In actuality, if interest rates went down by 2 percent, the 8 percent, 20-year bond would go up by 18.5 percent, while the 12 percent, 25-year bond would only increase by 17.9 percent.

■ DURATION AND ZERO-COUPON BONDS

Characteristics of zero-coupon bonds were briefly described in Chapter 11. As previously mentioned, Figure 13–1 depicts the duration of zero-coupon bonds as a 45-degree line relative to years to maturity. This graphically indicates that the duration of a zero-coupon bond equals the number of years it has to maturity. For all bonds of equal risk and maturity, the zero-coupon bond has the greatest duration and therefore the greatest price sensitivity. This price risk is one that is often lost in the image of safety that CATs, RATs, TIGRs, COUGARs, and other zero-coupons have when backed by U.S. government securities.

---

[5]As previously indicated, if we vary the market rate of interest, we can also influence the outcome to our question.

Table 13–8	Duration of Zero-Coupon versus 8 Percent Coupon Bonds (Market Rate of Interest Is 12 Percent)			
(1) Years to Maturity	(2) Duration of Zero-Coupon Bond	(3) Duration of 8 Percent Coupon Bond	(4) Relative Duration of Zero-Coupon to 8 Percent Coupon Bonds (2) ÷ (3)	
10	10	6.8374	1.4625	
20	20	8.9390	2.2374	
30	30	9.3662	3.2030	
40	40	9.3972	4.2566	
50	50	9.3716	5.3353	

A headline in *The Wall Street Journal* on June 1, 1984, appeared as follows: "Zero-Coupon Bonds' Price Swings Jolt Investors Looking for Security."[6] It was reported that between March 31, 1983, and March 31, 1984, Salomon Brothers' 30-year CATs declined 25 percent in price, while returns on conventional 30-year government bonds declined only a few percentage points. The article cited one client buying $100,000 of zero coupons, thinking they were similar to short-term Treasury bill investments, only to find out four weeks later that his zero-coupon bonds had declined in value by $24,000.

To put the volatility of a zero-coupon bond into better perspective, we compare the duration of a zero-coupon bond to that of an 8 percent coupon bond for several maturities in Table 13–8.

The far right column in Table 13–8 indicates the ratio of duration between zero-coupon and 8 percent coupon rate bonds. As stressed throughout the chapter, duration represents a measure of price sensitivity. Thus, for a 10-year maturity period, a zero-coupon bond is almost 1½ times as price sensitive as an 8 percent coupon rate bond (the ratio in the last column is 1.4625). For a 20-year maturity period, it is over two times more price sensitive (2.2374), and for 50 years the price sensitivity ratio is over five times greater (5.3353). This might explain why zero-coupons were much more sensitive to rising interest rates during 1983–84 as described in the story in *The Wall Street Journal*. Of course, tremendous profits can be made in zero-coupon bonds when there is a sharp drop in interest rates as in early 1985 and again in 1991–92.

---

[6]Randall Smith, "Zero-Coupon Bonds' Price Swings Jolt Investors Looking for Security," *The Wall Street Journal*, June 1, 1984, p. 19.

■ THE USES OF DURATION

Duration is primarily used as a measure to judge bond price sensitivity to interest-rate changes. Since duration includes information on several variables (maturity, coupon rate, and market rate of interest), it captures more information than any one of them. It therefore allows more accurate decisions for complex bond strategies. One such strategy involves the timing of investment inflows to provide a needed cash outlay at a known future date. Perhaps $1 million is needed after five years. Everything is tailored to this five-year time horizon. If interest rates go up, there will be a decline in the value of the portfolio but a higher reinvestment rate opportunity for inflows. Similarly, if interest rates go down, there will be capital appreciation for the portfolio but a lower reinvestment rate opportunity. By tying all the investment decisions to a duration period, the portfolio manager can take advantage of these counter forces to ensure a necessary outcome. This strategy is called **immunization** and is used by insurance companies, pension funds, and other institutional money managers to protect their portfolios against swings in interest rates. For a more comprehensive discussion of immunization strategies, an article by Fisher and Weil is an appropriate source.[7] For an excellent criticism of duration and immunization strategy, see Yawitz and Marshall.[8] One of the problems with duration analysis is that it often assumes a parallel shift in yield curves. Although long-duration bonds are clearly more price sensitive than shorter-duration bonds, there is no assurance that long- and short-term interest rates will move by equal amounts.

■ BOND REINVESTMENT ASSUMPTIONS AND TERMINAL WEALTH ANALYSIS

Reinvestment Assumptions

As indicated in the previous section, one concern an investor may have when purchasing bonds is that the interest income will not be reinvested to earn the same return the coupon payment represents. This may not be a problem for an individual consuming the interest payments, but it could be a serious concern for individuals building a retirement portfolio or a pension fund manager accumulating funds for future payout to retirees. The crucial issue is the amount of money accumulated at the time the retirement fund will be used to cover living expenses. One major determinant of the ending value of a retirement fund is the rate of return on coupon payments as they are reinvested.

---

[7]Lawrence Fisher and Roman L. Weil, "Coping with Risk of Interest Rate Fluctuations: Returns to Bondholders from Naive and Optimal Strategies," *Journal of Business,* October 1971, pp. 408–31.

[8]Jess B. Yawitz and William O. Marshall, "The Shortcomings of Duration as a Risk Measure for Bonds," *Journal of Financial Research,* Summer 1981, pp. 91–101.

Table 13–9   Compound Sum of $1.00 (From Appendix A)

Period	7 Percent	8 Percent	9 Percent	10 Percent	11 Percent	12 Percent
10	$ 1.967	$ 2.159	$ 2.367	$ 2.594	$ 2.839	$ 3.106
20	3.870	4.661	5.604	6.727	8.062	9.646
30	7.612	10.063	13.268	17.449	22.892	29.960
40	14.974	21.725	31.409	45.259	65.001	93.051

Since the late 1960s, interest rates have been much higher and more volatile than during previous periods. This has caused more emphasis on the management of fixed-income securities, not only in the selection of maturity but also in the switching from short- to long-term securities. These volatile high rates have caused more emphasis on concepts like duration to measure bond price sensitivity and on total return as a measure of bond management success. Given that interest rates change daily and by large amounts over a year, what impact would a lower or higher **reinvestment assumption** have on the outcome of your retirement nest egg?

First, let us look at a partial reproduction of Appendix A at the back of the text (reproduced in Table 13–9). The material covers the compound sum of $1. Appendix A assumes all interest is reinvested at the stated rate in order to find the ending value of $1 invested to maturity. For our current analysis, we are assuming annual interest (though the answer changes only slightly if we use semiannual interest).

The table values are given in $1 amounts, so for a $1,000 bond we would just move the decimal three places to the right. A $1,000 bond having a 12 percent coupon rate with interest being reinvested at 12 percent would compound to $93,051 over 40 years, while a 7 percent coupon bond reinvested at 7 percent would compound to only $14,974 over a similar period. A difference of 5 points in the rates creates a total difference of $78,077. This is quite a large difference. Notice that the longer the compounding period, the larger the amount. From further inspection of Table 13–9, other comparisons can be made between years and total ending values.

The importance of the reinvestment assumption can also be viewed from the perspective of its contribution to total wealth. For example, an investor owning a 40-year bond with a 12 percent coupon rate and an assumed reinvestment rate of 12 percent will have an accumulated value of $93,051. In terms of payout, $4,800 (40 × $120) comes directly from 40 years of 12 percent interest payments, $1,000 comes from principal, and the balance of $87,251 comes from interest that is earned on the annual interest payments. In this case, interest on interest represents 93.8 percent of the overall return ($87,251/$93,051).

Terminal Wealth Analysis

Now, we will assume a reinvestment assumption different from the coupon rate. Take the two extreme values from Table 13–9 of 12 percent and 7 percent. Assume you buy a bond having a 12 percent coupon rate, but the interest can only be reinvested at 7 percent. To find the ending value of this investment, we will need to use a **terminal wealth table.**

Table 13–10 is called a terminal wealth table because it generates the ending value of the investment at the end of each year, assuming the bond has a *maturity* date corresponding to that year. Let's use 10 years as an example in examining Table 13–10. If the bond matures in 10 years, the $1,000 principal in column (2) will be recovered. Also the investor will receive $120 in annual interest (12 percent of $1,000) in year 10 as indicated in column (3). In column (4), the accumulated interest up to the *beginning* of year 10 is shown. The reinvestment rate on this previously accumulated interest is a mere 7 percent as indicated in column (5). The interest on the previously accumulated interest is $100.62 (0.07 × $1,437.38). Finally, the total interest for year 10 is shown in column (7). This consists of the coupon interest of $120 and the interest on interest of $100.62 and totals to $220.62. The total ending value of the portfolio is shown in column (8). The ending value consists of the recovered principal of $1,000 plus the accumulated interest of $1,437.38 up to the beginning of year 10 plus the total interest paid in year 10 of $220.62. The ending wealth value (portfolio sum) thus shown in column (8) is $2,658.00. The value is summarized below.

Recovered principal	$1,000.00	Column (2)
Accumulated interest (beginning of year 10)	1,437.38	Column (4)
Total annual interest (during year 10)	220.62	Column (7)
Ending wealth value (portfolio sum)	$2,658.00	Column (8)

A $1,000 investment that grows to $2,658.00 after 10 years is the equivalent of a $1 investment that grows to 2.65800 as indicated in column (9). The annual percentage return for a $1 investment that grows to 2.65800 after 10 years is 10.26 percent as indicated in column (10).

A similar analysis can be done for all other maturity periods running from 1 to 40 years. One thing to notice from Table 13–10 is that the longer the maturity period of the bond, the greater the effect the low 7 percent reinvestment rate has on the bond. For 5 years, the annual percentage return (column 10) is 11.06 percent; for 15 years, 9.71 percent; and for 40 years, 8.37 percent.

What is the actual difference between the ending value for a 40-year, 12 percent coupon rate bond assuming a *12 percent* reinvestment rate and the 40-year, *7 percent* reinvestment rate just presented in Table 13–10? Earlier in this section we saw in using Table 13–9 that a 12 percent coupon rate bond with an assumed 12 percent reinvestment rate for 40 years would grow to

Table 13–10   Terminal Wealth Table (12 Percent Coupon with 7 Percent Reinvestment Rate on Interest)

(1)	(2)	(3)	(4)	(5)	(6)	(7)	(8)	(9)	(10)
Years to Maturity	Principal	Annual Coupon Interest	Accumu- lated Interest*	Reinvest- ment Rate on Interest	Interest on Interest	Total Annual Interest	Portfolio Sum	Compound Sum Factor	Annual Percentage Return
0.0	$1,000.00								
1.0	1,000.00	$120.00	$ 0.00			$ 120.00	$ 1,120.00	1.12000	12.00%
2.0	1,000.00	120.00	120.00	.07	$ 8.40	128.40	1,248.40	1.24840	11.73
3.0	1,000.00	120.00	248.40	.07	17.39	137.39	1,385.79	1.38579	11.48
4.0	1,000.00	120.00	385.79	.07	27.01	147.01	1,532.80	1.53280	11.26
5.0	1,000.00	120.00	532.80	.07	37.30	157.30	1,690.10	1.69010	11.06
6.0	1,000.00	120.00	690.10	.07	48.31	168.31	1,858.41	1.85841	10.86
7.0	1,000.00	120.00	858.41	.07	60.09	180.09	2,038.50	2.03850	10.71
8.0	1,000.00	120.00	1,038.50	.07	72.70	192.70	2,231.20	2.23120	10.55
9.0	1,000.00	120.00	1,231.20	.07	86.18	206.18	2,437.38	2.43738	10.40
10.0	1,000.00	120.00	1,437.38	.07	100.62	220.62	2,658.00	2.65800	10.26
11.0	1,000.00	120.00	1,658.00	.07	116.06	236.06	2,894.06	2.89406	10.14
12.0	1,000.00	120.00	1,894.06	.07	132.58	252.58	3,146.64	3.14664	10.02
13.0	1,000.00	120.00	2,146.64	.07	150.26	270.26	3,416.90	3.41690	9.91
14.0	1,000.00	120.00	2,416.90	.07	169.18	289.18	3,706.08	3.70608	9.80
15.0	1,000.00	120.00	2,706.08	.07	189.43	309.43	4,015.51	4.01551	9.71
16.0	1,000.00	120.00	3,015.51	.07	211.09	331.09	4,346.60	4.34660	9.61
17.0	1,000.00	120.00	3,346.60	.07	234.26	354.26	4,700.86	4.70086	9.54
18.0	1,000.00	120.00	3,700.86	.07	259.06	379.06	5,079.92	5.07992	9.44
19.0	1,000.00	120.00	4,079.92	.07	285.59	405.59	5,485.51	5.48551	9.37
20.0	1,000.00	120.00	4,485.51	.07	313.99	433.99	5,919.50	5.91950	9.29
21.0	1,000.00	120.00	4,919.50	.07	344.37	464.37	6,383.87	6.38387	9.22
22.0	1,000.00	120.00	5,383.87	.07	376.87	496.87	6,880.74	6.88074	9.16
23.0	1,000.00	120.00	5,880.74	.07	411.65	531.65	7,412.39	7.41239	9.09
24.0	1,000.00	120.00	6,412.39	.07	448.87	568.87	7,981.26	7.98126	9.04
25.0	1,000.00	120.00	6,981.26	.07	488.69	608.69	8,589.95	8.58995	8.98
26.0	1,000.00	120.00	7,589.95	.07	531.30	651.30	9,241.25	9.24125	8.92
27.0	1,000.00	120.00	8,241.25	.07	576.89	696.89	9,938.14	9.93814	8.87
28.0	1,000.00	120.00	8,938.14	.07	625.67	745.67	10,683.81	10.68381	8.82
29.0	1,000.00	120.00	9,683.81	.07	677.87	797.87	11,481.68	11.48168	8.78
30.0	1,000.00	120.00	10,481.68	.07	733.72	853.72	12,335.40	12.33540	8.73
31.0	1,000.00	120.00	11,335.40	.07	793.48	913.48	13,248.88	13.24888	8.69
32.0	1,000.00	120.00	12,248.88	.07	857.42	977.42	14,226.30	14.22630	8.65
33.0	1,000.00	120.00	13,226.30	.07	925.84	1,045.84	15,272.14	15.27214	8.61
34.0	1,000.00	120.00	14,272.14	.07	999.05	1,119.05	16,391.19	16.39119	8.57
35.0	1,000.00	120.00	15,391.19	.07	1,077.38	1,197.38	17,588.57	17.58857	8.53
36.0	1,000.00	120.00	16,588.57	.07	1,161.20	1,281.20	18,869.77	18.86977	8.50
37.0	1,000.00	120.00	17,869.77	.07	1,250.88	1,370.88	20,240.65	20.24065	8.46
38.0	1,000.00	120.00	19,240.65	.07	1,346.85	1,466.85	21,707.50	21.70750	8.43
39.0	1,000.00	120.00	20,707.50	.07	1,449.53	1,569.53	23,277.03	23.27703	8.40
40.0	1,000.00	120.00	22,277.03	.07	1,559.39	1,679.39	24,956.42	24.95642	8.37

*At beginning of year.

$93,051. In Table 13–10, we see a 12 percent coupon rate bond with a 7 percent reinvestment rate will grow to only $24,956.42 after 40 years. It should be evident that it is not only the coupon rate that matters but the reinvestment rate as well.

If the bond were not held to maturity in our analysis, then we would have to rely on the realized rate of return analysis developed in Chapter 12. The realized rate of return approach would assume the bond is not held to maturity and it is sold at either a gain or a loss. In the case of the bond analyzed in the terminal wealth table (13–10), we know that since interest rates are assumed to decline, any sale of the bond before maturity should result in a capital gain. How large that capital gain would be will be dependent on its duration. Terminal wealth analysis is a way of analyzing the reinvestment assumption when bonds are held to maturity, while the realized yield approach assumes bonds are actively traded to take advantage of interest-rate swings.

Zero-Coupon Bonds and Terminal Wealth

One of the benefits of zero-coupon bonds is that they lock in a compound rate of return (or reinvestment rate) for the life of the bond *if held to maturity.* There are no coupon payments during the life of the bond to be reinvested, so the originally quoted rate holds throughout if held to maturity. If a $1,000 par value, 15-year zero-coupon bond is quoted at a price of $183 to yield 12 percent, you truly have locked in a 12 percent reinvestment rate. Some would say you have not only locked in 12 percent but have thrown away the key. In any event, zero-coupon bonds allow you to predetermine your reinvestment rate.

Of course, if a zero-coupon bond is sold before maturity, there could be large swings in the sales price of the bond because of its high duration characteristics. Under this circumstance, the locked-in reinvestment concept for the zero-coupon bond loses much of its meaning. It is valid only when the zero-coupon bond is held to maturity.

■ SUMMARY

In Chapter 13, we have taken the concepts developed in Chapter 12 and expanded on the principles of bond price volatility and total return. We developed the concept of duration so that the student has a basic understanding of what it means and some of its applications. In general, we have shown that duration is the number of years, on a present-value basis, that it takes to recover an initial investment in a bond. More specifically, each year is weighted by the present value of the cash flow as a proportion to the present value of the bond, and is then summed. The higher the duration, the more sensitive the bond price is to a change in interest rates. Duration as one number captures the three variables—maturity, coupon rate, and market rate of

interest—to indicate the price sensitivities of bonds with unequal characteristics. Generally, bond duration increases with the increase in number of years to maturity. Duration also increases as coupon rates decline to zero, and finally, duration declines as market interest rates increase.

Zero-coupon bonds are highlighted as the most price sensitive of bonds to a change in market interest rates, and comparisons are made between zero-coupon bonds and coupon bonds. Duration's primary use is in explaining price volatility, but it also has applications in the insurance industry and other areas of investments where interest-rate risk can be reduced by matching duration with predictable cash outflows in a process called immunization.

An important concept has to do with the reinvestment of interest at rates other than the coupon rate. The method used to explain the effect on the total return is terminal wealth analysis, which assumes the investment is held to maturity, and all proceeds over the life of the bond are reinvested at the reinvestment rate. In general, the longer the maturity, the more total annualized return approaches the reinvestment rate. If the reinvestment rate is significantly different from the coupon rate, the annualized return can differ greatly from the coupon rate in as little as five years.

IMPORTANT WORDS AND CONCEPTS

weighted average life 427
duration 428
immunization 439

reinvestment assumption 440
terminal wealth table 441

DISCUSSION QUESTIONS

1. Why is the weighted average life of a bond less than the maturity date?
2. Define duration.
3. How can duration be used to determine a rough measure of the percentage change in the price of a bond as a result of interest-rate changes?
4. Comment on the statement, "It is possible that a bond with a shorter maturity than another bond may actually have a longer duration and be more price sensitive to interest-rate changes." Explain why a bond with a shorter maturity than another bond could have a longer duration.
5. As market rates of interest become higher, what impact does this have on duration?
6. What happens to duration as the coupon rate on a bond issue declines from 12 percent to 0 percent with the maturity date remaining constant?

7. Why is the maturity date and duration the same for a zero-coupon bond?

8. Should an investor who thinks interest rates are going down seek low or high coupon rate bonds? Relate your answer to duration and price sensitivity.

9. Why are zero-coupon bonds the most price sensitive of any type of bond issue?

10. Why is the reinvestment rate assumption critical to bond portfolio management?

11. What is a terminal wealth table? How is terminal wealth analysis different from the realized yield approach in Chapter 12?

12. Why is it said that zero-coupon bonds lock in the reinvestment rate?

13. Is the locked-in reinvestment assumption valid for zero-coupon bonds if they are sold before maturity? Explain.

■ PROBLEMS

Weighted average life

1. Compute the simple weighted average life for the following data. Use an approach similar to that in Table 13–1.

Year	Cash flow
1	$ 115
2	115
3	115
4	115
5	115
5	1,000

Duration

2. Compute the duration for the data in Problem 1. Use an approach similar to that in Table 13–2. A discount rate of 14 percent should be applied.

Price sensitivity

3. As part of your answer to Problem 2, you computed the price of the bond (column 4). This is the same as the PV of cash flows.

   a. Recompute the price of a bond based on a 12 percent discount rate (market rate of interest).

   b. What is the percentage change in the price of the bond as interest rates decline from 14 percent to 12 percent?

   c. Approximate this same value by multiplying the duration computed in Problem 2 times the change in interest rates (2 percent). The answer in part *c* should come reasonably close to the answer in part *b*. However, they will not be exactly the same.

Comparative
duration

4. *a.* Compute the duration for the following data. Use a discount rate of 14 percent.

Year	Cash flow
1	$ 60
2	60
3	60
4	60
5	60
5	1,000

b. Explain why the answer to 4*a* is higher than the answer to Problem 2.

c. If in part 4*a*, the discount rate were 10 instead of 14 percent, would duration be longer or shorter? You do not need to actually compute a value; merely indicate an answer based on the discussion material in the text.

Comparative
duration

5. You are considering the purchase of two $1,000 bonds, both issued by Lotus Incorporated. Your expectation is that interest rates will drop and you want to buy the bond that provides the maximum capital gains potential. The first Lotus bond has a coupon rate of 5 percent with four years to maturity, while the second has a coupon rate of 14 percent and comes due six years from now. The market rate of interest (discount rate) is 10 percent. Which bond has the best price movement potential? Use duration to answer the question.

Comparative
duration

6. Assume you desire maximum duration to take advantage of anticipated interest rate declines. Answer the following questions based on information taken from Table 13–6 and Table 13–7.

a. Would you prefer an 8 percent coupon rate bond with a 20-year maturity or a 4 percent coupon rate bond with a 25-year maturity? The market rate of interest is 10 percent.

b. Would you prefer an 8 percent coupon rate bond with a 20-year maturity or a 12 percent coupon rate bond with a 25-year maturity? The market rate of interest is 12 percent.

c. Would you prefer an 8 percent coupon rate bond with a 20-year maturity or a 12 percent coupon rate bond with a 25-year maturity? The market rate of interest is 6 percent.

Zero-coupon
bond and
duration

7. A 25-year, $1,000 par value zero-coupon bond provides a yield of 12 percent.

a. Compute the current price of the zero-coupon bond. (Hint: simply take the present value of the ending $1,000 payment).

b. What is the duration of the bond?

    c. Does the bond have a longer or shorter duration than a 50-year, 8 percent coupon rate bond, where the duration on the latter bond is based on a 10 percent market rate of interest (consult Table 13–6).

    d. Assume you were going to put the zero-coupon bond(s) in a nontaxable IRA. If you wish to have $30,000 after 25 years, how much would you need to invest today?

    e. If a $1,000 par value zero-coupon rate bond had a 40-year maturity and provided a yield of 12 percent, what would be the current price of the zero-coupon bond?

Return on zero-coupon bond

8. Assume you buy a 15-year, $1,000 par value zero-coupon bond that provides a 12 percent yield. Almost immediately after you buy the bond, yields go down to 11 percent. What will be your gain on the investment?

Reinvestment assumption

9. You have invested $1,000 in a 14 percent coupon bond that matures in five years. This bond is held in your individual retirement account, and you are not concerned about tax consequences. You are investing the interest income in a money market fund earning 9 percent. At the end of five years, what will be your portfolio sum? Follow the procedure in Table 13–10.

Annual return with reinvestment assumption

10. In Problem 9, what is the annual percentage return? Use Appendix A at the end of the book to help you find the answer. An approximation will be sufficient.

■ CFA MATERIAL

The following material contains sample questions and solutions from a prior Level I CFA exam. While the terminology is slightly different from that in this text, you can still view the skills that are necessary for the CFA exam.

CFA Exam Question

Question 7 is composed of two parts, for a total of 10 minutes.

7. You are asked to consider the following bond for possible inclusion in your company's fixed-income portfolio:

Issuer	Coupon	Yield to Maturity	Maturity	Duration
Wiser Company	8%	8%	10 Years	7.25 years

    a. (I) Explain why the Wiser bond's duration is less than its maturity.
       (II) Explain whether a bond's duration or its maturity is a better measure of the bond's sensitivity to changes in interest rates.
    (4 minutes)

   b. Briefly explain the impact on the duration of the Wiser Company bond under *each* of the following conditions:
       I. The coupon is 4 percent rather than 8 percent.
       II. The yield to maturity is 4 percent rather than 8 percent.
       III. The maturity is 7 years rather than 10 years.
   (6 minutes)

Solution—Question 7—Morning Section (10 points)

a.   I. The Wiser bond's duration is less than its maturity because some of the bond's cash flow payments (i.e., the coupons) occur before maturity. Since duration measures the weighted average time until cash flow payment, its duration is less than its maturity. Bond duration is defined as

$$D = \frac{\sum\limits_{t=1}^{N} PVCF_t \times t}{\sum\limits_{t=1}^{N} PVCF_t}$$

    II. For coupon bonds, duration is a better measure of the bond's sensitivity to changes in interest rates. Using the bond's maturity is deficient as a benchmark because it measures only when the final cash flow is paid and ignores all of the interim flows. Duration is a better measure because it measures the weighted average time until cash flow and thus is a more representative measure of the bond's overall cash flow sensitivity to interest-rate changes. Duration takes into account coupon (inverse relationship) and yield to maturity (inverse relationship) as well as time to maturity.

b.   I. Duration will increase. As the coupon decreases, a proportionately higher weight is given to the redemption payment, and therefore, the duration increases.

    II. Duration will increase. As rates decline, all of the cash flows increase in value, but the longest ones increase at the greatest rate. Therefore, the redemption payment has much greater effect, causing the duration to increase.

    III. Duration will decrease. The elapsing of time is accompanied by the reduction of total coupon payments and the shortening of time until the redemption payment. Therefore, because the redemption payment comes sooner, the duration decreases.

SELECTED REFERENCES

Duration and Price Volatility

Babcock, Guilford C. "Duration as a Link between Yield and Value." *Journal of Portfolio Management,* Summer 1984, pp. 58–65.

Fabozzi, Frank J., and Irving M. Pollack, eds. "Bond Yield Measures and Price Volatility Properties." chap. 4 in *The Handbook of Fixed Income Securities.* Homewood, Ill.: Dow-Jones Irwin, 1983, pp. 53–90.

Fuller, Russell J., and John W. Settle. "Determinants of Duration and Bond Volatility." *Journal of Portfolio Management,* Summer 1984, pp. 66–72.

Hopewell, Michael H., and George G. Kaufman. "Bond Price Volatility and Term to Maturity: A Generalized Respecification." *American Economic Review,* September 1973, pp. 749–53.

Applications of Duration

Arak, Marcelle; Laurie S. Goodman; and Joseph Snailer. "Duration Equivalent Bond Swaps: A New Tool." *Journal of Portfolio Management,* Summer 1986, pp. 26–32.

Bierwag, G. O., and George G. Kaufmann. "Durations of Non-Default-Free Securities." *Financial Analysts Journal,* July–August 1988, pp. 39–46.

Dunetz, Mark L., and Mahoney, James M. "Using Duration and Convexity in the Analysis of Callable Bonds." *Financial Analysts Journal,* May–June 1988, pp. 53–72.

Nawalkha, Sanjoy K. "Convexity of Bonds with Special Cash Flow Streams." *Financial Analysts Journal,* January–February 1991, pp. 80–87.

Reilly, Frank K., and Rupindner S. Sidha. "The Many Uses of Bond Duration." *Financial Analysts Journal,* July–August 1980, pp. 58–72.

Yawitz, Jess B., and William J. Marshall. "The Use of Futures in Immunized Portfolios." *Journal of Portfolio Management,* Winter 1985, pp. 51–58.

Shortcomings in the Use of Duration Analysis

Yawitz, Jess B., and William J. Marshall, "The Shortcomings of Duration as a Risk Measure for Bonds." *Journal of Financial Research,* Summer 1981, pp. 91–101.

The Reinvestment Assumption

Bernstein, Peter L. "How to Take Reinvestment Risk without Really Trying." *Journal of Portfolio Management,* Spring 1984, p. 4.

14

Convertible Securities and Warrants

An investment in convertible securities or warrants offers the market participant special opportunities to meet investment objectives. For conservative investors, convertible securities can offer regular income and potential downside protection against falling stock prices. Convertibles also offer capital gains opportunities for an investor desiring the appreciation potential of an equity investment. Warrants are more speculative securities and offer the chance for leveraged returns.

These securities have been used as financing alternatives by corporations in periods of high interest rates or tight money. Also, convertibles have been utilized as a medium of exchange for acquiring other companies' stock in mergers and acquisitions. Convertibles and warrants have advantages to the corporation and to the owner of the security. It is important to realize as we go through this chapter that what is an advantage to the corporation is often a disadvantage to the investor, and vice versa. These securities involve trade-offs between the buyer and the corporation that are considered in the pricing of each security.

■ CONVERTIBLE SECURITIES

A **convertible security** is a bond or share of preferred stock that can be converted into common stock at the option of the holder. Thus, the owner has a fixed-income security that can be transferred to common stock if and when the performance of the firm indicate such a conversion is desirable.

For purposes of our discussion, we will use a Home Depot 6 percent convertible note. The Home Depot convertible security was originally a seven-year obligation as opposed to a long-term bond, but it demonstrates the benefits and perils of owning any convertible security. During the first 17 months of its existence (June 15, 1990, through November 4, 1991) the price ranged between $850 and $1,815.

In general, the best time to buy convertible bonds is when interest rates are high (bond prices are depressed) and when stock prices are relatively low. A purchase at times like these increases the probability of a successful investment because rising stock prices and falling interest rates both exert upward pressure on the price of a convertible security. This will become more apparent as we proceed through the chapter.

■ CONVERSION PRICE AND CONVERSION RATIO

The following quote from the footnotes to the Home Depot's *1990 Annual Report* indicates the kind of information available to the bond- or stockholder.

(The Home Depot) 6 percent convertible subordinated notes,[1] due June 15, 1997, (are) convertible into shares of common stock of the company at a conversion price

---

[1]The terms *notes* and *bonds* are used interchangeably in this discussion.

of $32.11 per share. The bonds are redeemable by The Company at a premium, plus accrued interest, beginning June 30, 1992.

While there is standard information about the coupon being 6 percent and the maturity date being June 15, 1997, one piece of information is not answered directly. How many shares of common stock are you entitled to receive on conversion? The annual report states the bonds are convertible at $32.11 per share. This is called the **conversion price.**

The face value ($1,000) or par value never changes (the market price does), so by dividing the face value by the conversion price, we get the number of shares received on conversion of one $1,000 bond. This is called the **conversion ratio.**

$$\frac{\text{Face value}}{\text{Conversion price}} = \text{Conversion ratio} \qquad (14\text{--}1)$$

For the Home Depot convertible bond, an investor would receive 31.14 shares for each bond.

$$\frac{\$1,000 \text{ (Face value)}}{\$32.11 \text{ per share (Conversion price)}} = \frac{31.14 \text{ shares}}{\text{(Conversion ratio)}}$$

Value of the Convertible Bond

The Home Depot bond was originally sold at $1,000, and the common stock price on the New York Stock Exchange on the day of this offering closed at $25.75. If the bondholder converted the bond into 31.14 shares of common stock, what would be the market value of the common stock received? We can find this by multiplying the conversion ratio by the market price per share of the common stock, and we get a value of $801.88, which we round to $802.

$$(14\text{--}2)$$

$$
\begin{array}{lll}
\text{Conversion ratio} & \times \text{ Common stock price} & = \text{Conversion Value} \\
31.14 \text{ shares} & \times \ \$25.75 & = \$801.86
\end{array}
$$

This value is called the **conversion value** and indicates the value of the underlying shares of common stock each bond represents.

The convertible bond also has what is called a **pure bond value.** This represents its value as a straight bond (nonconvertible). In the case of Home Depot, straight bonds of similar risk (BBB rating) had a yield to maturity of about 10.9 percent at the time of issue. If the Home Depot 6 percent convertible bond were valued at a 10.9 percent yield to maturity, the pure bond value would be $764.[2] This pure bond value is considered the **floor value,** or minimum value, of the bond. The conversion value and the pure bond value can

---

[2]Using present value procedures from Chapter 12, the interest payment of $60 per year ($30 semiannually) for seven years would have a present value at 10.9% compounded semiannually of $288.60, and the principal of $1,000 would have a present value of $475.76 for a total value of $764.36. We round to $764.

be seen in Figure 14–1, which depicts the Home Depot convertible note. The reader should be aware that it is possible for the pure bond value to change if interest rates in the market change. In other words, the pure bond value will be inversely related to changes in interest rates just like any other fixed-income security. This point is not reflected in Figure 14–1.

In examining Figure 14–1, you can see that the market price of the bond will not go below the pure bond value regardless of what happens to the price of the common stock. If the stock price went down to $10 and the conversion value fell to $311.40 ($10 times 31.14 shares), the market value of the bond would at least equal its pure bond value of $764. The convertibility of the bond loses much of its meaning at low stock prices, and the pure bond value is the controlling factor on price. Of course, if the common stock goes up to $55 or $60 per share, the market price of the bond will approach $2,000 because of the attractive conversion feature. At a high bond price, the pure bond value of $764 loses much of its meaning. When a bond is selling at $2,000, it is little comfort to know the bond has a pure bond value or floor price of $764. You would lose $1,236 before the bond got down to the floor price.

In summary, you can see in Figure 14–1 that if the stock price is low or declining, pure bond value is very important in determining the bond price. When stock prices are booming, the conversion value is the controlling factor.

Bond Price and Premiums

You may wonder how a company can originally sell a bond for $1,000 with both a conversion value of $802 (rounded) and pure bond value of $764. Let's examine these values. The difference between the bond's market price ($1,000) and the conversion value ($802) is a premium of $198; it is usually expressed as a percentage of the conversion value and thus is called the **conversion premium.** In this case, the conversion premium at issue was 24.69 percent.

$$(14–3)$$

$$\text{Conversion premium} = \frac{\text{Market price of bond} - \text{Conversion value}}{\text{Conversion value}}$$

$$= \frac{\$1,000 - \$802}{\$802} = \frac{\$198}{\$802}$$

$$= 24.69\%$$

The $198 premium indicates the extra amount paid for the 31.14 shares of stock. Remember, in essence, you paid $32.11 per share for 31.14 shares by purchasing the bond at $1,000; you could have had the same number of shares purchased on the NYSE for $25.75 and had $198 in cash left. Instead, the investor buying the convertible security paid a premium for the benefits this type of security offers.

People pay the conversion premium for several reasons. In the case of Home Depot's convertible note, the premium is somewhat larger than the usual 20

Figure 14–1   Home Depot 6% Convertible Bond on Day of Issue (June 29, 1990)

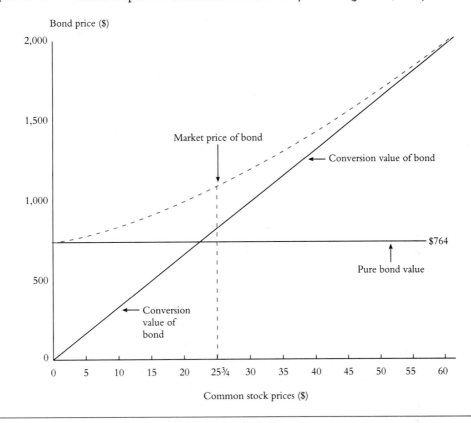

On the day of issue, the conversion value and pure bond value were both $802.

percent. First, at the time, Home Depot common stock paid $.08 per share in dividends ($.08 × 31.14) or approximately $2.50 per year for 31.14 shares. The bond paid $60 per year. If the bondholder owns the bond for a little over three years, he recovers almost all the premium through the differential between interest and dividend income. This analysis of interest income versus dividend income is always important in comparing a stock purchase to a convertible bond purchase.

Additionally, the bond price will rise as the stock price rises because of the convertible feature, but there is a downside limit if the stock should decline in price. This **downside limit** is established by the pure bond value, which in this case is $764. This downside protection is further justification for the conversion premium. One way to compute this downside protection is to calculate the difference between the market price of the bond and pure bond value as a percentage of the market price. We call this measure **downside risk.**

$$\text{Downside risk} = \frac{\text{Market price of bond} - \text{Pure bond value}}{\text{Market price of bond}} \quad (14\text{--}4)$$

$$= \frac{\$1,000 - \$764}{\$1,000}$$

$$= \frac{\$236}{\$1,000} = 23.60\%$$

Home Depot has a downside risk of 23.60 percent, which is the maximum percentage the bond will decline in value if the stock price falls. One important warning is necessary—the pure bond value is sensitive to market interest rates. As competitively rated BBB bond interest rates rise, the pure bond value will decline. Therefore, downside risk can vary with changing interest rates.

The conversion premium is also affected by several other variables. The more volatile the stock price as measured by beta or standard deviation of returns, the higher the conversion premium. This occurs because the potential for capital gains is larger than on less volatile stocks. The longer the term to maturity, the higher the premium—because there is a greater chance the stock price could rise, making the bond more valuable.

Figure 14–2 presents a graph of the Home Depot convertible note and depicts the conversion premium in panel (*a*) and the downside risk in panel (*b*). Note in panel (*a*), as the stock price gets higher, the conversion premium the investor is willing to pay becomes lower. This is because the investor is getting almost no downside protection. This is confirmed by the presence of large downside risk at high stock prices in panel (*b*).

You can track the actual performance of the Home Depot bonds in Table 14–1. The analysis is over a 16-month period.

Note between June 29, 1990, and October 12, 1990, the common stock price fell sharply from $25.75 to $19.16. That's a decline of $6.59, or 25.59 percent. Because the conversion ratio remained constant at 31.14, the conversion value fell by an equal percentage amount. However, the actual bonds only

Table 14–1   Home Depot Convertible Bond Price Performance

	June 29, 1990	October 12, 1990	November 4, 1991
Market price of bonds	$1,000.00	$860.00	$1,745.00
Common stock price	$ 25.75	$ 19.16	$ 55.50
Conversion ratio	31.14	31.14	31.14
Conversion value	$ 802.00	$596.64	$1,728.27
Conversion premium	24.69%	44.14%	0.97%
Pure bond value	$ 764.00	$780.00	$ 910.00
Downside risk	23.60%	9.30%	47.85%

Figure 14–2   Home Depot Convertible Bond—6 Percent, 1997 Maturity (Convertible into 31.14 Shares of Common Stock)

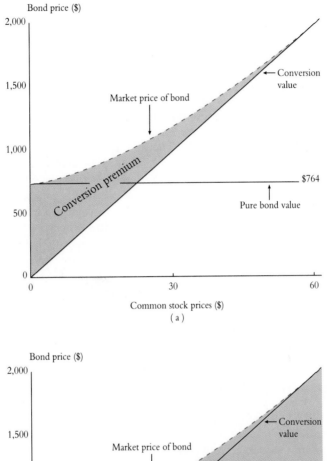

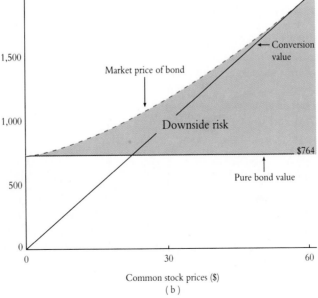

fell 14 percent from $1,000 to $860. That's because they had the security of a pure bond value on October 12, 1990, of $780 to back them up.

By November 4, 1991, the stock had demonstrated a superior performance, increasing from $19.16 on October 12, 1990, to $55.50 in November of the following year. This increase in stock value helped trigger an increase in the convertible bond value to $1,745.00. At this lofty price, the conversion premium declined to a mere 0.97 percent. One primary reason was that the downside risk measure was up to 47.85 percent. No one wants to pay much of a premium for so little protection.

Notice also that the pure bond value increased over the period of this analysis, indicating a general decline in interest rates.

In November 1991, the bonds were callable at 104 (104 percent of par) or $1,040. Suppose Home Depot calls the bonds; what action would an owner take? You have the choice of receiving 31.14 shares worth $1,728.27 or receiving $1,040 in cash. It should be obvious that the 31.14 shares are the best choice. If the company would call the bonds, all convertible bondholders would be "forced" to take the shares of common stock to maximize their value. This is called a **forced conversion** when the company calls the convertible security knowing the owners will take stock and thus convert debt to equity. The advantage to the company's balance sheet is an obvious reduction in the debt-to-equity ratio and less financial risk.

Comparison to Common Stock

Would you have been better off putting $1,000 in Home Depot common stock on June 29, 1990, or $1,000 in the convertible note? One thousand dollars in Home Depot stock at $25.75 would have purchased 38.83 shares, while $1,000 invested in the note got the investor 31.14 shares. On November 4, 1991, a stock investment would have been worth $2,155 plus $4.14 in dividends for a total of $2,159, and the convertible note would be worth $1,728 plus approximately $80 in interest income over the 16 months for a total of $1,808. The common stock investor would have been better off, but if the stock had gone down sharply, then the convertible with its floor value would have been the better investment. Table 14–2 shows the comparison between a stock investment and the convertible bond investment.

Table 14–2		Comparative Home Depot Incorporated Investments				
	Amount Invested June 1990	Shares	Stock Prices November 1991	Ending Value	Total Dividends or Interest	Total Value
Stock	$1,000	38.83	$55.50	$2,155	$ 4.14	$2,159
Bond	$1,000	31.14	$55.50	$1,728	$80.00	$1,808

Table 14–3 Selected Convertible Bonds and Preferred Stock

Selected Convertible Bonds—October 1991

Issue	Coupon	Maturity	Moody's Bond Rating	Bond Price	Conversion Price	Conversion Ratio	Common Stock Price	Conversion Value	Conversion Premium	Pure Bond Value	Stock Dividend Yield	Current Bond Yield	Call Price*
Ames Department Stores	7.5%	2014	Ca	$ 72.50	$21.50	46.51	$ 1.00	$ 46.50	56%	NMF	nil	NMF	NMF
Avnet	6	2012	A2	822.50	43.00	23.26	25.25	587.20	40	$730.00	2.4%	7.3%	$103.60
Bally MFG Corp.	10	2006	Ca	550.00	32.68	30.60	3.63	110.90	396	NMF	nil	NMF	103.97
Bank of Florida	9	2003	N.R.	447.50	22.16	45.13	2.88	129.70	245	450.00	nil	20.1	101.80
Bolt, Bernack, and Newman	6	2012	B2	628.80	30.00	33.33	5.75	191.70	228	560.00	1.0	9.5	103.60
Businessland	5.5	2007	Caa	492.50	20.50	48.78	.88	42.70	1053	NMF	nil	11.2	103.30
Champion Int'l Group	5	2011	Baa2	938.80	34.75	28.78	25.75	741.00	27	740.00	.8	6.9	103.25
Circle K Corp.	8.3	2005	C	75.00	13.36	74.85	.94	70.02	7	NMF	nil	NMF	103.30
Dana Corp.	5.9	2006	Baa1	732.50	50.43	19.83	28.38	562.60	30	570.00	5.6	8.0	100.00

Selected Convertible Preferred Stocks—October 1991

Issue	Dividend	Call Date	Preferred Stock Price	Common Stock Price	Conversion Ratio	Conversion Value	Conversion Premium	Pure Value†	Common Stock Dividend Yield	Preferred Stock Dividend Yield
Cooper Industries	$1.60	12-31-94	$31.25	$50.75	.550	$27.91	12%	$18.00	2.3%	5.1%
Metropolitan Financial Corp.	2.00	10-31-96	32.00	19.25	1.565	30.13	6	15.00	2.2	6.3
Norwest Corp.	3.50	09-01-95	53.75	32.75	1.372	44.93	20	40.00	2.8	6.5
Sea Containers	4.00	07-15-94	23.63	23.63	1.730	40.87	23	33.00	3.0	8.0
Tosco Corp.	4.38	08-15-94	22.25	22.25	2.083	46.35	31	30.00	2.7	7.2

*Percent of par value of $1,000.
†Value based strictly on dividend-paying level of the preferred stock.
Sources: *Moody's Bond Record* and *Value Line Convertible Index.*

459

The trade-off the investor makes in the stock versus the convertible security decision is whether to buy stock receiving more shares and a lower cash flow from dividends or to buy the convertible security with its option of fewer shares but higher cash flow from interest payments. In this case, the cash flow difference between dividends and interest was approximately $76 over this time period.

Table 14–3 presents a selection of convertible bonds and preferred stock and helps to illustrate several basic points. First, notice no bonds are rated Aa, or Aaa. While an occasional convertible bond like the Avnet 6%, 2012 carries an A2 rating, in general, convertible bonds are usually lower-quality subordinated debentures. Notice a number of bonds have conversion premiums of over 200 percent. This indicates the stock price has fallen since the original issue and the bond price is trading based on its pure bond value (investment value) or interest-paying ability rather than the stock price. The conversion value is extremely low relative to the bond price, and the common stock price would have to go up sharply before an investor would begin to benefit from an increased bond price.

The Circle K Corp. bond and the Metropolitan Financial Corp. preferred stock (bottom of table) both have very low conversion premiums of about 6 to 7 percent, which indicates these securities are selling close to their conversion value. In the case of Circle K, the bond is selling almost entirely on its stock price because it is the expectation that this C-rated bond will not pay its interest of $83, which by itself would be worth more than the bond price of $75.

Disadvantages to Convertibles

It has been said that everything has a price, and purchasing convertible securities at the wrong price can eliminate one of their main advantages. For example, once convertible bonds begin going up in value, or the pure bond value declines substantially, the downside protection becomes meaningless. In the case of Champion International Group, in Table 14–3, the market price of the bond is $938.80, while the pure bond value is $740. If the investor buys the bond at $938.80 and the common stock declines significantly, the investor is exposed to a potential decline of almost $200 (hardly adequate protection for a true risk averter). Also, don't forget that if market yields rise, the floor price or pure bond value could decline from $740, thus creating even greater downside risk.

Another drawback with convertible bonds is that the purchaser is invariably asked to accept below-market yields on the debt instrument. The interest rate on convertibles is generally one third below that for instruments in a similar risk class (perhaps 6 percent instead of 9 percent). Figure 14–3 (upper part) illustrates the yield spreads between corporate BBB bonds, corporate AAA bonds, 6-month Treasury bills, and the Value Line's Convertible Index. As indicated in the bottom panel of the figure, the yield spread between corporate BBB and convertibles was between 200 and 700 basis points between 1984 and

Figure 14–3   Yield Spreads

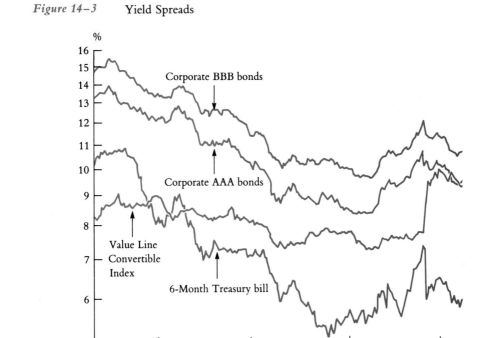

Interest rates

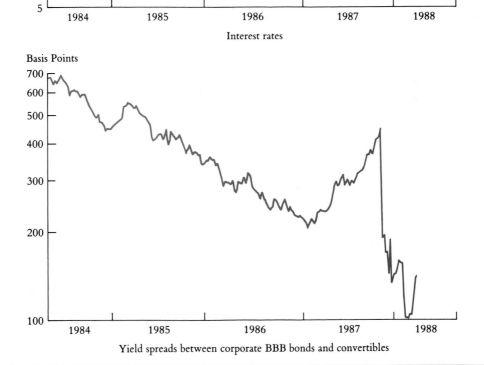

Yield spreads between corporate BBB bonds and convertibles

1987, but the crash of 1987 forced up the yields on convertibles to within 100 basis points of BBB bonds. This relationship is quite unusual because convertible bonds are usually priced to yield substantially less than straight corporate bonds. Since convertibles are generally high-risk bonds, the fear generated by the crash caused the normal yield relationships to vanish as investors refused to hold convertibles at substantially lower yields.

Recall that the purchaser of a convertible bond pays a premium over the conversion value. For example, if a $1,000 bond were convertible into 20 shares of common at $45 per share, a $100 conversion premium would be involved initially. If the same $1,000 were invested directly in common stock at $45 per share, 22.2 shares could be purchased. If the shares go up in value, we have 2.2 more shares on which to garner a profit.

From the institutional investor's standpoint, many convertible securities lack liquidity because of small trading volume or even the small amount of convertibles issued by one company. The institutions tend to stick with convertible issues of $100 million or more when they can be found.

When to Convert into Common Stock

Convertible securities generally have a call provision, such as the Home Depot bond had (in the earlier description), which gives the corporation the option of redeeming the bond at a specified price before maturity. The call price is usually at a premium over par value ($1,000) in the early years of callability, and it generally declines over time to par value. We know that as the price of the common stock goes up, the convertible security will rise along with the stock so the investor has no incentive to convert bonds into stock. However, the corporation may use the call privilege to force conversion before maturity. Companies usually force conversion when the conversion value is well above the call price. Investors will take the shares rather than the call price since the shares are worth more. This enables the company to turn debt into equity on its balance sheet and makes new debt issues a better risk for future lenders because of higher interest coverage and a lower debt-to-equity ratio.

Corporations may also encourage voluntary conversion by using a step-up in the conversion price over time. When the bond is issued, the contract may specify the following conversion provisions.

	Conversion Price	Conversion Ratio
First five years	$40	25.0 shares
Next three years	45	22.2 shares
Next two years	50	20.0 shares
Next five years	55	18.2 shares

At the end of each time period, there is a strong inducement to convert rather than accept an adjustment to a higher conversion price and a lower conversion ratio. This is especially true if the bond's conversion value is the dominating influence on the market price of the bond. In the case where the conversion value is below the pure bond value and where the interest income is greater than the dividend income, an investor will most likely not be induced to convert through the step-up feature.

About the only other reason for voluntarily converting is if the dividend income received on the common stock is greater than the interest income on the bond. Even in this case, risk-averse investors may want to hold the bond because interest is guaranteed, whereas dividends may be reduced. As with most investment decisions, investors must consider their expectations of future corporate and market conditions. Hard-and-fast rules are difficult to find, and different investors may react according to their own risk aversion and objectives.

■ ADVANTAGES AND DISADVANTAGES TO THE ISSUING CORPORATION

Having established the fundamental characteristics of the convertible security from the investor viewpoint, let us now examine the factors a corporate financial officer must consider in weighing the advisability of a convertible offer for the firm.

It has been established that the interest rate paid on convertible issues is lower than that paid on a straight debt instrument. Also, the convertible feature may be the only device for allowing smaller corporations access to the bond market. In this day of debt-ridden corporate balance sheets, investor acceptance of new debt may be contingent on a special sweetener, such as the ability to convert to common stock.

Convertible bonds are also attractive to a corporation that believes its stock is undervalued. For example, assume a corporation's $1,000 bonds are convertible into 20 shares of common stock at a conversion price of $50. Also assume the company's common stock has a current price of $45, and new shares of stock might be sold at only $44.[3] Thus, the corporation will effectively receive $6 over current market price, assuming future conversion. Of course, one can also argue that if the firm had delayed the issuance of common stock or convertibles for a year or two, the stock might have gone up from $45 to $60 or $65, and new common stock might have been sold at this lofty price.

To translate this to overall numbers for the firm, if a corporation needs $10 million in funds and offers straight stock now at a new price of $44, it must issue 227,272 shares ($10 million/$44 per share). With convertibles, the number of shares potentially issued is only 200,000 shares ($10 million/$50 per share). Finally, if no stock or convertible bonds are issued now and the stock

---

[3]There is always a bit of underpricing to ensure the success of a new offering.

goes up to a level at which new shares can be offered at a price of $60, only 166,667 will be required ($10 million/$60).

Another matter of concern to the corporation is the accounting treatment accorded to convertibles. In the funny-money days of the 1960s' conglomerate merger movement, corporate management often chose convertible securities over common stock because the convertibles had a nondilutive effect on earnings per share. As is indicated in the following section on reporting earnings for convertibles, the rules were changed in 1969.

■ ACCOUNTING CONSIDERATIONS WITH CONVERTIBLES

Before 1969, the full impact of the conversion privilege as it applied to convertible securities, warrants (long-term options to buy stock), and other dilutive securities was not adequately reflected in reported earnings per share. Since all of these securities may generate additional common stock in the future, the potential effect of this **dilution** should be considered. Let us examine the unadjusted (for conversion) financial statements of the XYZ Corporation in Table 14–4.

An analyst would hardly be satisfied in accepting the unadjusted earnings per share figure of $1.50 for the XYZ Corporation. In computing earnings per share, we have not accounted for the 400,000 additional shares of common stock that could be created by converting the bonds. How then do we make this full disclosure? According to *APB Opinion No. 15,* issued by the American Institute of Certified Public Accountants in 1969, we need to compute earnings per share using two different methods when there is potential dilution: **primary earnings per share** and **fully diluted earnings per share.**

1. Primary earnings per share

$$= \frac{\text{Adjusted earnings after taxes}}{\text{Shares outstanding} + \text{Common stock equivalents}} \qquad (14\text{--}5)$$

Common stock equivalents include warrants, other options, and any convertible securities that paid less than two thirds of the going interest rate at time of issue.[4]

2. Fully diluted earnings per share

$$= \frac{\text{Adjusted earnings after taxes}}{\substack{\text{Shares outstanding} + \text{Common stock equivalents} \\ + \text{ All convertibles regardless of the interest rate}}} \qquad (14\text{--}6)$$

The intent in computing both primary and fully diluted earnings per share is to consider the effect of potential dilution. Common stock equivalents represent those securities that are capable of generating new shares of common stock in the future. Note that convertible securities may or may not be re-

---

[4]The going interest rate was initially defined as the prime interest rate in *APB Opinion No. 15* (1969). In 1982, the Financial Accounting Standards Board defined the going interest rate as the average Aa bond yield at the time of issue.

Table 14–4   XYZ Corporation

1. Capital section of balance sheet:

   Common stock (1 million shares at $10 par) $10,000,000

   4.5% convertible debentures (10,000 debentures of $1,000;
   convertible into 40 shares per bond, or a total of 400,000 shares) 10,000,000

   Retained earnings 20,000,000

   Net worth $40,000,000

2. Condensed income statement:

   Earnings before interest and taxes .... $ 2,950,000

   Interest (4.5% of $10 million of convertibles) 450,000

   Earnings before taxes .... $ 2,500,000

   Taxes (40%) 1,000,000

   Earnings after taxes .... $ 1,500,000

3. Earnings per share (unadjusted):

$$\frac{\text{Earnings after taxes}}{\text{Shares of common stock}} = \frac{\$1,500,000}{1,000,000} = \$1.50$$

---

quired in computing primary earnings per share depending on rates, but they must be included in computing fully diluted earnings per share.

In the case of the XYZ Corporation in Table 14–4, the convertibles pay 4.5 percent interest. We assume the going interest rate was 9 percent at the time they were issued, so they are considered as common stock equivalents and are included in both primary and fully diluted earnings per share.

We get new earnings per share for the XYZ Corporation by assuming 400,000 new shares will be created from potential conversion, while at the same time, allowing for the reduction in interest payments that would occur as a result of the conversion of the debt to common stock. Since before-tax interest payments on the convertibles are $450,000, the after-tax interest cost ($270,000) will be saved and can be added back to income. After-tax interest cost is determined by multiplying interest payments by one minus the tax rate or $450,000 (1 − .4) = $270,000. Making the appropriate adjustments to the numerator and denominator, we show adjusted earnings per share.

$$\frac{\text{Primary earnings}}{\text{per share}^5} = \frac{\text{Adjusted earnings after taxes}}{\text{Shares outstanding} + \text{Common stock equivalents}}$$

$$= \frac{\overset{\text{Reported earnings}}{\$1,500,000} + \overset{\text{Interest savings}}{\$270,000}}{1,000,000 + 400,000} = \frac{\$1,770,000}{1,400,000} = \$1.26$$

---

[5]Same as fully diluted in this instance.

We see a 24-cent reduction from the earnings per share figure of $1.50 in Table 14–4. The new figure is the value that a sophisticated security analyst would utilize.

■ INNOVATIONS IN CONVERTIBLE SECURITIES

Not all convertible securities are convertible into the common stock of the company issuing the convertible. Some convertibles are convertible into bonds, preferred stock, stock of another company, or another type of asset.

Another type of new convertible security bears mentioning. For many companies recovering from years of losses and having tax-loss carryforwards, "convertible exchangeable preferred stock" is a security that can improve the firm's balance sheet and provide high returns to investors. A firm with losses does not need tax-deductible interest expenses but does need balanced financing. Since no taxes are due, preferred dividends are no different than interest expenses to the issuing company. When the issuing firm becomes taxable again, it can exchange the preferred stock for debt with the same conversion ratio and then can utilize the tax savings from the deductible interest expense. The exchange occurs without the cost of new underwriting fees.

■ SPECULATING THROUGH WARRANTS

A **warrant** is an option to buy a stated number of shares of stock at a specified price over a given time period. The nine warrants listed in Table 14–5 demonstrate the relationships discussed in the following sections. For example, Go-Video, a once hot stock listed as number 6 in Table 14–5, is selling for $.75 per share on October 21, 1991. The table lists a warrant currently available for the firm that allows the holder to buy the stock for $8.25 (column 4) until March 9, 1995. The common stock price would have to rise considerably for the warrant to have any value. If Go-Video can return to profitability, the common stock could rise above $8.25 per share, and the warrants could become valuable. If the stock does not eventually rise above the option price, Go-Video could extend the expiration date of the warrant. Some investors are willing to pay $.38 (column 2) for each warrant with the hope that the stock price will be over $8.25 before the warrant expires. Anything can happen in the stock market, and someone is willing to place bets on Go-Video.

Warrants are usually issued as a sweetener to a bond offering, and they may enable the firm to issue debt when this would not be feasible otherwise. The warrants allow the bond issue to carry a lower coupon rate and are usually detachable from the bond after the issue date. After being separated from the bond, warrants have their own market price and may trade on a different market than the common stock. After the warrants are exercised, the initial debt with which they were sold remains in existence.

The financial company Bache Group (now Prudential Securities) had a bond offering October 30, 1980. It offered 35,000 units of $1,000 debentures due in

Table 14–5   Selected Warrants as of October 21, 1991

(1) Name of Firm, Place of Warrant Listing, and Stock Listing*	(2) Warrant Price	(3) Per Share Stock Price	(4) Per Share Option Price	(5) Intrinsic Value† [(3) − (4)]	(6) Speculative Premium [(2) − (5)]	(7) Percentage Stock Must Rise to Break Even	(8) Number of Shares per Warrant	(9) Due Date
1. Allou Health and Beauty Care, ASE, ASE	$ 2.00	$ 6.63	$ 5.00	$ 1.63	$ .37	5.6%	1	07/10/94
2. BankAmerica, NYSE, OTC	21.50	40.13	17.50	22.63	0	−2.8%	1	10/22/97
3. Bank of New York, NYSE, OTC	3.00	31.63	62.00	0	3.00	105.5%	1	11/29/98
4. Biogen, OTC, OTC	20.00	36.00	20.00	16.00	4.00	11.1%	1	06/30/94
5. Canyon Resources, OTC, OTC	.50	1.81	3.50	0	.50	121.0%	1	12/31/94
6. Go-Video, ASE, ASE	.38	.75	8.25	0	.38	1050.7%	1	03/09/95
7. Hotel Investors, ASE, NYSE	.05	1.50	16.95	0	.05	1033.3%	1	09/14/96
8. Manville, NYSE, NYSE	2.00	6.50	9.40	0	2.00	75.4%	1	06/05/96
9. Wheeling-Pittsburgh, NYSE, NYSE	1.63	6.50	6.39	.11	1.52	23.4%	1	01/31/96

*OTC = Over-the-counter market, NYSE = New York Stock Exchange, ASE = American Stock Exchange
†When column 4 is larger than column 3, the intrinsic value will calculate as a negative number. Since the intrinsic value of a warrant cannot be less than worthless, we put a zero in column 5 in these cases.
Source: *Value Line Convertible Index*

the year 2000 with a coupon interest rate of 14 percent. To each bond, 30 warrants were attached. Each warrant allowed the holder to buy one share of stock at $18.50 until November 1, 1985. At the time of issue, the warrant had no true value since the common stock was selling below $18.50. During 1981, however, the stock went up as several merger offers were made for retail brokerage companies. On May 29, 1981, Bache common stock was selling at 31½, and each warrant traded at 13⅝. The 30 warrants received with each bond were now worth $408.75 and provided the sweetener every bondholder had hoped for.

Because a warrant is dependent on the market movement of the underlying common stock and has no "security value" as such, it is highly speculative. If the common stock of the firm is volatile, the value of the warrants may change dramatically.

Valuation of Warrants

Because the value of a warrant is closely tied to the underlying stock price, we can develop a formula for the minimum or intrinsic value of a warrant.

$$I = (M - OP) \times N \tag{14-7}$$

where:

I = The intrinsic or minimum value of the warrant

M = The market value of the common stock

OP = The option or exercise price of the warrant

N = The number of shares each warrant entitles the holder to purchase

Assume the common stock of the Graham Corporation is $25 per share, and each warrant carries an option to purchase one share at $20 over the next 10 years. The purchase price stipulated in the warrant is the **option** or **exercise price.** Using Formula 14–7, the intrinsic value is $5 [($25 − $20) × 1]. The **intrinsic value** in this case is equal to the market price of the common stock minus the option price of the warrant. Since the warrant has 10 more years to run and is an effective vehicle for speculative trading, it may well trade for over $5. If the warrant were selling for $9, we would say it had an intrinsic value of $5 and a speculative premium of $4. The **speculative premium** is equal to the price of the warrant minus the intrinsic value.

Even if the stock were trading at less than $20 (the option price on the warrant), the warrant might still have some value in the market. Speculators might purchase the warrant in the hope that the common stock value would increase sufficiently to make the option provision valuable. If the common stock were selling for $15 per share, thus giving the warrant a negative intrinsic value of $5, the warrant might still command a value of $1 or $2 in anticipation of increased common stock value.

Figure 14–4 Market Price Relationships for a Warrant

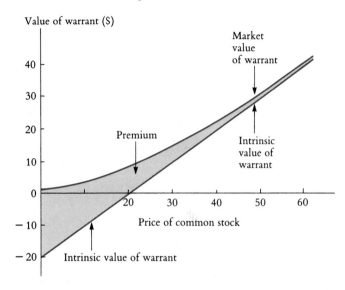

In many cases, firms would have negative intrinsic values because the stock price is below the warrant's option price, but a warrant cannot be more than worthless, so a zero value is denoted for the intrinsic value, as shown in Table 14–5 on page 467. In many cases, firms with zero intrinsic values still have large speculative premiums. This is true even when the stock price has to more than double in price by expiration before the warrant breaks even on the original investment. This **warrant break-even** can be calculated by adding the speculative premium to the option price (exercise price).

As an example of an extreme case, the Bank of New York's common stock was trading $30.37 below the exercise price of $62.00 on the warrant, and yet the warrant still traded for $3. Bank of New York common stock would have to rise $33.37 ($30.37 + $3.00) before the warrant holder would break even. This would be a 105 percent increase on the $31.63 stock price. The Bank of New York warrant is due to expire November 29, 1998, so a warrant holder has seven years to wait for a profit. If the economy recovers and banks return to profitability, a doubling in price could take much less than seven years and handsomely reward the warrant holder for the $3 investment.

The typical relationship between the market price and the intrinsic value of a warrant is depicted in Figure 14–4. We assume the warrant entitles the holder to purchase one new share of common stock at $20.

Although the intrinsic value of the warrant is theoretically negative at a common stock price between 0 and $20, the warrant still carries some value in

Table 14–6	Leverage in Valuing Warrants

(A)	(B)
Stock price = $25; warrant price = $5* + 10-point movement in stock price. New warrant price = $15 (10-point gain)	Stock price = $50; warrant price = $30 + 10-point movement in stock price. New warrant price = $40 (10-point gain)
$$\text{Percentage gain in warrant} = \frac{\$10}{\$5} \times 100 = 200\%$$	$$\text{Percentage gain in warrant} = \frac{\$10}{\$30} \times 100 = 33\%$$

*The warrant price would, of course, be greater than $5 because of a premium. Nevertheless, we use $5 for ease of computation.

the market. Also, observe that the difference between the market price of the warrant and its intrinsic value is diminished at the upper ranges of value. Two reasons may be offered for this declining premium.

First, the speculator loses the ability to use leverage to generate high returns as the price of the stock goes up. When the price of the stock is relatively low, say, $25, and the warrant is in the $5 to $10 range, a 10-point movement in the stock could mean a 200 percent gain in the value of the warrant, as indicated in Part A of Table 14–6. At the upper levels of stock value, much of this leverage is lost, as indicated in Part B of the table. At a stock value of $50 and a warrant value of approximately $30, a 10-point movement in the stock would produce only a 33 percent gain in the warrant.

Another reason speculators pay a very low premium at higher stock prices is that there is less downside protection. A warrant selling at $30 when the stock price is $50 is more vulnerable to downside movement than is a $5 to $10 warrant when the stock is in the 20s.

Warrant premiums are also influenced by the same factors that affect convertible bond premiums. More volatile common stocks will have greater potential to create short-run profits for warrant speculators, so the higher the price volatility, the greater the premium. Also, the longer the option has before expiration, the higher the premium will be. This "time premium" is worth more the longer the common stock has to reach and surpass the option price of the warrant.

Use of Warrants by Corporations

As previously indicated, warrants may allow for the issuance of debt under difficult circumstances. While a straight debt issue may not be acceptable or may be accepted only at extremely high rates, the same security may be well received because detachable warrants are included. Warrants may also be included as an add-on in a merger or acquisition agreement. A firm might offer $20 million in cash plus 10,000 warrants in exchange for all the outstanding shares of the acquisition candidate.

The use of warrants has traditionally been associated with such aggressive, "high-flying" firms as biotechs, airlines, and conglomerates.

As a financing device for creating new common stock, warrants may not be as desirable as convertible securities. A corporation with convertible bonds outstanding may force the conversion of debt to common stock through a call, while no similar device is available to the firm with warrants. The only possible inducement might be a step up in the option price—whereby the warrant holder must pay a progressively higher option price if he does not exercise by a given date.

The capital structure of the firm after the exercise of a warrant also is somewhat different from that created after the conversion of a debenture. In the case of a warrant, the original debt outstanding remains in existence after the detachable warrant is exercised, whereas the conversion of a debenture extinguishes the former debt obligation.[6]

■ ACCOUNTING CONSIDERATIONS WITH WARRANTS

As with convertible securities, the potential dilutive effect of warrants must be considered. Warrants are generally included in computing both primary and fully diluted earnings per share.[7] The accountant must compute the number of new shares that could be created by the exercise of all warrants, with the provision that the total can be reduced by the assumed use of the cash proceeds to purchase a partially offsetting amount of shares at the market price. Assume that warrants to purchase 10,000 shares at $20 are outstanding and the current price of the stock is $50. We show the following:

1. New shares created	10,000
2. Reduction of shares from cash proceeds (computed below)	4,000
Cash proceeds—10,000 shares at $20 = $200,000	
Current price of stock—$50	
Assumed reduction in shares outstanding from cash proceeds = $200,000/$50 = 4,000	
3. Assumed net increase in shares from exercise of warrants (10,000 − 4,000)	6,000

In computing earnings per share, we will add 6,000 shares to the denominator with no adjustment to the numerator, which will lower earnings per share. If earnings per share had previously been $1 based on $100,000 in earnings and 100,000 shares outstanding, EPS would now be reduced to $.943.

---

[6]A number of later financing devices can blur this distinction. See Jerry Miller, "Accounting for Warrants and Convertible Bonds," *Management Accounting,* January 1973, pp. 36–38.

[7]Under some circumstances, where the market price is below the option price, dilution need not be considered (*APB Opinion No. 15*).

$$\frac{\text{Earnings}}{\text{Shares}} = \frac{\$100,000}{106,000} = \$.943$$

With warrants included in computing both primary and fully diluted earnings per share, their impact on reported earnings is important from both the investor and corporate viewpoints.

■ SUMMARY

Convertible securities and warrants offer the investor an opportunity for participating in increased common stock values without owning common stock directly. Convertible securities may be in the form of debt or preferred stock, though most of our examples refer to debt.

Convertible securities provide a guaranteed income stream and a floor value based on required yield on the investment. At the same time, they have an established conversion ratio to common stock (par value/conversion price). The conversion value of an issue is equal to the conversion ratio times the current value of a share of common stock. The conversion value is generally less than the current market price of the convertible issue. Actually, the difference between the market price of the convertible issue and the conversion value is referred to as the conversion premium. The conversion premium is influenced by the volatility of the underlying common stock, the time to maturity, the dividend payment on common stock relative to the interest rate on the convertibles, and other lesser factors. Generally, when the common stock price has risen well above the conversion price (and the convertible is trading well above par), the conversion premium will be quite small, as indicated in the left-hand portion of Figure 14–2. The small premium is attributed to the fact that the investor no longer enjoys significant downside protection.

A convertible issue is considered to be potentially dilutive to the reported earnings of the corporation, and since 1969, primary and/or fully diluted earnings per share must consider the impact of potential conversion. Actually, the corporation may ultimately have the opportunity to force conversion through calling the issue at slightly over par when, in fact, it is selling at a substantially higher price. In the absence of a call, there is generally little incentive to convert since the convertible security will move up and down with the common stock issue.

A warrant is an option to buy a stated number of shares of stock (usually one) at a specified price over a given time period. Warrants are often issued as a sweetener to a bond issue and may allow the firm to issue debt where it would not normally be feasible. The warrants are generally detachable from the bond issue. Thus, if the warrants are exercised, the bond issue still remains in existence (this is clearly different from a convertible security). The difference between the market price of a warrant and its minimum or intrinsic value represents a premium that the investor is willing to pay. This premium rep-

resents the speculative potential in the warrant. Warrants are dilutive to earnings and must generally be considered in computing primary and fully diluted earnings per share.

IMPORTANT WORDS AND CONCEPTS

convertible security 452	dilution 464
conversion price 453	primary earnings per share 464
conversion ratio 453	fully diluted earnings per share 464
conversion value 453	warrant 466
pure bond value 453	option price (of warrant) 468
floor value 453	exercise price (of warrant) 468
conversion premium 454	intrinsic value (of warrant) 468
downside limit 455	speculative premium 468
downside risk 455	warrant break-even 469
forced conversion 458	

DISCUSSION QUESTIONS

1. Why would an investor have an interest in convertible securities? (What do they offer to the investor?)
2. What are the disadvantages of investing in convertible securities?
3. When is the best time to buy convertible bonds?
4. How can you determine the conversion ratio from the conversion price?
5. How do you determine the conversion value?
6. What is meant by the pure bond value?
7. For bonds that have conversion premiums in excess of 100 percent, what can you generally infer about the stock price?
8. How does the volatility of a stock influence the conversion premium?
9. How might a step up in the conversion price force conversion?
10. Why do corporations use convertible bonds?
11. What is meant by the dilutive effect of convertible securities?
12. What is a warrant?
13. For what reasons do firms issue warrants?
14. Why are warrants highly speculative?
15. Why do investors tend to pay a smaller premium for a warrant as the price of the stock goes up?

16. If warrants were initially a detachable part of a bond issue, will the amount of debt be reduced if the warrants are eventually exercised? Contrast this with a convertible security.

17. What type of firm generally issues warrants?

■ PROBLEMS

Conversion terms

1. A convertible bond has a face value of $1,000 and the conversion price is $40 per share. The stock is selling at $33 per share. The bond pays $70 per year interest and is selling in the market for $960. It matures in 10 years. Market rates are 12 percent per year.

   a. What is the conversion ratio?

   b. What is the conversion value?

   c. What is the conversion premium (in dollars and percent)?

   d. What is the floor value or pure bond value? (You may wish to review material in Chapter 12 for computing bond values.)

Downside risk

2. Compute the downside risk as a percentage in Problem 1. What does this mean?

Downside risk

3. Under what circumstances might the downside risk increase? Relate your answer to interest rates in the market.

Conversion premium

4. Alvin Motor Corporation has a $1,000 face value convertible bond outstanding that has a market value of $1,030. It has a coupon rate of 6 percent and matures in five years. The conversion price is $50. The common stock currently is selling for $44.

   a. What is the conversion premium (in percentage)?

   b. At what price does the common stock need to sell for the conversion value to be equal to the current bond price?

Pure bond value

5. In Problem 4, market rates of interest for comparable bonds are 10 percent and the pure bond value is $845.66. What will happen to the pure bond value if market rates of interest go to 12 percent? (Once again, you may wish to consult Chapter 12 for computing bond values.)

Comparative analysis of stock and convertible bond

6. Assume you bought a convertible bond two years ago for $900. The bond has a conversion ratio of 32. When the bond was purchased, the stock was selling for $25 per share. The bond pays $75 in annual interest. The stock pays no cash dividend. Assume after two years the stock price rises to $35 and the firm forces investors to convert to common stock by calling the bond (there is no conversion premium at this point).

   Would you have been better off if you (a) had bought the stock directly or (b) bought the convertible bond and eventually converted it to common stock? Assume you would have invested $900 in either

case. Disregard taxes, commissions, etc. Hint: consider appreciation in value plus any annual income received. See Table 14–2 on page 458 for an example.

EPS and convertibles

7. Given the following data, compute unadjusted earnings per share and fully diluted earnings per share. There are no other potentially dilutive securities outstanding, and the 8 percent interest is greater than two thirds of the going interest rate at time of issue.

Common stock (500,000 shares at $5 par) =	$2,500,000
Eight percent convertible debentures (5,000 bonds at $1,000 each; convertible into 50 shares per bond)	5,000,000
Retained earnings	5,000,000
Earnings before interest and taxes	2,800,000
Interest	400,000
Earnings before taxes	$2,400,000
Earnings after taxes (50 percent)	$1,200,000

Valuing warrants

8. Assume a firm has warrants outstanding that permit the holder to buy one new share of stock at $30 per share. The market price of the stock is now $36.

   a. What is the intrinsic value of the warrant?

   b. Why might the warrant sell for $2 on the market even if the stock price is $28?

Valuing warrants

9. Morgan Donuts has warrants outstanding that allow the holder to purchase 1.85 shares of stock per warrant at $18 per share (option price). The common stock is currently selling for $21. The warrant has a market value of $7.

   a. What is the intrinsic value of the warrant?

   b. If the stock sold for $16.50, how large would the negative intrinsic value be?

Valuing warrants

10. Assume in Table 14–5 that Allou Health and Beauty Care had a warrant price of $3.00 instead of $2.00 in column (2). The per share stock price in column (3) remains at $6.63, and the per share option price is still $5 in column (4). Based on the new information, compute the following three items.

   a. Intrinsic value (does it change?)

   b. Premium (warrant price minus intrinsic value)

   c. Percent the stock must rise to break even (first determine what price the stock must go to for the warrant to equal $3; then determine how large a growth that is from the current stock value). This assumes no premium.

Comparative
analysis of stock
and warrants

11. A firm has warrants outstanding that allow the holder to buy one share of stock at $30 per share. The stock is selling for $35 per share, and the warrants are now selling for $7 per warrant (this, of course, is above intrinsic value). You can invest $1,000 in the stock or the warrants (for purposes of the computation, round to two places to the right of the decimal point). Assume the stock goes to $42, and the warrants trade at their intrinsic value when the stock goes to $42. Would you have a larger total dollar profit by initially investing in the stocks or the warrants?

EPS and warrants

12. Assume a corporation has $300,000 in earnings and 150,000 shares outstanding ($2 in earnings per share). Also assume there are warrants outstanding to purchase 25,000 shares at $30 per share. The stock is currently selling at $50 per share. In considering the effect of the warrants outstanding, what would revised earnings per share be?

CFA MATERIAL

The following material contains a sample question and solution from a prior Level I CFA exam. While the terminology is slightly different from that in this text, you can still view the skills that are necessary for the CFA exam.

CFA Exam Question

6. In examining a company's straight debentures and subordinated convertible debentures, both issued at the same time with the same maturity and at par, you note that the coupon and yield for the subordinated convertible debenture is lower than for the straight debenture. *Discuss* the return potential for the convertible bond in an environment of stable interest rates and rising stock prices that would explain its lower coupon and yield.

   (5 minutes)

Solution—Question 6—Morning Section (5 points) The reason for the lower coupon and yield is that convertible bonds and preferred stock have the ability to act like common stock on the upside and be valued as a straight bond on the downside. This is demonstrated by the graph in Figure 14–5 on page 477.

   As shown, it has the upside potential of common stock and the downside protection of a bond. Thus, it could have a rate of return approaching common stock with substantially lower risk because it is protected on the downside. Also, the convertible bond has an income advantage relative to common stock until the point at which parity value drives the current yield below the dividend yield.

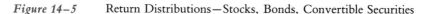

Figure 14–5   Return Distributions—Stocks, Bonds, Convertible Securities

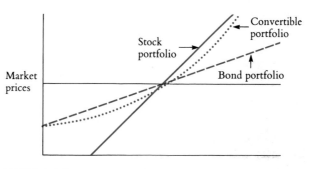

SELECTED REFERENCES

Innovations in Convertible-Type Securities

Chen, A. H., and J. W. Kensinger. "Puttable Stock: A New Innovation in Equity Financing." *Financial Management,* Spring 1988, pp. 27–37.

Heston, C. "How to Get Stocks and Bonds in One Package." *Futures,* September 1986, pp. 50–51.

Pershing, A. C. "Rupert Murdoch's New Convertible." *Institutional Investor,* August 1986, p. 27.

Valuing Convertibles

Alexander, Gordon J., and Roger D. Stover. "Pricing in the New Issue Convertible Debt Market." *Financial Management,* Fall 1977, pp. 35–39.

Brennan, M. J., and E. S. Schwartz. "Convertible Bonds: Valuation and Optimal Strategies for Call and Conversion." *Journal of Finance,* December 1977, pp. 1699–1715.

Hoffmeister, J. R. "Conditions Affecting the Timing of Convertible Bond Sales." *Journal of Business Research,* February 1987, pp. 101–6.

Leverage Considerations with Convertibles

Janjigian, V. "The Leverage Changing Consequences of Convertible Debt Financing." *Financial Management,* Autumn 1987, pp. 15–21.

Call Features with Convertibles

Ingersoll, Jonathan. "An Examination of Corporate Call Policies on Convertible Securities." *Journal of Finance,* May 1977, pp. 463–78.

Singh, Ajai; Arnold R. Cowan; and Nandkumer Nayar. "Underwritten Calls of Convertible Bonds." *Journal of Financial Economics,* March 1991, pp. 173–96.

Accounting Issues and Convertibles

Hagler, J. L., and P. B. Thomas. "Should FASB 84-Induced Conversions of Convertible Debt Apply to Convertible Preferred Stock?" *CPA Journal*, May 1986, pp. 86–88.

King, T. E., and A. K. Ortegren. "Accounting for Hybrid Securities: The Case of Adjustable-Rate Convertible Notes." *The Accounting Review*, July 1988, pp. 522–35.

Investing in Warrants

Miller, Jerry D. "Effects of Longevity on Values of Stock Purchase Warrants." *Financial Analysts Journal*, November–December 1971, pp. 78–85.

Rush, David F., and Ronald W. Melicher. "An Empirical Examination of Factors which Influence Warrant Prices." *Journal of Finance*, December 1974, pp. 1449–66.

Stone, Bernell K. "Warrant Financing." *Journal of Financial and Quantitative Analysis*, March 1976, pp. 143–53.

Part Five

Derivative Products

Outline

The futures markets (and options as well) allow us to take the pulse of investors about their expectations. We see what they are betting the price of a commodity will be months into the future. While they are not always right, they are still sharing their crystal ball with us.

When there is a potential oil crisis, such as when Saddam Hussein invaded Kuwait in the early 1990s, there tends to be a panic in the oil market. The best place to find out how a Middle East crisis is going to affect oil prices is through the futures market.

Some compare the futures market to a racetrack. Gamblers bet money based on their predictions; as they bet, prices constantly change, reflecting the best current guesses about the outcome of the race. The final odds represent the collective wisdom about what is going to happen. Basically, the same phenomenon occurs in the futures market. But instead of betting on Lazy Susan in the fourth, these gamblers are betting on light crude (or some other commodity) and what its price is likely to be in the future.

Back to the example of Saddam Hussein. At the time of the Iraqi invasion of Kuwait, some believed an embargo of oil shipments from Iraq and Kuwait could severely damage the world's oil supply. There was no immediate problem; this was all speculation about the future.

Nevertheless, the price of oil futures almost doubled overnight. An oil trader on the New York Mercantile Exchange proclaimed, "I have been in this business my whole life. My dad was a trader for 40 years, and I have been one now for 14 years, and I have never seen a market like this." What was driving the market was not what was actually happening (there was plenty of oil), but fear about what might happen.

But remember, the futures market is like any other market in that a transaction can occur only if there is a willing buyer and a willing *seller*. Despite the immediate panic, some calmer heads bet that the price of oil was about to plunge. At the time, the Venezuelans had about 600,000 barrels a day of unused capacity, and it was to their advantage to increase production if necessary. Furthermore, a rapid end to the war in the Middle East would quickly reverse the upward trend in oil prices.

How did the story end? This "horse race" was won by the sellers in the oil futures market as prices plunged to their pre-war levels. ■

15

Put and Call Options

The word **option** has many different meanings, but most of them include the ability or right to choose a certain alternative. One definition provided by *Webster's* is "the right, acquired for a consideration, to buy or sell something at a fixed price within a specified period of time." This definition is very general and applies to puts, calls, warrants, real estate options, or any other contracts entered into between two parties where a choice of action or decision can be put off for a limited time at a cost. The person acquiring the option pays an agreed-upon sum to the person providing the option. For example, someone may want to buy your house for its sale price of $75,000. The buyer does not have the money but will give you $2,000 in cash if you give him the right to buy the house for the next 60 days at $75,000. If you accept, you have given the buyer an option and have agreed not to sell the house to anyone else for the next 60 days. If the buyer raises $75,000 within the 60-day limit, he may buy the house, giving you the $75,000. Perhaps he finds the $75,000 but also finds another house he likes better for $72,000. He will not buy your house, but you have $2,000 and must now find someone else to buy your house. By selling the option, you tied up the sale of your house for 60 days, and if the option is not exercised, you have forgone an opportunity to sell the house to someone else.

The most widely known options are puts and calls on common stock. A **put** is an option to sell 100 shares of common stock at a specified price for a given period. **Calls** are the opposite of puts and allow the owner the right to buy 100 shares of common stock from the option seller (writer). Contracts on listed puts and calls have been standardized and can be bought on several different exchanges.

■ OPTIONS MARKETS

Before the days of options trading on exchanges, puts and calls were traded over-the-counter by the Put and Call Dealers Association. These dealers would buy and sell puts and calls for their own accounts for stocks traded on the New York Stock Exchange and then try to find an investor, hedger, or speculator to take the other side of the option. For example, if you owned 1,000 shares of General Motors and you wanted to write a call option giving the buyer the right to buy 1,000 shares of General Motors at $40 per share for six months, the dealer might buy the calls and look for someone who would be willing to buy them from him.

This system had several disadvantages. Dealers had to have contact with the buyers and sellers, and the financial stability of the option writer had to be endorsed (guaranteed) by a brokerage house. The option writer either had to keep the shares on deposit with the brokerage firm or put up a cash margin. Options in the same stock could exist in the market at various strike prices (price at which the option could be exercised) and scattered expiration dates. This meant that when an option buyer wanted to exercise or terminate the contract before expiration, he or she would have to deal directly with the

option writer. This does not make for an efficient, liquid market. Unlisted options also reduced the striking price of a call by any dividends paid during the option period, which did not benefit the writer of the call.

Listed Options Exchanges

The Chicago Board Options Exchange was established in 1973 as the first exchange for call options. The market response was overwhelming, and within three years, the American, Pacific, and Philadelphia exchanges were also trading call options. By 1991, the list of stocks with available option contracts increased dramatically from the original list of 16 companies to 1,600 companies, and puts as well as calls were traded for many companies. On many days, the number of underlying shares of stock represented by options traded on the option exchanges is greater than the number of actual shares traded on the NYSE in those same issues.

Table 15–1, from the *Chicago Board Option Exchange's Market Statistics,* shows the growth in options trading since 1973. Besides the Chicago Board

Table 15–1 — Total Options Contract Volume by Exchange (For Individual Stocks)

	CBOE	AMEX	PHLX	PSE	NYSE	MSE*	NASD	Total
1990	129,500,018	40,914,962	22,808,688	13,881,269	2,817,811	—	—	209,922,748
1989	126,765,253	49,873,264	27,970,765	18,091,434	4,315,944	—	—	227,016,660
1988	111,784,045	45,022,497	23,165,112	13,349,148	2,627,789	—	—	195,948,591
1987	182,112,636	70,988,990	29,155,308	19,410,875	3,499,095	—	—	305,166,904
1986	180,357,774	65,440,500	24,467,468	14,075,872	4,823,782	—	45,239	289,210,635
1985	148,889,091	48,559,122	18,134,575	12,793,451	4,426,855	—	107,453	232,910,547
1984	123,273,736	40,104,605	16,109,050	11,366,056	4,093,816	—	—	194,947,263
1983	82,468,750	38,967,725	16,808,125	11,155,906	656,480	—	—	150,056,986
1982	75,735,739	38,790,852	13,466,652	9,309,563	—	—	—	137,302,806
1981	57,584,175	34,859,475	10,009,565	6,952,567	—	—	—	109,405,782
1980	52,916,921	29,048,323	7,758,101	5,486,590	—	1,518,611	—	96,728,546
1979	35,379,600	17,467,018	4,952,737	3,856,344	—	2,609,164	—	64,264,863
1978	34,277,350	14,380,959	3,270,378	3,289,968	—	2,012,363	—	57,231,018
1977	24,838,632	10,077,578	2,195,307	1,925,031	—	600,780	—	39,637,328
1976	21,498,027	9,035,767	1,274,702	550,194	—	15,237	—	32,373,927
1975	14,431,023	3,530,564	140,982	—	—	—	—	18,102,569
1974	5,682,907	—	—	—	—	—	—	5,682,907
1973	1,119,177	—	—	—	—	—	—	1,119,177

*The Midwest Stock Exchange Options Program was consolidated with the CBOE on June 2, 1980.
Source: *The Chicago Board Option Exchange's Market Statistics,* 1990, p. 33.

Options Exchange (CBOE), the American Exchange (AMEX), the Philadelphia Exchange (PHLX), the Pacific Coast Exchange (PSE), and the New York Stock Exchange (NYSE) currently trade options.

One can now also buy a put or call option on *stock indexes*. For example, the Standard & Poor's 500 Stock Index or the S&P 100 Stock Index are traded on the CBOE and options on the New York Stock Exchange Index are traded on the NYSE. Options on stock indexes are covered in detail in Chapter 17, while this chapter concentrates on options on individual common stocks.

There are several reasons the listed options markets are so desirable compared to the previous method of over-the-counter trading for options. The contract period was standardized with three-, six-, and nine-month expiration dates on three calendar cycles.

Cycle 1: January/April/July/October.

Cycle 2: February/May/August/November.

Cycle 3: March/June/September/December.

The use of three cycles spreads out the expiration dates for the options so that not all contracts come due on the same day. Each contract expires at 11:59 P.M. Eastern time on the Saturday immediately following the third Friday of the expiration month. For all practical purposes, any closing out of positions must be done on that last Friday while the markets are open.

In an attempt to satisfy demand for longer-term options, **long-term equity anticipation securities (LEAPS)** were added and provided options with up to two years of expiration. LEAPS have generally been limited to blue-chip stocks such as Coca-Cola, Dow Chemical, General Electric, IBM, and others. LEAPS have the same characteristics as the short-term options, but because of their length they have higher premiums.

Another important feature of option trading is the standardized **exercise price** (strike price). This is the price the contract specifies for a buy or sell. For all stocks over $25 per share, the striking price changes by $5 intervals, and for stocks selling under $25 per share, the strike price changes by $2.50 a share. As the underlying stocks change prices in the market, options with new striking prices are added. For example, a stock selling at $30 per share when the January option is added will have a striking price of 30, but if the stock gets to 32½ (halfway to the next striking price), the exchange may add another option (to the class of options) with a 35 strike price.

This standardization of expiration dates and strike prices creates more certainty when buying and selling options in a changing market and allows more efficient trading strategies because of better coordination between stock prices, strike prices, and expiration dates. Dividends no longer affect the option contract as they did in the unlisted market. Transactions occur at arm's length between the buyer and seller without any direct matchmaking needed on the part of the broker. The ultimate result of these changes in the option market is a highly liquid, efficient market where speculators, hedgers, and arbitrageurs all operate together.

Table 15–2		\multicolumn{3}{c}{January 7, 1992, General Electric Options}			

Stock Price Close	Strike Price	Calls–Last			Puts–Last		
		January	February	March	January	February	March
Gen El.							
75⅞	65	10⅞	r	11¼	¹⁄₁₆	r	⁷⁄₁₆
75⅞	70	6⅜	6⅛	7¼	r	⁹⁄₁₆	1
75⅞	75	2	3¼	3⅞	1	2	2⅝
75⅞	80	⅛	1	1⅜	r	4¾	r

r = not traded

General Electric put and call options are presented in Table 15–2 as an example of different strike prices (65, 70, 75, 80) and expiration months. The expiration months demonstrate the first month in each expiration cycle (January, February, March). General Electric common stock closed at 75⅞ on January 7, 1992. The values within Table 15–2, such as 10⅞ or 6⅜, reflect the price of the various option contracts. This information will take on greater meaning as we go through the chapter.

■ THE OPTIONS CLEARING CORPORATION

Much of the liquidity and ease of operation of the option exchanges is due to the role of the **Options Clearing Corporation,** which functions as the issuer of all options listed on the five exchanges—the CBOE, the AMEX, the Philadelphia Exchange, the Pacific Coast Exchange, and the NYSE. Investors who want to trade puts and calls need to have an approved account with a member brokerage firm; on opening an account, they receive a prospectus from the Options Clearing Corporation detailing all aspects of option trading.

Options are bought and sold through a member broker the same as other securities. The exchanges allow special orders, such as limit, market, and stop orders, as well as orders used specifically in options trading, like spread orders and straddle orders. The order process originates with the broker and is transacted on the floor of the exchange. Remember that for every order there must be a buyer and seller (writer) so that the orders can be "matched." Once the orders are matched, they are filed with the Options Clearing Corporation, which then issues the necessary options or closes the position. Four basic transactions are handled:

Opening purchase transaction—A transaction in which an investor intends to become the holder of an option.

Opening sale transaction—A transaction in which an investor intends to become the writer (seller) of an option.

Closing purchase transaction—A transaction in which an investor who is obligated as a writer of an option intends to terminate his obligation as a writer. This is accomplished by "purchasing" an option in the same series as the option previously written. Such a transaction has the effect, upon acceptance by the Options Clearing Corporation, of canceling the investor's preexisting position as a writer.

Closing sale transaction—A transaction in which an investor who is the holder of an outstanding option intends to liquidate his position as a holder. This is accomplished by "selling" an option in the same series as the option previously purchased. Such a transaction has the effect, upon acceptance by the Options Clearing Corporation, of liquidating the investor's preexisting position as a holder of the option.

In a transaction, holders and writers of options are not contractually linked but are committed to the Options Clearing Corporation. Since no certificates are issued for options, a customer must maintain a brokerage account as long as he or she holds an option position and must liquidate the option through the broker originating the transaction unless a brokerage transfer is completed before an ensuing transaction. If an option is traded on more than one exchange, it may be bought, sold, or closed on any exchange and cleared through the Options Clearing Corporation. Basically, the aggregate obligation of the option holders is backed up by the aggregate obligation of the option writers. If holders choose to exercise their options, they must do so through the Clearing Corporation, which randomly selects a writer from all Clearing member accounts in the same option series.[1] This would be true whether the holder chooses to exercise early or at expiration. Upon notice from the Options Clearing Corporation, a call writer must sell 100 shares of the underlying common stock at the exercise price, while the put writer must buy 100 shares from the holder exercising the put.

All option contracts are adjusted for stock splits, stock dividends, or other stock distributions. For example, a two-for-one stock split for a stock selling at 60, with options available at 70, 60, and 50 strike prices, would cause the stock to trade at 30 and the strike prices to be 35, 30, and 25.

■ OPTION PREMIUMS

Before investors or speculators can understand various option strategies, they must be able to comprehend what creates option premiums (prices). In Table 15–3, using Gap as an example, we can see that the common stock closed at $59 per share on the NYSE and that calls and puts are available for the following strike prices—45, 50, 55, and 60. The January 50 call closed at 8⅞

---

[1]Few option holders choose to exercise their options and take possession of securities. During the 1980s approximately 15 percent of all call options were exercised while only 7 percent of put options were exercised. Assuming the option holder does not want to exercise the option, he may close out the position on the open market through a closing sale transaction.

Table 15–3

LISTED OPTIONS QUOTATIONS

Monday, January 6, 1992

Options closing prices. Sales unit usually is 100 shares.
Stock close is New York or American exchange final price.

CHICAGO BOARD

Option & NY Close	Strike Price	Calls-Last Jan	Calls-Last Feb	Calls-Last Mar	Puts-Last Jan	Puts-Last Feb	Puts-Last Mar
ADT Ltd	5	2 3/8	r	r	r	r	r
7	7 1/2	r	r	3/4	r	r	r
7	10	r	1/8	1/8	r	r	r
APwrCv	15	s	s	14	s	s	r
28 3/4	17 1/2	r	s	11 1/2	r	s	r
28 3/4	20	r	9	r	r	r	r
28 3/4	22 1/2	5 1/8	r	7 1/2	1/8	r	r
28 3/4	25	3 1/2	5 5/8	4 5/8	3/8	1 1/4	1 3/4
28 3/4	30	1	2 3/8	3 1/8	r	r	r
ApiMag	5	r	1 1/4	r	r	r	r
6 3/8	7 1/2	r	r	1/2	r	r	r
Baybks	15	4 5/8	r	r	r	r	r
19 1/8	20	r	1	1 1/2	r	r	r
Blkbst	10	3 1/4	3 3/8	3 5/8	r	1/8	1/4
13 1/4	12 1/2	15/16	1 1/4	1 3/4	1/2	1/2	r
13 1/4	15	r	r	1/2	r	r	2
BrMSq	75	r	r	14 1/4	r	r	1/4
88 5/8	80	8 1/4	8 1/2	9 1/2	r	r	11/16
88 5/8	85	4	4 7/8	5 3/4	1/4	1 3/8	1 5/8
88 5/8	90	3/4	2	3	2 1/2	3 1/2	r
Bruns	12 1/2	1 3/8	1 3/4	2	r	r	9/16
14	15	1/4	1/4	9/16	r	1 1/8	r
Catels	10	r	r	1 1/16	r	r	r
Chamin	25	5/8	r	1 1/8	r	1	r
Cirrus	12 1/2	r	r	r	r	3/8	r
16 1/8	15	r	r	r	1/2	7/8	r
16 1/8	17 1/2	r	1 1/2	r	r	2 5/16	r
CompSc	65	r	r	13 3/4	r	r	r
78 1/4	70	7 1/2	r	r	r	1 1/8	1 5/8
78 1/4	80	r	2 1/2	r	r	r	5 3/4
78 1/4	85	r	r	r	r	8 1/4	r
ContBk	10	r	7/16	3/4	r	r	1
9 3/4	12 1/2	r	s	r	r	s	2 7/8
CypSem	15	3	r	r	1/8	r	r
17 7/8	17 1/2	3/4	1 5/8	2	r	1 1/4	r
17 7/8	20	r	r	1 1/4	r	r	r
17 7/8	22 1/2	s	s	3/8	s	s	r
17 7/8	25	s	s	1/4	s	s	r
Dow Ch	50	2 7/16	3 1/8	4 3/4	3/8	1	1 3/8
51 7/8	55	1/8	7/8	1 1/8	3 1/8	3 5/8	r
51 7/8	60	s	s	1/2	s	s	r
Duracl	30	4 1/2	r	4 7/8	r	r	1/2
EleArt	35	5 1/2	r	r	r	r	r
40 3/4	40	2	r	r	r	r	r
Entrgy	30	r	r	11/16	r	r	r
FHP s	20	r	s	r	r	s	6
FFB	35	1/4	r	r	r	r	r
Ford	22 1/2	r	r	9	r	r	1/16
30 3/4	25	6	r	6 1/8	1/16	1/4	5/16
30 3/4	30	1 3/16	1 15/16	2 5/16	7/16	1 1/4	1 7/16
30 3/4	35	s	3/8	11/16	s	4 3/8	4
30 3/4	40	s	s	1/4	s	s	9 1/4
Fuqua	12 1/2	r	2 3/16	r	r	r	r
14 1/8	15	r	1/2	13/16	r	r	r
Gap	45	14	r	14 1/4	1/16	r	r
59	50	8 7/8	9 3/4	10 5/8	1/16	5/8	1 1/16
59	55	4 1/4	5 3/4	6 5/8	3/8	1 5/8	2 1/2
59	60	1 3/8	3	4	2 3/8	3 3/4	4 1/2
Gencp	10	1 3/16	r	r	r	r	r
Gen El	60	r	s	r	r	s	3/16
75 7/8	65	10 7/8	r	11 1/4	1/16	r	7/16
75 7/8	70	6 3/8	6 1/8	7 1/4	r	9/16	1
75 7/8	75	2	3 1/4	3 7/8	1	2	2 5/8
75 7/8	80	1/8	1	1 3/8	r	4 3/4	r
G M	25	8 1/4	r	8 3/8	r	1/8	3/16
33 1/2	30	3 5/8	4 1/8	4 3/8	1/8	5/8	1
33 1/2	35	9/16	1 5/16	1 13/16	1 11/16	3	3 3/8
33 1/2	40	1/16	s	9/16	r	s	6 3/4
33 1/2	45	s	s	3/16	s	s	r
Gensia	45	13 1/4	14	15 1/2	1/4	r	r
59	50	10	10 5/8	r	r	r	r
59	55	5 1/2	7 3/4	10	1 3/16	r	5
59	60	s	5 3/4	7 3/4	s	r	r
GtLCh	100	r	r	17	r	r	r
115 3/4	105	r	r	13 1/8	r	r	r
115 3/4	110	r	r	r	[illegible]	1 13/16	r
115 3/4	115	2 3/8	[illegible]				
115 3/4	120						

Option & NY Close	Strike Price	Calls-Last Jan	Calls-Last Feb	Calls-Last Apr	Puts-Last Jan	Puts-Last Feb	Puts-Last Apr
14	20	1/16	s	r	r	s	r
Biogen	30	12 7/8	s	r	r	s	r
42 3/4	35	7 1/2	r	r	1/4	r	r
42 3/4	40	3 5/8	r	6 1/4	1 1/8	r	4
42 3/4	45	1	3	4 1/8	3 1/4	r	6 7/8
42 3/4	50	1/4	s	3 1/4	r	s	r
Biomet	22 1/2	r	r	8 1/4	1/16	r	r
30 1/4	25	5 1/4	5 3/4	6 3/8	r	r	r
30 1/4	27 1/2	2 5/8	s	r	r	s	r
30 1/4	30	1 1/8	2	3 1/2	r	2 1/4	3
30 1/4	35	r	3/4	1 1/2	r	r	r
Borind	40	37 1/2	s	r	r	s	r
80	50	30	s	r	r	s	r
80	55	24 3/8	s	r	r	s	r
80	60	19 7/8	s	r	1/8	s	1 1/2
80	65	r	s	r	r	s	2 1/2
80	70	9 7/8	r	13 1/2	1/2	1 11/16	4 1/8
80	75	5 3/4	r	10 7/8	1 3/16	3 7/8	6
80	80	3 1/8	6 1/8	8 1/4	3 3/8	6 1/8	7 3/4
80	85	1	3 7/8	6 3/8	6 7/8	10	11 7/8
80	90	s	r	4 5/8	s	r	r
BurlN	30	r	r	10 3/4	r	r	r
41	35	r	r	r	r	r	1/2
41	40	1 7/16	2 1/8	r	r	r	r
41	45	r	5/8	1 1/8	r	r	r
CIGNA	50	9 3/4	r	r	1/16	r	r
59 5/8	55	4 1/2	r	r	1/4	r	r
59 5/8	60	r	2 7/16	r	15/16	2 11/16	r
59 5/8	65	r	r	1 5/8	r	r	r
CarnCr	20	r	r	r	r	r	1/2
26 1/8	22 1/2	r	r	r	1/16	r	r
26 1/8	25	1 3/8	r	r	7/16	r	r
Cntocr	30	r	s	r	r	s	1/4
58 3/8	32 1/2	25 1/8	s	s	r	s	s
58 3/8	35	22 5/8	s	22 5/8	1/16	s	3/8
58 3/8	40	17 5/8	s	18 7/8	1/16	s	7/8
58 3/8	45	13 1/4	14	15 1/2	1/8	11/16	1 3/4
58 3/8	50	8 3/8	10	11 1/4	1/4	1 5/8	3
58 3/8	55	4 3/8	7	8 3/4	1 1/8	3	5 1/8
58 3/8	60	1 15/16	4 1/2	6 3/4	3 1/2	5 7/8	7 7/8
ChamDv	30	3 7/8	r	r	r	r	r
Chiron	60	6 7/8	r	r	3/8	r	3 1/2
66 1/4	65	3 1/2	r	r	1 1/4	r	r
66 1/4	70	1 1/8	r	r	4 3/8	6 3/8	r
66 1/4	75	r	2	r	r	r	r
66 1/4	85	r	s	1 1/2	r	s	r
Chryslr	7 1/2	r	r	r	r	r	1/8
13 5/8	10	3 7/8	r	4	1/16	r	r
13 5/8	12 1/2	1 7/16	1 7/8	2 1/4	3/16	7/16	7/8
13 5/8	15	3/16	1/2	7/8	1 3/8	1 7/16	2
13 5/8	17 1/2	r	s	s	3 5/8	s	s
CinBel	17 1/2	r	r	r	r	r	7/16
19 1/8	20	r	3/8	11/16	1 5/16	r	1 1/2
19 1/8	22 1/2	r	s	r	r	s	3 5/8
Cisco	45	21 5/8	s	22 1/2	r	s	r
67 1/4	50	r	r	18 1/4	r	r	r
67 1/4	55	r	r	13 3/4	r	1/4	r
67 1/4	60	7	r	9 7/8	1/8	r	r
67 1/4	65	2 3/4	5 1/8	r	1 1/8	r	r
67 1/4	70	r	r	4 3/8	r	r	r
Citicp	7 1/2	r	r	r	1/16	r	5/16
10 3/4	10	7/8	1 5/16	1 1/2	3/16	9/16	13/16
10 3/4	12 1/2	1/16	5/16	5/8	1 7/8	1 13/16	2 1/8
10 3/4	15	1/16	s	1/4	r	s	r
CmprsL	17 1/2	r	r	r	r	r	3/8
28 7/8	20	8 5/8	9 1/2	9 1/2	1/16	r	r
28 7/8	22 1/2	6 1/8	r	8 1/8	r	3/4	1 1/2
28 7/8	25	4 1/8	s	6 1/2	3/8	s	2 1/8
28 7/8	30	1 3/16	s	3 3/4	1 15/16	s	r
CmpAsc	7 1/2	3 3/4	r	r	r	r	1/16
11	10	1	1 1/4	1 3/4	1/16	r	r
11	12 1/2	1/8	3/8	1/2	r	r	1 9/16
CyprMn	20	2 9/16	r	3	r	r	r
22 1/2	22 1/2	3/8	r	r	r	1 1/8	r
22 1/2	25	r	r	r	r	r	3 3/8
Delta	55	r	r	15 1/8	r	r	r
71	60	9 3/8	r	12	1/16	5/16	11/16
71	65	4 7/8	6	7 1/4	[illegible]	[illegible]	[illegible]
71	70	2 1/8	2 3/4	[illegible]			
71	75	3/16	[illegible]				

Option & NY Close	Strike Price	Calls-Last Jan	Calls-Last Feb	Calls-Last Apr	Puts-Last Jan	Puts-Last Feb	Puts-Last Apr
48 3/4	45	3 1/2	r	r	r	r	r
48 3/4	50	7/8	r	r	r	r	r
Sizzlr	10	2 1/2	r	r	r	r	r
12 3/8	12 1/2	r	r	13/16	r	r	r
T J X	15	1 5/8	r	r	r	r	r
16 3/8	17 1/2	r	1/2	1 1/16	r	r	r
Teldyn	15	r	s	9 1/4	r	s	r
24 1/2	17 1/2	5 3/4	r	r	r	r	r
24 1/2	20	4 3/8	4	4 5/8	1/16	r	r
24 1/2	22 1/2	1 7/8	2 1/2	3 1/8	3/8	r	1 7/16
Terdta	22 1/2	8 1/4	s	r	r	s	r
31 3/8	25	r	r	7	r	r	1/16
31 3/8	30	1 1/8	1 1/2	r	r	r	r
Tex In	25	8 1/4	8	8 1/2	r	r	r
33 1/8	30	3 1/4	3 3/8	4 3/4	1/8	3/4	1 1/8
33 1/8	35	3/8	1 1/4	2 1/4	2 1/8	r	3 1/4
33 1/8	40	1/16	s	s	r	s	s
33 1/8	45	r	s	s	12 5/8	s	s
UJB Fn	12 1/2	2 7/8	r	r	r	r	r
15 1/4	15	5/8	1 1/4	1 11/16	r	r	r
15 1/4	17 1/2	r	r	7/8	r	r	r
Unitrn	40	r	r	7/8	r	r	r
Upjohn	35	r	r	r	r	r	7/16
41 7/8	40	2 1/16	3 1/8	3 3/4	3/16	13/16	1 5/8
41 7/8	45	1/8	3/4	1 1/2	3 1/4	3 1/2	4 1/4
41 7/8	50	1/16	1/4	9/16	r	8	r
VLSI	5	r	3 1/2	r	r	r	r
8 3/8	7 1/2	1 1/8	r	1 11/16	r	r	r
Weyerh	25	3	3 1/8	3 1/8	r	5/8	5/8
27 3/8	30	1/4	5/16	5/8	r	r	r
WinDix	35	4 1/2	4 3/4	r	r	r	r
Xerox	55	12 1/2	s	r	r	s	r
67 1/2	60	7 3/8	r	8 1/2	1/16	r	r
67 1/2	65	3 1/4	r	5 3/4	1/2	1 3/8	2 3/4
67 1/2	70	1/2	1 1/2	2 7/8	r	r	r
		Jan	**Feb**	**May**	**Jan**	**Feb**	**May**
AirbFr	22 1/2	r	1 7/8	r	r	r	r
AlexAl	20	r	7/8	r	r	r	r
AllanP	20	r	14 1/8	r	r	r	r
34	22 1/2	r	r	13 1/4	r	r	r
34	25	9 3/8	9 7/8	r	1/4	15/16	2 9/16
34	30	5 1/8	6 5/8	8 7/8	7/8	2 5/16	4 1/4
Amdahl	12 1/2	3 1/4	r	r	r	3/16	1/2
15 7/8	15	r	1 1/2	2 1/4	r	9/16	1 1/8
15 7/8	17 1/2	r	3/16	1 1/16	r	r	r
A E P	35	1/16	r	r	r	r	r
AInGrp	95	r	5 7/8	r	3/4	1 1/2	r
98 1/8	100	3/4	2 9/16	5 1/8	r	r	r
Amoco	45	r	r	5 3/4	r	3/8	r
49 1/2	50	r	1 3/8	2	3/4	1 3/4	r
49 1/2	55	r	3/16	1/2	r	r	r
A M P	55	4 1/4	r	6 1/8	r	r	r
59 1/4	60	r	1 5/8	3 1/8	r	r	r
Anadrk	25	r	r	r	r	r	2 11/16
BMC Sft	55	14 7/8	15	r	r	r	r
69 3/4	60	9 7/8	r	r	r	r	3 1/2
69 3/4	65	5 1/4	6 3/8	r	3/4	r	r
69 3/4	70	2 1/4	r	7 7/8	r	6	r
Baxter	35	5 1/8	5 1/2	5 3/8	r	1/4	3/4
40 1/8	40	3/4	1 1/2	2 5/8	r	1 7/8	2
40 1/8	45	r	r	15/16	r	r	r
BioTcG	7 1/2	1 7/8	2 3/8	3 1/4	r	7/16	r
9 3/8	10	3/8	1 1/8	1 3/4	1	r	r
Blk Dk	12 1/2	r	r	5 3/8	r	r	r
17 3/4	15	2 3/4	3	r	1/16	1/4	5/8
17 3/4	17 1/2	3/4	1 1/8	1 3/4	1/2	r	1 1/2
17 3/4	20	r	3/8	7/8	r	r	r
Boeing	40	7 3/4	7 5/8	8 3/4	1/8	1/8	5/8
47 3/8	45	2 7/8	3 3/8	4 5/8	1/8	7/8	1 3/4
47 3/8	50	3/16	13/16	1 7/8	r	3 3/8	r
47 3/8	55	s	1/8	11/16	s	r	r
Bois C	20	r	r	4 1/4	r	r	r
23 3/8	25	1/4	9/16	1 5/16	r	r	r
Brunos	15	r	1/2	r	r	r	r
C B S	125	r	r	r	r	7/8	2 3/4
137 5/8	135	r	r	r	1 1/2	3 1/2	5 7/8
137 5/8	140	2 1/8	r	8 1/2	r	6 1/8	7 3/4
137 5/8	145	3/4	3 3/8	6 3/4	6 1/2	r	11
[illegible]	150	1/8	r	r	r	r	r
	[illegible]	r	r	3	r	r	r
		r	r	1 3/8	r	[illegible]	

Source: *The Wall Street Journal*, January 7, 1992, p. C13. Reprinted by permission of *THE WALL STREET JOURNAL*, © 1992 by Dow Jones & Company, Inc. All Rights Reserved Worldwide.

($887.50 for one call on 100 shares), while the January 55 call closed at 4¼. The 45, 50, and 55 call options are said to be **in the money** because the market price (59) is above the strike (or purchase) price of 45 or 55. The 60 call is **out of the money** since the strike price is above the market price. If Gap common were trading at 60, the 60 call and put would be at the money. Let's once again assume the stock is selling for 59. Since a put allows you to sell the stock at the strike price, in the money *puts* would be at the 60 strike price, and out of the money puts would be at 45, 50, and 55.

Intrinsic Value

In the money *call* options have an **intrinsic value** equal to the market price minus the strike price. In the case of the Gap March 50 call, the intrinsic value is 9 as indicated by Formula 15–1.

$$\text{Intrinsic value (call)} = \text{Market price} - \text{Strike price} \qquad (15\text{--}1)$$

$$\text{Intrinsic value} = 59 - 50$$

$$= 9 \text{ (Gap 50 March call)}$$

Options that are out of the money have no positive intrinsic value. If we use Formula 15–1 for the Gap 60 call, we calculate a negative $1 intrinsic value. When the market price minus the strike price is negative, the negative value represents the amount the stock price must increase to have the option at the money where the strike price and market price are equal.

The intrinsic value for the in the money *put* options equals the strike price minus the market price. In the case of the Gap 60 March put, the intrinsic value is 1 as indicated by Formula 15–2.

$$\text{Intrinsic value put} = \text{Strike price} - \text{Market price} \qquad (15\text{--}2)$$

$$\text{Intrinsic value} = 60 - 59$$

$$= 1 \text{ (Gap 60 March put)}$$

Since puts allow the owner to sell stock at the strike price, in the money put options exist where the strike price is above the market price of the stock. Out of the money puts have market prices for common stock above the strike price.

Speculative Premium

Returning to the Gap 50 March call, we see in Table 15–3 that the total premium is 10⅝, while the previously computed intrinsic value is 9. This call option has an additional speculative premium of 1⅝ due to other factors. The total premium (option price) is a combination of the intrinsic value plus a **speculative premium.** This relationship is indicated in Formula 15–3 and shown in Figure 15–1.

Figure 15–1   Components of the Total Premium on a Call Option

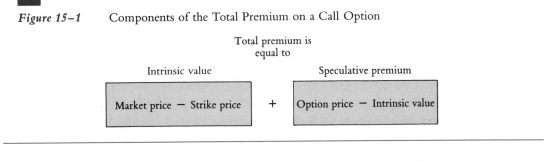

$$\text{Total premium} = \text{Intrinsic Value} + \text{Speculative premium} \qquad (15\text{–}3)$$
$$10\tfrac{5}{8} \quad = \quad 9 \quad + \quad 1\tfrac{5}{8}$$

Generally, the higher the volatility of the common stock—as measured by its stock price's standard deviation or by its beta—and the lower the dividend yield, the greater the speculative premium.[2] The longer the exercise period, the higher the speculative premium, especially if market expectations over the duration of the option are positive. Finally, the deeper the option is in the money, the smaller the leverage potential and therefore the smaller the speculative premium. Most often, we examine the speculative premium separately to see if it is a reasonable premium to pay for the possible benefits.

The speculative premium can be expressed in dollars or as a percentage of the common stock price. A speculative premium expressed in percent indicates the increase in the stock price needed for the purchaser of a call option to break even on the expiration date. Table 15–4 shows this point.[3] Notice that the Gap March 45 call option, which is deep in the money, has the lowest speculative

Table 15–4   Speculative Premiums on January 7, 1992, for Gap Options

Market Price	Gap Strike Price	Total Premium (Price)	–	Intrinsic Value	=	Speculative Premium	Speculative Premium as a Percent of Stock Price
$59	45 March Call	14¼		14		¼	.42%
59	50 March Call	10⅝		9		1⅝	2.75
59	55 March Call	6⅝		4		2⅝	4.45
59	60 March Call	4		(1)		5	8.47

---

[2] Some people refer to the speculative premium as the time premium because time may be the overriding factor affecting the speculative premium.

[3] As applied to put options, the speculative premium indicates the decrease in stock price needed for the purchaser of a put option to break even on the expiration date.

		January Total Premium* (Price)	Speculative Premium		February Total Premium† (Price)	Speculative Premium		March Total Premium‡ (Price)	Speculative Premium	
Market Price	Strike Price		Dollars	Percent		Dollars	Percent		Dollars	Percent
$59.00	$45	$14	$ 0	0%	r	—	—	14¼	$ .25	.42%
59.00	50	8⅞	−.13	−.22	9¾	$ .75	1.27%	10⅝	1.63	2.76
59.00	55	4¼	.25	.42	5¾	1.75	2.97	6⅝	2.63	4.46
59.00	60	1⅜	.38	.64	3	2.00	3.39	4	3.00	5.08

Table 15–5   Speculative Premiums over Time (Gap Calls, January 7, 1992)

* January—11 days to expiration
† February—46 days to expiration
‡ March—74 days to expiration
r = not traded

premium, while the 60 call option has the highest. Realize that the 60 call option has a cash value of only 4 (the total premium), and the other 1 represents the required increase in the stock price for the market price and the strike price to be equal. The 8.47 percent speculative premium for March 60 call options represents the percentage movement in stock price by the expiration date for a break-even position. At expiration, there will be no speculative premium. The option will reflect only the intrinsic value and possibly even a discount because of commission expenses incurred on exercise.

Speculative Premiums and the Time Factor Table 15–5 provides a look at premiums for the in the money and out of the money call options with varying times to expiration. Since the quotes are as of January, the January options will expire first, then the February options, and finally the March options. The option premiums increase with more time to expiration.

The Gap's speculative premiums in Table 15–5 demonstrate that percentage speculative premiums increase with time across all series of strike prices. The speculative premiums are lowest with the in the money 45, 50, and 55 calls because of the low leverage potential and the downside risk if the stock declines. The 60 call option has a high speculative premium, but an option writer (seller) would *not reap much cash inflow.* Generally, out of the money call options have high speculative premiums, but little of the premium may be in the form of cash. For example, the Gap January 60 call has a total premium of 1⅜ and a speculative premium of ⅜. The fact that the cash premium is only 38 cents is an important consideration for an option writer.

Speculative Premiums, Betas, and Dividend Yields Table 15–6 demonstrates the relationship of betas and dividend yields to the speculative premium. The four options listed are all January calls from Table 15–3. Ford Motor and Dow Chemical are in the money, and Texas Instruments and Biogen Inc. are out of the money. It would be better to have all of them at the

				Speculative Premium			Expected Dividend Yield
	January Strike	Market Price	Total Premium	Dollars	Percent	Beta	
Ford Motor	$25	$30¾	$6	$ .25	.81%	1.10	6.7%
Dow Chemical	50	51⅞	2⁷⁄₁₆	.56	1.08	1.25	5.1
Texas Instruments	35	33⅛	⅜	2.25	6.79	1.45	2.4
Biogen Inc.	45	42¾	1	3.25	7.60	1.70	nil

Table 15–6   Speculative Premiums Related to Betas and Dividend Yields

money so the comparison would not be biased by differences between the strike price and market price. In general, the speculative premiums (in percent) are higher for the high-beta, low-dividend yield stocks, and lower for the low-beta, high-dividend stocks.

High-beta stocks have a greater probability of participating in a market upturn, and so speculators will pay a higher speculative premium on a call for the chance to participate in an up market. High-dividend-yield stocks are the ones favored by call writers, and therefore, the speculative premiums are lower because there is a larger number of call writers for these stocks. Other factors, such as market attitudes or individual company conditions, can also have a strong bearing on the speculative premium.

Speculative Premiums per Day   Speculative premiums can be deceiving. The novice may attempt to write the options with the highest total premium or speculative premium, while the buyer may think the smallest dollar investment provides the greatest advantage. These are not usually true if we look at speculative premiums on a per day basis. For example, the Gap calls in Table 15–5 have the following speculative premiums per day. Note the speculative premium per day is divided by the number of days to expiration.

Month	Strike	Speculative Premium	÷	Days to Expiration	=	Speculative Premium per Day
January	55	.42%		11 days		.0382 per day
February	55	2.97		46 days		.0646 per day
March	55	4.46		74 days		.0602 per day

An examination of daily premiums would suggest that call writers should write short-lived calls on a continuous basis to get a maximum return. In this case the February calls give the maximum premium per day. The January calls are so close to expiration, the premium is starting to decay and most call writers would avoid the January 55. On the other hand, call buyers get more time for less premium by purchasing the March calls.

Understanding option premiums is important to make sense out of option strategies. Various strategies involving calls and puts are covered in the next section. Appendix 15–A presents the Black-Scholes option pricing model, a much more sophisticated way of analyzing option prices and their time premiums and speculative premiums. This appendix is primarily designed for those who wish to achieve a more advanced understanding of the theoretical basis for option pricing and is not essential for the standard reading of the text.

■ BASIC OPTION STRATEGIES

Option strategies can be very aggressive and risky, or they can be quite conservative and used as a means of reducing risk. Option buyers and writers both attempt to take advantage of the option premiums discussed in the preceding section. In theory, many option strategies can be created, but in practice, the market must be liquid to execute these strategies. After a decade of explosive growth, option volume on individual common stocks has not expanded as much in the late 1980s and early 1990s as in the first years of the Chicago Board Options Exchange. Although volume on the underlying common stock has continued to increase, much of the option activity has been absorbed by options on the Standard & Poor's 100 and 500 Stock Indexes, where large institutional investors can transact portfolio strategies on the market rather than on individual stocks.

A reduction of individual option trading reduces the ability to create workable strategies for specific companies. For example, the lack of a liquid market can keep institutional investors from executing hedging strategies involving several hundred thousand shares. Even with these limitations in mind, the average investor can still find many opportunities for option strategies. In this section, we discuss the possible uses of calls and puts to achieve different investment goals. Table 15–7 provides option quotes at three time periods for our examples. We have ignored commissions in most examples, but commissions can be a significant hidden cost in some types of option strategies.

Buying Call Options

The Leverage Strategy Leverage is a very common reason for buying call options when the market is expected to rise during the exercise period. The use of calls in this way is similar to warrants discussed in Chapter 14, but calls have shorter lives. The call option is priced much lower than the common stock, and the leverage is derived from a small percentage change in the price of the common stock that can cause a large percentage change in the price of the call option. For example, on November 29, 1991, Bristol-Myers Squibb

Table 15–7 Option Quotes

Prices, Nov. 29, 1991

Expire date Strike price	Sales	Open Int.	Week's High	Low	Price	Net Chg.	N.Y. Close
Blkbst Dec 15	407	13187	1/16	1/16	1/16	...	11 3/8
Blkbst Jan 10	268	255	2	1 7/8	2	+2	11 3/8
Blkbst Jan 12 1/2	1206	1685	9/16	3/8	7/16	−1/16	11 3/8
Blkbst Jan 12 1/2 p	180	110	1 3/8	1 3/8	1 3/8	−1/4	11 3/8
Blkbst Mar 10	1077	3619	2 5/8	2 5/16	2 5/16	...	11 3/8
Blkbst Mar 12 1/2	1576	3906	1 3/16	3/4	3/4	−1/8	11 3/8
Boeing Dec 45	523	1591	1 1/4	5/8	13/16	−1/16	44 1/4
Boeing Dec 45 p	830	1092	2 1/8	1	1 1/2	−5/8	44 1/4
Boeing Dec 50	402	2880	1/8	1/16	1/16	−1/16	44 1/4
Boeing Jan 40 p	487	160	5/8	3/8	1/2	−1/8	44 1/4
Boeing Jan 45	220	536	1 3/4	1 3/8	1 1/2	+1/8	44 1/4
Boeing Feb 40 p	103	1452	15/16	9/16	5/8	−5/16	44 1/4
Boeing Feb 45	438	4637	2 1/2	1 13/16	2 1/4	+1/4	44 1/4
Boeing Feb 45 p	224	4231	3	2 3/8	2 3/8	−5/8	44 1/4
Boeing Feb 50	445	7095	3/4	9/16	5/8	...	44 1/4
Boeing Feb 55	122	4425	1/4	3/16	1/4	...	44 1/4
Boeing May 45	187	691	3 5/8	3 1/8	3 3/8	+1/4	44 1/4
Boeing May 45 p	105	895	3 1/2	3 1/8	3 1/4	−3/8	44 1/4
Boeing May 50	183	1064	1 5/8	1 5/16	1 7/16	+1/16	44 1/4
Boeing May 55	105	1691	5/8	1/2	9/16	−1/16	44 1/4
Bois C Jan 22 1/2 p	111	112	1 7/8	15/16	1 7/8	+1 1/8	21 5/8
Borlnd Dec 65 p	369	760	1 5/8	5/8	11/16	−3/16	73 1/2
Borlnd Dec 70	400	2921	7	2 7/8	5 3/8	−5/8	73 1/2
Borlnd Dec 70 p	441	234	3 3/4	1 9/16	1 5/8	−3/8	73 1/2
Borlnd Dec 75	592	659	3 1/2	1 3/8	2 3/4	−1/2	73 1/2
Borlnd Dec 75 p	179	529	6 1/4	3 3/8	4 3/4	...	73 1/2
Borlnd Dec 80	432	794	1 7/8	1/2	1 1/8	−9/16	73 1/2
Borlnd Jan 60 p	369	182	1 3/8	7/8	1 1/4	+1/2	73 1/2
BrMSq Dec 70	666	2918	9 3/8	5 3/4	9 1/4	−1 1/2	78 5/8
BrMSq Dec 70 p	932	3078	5/8	1/8	3/16	+1/16	78 5/8
BrMSq Dec 75	916	2443	5	2	4 3/4	−1 3/8	78 5/8
BrMSq Dec 75 p	2339	2336	2 3/8	3/8	11/16	+3/16	78 5/8
BrMSq Dec 80	4997	4154	2	1/2	1 1/4	−1 1/8	78 5/8
BrMSq Dec 80 p	1067	2840	5 3/8	2	2 5/8	+5/8	78 5/8
BrMSq Dec 85	1682	5543	1/2	1/16	3/8	−1/4	78 5/8
BrMSq Dec 85 p	148	1067	10 1/8	5 7/8	6 5/8	+1 5/8	78 5/8
BrMSq Dec 90	200	3150	1/8	1/16	1/8	...	78 5/8
BrMSq Dec 90 p	200	299	13 3/4	13 3/4	13 3/4	+3 3/4	78 5/8
BrMSq Jan 75	625	384	5 3/4	2 7/8	5 1/4	−3/4	78 5/8
BrMSq Jan 75 p	127	254	2 3/4	1 1/4	1 5/8	+1/2	78 5/8
BrMSq Jan 80	1449	1273	3	1 1/16	1 7/8	−1 1/4	78 5/8
BrMSq Jan 85	518	914	1	1/2	11/16	−7/16	78 5/8
BrMSq Mar 75	193	1126	7	4 1/2	6 1/2	−1 1/4	78 5/8
BrMSq Mar 75 p	314	836	3 5/8	2	2 1/8	+1/4	78 5/8
BrMSq Mar 80	463	2493	4 1/4	2 9/16	4	−5/8	78 5/8
BrMSq Mar 85	1258	2961	2 3/8	1 1/4	2	−5/8	78 5/8
BrMSq Mar 90	191	1258	1 1/8	9/16	7/8	−1/4	78 5/8
BrMSq Jun 75	151	142	8	5 3/4	8	−3 1/4	78 5/8
BrMSq Jun 75 p	107	200	4 5/8	3 3/8	4 1/8	+1 1/4	78 5/8
BrMSq Jun 80	243	485	5 3/4	4	4 3/4	−7/8	78 5/8
C B S Dec 135	102	110	4 1/4	2 5/8	2 5/8	−2 5/8	132 1/4
C B S Dec 135 p	114	89	3 7/8	2 11/16	3 7/8	+1 7/8	132 1/4
C B S Dec 140	223	630	2 3/16	1 1/4	1 1/4	−2 1/8	132 1/4
C B S Dec 140 p	153	91	7 1/4	4 3/4	7	+3	132 1/4
C B S Dec 145 p	143	641	10 1/8	8	9 3/4	+2 5/8	132 1/4
C B S Dec 150 p	335	264	15 1/8	12 7/8	13 7/8	+2 7/8	132 1/4
C B S Jan 140 p	140	97	8 1/2	6 7/8	8 1/2	+4 3/8	132 1/4
C B S Feb 150	157	497	2 9/16	2 1/8	2 1/8	−7/8	132 1/4
CIGNA Dec 55 p	150	410	4 3/8	4 1/4	4 1/4	−1/4	52 1/8
CamBio Feb 12 1/2	194	480	5/8	9/16	9/16	+1/16	9 5/8
CamBio May 12 1/2	133	963	1	1	1	+1/16	9 5/8
CarnCr Jan 22 1/2	649	926	1 5/8	1 3/8	1 5/8	−1/4	23 1/8
Cntocr Dec 40 p	206	984	1/2	1/4	1/4	−3/8	49
Cntocr Dec 45	261	1884	6 1/2	4 3/4	5 1/8	−1	49
Cntocr Dec 45 p	398	2150	1 3/8	7/8	7/8	−1/2	49
Cntocr Dec 50	2048	5559	2 3/4	1 3/4	2 1/8	−1/4	49
Cntocr Dec 50 p	296	4061	3 1/2	2 9/16	2 3/4	−3/4	49
Cntocr Dec 55	1359	3405	1 3/8	5/8	3/4	−1/4	49
Cntocr Jan 45	137	1680	7	6 1/4	6 1/4	−1/2	49
Cntocr Jan 45 p	160	1431	2 7/8	2 1/4	2 1/4	−1/2	49
Cntocr Jan 50	348	3523	4 5/8	3 5/8	4	−1/8	49
Cntocr Jan 50 p	193	1091	5 1/8	4 1/2	4 3/4	+1/2	49
Cntocr Jan 55	251	3549	2 5/8	1 5/8	2 3/8	+1/8	49
Cntocr Jan 60	489	1787	1 3/8	11/16	1 1/8	−1/4	49
Cntocr Apr 35 p	138	462	2 1/16	1 3/4	2	+3/16	49
Cntocr Apr 40	251	951	13 1/4	13	13 1/8	+1/8	49
Chryslr Dec 10	210	170	1 15/16	1 7/8	1 7/8	+1/4	11 5/8
Chryslr Dec 12 1/2	791	1663	5/16	1/8	1/8	−1/8	11 5/8
Chryslr Dec 15 p	1000	1036	3 1/2	3 3/8	3 1/2	+1/2	11 5/8
Chryslr Jan 10	155	678	2 1/8	1 3/4	1 3/4	−1/8	11 5/8
Chryslr Jan 10 p	304	4416	5/16	3/16	3/16	...	11 5/8
Chryslr Jan 12 1/2	141	3442	9/16	7/16	1/2	−1/16	11 5/8
Chryslr Jan 12 1/2 p	237	1789	1 7/16	1 3/16	1 7/16	+1/16	11 5/8
Chryslr Jan 15 p	275	1367	3 3/8	3 1/4	3 1/4	...	11 5/8
Cisco Dec 45	110	595	5 3/8	4 7/8	5 3/8	+1/8	49 1/2
Cisco Dec 50	196	995	2 5/16	1 11/16	2 1/8	−1/16	49 1/2
Cisco Dec 50 p	110	141	2 7/8	2 13/16	2 7/8	+1/8	49 1/2
Cisco Dec 55	130	1556	5/8	3/8	9/16	+1/16	49 1/2
Cisco Jan 45	110	349	6 3/8	6 3/8	6 3/8	−1 1/8	49 1/2
Cisco Jan 50	229	1116	3 5/8	2 3/4	3 1/8	−1/8	49 1/2
Cisco Apr 55	104	150	3 3/8	3 1/4	3 3/8	−1/4	49 1/2
Citicp Dec 10 p	146	1418	1/4	3/16	1/4	...	10 5/8
Citicp Dec 12 1/2	136	2083	1/8	1/16	1/16	−1/16	10 5/8
Citicp Dec 12 1/2 p	2000	1284	1 7/8	1 11/16	1 7/8	+1/16	10 5/8
Citicp Jan 10 p	383	3175	1/2	1/4	1/2	+1/8	10 5/8
Citicp Jan 12 1/2	656	6055	3/8	3/16	5/16	+1/16	10 5/8
Citicp Jan 12 1/2 p	176	5014	2 3/16	1 3/4	2	...	10 5/8
Citicp Jan 15	379	9944	1/8	1/16	1/16	...	10 5/8
Citicp Apr 10	269	1306	2 1/8	1 9/16	1 9/16	−3/8	10 5/8
Citicp Apr 10 p	104	3584	15/16	5/8	15/16	+1/8	10 5/8
Citicp Apr 12 1/2	297	3662	3/4	9/16	5/8	−1/16	10 5/8
Citicp Apr 12 1/2 p	166	3236	2 7/16	2	2 7/16	+1/4	10 5/8
Citicp Apr 15	279	3171	1/4	3/16	3/16	−3/16	10 5/8
Coke Dec 60 p	132	1132	1/8	1/16	1/16	−1/16	69 3/8
Coke Dec 65	434	1861	5 7/8	3 3/4	5 1/8	+1	69 3/8
Coke Dec 65 p	618	2240	13/16	1/4	3/8	−1/4	69 3/8
Coke Dec 70	1947	2360	2 1/8	3/4	1 3/8	...	69 3/8
Coke Dec 70 p	1031	841	2 7/8	1 1/4	1 3/4	−1/4	69 3/8
Coke Dec 75	407	383	7/16	3/16	1/4	−1/8	69 3/8
Coke Jan 65	810	910	5 7/8	4 5/8	5 7/8	+1 3/8	69 3/8
Coke Jan 65 p	288	441	1 5/16	5/8	3/4	−1/2	69 3/8
Coke Jan 70	428	852	3 3/8	1 5/8	2 3/4	+3/8	69 3/8

Prices, November 29, 1991
Barron's, December 2, 1991

Prices, Jan. 3, 1992

Expire date Strike price	Sales	Open Int.	Week's High	Low	Price	Net Chg.	N.Y. Close
BellAtl Jul 50	218	773	1 3/4	1	1 3/4	+3/8	48 1/2
Beth S Jan 15	261	838	5/16	3/16	1/4	+1/8	14 1/2
Beth S Apr 15	207	569	1	3/4	1	+3/8	14 1/2
Biogen Jan 35	217	887	6 3/4	4 1/2	6 3/8	+1	41 1/4
Biogen Jan 40	418	1355	3 1/4	1 7/16	2 11/16	+9/16	41 1/4
Biogen Jan 40 p	235	673	2 3/4	1 3/4	1 13/16	−13/16	41 1/4
Biogen Jan 45	275	1121	1	1/4	3/4	+3/8	41 1/4
Biomet Jan 25	485	1404	7	4	4 5/8	+3/8	30
Biomet Jan 25 p	316	774	1/4	1/16	1/8	−1/8	30
Biomet Jan 27 1/2	622	839	4 5/8	2	2 1/2	+1/8	30
Biomet Jan 30	928	728	2 1/2	7/8	1	−1/4	30
Biomet Jan 30 p	460	486	1 3/4	3/4	1 1/8	−3/4	30
Biomet Feb 30	1834	756	3 7/8	1 3/4	2 1/8	...	30
Biomet Feb 35	425	277	1 5/8	3/4	3/4	+3/4	30
Biomet Apr 20 p	232	308	1/4	3/16	1/4	−1/2	30
Biomet Apr 30	463	449	4 1/2	3 1/8	3 1/4	...	30
Biomet Jul 30	282	129	6	3 7/8	4 1/4	+3/8	30
Biomet Jul 35	458	231	3 7/8	2 1/2	2 7/8	+2 7/8	30
BioTcG Feb 10	356	621	1	3/4	7/8	+1/8	8 7/8
Blk Dk Jan 17 1/2	452	721	9/16	3/8	1/2	+1/8	17 3/8
Blk Dk Feb 15	256	701	2 3/4	2 1/8	2 9/16	+7/16	17 3/8
Blk Dk Feb 17 1/2	378	2071	15/16	5/8	3/4	...	17 3/8
Blkbst Jan 10	388	1053	2 5/16	1 5/16	2 5/16	+1 5/16	12 3/8
Blkbst Jan 12 1/2	1565	3040	3/8	1/8	3/8	+1/4	12 3/8
Blkbst Feb 10	327	470	2 1/2	1 7/8	2 1/2	+7/8	12 3/8
Blkbst Feb 12 1/2	1672	1758	3/4	5/16	3/4	+7/16	12 3/8
Blkbst Mar 10	456	3756	2 9/16	1 5/8	2 3/8	+11/16	12 3/8
Blkbst Mar 12 1/2	1017	5018	1	5/8	1	+7/16	12 3/8
Blkbst Jun 12 1/2	262	867	1 1/2	1	1 1/2	+5/8	12 3/8
Boeing Jan 45	721	2192	3	1 11/16	2 5/8	+11/16	47 1/8
Boeing Jan 45 p	308	915	5/8	1/4	1/4	−7/16	47 1/8
Boeing Jan 50	778	2157	5/16	1/8	3/16	...	47 1/8
Boeing Feb 45	746	5107	3 5/8	2 1/2	3 1/4	+3/4	47 1/8
Boeing Feb 45 p	566	4254	15/16	13/16	15/16	−7/16	47 1/8
Boeing Feb 50	2066	8372	15/16	9/16	3/4	+1/8	47 1/8
Boeing May 45	369	2252	4 3/4	3 3/4	4 1/2	+3/4	47 1/8
Boeing May 50	994	2724	2 1/16	1 9/16	1 13/16	+3/16	47 1/8
Boeing Aug 55	334	7080	1 1/2	1 1/4	1 1/2	+1/16	47 1/8
Bois C Feb 22 1/2	204	222	1 13/16	3/8	1 13/16	+1 5/16	23 3/8
Borlnd Jan 60	1965	2245	20 3/8	20	20	+6 1/4	83 1/4
Borlnd Jan 60 p	1961	2125	3/16	1/16	1/16	−1/16	83 1/4
Borlnd Jan 75	792	2426	11 5/8	6	9 1/8	+2 1/2	83 1/4
Borlnd Jan 75 p	322	533	1 11/16	7/16	3/4	−1	83 1/4
Borlnd Jan 80	945	595	7 7/8	3	5 1/4	+1 5/8	83 1/4
Borlnd Jan 80 p	419	955	3 5/8	1 7/16	2 3/16	−1 9/16	83 1/4
Borlnd Jan 85	1249	539	4 1/4	1 1/4	2 3/4	+1 3/8	83 1/4
Borlnd Jan 85 p	242	244	5 7/8	3 1/8	3 1/2	−2 1/8	83 1/4
Borlnd Feb 80 p	239	248	5 1/2	3 5/8	4 1/2	...	83 1/4
BrMSq Jan 80	773	1469	9	5 7/8	8 1/2	+3	88 3/8
BrMSq Jan 85	1649	1208	4 7/8	1 1/2	3 5/8	+1 7/8	88 3/8
BrMSq Jan 85 p	713	347	1 5/8	3/8	3/8	−7/8	88 3/8
BrMSq Jan 90	3278	1534	1 3/4	1/4	13/16	+7/16	88 3/8
BrMSq Feb 85	309	420	5 3/4	2 7/8	4 5/8	+1 1/2	88 3/8
BrMSq Feb 85 p	342	303	2	1 1/4	1 3/8	−3/4	88 3/8
BrMSq Feb 90	1343	788	2 3/4	1	2 1/8	+2 1/8	88 3/8
BrMSq Mar 80	565	2808	10 1/2	6 3/4	9 1/2	+2 1/2	88 3/8
BrMSq Mar 80 p	638	1573	1 1/4	1/2	5/8	−5/8	88 3/8
BrMSq Mar 85	712	3702	6 5/8	3 3/4	5 7/8	+2 1/8	88 3/8
BrMSq Mar 85 p	266	711	2 3/4	1 3/4	1 3/4	−3/4	88 3/8
BrMSq Mar 90	2802	2925	3 1/2	1 1/2	2 7/8	+1 3/16	88 3/8
BrMSq Jun 90	486	592	5	2 3/4	4 3/4	+1 3/4	88 3/8
Bruns Jan 15	583	111	7/16	1/8	1/4	+3/16	14 3/8
Bruns Feb 15	492	15	13/16	1/4	5/8	+5/8	14 3/8
Bruns Mar 15	842	1262	1	1/4	13/16	+9/16	14 3/8
Bruns Jun 15	517	516	1 1/4	9/16	1 1/4	+3/4	14 3/8
C B S Jan 125	212	205	18 5/8	13 1/4	15 1/2	+1/2	138 7/8
C B S Jan 125 p	220	222	1/4	3/16	1/4	−1/4	138 7/8
CarnCr Feb 30	245	230	3/8	3/16	3/8	+3/8	26
Cntocr Jan 40	543	1348	17 3/8	9 3/4	17 1/4	+8 3/8	57
Cntocr Jan 40 p	228	1742	1/2	1/16	1/16	−7/16	57
Cntocr Jan 45	1010	1920	12 3/8	5 1/4	12	+7	57
Cntocr Jan 45 p	730	2187	1 3/8	1/8	3/16	−1 5/16	57
Cntocr Jan 50	5533	4931	7 7/8	2 1/4	7 1/4	+5 1/16	57
Cntocr Jan 50 p	911	1290	3	3/8	1/2	−3	57
Cntocr Jan 55	5059	6591	3 7/8	1	3 1/4	+2 1/2	57
Cntocr Jan 55 p	516	486	6 1/4	1 1/2	1 1/2	−6 1/2	57
Cntocr Jan 60	2282	2590	1 5/8	7/16	1 1/4	+7/8	57
Cntocr Feb 50	869	1005	9 1/4	4 3/8	9	+5 1/8	57
Cntocr Feb 50 p	447	228	4 5/8	1 3/4	2	−2 3/4	57
Cntocr Feb 55	1675	810	6 1/8	2 5/8	6	+3 5/8	57
Cntocr Feb 60	864	...	4	3 1/4	3 3/4	+3 3/4	57
Cntocr Apr 35 p	283	941	1 1/16	3/8	5/8	−1 1/16	57
Cntocr Apr 40	349	1043	18 3/4	12	18 1/4	+7 1/4	57
Cntocr Apr 45	452	1135	14 3/4	9 1/2	14 3/4	+6 3/4	57
Cntocr Apr 50	1078	1479	11 1/2	6 1/2	10 3/4	+5 1/8	57
Cntocr Apr 50 p	246	914	6	3 1/2	3 3/4	−3	57
Cntocr Apr 55	1604	1471	8 3/4	4 3/8	8 3/8	+4 3/8	57
Cntocr Apr 60	1143	1393	6 3/8	3	6 1/8	+3 1/8	57
Chiron Jan 70	404	1173	2 7/8	7/8	1 3/16	...	66 1/4
Chryslr Jan 10	388	951	3 1/2	1 1/2	3 1/2	+1 3/4	13 3/8
Chryslr Jan 10 p	245	5263	1/4	1/16	1/16	−3/16	13 3/8
Chryslr Jan 12 1/2	2320	3781	1 1/8	1/8	1 1/8	+15/16	13 3/8
Chryslr Jan 12 1/2 p	555	2349	1 15/16	1/8	3/16	−1 1/2	13 3/8
Chryslr Jan 15	807	2946	3/16	1/16	1/8	+1/16	13 3/8
Chryslr Jan 15 p	1066	982	3 3/8	1 3/8	1 3/4	−2 1/4	13 3/8
Chryslr Feb 12 1/2	816	482	1 5/8	3/8	1 1/2	+1	13 3/8
Chryslr Feb 15 p	918	...	2 3/16	2	2	+2	13 3/8
Chryslr Apr 12 1/2	1368	1840	1 7/8	7/8	1 7/8	+7/8	13 3/8
Chryslr Apr 12 1/2 p	312	509	2 1/4	7/8	7/8	−1	13 3/8
Chryslr Apr 15	613	1261	13/16	5/16	3/4	+1/2	13 3/8
Chryslr Jul 12 1/2	312	517	2 1/4	1 1/8	2 1/4	+1	13 3/8
Chryslr Jul 15	247	133	1 3/16	5/8	1 1/8	+1/2	13 3/8
Cisco Jan 50	523	810	18 1/8	14 3/4	17	+3 1/8	67
Cisco Jan 55	330	631	12 3/4	10	11 1/2	+2 5/8	67
Cisco Jan 60 p	260	797	1/2	3/16	1/4	−1/2	67
Cisco Jan 65	246	251	4 1/8	2 1/4	3	+3/4	67
Cisco Jan 65 p	876	527	2	1 1/8	1 3/16	−1 7/16	67
Cisco Feb 65	774	700	5 7/8	3 7/8	4 7/8	+1	67
Cisco Feb 70	270	112	3 3/8	2	2 7/16	+2 7/16	67
Citicp Jan 10	2232	9261	1 1/8	1/2	1	+1/16	10 7/8
Citicp Jan 10 p	1992	8558	1/2	3/16	1/4	−1/8	10 7/8
Citicp Jan 12 1/2	350	6349	3/16	1/16	1/16	−1/16	10 7/8

Prices, January 3, 1992
Barron's, January 6, 1992

Prices, Jan. 31, 1992

Expire date Strike price	Sales	Open Int.	Week's High	Low	Price	Net Chg.	N.Y. Close
Blk Dk May 20 p	558	558	1	11/16	11/16	−13/16	22 3/8
Blk Dk May 22 1/2	260	338	2 5/8	5/8	2 1/8	+1 7/16	22 3/8
Blk Dk Aug 22 1/2	364	338	3	1 3/4	2 1/2	+1	22 3/8
Blkbst Feb 12 1/2	370	3829	1 15/16	7/8	7/8	−1/4	13
Blkbst Feb 12 1/2 p	279	837	3/16	1/16	1/8	−1/8	13
Blkbst Feb 15	1388	3390	3/8	1/16	1/8	−1/16	13
Blkbst Mar 7 1/2	225	1145	6 5/8	5 3/4	5 3/4	+1/8	13
Blkbst Mar 10	697	2573	4 1/4	3 3/4	3 3/4	+1/4	13
Blkbst Mar 12 1/2	486	5049	2	1 1/4	1 1/4	−3/8	13
Blkbst Mar 15	818	5563	11/16	1/4	3/8	−1/16	13
Blkbst Jun 10	521	2571	4 1/2	3 7/8	4 1/8	−1/8	13
Blkbst Jun 12 1/2	433	1481	2 3/4	1 7/8	1 7/8	−7/16	13
Blkbst Jun 15	987	5401	1 5/16	13/16	13/16	−1/4	13
Blkbst Sep 12 1/2 p	603	546	1 5/16	1	1 5/16	+1/4	13
Blkbst Sep 15	215	222	1 13/16	1 3/16	1 3/16	−1/4	13
Boeing Feb 45	677	4159	9 7/8	6	6 1/2	−1 5/8	50 7/8
Boeing Feb 45 p	552	4117	3/16	1/16	1/16	−1/16	50 7/8
Boeing Feb 50	4585	12083	4 3/4	1 3/4	2	−1 1/4	50 7/8
Boeing Feb 50 p	3060	3441	1 3/8	3/8	1	+1/4	50 7/8
Boeing Feb 55	7791	7755	1 3/8	5/16	3/8	−3/8	50 7/8
Boeing Feb 55 p	818	298	4 3/8	2	3 7/8	+5/8	50 7/8
Boeing Mar 50	876	1052	5	2 7/8	2 7/8	−1 1/8	50 7/8
Boeing Mar 50 p	639	421	1 15/16	11/16	1 13/16	+11/16	50 7/8
Boeing Mar 55	2795	1733	2 1/8	3/4	7/8	−3/8	50 7/8
Boeing May 45	205	2558	10	6 7/8	7 3/8	−1 3/8	50 7/8
Boeing May 50	1872	4647	6	3 1/2	4	−3/4	50 7/8
Boeing May 50 p	796	1667	2 1/2	1 3/8	2 1/2	+5/8	50 7/8
Boeing May 55	3712	5743	3	1 1/2	1 13/16	−5/16	50 7/8
Boeing May 55 p	284	333	5 1/2	3 1/8	5 3/8	−5/8	50 7/8
Boeing May 60	276	188	1 1/8	3/4	13/16	...	50 7/8
Boeing Aug 35	259	2142	19 1/2	17 1/8	17 1/8	−1	50 7/8
Boeing Aug 50	1490	1188	7	4 1/2	5 1/8	−7/8	50 7/8
Boeing Aug 55	1623	7087	4 1/8	2 1/2	2 3/4	−3/8	50 7/8
Bois C Feb 22 1/2	552	553	2 1/2	15/16	2 1/2	+1 1/2	23 1/4
Borlnd Feb 70 p	374	568	2 3/8	7/8	1 1/8	−1 1/4	76
Borlnd Feb 75	700	1145	4 1/4	2 1/2	4	+1 1/4	76
Borlnd Feb 80	594	804	2	15/16	2	+1	76
Borlnd Feb 80 p	772	985	8 1/4	6	6 1/4	−3 1/8	76
Borlnd Mar 65 p	317	205	2 1/8	1 3/4	1 3/4	−13/16	76
Borlnd Mar 70 p	471	97	4 1/4	3 1/4	3 1/4	−1 3/8	76
Borlnd Mar 75	728	548	5 5/8	4 3/4	5 5/8	+1 5/8	76
Borlnd Mar 80	269	115	3 3/4	2 3/4	3 3/4	+5/8	76
Borlnd Apr 50 p	255	384	5/8	3/8	5/8	−1/16	76
Borlnd Apr 60 p	1354	1426	2 3/8	1 3/4	1 3/4	−3/8	76
Borlnd Apr 75	610	640	7 1/4	6	7 1/4	+1 5/8	76
BrMSq Feb 80	1122	784	4 1/2	1 5/8	1 13/16	−1 13/16	79 7/8
BrMSq Feb 80 p	698	1165	2	7/8	1 1/4	+1/4	79 7/8
BrMSq Feb 85	639	2393	1 1/2	5/16	3/8	−5/8	79 7/8
BrMSq Feb 85 p	301	743	6	4	5 1/8	+2 1/8	79 7/8
BrMSq Mar 75 p	233	1113	7/8	1/2	3/4	+1/4	79 7/8
BrMSq Mar 80	463	2917	5 1/4	2 7/8	3	−2 3/8	79 7/8
BrMSq Mar 80 p	370	1982	3	1 3/8	2 1/8	+1/2	79 7/8
BrMSq Mar 85	1330	5474	2 3/8	1	1 1/8	−1 1/8	79 7/8
BrMSq Mar 90	200	4117	7/8	3/8	1/2	−1/8	79 7/8
BrMSq Jun 75 p	343	602	2 3/8	1 3/8	2	+1/2	79 7/8
BrMSq Jun 80 p	326	822	4 1/4	2 3/4	4	+7/8	79 7/8
BrMSq Jun 85	263	1123	4 1/2	2 9/16	3	−1 1/8	79 7/8
BrMSq Jun 90	212	954	2 1/4	1 1/2	1 1/2	−1/2	79 7/8
BrMSq Sep 75	277	1349	11 5/8	9 1/2	9 5/8	−7/8	79 7/8
Bruns Mar 15	377	1971	1 7/8	3/4	3/4	−5/16	15
Bruns Jun 15	232	1134	2 3/8	1 1/4	1 3/8	−1/4	15
Bruns Jun 17 1/2	487	490	1 1/16	1/2	13/16	+1/16	15
BurlN Feb 40 p	230	470	3/4	11/16	3/4	−1/8	40
BurlN Mar 40 p	360	410	1 5/8	1 1/2	1 9/16	+3/16	40
C B S Feb 145	247	238	3 1/2	2	2	−1 1/4	137 1/2
C B S Feb 150	715	1117	1 13/16	11/16	11/16	−1 1/4	137 1/2
C B S Feb 160	201	574	11/16	1/2	1/2	−1/4	137 1/2
CIGNA Feb 55 p	289	233	2 1/4	13/16	2	+1 3/16	54
CIGNA Feb 60	315	492	13/16	1/4	5/16	−3/4	54
Cadenc Feb 30	557	926	1 3/8	11/16	11/16	+1/8	27 3/8
Cadenc May 15	270	445	14 1/4	14 1/4	14 1/4	+4 5/8	27 3/8
Cadenc Aug 20	270	645	10 1/2	10 1/2	10 1/2	...	27 3/8
Cntocr Feb 45	276	573	9	5 1/4	6 1/4	−2 1/4	50
Cntocr Feb 45 p	1294	1161	1 7/8	9/16	1 1/4	+3/4	50
Cntocr Feb 50	3579	3232	5 3/8	2 3/4	2 3/4	−2 1/2	50
Cntocr Feb 50 p	1555	1912	4	1 3/4	3 1/8	+1 1/8	50
Cntocr Feb 55	3082	5827	2 3/4	1 1/8	1 1/8	−1 1/2	50
Cntocr Feb 55 p	305	713	7	4 3/8	5 1/4	+1 1/4	50
Cntocr Feb 60	1669	5110	1 1/8	7/16	1/2	−3/4	50
Cntocr Mar 45 p	299	279	2 11/16	1 1/2	1 3/4	+1/4	50
Cntocr Mar 50	829	652	6 1/4	4 1/4	4 1/2	−3 1/8	50
Cntocr Mar 55	802	854	3 7/8	2 3/8	2 9/16	−1 15/16	50
Cntocr Mar 60	401	434	2 1/2	1 3/8	1 1/2	−1	50
Cntocr Apr 40	222	1137	13 1/8	10 3/4	12	−4	50
Cntocr Apr 40 p	288	908	2 1/8	1 1/4	1 3/8	+1/8	50
Cntocr Apr 45	490	962	10 1/2	7 5/8	8 1/4	−2	50
Cntocr Apr 45 p	212	978	3 1/2	2 3/16	2 3/4	+3/4	50
Cntocr Apr 50	580	1877	7 1/2	5 1/2	5 3/4	−2 3/4	50
Cntocr Apr 50 p	455	859	6 1/4	4 1/8	4 3/4	+3/4	50
Cntocr Apr 55	673	1682	5 3/4	3 3/8	4	−1 5/8	50
Cntocr Apr 60	628	2587	3 1/4	2 1/8	2 3/8	−7/8	50
Cntocr Jul 50	1005	516	10	7 5/8	8 1/2	−2 1/8	50
Cntocr Jul 55	243	856	8 1/4	6	6 1/2	−2	50
Chamin Feb 25	648	925	1 7/8	1 1/4	1 3/8	−1/2	25 1/2
Chiron Feb 55 p	446	1114	2 7/8	1 5/16	1 5/8	+5/8	58
Chiron Feb 60	328	593	4	1 13/16	2 3/16	−3 7/16	58
Chiron Feb 65	507	1210	2 1/2	11/16	11/16	−2 1/16	58
Chiron Feb 70	205	1528	13/16	5/16	3/8	−7/8	58
Chryslr Feb 7 1/2	400	...	7	7	7	...	14 3/8
Chryslr Feb 10	411	46	5 5/8	4 1/2	4 1/2	+1 1/4	14 3/8
Chryslr Feb 12 1/2	404	955	3	1 7/8	2	+5/8	14 3/8
Chryslr Feb 12 1/2 p	324	973	1/4	1/8	3/16	−1/8	14 3/8
Chryslr Feb 15	3282	2362	1 1/8	3/8	7/16	+3/16	14 3/8
Chryslr Feb 15 p	1148	1581	1 1/4	1/2	1 1/16	−7/8	14 3/8
Chryslr Feb 17 1/2	214	138	1/4	3/16	3/16	...	14 3/8
Chryslr Mar 12 1/2 p	647	644	9/16	3/8	7/16	−3/16	14 3/8
Chryslr Mar 15	595	486	1 1/2	3/4	15/16	+5/16	14 3/8
Chryslr Apr 10 p	267	1169	1/8	1/8	1/8	−1/16	14 3/8
Chryslr Apr 12 1/2	404	2185	3 3/8	2 3/8	2 1/2	+1 3/16	14 3/8
Chryslr Apr 12 1/2 p	621	1705	3/4	7/16	1/2	−3/8	14 3/8
Chryslr Apr 15	2396	4172	1 3/4	1	1 1/8	+7/16	14 3/8
Chryslr Apr 15 p	947	940	1 15/16	1 1/4	1 15/16	−1/2	14 3/8

Prices, January 31, 1992
Barron's, February 3, 1992

common stock closed at $78.625 per share and the March 80 call closed at $4.00 (see Table 15–7 for the abbreviated BrMSq Mar 80 quote).[4]

One month later, on January 3, 1992, the stock closed at $88.375 for a $9.75 point gain of 12.4 percent. The March 80 call closed at $9.50 for a $5.50 gain of 138 percent. The call option increased by more than 11 times the percentage move in the common stock. The relationship is indicated below.

Bristol-Myers Squibb

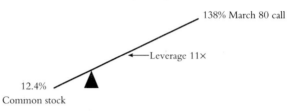

Figure 15–2 depicts the relationship between profit and loss opportunities for the Bristol-Myers Squibb March 80 call option, assuming the option is held until the day of expiration (no speculative premium exists at expiration).

As long as the common stock closes under $80, the call buyer loses the whole premium of $4 (or 100 shares times $4 equals $400). At a price of $84, the call buyer breaks even as the option is worth an intrinsic value of $4. As the stock increases past $84, the profit starts accumulating. At a price of $89, the profit equals $500 at expiration. If the option is sold before expiration, a speculative premium may increase the profit potential.

An investor striving for maximum leverage will generally buy options that are out of the money or slightly in the money. Buying high-priced options for $10 or $15 that are well in the money limits the potential for leverage. You may have to invest almost as much in the options as you would have in the stock.

Playing the leverage game doesn't always work. If a speculator on January 3, 1992, had assumed Centocor (CNTOCR) would go up and bought the February 55 call for $6, almost one month later on January 31, 1992, the Centocor February 55 call option would have been worth $1.125. A $4.875 point loss has occurred. The decline in Centocor common stock from $57 to $50 would have caused a $4.875 loss (100 shares × $4.875 = $487.50) for the option buyer. Although the stock declined only $7, or 12.3 percent, the call declined $4.875 points, or 81.25 percent. If the stock price stays at $50 until expiration, the owner of the 55 call can expect to lose the current call premium of $1.125 because the intrinsic value at a market price of $50 is zero. It is not hard to lose all your money under these circumstances—leverage works in reverse, too.

---

[4] Do not use the March 80 p as that refers to put options rather than call options.

Figure 15–2   Bristol-Myers Squibb March 80 Call Buy 1 Option (Excludes Commissions)

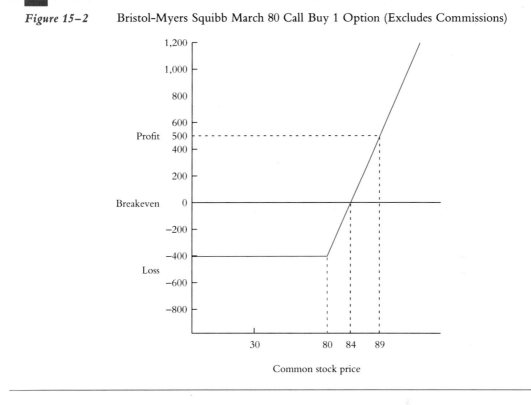

Call Options Instead of Stock Many people do not like to risk losing large amounts of money and view call options as a way of controlling 100 shares of stock without a large dollar commitment. For example, using Table 15–7 for the January 3, 1992, prices, Centocor common stock could have been purchased at $57 or $5,700 for 100 shares. An April 50 call purchased on January 3, 1992, could also be bought for $10.75 ($1,075), which would leave $4,625 ($5,700 − $1,075), for an investment elsewhere while still controlling 100 shares of Centocor at 50 through the option.

Assume the call is purchased for $1,075 and the $4,625 is left to be invested in a money market fund at 5 percent until January 31, 1992. The interest income would be about $17.75 for the 28 days.[5]

During this time, the stock declined from $57 to $50 for a loss of $7, or $700. As would be expected, the call option also went down from $10.75 to $5.75. That's a loss of $500 that was partially offset by the $17.75 of interest income from the investment of leftover cash in a money market fund. The net

---

[5] The approximate calculation is $4,625 × 5% × (28 days/365) = $17.75.

loss associated with the call option is $482.25 ($500 − $17.75). The net loss on the call option of $482.25 is certainly less than the net loss of $700 on the stock purchased. The overall effect is demonstrated in Table 15–8. An additional unspecified cost consideration is that the investor probably saved another $25 to $50 in commissions since stock trading is more expensive than option trading.

Had the stock really declined in value, say to $40, the advantage of the limited dollar loss exposure of the option would be even more apparent. The purchaser of 100 shares of stock would have lost $1,700 as the stock declined from $57 to $40. The purchaser of the option cannot lose more than the initial purchase price of $1,075 ($10.75 × 100). Even this loss is slightly offset by the $17.75 of interest from the investment of leftover cash in a money market account.[6]

Of course, if the stock rises to $80 or $90, both the stock purchaser and option buyer will show substantial profits.

Protecting a Short Position   Calls are often used to cover a short sale against the risk of rising stock prices. This is called hedging your position; by purchasing a call, the short seller guarantees a loss of no more than a fixed amount while at the same time reducing any potential profit by the total premium paid for the call. Again refer to Table 15–7 and assume you sold 100 shares of Boeing short at $44.25 on November 29, 1991, and bought a May 50 call for $1.4375 (1⅞₆) as protection against a rise in the price of the stock. By January 31, 1992, the stock has risen to $50.875 for a $6.625 loss on the short position. This loss has been partially offset by an increase in the May 50 call option price from $1.4375 to $4.00, or a $2.5625 gain. Instead of losing $6.6250, the short position is only out $4.0625 so far ($6.6250 − $2.5625). This is the loss of $6.625 on the short position less the gain of $2.5625 on the call option.

The initial $1.4375 is a speculative premium paid for the May 50 call; the speculative premium evaporates at expiration, but otherwise after the stock reaches $50, the call goes up dollar for dollar with the stock. If the investor thinks Boeing is a good short at $50.875 on January 31, 1992, he may sell the May 50 call for $4 on January 31, 1992, and be left with an unprotected short position hoping the stock will eventually decline from its current price.

Consider the initial $1.4375 call premium. If the stock goes up, the call limits your loss, but if the stock goes down as expected, your profit on the short position is reduced by the call premium. In the case of Boeing, the stock would have to decline to $42.8125 ($44.25 − $1.4375) before the short seller with call protection would break even. In other words, a decline of only 3.25 percent in the stock price would have to occur before the short seller would begin to profit, and this ignores commissions. As is true of most option plays, there are advantages and disadvantages to most strategies.

---

[6] It should be pointed out we are talking about *absolute* dollar losses. On a percentage basis, the options would be the bigger losers.

Table 15–8	Comparison of Call Option to Stock Purchase (Centocor)	
Buy Stock*:		**Buy Call:**
January 3, 1992		January 3, 1992
−$5,700 (100 × $57) investment		−$1,075 (100 × $10.75)
January 31, 1992		January 31, 1992
+$5,000 (100 × $50) Stock value		+$ 575 (100 × $5.75) Option value
+ 0 Dividend		+$ 17.75 Interest
$5,000 Total value		$ 592.75 Total value
$700 Loss ($5,000 − $5.700)		$ 482.25 Loss ($592.75 − $1,075)

*Note: The stock pays no dividend.

Guaranteed Price   Often, an investor thinks a stock will rise over the long term but does not currently have the cash available to purchase the stock. The important point for this strategy is that the investor wants to own this stock eventually but does not want to miss out on a good buying opportunity now (based on expectations). Perhaps the oil stocks are depressed or semiconductors have hit bottom. A call option can be utilized. The investor could be anticipating a cash inflow in the future when he plans to exercise the call option with a tax refund, a book royalty, or even the annual Christmas bonus.

For example, on November 29, 1991, Carrie Nowakowski buys a Coca-Cola (Coke) January 70 call option for $2.75, which is all speculative premium since Coke is selling for $69.375 per share on that date. By January 3, 1992, she has received her $7,000 royalty check and exercises the option to buy the stock when the stock is selling at $83.25. For tax purposes, the cost or basis of these 100 shares of Coke is the strike price ($70) plus the option premium ($2.75), or $72.75 per share. Since most investors will not pursue this strategy if they expect prices to fall, they will usually seek out the deepest in the money option they can afford because it is likely to have the lowest speculative premium. For example, Carrie could have bought the January 65 call with a price of $5.875, and the final cost would be $70.875 rather than $72.75 per share.

Writing Call Options

Writers of call options take the opposite side of the market from the buyers. The writer is similar to a short seller in that he or she expects the stock to decline or stay the same. For short sellers to profit, prices may decline, but since writers of call options receive a premium, they can make a profit if prices stay the same or even rise less than the speculative premium. Option writers can write **covered options,** meaning they own the underlying common stock, or they can write **naked options,** meaning they do not own the underlying stock.

Writing covered call options is often considered a hedged position because if the stock price declines, the writer's loss on the stock is partially offset by the option premium. A potential writer of a covered call must decide if he is willing to sell the underlying stock if it closes above the strike price and the option is exercised.

Returning to Table 15–7 for another set of option quotes, find Bristol-Myers Squibb (BrMSq) options on January 3, 1991. The market price of the common stock is 88.375 and the writer for a March call option can choose from the strike prices reprinted in Table 15–9 at the top of the next page.

Remember, the writer agrees to sell 100 shares at the strike price for the consideration of the premium. The 80 strike price has the highest premium and would be a good write if the stock closed at less than 80 because the call would not get exercised and the writer would profit by the amount of the 9½ premium. If the stock closed at 80 or higher, then the call could get exercised, and the writer would have to deliver 100 shares at 80. More likely, the option writer would buy back the option for its price in the market to avoid having the option exercised. If the ending value of the stock were 85, the option writer could buy back the 80 call option for 5 and still have a $4.50 profit before commissions. If the stock closed at more than $89.50, the call writer would buy back the option at a loss. Figure 15–3 shows this relationship between profit and loss and the common stock price in writing an option.

By January 31, 1992, Brystol-Myers Squibb stock closed at $79.875 and the March 80 option was worth $3. If the position were closed out at that point, the covered call writer would lose money and a naked option writer would make a profit. The covered option writer is assumed to have bought 100 shares at 88.375 at the time he wrote the option for $9.50 on January 3. The naked option writer merely sold the option for $9.50. It is further assumed the covered option writer would receive a $69 quarterly dividend. The analysis is presented below.

Covered Writer		**Naked Writer**	
− Initial investment (100 × 88.375)	$(8,837.50)	− Margin (30% of stock price)	$(2,651.25)
+ Option premium ($9.50)	950.00	+ Option premium ($9.50)	950.00
+ Dividend	69.00	(no dividends received)	—
+ Ending value stock	7,987.50	+ Ending value margin	2,651.25
− Repurchase of option	(300.00)	− Repurchase of option	(300.00)
Loss	− $ 131.00	Profit	$ 650.00
Percent return (loss) on		Percent return on	
initial investment	− 14.82%	initial investment	24.5%

The covered writer hedged the loss on his stock from $850 to a loss of $131 through profits from the option and a dividend. The naked option writer made money and a high percentage return on his initial margin (24.5 percent) for less than a one-month investment or close to a 294 percent annualized return. The

Table 15–9	Bristol-Myers Squibb March Strike Prices and Option Prices		
January 3, 1992	**Market Price**	**Strike Price**	**Option Price**
Bristol-Myers	$88.375	$80	$9.50
Bristol-Myers	$88.375	$85	$5.875
Bristol-Myers	$88.375	$90	$2.875

Figure 15–3   Bristol-Myers Squibb March 80 Calls
Write 1 Call (Excludes Commissions)

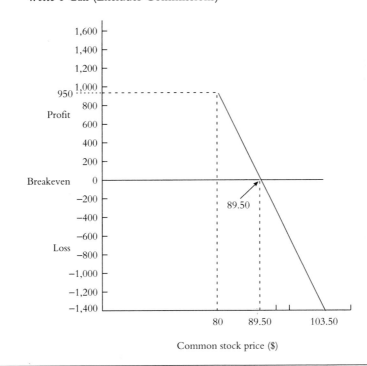

Common stock price ($)

naked writer was required to put up margin on 30 percent of the value of the stock to ensure his ability to close out the option write if the stock should rise significantly. The capital was returned to him when it was no longer needed as collateral. If the stock price had risen, the naked writer was exposed to un-limited risk as he either had to close out his position at a loss or purchase the stock above the strike price and deliver it at a loss. The covered writer had limited risk because he owned the stock and could deliver it or close out his position before it is called.

Another critical decision for a call writer is the choice of months. In the section on option premiums, we examined percentage premiums per day and found that the shortest expiration dates usually provided the highest daily speculative premium. In most cases, the call writer will choose the short-term options and, as they expire, write another short-term option. *Annualized* returns of 12 to 15 percent are not uncommon for continuously covered writing strategies.

Buying Put Options

The owner (buyer) of a put may sell 100 shares of stock to the put writer at the strike price. The strategy behind a put is similar to selling short or writing a call except losses are limited to the total investment (premium), and no more risk exposure is possible if the stock rises. Buying a put in anticipation of a price decline is one method of speculating on market price changes. The same factors influencing call premiums also apply to put premiums except that expectations for the direction of the market are the opposite.

On January 3, 1992, Bristol-Myers Squibb (BrMSq) common stock was 88.375, and an 80 March put could be purchased for ⅝ or $0.625 (see Table 15–7 and look for put prices as designated by a p rather than call prices). The put was out of the money by $8.375. Two-and-one-half months remained until expiration. The buyer of the put would expect a price decline with the idea that the intrinsic value of the put would increase. By January 31, 1992, Bristol-Myers Squibb declined to 79.875 with the March 80 put trading at $2⅛. The intrinsic value was now $.125 (80 − 79.875), and the speculative premium was $2. At this time, the owner of the put had a $1.50 gain on a $.625 investment (or a 240 percent return) while the stock had declined only 9.62 percent.

Puts can make money in a down market and also possibly help offset a loss in the value of the common stock. As an example of the latter case, an owner of 100 shares of Bristol-Myers Squibb could have bought a put to hedge against a loss in the value of the stock. Bristol-Myers Squibb dropped $8.50 (88.375 − 79.875), and the gain of $1.50 on the put would have offset some of the loss suffered on the common stock.

Hedges do not always work as expected. For example, assume on November 29, 1992, an owner of 100 shares of Bristol-Myers Squibb stock thought the stock was going to decline because of expectations of rising interest rates, but he did not want to sell the stock and pay a capital gains tax on these shares held for many years. Instead, he bought a January 75 put for $1.625 when the stock was trading at $78.625. One month later, Bristol-Myers Squibb was up to $88.375 (the decline never materialized), and the January 75 put was worthless, providing a loss of $162.50 on the put. This $162.50 loss partially offset the $9.75 (per share or $975 total) gain on the stock and reduced the total profit. Of course, one can think of the $162.50 loss as insurance against a price decline that never happened. Much like auto insurance, we pay a premium for something we hope never happens.

■ USING OPTIONS IN COMBINATIONS

Spreads

Now that you have studied puts and calls from both the buyer's and writer's perspectives, we proceed with a discussion of spreads. Most combinations of options are called **spreads** and consist of buying one option (going long) and writing an option (going short) on the same underlying stock. Spreads are for the sophisticated investor and involve many variations on a theme. Vertical spreads involve buying and writing two contracts at different striking prices with the same month of expiration. Horizontal spreads consist of buying and writing two options with the same strike price but different months, and a diagonal spread is a combination of the vertical and horizontal spread. Table 15–10 presents an example of XYZ Corporation demonstrating the options, months, and strike prices involved in each type of spread. There are more complicated spreads than these, such as the butterfly spread, variable spread, and domino spread. We cannot attempt to explain all of these spreads in the space available, so we will concentrate on vertical bull spreads and vertical bear spreads.

Since spreads require the purchase of one option and the sale of another option, a speculator's account will have either a debit or credit balance. If the cost of the long option position is greater than the revenue from the short option position, the speculator has a net cash outflow and a debit in his ac-

Table 15–10   Spreads (Call options)

Vertical spreads

	Market Price	Strike Price	October	*Option prices* January	April
XYZ	36⅜	35	4	6	6½
	36⅜	40	2	3⅜	4
	36⅜	45	11/16	1½	6

Horizontal spread

	Market price	Strike Price	October	January	April
XYZ	36⅜	35	4	6	6½
	36⅜	40	2	3⅜	4
	36⅜	45	11/16	1½	6

Diagonal Spread

	Market Price	Strike Price	October	January	April
XYZ	36⅜	35	4	6	6½
	36⅜	40	2	3⅜	4
	36⅜	45	11/16	1½	6

Table 15–11   Profit on Vertical Bull Spread

XYZ October 35		XYZ October 40		Price Spread
Bought at	4	Sold at	2	2
Sold at	7½	Bought at	4½	3
Gain	3½	(Loss)	(2½)	1
		Net gain	$100	
		Investment	$200	
		Return	50%	

count. When your spread is put on with a debit, it is said you have "bought the spread." You have "sold the spread" if the receipt from writing the short option position is greater than the cost of buying the long option position and you have a credit balance. For example, the difference between the option prices for a vertical spread on XYZ Corporation in Table 15–10 with October strike prices of 35 and 40 is $2 ($4 − $2). The $2 difference between these two option prices could be either a debit or credit, depending on whether a bull or bear spread is used. In either case, the profit or loss from a spread position results in the change between the two option prices over time as the price of the underlying stock goes up or down.

Vertical Bull Spread   In a bull spread, the expectation is that the common stock price will rise. The speculator can buy the common stock outright, or if he wants to profit from an expected price increase but reduce his risk of loss, he can enter into a bull spread. Vertical bull spreads limit both the maximum gain and maximum loss available. They are usually debit positions because the spreader buys the higher-priced, in the money option and shorts (writes) an inexpensive, out of the money option. Using Table 15–10 for an XYZ October vertical bull spread, we would buy the October 35 at 4 and sell the October 40 at 2 for a debit of 2 (price spread). This represents a $200 investment. Assume that three weeks later, XYZ stock rises from 36⅜ to 42 with the October 35 selling at 7½ (previously purchased at 4) and the October 40 at 4½ (previously sold at 2). Table 15–11 shows the result of closing out the spread.

Because the investment was only $200, the total return of $100 provided a 50 percent return. However, returns on spreads can be greatly altered by commissions. If the following spread incurred commissions of $25 in and $25 out, the percentage return could be cut in half to 25 percent.

The maximum profit at expiration is equal to the difference in strike prices ($5 in this case) minus the initial price spread ($2 in this case). For the XYZ vertical bull spread, the maximum profit is $300, and the maximum loss is the original debit of $200. At expiration, all speculative premiums are gone, and

Table 15–12   XYZ Vertical Bull Spread

XYZ Stock Price at Expiration 35				XYZ Stock Price at Expiration 40				XYZ Stock Price at Expiration 45			
October 35		October 40		October 35		October 40		October 35		October 40	
Bought at	4	Sold at	2	Bought at	4	Sold at	2	Bought at	4	Sold at	2
Expired at★	0	Expired at★	0	Sold at★	5	Expired at★	0	Sold at★	10	Bought at★	5
(Loss)	(4)	Gain	2	Gain	1	Gain	2	Gain	6	Loss	(3)
(Net loss) (2)				Net gain 3				Net gain 3			
($200) = 100 percent loss				$300 = 150 percent gain				$300 = 150 percent gain			

★All call options on date of expiration equal their intrinsic value.

each option sells at its intrinsic value. Table 15–12 shows maximum profit and loss at various closing market prices at expiration. Remember, our initial investment is $200.

As Table 15–12 indicates, profit does not increase after the stock moves through the 40 price range. Every dollar of increased profit on the long position is offset by $1 of loss on the short position after the stock passes a price of 40. One of the important but difficult aspects of spreading is forecasting a range of prices rather than just the direction prices will move. If a speculator is bullish, he or she may buy a call instead of spreading. The potential loss is higher with the call but still limited, while the possible gain is unlimited. The relationship between long calls and bull spreads starts in the *bottom* of Figure 15–4. Note the maximum loss with the bull spread is $200 and $400 with a long call. The break-even point is also $2 less for the bull spread ($37 versus $39). However, the long call has unlimited profit potential, and the bull spread is locked in at $300 at a stock price of $40 or higher. The spread position lowers the break-even point by $2 per share but also limits potential returns—a classic case of risk-return trade-off.

Vertical Bear Spread   The speculator enters a bear spread anticipating a decline in stock prices. Instead of selling short or writing a call with both having unlimited risk, he spreads by selling short the call with the lower strike price (highest premium) and covers the upside risk with the purchase of a call having a higher strike price. This creates a credit balance. In a sense, the bear spread does the opposite of the vertical bull spread as seen in Table 15–13 in which we show profits and losses from the strategy if XYZ ends up at 35 or at 40. With a bear spread, the price spread of 2 is the maximum gain if the stock closes at 35 or less at expiration, while the maximum loss equals 3, the difference between the exercise prices minus the price spread. The relationship between bear spreads and writing a call option is also demonstrated in Figure 15–4 (the comparison starts at the *top* of the figure).

Figure 15–4   Profit and Loss Relationships on Spreads and Calls

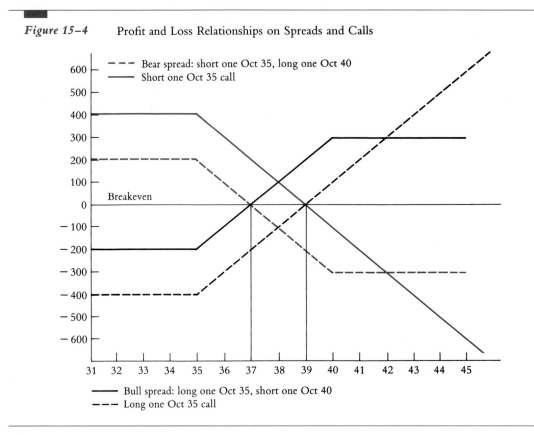

Bear spread: short one Oct 35, long one Oct 40
Short one Oct 35 call

Bull spread: long one Oct 35, short one Oct 40
Long one Oct 35 call

Table 15–13   XYZ Vertical Bear Spread

XYZ Stock Price at Expiration 35				XYZ Stock Price at Expiration 40			
October 35		**October 40**		**October 35**		**October 40**	
Sold at	4	Bought at	2	Sold at	4	Bought at	2
Expired at	0	Expired at	0	Bought at	5	Expired at	0
Gain	4	(Loss)	(2)	(Loss)	1	(Loss)	2
		Net gain 2				Net loss (3)	
		$200				$(300)	

Straddles

A **straddle** is a combination of a put and call on the same stock with the same strike price and expiration date. It is used to play wide fluctuations in stock prices and is usually applied to individual stocks with high betas and a history of large, short-term fluctuations in price. The speculator using a straddle may be unsure of the direction of the price movement but may be able to make a large enough profit on one side of the straddle to cover the cost of both options even if one option expires worthless.

For example, assume a put and a call can be bought for $5 apiece on an ABC October 50 when ABC Corporation is selling at 50 with six months to expiration. The total investment is 10 ($1,000). If the stock should rise from 50 to 65 at expiration, the call would provide a profit of 10 (15 value − 5 cost), and the put would be left to expire worthless for a loss of 5. This would provide a net gain of 5, or $500. The same type of example can be drawn if the price goes way down. Some who engage in spreads or straddles might attempt to close out one position before the other. This expands the profit potential but also increases the risk.

■ OTHER OPTION CONSIDERATIONS

Many factors have not been covered in detail because of their changing nature over time. Tax laws relating to options are constantly changing, and some items, such as capital gains, have been revised several times in the last few years. We do know that the tax laws have a significant impact on spread positions and also on the tax treatment where put options are involved. The recognition of the year in which a gain or loss is declared can still be affected by option strategies in combination with stock positions. The best advice we can give is to check the tax consequences of any option strategy with your accountant or stockbroker.

Commissions vary among brokerage houses and are not easy to pinpoint for option transactions since quantity discounts exist. Because many option positions involve small dollar investment outlays, commissions of $25 to $50 for buying and selling can significantly alter your returns and even create losses. Commissions on acquiring common stock through options are higher than the transaction costs of options, and this is a motivating force in closing out option transactions before expiration. Overall, commissions on options tend to be more significant than commissions on commodities or other highly leveraged investments.

■ SUMMARY

Put and call options are an exciting area of investment and speculation. We have discussed the past history of over-the-counter options trading and more recent trading of options on the listed options exchanges, such as the CBOE. The markets are more efficient, and the standardized practices of the listed

exchanges have made options more usable for many investors and widened the number of option strategies that can be employed.

Option premiums (option prices) are affected by many variables such as time, market expectations, stock price volatility, dividend yields, and in the money, out of the money relationships. The total premium consists of an intrinsic value plus a speculative premium that declines to zero by the expiration date. Calls are options to buy 100 shares of stock, while puts are options to sell 100 shares of stock.

Understanding the benefits and risks of trading options is complicated. Options can be risky or used to reduce risk. Calls can be bought for leverage, to cover a short position, or as an alternative to investing in the underlying common stock while buying time to purchase the stock (waiting for the financial resources to exercise the call). Calls are written either as a hedge on a long position in the underlying stock or to speculate on a price decline. Puts are bought to hedge a long position against a price decline or as an alternative to selling short. A writer of a put may speculate on a price increase or use the write as a hedge against a short position (if the price goes up, he will come out ahead on the writing of the put to partially offset the loss on the short sale).

Spreads are combinations of buying and writing the same options for an underlying common stock. In general, spreads reduce the risk of loss while limiting the gain. Spreads can be created to profit from rising prices, falling prices, or no price change. The important part is having the correct expectations. Straddles are a combination of a put and a call option in a stock at the same exercise date and strike price. They are used to profit from stocks showing large, short-term price fluctuations.

Other factors affect option profitability, such as taxes and commissions, and in general, each investor or speculator should check out his or her own situation and factor in the appropriate information with regard to taxes and commissions.

IMPORTANT WORDS AND CONCEPTS

option 484
put 484
calls 484
long-term equity anticipation securities
  (LEAPS) 486
exercise price 486
Options Clearing Corporation 487
opening purchase transaction 487
opening sale transaction 487
closing purchase transaction 488

closing sale transaction 488
in the money 490
out of the money 490
intrinsic value 490
speculative premium 490
covered options 499
naked options 499
spreads 503
straddle 507

■ DISCUSSION QUESTIONS

1. What exchanges trade in stock options?
2. How has the option market been expanded to go beyond individual stocks?
3. What is meant by the exercise or strike price on an option?
4. Explain how the Options Clearing Corporation operates.
5. What factors influence a speculative premium on an option?
6. Why might an option price reflect a discount at expiration?
7. Why does an option that is deep in the money often have a low speculative premium?
8. Why would a high-beta stock often have a greater speculative premium than a low-beta stock?
9. Comment on the statement, "The novice may attempt to write the options with the highest total premium or speculative premium, while the buyer may think the smallest investment provides the greatest leverage."
10. What does the speculative premium as a percent of stock price indicate for a call option?
11. Comment on how leverage works in purchasing a call option.
12. Assume you wish to control the price movement of 100 shares of stock. You may buy 100 shares of stock directly or purchase a call option on the 100 shares. Which strategy is likely to expose you to the larger potential dollar amount of loss? Which strategy is likely to expose you to the larger potential percentage loss on your investment?
13. Explain how options can be used to protect a short position.
14. What are two option strategies to take advantage of an anticipated decline in stock prices? (Relate one to call options and the other to put options.)
15. What is the difference between a covered and a naked call option write?
16. In general, if the price of the underlying stock is going up, what will happen to the price of a put option? Briefly explain.
17. What is a vertical spread? A horizontal spread? A diagonal spread?
18. Is a vertical bear spread likely to be more or less risky than selling short or writing a naked call option?
19. What is a straddle? Why is it used?
20. Why might small commissions of $25 to $50 be important in option trades?

PROBLEMS

Option trading
prices

1. Look at the option quotes in Table 15–2.

   a. What is the closing price of the common stock of General Electric (Gen El)?

   b. What is the highest strike price listed?

   c. What is the price of a March 75 call option?

   d. What is the price of a March 75 put option?

   e. Explain the reason for the difference between the prices of the call and the put.

Option trading
terms

2. Assume a stock is selling for $51.50 with options available at 40, 50, and 60 strike prices. The 50 call option price is at 4½.

   a. What is the intrinsic value of the 50 call?

   b. Is the 50 call in the money?

   c. What is the speculative premium on the 50 call option?

   d. What percent does the speculative premium represent of common stock price?

   e. Are the 40 and 60 call options in the money?

Option trading
terms

3. In the case of Dow Chemical (Dow Ch) in Table 15–3:

   a. What is the intrinsic value of the March 50 call?

   b. What is the total premium?

   c. What is the speculative premium?

Option trading
terms

4. In the case of Upjohn in Table 15–3:

   a. What is the intrinsic value of the April 45 call?

   b. How much is the speculative premium?

   c. By what percent does the stock need to go up by expiration to break even on the call option?

Speculative
premium per day

5. Assume on May 1, you are considering a stock with three different expiration dates for the 60 call options. The percentage speculative premium for each date is as follows:

May	2.6%
August	6.9%
November	11.2%

Each contract expires at 11:59 P.M. Eastern time on the Saturday immediately following the third Friday of the expiration month. For purposes of this problem, assume the May option has 21 days to run, the August option has 112 days, and the November option has 203 days.

a. Compute the percentage speculative premium per day for each of the three dates.

b. From the viewpoint of a call option purchaser, which expiration date appears most attractive (all else being equal)?

c. From the viewpoint of a call option writer, which expiration date appears most attractive (all else being equal)?

Leverage strategy

6. In Table 15–7, calculate the leverage from holding a Centocor (Cntocr) call option (Jan 50) from November 29, 1991, to January 3, 1992. (The best approach for doing this is to compute the percentage gain from holding the option, then compute the percentage gain from holding the stock, and finally, divide the first value by the second value.)

Naked call options

7. Assume an investor writes a call option for 100 shares at a strike price of 40 for a premium of 6½. This is a naked option.

a. What would the gain or loss be if the stock closed at 35?

b. What would the break-even point be in terms of the closing price of the stock?

Covered call options

8. Assume you purchase 100 shares of stock at $73 per share and wish to hedge your position by writing a 100-share call option on your holdings. The option has a $70 strike price and a premium of $8. If the stock is selling at $68 at the time of expiration, what will be the overall gain or loss on this covered option play? (Consider the change in stock value as well as the gain or loss on the option.) Note that the stock does not pay a cash dividend.

Covered call options

9. In Problem 8, what would be the overall gain or loss if the stock ended up at (*a*) $70, (*b*) $48, (*c*) $85, (*d*) $100 (disregard the stock being called away in (*a*) and (*c*).

Commission considerations

10. Though commissions are not explicitly considered in Problems 7 through 9, might they be significant?

Put options

11. Assume a 40 July put option is purchased for 5½ on a stock selling at $36 per share. If the stock ends up on expiration at $29½, what will be the value of the put option?

Put options

12. In Problem 11, at what ending stock price would the investor break even?

Vertical bull spread

13. Vertical bull spread: a stock is selling for $57. You buy a July 55 call option for 3¼ and short (write) a July 60 call option for 1. If the stock is $64 at expiration, what will your profit or loss be on the spread? (Note: you do not own any stock directly.)

Protecting a short position with options

14. Assume you sell 100 shares of Bowie Corporation short at $61. You also buy a 60 call option for 3½ to protect against the stock price going up.

    a. If the stock ends up at $80, what will be your overall gain or loss?

    b. If the stock ends up at $40, what will be your overall gain or loss?

    c. What is the most you can lose under this short sale-call option plan?

    d. If you had an unprotected short sale position (no call option), what is the most you could lose?

SELECTED REFERENCES

General Material

Exchange Traded Options. Chicago: Chicago Board Options Exchange, March 1991.

Option Trading Strategy

Black, Fisher. "Fact and Fantasy in the Use of Options." *Financial Analysts Journal,* July–August 1975, pp. 36–41.

Degler, William. "Option for Professionals: Tools of the Trade." *Futures,* April 1987, pp. 52–55.

_____. "Simple Options Strategies: The Versatile Bull Spread." *Futures,* August 1986, pp. 56–59.

Finucane, Thomas J. "Put-Call Parity and Expected Returns." *Journal of Financial and Quantitative Analysis,* December 1991, pp. 445–57.

French, Dan W., and Glenn V. Henderson. "Substitute Hedged Option Portfolios: Theory and Evidence." *Journal of Financial Research,* Spring 1981, pp. 21–31.

Gambola, Michael J.; Rodney L. Roenfeldt; and Philip L. Cooley. "Spreading Strategies in CBOE Options: Evidence on Market Performance." *Journal of Financial Research,* Winter 1978, pp. 35–44.

Hauser, R. J., and J. S. Eales. "On Marketing Strategies with Options: A Technique to Measure Risk and Return." *Journal of Futures Markets,* Summer 1986, pp. 273–78.

Labuszewski, John. "Setting up Your Options Trading Battle Plan." *Futures,* November 1988, pp. 44–45.

Merton, Robert C.; Myron S. Scholes; and Mathew L. Gladstein. "The Returns and Risk of Alternative Call Option Investment Strategies." *Journal of Business,* April 1978, pp. 183–242.

"Options—A Pension Management Tool for Controlling Risk and Return." *Financial Executive,* March 1979, pp. 37–43.

Rendleman, Richard J., Jr. "Optional Long-Run Option Investment Strategies." *Financial Management,* Spring 1981, pp. 61–76.

Valuing Options

Black, Fischer, and Myron Scholes. "The Valuation of Option Contracts and a Test of Market Efficiency." *Journal of Finance,* May 1972, pp. 399–417.

_____. "The Pricing of Options and Corporate Liabilities." *Journal of Political Economy,* May–June 1973, pp. 637–54.

Geske, Robert, and Kuldeep Shastri. "Valuation by Approximation: A Comparison of Alternative Option Valuation Techniques." *Journal of Financial and Quantitative Analysis,* March 1985, pp. 45–71.

Woodward, R. S. "The Effect of Monetary Surprises on Financial Futures Prices." *Journal of Futures Markets,* Fall 1986, pp. 375–84.

Option-Market Efficiency

Finnerty, Joseph E. "The Chicago Board Options Exchange and Market Efficiency." *Journal of Financial and Quantitative Analysis,* March 1978, pp. 29–38.

Galai, Dan. "Tests of Market Efficiency of the Chicago Board Options Exchange." *Journal of Business,* April 1977, pp. 167–97.

Appendix 15–A: The Black-Scholes Option Pricing Model*

■ THEORY

In 1973, Fischer Black and Myron Scholes published their derivation of a theoretical option pricing model. They started with three securities: riskless bonds, shares of common stock, and call options. The shares of common stock and call options were combined to form a riskless hedge that, by definition, had to duplicate the return of a discount bond with the same maturity length as the option. Using the riskless-hedge concept as a basis, Black and Scholes then proceeded with their model derivation.

Black and Scholes made the following assumptions:

1. Markets are frictionless. This means there are no taxes or transactions costs; all securities are infinitely divisible; all market participants may borrow and lend at the known and constant riskless rate of interest; there are no penalties for short selling.
2. Stock prices are lognormally distributed, with a constant variance for the underlying returns.
3. The stock neither pays dividends nor makes any other distributions.
4. The option may be exercised only at maturity.

Given the above assumptions and the riskless hedging strategy, Black and Scholes derived a call option pricing model that may be expressed as:

$$c = (S)(N(d_1)) - (X)(e^{-rt})(N(d_2)) \qquad (15A-1)$$

where:

$$d_1 = \frac{\ln(S/X) + (r + (\sigma^2/2))(T)}{(\sigma)(\sqrt{T})} \qquad (15A-2)$$

$$d_2 = d_1 - (\sigma)(\sqrt{T}) \qquad (15A-3)$$

The terms are defined as follows:

c = Price of the call option

S = Prevailing market price of a share of common stock on the date the call option is written

---

* This appendix was developed by Professor Carl Luft of DePaul University in consultation with the authors.

X = Call option's striking price (exercise price)

r = Annualized prevailing short-term riskless rate of interest

T = Length of the option's life expressed in annual terms

σ^2 = Annualized variance associated with the underlying security's price changes

$N(\cdot)$ = Cumulative normal density function

At maturity ($T = 0$), so the call option must sell for either its intrinsic value or zero, whichever is greater. This boundary condition may be expressed mathematically as:

$$c = \text{Max}\,(0,\, S - X) \tag{15A-4}$$

It can be shown that given a put option and a call option, with the same striking price, and one share of the underlying stock, one can form a portfolio that will earn an amount equal to the option's striking price no matter what value the stock takes at expiration. From this relationship, the value of a put option can be determined mathematically as:

$$p = (X)(e^{-rt}) - S + c \tag{15A-5}$$

with the boundary condition,

$$p = \text{Max}(0,\, X - S) \tag{15A-6}$$

Formula 15A–5 is known as the put-call parity relationship, and Formula 15A–6 shows that at maturity the put must sell for either its intrinsic value or zero.

Inspection of Formulas 15A–1 through 15A–6 reveals that both the call and put option prices are a function of only five variables: S, the underlying stock's market price; X, the striking price; T, the length of the option's life; σ^2, the volatility of the stock price changes; and r, the riskless rate of interest. All of these variables are easily observed or estimated. Previously developed option pricing models relied on variables that were based on individual investor risk preferences or on expected values of the stock price. Since the Black-Scholes model does not rely on such variables, it is superior to prior models.

To understand the behavior of options, it is necessary to examine the relationship of the option price to each of the five inputs. For call options, the price is positively related to the stock's price, the riskless rate of interest, the volatility, and the time to maturity; whereas an inverse relationship exists between the call option price and the striking price. Put options exhibit positive relationships with the striking price and volatility, negative relationships with the underlying stock price and riskless rate, and either a positive or negative relationship with time.

These relationships are easy to grasp if one realizes that options will not be exercised unless they have an intrinsic value. Consider first the price of the underlying stock. As it increases, calls go in the money and gain intrinsic value

while puts fall out of the money and lose intrinsic value. If the stock price declines, then the reverse is true. This explains the positive relationship between the call price and the stock price and the inverse relationship between the put price and the stock price. Higher striking prices cause lower intrinsic values for call options but result in greater intrinsic values for put options. In this case, the loss of intrinsic value causes the inverse relationship between the call option and striking price, while the gain in intrinsic value causes the positive relationship between the put price and the striking price. The positive relationship of both put and call prices to the volatility can be explained by the fact that options written on higher-volatility stocks have a relatively better chance of being in the money at expiration than do options written on lower-volatility stocks. The positive relationship of the call price to the risk-free rate reflects the fact that the intrinsic value increases because the present value of the exercise price decreases as the risk-free rate rises. For put options, such rate increases and declining present values of exercise prices cause a loss of intrinsic value and account for the inverse relationship between the put option price and risk-free rate. Finally, the positive relationship of the call price to time is caused by an increasing intrinsic value due to lower present values of the exercise price for longer time periods. A more complex relationship exists for put options.

Intuitively, one might expect a strictly positive relationship between the put option price and time. Such a relationship will occur if the put is at the money or out of the money, while a negative relationship can exist for deep in the money puts. The reason for this inverse relationship lies embedded in the stock's price behavior. Since stock prices cannot be less than zero, the put option has a maximum value that equals the strike price. Investors who own deep in the money put options that are close to their maximum value because of extremely low stock prices are prohibited from exercising these options by assumption 4. Thus, time is working against these investors since they run the risk of losing intrinsic value if the stock price rises before expiration.

After deriving the model, Black and Scholes subjected it to empirical testing. They implemented the riskless-hedging strategy by combining options and stock in proportions dictated by the model and comparing these hedged returns to observed Treasury bill returns. They hypothesized that if the model provided equilibrium, or fair option prices, then the hedged returns should equal the returns generated by the investment in riskless securities. In effect, they attempted to create a synthetic Treasury bill by combining options and stock. If the returns from the option-stock hedge were not equal to the Treasury bill return, it meant the model was unable to provide equilibrium option prices. On the other hand, if there was no significant difference between the hedge and Treasury bill returns, then it could be concluded that the model provided equilibrium prices. The results of the Black-Scholes empirical test showed no significant difference between the option-stock hedged returns and the Treasury bill returns. Thus, Black and Scholes concluded the model did provide equilibrium prices.

The theoretical derivation and empirical justification of an option pricing model by Black and Scholes was an extremely important accomplishment with far-reaching implications. Basically, it meant model-generated prices could be considered being the equilibrium, or correct, prices. Thus, an investor could use the model to determine whether the market had mispriced an option. Mispriced options spawn arbitrage opportunities. Given such an opportunity, the most obvious way to benefit is to form a riskless hedge by combining options and stock and then maintaining the hedge until the option's market price adjusts to the equilibrium model price. This strategy will provide arbitrage profits since the level of risk that is being assumed equals that of a Treasury bill, but the profits earned when the mispriced option adjusts to the equilibrium, or model price, will exceed the profits earned from investing in a Treasury bill.

■ APPLICATION

The data in Table 15A–1 illustrate the mechanics of the Black-Scholes option pricing model.

Column (1) simply denotes the stock's ticker symbol, while columns (2) through (7) provide the required inputs for the model. Notice that the option maturity is expressed in calendar days and the volatility is given as the standard deviation of returns. The call and put option prices (for both stocks) implied by the data will not be computed.

When the values from Table 15A–1 for CFL stock are used in Formulas 15A–2 and 15A–3, we obtain the following answers for d_1 and d_2:

$$d_1 = \frac{\ln(33/35) + (.09 + (.04/2))(.4932)}{(.2)(\sqrt{.4932})}$$

$$= \frac{-.0588 + .0543}{.1405}$$

$$= -.032$$

$$d_2 = -.032 - .1405$$

$$= -.1725$$

To obtain values for $N(d_1)$ and $N(d_2)$, the Standard Normal Distribution Function Table (Table 15A–2) must be used. The $N(d_1)$ and $N(d_2)$ values are found by first locating the row and column entries in the table that correspond to the computed d_1 and d_2 values. For CFL stock, the row entry is $-.0$, and the column entry is 3. This value of $-.03$ approximates the computed d_1 value of $-.032$. For d_2, the row entry is $-.1$, and the column entry is 7, yielding a value of $-.17$, approximating the computed value of $-.1725$ for d_2.

Locating the d_1 and d_2 values yield the table entries that define the values of $N(d_1)$ and $N(d_2)$. For CFL stock, the $N(d_1)$ value is .4880, while the $N(d_2)$

(1)	**(2)**	**(3)**	**(4)** _(T)_	**(5)**	**(6)** _(σ)_	**(7)** _(σ²)_
Stock Symbol	**(S)** **Stock Price**	**(X)** **Strike Price**	**Days to Maturity Divided by Days in Year**	**(r)** **Risk-Free Rate**	**Standard Deviation of Returns**	**Variance of Stock Returns**
CFL	33	35	180/365	.09	.20	.04
GAH	42	40	50/365	.10	.23	.0529

Table 15A–1   Illustrative Data for Black-Scholes Option Model

value is .4325. In this example, these values are only approximations, since $-.03$ and $-.17$ are approximations. If one desires more precise $N(d_1)$ and $N(d_2)$ values, they can be obtained through interpolation. For these examples, the approximations are sufficient.

At this point, all the necessary values for computing the option price have been found. Determining the options' prices via Formulas 15A–1 and 15A–5 is all that remains to be done. Thus, the CFL call option price is:

$$c = (33)(.4880) - (35)(e^{-(.09)(.4932)})(.4325)$$
$$= 16.1040 - (35)(.9566)(.4325)$$
$$= 16.1040 - 14.4805$$
$$= 1.6235$$

and the CFL put option price is:

$$p = (35)(e^{-(.09)(.4932)}) - 33 + 1.6235$$
$$= (35)(.9566) - 33 + 1.6235$$
$$= 2.1045$$

Since each option controls 100 shares of stock, the theoretical call price is $162.35, while the put's theoretical price is $210.45.

A second example (using GAH stock) again uses the variables from Table 15A–1 and substitutes them into Formulas 15A–2 and 15A–3 to derive d_1 and d_2 as follows:

$$d_1 = \frac{\ln(42/40) + (.10 + (.0529/2))(.1370)}{(.23)(\sqrt{.1370})}$$
$$= \frac{.0488 + .0173}{.0851}$$
$$= .7767$$
$$d_2 = .7767 - .0851$$
$$= .6916$$

Table 15A–2 Standard Normal Distribution Function

t	0	1	2	3	4	5	6	7	8	9
−3.	.0013									
−2.9	.0019	.0018	.0017	.0017	.0016	.0016	.0015	.0015	.0014	.0014
−2.8	.0026	.0025	.0024	.0023	.0023	.0022	.0021	.0021	.0020	.0019
−2.7	.0035	.0034	.0033	.0032	.0031	.0030	.0029	.0028	.0027	.0026
−2.6	.0047	.0045	.0044	.0043	.0041	.0040	.0039	.0038	.0037	.0036
−2.5	.0062	.0060	.0059	.0057	.0055	.0054	.0052	.0051	.0049	.0048
−2.4	.0082	.0080	.0078	.0075	.0073	.0071	.0069	.0068	.0066	.0064
−2.3	.0107	.0104	.0102	.0099	.0096	.0094	.0091	.0089	.0087	.0084
−2.2	.0139	.0136	.0132	.0129	.0125	.0122	.0119	.0116	.0113	.0110
−2.1	.0179	.0174	.0170	.0166	.0162	.0158	.0154	.0150	.0146	.0143
−2.0	.0227	.0222	.0217	.0212	.0207	.0202	.0197	.0192	.0188	.0183
−1.9	.0287	.0281	.0274	.0268	.0262	.0256	.0250	.0244	.0239	.0233
−1.8	.0359	.0351	.0344	.0336	.0329	.0322	.0314	.0307	.0300	.0294
−1.7	.0446	.0436	.0427	.0418	.0409	.0401	.0392	.0384	.0375	.0367
−1.6	.0548	.0537	.0526	.0516	.0505	.0495	.0485	.0475	.0465	.0455
−1.5	.0668	.0655	.0643	.0630	.0618	.0606	.0594	.0582	.0571	.0559
−1.4	.0808	.0793	.0778	.0764	.0749	.0735	.0721	.0708	.0694	.0681
−1.3	.0968	.0951	.0934	.0918	.0901	.0885	.0869	.0853	.0838	.0823
−1.2	.1151	.1131	.1112	.1093	.1075	.1056	.1038	.1020	.1003	.0985
−1.1	.1357	.1335	.1314	.1292	.1271	.1251	.1230	.1210	.1190	.1170
−1.0	.1587	.1562	.1539	.1515	.1492	.1469	.1446	.1423	.1401	.1379
−.9	.1841	.1814	.1788	.1762	.1736	.1711	.1685	.1660	.1635	.1611
−.8	.2119	.2090	.2061	.2033	.2005	.1977	.1949	.1921	.1894	.1867
−.7	.2420	.2389	.2358	.2326	.2297	.2266	.2236	.2206	.2177	.2148
−.6	.2743	.2709	.2676	.2643	.2611	.2578	.2546	.2514	.2483	.2451
−.5	.3085	.3050	.3015	.2981	.2946	.2912	.2877	.2843	.2810	.2776
−.4	.3446	.3409	.3372	.3336	.3300	.3264	.3228	.3192	.3156	.3121
−.3	.3821	.3783	.3745	.3707	.3669	.3632	.3594	.3557	.3520	.3483
−.2	.4207	.4168	.4129	.4090	.4052	.4013	.3974	.3936	.3897	.3859
−.1	.4602	.4562	.4522	.4483	.4443	.4404	.4364	.4325	.4286	.4247
−.0	.5000	.4960	.4920	.4880	.4840	.4801	.4761	.4721	.4681	.4641

t	0	1	2	3	4	5	6	7	8	9
.0	.5000	.5040	.5080	.5120	.5160	.5199	.5239	.5279	.5319	.5359
.1	.5398	.5438	.5478	.5517	.5557	.5596	.5636	.5675	.5714	.5753
.2	.5793	.5832	.5871	.5910	.5948	.5987	.6026	.6064	.6103	.6141
.3	.6179	.6217	.6255	.6293	.6331	.6368	.6406	.6443	.6480	.6517
.4	.6554	.6591	.6628	.6664	.6700	.6736	.6772	.6808	.6844	.6879
.5	.6915	.6950	.6985	.7019	.7054	.7088	.7123	.7157	.7190	.7224
.6	.7257	.7291	.7324	.7357	.7389	.7422	.7454	.7486	.7517	.7549
.7	.7580	.7611	.7642	.7673	.7704	.7734	.7764	.7794	.7823	.7852
.8	.7881	.7910	.7939	.7967	.7995	.8023	.8051	.8079	.8106	.8133
.9	.8159	.8186	.8212	.8238	.8264	.8289	.8315	.8340	.8365	.8389
1.0	.8413	.8438	.8461	.8485	.8508	.8531	.8554	.8577	.8599	.8621
1.1	.8643	.8665	.8686	.8708	.8729	.8749	.8770	.8790	.8810	.8830
1.2	.8849	.8869	.8888	.8907	.8925	.8944	.8962	.8980	.8997	.9015
1.3	.9032	.9049	.9066	.9082	.9099	.9115	.9131	.9147	.9162	.9177
1.4	.9192	.9207	.9222	.9236	.9251	.9265	.9279	.9292	.9306	.9319
1.5	.9332	.9345	.9357	.9370	.9382	.9394	.9406	.9418	.9429	.9441
1.6	.9452	.9463	.9474	.9484	.9495	.9505	.9515	.9525	.9535	.9545
1.7	.9554	.9564	.9573	.9582	.9591	.9599	.9608	.9616	.9625	.9633
1.8	.9641	.9649	.9656	.9664	.9671	.9678	.9686	.9693	.9700	.9706
1.9	.9713	.9719	.9726	.9732	.9738	.9744	.9750	.9756	.9761	.9767
2.0	.9773	.9778	.9783	.9788	.9793	.9798	.9803	.9808	.9812	.9817
2.1	.9821	.9826	.9830	.9834	.9838	.9842	.9846	.9850	.9854	.9857
2.2	.9861	.9864	.9868	.9871	.9875	.9878	.9881	.9884	.9887	.9890
2.3	.9893	.9896	.9898	.9901	.9904	.9906	.9909	.9911	.9913	.9916
2.4	.9918	.9920	.9922	.9925	.9927	.9929	.9931	.9932	.9934	.9936
2.5	.9938	.9940	.9941	.9943	.9945	.9946	.9948	.9949	.9951	.9952
2.6	.9953	.9955	.9956	.9957	.9959	.9960	.9961	.9962	.9963	.9964
2.7	.9965	.9966	.9967	.9968	.9969	.9970	.9971	.9972	.9973	.9974
2.8	.9974	.9975	.9976	.9977	.9978	.9978	.9979	.9980	.9980	.9981
2.9	.9981	.9982	.9982	.9983	.9984	.9984	.9985	.9985	.9986	.9986
3.	.9987									

The $N(d_1)$ and $N(d_2)$ values from the Standard Normal Distribution Table (15A–2) are .7823 and .7549, respectively. As mentioned in the previous example, greater precision is possible through interpolation.

Given the above values, the GAH call and put prices are computed as:

$$c = (42)(.7823) - (40)(e^{-(.10)(.1370)})(.7549)$$
$$= 32.8566 - (40)(.9864)(.7549)$$
$$= 32.8566 - 29.7853$$
$$= 3.0713$$
$$p = (40)(e^{-(.10)(.1370)}) - 42 + 3.0713$$
$$= (40)(.9864) - 42 + 3.0713$$
$$= .5273$$

These calculations indicate the theoretically correct price (for 100 shares) for the call is $307.13 and that $52.73 is the theoretically correct price for the put.

Suppose the market had priced the GAH call at $262.50. How would you be able to earn arbitrage profits? According to Black and Scholes, you would buy the undervalued calls at $262.50 and sell shares of GAH stock at $42 per share to form a riskless hedge and thus obtain arbitrage profits when equilibrium is established. However, to implement such a strategy, an investor must know how many shares to combine with each option to form the riskless hedge. This information is provided by $N(d_1)$ and is known as the hedge ratio or delta.

Since each option controls 100 shares of stock, the appropriate arbitrage activity in this example is to sell .7823 shares of GAH stock for every option purchased. Practically speaking, one cannot buy and sell fractional shares. Thus, 78 shares should be sold for each option that is purchased. If the market had overpriced the option, then the arbitrageur would sell options and purchase 78 shares for each option sold. In either case, the hedge's risk level will equal that of a Treasury bill, but the hedge's returns will exceed the Treasury bill's return, thus generating arbitrage profits.

16

Commodities and Financial Futures

What do pork bellies, soybeans, Japanese yen, and Treasury bills have in common? They are all items on which contracts may be traded in the commodities and financial futures markets.

A **futures contract** is an agreement that provides for the delivery of a specific amount of a commodity at a designated time in the future at a given price. An example might be a contract to deliver 5,000 bushels of corn next September at $2.50 per bushel. The person who sells the contract does not need to have actual possession of the corn, nor does the purchaser of the contract need to plan on taking possession of the corn. Almost all commodities futures contracts are closed out or reversed before the actual transaction is to occur. Thus, the seller of a futures contract for the delivery of 5,000 bushels of corn may simply later buy back a similar contract for the purchase of 5,000 bushels and close out his position. The initial buyer also reverses his position. Over 97 percent of all contracts are closed out in this fashion rather than through actual delivery. The commodities futures market is similar to the options market in that there is a tremendous volume of activity, but very few actual items ever change hands.

The futures markets were originally set up to allow grain and livestock producers and processors to **hedge** (protect) their positions in a given commodity. For example, a wheat producer might have a five-month lead time between the planting of his crop and the actual harvesting and delivery to the market. While the current price of wheat might be $3 a bushel, there is a tremendous risk that the price might change before delivery to the market. The wheat farmer can hedge his position by offering to sell futures contracts for the delivery of wheat. Even though he will probably close out or reverse these futures contracts before the call for actual delivery, he will still have effectively hedged his position. Let's see how this works. If the price of wheat goes down, he will have to sell his crop for less than he anticipated when he planted the wheat, but he will make up the difference on the wheat futures contracts. That is, he will be able to buy back the contracts for less than he sold them. Of course, if the price of the wheat goes up, the extra profit he makes on the crop will be lost on the futures contracts as he now has to buy back the contracts at a higher price.[1]

A miller who uses wheat as part of his processing faces the opposite dilemma in terms of pricing. The miller is afraid the price of wheat might go up and ultimately cut into his profit margin when he takes actual delivery of his product. He can hedge his position by buying futures contracts in wheat. If the actual price of wheat does go up, the extra cost of producing his product will be offset by the profits he makes on his futures contracts.

The commodities market allows the many parties in need of hedging opportunities to acquire contracts. While some of this could be accomplished on a private basis (one party in Kansas City calls another party in Chicago on the

---

[1]The hedger not only reduces risk of loss but also eliminates additional profit opportunities. This may be appropriate for farmers since they are not in the risk-taking business but rather in agriculture.

advice of his banker), this would be virtually impossible to handle on a large-scale basis. Liquid, fluid markets such as those provided by the commodity exchanges are necessary to accomplish this function.

While the hedgers are the backbone and basic reason for existence of the commodity exchanges, they are not the only significant participants. We also have the speculators who take purely long or short positions without any intent to hedge actual ownership. Thus, there is the speculator in wheat or silver who believes the next major price move can be predicted to such an extent that a substantial profit can be made. Because commodities are purchased on the basis of a small investment in the form of **margin** (usually running 3 to 10 percent of the value of the contract), there is substantial leverage on the investment, and percentage returns and losses are greatly magnified. The typical commodities trader often suffers many losses with the anticipation of a few very substantial gains. Commodities speculation, as opposed to hedging, represents somewhat of a gamble, and stories have been told of reformed commodities speculators who gave up the chase to spend the rest of their days merely playing the slot machines. Nevertheless, commodity speculators are quite important to the liquidity of the market.

The volatility of commodity prices can be seen in Figure 16–1 on page 524. While the price trend for the 27 commodities in the index has been upward, note the up and down patterns, particularly in the 1980s.

■ TYPES OF COMMODITIES AND EXCHANGES

Commodities and financial futures can be broken down into a number of categories based on their essential characteristics. As indicated in Table 16–1 on page 525, there are six primary categories. In each case, we show representative items that fall under the category.

The first five categories represent traditional commodities, but category six came into prominence in the 1970s and 1980s, with foreign exchange futures originating in 1972, interest rate futures beginning in 1975, and stock index futures in 1982. Because many financial futures have tremendous implications for financial managers, we will give them special attention later in this chapter. We will defer discussion of stock index futures to Chapter 17 so that they can be given *complete coverage* as a separate topic.

The commodities listed in Table 16–1 trade on various commodity exchanges in the United States and Canada (see Table 16–2 on page 525). While the exchanges are well organized and efficient in their operation, they are still run by an open auction complete with outcries of bids and various hand-signal displays.

The largest commodity exchange is the Chicago Board of Trade (CBT) with the Chicago Mercantile Exchange (CME) in second place. While some exchanges are highly specialized, such as the New York Cotton Exchange, most exchanges trade in a number of securities. For example, the Chicago Board of Trade deals in such diverse products as corn, oats, soybeans, wheat, silver, and Treasury bonds.

Figure 16-1

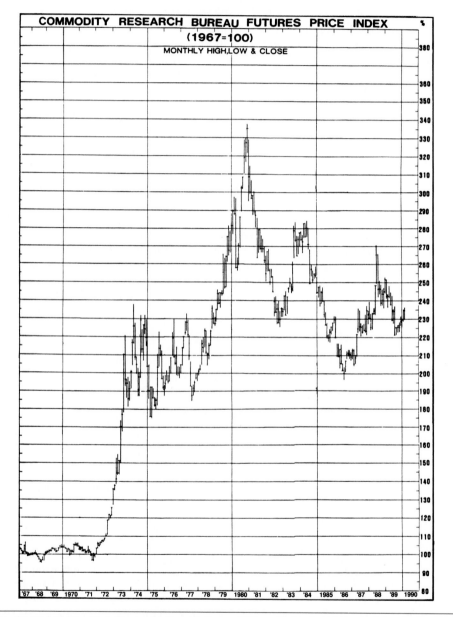

COMMODITY RESEARCH BUREAU FUTURES PRICE INDEX
(1967=100)
MONTHLY HIGH,LOW & CLOSE

Source: *Commodity Yearbook* (New York: Commodity Research Bureau, 1990), p. 70. Reprinted with permission © 1992 Commodity Research Bureau, 30 S. Wacker, Chicago, IL 60606.

Table 16–1 Categories of Commodities and Financial Futures

(1)	(2)	(3)
Grains and oilseeds:	Livestock and meat:	Food and fiber:
Corn	Cattle—feeder	Cocoa
Oats	Cattle—live	Coffee
Soybeans	Hogs—live	Cotton
Wheat	Pork bellies	Orange juice
Barley	Turkeys	Potatoes
Rye	Broilers	Sugar
		Rice
		Butter

(4)	(5)	(6)
Metals and petroleum:	Wood:	Financial futures:
Copper	Lumber	*a.* Foreign exchange:
Gold	Plywood	Pound, yen, franc, etc.
Platinum		*b.* Interest rate futures:
Silver		Treasury bonds
Mercury		Treasury bills
Heating oil no. 2		Certificates of
		deposit
		Municipal bonds
		Eurodollars
		c. Stock index futures:
		S&P 500
		Value Line

Table 16–2 Major United States and Canadian Commodity Exchanges

American Commodities Exchange (ACE)

Chicago Board of Trade (CBT)

Chicago Mercantile Exchange (CME)

   Also controls International Monetary Market (IMM)

Commodity Exchange (CMX)

Kansas City Board of Trade (KC)

Minneapolis Grain Exchange (MPLS)

New Orleans Commodity Exchange

New York Coffee, Sugar, and Cocoa Exchange (CSCE)

New York Cotton Exchange (CTN)

New York Futures Exchange (NYFE)

   Subsidiary of the New York Stock Exchange

New York Mercantile Exchange (NYM)

Pacific Commodities Exchange (PCE)

Winnipeg Grain Exchange (WPG)

Table 16-3	Size of Commodity Contracts	
Contract	**Trading Units**	**Size of Contract Based on Mid-1991 Prices (in dollars)**
Corn	5,000 bushels	$ 12,500
Oats	5,000 bushels	5,600
Wheat	5,000 bushels	15,000
Pork bellies	38,000 pounds	20,520
Coffee	37,500 pounds	31,900
Cotton	50,000 pounds	39,600
Sugar	112,000 pounds	23,500
Copper	25,000 pounds	25,125
Gold	100 troy ounces	37,100
Silver	5,000 troy ounces	22,200
Treasury bonds	$100,000	92,310
Treasury bills	$1,000,000	944,200

The activities of the commodity exchanges are primarily regulated by the Commodity Futures Trading Commission (CFTC), a federal regulatory agency established by Congress in 1975. The CFTC has had a number of jurisdictional disputes with the SEC over the regulation of financial futures.

Types of Commodities Contracts

The commodity contract lists the type of commodity and the denomination in which it is traded (bushels, pounds, troy ounces, metric tons, percentage points, etc.). The contract will also specify the standardized unit for trade (5,000 bushels, 30,000 pounds, etc.). A further designation will indicate the month in which the contract ends, with most commodities having a whole range of months from which to choose. Typically, contracts run as far as a year into the future, but some interest rate futures contracts extend as far as three years.

Examples of the sizes of futures contracts are presented in Table 16-3. Be aware that there may be many different forms of the same commodity (such as spring wheat or amber/durum wheat).

■ ACTUAL COMMODITIES CONTRACT

To examine the potential gain or loss in a commodities contract, let's go through a hypothetical investment. Assume we are considering the purchase of a December wheat contract (it is now May 1). The price on the futures

contract is $3 per bushel. Since wheat trades in units of 5,000 bushels, the total price is $15,000. As we go through our example, we will examine many important features associated with commodity trading—beginning with margin requirements.

Margin Requirements

Commodity trading is based on the use of margin rather than on actual cash dollars. Margin requirements are typically 3 to 10 percent of the value of the contract and may vary over time or even among exchanges for a given commodity. For our example, we will assume a $600 margin requirement on the $15,000 wheat contract.[2] That was the specified margin in 1991. The $600 would represent 4 percent of the value of the contract ($15,000).

Margin requirements on commodities contracts are much lower than those on common stock transactions, where 50 percent of the purchase price has been the requirement since 1974. Furthermore, in the commodities market, the margin payment is merely considered to be a good-faith payment against losses. There is no actual borrowing or interest to be paid.[3]

In addition to the initial margin requirements, **margin maintenance requirements** (minimum maintenance standards) run 60 to 80 percent of the value of the initial margin. In the case of the wheat contract, the margin maintenance requirement might be $400 (67% × $600). If our initial margin of $600 is reduced by $200 due to losses on our contract, we will be required to replace the $200 to cover our margin position. If we do not do so, our position will be closed out, and we will take our losses.

The margin requirement, relative to size, is even less for financial futures. For example, on a $1 million Treasury bill contract, the investor generally must post only an initial margin of $540. Similar requirements exist for other types of financial futures.

Note that the high risk inherent in a commodities contract is not so much a function of volatile price movements as it is the impact of high leverage made possible by the low initial margin requirements. A 5 percent price move may equal or exceed the size of our initial investment in the form of the margin deposit. This is similar to the type of leverage utilized in the options market as described in Chapter 15. However, the action in the commodities market is much quicker. You can be asked to put up additional margin within hours after you establish your initial position.

---

[2]The amount of margin required also differs between speculative and hedging activities. For example, $600 represents the margin for speculation. The margin for hedging is $400 in this case.

[3]It should also be pointed out that a customer may need a minimum account balance of $5,000 or greater to open a commodity account.

Market Conditions

Because the price of every commodity moves in response to market conditions, each investor must determine the key market variables that influence the value of his or her contract. In the case of wheat, the investor may be particularly concerned about such factors as weather and crop conditions in the Midwest, the price of corn as a substitute product, the carryover of wheat supply from the previous year, and potential wheat sales to other countries.

Gains and Losses

In the present example, assume we guessed right in our analysis of the wheat market; we purchased a December futures contract for $3 per bushel, and the price goes to $3.12 per bushel (recall that the contract was for 5,000 bushels). With a 12-cent increase per bushel, we have established a dollar gain of $600 (5,000 bushels × $.12 per bushel profit). With an initial margin requirement of $600, we have made a percentage profit of 100 percent as indicated in the following formula.[4]

$$\frac{\text{Dollar gain}}{\text{Amount of margin deposit}} = \frac{\$600}{\$600} \times 100 = 100\%$$

If this transaction occurred over one month, the annualized gain would be 1,200 percent (100% × 12 = 1,200%). Note that this was all accomplished by a 12-cent movement in the price of a December wheat contract from $3 to $3.12.

Actually, we may choose to close out the contract or attempt to let the profits run. We also may use the profits to establish the basis for margin on additional futures contracts. A paper gain of $600 is enough to provide the $600 margin on another wheat contract.

We are now in a position to use an inverse pyramid to expand our position. With two contracts outstanding, a mere 6-cent price change will provide $600 in profits.

$$
\begin{array}{r}
\$\ .06 \text{ Price change} \\
\times\ \underline{10,000} \text{ Bushels (two contracts)} \\
\$600 \text{ Profits (can be applied to third contract)}
\end{array}
$$

The new $600 in profits can be used to purchase a third contract, and now with 15,000 bushels under control, a 4-cent price change will generate enough profits for a fourth contract.

---

[4]This does not include commissions, which are generally less than $100 for a complete transaction (buy and sell).

$ .04 Price change
× 15,000 Bushels (three contracts)
$600 Profits (can be applied to fourth contract)

Inverse pyramiding begins to sound astounding since eventually a 1-cent or ½-cent change in the price of wheat will trigger enough profits for a new contract. Of course, great risks are associated with such a process. It is like building a house with playing cards. If one tumbles, the whole house comes down. The investor can become so highly leveraged that any slight reversal in price can trigger off margin calls. While it is often wise to let profits run and perhaps do some amount of pyramiding, prudence must be exercised.

Our primary attention up to this point has been on contracts that are making money. What are the implications if there is an immediate price reversal after we have purchased our December wheat contract? You will recall there was a margin maintenance requirement of $400 based on our initial margin of $600. In this case, a $200 loss would call for an additional deposit to bring our margin position up to $600. How much would the price of wheat have to decline for us to get this margin call to increase our deposit? With a 5,000-bushel contract, we are talking about a mere decline of 4 cents per bushel.

$$\frac{\$200 \text{ loss}}{5,000 \text{ bushels}} = \$.04 \text{ per bushel}$$

This could happen in a matter of minutes or hours after our initial purchase. When we get the margin call, we can either elect to put up the additional $200 and continue with the contract or tell our commodities broker to close out our contract and take our losses. If we put up the $200, our broker could still be on the phone a few minutes later asking for more margin because the price has shown further deterioration. Because investors often buy multiple contracts, such as 10 December wheat contracts, the process can be all the more intense. In the commodities market, the old adage of "cut your losses short and let your profits run" probably has its greatest significance. Even a seasoned commodities trader might determine that he is willing to lose 80 percent of the time and win only 20 percent of the time, but those victories will represent home runs and the losses mere outs.

Price Movement Limitations

Because of the enormous opportunities for gains and losses in the commodities markets, the commodity exchanges do limit maximum daily price movements in a commodity. Some examples are shown in Table 16–4.

These daily trading limits obviously must affect the efficiency of the market somewhat. If market conditions indicate the price of wheat should decline by 30 cents and the daily limit is 20 cents, then obviously the price of wheat is not in equilibrium as it opens the following morning. However, the desire to stop market panics tends to override the desire for total market efficiency in the

Table 16–4   Maximum Daily Price Changes

Commodity	Exchange	Normal Price Range	Maximum Daily Price Change (from Previous Close)*
Corn	CBT	$2.30–$3.00	$ .10 per bushel
Oats	CBT	1.00– 1.75	$ .10 per bushel
Wheat	CBT	2.50– 3.50	$ .20 per bushel
Pork bellies	CBT	0.50– 0.75	$ .02 per pound
Copper	CMX	0.90– 1.30	$ .03 per pound
Silver	CBT	3.50– 6.50	$1.00 per ounce
Treasury bills	IMM of CME	85% of par and up	No limit

*These values may change slightly from exchange to exchange and are often temporarily altered in response to rampant speculation.

commodity markets. Nevertheless, the potential intra-day trading range is still large. Recall, for example, that a 20-cent change in the price of wheat, which is the daily limit, is more than enough to place tremendous pressure on the investor to repeatedly increase his margin position. On the typical 5,000-bushel contract, this would represent a daily loss of $1,000.

■ READING MARKET QUOTES

We turn our attention to interpreting market quotes in the daily newspaper. Table 16–5 shows an excerpt from the July 16, 1991, edition of *The Wall Street Journal* covering 21 different types of contracts (this represents about 40 percent of the contracts reported for that day).

In each case, we see a wide choice of months for which a contract may be purchased. For example, corn, which trades on the Chicago Board of Trade (CBT), has futures contracts for July, September, December, March, and May. Some commodities offer a contract for virtually every month. To directly examine some of the terms in the table, we produce a part of the corn contract (CBT) in Table 16–6.

The second line in the table indicates we are dealing in corn traded on the CBT. We then note that corn is traded in 5,000-bushel units and quoted in cents per bushel. Quotations in cents per bushel require some mental adjustment. For example, 200 cents per bushel would actually represent $2 per bushel. We generally move the decimal point two places to the left and read the quote in terms of dollars. For example, the July 1991 opening price was 235¾, or $2.3575 per bushel.

Across the top of the table we observe that we are given information on the open, high, low, settle (close), and change from the previous day's close as well as the lifetime high and low for that particular contract. The last column represents the open interest, or the number of actual contracts presently outstanding for that delivery month.

Table 16–5 Examples of Price Quotes on Commodity Futures

Monday, July 15, 1991.

Open Interest Reflects Previous Trading Day.

	Open	High	Low	Settle	Change	Lifetime High	Lifetime Low	Open Interest
–GRAINS AND OILSEEDS–								
CORN (CBT) 5,000 bu.; cents per bu.								
July	235¾	238½	235	237½	+ 4½	308¼	223	4,131
Sept	227	229	226	228	+ 3¾	287½	218½	58,917
Dec	230	231½	228¾	229½	+ 2½	275	220	101,370
Mr92	237¾	239½	236½	237½	+ 2½	275¼	228½	19,621
May	246	246	242¾	243	+ 2	279½	234¾	5,423
July	250	250	247	248	+ 1¾	282	239½	3,825
Sept	241	242	241	241	+ 1½	259	236½	101
Dec	241¼	242½	241	241	+ 1¾	262½	236½	259
Est vol n.a.; vol Fri 5,175; open int 193,647, +1,872.								
OATS (CBT) 5,000 bu.; cents per bu.								
July	127½	127½	126	127	+ 2½	164¾	103½	140
Sept	130	130½	128½	129¾	+ 2½	153	109½	6,586
Dec	136¼	136¼	134	135¼	+ 2	151½	118½	4,168
Mr92	142	142	141	141½	+ 2	157	126½	228
Est vol n.a.; vol Fri 2,002; open int 11,221, +220.								
SOYBEANS (CBT) 5,000 bu.; cents per bu.								
July	534	534	530	531½	+ 4½	718	518½	2,711
Aug	530	532	528	528¾	+ 4	695	515	21,395
Sept	531½	533	528½	528¾	+ 3¼	670	513½	13,928
Nov	536	538¾	533¾	534½	+ 3½	674	517	43,090
Ja92	546½	548¼	543½	544	+ 2¾	649½	527½	6,244
Mar	556	558¼	553½	553½	+ 2¼	660	538	3,413
May	565½	566½	562½	562¾	+ 3¾	662½	547	1,126
July	571	573½	569½	569½	+ 3¼	666	554	676
Nov	568	570	567	568	+ 5	620¾	552	326
Est vol n.a.; vol Fri 36,006; open int 92,909, +2,642.								
SOYBEAN MEAL (CBT) 100 tons; $ per ton.								
July	163.80	163.80	162.20	163.10	+ 1.00	209.00	158.60	2,080
Aug	164.50	164.70	163.30	164.20	+ 1.40	199.00	159.70	17,007
Sept	164.80	165.00	163.80	164.40	+ 1.30	193.50	160.00	8,218
Oct	164.80	165.00	163.80	164.20	+ 1.30	190.00	159.90	5,426
Dec	165.50	166.00	164.60	165.10	+ 1.40	191.50	160.00	19,899
Ja92	166.50	167.00	165.90	166.20	+ 1.30	190.50	161.30	3,133
Mar	169.00	169.00	167.50	168.20	+ 1.50	187.50	163.60	1,809
May	170.00	170.00	170.00	170.00	+ 2.00	191.00	165.00	220
July	171.00	171.00	171.00	171.00	+ 2.00	191.00	166.00	160
Est vol n.a.; vol Fri 17,284; open int 57,952, –26.								
SOYBEAN OIL (CBT) 60,000 lbs.; cents per lb.								
July	18.58	18.60	18.45	18.45	+ .12	25.70	18.15	1,129
Aug	18.55	18.65	18.43	18.44	+ .07	25.50	18.18	18,921
Sept	18.77	18.81	18.59	18.59	+ .11	25.10	18.37	14,817
Oct	18.92	18.98	18.78	18.79	+ .14	24.90	18.50	10,726
Dec	19.28	19.35	19.12	19.12	+ .09	24.75	18.81	19,792
Ja92	19.43	19.45	19.30	19.30	+ .14	24.15	19.00	4,081
Mar	19.80	19.80	19.70	19.60	+ .09	23.55	19.32	1,983
May	20.10	20.10	20.00	19.81	+ .05	23.80	19.62	1,523
July	20.35	20.35	20.30	19.95	– .01	23.70	19.90	378
Est vol n.a.; vol Fri 13,845; open int 73,412, +409.								
WHEAT (CBT) 5,000 bu.; cents per bu.								
July	273	273	266	266	– 3	355	250	258
Sept	275	276½	271	271¼	– 2¼	326	258½	23,056
Dec	286	288½	282	282¼	– 3¼	325	272½	23,515
Mr92	293	293½	288½	288¾	– 2½	332½	279	5,146
May	291	292	285	285	– 4½	331	280½	1,126
July	284½	285	282	282	– 1½	311	279½	1,909
Est vol n.a.; vol Fri 12,643; open int 55,010, +534.								
WHEAT (KC) 5,000 bu.; cents per bu.								
July	272	272½	270¾	270¾	– 1¼	320½	261	99
Sept	274	275	271	271¼	– 1½	307¼	262	17,044
Dec	283	283¾	279	279¼	– 2¾	318¼	272¼	14,791
Mr92	288	288	284	284	– 2¼	319	275½	3,797
May	284	284	280	280½	– 1½	316½	273	680
July	279	280	278½	278½	– ½	305½	272	1,221
Est vol n.a.; vol Fri 9,203; open int 37,632, +1,360.								
WHEAT (MPLS) 5,000 bu.; cents per bu.								
July	266	266	265¾	265¾	+ 1¾	306	254½	502
Sept	269	269½	266½	266½	– 1½	309½	257	9,073
Dec	280	280½	277¼	277¾	– 1¾	319½	269½	2,903
Mr92	289	289½	288	288	– ½	327	279½	6,936
Est vol n.a.; vol Fri 3,379; open int 19,491, +802.								
BARLEY (WPG) 20 metric tons; Can. $ per ton								
July	75.00	76.10	74.80	75.00	+ 1.00	102.00	72.70	194
Oct	77.00	78.80	76.80	77.00	+ 1.00	94.50	74.70	3,615
Dec	79.00	81.00	79.00	79.40	+ .90	95.80	77.20	2,029
Mr92	83.00	84.70	82.80	83.00	+ 1.10	97.50	81.00	383
Est vol 1,290; vol Fri 424; open int 6,221, +102.								
FLAXSEED (WPG) 20 metric tons; Can. $ per ton								
July	....	....	....	185.20	+ 3.70	296.00	177.50	0
Oct	192.20	194.50	192.20	192.50	+ 2.50	292.00	183.00	2,469
Dec	198.50	198.50	196.00	196.20	+ 2.20	272.50	187.10	1,663
Mr92	202.20	203.80	202.00	202.00	+ 2.80	234.50	193.20	670
May	....	....	....	206.50	+ 4.00	216.90	200.70	375
Est vol 375; vol Fri 280; open int 5,177, –34.								
CANOLA (WPG) 20 metric tons; Can. $ per ton								
Sept	260.00	263.00	260.00	262.10	+ 3.90	339.00	250.00	7,107
Nov	258.50	259.00	257.50	257.70	+ 2.70	326.50	247.60	13,086
Ja92	263.50	264.70	263.50	263.80	+ 2.70	317.50	253.40	5,487
Mar	268.00	270.00	[illegible]	[illegible]	[illegible]	[illegible]	261.60	1,366
[illegible]	278.50	[illegible]	[illegible]	[illegible]	[illegible]	[illegible]	[illegible]67.00	455
Fb92	48.60	49.20	47.70	48.77	+ .45	63.15	45.10	1,868
Est vol 3,146; vol Fri 2,750; open int 7,546, –289.								
–FOOD & FIBER–								
COCOA (CSCE)–10 metric tons; $ per ton.								
July	913	930	913	918	+ 13	1,590	860	134
Sept	960	978	955	967	+ 13	1,515	893	18,933
Dec	1,009	1,025	1,004	1,016	+ 13	1,535	953	13,681
Mr92	1,054	1,063	1,051	1,059	+ 13	1,538	997	8,894
May	1,082	1,091	1,080	1,088	+ 14	1,385	1,036	3,778
July	1,109	1,116	1,107	1,116	+ 12	1,385	1,056	3,948
Sept	1,136	1,145	1,133	1,145	+ 12	1,220	1,080	3,301
Dec	1,185	1,185	1,185	1,185	+ 13	1,185	1,119	1,025
Est vol 5,419; vol Fri 6,276; open int 53,698, +699.								
COFFEE (CSCE)–37,500 lbs.; cents per lb.								
July	83.75	83.75	82.00	81.90	– 2.85	111.50	82.00	722
Sept	84.20	84.70	83.05	83.25	– 1.95	113.50	83.05	26,912
Dec	87.80	88.10	86.55	86.65	– 2.00	116.00	86.55	10,818
Mr92	91.25	91.25	89.80	89.80	– 2.20	107.50	89.80	2,119
May	92.80	92.80	92.05	92.05	– 2.25	106.00	92.05	388
July	....	....	....	94.65	– 2.35	108.00	95.00	351
Sept	96.50	96.50	96.50	96.65	– 2.50	108.00	96.50	233
Est vol 8,407; vol Fri 10,522; open int 41,545, –1,163.								
SUGAR–WORLD (CSCE)–112,000 lbs.; cents per lb.								
Oct	9.16	9.29	9.05	9.05	– .19	14.40	7.45	63,868
Mr92	8.75	8.80	8.64	8.64	– .16	10.14	7.56	39,229
May	8.78	8.82	8.68	8.68	– .15	9.77	7.67	6,687
July	....	....	....	8.76	– .09	9.05	7.85	365
Est vol 11,604; vol Fri 8,685; open int 110,192, +336.								
SUGAR–DOMESTIC (CSCE)–112,000 lbs.; cents per lb.								
Sept	21.20	21.25	21.20	21.24	+ .04	23.35	21.19	4,727
Nov	21.59	21.62	21.59	21.62	+ .03	23.14	21.58	3,757
Ja92	21.84	21.86	21.84	21.86	+ .02	23.01	21.81	1,851
Mar	21.84	21.86	21.84	21.85	+ .05	22.80	21.80	1,797
May	21.99	22.00	21.99	22.00	+ .02	22.30	21.97	681
July	....	....	....	22.11	+ .01	22.39	22.05	550
Sept	....	....	....	22.14	....	22.35	22.15	110
Est vol 330; vol Fri 133; open int 13,476, –7.								
COTTON (CTN)–50,000 lbs.; cents per lb.								
Oct	69.50	69.80	68.60	68.66	– 1.75	83.30	66.75	10,303
Dec	68.65	68.90	68.20	68.29	– 1.15	76.35	63.85	17,776
Mr92	70.15	70.20	69.60	69.78	– .92	77.15	64.70	6,601
May	70.75	70.75	70.50	70.57	– .68	77.30	65.10	2,847
July	71.50	71.50	71.15	71.20	– .85	77.70	65.50	2,120
Oct	69.20	69.20	69.20	68.77	– .50	70.60	68.00	190
Dec	67.80	67.80	67.65	67.65	– .23	69.00	67.20	470
Est vol 7,500; vol Fri 3,895; open int 40,307, –267.								
ORANGE JUICE (CTN)–15,000 lbs.; cents per lb.								
July	119.50	119.50	119.00	118.25	– .75	180.00	102.50	146
Sept	120.65	120.75	118.00	118.50	– 1.25	127.00	106.00	2,739
Nov	119.60	119.80	117.40	117.40	– 1.65	121.00	111.00	619
Ja92	119.40	119.50	117.50	117.65	– 1.25	120.25	113.40	1,144
Mar	119.25	119.25	117.90	117.75	– 1.25	120.80	113.60	714
Est vol 1,000; vol Fri 696; open int 5,401, +136.								
–METALS & PETROLEUM–								
COPPER-HIGH (CMX)–25,000 lbs.; cents per lb.								
July	97.90	98.50	97.80	98.30	– .35	113.50	96.05	2,751
Aug	98.00	98.25	98.00	98.25	– .55	109.00	96.10	702
Sept	97.85	98.50	97.50	98.25	– .25	110.50	95.40	15,421
Oct	....	....	....	98.00	– .15	106.90	95.30	663
Nov	....	....	....	97.65	– .20	105.00	95.10	344
Dec	97.00	97.50	96.90	97.35	– .15	108.50	94.50	6,484
Ja92	97.00	97.00	97.00	96.95	– .15	104.50	95.00	255
Feb	....	....	....	96.55	– .15	105.10	95.00	138
Mar	95.90	96.40	95.90	96.20	– .10	106.80	93.90	1,958
Apr	....	....	....	95.80	– .10	99.10	93.50	168
May	95.40	95.40	95.30	95.40	– .10	106.20	93.30	1,364
July	94.80	94.80	94.60	94.70	– .10	103.80	92.80	1,150
Sept	94.00	94.15	94.00	94.00	– .10	103.45	92.80	663
Dec	93.70	93.80	93.50	93.55	– .10	100.50	91.60	568
Mr93	93.40	93.50	93.40	93.05	– .10	96.65	92.80	257
Est vol 4,500; vol Fri 7,714; open int 32,918, +132.								
GOLD (CMX)–100 troy oz.; $ per troy oz.								
July	369.00	369.00	368.60	369.10	+ .50	371.00	357.00	9
Aug	370.50	370.80	368.50	370.10	+ .50	468.00	355.80	48,297
Oct	374.30	374.30	372.60	373.70	+ .60	476.00	359.30	4,603
Dec	377.40	378.00	375.80	377.20	+ .60	483.00	362.00	15,047
Fb92	380.30	380.40	379.60	380.60	+ .60	456.50	366.00	6,264
Apr	....	....	....	383.90	+ .60	446.00	369.70	6,056
June	....	....	....	387.30	+ .60	467.00	375.00	5,546
Aug	....	....	....	390.90	+ .60	426.50	377.50	1,914
Oct	....	....	....	394.60	+ .60	410.80	389.50	1,086
Dec	....	....	....	398.60	+ .60	431.00	383.50	2,139
Fb93	....	....	....	402.90	+ .60	....	....	564
Apr	[illegible]	[illegible]	[illegible]	[illegible]10	+ .60	410.00	404.50	684
June	[illegible]	[illegible]	[illegible]	[illegible]	[illegible] .50	418.50	405.50	1[illegible]
[illegible] int 94,053, –[illegible]								

Source: *The Wall Street Journal,* July 16, 1991, p. C13. Reprinted by permission of *THE WALL STREET JOURNAL,* © 1991 by Dow Jones & Company, Inc. All Rights Reserved Worldwide.

(1)						Lifetime		Open
	Open	High	Low	Settle	Change	High	Low	Interest

Table 16–6 Price Quotes for Corn Contracts

(1)	Open	High	Low	Settle	Change	High	Low	Open Interest
(2) Corn (CBT) — 5,000 bu.; cents per bu.								
July	235¾	238½	235	237½	+4½	308¼	223	4,131
Sept	227	229	226	228	+3¾	287½	218½	58,917
Dec	230	231½	228¾	229½	+2½	275	220	101,370
Mar 92	237¾	239½	236½	237½	+2½	275¼	228½	19,621

Source: *The Wall Street Journal,* July 16, 1991, p. 16C. Reprinted by permission of *THE WALL STREET JOURNAL,* © 1991 by Dow Jones & Company, Inc. All Rights Reserved Worldwide.

■ THE CASH MARKET AND THE FUTURES MARKET

Many commodity futures exchanges provide areas where buyers and sellers can negotiate **cash** (or **spot**) **prices.** The cash price is the actual dollar value paid for the immediate transfer of a commodity. Unlike a futures contract, there must be a transfer of the physical possession of the goods. Prices in the cash market are somewhat dependent on prices in the futures market. Thus, it is said that the futures markets provide an important service as a price discovery mechanism. By cataloging price trends in everything from corn to cattle, the producers, processors, and handlers of over 50 commodities are able to observe price trends in categories of interest.

■ THE FUTURES MARKET FOR FINANCIAL INSTRUMENTS

The major event in the commodities markets for the last two decades has been the development of financial futures contracts. With the great volatility in the foreign exchange markets and in interest rates, corporate treasurers, investors, and others have felt a great need to hedge their positions. Financial futures also appeal to speculators because of their low margin requirements and wide swings in value.

Financial futures may be broken down into three major categories, currency futures, interest-rate futures, and stock index futures (the latter is covered in depth in Chapter 17). Trading in currency futures began in May 1972 on the International Monetary Market (part of the Chicago Mercantile Exchange). Interest-rate futures started trading on the Chicago Board of Trade in October 1975 with the GNMA certificate. Trading in financial futures, regardless of whether they are currency or interest-rate futures, is very similar to trading in traditional commodities such as corn, wheat, copper, or pork bellies. There is a stipulated contract size, month of delivery, margin requirement, and so on. We will first look at currency futures and then shift our attention to interest-rate futures.

Goldman, Sachs Gives Its Blessings to Futures

In the summer of 1991, Goldman, Sachs & Co., the old-line prestigious investment banking house, gave its special blessings to the commodities futures market. It announced the development of the Goldman, Sachs Commodity Index. Traditionally, Goldman, Sachs has been associated with the stock and bond markets, specializing in underwriting new security issues for Fortune 500 companies. It also is a major advisor to firms in the area of corporate finance and mergers and acquisitions.

Now it is bringing pork bellies, soybeans, and other commodities under its area of expertise. The message to large institutional investors, such as pension funds, mutual funds, and bank trust departments, is that futures are a legitimate area for investment and henceforth would be tracked by Goldman, Sachs.

Goldman, Sachs also intends to give a boost to its own efforts to establish itself in the commodities business. Knowing more about the index for measurement than anyone else gives the firm a leg up when its salespeople call on accounts to do commission business. It is partially accomplishing this through J. Aron, a subsidiary, which is a key player in the commodities area.

Goldman, Sachs's index is value-weighted, which means each of the 18 items in the index is weighted in proportion to its representation to total world production. This is not true of currently existing indexes where commodities are equally weighted, and orange juice, for example, has the same importance as oil. In other indexes, an overnight freeze in Florida may carry the same effect on the index as the bombing of a major oil field.

■ CURRENCY FUTURES

Futures are generally available in the currencies listed below.

British pound	Swiss franc
Australian dollar	German mark
Canadian dollar	French franc
Japanese yen	

The futures market in currencies provides many of the same functions as the older and less formalized market in foreign exchange operated by banks and specialized brokers, who maintain communication networks throughout the world. In either case, one can speculate or hedge. The currency futures market, however, is different in that it provides standardized contracts and a strong secondary market.

Let's examine how the currency futures market works. Assume you wish to purchase a currency futures contract in Japanese yen. The standardized contract is 12.5 million yen. The value of the contract is quoted in cents per yen. Assume you purchase a December futures contract in May, and the price on the contract is .007292 per yen. The total value of the contract is $91,150 (12.5 million yen × $.007292). The typical margin on a yen contract is $2,100.

We will assume the yen strengthens relative to the dollar. This might happen because of decreasing U.S. interest rates, declining inflation in Japan, or any

Table 16–7	Contracts in Currency Futures		
Currency		**Trading Units**	**Size of Contract Based on Mid-1991 Prices**
British pound		62,500	$102,500
Canadian dollar		100,000	86,800
Swiss franc		62,500	40,269
German mark		125,000	69,288

number of other reasons. Under these circumstances, the currency might rise to $.007406 per yen (the yen is now worth more cents than it was previously). The value of the contract has now risen to $92,575 (12.5 million × $.007406). This represents an increase in value of $1,425.

$$
\begin{array}{ll}
\text{Current value} & \$92,575 \\
\text{Original value} & - \ \underline{91,150} \\
\text{Gain} & \$ \ 1,425
\end{array}
$$

With an original margin requirement of $2,100, this represents a return of 67.9 percent.

$$\frac{\$1,425}{\$2,100} \times 100 = 67.9\%$$

On an annualized basis, it could even be higher. Of course, the contract could produce a loss if the yen weakens against the dollar as a result of higher interest rates in the United States or increasing inflation in Japan. With a normal margin maintenance requirement of $1,500, a $600 loss on the contract will call for additional margin.

Corporate treasurers often try to hedge an exposed position in their foreign exchange dealings through the currency futures market. Assume a treasurer closes a deal today to receive payment in two months in Japanese yen. If the yen goes down relative to the dollar, he will have less value than he anticipated. One solution would be to sell a yen futures contract (go short). If the value of the yen goes down, he will make money on his futures contract that will offset the loss on the receipt of the Japanese yen in two months.

Table 16–7 lists the typical size of contracts for four other foreign currencies that trade on the International Monetary Market.

■ INTEREST-RATE FUTURES

Since the inception of the interest-rate futures contract with GNMA certificates in October 1975, the market has been greatly expanded to include Treasury bonds, Treasury bills, Treasury notes, commercial paper, certificates of

deposit, and Eurodollars. There is almost unlimited potential for futures contracts on interest-related items.

Interest-rate futures trade on a number of major exchanges, including the Chicago Board of Trade, the International Monetary Market of the Chicago Mercantile Exchange, and the New York Futures Exchange. There is strong competition between Chicago and New York City for dominance in this business, with Chicago being not only the historical leader but also the current leader.

Table 16–8 shows examples of quotes on interest-rate futures. Direct your attention to the first category, Treasury bonds (CBT), trading on the Chicago Board of Trade.

The bonds trade in units of $100,000, and the quotes are in percent of par value taken to 32nds of a percentage point. Although it is not shown in these data, the bonds on which the futures are based are assumed to be new, 15-year Treasury instruments paying 8 percent interest. In the first column for the September contract for Treasury bonds, we see a price of 92-27. This indicates a value of $92\frac{27}{32}$ percent of stated (par) value. We thus have a contract value of $92,843.75 ($92\frac{27}{32} \times$ $100,000). This represents the opening value. The entire line in Table 16–8 would read as follows:

	Open	High	Low	Settle	Chg.	Yield Settle	Chg.	Open Interest
Sept	92-27	93-12	93-21	93-11	+18	8.708	−.064	244,738

We see the **settle,** or closing, **price** is 93-11, which represents a change (chg.) of $\frac{18}{32}$ths from the close for the previous day. The close for the previous day is not always the same as the open for the current day.[5] We also see what yield the settle (closing) price represents on a 15-year bond paying an 8 percent coupon rate. In this case, it is 8.708 percent, which is a decline in yield from the previous day of 0.064. The decline in yield is consistent with the increase in settle price (and vice versa). Finally, we see there is an open interest of 244,738 indicating the number of contracts that are presently outstanding for September.

Assume we buy a September futures contract for $93\frac{11}{32}$ or $93,348.75 ($93\frac{11}{32} \times$ $100,000). The margin requirement for this contract on the Chicago Board of Trade is $2,700 with a $2,000 margin maintenance requirement. In this case, it may be that we bought the futures contract because we anticipate easier monetary policy by the Federal Reserve, which will trigger a decline in interest rates and an increase in bond prices. If interest rates decline by 0.6 percent (60 basis points), Treasury bond prices will increase by approximately

---

[5]A number of overnight events can cause the difference. In this case, we can assume the close for the previous day was 92–25.

Table 16–8   Examples of Price Quotes on Interest-Rate Futures

						Yield		Open
	Open	High	Low	Settle	Chg	Settle	Chg	Interest
TREASURY BONDS (CBT)—$100,000; pts. 32nds of 100%								
Sept	92-27	93-12	92-21	93-11 +	18	8.708 −	.064	244,738
Dec	92-04	92-20	92-00	92-20 +	19	8.790 −	.067	15,985
Mr92	91-19	92-01	91-15	92-01 +	19	8.857 −	.069	3,228
June	....	....	....	91-15 +	19	8.922 −	.069	3,832
Sept	90-22	90-31	90-18	90-31 +	19	8.980 −	.070	704
Dec	90-07	90-17	90-07	90-17 +	19	9.031 −	.071	169
Est vol 240,000; vol Wed 186,851; op int 268,656, −2,485.								
TREASURY BONDS (MCE)—$50,000; pts. 32nds of 100%								
Sept	92-27	93-12	92-22	93-11 +	15	8.708 −	.053	13,617
Est vol 5,600; vol Wed 4,319; open int 13,645, −80.								
T—BONDS (LIFFE) U.S. $100,000; pts of 100%								
Sept	92-29	93-05	92-24	n.a.	....	95-11	92-09	n.a.
Est vol 1,522; vol Wed 1,065; open int n.a., n.a..								
GERMAN GOV'T. BOND (LIFFE)								
250,000 marks; $ per mark (.01)								
Sept	84.63	84.64	84.38	84.44 −	.14	86.91	83.60	n.a.
Dec	84.65	84.76	84.65	84.64 −	.12	86.08	84.51	n.a.
Est vol 39,341; vol Wed 35,812; open int n.a., n.a..								
TREASURY NOTES (CBT)—$100,000; pts. 32nds of 100%								
Sept	97-01	97-11	96-30	97-11 +	12	8.398 −	.057	82,554
Dec	96-11	96-22	96-11	96-22 +	12	8.498 −	.058	1,152
Est vol 15,000; vol Wed 11,859; open int 83,707, +305.								
5 YR TREAS NOTES (CBT)—$100,000; pts. 32nds of 100%								
Sept	99-17	99-235	99-155	99-235 +	7.5	8.07 −	.05	71,893
Dec	....	....	....	99-045 +	7.5	8.21 −	.06	705
Est vol 10,500; vol Wed 5,706; open int 72,598, +197.								
2 YR TREAS NOTES (CBT)—$200,000; pts. 32nds of 100%								
Sept	101-05	101-07	01-045	101-07 +	2½	7.334 −	.042	15,440
Est vol 600; vol Wed 259; open int 15,441, +49.								
30-DAY INTEREST RATE (CBT)–$5 million; pts. of 100%								
July	94.15	94.16	94.15	94.15 +	.01	5.85 −	.01	1,608
Aug	94.13	94.14	94.13	94.14 +	.01	5.86 −	.01	1,052
Sept	94.05	94.07	94.05	94.07 +	.03	5.93 −	.03	1,121
Oct	93.97	94.00	93.97	94.00 +	.04	6.00 −	.04	522
Nov	93.88	93.90	93.88	93.90 +	.04	6.10 −	.04	395
Dec	93.63	93.67	93.63	93.67 +	.06	6.33 −	.06	428
Est vol 700; vol Wed 189; open int 5,156, +6.								
TREASURY BILLS (IMM)—$1 mil.; pts. of 100%								
						Discount		Open
	Open	High	Low	Settle	Chg	Settle	Chg	Interest
Sept	94.44	94.46	94.41	94.45 +	.02	5.55 −	.02	47,997
Dec	94.05	94.07	94.02	94.07 +	.02	5.93 −	.02	9,000
Mr92	....	....	....	93.98 +	.03	6.02 −	.02	1,100
June	....	....	....	93.63 +	.06	6.37 −	.06	154
Est vol 5,476; vol Wed 5,628; open int 58,252, −458.								

$1^{17}/_{32}$.[6] On a $100,000 par value futures contract, this would represent a gain of $1,531.25 as indicated below.

$$\begin{array}{r} \$\,100,000 \\ \times\ \underline{\quad 1^{17}/_{32}\% \ (1.53125\%)} \\ \$1,531.25 \end{array}$$

With a $2,700 initial margin, the $1,531.25 profit represents an attractive return of 56.71 percent. Note, however, that if interest rates go up by even a small amount, our Treasury bond futures contract value will fall, and there may be a margin call.

---

[6]This is derived from a standard bond table and not explicitly calculated in the example.

As is true of other commodities, when we trade in interest rate futures, we do not take actual title or possession of the commodity unless we fail to reverse our initial position. The contract merely represents a bet or hedge on the direction of future interest rates and bond prices.

Quotes on Treasury Bill Futures

One type of interest-rate futures contract that requires special attention is the Treasury bill future. Particular reference in this case is made to the 90-day, $1 million, T-bill futures contract that trades on the International Monetary Market of the Chicago Mercantile Exchange and is shown on the bottom portion of Table 16–8. We reproduce the first line below.

	Open	High	Low	Settle	Chg.	Discount Settle	Discount Chg.	Open Interest
Sept	94.44	94.46	94.41	94.45	+.02	5.55	−.02	47,997

The items of particular interest are the settle price of 94.45 and the settle discount of 5.55 percent. Unlike other interest-rate futures, such as Treasury bonds, we cannot simply multiply the settle price of 94.45 (percent) times the par value of $1 million to get the value of the contract. This Treasury bill represents a 90-day instrument, and the annual yield of 5.55 percent must be converted to a 90-day rate to determine value. We thus take the annual rate of 5.55 percent and multiply it by $90/360$ to get an equivalent 90-day yield of 1.39%.

$$5.55 \times \frac{90}{360} = 1.39\%$$

We then subtract this value from 100 percent to get the appropriate percentage to multiply times par value to get the value of the contract. For the $1 million Treasury bill, the actual converted price is:

$$(100\% - 1.39\%) \times \$1,000,000$$
$$98.61\% \times \$1,000,000 = \$986,100$$

Each time the yield on a Treasury bill changes by 0.01 percent ($1/100$ of 1 percent or 1 **basis point**), the price of the T-bill future will change by $25 as indicated in the two steps below:

$$.01\% \text{ of } \$1,000,000 = \$100$$

We convert this from an annual amount to a 90-day amount by multiplying by $90/360$.

$$\$100 \times \,^{90}/_{360} = \$25$$

Thus, if you buy a Treasury bill futures contract and interest rates on Treasury bills change by 0.50 percent (50 basis points), you will gain or lose $1,250.

$25 for each .01% or basis point
$$\times\ \underline{50}\ \text{Basis points}$$
$$\overline{\$1,250}$$

The initial margin requirement for a $1 million Treasury bill on the International Money Market of the Chicago Mercantile Exchange is only $540, with a $400 margin maintenance requirement (in July 1991). A 50 basis point move would provide a return or loss on the initial margin of 231 percent.

Hedging with Interest-Rate Futures

Interest-rate futures have opened up opportunities for hedging that can only be compared to the development of the traditional commodities market over a century ago. Consider the following potential hedges against interest-rate risks.

a. A corporate treasurer is awaiting a new debt issue that will occur in 60 days. The underwriters are still putting the final details together. The great fear is that interest rates will rise between now and then. The treasurer could hedge his or her position in the futures market by selling a Treasury bond or other similar security short. If interest rates go up, the price to buy back the interest-rate futures will go down, and a profit will be made on the short position. This will partially or fully offset the higher interest costs on the new debt issue.

b. A corporate treasurer is continually reissuing commercial paper at new interest rates or borrowing under a floating prime agreement at the bank. He or she fears that interest rates will go up and make a big dent in projected profits. By selling (going short on) interest-rate futures, the corporate treasurer can make enough profit on interest-rate futures if interest rates go up to compensate for the higher costs of money.

c. A mortgage banker has made a forward commitment to provide a loan at a set interest rate one month in the future. If interest rates go up, the resale value of the mortgage in the secondary market will go down. He or she can hedge the position by selling or going short on an interest rate futures contract.

d. A pension fund manager has been receiving a steady return of 8 percent on his short-term portfolio in 90-day Treasury bills. He is afraid interest rates will go down and he will have to adjust to receiving lower returns on the managed funds. His strategy might be to buy (go long on) a Treasury bill futures contract. If interest rates go down, he will make a profit on his futures contract that will partially or fully off-set his decline in interest income for one period. Of course, if he is heavily invested in long-term securities and fearful of an interest-rate rise, a sell or short

position that would provide profits on an interest-rate rise would be advisable. This, of course, would offset part of the loss in the portfolio value due to increasing interest rates.

e. A commercial banker has most of his loans on a floating prime basis, meaning the rate he charges will change with the cost of funds. However, some of the loans have a fixed rate associated with them. If the cost of funds goes up, the fixed-rate loans will become unprofitable. By selling or going short interest-rate futures, the danger of higher interest rates can be hedged away by the profits he will make on the interest-rate futures. Similarly, a banker may make a commitment to pay a set amount of interest on certificates of deposit for the next six months. If interest rates go down, the banker may have to lend the funds at a lower rate than he is currently paying. If he buys a futures contract, then lower interest rates will increase the value of the contract and provide a profit. This will offset the possible negative profitability spread described above.

An Actual Example

Assume an industrial corporation has a $10 million, 15-year bond to be issued in 60 days. Long-term rates for such an issue are currently 10.75 percent, and there is concern that interest rates will go up to 11 percent by the time of the issue. The corporate treasurer has figured out that the extra ¼ point would have a present value cost of $179,775 over the life of the issue (on a before-tax basis).

$$
\begin{array}{rl}
\$10,000,000 & \\
\times \quad \frac{1}{4}\% & \\
\hline
\$ \quad 25,000 & \\
\times \quad 7.191 & \text{Present value factor for 15 years at 11 percent} \\
\hline
\$ \quad 179,775 & \text{Present value of futures costs}
\end{array}
$$

To establish a hedge position, he sells 109 Treasury bond futures short. We assume they are currently selling at 92 (92 percent of $100,000), equaling $92,000 each. The total value of the hedge would be $10,028,000. This is roughly equivalent to the $10 million size of the corporate bond issue. If interest rates go up by ¼ point, the profit on the Treasury bond futures contract (due to falling prices with a short position) will probably offset the present value of the increased cost of the corporate bond issue.

Of course, we do not suggest that both rates (on Treasury bonds and corporate bonds) would move exactly together. However, the general thrust of the example should be apparent. We are actually establishing a **cross-hedging** pattern by using one form of security (Treasury bonds) to hedge another form of security (corporate bonds). This is often necessary. Even when the same security is used, there may be differences in maturity dates so that a perfect hedge is difficult to establish.

Many financial managers prefer **partial hedges** to complete hedges. They are willing to take away part of the risk but not all of it. Others prefer no hedge at all because it locks in their position. While a hedge ensures them against loss, it precludes the possibility of an abnormal gain.

Nevertheless, in a risk-averse financial market environment, most financial managers can gain by hedging their position as described in the many examples in this section. Companies such as Burlington Northern, Eastman Kodak, and McDonald's Corp. have established reputations for just such actions. Others have not yet joined the movement because of a lack of appreciation or understanding of the highly innovative financial futures market. Much of this will change with the passage of time.

■ OPTIONS AS WELL AS FUTURES

In late 1982, many exchanges began offering options on financial instruments and commodities. For example, the Chicago Board Options Exchange began listing put and call options on Treasury bonds. Also, the American Stock Exchange started trading options on Treasury bills and Treasury notes, and the Philadelphia Exchange offered foreign currency options. The Chicago Board of Trade, the Chicago Mercantile Exchange, and the Comex have also attached options to commodity plays. The relationship, similarities, and dissimilarities between option contracts and futures contracts are given much greater attention in the following chapter. For now it will suffice to say that the futures contract requires an initial margin, which can be parlayed into large profits or immediately wiped out, whereas an option requires the payment of an option premium, which represents the full extent of an option purchaser's liability. In Chapter 17, we will also see there are options to purchase futures, which combine the elements of both types of contracts.

■ SUMMARY

In this chapter, we broke down the commodities futures market into traditional commodities (such as grains, livestock, and meat) and financial futures primarily in currencies and interest rates.

A commodities futures contract is an agreement that provides for the delivery of a specific amount of a commodity at a designated time in the future. It is not intended that the purchaser of a contract take actual possession of the goods but, rather, that he or she reverse or close out the contract before delivery is due. The same is true for the seller.

Primary participants in the commodities market include both speculators and hedgers. We first examine speculators. A speculator buys a commodities

contract (goes long) or sells a commodities contract (goes short) because he believes he can anticipate the direction in which the market is going to move. Because of low margin (initial deposit) requirements of 3 to 10 percent, large profits or losses are possible with small price movements. If the market moves against someone who has a commodity contract, that person may be asked to put up additional margin.

A hedger buys or sells a commodities futures contract to protect an underlying position he or she might have in the actual commodity. For example, a wheat farmer may sell (go short on) a futures contract in wheat to protect against a price decline. If prices go down, he can buy back his contract at a lower price than he sold it and record a profit on the transaction. This may offset any losses he incurs as a result of selling wheat at a lower price to its intended user. Of course, if the price goes up, he will lose on his futures contract but make up the difference on the actual sale of wheat. Millers or bakers who know they will have to purchase wheat in the future may buy (go long on) a futures contract. If the price goes up, they will make money on the contract, and this will offset the added production costs.

Many commodity futures exchanges provide areas where buyers and sellers can negotiate cash (or spot) prices. The cash price is the actual dollar paid for the immediate delivery of the goods. Near-term futures prices and cash prices tend to approximate each other.

Currency and interest rate futures represent important financial futures. Although these markets only came into existence in the 1970s, they have seen explosive growth. The contract on financial futures is very similar to that on basic, traditional commodities; only the items traded and units of measurement are different.

Currency futures relate to many different currencies and enable financial managers to hedge their position in foreign markets. There is also active participation by speculators.

Interest-rate futures cover Treasury bonds, Treasury bills, Treasury notes, certificates of deposit, and similar items. Many other items are on the drawing board. Interest-rate futures generally trade in units of $100,000 or $1 million with extremely low margin requirements. There is a battle between the traditional commodity exchanges in Chicago and the New York Futures Exchange (part of the New York Stock Exchange) and the Amex Commodity Exchange (part of the American Stock Exchange) to see which will ultimately have a dominant position in the financial futures markets.

In the current environment of volatile interest rates, interest-rate futures offer an excellent opportunity to hedge dangerous interest-rate risks. Possible hedgers include corporate financial officers, pension fund managers, mortgage bankers, and commercial bankers. As sophistication and understanding in the use of these hedging techniques increase, the market in financial futures will continue to grow. In Chapter 17, we expand the discussion of futures to include stock index futures and options.

IMPORTANT WORDS AND CONCEPTS

futures contract 522
hedge 522
margin 523
margin maintenance requirements 527
cash or spot prices 532

financial futures 532
settle price 535
basis point 537
cross-hedging 539
partial hedge 540

DISCUSSION QUESTIONS

1. What is a futures contract?
2. Do you have to take delivery or deliver the commodity if you are a party to a futures contract?
3. Explain what hedging is.
4. Why is there substantial leverage in commodity investments?
5. What are the basic categories of items traded on the commodity exchanges?
6. What group has primary regulatory responsibility for the activities of the commodity exchanges?
7. How does the concept of margin on a commodities contract differ from that of margin on a stock purchase?
8. Indicate some factors that might influence the price of wheat in the commodities market.
9. What is meant by a daily trading limit on a commodities contract?
10. Refer to Table 16–5 and explain the quotation for March (Mr) 1992 corn on the Chicago Board of Trade (CBT).
11. How does the cash market differ from the futures market for commodities?
12. What are the three main categories of financial futures? Which two are discussed in this chapter?
13. How does the currency futures market differ from the foreign exchange market?
14. Describe the Treasury bonds that are part of the futures contract that trades on the Chicago Board of Trade (size of units, maturity, assumed initial interest rate).
15. If you purchase a Treasury bill futures contract and interest rates change by 25 basis points, how much does this represent in dollars?
16. How can using the financial futures markets for interest rates and foreign exchange help financial managers through hedging? Briefly explain and give one example.

PROBLEMS

1. You purchase a 5,000-bushel contract for corn at $2.40 per bushel with an initial margin requirement of 8 percent. The price goes up to $2.49 in one month. What is your percentage profit and the annualized gain?

2. An investor purchases a 25,000-pound contract for copper at $.96 per pound with an initial margin requirement of 6 percent. The price goes up to $1 in three months. What is the percentage profit and the annualized gain?

3. Farmer William Cropley anticipates taking 100,000 bushels of oats to the market in four months. The current cash price for oats is $1.29. He can sell a four-month futures contract for oats at $1.33. He decides to sell ten 5,000-bushel futures contracts at that price. Assume in four months when Farmer Cropley takes the oats to market and also closes out the futures contracts (buys them back), the price of oats has tumbled to $1.15.

   a. What is his total loss in value over the three months on the actual oats he produced and took to market?

   b. How much did his hedge in the futures market generate in gains?

   c. What is his overall net loss considering the answer in Part *a* and the partial hedge in Part *b*?

4. The Midwestern Grain Miller's Corporation anticipates the need to purchase 70,000 bushels of wheat in six months to use in its products. The current cash price for wheat is $2.80 a bushel. A six-month futures contract for wheat can be purchased at $2.84.

   a. Explain why Midwestern Grain Miller's Corporation might need to purchase futures contracts to hedge its position.

   b. To attempt to completely hedge its exposure, how many contracts will it need to purchase? (Consult Table 16–3 for the size of the trading units in a contract.)

   c. If the price of wheat ends up at $3.06 per bushel after six months, by how much will the actual cost of 70,000 bushels of wheat have gone up?

   d. After the futures contracts are closed out (sold) at $3.06 also, what will be the gain on the futures contracts?

   e. Considering the answers to Parts *c* and *d,* what is Midwestern Grain Miller's net position?

   f. Given the number of wheat futures contracts it controls, what is the most it can lose in the futures markets on any given day? You may want to consult Table 16–4 for part of the answer.

5. With a 5,000-bushel contract for $15,000, assume the margin requirement is $1,000 and the maintenance margin is 70 percent of the

margin requirement. How much would the price per bushel have to fall before additional margin is required?

Generating margin

6. If contracts are written on a 5,000-bushel basis requiring $1,000 of margin and you control four contracts, how much would the price per bushel have to change to generate enough profit to purchase an additional contract?

Pyramiding

7. Referring to Problem 6, how many contracts would need to be controlled to generate enough profit for a new margin contract if the price changed by only 1 cent per bushel?

Currency futures

8. You purchase a futures contract in German marks for $72,000. The trading unit is 125,000 marks.

   a. What is the ratio of cents to marks in this contract? (Divide the dollar contract size by the size of the trading unit.)

   b. Assume you are required to put up $2,200 in margin and the mark increases by 3 cents (per mark). What will be your return as a percentage of margin?

Treasury bond futures

9. Hogan Securities buys a $100,000 par value, March 1992 Treasury bond contract on the Chicago Board of Trade (CBT) at the quoted settle price in Table 16–8.

   a. What is the dollar value of the contract? Use the settle price in your calculation.

   b. There is an initial margin requirement of $2,700 and a margin maintenance requirement of $2,000. If an interest rate increase causes the bond to go down by 0.9 percent of *par value,* will Hogan be called on to put up more margin?

   c. Assume Hogan's investment is for six months. To have a 100 percent annualized return on the initial $2,700 margin, by what percent of par value must the bond increase to achieve this?

Treasury bill quotes

10. What is the value of the June 1992 Treasury bill contract in Table 16–8? Remember to convert settle yield (6.37 percent) from an annual basis to a 90-day basis as the first step in the calculation. The contract is based on a $1,000,000 par value.

Treasury bill futures

11. Assume a Treasury bill futures contract is up 30 basis points each day for six straight days. What will be the dollar return to the investor?

Hedging by corporate treasurer

12. The treasurer of the Atlas Corporation, Wanda Zinke, is going to bring a $10 million issue to the market in 45 days. It will be a 25-year issue. The interest-rate environment is highly volatile, and even though interest rates are currently $10\frac{1}{4}$ percent, there is a fear that interest rates will be up to 11 percent by the time the bonds get to the market.

   a. If interest rates go up by $\frac{3}{4}$ point what is the present value of the extra interest this increase will cost the corporation? Use an 11 percent discount rate and disregard tax considerations.

b. Assume the corporation is going to short September 1991 Treasury bonds as quoted at the top of Table 16–8. Based on the settle price, how many contracts must the corporation sell to equal the $10 million exposed position? Round to the nearest whole number of contracts.

c. Based on your answer in Part *b,* if Treasury bond prices increase by 2.8 percent of par value in each contract in response to an unexpected ½ point decline in interest rates over the next 45 days, what will be the total dollar loss on the futures contracts?

Hedging by corporate treasurer

13. Should the treasurer of the Atlas Corporation think she has failed in her tasks if the circumstance in Part *c* of Problem 12 occurs?

■ CRITICAL THOUGHT CASE

Ever since the market crash of October 1987, the investment industry regulators have scrutinized the rules governing exchanges and the activities of brokers and traders. Dual trading has been a hot issue for some time, and it looks as though changes will be made. Dual trading allows brokers to execute trades for their own accounts in addition to customer accounts on the same day.

Many believe brokers execute their own personal orders before customer orders, thus getting better fills (price levels), when in fact, the customers' orders should always be filled before the broker's orders. Some say an easy answer to this problem is just to ban dual trading. This would be fine if dual trading did not serve a purpose on the floor, but allowing brokers to dual trade provides liquidity and price competitiveness to the market. Brokers fear that if dual trading is banned, customers will not get the best possible price for their orders. Also, this would cut a big chunk out of brokers' profits.

Another related issue is broker associations' trading practices. Broker associations are groups of floor brokers that work together to fill customer orders. An association can have as few as 2 brokers or more than 100 brokers. The brokers within the group can cover for each other if one leaves the floor, goes out for lunch, or takes a vacation. These groups are found on the floors of all the exchanges and play an integral part in its daily operations. A group can share the costs of brokering on the floor as well as profits. There have been complaints that these broker associations have become too big, too powerful, and too intimidating. They are accused of trading only among themselves and not directing any business to the locals on the floor. Since locals do not have any outside customers (they trade only for their own account), a ban on dual trading would benefit them and put them on a more even keel with the broker groups. But a ban would mean broker groups would have to trade exclusively for either their own accounts or their customer accounts, which, according to them, means less profits due to lost commissions and fees. So the question still remains, "Should dual trading be banned?"

The Commodity Futures Trading Commission (CFTC) and the Securities and Exchange Commission (SEC) have been investigating dual trading since the October 1987 market crash. Some firmly believe that, on the day of the crash, dual trading is what saved the Standard & Poor's 500 Index futures (S&P) pit from demise. The broker associations had the capital base to handle the barrage of customer orders and thus helped in maintaining the liquidity in the market.

The Chicago Mercantile Exchange (CME) has studied the issue extensively, and in April 1990, banned dual trading for those contracts that were close to maturity and had high trading volume. Despite the ruling, the issue has not been laid to rest. Many brokers resent the ruling and have bombarded the CME board of governors with requests that the issue be readdressed. In the meantime, the CFTC is awaiting approval by Congress on its prospective legislation for banning, or at least curbing, dual trading.

Questions

1. If the CFTC's proposal is approved and dual trading is banned, what will that do to the liquidity of high-volume pits such as the S&P and low-volume pits such as sugar?
2. Is there a conflict of interest in dual trading?
3. Is the government overregulating the industry?

SELECTED REFERENCES

General Source

Extensive bibliography presented regularly by Robert T. Diagler in the *Journal of Futures Markets.*

Trading Strategy and Hedging

Bell, David, and William Krasker. "Estimating Hedge Ratios." *Financial Management,* Summer 1986, pp. 34–49.

Block, Stanley B., and Timothy J. Gallagher. "How Much Do Bank Trust Departments Use Derivatives?" *Journal of Portfolio Management,* Fall 1988, pp. 12–16.

Geske, Robert, and Dan Peiptea. "Hedging with Interest Rate Futures: A Stochastic Process Approach." Working Paper No. 132, Center for the Study of Futures Markets, Columbia University, Spring 1986.

Miller, Merton. "Financial Innovation: The Last Twenty Years and the Next." *Journal of Financial and Quantitative Analysis,* December 1986, pp. 459–71.

Schroeder, Edmund. "Will Off-Exchange Contracts Set Off Industry War?" *Futures,* March 1987, pp. 54–55.

Returns on Futures

Cox, John; Jonathan Ingersoll, Jr.; and Stephen Ross. "The Relation between Forward and Futures Prices." *Journal of Financial Economics,* December 1981, p. 346.

Nelson, Ray, and Robert Collins. "A Measure of Hedging Performance." *Journal of Futures Markets,* Spring 1985, pp. 45–56.

Thomas, Lee R., III. "Random Walk Profits in Currency Futures Trading." *Journal of Futures Markets,* Spring 1986, pp. 109–66.

Treasury Futures

Easterwood, John, and A. J. Senchack, Jr. "Arbitrage Opportunities with T-Bill/T-Bond Futures Combinations." *Journal of Futures Markets,* Fall 1986, pp. 433–42.

Hegde, Shantaram P., and Bill McDonald. "On the Information Role of Treasury Bill Futures." *Journal of Futures Markets,* Winter 1986, pp. 629–45.

Kane, Alex, and Alan J. Marcus. "The Quality Option in the Treasury Bond Futures Market: An Empirical Assessment." *Journal of Futures Markets,* Summer 1986, pp. 231–48.

Simpson, W. Gary, and Timothy C. Ireland. "The Impact of Financial Futures on the Cash Market for Treasury Bills." *Journal of Financial and Quantitative Analysis,* September 1985, pp. 371–79.

Foreign Currency Futures

Nesbitt, Stephen L. "Currency Hedging Plans for Plan Sponsors." *Financial Analysts Journal,* March–April 1991, pp. 73–81.

Shastri, Kuldeep, and Kishore Tandon. "Valuation of Foreign Currency Options: Some Empirical Tests." *Journal of Financial and Quantitative Analysis,* June 1986, pp. 145–60.

17

Stock Index Futures and Options

In February 1982, the Kansas City Board of Trade began trading futures on a stock index, the Value Line Index. This event ushered in a new era of futures and options trading.

A future or option on an index allows the investor to participate in the movement of an entire index rather than an individual security. Currently, futures and options relate to such indexes as the Standard & Poor's 500 Stock Index, the Standard & Poor's 100 Stock Index, the New York Stock Exchange Composite Index, the Major Market Index, the Value Line Index, and many other old and new market measures.[1]

If an investor purchases a **futures contract on a stock market index,** he puts down the required margin and gains or loses on the transaction based on the movement of the index. For example, an investor may purchase a futures contract on the Standard & Poor's 500 Stock Index with $22,000 in margin. The actual contract value is based on the index value times 500. If the S&P 500 Futures Index were at 390, the initial contract value would be $195,000 (500 × 390). If the index went up or down by 2 points, the investor would gain or lose $1,000 (500 × ± 2). Because the initial investment is $22,000 in margin, we see a gain or loss of 4.6 percent (4.6 percent = $1,000/$22,000). Since this might happen over a one- or two-day period, the annualized return or loss could be high.

If the investor is trading in **stock index options** instead of futures, he may choose to participate in the Standard & Poor's 100 Stock Index. The S&P 100 Index is a smaller version of the S&P 500 Index and is composed of 100 blue-chip stocks on which the Chicago Board Options Exchange currently has individual option contracts. Included in the S&P 100 Index are such firms as IBM, General Motors, AT&T, and so on. The value of the S&P 100 Index tends to be about 20 points lower than the S&P 500 Index. If the S&P 100 Index were at 370 at a given time, an option to purchase the index at a strike price of 370 in two months might carry a premium (option price) of $5. The option price is multiplied by 100 to get a total value for the option of $500 (100 × $5). If the S&P 100 Index closed out at 379 on expiration, the option price will be $9, and a profit of $400 will be achieved over the two months.

Final value (100 × $9)	$900
Purchase price (100 × $5)	−500
Profit	$400

As we go further into the chapter, you will see there are not only futures and options on stock market indexes, but also **options to purchase futures** on

---

[1] To date, there is no contract on the Dow Jones Industrial Average because Dow Jones & Company has resisted having its venerable index used for this purpose.

stock market indexes. This represents a combination of a futures and option contract.

Stock index futures have grown faster than any new futures trading outlet in history. In their first six months of trading, the average daily volume was 4.5 times as great as the volume on Treasury bond futures during a comparable period of infancy. The same sort of pattern has occurred in index option trading.

■ THE CONCEPT OF DERIVATIVE PRODUCTS

Trading in stock index futures and options has had a tremendous impact on the financial markets in the United States. Stock index futures and options are sometimes referred to as **derivative products** because they derive their existence from actual market indexes, but have no intrinsic characteristics of their own.[2] These derivative products are thought to make market movements more volatile. The primary reason is that enormous amounts of securities can be controlled by relatively small amounts of margin payments or option premiums. Also, these derivative products are often used as part of program trading. As discussed in Chapter 2, **program trading** means that computer-based trigger points are established in which large volume trades are initiated by institutional investors. Stock index futures and options facilitate program trading because a large volume of securities can be controlled. The presence of program trading, as supported by the use of stock index futures and options, was blamed by many for the market crash of 508 points in the Dow Jones Industrial Average on October 19, 1987. It was thought that too many institutional investors were moving in the same direction (to sell) at one time. Increased stock price volatility since the market crash has also been blamed on program trading and the use of stock index futures and options.

Actually, these are somewhat controversial topics. A study by the Chicago Mercantile Exchange suggests program trading and the use of derivative products has no negative effect on the market volatility per se. These trading tools merely help the market reach a new equilibrium level (in terms of value) more quickly.[3]

It is the contention of the authors that stock index futures and options have many useful purposes, which we will cover throughout the chapter. We will also try to point out potential negatives where they exist.

Before going into further discussion of futures and options on stock market indexes, the student should have read Chapter 15, Put and Call Options, and Chapter 16, Commodities and Financial Futures.

---

[2] Interest-rate futures and options are also considered to be derivative products.

[3] *Report of the Committee of Inquiry Appointed by the Chicago Mercantile Exchange to Examine the Events Surrounding October 19, 1987* (Chicago: The Chicago Mercantile Exchange, December 17, 1987).

■ TRADING STOCK INDEX FUTURES

There are major stock index futures contracts on the S&P 500 Index (Chicago Mercantile Exchange), the Nikkei 225 Stock Average (Chicago Mercantile Exchange), the New York Composite Index (New York Financial Exchange[4]), and the Major Market Index (Chicago Board of Trade). An example of these stock index futures contracts is shown in Table 17–1.[5]

We mentioned some of these indexes in Chapter 3 with the exception of the Nikkei 225 Stock Average and the Major Market Index. The Nikkei 225 Stock Average tracks movement on the Tokyo Stock Exchange. In the past five years, it has traded between 16,000 and 40,000. Trading stock index futures on the Nikkei 225 is a way to play movements in the Japanese market without becoming involved with individual stocks.

The Major Market Index (MMI) is a price-weighted index composed of 20 of the largest firms in the United States. It is a convenient way to imitate movements in the Dow Jones Industrial Average and has a 97 percent correlation with that average (although its price movements are from a different base). Since Dow Jones & Company has prohibited the use of the Dow Jones Industrial Average for futures and options trading, this is an alternative way to play the game. Seventeen of the firms in the Major Market Index are part of the Dow Jones Industrial Average.

You will note in Table 17–1 that the title line for each contract (such as the S&P 500 Index) indicates the appropriate multiple times the value in the table. For the S&P 500 Index and the NYSE Composite Index, the multiplier is 500, while for the Major Market Index, it is 250, and for the Nikkei Stock Average, it is 5. Looking at the September settle price in each of the four indexes, we see the value of the contracts in Table 17–2.

With a margin requirement ranging from $9,000 on the New York Futures Exchange to $22,000 on the Chicago Mercantile Exchange, the investor can engage in a futures trade. (These margin values apply to August 1991 and change occasionally.)

If the investor thinks the market is going up, he will purchase a futures contract. If he thinks the market is going down, he will sell a futures contract and hope the market will decline so that the contract can be closed out (repurchased) at a lower value than the sales price. Selling futures contracts can also be used to hedge a large stock portfolio. If the market goes down, what you lose on your portfolio you recoup in your futures contract.

In the example in Table 17–2, the investor has four indexes from which to choose.

---

[4] The NYFE (New York Financial Exchange) is a division of the New York Stock Exchange.

[5] The Kansas City Board of Trade also continues to trade contracts on the Value Line Index (though the volume is relatively low).

Table 17–1   Stock Index Futures (August 12, 1991, Prices)

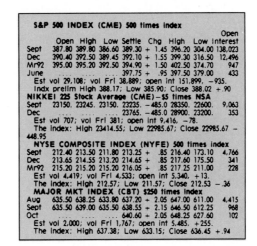

Source: *The Wall Street Journal,* August 13, 1991, p. 21C. Reprinted by permission of *THE WALL STREET JOURNAL,* © 1991 by Dow Jones & Company, Inc. All Rights Reserved Worldwide.

Table 17–2   Value of Contracts

	September 1991 Settle Price	Multiplier	Contract Value
S&P 500 Index	389.30	500	$194,650
Nikkei 225 Stock Average	23,235.00	5	116,175
NYSE Composite Index	213.25	500	106,625
Major Market Index	638.55	250	159,638

We shall direct our attention for now to the S&P 500 Index futures contract (though the same basic principles would apply to other indexes). Part of the material from Table 17–1 that pertains to the S&P 500 Index futures contract is reproduced in Table 17–3 so we can examine a number of key features related to the contract.

Trading Cycle

The trading cycle in the table is made up of the four months of September, December, March, and June. The last day of trading for a contract is the third Thursday of the ending month. The contracts in Table 17–3 extend 10 months into the future.

Table 17–3   S&P 500 Index Futures Contract (CME), 500 Multiplier (August 12, 1991)

Contract Month	Open	High	Low	Settle	Change
September 1991	387.80	398.80	386.60	389.30	+1.45
December	390.40	392.50	389.45	392.10	+1.55
March 1992	395.00	395.20	392.50	394.90	+1.50
June	. . . . .	. . . . .	. . . . .	397.75	+ .95

Value of S&P Stock Index (August 12, 1991) = 388.02

Margin Requirement

As previously mentioned, the basic margin requirement for buying or selling an S&P 500 Index futures contract on the Chicago Mercantile Exchange was $22,000 in 1991. Based on the September 1991 contract value of $194,650 (found on the top line in Table 17–2), this represents a margin requirement of 11.30 percent ($22,000 ÷ $194,650). There is also a margin maintenance requirement of $9,000. Thus, if the initial margin or equity in the account falls to this level, the investor will be required to supply sufficient cash or securities to bring the account back up to $22,000. Since the contract trades at 500 times the index, a decline of 26 points in the S&P contract value would cause a loss of $13,000. In this instance, the margin position would be reduced from $22,000 to $9,000, and the investor would be asked to supply $13,000 in funds.

If the investor can prove he is hedging a long position, the margin requirement will be less. For example, if an investor owns a portfolio of stocks that roughly equals the value of the index futures contract ($194,650 in this case), the initial margin requirement is only $9,000 (though the margin maintenance requirement remains at $9,000). Since a hedged position is not as risky as a speculative position, less initial margin is required. Of course, it is sometimes difficult to prove that a truly hedged position is in place.[6]

One of the developments following the market crash of October 1987 was to raise the margin requirements on stock index futures contracts. At that time it was 7.5 percent. In mid-1991, it was 11.30 percent of the contract value. Although the margin requirement will undoubtedly change again, the exchanges and regulatory authorities intend to keep the margin on stock index futures relatively high as compared to the margin on interest-rate futures and many other commodities. This once again pertains to a fear that stock index futures have contributed to new trading patterns that have increased the volatility of stock prices and driven some small investors from the marketplace.

---

[6] For an investor initiating a spread position (buying and selling comparable but somewhat different contracts at the same time), the margin requirement is even lower.

Minimum Price Change

The minimum price change per trade for the S&P 500 Futures Index contract is .05. Thus, if the September futures contract is at 389.30, the smallest possible price move would be down to 389.25 or up to 389.35. Since the contract is multiplied by 500 to determine value, an index movement of .05 represents $25 (500 × .05 = $25). Therefore, the smallest possible price change is $25.

Cash Settlement

In traditional commodity futures markets, the potential for physical delivery exists. One who is trading in wheat could actually decide to deliver the commodity to close out the contract. As discussed in Chapter 16, this happens only a very small percentage of the time, but it is possible. The stock index futures market, on the other hand, is purely a **cash-settlement** market. There is never the implied potential for future delivery of the Standard & Poor's 500 Stock Index. An investor simply closes out (or reverses) his position before the settlement date. If he does not, his account is automatically credited with his gains or debited with his losses, and the transaction is completed.[7]

One of the advantages of a cash-settlement arrangement is that it makes it impossible for a "short squeeze" to develop. A short squeeze occurs when an investor attempts to corner a market in a commodity, such as silver, so that it is not possible for those who have short positions to make physical delivery. Clearly, with a cash-settlement position, this can never happen.

Basis

The term **basis** represents the difference between the stock index futures price and the value of the actual underlying index.[8] We can now turn back to Table 17–3 to see a numerical example of basis. On the date of the table, the S&P 500 futures contract for September was quoted at a settle (closing) price of 389.30 (second item from the right in the first row). The actual S&P 500 Stock Index, as shown at the bottom of Table 17–3, closed at 388.02. The basis, or difference, between the futures price and the actual underlying index was 1.28.

Stock index futures price	389.30
Actual underlying index	− 388.02
Basis	1.28

Moving to the December 1991 contract in Table 17–3, the basis is the difference between the December contract settle value of 392.10 and the value

---

[7] Actually, the account is adjusted daily to reflect the gains and losses. This is known as marking the customer's position to market.

[8] The same concept can be applied to other types of futures contracts.

Table 17–4   Specifications for Stock Index Futures Contracts

Index and Exchange	Index	Contract Size and Value (in dollars)	Contract Months
S&P 500 Index Index and Options Market (IOM) of Chicago Mercantile Exchange (CME)	Value of 500 selected stocks on NYSE, AMEX, and OTC, weighted to reflect market value of issues	500 × S&P 500 Index	March June September December
Nikkei 225 Stock Average Index and Options Market (IOM) of Chicago Mercantile Exchange (CME)	Index of 225 Japanese stocks, weighted to reflect market value	5 × Nikkei Stock Average	March June September December
NYSE Composite Index New York Futures Exchange (NYFE) of the New York Stock Exchange	Index of 1,550 NYSE stocks, weighted to reflect market value	500 × NYSE Composite Average	March June September December
Major Market Index Chicago Board of Trade (CBT)	Index of 20 major stocks, weighted to reflect market value	250 × Major Market Index (MMI)	March June September December

of the underlying index, which, of course, is still 388.02. The difference is 4.08. For the data in Table 17–3, the basis indicates a premium is being paid over the actual underlying index value, and furthermore, the premium expands with the passage of time. This is generally thought to be a positive sign. If the index futures price is below the actual underlying index, there is a negative basis.

An excellent discussion of the ability of stock index futures to forecast the actual underlying index is presented in an article by Zeckhauser and Niederhoffer in the *Financial Analysts Journal*.[9] A part of their thesis is that futures contracts move instantaneously to reflect market conditions, whereas

---

[9] Richard Zeckhauser and Victor Niederhoffer, "The Performance of Market Index Futures Contracts," *Financial Analysts Journal*, January–February 1983, pp. 59–65.

the actual underlying index moves more slowly. If the market makes an important move, some of the stocks that are part of the actual underlying index will not yet have reacted. Thus, initial, significant, and potentially predictive information may be found in the futures market quotes.

Also, at times, futures or options markets stay open later or begin trading earlier than the actual underlying stock markets. This can be very beneficial not only in providing lead time information on market movements, but also in giving the trader an opportunity to take a position before the opening or after the closing of the stock market.

Overall Features

Many of the important features related to stock index futures on the various exchanges are presented in Table 17–4. This table can serve as a ready reference guide to trading commodities in various markets.

■ USE OF STOCK INDEX FUTURES

There are a number of actual and potential users of stock index futures. As is true of most commodity futures contracts, the motivation may be either speculation or the opportunity to hedge.

Speculation

The speculator may use stock index futures in an attempt to profit from major movements in the market. He or she may have developed a conviction about the next move in the market through utilizing fundamental or technical analysis. For example, those who utilize fundamental analysis may determine that P/E ratios are at a 10-year low or that earnings performance should be extremely good in the next two quarters, so they wish to bet on the market moving upward. Market technicians might observe that a resistance or support position in the market is being penetrated and that it is time to take a position based on the anticipated consequences of that penetration.

While the market participant could put his or her money in individual stocks, it might be more efficient and less time-consuming to simply invest in stock index futures. In buying futures on the S&P 500 Index, the investor is capturing the performance of 500 securities; with the New York Stock Exchange Index 1,500 securities; and 225 Japanese stocks with the Nikkei Average.

As discussed in Chapter 1, two types of risks are associated with investments: systematic or market-related risks, and unsystematic or firm-related risks. Since only systematic risk is assumed to be rewarded in an efficient capital market environment (unsystematic risk can be diversified away), the investor may wish to be exposed only to systematic risk. Stock index futures represent an efficient approach to only taking systematic, market-related risk.

Another advantage of stock index futures is that there is less manipulative action and insider trading than with individual securities. While it is possible (though not legal) for "informed" insider trading to cause an individual stock to move dramatically in the short term, such activity is not as likely for an entire index. This advantage, however, should not be overstated. Unusual trading activity of stock index futures comes under the scrutiny of federal regulators from time to time.

Stock index futures also offer leverage potential. A $190,000 to $200,000 S&P futures contract can be established for $22,000 in margin and with no interest on the balance.[10] If you were investing $200,000 in actual stocks through margin, you would have to put up a minimum of $100,000 (50 percent) in margin and pay interest on the balance. While we previously said the margin on stock index futures is relatively high in comparison to interest-rate futures (and other commodities), and was raised following the market crash in October 1987, we see the margin requirement is still considerably lower than that on an outright stock purchase. Also, the commissions on a stock index futures contract are minuscule in comparison to commissions on securities of comparable value.

Volatility and Profits or Losses Before the market crash of 1987, the average daily move on the S&P 500 Index was approximately 0.50 (one half of a point per day). Since the crash, the average daily movement has been in the 0.75 to 1.00 range. A 0.90 upward move in an S&P 500 futures contract (say from 389 to 389.90) means a daily gain of $450 (recall the contract has a multiplier of 500). With a margin requirement of $22,000, that's a 2.05 percent one-day return on your money.

Gain in futures contract	$ .90
Multiplier	× 500
Dollar gain	$ 450
Margin	$22,000
Percentage gain	2.05%

This translates into a 738 percent annualized return (2.05 percent × 360). By contrast if the $22,000 were invested in a 6 percent certificate of deposit, only $3.67 in interest would accrue on a daily basis. The difference here, of course, is that the $450 average daily movement related to the index may be up or down, whereas the $3.67 is only up.

Actually, from January 1 to early October 1987, the S&P 500 Index (and futures contracts) went up by 100 points as indicated in Figure 17–1. That represents a gain of $50,000 (500 × 100) on a typical margined investment of

---

[10] As mentioned in Chapter 16, margin on futures contracts merely represents good-faith money, and there is never any interest on the balance.

Figure 17–1   Price Movements in the S&P 500 Index

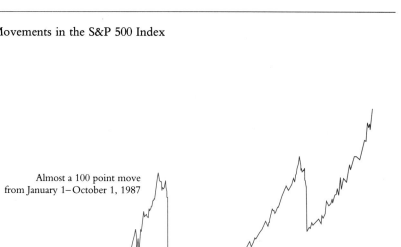

Closing prices

Almost a 100 point move
from January 1–October 1, 1987

$22,000. However, the S&P 500 Index fell 57.86 points on October 19th, 1987, and related futures contracts declined by 80 points (that meant an incredible negative basis of 22.14 points). An investor in an S&P 500 contract lost $40,000 (500 × 80) in one day if he held his position. Based on $22,000 margin, that's a 182 percent loss in one day.[11]

When a stock index futures contract starts to run against an investor, he or she can bail out and cut losses. If the contract value is going down rapidly, the investor will be continually called on to put up more margin as the margin

---

[11] This assumes the investor continued to maintain margin and did not close out his or her position.

position is being depleted. That puts tremendous pressure on the investor. He or she must decide whether to put up more margin and hold the position in hopes of a comeback or close out the position and take a loss.

Not all speculation in stock index futures must necessarily be based on the market going up. You can also speculate that the market will go down. You simply sell a contract with the anticipation of repurchasing it at a lower price later. Margin requirements are similar, and gains come from a declining market and losses from an increasing market. If the index goes up rapidly, the investor will be called on to put up more margin.

Hedging

Up to now our discussion of stock index futures has mainly related to speculating (or anticipating the next major move in the market). Perhaps the most important use of stock index futures is for hedging purposes. One who has a large diversified portfolio may think the market is about to decline. A portfolio manager who suffers a 20 percent decline in his or her portfolio actually requires a 25 percent gain from the new lower base to break even.

A portfolio manager faced with the belief that a declining market is imminent may be inclined to sell part or all of the portfolio. The question becomes, is this realistic? First, large transaction costs are associated with selling part or all of a portfolio and then repurchasing it later. Second, it may be difficult to liquidate a position in certain securities that are thinly traded. For example, a mutual fund or pension fund that tries to sell 10,000 shares of a small over-the-counter stock may initially find a price quote of $25, but only be able to close out its relatively large position at $23.50. A $15,000 loss would be suffered. Furthermore, the fund might find the same type of problem in reacquiring the stock after the overall market decline is over. This problem could be multiplied by 25 or 50 times, depending on the number of securities in the portfolio. Though larger, more liquid holdings would be easier to trade, significant transactions costs are still involved.

A more easily executed defensive strategy would be to sell one or more stock index futures as a hedge against the portfolio. If the stock market does go down, the loss on the portfolio will be partially or fully offset by the profit on the stock index futures contract(s) because they are bought back at a lower price than the initial sales price.

As an example, assume a corporate pension fund has $20 million in stock holdings. The investment committee for the fund is very bearish in its outlook, fearing that the overall market could go down by 20 percent in the next few months and a $4 million loss would be suffered. The pension fund decides to fully hedge its position.

The fund is going to use S&P 500 Index futures for the hedge. We shall assume the futures can be sold for 390, with a settlement date in three months. Before the number of contracts for execution is determined, the portfolio

manager must consider the relative volatility of his portfolio. If the portfolio is more volatile than the market, this must be factored into the decision-making process. As discussed in Chapter 1, the beta coefficient indicates how volatile a stock is relative to the market. If a stock has a beta of 1.20, it is 20 percent more volatile than the market (or market index). We shall assume the $20 million portfolio discussed above has a weighted average beta of 1.15 (that is, the portfolio is 15 percent more volatile than the market).

To determine the number of contracts necessary to hedge the position, we use the following formula:

$$\frac{\$ \text{ Value of portfolio}}{\$ \text{ Value of contract}} \times \frac{\text{Weighted beta}}{\text{of portfolio}} = \frac{\text{Number of}}{\text{contracts}} \qquad (17\text{--}1)$$

In the example under discussion, we would show:

$$\frac{\$20,000,000}{390 \times 500} \times 1.15 = \text{Number of contracts}$$

In the first term of the formula, the numerator is the size of the portfolio being hedged. The denominator is the size of each contract and, in this example, is found by multiplying the S&P futures contract value of 390 by 500. The first term is then multiplied by the weighted beta value of 1.15. The answer works out as:

$$\frac{\$20,000,000}{\$195,000} \times 1.15 = 102.56 \times 1.15 = 118 \text{ contracts}$$

The portfolio can be effectively hedged with 118 contracts.

Assume the market does go down but only by 10 percent instead of the 20 percent originally anticipated. Let's demonstrate that the hedge has worked. Since the portfolio has a beta of 1.15, its decline would be 11.5 percent (10 percent × 1.15). With a $20 million portfolio, the loss would be $2.3 million. To offset this loss, we will have a gain on 118 contracts. The gain is shown as follows:

S&P Index futures contract (sales price)	390.0
Decline in price on the futures contract	
(10% × 390)	− 39.0
Ending value (purchase price)	351.0

The 39-point decline on the index futures contract indicates the profit made on each contract.[12] They were sold for 390.0 and repurchased for 351.0. With 118 contracts, the profit on the stock index futures contracts comes out as $2,301,000.

---

[12] Note that the futures contract is assumed to move on a one-to-one basis with the market. The actual relationship may not be this precise.

Profit per contract (39.0 × 500)	$ 19,500
Number of contracts	× 118
Total profit	$2,301,000

The gain of $2,301,000 on the stock index futures contracts offsets the loss of $2.3 million on the portfolio. The small difference between the two values represents rounding. Actually, executing a perfect hedge may be further complicated by a number of other factors such as the lack of an appropriate index to match against the portfolio and the change in basis over time. Also, the portfolio may not move exactly in accordance with the beta. No doubt, many real-world factors can complicate any hedge.

While a stock index futures hedge offers the advantage of protecting against losses, it takes away the upside potential. If the market goes up by 10 percent instead of down, the gain on the portfolio may be wiped out by the loss on the stock index futures contracts. The investor could be forced to buy back the futures contract for 10 percent more than the selling price. Because some portfolio managers are afraid of losing all their upside potential in a hedged position, they may wish to hedge less than 100 percent of their portfolio.

While the hedging procedure just described can be potentially beneficial to portfolio managers, it can be potentially detrimental to the market in general if overused. Actually, protecting a large portfolio against declines is sometimes referred to as **portfolio insurance.** It is potentially a good strategy, but what if many investors initiate their portfolio-insurance strategies at the same time? Perhaps they are worried because there has been an increase in the prime rate or a bad report on inflation. An overload of stock index futures sales hitting the market at the same time drives down not only stock index futures prices but the stocks in the indexes as well (such as those in the S&P 500 Stock Index). An overall panic can result. The chain reaction is that a whole new round of portfolio-insurance-induced sales are triggered.

Partially to protect against a recurrence of the events that were part of the market crash of 1987, the Chicago Mercantile Exchange and New York Stock Exchange introduced so-called circuit breakers in 1990. **Circuit breakers** call for the temporary halt in trading of futures contracts when the market is tumbling. For example, the Chicago Mercantile Exchange has a rule that prevents market participants from trading Standard & Poor's 500 Stock Index futures at lower prices for 30 minutes after the S&P 500 Index has fallen 12 points. The New York Stock Exchange temporarily bars most program-trading-related activities any time the Dow Jones Industrial Average falls by 50 points.[13] While these circuit breakers have worked effectively since their in-

---

[13] Under Rule 80A, the New York Stock Exchange mandates that stock index arbitrage, in which computer-assisted traders rapidly buy or sell stocks in New York with offsetting trades in stock futures in Chicago, must be conducted in a technically stabilizing way once the Dow Jones Industrial Average swings 50 points.

troduction in the summer of 1990, they have not been fully tested. In a true panic, the circuit breakers themselves could add to fear as traders and hedgers are not able to execute their transactions.

Other Uses of Hedging   Hedging with stock index futures has a number of other uses besides attempting to protect the position of a long-term investment portfolio. These include:

Underwriter Hedge   As described in Chapter 10, the investment banker (underwriter) has a risk exposure from buying stock from the issuing corporation with the intention of reselling it in the public markets. If there is weakness during the distribution period, the potential resale price could fall below the purchase price, and the underwriter's profit would be wiped out. To protect against this market risk, the underwriter could sell stock index futures contracts. If the market goes down, presumably, the loss on the stock will be compensated for by the gain on the stock index futures contract as a result of being able to repurchase it at a lower price. This, of course, is not a perfect hedge. It is possible that the stock could go down while the market is going up, and losses on both the stock and stock index futures contract would occur (writing options directly against the stock might be more efficient, but in many cases such options are not available).

Specialist or Dealer Hedge   As indicated in Chapter 2, a specialist on an exchange or a dealer in the over-the-counter market buys and sells stocks for his own inventory for temporary holding. He may, at times, assume a larger temporary holding than desired, with all the risks associated with that exposure. Stock index futures can reduce the market (or systematic) risk, although the futures cannot reduce the specific risk associated with a security.

Retirement or Estate Hedge   As we move into the next two or three decades, large retirement funds will be accumulated from voluntary retirement plans. A retirement plan participant who has accumulated a large sum in an equity fund may feel a need to hedge his or her position in certain time periods in the economy (where liquidation is neither legal nor possible). A futures contract may provide that hedge. Also, a person with responsibility for an estate may be locked into a portfolio during the period of probate (validation of the will process) and wish to hedge his or her position with a stock index futures contract.

Tax Hedge   An investor may have accumulated a large return on a diversified portfolio in a given year. To maintain the profitable position but defer the taxable gains until the next year, futures contracts may be employed.

Arbitraging

While stock index futures started out as a major tool for speculating and hedging, they are now also widely used for arbitraging. Basically, an **arbitrage** is set up when a simultaneous trade (a buy and a sell) occurs in two different markets and a profit is locked in. Assume the S&P 500 Stock Index has a value of 389 based on the market value of all the stocks in the index. Also, assume the S&P 500 Stock Index futures contract, due to expire in two months, is selling for 390. There is a one-point positive basis between the futures contract and the underlying index. A sophisticated institutional investor may decide to arbitrage based on this difference. He or she will simultaneously sell a futures contract for 390 and buy a basket of stocks that matches the S&P 500 Stock Index for 389.[14] Because at expiration, the futures contract and underlying index will have the same value, a one-point profit is locked in at the time of arbitraging. For example, if at expiration, the S&P 500 Stock Index has a value of 387, a gain of three will occur on the sale, and a loss of two will be associated with the purchase for a net profit of one. If thousands of such contracts are involved, the profits can be substantial, and the potential for losses in a true arbitrage are nonexistent.

As you might assume, index arbitraging is in the exclusive providence of wealthy, sophisticated investors. For this reason, many smaller investors are somewhat resentful of the process and claim it tends to disrupt the normal operations of the marketplace. While there is nothing inherently wrong with arbitraging and it may even make the markets more efficient, it is sometimes a target for criticism by regulators. This is because it involves the process of program trading, discussed earlier in the chapter.

■ TRADING STOCK INDEX OPTIONS

Stock index options also allow the market participant to speculate or hedge against major market movements, though there is no opportunity for arbitraging. Stock index options are similar in many respects to the standard put and call options on individual stocks discussed in Chapter 15. The purchaser of an option pays an initial premium and then closes out the option at a given price in the future. One essential difference between stock index options and options on individual securities is that in the former case, there is only a cash settlement of the position, whereas in the latter case (individual securities), you can force the option writer to deliver the securities.

---

[14] Actually, arbitraging has become sufficiently sophisticated through mathematics and computer analysis that all 500 stocks do not actually have to be purchased. Perhaps 10 or 15 key stocks bought in large quantities will be sufficient to adequately represent the S&P 500 Index. Commissions on such transactions tend to be extremely small.

Examples of stock index options are presented in Table 17–5. The key option contracts on broad market indexes relate to:

Standard & Poor's 100 Index (Chicago Board Options Exchange).

Standard & Poor's 500 Index (Chicago Board Options Exchange).

Major Market Index (American Stock Exchange).

Institutional Index (American Stock Exchange).

Japan Index (American Stock Exchange).

Value Line Index (American Stock Exchange).

Financial News Coast Composite Index (Pacific Coast Exchange).

NYSE Index (New York Stock Exchange).

We have discussed many of these indexes either in Chapter 3 or in this chapter. One item to observe is that the stock index option contract often trades on a different exchange than the previously discussed stock index futures contract. For example, the Standard & Poor's 500 Index *option* contract trades on the Chicago Board Options Exchange while the *futures* contract on the same index trades on the Chicago Mercantile Exchange (CME). Similarly, the option contract on the Major Market Index trades on the American Stock Exchange, and the futures contract trades on the Chicago Board of Trade (CBT). Other examples could also be cited. The point is that some exchanges have greater expertise in options (such as the Chicago Board Options Exchange and the American Stock Exchange), while others specialize in futures (the Chicago Mercantile Exchange and the Chicago Board of Trade). There is tremendous competition to find the appropriate niche in stock index futures and options.

Actual Trade in the S&P 100 Index

Let's take a closer look at the most popular of the stock index options, the Standard & Poor's 100 Index options trading on the Chicago Board Options Exchange. We reproduce a part of Table 17–5 covering this index in Table 17–6. You will recall from an earlier discussion that the S&P 100 Index is composed of 100 blue-chip stocks on which the Chicago Board Options Exchange currently has individual option contracts. It is a smaller version of the S&P 500 Index and generally has a value of about 20 points less (though it closely parallels the overall movements of the S&P 500). Both indexes are value-weighted.

Note at the bottom of Table 17–6 that the S&P 100 Index closed on August 12, 1991, at 368.28. With this value in mind, we can examine the strike prices and premiums for the various contracts. The premium in each case is multiplied by 100 to determine the total cash value involved.[15] Let's read down

---

[15] The 100 multiplier applies to all the other option contracts listed in Table 17–5 as well.

Table 17–5 Stock Index Options

INDEX TRADING

Monday, August 12, 1991

OPTIONS

CHICAGO BOARD

S&P 100 INDEX-$100 times index

Strike Price	Calls–Last Aug	Calls–Last Sep	Calls–Last Oct	Puts–Last Aug	Puts–Last Sep	Puts–Last Oct
335	33⅝	....	36¾	1/16	9/16	1⅞
340	29	29¼	....	1/16	¾	2½
345	23⅜	....	28	1/16	1⅛	2¾
350	17¾	20	24	⅛	1⅝	3⅝
355	9⅝	17	20⅛	3/16	2 5/16	4⅝
360	4⅞	13⅜	16	⅜	3⅜	5⅝
365	1¾	9⅝	12¾	15/16	4⅞	7½
370	⅜	6½	9⅛	2⅞	6⅞	9⅝
375	1/16	4¼	7	6¾	10	13¼
380	1/16	2 9/16	5	12	14	16
385	....	1 7/16	3¼	17¾	18¾	....
390	....	¾	2 1/16	....	....	22½

Total call volume 90,294 Total call open int. 347,289
Total put volume 84,269 Total put open int. 405,218
The index: High 368.56; Low 366.23; Close 368.28, +0.84

S&P 500 INDEX-$100 times index

Strike Price	Calls–Last Aug	Calls–Last Sep	Calls–Last Dec	Puts–Last Aug	Puts–Last Sep	Puts–Last Dec
325	....	....	....	....	3/16	2⅛
345	....	....	....	....	....	4
350	....	....	....	....	⅜	4½
355	....	....	....	....	15/16	....
360	26	....	....	....	1	5⅞
365	....	....	....	1/16	1⅜	....
370	16½	20½	....	⅛	1⅞	....
375	13¼	16½	....	⅛	2⅝	9¼
380	7¼	11⅞	....	⅜	4	10½
385	4⅛	9	17¾	1 3/16	5⅛	11⅞
390	1⅜	6¼	15½	3¼	7½	....
395	⅜	3⅞	12⅛	8⅝	11⅝	....
400	1/16	2 7/16	10⅛	13⅞	14	18⅛
405	....	1⅜	....	....	....	....
410	....	11/16	....	....	....	....

Total call volume 28,770 Total call open int. 366,871
Total put volume 34,411 Total put open int. 480,326
The index: High 388.17; Low 385.90; Close 388.02, +0.90

LEAPS-S&P 100 INDEX

Strike Price	Calls–Last Dec 92	Calls–Last Dec 93		Puts–Last Dec 92	Puts–Last Dec 93	
30	8½	....	....	⅞	1½	....
32½	....	....	....	1 9/16	....	....
35	....	....	....	2 3/16	2⅞	....

Total call volume 10 Total call open int. 22,493
Total put volume 208 Total put open int. 69,278
The index: High 36.86; Low 36.62; Close 36.83, +0.09

LEAPS-S&P 500 INDEX

Strike Price	Calls–Last Dec 92	Calls–Last Dec 93		Puts–Last Dec 92	Puts–Last Dec 93	
30	....	....	....	....	....	15/16
37½	....	6	....	....	2½	....

Total call volume 50 Total call open int. 26,323
Total put volume 111 Total put open int. 59,999
The index: High 38.82; Low 38.59; Close 38.80, +0.09

AMERICAN

MAJOR MARKET INDEX

Strike Price	Calls–Last Aug	Calls–Last Sep	Calls–Last Oct	Puts–Last Aug	Puts–Last Sep	Puts–Last Oct
540	....	....	....	....	5/16	1
560	....	....	....	....	....	1⅜
570	....	....	....	....	¾	....
580	56⅛	....	....	1/16	....	....
590	44¼	....	....	⅛	....	3⅞
600	....	....	43¾	3/16	2¼	5
605	....	....	....	¼	2¾	....
610	....	....	....	3/16	3⅜	....
615	....	....	32⅜	¼	....	....
620	15⅞	....	....	7/16	....	....
625	12¾	18¼	....	¾	7	....
630	8⅝	16	....	1⅜	9	....
635	5⅛	12⅜	....	2⅞	11¼	....
640	2 9/16	10⅛	....	5⅜	13⅜	17
645	1⅛	8	....	8¾	16½	....
650	7/16	6⅛	....	14⅝	....	....
655	3/16	....	....	....	....	....
660	1/16	3¼	6⅞	23¾	26⅝	....
680	....	¾	2 3/16	....	....	....

Total call volume 5,242 Total call open int. 34,542
Total put volume 3,246 Total put open int. 35,607
The index: High 637.38; Low 633.15; Close 636.45, +0.94

LT-20 INDEX

Strike Price	Calls–Last Dec 92	Calls–Last Dec 93		Puts–Last Dec 92	Puts–Last Dec 93	
30	....	5⅜	....	....	....	....

Total call volume 3,000 Total call open int. 59,788
Total put volume 0 Total put open int. 125,356
The index: High 31.87; Low 31.66; Close 31.82, +0.04

INSTITUTIONAL INDEX

Strike Price	Calls–Last Aug	Calls–Last Sep	Calls–Last Oct	Puts–Last Aug	Puts–Last Sep	Puts–Last Oct
300	....	....	....	....	....	⅛
335	....	....	....	....	⅛	....
350	....	....	....	....	....	1 1/16
355	....	....	....	....	⅜	1 5/16
365	....	....	....	....	....	1 15/16
375	....	30⅛	....	1/16	1⅛	2 9/16
380	....	....	....	....	1 7/16	....
385	....	....	....	3/16	2¼	....
395	7½	....	....	7/16	....	....
400	5⅛	....	....	1 1/16	....	....
405	2 5/16	7⅛	....	3⅛	....	....
410	½	4¾	....	6⅜	....	....
415	⅛	3	....	....	....	....

Total call volume 114 Total call open int. 1,635
Total put volume 24 Total put open int. 1,184
The index: High 84.39; Low 83.27; Close 83.39, −1.20

VALUE LINE INDEX OPTIONS

Strike Price	Calls–Last Aug	Calls–Last Sep	Calls–Last Oct	Puts–Last Aug	Puts–Last Sep	Puts–Last Oct
300	....	....	....	⅛	1⅞	....
310	6⅛	8½	....	⅜	3⅞	6
315	1¼	4⅜	8	2⅛	6⅜	8⅛
335	....	11/16	....	....	....	....

Total call volume 2,409 Total call open int. 7,798
Total put volume 2,457 Total put open int. 8,080
The index: High 315.13; Low 314.10; Close 315.11, +0.44

UTILITIES INDEX

Strike Price	Calls–Last Aug	Calls–Last Sep	Calls–Last Oct	Puts–Last Aug	Puts–Last Sep	Puts–Last Oct
225	9½	....	....	....	....	....
235	....	....	3⅞	....	....	....

Total call volume 180 Total call open int. 1,664
Total put volume 0 Total put open int. 4,033
The index: High 235.04; Low 233.73; Close 234.91, +0.25

PACIFIC

FINANCIAL NEWS COMPOSITE INDEX

Strike Price	Calls–Last Aug	Calls–Last Sep	Calls–Last Dec	Puts–Last Aug	Puts–Last Sep	Puts–Last Dec
250	....	....	....	....	1 11/16	....
255	7¾	10⅛	....	....	2⅝	....
260	3¼	....	....	....	3⅞	....
265	¾	4	....	3⅜	6½	....
270	3/16	....	....	7⅜	....	....
275	....	1⅛	....	....	....	....

Total call volume 230 Total call open int. 2,866
Total put volume 212 Total put open int. 810
The index: High 262.79; Low 261.33; Close 262.54, +0.03

NEW YORK

NYSE INDEX OPTIONS

Strike Price	Calls–Last Aug	Calls–Last Sep	Calls–Last Oct	Puts–Last Aug	Puts–Last Sep	Puts–Last Oct
205	8	8¾	....	....	....	....
210	3	....	7	⅜	2 15/16	....
212½	1¼	....	....	1¼	....	....
215	3/16	....	....	3⅛	....	3⅛
220	....	....	2⅛	....	....	....

Total call volume 170 Total call open int. 2,366
Total put volume 109 Total put open int. 2,238
The index: High 212.57; Low 211.57; Close 212.53, +0.36

Source: *The Wall Street Journal,* August 13, 1991, p. 21C. Reprinted by permission of *THE WALL STREET JOURNAL,* © 1991 by Dow Jones & Company, Inc. All Rights Reserved Worldwide.

Table 17–6 S&P 100 Index Stock Options (Chicago Board Options Exchange, August 12, 1991)

Strike Price	Calls			Puts		
	August	September	October	August	September	October
335	33⅝	—	36¾	1/16	9/16	1⅞
340	29	29¼	—	1/16	¾	2½
345	23⅜	—	28	1/16	1⅛	2¾
350	17¾	20	24	⅛	1⅝	3⅝
355	9⅜	17	20⅛	3/16	2 5/16	4⅝
360	4⅞	13⅜	16	⅜	3⅜	5⅝
365	1¾	9⅝	12¾	15/16	4⅞	7½
370	⅜	6½	9⅛	2⅞	6⅞	9⅝
375	1/16	4¼	7	6¾	10	13¼
380	1/16	2 9/16	5	12	14	16
385	—	1 7/16	3¼	17¾	18¾	—
390	—	¾	2 1/16	—	—	22½

The multiplier times the premium is 100.
Value of the S&P 100 Index (August 12, 1991) = 368.28.

to the 370 strike price and across to the September call option (second monthly column). The premium is 6½ (6.50).

Assume an investor bought a September 370 contract for a 6.50 premium on August 12, 1991, and that when the September contract expired, the S&P 100 Index was 388 under our optimistic assumption, and that under our pessimistic assumption it was 352. At an index value of 388, the option value is 18 (388 − 370). The ending or expiration price is 18 points higher than the strike price. Keep in mind the option cost of 6.50. The profit is shown below to be $1,150.

At an ending value of 352 (pessimistic assumption), the option is worthless, and there is a loss of $650. Remember these are 370 call options.

388 Optimistic Assumption		352 Pessimistic Assumption
Final value (100 × 18)	$1,800.00	$ 0.00
Purchase price (100 × 6.50)	−650.00	−650.00
Profit or loss	$1,150.00	$−650.00

We have been working with call options. Now, let's shift our attention to put options. If a 370 put option (the option to sell at 370 rather than buy at 370) had been acquired on August 12, 1991, we can see in Table 17–6

(September put column, fifth row from the bottom) that the initial price of the put option would be 6⅞ ($687.50). Let's assume that when the September put contract expired, the S&P 100 Index was 388 under what is now our pessimistic assumption and 352 under what is now our optimistic assumption.

At an index value of 388, no value is associated with a put option that allows you to sell at only 370. Since the put option cost 6⅞, there is a $687.50 loss. At a final value of 352, the put option to sell at 370 has a value of 18. With a cost of 6⅞, a profit of $1,112.50 occurs. The profit and losses are indicated below.

388 Pessimistic Assumption		352 Optimistic Assumption	
Final Value	0.00	(100 × 18)	$1,800.00
Purchase price (100 × 6⅞)	−687.50	(100 × 6.875)	687.50
Profit or loss	$−687.50		$1,112.50

■ HEDGING WITH STOCK INDEX OPTIONS

The discussion of stock index options thus far has pertained to speculation about market moves. Stock index options can also be used for hedging. Like stock index futures, stock index options can be used to protect a portfolio or for special purposes by underwriters, specialists, dealers, tax planners, and others.

At times, options may offer a hedging advantage over futures to investors who are limited by law from purchasing futures contracts. On the other hand, futures generally allow for a more efficient hedge than options. If the market goes down by 20 or 25 percent, chances are good that a completely hedged short futures position (selling futures contracts) will compensate fully, or to a reasonable degree, losses in a portfolio. An option write, used to hedge a portfolio, may be inadequate. Perhaps the option premium income represents 10 percent of the portfolio, but the market goes down by 25 percent. Fifteen percent of the loss will be unprotected. Buying a put option may overcome this problem, but the cash outflow to purchase the put option could involve substantial funds. Clearly, both futures and options have their advantages and disadvantages.

■ OPTIONS ON STOCK INDEX FUTURES

We have discussed *stock index futures* and *stock index options,* so a natural extension of our discussion is to consider the third form of stock index trading,

Figure 17–2   Comparison of Option Contracts

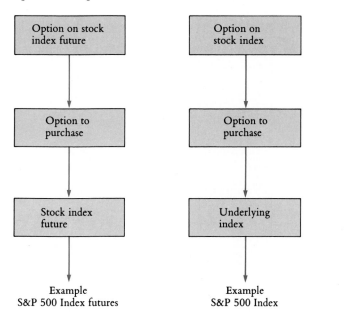

options on stock index futures. The three forms of index trading are listed below for future reference.

1. Stock index futures.
2. Stock index options.
3. Options on stock index futures.

An option on stock index futures (item 3) gives the holder the right to purchase the stock index *futures contract* at a specified price over a given period. This is slightly different from the stock index option (item 2) that gives the holder the right to purchase the *underlying index* at a specified price over a given time period.[16] The contrast is shown in Figure 17–2.

The primary topic for discussion in this section is represented by the lefthand column in Figure 17–2, an option on a stock index futures contract. The value of an option to purchase a stock index futures contract will depend

---

[16] Because of cash-settlement procedures, the actual index will never actually be purchased, and the gain or loss will be settled for cash.

Table 17–7   Options on Stock Index Futures
(August 12, 1991)

```
┌─────────────────────────────────────────────────────┐
│ S&P 500 STOCK INDEX (CME) $500 times premium         │
│ Strike        Calls – Settle         Puts – Settle   │
│ Price     Aug-c  Sep-c  Dc-c    Aug-p  Sep-p  Dec-p  │
│ 380        9.65  12.80  22.00    0.35   3.55  10.10  │
│ 385        5.25   9.35  18.65    0.95   5.05  11.65  │
│ 390        2.05   6.45  15.40    2.75   7.10  13.45  │
│ 395        0.50   4.20  12.60    6.20   9.85  15.45  │
│ 400        0.10   2.50  10.05   10.80  13.15  17.80  │
│ 405        0.05   1.45   7.85    ....  17.00   ....  │
│ Est. vol. 5,325; Fri vol. 2,200 calls; 3,120 puts    │
│ Open Interest Fri; 30,999 calls; 55,814 puts         │
│                                                       │
│           OTHER FUTURES OPTIONS                       │
│                                                       │
│ NYSE COMPOSITE INDEX (NYFE) $500 times premium       │
│ Strike        Calls – Settle         Puts – Settle   │
│ Price     Aug-c  Sep-c  Dec-c   Aug-p  Sep-p  Dec-p  │
│ 214        0.75   2.95   5.15    1.55   3.80   4.75  │
│ Est. vol. 87, Fri vol. 36 calls, 19 puts             │
│ Open Interest Fri 865 calls, 950 puts                │
│ NIKKEI 225 STOCK AVERAGE (CME) $5 times NSA          │
│ Strike        Calls – Settle         Puts – Settle   │
│ Price     Aug-c  Sep-c  Dec-c   Aug-p  Sep-p  Dec-p  │
│ 24000.      50    245    ....    ....  1005   1160   │
│ Est. vol. 113, Fri vol. 63 calls, 4 puts             │
│ Open Interest Fri 693 calls, 785 puts                │
│ CBT – Chicago Board of Trade. CME – Chicago Mercantile│
│ Exchange. NYFE – New York Futures Exchange, a unit of │
│ the New York Stock Exchange.                          │
└─────────────────────────────────────────────────────┘
```

Source: *The Wall Street Journal,* August 12, 1991, p. 21C. Reprinted by permission of *THE WALL STREET JOURNAL,* © 1991 by Dow Jones & Company, Inc. All Rights Reserved Worldwide.

on the outlook for the futures contract. Quotes on options to purchase stock index futures are shown in Table 17–7.[17]

As indicated in Table 17–7, options on stock index futures are available for the S&P 500 Stock Index, the NYSE Composite Index, and the Nikkei 225 Stock Average. Let's look at the quotes on the S&P 500 Stock Index at the top of the table. A call option to buy a September S&P 500 Stock Index futures contract at a price of 395 has a premium of 4.20. On these option contracts, the premium is multiplied by 500 to get the value of the contract. Thus, the cost of the contract is $2,100 (500 × 4.20).

In examining Table 17–7, note that the premiums on the call options increase substantially with the passage of time from August to December. This gain in value is not only a function of the extended time period associated with the option, but is also due to the fact that the S&P futures contract has a higher value with the passage of time.[18] For example on August 12, 1991, the S&P 500 September contract traded at 389.30, while the December contract traded at 392.10. Thus, options on stock index futures not only have a time premium

---

[17] These quotes generally appear in the futures section of *The Wall Street Journal* rather than in the options section. This can be confusing.

[18] Of course, if the market outlook were highly pessimistic, there would be a decline in the S&P futures contract with the passage of time.

Commodity Trading: Make Room for the Newest Players

No job in the commodities market is tougher than being a trader. You are constantly buying and selling futures contracts in the trading pits with some of the pushiest people in the world. But according to a September 13, 1991, *Wall Street Journal* article, women are making their presence known in this rock-em, sock-em world of finance. The article stated, "Many women traders are earning far more than they did in their previous careers: It's not unusual for traders to earn $100,000 or more a year, and the sky's the limit for very good or very lucky traders."[19]

The traders stand toe to toe using hand signals to indicate their buy or sell intentions for stock index futures, pork bellies, soybeans, and other items. Although there are Andrew Dice Clay sexist jokes floating around and locker room talk is often the mode of communication, women are holding their own. Why? When all is said and done, all that counts is performance. It is very easy to measure success, the bottom line, and it shows up every day of trading. Often, the article pointed out, women are better suited to trading because they do not let egos get in their way. They simply use straight logic to get the job done.

(as all options do), but may also have an additional premium (or discount) depending on the relationship of the far-term futures market to the near-term futures market.

Options on stock index futures may be settled on a cash basis, or the holder of a call option may exercise the option and force the option writer to produce a specified futures contract.

SUMMARY

For the investor who wishes to trade in stock indexes, there are three basic types of securities: stock index futures, stock index options, and options on stock index futures.

Stock index futures and options offer the potential for speculation as well as for hedging. With stock index futures, the margin is relatively low, which allows for a strong leverage potential. In hedging a portfolio position, the investor should consider the beta of his or her portfolio and adjust the number of contracts accordingly. Basis in the futures market represents the difference between the stock index futures price and the value of the actual underlying index. Basis may present the investor with a potential clue about the future direction of the market. The stock index futures market and the stock index

[19] Elyse Tanouye, "Women Traders Make Headway on the Futures Floor," *The Wall Street Journal,* September 3, 1991, p. C1.

option market trade on a cash-settlement basis. No securities ever change hands as the settlement is always in cash.

Investors in stock index futures may also engage in arbitraging procedures in which a simultaneous trade (a buy and a sell) occurs in the stock index futures contract and in the underlying securities in the index. This allows the investor to lock in a profit. The use of arbitraging, portfolio insurance, and program trading has been blamed by some for the market crash in October 1987 and the subsequent volatility in the market after the crash. This is subject to debate. Nevertheless, the Chicago Mercantile Exchange and the New York Stock Exchange have established circuit breakers that call for the temporary halt in trading of futures contracts when the market is tumbling.

The stock index option contract is generally similar to the option contract on individual securities. The investor has an opportunity to buy puts and calls, and the premium is related to the future prospects for the index.

The third form of stock index contracts, an option on stock index futures, combines the option concept with the futures market. Instead of an option on an actual index, you have an option on a stock index futures contract. The contract may be settled either with cash or with securities.

The two forms of option contracts offer an investment outlet to some investors who are constrained by law from investing in commodity contracts and thus cannot participate in stock index futures. On the other hand, stock index futures do provide a more efficient hedging device in that the gain on the futures contract may offset the loss on the portfolio. With an option, this may be more difficult or expensive to establish.

IMPORTANT WORDS AND CONCEPTS

futures contract on a stock market index (stock index futures) 550

stock index options 550

options to purchase futures 550

derivative products 551

program trading 551

cash settlement 555

basis 555

portfolio insurance 562

circuit breakers 562

arbitrage 564

DISCUSSION QUESTIONS

1. Why are stock index futures and options sometimes referred to as derivative products? Why do some believe derivative products make the markets more volatile?

2. How many stocks are in the Major Market Index? With what other market average does it closely correlate?

3. Why does a hedging position require less initial margin than a speculative position?

4. What is meant by the concept of cash settlement?

5. What does the term *basis* mean in the futures market? If there is a premium and it expands with the passage of time, what is the general implication?

6. Why does a down market put tremendous pressure on a speculator if he or she is the purchaser of a contract in anticipation of a market increase? Relate this answer directly to margin.

7. Why is it unrealistic for a portfolio manager to sell a large portion of his portfolio if he thinks the market is about to decline?

8. How does the beta of a portfolio influence the number of contracts that must be used in the hedging process?

9. What are some complicating factors in attempting to hedge a portfolio?

10. Why might the overuse of portfolio insurance be dangerous to the market?

11. What is an arbitrage position?

12. What is an essential difference between stock index options and options on individual securities in terms of settlement procedures?

13. Under what circumstance might a portfolio manager be more likely to use index option contracts instead of futures contracts to hedge a portfolio? What is the counter argument for futures contracts over index options?

14. Explain the difference between a stock index option and an option on stock index futures.

15. Suggest two reasons why an option on a stock index futures contract that has a distant expiration date might have a high premium.

PROBLEMS

Stock index futures

1. Based on the information in Table 17–1, what is the total value of an S&P 500 Index futures contract for December 1991? Use the settle price and the appropriate multiplier. Also, if the required margin is $22,000, what percent of the contract value does margin represent?

Gain on S&P futures

2. In Problem 1, if the S&P Index futures contract goes up to 400.80, what will be the total dollar profit on the contract? What is the percent return on the initial margin? If this price change occurred over four months, what is the annualized return?

Loss on S&P futures and margin

3. Return to Problem 1 and assume that margin must be maintained at a minimum level of $9,000. If the S&P Index futures contract goes from its initial value down to 364.80, will there be a call for more margin?

Computing settle price

4. Based on the information in Table 17–1, assume you buy a Major Market Index September contract at the settle price. You hold the contract for one month and enjoy a gain in value of $10,000. What was the settle price after one month?

<table>
<tr><td>Computing basis</td><td>5. Examine Table 17–3. Using settle prices, what is the value of the basis for the December 1991 and June 1992 contracts?</td></tr>
</table>

Computing basis

5. Examine Table 17–3. Using settle prices, what is the value of the basis for the December 1991 and June 1992 contracts?

Hedging and basis

6. Western States Life Insurance Company has a $12 million stock portfolio. The company is very aggressive, and the portfolio has a weighted beta of 1.25.

   a. Assume they use S&P 500 Index futures contracts to hedge the portfolio for the next 60 days and the contracts can be sold at 392. The contracts have a multiplier of 500. With the appropriate beta adjustment factor, how many contracts should be sold? Round your final answer to the nearest whole number.

   b. If NYSE Composite Index contracts selling at 215 were used instead, how many contracts should be sold? These contracts also have a multiplier of 500. Once again, consider the appropriate beta adjustment factor and round your final answer to the nearest whole number.

Hedging and betas

7. The 21st Century Pension Fund decides to hedge its $30 million stock portfolio on September 1. The portfolio has a beta of 1.10. It will use Major Market Index futures contracts selling at 638 to hedge. These contracts have a multiplier of 250. The fund intends to hedge the portfolio for the next 90 days.

   a. With the appropriate beta adjustment factor and rounding the final answer to the nearest whole number, how many contracts should be sold?

   b. Assuming that by December 1, the market has gone down by 20 percent and the stock portfolio moves in accordance with its beta, what will be the total dollar decline in the portfolio?

   c. Assume the Major Market Index futures contracts decline by 20 percent from 638. What will be the total dollar gain on the futures contracts? In the process, compare the sales price of 638 to the current value, multiply by 250, and then multiply this value by the number of contracts.

   d. Now assume that because of changing basis, the stock index futures contract does not move in parallel with the market. Although the market goes down by 20 percent, the stock index futures decline by only 15 percent. What will be the gain on the futures contracts? How does this compare to the loss in portfolio value in Part *b*?

S&P 100 call options

8. The following problem relates to data in Table 17–6. Assume you purchase an October 370 (strike price) S&P 100 call option. Compute your total dollar profit or loss if the index has the following values at expiration.

   a. 396

   b. 374

   c. 315

S&P 100 call
options

9. Using data from Table 17–6, assume you purchase an October 365 (strike price) S&P 100 put option. Compute your total dollar profit or loss if the index has the following values at expiration.

   a. 390

   b. 360

   c. 313

Hedging with the
Major Market
Index

10. The Topps Company has a $1 million funded pension plan for its employees. The portfolio beta is equal to 1.14. Assume the company sells (writes) 20 September 630 (strike price) call option contracts on the American Exchange Major Market Index as shown in Table 17–5. (Each contract trades in units of 100.) At the time the options were written, the index had a value of 636.45.

   a. What are the proceeds from the sale of the call options?

   b. Assume the market goes down by 12 percent. Considering the portfolio beta, what will be the total dollar decline in the portfolio?

   c. Assume the American Exchange Major Market Index also goes down by 12 percent at expiration. What will be the value of the index at that time?

   d. Based on your answer to Part *c*, what will be your profit on the option writes?

   e. Considering your answers to Parts *b* and *d*, what is your net gain or loss?

Using puts to
hedge

11. Assume that in Problem 10 you had purchased 20 September 630 put option contracts on the American Exchange Major Market Index listed in Table 17–5 instead of the call options. If the American Exchange Major Market Index goes down by 12 percent at expiration:

   a. What will be your profit on the puts? Comparing that to your loss on the stock portfolio in Problem 10*b*, what is your net overall gain or loss?

   b. Compare the protection afforded by the call-writing hedge in Problem 10 to the protection afforded by the put purchase in this problem.

   c. Suggest any modifications to the call writing or put purchase strategy that would allow you to increase your protection even more. A general statement is all that is required.

Using calls and
puts to hedge

12. Newman Money Management Incorporated is in charge of a $50 million portfolio. Its beta is equal to the market. To hedge its position, it sells (writes) 900 October 375 call option contracts on the S&P 100 Stock Index as shown in Table 17–5. It also buys 800 October 380 put option contracts on the same index shown in Table 17–5. Instead of going down, the market goes up by 10 percent (as does the portfolio), and the S&P 100 Stock Index ends up at 408.

   Consider the change in the portfolio value and the gains or losses on the call and put options. Each option contract trades in units of 100.

What is the overall net gain or loss of Newman Money Management as a result of the changes in the market?

Options on stock index futures

13. The State College retirement fund purchases a call on a stock option futures contract. The quote can be found in Table 17–7. The option is on the S&P 500 Stock Index. It has a strike price of 385 for September (1991). In the table, call options have a *c* after the month and put options a *p*.

   a. What is the quoted option premium (price)?

   b. Referring to Table 17–1, what is the quote for the September 1991 (futures) contract for the S&P 500 Stock Index? (Use the settle price.)

   c. Also referring to Table 17–1, what was the actual quote (value) for the S&P 500 Stock Index? (Use the closing price at the bottom of the S&P 500 Stock Index data.)

   d. By how much does the futures quote (Part *b*) exceed the actual index quote (Part *c*)? That is, how much is the basis?

   e. By how much does the quoted option premium (Part *a*) exceed the basis (Part *d*)?

   f. If the basis were to suddenly go to zero and the option declined by a similar amount, what would the new option premium be?

■ SELECTED REFERENCES

Use of Stock Index Futures and Options

Castelino, Mark G.; Jack C. Francis; and Avner Wolf. "Cross Hedging: Basis Risk and Choice of the Optimal Hedging Vehicle." *Financial Review,* May 1991, pp. 179–210.

Donnelly, Barbara. "Playing the Stock Index Arbitrage Game." *Institutional Investor,* February 1985, pp. 149–50, 156.

Fabozzi, Frank J., and Gregory M. Kipnis. *Stock Index Futures.* Homewood, Ill.: Dow Jones-Irwin, 1984.

Figlewski, Stephen. "Hedging with Stock Index Futures: Theory and Application in a New Market." *Journal of Futures Markets,* Summer 1985, pp. 183–200.

Holden, Craig W. "Index Arbitrage and the Media." *Financial Analysts Journal,* September–October 1991, pp. 8–9.

Junkus, Joan C., and Cheng F. Lee. "Use of Three Stock Index Futures in Hedging Decisions." *Journal of Futures Markets,* Summer 1985, pp. 201–22.

Nordhauser, Fred. "Using Stock Index Futures to Reduce Market Risk." *Journal of Portfolio Management,* Spring 1984, pp. 56–69.

Valuation of Stock Index Futures and Options

Cornell, Bradford. "Taxes and the Pricing of Stock Index Futures: Empirical Results." *Journal of Futures Markets,* Spring 1985, pp. 89–102.

Modest, David M. "On the Pricing of Stock Index Futures." *Journal of Portfolio Management,* Summer 1984, pp. 51–57.

Pitts, Mark. "The Pricing of Options on Debt Securities." *Journal of Portfolio Management,* Winter 1985, pp. 41–50.

Shastri, Kuldeep, and Kishore Tandon. "Options on Futures Contracts: A Comparison of European and American Pricing Models." *Journal of Futures Markets,* Winter 1986, pp. 593–618.

Program Trading

Kritzman, Mark. "What's Wrong with Portfolio Insurance." *Journal of Portfolio Management,* Fall 1986, pp. 13–16.

Stoll, Hans, and Robert Whaley. "Program Trading and Expiration-Day Effects." *Financial Analysts Journal,* March–April 1987, pp. 16–28.

Wunsch, Steven. "A New Idea: Public Announcements for Program Trades and Stock Indexes." *Intermarket,* May 1986, pp. 59–60.

Systematic Risk and Dividend Yield

Graham, David, and Robert Jennings. "Systematic Risk, Dividend Yield and the Hedging Performance of Stock Index Futures." *Journal of Futures Markets.* February 1987, pp. 1–14.

Part Six

Broadening the Investment Perspective

Outline

Nomura Securities is the most profitable brokerage house in the world. If you want to work there, plan to get to work early and stay late. The Japanese are among the best savers in the world, and in recent times, much of their funds have gone into equities. The rest of the world better hope they do not lose their appetite for investments.

Wall Street is the main place for securities trading in the United States. Kibudatu is the financial district of Tokyo. It is where you will find the Tokyo Stock Exchange.

The most profitable stock brokerage house in the world is Nomura Securities. If you were to work there, you would need to set your alarm for 6 A.M. and hit the ground running the moment it goes off. "Work harder" is the battle cry of Nomura. Brokers are held to rigorous sales quotas and are publicly humiliated if they fail to meet them. The company isn't afraid to trumpet the pressure it puts on its people. A new employee is expected to meet at least a thousand clients during the first three months with the company.

Many relationships with customers are long-standing. For example, Fumie Mitobe is part of the female sales force at Nomura. She has been selling Nomura's products door to door since the end of World War II. In the 1950s, she would visit the families in her neighborhood and give them a savings box, and she would keep the key. A month later, she would return, remove whatever money had been saved and invest for the family, usually in securities. She and others like her helped build a huge client base.

Among working-age people in Japan, 8 out of 10 own stock. This is not surprising, as the Japanese people are the world's greatest savers, putting away a quarter of their income. In the United States, the individual savings rate is closer to 5 percent.

Over the decades, Japanese savers have transferred much of their savings from low-yielding bank accounts to stocks and bonds. This was a great strategy as long as the market climbed to even higher levels. But in the early 1990s, the Tokyo Nikkei Average fell by 50 percent. The decline was caused by the unusually high valuation assigned in the marketplace to Japanese securities. At one time, price-earnings ratios of 70-80 were the norm.

Still, the rest of the world (and particularly the United States) continues to closely watch the developments in the Tokyo markets. We have all become dependent on the Japanese saver to provide part of our capital. If these funds are withdrawn, who will help finance the U.S. deficit of hundreds of billions of dollars a year? ■

18

International Securities Markets

In Chapter 1, we discussed the advantage of diversification in terms of risk reduction. To reduce risk exposure, the investor may desire a broad spectrum of securities from which to choose. An investor who lives in California would hardly be expected to limit all his investments to that geographic boundary. The same might be said for an investor living in the United States or Germany or Japan. The advantages of crossing international boundaries may be substantial in terms of diversification benefits.

Companies operating in different countries will be affected differently by international events such as crop failures, energy prices, wars, tariffs, trade between countries, and the value of local currencies relative to other currencies, especially the U.S. dollar. Furthermore, despite the up and down markets in the United States, there is almost certain to be a bull market somewhere in the world for the investor who likes to keep his chips on the table at all times.

The main drawback to investing in international securities would appear to be the more complicated nature of the investment. Currently, one cannot simply pick up the phone and ask a broker to buy 100 shares of Banco Bilbao on the Spanish Stock Exchange (this may change in the future). Nevertheless, the difficulties of participating in international securities are not as great as one might initially expect. As will be suggested later in this chapter, an investor has a number of feasible and easily executed routes to follow in participating in the international markets.

The primary attention in this chapter is to international equities, although investments may certainly include fixed-income securities and real assets. We shall examine the composition of world equity markets, the diversification and return benefits that can be derived from foreign investments, the obstacles that are present, and finally, the methods of participating in foreign investments, directly and indirectly.

■ THE WORLD EQUITY MARKET

The world markets have grown dramatically since the last edition of this book in 1989, and Japan and the United States have been going back and forth as the largest securities markets in terms of total market valuation. Table 18–1 lists the major developed markets at year-end 1981 and 1990 by their market capitalizations. Japan and the United States are far ahead of the other countries in terms of total market values. The U.S. share of the world market contracted significantly from 53 percent to 33 percent while Japan increased from 17 percent to 32 percent.

Figure 18–1 on page 584 depicts the geographical breakdown of major developed markets showing Europe, North America, and the Pacific region.

While the developed world securities markets continue to expand, major growth in securities markets has occurred in what has become known as the "emerging" markets such as Argentina, Brazil, Chile, Nigeria, Taiwan, Turkey, and Zimbabwe. Additionally, the Eastern European countries of Poland, Czechoslovakia, and Hungary have instituted capitalistic economic reforms

| Table 18–1 | Market Capitalization of Developed Countries (in Millions of U.S. Dollars) | | | |

Country	Year-End 1981	Percent of Total	Year-End 1990	Percent of Total
New Zealand	—	0.00%	$ 8,835	0.10%
Luxembourg	$ 4,457	0.18%	$ 10,456	0.12%
Israel	$ 6,972	0.28%	$ 10,560	0.12%
Finland	—	0.00%	$ 22,721	0.25%
Norway	$ 3,334	0.13%	$ 26,130	0.29%
Austria	$ 1,600	0.06%	$ 26,230	0.29%
Singapore	$ 34,808	1.39%	$ 34,308	0.38%
Denmark	$ 6,200	0.25%	$ 39,063	0.43%
Belgium	$ 8,400	0.34%	$ 65,449	0.72%
Hong Kong	$ 38,912	1.56%	$ 83,397	0.92%
Sweden	$ 17,200	0.69%	$ 92,102	1.02%
Australia	$ 54,400	2.17%	$ 106,915	1.18%
Spain	$ 16,700	0.67%	$ 111,404	1.23%
South Africa	$ 74,900	2.99%	$ 137,540	1.52%
Netherlands	$ 23,000	0.92%	$ 148,521	1.64%
Italy	$ 24,000	0.96%	$ 148,766	1.64%
Switzerland	$ 35,200	1.41%	$ 165,913	1.83%
Canada	$ 105,500	4.22%	$ 241,920	2.67%
France	$ 38,100	1.52%	$ 341,695	3.77%
Germany	$ 62,600	2.50%	$ 379,399	4.19%
United Kingdom	$ 180,600	7.22%	$ 867,599	9.58%
Japan	$ 431,387	17.24%	$2,917,679	32.21%
United States	$1,333,385	53.30%	$3,072,303	33.91%
Total	$2,501,655	100.00%	$9,058,905	100.00%

Source: *Emerging Stock Markets Factbook, 1991* (Washington, D.C.: International Finance Corporation, 1991), pp. 50–51.

including fledgling equity markets. East Germany and West Germany united to create a new German state that already had the benefits of a developed capital market. Table 18–2 on page 585 lists the market capitalizations of the emerging markets. Their total value of $475 billion would rank them in fourth place among developed countries. Some of these emerging markets, such as Korea and Taiwan-China, are bigger than markets in developed countries, but because these countries have low per capita gross domestic product, they are listed with the emerging economies.

A geographical breakdown of the emerging markets is depicted in Figure 18–2 on page 586 for 1981 and 1990. The relationships among the emerging countries have changed dramatically. Latin America fell from 46 percent to 17 percent of the total emerging market capitalization as the economies of this region suffered from high inflation, too much debt, and slow real economic

Figure 18–1   Developed Markets by Geographical Region (Market Capitalization in U.S. Dollars in Billions)

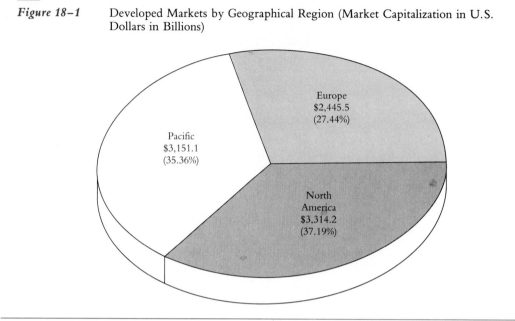

Source: Data From *Emerging Stock Markets Factbook, 1991* (Washington, D.C.: International Finance Corporation, 1991).

growth. Many international banks know all too well the problems of Latin America and the loan defaults in many countries of this region. A rising share of market value in the emerging markets goes to the high growth countries of East Asia (from 14 percent to 46 percent) and to smaller countries in Europe (from 4 percent to 9 percent). The total value of these markets increased from $83 billion to $470 billion over this 10-year period, an increase of over five times or an annual growth of over 20 percent per year. As emerging markets have grown, there are more opportunities to own equity positions. It is useful to look at the different market structures and institutional characteristics of these markets.

In 1988, Richard Roll published an article in the *Financial Analysts Journal* that analyzed the different institutional distinctions in many of the world's capital markets after the market crash in October 1987.[1] Table 18–3 on page 587 shows the institutional arrangements in world markets. Continuous auction markets (second column) are the standard in markets like the United States, Japan, United Kingdom, Germany, Canada, Hong Kong, and others. Table 18–3 also summarizes the use of specialists, the use of forward contracts, automated quotations, and many other factors.

[1]Richard Roll, "The International Crash of 1987," *Financial Analysts Journal,* September–October 1988, pp. 19–35.

Table 18-2   Market Capitalization of Emerging Markets (in Millions of U.S. Dollars)

Country	Year-End 1990	Percent of Total
Argentina	$ 3,268	0.69%
Bangladesh	$ 321	0.07%
Brazil (Sao Paulo)	$ 16,354	3.44%
Chile	$ 13,645	2.87%
Colombia	$ 1,416	0.30%
Costa Rica	—	0.00%
Cote d'Ivoire	$ 549	0.12%
Egypt (Cairo)	—	0.00%
Greece	$ 15,228	3.21%
India (Bombay)	$ 38,567	8.12%
Indonesia	$ 8,081	1.70%
Jamaica	$ 911	0.19%
Jordan	$ 2,001	0.42%
Kenya	$ 448	0.09%
Korea	$110,594	23.28%
Kuwait	—	0.00%
Malaysia	$ 48,611	10.23%
Mexico	$ 37,725	7.94%
Morocco	$ 966	0.20%
Nigeria	$ 1,372	0.29%
Pakistan	$ 2,985	0.63%
Peru	$ 848	0.18%
Philippines	$ 5,927	1.25%
Portugal	$ 9,201	1.94%
Sri Lanka	$ 917	0.19%
Taiwan, China	$100,710	21.20%
Thailand	$ 23,896	5.03%
Trinidad and Tobago	$ 696	0.15%
Turkey	$ 19,065	4.01%
Uruguay	—	0.00%
Venezuela	$ 8,361	1.76%
Zimbabwe	$ 2,395	0.50%
IFC Composite Index	$464,402	
All emerging markets	$475,058	100.00%

Source: *Emerging Stock Markets Factbook, 1991* (Washington, D.C.: International Finance Corporation, 1991), p. 51.

Figure 18–2   Regional Weights of Emerging Markets (Based on Market Capitalization in U.S. Dollars)

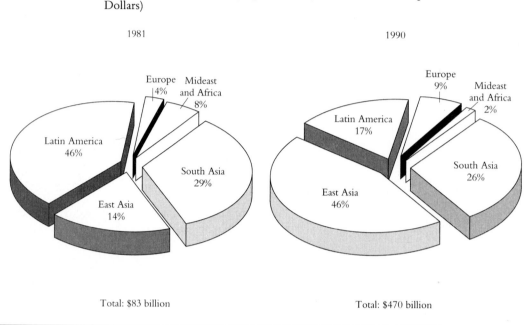

1981

Europe 4%   Mideast and Africa 8%

Latin America 46%

East Asia 14%

South Asia 29%

Total: $83 billion

1990

Europe 9%   Mideast and Africa 2%

Latin America 17%

East Asia 46%

South Asia 26%

Total: $470 billion

Source: *Emerging Stock Market Factbook, 1991* (Washington, D.C.: International Finance Corporation, 1991), p. 53.

While the next section points out the benefits of diversification using foreign securities, the crash of 1987 was an international phenomenon where 19 out of 23 markets declined more than 20 percent. This is unusual given the low degree of correlation between the historical returns of different countries. Richard Roll's article points out that the most significant factor relating to the size of the market decline in each country was the beta of that market to the world market index.

■ DIVERSIFICATION BENEFITS

Not all foreign markets move in the same direction at any point in time. In Table 18–4 on page 588, we see the stock market movements for a number of key countries over 15 years. Each year there is a wide range of performance numbers among these nine countries; the highest and lowest yearly returns are highlighted in bold. There are several issues worth noting. First, no country continually outperforms the others on an annual basis. Hong Kong has the highest returns 4 out of 15 years, while Canada never has had the highest return. Second, in all but four years (1978, 1986, 1988, 1989), one of these countries in the table had a loss.

Table 18–3 Institutional Arrangements in World Markets

Country	Auction	Official Special-ists	Forward Trading on Ex-change	Auto-mated Quota-tions	Computer-Directed Trading	Options/Futures Trading	Price Limits	Transac-tion Tax (Round Trip)	Margin Require-ments	Trading Off Exchange
Australia	Continuous	No	No	Yes	No	Yes	None	0.6%	None	Infrequent
Austria	Single	Yes	No	No	No	No	5%	0.3%	100%	Frequent
Belgium	Mixed	No	Yes	No	No	No[a]	10%/None[b]	0.375%/0.195%	100%/25%[b]	Occasional
Canada	Continuous	Yes	No	Yes	Yes	Yes	None[c]	0	50%[d]	Prohibited
Denmark	Mixed	No	No	No	No	No	None	1%	None	Frequent
France	Mixed	Yes	Yes	Yes	Yes	Yes	4%/7%[e]	0.3%	100%/20%[f]	Prohibited
Germany	Continuous	Yes	No	No	No	Options	None	0.5%	None	Frequent
Hong Kong	Continuous	No	No	Yes	No	Futures	None[g]	0.6%+	None	Infrequent
Ireland	Continuous	No	No	Yes	No	No	None	1%	100%	Frequent
Italy	Mixed	No	Yes	No	No	No	10–20%[h]	0.3%	100%	Frequent
Japan	Continuous	Yes	No	Yes	Yes	No[i]	–10%	0.55%	70%[j]	Prohibited
Malaysia	Continuous	No	No	Yes	No	No	None	0.03%	None	Occasional
Mexico	Continuous	No	Yes	No	No	No	10%[k]	0	None	Occasional
Netherlands	Continuous	Yes	No	No	No	Options	Variable[l]	2.4%[m]	None	Prohibited
New Zealand	Continuous	No	No	No	No	Futures	None	0	None	Occasional
Norway	Single	No	No	No	No	No	None	1%	100%	Frequent
Singapore	Continuous	No	No	Yes	No	No[n]	None	0.5%	71%	Occasional
South Africa	Continuous	No	No	Yes	No	Options	None	1.5%	100%	Prohibited
Spain	Mixed[o]	No	No	No	No	No	10%[p]	0.11%	50%[p]	Frequent
Sweden	Mixed	No	No	Yes	No	Yes	None	2%	40%	Frequent
Switzerland	Mixed	No	Yes	Yes	No	Yes	5%[q]	0.9%	None	Infrequent
United Kingdom	Continuous	No	No	Yes	Yes	Yes	None	0.5%	None	Occasional
United States	Continuous	Yes	No	Yes	Yes	Yes	None	0	Yes	Occasional

[a]Calls only on just five stocks.
[b]Cash/forward
[c]None on stocks; 3–5% on index futures.
[d]10% (5%) for uncovered (covered) futures.
[e]Cash/forward, but not always enforced.
[f]Cash/forward; 40% if forward collateral is stock rather than cash.
[g]"Four Spread Rule": offers not permitted more than four ticks from current bids and asks.
[h]Hitting limit suspends auction; auction then tried a second time at end of day.
[i]Futures on the Nikkei Index are traded in Singapore.
[j]Decreased to 50% on October 21, 1987, "to encourage buyers."

[k]Trading suspended for successive periods, 15 and then 30 minutes; effective limit: 30–40%.
[l]Authorities have discretion. In October, 2% limits every 15 minutes used frequently.
[m]For nondealer transactions only.
[n]Only for Nikkei Index (Japan).
[o]Groups of stocks are traded continuously for 10 minutes each.
[p]Limits raised to 20% and margin to 50% on October 27.
[q]Hitting limit causes 15-minute trading suspension. Limits raised to 10–15% in October.
Source: Richard Roll, "The International Crash of 1987," *Financial Analysts Journal,* September–October 1988, p. 29.

	Germany	Switzer-land	United Kingdom	Australia	Hong Kong	Japan	Singapore/Malaysia	Canada	United States
1976	6.6	10.5	(12.7)	(10.2)	**40.7**	25.6	13.9	9.7	23.8
1977	25.8	28.7	**58.0**	11.9	(11.2)	15.9	5.9	(2.1)	(7.2)
1978	26.9	21.9	14.6	21.8	18.5	**53.3**	45.1	20.4	6.5
1979	(2.2)	12.1	22.1	43.6	**83.5**	(11.9)	28.5	51.8	18.5
1980	(9.1)	(7.3)	41.1	55.3	**72.7**	30.3	62.8	22.6	32.4
1981	(8.2)	(9.5)	(10.6)	(23.9)	(15.8)	15.8	**18.3**	(10.7)	(4.9)
1982	12.3	3.4	9.2	(22.6)	(44.5)	(0.5)	(16.7)	2.4	**21.5**
1983	25.9	19.3	17.2	**56.0**	(3.0)	24.9	31.7	33.4	22.2
1984	(3.8)	(11.1)	5.4	(12.6)	**46.8**	17.1	(25.9)	(7.6)	6.2
1985	**139.2**	107.4	52.8	20.9	51.6	43.4	(22.2)	15.9	31.6
1986	37.2	34.3	27.1	43.8	56.0	**99.7**	45.2	10.7	18.2
1987	(23.4)	(8.8)	36.5	10.3	(4.1)	**43.2**	2.3	14.6	5.2
1988	23.1	**7.1**	**7.1**	**38.0**	28.0	35.5	33.3	18.0	16.5
1989	**48.8**	27.1	23.1	10.8	8.3	1.8	42.2	25.2	31.4
1990	(10.8)	(7.8)	**6.0**	(21.0)	3.7	(36.4)	(13.1)	(15.3)	(5.6)

Table 18–4   The Best Performing Equity Markets, 1976–1990

Note: Numbers represent total return, assuming reinvestment of dividends in U.S. dollars of the Morgan Stanley Capital International Index for each country. (Bold color numbers represent lowest returns and bold black numbers represent highest returns.)
Source: Templeton International.

Let us look at a U.S. investor based on the data in table 18–4. In 1976, a 23.8 percent return could be earned in the United States, while a 12.7 percent loss occurred in the United Kingdom. In 1977, this situation was reversed with a 7.2 percent loss in the United States and a 58 percent return in the United Kingdom. If an investor had held equal positions in both countries, returns would have been less volatile (risky), and a U.S. investor would have had a greater total return. Diversification reduces portfolio volatility and at the same time offers opportunities for higher returns than a single country portfolio.

Another way to consider **diversification benefits** is to measure the extent of correlation of stock movements. The correlation coefficient measures the movement of one series of data over time to another series of data, in this case stock market returns. The correlation coefficient can be between -1 and $+1$. A coefficient of $+1$ indicates a perfect positive relationship as the two variables move together up and down. A coefficient of -1 indicates a perfect negative relationship as the two variables move opposite of each other. A zero coefficient describes a series that has no relationship. Any time you can diversify into assets that have a correlation coefficient of less than $+1$, you reduce the amount of risk assumed. Such a measure is presented in Table 18–5, in which

Table 18-5   Correlation of Foreign Stock Movements with U.S. Stock Movements

Country	Correlation 1960–1980	Correlation June 1981– September 1987
United States	1.000	1.000
Hong Kong	.814 (1)	.114 (17)
Netherlands	.730 (2)	.473 (4)
Canada	.710 (3)	.720 (1)
Australia	.699 (4)	.328 (9) median
United Kingdom	.617 (5)	.513 (2)
Singapore	.579 (6)	.377 (6)
Switzerland	.454 (7)	.500 (3)
Sweden	.398 (8)	.279 (11)
Belgium	.389 (9) median	.250 (12)
Denmark	.243 (10)	.351 (8)
Japan	.216 (11)	.326 (10)
France	.214 (12)	.390 (5)
Germany	.210 (13)	.209 (15)
Italy	.208 (14)	.224 (13)
Norway	.009 (15)	.356 (7)
Austria	− .076 (16)	.138 (16)
Spain	− .115 (17)	.214 (14)

Source: Roger G. Ibbotson, Richard C. Carr, and Anthony W. Robinson, "International Equity and Bond Returns," *Financial Analysts Journal,* July–August 1982, p. 71; and Richard Roll, "The International Crash of 1987," *Financial Analysts Journal,* September–October 1988, pp. 20–21.

stock movements for a number of developed countries are compared to those of the United States. Two sets of correlation coefficients are presented, one long-term set from 1960 through 1980 and a short-term set of data from June 1981 through September 1987. The countries are listed from the highest correlation to the lowest based on 1960–80 data. By comparing the two sets of correlations, we can see there is not a great amount of stability between the two time periods, with some countries like Hong Kong going from the top of the list to the bottom. However, correlations of returns with the U.S. market are still quite low on average, with the median correlation being .389 in the first period and .328 in the second period.

The best risk-reduction benefits can be found by combining U.S. securities with those from countries having low correlations such as Spain and Austria in both periods. Countries with high correlations provide the least benefit from diversification. Even though countries like Germany and Italy have fairly stable

Table 18–6   Correlation Coefficient Matrix of Total Return Indexes (Five Years Ending December 1990)

	USA	EAFE	FTEP	IFCC	IFCL	IFCA	Arg	Bra	Chi	Col	Gre	Ind	Idn	Jor	Kor	Mal	Mex	Nig	Pak	Phi	Por	Tai	Tha	Tur	Ven	Zim
• USA	1.00																									
• EAFE	0.45	1.00																								
• FTEP	0.45	1.00	1.00																							
IFCC	0.37	0.26	0.27	1.00																						
IFCL	0.31	0.20	0.21	0.67	1.00																					
IFCA	0.36	0.26	0.27	0.89	0.33	1.00																				
Arg	0.03	-0.14	-0.14	0.00	-0.04	-0.03	1.00																			
Bra	0.03	0.07	0.08	0.00	0.11	0.11	-0.21	1.00																		
Chi	0.34	0.10	0.07	0.44	0.36	0.37	-0.08	0.09	1.00																	
Col	0.16	0.12	0.12	0.09	0.06	0.06	-0.14	0.04	0.42	1.00																
Gre	0.13	0.08	0.07	0.00	0.00	-0.04	0.10	0.01	0.14	0.33	1.00															
— Ind	-0.11	-0.18	-0.18	-0.05	-0.02	-0.16	0.31	-0.03	-0.07	-0.08	-0.03	1.00														
Idn	0.20	-0.11	-0.11	0.22	-0.15	0.19	-0.07	-0.16	0.42	0.23	0.20	-0.07	1.00													
Jor	0.02	0.14	0.13	0.01	-0.19	0.03	-0.13	-0.14	-0.13	0.12	0.16	-0.08	0.24	1.00												
Kor	0.30	0.34	0.36	0.20	0.17	0.21	-0.17	0.06	0.06	0.00	-0.27	-0.11	-0.16	-0.20	1.00											
Mal	0.66	0.37	0.37	0.44	0.29	0.50	0.00	0.07	0.25	0.01	0.02	-0.03	0.37	0.03	0.19	1.00										
Mex	0.46	0.20	0.20	0.48	0.37	0.48	0.11	-0.08	0.35	0.18	0.16	0.04	0.18	-0.07	0.22	0.45	1.00									
Nig	0.07	0.04	0.05	0.01	-0.02	-0.23	0.10	-0.03	0.05	0.06	0.13	0.03	0.09	-0.10	0.03	-0.21	-0.14	1.00								
— Pak	-0.17	0.10	0.10	0.13	-0.03	0.01	0.10	-0.04	0.06	0.08	-0.11	0.22	-0.03	0.07	-0.03	0.03	0.04	0.01	1.00							
Phi	0.28	0.32	0.32	0.37	0.07	0.15	0.10	0.11	0.23	0.18	0.05	-0.10	0.63	0.15	0.12	0.26	0.07	0.07	0.01	1.00						
Por	0.17	0.38	0.37	0.82	0.28	0.32	-0.15	0.09	0.21	0.06	0.42	-0.12	0.16	-0.02	0.26	0.22	0.39	-0.23	0.09	0.04	1.00					
Tai	0.18	0.19	0.19	0.27	0.27	0.91	-0.01	0.09	0.36	0.11	0.04	-0.14	0.04	0.09	-0.03	0.24	0.38	-0.23	0.02	0.02	0.39	1.00				
Tha	0.43	0.39	0.39	0.46	0.26	0.49	0.15	0.07	0.29	0.33	0.28	-0.03	0.45	-0.11	-0.07	0.52	0.46	-0.10	0.14	0.23	0.40	0.43	1.00			
Tur	0.01	0.03	0.03	0.25	0.14	0.14	0.20	0.18	0.09	0.14	0.14	0.27	0.06	-0.05	-0.18	0.24	0.20	0.14	0.05	-0.04	0.17	0.09	0.18	1.00		
— Ven	-0.10	-0.23	-0.23	-0.35	-0.30	-0.30	0.03	-0.31	-0.20	-0.14	-0.10	0.17	0.13	-0.18	-0.17	-0.13	-0.12	-0.01	0.06	-0.24	-0.08	-0.27	-0.25	-0.17	1.00	
— Zim	-0.32	-0.05	-0.04	-0.23	-0.19	-0.20	-0.24	-0.06	0.00	0.00	0.05	0.12	0.05	0.12	-0.17	-0.11	-0.11	-0.02	0.17	-0.01	0.15	-0.08	-0.11	0.00	0.02	1.00
	USA	EAFE	FTEP	IFCC	IFCL	IFCA	Arg	Bra	Chi	Col	Gre	Ind	Idn	Jor	Kor	Mal	Mex	Nig	Pak	Phi	Por	Tai	Tha	Tur	Ven	Zim

Notes:
• S&P 500 for USA, MSCI for EAFE (Europe, Australia and Far East), and FT-Actuaries for FTEP(FT EuroPacific).
• Portugal starts January 1986, Turkey starts December 1986, and Indonesia starts December 1989.

Source: *Emerging Stock Markets Factbook, 1991* (Washington, D.C.: International Finance Corporation, 1991), p. 93.

correlations between the two periods, France and Norway display a switching of rankings between the two periods. According to one researcher, Bruno Solnik, a well-diversified international portfolio can achieve the same risk-reduction benefits as a pure U.S. portfolio that is twice the size in terms of securities.[2]

In Table 18–5, we examined developed countries. Using Table 18–6 for emerging markets and several regional indexes, we see a correlation matrix using data for five years ending in 1990. Looking down the first column of numbers gives each country's correlation coefficient against the U.S. market as measured by the Standard & Poor's 500 Index. Four countries (India, Pakistan, Venezuela, Zimbabwe) have negative correlations with the United States, and the highest positive correlation with the United States is 0.66 for Malaysia. It is interesting to note that Morgan Stanley Capital International's EAFE Index (Europe, Australia, and Far East) and the FTEP (Financial Times EuroPacific Index) both have correlation coefficients of 0.45 against the U.S. market. These two indexes compared with the U.S. market indicate the scope of diversification available to today's investors.

▪ RETURN POTENTIAL IN INTERNATIONAL MARKETS

Actually, risk reduction through effective international diversification is only part of the story. Not only does the investor have less risk exposure, but there is also the potential for higher returns in many foreign markets. Why? A number of countries have had superior growth rates to that of the United States in terms of real GDP. These would include Japan, Norway, Singapore, and Hong Kong. Second, many countries have become highly competitive in traditional U.S. products such as automobiles, steel, and consumer electronics. Third, many nations (Germany, Japan, France, Canada) enjoy higher individual savings rates than the United States, and this leads to capital formation and potential investment opportunity. This is not to imply that the United States does not have the strongest and best regulated securities markets in the world. It clearly does. However, it is a more mature market than many others, and there may be abundant opportunities for superior returns in a number of foreign markets.

We have already presented the annual returns for nine developed countries in Table 18–4. However, we present five different international indexes of investment performance in Figure 18–3 on page 592 showing the wealth that would have accumulated by the end of 1990 from an investment of $1 in each index at the beginning of 1970. The Pacific region has performed much better than the others, while the North American index (Canada and the United

---

[2]Bruno H. Solnik, "Why Not Diversify Internationally Rather than Domestically?" *Financial Analysts Journal,* July–August 1974, pp. 48–54.

Figure 18–3   U.S. Dollar-Adjusted Cumulative Wealth Indexes of World Equities: 1970–1990

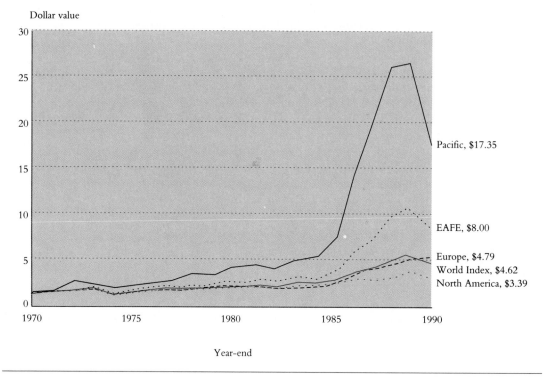

States) was at the bottom. The annualized rates of return for each index over this 20 years are as follows:

Region	Annualized Rate of Return
Pacific	15.34%
EAFE	10.95
Europe	8.15
World Index	7.95
North America	6.29

Figure 18–3 represents a long-term perspective. There are, of course, time periods when the United States outperforms foreign markets. The performance figures represent the rapid growth experienced in the Pacific region between 1985 and 1988 and the subsequent 34 percent decline in 1990. The U.S. markets suffered greatly in 1973 (17.6 percent decline) and 1974 (29.86

percent decline). By 1978, the $1 invested in the North American market was worth only $1.03. If we measure returns from 1978 to 1990, the North American annualized return increases to 10.46 percent versus 15.27 percent over this same time for the Pacific region. This is still a lower return but not in such great proportions as the 20-year period.

Current Quotations on Foreign Market Performance

To track the current performance of selected world markets, *The Wall Street Journal* provides daily quotes of price movements, while *Barron's* presents a weekly summary of the major global markets. The closing quotes of January 23, 1992, for *Barron's* are presented in Table 18–7 on page 594.

The quotes are shown in local currencies as well as in U.S. dollars. For a U.S. investor, the returns in U.S. dollars are the best comparative measure for an investment in U.S. stocks. Under the U.S. dollars columns, you can first observe the percentage change from the last weekly quote. Next observe the index values shown under the 1/23 column (third column from the right) for U.S. dollar values. The base period for the index is 1970. Over the 21 years, the indexes of Japan (2720.5) and Hong Kong (2409.9) have substantially outperformed the United States (387.8). The wide disparity in index values over time indicates the differing movements in foreign markets. For example, in the last edition of this book, this table for November 24, 1988, listed Japan's index value at 4095, Hong Kong at 1417, and the U.S. index value at 248.

At the top of Table 18–7 is the **World Index,** which is a value-weighted index of the performance in 19 major countries as compiled by Morgan Stanley Capital International Perspective, Geneva, Switzerland.

Other Market Differences

There are large differences among cultures, including willingness to take risk, desire for dividend income versus growth in share value, the number and type of companies available to stockholders, and bureaucratic differences such as accounting conventions and government regulation of markets. In a book of this type, we do not intend to cover each issue but simply bring them to your attention. Table 18–8 on page 595 presents differences in price-earnings ratios, price-to-book value ratios, and dividend yields from the *Emerging Stock Market Factbook, 1991,* published by International Finance Corporation of Washington, D.C.

Many developing countries have higher price-earnings ratios in their stock markets than the rest of the World. For example, Taiwan-China has an average P/E of 44.4 versus 15.30 for the World Index at year-end 1990. However, the P/E ratios in Latin America vary widely from country to country ranging from 3.11 in Argentina to 29.31 in Venezuela. Clearly, individual country differences account for these disparities, but in all cases, those countries with high expected growth in "real" earnings and dividends will have higher price-

Table 18–7   Global Stock Markets

Index	In Local Currencies				In U.S. Dollars*			
	Percent Change	1/23	52-Week Range		Percent Change	1/23	52-Week Range	
			High	Low			High	Low
The World	−0.3	406.0	420.5–	358.2	1.2	527.7	543.5–	467.9
EAFE†	−0.1	498.3	550.8–	466.2	2.5	850.1	905.7–	752.1
Australia	−2.4	346.3	363.5–	266.6	−2.0	230.9	254.9–	185.4
Austria	0.2	396.6	511.0–	372.7	1.8	920.5	1206.6–	793.1
Belgium	2.0	413.4	416.9–	338.2	3.6	630.1	647.5–	497.6
Canada	−0.7	410.3	413.2–	361.1	−0.7	384.3	388.0–	337.5
Denmark	−0.6	818.0	859.2–	667.4	1.2	994.1	1029.1–	836.5
Finland	−4.0	62.2	81.8–	53.9	−2.4	56.6	81.9–	50.3
France	−0.7	522.1	529.3–	427.5	1.0	533.5	549.5–	422.2
Germany	0.7	258.8	271.4–	222.0	2.3	594.9	624.6–	467.9
Hong Kong	5.1	3366.5	3366.5–	2263.0	5.2	2409.9	2409.9–	612.9
Italy	−0.2	397.4	442.4–	342.5	1.5	207.3	233.2–	168.4
Japan	0.0	934.3	1155.1–	910.5	3.6	2720.5	3096.7–	2475.3
Netherlands	0.5	338.3	340.5–	269.6	2.2	683.5	691.1–	569.0
New Zealand	−3.2	72.5	76.6–	57.8	−2.9	59.6	68.4–	52.4
Norway	−3.8	670.5	842.0–	554.2	−1.9	766.3	958.3–	625.7
Sing/Malays	0.2	780.3	810.4–	655.1	0.8	1469.5	1473.9–	1167.7
Spain	−2.7	208.5	237.8–	180.9	−0.5	145.1	163.1–	125.5
Sweden	0.6	1169.0	1391.2–	1031.3	2.4	1045.3	1174.2–	946.8
Switzerland	0.0	217.1	218.3–	170.1	1.7	660.4	668.1–	542.2
United Kingdom	−0.6	747.3	801.8–	628.4	1.8	561.0	585.2–	487.4
United States	−0.6	387.8	392.7–	312.0	−0.6	387.8	392.7–	312.0

Base: January 1, 1970 = 100
*Adjusted for foreign exchange fluctuations relative to the U.S. dollar.
†Europe, Australia, Far East Index.
Source: Morgan Stanley Capital International Perspective, Geneva.

earnings ratios than those with lower expected growth. This is the same impact found in the U.S. market as discussed in Chapter 7.

To some extent, the price-to-book-value ratio in each country corresponds to each country's P/E ratio. Countries with high P/Es have high P/BV ratios and vice versa. The dividend yields show a wide difference with Nigeria having a yield of 11.97 percent and Taiwan-China having a zero dividend yield. This wide difference is mostly attributable to country differences, inflation rates, different accounting methods, and risk-return preferences of the stockholders.

Table 18–8 Comparative Valuations of Emerging Countries★

Market	Price-Earnings Ratio			Price-Book Value Ratio			Dividend Yield		
	End 1990	Relative to World[†]	End 1989	End 1990	Relative to World[†]	End 1989	End 1990	Relative to World[†]	End 1989
Latin America									
• Argentina	3.11	0.20	22.14	0.37	0.20	1.64	0.89	0.29	4.69
Brazil	5.34	0.35	8.30	0.75	0.41	1.34	9.44	3.05	0.66
Chile	8.86	0.58	5.82	1.42	0.78	1.33	5.00	1.61	9.50
Colombia	10.66	0.70	6.96	1.35	0.74	1.08	7.60	2.45	7.05
Mexico	13.20	0.86	10.66	1.29	0.71	1.03	3.41	1.10	2.10
• Venezuela	29.31	1.92	6.44	5.94	3.26	1.37	0.72	0.23	2.21
East Asia									
Korea	21.48	1.40	38.57	1.47	0.81	2.50	0.48	0.15	1.26
Philippines	24.51	1.60	18.50	3.37	1.85	4.35	2.28	0.74	1.10
• Taiwan-China	44.41	2.90	51.17	6.54	3.59	6.55	0.00	0.00	0.58
South Asia									
India	20.59	1.35	18.34	4.02	2.21	3.46	1.89	0.61	1.93
Indonesia	30.84	2.02	41.50	4.24	2.33	7.50	0.53	0.17	—
Malaysia	23.01	1.50	30.75	3.08	1.69	3.34	2.20	0.71	2.19
Pakistan	8.53	0.56	8.44	1.98	1.09	1.80	5.61	1.81	8.26
Thailand	10.90	0.71	23.07	3.71	2.04	8.06	4.18	1.35	7.94
Europe/Mideast/Africa									
Greece	26.23	1.71	24.30	4.87	2.68	3.12	4.96	1.60	4.62
Jordan	8.15	0.53	14.93	1.68	0.92	1.88	6.47	2.09	2.38
• Nigeria	7.01	0.46	6.99	1.77	0.97	1.83	11.97	3.86	7.33
Portugal	15.47	1.01	21.42	2.06	1.13	3.79	2.66	0.86	1.87
Turkey	22.50	1.47	17.64	3.70	2.03	7.18	5.47	1.76	3.61
Zimbabwe	12.01	0.78	7.00	1.98	1.09	1.27	4.02	1.30	9.75
Developed Markets[‡]									
France	9.30	0.61	12.50	1.38	0.76	2.09	4.00	1.29	2.70
Germany	12.60	0.82	17.80	1.75	0.96	2.39	4.00	1.29	2.90
Japan	31.00	2.03	51.90	2.52	1.38	4.79	0.80	0.26	0.40
United Kingdom	10.90	0.71	11.70	1.54	0.85	1.95	5.70	1.84	4.50
United States	14.10	0.92	14.10	1.92	1.05	2.16	3.70	1.19	3.30
• World	15.30	1.00	19.30	1.82	1.00	2.60	3.10	1.00	2.20

—Not available.
★The composite P-E and P-BV are averages of the companies in the IFC indexes weighted by market capitalization; the dividend yield represents a 12 month moving yield for the indexes.
[†]Relative to the MSCI World Index.
[‡]Source for developed markets: MSCI
Source: *Emerging Stock Markets Factbook, 1991* (Washington, D.C.: International Finance Corporation, 1991), p. 62.

■ CURRENCY FLUCTUATIONS AND RATES OF RETURN

We must explicitly consider the effect of **currency fluctuations** (changes in currency values) as well as rates of return in different countries. For example, assume an investment in France produces a 10 percent return. But suppose at the same time the French franc declines in value by 5 percent against the U.S. dollar. The French franc profits are thus worth less in dollars. In the present case, the gain on the investment would be shown as follows:

110%	(Investment with 10% profit)
× .95	(Adjusted value of French franc relative to U.S. dollar)
104.5%	Percent of original investment

The actual return in U.S. dollars would be 4.5 percent instead of 10 percent. Of course, if the French franc appreciated by 5 percent against the dollar, the French franc profits converted to dollars would be worth considerably more than 10 percent. The values are indicated below.

110%	(Investment with 10% profit)
× 1.05	(Adjusted value of French franc relative to U.S. dollar)
115.5%	Percent of original investment

The 10 percent gain in the French franc investment has produced a 15.5 percent gain in U.S. dollars. A U.S. investor in foreign securities must consider not only the potential trend of security prices but also the trend of foreign currencies against the dollar. This point will become more apparent as we look at Table 18–9.

Let's examine currency effects in London. In this instance, the one-year return in the local currency was 15.2 percent (second column), but the currency (British pound) declined 16.9 percent (5th column) against the U.S. dollar for the one-year period, causing an overall *loss* on the investment of 4.3 percent (second column from the right for London). The values are computed as follows:

115.2%	(Investment with 15.2% profit)
	(Adjusted value of British pound to the U.S. dollar)
× .831	(1.000 − .169 decline in currency)
95.7%	Percent of original investment

The ending value of 95.7 percent indicates a loss of 4.3 percent from the initial value of 100 percent.[3] If one were merely to subtract the foreign currency loss of 16.9 percent from the 15.2 percent profit, the answer would be a loss of 1.7 percent, but this is not the correct procedure. The gain of 15.2 percent was on an initial base of 100 percent, but the foreign currency loss of

---

[3]Due to rounding and other statistical adjustments, not all values adjusted to U.S. dollars come out as precisely as this.

Table 18–9		Return on World Stock Markets (through March 1983)							
	Return in Each Currency (Percent)			Currency Valuation (Percent)			Return in U.S. Dollars (Percent)		
	3 Months	1 Year	5 Years	3 Months	1 Year	5 Years	3 Months	1 Year	5 Years
New York	8.8%	36.6%	11.4%	0.0%	0.0%	0.0%	8.8%	36.6%	11.4%
Tokyo	4.0	15.7	8.7	−2.0	3.5	−1.7	1.9	19.8	6.8
—London	9.8	15.2	7.2	−8.3	−16.9	−4.5	0.6	−4.3	2.4
Toronto	10.1	36.6	15.2	−0.7	−0.8	−1.7	9.3	35.5	13.2
Frankfurt	19.1	26.5	2.7	−2.2	−0.7	−3.9	16.5	25.6	−1.3
Sydney	5.6	11.0	10.8	−11.9	−17.7	−5.4	−6.9	−8.7	4.8
Paris	20.5	10.8	8.6	−7.4	−13.9	−9.1	11.6	−4.5	−1.3
Zurich	9.0	22.4	1.3	−3.7	−7.2	−2.6	5.0	13.7	−1.3
Hong Kong	27.1	14.6	17.3	−3.7	−13.0	−7.2	22.4	−25.7	8.8
Milan	28.5	4.8	28.5	−5.3	−8.4	−10.1	21.7	−4.0	15.6
Amsterdam	29.4	49.9	7.1	4.0	−2.0	−4.6	24.1	47.0	2.2
Singapore	18.5	19.3	24.9	1.1	2.3	2.1	19.8	22.0	27.5

16.9 percent was on an ending value of 115.2 percent (which comes out to an actual loss in currency value of 19.5 percent).

Those who track the performance in foreign markets usually make adjustments so that the reported returns are in U.S. dollars that have already been adjusted for **foreign currency effects.** For example, most of the returns in prior tables of this chapter have already been adjusted for the foreign currency effect.

One might justifiably ask, how important is the foreign currency effect in relation to the overall return performance in the foreign currency? Do events in foreign exchange markets tend to overpower actual returns achieved in specific investments in foreign countries? Normally, the foreign currency effect is only about 10 to 20 percent as significant as the actual return performance in the foreign currency.[4] However, when the dollar is rising or falling rapidly over a short period, the impact can be much greater. For example, the returns to U.S. investors in Japanese securities between 1985 and 1988 were increased by 50 percent from the gain in the yen against the dollar.

In a well-diversified international portfolio, the changes in foreign currency values in one part of the world normally tend to cancel changes in other parts of the world. Also, those who do not wish to have foreign currency exposure

---

[4]Bertrand Jacquillat and Bruno Solnik, "Multinationals Are Poor Tools for Diversification," *Journal of Portfolio Management,* Winter 1978, pp. 8–12.

of any sort may use forward exchange contracts, futures market contracts, or put options on foreign currency to hedge away the risk. Finally, there are those who believe in parity theories that suggest one should get additional compensation in local returns to make up for potential losses in foreign currency values. This latter point is a purely theoretical matter that provides little comfort in the short run.

The authors would suggest that those considering international investments be sensitive to the foreign currency effect, but not be overly discouraged by it. The superior return potential from foreign investments previously shown in Figure 18–3 (and most other places in this chapter) are constructed *after* considering the foreign exchange effect on U.S. dollar returns. While foreign currency swings have been *wider* in recent times, they are still not a major deterrent to an internationally diversified portfolio.

■ OTHER OBSTACLES TO INTERNATIONAL INVESTMENTS

Other problems are peculiar to international investments. Let us consider some of them.

Political Risks

Many firms operate in foreign political climates that are more volatile than that of the United States. There is the danger of nationalization of foreign firms or the blockage of capital flows to investors. There also may be the danger of a violent overthrow of the political party in power. Furthermore, many countries have been unable to meet their foreign debt obligations, and this has important political implications.

The informed investor must have some feel for the political/economic climate of the foreign country in which he or she invests. Of course, problems sometimes create opportunities. Local investors may overreact to political changes occurring in their environment. Because all their eggs are in one basket, they may engage in an oversell in regard to political changes. A less-impassioned outside investor may identify an opportunity for profit.

Nevertheless, political risk represents a potential deterrent to foreign investment. The best solution for the investor is to be sufficiently diversified around the world so that a political or economic development in one foreign country does not have a major impact on his or her portfolio (this can be accomplished through a mutual fund or through other means discussed later in the chapter).

Tax Problems

Many major foreign countries may impose a 7.5 percent to 15 percent withholding tax against the dividends or interest paid to nonresident holders of equity or debt securities. However, it is often possible for *tax-exempt* U.S. investors to secure an exemption or rebate on part or all of the withholding

tax. Also, taxable U.S. investors can normally claim a U.S. tax credit for taxes paid in foreign countries. The problem is more likely to be one of inconvenience and paper shuffling rather than loss of funds.

Lack of Market Efficiency

U.S. capital markets tend to be the most liquid and efficient in the world. Therefore, an investor who is accustomed to trading on the New York Stock Exchange may have some difficulties adjusting to foreign markets. A larger spread between the bid (sell) and asked (buy) price in foreign countries is likely. Also, an investor may have more difficulty handling a large transaction (the seller may have to absorb a larger discount in executing the trade). Furthermore, as a general rule, commission rates are higher in foreign markets than in the United States.

Administrative Problems

There can also be administrative problems in dealing in foreign markets in terms of adjusting to the various local systems. For example, in the Hong Kong, Swiss, and Mexican stock markets, you must settle your account one day after the transaction; in London, there is a two-week settlement procedure; and in France, there are different settlement dates for cash and forward markets. The different administrative procedures of foreign countries simply add up to an extra dimension of difficulty in executing trades. (As implied throughout this chapter, there are ways to avoid most of these difficulties by going through mutual funds and other investment outlets.)

Information Difficulties

The U.S. securities markets are the best in the world at providing investment information. The Securities and Exchange Commission, with its rigorous requirements for full disclosure, is the toughest national regulator of investment information. Also, the United States has the Financial Accounting Standards Board (FASB) continually providing pronouncements on generally accepted accounting principles for financial reporting. Publicly traded companies are required to provide stockholders with fully audited annual reports. In the United States, we are further spoiled by the excellent evaluative reports and ratings generated by Moody's, Standard & Poor's, Value Line, and other firms. We also have extensive economic data provided by governmental sources such as the Department of Commerce and the Federal Reserve System.

Many international firms, trading in less sophisticated foreign markets, simply do not provide the same quantity or quality of data. This would be particularly true of firms trading in some of the smaller foreign markets. Even when the information is available, there may be language problems for the analyst who does not speak German, French, Portuguese, and so on.

Also, the analyst must be prepared to analyze the firm in light of the standards that are generally accepted in the foreign market in which the company operates. For example, Japanese companies often have much higher debt ratios than U.S. firms. A debt-to-equity ratio of three times is not unusual in Japan, whereas in the United States, the standard is closer to 1 : 1. The analyst may be inclined to "mark down" the Japanese firm for high debt unless he or she realizes the different features at play in the Japanese economy. For example, in Japan there are normally very close relationships between the lending bank and the borrower, with the lender perhaps having an equity position in the borrower and with interlocking boards between the two. This diminishes the likelihood of the lender calling in the loan in difficult economic periods. Also, the Japanese make extensive use of reserve accounts that tend to give the appearance of a smaller asset or equity base than actually exists. This pattern of understatement is further aided by a strict adherence to historical cost valuation even though Japanese land values have increased more rapidly than almost anywhere else in the world since the end of World War II. When appropriate adjustments are made for these effects on financial reporting, a Japanese debt-to-equity ratio of 3 : 1 may not be a matter of any greater concern than a U.S. debt-to-equity ratio of 1 : 1.

■ METHODS OF PARTICIPATING IN FOREIGN INVESTMENTS

The avenues to international investment include investing in firms in their own foreign markets, purchasing the shares of foreign firms trading in the United States, investing in mutual funds and closed-end funds with a global orientation, buying the shares of multinational corporations, and entrusting funds to private money managers who specialize in international equities. We shall examine each of these alternatives.

Direct Investments

The most obvious but least likely alternative would be to directly purchase the shares of a firm in its own foreign market through a foreign broker or an overseas branch of a U.S. broker. The investor might consider such firms as Toshiba or Fanuc on the Tokyo Stock Exchange, Consolidated Rutile on the Sydney Stock Exchange, or Hoechst on the Frankfort Stock Exchange. This approach is hampered by all the difficulties and administrative problems associated with international investments. There could be information-gathering problems, tax problems, stock-delivery problems, capital-transfer problems, and communication difficulties in executing orders. Only the most sophisticated money manager would probably follow this approach (though this may change somewhat in the future as foreign markets become better coordinated).

A more likely route to direct investment would be to purchase the shares of foreign firms that actually trade in U.S. securities markets. Hundreds of foreign firms actively trade their securities in the United States. A listing of some key participants is presented in Table 18–10.

Table 18-10   Foreign Firms Trading on the New York Stock Exchange (December 31, 1990)

Country	Company	Industry
Africa	ASA Limited	Closed-end inv. co.—gold mining
Australia	Broken Hill Proprietary Company Limited★	Petroleum; minerals; steel
	Coles Myer Ltd.★	Australian retailer
	FAI Insurances Limited★	Insurance; financial services—Australia
	National Australia Bank Limited★	Holding co.—bank
	News Corporation Ltd.★ (2 issues)	Publishing; broadcasting
	Western Mining Corp. Holdings Ltd.★	Mineral & petroleum exploration, development
	Westpac Banking Corporation★ (2 issues)	Commercial banking—Australia
British W.I.	Bond International Gold, Inc.	Gold mining, exploration
	Club Med, Inc.	Hotel, resort operator
Canada	Abitibi-Price Inc.	Newsprint, uncoated papers
	Alcan-Aluminum Limited	Aluminum producer
	American Barrick Resources Corp.	Gold mining
	Avalon Corporation	Oil & gas exploration, production
	BCE Inc.	Holding co.—telecommunications services
	Campbell Resources Inc.	Diversified natural resources
	Canadian Pacific Limited	Transportation; oil & gas; forest products
	Cineplex Odeon Corporation	Motion pictures theatres operator
	Curragh Resources Inc.	Zinc & lead concentrates
	Domtar Inc.	Pulp, paper, packaging; construction prods.
	Horsham Corporation	Holding co.—petroleum refiner & marketer
	Inco Limited	Nickel, copper producer
	InterTAN Inc.	Holding co.—consumer electronics retailer
	LAC Minerals Ltd.	Gold mining
	Laidlaw Inc. (2 issues)	School transportation services; waste services
	Mitel Corporation	Telecommunications equipment
	Moore Corporation Limited	Business forms
	Northern Telecom Limited	Telecommunications equipment
	Northgate Exploration Limited	Holding co.—metal producer
	NOVA Corporation of Alberta	Petrochemicals; gas transmission
	Placer Dome Inc.	Gold, silver, copper mining
	Potash Corporation of Saskatchewan Inc.	Potash
	Ranger Oil Limited	Oil & gas exploration, production
	Seagram Company Ltd.	Distilled spirits & wine
	TransCanada PipeLines Limited	Natural gas transmission
	United Dominion Industries Limited	Construction services; industrial products
	Varity Corporation (2 issues)	Farm & industrial machinery
	Westcoast Energy Inc.	Natural gas distributor
Chile	Compania de Telefonos de Chile S.A.★	Telecommunications—Chile
Denmark	Novo-Nordisk A/S★	Industrial enzymes; pharmaceuticals
France	Rhone-Poulenc S.A.★ (3 issues)	Diversified chemicals

Table 18–10   Foreign Firms Trading on the New York Stock Exchange   *(continued)*

Country	Company	Industry
Hong Kong	Hong Kong Telecommunications Ltd.★	Holding co.—telecommunications services, equip.
	Universal Matchbox Group Ltd.	Designs & manufactures toys
Ireland	Allied Irish Banks plc★ (2 issues)	Merchant banking
Israel	Elscint Limited	Diagnostic medical imaging equipment
Italy	Benetton Group S.p.A.★	Casual apparel
	Fiat S.p.A.★ (3 issues)	Automobiles
	Luxottica Group S.p.A.★	Eyeglass frames
	Montedison S.p.A.★ (2 issues)	Diversified chemicals; pharmaceuticals
Japan	Hitachi, Ltd.★	Electronic equip.; machinery; consumer prods.
	Honda Motor Co., Ltd.★	Automobile & motorcycle manufacturer
	Kubota Corporation★	Agricultural equipment; pipe manufacturer
	Kyocera Corporation★	Ceramic products; electronic equipment
	Matsushita Electric Industrial Co., Ltd.★	Consumer electronic & electric products
	Mitsubishi Bank Ltd.★	Commercial banking
	Pioneer Electronic Corporation★	Consumer electronics
	Sony Corporation★	Consumer electronics
	TDK Corporation★	Electronic materials & components; magnetic tapes
Netherlands	KLM Royal Dutch Airlines†	Air transportation
	Philips N.V.†	Electronics, appliances; professional prods.
	PolyGram N.V.†	Recorded music
	Royal Dutch Petroleum Co.†	Holding co.—integrated int'l oil co.
	Unilever N.V.†	Holding co.—branded foods
Netherlands Antilles	Schlumberger Limited	Oilfield services
Norway	Norsk Hydro a.s.★	Agriculture; oil & gas
Philippines	Benguet Corporation	Mining; industrial construction
Spain	Banco Bilbao Vizcaya, S.A.★	Commercial bank
	Banco Central, S.A.★	Holding co.—bank
	Banco Santander★	Holding co.—bank
	Empresa Nacional de Electricidad, S.A.★	Electricity producer—Spain
	Repsol, S.A.★	Integrated oil company
	Telefonica de Espana, S.A.★	Telephone service—Spain
United Kingdom	Barclays PLC★ (4 issues)	Holding co.—bank
	Bass plc★	Beverages; hotels; restaurants
	Beazer PLC★	International construction
	BET Public Limited Company★	Industrial; transport; construction servs.
	British Airways Plc★	Passenger airline
	British Gas plc★	Natural gas distributor
	British Petroleum Co. p.l.c.★	Holding co.—integrated int'l oil
	British Steel plc★	Steel producer

Table 18–10   Foreign Firms Trading on the New York Stock Exchange   *(concluded)*

Country	Company	Industry
United Kingdom *(continued)*	British Telecommunications plc★	Telecommunications services & products
	Cable and Wireless Public Limited Co.★	International telecommunications
	Glaxo Holdings p.l.c.★	Holding co.—pharmaceuticals
	Hanson PLC★	Holding co.—consumer goods; building products
	Huntingdon International Holdings plc★	Research-life sciences; engineering servs.
	Imperial Chemical Industries PLC★	Diversified chemical producer
	Manpower PLC★	Holding co.—employment agency
	National Westminster Bank PLC★	Holding co.—bank
	Racal Telecom Plc★	Mobile telecommunications services—U.K.
	Royal Bank of Scotland Group plc★	Holding co.—diversified financial services
	RTZ Corporation PLC★	International natural resources
	Saatchi & Saatchi Company PLC★	Advertising; consulting
	"Shell" Transport & Trading Co., p.l.c.★	Holding co.—integrated int'l oil
	SmithKline Beecham plc★ (2 issues)	Pharmaceuticals; healthcare products
	Unilever PLC★	Holding co.—branded foods
	Willis Corroon plc★	Insurance

★ American depository receipts/shares.
† N.Y. shares and/or guilder shares.
Source: *New York Stock Exchange Fact Book* (New York: New York Stock Exchange, 1991) pp. 30–31.

Firms such as Alcan Aluminium Ltd., Campbell Resources Inc., and Ranger Oil Limited trade their stocks *directly* on the New York Stock Exchange. Most of the other firms in the table (as well as other large foreign firms) trade their shares in the United States through *American Depository Receipts (ADRs)*. The ADRs represent the ownership interest in a foreign company's common stock. In Table 18–10, such firms have an asterisk after their names. The process is as follows: The shares of the foreign company are purchased and put in trust in a foreign branch of a New York bank. The bank receives and can issue depository receipts to the American shareholders of the foreign firm. These ADRs (that is, depository receipts) allow foreign shares to be traded in the United States.

When you call your broker and ask to purchase Sony Corporation or Honda Motor Co., Ltd. (which are represented by ADRs), you will notice virtually no difference between this transaction and buying shares of General Motors or Eastman Kodak. You can receive a certificate that looks very much like a U.S. stock certificate. You'll receive your dividends in dollars and get your reports about the company in English. Generally, you will pay your normal commission rates.

Table 18–11 shows a page from *Standard & Poor's Stock Guide* that includes Sony Corporation's ADRs. Note the financial information is basically the same as that for other U.S. corporations trading on a major exchange or over-the-counter. The Sony ADRs also receive coverage from Value Line and

Table 18–11 Sample Page from *Standard & Poor's Stock Guide*

188 SOF-SPI

Standard & Poor's Corporation

¶ S&P 500 · # MidCap 400 · • Options

Index	Ticker Symbol	Name of Issue (Call Price of Pfd. Stocks)	Market	Com. Rank. & Pfd. Rating	Par Val.	Inst. Hold Cos	Inst. Hold Shs. (000)	Principal Business	Price Range 1971-89 High	1971-89 Low	1990 High	1990 Low	1991 High	1991 Low	Dec. Sales in 100s	December, 1991 Last Sale Or Bid High	Low	Last	%Div Yield	P-E Ratio
1	SSPE	**Software Spectrum**	OTC	NR	1¢	15	607	Reseller of business software	...	...	...	...	17¾	9½	12400	17¾	12⅞	17½B	...	18
2	TWRX	**Software Toolworks**	OTC,M	NR	1¢	28	6468	Dvlp/dstr computer software	7⅝	2⅛	24⅜	1¾	8½	1¾	74575	7⅛	4½	5B	...	d
3	SLTN	**Solectron Corp**	OTC	NR	No	35	2342	Mfr computer prod/subsys	7⅜	6	17½	6⅞	36½	8⅝	22673	36½	27	34¾B	...	21
4	SOD	**Solitron Devices**	NY,B,M,P,Ph	C	1¢	10	475	Semiconductors-microwave	19⅜	¾	2	⅜	2⅝	⅜	3650	⅝	⅜	7/16	...	d
5	SMTG	**Somatogen Inc**	OTC	NR	0.001	41	2228	Dvlp stge:human blood subst	...	...	...	...	44½	19	12544	44½	32½	43B	...	d
6	SOMR	**Somerset Group**	OTC	NR	No	8	275	Concrete,radio,svgs bank	11	6	7¾	5½	7¾	5	810	5¾	5	5B	...	7
¶7•[1]	SNT	**Sonat, Inc**	NY,B,C,M,P,Ph	B	1	307	28774	Nat'l gas P.L.: drill'g o&g	50⅜	6¾	55⅞	43	47⅜	31	26329	35⅜	31	33	6.1	19
8	SONC	**Sonic Corp**	OTC	NR	1¢	48	3057	Oper fast food drive-in restr	...	...	...	...	31½	12¼	10782	31½	22½	31¼B	...	54
#9	SONO	**Sonoco Products**	OTC	A	No	123	12051	Mfr paper packaging products	39	1 3/16	38¼	25¼	38¾	28½	29809	34¾	28½	34½B	2.7	15
10	SNE	**Sony Corp ADR**	NY,B,C,M,P,Ph,Mo,To	NR	[52]..	54	1448	Color TV sets,tape rec,radio	59¾	2⅝	55⅞	36⅝	49⅞	31⅜	6342	34⅝	31⅜	34⅝	0.9	20
#11•[2]	BID	**Sotheby's Hldgs Cl'A'**	NY,M	NR	10¢	98	10363	Worlds largest art auctioneer	37	7¾	26½	8⅞	15¼	9⅝	13415	12	9¾	12	e5.0	32
12	SUND	**Sound Advice**	OTC	B	1¢	23	1413	Retails consumer electr prod	12⅞	2⅝	7½	3⅞	15	5	6112	8	5	7¾B	...	10
13	SOR	**Source Capital**	NY,M	NR	1	22	92	Equity/equity related inv co	45⅞	5⅝	43⅜	35⅛	45¼	36⅝	648	45¼	41	44¼	8.1	..
14	SJI	**South Jersey Indus**	NY,B,M,Ph	B+	1.25	42	1442	Hldg co: gas, fuel oil, sand	23⅜	4⅝	21	16¾	20¾	17¾	1025	20¾	19½	19⅞	7.2	17
#15	SDW	**Southdown, Inc**	NY,M,Ph	B	1¼	75	9395	Cement:concrete:environ'l svc	29¼	1⅜	31½	9½	19⅞	11⅛	4012	13⅝	12	13⅝	...	d
16	SMGS	**Southeastern Mich Gas Ent**	OTC	A	1	17	416	Integrated natural gas sys	18⅛	2⅝	18⅛	11⅞	19½	12⅞	1015	16½	14½	15¼B	s5.2	19
17	SWTR	**Southern Cal Water**	OTC	A−	5	30	749	Water supply, some elec	35	8½	31½	25¼	35¾	27¼	732	35	32	33½B	6.6	8
¶18•[3]	SO	**Southern Co**	NY,B,C,M,P,Ph	A−	5	444	97824	Elec util hldg:Southeast	29¾	7⅞	29⅜	23	34¾	25¾	93119	34¾	30⅞	34⅜	6.2	14
19	SIG	**Southern Indiana G&E**	NY,M,Ph	A	No	89	2526	Utility:elec/gas,Evansville	32⅛	5½	33⅜	27⅞	45⅛	31¼	2037	45⅛	41⅛	45⅛	4.4	14
20	SNB	**Southern National**	NY	A	5	20	1084	Comm'l bkg,North&So.Carolina	15½	2¾	14½	8	16¼	8¾	2319	16¼	13⅝	13⅞	3.5	12
#21•[4]	SNG	**Southern New Eng Telecom**	NY,B,M,Ph	A	1	187	19471	Supplies telecommunic svcs	46½	6⅜	46¼	26	35⅞	29	13340	31¾	29	31⅝	5.6	14
22	SUG	**Southern Union**	AS,B,M	NR	1	32	2149	Natural gas dstr: oil & gas	...	...	20⅜	12	16⅝	12⅛	1979	15⅝	13¼	15¼	...	34
#23•[5]	SOTR	**SouthTrust Corp**	OTC	A	2½	72	10437	Commercial bkg,Alabama	25¼	1 15/16	23¼	12⅞	38¾	15	18356	38¾	30¾	37½B	2.9	12
24	SWTX	**Southwall Technologies**	OTC	NR	.001	20	1758	Produces thin film coatings	12	4	8¾	3¾	6¼	2⅞	3724	3¾	3⅛	3⅜B	...	d
#25•[6]	LUV	**Southwest Airlines**	NY,B,M,P,Ph	B+	1	189	31313	Airline in Texas	23½	⅛	20	12¾	35	16⅜	45605	35	28¼	34⅛	0.3	57
26	TXMX	**Southwest Cafes**	OTC	NR	10¢	13	886	Mexican restaur'ts:franch	14¾	2¾	3⅞	2½	4½	2½	1909	4	3⅜	3¾B	...	11
27	SWX	**Southwest Gas**	NY,B,M,P,Ph	A−	1	59	4075	Natural gas,banking,R.E. dvlp	26¾	6⅛	18½	11¾	17½	9	9359	11½	10⅛	10⅝	6.6	d
28	SWL	**Southwest Realty (Dep)**	AS,M,P	NR	No	..	...	Lmtd ptnshp: real estate	15½	½	1⅝	1	1¾	⅞	497	1⅛	⅞	15/16	...	d
29	SWST	**Southwest Securities Grp**	OTC	NR	10¢	..	...	Securities/brokerage svcs	...	...	...	...	11	8½	2888	9⅛	8½	8¾B	1.1	7
30	SWWC	**Southwest Water Co**	OTC	B+	1	21	325	Water utility:serves CA,NM,TX	24	2½	18	11¾	18½	12½	1280	16¼	12½	13¾B	6.2	21
¶31•[7]	SBC	**Southwestern Bell Corp**	NY,B,M,P,Ph	A−	1	740	116870	Tel svc:Ark,Kan,Mo,Okl,Tex	64⅜	18⅜	64¾	47¼	65⅞	49	90086	65⅞	56¼	64⅝	4.4	17
32	SWEL	**Southwestern Elec Sv**	OTC	A	1	17	104	Small utility in Texas	43	11	42	38	51½	41¼	45	50½	47	47B	5.2	9
33	SWN	**Southwestern Energy**	NY,M,Ph	A−	2½	89	4745	Hldg gas utility,Ark: o & g	33¼	1 13/16	36⅛	28¼	38⅛	27¼	1913	33⅜	31¼	31½	1.8	14
#34	SPS	**Southwestern Pub Sv**	NY,B,M,P,Ph	A	1	177	10631	Electric util:Texas,Okl,N.M.	37⅞	8⅛	30⅞	25⅛	34⅜	27⅛	6450	34⅜	32	34⅛	6.4	13
35	SWH	**Spaghetti Warehouse**	NY,Ph	B	1¢	63	3732	Family-style Italian rest'ts	10⅞	1¼	13¾	7⅛	30¾	10	9480	29	21¼	25⅜	...	31
36	SNF	**Spain Fund**	NY,M,Ph	NR	1¢	3	2	Closed-end investment co	39	9	31¾	10¼	17¼	10½	3531	13⅞	12⅛	13	⊙1.5	..
37	SPAN	**Span-America Med Sys**	OTC	B	No	11	819	Foam pads for health care ind	13	1½	6⅛	2⅝	9⅛	3	4855	9⅛	5½	8⅝B	1.2	17
38	SPAR	**Spartan Motors**	OTC	B	No	32	2643	Mfg heavy truck chassis	5	9/16	3⅞	2 3/16	24¾	2 5/16	21310	19½	14⅞	19B	0.2	25
39	SEH	**Spartech Corp**	AS	C	75¢	10	371	PVC compounds,plastic sheet	22⅝	1 7/16	4¾	1⅛	2⅝	1	426	1¾	1¼	1½	...	d
40	SPA	**Sparton Corp**	NY,M,Ph	B−	1¼	24	1935	Sonobuoys: conveyors,auto eq	24	1	6⅞	2½	9⅛	2⅞	1289	8⅝	6½	8	...	11
41	SPEK	**Spec's Music**	OTC	B−	1¢	20	1462	Retails music & video prod	9⅛	2⅜	8¾	2½	5½	2¾	2388	5¼	4¼	4¾B	...	13
42	SDII	**Special Devices**	OTC	NR	1¢	16	843	Design/mfr pyrotechnic devices	...	...	...	...	13¼	9	3916	12½	9	10⅞B	...	38
43	SPEC	**Spectrum Control**	OTC	C	No	11	1063	Electronic pollution controls	13¾	5/16	2⅝	¼	1 11/16	5/16	4186	1 1/16	11/16	⅞B	...	d
44	SBM	**Speed-O-Print Bus Mach**	AS	C	1	4	12	Dstr office eqp:radio brdcstg	9⅝	¾	4⅝	2½	3⅜	2⅜	127	2⅝	2⅜	2⅝B	...	d
45	SP	**Spelling Entertainment**	AS,M,P	NR	1¢	21	29550	Dvlp/prod TV series,movies	16⅞	4⅛	12⅞	2⅝	5⅞	3⅜	1485	4⅞	4⅛	4⅞	...	27
46	SPI	**SPI Pharmaceuticals**	AS,M,Ph	NR	1¢	21	1245	Mfr specialty/generic prod	28⅝	2⅝	9⅜	4⅜	32¼	7	16807	32¼	26⅝	31¼	3.2	23

Uniform Footnote Explanations-See Page 1. Other: [1]ASE:Cycle 1. [2]ASE,CBOE,P:Cycle 1. [3]CBOE:Cycle 2. [4]NY:Cycle 1. [5]P:Cycle 3. [6]CBOE:Cycle 3. [7]P:Cycle 1. [51]®$2.57,'90. [52]ADR equal 1 ord shr, 50y. [53]Incl $1.7543 non-taxable,'90. [54]Subsid Pfd. [55]Excl $1344M subsid Pfd. [56]Return of capital. [57]Current value basis $9.15 at 12-31-90. [58]®$1.40,'90. [59]®$0.79,'91. [60]Incl foreign curr gains:©$0.18,'92. [61]©$1.03,'91. [62]Incl cap gains:short $0.55,long $0.18,'90.

Source: *Standard & Poor's Stock Guide*, January 1992, p. 188.

Foreign Perils: Language, Customs, and Currency Shifts Tax the Wits of Global-Fund Managers

Mutual-fund trader Madis Senner thought he had found one of the world's best bond markets—in Ireland. In January 1987, yields on Irish government securities were a robust 12 percent. What's more, the Irish pound, as part of the European Monetary System, seemed likely to benefit from a dollar slump. As head bond trader at New York-based Clemente Capital Inc., Mr. Senner bought about $5 million of Irish bonds. He largely cashed out a few months later at a profit. But what he kept gave him fits.

A surge in global interest rates sent the Irish market into a tailspin. Mr. Senner tried to sell, but "there were no bids," he recalls. "Although the Irish government is the marketmaker for bonds, it would have taken two days to sell a million of them," Mr. Senner says. So he had to hang on in a market he would have preferred to be out of.

Such is the life of a global trader. Mutual funds that invest abroad have soared in popularity, particularly when dollar weakness has helped foreign stocks and bonds. Small U.S. investors in effect rely on pros like Mr. Senner

to help them invest in foreign markets without having to sort out all the different time zones, languages, and customs.

For the folks at Clemente Capital, however, there's no escaping the quirks of dozens of overseas markets, none of which functions quite according to U.S. rules. English brokers, for instance, "don't show us their whole hand because . . . they see us as the competition, not as the client," says Mr. Senner. And in Asian markets, getting into the early stages of the rumor mill counts for a lot more than the detailed number-crunching that's practiced on public data in the United States.

Clemente's $148 million Freedom Global Income Plus mutual fund, which Mr. Senner helps manage, has been a standout among long-term bond funds. Competing mutual funds in 1988 averaged small losses while Freedom Global had a 4.32 percent gain over a nine-month period.

Source: Matthew Winkler, *The Wall Street Journal*, September 23, 1988, p. 23R. Reprinted by permission of *THE WALL STREET JOURNAL*, © 1988 by Dow Jones & Company, Inc. All Rights Reserved Worldwide.

other reporting services. *The Wall Street Journal* has daily quotes just as it would have for any company. Since these ADRs trade on the New York Stock Exchange, the quote would be found in that section of the paper.

Indirect Investments

The forms of indirect investments in the international securities include *(a)* purchasing shares of multinational corporations, *(b)* purchasing mutual funds or closed-end investment funds specializing in worldwide investments, and *(c)* engaging the services of a private firm specializing in foreign investment portfolio management.

Purchasing Shares of Multinational Corporations The **multinational corporations,** that is, firms with operations in a number of countries, represent an opportunity for international diversification. For example, the major oil companies have investments and operations throughout the world.

The same can be said for large banking firms and mainframe computer manufacturers. When one buys Exxon, to some extent one is buying exposure to the world economy (74.9 percent of sales are foreign for this firm). A list of the 20 largest U.S. multinational firms is presented in Table 18–12. Of particular interest is the third column from the left, which represents foreign revenue as a percentage of total revenue, and the fourth column from the right, which represents foreign profit as a percentage of total profit.

Although buying shares in a U.S. multinational firm is an easy route to take to experience worldwide economic effects, some researchers maintain that multinationals do not provide the major *investment* benefits that are desired. Jacquillat and Solnik found that multinationals provide very little risk reduction over and above purely domestic firms (perhaps only 10 percent).[5] The prices of multinational shares tend to move very closely with U.S. financial markets despite their worldwide investments. Thus, U.S. multinationals may not do well in a U.S. bear market even if they have investments in strong markets in other countries. This leaves us to turn to mutual funds and closed-end investment companies as potential international investments.

Mutual Funds and Closed-End Investment Companies As will be described in Chapter 19, mutual funds offer the investor an opportunity for diversification as well as professional management. Nowhere is the mutual fund concept more important than in the area of international investments. Those who organize the funds usually have extensive experience in investing overseas and are prepared to deal with the administrative problems. This, of course, does not necessarily lead to superior returns, but the likelihood for inexperienced blunders is reduced.

One may also invest in closed-end investment companies specializing in international equity investments. As later described in Chapter 19, a closed-end investment company has a fixed supply of shares outstanding and trades on a national exchange or over-the-counter, much as an individual company does. It may trade at a premium or discount from its net asset value. An example is the Japan Fund.

A listing of internationally oriented funds is presented in Table 19–7 of the next chapter. The addresses of these funds can be found in *Forbes* magazine or the Wiesenberger Investment Companies Service (also discussed in the next chapter).

Specialists in International Securities The large investor may consider the option of engaging the services of selected banks and investment counselors with specialized expertise in foreign equities. Major firms include Morgan

---

[5]Jacquillat and Solnik, "Multinationals Are Poor Tools for Diversification," pp. 8–12.

Table 18–12   Large U.S. Multinational Corporations

1990 Rank	Company	Revenue			Net Profit[a]			Assets		
		Foreign ($million)	Total ($million)	Foreign as Percent of Total	Foreign ($million)	Total ($million)	Foreign as Percent of Total	Foreign ($million)	Total ($million)	Foreign as Percent of Total
1	Exxon	79,015	105,519	74.9	4,184	5,010	83.5	51,586	87,707	58.8
2	IBM	41,886	69,018	60.7	4,548	6,020	75.5	45,692	87,568	52.2
3	General Motors	37,738	124,705	30.3	2,585	–1,986	n.a.	52,621	179,976	29.2
4	Ford Motor	35,879	97,650	36.7	232	860	27.0	55,161	173,611	31.8
5	Mobil	32,515[b]	58,770[b]	55.3	2,132[c]	2,547[c]	83.7	22,296	41,665	53.5
6	Citicorp	21,072	38,385	54.9	178	318	56.0	99,007[d]	231,788[d]	42.7
7	Texaco	17,520	40,899	42.8	936[c]	1,993[c]	47.0	7,818	25,975	30.1
8	El du Pont de Nemours	17,413[c]	40,047[c]	43.5	948	2,310	41.0	11,878	38,128	31.2
9	ITT[f]	11,628	25,734	45.2	540[g]	900[g]	60.0	12,762	52,588	24.3
10	Philip Morris Cos.	10,468	44,323	23.6	960	3,540	27.1	12,510	46,569	26.9
11	Dow Chemical	10,279	19,773	52.0	543[g]	1,585[g]	34.3	10,879	23,953	45.4
12	Procter & Gamble	9,618	24,081	39.9	467	1,602	29.2	6,516	18,487	35.2
13	Chevron	8,592	38,607	22.3	1,311	2,157	60.8	8,406	35,089	24.0
14	General Electric	8,272[b]	58,414[b]	14.2	490	4,303	11.4	16,461	153,884	10.7
15	Eastman Kodak	8,245	18,908	43.6	605	703	86.1	7,107	24,125	29.5
16	Amoco	8,227[b]	29,201[b]	28.2	975	1,913	51.0	10,570	32,209	32.8
17	Xerox[f]	8,105	19,188	42.2	531[g]	792[g]	67.0	8,659	32,177	26.9
18	United Technologies	7,840[b]	21,783[b]	36.0	434[g]	812[g]	53.4	4,379	15,918	27.5
19	Hewlett-Packard	7,208	13,233	54.5	361	739	48.8	5,088	11,395	44.7
20	Digital Equipment	7,119	12,943	55.0	374	74	505.4	5,085	11,655	43.6

[a]From continuing operations.
[b]Includes other income.
[c]Net income before corporate expense.
[d]Average assets.
[e]Includes excise taxes.
[f]Includes proportionate interest in unconsolidated subsidiaries or affiliates.
[g]Net income before minority interest.
n.a. = not available
Source: *Forbes,* July 22, 1991 pp. 286–87.

Guaranty Trust Co., State Street Bank and Trust Co., Batterymarch Financial Management, and Fidelity Trust Company of New York. These firms provide a total range of advisory and management services. However, they often require a minimum investment well in excess of $100,000 and are tailored to the needs of the large institutional investor.

SUMMARY

Investments in international securities allow the investor to diversify a portfolio beyond the normal alternatives. Because different foreign markets are influenced by varying and often contradictory factors, effective risk reduction can be provided. An example might be a sharp and unexpected increase in energy prices. The negative impact on oil importers will likely be offset by the positive impact on oil exporters.

Investments in selected foreign equity markets may also provide excellent return opportunities. A number of countries have had superior real GDP growth performance in comparison to the United States. They may also have greater savings rates and higher capital formation. Furthermore, a number of countries are becoming more competitive in traditional U.S. products such as automobiles, steel, and consumer electronics. Emerging countries may offer even greater return and risk-reduction benefits than investments in better-established markets. However, many of the problems of international investments can surface in these less-developed countries.

The impact of currency fluctuations on returns is an added dimension to international investments. Not only must the investor determine whether the security will provide a positive return, but he or she must also evaluate the possibility of the return being enhanced or diminished by changes in currency relationships with the U.S. dollar.

Other obstacles to foreign investment include political risks associated with foreign nations, tax problems, market efficiency and liquidity concerns, administrative problems, and gaps in information transference. The latter issue draws attention because of the comprehensive reporting system in the United States compared to the rest of the world. Also, the analyst must evaluate a security within the norms of the country in which the firm resides. This can be a problem for the uninitiated investor.

Fortunately, most of these obstacles can be overcome by appropriate investment routes into foreign markets. ADRs (American Depository Receipts) represent the ownership interest in a foreign company's common stock. The shares of the foreign company are put in trust in the foreign branch of a New York bank. The bank receives and can issue depository receipts to the American shareholders of the foreign firm. These ADRs allow foreign shares to be traded in the United States.

Indirect means of participation include the purchase of shares in multinational firms or, more importantly, investing in mutual funds or closed-end

investment companies specializing in foreign securities. An international fund offers the advantages of partial or comprehensive worldwide diversification and the removal of administrative and information-gathering problems.

The reader can readily observe that one who wishes to participate in foreign equities has many feasible alternatives.

IMPORTANT WORDS AND CONCEPTS

diversification benefits 588	foreign currency effects 597
World Index 593	American Depository Receipts 603
currency fluctuations 596	multinational corporations 605

DISCUSSION QUESTIONS

1. Does an investor who achieves international diversification through foreign investments necessarily have to accept lower returns?

2. Why does Canada represent a relatively poor outlet for achieving risk reduction for U.S. investors? (Merely use your own judgment in answering this question.)

3. In discussing return potential in foreign markets, indicate why a number of foreign countries may have higher return possibilities than the United States.

4. According to researcher Bruno Solnik, how much larger would a pure U.S. portfolio have to be in relation to a well-diversified international portfolio to achieve the same risk-reduction benefits?

5. Examine Table 18–8 and indicate which emerging country has firms with the highest average P/E ratios and the lowest dividend yields.

6. Explain how currency fluctuations affect the return on foreign investments.

7. Suggest two types of strategies to reduce or neutralize the impact of currency fluctuations on portfolio returns.

8. Suggest how foreign political risk may create a potential investment opportunity.

9. Are foreign markets likely to be more or less efficient than U.S. markets? What effect does this have on bid-ask spreads and the ability to absorb large transactions?

10. Explain why high debt ratios in Japan may not be as great a problem as one might first assume.

11. What are some of the key problems in investing directly in foreign securities?

12. Explain the concept of an ADR.

13. Why did Jacquillat and Solnik indicate that multinational firms may provide very little risk-reduction benefits in comparison to domestic firms?

14. Why might mutual funds be particularly beneficial in the international area?

PROBLEMS

Foreign currency effects

1. Assume you invest in the German equity market and have a 15 percent return (quoted in German marks).
   a. If during this period the mark appreciated by 10 percent against the dollar, what would be your actual return translated into U.S. dollars?
   b. If the mark declined by 10 percent against the dollar, what would your actual return be translated into dollars?
   c. Recompute the answer based on a 25 percent decline in the mark against the dollar.

Foreign currency effects

2. Assume you invest in the Japanese equity market and you have a 12 percent return (quoted in yen). However, during the course of your investment, the yen declines versus the dollar. By what percent could the yen decline relative to the dollar before all your gain is eliminated?

CFA MATERIAL

The following material contains a sample question and solution from a prior Level I CFA exam. While the terminology is slightly different from that in this text, you can still view the skills that are necessary for the CFA Exam.

CFA Exam Question

2. Unique risks are associated with international investing. Briefly describe *four* such risks.
   (5 minutes)

Solution: Question 2—Morning Section (5 points)

Four primary risks are:

1. *Currency fluctuations.* If the value of the investors' domestic currency strengthens after the purchase of foreign securities, the value of the investment declines.

2. *Availability of information.* Quality information about foreign companies may be less readily available to analysts than information about domestic

companies. This results because of varying requirements for corporate disclosure, less exhaustive analysis conducted by the foreign financial community, and the use of accounting conventions that differ from those in the country of the investor.

3. *Liquidity.* Foreign equity issues may tend to be smaller (or larger) than those in the investor's country making the accumulation of substantial positions more (or less) difficult.

4. *Sovereign risks.* These risks include the potential for disruptive political, sociological, or psychological developments. Examples of political risk are the possibility of nationalization of local companies, expropriation of assets owned by foreign investors, punitive taxation, and restrictions on the withdrawal of capital.

Other unique risks that might be addressed are:

5. High transaction costs, including taxes.
6. Administrative cost/settlement problems.
7. Difficulty in assessing manager skill and high fee structure.

MARKETBASE-E EXERCISES

1. *a.* MarketBase-E includes a number of international firms. Find 10 of those companies. (There is no means of doing this automatically. You must manually go through the database looking for companies whose accounting information is translated from native currency. This information appears as a note on a company's first screen of information.) As examples, consider companies such as Honda, Philips, Royal Dutch Petroleum, Sony, and Thomson CSF.
   b. Compare the price-earnings ratios of these companies with the MarketBase-E average.
   c. Compare the dividend yields of these companies with the MarketBase-E average.
   d. Compare the price-sales ratios of these companies with the MarketBase-E average.

SELECTED REFERENCES

Risk and Return Considerations

Alexander, Gordon J.; Cheol S. Eun; and S. Janakiramanan. "International Listings and Stock Returns: Some Empirical Evidence." *Journal of Financial and Quantitative Analysis,* June 1988, pp. 135–52.

Bergstrom, Gary L. "A New Route to Higher Returns and Lower Risks." *Journal of Portfolio Management,* Fall 1975, pp. 30–38.

Bergstrom, Gary L.; John K. Koeneman; and Martin J. Siegel. "International Security Market." In *Readings in Financial Management,* ed. Frank J. Fabozzi. Homewood, Ill.: Richard D. Irwin, 1983.

Bostock, Paul, and Paul Woolley. "A New Way to Analyze International Equity Performance." *Financial Analysts Journal,* January–February 1991, pp. 32–38.

French, Kenneth R., and James M. Toberba. "Were Japanese Stock Prices Too High?" *Journal of Financial Economics,* October 1991, pp. 337–63.

Ibbotson, Roger G.; Richard C. Carr; and Anthony W. Robinson. "International Equity and Bond Returns." *Financial Analysts Journal,* July–August 1982, pp. 61–83.

Ibbotson, Roger G., and Laurence B. Siegel. "The World Market Wealth Portfolio." *Journal of Portfolio Management,* Winter 1983, pp. 5–17.

Lessard, Donald R. "World, Country and Industry Relationships in Equity Returns." *Financial Analysts Journal,* January–February 1976, pp. 32–38.

Logue, Dennis E. "An Experiment in International Diversification." *Journal of Portfolio Management,* Fall 1982, pp. 22–27.

Maldanado-Bear, Rita, and Anthony Sanders. "International Portfolio Diversification and the Stability of International Stock Market Relationships, 1957–1980." *Financial Management,* Autumn 1981, pp. 54–63.

Reinganum, Marc R., and Alan C. Shipiro. "Taxes and Stock Return Seasonality: Evidence from the London Stock Exchange." *Journal of Business,* April 1987, pp. 281–98.

Solnik, Bruno. "Why Not Diversify Internationally Rather than Domestically?" *Financial Analysts Journal,* July–August 1974, pp. 48–54.

Stanley, Marjorie. "Capital Structure and Cost of Capital for the International Firm." *Journal of International Business Studies,* Spring–Summer 1981, pp. 103–20.

Emerging Markets

Errunza, Vihang R. "Emerging Markets: A New Opportunity for Improving Global Portfolio Performance." *Financial Analysts Journal,* September–October 1983, pp. 51–58.

Larson, John C., and Joel N. Morse. "Intervalling Effects in Hong Kong Stocks." *Journal of Financial Research,* Winter 1987, pp. 353–62.

Ryan, Collen. "Stock Markets: Sapped in Sydney." *Institutional Investor,* February 1988, pp. 173–74.

Currency Considerations

Chang, Jack, and Latha Shanker. "Hedging Effectiveness of Currency Options and Currency Futures." *Journal of Futures Markets,* Summer 1986, pp. 289–306.

Perold, Andre F., and Evan C. Schulman. "The Free Lunch in Currency Hedging: Implications for Investment Policy and Performance Standards." *Financial Analysts Journal,* May–June 1988, pp. 44–52.

Thomas, Lee R., III. "Currency Risks in International Equity Portfolios." *Financial Analysts Journal,* March–April 1988, pp. 68–70.

International Market Crash of 1987

Roll, Richard. "The International Crash of 1987." *Financial Analysts Journal,* September–October 1988, pp. 19–35.

19

Mutual Funds

Of over 50 million investors in the United States, approximately one third participate through the purchase of mutual funds rather than directly through the ownership of common stock or other securities.

The concept of a mutual fund is best understood by an example. Suppose you and your friends are too busy to develop the expertise needed to manage your own assets. One of your neighbors, however, has studied investments and security markets extensively. He has also had years of hands-on experience as a trustee of his company's pension fund. You and your friends decide to pool your money and have this experienced investor act as your investment advisor. He will be compensated by receiving a small percentage of the average amount of assets under his management during the forthcoming year.

By common agreement, the pooled money is to be invested in the common stock of large, stable companies with the objective of capital appreciation and moderate dividend income; funds not so invested are to be placed in short-term T-bills to earn interest. Group members collectively contribute $100,000 and decide to issue shares in the fund at a rate of one share for each $10 contributed—a total of 10,000 shares. Since you put in $10,000, you receive 1,000 shares of the fund—or 10 percent of the fund's shares. Over the next few weeks, your investment advisor uses $90,000 to purchase common stock in a number of companies representing several different industries and puts $10,000 in T-bills. The portfolio looks like this:

Common stocks grouped by industry:

Computers:
  Hewlett-Packard
  IBM
  Digital Equipment
Financial services:
  Chemical Bank
  Merrill Lynch
  Northwestern National Life Insurance Co.
Consumer retail:
  K mart
  Toys R Us
  Dayton Hudson
Treasury bills:
  $10,000

Since you own 10 percent of this portfolio, you are entitled to 10 percent of all income paid out to shareholders and 10 percent of all realized capital gains or losses.

The initial value of the portfolio is $100,000, or $10 per share. Assume your investment manager picked some winning stocks, and the portfolio rises to $115,000. Now each share is worth $11.50 per share.

Your group of investors has many characteristics of a mutual fund: ownership interest represented by shares, professional management, stated investment objectives, and a diversified portfolio of assets. A billion-dollar mutual fund would operate with many of the same concepts and principles—only the magnitude of the operation would be thousands of times larger.

■ ADVANTAGES AND DISADVANTAGES OF MUTUAL FUNDS

Mutual funds offer an efficient way to diversify your investments. For many small investors, diversification may be difficult to achieve. The normal trading unit for listed stocks—the "round lot"—is 100 shares. If proper diversification required a portfolio of at least 10 different stocks, the investor should purchase 100 shares of each of them. If each stock had a market value of $30, cost would be (excluding commission) $30,000 ($30 × 100 × 10). That's a big bite for most individuals just to get started.

With a mutual fund, you are also buying the expertise of the fund management. In many cases, fund managers have a long history of investment experience and may be specialists in certain areas such as international securities, gold stocks, or municipal bonds. By entrusting your funds to capable hands, you are freeing your time for other pursuits. This may be particularly important to people such as doctors or lawyers who may be capable of earning $150 to $200 an hour in their normal practice but are novices in the market.

As will be demonstrated throughout the chapter, you have a multitude of funds from which to choose to satisfy your investment objectives. Thus, another advantage of mutual funds is that they can be used to buy not only stocks, but also U.S. government bonds, corporate bonds, municipal securities, and so on. Also, they represent an efficient way to invest in foreign securities.

With many of these advantages in mind, it is not surprising that mutual funds have enjoyed enormous growth in the last decade. The amount of funds in existence grew from 300 in the 1970s to over 3,000 in 1991. The amount of assets being managed increased fifteenfold.

Having stated some of the advantages of mutual funds, let's look at the disadvantages. First, mutual funds, on average, do not outperform the market. That is to say, over long periods, they do no better than the Standard & Poor's 500 Stock Index, the Dow Jones Industrial Average, and so on. Nevertheless, they provide an efficient means for diversifying your portfolio. Also, a minority of funds have had exceptional returns over time (many of these have had exposure to international investments).

Some mutual funds can be expensive to purchase. However, this factor should not overly concern you because a high commission can often be avoided. As you read further into the chapter, you will become very proficient at identifying the absence or presence of a commission and whether it is justified.

An investor in mutual funds must also be sensitive to the excessive claims sometimes made by mutual fund salespeople. Often, potential returns to the investor are emphasized without detailing the offsetting risks. The fact that a fund made 20 to 25 percent last year in no way ensures such a return in the future. Although the Securities and Exchange Commission has begun clamping down on false or overly enthusiastic advertising practices by members of the industry, the buyer still needs to beware. We will also help develop your skills in measuring actual performance as we progress through the chapter.

A final potential drawback to mutual funds is actually a reverse view of an advantage. With over 3,000 mutual funds from which to choose, an investor has as much of a problem in selecting a mutual fund as a stock. For example, there are approximately 1,500 stocks on the New York Stock Exchange, considerably less than the number of mutual funds in existence. Nevertheless, if you sharpen your goals and objectives, you will be able to focus on a handful of funds that truly meet your needs.

Having discussed the general nature of mutual funds and some of the potential advantages and disadvantages, we now examine the actual mechanics. In the remainder of this chapter, we shall discuss closed-end versus open-end funds, load versus no-load funds, fund objectives, considerations in selecting a fund, and measuring the return on a fund. There is also a brief description of unit investment trusts (UITs) in Appendix 19–A. UITs have some attributes similar to mutual funds.

■ CLOSED-END VERSUS OPEN-END FUNDS

There are basically two types of investment funds, the closed-end fund and the open-end fund. We shall briefly discuss the closed-end fund and then move on to the much more important type of arrangement, the open-end fund.

Actually, these terms refer to the manner in which shares are distributed and redeemed. A **closed-end fund** has a fixed number of shares, and purchasers and sellers of shares must trade with each other. You cannot buy the shares directly from the fund (except at the inception of the fund) because of the limitation on shares outstanding. Furthermore, the fund does not stand ready to buy the shares back from you.

As we shall eventually see, an open-end fund represents exactly the opposite concept. The **open-end fund** stands ready at all times to sell you new shares or buy back your old shares. Having made this distinction, let's stay with the closed-end fund for now. The shares of closed-end funds trade on security exchanges or over-the-counter just as any other stock might. Instead of the

Table 19–1 A Closed-End Fund Quote on the New York Stock Exchange

52 Weeks Hi	Lo	Stock	Sym	Div	Yld %	PE	Vol 100s	Hi	Lo	Close	Net Chg
70	48¾	ReynMetl	RLM	1.80	2.9	15	3982	61⅝	59¾	61⅝	+1½
3	**1/16**	**RhonPoulnc wt**			...	...	**51**	11/16	11/16	11/16	+ ⅛
18½	8¾	RhonPoulnc pfA		1.60e	11.6	...	279	14⅜	13¾	13¾	– ⅝
20⅝	9⅛	RhonPoulnc	RPU	1.60e	10.7	...	27	15½	15	15	– ⅜
42¾	28⅛	RhonPlRorer	RPR		...	415	607	41⅝	41¼	41½	– ⅛
47¾	29½	RiteAid	RAD	.50	1.2	16	833	42⅝	41⅝	41¾	–1
15¾	7	RobtHalfInt	RHI		...	17	37	11	10⅞	11	+ ⅛
20¾	16⅞	RochG&E	RGS	1.62	8.3	11	182	19⅝	19¼	19⅝	+ ⅜
35¼	24⅝	RochTele	RTC	1.50	5.0	17	114	30	29⅝	29⅞	– ⅛
20¼	15¼	RockeCtr	RCP	1.92	10.0	19	329	19¼	18⅞	19⅛	+ ¼
29¼	20½	Rockwell	ROK	.86	3.1	11	1875	27⅞	27½	27¾	+ ⅛
46⅜	24¼	RohmHaas	ROH	1.24	2.8	15	303	44⅛	43½	44⅛	+ ⅜
25¾	11½	RohrInd	RHR		...	16	437	24	23⅜	24	+ ¾
15¼	7¼	RollinsEnvr	REN	.09	1.0	19	1590	8⅞	8½	8⅞	+ ¼
25	16	RollinsInc	ROL	.58	2.7	18	177	21¾	21⅝	21⅝	+ ⅛
13⅛	5¾	RollinsLeas	RLC	.20	1.5	13	1020	13⅛	12¾	13	+ ⅜
15⅞	8¼	RowanCos	RDC		...	...	1311	8⅜	8⅛	8¼	– ⅛
25⅛	19⅝	RoylBkScot adr		2.81e	11.5	...	111	24⅜	24	24⅜	+ ¼
87	73	RoylDutchP	RD	4.23e	5.4	11	5107	78¾	77¾	77¾	–1⅛
11	7	RoyceValTr	RVT	.32e	3.2	...	176	10⅛	9¾	9⅞	...
54¼	32¼	Rubbermaid	RBD	.60	1.2	28	857	51¼	50½	51	+ ⅝
15⅛	**9½**	**Ruddick**	**RDK**	**.24**	**1.6**	**12**	**364**	**14¾**	**13¾**	**14¾**	**+1**
18⅜	13½	RussBerr	RUS	.60a	4.5	11	95	13½	13⅛	13¼	– ⅜
9⅞	4	RussTogs	RTS		...	...	139	5¼	5⅛	5⅛	– ⅛
31	16	Russell	RML	.32	1.3	17	494	24¼	23¾	24	– ⅛
22⅝	12¼	RyderSys	R	.60	3.1	24	733	19½	19	19½	+ ⅛
21⅞	14¼	Rykoff	RYK	.60	2.9	20	142	21	20¾	21	+ ⅛
25¼	9½	RylandGp	RYL	.60	3.0	32	221	20	19⅝	20	+ ⅛
10½	3¾	Rymer	RYR		...	...	29	8¼	8	8¼	– ¼
9¼	4½	Rymer pf		1.17	14.4	...	2	8⅛	8⅛	8⅛	+ ⅛

Source: *The Wall Street Journal,* July 3, 1991, p. 15. Reprinted by permission of *THE WALL STREET JOURNAL,* © 1991 by Dow Jones & Company, Inc. All Rights Reserved Worldwide.

firm being involved in the manufacturing of automobiles or the discovery of new drugs, it is involved in the investment and management of a security portfolio. An example of a closed-end fund that trades on a security exchange is shown in Table 19–1. Note the Royce Value Trust Fund, a closed-end fund specializing in high-grade equities, is presented the same as any other common stock, such as Royal Dutch Petroleum shown directly above it. If you wish to buy or sell shares in the Royce Value Trust Fund, you call your broker and place your order.

One of the most important considerations in purchasing a closed-end fund is whether it is trading at a discount or premium from net asset value. First, let's look at the formula for net asset value.

$$\text{Net asset value (NAV)} = \frac{\text{Total value of securities} - \text{Liabilities}}{\text{Shares outstanding}} \qquad (19\text{–}1)$$

The **net asset value (NAV)** is equal to the current value of the securities owned by the fund minus any liabilities divided by the number of shares

Table 19–2   Premiums or Discounts from Net Asset Value

INVESTMENT COMPANY INSTITUTE LIST

Friday, May 10, 1991

Fund Name	Stock Exch.	N.A. Value	Stock Price	% Diff.
Diversified Common Stock Funds				
Adams Express	NYSE	19.38	17 ½	− 9.70
Baker Fentress	NYSE	21.16	17 ⅝	− 16.71
Blue Chip Value	NYSE	7.75	7 ¼	− 6.45
Clemente Global Gro	NYSE	b11.03	9 ¼	− 16.14
Gemini II Capital	NYSE	15.75	13 ¼	− 15.87
Gemini II Income	NYSE	9.38	12 ⅝	+ 34.59
General Amer Invest	NYSE	25.79	22 ¼	− 13.73
Growth Stock Outlook	NYSE	10.46	9 ¾	− 6.79
Liberty All-Star Eqty	NYSE	10.16	9 ⅜	− 7.73
Niagara Share Corp.	NYSE	16.09	13 ⅝	− 15.32
Nicholas-Applegate	NYSE	12.34	12 ¼	− 0.73
Quest For Value Cap	NYSE	19.71	13 ⅞	− 29.60
Quest For Value Inco	NYSE	11.64	13 ⅝	+ 17.05
Royce Value Trust	NYSE	10.71	10 ⅛	− 5.46
Salomon Fd	NYSE	15.17	12 ¾	− 15.95
Source Capital	NYSE	40.72	42 ¼	+ 3.76
Tri-Continental Corp.	NYSE	27.69	24 ¾	− 10.62
Worldwide Value	NYSE	16.87	14	− 17.01
Zweig Fund	NYSE	11.37	12 ⅝	+ 11.04

Source: *Barron's,* May 13, 1991, p. 101. Reprinted by permission of *Barron's,* © 1991 by Dow Jones & Company, Inc. All Rights Reserved Worldwide.

outstanding. For example, assume a fund has securities worth $140 million, liabilities of $5 million, and 10 million shares outstanding. The NAV is $13.50.

$$\text{NAV} = \frac{\$140 \text{ million} - \$5 \text{ million}}{10 \text{ million shares}} = \frac{\$135 \text{ million}}{10 \text{ million}} = \$13.50$$

The NAV is computed at the end of each day for a fund.

Intuitively, one would expect a closed-end fund to sell at its net asset value, but that is not the case. Many funds trade at a discount from NAV because they have a poor record of prior performance, are heavily invested in an unpopular industry, or are thinly traded (illiquid). A few trade at a premium because of the known quality of their management, the nature of their investments, or the fact they have holdings in nonpublicly traded securities that are believed to be undervalued on their books. Note in Table 19–2 the predominance of common stock funds trading at discounts from NAV in May 1991 (last column). This has normally been the case over the last decade. Some researchers even use the fact that closed-end funds do not sell for what they are worth (in terms of their holdings) as evidence that the market is something less than truly efficient in valuing securities (see the accompanying box on naive investors).

How Naive Can Investors Be?

It is assumed the stock market is reasonably efficient; that is, information is quickly absorbed by investors and impounded into the value of securities. An associated feature of market efficiency is that stocks tend to be correctly priced at any point in time. Forget it! While IBM and General Motors might be correctly priced, such is not the case with closed-end investment companies. Clearly, the true value per share of a closed-end investment company is the total current value of the stock holdings (less any liabilities) divided by the number of shares outstanding. If a fund has a net asset value of $10, but is selling at a 15 percent discount for $8.50, all the fund management has to do is liquidate the assets of the fund and give each stockholder $10 per share. Forget about whether the fund is popular or not; its assets still have an immediate liquidation value of $10.

It is indeed surprising that 75 to 80 percent of closed-end funds sell at a discount from actual value (normally 10 to 15 percent below). The discount tends to be well in excess of the relatively small costs to liquidate the fund or simply convert it into an open-end fund (where it immediately trades at full net asset value).

Even more surprising is the fact that closed-end funds are almost always initially issued at a premium above net asset value. Then, within the first couple of weeks of trading, they slip to a discount. Why would anyone buy a fund with such a high probability of a loss? To directly quote *Forbes* magazine, "How Dumb Can Investors Be?"[*] If an investor wants to invest in a closed-end fund, why not buy an existing one at a discount and hope for a liquidation. Why pay the initial premium and then wait to take a beating?

The most plausible answer, according to *Forbes* and other sources, is that this is the least sophisticated part of the investment community. Naive investors engage in a mass misunderstanding about their own self-interest when they buy into an initial distribution of a closed-end fund. Rest assured there are very few institutional investors or enlightened finance majors playing this game.

[*]Mark Fadiman, "Muni Mystery," *Forbes,* September 3, 1990, p. 174.

■ INVESTING IN OPEN-END FUNDS

As previously indicated, an open-end fund stands ready at all times to sell new shares or buy back old shares from investors. You do not deal with other shareholders. Over 95 percent of the investment funds in the United States are open-ended. Actually, the term *mutual fund* applies specifically to *open-end* investment companies, although closed-end funds are sometimes loosely labeled as mutual funds as well. We shall be careful to make the distinction where appropriate.

Transactions with open-end funds are made at the net asset value as described in Formula 19–1 on page 619 (though there may be an added commission). If the fund has 100 million shares outstanding at a NAV of $10 per share ($1 billion) and sells 20 million more shares at $10 per share, the new funds ($200 million) are redeployed in investments worth $200 million, and the NAV remains unchanged. The only factor that changes the NAV is the up and down movement of the securities in the fund's portfolio. The primary

Table 19–3	Distinctions between Closed-End and Open-End Funds		
	Method of Purchase	**Number of Shares Outstanding**	**Shares Traded at Net Asset Value**
Closed-end fund	Stock exchange or over-the-counter	Fixed	No—there may be a discount or premium from NAV
Open-end fund (mutual fund)	Direct from fund or fund salesperson	Fluctuates	Yes—but there may be a commission

distinctions between closed-end and open-end funds are presented in Table 19–3. All of our subsequent discussion will be about open-end (mutual) funds. These include such established names as Fidelity, Dreyfus, Vanguard, IDS, T. Rowe Price, and Templeton.

Load versus No-Load Funds

Some funds have established selling agreements with stockbrokers, financial planners, insurance agents, and others licensed to sell securities. These selling agents receive a commission for selling the funds. The funds are termed **load funds** because there is a commission associated with the purchase of the fund shares. The commission may run as high as 8.5 percent.

Several stock funds are referred to as **low-load funds** because their sales charges are 3 to 4 percent instead of 8.5 percent. In recent years, a number of funds have also introduced a back-end load provision. While there may or may not be a front-end load in buying such a fund, there is an exit fee in selling a fund with a **back-end load** provision. The fee may be 3 to 5 percent of the selling price, but typically declines with the passage of time.

No-Load Funds

No-load funds do not charge commissions and are sold directly by the investment company through advertisements, prospectuses, and 800-number telephone orders. As of mid-1991, no-load funds made up about 32 percent of all mutual fund assets. Some wonder how no-load funds justify their existence since they charge no commission to purchase their shares. The answer is because of the fee they charge to manage the assets in the fund. This normally totals 1 to 1.5 percent. On a billion-dollar fund, this represents $10 million to $15 million a year and can be more than adequate to compensate the fund managers. It should also be pointed out that load funds also have similar management fees.

The question then becomes, why pay the load (commission)? Studies indicate there is no significant statistical difference in the investment performance of load and no-load funds. Consequently, most astute investors shop around for a no-load fund to fit their needs rather than pay a commission. This statement is not intended to dismiss the possibility that apprehensive or uncomfortable investors may benefit from the consultation and advice of a competent mutual fund salesman or financial advisor, and thus receive a commensurate service from paying the commission. Also, some specialized funds may exist only in the form of load funds. However, whenever possible, investors are better off using the commission toward the purchase of new shares rather than the payment of a sales fee.

If you invest $1,000 in a mutual fund and pay an 8.5 percent commission, only 91.5 percent will go toward purchasing your shares. A $1,000 investment will immediately translate into a holding of $915. This means the fund must go up by $85, or 9.29 percent, just for you to break even.

$$\frac{\$85}{\$915} = 9.29 \text{ percent}$$

With these thoughts in mind, you should become proficient in recognizing funds that are charging a load and those that are not. To accomplish this goal, observe Table 19–4, which is an excerpt on mutual fund quotations from *The Wall Street Journal*.

The bold letters in the table represent the name of the mutual fund sponsor. For example, AARP (the second listed group) has six different mutual funds dedicated to serving diverse needs ranging from Capital Growth (CaGr) to Tax-Free Short-Term investments (TXFSh). The table has three primary columns that allow us to determine whether a fund is a load or a no-load. As examples of load funds, observe the AAL Mutual Funds at the top of the table or the Alliance Capital group at the bottom of the first column. In each case, the NAV (net asset value) is different from the offer price. This means a commission must be paid. For example, for the second fund in the Alliance Capital group (Balan), the NAV is $12.36, and the offer price is $13.08. This means the fund has a net asset value of $12.36 per share but is offered to the public for $13.08. The difference between $13.08 and $12.36 of $.72 represents the commission.

Offer price	$13.08
NAV (net asset value)	12.36
Commission	$ .72

In this case, the commission represents 5.5 percent of the offer price ($.72/$13.08 = 5.5%).[1] You will buy a fund valued at $12.36 for $13.08

---

[1]It also represents 5.83 percent of the net asset value ($.72/$12.36).

Table 19–4 Mutual Fund Quotations

MUTUAL FUND QUOTATIONS

Tuesday, June 11, 1991

Price ranges for investment companies, as quoted by the National Association of Securities Dealers. NAV stands for net asset value per share; the offering includes net asset value plus maximum sales charge, if any.

	NAV	Offer Price	NAV Chg.
AAL Mutual:			
CaGr p	12.68	13.31	+.07
Inco p	9.67	10.15	...
MuBd p	10.06	10.56	−.02
AARP Invst:			
CaGr	28.14	NL	−.03
GinIM	15.20	NL	...
GthInc	26.28	NL	+.12
HQ Bd	15.03	NL	...
TxFBd	16.74	NL	−.04
TxFSh	15.22	NL	−.01
ABT Funds:			
Emrg p	9.86	10.35	+.01
FL TF	10.27	10.78	−.01
GthIn p	9.66	10.14	+.03
UtilIn p	11.95	12.55	+.07
AdsnCa p	19.49	20.09	+.10
AEGON USA:			
CapApp	4.08	4.28	+.01
HiYld	9.67	10.15	+.01
Gwth	5.98	6.28	+.02
AFA NAv	10.68	11.21	+.05
AFA Tele	15.02	15.77	+.03
AHA Bal	11.19	NL	+.05
AHA LtM	10.09	NL	...
AIM Funds:			
Chart p	7.74	8.19	+.03
Const p	10.17	10.76	+.06
CvYld p	11.47	12.04	+.04
HiYld p	5.13	5.39	...
LimM p	9.91	10.09	...
Sumit	9.03	....	+.06
Weing p	14.65	15.50	+.10
A M A Family:			
ClaGt p	8.13	8.54	+.01
GlbGt p	22.24	23.35	+.08
GlbIn p	18.52	19.44	+.01
USGv p	8.60	9.03	...
AMEV Funds:			
AstAl p	12.44	13.03	+.03
Capitl p	15.29	16.05	+.06
CaAp p	16.56	17.34	+.07
Fidcr p	24.63	25.79	+.09
GvTR p	8.87	9.29	...
Grwth p	22.13	23.23	+.10
HiYld p	7.15	7.49	...
TF MN	9.75	10.21	−.02
TF Nat	9.95	10.42	−.01
TF NY	10.52	11.02	−.02
US Gvt	9.61	10.06	...
AMF Funds:			
Cp Bd	9.22	NL	...
IntlLiq	10.46	NL	−.01
MtgSc	10.84	NL	+.01
ASO Eq	12.69	13.08	+.06
AcornF	41.59	41.59	−.04
Afuture	11.84	NL	−.14
Advance America:			
EqInc	9.86	10.35	+.03
TF In p	9.80	10.29	−.01
US Gv p	9.18	9.64	+.01
Advest Advant:			
Govt p	8.47	8.47	...
Gwth p	14.86	14.86	+.08
HY Bd p	7.54	7.54	...
Inco p	10.84	10.84	+.03
Spcl p	13.50	13.50	+.06
AlgrSCp t	19.04	19.04	+.12
AlgerG t	16.18	16.18	+.08
Alliance Cap:			
Allan p	6.24	6.60	+.02
Balan p	12.36	13.08	+.02
Canad p	6.04	6.39	+.03
Count p	18.18	19.24	+.03
GlbSA p	10.19	10.78	+.02
Govt p	7.98	8.38	...
GrInc p	2.47	2.61	+.01
HiYld p	5.15	5.41	−.01
IntlA p	14.68	15.53	+.06
ICalT p	12.44	13.03	+.02
InsMu	9.60	10.05	−.01
MonIn p	11.22	11.78	+.01
Mortg p	8.70	9.13	+.01
MltIn	2.00	2.00	...
MMS A	9.94	10.25	−.01
MuCA	9.73	10.19	−.01
MuNY	9.03	9.46	−.01
NtlMu	9.72	10.18	−.01
NEur p	8.95	9.47	+.02
QusrA p	20.43	21.62	+.05
MMS B	9.94	9.94	−.01
ST Mla p	9.87	10.18	...
ST Mi			.01
Capstone Group:			
CshFr	9.82	10.31	+.01
Fd SW	15.34	16.10	+.07
GvtInc	4.64	4.64	...
MedRs	16.16	16.97	+.05
PBHG	11.48	12.05	−.01
Ray EI	6.59	6.92	+.02
Trend	13.83	14.52	+.09
CarilCa	12.07	12.71	+.01
Carneg Cappiello:			
EmGr p	10.41	10.90	+.02
Grow p	18.36	19.23	−.09
TRetn p	11.17	11.70	−.07
Carnegie Funds:			
Govt p	9.09	9.52	...
TEOhG	9.21	9.64	−.02
TENHI	9.57	10.02	...
Cardnl	11.66	12.74	+.05
CrdnlGv	8.85	9.27	...
Cnt Shs	19.97	NL	−.02
ChartBC	11.19	11.19	+.11
Chestnt	110.66	NL	+.41
CIGNA Funds:			
Agrsv p	15.70	16.53	−.02
GvSc p	9.90	10.42	...
Grth p	14.74	15.52	+.04
HiYld p	8.16	8.59	...
Inco p	7.46	7.85	...
MunB p	7.74	8.15	−.02
Util p	12.52	13.18	+.06
Value p	16.44	17.31	+.06
Citibank IRA-CIT:			
Balan f	2.50	NL	...
Equit f	2.81	NL	...
Incom f	2.16	NL	...
ShtTr f	1.80	NL	...
Clipper	44.57	44.57	+.03
Colonial Funds:			
AGold p	16.30	17.29	+.01
CalTE	6.99	7.34	...
CpCsh p	44.58	45.49	−.02
DvsdIn	6.70	7.03	...
Fund p	20.68	21.94	+.06
GvSec p	10.41	10.93	...
Gwth p	13.03	13.82	+.03
HiYld p	5.42	5.69	−.01
Incom p	6.14	6.45	...
IntEq p	15.98	16.95	+.06
MATx	7.15	7.51	−.01
MI TE	6.55	6.88	...
MN TE	6.89	7.23	−.01
NY TE	6.61	6.94	...
OhTE	6.86	7.20	−.01
SmlIn p	12.26	13.01	+.03
TXIns p	7.72	8.10	−.01
TxEx p	12.93	13.57	−.01
US Gv p	6.95	7.30	+.01
US Id p	18.74	19.88	+.13
Colonial VIP:			
DvRet t	11.07	11.07	+.01
FdSec t	9.81	9.81	+.01
Gwth t	11.60	11.60	−.03
HiInc t	8.61	8.61	−.01
HYMu t	9.61	9.61	...
InfHd t	10.32	10.32	+.02
Columbia Funds:			
Fixed	12.73	NL	...
Govt	8.44	NL	...
Grth	25.86	NL	+.03
Muni	11.82	NL	−.01
Specl	47.08	NL	−.04
Common Sense:			
Govt	10.93	11.72	...
Grwth	14.50	15.85	+.08
GrInc	14.01	15.31	+.09
MunB	12.48	13.10	−.02
CwlthBl	2.06	2.23	...
Compass Capital:			
EqInc	11.57	NL	+.03
FxdIn	10.02	NL	...
Grwth	11.89	NL	+.06
ShInt	10.14	NL	...
Composite Group:			
BdStk p	11.16	11.63	+.05
Gwth p	11.97	12.47	+.07
InFd p	8.38	8.73	...
NW50 p	26.90	28.17	+.05
TxEx p	7.19	7.49	−.01
USGv p	10.10	10.52	...
Conn Mutual:			
Govt	10.69	11.19	...
Grwth	13.82	14.74	+.03
TotRet	13.47	14.37	+.01
oley	14.46	NL	+.0
	19.04	NL	
USGv t	8.87	8.87	...
EqStrat	29.07	NL	+.05
Evergreen Funds:			
Evgrn	12.99	NL	+.05
TotRtn	18.25	NL	+.04
ValTm	12.48	NL	+.03
LtdMk	18.72	NL	+.04
ExcelMid	2.59	2.71	...
ExcHY p	6.58	6.91	...
FBL Gth t	11.76	11.76	+.01
FPA Funds:			
Capit	15.53	16.61	−.15
NwInc	10.14	10.62	−.01
Parmt	14.10	15.08	+.03
Peren	21.28	22.76	+.05
Fairmt	15.50	NL	+.05
Federated Funds:			
Exch	58.58	NL	+.16
FBF	9.24	NL	...
FIGT	9.81	NL	...
FFRT	9.07	NL	+.01
GNMA	11.19	NL	+.01
FGRO	20.69	NL	+.05
FHYT	7.81	NL	−.01
FIT	10.35	NL	−.01
FIMT	10.02	NL	−.01
FSIMT	10.19	NL	...
FSIGT	10.10	NL	−.01
FSBF	15.30	NL	+.03
FST	23.28	NL	+.08
FGVT	9.38	NL	...
SP 500	10.82	NL	+.08
Tg2Yr p	9.98	NL	...
Fenimre	14.12	14.86	−.06
Fidelity Invest:			
AgTF r	11.43	11.43	−.01
A Mgr	12.53	NL	+.02
Balanc	11.99	NL	...
BluCh	17.78	18.33	+.11
CA TF	11.28	NL	...
CA In	9.69	NL	−.01
Canad	16.43	16.94	+.03
CapAp	16.02	16.52	−.01
CpInc r	6.91	NL	...
CngS	132.05	....	+.51
Contra	22.79	23.49	+.10
CnvSc	12.73	NL	+.04
DestI	15.81	....	+.08
DestII	24.64	....	+.10
DisEq r	15.76	NL	+.05
EmgGr	13.45	NL	+.04
Eq Inc	25.14	25.65	+.12
EqIdx	14.49	NL	+.10
Europ	15.81	16.30	−.01
Exch	87.93	....	+.61
Fidel	19.34	NL	+.08
FlexB	6.77	NL	...
GloBd	11.78	NL	−.01
GNMA	10.51	NL	+.01
GovtSc	9.51	NL	...
GroInc	19.86	20.27	+.07
GroCo	24.72	25.48	+.09
HiYld	12.48	NL	−.01
InsMu	11.15	NL	−.01
IntBd	9.96	NL	...
IntGr	13.65	13.93	+.07
LtdMn	9.36	NL	−.01
LowP r	12.57	NL	−.02
Magin	65.14	67.15	+.35
MI TF	10.89	NL	−.02
MA TF	11.18	NL	−.01
MN TF	10.56	NL	−.01
MtgSc	10.36	NL	...
MunBd	8.18	NL	−.01
Oh TF	10.89	NL	−.01
NY HY	11.69	NL	−.01
NY Ins	10.95	NL	−.01
OTC	23.52	24.25	+.03
Ovrse	25.26	26.04	−.02
PcBas	12.73	13.12	+.11
Puritn	13.63	13.91	+.05
RealEs	10.02	NL	+.01
RetGr	15.72	NL	+.02
ShtBd	9.18	NL	+.01
SpcSit	20.85	21.89	+.07
StkSlc	14.49	NL	+.05
Trend	46.09	NL	−.02
USBI	10.26	10.26	−.01
UtilInc	11.93	NL	+.05
Value	29.07	NL	+.09
Wrldw	9.21	NL	−.01
Fidl Inv Instit:			
CTAR r	8.49	NL	...
EqP G	23.06	NL	+.05
EqP I	11.25	NL	+.06
IP LTD	10.15	NL	...
IP SG	9.54	NL	...
TE Ltd	10.68	NL	−.01
QualD t	11.31	NL	+.05
Fidelity S			
NC TF	10.85	11.30	−.02
OhioI	11.34	11.81	−.01
ORTF	10.73	11.18	−.02
PaTF	9.51	9.91	−.01
PrmRt	4.85	5.05	+.02
PR TF	10.85	11.30	−.01
SI Gov	10.24	10.40	...
SpEq	11.64	12.13	+.06
TA Gov	10.23	10.66	...
TxAHY	7.19	7.49	−.01
TX TF	10.78	11.23	−.01
Utils	8.13	8.47	+.03
US Gov	6.94	7.23	...
VA TF	10.68	11.13	−.02
Franklin Mgd Tr:			
CpQul p	20.99	21.31	+.02
InvGd p	8.45	8.80	−.01
RisDv p	13.57	14.14	+.01
Freedom Funds:			
Envrn p	9.42	9.86	−.02
EqVal t	11.15	11.15	+.05
Globl t	10.62	10.62	+.05
GlbIn t	10.14	10.14	−.01
Gold t	14.33	14.33	...
GvtIn t	9.89	9.89	...
MgTE t	10.79	10.79	−.03
RgBk t	12.09	12.09	...
ST Wld	10.08	10.08	...
FmntCA	10.24	NL	−.01
FmntMA	11.05	NL	+.05
FundTrust:			
Aggr fp	14.14	14.36	−.05
Grth fp	13.55	13.76	−.04
GroI fp	14.08	14.29	−.03
Inco f	9.32	9.46	...
GAM Funds:			
Glbl	108.01	113.69	+.52
Intl	130.52	137.39	+.56
PcBas	129.10	135.89	+1.00
GIT Invst:			
EqSpc	19.06	NL	+.01
HiYd	10.55	NL	−.01
InMax	6.84	NL	...
TFVA	11.07	NL	−.01
GNA t	9.69	9.69	...
GS CapG	12.57	13.30	−.01
GT Global:			
Amer p	13.92	14.61	+.02
Bond p	10.77	11.31	...
Euro p	9.88	10.37	+.04
GvInc p	10.09	10.59	+.01
GrInc	5.22	5.48	+.01
HltCr p	16.70	17.53	+.10
Intl p	8.85	9.29	+.02
Japan p	12.84	13.48	+.14
Pacif p	12.04	12.64	+.04
Wldw p	13.50	14.17	+.03
GW Sierra Tr:			
CalBd p	10.06	10.53	...
CpInc p	9.84	10.30	...
GvSec p	10.01	10.48	+.01
GrInc p	10.92	11.43	+.06
StIntl p	8.73	9.14	+.05
NtMu p	10.13	10.61	−.01
Gabelli Funds:			
Asset p	17.69	NL	+.02
CnvSc	11.32	11.85	+.02
Gwth p	18.51	NL	+.10
Value p	9.79	10.36	+.06
Galaxy Funds:			
EqGth	11.66	NL	+.06
EqtVal	11.53	NL	+.07
HiQ Bd	9.85	NL	+.01
IntBd	10.04	NL	...
GatwyGr	13.22	NL	+.05
GatwyIn	14.72	NL	+.02
Gelco fp	....	....	...
Gen Elec Inv:			
ElfDiv	12.27	NL	+.01
ElfGl	12.09	NL	+.08
ElfnIn	11.03	NL	...
ElfnTr	31.45	NL	+.10
ElfnTx	11.08	NL	−.01
S&S	....	....	...
S&S Lg	11.22	NL	...
GenSec	12.69	13.36	...
Gintel Group:			
CaAp p	14.63	NL	...
Erisa p	33.64	NL	+.20
Gintel	77.83	NL	+.01
GS ST Gv	10.01	10.01	...
Gradison Funds:			
EstGr p	18.41	NL	+.05
GvIn p	12.81	13.07	+.01
OpGr p	14.98	NL	+.04
Grnspg	12.83	NL	+.03
GwWsh p	12.68	13.48	+.10
Guardian Funds:			
Bond	12.04	NL	...
ParkA	22.12	23.16	−.03
	21.76	NL	−.02
	.58	12.13	+.04

because of the sales charge. What if you decided to sell the fund on the same day you bought if for an unanticipated reason? You would receive the net asset value of $12.36 and be out $.72.

Contrast this with no-load funds. With no-load funds, you buy and sell at the same price. You can identify no-load funds by the symbol NL under the offer price column in Table 19–4. For example, the AARP group (second listed funds) are no-loads, and you will see NL (no-load) under the offer price column. Looking at the Capital Growth (CaGr) fund under the AARP group, the offering price is the same as the NAV of $28.14 because there is no commission. (Incidently, the third column in the table indicates whether the NAV changed for the day.)

Another way to determine whether a fund is load or no-load is by examining the *Forbes* annual mutual fund survey published each September. An excerpt from approximately 50 pages of data is presented in Table 19–5. Observe the maximum sales charge is shown in the second column from the right. Clearly, the term *none* indicates a no-load.

As you can see, you will get a great deal of other information from Table 19–5 as well. This can be important if you are trying to pick an appropriate no-load fund because you will have to select the fund and initiate the action on your own. Remember, there is no salesperson to call on you with a no-load fund. (But opening a no-load fund is an easy, routine process.)

Some of the information from *Forbes* in Table 19–5 will be discussed later in the chapter, but note for now that you get a rating on performance in up and down markets (left margin), average annual return data for a decade (November 1980 to June 1991), returns for the latest 12 months, yield, size of total assets, maximum sales charges, and annual expenses per $100. Although not specifically listed, most of these funds have an initial minimum investment of $500 to $1,000, but the amount may vary from fund to fund (later additional contributions may be smaller).

Assume you select a number of funds that interest you from the funds listed in *Forbes* or some other source. The next step is to contact the fund by mail or telephone (most have toll-free numbers). You can then ask any questions, and you will receive a detailed prospectus describing the fund.

The same September *Forbes* issue that provided financial information on funds in Table 19–5 also supplies information about mailing addresses and telephone numbers for all major funds. An excerpt is presented in Table 19–6. Other sources of similar mutual fund information include *Consumer Reports, Business Week, Financial World,* and *Money* magazine. For more comprehensive information to use in screening a fund, you may wish to consult the *Wiesenberger Investment Companies Service* publication (produced annually by Warren, Gorham and Lamont, Boston). This hardback, oversized book has a complete page of information on all mutual funds and can be found in most libraries. An excerpt is presented in Figure 19–1. This presents data on the T. Rowe Price

Table 19–5   *Forbes* Mutual Fund Information

STOCK FUNDS
FUND SURVEY

Performance UP markets	Performance DOWN markets	Fund/distributor	Total return — Annual average 11/80 to 6/91	Total return — Last 12 months	Yield	Assets 6/30/91 ($mil)	Assets % change 91 vs 90	Maximum sales charge	Annual expenses per $100
		Standard & Poor's 500 stock average	14.2%	7.4%	3.3%				
		Forbes stock fund composite	12.2%	6.0%	2.6%				$1.29
A+	F	Axe-Houghton Growth/USF&G	9.9%	19.1%	0.6%	$79	12%	5.75%	$1.52
		Babson Enterprise Fund/Jones & Babson	—*	3.0	1.0	113	17	none	1.22
C	D	Babson Growth Fund/Jones & Babson	10.4	3.0	2.2	236	–9	none	0.86
		Babson Value Fund/Jones & Babson	—*	6.9	3.7	27	9	none	1.04
		Baird Blue Chip Fund/Baird	—*	7.8	1.6	44	30	5.75	1.55
D	B	Baker, Fentress & Co/closed-end	9.9	–6.3	3.3	394	–12	NA	0.68
		Baron Asset Fund/Baron	—*	–2.0	1.4	46	–16	2.00b	1.80p
■D	■A	Bartlett Capital-Basic Value/Bartlett	—*	0.3	3.7	93	–15	none	1.21
A	D	Berger One Hundred/Berger	12.2	17.7	none	37	100	none	2.62p
A	A	Bergstrom Capital/closed-end	19.2	29.2	2.2	89	22	NA	0.99
C	C	Wm Blair–Growth/Wm Blair	11.6	5.9	1.6	72	2	none	0.90
		Blue Chip Value Fund/closed-end	—*	8.7	9.7	71	–2	NA	1.45
C	C	Boston Co Capital Appreciation/Boston Co	12.0	–3.4	1.9	478	–21	none	1.18
		Boston Co Special Growth Fund/Boston Co	—*	9.6	0.2	36	–16	none	1.77
		Brandywine Fund/Brandywine	—*	1.3	1.6	445	55	none	1.12
D	D	Bull & Bear Capital Growth/Bull & Bear	4.3	–26.0	none	44	–38	none	2.40
D	A	Burnham Fund/Burnham	12.2	4.7	5.4	122	–9	5.00	1.10
		Calvert-Ariel Appreciation Fund/Calvert	—*	9.0	1.0	48	187	4.75	0.70p

Forbes Mutual Fund Information (concluded)

		Calvert-Ariel Growth Fund/Calvert	—*	0.5	1.0	248	0	†	*1.31*
		Calvert Social Inv–Equity/Calvert	—*	5.1	0.6	37	68	4.75	*1.00p*
		Capital Income Builder/American Funds	—*	14.9	5.1	416	87	5.75	*1.01*
C	B	Cardinal Fund/Cardinal	14.1	8.1	3.4	212	7	8.50	0.69
		Carnegie-Cappiello–Growth/Carnegie	—*	3.6	1.1	78	0	4.50	*1.78*
		Carnegie-Cappiello–Total Return/Carnegie	—*	-0.6	5.6	64	-21	4.50	*1.58*
C	D	Central Securities/closed-end	8.7	6.0	1.7	123	0	NA	0.98
B	A	Century Shares Trust/Century Shares	16.3	9.2	2.6	147	3	none	1.03
A+	B	CGM Capital Development/TNE	20.5	22.4	0.4	238	14	†	0.94
C	C	Cigna Growth Fund/Cigna	11.1	0.6	1.4	166	-11	5.00	*1.19*
		Cigna Utilities Fund/Cigna	—*	3.6	5.6	73	10	5.00	*1.27*
		Cigna Value Fund/Cigna	—*	2.8	1.6	110	21	5.00	*1.24*
		Clipper Fund/Pacific Finl	—*	6.0	2.6	137	-9	none	1.18
B	D	Colonial Growth Shares Trust/Colonial	12.0	2.4	1.8	129	-3	5.75	*1.03*
		Colonial Small Stock Index Trust/Colonial	—*	-14.3	0.4	29	-33	5.75	*1.69*
		Colonial US Equity Index Trust/Colonial	—*	6.1	1.8	42	11	5.75	*1.62*
		Colonial VIP Equity–Diversified Ret/Colonial	—*	0.5	3.9	31	16	5.00b	*2.25p*
A	C	Columbia Growth Fund/Columbia	14.3	5.8	1.9	380	15	none	0.88
		Columbia Special Fund/Columbia	—*	0.5	0.1	202	42	none	*1.21*

■ Fund rated for two periods only: maximum allowable grade A.   * Fund not in operation for full period.   † Closed to new investors.   § Distributor may impose redemption fee, which proceeds revert to the fund.   *Expense ratio is in italics if the fund has a shareholder-paid 12b-1 plan exceeding 0.1% (hidden load) pending or in force.*   b: Includes back-end load that reverts to distributor.   p: Net of absorption of expenses by fund sponsor.   NA: Not applicable or not available.   †Formerly Growth Industry Shares.

Table 19–6 Addresses of Mutual Funds (Fund Distributors)

Fund	Type
Alliance Global–Small Cap Fund	ST
Alliance Growth & Income	ST
Alliance International Fund	FS
Alliance Mortgage Securities Income	BD
Alliance Muni Income–California	MU
Alliance Muni Income–Ins Natl	MU
Alliance Muni Income–National	MU
Alliance Muni Income–New York	MU
Alliance New Europe Fund	FS
Alliance Quasar Fund	ST
Alliance Short-Term Multi-Market	GB
Alliance Technology Fund	ST
AMA Investment Advisers PO Box 1111 Blue Bell, PA 19422 (800) 523-0864	
AMA Family of Funds–Classic Growth	ST
AMA Family of Funds–Global Growth	GS
American Capital Marketing 2800 Post Oak Boulevard Houston, TX 77056 (800) 421-5666	
American Capital Comstock Fund	ST
American Capital Corp Bond Fund	BD
American Capital Emerging Growth	ST
American Capital Enterprise Fund	ST
American Capital Equity Income	BA
American Capital Government Secs	BD
American Capital Growth & Income	ST
American Capital Harbor Fund	BA
American Capital High Yield Inv	JU
American Capital Muni Bond Fund	MU
American Capital Pace Fund	ST
American Capital Tax-Ex–High Yld	MU
American Funds Group 333 South Hope Street Los Angeles, CA 90071 (714) 671-7000* (local); (800) 421-0180	
Amcap Fund	ST
American Balanced Fund	BA
American High-Income Trust	JU
American Mutual Fund	ST
Bond Fund of America	BD
Capital Income Builder	ST
Capital World Bond Fund	GB
EuroPacific Growth Fund	FS
Fundamental Investors	ST
Growth Fund of America	ST
Income Fund of America	BA
Intermediate Bond Fund of America	BD
Investment Co of America	ST
New Economy Fund	ST
New Perspective Fund	GS
Smallcap World Fund	GS
Tax-Exempt Bond Fund of America	MU
Tax-Exempt Fund of California	MU
US Government Securities	BD
Washington Mutual Investors	ST
American Growth Fund Sponsors 410 17th Street Suite 800 Denver, CO 80202 (303) 623-6137* (local); (800) 525-2406	
American Growth Fund	ST
American Investors PO Box 2500 Greenwich, CT 06836 (800) 243-5353	
American Investors Growth Fund	ST
American Pension Distributors PO Box 2529 Lynchburg, VA 24501 (800) 544-6060	
API Trust–Growth	ST
AMEV Investors 500 Bielenberg Drive Woodbury, MN 55125 (612) 738-4000* (local); (800) 800-2638	
AMEV Advantage–Asset Allocation	BA
AMEV Capital Fund	ST
AMEV Fiduciary Fund	ST
AMEV Growth Fund	ST
AMEV US Govt Securities Fund	BD
Amway Management Co 7575 East Fulton Road Ada, MI 49355 (800) 346-2670	
Amway Mutual Fund	ST
Analytic Optioned Equity Fund 2222 Martin Street Suite 230 Irvine, CA 92715 (714) 833-0294*	
Analytic Optioned Equity Fund	ST
Angeles Securities 10301 West Pico Boulevard Los Angeles, CA 90064 (213) 277-4900* (local); (800) 421-4374	
FPA Capital Fund	ST
FPA Paramount Fund	ST
FPA Perennial Fund	ST
Aquila Distributors 380 Madison Avenue Suite 2300 New York, NY 10017 (800) 228-4227	
Hawaiian Tax-Free Trust	MU
Tax-Free Fund of Colorado	MU
Tax-Free Trust of Arizona	MU
Tax-Free Trust of Oregon	MU
Associated Planners Security 1925 Century Park East Suite 1900 Los Angeles, CA 90067 (213) 553-6740 (local); (800) 950-2748	
Associated Planners Stock Fund	ST
Bailard, Biehl & Kaiser 2755 Campus Drive Suite 300 San Mateo, CA 94403 (800) 882-8383	
Bailard Biehl & Kaiser Diversa Fund	GS
Robert W Baird & Co 777 East Wisconsin Avenue Milwaukee, WI 53202 (800) 792-2473	
Baird Blue Chip Fund	ST
Baron Asset Fund 450 Park Avenue Suite 2802 New York, NY 10022 (800) 992-2766	
Baron Asset Fund	ST
Bartlett Capital Trust 36 East Fourth Street Cincinnati, OH 45202 (513) 621-4612 (local); (800) 800-4612	
Bartlett Capital Trust–Basic Value	ST
Bartlett Capital Trust–Fixed Income	BD
Baxter Financial 1200 North Federal Highway Suite 424 Boca Raton, FL 33432 (800) 749-9933	
Philadelphia Fund	ST
Benham Capital Management 1665 Charleston Road Mountain View, CA 94043 (800) 472-3389	

Fund	Symbol
Balanced	BA
Foreign Stock	FS
Global Bond	GB
Global Stock	GS
Junk Bond	JU
Money Market	MM
Municipal Bond	MU
Stock	ST
Taxable Bond	BD

*Will accept collect calls.

Source: Reprinted by permission of *Forbes,* September 2, 1991, p. 295.

Figure 19–1   Wiesenberger Investment Companies Service Reports

T. ROWE PRICE NEW ERA FUND, INC.

The investment objective of the fund is long-term growth of capital. It may seek this in any industry, but its current portfolio consists largely of securities of companies in the energy sources area, precious metals and other metals and minerals, other basic commodities, and companies which own or develop land. Investments in companies which provide consumer products and services are included, as well as companies operating in technological areas, such as the manufacture of labor-saving machinery and instruments.

At the 1989 year-end, the fund had 89.2% of its assets in common stocks with major commitments in integrated oils (21.3%); diversified resources (12.9%); precious metals (11.7%); chemicals (7.7%), and diversified metals (6.2%). The largest individual stock commitments were Mobil (4.9%); Cyprus Minerals (4.3%); Dow Chemical (3.4%), and Amoco and Newmont Mining (3.2% each). Portfolio turnover during the year was 18.6% of average assets. Unrealized appreciation at the year-end was 30.5% of total net assets.

Statistical History

						% of Assets in							
Year	Total Net Assets ($)	Number of Share-holders	Net Asset Value Per Share ($)	Yield (%)	Cash & Gov't	Bonds & Pre-ferreds	Com-mon Stocks	Income Div-idends ($)	Capital Gains Distribu-tion ($)	Expense Ratio (%)	Offering Price ($) High	Low
1989	826.582.185	55.405	21.73	2.5	11	—	89	0.56	1.05†	0.83	23.46	18.67
1988	726,475,776	61,822	18.79	2.7	8	1	91	0.53	0.61	0.89	20.60	17.37
1987	756,549,196	66,516	18.08	4.9	15	—	85	0.98	1.77	0.82	25.17	17.10
1986	496,242,331	39,248	17.76	2.4	15	—	85	0.50	3.25	0.73	20.84	17.45
1985	529,469,479	42,102	18.67	3.4	8	—	92	0.68	1.41†	0.69	18.87	15.67
1984	471,995,371	45,828	17.13	3.3	10	—	90	0.61	1.29†	0.68	18.94	15.14
1983	485,072,775	47,214	18.44	4.4	12	6	82	0.81	0.072	0.68	18.60	14.97
1982	411,506,259	46,422	15.53	4.6	11	—	89	0.863	3.045	0.71	19.35	11.38
1981	436,197,041	44,712	19.34	3.4	20	—	80	0.672	1.489	0.64	25.53	17.87
1980	571,568,790	41,463	25.27	1.9	10	1	89	0.47	0.362	0.63	27.23	14.58
1979	330,817,793	30,172	17.45	2.3	15	—	85	0.38	0.388	0.67	17.45	11.15

† Includes short-term capital gains of $0.45 in 1984; $0.67 in 1985; $0.26 in 1989.

An assumed investment of $10,000 in this fund, with capital gains accepted in shares and income dividends reinvested, is illustrated below. The explanation in the introduction to this section must be read in conjunction with this illustration.

T. ROWE PRICE NEW ERA FUND, INC

Cost of Investment January 1, 1980 $10,000

(Initial Net Asset Value $10,000)

December 29, 1989

*Includes Value of Shares Accepted as Capital Gains $18,370; Reinvested Income Dividends $8,505.

$39,328 Total Value of Investment

$12,453 Value of Original Shares

	1980	1981	1982	1983	1984	1985	1986	1987	1988	1989			
Value of Shares Initially Acquired Through Investment of $10,000	$14,481	$11,083	$8,900	$10,567	$9,817	$10,699	$10,178	$10,361	$10,768	$12,453			
Value of Shares Resulting From Reinvestment of Capital Gains and Income Dividends (Cumulative)	721	1,713	4,213	5,885	7,186	10,285	14,162	18,321	20,874	26,875*			
Total Return	15,202	12,796	13,113	16,452	17,003	20,984	24,340	28,682	31,642	39,328			

Dollar amounts of distributions reinvested:

	Capital Gains	Income Dividends
1980	$ 207	$ 269
1981	896	405
1982	2,014	571
1983	61	684
1984	1,151	544
1985	1,400	675
1986	3,858	562
1987	2,506	1,383
1988	968	841
1989	1,768	943
Total	$14,829	$6,877

Results Taking Capital Gains in SHARES and Income Dividends in CASH

Initial Investment At Offering Price, January 1, 1980	$10,000
Value as of 12.29.89 of Shares Initially Acquired	$12,453
Value of Shares Accepted as Capital Gains Distributions	$15,094 ₤
Total Value as of December 29, 1989	$27,547
Total Dividends PAID From Investment Income	$ 5,650

₤ Dollar Amount of these distributions at the time shares were acquired: $12,100

Results Taking All Dividends and Distributions in CASH

Initial Investment At Offering Price, January 1, 1980	$10,000
Total Value as of December 29, 1989	$12,453
Distributions From Capital Gains	$ 8,222
Dividends From Investment Income	$ 3,825

New Era Fund, Inc. Finally, you may wish to contact the Investment Company Institute to get its annual directory of mutual funds.[2]

DIFFERING OBJECTIVES AND THE DIVERSITY OF MUTUAL FUNDS

Recognizing that different investors have different objectives and sensitivities to risk, the mutual fund industry offers a large group of funds from which to choose. In 1992, there were over 3,000 mutual funds, each unique in terms of stated objectives, investment policies, and current portfolio. To make some sense out of this much variety, funds can be classified in terms of their stated objectives.

Money Market Funds   Money market funds have been the phenomenon of the last two decades. (*Forbes* Mutual Fund Survey lists 200.) Money market mutual funds invest in short-term securities, such as U.S. Treasury bills and Eurodollar deposits, commercial paper, jumbo bank certificates of deposit (CDs), and repurchase agreements.

Money market funds are no-load, and most require minimum deposits of $500 to $1,000. Most have check-writing privileges, but usually the checks must be written for at least $250 to $500.

Because the maturities of assets held in money market portfolios generally range from 20 to 50 days, the yields of these funds closely track short-term market interest rates. Money market funds give small investors an opportunity to invest in securities that were once out of reach.

Growth Funds   The pursuit of capital appreciation is the emphasis here. This class of funds includes those called aggressive growth funds and those concentrating on more stable and predictable growth. Both types invest primarily in common stock. Aggressive funds concentrate on speculative issues, emerging small companies, and "hot" sectors of the economy and frequently use financial leverage to magnify returns. Regular growth funds generally invest in common stocks of more stable firms. They are less inclined to stay fully invested in stocks during periods of market decline, seldom use aggressive techniques like leverage, and tend to be long-term in orientation.

The best way to determine the type of growth fund is to carefully examine the fund's prospectus and current portfolio.

Growth with Income   A number of large, growing firms pay steady dividends. Their stocks are attractive to investors interested in capital growth potential with a base of dividend or interest income. Funds that invest in such

---

[2]The price is approximately $5. The address is the Investment Company Institute, P.O. Box 66140, Washington, D.C. 20035-6140. The phone number is (202) 293-7700.

stocks are less volatile and risky than growth funds investing in small companies paying low or no dividends.

Balanced Funds These funds combine investments in common stock and bonds and often preferred stock. They try to provide income plus some capital appreciation. Funds that invest in convertible securities are also considered balanced, since the convertible security is a hybrid fixed-income security with the opportunity for appreciation if the underlying common stock rises.

Bond Funds Income-oriented investors have always been attracted to bonds. Because bonds represent a contractual obligation on the part of the issuer to the bondholder, they normally offer a certain return. But as pointed out in Chapter 12, rising interest rates can undercut the market value of all classes of fixed-income securities. During the 1970s and early 1980s, a time of intense interest-rate fluctuations, many bondholders watched the principal value of even their "safe" government bonds drop to 75 percent of face value. Bonds held in mutual funds were affected by the same market forces. Returns from bonds are historically lower than those from stocks, and bond funds are no exception.

Bond mutual funds can be roughly subdivided into corporate, government, and municipal funds.

Some corporate bond funds are particularly targeted to low-rated, high-yielding bonds. These funds are termed *junk bond funds*. They may have a yield 4 or 5 percent over the typical corporate bond fund but also possess greater risk in terms of potential default by the securities in the bond portfolio. Just how much greater that risk is was discovered in the fall of 1989 when a number of low-rated bonds in these funds defaulted on their interest payments and prices for all junk bonds fell.

Because municipal bond funds buy only tax-exempt securities, interest income to shareholders is free of federal tax. Special tax-exempt funds also have been established for the benefit of investors in states with high state and local income taxes. For example, fund managers of New York municipal bond funds establish portfolios of tax-exempt securities issued within the boundaries of that state. Under current tax law, interest income from these funds is exempt from federal, state, and local taxes for New York residents—a very appealing feature to high-bracket taxpayers.

Sector Funds Special funds have been created to invest in specific sectors of the economy. Sector funds exist for such areas as energy, medical technology, computer technology, leisure, and defense.

Because stock performance of companies within a particular industry, or sector, tend to be positively correlated, these funds offer investors less diversification and higher loss/reward potential.

Investors should be cautious of the initial offering of new sector funds. An initial offering usually occurs after the sector has already been the subject of

intense interest based on recent spectacular performance. As a result, stocks in that sector are often fully priced or overpriced.

Foreign Funds As noted in Chapter 18, investors seeking participation in foreign markets and foreign securities confront a number of obstacles, but the rewards can be remarkable. The mutual fund industry has made overseas investing convenient by establishing funds whose policies mandate investing on a global basis (Templeton World Fund), within the markets of a particular locale (Canadian Fund, Inc.), or within a region (Merrill Lynch Pacific). One fund even specializes in Third World countries.

Foreign funds as a group outperformed all other kinds of mutual funds in the last decade. A listing of some important international funds is presented in Table 19–7.

Specialty Funds Some mutual funds have specialized approaches that do not fit neatly into any of the preceding categories. Their names are often indicative of their investment objectives or policies: the Sunbelt Fund, the Phoenix Fund (rising from the ashes?), the Calvert Social Investment Fund, and United Services Gold Shares, to name just a few.

There is even a "fund of funds" (FundTrust) that manages a portfolio of different mutual fund shares.

Owing to some fund managers' poor record in attempting to outperform the market, a number of funds have taken up the maxim that "if you can't beat 'em, join 'em!" Calling themselves index funds, these mutual funds establish portfolios that replicate some major market index, such as the S&P 500. Fund performance is almost exactly correlated with performance of "the market."

Matching Investment Objectives with Fund Types

Investors must consider how much volatility of return they can tolerate. Investors who require safety of principal with very little deviation of returns should choose money market funds first and bond funds second. They should also expect to receive lower returns based on historical evidence. While aggressive growth stock funds provide the highest return, they also have the biggest risk.

Liquidity objectives are met by all mutual funds since redemption can occur any time. If investors need income, bond funds provide the highest annual current yield, while aggressive growth funds provide the least. Growth-income and balanced funds are most appropriate for investors who want growth of principal with moderate current income.

Many investors diversify by fund type. For example, at one stage in the business cycle, an investor may want to have 50 percent of assets in common stocks, 35 percent in bonds, 10 percent in money market funds, and 5 percent in an international stock fund. These percentages could change as market conditions change. If interest rates are expected to decline, it would be better to have

Table 19-7   Internationally Oriented Funds

Name of Fund	Open- or Closed-End	Load (L) No-Load (NL)	Where Invested
Canadian Fund, Inc.	Open	L	Canada
International Investors Incorporated	Open	L	Gold mines
G. T. Pacific Fund, Inc.	Open	NL	Asia (Japan, Hong Kong, etc.)
Fidelity Overseas Fund	Open	L	Worldwide
Kemper International Fund, Inc.	Open	L	Worldwide
Merrill Lynch Pacific	Open	L	Far East
Merrill Lynch International Holdings	Open	L	Worldwide
Putnam International Equities Fund	Open	L	Worldwide
Research Capital Fund, Inc.	Open	L	Foreign mining
T. Rowe Price International Fund, Inc.	Open	NL	Worldwide
Scudder International Fund, Inc.	Open	NL	Worldwide
Strategic Investments Fund, Inc.	Open	L	South African gold mines
Templeton World Fund, Inc.	Open	L	Worldwide
Transatlantic Fund, Inc.	Open	NL	Worldwide
United International Growth Fund	Open	L	Worldwide
ASA Limited	Closed	Commission	South African gold mines
Mexican Fund	Closed	Commission	Mexico
U.S. and Foreign Securities	Closed	Commission	Worldwide

a higher percentage of bonds and fewer money market securities. Investing with a "family of funds" allows the investor a choice of many different types of funds and the privilege of switching between funds at no or low cost. Some of the larger families of funds are managed by American Capital, Dreyfus Group, Federated Funds, Fidelity Investments, T. Rowe Price Funds, and the Vanguard Group. In addition, most major retail brokerage firms, such as Merrill Lynch, Dean Witter, Prudential, and Shearson Lehman have families of mutual funds.

Each mutual fund has a unique history and management team. There is no guarantee that past performance will be repeated. Investors should check on a fund's longevity of management, historical returns, trading history, and management expenses. A very key instrument in providing information in this regard is the fund prospectus.

■ THE PROSPECTUS

The Investment Companies Act of 1940, which established the standard of practice for all investment companies, requires that the purchaser of fund shares be provided with a current prospectus. The **prospectus** contains information deemed essential by the SEC in providing "full disclosure" to potential investors regarding the fund's investment objectives and policies, risks, management, expenses, and current portfolio. The prospectus also provides information on how shares can be purchased and redeemed, sales and redemption charges (if any), and shareholders' services. Other fund documents are available to the public on request including the Statement of Additional Information and the fund's annual and quarterly reports.

While it is beyond the scope of this chapter to provide a complete discourse on interpreting a prospectus, investors need to understand the following essentials.

Investment Objectives and Policies   This section is always found in the beginning of the prospectus. It usually describes the fund's basic objectives such as:

> The Fund will invest only in securities backed by the full faith and credit of the U.S. Government. At least 70% of the Fund's assets will be invested in certificates issued by the Government National Mortgage Association (GNMA). It may also purchase other securities issued by the U.S. Government, its agencies, or instrumentalities as long as these securities are backed by the full faith and credit of the U.S. Government.

The prospectus normally goes on to detail investment management policies under which it intends to operate—typically with regard to the use of borrowed money, lending of securities, or something like the following:

> The Fund may, under certain circumstances, sell covered call options against securities it is holding for the purpose of generating additional income.

Portfolio (or "Investment Holdings")   This section lists the securities held by the fund as of the date indicated. Since investment companies are only required to publish their prospectuses every 16 months, the information is probably dated. Still, the portfolio should be compared to the stated objectives of the fund to see if they are consistent.

Management Fees and Expenses   Besides sales and redemption charges, the prospectus also provides information and figures on fund managers' reimbursement and the fund's housekeeping expenses. Annual fees for the investment advisor are expressed as a percentage of the average daily net assets during the year (usually 0.50 percent). Other expenses include legal and auditing fees, the cost of preparing and distributing annual reports and proxy statements, directors' fees, and transaction expenses. When lumped together

with investment advisory fees, a fund's total yearly expenses typically range from 1 to 1.5 percent of fund assets. Experienced mutual fund investors cast a jaundiced eye on funds with expense ratios that exceed this figure.

A controversial SEC ruling—Rule 12b-1—allows mutual funds to use fund assets for marketing expenses. Since marketing expenses have nothing to do with advancing shareholders' interests and everything to do with increasing the managers' fees, investors should be alert to this in the prospectus.

Turnover Rate A number of mutual funds trade aggressively in pursuit of profits; others do just the opposite. In one year, the Fidelity Contrafund had a 243 percent turnover rate; the rate for the Oppenheimer Special Fund was 9 percent.

In reality, transaction costs amount to more than just commissions, and they are not always accounted for in the expense ratio. When fund assets are traded over-the-counter, the dealer's spread between the bid and asked price is not considered. Nor is the fact that large block trades—the kind mutual funds usually deal in—are made at less favorable prices than are smaller volume transactions.

The prospectus also contains audited data on the turnover rate, the expense ratio, and other important data in the section on per-share income and capital changes.

■ DISTRIBUTION AND TAXATION

The selling of securities by a mutual fund's portfolio results in capital losses or gains for the fund. After netting losses against gains, most mutual funds distribute capital gains to shareholders annually.

Funds with securities that pay dividends or interest also have a source of investment income. The fund, in turn, distributes such income to shareholders either quarterly or annually.

A fund that distributes at least 90 percent of its net investment income and capital gains is not subject, as an entity, to federal income tax. It is simply acting as a "conduit" in channeling taxable sources of income from securities held in the portfolio to the fund's shareholders. Most funds operate this way. But while the mutual fund may not be subject to taxation, its shareholders are.

At the end of every calendar year, each fund shareholder receives a Form 1099-DIV. This document notifies the shareholder of the amount and tax status of his or her distributions.

When the investor actually sells (redeems) shares in a mutual fund, another form of taxable event occurs. It is precisely the same as if stocks or bonds or other securities were sold. The investor must consider the cost basis, the selling price, and any gain or loss and appropriately report the tax consequences on his or her tax form.

■ SHAREHOLDER SERVICES

Most mutual funds offer a number of services to their shareholders. Some can be used in the investor's strategy. Common services include:

Automatic reinvestment. The fund reinvests all distributions (usually without sales charge). Shares and fractional shares are purchased at the net asset value. Purchases are noted on annual and periodic account statements.

Safekeeping. While shareholders are entitled to receive certificates for all whole shares, it is often convenient to let the fund's transfer agent hold the shares.

Exchange privilege. Many large management companies sponsor a family of funds. They may have five or more funds, each dedicated to a different investment objective. Within certain limits, shareholders are free to move their money between the different funds in the family on a net asset value basis. Transfers can often be done by telephone; a minimal charge is common to cover paperwork. These exchanges are taxable events.

Pre-authorized check plan. Many people lack the discipline to save or invest regularly. Those who recognize this trait in themselves can authorize a management company to charge their bank account for predetermined amounts on a regular basis. The amounts withdrawn are used to purchase new shares.

Systematic withdrawal plan. Every shareholder plans to convert shares into cash at some time. The investor who wants to receive a regular amount of cash each month or quarter can do so by arranging for such a plan. The fund sells enough shares on a periodic basis to meet the shareholder's cash requirement.

Checking privileges. Most money market mutual funds furnish shareholders with checks that can be drawn against the account, provided that the account balance is above a minimum amount (usually $1,000). A per-check minimum of $250 to $500 is common.

■ INVESTMENT FUNDS, LONG-TERM PLANNING, AND DOLLAR-COST AVERAGING

Perhaps more than anything else, the liquidity and conveniences inherent in mutual funds lend themselves best to financial-planning activities. The most important of these is the gradual accumulation of capital assets.

Using the pre-authorized check plan, investors can have fixed amounts regularly withdrawn from their checking accounts to purchase fund shares. Just as savers can have their banks channel a specific amount from their paychecks into savings accounts, so too can investors make regular, lump-sum

Table 19–8 Dollar-Cost Averaging

(1) Month	(2) Investment	(3) Share Price	(4) Shares Purchased
January	$ 200	$12	16.66
February	200	14	14.28
March	200	16	12.50
April	200	19	10.52
May	200	15	13.33
June	200	12	16.66
Totals	$1,200	$88	83.95

fund share purchases on an "out of sight, out of mind" basis. Reinvestment of distributions enhances this strategy.

What distinguishes the mutual fund from the bank savings strategy is the fact that fund shares are purchased at different prices. The investor can even use a passive strategy known as dollar-cost averaging. Under **dollar-cost averaging,** the investor buys a fixed dollar's worth of a given security at regular intervals regardless of the security's price or the current market outlook. By using such a strategy, investors concede they cannot outsmart the market. The intent of dollar-cost averaging is to avoid the common practice of buying high and selling low. In fact, investors are forced to do the opposite. Why? They commit a fixed-dollar amount each month (or year) and buy shares at the current market price. When the price is high, they are buying relatively fewer shares; when the price is low, they are accumulating more shares. An example is presented in Table 19–8. Suppose we use the preauthorized check plan to channel $200 per month into a mutual fund. The price ranges from a low of $12 to a high of $19.

Note that when the share price is relatively low, such as in January, we purchased a larger number of shares than when the share prices were high, as in April. In this case, the share price ended in June at the same price it was in January ($12).

What would happen if the price merely ended up at the average price over the six-month period? The values in column 3 total $88, so the average price over six months is $14.67 ($88/6). Actually, we would still make money under this assumption because the average *cost* is less than this amount. Consider that we invested $1,200 and purchased 83.95 shares. This translates to an average cost of only $14.29.

$$\frac{\text{Investment}}{\text{Shares purchased}} = \frac{\$1,200}{83.95} = \$14.29$$

Some Funds Don't Like Quick-Change Artists

A few mutual funds are starting to discourage the troublesome clients that most people in the industry regard as Fund Enemy No. 1.

These pesky customers are the market timers—money managers who dash in and out of mutual funds with the aim of catching broad market swings.

The chief complaint about timers is that their frenzied switching forces funds to buy and sell huge blocks of securities, penalizing other, often smaller, shareholders. Many fund groups have accelerated their anti-timer campaigns in recent months by imposing limits and fees on switches.

Timers are drawn most often to no-load fund groups—which don't levy an upfront sales charge—because they offer the fastest and cheapest way to switch in and out of stocks.

Fund operators over the years have abruptly kicked out a number of timers who have failed to heed pleas to curb switching. Fidelity Investments of Boston has responded with a series of ever-tighter restrictions on switches. They now are limited to four a year for most funds and five a month for its select funds, which usually invest in one industry and are intended to handle much faster turnover.

The timers' strategy continues to pose a basic dilemma. Says the president of one investment management firm: "If we trade too often, we get kicked out by the funds. And if we don't perform, we get kicked out by our clients."

Source: *The Wall Street Journal*, November 22, 1988, p. C1. Reprinted by permission of *THE WALL STREET JOURNAL*, © 1988 by Dow Jones & Company, Inc. All Rights Reserved Worldwide.

The average cost ($14.29) is less than the average price ($14.67) because we bought relatively more shares at the lower price levels, and they weighed more heavily in our calculations. Thus, under dollar-cost averaging, investors can come out ahead over a period of investing fixed amounts, even if the share price ends up less than the average price paid on each transaction.[3]

The only time investors lose money is if the eventual price falls below the average cost ($14.29) and they sell at that point. While dollar-cost averaging has its advantages, it is not without criticism. Clearly, if the share price continues to go down over a long period, it is hard to make a case for continued purchases. However, the long-term performances of most diversified mutual funds has been positive, and long-term investors may find this strategy useful in accumulating capital assets for retirement, children's education funds, or other purposes.

■ EVALUATING FUND PERFORMANCE

Throughout this chapter, we referred to mutual fund performance. We will now consider the issue more directly by actually comparing mutual fund

---

[3]This does not consider any sales charges or commissions, which could be important.

performance to the market in general. This topic will also be considered more fully in Chapter 22.

A good place to start the current discussion is to return to Table 19–5, on page 626, which covers *Forbes* mutual fund information. Direct your attention to total returns in the middle two columns of the table. The first column shows the average annual total return over an 11-year period (1980–1991).[4] This total return figure is composed of capital appreciation plus dividend income. Notice toward the top of the table that the Standard & Poor's 500 Stock Average (a measure of the total market) had an average annual return of 14.2 percent, while the Forbes Stock Fund Composite (a measure of mutual funds) had a value of 12.2 percent.

The next column shows return data for the most recently reported 12 months. The Standard & Poor's 500 Stock Average was up 7.4 percent, while the Forbes Stock Fund Composite showed a gain of 6.0 percent. Over the time periods shown in Table 19–5, the Standard & Poor's 500 Stock Average outperformed the Forbes Stock Fund Composite. However, this is not always the case. If we were to look at other time periods (such as 1978–1988), the Forbes Stock Fund Composite outperformed the Standard & Poor's 500 Stock Average. In some periods, mutual funds as a group beat the popular market averages; while in other periods they do not.

You can also identify the performance of individual funds in Table 19–5. An example of a strong performer is *CGM Capital Development/CNE* (middle of page 627) and an obvious underperformer is *Bull and Bear Capital Growth/Bull & Bear* (toward the bottom of page 626).

Notice that grades are assigned to fund performance in the first two columns on the far left side of Table 19–5. The grades are based on how the funds performed in up and down markets over the last 10 years. The grades theoretically range from A+ to F. Most investors like funds that do reasonably well in both types of markets. Of course, if you feel strongly that the market is about to move in one direction rather than another, you will adjust your emphasis accordingly.

One warning: Past performance in no way guarantees future performance. A fund that did well in the past may do poorly in the future and vice versa.[5] Nevertheless, all things being equal, investors generally prefer funds that have a prior record of good performance. Investors do not know whether the funds can reproduce the performance, but at least the funds have indicated the capacity for good returns in the past. The same cannot be said for underperformers.

Lipper Mutual Fund Performance Averages

As you can see in Table 19–9, mutual fund performance can also be broken down by type of fund (this information was previously presented in Chapter

---

[4]The period covers November 1980 to June 1991.

[5]The factor is covered more fully in Chapter 22.

Table 19–9   Lipper Mutual Fund Performance Average

Weekly Summary Report
May 9, 1991

General Equity Funds NAV Mil. $	No. Funds	Dividends Reinvested Cumulative Performances	10/11/90- 05/09/91	07/12/90- 05/09/91	05/10/90- 05/09/91	12/31/90- 05/09/91	05/02/91- 05/09/91
20,341.4	145	Capital Appreciation	+ 34.27%	+ 5.17%	+ 13.06%	+ 20.77%	+ 0.91%
83,972.1	271	Growth Funds	+ 34.93%	+ 5.98%	+ 14.73%	+ 20.34%	+ 0.91%
13,031.6	91	Small Company Growth	+ 47.66%	+ 6.83%	+ 16.13%	+ 28.47%	+ 1.16%
87,037.6	216	Growth and Income	+ 29.32%	+ 7.01%	+ 13.46%	+ 16.78%	+ 0.76%
24,577.9	74	Equity Income	+ 24.33%	+ 6.97%	+ 10.85%	+ 13.96%	+ 0.58%
228,960.6	797	Gen. Equity Funds Avg.	+ 33.79%	+ 6.29%	+ 13.89%	+ 19.79%	+ 0.87%
Other Equity Funds							
2,814.8	9	Health/Biotechnology	+ 57.58%	+ 32.60%	+ 54.99%	+ 32.68%	+ 1.39%
1,986.4	20	Natural Resources	+ 5.74%	− 2.45%	+ 1.63%	+ 7.59%	+ 0.87%
293.5	7	Environmental	+ 29.54%	− 6.90%	+ 4.58%	+ 15.69%	− 0.45%
2,040.9	21	Science & Technol.	+ 53.46%	+ 6.45%	+ 16.61%	+ 26.95%	+ 1.85%
1,603.3	32	Specialty/Misc.	+ 33.83%	+ 2.55%	+ 7.68%	+ 19.61%	+ 0.72%
7,356.7	23	Utility Funds	+ 15.06%	+ 9.31%	+ 11.40%	+ 6.06%	− 0.13%
309.0	9	Financial Services	+ 53.83%	+ 14.78%	+ 19.21%	+ 31.96%	+ 0.39%
152.4	5	Real Estate	+ 32.08%	+ 6.13%	+ 9.52%	+ 25.70%	+ 0.09%
1,782.0	9	Option Income	+ 25.02%	+ 5.91%	+ 9.93%	+ 12.57%	+ 0.74%
14,990.7	51	Global Funds	+ 15.62%	− 3.91%	+ 3.45%	+ 12.50%	+ 0.25%
10,553.9	64	International Funds	+ 7.77%	− 8.45%	− 1.66%	+ 8.92%	− 0.14%
3,916.6	22	European Region Fds	+ 0.45%	− 13.30%	− 8.72%	+ 1.54%	− 0.59%
1,561.9	17	Pacific Region Funds	+ 12.44%	− 5.88%	+ 5.48%	+ 15.71%	− 0.20%
2,954.1	37	Gold Oriented Funds	− 8.93%	− 14.17%	− 18.63%	− 7.49%	+ 0.16%
280,983.3	1116	All Equity Funds Avg.	+ 29.10%	+ 3.93%	+ 11.02%	+ 17.36%	+ 0.70%
Other Funds							
4,357.2	50	Flexible Portfolio	+ 21.15%	+ 6.73%	+ 11.88%	+ 11.69%	+ 0.37%
1,454.2	13	Global Flex Port.	+ 12.07%	+ 1.87%	+ 6.54%	+ 7.64%	+ 0.08%
14,977.8	60	Balanced Funds	+ 21.40%	+ 8.28%	+ 13.58%	+ 11.80%	+ 0.47%
2,247.9	32	Conv. Securities	+ 22.53%	+ 3.97%	+ 9.10%	+ 15.91%	+ 0.44%
4,194.5	13	Mixed Income Funds	+ 17.78%	+ 8.99%	+ 12.75%	+ 10.76%	+ 0.17%
4,194.5	13	Income Funds	+ 17.78%	+ 8.99%	+ 12.75%	+ 10.76%	+ 0.17%
16,905.8	66	World Income Funds	+ 2.05%	+ 8.37%	+ 12.98%	+ 0.72%	− 0.02%
163,887.9	555	Fixed Income Funds	+ 10.24%	+ 8.32%	+ 11.87%	+ 6.10%	− 0.17%
489,884.0	1918	Total Long-Term Funds					
		Long-Term Average	+ 22.06%	+ 5.55%	+ 11.37%	+ 13.08%	+ 0.39%
		Long-Term Median	+ 20.00%	+ 7.60%	+ 12.40%	+ 12.70%	+ 0.30%
		Funds with % Change					
Lipper Indexes							
553.96	30	Growth Fund Index	+ 35.21%	+ 6.61%	+ 15.85%	+ 20.00%	+ 0.82%
835.76	30	Growth & Income Index	+ 28.60%	+ 7.07%	+ 12.78%	+ 16.66%	+ 0.73%
533.84	30	Equity Income Index	+ 23.78%	+ 7.77%	+ 11.67%	+ 14.25%	+ 0.58%
645.65	10	Balanced Fund Index	+ 23.22%	+ 8.66%	+ 14.59%	+ 13.12%	+ 0.43%
133.95	10	Gold Fund Index	− 5.48%	− 11.16%	− 16.31%	− 3.92%	+ 0.37%
207.86	10	Sci & Tech Index	+ 51.06%	+ 5.06%	+ 15.33%	+ 26.23%	+ 1.89%
338.91	10	International Index	+ 7.23%	− 8.29%	− 0.74%	+ 8.87%	+ 0.07%
Value 03/31/91			03/31/76- 03/31/91	03/31/81- 03/31/91	03/31/86- 03/31/91	03/31/90- 03/31/91	12/31/90- 03/31/91
375.22		S&P 500 Reinvested	+ 606.48%	+ 315.81%	+ 86.33%	+ 14.40%	+ 14.51%
2,913.86		Dow Jones Reinvested	+ 503.01%	+ 353.81%	+ 92.94%	+ 11.78%	+ 11.61%

Source: *Barron's*, May 13, 1991, p. 131. Reprinted by permission of *Barron's*, © 1991 by Dow Jones & Company, Inc. All Rights Reserved Worldwide.

3 under the discussion of stock market index and averages, but now takes on greater meaning in the current context of mutual fund evaluation). You can observe how certain types of funds did better or worse and how their performance changed with differing periods for measurement. The Lipper Mutual Fund Performance Averages shown above are published weekly in *Barron's*.

Computing Total Return on Your Investment

Assume you own a fund for a year and want to determine the total return on your investment. There are three potential sources of return:

Change in net asset value (NAV).

Dividends distributed.

Capital gains distributed.[6]

Assume the following:

Beginning NAV	$14.05
Ending NAV	15.10
Change in NAV (+)	1.05
Dividends distributed	.40 ⎫
Capital gains distributed	.32 ⎬ $.72
Total return	$ 1.77

In this instance, there is a total return of $1.77. Based on a beginning NAV of $14.05, the return is 12.60 percent.

$$\frac{\text{Total return}}{\text{Beginning NAV}} = \frac{\$1.77}{\$14.05} = 12.60 \text{ percent}$$

As a further consideration, assume that instead of taking dividends and capital gains income in cash, you decide to automatically reinvest the proceeds to purchase new mutual fund shares. To compute the percentage return in this instance, you must compare the total value of your ending shares to the total value of your beginning shares. Assume you owned 100 shares to start, and you received 72 cents in dividends plus capital gains per share (see prior example). This would allow you to reinvest $72 (100 shares × $.72 per share). Further assume you bought new shares at an average price of $14.40 per share. This would provide you with five new shares.[7]

$$\frac{\text{Dividends and capital gains allocated to the account}}{\text{Average purchase price of new shares}} =$$

$$\frac{\$72}{\$14.40} = 5 \text{ new shares}$$

---

[6]This represents net capital gains that the fund actually had as a result of selling securities. They are distributed to shareholders.

[7]In this case, the number of new shares came out to be a whole number. It is also possible to buy fractional shares in a mutual fund.

In comparing the ending and beginning value of the investment based on the example in this section, we show the following:

$$\text{Total return} = \frac{\left(\begin{array}{c}\text{Number of}\\\text{ending shares}\\\times \text{ Ending price}\end{array}\right) - \left(\begin{array}{c}\text{Number of}\\\text{beginning shares}\\\times \text{ Beginning price}\end{array}\right)}{\text{Number of beginning shares} \times \text{ Beginning price}} \quad (19\text{--}2)$$

$$= \frac{(105 \times \$15.10) - (100 \times \$14.05)}{(100 \times \$14.05)}$$

$$= \frac{\$1,585.50 - \$1,405}{\$1,405}$$

$$= \frac{\$180.50}{\$1,405} = 12.85\%$$

In determining whether the returns computed in this section are adequate, you must compare your returns to the popular market averages and to the returns on other mutual funds. You must also consider the amount of risk you are taking. While the returns might be considered quite good for a conservative fund, such might not be the case for an aggressive, growth-oriented fund. These factors are more fully developed in the chapters on portfolio management.

■ SUMMARY

Investment funds allow investors to pool their resources under the guidance of professional managers. Some funds are closed-end, which means there is a *fixed* number of shares, and purchasers and sellers of shares must deal with each other. They normally cannot buy new shares from the fund. Much more important is the open-end fund, which stands ready at all times to sell new shares or buy back old shares. Actually, it is the open-end investment fund that technically represents the term *mutual fund*.

An important consideration with an open-end fund is whether it is a load fund or a no-load fund. The former requires a commission that may run as high as 8.5 percent, while the latter has no such charge. Because there is no proof that load funds deliver better performance than no-load funds, the investor should think long and hard before paying such a commission. Important sources of information on mutual funds include the *Forbes* annual September issue and the *Wiesenberger Investment Companies Service* guide. *Consumer Reports, Business Week, Financial World,* and *Money* also provide good mutual fund information.

Mutual funds may take many different forms such as those emphasizing money market management, growth in common stocks, bond portfolio management, special sectors of the economy (such as energy or computers), or

foreign investments. The funds with an international orientation have enjoyed strong popularity in the last decade.

Through examining a fund's prospectus, the investor can become familiar with the fund's investment objectives and policies, its portfolio holdings, its turnover rate, and the fund's management fees. The investor can also become aware of whether the fund offers such special services as automatic reinvestment of distributions (when desired), exchange privileges among different funds, systematic withdrawal plans, and check-writing privileges.

Some investors use mutual funds as part of a strategy for long-term investment planning and may purchase the fund on a dollar-cost averaging basis, in which fixed amounts are placed in the fund on a regular basis regardless of present net asset value or the short-term economic outlook.

Return to fund holders may come in the form of capital appreciation or yield. Over the long term, mutual funds have not outperformed the popular market averages. However, they do offer an opportunity for low-cost, efficient diversification, and they normally have experienced management. Also, a minority of funds have turned in above-average performances.

◼ IMPORTANT WORDS AND CONCEPTS

closed-end fund 618
open-end fund 618
net asset value (NAV) 619
load funds 622
low-load funds 622

back-end load 622
no-load funds 622
prospectus 634
dollar-cost averaging 637

◼ DISCUSSION QUESTIONS

1. Do mutual funds, on average, outperform the market?
2. Do mutual funds generally provide efficient diversification?
3. Explain why the vast array of mutual funds available to the investor may be a partial drawback and not always an advantage.
4. What is the basic difference between a closed-end fund and an open-end fund?
5. Define net asset value. Do closed-end funds normally trade at their net asset value? What about open-end funds?
6. Is it mandatory that you pay a load fee when purchasing an open-end mutual fund? What is a low-load fund?
7. Should you get better performance from a load fund in comparison to a no-load fund?
8. If there is a difference between the net asset value (NAV) and the offer price for a mutual fund, what does that tell us about the fund?

9. How can you distinguish between regular growth funds and aggressive growth funds?

10. What type of fund is likely to invest in convertible securities?

11. Why might there be some potential danger in investing in sector funds?

12. What does Rule 12b-1 enable mutual funds to do? Is this normally beneficial to current mutual fund shareholders?

13. Are earnings of mutual funds normally taxed at the fund level or the shareholder level?

14. What is the advantage of investing in a mutual fund that offers an exchange privilege?

15. What is dollar-cost averaging? If you were a particularly astute investor at timing moves in the market, would you want to use dollar-cost averaging?

16. How does *Forbes* magazine rate fund performance in up and down markets?

■ PROBLEMS

Net asset value

1. The New Frontier closed-end fund has $420 million in securities, $6 million in liabilities, and 20 million shares outstanding. It trades at a 10 percent discount from net asset value (NAV).

   a. What is the net asset value of the fund?

   b. What is the current price of the fund?

   c. Suggest two reasons the fund may be trading at a discount from net asset value.

Load funds

2. An open-end fund is set up to charge a load. Its net asset value is $11.80, and its offer price is $12.40.

   a. What is the dollar value of the load (commission)?

   b. What percent of the offer price does the load represent?

   c. What percent of the net asset value does the load represent?

   d. Do load funds necessarily outperform no-load funds?

   e. How do no-load funds earn a return if they do not charge a commission?

Load funds

3. In Problem 2, assume the fund increased in value by 20 cents the first month after you purchased 200 shares.

   a. What is your total dollar gain or loss? (Compare the total current value to the total purchase amount.)

   b. By what percent would the net asset value of the shares have to increase for you to break even?

Loads versus
no-loads

4. Examine Table 19–4 on page 624 and fill in the table below.

	Load or No-Load	If Load, Percent of Offer Price Load Represents
AEGON USA—Growth		
Columbia Funds—Fixed		
Common Sense—Govt		

Back-end load

5. The Horizon Investment Fund does not have a front-end load but does have back-end load provision. The back-end load starts at 5 percent of total proceeds received and goes down by 1 percent each year the fund is held. It is eliminated after five years. Assume you buy 200 shares at $16.75 per share and sell them three years later at a gain of $2.25. After you pay the back-end load, what will your total proceeds be?

Comparative fund performance and loads

6. Use Table 19–9 on page 640 for this problem:

   a. What was the strongest performing industry between October 11, 1990, and May 9, 1991? (First column.) What was the percent gain?

   b. If you purchased a low-load fund in this group at $10.40 and it had a net asset value of $10.00, what is the percent load (as a percent of purchase price)?

   c. If the fund's performance percentagewise equaled that of the rest of the group, what would its new net asset value be? (Refer back to Part *a*.)

   d. What is your dollar profit or loss per share based on your purchase price?

   e. What is your percentage return on your purchase price?

Total returns to a fund

7. An investor buys shares in the no-load Atlas World Fund on January 1 at a net asset value of $22.10. At the end of the year, the price is $26.50. Also, the investor receives 60 cents in dividends and 30 cents in capital gains distributions. What is the total percentage return on the beginning net asset value? (Round to two places to the right of the decimal point.)

Total returns to a fund

8. Dale Hansen purchases shares in the no-load 21st Century Fund at a net asset value of $12.20. During the year, he receives 55 cents in dividends and 17 cents in capital gains distributions. At the end of the year, the fund's price is $11.80. What is the total percentage return or loss on the beginning net asset value? (Round to two places to the right of the decimal point.)

Total returns with reinvestment

9. Anna Gomez had 200 shares of the Discovery Fund on January 1. The shares had a value of $12.60. During the year she received $80 in dividends and $206 in capital gains distributions. She used the new funds to purchase shares at an average price of $13 per share. By

the end of the year, the shares were up to $13.40. What is her percentage total return? Use Formula 19–2 and round to two places to the right of the decimal point. Recall you first must determine the number of new shares.

Dollar-cost averaging

10. Under dollar-cost averaging, an investor will purchase $9,000 worth of stock each year for three years. The stock price is $60 in year 1, $45 in year 2, and $75 in year 3.

  a. Compute the average price per share.

  b. Compute the average cost per share.

  c. Explain why the average cost is less than the average price.

■ CRITICAL THOUGHT CASE

Al Harris was particularly glad he had an opportunity to visit with Mildred Frazier. Al had been selling mutual funds for the last five years, and he believed he was about to make his best sale of the year.

Mildred, age 70, had inherited $500,000 on the death of her husband four months ago. Her husband had been a successful businessman and had managed their financial affairs up to the time of his death. Although their home mortgage had been paid, Mildred had $500,000 in CDs, money market funds, and widely diversified stocks and bonds to manage. Her first inclination was to turn over the assets to the trust department of the largest bank in town and let it manage the funds for a 1½ percent fee.

She mentioned this plan to Al at a church gathering when he responded that bank trust departments were so conservative in their management policies that she probably would not get a return high enough to keep up with inflation.

He suggested she put her $500,000 in the New Era Science and Technology fund. He emphasized the fund had enjoyed an increase in net asset value of 20 percent per year over the past five years for a total compounded gain of 148.8 percent. He suggested a $500,000 investment could easily be worth $1,244,000 five years from now as the same pattern was likely to persist.

When she asked if there were any expenses involved in buying the fund, Al said there was a courtesy commission of 8½ percent at the time of purchase. Also, there was a back-end fee of 5 percent if she decided to sell the fund. He stressed that the 8½ percent commission was insignificant when one considered the enormous return potential. Furthermore, he said the 5 percent back-end sales commission would be reduced by 1 percent each year and would be eliminated after five years.

Mildred was excited about the information Al had given her and promised to consider it very carefully.

Question

1. Comment on the practices Al Harris has used.

SELECTED REFERENCES

Investment Strategy

Brealey, Richard A. "How to Combine Active Management with Index Funds." *Journal of Portfolio Management,* Winter 1986, pp. 4–10.

Fisher, David. "Lessons from the Third World." *Institutional Investor,* October 1988, pp. 243–45.

Gordon, Marion, and Janice Horowitz. "Inside Moves: Market Timing with Mutual Funds." *Personal Investor,* July 1985, pp. 32–39.

Herkinson, Roy D. "Market Timing and Mutual Fund Performance: An Empirical Investigation." *Journal of Business,* January 1984, pp. 73–96.

Irwin, Scott H., and B. Wade Brorsen. "Public Futures Funds." *Journal of Futures Markets,* Summer 1985, pp. 149–72.

Ruth, Simon. "Why Good Brokers Sell Bad Funds." *Money,* July 1991, pp. 94–99.

Simonds, Richard R. "Mutual Fund Strategies for IRA Investors." *Journal of Portfolio Management,* Winter 1986, pp. 40–43.

Mutual Fund Performance

Gallagher, Timothy J. "Mutual Fund Size and Risk-Adjusted Performance." *Illinois Business Review,* August 1988, pp. 11–13.

Jensen, Michael C. "Risk, Capital Assets and Evaluation of Portfolios." *Journal of Business,* April 1969, pp. 167–247.

Kon, Stanley J. "The Market Timing of Mutual Fund Managers." *Journal of Business,* July 1983, pp. 323–47.

Kon, Stanley J., and Frank C. Jen. "The Investment Performance of Mutual Funds: An Empirical Investigation of Timing, Selectivity, and Market Efficiency." *Journal of Business,* April 1979, pp. 263–89.

Mutual Fund Guides and Surveys

"A Guide to Mutual Funds." *Consumer Reports* (published annually).

"Tallying the Totals: Mutual Fund Scorecard." *Financial World* (published annually).

"The Money Ranking of Mutual Funds." *Money* (published annually).

"The Mutual Fund Survey." *Forbes* (published annually).

Wiesenberger Investment Companies Service. Boston: Warren, Gorham and Lamont, published annually.

Closed-End Funds

Anderson, Seth Copeland. "Closed-End Funds vs. Market Efficiency." *Journal of Portfolio Management,* Fall 1986, pp. 63–65.

Appendix 19–A: Unit Investment Trusts (UITs)

Unit investment trusts (UITs) are investment companies organized for the purpose of purchasing a pool of securities—usually tax-exempt municipal bonds. UITs issue units to investors, representing a proportionate interest in the assets of the trust. Investors also receive a proportionate share in the interest or dividends received by the trust.

Unit investment trusts are passive investments. They normally purchase assets and hold them for the benefit of owners for a specified period.

To understand UITs better, consider the following hypothetical example. Nuveen, Inc.—a prominent firm in this field—announces the formation of the next in its series of tax-exempt unit trusts: Nuveen Series 200. Through advertising and selling agents, Nuveen will raise $4 million; investors will pay approximately $1,000 per unit. After deducting 3 to 4 percent for sales commissions, Nuveen will use the remaining cash to purchase large blocks of municipal securities from 10 to 20 different issuers. Once this diversified pool of bonds is acquired, Nuveen will play a passive role. It will collect and pass on to unit holders all interest payments received and all principal repayments resulting from maturing or recalled bonds. While UITs usually hold bonds until maturity, the trust custodian may sell off bonds whose future ability to pay interest and principal is altered by events.

The majority of UITs formed in the past decade have invested in tax-exempt securities. Often, trusts are formed to purchase tax-exempt securities from issuers in specific, high-tax states, such as New York, Massachusetts, and Minnesota. Unit holders residing in these states expect to receive a stream of income exempt from federal, state, and local taxation.

Even unit investment trusts dedicated to tax-exempt bonds have different investment objectives. Some deal strictly in long-term, high-rated issues. Others seek higher yields by purchasing issues with low ratings.

Units of a trust are redeemable under terms set forth in the prospectus. In most cases, this means a unit holder can sell units back to the trust at their net asset value, which is the current market value of each trust unit.

A secondary market for unit trusts is evolving among broker-dealers. Investors seeking to acquire or sell units can sometimes find a better deal in this market. However, most investors in UITs do not intend to redeem early.

Investors in UITs benefit by professional selection of securities, by diversification, and by avoiding the housekeeping chores of collecting coupon payments. As a large buyer, a UIT can usually purchase securities at a better price than the individual who buys in small lots.

Essential Difference between a Unit Investment Trust and a Mutual Fund

There is an important difference between UITs and mutual funds. UITs are formed with the intention of keeping all the initially purchased assets until maturity. The investment strategy, as described above, is strictly passive. A UIT of $4 million with a 10-year life will draw interest over that time period, while only cashing in bonds as they mature and returning the funds to the investors. The UIT will cease to exist after 10 years. Because of the features just described, there is very little interest-rate risk associated with UITs. Since all bonds are intended to be held until maturity, the investor can be reasonably well assured of recovering his initial investment (plus interest). The fact that interest rates and bond prices are changing at any point in time during the life of the UIT makes little difference.[1]

A bond-oriented mutual fund has no such assurance of recovering the initial investment. First, mutual funds have no stipulated life. Second, the bonds in the portfolio are actively managed and frequently sold off before their maturity dates at large profits or losses. Thus, the purchaser of a bond-oriented mutual fund may experience large capital gains or losses as well as receiving interest income.

The message is that if preservation of capital is of paramount importance to the investor, the UIT may be a better investment than a mutual fund. Of course, if one thinks interest rates are going down and bond prices up, the bond-oriented mutual fund would be a better investment.

---

[1] Of course, if the investor needs to redeem shares before the end of the life of the trust, there will be fluctuations in value.

20

Investments in Real Assets

In this chapter, we turn our attention to **real assets;** that is, tangible assets that may be seen, felt, held, or collected. Examples of such assets are real estate, gold, silver, diamonds, coins, stamps, and antiques. This is no small area from which to consider investments. For example, the total market value of all real estate holdings in the United States in the early 1990s was in excess of $5 trillion.

As further evidence of value, in the late 1980s, a Van Gogh painting sold for $40 million, and a 132-carat diamond earring set sold for $6.6 million. Coins and stamps also sold for values well into the hundreds of thousands.

A number of the traditional stock brokerage houses have moved into the area of real estate. Also, 25 million people in the United States are stamp collectors, and 8 million collect and invest in coins.

As was pointed out in Chapter 1, in inflationary environments, real assets have at times outperformed financial assets (such as stocks and bonds). With this in mind, the reader is well advised to become familiar with these invest-ment outlets—not only to take advantage of the investment opportunities but also to be well aware of the pitfalls. A money manager who is challenged by clients to include real assets in a portfolio (such as real estate or precious metals) must be conversant not only with the opportunities but also with the drawbacks.

■ ADVANTAGES AND DISADVANTAGES OF REAL ASSETS

As previously mentioned, real assets may offer an opportunity as an inflation hedge because inflation means higher replacement costs for real estate, precious metals, and other physical items. Real assets also serve as an investment hedge against the unknown and feared. When people become concerned about world events, gold and other precious metals may be perceived as the last safe haven for investments.

Real assets also may serve as an effective vehicle for portfolio diversifica-tion. Since financial and real assets at times move in opposite directions, some efficient diversification may occur. A study by Robichek, Cohn, and Pringle in the *Journal of Business* actually indicates that movements between various types of real and monetary assets are less positively correlated than are those for monetary assets alone.[1] The general findings indicate that enlarging the uni-verse of investment alternatives would benefit the overall portfolio construc-tion in terms of risk-return alternatives.

A final advantage of an investment in real assets is the psychic pleasure that may be provided. One can easily relate to a beautiful painting in the living room, a mint gold coin in a bank lockbox, or an attractive real estate development.

There are many disadvantages to consider as well. Perhaps the largest draw-back is the absence of large, liquid, and relatively efficient markets. Whereas stocks or bonds can generally be sold in a few minutes at a value close to the

---

[1]Alexander A. Robichek, Richard A. Cohn, and John J. Pringle, "Return on Alternative Media and Implica-tions for Portfolio Construction," *Journal of Business,* July 1972, pp. 427–43.

latest quoted trade, such is not likely to be the case for real estate, diamonds, art, and other forms of real assets. It may take many months to get the desired price for a real asset, and even then, there is an air of uncertainty about the impending transaction until it is consummated.

Furthermore, there is the problem of dealer spread or middleman commission. Whereas in the trading of stocks and bonds, spreads or commissions are very small (usually 1 or 2 percent), dealer spreads for real assets can be as large as 20 to 25 percent or more. This is particularly true for small items that do not have great value. On more valuable items, such as rare paintings, valuable jewels, or mint gold coins, the dealer spread tends to be smaller (perhaps 5 to 10 percent) but still more than that on securities.

The investor in real assets generally receives no current income (with the possible exception of real estate) and may incur storage and insurance costs. Furthermore, there may be the problem of high unit cost for investments. You cannot easily acquire multiple art masterpieces.

A final drawback or caveat in real assets is the hysteria or overreaction that tends to come into the marketplace from time to time. Gold, silver, diamonds, and coins may be temporarily bid all out of proportion to previously anticipated value. The last buyer, who arrives too late, may end up owning a very unprofitable investment. The trick is to get into the recurring cycle early enough to take advantage of the large capital gains opportunities that regularly occur for real assets. Also, you should buy items of high enough quality so that you can ride out the setbacks if your timing is incorrect.

In the remainder of this chapter, we will examine real estate, gold, silver, diamonds, and other collectibles as investment outlets. Because real estate lends itself more directly to analytical techniques familiar to students of finance, it will receive a proportionately larger share of our attention.

■ REAL ESTATE AS AN INVESTMENT

Approximately half the households in the United States own real estate as a home or investment. Also, many firms in the brokerage and investment community have also moved into real estate. As examples, Merrill Lynch and Shearson Lehman have acquired real estate affiliates to broker property, conduct mortgage banking activities, or package real estate syndications. While only 2 to 3 percent of pension fund assets are currently in real estate, the number may grow to 10 percent or more by the mid-1990s.

Some insight into changing real estate values may be gained from viewing Figure 20–1. We see the gain for a dollar invested in real estate in 1946 (as compared to fixed-income investments).

Real estate investments may include such outlets as your own home, duplexes and apartment buildings, office buildings, shopping centers, industrial buildings, hotels and motels, as well as undeveloped land. The investor may participate as an individual, as part of a limited partnership real estate syndicate, or through a real estate investment trust. These forms of ownership will receive further coverage toward the end of this section.

Figure 20–1   Growth in Value: 1946–1991 ($1 of Investment)

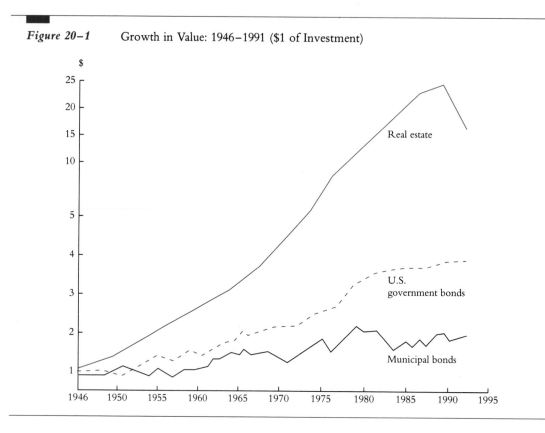

Throughout the rest of the section, we will consider the effect of tax reform on real estate projects, evaluate a typical real estate investment, consider new methods of real estate financing, and examine limited partner syndicates and real estate investment trusts.

Tax Reform, Economic Conditions, and Real Estate Investments

With the Tax Reform Act of 1986, the life over which a real estate investor can write off depreciation deduction for tax purposes was extended from 19 years to 27½ years for residential rental property and to 31½ years for commercial property. This means you have to wait longer to take full advantage of tax deductions. Furthermore, the lowering of the marginal tax rate under the Tax Reform Act of 1986 and the Deficit Reduction Act of 1990 reduced the incentive to invest in real estate as a tax shelter. A maximum tax rate of 31 percent[2]

---

[2]The marginal rate may be slightly higher for wealthy individuals because of limitations on itemized deductions and the phase out of personal exemptions.

gives much less incentive to utilize tax write-offs than a 50 percent rate. Finally, real estate investors not actively involved in the management of property are very limited in writing off paper losses created through limited partnerships against other forms of income.

The effect of tax reform is to make real estate a less attractive investment, at least for now. Because of the loss of many traditional tax benefits for real estate, some existing properties have less value, and new construction is proceeding at a slower pace.

The initial negative impact of tax reform on real estate was also associated with declining economic conditions in various sections of the country during the late 1980s and early 1990s. First, the Southwest (and Texas in particular) was hit with a 70 percent plunge in oil prices in 1986. This meant office buildings, shopping centers, and homes built on an assumption of increasing energy prices to stimulate economic growth went begging for buyers. It was not unusual for a home that was purchased in Dallas, Oklahoma City, or Denver for $300,000 in 1986 to be sold at 50 to 60 percent of that amount five years later. Even as the southwestern economy began to slowly recover in the early 1990s, real estate-related problems moved into the Northeast, with Massachusetts being hit particularly hard. The next area to suffer was the supposedly immune West Coast. Few thought it possible that the ever-growing state of California would see the real estate bubble burst in such dynamic areas as Los Angeles and the San Francisco Bay area.

Not only were real estate investors and home buyers hurt, but so were the financial institutions that loaned money to them. In 1989, the Resolution Trust Corporation (RTC) was formed by Congress in an attempt to help savings and loans liquidate their bad real estate loans. The eventual cost to the government (and taxpayers) is likely to be $200 billion to $300 billion. By 1992, banks were facing the same problems with First Interstate, Bank of America, and others holding large chunks of bad real estate in their portfolios.

Over the long term, however, real estate may still be a good investment. Why? With fewer new properties being developed as a result of tax reform and economic conditions, the glut in office space and apartments in certain sections of the country will eventually disappear. Furthermore, with fewer new properties brought to the market, rents will eventually go up on existing properties. The increased rents will also be necessary to provide adequate cash returns to investors who previously received a large portion of their total return from tax-shelter benefits but no longer do. The eventual impact of higher rents will be higher valuation, perhaps by the mid-1990s.

The above comments about real estate apply primarily to real estate investments (apartments, shopping centers, and so on) as opposed to homeownership. All the benefits of homeownership basically remain in effect after tax reform. There is no depreciation deduction on your personal residence, so this is really not an issue. The only slight disadvantage to homeownership as a result of tax reform is that marginal tax rates are now lower so there is somewhat less benefit in taking tax deductions. Nevertheless, the overall tax

advantages of owning your own home still remain firmly in place. Home-ownership was simply too much a part of the American way of life to be attacked by tax reformers in Congress.

An Actual Example

Let's look at an actual real estate investment example. Assume we are considering investing $170,000 in a new fourplex (four-unit apartment housing project). The land costs will be $30,000, and the actual physical structure will cost $140,000. This latter amount will be the value to be depreciated. We will assume we borrow 75 percent of the total property value of $170,000, which represents a loan of $127,500. Though we are dealing with relatively small numbers for ease of computation, the same types of considerations would apply to a multimillion-dollar shopping center or office building. Before we actually evaluate our cash inflows and outflows, we will consider tax and accounting factors related to depreciation in real estate.

Depreciation Effects

In the present case, we can write off depreciation on residential real estate property over 27½ years. You will recall the depreciation period for commercial property (shopping centers, for example) is 31½ years. Furthermore, under the Tax Reform Act of 1986, only **straight-line depreciation** (equal annual depreciation) can be applied to any form of real estate investment. There is no potential for accelerated depreciation as there was before the passage of this act.

Returning to our example, the $140,000 physical structure would be depreciated over 27½ years using straight-line depreciation.[3] The annual depreciation charge would be $5,091.

$$\frac{\$140,000}{27.5} = \$5,091 \text{ annual depreciation}$$

Cash Flow Considerations

The only aspect of our investment we have considered so far is depreciation. We have established the fact that on a $170,000 investment with $30,000 in land and $140,000 in the building, we could take annual depreciation of $5,091. Depreciation is a noncash tax-deductible item that is used to lower tax obligations. We now must consider various cash flow items, such as the receipt of the rent, the payment of interest, property taxes, insurance, maintenance ex-

---

[3]The time period may vary slightly from this due to midmonth conventions. The impact is too small to be considered.

Table 20–1   Cash Flow Analysis for an Apartment (Fourplex) Investment

Gross annual rental (4 units at $490 per month or $5,880 per year for each unit)		$23,520
Less 5 percent vacancy		1,176
Net rental income		$22,344
Interest expense on a loan of 75 percent of property value at 12 percent interest: (75%) × $170,000 = $127,500 (12%) × $127,500 = $15,300	$15,300	
Property taxes	2,000	
Insurance	750	
Maintenance	1,000	
Depreciation	5,091	
Total expenses		24,141
Before-tax income or (loss)		$(1,797)
Tax benefit (assumes 33 percent tax rate)		557
Depreciation		5,091
Cash flow		$ 3,851

penses, and so on. An overall example of cash flow analysis is presented in Table 20–1. This is assumed to represent the first year of the investment.

We see in Table 20–1 that we have a loss of $1,797 before federal income tax, and this provides a tax-shelter benefit of $557 against other income.[4] We also add depreciation of $5,091 back in to get cash flow because, although it was subtracted out, it is really a noncash item. The negative and two positive values at the bottom of the table provide a positive cash flow of $3,851.

In terms of investor return in the first year, the initial cash investment is $42,500. This is based on the total value of the property of $170,000 minus the initial loan of $127,500, requiring the investor to put up $42,500 in cash. With a cash inflow of $3,851 in the first year, the cash-on-cash return in the first year is 9.06 percent ($3,851/$42,500).

---

[4]The assumption in this case is that we have an active participation in the property and are allowed to deduct the tax loss. This is a tricky matter in real estate because some real estate losses are considered to be passive and nondeductible. However, there are exemptions. If the investor is actively involved in the management of the property and has adjusted gross income of $100,000 or less, up to $25,000 in losses can be claimed. For income over $100,000, the $25,000 write-off is phased out up to income levels of $150,000. In a later discussion on limited partnerships, we will examine circumstances in which tax losses on real estate cannot be claimed on an individual's tax return regardless of income level.

Table 20–2	Interest Payments for a 20-Year Loan (Principal Amount Equals $127,500)				
	8 Percent	**10 Percent**	**12 Percent**	**14 Percent**	**16 Percent**
Annual payment	$ 12,986	$ 14,975	$ 17,070	$ 19,251	$ 21,504
First year interest	10,200	12,750	15,300	17,850	20,400
Total interest over the life of the loan	132,220	172,000	213,900	257,520	302,580

However, we should point out that in considering the cost of the loan in Table 20–1, we have evaluated only interest payments. We might wish to consider repayment of principal as well. In the present case, we are assuming that in the first year we are paying 12 percent on a loan balance of $127,500, or $15,300 in interest (as shown in Table 20–2). Assuming a 20-year loan (it is not unusual for the life of the loan to be different from the depreciation period), the total first-year payment for interest and principal is $17,070, indicating that $1,770 is applied toward the repayment of principal.

$$\text{Payment} - \text{Interest} = \text{Repayment of principal}$$
$$\$17,070 - \$15,300 = \$1,770$$

On this basis, our net cash flow figure will be reduced to $2,081.

$$\text{Cash flow} - \text{Repayment of principal} = \text{Net cash flow}^5$$
$$\$3,851 \quad - \quad \$1,770 \qquad\qquad = \$2,081$$

With a net cash flow of $2,081 (after repayment of principal), the cash-on-cash return in the first year is 4.90 percent ($2,081/$42,500). This value will be different from year to year as rental income, expenses, and repayment of principal change.

While the return appears to be low, it should be pointed out that the investor will build up equity or ownership interest by the amount of repayment toward principal each year as well as any increase in property value resulting from inflation. If the property increases by 5 percent in the first year, this represents an added benefit of $8,500 (5 percent times the $170,000 value of the property). Actually, return benefits associated with price appreciation may exceed all other considerations. An investor may be willing to accept relatively low cash

---

[5]One could argue that we are building up equity or ownership interest through the repayment of principal. However, our focus for now is simply on the amount of cash flow going in and out. We will consider buildup in equity in the bottom paragraph.

flow if he or she can enjoy inflation-related gains. Note in the present case, the $8,500 gain from price appreciation alone would represent a first-year return on cash investment of 20 percent ($8,500/$42,500).

This gain is particularly relevant because most of the tax advantages of real estate have been largely reduced, so there is a dependence on cash generation and *inflation*.

You can readily see the twin factors that make real estate potentially attractive are depreciation write-offs and appreciation in value due to price appreciation. Apartments, office buildings, warehouses, and shopping centers have served particularly well as good performers in inflationary environments. However, the clear downside is that in a weak economic environment there may not be enough cash inflow to cover the financial obligations associated with the investment. As previously mentioned, this happened all too often in various sections of the country during the late 1980s and early 1990s.

■ FINANCING OF REAL ESTATE

One of the essential considerations in any real estate investment analysis is the cost of financing. In the prior example, we said a loan for $127,500 over 20 years at 12 percent interest would have yearly payments of $17,070. Note in Table 20–2 the effects of various interest rates on annual payments.

We see the difference in annual payments ranges from $12,986 at 8 percent up to $21,504 at 16 percent. Even more dramatic is the increase in total interest paid over the life of the loan; it goes from $132,220 at 8 percent to $302,580 at 16 percent. (Keep in mind that the total loan was only $127,500.)

An investor who has the unlikely opportunity to shift out of the loan at 16 percent into one at 8 percent might be willing to pay as much as $83,692.72 for the privilege. (Tax effects are not specifically considered here.)

$$16 \text{ percent interest} - 8 \text{ percent interest} = \text{Dollar difference in annual payments}$$

$$\$21,504 - \$12,986 \qquad = \$8,518$$

The present value of $8,518 over 20 years assuming an 8 percent discount rate (see Appendix D at the end of the book) is:

$$\$8,518 \times 9.818 = \$83,629.72$$

Thus, it is easy to appreciate the role of interest rates in a real estate investment decision. No industry is more susceptible to the impact of changing interest rates than real estate. Each time the economy overheats and interest rates skyrocket, the real estate industry comes to a standstill. With the eventual easing of interest-rate pressures, the industry once again enjoys a recovery.

New Types of Mortgages

In actuality, a whole new set of mortgage arrangements has appeared as alternatives to the fixed-interest-rate mortgage (particularly for home mortgages). The borrower must now be prepared to consider such alternative lending arrangements as the **adjustable rate mortgage,** the **graduated payment mortgage,** and the **shared appreciation mortgage.**

Adjustable Rate Mortgage (ARM)   Under this mortgage arrangement, the interest rate is adjusted regularly. If interest rates go up, borrowers may either increase their normal payments or extend the maturity date of the loan at the same fixed-payment level to fully compensate the lender. Similar downside adjustments can also be made if interest rates fall. Generally, adjustable rate mortgages are initially made at rates 1 to 2 percent below fixed-interest-rate mortgages because the lender enjoys the flexibility of changing interest rates and is willing to share the benefits with the borrower. Adjustable rate mortgages currently account for over half of the residential mortgage market. Although adjustable rate mortgages usually have an upper boundary (such as 15 or 18 percent), there is a real possibility of default for many borrowers if interest rates reach high levels.

Graduated Payment Mortgage (GPM)   Under this type of financial arrangement, the payments start out on a relatively low basis and increase over the life of the loan. This type of mortgage may be well suited to the young borrower who has an increasing repayment capability over the life of the loan. An example would be a 30-year, $50,000 loan at 12 percent that would normally require monthly payments of $503.20 under a standard fixed-payment mortgage. With a graduated payment mortgage, monthly payments might start out as $350 or $400 and eventually progress to over $600. The GPM plan has been referred to by a few of its critics as the "gyp em" plan, in that early payments may not be large enough to cover interest, and therefore, later payments must cover not only the amortization of the loan but also interest on the accumulated, unpaid, early interest. This is not an altogether fair criticism, but merely an interpretation of what the graduated payment stream represents.

Shared Appreciation Mortgage (SAM)   Perhaps the newest and most innovative of the mortgage payment plans is the shared appreciation mortgage. This provides the lender with a hedge against inflation because he directly participates in any increase in value associated with the property being mortgaged. The lender may enjoy as much as 30 to 40 percent of the appreciation in value over a specified time period, such as 10 years. The lender may take his return from the selling of the property or from the refinancing of the appreciated property value with a new lender. In return for this appreciation-potential privilege, the lender may advance funds at well below current market rates (perhaps at three quarters of current rates). The shared appreciation mortgage is not yet legal in all states.

The Reverse Mortgage Loan—The Mortgage of the 21st Century

According to the 1990 census, 32 million people in the United States are 65 years or older. By the year 2030, 55 million people will be in this category. For many of these people, their homes are their most important asset.

Many of these elderly citizens are home rich and cash poor. There is about a 50-50 chance you will have a parent or grandparent fall into this category. What advice can you give?

One approach might be to sell the valuable house (or farm), and use the proceeds to live on. Of course, this calls for uprooting people from their home and neighborhood. There also may be high commissions and, in some cases, taxes involved.

Another alternative is to remain in the home and borrow through a conventional mortgage on the property. In many cases, the property is paid for, and the homeowner has 100 percent equity in the property. The only problem is that the mortgage (say for $80,000) must be repaid over the life of the loan. For people on fixed or low income, this may be a monthly burden they are unprepared to face. They get more cash than they need on the front-end and then must be prepared to manage it wisely enough to make their monthly mortgage payments or lose the property.

Enter the reverse mortgage, the so-called mortgage of the 21st century. Under this plan, the lender pays the homeowners a monthly annuity based on the equity value of the property. Essentially, the homeowners are withdrawing their equity over a period expected to coincide with their remaining life span. The withdrawal is actually a loan that carries interest, but for purposes of financial planning can be thought of as an annuity to cover everyday living expenses.

On death of the occupants, the executor of the estate sells the home and pays off the reverse mortgage. To be safe, the applicant(s) for a reverse home mortgage should set up a loan and annuity payout schedule that far exceeds their anticipated remaining life so they are not caught with the burden of paying off the loan. Sound financial advice is that one should not outlive the reverse mortgage.

The Department of Housing and Urban Development (800-245-2691) provides free information on reverse mortgages and a list of approved FHA lenders in all states.

Other Forms of Mortgages Somewhat similar to the shared appreciation mortgage is the concept of equity participation that is popular in commercial real estate. Under an **equity participation** arrangement, the lender not only provides the borrowed capital but part of the equity or ownership funds as well. A major insurance company or savings and loan thus may acquire an equity interest of 10 to 25 percent (or more). This financing arrangement becomes popular each time inflation rears its head. Some lenders are simply unwilling to commit capital for long periods without a participation feature.

Borrowers may also look toward a *second mortgage* for financing. Here, a second lender provides additional financing beyond the first mortgage in return for a secondary claim or lien. The second mortgage is generally for a shorter period of time than the initial mortgage. Primary suppliers of second mortgages in recent times have been sellers of property. Often, to consummate a sale, it is necessary for the seller to supplement the financing provided by a financial institution. Sellers providing second mortgages generally advance the funds at rates below the first mortgage rate to facilitate the sale, whereas other

second mortgage lenders (nonsellers) will ask for a few percentage points above the first mortgage rate to compensate for the extra risk of being in a secondary claim position.

In some cases, sellers may actually provide all the financing to the buyer. Usually the terms of the mortgage are for 20 to 30 years, but the seller has the right to call in the loan after three to five years if so desired. The assumption is that the buyer may have an easier time finding his own financing at that point in time. This may or may not be true.

■ FORMS OF REAL ESTATE OWNERSHIP

Ownership of real estate may take many forms. The investor may participate as an individual, in a regular partnership, through a real estate syndicate (generally a limited partnership), or through a real estate investment trust (REIT).

Individual or Regular Partnership

Investing as an individual or with two or three others in a regular partnership offers the simplest way of getting into real estate from a legal viewpoint. The investors pretty much control their own destinies and can take advantage of personal knowledge of local markets and changing conditions to enhance their returns.

As is true with most smaller and less complicated business arrangements, there is a well-defined center of responsibility that often leads to quick corrective action. However, there may be a related problem of inability to pool adequate capital to engage in large-scale investments as well as the absence of expertise to develop a wide range of investments. Furthermore, there is unlimited liability to the investor(s).

Syndicate or Limited Partnership

To expand the potential for investor participation, a syndicate or limited partnership has traditionally been formed.[6] The **limited partnership** works as follows: A general partner forms the limited partnership and has unlimited liability for the partnership liabilities. The general partner then sells participation units to the limited partners whose liability is generally limited to the extent of their initial investment (such as $5,000 or $10,000). Limited liability is particularly important in real estate because mortgage debt obligations may exceed the net worth of the participants. The general partner is normally responsible for managing the property, while the limited partners are merely investors.

Although the restricted liability feature of the limited partnership remains attractive, the Tax Reform Act of 1986 generally restricted the use of limited

---

[6]A syndicate may take the form of a corporation, but this is not common. The term *real estate syndicate* has become virtually synonymous with the limited partnership form of operation.

partnerships as tax shelters. Historically, real estate limited partnerships generated large paper losses through accelerated depreciation (though not cash losses), and these paper losses were used to shelter other forms of income (such as a doctor's salary) from taxation. Under the Tax Reform Act of 1986, a taxpayer is no longer allowed to use passive losses to offset other sources of income such as salary or portfolio income. Such losses can only be used to offset income from other passive investments.

It is easy to see why the Tax Reform Act of 1986 had a damaging effect on real estate values. Investors who had bought into real estate limited partnerships a number of years before the act was passed had their tax write-off privileges rapidly phased out after the passage of the act. All of a sudden, investors in existing real estate limited partnerships were bailing out. They were refusing to make required annual payments into the partnership, and as a result, many of the limited partnerships (as well as their investors) were disposing of property at fire-sale prices.

As previously mentioned, the initial impact of the act has already occurred, so real estate has the potential to be a bargain in the future. Real estate limited partnerships still exist but more for limited liability than for tax reasons. The successful partnerships stress strong cash flow generation and capital appreciation potential. In the analysis in Table 20–1, a limited partnership was not involved, and the investor actively participated in managing the property. Some small tax write-offs were allowed, but note that the success of the project was much more dependent on cash flow and potential capital appreciation.

If you decide to invest in a limited partnership, you should follow certain guidelines. You must be particularly sensitive to the front-end fees and commissions the general partner might charge. These can vary anywhere from 5 to 10 percent to as large as 20 to 25 percent. The investor must also be sensitive to any double-dealing the general partner might be doing. An example would be selling property between different partnerships the general partner has formed and taking a commission each time. The inflated paper profits may prove quite deceptive and costly to the uninformed limited partner.

In assessing a general partner and his associated real estate deal, the investor should look at a number of items. First, he should review the prior record of performance of the general partner. Is this the 1st or 10th deal that the general partner has put together? The investor will also wish to be sensitive to any lawsuits against the general partner that might exist. The investor might also wish to ascertain whether he or she is investing in a **blind pool** arrangement where funds are provided to the general partner to ultimately select properties for investment or if specific projects have already been identified and analyzed.

Finally, the investor may have to decide whether to invest in a limited partnership/syndication that is either *public* or *private* in nature. A public offering generally involves much larger total amounts and has gone through the complex and rigorous process of SEC registration. Of course, SEC registration only attempts to ensure that full disclosure has occurred—it does not judge the prudence of the venture. A private offering of a limited partnership syndication is usually local in scope and restricted to a maximum of 35 investors.

Secondary (resale) markets for both public and private limited partnerships exist, but the dealer spreads and commissions tend to be very high. The spreads on desirable property are perhaps 10 to 15 percent; on less desirable property, 20 to 30 percent or more. Really bad property may approach total illiquidity. As you might anticipate, a public limited partnership has much more resale potential than a private one.

Real Estate Investment Trust

Another form of real estate investment is the **real estate investment trust (REIT)**. REITs are similar to mutual funds or investment companies and trade on organized exchanges or over-the-counter. They pool investor funds, along with borrowed funds, and invest them directly in real estate or use them to make construction or mortgage loans to investors.

The advantage to the investor of a REIT is that he or she can participate in the real estate market for as little as $5 to $10 per share. Furthermore, this is the most liquid type of real estate investment because of the large secondary market for the shares.

REITs were initiated under the Real Estate Investment Trust Act of 1960. Like other investment companies, they enjoy the privilege of single taxation of income (only the stockholder pays and not the trust). To qualify for the tax privilege of a REIT, a firm must pay out at least 90 percent of its income to shareholders, have no less than 75 percent of its assets in real estate, and concurrently obtain at least 75 percent of its income from real estate.

REITs may take any of three different forms or combinations thereof. **Equity trusts** buy, operate, and sell real estate as an investment; **construction and development trusts** make short-term loans to developers during their construction period; and **mortgage trusts** make long-term loans to real estate investors. REITs are generally formed and advised by affiliates of commercial banks, insurance companies, mortgage bankers, and other financial institutions. Representative issues include Bank American Realty, Continental Illinois Property, and Connecticut General Mortgage.

Although REITs were enormously popular investments during the 1960s and early 1970s, the bottom fell out of the REIT market in the mid-1970s. Many had made questionable loans that came to the surface in the tight money, recessionary period of 1973–75. Nevertheless, REITs have now regained some of their earlier popularity. The investor in REITs normally hopes to receive a reasonably high yield because 90 percent of income must be paid out in the form of dividends plus a modest capital appreciation in stock value. In some cases, outside investors have taken over REITs with the intention of liquidating assets at higher than current stock market values.

There are over 200 REITs from which the investor may choose. Further information on REITs may be acquired from the National Association of Real Estate Investment Trusts, 1101 17th St., N.W., Washington, D.C. 20036. In Figure 20–2, a Value Line data sheet is presented for BRE Properties, a typical REIT.

Figure 20–2   Data Sheet for a REIT

BRE PROPERTIES NYSE-BRE | RECENT PRICE **29** | P/E RATIO **14.1** (Trailing: 14.6 Median: NMF) | RELATIVE P/E RATIO **.95** | DIV'D YLD **8.3%** | VALUE LINE **1172**

TIMELINESS **3** Average (Relative Price Performance Next 12 Mos.)

SAFETY **2** Above Average (Scale: 1 Highest to 5 Lowest)

BETA .60 (1.00 = Market)

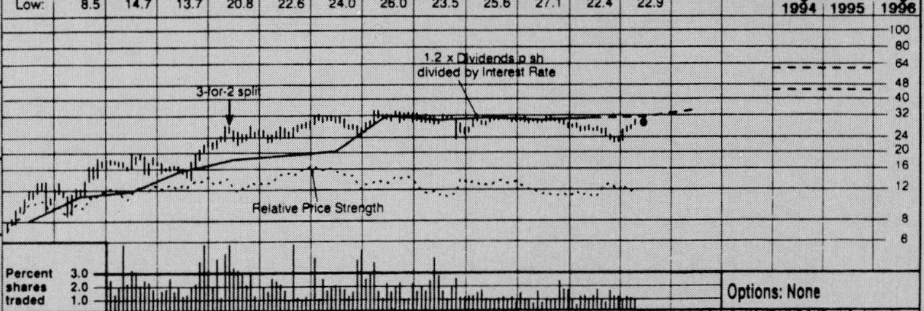

1994-96 PROJECTIONS

	Price	Gain	Ann'l Total Return
High	60	(+105%)	25%
Low	45	(+55%)	18%

Insider Decisions

	J	A	S	O	N	D	J	F	M
to Buy	0	0	1	0	1	1	0	1	1
Options	0	0	0	0	0	0	0	0	0
to Sell	0	0	0	0	0	0	0	0	0

Institutional Decisions

	2Q'90	3Q'90	4Q'90
to Buy	8	6	6
to Sell	10	7	6
Hld's(000)	4123	4073	4079

Options: None

© VALUE LINE PUB., INC.

Target Price Range 1994 1995 1996

3-for-2 split

1.2 x Dividends per sh divided by Interest Rate

Relative Price Strength

CAPITAL STRUCTURE as of 1/31/91

ST Debt Nil   Due in 5 Yrs $4.0 mill.

LT Debt $66.2 mill.   LT Interest $6.2 mill.

(Total interest coverage in fiscal '90: 3.4x)

Incl. $.1 mill. 9½% ('00), call. 108.55, each conv. into $7.34 shs. at $17.44; $46.9 mill. 9½% debs. ('08), callable 103.8, each conv. into 32.26 shs. at $31.00.   (32% of Cap'l)

Pfd Stock None

Common Stock 7,912,048 shs.   (68% of Cap'l)
(9.4 mill. fully diluted shs.)

FUNDS FLOW ($mill.)

	1988	1989	1990
Net Profit Plus			
Noncash charges	18.2	19.0	33.9
Investments Repaid	2.9	6.1	26.3
Net New Debt	(.7)	3.7	(8.6)
New Equity	(.5)	.2	.1
Investments Funded	10.9	7.3	10.3
Dividends Declared	18.9	18.9	18.9

FINANCIAL POSITION

	1/31/90	1/31/91
Senior Debt	$20.1 mill.	$19.2 mill.
Subordinated Debt	$48.6 mill.	$47.0 mill.
Sr Debt/Cap'l Funds	.10:1	.10:1
Total Debt/Equity	.44:1	.46:1

PORTFOLIO CONDITION

	Year Ago	Latest
Mtges Repaid in Quarter	$.1 mill.	$7.7 mill.
Loss Reserve – %/Invests.	.5%	.5%
Non-Earn Assets – %/Invests.	NA	NA

LOANS & REAL ESTATE ($ mill.) [A][B]

Fiscal Year Ends	Oct. 31	Jan. 31	Apr. 30	July 31
1988	193.7	194.2	199.0	198.7
1989	192.1	202.2	201.3	200.4
1990	202.9	201.8	200.9	200.1
1991	199.7	191.9	200	205
1992	210	215	220	225

EARNINGS PER SHARE [A][C]

Fiscal Year Ends	Oct. 31	Jan. 31	Apr. 30	July 31	Full Fiscal Year
1988	.40	.48	.44	.55	1.87
1989	.52	.48	.48	.55	2.03
1990	2.24	.45	.50	.55	3.74
1991	.41	.53	.50	.51	1.95
1992	.51	.52	.53	.54	2.10

QUARTERLY DIVIDENDS PAID [D]

Calendar	Mar. 31	Jun. 30	Sept. 30	Dec. 31	Full Year
1987	.60	.60	.60	.60	2.40
1988	.60	.60	.60	.60	2.40
1989	.60	.60	.60	.60	2.40
1990	.60	.60	.60	.60	2.40
1991	.60				

1975	1976	1977	1978	1979	1980	1981	1982	1983	1984	1985	1986	1987	1988	1989	1990	1991	1992	©VALUE LINE 94-96	
9.83	9.77	10.20	11.28	11.58	11.76	12.40	12.68	14.52	16.09	16.03	17.74	17.86	17.30	16.93	18.26	17.50	17.65	Book Value per sh [A][B]	16.30
d2.28	.43	.98	1.70	1.12	1.14	2.07	1.93	2.26	2.22	2.43	2.55	2.23	2.32	2.54	2.96	2.60	2.75	"Cash Flow" per sh [C]	3.70
d2.46	.15	.70	1.51	.97	.96	1.87	1.69	2.60	3.49	2.29	4.12	2.52	1.87	2.03	3.74	1.95	2.10	Earnings per sh [C]	2.90
.67	.20	.27	.43	.67	.80	1.27	1.47	1.70	1.95	2.35	2.40	2.40	2.40	2.40	2.40	2.40	2.50	Div'ds Decl'd per sh [D]	3.50
48.16	47.27	40.02	31.52	31.43	23.40	30.93	31.15	22.40	23.40	22.84	24.54	24.67	25.26	25.44	25.29	25.65	26.45	Loans & Real Est per sh [B]	28.95
5.32	5.32	5.32	5.32	5.32	5.36	5.44	5.52	7.53	7.73	7.86	7.86	7.87	7.87	7.88	7.91	8.00	8.50	Common Shs Outst'g [E]	9.50
-54%	-57%	-40%	-33%	-22%	0%	38%	31%	61%	62%	82%	64%	64%	69%	77%	54%	Bold figures are Value Line estimates		Premium Over Book	220%
- -	28.6	8.7	4.9	9.3	12.0	9.0	9.7	8.4	7.1	12.8	7.1	7.1	15.6	14.8	7.5			Avg Ann'l P/E Ratio	17.5
- -	3.66	1.14	.67	1.35	1.59	1.09	1.07	.71	.66	1.08	.48	.48	1.29	1.18	.54			Relative P/E Ratio	1.45
12.5%	4.8%	4.5%	5.9%	7.4%	6.9%	7.6%	8.9%	7.8%	7.8%	8.0%	8.2%	8.3%	8.3%	8.0%	8.5%			Avg Ann'l Div'd Yield	6.7%
29.0	29.9	33.5	44.0	33.1	51.5	39.9	36.8	38.9	53.7	41.0	45.0	Gross Income ($mill) [A]	63.0						
10.1	9.3	15.6	26.7	17.8	32.3	19.9	14.7	16.0	29.5	16.0	17.0	Net Profit ($mill)	28.0						
35.0%	31.3%	46.7%	60.6%	53.8%	62.6%	49.8%	39.9%	41.1%	54.9%	39.0%	37.8%	Net Profit Margin	44.4%						
168.3	171.9	168.7	180.9	178.6	192.9	194.2	198.7	200.4	200.1	205	225	Loans & Real Est ($mill) [B]	275						
2.0	2.5	2.0	1.2	1.0	1.0	1.0	1.0	1.0	1.0	1.0	1.0	Loss Reserve ($mill)	1.5						
11.1%	11.7%	9.3%	9.4%	9.4%	9.5%	9.1%	9.0%	9.1%	9.3%	9.5%	9.5%	Avg Interest Paid	9.0%						
29.0	32.5	- -	- -	- -	- -	- -	3.3	2.0	.7	Nil	Nil	Short-Term Debt ($mill)	Nil						
71.8	69.9	72.6	69.3	68.2	71.6	73.4	69.4	74.0	66.7	70.0	75.0	Long-Term Debt ($mill)	120						
67.5	69.9	109.3	124.4	125.3	139.4	140.6	136.1	133.4	144.4	140	150	Net Worth ($mill)	155						
65.6%	64.7%	91.2%	91.8%	91.5%	90.3%	89.5%	89.5%	87.9%	90.4%	90.5%	89.0%	% Cap Funds to Tot Cap	77.0%						
1.5%	1.6%	2.0%	1.7%	1.8%	3.6%	3.2%	3.8%	4.1%	4.6%	3.5%	3.5%	% Expenses to Assets	3.0%						
12.8%	12.4%	14.1%	17.7%	12.5%	19.2%	12.5%	10.1%	10.9%	16.8%	11.0%	11.0%	% Earned Total Cap'l	14.0%						
15.5%	13.5%	19.4%	22.8%	14.2%	24.0%	14.3%	10.6%	11.9%	20.5%	11.0%	11.5%	% Earned Net Worth	17.5%						

High: 18.3 19.8 23.3 28.0 29.9 32.5 34.3 33.0 31.9 31.9 28.8 30.0
Low: 8.5 14.7 13.7 20.8 22.6 24.0 26.0 23.5 25.6 27.1 22.4 22.9

Percent shares traded 3.0 2.0 1.0

BUSINESS: BRE Properties, Inc., formerly BankAmerica Realty, is a real estate investment trust with an emphasis on income producing real estate. Portfolio at 7/31/90: real property, 93%; mortgages, 7%. Real estate owned by type: shopping centers, 26% at cost (22% on appraised values); apartments, 36% (52%); office buildings, 7% (5%); industrial, 29% (18%); hotels and other, 2% (3%). Major investment locations: California, 70%; Washington, 26%. Has about 5,824 shareholders. Insiders own 1.7% of fully diluted shares; State Farm Insurance, about 25%. Organized: California. Chairman: Eugene P. Carver. President & C.E.O.: Arthur G. Von Thaden. Address: Suite 2500, Telesis Tower, One Montgomery St., San Francisco, CA 94104. Telephone: 415-445-6530.

BRE's February-quarter share net had a healthy rebound from the trust's depressed showing in the first quarter of fiscal 1991 (ends July 31st). The upturn in profits is not as vibrant as it appears, however. October-quarter results were depressed by the one-time capitalization of improvements equal to about 8¢ a share at two apartment projects, while the January quarter included profits of about 2¢ a share accruing from a litigation settlement. Nonetheless, we are encouraged by the net 2¢ consecutive-quarter improvement in share profit, especially given the presently difficult environment for most property owners.

The retail portfolio continues to perform well in a sluggish environment. Occupancy at the trust's showpiece shopping center recently slipped below 90% for the first time in recent memory, but has since bounced back, and now appears headed modestly higher. Occupancy at BRE's other shopping center is a strong 93%, and, in response, designs are being drafted for an expansion that may get under way, assuming successful pre-leasing, before the end of the year.

The trust is still trying to fill a pending vacancy at a light industrial facility and an empty warehouse-distribution project. Near-term prospects for leasing the former, at a rent rate equal to about two times the former level, are fairly good. However, due to the uniqueness of the other facility, which has been vacant for over a year, it may be some time before the space is filled.

BRE's Washington State properties are going great guns. The regional economy is still quite strong, and due to major plant expansions by two large area employers, we think there will be strong upward movements in rent rates over the next few years.

BRE stock is a good selection for respectable long-haul total returns. With cash flow coverage of the dividend at about 108%, the payout appears secure. And the seasoning of existing investments, plus what we gauge as excellent prospects for planned projects, seems likely to provide a growing stream of distributable funds over the pull to 1994–96.

William Acheson   *May 10, 1991*

(A) Fiscal year ends July 31st. (B) At 7/31/90 estimated asset value (incl. real estate at market value rather than book value) was $37.75/fully diluted share. (C) Based on average shares outstanding. Next earnings report due late May. In '90, includes nonrecurring gain from litigation settlement, 43¢; property sale gain, $1.32. (D) Next dividend meeting about May 20. Goes ex about May 26. Approx. dividend payment dates: 20th of Mar., Jun., Sept., Dec. (E) In millions, adjusted for stock split.

Company's Financial Strength **B++**
Stock's Price Stability **100**
Price Growth Persistence **25**
Earnings Predictability **45**

Factual material is obtained from sources believed to be reliable, but the publisher is not responsible for any errors or omissions contained herein.

Figure 20–3   Dollar per Troy Ounce

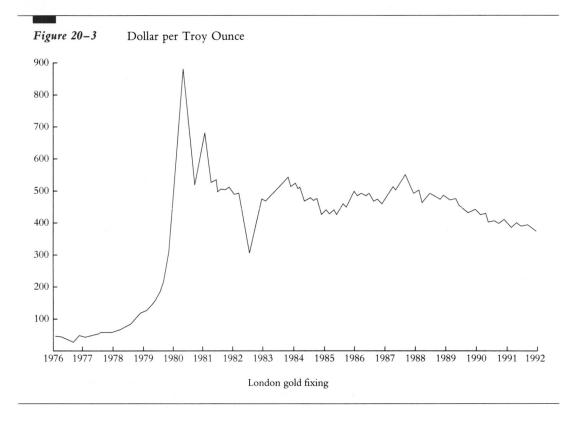

London gold fixing

■ GOLD AND SILVER

We now examine a number of other forms of real asset investments. Precious metals represent the most volatile of the investment alternatives. Gold and silver tend to move up in troubled times and show a decline in value during stable, predictable periods. Observe the movement in the price of gold between January 1976 and July 1992 in Figure 20–3.

Gold

Major factors that tend to drive up gold prices are fear of war, political instability, and inflation (these were particularly evident in 1979 with the takeover of U.S. embassies in Iran and double-digit inflation). Conversely, moderation in worldwide tensions and lower inflation cause a decline in gold prices. High interest rates are also a negative influence on gold prices. When interest rates are high, it may be very expensive to carry gold as an investment.

Gold may be owned in many different forms, and a survey by *Changing Times* indicated 30 percent of the U.S. population with incomes over $30,000 per year owned gold (directly or indirectly) or other forms of precious metals. Let's examine the different forms of gold ownership.

Gold Bullion Gold bullion includes gold bars or wafers. The investor may own anywhere from 1 troy ounce to 10,000 troy ounces (valued at approximately $3.6 million in 1991). Smaller bars generally trade at a 6 to 8 percent premium over pure gold bullion value, with larger bars trading at a 1 to 2 percent premium. Gold bullion may provide storage problems, and unless the gold bars remain in the custody of the bank or dealer who initially sells them, they must be reassayed before being sold.

Gold Coins Many of the storing and assaying costs associated with gold bullion can be avoided by investing directly in gold coins. There are three basic outlets for investing in gold coins. First, there are *gold bullion coins,* such as the South African Krugerrand, the Mexican 50 peso, and the Canadian Maple Leaf. These coins trade at a small premium of 2 to 3 percent over pure bullion value and afford the investor an excellent outlet for taking a position in the market. A second form is represented by *common date gold coins* that are no longer minted, such as the U.S. double eagle, the British sovereign, or the French Napoleon. These coins may trade at as much as 50 to 100 times their pure gold bullion value. Finally, there are gold coins that are *old* and *rare* and that may trade at a numismatic value into the thousands or hundreds of thousands of dollars.

Gold Stocks In addition to gold bullion and gold coins, the investor may take a position in gold by simply buying common stocks that have heavy gold-mining positions. Examples of companies listed on U.S. exchanges include Battle Mountain (U.S. based), Placer Dome Inc. (Canadian based), and Homestake Mining (U.S. based). Because these securities often move in the opposite direction of the stock market as a whole, they may provide excellent portfolio diversification.

Gold Futures Contracts Finally, the gold investor may consider trading in futures contracts. Gold futures are traded on five different U.S. exchanges and on many foreign exchanges.[7]

Silver

Silver has many of the same investment characteristics as gold in terms of being a hedge against inflation and a safe haven for investment during troubled times. Silver moved from $4 a troy ounce in 1976 to over $50 an ounce in early 1980 and then back to $4 an ounce in the early 1990s.

More so than gold, silver has heavy industrial and commercial applications. Areas of utilization include photography, electronic and electrical manufacturing, electroplating, dentistry, and silverware and jewelry. It is estimated that

---

[7]There are also options on gold futures on the Comex.

industrial uses of silver exceed annual production by 150 million ounces per year. Furthermore, the supply of silver does not necessarily increase with price because silver is a by-product of copper, lead, zinc, and gold. Because of the undersupply factor, many consider silver to be appropriate for long-term holding.

Investment in silver can also take many different forms. Some may choose to buy *silver bullion* in the form of silver bars. Because the price of silver generally is ⅟₂₅th to ⅟₇₅th the price of gold and larger bulk is involved for an equivalent dollar size investment, the storage and carrying costs can be quite high. Second, *silver coins* may be bought in large bags or as rare coins for their numismatic value. Keep in mind that dimes, quarters, and half-dollars minted during and before 1965 were 90 percent pure silver. As a third outlet, the investor may wish to consider *silver futures contracts*. Finally, the investor may purchase *stocks* of firms that have interests in silver mining, such as Callahan Mining, Hecla Mining, or Sunshine Mining.

PRECIOUS GEMS

Precious gems include diamonds, rubies, sapphires, and emeralds. Diamonds and other precious gems have appeal to investors because of their small size, easy concealment, and great durability. They are particularly popular in Europe because of a long-standing distrust of paper currencies as a store of value.

The reason diamonds are so valuable can be best understood by considering the production process. It is estimated that 50 to 200 *tons* of rock or sand is required to uncover one carat (⅟₁₄₂ of an ounce) of quality diamonds.

The distribution of diamonds is under virtual monopolistic control by De Beers Consolidated Mines of South Africa, Ltd. It controls the distribution of approximately 80 percent of the world's supply and has a stated policy of maintaining price control. Diamonds have generally enjoyed a steady, somewhat spectacular movement in price. For example, the price of a "D" color, one-carat, flawless, polished diamond increased over tenfold between 1974 and 1980.

Of course, not all diamonds have done so well. Furthermore, there have been substantial breaks in the market, such as in 1974 and 1980–82 when diamond prices declined by one fourth and more. Even with large increases in value, the diamond investor does not automatically come out ahead. Dealer markups may be anywhere from 10 percent to 100 percent so three to five years of steady gain may be necessary to show a substantial profit.

In no areas of investment is product and market knowledge more important. Either you must be an expert yourself or know that you are dealing with an "honest" expert. Diamonds are judged on the basis of the four *c*'s (color, clarity, carat weight, and cut), and the assessment of any stone should be certified by the Gemological Institute of America. As is true of most valuable items, the investor is well advised to purchase the highest quality possible. You are considerably better off using the same amount of money to buy a higher-quality, smaller-carat diamond than a lesser-quality, high-carat diamond.

Baseball Cards Continue to Increase in Value

Although we most often associate baseball cards with the 10-year-old child who coaxes 50 cents from his parents to buy a pack of cards in the drugstore, there is actually a half-billion-dollar a year industry out there. There are 100,000 serious baseball card collectors and millions of child arbitragers doing business on a daily basis.

And why not? In a Sotheby's Holdings Inc.'s New York auction in March 1991, a Honus Wagner 1910 tobacco baseball card sold for $451,000. Only three years ago in the 3rd edition of this book, the card had reportedly been sold for the then seemingly unbelievable sum of $110,000. Why is this card so valuable? Wagner did not approve of smoking and when his card appeared in a tobacco-related set around 1910, he forced the American Tobacco Company to pull all but 100 off the market. Now, only 40 known Wagner cards exist, and the one sold at the Sotheby's auction was in exceptional condition. The law of demand and supply has clearly set in over the decades.

Among other items, a Mickey Mantle Topps card that could be purchased for one cent in 1952 as part of a gum pack went for $49,500 at the same auction.

If you are a Nolan Ryan fan, be prepared to pay $2,000 for his rookie card in mint condition. For the modern collector, such stars as Cecil Fielder, Frank Thomas, and Dave Justice promise appreciation in value. In fact, any hot rookie prospect will do.

Other forms of sports memorabilia have value as well. A baseball clearly autographed by Babe Ruth is worth about $2,500. An authentic Lou Gehrig game-worn uniform carries a $125,000 price tag. A truly enterprising collector went so far as to pay $500 for the dental records of Eddie Cicotte, a long-deceased pitcher for the infamous Chicago Black Sox of 1919.

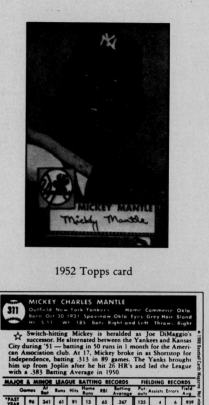

1952 Topps card

■ OTHER COLLECTIBLES

A listing of other collectibles for investment might include art, antiques, stamps, Chinese ceramics, rare books, and other items that appeal to various sectors of our society. Each offers psychic pleasure to the investor as well as the opportunity for profit.

Anyone investing in a collectible should have some understanding of current market conditions and of the factors that determine the inherent worth of the item. Otherwise, you may be buying someone else's undesirable holding at a premium price. It is important not to get swept away in a buying euphoria. The best time to buy art, antiques, or stamps is when the bloom is off the market and dealers are overburdened with inventory, not when there is a weekly story in *The Wall Street Journal* or *Business Week* about overnight fortunes being made. There seems to be a pattern or cycle in the collectibles market the same as in other markets (arts, antiques, and stamps actually do move together).

As is true of other markets, the wise investor in the collectibles market must be sensitive to dealer spreads. A price guide that indicates a doubling in value every two or three years may be meaningless if the person with whom you are dealing sells for $100 and buys back for $50. The wise investor/collector can best maintain profits by dealing with other collectors or investors and eliminating the dealer or middleman from the transaction where possible.

Such periodicals as *Money* magazine and the *Collector/Investor* provide excellent articles on the collectibles market. Specialized periodicals, such as *American Arts and Antiques, Coin World, Linn's Stamp News, The Sports Collectors Digest,* and *Antique Monthly,* also are helpful. The interested reader can find books on almost any type of collectible in a public library or large bookstore.

■ SUMMARY

Investments in real assets must be considered in a total portfolio concept. They offer a measure of inflation protection, an opportunity for efficient diversification, and psychic pleasure to the investor.

A disadvantage is the absence of a large, liquid market such as that provided by the securities markets. There also may be a large dealer or middleman spread, and the investor may have to forgo current income.

The hysteria that grips these markets from time to time not only creates substantial opportunities for profit but also dictates the investor must be particularly cautious about market timing. It can be quite expensive to be the last buyer in a gold or silver boom.

Investors in real estate should be aware of the impact the Tax Reform Act of 1986 had on real estate values. The combined effect of lengthening the depreciation write-off, lowering the marginal tax rate, and disallowing passive losses to be written off against other forms of income drove down commercial

real estate values across the country. However, all markets tend to adjust over time, and some bargain opportunities may exist in real estate in the 1990s. Because of the disallowance of many tax advantages in real estate, the emphasis now is on cash flow generation and the potential for capital appreciation.

The financing of real estate is becoming increasingly complicated as lenders seek alternatives to fixed-rate mortgages. Thus, we have seen the creation of the adjustable rate mortgage (ARM) and other floating-rate plans, the graduated payment mortgage (GPM), and the shared appreciation mortgage (SAM).

Gold and silver represent two highly volatile forms of real assets in which price movements often run counter to events in the economy and the world. Bad news is good news (and vice versa) for precious-metal investors. Gold and silver may generally be purchased in bullion or bulk form, as coins, in the commodities futures market, or indirectly through securities of firms specializing in gold or silver mining.

Precious gems and other collectibles, such as art, antiques, stamps, Chinese ceramics, and rare books, have caught the attention of investors in recent times. Although there are many warning signs, the wise and patient investor can do well over the long run. The investor should understand the factors that determine value before taking a serious investment position.

IMPORTANT WORDS AND CONCEPTS

real assets 652

straight-line depreciation 656

adjustable rate mortgage 660

graduated payment mortgage 660

shared appreciation mortgage 660

equity participation 661

limited partnership 662

blind pool 663

real estate investment trust (REIT) 664

equity trusts 664

construction and development trusts 664

mortgage trusts 664

DISCUSSION QUESTIONS

1. Why might real assets offer an opportunity as an inflation hedge?
2. Explain why real assets might add to effective portfolio diversification.
3. What are some disadvantages of investing in real estate.
4. In what way does real estate provide for a high degree of leverage?
5. What is an adjustable rate mortgage?
6. For what type of borrower is the graduated payment mortgage best suited?
7. Explain a shared appreciation mortgage.
8. What is meant by a seller loan with a call privilege?
9. How is liability handled in a limited partnership?

10. What are REITs? What are the various types of REITs?

11. What are some factors that drive up the price of gold? What are factors that drive it down?

12. What are three different ways to invest in gold coins?

13. Suggest some commercial and industrial uses of silver. What forms can silver investments take?

14. Explain how the dealer spread can affect the rate of return on a collectible item.

PROBLEM

Real estate
investment
analysis

1. An investor has a rental duplex with land valued at $30,000 and the building valued at $90,000. Straight-line depreciation over 27½ years will be taken. The investor will be actively involved in the management of the property. He is in a 31 percent tax bracket.

a. What is the annual depreciation deduction? (Round to the nearest dollar.)

b. Assume revenue minus all other expenses besides depreciation provides $2,800 of net income in the first year. Now, considering the depreciation computed in Part a, how much will cash flow be in the first year? Add together lines (3), (4), and (5) below to get your answer.

(1) Net income before depreciation	$2,800
(2) − Depreciation	_____
(3) Before-tax income (or loss)	_____
(4) + Tax benefit (31% rate)	_____
(5) + Depreciation	_____
(6) Cash flow	_____

c. Assume a 25-year loan equal to 70 percent of the total value of the property at 10 percent interest. Annual payments will be $9,254. How much of the annual payment will go toward interest and how much will go toward the repayment of principal in the first year?

d. Based on the information in Parts b and c, compute net cash flow.

Cash flow (line (6) of Part b)	_____
− Repayment of principal	_____
Net cash flow	_____

e. What is the ratio of net cash flow to initial cash investment? Initial investment equals total investment minus the loan?

f. If there is 3.5 percent inflation related to total property value in the first year, what will be the ratio of inflationary gains to initial cash investment?

g. Comment on the comparative importance of your answers to Parts e and f.

SELECTED REFERENCES

Portfolio Considerations with Real Assets

Robichek, Alexander A.; Richard A. Cohn; and John J. Pringle. "Return on Alternative Media and Implications for Portfolio Construction." *Journal of Business,* July 1972, pp. 427–43.

Van Caspel, Venita. *Money Dynamics for the New Economy.* New York: Simon & Schuster, 1986.

Investments in Real Estate

Alpert, Mark. "Office Buildings for the 1990s." *Fortune,* November 18, 1991, pp. 140–42.

Folger, H. Russell. "20% in Real Estate: Can Theory Justify It?" *Journal of Portfolio Management,* Winter 1984, pp. 6–13.

Grissom, Terry V.; James L. Kuhle; and Carl H. Walther. "Diversification Works in Real Estate, Too." *Journal of Portfolio Management,* Winter 1987, pp. 66–71.

Kaplan, Howard M. "Farmland as a Portfolio Investment." *Journal of Portfolio Management,* Winter 1985, pp. 73–79.

Kopcke, Richard W., and Peter C. Aldrich. "A Real Estate Crisis: Averted or Just Postponed?" *Journal of Portfolio Management,* Spring 1984, pp. 21–29.

Lipscomb, Joseph. "Discount Rates for Cash Equivalent Analysis." *Appraisal Journal,* January 1981, pp. 23–33.

Meyers, William. "Real Estate: A High Water Mark?" *Institutional Investor,* January 1988, pp. 129–36.

───── . "Real Estate: Shuwa's Great American Gamble." *Institutional Investor,* February 1988, pp. 136–38.

Precious Metals and Precious Gems

Regular articles featured in: *Money, Personal Investor, Consumer Reports,* and *Changing Times.*

Collectibles

Periodicals: *American Arts and Antiques, Antique Monthly, Coin World, Collector/Investor, Linn's Stamp News,* and *Sports Collectors Digest.*

Part Seven

Introduction to Portfolio Management

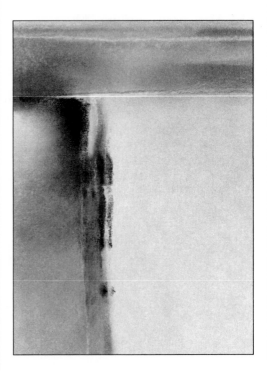

Outline

Modern portfolio managers are being held accountable not only for the return they make, but also for the risk of their portfolio. One way to reduce this risk is through portfolio insurance (insuring a portfolio against decline), but does this technique really work?

Suppose you bought a beautiful new BMW or Mercedes (no, this is not a fairy tale). One of your first concerns, besides being sure that everyone on campus saw you behind the wheel of your treasured automobile, would be that you had adequate insurance to protect against an unexpected event. This might include a crash with another car, a burglary, a fire, and so on.

The same need for insurance applies to those who manage large pools of money. Although professional money managers normally hope the market will go up, they need financial protection against a sharp drop in the market. Although the protection involves some expense, the cost is justified just as the auto insurance premium you pay can normally be justified as a prudent business expense.

Actually, specialized computer programs that assist the money manager represent a form of portfolio insurance. These programs keep an eye out for a downturn in the market; when the market drops, the program automatically pre-sells baskets of stocks in the futures market. That selling action protects the money manager against a crash.

A money manager who has $100 million in a diversified stock portfolio would normally absorb a loss of $20 million if the market went down by 20 percent. But with portfolio insurance, the manager is simultaneously selling futures contracts that can be bought back at a lower price as the market falls. Thus, the manager is insured (hedged) against the consequences of a falling market.

The popularity of portfolio insurance can be linked to the development of modern portfolio theory in which money managers are held accountable not only for the return they generate, but also for the risks they take in generating that return. Portfolios that have widely changing values from quarter to quarter are thought to be much less desirable than steadily performing portfolios even though their total return might be equal over 5 or 10 years.

Portfolio insurance may be a good approach for lessening risk if only a handful of portfolio managers are using it, but what happens if a large number of portfolio managers are committed to a similar plan?

Event number one: The stock market falls sharply due to bad economic news for a variety of reasons.

Event number two: The money managers' computer programs see the drop and automatically pre-sell a number of baskets of stocks in the futures market as insurance against the crash.

Event number three: The stock market continues to plummet, partially as a result of the activation of the portfolio insurance sell programs.

Event number four: The computer programs kick in again and pre-sell more baskets of stocks. And on and on!

Where does this all end? Does the initial protection provided by portfolio insurance actually create a new round of larger losses by the actual presence of the insurance? Market researchers are very concerned about this. ∎

21

A Basic Look at Portfolio Management and Capital Market Theory

In this chapter, we develop a more complete understanding of how the investor perceives risk and demands compensation for it. We eventually build toward a theory of portfolio management that incorporates these concepts. While the use of mathematical terms is an essential ingredient to a basic understanding of portfolio theory, more involved or complicated concepts are treated in appendixes at the end of the chapter.

As indicated in Chapter 1, risk is generally associated with uncertainty about future outcomes. The greater the dispersion of possible outcomes, the greater the risk. We also observed in Chapter 1 that most investors tend to be risk-averse; that is, all things being equal, investors prefer less risk to more risk and will increase their risk-taking position only if a premium for risk is involved. Each investor has a different attitude toward risk. The inducement necessary to cause a given investor to withdraw funds from a savings account to drill an oil well may be quite different from yours. For some, only a very small premium for risk is necessary, while others may not wish to participate unless there are exceptionally high rewards. We begin the chapter with a formal development of risk measures.

■ FORMAL MEASUREMENT OF RISK

Having defined risk as uncertainty about future outcomes, how do we actually measure risk? The first task is to design a probability distribution of anticipated future outcomes. This is no small task. The possible outcomes and associated probabilities are likely to be based on economic projections, past experience, subjective judgments, and many other variables. For the most part, we are forcing ourselves to write down what already exists in our head. Having established the probability distribution, we then determine the expected value and the dispersion around that expected value. The greater the dispersion, the greater the risk.

Expected Value

To determine the **expected value**, we multiply each possible outcome by its probability of occurrence. Assume we are considering two investment proposals where K represents a possible outcome and P represents the probability of that outcome based on the state of the economy. If we were dealing with stocks, K would represent the price appreciation potential plus the dividend yield (total return). Table 21–1 presents the data for two investments, i and j.

We will say that $\overline{K}_i$ (the expected value of investment i) equals $\Sigma K_i P_i$. In this case, the answer would be 10.0 percent, as shown under Formula 21–1 on page 679.

Table 21–1		Return and Probabilities for Investments *i* and *j*		
Investment i			*Investment j*	
	P_i (Probability of K_i Occurring)	Possible State of the Economy		P_j (Probability of K_j Occurring)
5%	.20	Recession	20%	.20
7	.30	Slow growth	8	.30
13	.30	Moderate growth	8	.30
15	.20	Strong economy	6	.20

$$\overline{K}_i = \Sigma K_i P_i \tag{21–1}$$

K_i	P_i	$K_i P_i$
5%	.20	1.0%
7	.30	2.1
13	.30	3.9
15	.20	3.0
		10.0% $= \Sigma K_i P_i$

Standard Deviation

The commonly used measure of dispersion is the **standard deviation,** which is a measure of the spread of the outcomes around the expected value. The formula for the standard deviation is:

$$\sigma_i = \sqrt{\Sigma(K_i - \overline{K}_i)^2 P_i} \tag{21–2}$$

Let's determine the standard deviation for investment *i* around the expected value $(\overline{K}_i)$ of 10 percent.

K_i	$\overline{K}_i$	P_i	$(K_i - \overline{K}_i)$	$(K_i - \overline{K}_i)^2$	$(K_i - \overline{K}_i)^2 P_i$
5%	10%	.20	-5%	25%	5.0%
7	10	.30	-3	9	2.7
13	10	.30	$+3$	9	2.7
15	10	.20	$+5$	25	5.0
					15.4% $= \Sigma(K_i - \overline{K}_i)^2 P_i$

$$\sigma_i = \sqrt{\Sigma(K_i - \overline{K}_i)^2 P_i}, = \sqrt{15.4\%} = 3.9\%$$

The standard deviation of investment i is 3.9 percent (rounded). To have some feel for the relative risk characteristics of this investment, we compare it to a second proposal, investment j.

We assume investment j is a countercyclical investment. It does well during a recession and poorly in a strong economy. Perhaps it represents a firm in the housing industry that is most profitable when the economy is sluggish and interest rates are low. Under these circumstances, people will avail themselves of low-cost financing to purchase a new home, and the stock of the firm will do well. In a booming economy, interest rates will advance rapidly, and the financing of housing will become expensive. Thus, we have a countercyclical investment. The outcomes and probabilities of outcomes for investment j are as follows: The expected value for investment j is:

$$\overline{K}_j = \Sigma K_j P_j$$

K_j	P_j	$K_j P_j$
20%	.20	4.0%
8	.30	2.4
8	.30	2.4
6	.20	1.2
		$\overline{K}_j = 10.0\%$

The standard deviation for investment j is:

$$\sigma_j = \sqrt{\Sigma(K_j - \overline{K}_j)^2 P_j}\,,$$

K_j	$\overline{K}_j$	P_j	$(K_j - \overline{K}_j)$	$(K_j - \overline{K}_j)^2$	$(K_j - \overline{K}_j)^2 P_j$
20%	10%	.20	+10%	100%	20.0%
8	10	.30	−2	4	1.2
8	10	.30	−2	4	1.2
6	10	.20	−4	16	3.2
					$25.6\% = \Sigma(K_j - \overline{K}_j)^2 P_j$

$$\sigma_j = \sqrt{\Sigma(K_j - \overline{K}_j)^2 P_j} = \sqrt{25.6\%} = 5.1\% \text{ (rounded)}$$

We now see we have two investments, each with an expected value of 10 percent but with varying performances in different types of economies and different standard deviations (3.9 percent versus 5.1 percent).[1]

---

[1]Actually, rather than use the standard deviation, we can also use its squared value, termed the *variance,* to describe risk. That is, we may use σ^2 (the standard deviation squared) to describe risk in an individual security.

■ PORTFOLIO EFFECT

An investor who is holding only investment i may wish to consider bringing investment j into the portfolio. If the stocks are weighted evenly, the new portfolio's expected value will be 10 percent. We define K_p as the expected value of the portfolio.

$$K_p = X_i \overline{K}_i + X_j \overline{K}_j \qquad (21-3)$$

The X values represent the weights assigned by the investor to each component in the portfolio and are 50 percent for both investments in this example. The $\overline{K}_i$ and $\overline{K}_j$ values were previously determined to be 10 percent. Thus we have:

$$K_p = .5(10\%) + .5(10\%) = 5\% + 5\% = 10\%$$

What about the standard deviation for the combined portfolio (σ_p)? If a weighted average were taken of the two investments, the new standard deviation would be 4.5 percent.

$$X_i \sigma_i + X_j \sigma_j$$
$$.5(3.9\%) + .5(5.1\%) = 1.95\% + 2.55\% = 4.5\%$$

The interesting element is that the investor in investment i would appear to be losing from the combined investment. His expected value remains at 10 percent, but his standard deviation has increased from 3.9 percent to 4.5 percent. Given that he is risk-averse, he appears to be getting more risk rather than less risk by expanding his portfolio.

There is one fallacy in the analysis. The standard deviation of a portfolio is not based on the simple weighted average of the individual standard deviations (as the expected value is). Rather, it considers significant interaction between the investments. If one investment does well during a given economic condition while the other does poorly and vice versa, there may be significant risk reduction from combining the two, and the standard deviation for the portfolio may be less than the standard deviation for either investment (this is the reason we do not simply take the weighted average of the two).

Note in Figure 21–1 on page 682 the risk-reduction potential from combining the two investments under study. Investment i alone may produce outcomes anywhere from 5 to 15 percent, and investment j, from 6 to 20 percent. By combining the two, we narrow the range for investment (i, j) to from 7.5 to 12.5 percent. Thus, we have reduced the risk while keeping the expected value constant at 10 percent. We now examine the appropriate standard deviation formula for the two investments.

Figure 21–1   Investment Outcomes under Different Conditions

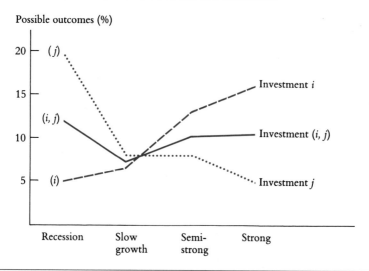

Standard Deviation for a Two-Asset Portfolio

The standard deviation for a two-asset portfolio is presented in Formula 21–4.[2]

$$\sigma_p = \sqrt{X_i^2 \sigma_i^2 + X_j^2 \sigma_j^2 + 2X_i X_j r_{ij} \sigma_i \sigma_j} \qquad (21\text{–}4)$$

The only new term in the expression is r_{ij}, the **correlation coefficient** or measurement of joint movement between the two variables. The value for r_{ij} can be from -1 to $+1$, although for most variables, the correlation coefficient falls somewhere in between these two values. Figure 21–2 demonstrates the concept of correlation. In Panel A, assets i and j are perfectly correlated, with r_{ij} equal to $+1$. As i increases in value, so does j in exact proportion to i. In Panel B, assets i and j exhibit a perfect negative correlation, with r_{ij} equal to -1. As i increases, j decreases in exact proportion to i. Panel C demonstrates assets i and j having no correlation at all, with r_{ij} equal to 0.

The actual computation of the correlation coefficient for investments i and j is covered in Appendix 21–A. It is not necessary to go through Appendix 21–A before proceeding with our discussion, though some readers may wish

---

[2]For a multiple asset portfolio, the expression is written as:

$$\sigma_p = \sqrt{\sum_{i=1}^{N} X_i^2 \sigma_i^2 + 2 \sum_{i=1}^{N-1} \sum_{j=1+1}^{N} X_i X_j r_{ij} \sigma_i \sigma_j}$$

N is the number of securities in the portfolio.

Figure 21-2   Correlation Analysis

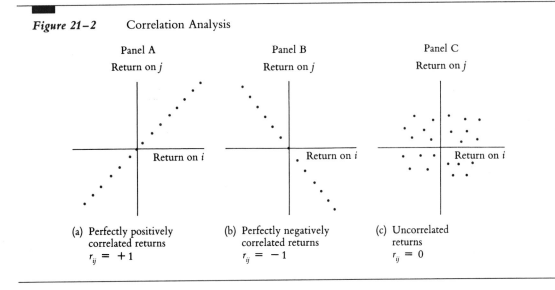

Panel A	Panel B	Panel C
Return on *j*	Return on *j*	Return on *j*

(a) Perfectly positively correlated returns
$r_{ij} = +1$

(b) Perfectly negatively correlated returns
$r_{ij} = -1$

(c) Uncorrelated returns
$r_{ij} = 0$

to do so. As indicated in Appendix 21–A, the correlation coefficient (r_{ij}) between our investment *i* and investment *j* is $-.70$. This indicates the two investments show a high degree of negative correlation. Plugging this value into Formula 21–4, along with other previously determined values, the standard deviation (σ_p) for the two-asset portfolio can be computed.[3]

$$\sigma_p = \sqrt{X_i^2\sigma_i^2 + X_j^2\sigma_j^2 + 2X_iX_jr_{ij}\sigma_i\sigma_j} \qquad (21\text{–}4)$$

where:

$$X_i = .5, \ \sigma_i = 3.9$$
$$X_j = .5, \ \sigma_j = 5.1$$
$$r_{ij} = -.70$$
$$\begin{aligned}
\sigma_p &= \sqrt{(.5)^2(3.9)^2 + (.5)^2(5.1)^2 + 2(.5)(.5)(-.7)(3.9)(5.1)} \\
&= \sqrt{(.25)(15.4) + (.25)(25.6) + 2(.25)(-.7)(19.9)} \\
&= \sqrt{3.85 + 6.4 + (.5)(-13.93)} \\
&= \sqrt{3.85 + 6.4 - 6.97} \\
&= \sqrt{3.28} = 1.8\%
\end{aligned}$$

The standard deviation of the portfolio of 1.8 percent is less than the standard deviation of either investment *i* (3.9 percent) or *j* (5.1 percent). Any time

---

[3]Note that the squared values, such as $(3.9)^2 = 15.4$, are the reverse of earlier computations. Previously, we found the square root of 15.4 to be 3.9 (see computation under Formula 21–2). The use of rounding introduces slight discrepancies where we square numbers for which we previously found the square root.

two investments have a correlation coefficient (r_{ij}) less than $+1$ (perfect positive correlation), some risk reduction will be possible by combining the assets in a portfolio. In the real world, most items are positively correlated; the extent that we can still get risk reduction from positively correlated items gives extra meaning to portfolio management. Note the impact of various assumed correlation coefficients for the two investments previously described in terms of individual standard deviations.[4]

Correlation Coefficient (r_{ij})	Portfolio Standard Deviation (σ_p)
$+1.0$	4.5
$+ .5$	3.9
$.0$	3.2
$- .5$	2.3
$- .7$	1.8
-1.0	0.0

The conclusion to be drawn from our portfolio analysis discussion is that the most significant risk factor associated with an individual investment may not be its own standard deviation but how it affects the standard deviation of a portfolio through correlation. As we shall later observe in this chapter, there is not considered to be a risk premium for the total risk or standard deviation of an individual security, but only for that risk component that cannot be eliminated by various portfolio diversification techniques.

■ DEVELOPING AN EFFICIENT PORTFOLIO

We have seen how the combination of two investments has allowed us to maintain our return of 10 percent but reduce the portfolio standard deviation to 1.8 percent. We also saw in the preceding table that different coefficient correlations produce many different possibilities for portfolio standard deviations. A shrewd portfolio manager may wish to consider a large number of portfolios, each with a different expected value and standard deviation, based on the expected values and standard deviations of the individual securities and, more importantly, on the correlations between the individual securities. Though we have been discussing a two-asset portfolio case, our example may be expanded to cover 5-, 10-, or even 100-asset portfolios.[5] The major tenets

---

[4]Each is assumed to represent 50 percent of the portfolio.

[5]The incremental benefit from reduction of the portfolio standard deviation through adding securities appears to diminish fairly sharply with a portfolio of 10 securities and is quite small with a portfolio as large as 20. A portfolio of 12 to 14 securities is generally thought to be of sufficient size to enjoy the majority of desirable portfolio effects. See W. H. Wagner and S. C. Lau, "The Effect of Diversification on Risk," *Financial Analysts Journal,* November–December 1971, pp. 48–53.

of portfolio theory that we are currently examining were developed by Professor Harry Markowitz in the 1950s, and so we refer to them as Markowitz portfolio theory.

Assume we have identified the following risk-return possibilities for eight different portfolios (there may also be many more, but we will restrict ourselves to this set for now).

Portfolio	K_p	σ_p
A	10%	1.8%
B	10	2.1
C	12	3.0
D	13	4.2
E	13	5.0
F	14	5.0
G	14	5.8
H	15	7.2

In diagramming our various risk-return points, we show the values in Figure 21–3 on page 686.

Though we have only diagrammed eight possibilities, we see an efficient set of portfolios would lie along the ACFH line. This line is efficient because the portfolios on this line dominate all other attainable portfolios. This line is called the **efficient frontier** because the portfolios on the efficient frontier provide the best risk-return trade-off. That is, along this efficient frontier we can receive a maximum return for a given level of risk or a minimum risk for a given level of return. Portfolios do not exist above the efficient frontier, and portfolios below this line do not offer acceptable alternatives to points along the line. As an example of *maximum return* for a given level of risk, consider point F. Along the efficient frontier, we are receiving a 14 percent return for a 5 percent risk level, whereas directly below point F, portfolio E provides a 13 percent return for the same 5 percent standard deviation.

To also demonstrate that we are getting *minimum risk* for a given return level, we can examine point A in which we receive a 10 percent return for a 1.8 percent risk level, whereas to the right of point A, we get the same 10 percent return from B, but a less desirable 2.1 percent risk level. One portfolio can consist of various proportions of two assets or two portfolios. For example, we can connect the points between A and C by generating portfolios that combine different percentages of portfolio A and portfolio C and so on between portfolio C and F and portfolio F and H. Though we have shown but eight points (portfolios), a fully developed efficient frontier may be based on a virtually unlimited number of observations as is presented in Figure 21–4.

In Figure 21–4, we once again view the efficient frontier in relationship to the feasible set and note certain risk-return possibilities are not attainable (and

Figure 21–3   Diagram of Risk-Return Trade-Offs

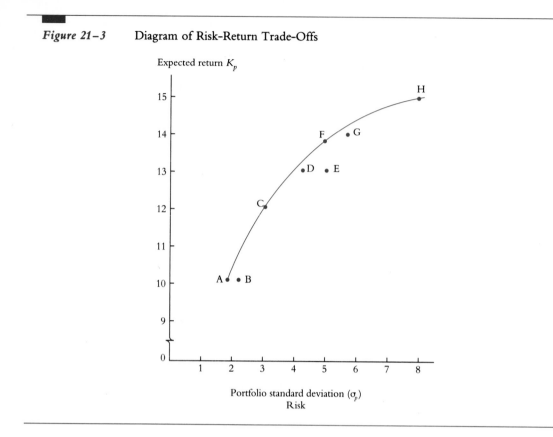

should be disregarded). At this point in the analysis, we can stipulate that the various points along the efficient frontier are all considered potentially optimal and a given investor must choose the most appropriate single point based on individual risk-return trade-off desires. We would say that a low-risk-oriented investor might prefer point A in Figure 21–3, whereas a more-risk-oriented investor would prefer point F or H. At each of these points, the investor is getting the best risk-return trade-off for his or her own particular risk-taking propensity.

Risk-Return Indifference Curves

To actually pair an investor with an appropriate point along the efficient frontier, we look at his or her indifference curve as illustrated in Figure 21–5.

The **indifference curves** show the investor's trade-off between risk and return. The steeper the slope of the curve, the more risk-averse the investor is.

Figure 21–4   Expanded View of Efficient Frontier

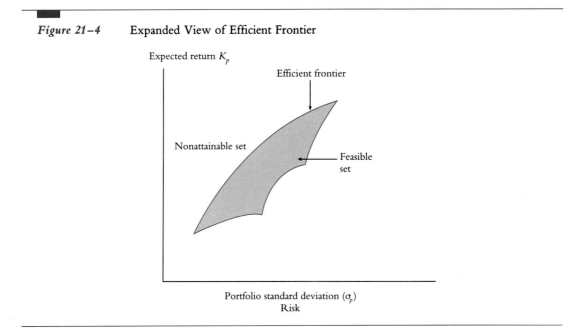

Expected return K_p

Efficient frontier

Nonattainable set

Feasible
set

Portfolio standard deviation (σ_p)
Risk

Figure 21–5   Risk-Return Indifference Curves

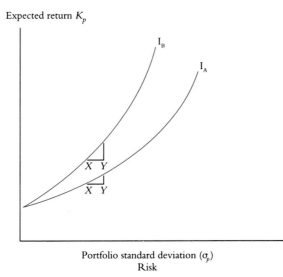

Expected return K_p

I_B

I_A

$\overline{X \quad Y}$

$\overline{X \quad Y}$

Portfolio standard deviation (σ_p)
Risk

Figure 21–6   Indifference Curves for Investor A

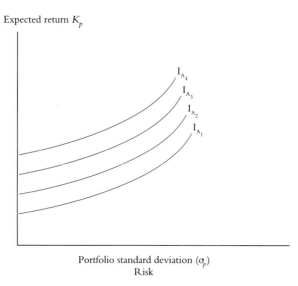

For example, in the case of investor B (I_B in Figure 21–5), the indifference curve has a steeper slope than that for Investor A (I_A). This means investor B will require more incremental return (more of a risk premium) for each additional unit of risk. Note that to take risks, investor B requires approximately twice as much incremental return as investor A between points X and Y. Investor A is still somewhat risk-averse and perhaps represents a typical investor in the capital markets.

Once the shape of an investor's indifference curve is determined, a second objective can be established—to attain the highest curve possible. For example, investor A, initially shown in Figure 21–5, would have a whole set of similarly shaped indifference curves as presented in Figure 21–6.

While he is indifferent to any point along a given curve (such as I_{A_4}), he is not indifferent to achieving the highest curve possible (I_{A_4} is clearly superior to I_{A_1}). I_{A_4} provides more return at all given risk levels. The only limitation to achieving the highest possible indifference curve is the feasible set of investments available.

Optimum Portfolio

The investor must theoretically match his own risk-return indifference curve with the best investments available in the market as represented by points on the efficient frontier. We see in Figure 21–7 that investor A will achieve the highest possible indifference curve at point C along the efficient frontier.

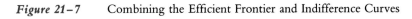

Figure 21–7   Combining the Efficient Frontier and Indifference Curves

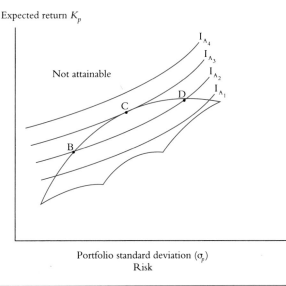

This is the point of tangency between his own indifference curve (I_{A_3}) and the efficient frontier. Both curves have the same slope or risk-return characteristics at this point. While a point along indifference curve (I_{A_4}) might provide a higher level of utility, it is not attainable. Also, any other point along the efficient frontier would cross a lower-level indifference curve and be inferior to point C. For example, points B and D cross I_{A_2}, providing less return for a given level of risk than I_{A_3}. Investors must relate the shape of their *own* risk-return indifference curves to the efficient frontier to determine that point of tangency providing maximum benefits.

■ CAPITAL ASSET PRICING MODEL

The development of the efficient frontier in the previous section gives insight into optimum portfolio mixes in an appropriate risk-return context. Nevertheless, the development of multiple portfolios is a rather difficult and tedious task. Professors Sharpe, Lintner, and others have allowed us to take the philosophy of efficient portfolios into a more generalized and meaningful context through the **capital asset pricing model.** Under this model, we examine the theoretical underpinnings through which assets are valued based on their risk characteristics.

The capital asset pricing model (CAPM) takes off where the efficient frontier concluded through the introduction of a new investment outlet, the risk-free asset (R_F). A risk-free asset has no risk of default and a standard deviation

Figure 21–8   Basic Diagram of the Capital Asset Pricing Model

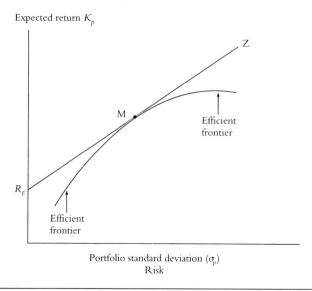

of 0 ($\sigma_{R_F} = 0$) and is the lowest assumed safe return that can be earned. A U.S. Treasury bill or Treasury bond is often considered representative of a risk-free asset. Under the capital asset pricing model, we introduce the notion of combining the risk-free asset and the efficient frontier with the development of the $R_F MZ$ line as indicated in Figure 21–8.

The $R_F MZ$ line opens up the possibility of a whole new set of superior investment opportunities. That is, by combining some portion of the risk-free asset as represented by (R_F) with M (a point along the efficient frontier), we create new investment opportunities that will allow us to reach higher indifference curves than would be possible simply along the efficient frontier. The only point along the efficient frontier that now has significance is point M, where the straight line from R_F is tangent to the old efficient frontier. Let us further examine the $R_F MZ$ line.

We can reach points along the $R_F MZ$ line in a number of different ways. To be at point R_F, we would simply buy a risk-free asset. To be at a point between R_F and M, we would buy a combination of R_F and the M portfolio along the efficient frontier. To be at a point between M and Z, we buy M with our available funds and then borrow additional funds to further increase our purchase of the M portfolio (an example of this would be to be at point P in Figure 21–9). To the extent that M is higher than R_F and we can borrow at a rate equal to R_F or slightly higher, we can get larger returns with a combination of buying M and borrowing additional funds to buy M. (Of course, this calls for greater risk as well.)

Figure 21–9   The CAPM and Indifference Curves

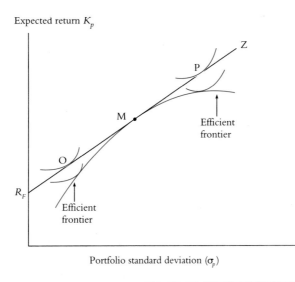

We also note that point M is considered the optimum "market basket" of investments available (though you may wish to combine this market basket with risk-free assets or borrowing). If you took all the possible investments that investors could acquire and determined the optimum basket of investments, you would come up with point M (because it is along the efficient frontier and tangent to the R_F line). Point M can be measured by the total return on the Standard & Poor's 500 Stock Average, the Dow Jones Industrial Average, the New York Stock Exchange Index, or similar measures. If point M or the market were not represented by the optimum risk-return portfolio for all investments at a point in time, then it is assumed there would be an instantaneous change, and the market measure (point M) would once again be in equilibrium (be optimal).

Capital Market Line

The previously discussed R_FMZ line is called the **capital market line (CML)** and is once again presented in Figure 21–10.

The formula for the capital market line in Figure 21–10 may be written as:

$$K_P = R_F + \left(\frac{K_M - R_F}{\sigma_M - 0}\right) \sigma_P$$

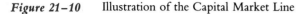

Figure 21–10   Illustration of the Capital Market Line

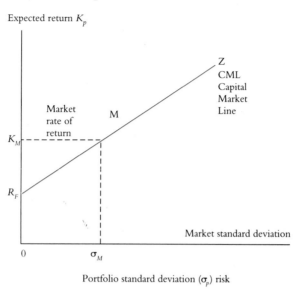

We indicate that the expected return on any portfolio (K_P) is equal to the risk-free rate of return (R_F), plus the slope of the line times a value along the horizontal axis (σ_P) indicating the amount of risk undertaken. We can relate the formula for the capital market line to the basic equation for a straight line as follows:

$$\text{Straight line } Y = a + b \cdot X$$

$$\text{Capital market line } K_P = R_F + \left(\frac{K_M - R_F}{\sigma_M}\right) \cdot \sigma_P$$

In using the capital market line, we start with a minimum rate of return of R_F and then say any additional return is a reward for risk. The reward for risk or risk premium is equal to the market rate of return (K_M) minus the risk-free rate (R_F) divided by the market standard deviation (σ_M). If the market rate of return (K_M) is 9 percent and the risk-free rate of return (R_F) is 6 percent, with a market standard deviation (σ_M) of 10 percent, there is a risk premium of .3. Then if the standard deviation of our portfolio (σ_P) is 14 percent, we can expect a return of 10.2 percent along the CML computed as follows:

$$K_P = R_F + \left(\frac{K_M - R_F}{\sigma_M}\right) \sigma_P \qquad (21\text{--}5)$$

$$K_P = 6\% + \left(\frac{9\% - 6\%}{10\%}\right) 14\%$$

$$= 6\% + \left(\frac{3\%}{10\%}\right) 14\%$$

$$= 6\% + (.3)14\%$$

$$= 6\% + 4.2\% = 10.2\%$$

The essence of the capital market line is that the way to get larger returns is to take increasingly higher risks. Thus, the only way to climb up the K_P *return* line in Figure 21–10 is to extend yourself out on the σ_P *risk* line. Portfolio managers who claim highly superior returns may have taken larger than normal risks and thus may not really be superior performers on a risk-adjusted basis. We shall see in the following chapter that the best way to measure a portfolio manager is to evaluate his returns relative to the risks taken. Average to slightly above average returns based on low risk may be superior to high returns based on high risk. One does not easily exceed market-dictated constraints for risk and return.

■ RETURN ON AN INDIVIDUAL SECURITY

We have been examining return expectations for a portfolio; we now turn our attention to an individual security. Once again the return potential is closely tied to risk. However, when dealing with an individual security, the premium return for risk is not related to *all* the risk in the investment as measured by the standard deviation (σ). The reason for this is that the standard deviation is made up of two types of risk, but only one is accorded a premium return under the capital asset pricing model.

We now begin an analytical process that allows us to get at the two forms of risk in an individual security. The first form of risk is measured by the beta coefficient.

Beta Coefficient In analyzing the performance of an individual security, it is first important to measure its relationship to the market through the **beta coefficient.** Let us lay the groundwork for understanding beta. In the case of a potential investment, stock i, we can observe its relationship to the market by tracing its total return performance relative to market total return over the last five years.[6]

---

[6]Though monthly calculations would be desirable, we can satisfy our same basic objectives with annual data.

Year	Stock *i* Return (*K*)	Market Return (*K*$_M$)
1	4.8%	6.5%
2	14.5	11.8
3	19.1	14.9
4	3.7	1.1
5	15.6	12.0

We see that stock *i* moves somewhat with the market. Plotting the values in Figure 21–11, we observe a line that is upward sloping at slightly above a 45-degree angle.

A straight line of best fit has been drawn through the various points representing the following formula:

$$K_i = a_i + b_i K_M + e_i \qquad (21\text{–}6)$$

K_i represents the anticipated stock return based on the formula; a_i (alpha) is the point at which the line crosses the vertical axis; b_i (beta) is the slope of the line; K_M is the independent variable of market return; and e_i is the random error term. The $a_i + b_i K_M$ portion of the formula describes a straight line, and e_i represents deviations or random, nonrecurring movements away from the straight line. In the present example, the formula for the straight line is $K_i = .42 + 1.20\,K_M$ (indicating a beta or line slope of 1.2). These values can be approximated by drawing a line of best fit as indicated in Figure 21–11 or through the use of least squares regression analysis presented in Appendix 21–B. Basically, the equation tells us how volatile our stock is relative to the market through the beta coefficient. In the present case, if the market moves up or down by a given percent, our stock is assumed to move 1.2 times that amount.

Since beta measures the correlation of a stock's total return to a market index, the beta of the market when regressed on itself will always be 1.0. With a beta of 1.2, our stock is considered to be 20 percent more volatile than the market and therefore riskier. A stock with average volatility would have a beta of 1.0, the same beta as the market. A stock having a beta of less than 1.0 would have less risk than the market.

Systematic and Unsystematic Risk

Previously, we mentioned the two major types of risk associated with a stock. One is the market movement or beta (b_i) risk. If the market moves up or down, a stock is assumed to change in value. This type of risk is referred to as **systematic risk** and was introduced in Chapter 1. The second type of risk is represented by the error term (e_i) and indicates changes in value not associated with market movement. It may represent the temporary influence of a competitor's new product, changes in raw material prices, or unusual economic

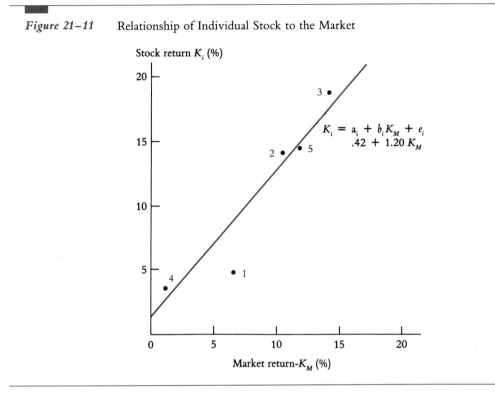

Figure 21–11   Relationship of Individual Stock to the Market

and government influences on a given firm. These changes are peculiar to an individual security or industry at a given point and are not directly correlated with the market. This second type of risk is referred to as **unsystematic risk.**

Since unsystematic risk is associated with an individual company or industry, it may be diversified away in a large portfolio and is not a risk inherent in investing in common stocks. Thus, by picking stocks that are less than perfectly correlated, unsystematic risk may be eliminated. For example, the inherent risks of investing in cyclical semiconductor stocks may be diversified away by investing in countercyclical housing stocks. Researchers have indicated that all but 15 percent of unsystematic risk may be eliminated with a carefully selected portfolio of 10 stocks, and all but 11 percent, with a portfolio of 20 stocks.[7]

The systematic risk (beta) cannot be diversified away even in a large portfolio, and therefore, the market compensates an investor with a higher expected return when that investor buys securities with a high beta, or a lower expected return than the market when the investor buys securities with a beta

---

[7]Wagner and Lau, "The Effect of Diversification on Risk."

less than the market. Using this method of risk adjustment, the capital asset pricing model creates a linear risk-return trade-off using the market as the reference point for risk and return.

Since unsystematic risk can be diversified away, systematic risk (b_i) is the only relevant risk under the capital asset pricing model. Thus, even though we can describe total risk as:

$$\text{Total risk} = \text{Systematic risk} + \text{Unsystematic risk}$$

In a diversified portfolio, unsystematic risk approaches 0.

Security Market Line

We actually express the trade-off between risk and return for an *individual stock* through the **security market line (SML)** in Figure 21–12. Whereas in Figure 21–11, we graphed the relationship that allowed us to compute the beta (b_i) for a security, in Figure 21–12 we now take that beta and show what the anticipated or required return in the marketplace is for a stock with that characteristic. The security market line (SML) shows the risk-return trade-off for an individual stock in Figure 21–12 just as the capital market line (CML) accomplished that same objective for a portfolio in Figure 21–10.

Once again, we stress that the return is not plotted against the total risk (σ) for the individual stock but only that part of the risk that cannot be diversified away, commonly referred to as the systematic or beta risk. The actual formula for the security market line (SML) is:

$$K_i = R_F + b_i(K_M - R_F) \tag{21–7}$$

The mathematical derivation of the formula is presented in Appendix 21–C. As we did with the capital market line for portfolio returns, with the security market line, we start out with a basic rate of return for a risk-free asset (R_F) and add a premium for risk. In this case, the premium is equal to the beta on the stock times the difference between the market rate of return (K_M) and the risk-free rate of return (R_F). If $R_F = 6\%$, $K_M = 9\%$, and the stock has a beta (b_i) of 1, the anticipated rate of return, using Formula 21–7, would be the same as that in the market, or 9 percent.

$$K_i = 6\% + 1(9\% - 6\%) = 6\% + 3\% = 9\%$$

Since the stock has the same degree of risk as the market in general, this would appear to be logical. If the stock has a beta of 1.5, the added systematic risk would call for a return of 10.5 percent, whereas a beta of .5 would indicate the return should be 7.5 percent. The calculations are indicated below.

Beta $= 1.5$

$$K_i = 6\% + 1.5(9\% - 6\%) = 6\% + 1.5(3\%) = 6\% + 4.5\% = 10.5\%$$

Beta $= .5$

$$K_i = 6\% + .5(9\% - 6\%) = 6\% + .5(3\%) = 6\% + 1.5\% = 7.5\%$$

Figure 21–12   Illustration of the Security Market Line

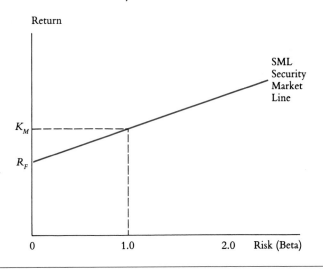

Since the beta factor is deemed to be important in analyzing potential risk and return, much emphasis is placed on knowing the beta for a given security. Merrill Lynch, Value Line, and various brokerage houses and investment services publish information on beta for a large number of securities. A representative list is presented in the table below.

Corporation	Beta (September 1991)
Merrill Lynch & Co.	1.35
Georgia-Pacific	1.30
Digital Equipment	1.20
Ford Motor	1.15
Colgate-Palmolive	1.00
Cincinnati Gas and Electric	.70
Echo Bay Mines	.60

■ ASSUMPTIONS OF THE CAPITAL ASSET PRICING MODEL

Having evaluated some of the implications of the CAPM, it is important that the student be aware of some of the assumptions that go into the model.

1. All investors can borrow or lend an unlimited amount of funds at a given risk-free rate.
2. All investors have the same one-period time horizon.

3. All investors wish to maximize their expected utility over this time horizon and evaluate investments on the basis of means and standard deviations of portfolio returns.

4. All investors have the same expectations—that is, all investors estimate identical probability distributions for rates of return.

5. All assets are perfectly divisible—it is possible to buy fractional shares of any asset or portfolio.

6. There are no taxes or transactions costs.

7. The market is efficient and in equilibrium or quickly adjusting to equilibrium.

Listing these assumptions indicates some of the necessary conditions to create the CAPM. While at first they may appear to be severely limiting, they are similar to those often used in the standard economic theory of the firm and in other basic financial models.

The primary usefulness in examining this model or similar risk-return trade-off models is to provide some reasonable basis for relating return opportunity with risk on the investment. Portfolio managers find risk-return models helpful in explaining their performance or the performance of their competitors to clients. A competitor's portfolio that has unusually high returns may have been developed primarily on the basis of high-risk assets. To the extent that this can be explained on the basis of capital market theory, the competitor's performance may look less like superior money management and more like a product of high risk taking. As we shall see in Chapter 22, many of the techniques for assessing portfolio performance on Wall Street are explicitly or implicitly related to the risk-return concepts discussed in this chapter.

Though empirical tests have somewhat supported the capital asset pricing model, a number of testing problems remain. To develop the SML in which stock returns (vertical axis) can be measured against beta (horizontal axis), an appropriate line must be drawn. Researchers have some disagreement about R_F. (Is it represented by short-term or long-term Treasury rates?) There is also debate about what is the appropriate K_M, or market rate of return. Some suggest the market proxy variable will greatly influence the beta and that difficulties in dealing with this problem can bring the whole process under attack.[8]

When empirical data are compared to theoretical return expectations, there is some discrepancy in that the theoretical SML may have a slightly greater slope than the actual line fitted on the basis of real-world data as shown in Figure 21–13.[9]

---

[8]Richard Roll, "A Critique of the Asset Pricing Theory's Test," *Journal of Financial Economics,* March 1977, pp. 129–76. Also, "Ambiguity When Performance Is Measured by the Securities Market Line," *Journal of Finance,* September 1978, pp. 1051–69.

[9]Franco Modigliani and Gerald A. Pogue, "An Introduction to Risk and Returns," *Financial Analysts Journal,* March–April 1974, pp. 68–86, and May–June 1974, pp. 69–86.

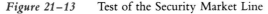

Figure 21–13   Test of the Security Market Line

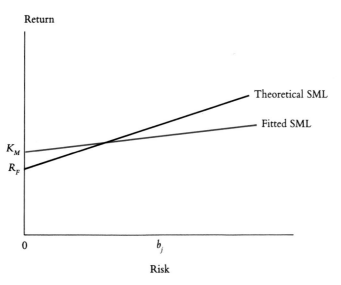

There may also be a possible problem in that betas for individual securities are not necessarily stable over time (rather than remaining relatively constant at 1.3 or perhaps 0.7, they tend to approach 1 over time). Thus, a beta based on past risk may not always reflect current risk.[10] Because the beta for a portfolio may be more stable than an individual stock's beta, portfolio betas are also used as a systematic risk variable. A portfolio beta is simply the weighted average of the betas of the individual stocks. We can say:

$$b_P \text{ (portfolio beta)} = \sum_{i=1}^{n} x_i b_i \qquad (21\text{–}8)$$

and

$$K_P = R_F + b_P(K_M - R_F) \qquad (21\text{–}9)$$

By examining portfolio betas rather than individual stock betas, we overcome part of the criticism leveled at the instability of betas in the capital asset pricing model. Many of the other criticisms have also evoked new research that may provide different approaches or possible solutions to past deficiencies in the model.

---

[10]Robert A. Levy, "On the Short-Term Stationary of Beta Coefficients," *Financial Analysts Journal,* November–December 1971, pp. 55–62. Also, Marshall E. Blume, "Betas and Their Regression Tendencies," *Journal of Finance,* June 1975, pp. 785–95.

■ ARBITRAGE PRICING THEORY

Another theory for explaining stock prices and stock returns is arbitrage pricing theory (APT). This is a fairly sophisticated theory and will be of interest only to those who wish to learn more about asset pricing.

Arbitrage pricing theory assumes a linear return generating model that makes the return on an investment a function of more than one factor. The capital asset pricing model also uses a linear return generating model but assumes that returns are a function of a stock's sensitivity to the equity risk premium. APT acknowledges that a stock's return may be a function of many factors. The arbitrage pricing model is a more generalized model than the CAPM and less restrictive in its assumptions; it does not assume equilibrium markets or make assumptions about investor preferences. However, the concept of arbitrage behavior will drive markets to equilibrium as investors try to make risk-free profits.

Arbitrage behavior assumes one good should have the same price. If two different prices are found for gold in London and New York, an arbitrageur could sell short the high-priced gold and buy the low-priced gold. This behavior would drive the price of high-priced gold down and the price of low-priced gold up until the price of gold was the same. Theoretically, by selling short, the investor can use the proceeds from the short sale to buy long, and therefore, the transaction can be made without any investment. This makes the transaction a no-cost riskless transaction. Arbitrage relies on the behavior of market participants to take advantage of prices in disequilibrium, and through this arbitrage mechanism, prices will move into equilibrium.

The arbitrage pricing model describes the expected return on a stock as a function of several factors. While there is no universal agreement on what factors have the greatest impact on stock returns, Chen[11] and Roll and Ross[12] suggest there are a few major factors. These are changes in expectations about:

1. Interest-rate risk.
2. Business-cycle risk.
3. Inflation.
4. The risk of changing risk premiums.

The return-generating process using the APT model appears in Formula 21–10. We have listed four factors here, but there could be as few as one factor or many other factors. Three or four factors probably capture the most significant return sensitivities.

---

[11]Nai-fu Chen, "Some Empirical Tests of the Theory of Arbitrage Pricing," *Journal of Finance,* December 1983, pp. 1393–1414.

[12]Richard Roll and Stephen A. Ross, "An Empirical Investigation of the Arbitrage Pricing Theory," *Journal of Finance,* December 1980, pp. 1073–1103.

$$K_{i,t} = a_i + b_{i,1}F_{1,t} + b_{i,2}F_{2,t} + b_{i,3}F_{3,t} + b_{i,4}F_{4,t} + e_{i,t} \qquad (21\text{-}10)$$

Where:

$K_{i,t}$ = Return on stock i at time t

a_i = Expected return on stock i

b_i = Constants unique to stock i; reflect the sensitivity of each separate factor

F = Factors common to all stocks

e_i = Random term unique to stock i

If a_i is the expected return on the stock, then the effect of the factors is expected to be zero (0). In other words, the market has already incorporated expectations about these factors into the stock's price. What will affect the actual return on stock i are any surprises in these factors that were not anticipated. For example, if factor 1 is changing real GDP, and real GDP goes up more than expected, stocks that are sensitive to changes in real GDP will go up, while those stocks that are not sensitive to the business cycle will be unaffected. Conversely, if inflation is factor 2, and it increases more than expected, stocks that are subject to inflationary pressures will decline in price, while those that are not sensitive to changes in inflation will not be affected. The sensitivity to these various factors shows up in the b_i for each factor.

The random term e_i represents the unexpected portion of the return on security i, which is not explained by the factors. It captures unexpected events unique to firm i. For example, a new product announcement, a merger, or a takeover will affect firm i only. These unexpected events were not impounded into the stock's expected return, a_i.

The b_is (factor sensitivities) reflect the sensitivity of the factor on the stock's return. Like the capital asset pricing model, the factor sensitivity for a portfolio is the sum of the weighted beta for each factor based on the percentage of market value that each stock contributes to the portfolio.

Let us take two stocks, x and y. Two factors affect the returns of both stocks, and the random variable e_i is eliminated because we assume that in a diversified portfolio, e_i approaches zero (0).

$$K_x = 12\% + 3F_{1,t} - 2F_{2,t}$$
$$K_y = 15\% + 1F_{1,t} - 6F_{2,t}$$

Each factor will have an impact on portfolio risk in proportion to the amount invested in each stock and the sensitivity of each factor on the stock's return. For example, if factor 1 represents the impact of changing real GDP (the business cycle risk), an unexpected increase in real GDP would increase the return on stock x by 3 percent. The same 1 percent unexpected change in GDP would increase the return on stock y by 1 percent. These effects show up in the factor sensitivities (b_i) of 3 for K_x and 1 for K_y.

If the second factor represents inflation, we can see that a 1 percent unexpected increase in inflation will cause a reduction in return of 2 percent for stock x and 6 percent for stock y. When we combine stocks x and y into a portfolio weighted 40 percent stock x and 60 percent stock y, we end up with portfolio risk dependent on the percentage of each stock in the portfolio and each stock's sensitivity to factors affecting risk. We multiply both sides of the return equations by the portfolio weights.

$$(0.4) \, K_x = (.40) \times 12\% + (.40) \times (3)F_{1,t} - (.40) \times (2)F_{2,t}$$
$$(0.4) \, K_x = 4.8\% \qquad\qquad + 1.2F_{1,t} \qquad\qquad - .8F_{2,t}$$

Forty percent of stock x will contribute 4.8 percent expected return to the portfolio and will have a factor sensitivity of 1.2 to the business-cycle risk and a negative factor sensitivity of .8 to the inflation risk.

$$(0.6) \, K_y = (.60) \times 15\% + (.60) \times (1)F_{1,t} - (.60) \times (6)F_{2,t}$$
$$(0.6) \, K_y = 9.0\% \qquad\qquad + .6F_{1,t} \qquad\qquad - 3.6F_{2,t}$$

Sixty percent of stock y will contribute 9.0 percent expected return to the portfolio and will have a factor sensitivity of .6 to the business-cycle risk and a negative factor sensitivity of 3.6 to the inflation risk. When we combine the two stocks into a portfolio, we end up with a portfolio having an expected return of 13.8 percent and having a sensitivity to factor 1 (business-cycle risk) of 1.8 and a negative sensitivity to factor 2 (inflation risk) of 4.4.

$$\text{Portfolio return } K_p = (4.8\% + 9\%) + (1.2 + .6) - (.8 + 3.6)$$
$$K_p = 13.8\% \qquad\qquad + 1.8F_{1,t} \qquad - 4.4F_{2,t}$$

We have structured a portfolio that will be moderately sensitive to any unexpected events having to do with changes in real GDP and highly susceptible to unexpected changes in inflation.

It is important to understand that the sign in front of the factor sensitivity indicates whether the unexpected event is directly related to returns or inversely related to returns. For example, we assume unexpected increases in inflation reduce stock returns while unexpected decreases in inflation increase stock returns. Thus, we have a minus sign before the second factor.

Application to Portfolio Management

From the portfolio manager's point of view, the arbitrage pricing theory can help measure the sensitivity of a portfolio to various macro factors that could potentially affect the actual return on one stock or a portfolio. This model allows investment managers to structure portfolios that either are highly sensitive or insensitive to certain kinds of risk exposures. If a manager were concerned about a recession and this information were not yet factored into stock prices, he or she could create a portfolio that insulated the returns on the portfolio from unpleasant surprises. On the other hand, if the market had

factored in expectations for a recession and the manager expected good business-cycle news, he or she could buy stocks sensitive to business-cycle news.

Let us look at one last arbitrage case that for simplicity assumes one factor affects two stocks.

$$K_{a,t} = 19\% + 3F$$

$$K_{b,t} = 13\% + 2F$$

Stock *a* has an expected return of 19 percent and a factor risk of 3, while stock *b* has an expected return of 13 percent and a factor risk of 2. Stock *b* has less risk than stock *a* because its factor sensitivity is 2 versus 3. To create a portfolio of equal risk to stock *b*, we can structure a portfolio consisting of two thirds of stock *a* and one third of a risk-free asset. If we can borrow at a risk-free rate of 6 percent, we can arbitrage our portfolio and increase our return. We would sell a portfolio consisting of only security *b* and buy a portfolio consisting of two thirds of security *a* and one third of the risk-free security. The portfolio we bought now has a factor sensitivity of 2 from the combined risk of stock *a* and the risk-free asset [(⅔ × 3F) + (⅓ × 0)]. This risk of 2 for the risk factor *F* is the same risk as security *b*. This is because the risk-free security has no factor risk at all, and two thirds of the factor risk in security *a* equals 2. What happens to our return? It goes up to 14.7 percent (two thirds of 19 percent from stock *a* plus one third of 6 percent from the risk-free asset). Since we sold security *b* and bought security *a* and a risk-free security equal to the sales price of security *b*, we have increased the expected return from 13 percent to 14.7 percent without increasing our investment or risk. If opportunities like this one become available, arbitrageurs will follow the same strategy outlined and drive the price of security *b* down and the price of security *a* up until the two are in equilibrium with respect to their risk and return expectations.

Arbitrage pricing theory shows that market participants using arbitrage will create a unique equilibrium price of risk for each factor so that the expected return is a function of all the expected returns attributable to each factor.

◾ SUMMARY

The investor is basically risk-averse and therefore will demand a premium for incremental risk. In an efficient market context, the ability to achieve high returns may be more directly related to absorption of additional risk than superior ability in selecting stocks (this remains a debatable point that proponents of fundamental and technical analysis would argue).

Risk for an individual stock is measured in terms of the standard deviation (σ_i) around a given expected value ($\overline{K}_i$). The larger the standard deviation, the greater the risk. For a portfolio of stocks, the expected value (K_P) is the weighted average of the individual returns; but this is not true for the portfolio

standard deviation (σ_P). The portfolio standard deviation is also influenced by the interaction between the stocks. To the extent the correlation coefficient (r_{ij}) is less than $+1$, there will be some reduction from the weighted average of the standard deviation of the individual stocks that we are combining. A negative correlation coefficient will provide substantial reduction in the portfolio standard deviation.

Under classic Markowitz portfolio theory, we look at a large array of possible portfolios in an attempt to construct an efficient frontier that represents the best possible risk-return trade-off at different levels of risk. Individuals then match their own risk-return indifference curves with the efficient frontier to determine where they should be along this optimal scale.

This was the prevailing theory until the capital asset pricing model (CAPM) was developed. The CAPM supersedes some of the findings of classic portfolio theory with the introduction of the risk-free asset as represented by (R_F) into the analysis. The assumption is that an individual can choose an investment combining the return on the risk-free asset with the market rate of return, and this will provide superior returns to the efficient frontier at all points except M, where they are equal. The investor may invest in any combination of R_F and M to achieve the risk-return positions described by the capital market line in Figure 21–10.

The capital market line describes the general trade-off between risk and return for portfolio managers in the economy. Any attempt to get higher portfolio returns must be matched by higher portfolio risks. Although the portfolio manager is investing in stocks and bonds, the general pattern set out for the risk-free asset and market combination is perceived to establish the limits for investment performance of any nature. Any increase in portfolio returns (K_P) must be associated with an increase in the portfolio standard deviation (σ_P).

The capital asset pricing model also calls for an evaluation of individual assets (rather than portfolios). The security market line in Figure 21–12 shows the same type of risk-return trade-off for individual securities as the capital market line did for portfolios. Investors in individual assets are only assumed to be rewarded for systematic, market-related risk, known as the beta (b_i) risk. All other risk is assumed to be susceptible to diversification.

A number of assumptions associated with the capital asset pricing model are subject to close review and challenge. Furthermore, there is some question about the appropriate measures for R_F and K_M as well as the stability of beta and the appropriate slope of the SML line. Nevertheless, the capital asset pricing model represents a generally useful device for portraying the relationship of risk and return in the capital markets over the long term.

Arbitrage pricing theory allows for several sources of systematic risk as opposed to one measure under the capital asset pricing model. It further assumes investors will appropriately hedge or arbitrage between securities and portfolios to establish expected returns. While arbitrage pricing theory offers some conceptual and empirical advantages over the capital asset pricing model, it is less widely used.

IMPORTANT WORDS AND CONCEPTS

expected value 678

standard deviation 679

correlation coefficient 682

efficient frontier 685

indifference curves 686

capital asset pricing model 689

capital market line (CML) 691

beta coefficient 693

systematic risk 694

unsystematic risk 695

security market line (SML) 696

arbitrage pricing theory 700

DISCUSSION QUESTIONS

1. Define risk.

2. What is an expected value?

3. What is the most commonly used measure of dispersion?

4. In a two-asset portfolio, is the portfolio standard deviation a weighted average of the two individual stocks' standard deviation? Explain.

5. What does the correlation coefficient (r_{ij}) measure? What are the two most extreme values it can take and what do they indicate? In the real world, are more variables positively or negatively correlated?

6. What are the two characteristics of points along the efficient frontier? Do portfolios exist above the efficient frontier?

7. What does the steepness of the slope of the risk-return indifference curve indicate?

8. Describe the optimum portfolio for an investor in terms of indifference curves and the efficient frontier.

9. What new investment variable or outlet allowed market researchers to go from the Markowitz portfolio theory (including the efficient frontier) to the capital asset pricing model?

10. In examining the *capital market line* as part of the capital asset pricing model, to increase portfolio return (K_P) what other variable must you increase?

11. In terms of the capital asset pricing model:

    a. Indicate the two types of risks associated with an individual security.

    b. Which of these two is the beta risk?

    c. What risk is assumed not to be compensated for in the marketplace under the capital asset pricing model? Why?

12. What can be assumed in terms of volatility for a stock that has a beta of 1.2?

13. What does the security market line indicate? In general terms, how is it different from the capital market line?

14. In regard to the capital asset pricing model, comment on disagreements or debates related to R_F (the risk-free rate) and K_M (market rate of return).

15. Are betas of individual stocks necessarily stable (constant) over time?

16. Arbitrage pricing theory is more generalized than the capital asset pricing model because it assumes an investment's return is related to more than just the one factor of risk. Suggest four factors that might influence return under arbitrage pricing theory as suggested by Chen and Roll and Ross.

17. Under arbitrage pricing theory, how does an investor attempt to take advantage of economic events that are not yet fully recognized in the marketplace?

18. How does arbitraging tend to create equilibrium in the marketplace?

■ PROBLEMS

Expected value and standard deviation

1. An investment has the following range of outcomes and probabilities.

Outcomes (Percent)	Probability of Outcomes
6%	.30
9	.40
12	.30

Calculate the expected value and the standard deviation (round to two places after the decimal point where necessary).

Portfolio expected value and standard deviation

2. Given another investment with an expected value of 13 percent and a standard deviation of 3.1 percent that is counter-cyclical to the investment in Problem 1, what is the expected value of the portfolio and its standard deviation if both are combined into a portfolio with 40 percent invested in the first investment and 60 percent in the second? Assume the correlation coefficient (r_{ij}) is $-.40$.

Portfolio standard deviation

3. What would be the portfolio standard deviation if the two investments in Problem 2 had a correlation coefficient (r_{ij}) of $+.40$?

Efficient frontier

4. Assume the following risk-return possibilities for 10 different portfolios. Plot the points in a manner similar to Figure 21−3 and indicate the approximate shape of the efficient frontier.

Portfolio Number	K_P	σ_P
1	10%	1.5%
2	10	2.5
3	9	3.0
4	12	4.0

Portfolio Number	K_P	σ_P
5	11	4.0
6	12	5.0
7	12	6.0
8	13.5	6.5
9	13	6.5
10	14	7.0

Capital market line

5. Using the formula for the capital market line (Formula 21–5), if the risk-free rate (R_F) is 7 percent, the market rate of return (K_M) is 12 percent, the market standard deviation (σ_M) is 10 percent, and the standard deviation of the portfolio (σ_p) is 13 percent, compute the anticipated return (K_p).

Capital market line

6. Recompute the answer to Question 5 based on a portfolio standard deviation of 16 percent. In terms of capital market theory, explain why K_p has increased.

Security market line

7. Using the formula for the security market line (Formula 21–7), if the risk-free rate (R_F) is 7 percent, the beta (b_i) is 1.15, and the market rate of return (K_M) is 12 percent, compute the anticipated rate of return (K_i).

Beta consideration

8. If another security had a lower beta than indicated in Question 7, would K_i be lower or higher? What is the logic behind your answer in terms of risk?

Plotting best fit of data

9. Assume the following values for a stock's return and the market return.

Year	Stock i Return (K)	Market Return (K_M)
1	15.5	14.9
2	2.8	1.1
3	17.7	12.0
4	15.1	10.1
5	6.0	3.2

Plot the data and draw a line of best fit similar to that in Figure 21–11.

Least squares regression analysis

10. Using the formulas in Appendix 21–B, compute a least squares regression equation for Problem 9. (Round beta and alpha to two places after the decimal point.)

Rate of return

11. Use the beta (b_i) from Problem 10 and plug into the formula for the security market line (Formula 21–7). Assume the risk-free rate (R_F) is 8 percent and the market rate of return (K_M) is 13.5 percent. What is the value of the anticipated rate of return (K_i)?

Arbitrage pricing theory

12. Under arbitrage pricing theory, assume two stocks have the following equations.

$$K_x = 14\% + 2F_{1,t} - 3F_{2,t}$$
$$K_y = 10\% + 1F_{1,t} - 4F_{2,t}$$

The first factor relates to unexpected increases in real GDP, and the second factor relates to unexpected increases in interest rates.

If a portfolio consists of 60 percent of stock x and 40 percent of stock y, what will be the equation for portfolio return (K_P)?

Arbitrage pricing theory

13. Assume the following two stocks are available for purchase. (There is only one risk factor.)

$$K_a = 20\% + 4F$$
$$K_b = 12\% + 3F$$

We will sell stock b and replace three fourths of its value with stock a and one fourth of its value with a risk-free asset yielding 6 percent.

a. What is the new weighted average for the risk factor?

b. What is the new weighted average return?

c. Has the investor benefited from a risk–return perspective?

■MARKETBASE-E EXERCISES

1. *a.* Use the American Association of Individual Investors' *Shadow Stock* criteria to identify small company stocks that are not held by a large number of institutions. [See the Chapter 10 MarketBase-E exercise and include the positive earnings requirement in part (*b*).] Pick the five stocks from this list with the highest ROE.

   b. Go to the newspaper and determine the prices of these stocks exactly one year ago. What rate of return has this portfolio offered?

   c. Compare the portfolio return on a risk-adjusted basis to the return offered by the Standard and Poor's 500 Stock Index over the same period. Did the portfolio earn excess returns or not?

2. *a.* Define the required rate of return for each company using the current rate on one-year Treasury bills as the risk-free return and 7% as the market-risk premium.

   b. Sort the companies by beta. Make two portfolios—one of the five highest beta stocks and one of the five lowest beta stocks. What are the CAPM portfolio returns for these two portfolios?

   c. Compare the CAPM portfolio return on a risk-adjusted basis to the actual return offered by these portfolios over the past year. Did the portfolios earn excess returns or not?

3. *a.* Sort the *Shadow Stocks* (from question 1) by market value in descending order. Take the first ten companies (the 10 largest) and sort by ROE. Is there any relationship between ROE rank and market value?

   b. Sort the *Shadow Stock* companies by beta. Make two portfolios—one of the five highest beta stocks and one of the five lowest beta stocks. What are the CAPM portfolio returns for these two portfolios?

   c. Look up the stocks' prices exactly one year ago and compute the return. Compare the CAPM portfolio return on a risk-adjusted basis to the actual return offered by these portfolios over the past year. Did the portfolios earn excess returns or not?

■ SELECTED REFERENCES

Portfolio Considerations

Blume, Marshall E., and Irwin Friend. "The Asset Structure of Individual Portfolios and Some Implications for Utility Functions." *Journal of Finance,* May 1975, pp. 585–603.

Fuller, Russell J., and G. Wenchi Wong. "Traditional vs Theoretical Risk Measures." *Financial Analysts Journal,* March–April 1988, pp. 52–57.

McEnally, Richard W. "Time Diversification: The Surest Route to Lower Risk?" *Journal of Portfolio Management,* Summer 1985, pp. 24–26.

Capital Asset Pricing Model

Friend, Irwin; Randolph Westerfield; and Michael Granito. "New Evidence on the Capital Asset Pricing Model." *Journal of Finance,* June 1978, pp. 903–17.

Graver, Robert R. "Further Ambiguity When Performance Is Measured by the Security Market Line." *Financial Review,* November 1991, pp. 569–85.

Jensen, Michael C., ed. *Studies in the Theory of Capital Markets.* New York: Praeger Publishers, 1972.

Roll, Richard. "Ambiguity When Performance Is Measured by the Securities Market Line." *Journal of Finance,* September 1978, pp. 1051–70.

Sharpe, William F. "Factor Models, CAPMs, and the APT." *Journal of Portfolio Management,* Fall 1984, pp. 21–25.

———. "Capital Asset Prices: A Theory of Market Equilibrium under Conditions of Risk." *Journal of Finance,* September 1964, pp. 425–42.

Beta Measurement

Carvell, Steven, and Paul Strebel. "A New Beta Incorporating Analysts' Forecasts." *Journal of Portfolio Management,* Fall 1984, pp. 81–84.

Elgers, Pieter T.; James R. Haltiner; and William H. Hawthorne. "Beta Regression Tendencies: Statistical and Real Causes." *Journal of Finance,* March 1979, pp. 261–63.

Elton, Edwin J.; Martin J. Gruber; and Thomas J. Ulrich. "Are Betas Best?" *Journal of Finance,* December 1978, pp. 1375–84.

Fabozzi, Frank J., and Jack Clark Francis. "Stability Tests for Alphas and Betas over Bull and Bear Market Conditions." *Journal of Finance,* September 1977, pp. 1093–99.

Fisher, Lawrence, and Jules H. Kamin. "Forecasting Systematic Risk: Estimates of 'Raw' Beta that Take Account of the Tendency of Beta to Change and the Heteroskedasticity of Residual Returns." *Journal of Financial and Quantitative Analysis,* June 1985, pp. 127–49.

Martin, John D., and Arthur Keown. "A Misleading Feature of Beta for Risk Measurement." *Journal of Portfolio Management,* Summer 1977, pp. 31–34.

Rosenberg, Barr. "Prediction of Common Stock Betas." *Journal of Portfolio Management,* Winter 1985, pp. 5–14.

Arbitrage Pricing Theory

Berry, Michael A.; Edwin Burmeister; and Marjorie B. McElroy. "Sorting Out Risks Using Known APT Factors." *Financial Analysts Journal,* March–April 1988, pp. 29–42.

Dhrymes, Phoebus. "Arbitrage Pricing Theory." *Journal of Portfolio Management,* Summer 1984, pp. 35–44.

Gehr, Adam. "Some Tests of the Arbitrage Pricing Theory." *Journal of the Midwest Finance Association,* Annual 1978 issue, pp. 91–105.

Roll, Richard. "A Critique of the Asset Pricing Theory's Test." *Journal of Financial Economics,* March 1977, pp. 129–76.

Roll, Richard, and Stephen A. Ross. "An Empirical Investigation of the Arbitrage Pricing Theory." *Journal of Finance,* December 1980, pp. 1073–1103.

Ross, Stephen A. "The Arbitrage Theory of Capital Asset Pricing," *Journal of Economic Theory,* December 1976, pp. 314–60.

Appendix 21–A: The Correlation Coefficient

There are a number of formulas for the correlation coefficient. We shall use the statement:

$$r_{ij} = \frac{\text{cov}_{ij}}{\sigma_i \sigma_j} \qquad (21A-1)$$

Cov$_{ij}$ (covariance) is an *absolute* measure of the extent to which two sets of variables move together over time. Once we have determined this value, we simply divide by $\sigma_i \sigma_j$ to get a relative measure of correlation (r_{ij}).

The formula for the covariance is:

$$\text{cov}_{ij} = \Sigma(K_i - \bar{K}_i)(K_j - \bar{K}_j)P \qquad (21A-2)$$

We take our K and P values from investment i and investment j in Chapter 21 to compute the following:

K_i	$\bar{K}_i$	$(K_i - \bar{K}_i)$	K_j	$\bar{K}_j$	$(K_j - \bar{K}_j)$	$(K_i - \bar{K}_i)(K_j - \bar{K}_j)$	P	$(K_i - \bar{K}_i)(K_j - \bar{K}_j)P$
5%	10%	−5%	20%	10%	+10%	−50%	.20	−10.0%
7	10	−3	8	10	−2	+6	.30	+1.8
13	10	+3	8	10	−2	−6	.30	−1.8
15	10	+5	6	10	−4	−20	.20	−4.0
								−14.0%

$$\text{cov}_{ij} = \Sigma(K_i - \bar{K}_i)(K_j - \bar{K}_j)P = -14.0\%$$

Using the values in the chapter for σ_i equal to 3.9 and σ_j equal to 5.1, we determine:

$$r_{ij} = \frac{\text{cov}_{ij}}{\sigma_i \sigma_j} = \frac{-14.0}{(3.9)(5.1)} = \frac{-14.0}{19.9} = -.70$$

Appendix 21–B: Least Squares Regression Analysis

We shall show how least squares regression analysis can be used to develop a linear equation to explain the relationship between the return on a stock and return in the market.

We will develop the terms in the expression:

$$K_i = a_i + b_i K_M + e_i$$

(e_i is the random error term and will not be quantified in our analysis).

Using the data from the chapter,

Year	K_i	K_M
1	4.8%	6.5%
2	14.5	11.8
3	19.1	14.9
4	3.7	1.1
5	15.6	12.0

The normal or mathematical equation to solve for b_i is:

$$b_i = \frac{N\Sigma K_i K_M - \Sigma K_i \Sigma K_M}{N\Sigma K_M^2 - (\Sigma K_M)^2} \qquad (21B-1)$$

For a_i, we use the following formula (which is dependent on a prior determination of b_i).

$$a_i = \frac{\Sigma K_i - b_i \Sigma K_M}{N} \qquad (21B-2)$$

We compute four columns of data and plug the values into our formulas.

K_i	K_M	$K_i K_M$	K_M^2
4.8	6.5	31.20	42.25
14.5	11.8	171.10	139.24
19.1	14.9	284.59	222.01
3.7	1.1	4.07	1.21
15.6	12.0	187.20	144.00
$\Sigma K_i = 57.7$	$\Sigma K_M = 46.3$	$\Sigma K_i K_M = 678.16$	$\Sigma K_M^2 = 548.71$

Also N (number of observations) $= 5$.

$$b_i = \frac{N\Sigma K_i K_M - \Sigma K_i \Sigma K_M}{N\Sigma K_M^2 - (\Sigma K_M)^2}$$

$$= \frac{5(678.16) - 57.7(46.3)}{5(548.71) - (46.3)^2}$$

$$= \frac{3390.80 - 2671.51}{2743.55 - 2143.69} = \frac{719.29}{599.86} = 1.20$$

Using our beta value, we now compute alpha:

$$a_i = \frac{\Sigma K_i - b_i \Sigma K_M}{N}$$

$$a_i = \frac{57.7 - 1.2(46.3)}{5}$$

$$a_i = \frac{57.7 - 55.6}{5} = \frac{2.1}{5} = .42$$

In summary:

$$K_i = a_i + b_i K_M$$
$$K_i = .42 + 1.20\, K_M$$

Appendix 21–C: Derivation of the Security Market Line (SML)

First, we graph the SML based on covariance (Figure 21C–1).[13]

Along the vertical axis we show return, and along the horizontal axis, covariance of return with the market.[14] We can describe our equation for the SML in terms of the slope of the line.

$$K_i = R_F + \frac{(K_M - R_F)}{(\sigma_M^2 - 0)} \text{cov}_{iM} \tag{21C-1}$$

We then rearrange our terms:

$$K_i = R_F + \left(\frac{\text{cov}_{iM}}{\sigma_M^2}\right)(K_M - R_F) \tag{21C-2}$$

The systematic risk of an individual asset is measured by its covariance with the market (cov_{iM}). We can convert this to a relative measure by dividing through by the market variance (σ_M^2). The *relative* systematic movement of an individual asset with the market is referred to as the beta regression coefficient. Thus, we show in Formula 21C–3

$$b_i = \frac{\text{cov}_{iM}}{\sigma_M^2} \tag{21C-3}$$

Substituting beta into Formula 21C–2, we show:

$$K_i = R_F + b_i(K_M - R_F) \tag{21C-4}$$

---

[13]The concept of covariance is described in Appendix 21–A.

[14]Actually, σ_M^2 represents the covariance of the market with the market (a bit redundant). The cov_{MM} equals σ_M^2. The covariance of a variable with itself is equal to the variance.

Figure 21C–1   Derivation of the SML

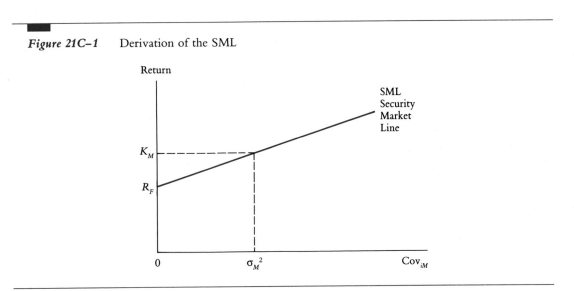

22

Measuring Risks and Returns of Portfolio Managers

In the bull market days of the mid-1980s, many portfolio managers turned in performances that were superior to the market averages. These high returns were often achieved by taking larger than normal risks through investing in small growth companies or concentrating in a limited number of high-return industries. These portfolio managers or their representatives proclaimed their superior ability in managing money and often extrapolated past returns into the future to indicate the potential returns to the investor. A typical statement might be: "The Rapid Growth Fund has earned 20 percent per year over the past 10 years. The investor who places funds with us has the possible opportunity to see the funds grow from a $100 investment today to $672.70 in 10 years at this historical growth rate of 20 percent." There was very little attempt to relate rate of return directly to risk exposure or to provide warnings about the likelihood of repeating past performance.

Thus, the bull market of the 1980s, like other bull markets, lulled investors into looking for the highest stock returns while paying little heed to the relative risk of individual stock portfolios. The crash of 1987 drove home risk-adjusted returns once more. If an investor had been invested in bonds rather than stock on October 19, 1987, he or she would have seen the value of bonds rise as the Federal Reserve pushed interest rates down by pumping liquidity into the market. Money market securities would have been another safe haven, but investors in common stock lost out during the crash on a worldwide basis.

In this chapter, we will examine actual studies of risk-return performance for professional money managers. We will evaluate the setting of objectives, the achievement of efficient diversification, and the measurement of return related to risk. In some of this discussion, we will relate back to the capital asset pricing model developed in Chapter 21.

Because mutual funds are professionally managed and publicly traded, much data are available to judge performance and evaluate risk-return objectives. For this reason, much of the research presented in this chapter relies on mutual fund data. However, there are many other important participants among professional money managers. These include pension funds, life insurance companies, property and casualty companies, bank trust departments, and endowment funds and foundations. These institutional investors are examined later in this chapter.

■ STATED OBJECTIVES AND RISK

A first question to be posed to a professional money manager is: Have you followed the basic objectives that were established? These objectives might call for maximum capital gains, a combination of growth plus income, or simply income (with many variations in between). The objectives should be set with an eye toward the capabilities of the money managers and the financial needs of the investors. The best way to measure adherence to these objectives is to evaluate the risk exposure the fund manager has accepted. Anyone who aspires to maximize capital gains must, by nature, absorb more risk. An income-oriented fund should have a minimum risk exposure.

Figure 22–1   Risk and Fund Objectives for 123 Mutual Funds, 1960–1969

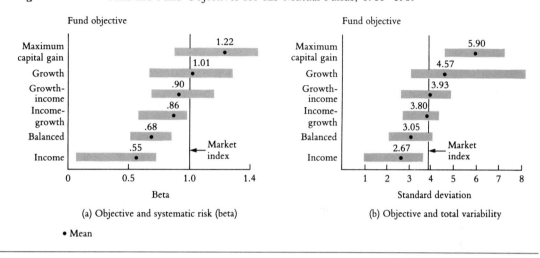

(a) Objective and systematic risk (beta)

(b) Objective and total variability

• Mean

Source: John G. McDonald, "Objectives and Performance of Mutual Funds, 1960–1969," *Journal of Financial and Quantitative Analysis,* June 1974, p. 316.

A classic study by John McDonald published in the *Journal of Financial and Quantitative Analysis* indicates mutual fund managers generally follow the objectives they initially set. As indicated in Figure 22–1, he measured the betas and standard deviations for 123 mutual funds and compared these to the funds' stated objectives. In Panel (a), we see the fund's beta dimension along the horizontal axis and the fund's stated objective along the vertical axis. Inside the panel, we see the association between the two. For example, funds with an objective of maximum capital gains had an average beta of 1.22, those with a growth objective had an average beta of 1.01, and so on all the way down to an average beta of 0.55 for income-oriented funds. In Panel (b) of Figure 22–1, a similar approach was used to compare the fund's objective to the portfolio standard deviation.

In both cases of using betas and portfolio standard deviations, we see that the risk absorption was carefully tailored to the fund's stated objectives. Funds with aggressive capital gains and growth objectives had high betas and portfolio standard deviations, while the opposite was true of balanced and income-oriented funds.

Adherence to objectives as measured by risk exposure is important in evaluating a fund manager because risk is one of the variables a money manager can directly control. While short-run return performance can be greatly influenced by unpredictable changes in the economy, the fund manager has almost total control in setting the risk level. He can be held accountable for doing what was specified or promised in regard to risk. Most lawsuits brought against money managers are not for inferior profit performance but for failure to adhere to stated risk objectives. Though it may be appropriate to shift the risk level in anticipation of changing market conditions (lower the beta at a perceived peak in the market), long-run adherence to risk objectives is advisable.

■ MEASUREMENT OF RETURN IN RELATION TO RISK

In examining the performance of fund managers, the return measure commonly used is excess returns. Though the term **excess returns** has many definitions, the one most commonly used is: total return on a portfolio (capital appreciation plus dividends) minus the risk-free rate.

$$\text{Excess returns} = \text{Total portfolio return} - \text{Risk-free rate}$$

Thus, excess returns represents returns over and above what could be earned on a riskless asset. The rate on U.S. government Treasury bills is often used to represent the risk-free rate of return in the financial markets (though other definitions are possible). Thus, a fund that earns 12 percent when the Treasury bill rate is 6 percent has excess returns of 6 percent.

Once computed, excess returns are then compared to risk. We look at three different approaches to comparing excess returns to risk: the **Sharpe approach**, the **Treynor approach**, and the **Jensen approach**.

Sharpe Approach

In the Sharpe approach,[1] the excess returns on a portfolio are compared to the portfolio standard deviation.

$$\text{Sharpe measure} = \frac{\text{Total portfolio return} - \text{Risk-free rate}}{\text{Portfolio standard deviation}} \qquad (22\text{--}1)$$

The portfolio manager is thus able to view excess returns per unit of risk. If a portfolio has a return of 10 percent, the risk-free rate is 6 percent, and the portfolio standard deviation is 18 percent, the Sharpe measure is .22.

$$\text{Sharpe measure} = \frac{10\% - 6\%}{18\%} = \frac{4\%}{18\%} = .22$$

This measure can be compared to other portfolios or to the market in general to assess performance. If the market return per unit of risk is greater than .22, then the portfolio manager has turned in an inferior performance. Assume there is a 9 percent total market return, a 6 percent risk-free rate, and a market standard deviation of 12 percent. Then the Sharpe measure for the overall market is:

$$\frac{9\% - 6\%}{12\%} = \frac{3\%}{12\%} = .25$$

The portfolio measure of .22 is less than the market measure of .25 and represents an inferior performance. Of course, a portfolio measure above .25 would have represented a superior performance.

---

[1]William F. Sharpe, "Mutual Fund Performance," *Journal of Business,* January 1966, pp. 119–38.

Treynor Approach

The formula for the second approach for comparing excess returns to risk (developed by Treynor[2]) is:

$$\text{Treynor measure} = \frac{\text{Total portfolio return} - \text{Risk-free rate}}{\text{Portfolio beta}} \quad (22\text{--}2)$$

The only difference between the Sharpe and Treynor approaches is in the denominator. While Sharpe uses the portfolio standard deviation—Formula 21–1, Treynor uses the portfolio beta—Formula 22–2. Thus, one can say that Sharpe uses total risk, while Treynor uses only the systematic risk, or beta. Implicit in the Treynor approach is the assumption that portfolio managers have diversified away unsystematic risk, and only systematic risk remains.

If a portfolio has a total return of 10 percent, the risk-free rate is 6 percent, and the portfolio beta is .9, the Treynor measure would be:

$$\frac{10\% - 6\%}{.9} = \frac{4\%}{.9} = \frac{.04}{.9} = .044$$

This measure can be compared to other portfolios or to the market in general to determine whether there is a superior performance in terms of return per unit of risk. Assume the total market return is 9 percent, the risk-free rate is 6 percent, and the market beta (by definition) is 1; then the Treynor measure as applied to the market is .03.

$$\frac{9\% - 6\%}{1.0} = \frac{3\%}{1.0} = \frac{.03}{1.0} = .030$$

This would imply the portfolio has turned in a superior return to the market (.044 versus .030). Not only is the portfolio return higher than the market return (10 percent versus 9 percent), but the beta is less (.9 versus 1.0). Clearly, there is more return per unit of risk.

Jensen Approach

In the third approach, Jensen emphasizes using certain aspects of the capital asset pricing model to evaluate portfolio managers.[3] He compares their actual excess returns (total portfolio return − risk-free rate) to what should be required in the market, based on their portfolio beta.

The required rate of excess returns in the market for a given beta is shown in Figure 22–2 as the **market line.** If the beta is 0, the investor should expect to earn no more than the risk-free rate of return since there is no systematic

---

[2]Jack L. Treynor, "How to Rate Management of Investment Funds," *Harvard Business Review,* January–February 1965, pp. 63–74.

[3]Michael C. Jensen, "The Performance of Mutual Funds in the Period 1945–1964," *Journal of Finance,* May 1968, pp. 389–416.

Figure 22–2   Risk-Adjusted Portfolio Returns

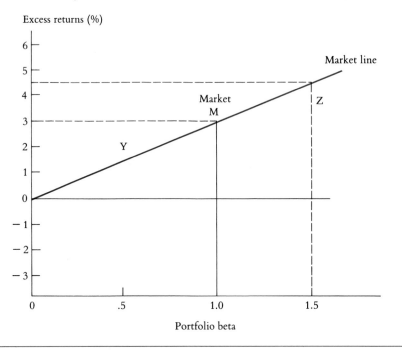

risk. If the portfolio manager earns only the risk-free rate of return, the excess returns will be 0. Thus, with a beta of 0, the expected excess returns on the market line are 0. With a portfolio beta of 1, the portfolio has a systematic risk equal to market, and the expected portfolio excess returns should be equal to market excess returns. If the market return (K_M) is 9 percent and the risk-free rate (R_F) is 6 percent, the market excess returns are 3 percent. A portfolio with a beta of 1 should expect to earn the market rate of excess returns $(K_M - R_F)$, equal to 3 percent. Other excess returns expectations are shown for betas ranging from 0 to 1.5. For example, a portfolio with a beta of 1.5 should provide excess returns of 4.5.

Adequacy of Performance

Using the Jensen approach, the adequacy of a portfolio manager's performance can be judged against the market line. Did he fall above or below the line? While it would appear that portfolio manager Y in Figure 22–2 had inferior returns in comparison to portfolio manager Z (approximately 2.1 percent versus 3.9 percent), this notion is quickly dispelled when one considers risk. Actually, portfolio manager Y performed above risk-return expectations as

Figure 22–3   Empirical Study of Risk-Adjusted Portfolio Returns—Systematic Risk and Return

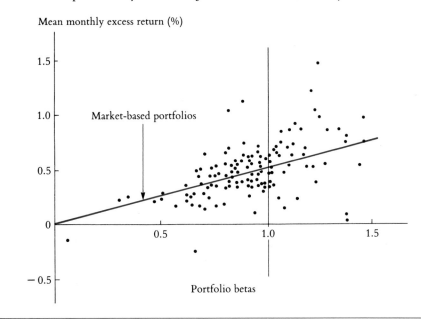

Source: John G. McDonald, "Objectives and Performance of Mutual Funds, 1960–1969," *Journal of Financial and Quantitative Analysis,* June 1974, p. 321.

indicated by the market line, while portfolio manager Z was below his risk-adjusted expected level. The vertical difference from a fund's performance point to the market line can be viewed as a measure of performance. This value, termed **alpha** or **average differential return,** indicates the difference between the return on the fund and a point on the market line that corresponds to a beta equal to the fund. In the case of fund Z, the beta of 1.5 indicated an excess return of 4.5 percent along the market line, and the actual excess return was only 3.9 percent. We thus have a negative alpha of 0.6 percent (3.9% − 4.5%). Clearly, a positive alpha indicates a superior performance, while a negative alpha leads to the opposite conclusion.

Key questions for portfolio managers in general are: Can they consistently perform at positive alpha levels? Can they generate returns better than those available along the market line, which are theoretically available to anyone? The results of a classic study conducted by John McDonald on 123 mutual funds are presented in Figure 22–3.

The upward-sloping line is the market line, or anticipated level of performance based on risk. The small dots represent performance of the funds. About as many funds underperformed (negative alpha below the line) as overperformed (positive alpha above the line). Although a few high-beta funds had an unusually strong performance on a risk-adjusted basis, there is no consistent pattern of superior performance.

Figure 22–4   Frequency Distribution of Estimated Alphas

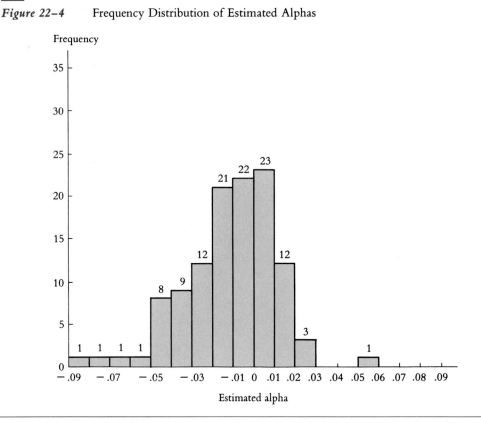

Source: Michael C. Jensen, "The Performance of Mutual Funds in the Period 1945–1964," *Journal of Finance,* May 1968, p. 404.

Other Studies

There are many other studies of a similar nature. Figure 22–4 shows the results of a landmark study by Michael Jensen in which he computed the alpha values of 115 mutual funds. The average alpha value was −1.1 percent per year, and only 39 out of 115 funds had a positive alpha.

A number of other important studies have been conducted by the Securities and Exchange Commission, Merrill Lynch, and various professors throughout the country (Friend, Blume, Crockett, Gentry, Schlarbaum, Williamson, etc.).[4] Although they worked with different data bases over varying time periods, their overall results were similar. Professional money managers have generally not outperformed the market over the long term on a risk-adjusted basis.

---

[4]Complete citations for these sources are presented under Selected References at the end of this chapter.

Those portfolio managers that do produce superior results (positive alphas) may attribute their performance to either superior market timing or excellence in security analysis and selection. As indicated in the next section, even when superior performance is achieved, it is not necessarily continued into the future.

■ PAST PERFORMANCE AND FUTURE PERFORMANCE

With this wealth of data available to investors, key questions that must still be considered are: How well does past performance indicate future performance? Will a fund that has provided high positive alphas or A's on the *Forbes* scale necessarily do the same in the future? Will a fund that has the most impressive record in the Wiesenberger survey necessarily do the best in the future?

Substantial research by the SEC and Jensen found that this is not necessarily the case. In Table 22–1, we observe results from the classic Jensen study of 115 mutual funds.

In the left-hand column of Table 22–1, we see the number of years selected funds beat a passive (unmanaged) portfolio with equal market risk. In the right-hand column, we see the percent of those funds that beat the same measure in the next year. Even for funds with good prior year's performance, the odds of beating the control group in the next year were not particularly high. For another look at the same phenomenon, observe in Table 22–2 the best fund performers over one quarter, one year, and five years. If you had bought Deleware Delcap because of its strong five-year performance, you would not have benefited in terms of strong performance in the first quarter of 1991. It did not even make the list of the best performers for the first quarter of 1991. Likewise, American Heritage, the top performer for the first quarter of 1991, has no prior record of superior performance over one year or five years. Very few funds appeared on all three lists.

Table 22–1   Relating Past and Future Performance

Number of Consecutive Years Funds' Performance Exceeded that of a Passive Portfolio with Similar Risk	Percentage of Group with Performance Exceeding that of a Passive Portfolio, with Similar Market Risk, in the Next Year
1	50.4%
2	52.0
3	53.4
4	55.8
5	46.4
6	35.3
7	25.0

Source: Michael C. Jensen, "Risk, Capital Assets, and Evaluation of Portfolios," *Journal of Business,* April 1969, p. 239.

Table 22-2   The Consistency of Fund Performance (From 1986–1991)

First Quarter (12/31/90 to 1/31/91)		One Year (1/31/90 to 1/31/91)		Five Year (3/31/86 to 3/31/91)	
Fund	Percent Change	Fund	Percent Change	Fund	Percent Change
American Heritage	54.17	Fidelity Sel Bio Tech	92.12	Delaware Delcap	342.70
Prudent Speculatr: Levrgd	48.32	Fidelity Sel Medical	79.94	Financial Port: Health	254.42
Oberweis Emerging Growth	43.85	Fidelity Sel Health	72.27	DFA: Japan Small Co	216.90
T Rowe Price Sci & Tech	43.58	Financial Port: Health	69.04	GT Global Japan	193.02
Fidelity Sel Medical	41.61	Twentieth Cent: Ultra Inv	60.91	GT Global Pacific	174.77
Twentieth Cent: Ultra Inv	40.75	Oppenheimer Glbl Bio-Tech	59.98	Transam Cap Appreciation	161.44
Fidelity Sel Bio Tech	40.42	Putnam Health Science	46.69	Fidelity Sel Health	156.93
Transam Cap Appreciation	40.02	Equity Port: Growth	46.60	Fidelity Sel Food	149.71
Montgomery: Small Cap	39.57	Phoenix Multi: Cap Apprec	43.84	Nomura Pacific Basin	145.53
Oppenheimer Glbl Bio-Tech	38.97	Founders: Discovery	42.53	First Inv Global	144.30
Equity Port: Growth	37.10	Amex: Equity Growth	41.98	Vanguard Spl: Health	143.55
FPA Capital	36.98	Pac Hzn: Aggressive Growth	41.20	Fidelity Sel Bio Tech	141.75
Security Ultra	36.65	GT Global Health Care	40.67	Twentieth Cent: Ultra Inv	137.03
Sherman, Dean	36.65	Vanguard Spl: Health	39.79	Equity Port: Growth	136.39
Shearson Small Cap	35.63	Rbrtsn Steph Emerging Gro	38.79	Vanguard Spl: Energy	135.04
Security Omni	35.21	Fidelity Sel Computer	37.47	Putnam Health Science	132.78
Seligman Comm & Informtn	35.18	MIM Mutual: Stock Apprec	37.39	Templeton: Foreign	131.54
Financial Port: Tech	34.76	CGM Cap Development	36.66	Merrill Pacific: A	127.99
Fidelity Sel Computer	34.47	Schield: Prog Envirnmnt	36.44	Hartwell Emerging Growth	123.40
Fidelity Sel Health	34.45	T Rowe Price Sci & Tech	35.45	Fidelity Destiny II	122.95
Harbor: Growth	34.37	Fidelity Sel Technology	35.33	Janus Venture	121.51
Vista: Growth & Income	33.98	USFG Axe-Hghtn: Growth	35.18	Idex Fund	120.93
CGM Cap Development	33.91	Westcore: Midco Growth	34.75	Berger 100	119.75
Twentieth Cent: Giftrust	33.88	New England: Growth	34.60	Fidelity Sel Telecomm	119.70
Keystone S-4	33.82	United New Concepts	33.62	Gabelli Asset	119.30

Source: *Barron's*, May 13, 1991, p. M20. Reprinted by permission of *Barron's*, © 1991 by Dow Jones & Company, Inc. All Rights Reserved Worldwide.

Though past performance does not offer significant promise for the future, historical perspective does take on some importance. Clearly, you would not wish to buy a fund that has had consistently negative alphas or performance below the norm measured on some other basis. They may be overtrading the portfolio or inefficiently diversifying. By the same token, you should be most hesitant about paying any kind of premium sales commission or high management fee purely on the basis of a fund's strong past performance, which may or may not be repeated in the future. A good rule to follow is to go for

the best performance, but pay no extra premium for it. This is often possible because money managers with prior success may have large asset bases and low percentage management fees.

■ DIVERSIFICATION

An important service a money manager can provide is effective diversification of asset holdings. Once we at least partially accept the fact that superior performance on a risk-adjusted basis is a difficult achievement, we begin to look hard at other attributes money managers may possess. We can ask: Are mutual fund managers effective diversifiers of their holdings?

As previously discussed in Chapter 21 and in this chapter, there are two measures of risk: systematic and unsystematic. Systematic risk is measured by the portfolio's (or individual stock's) beta. Under the capital asset pricing model, higher betas are rewarded with relatively high returns, and vice versa. As the market goes up 10 percent, our portfolio might go up 12 percent (beta of 1.2), and a similar phenomenon may occur on the downside. Unsystematic risk is random or nonmarket related and may be generally diversified away by the astute portfolio manager. Under the capital asset pricing model, there is no market reward for unsystematic risk since it can be eliminated through diversification.

The question for a portfolio manager then becomes: How effective have you been in diversifying away the nonrewarded, unsystematic risk? Put another way, to what extent can a fund's movements be described as market related rather than random in nature? If we plot a fund's excess returns over an extended period against market excess returns, we can determine the joint movement between the two as indicated in Figure 22–5. In Panel (a) we plot the fund's basic points. In Panel (b) we draw a regression line through these points. Of importance to the present discussion is the extent to which our line fits the data. If the points of observation fall very close to the line, the independent variable (excess market returns) is largely responsible for describing the dependent variable (excess returns for fund X).

The degree of association between the independent and dependent variables is measured by R^2 (**coefficient of determination**).[5] R^2 may take on a value anywhere between 0 and 1. A high degree of correlation between the independent and dependent variables will produce an R^2 of .7 or better. In Panel (b) it is assumed to be .90.

---

[5]R^2 also represents the correlation coefficient squared. Thus, we can square Formula 21A–1 in Chapter 21. Another statement is:

$$R^2 = 1 - \frac{\Sigma(y - y_c)^2/n}{\Sigma(y - \bar{y})^2/n}$$

where y_c represents points along the regression line, and y is the average value of the independent variable.

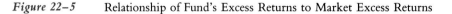

Figure 22–5   Relationship of Fund's Excess Returns to Market Excess Returns

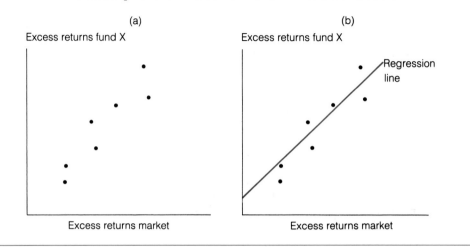

In Figure 22–6, the points do not fall consistently close to the regression line, and the R^2 value is assumed to be only .55. In this instance, we say the independent variable (excess market returns) was not the only major variable in explaining changes in the dependent variable (excess returns for fund Y).

The points in Figure 22–6 imply that the portfolio manager for fund Y may not have been particularly effective in his diversification efforts. Many other factors besides market returns appear to be affecting the portfolio returns of fund Y, and these could have been diversified away rather than allowed to influence returns. In this instance, we say there is a high degree of unsystematic, or nonmarket-related, risk. Since unsystematic risk is presumed to go unrewarded in the marketplace under the capital asset pricing model, there is evidence of inefficient portfolio diversification.

What does empirical data tell us about the effectiveness of portfolio managers in achieving diversification? How have they stacked up in terms of R^2 values for their portfolios? As indicated in Figure 22–7, their record is generally good.

The Merrill Lynch study of 100 mutual funds between 1970 and 1974 shows an average R^2 value of approximately .90 with very few funds falling below .70. The actual range is between .66 and .98. Studies by McDonald, Jensen, Gentry, and Williamson have led to similar conclusions (see Selected References for complete citations).

Although many mutual funds invest in 80 to 100 securities to achieve effective diversification, this is often more than is necessary. A high degree of diversification can be achieved with between 10 and 20 efficiently selected stocks, as is indicated in Table 22–3. The Wagner and Lau study shows the number of securities in the portfolio, the portfolio standard deviation, and correlation with return on the market index (R^2).

Figure 22–6   Example of Lower Correlation

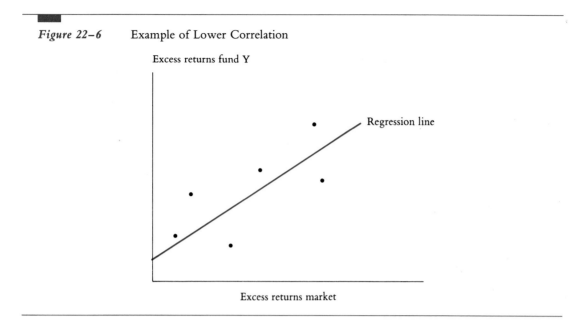

Excess returns fund Y

Regression line

Excess returns market

Figure 22–7   Quarterly Returns Attributable to Market Fluctuations: 100 Mutual Funds, 1970–1974

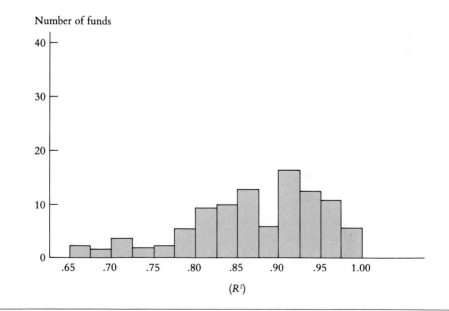

Number of funds

(R^2)

Source: Merrill Lynch, Pierce, Fenner & Smith, *Investment Performance Analysis, Comparative Survey*, 1974.

Table 22–3   Reduction in Portfolio Risk through Diversification

Number of Securities in Portfolio	Standard Deviation of Portfolio Returns, σ_p (Percent per Month)	Correlation with Return on Market Index*
1	7.0	0.54
2	5.0	0.63
3	4.8	0.75
4	4.6	0.77
5	4.6	0.79
10	4.2	0.85
15	4.0	0.88
20	3.9	0.89

*The market here refers to an unweighted index of all NYSE stocks.
Source: W. H. Wagner and C. S. Lau, "The Effect of Diversification on Risk," *Financial Analysts Journal*, November–December 1971, p. 53.

■ STABILITY OF BETAS

In Chapter 21, the lack of stability of the beta coefficient of an individual security was mentioned as a possible drawback to the use of the capital asset pricing model. Instability means prior beta values may not be reflective of future beta values. If this is the case, then use of a beta based on prior performance may not be accurate in reflecting future return potential. Since the beta coefficient is such an integral part of our analysis in Chapters 21 and 22, we must address this issue.

We break down our discussion on beta stability as it relates to individual stocks, industry groupings, and portfolios. In regard to individual stocks, a study by Blume provided evidence that the betas of individual stocks tend to regress or approach 1 over time.[6] That is, a stock with a beta of 1.5 may tend to have a beta of 1.4 in the next period, 1.3 in a subsequent period, and so on. Stocks with betas below 1 also tend to approach 1 over time. While this is not automatic, there is a tendency to follow this pattern.

The same pattern of instability would apply to betas for various industry groupings, as indicated in Table 22–4. The Valentine study shows the changing betas for different industry groupings over time. The pattern of typical change can be found in such industries as canned goods and department stores.

While betas of individual stocks and industries may not be particularly stable over time, there is some evidence portfolio betas are stable. This stability can be achieved with reasonably sized diversified portfolios of 10 to 20 stocks. We look to the classic research of Marshall Blume in Table 22–5 on page 732.

---

[6]Marshall E. Blume, "Betas and Their Regression Tendencies," *Journal of Finance*, June 1975, pp. 785–95.

Table 22–4   Industry Beta Values, 1951–1970

	1951–1955	1956–1960	1961–1965	1966–1970
Aerospace	.96247	.66585	.72409	1.31815
Agricultural machinery	.78687	.90875	.81422	1.14613
Aluminum	1.18617	1.60756	1.13980	1.21376
Apparel manufacturing	.50733	.47428	1.23344	1.52437
Auto parts and accessories	.87577	1.03116	.84302	1.17786
Autos	1.21383	1.00899	.87593	1.00869
Auto tires and rubber goods	1.18350	1.20016	1.16497	.97226
Auto trucks and parts	.96299	1.24551	1.21358	1.24255
Biscuit bakers	.34377	.18935	.76037	.68711
Bituminous coal	1.02612	1.14341	1.11203	.80200
Bread and cake bakers	.35396	.35301	.93734	1.91074
Brewers	.18364	.56817	.74847	1.03782
Business and office equipment	1.12362	1.12134	1.44912	1.09700
—Canned foods	.65238	.55939	1.04155	1.01861
Cement	1.01518	.87642	.82306	1.53511
Chemicals	1.06482	1.04785	.94006	.85256
Cigarettes	.29077	.23970	1.29410	.55432
Confectionery	.35793	.35514	1.04756	.59934
Construction and material handling machinery	1.14771	1.18300	.91518	1.19976
Copper	1.17911	.97515	.94643	1.08206
Corn refiners	.32177	.44286	1.02606	.93099
Crude oil producers	.69844	1.03158	1.12971	.95093
Dairy products	.40212	.35200	.98700	1.04501
—Department stores	.60589	.53718	.66176	1.21765
Distillers	.74801	.79331	.86246	.90287
Drugs	.54110	1.05861	1.29238	.95521
Electrical equipment	.96542	1.25540	1.04542	1.19990
Electrical household appliances	.76593	1.01648	.91009	1.15041
Electronics	.90328	1.31251	1.55722	1.56784
Food chain stores	.38349	.51301	1.00418	.73317
Gold mining	.54291	.63910	.06125	.07090
Heating and plumbing	.64976	.86583	.95464	1.27624
Home furnishings	.45473	.76023	1.18308	1.60301
Industrial machinery	.81678	1.18670	1.03285	1.33398
Integrated domestic oil companies	.79546	1.09107	.82772	.96288
Integrated international oil companies	1.05360	.98599	.70443	.73875
Lead and zinc	.91563	.99167	1.07584	.72259

Source: Jerome L. Valentine, "Investment Analysis and Capital Market Theory," *Occasional Paper No. 1* (Charlottesville, Va.: The Financial Research Foundation, 1975), p. 34.

Table 22–5   Correlation Coefficients of Betas for Portfolios of N Securities

Number of Securities per Portfolio	7/26–6/33 and 7/33–6/40	7/33–6/40 and 7/40–6/47	7/40–6/47 and 7/47–6/54	7/47–6/54 and 7/54–6/61	7/54–6/61 and 7/61–6/68
1	0.63	0.62	0.59	0.65	0.60
2	0.71	0.76	0.72	0.76	0.73
4	0.80	0.85	0.81	0.84	0.84
7	0.86	0.91	0.88	0.87	0.88
10	0.89	0.94	0.90	0.92	0.92
20	0.93	0.97	0.95	0.95	0.97
35	0.96	0.98	0.95	0.97	0.97
50	0.98	0.99	0.98	0.98	0.98

Source: Abstracted from Marshall Blume, "On the Assessment of Risk," *Journal of Finance,* March 1971, p. 7.

Table 22–6   Average Values of Beta for Stocks in Selected Industries, 1966–1974.

Industry	Beta Value	Industry	Beta Value
Air transport	1.80	Chemicals	1.22
Real property	1.70	Energy, raw materials	1.22
Travel, outdoor recreation	1.66	Tires, rubber goods	1.21
Electronics	1.60	Railroads, shipping	1.19
Miscellaneous finance	1.60	Forest products, paper	1.16
Nondurables, entertainment	1.47	Miscellaneous, conglomerate	1.14
Consumer durables	1.44	Drugs, medicine	1.14
Business machines	1.43	Domestic oil	1.12
Retail, general	1.43	Soaps, cosmetics	1.09
Media	1.39	Steel	1.02
Insurance	1.34	Containers	1.01
Trucking, freight	1.31	Nonferrous metals	.99
Producer goods	1.30	Agriculture, food	.99
Aerospace	1.30	Liquor	.89
Business services	1.28	International oil	.85
Apparel	1.27	Banks	.81
Construction	1.27	Tobacco	.80
Motor vehicles	1.27	Telephone	.75
Photographic, optical	1.24	Energy, utilities	.60
		Gold	.36

Source: Barr Rosenberg and James Guy, "Prediction of Beta from Investment Fundamentals," *Financial Analysts Journal,* July–August 1976, p. 66.

As indicated in Table 22–5, he measured the correlation between portfolio betas during different time periods. In each case, he compared one period to the next and determined the extent of correlation for different-sized portfolios. A high degree of correlation would indicate a stable beta as the past would be correlated with the future. For example, the last column shows the correlation of betas between the seven-year time periods of July 1954 to June 1961 and July 1961 to June 1968. With only one security, there was a correlation coefficient of .60; with 10 securities, .92; with 20 securities, .97; and finally with 50 securities, .98. The presumption is that reasonably large portfolios have stable betas over time, and this may be useful in assessing future risk considerations.

One further observation about betas. Over any given period, some industries tend to have higher betas than others and this can be important when you are compiling a portfolio. Firms in industries that are subject to the business cycle have highly variable earnings and this shows up in the average industry beta. Note in Table 22–6 the high industry betas that Rosenberg and Guy found for the air transport, real property (real estate), travel, and electronics industries. Firms that are in industries that provide necessities (and thus have less volatile earnings) have betas closer to 1. Examples are soaps and cosmetics, containers, and agriculture and food.

■ OTHER ASSETS AS WELL AS STOCKS

This chapter has dealt primarily with the ability to measure risk and return as it relates to portfolios of common stock. Unfortunately, most professionally managed funds have portfolios that are also diversified across asset classes. Brinson, Hood, and Beebower (BHB) examined 91 large corporate pension plans from 1974 to 1983 and found that the average plan included investments in stocks, bonds, T-bills, and real estate.[7] The combined asset mix makes performance evaluation more complex than the Sharpe, Treynor and Jensen measures discussed earlier in the chapter, which can be applied only to the stock portion of the portfolio.

BHB suggest that performance of portfolios diversified across asset classes be compared to a benchmark portfolio that consists of the pension plan's normal percentage distribution between asset classes. BHB use the Standard & Poor's 500 Index, the Shearson Lehman Government/Corporate Bond Index, and 30-day Treasury bills as the benchmark for each of these asset classes. For an investment manager to generate superior performance, he or she would have to outperform a passively managed portfolio maintaining the plan's mix of asset classes. If the plan manager can not outperform a passive portfolio through an active management strategy, then it is not worth paying for active portfolio management.

---

[7]Gary P. Brinson, Randolph Hood, and Gilbert L. Beebower, "Determinants of Portfolio Performance," *Financial Analysts Journal*, July–August 1986, pp. 39–44.

Table 22–7   Typical Weighted Portfolio for Money Managers

Asset Class	Weight	
Equities:		
Domestic large capitalization...........................	30%	
Domestic small capitalization	15	55%
International..	10	
Venture capital.......................................	5	
Fixed income:		
Domestic bonds......................................	15	
International dollar bonds	4	
Nondollar bonds.....................................	6	
Real estate..	15	
Cash equivalents	0	
	100%	

Source: Gary Brinson, Jeffrey J. Diermeier, and Gary C. Schlarbaum, "A Composite Portfolio Benchmark for Pension Plans," *Financial Analysts Journal,* March–April 1986, p. 15.

Ignoring real estate and focusing on stocks, bonds, and T-bills, BHB found that in general the actual mean average total return on portfolios over the period was 9.01 percent versus 10.11 percent for the benchmark portfolio. In other words, active management cost the pension plans 1.10 percent per year. Of course, other time periods could reflect superior results. Stressed throughout the BHB analysis is also the fact that determining the appropriate asset allocation mix (stocks versus bonds versus T-bills) is much more important than simply picking winning or losing stocks.

Asset managers lose their jobs not so much because they picked stock A over stock B, but because they had a poorly allocated portfolio under a given market condition. For example, Table 22–7 shows a typical portfolio composition for large pension fund managers. Equities of all types make up 55 percent of the portfolio. If in a bull market, one is only 40 percent invested in equities, he or she could be in real trouble even if individual stock selection was great.

■ THE MAKEUP OF INSTITUTIONAL INVESTORS

Having discussed measurement and portfolio management techniques for institutional investors, we will now take a more specific look at the participants. **Institutional investors** (as opposed to individual investors) represent organizations that are responsible for bringing together large pools of capital for reinvestment. Our coverage will center on investment companies (including mutual funds), pension funds, life insurance companies, bank trust departments, and endowments and foundations.

Table 22–8	Percentage of Institutional Market Held by Institutional Investors	
		Percent
1. Private noninsured pension funds		26.2%
2. Open-end investment companies		15.5
3. Other investment companies		2.0
4. Life insurance companies		6.1
5. Property-liability insurance companies		4.9
6. Personal trust funds		27.8
7. Common trust funds		1.7
8. Mutual savings banks		1.1
9. State and local retirement funds		4.6
10. Foundations		7.4
11. Educational endowments		2.7
		100.0%

Source: Compiled from a review of annual reports from the Securities and Exchange Commission and the New York Stock Exchange.

Investment Companies (Including Mutual Funds)

Investment companies take the proceeds of individual investors and reinvest them in other securities according to their specific objectives. Income and capital gains are generally distributed to stockholders and are subject to single taxation under Subchapter M of the Internal Revenue Code. Investment companies were discussed at some length in Chapter 19.

Other Institutional Investors

Other institutional investors (along with investment companies) and their extent of market participation are presented in Table 22–8. Total institutional holdings are over $5 trillion. We will briefly comment on pension funds, insurance companies, bank trust departments, and foundations and endowments.

Pension Funds Pension funds represent an important and growing sector of the institutional market and may be private or public. Private funds represent well over half of the pension fund market. The benefits that accrue under private pension funds may be insured or uninsured, with the latter arrangement occurring most frequently. Public pension funds are run for the benefit of federal, state, or local employees.

Insurance Companies Insurance companies may be categorized as either "life" or "property and casualty." Life insurance companies must earn a minimum rate of return assumed in calculating insurance premiums, and public

Students as Portfolio Managers

It started at the University of Wisconsin over two decades ago. Now, students manage part of the university endowment in over 25 colleges and universities. This is no simulation.

The largest such program is at Ohio State University where the students are enrolled in courses that allow them to manage over $5 million of the permanent endowment of the university. Other schools such as UCLA, Indiana University, the University of Missouri, Southern Methodist University, Notre Dame, Gannon College, Virginia Military Institute, De Paul University, and Texas Christian University have similar programs. For a complete listing of schools with programs, see E. C. Lawrence, "Learning Portfolio Management by Experience: University Student Investment Funds," *Financial Review,* February 1990, pp. 163–73.

The authors are most familiar with the student-managed fund at Texas Christian University, where they have both served as faculty advisors. The students manage $1.2 million in stock and bonds and have power to make their own investment decisions. The faculty advisors do not even have veto power (don't ask if they sweat a lot). The students receive six hours of academic credit for their work and do intensive work in analyzing securities and balancing the portfolio. The students also have their own committees operating in such areas as economics, accounting, and so on.

As would be true of other professional money managers, they provide quarterly reports, in which they compare their performance to their own goals as well as to the popular market averages.

policy emphasizes safety of assets. Part of life insurance company assets are in privately placed debt or mortgages, with the balance in bonds and stocks. Property and casualty insurance companies enjoy more lenient regulation of their activities and generally have a larger percentage of their assets in bonds and stocks.

Bank Trust Departments   The emphasis in bank trust departments is on managing other people's funds for a fee. Banks may administer individual trusts or commingled (combined) funds in a common trust fund. Often a bank will establish more than one common trust fund to serve varying needs and objectives. The overall performance of bank trust departments has been mixed, with the usual number of leaders and laggards. Bank trust management is highly concentrated with a relatively small number of trust departments holding the majority of funds. Out of approximately 4,000 bank trust departments, the top 10 hold one third of all assets, and the largest 60 hold two thirds.

Foundations and Endowments   Foundations represent nonprofit organizations set up to accomplish social, educational, or charitable purposes. They are often established through the donation of a large block of stock in which

the donor was one of the corporate founders. Examples include the Ford, Carnegie, and Rockefeller Foundations. Endowments, on the other hand, represent permanent capital funds that are donated to universities, churches, or civic organizations. The management of endowment funds is often quite difficult because of the pressure for current income to maintain operations (perhaps the university library) while at the same time there is a demand for capital appreciation. Measurement of performance for foundations and endowments has gone much more to a total-return basis (annual income plus capital appreciation) rather than the traditional interest-earned or dividend-received basis.

■ COMMENTS ON INSTITUTIONAL PERFORMANCE

Performance studies similar to those presented earlier in the chapter on mutual funds and pension funds have been conducted on other institutional portfolios by Gentry, Schlarbaum, Williamson, and others.[8] The conclusion of this research is very similar to that reached on mutual funds; that is, on a risk-adjusted basis, they have not provided performance superior to a generally accepted market average or a randomly selected portfolio.

Of equal concern is whether large institutional investors tend to control the movements in the market due to their large size. Prior studies (before the crash of 1987) tended to indicate this was not the case.[9] However, with the increased volatility in the market concurrent with and following the crash, the impact of institutional investors on the market may be much greater due to program trading, portfolio insurance, and other investing patterns.[10] There is certainly a strong public perception that institutional investors have a dominant position in the market, and only further research will be able to fully reconcile this issue.

■ SUMMARY

The ability of portfolio managers to meet various goals and objectives is considered in this chapter. Many portfolio managers appear to demonstrate superior performances during market boom years. However, when this performance is adjusted for risk, any perceived superiority may quickly vanish.

---

[8]Complete citations are provided under Selected References at the end of the chapter.

[9]Alan Kraus and Hans K. Stoll, "Parallel Trading by Institutional Investors," *Journal of Financial and Quantitative Analysis,* December 1972, pp. 2107–38. Also, Frank K. Reilly, "Institutions on Trial: Not Guilty!" *Journal of Portfolio Management,* Winter 1977, pp. 5–10.

[10]Stanley B. Block and Timothy J. Gallagher, "How Much Do Bank Trust Departments Use Derivatives?" *Journal of Portfolio Management,* Fall 1988, pp. 12–16.

Some concepts related to the capital asset pricing model may be used to evaluate the performance of money managers. Portfolio beta values are shown along the horizontal axis, while the market line indicates expected returns. Portfolio managers that are able to operate above the line (positive alphas) are thought to be superior managers, while the opposite would be true of those falling below the line. Research by McDonald, Jensen, and others indicates that, on average, portfolio managers do not beat the popular averages or random portfolios on a risk-adjusted basis. One possible reason is the high transaction costs involved in active portfolio management.

Empirical research has also indicated those funds that have done well in the past do not necessarily promise superior returns in the future. Although it may be helpful to examine past records to eliminate clearly unsatisfactory performers, the stars of the past may not necessarily be the stars of the future. Nevertheless, mutual funds (or other managed portfolios) do have some desirable attributes. As indicated by a Merrill Lynch study (and others as well), mutual funds tend to be very efficient diversifiers. Their average correlation with the market (R^2) tends to be approximately 90 percent, indicating only 10 percent unsystematic, or nonrewarded, risk. In general, mutual fund managers also do a good job of constructing portfolios that are consistent with their initially stated objectives (that is, maximum capital gains, growth, income, etc.).

The beta for a diversified portfolio also tends to be more stable than that for a given stock or group of stocks within an industry. Thus, the historical portfolio beta may be more reflective of current and future risk than would be the case with individual securities.

The market of institutional investors is made up of investment companies (closed-end and mutual funds), pension funds, insurance companies, foundations, endowments, and other participants. Although the great weight of empirical research has dealt with mutual funds, the same basic conclusions about risk-adjusted returns can be applied to other institutional investors. While research indicates that large institutional investors did not control the market in the past, the events of the late 1980s have called for serious reexamination of the potentially dominant role of the institutional investor in the marketplace.

◼ IMPORTANT WORDS AND CONCEPTS

excess returns 720	market line 721
Sharpe approach 720	alpha (average differential return) 723
Treynor approach 720	R^2 (coefficient of determination) 727
Jensen approach 720	institutional investors 734

DISCUSSION QUESTIONS

1. What is a risk-adjusted return?
2. In evaluating a mutual fund manager, what would be the first point to analyze?
3. How can adherence to portfolio objectives be measured?
4. How can risk exposure be measured?
5. How are excess returns defined?
6. What is the Sharpe approach to measuring portfolio risk? If a portfolio has a higher measure than the market in general under the Sharpe approach, what is the implication?
7. How does the Treynor approach differ from the Sharpe approach? Which of the two measures assumes unsystematic risk will be diversified away?
8. Under the Jensen approach, how is the market line related to the beta?
9. Explain alpha as a measure of performance.
10. What conclusions can be drawn from the empirical studies of portfolio (fund) managers' performances?
11. Is the past performance of portfolio managers of any significance?
12. If investment companies do not offer returns that are, on average, any better than the market in general, why would someone invest in them?
13. What is the meaning of beta instability versus stability? Relate this to individual firms, industries, and portfolios.
14. According to the Brinson, Hood, and Beebower (BHB) study, are asset allocation decisions (stocks versus bonds, etc.) more or less important than individual stock selection decisions?
15. What is meant by an institutional investor? Give some examples.

PROBLEMS

Sharpe approach to measuring performance

1. A firm that evaluates portfolios uses the Sharpe approach to measuring performance. How would it rank the following three portfolios?

	Portfolio Return	Risk-Free Rate	Portfolio Standard Deviation
Bowman Money Managers	11%	7%	20%
Donruss Group	15	7	25
Fleer Investment Company	10	7	14

Treynor approach
to measuring
performance

2. Assume a second firm that evaluates portfolios uses the Treynor approach to measuring performance. The firm is also evaluating the three portfolios in Problem 1. The portfolio betas are as follows:

	Portfolio Beta
Bowman Money Managers	1.08
Donruss Group	1.20
Fleer Investment Company	1.10

   a. Using the Treynor approach, how would the second firm rank the three portfolios?
   b. Explain why any differences have taken place in the rankings between Problem 1 and Problem 2a.
   c. If the Treynor approach is utilized, and the market return is 10 percent (with a risk-free rate of 7 percent), which of the portfolios outperformed the market?

Jensen approach
to measuring
performance

3. Assume the Jensen approach to portfolio valuation is being used.
   a. Draw a market line similar to that in Figure 22–2 (i.e., show 0 excess returns at a 0 portfolio beta and 3 percent (10 percent − 7 percent) at a portfolio beta of 1).
   b. Now graph the three portfolios. Which portfolio(s) over or underperformed the market?

■ MARKETBASE-E EXERCISES

1. a. Compute a Treynor return-risk measure for each security. Sort the stocks by the Treynor measure. Make two portfolios—one of the five highest Treynor and one of the five lowest Treynor. What are the CAPM portfolio returns for these two portfolios?
   b. Go to the newspaper and determine the prices of these stocks exactly one year ago. What rate of return have these portfolios offered?
   c. Compare the portfolio return on a risk-adjusted basis to the return offered by the Standard and Poor's 500 Stock Index over the same period. Did the portfolio earn excess returns or not?
2. a. Compute the Jensen excess return measure for each security you identified in problem (1).
   b. Sort the stocks by the Jensen measure you computed. Make two portfolios—one of the five highest Jensen measures and one of the five lowest Jensen measures. What differences do you observe between the rankings by Jensen measure and the rankings by the Treynor measure?

3. *a.* Sort the companies by beta in ascending order. Scroll through the companies until you get to one with a meaningful figure. How many companies do not have a meaningful beta measure? Can you determine why this is?

   b. In scrolling through the companies, you will find that there are some with negative betas. Select those companies. (Do not include companies with a zero beta.)

   c. Compute the Treynor measures for the negative beta companies.

   d. Save the companies with negative betas to a spreadsheet file. Include the following variables: ROE, DYL, MRK, ISH, ROA, PE, PS, and PB. Use the spreadsheet to compute average ratios for these companies. Compare these companies' averages with the overall MarketBase-E averages. Are any patterns discernible here?

■ SELECTED REFERENCES

Measuring Portfolio Performance

Brinson, Gary P.; Randolph Hood; and Gilbert L. Beebower. "Determinants of Portfolio Performance." *Financial Analysts Journal,* July–August 1986, pp. 39–44.

Brown, Keith C., and Gregory D. Brown. "Does the Market's Portfolio's Composition Matter?" *Journal of Portfolio Management,* Winter 1987, pp. 26–32.

French, Dan W., and Glenn V. Henderson, Jr. "How Well Does Performance Evaluation Perform?" *Journal of Portfolio Management,* Winter 1985, pp. 15–18.

Friend, Irwin; Marshall Blume; and Jean Crockett. *Mutual Funds and Other Institutional Investors.* New York: McGraw-Hill, 1970.

Gentry, James A. "Capital Market Line Theory, Insurance Company Portfolio Performance, and Empirical Anomalies." *Quarterly Review of Economics and Business,* Spring 1975, pp. 8–16.

Ibbotson, Roger G.; Laurence B. Siegel; and Kathryn S. Love. "World Wealth: Market Values and Returns." *Journal of Portfolio Management,* Fall 1985, pp. 4–23.

Jensen, Michael C. "The Performance of Mutual Funds in the Period 1945–1964." *Journal of Finance,* May 1968, pp. 389–416.

———. "Risk, Capital Assets, and Evaluation of Portfolios." *Journal of Business,* April 1969, pp. 167–247.

McDonald, John G. "Objectives and Performance of Mutual Funds, 1960–1969." *Journal of Financial and Quantitative Analysis,* June 1974, pp. 311–33.

Schlarbaum, Gary G. "The Investment Performance of the Common Stock Portfolios of Property-Liability Insurance Companies." *Journal of Financial and Quantitative Analysis,* January 1974, pp. 89–106.

Sharpe, William F. "Mutual Fund Performance." *Journal of Business,* January 1966, pp. 119–38.

Singer, Brian D., and Gilbert L. Beebower. "Determinants of Portfolio Performance II: An Update." *Financial Analysts Journal,* May–June 1991, pp. 40–48.

Treynor, Jack L. "How to Rate Management of Investment Funds." *Harvard Business Review,* January–February 1965, pp. 63–74.

Williamson, J. Peter. "Measuring Mutual Fund Performance." *Financial Analysts Journal,* November–December 1972, pp. 78–84.

Portfolio Strategy

Ezra, Don D. "Asset Allocation by Surplus Optimization." *Financial Analysts Journal,* January–February 1991, pp. 51–57.

Lerner, Eugene M., and Pochara Theerathorn. "The Returns of Different Investment Strategies." *Journal of Portfolio Management,* Summer 1983, pp. 26–28.

Lloyd, William P., and Naval K. Modani. "Stocks, Bonds, Bills, and Time Diversification." *Journal of Portfolio Management,* Spring 1983, pp. 7–11.

McEnally, Richard W. "Latane's Bequest: The Best Portfolio Strategies." *Journal of Portfolio Management,* Winter 1986, pp. 21–30.

Wagner, W. H., and S. C. Lau. "The Effect of Diversification on Risk." *Financial Analysts Journal,* November–December 1971, pp. 48–53.

Special Tools for Portfolio Management

Kritzman, Mark. "What's Wrong with Portfolio Insurance?" *Journal of Portfolio Management,* Winter 1987, pp. 13–18.

Labuszewski, John, and John Nyhoff. "How to 'Fence in' Your Profits with Options." *Futures,* November 1986, pp. 58–59.

Wolf, Avner. "Optimal Hedging with Futures Options." *Journal of Economics and Business,* May 1987, pp. 141–58.

Student-Managed Portfolios

Lawrence, E. C. "Learning Portfolio Management by Experience: University Student Investment Funds." *Financial Review,* February 1990, pp. 163–73.

Appendixes

Outline

Appendix A   Compound Sum of $1

Compound sum of $1

Percent

Period	1%	2%	3%	4%	5%	6%	7%	8%	9%	10%	11%
1	1.010	1.020	1.030	1.040	1.050	1.060	1.070	1.080	1.090	1.100	1.110
2	1.020	1.040	1.061	1.082	1.103	1.124	1.145	1.166	1.188	1.210	1.232
3	1.030	1.061	1.093	1.125	1.158	1.191	1.225	1.260	1.295	1.331	1.368
4	1.041	1.082	1.126	1.170	1.216	1.262	1.311	1.360	1.412	1.464	1.518
5	1.051	1.104	1.159	1.217	1.276	1.338	1.403	1.469	1.539	1.611	1.685
6	1.062	1.126	1.194	1.265	1.340	1.419	1.501	1.587	1.677	1.772	1.870
7	1.072	1.149	1.230	1.316	1.407	1.504	1.606	1.714	1.828	1.949	2.076
8	1.083	1.172	1.267	1.369	1.477	1.594	1.718	1.851	1.993	2.144	2.305
9	1.094	1.195	1.305	1.423	1.551	1.689	1.838	1.999	2.172	2.358	2.558
10	1.105	1.219	1.344	1.480	1.629	1.791	1.967	2.159	2.367	2.594	2.839
11	1.116	1.243	1.384	1.539	1.710	1.898	2.105	2.332	2.580	2.853	3.152
12	1.127	1.268	1.426	1.601	1.796	2.012	2.252	2.518	2.813	3.138	3.498
13	1.138	1.294	1.469	1.665	1.886	2.133	2.410	2.720	3.066	3.452	3.883
14	1.149	1.319	1.513	1.732	1.980	2.261	2.579	2.937	3.342	3.797	4.310
15	1.161	1.346	1.558	1.801	2.079	2.397	2.759	3.172	3.642	4.177	4.785
16	1.173	1.373	1.605	1.873	2.183	2.540	2.952	3.426	3.970	4.595	5.311
17	1.184	1.400	1.653	1.948	2.292	2.693	3.159	3.700	4.328	5.054	5.895
18	1.196	1.428	1.702	2.206	2.407	2.854	3.380	3.996	4.717	5.560	6.544
19	1.208	1.457	1.754	2.107	2.527	3.026	3.617	4.316	5.142	6.116	7.263
20	1.220	1.486	1.806	2.191	2.653	3.207	3.870	4.661	5.604	6.727	8.062
25	1.282	1.641	2.094	2.666	3.386	4.292	5.427	6.848	8.623	10.835	13.585
30	1.348	1.811	2.427	3.243	4.322	5.743	7.612	10.063	13.268	17.449	22.892
40	1.489	2.208	3.262	4.801	7.040	10.286	14.974	21.725	31.409	45.259	65.001
50	1.645	2.692	4.384	7.107	11.467	18.420	29.457	46.902	74.358	117.39	184.57

Appendix A   Compound Sum of $1 *(concluded)*

Compound sum of $1

							Percent				
Period	12%	13%	14%	15%	16%	17%	18%	19%	20%	25%	30%
1	1.120	1.130	1.140	1.150	1.160	1.170	1.180	1.190	1.200	1.250	1.300
2	1.254	1.277	1.300	1.323	1.346	1.369	1.392	1.416	1.440	1.563	1.690
3	1.405	1.443	1.482	1.521	1.561	1.602	1.643	1.685	1.728	1.953	2.197
4	1.574	1.630	1.689	1.749	1.811	1.874	1.939	2.005	2.074	2.441	2.856
5	1.762	1.842	1.925	2.011	2.100	2.192	2.288	2.386	2.488	3.052	3.713
6	1.974	2.082	2.195	2.313	2.436	2.565	2.700	2.840	2.986	3.815	4.827
7	2.211	2.353	2.502	2.660	2.826	3.001	3.185	3.379	3.583	4.768	6.276
8	2.476	2.658	2.853	3.059	3.278	3.511	3.759	4.021	4.300	5.960	8.157
9	2.773	3.004	3.252	3.518	3.803	4.108	4.435	4.785	5.160	7.451	10.604
10	3.106	3.395	3.707	4.046	4.411	4.807	5.234	5.696	6.192	9.313	13.786
11	3.479	3.836	4.226	4.652	5.117	5.624	6.176	6.777	7.430	11.642	17.922
12	3.896	4.335	4.818	5.350	5.936	6.580	7.288	8.064	8.916	14.552	23.298
13	4.363	4.898	5.492	6.153	6.886	7.699	8.599	9.596	10.699	18.190	30.288
14	4.887	5.535	6.261	7.076	7.988	9.007	10.147	11.420	12.839	22.737	39.374
15	5.474	6.254	7.138	8.137	9.266	10.539	11.974	13.590	15.407	28.422	51.186
16	6.130	7.067	8.137	9.358	10.748	12.330	14.129	16.172	18.488	35.527	66.542
17	6.866	7.986	9.276	10.761	12.468	14.426	16.672	19.244	22.186	44.409	86.504
18	7.690	9.024	10.575	12.375	14.463	16.879	19.673	22.091	26.623	55.511	112.46
19	8.613	10.197	12.056	14.232	16.777	19.748	23.214	27.252	31.948	69.389	146.19
20	9.646	11.523	13.743	16.367	19.461	23.106	27.393	32.429	38.338	86.736	190.05
25	17.000	21.231	26.462	32.919	40.874	50.658	62.669	77.388	95.396	264.70	705.64
30	29.960	39.116	50.950	66.212	85.850	111.07	143.37	184.68	237.38	807.79	2,620.0
40	93.051	132.78	188.88	267.86	378.72	533.87	750.38	1,051.7	1,469.8	7,523.2	36,119.
50	289.00	450.74	700.23	1,083.7	1,670.7	2,566.2	3,927.4	5,988.9	9,100.4	70,065.	497,929.

Appendix B Compound Sum of an Annuity of $1

Compound sum of an annuity of $1

Period	Percent										
	1%	2%	3%	4%	5%	6%	7%	8%	9%	10%	11%
1	1.000	1.000	1.000	1.000	1.000	1.000	1.000	1.000	1.000	1.000	1.000
2	2.010	2.020	2.030	2.040	2.050	2.060	2.070	2.080	2.090	2.100	2.110
3	3.030	3.060	3.091	3.122	3.153	3.184	3.215	3.246	3.278	3.310	3.342
4	4.060	4.122	4.184	4.246	4.310	4.375	4.440	4.506	4.573	4.641	4.710
5	5.101	5.204	5.309	5.416	5.526	5.637	5.751	5.867	5.985	6.105	6.228
6	6.152	6.308	6.468	6.633	6.802	6.975	7.153	7.336	7.523	7.716	7.913
7	7.214	7.434	7.662	7.898	8.142	8.394	8.654	8.923	9.200	9.487	9.783
8	8.286	8.583	8.892	9.214	9.549	9.897	10.260	10.637	11.028	11.436	11.859
9	9.369	9.755	10.159	10.583	11.027	11.491	11.978	12.488	13.021	13.579	14.164
10	10.462	10.950	11.464	12.006	12.578	13.181	13.816	14.487	15.193	15.937	16.722
11	11.567	12.169	12.808	13.486	14.207	14.972	15.784	16.645	17.560	18.531	19.561
12	12.683	13.412	14.192	15.026	15.917	16.870	17.888	18.977	20.141	21.384	22.713
13	13.809	14.680	15.618	16.627	17.713	18.882	20.141	21.495	22.953	24.523	26.212
14	14.947	15.974	17.086	18.292	19.599	21.015	22.550	24.215	26.019	27.975	30.095
15	16.097	17.293	18.599	20.024	21.579	23.276	25.129	27.152	29.361	31.772	34.405
16	17.258	18.639	20.157	21.825	23.657	25.673	27.888	30.324	33.003	35.950	39.190
17	18.430	20.012	21.762	23.698	25.840	28.213	30.840	33.750	36.974	40.545	44.501
18	19.615	21.412	23.414	25.645	28.132	30.906	33.999	37.450	41.301	45.599	50.396
19	20.811	22.841	25.117	27.671	30.539	33.760	37.379	41.446	46.018	51.159	56.939
20	22.019	24.297	26.870	29.778	33.066	36.786	40.995	45.762	51.160	57.275	64.203
25	28.243	32.030	36.459	41.646	47.727	54.865	63.249	73.106	84.701	98.347	114.41
30	34.785	40.588	47.575	56.085	66.439	79.058	94.461	113.28	136.31	164.49	199.02
40	48.886	60.402	75.401	95.026	120.80	154.76	199.64	259.06	337.89	442.59	581.83
50	64.463	84.579	112.80	152.67	209.35	290.34	406.53	573.77	815.08	1,163.9	1,668.8

Appendix B   Compound Sum of an Annuity of $1 *(concluded)*

Compound sum of an annuity of $1

Percent

Period	12%	13%	14%	15%	16%	17%	18%	19%	20%	25%	30%
1	1.000	1.000	1.000	1.000	1.000	1.000	1.000	1.000	1.000	1.000	1.000
2	2.120	2.130	2.140	2.150	2.160	2.170	2.180	2.190	2.200	2.250	2.300
3	3.374	3.407	3.440	3.473	3.506	3.539	3.572	3.606	3.640	3.813	3.990
4	4.779	4.850	4.921	4.993	5.066	5.141	5.215	5.291	5.368	5.766	6.187
5	6.353	6.480	6.610	6.742	6.877	7.014	7.154	7.297	7.442	8.207	9.043
6	8.115	8.323	8.536	9.754	8.977	9.207	9.442	0.683	9.930	11.259	12.756
7	10.089	10.405	10.730	11.067	11.414	11.772	12.142	12.523	12.916	15.073	17.583
8	12.300	12.757	13.233	13.727	14.240	14.773	15.327	15.902	16.499	19.842	23.858
9	14.776	15.416	16.085	16.786	17.519	18.285	19.086	19.923	20.799	25.802	32.015
10	17.549	18.420	19.337	20.304	21.321	22.393	23.521	24.701	25.959	33.253	42.619
11	20.655	21.814	23.045	24.349	25.733	27.200	28.755	30.404	32.150	42.566	56.405
12	24.133	25.650	27.271	29.002	30.850	32.824	34.931	37.180	39.581	54.208	74.327
13	28.029	29.985	32.089	34.352	36.786	39.404	42.219	45.244	48.497	68.760	97.625
14	32.393	34.883	37.581	40.505	43.672	47.103	50.818	54.841	59.196	86.949	127.91
15	37.280	40.417	43.842	47.580	51.660	56.110	60.965	66.261	72.035	109.69	167.29
16	42.753	46.672	50.980	55.717	60.925	66.649	72.939	79.850	87.442	138.11	218.47
17	48.884	53.739	59.118	65.075	71.673	78.979	87.068	96.022	105.93	173.64	285.01
18	55.750	61.725	68.394	75.836	84.141	93.406	103.74	115.27	128.12	218.05	371.52
19	63.440	70.749	78.969	88.212	98.603	110.29	123.41	138.17	154.74	273.56	483.97
20	72.052	80.947	91.025	102.44	115.38	130.03	146.63	165.42	186.69	342.95	630.17
25	133.33	155.62	181.87	212.79	249.21	292.11	342.60	402.04	471.98	1,054.8	2,348.80
30	241.33	293.20	356.79	434.75	530.31	647.44	790.95	966.7	1,181.9	3,227.2	8,730.0
40	767.09	1,013.7	1,342.0	1,779.1	2,360.8	3,134.5	4,163.21	5,529.8	7,343.9	30,089.	120,393.
50	2,400.0	3,459.5	4,994.5	7,217.7	10,436.	15,090.	21,813.	31,515.	45,497.	280,256.	1,659,731.

Appendix C   Present Value of $1

Present value of $1

Period	1%	2%	3%	4%	5%	6%	7%	8%	9%	10%	11%	12%
1	0.990	0.980	0.971	0.962	0.952	0.943	0.935	0.926	0.917	0.909	0.901	0.893
2	0.980	0.961	0.943	0.925	0.907	0.890	0.873	0.857	0.842	0.826	0.812	0.797
3	0.971	0.942	0.915	0.889	0.864	0.840	0.816	0.794	0.772	0.751	0.731	0.712
4	0.961	0.924	0.885	0.855	0.823	0.792	0.763	0.735	0.708	0.683	0.659	0.636
5	0.951	0.906	0.863	0.822	0.784	0.747	0.713	0.681	0.650	0.621	0.593	0.567
6	0.942	0.888	0.837	0.790	0.746	0.705	0.666	0.630	0.596	0.564	0.535	0.507
7	0.933	0.871	0.813	0.760	0.711	0.665	0.623	0.583	0.547	0.513	0.482	0.452
8	0.923	0.853	0.789	0.731	0.677	0.627	0.582	0.540	0.502	0.467	0.434	0.404
9	0.914	0.837	0.766	0.703	0.645	0.592	0.544	0.500	0.460	0.424	0.391	0.361
10	0.905	0.820	0.744	0.676	0.614	0.558	0.508	0.463	0.422	0.386	0.352	0.322
11	0.896	0.804	0.722	0.650	0.585	0.527	0.475	0.429	0.388	0.350	0.317	0.287
12	0.887	0.788	0.701	0.625	0.557	0.497	0.444	0.397	0.356	0.319	0.286	0.257
13	0.879	0.773	0.681	0.601	0.530	0.469	0.415	0.368	0.326	0.290	0.258	0.229
14	0.870	0.758	0.661	0.577	0.505	0.442	0.388	0.340	0.299	0.263	0.232	0.205
15	0.861	0.743	0.642	0.555	0.481	0.417	0.362	0.315	0.275	0.239	0.209	0.183
16	0.853	0.728	0.623	0.534	0.458	0.394	0.339	0.292	0.252	0.218	0.188	0.163
17	0.844	0.714	0.605	0.513	0.436	0.371	0.317	0.270	0.231	0.198	0.170	0.146
18	0.836	0.700	0.587	0.494	0.416	0.350	0.296	0.250	0.212	0.180	0.153	0.130
19	0.828	0.686	0.570	0.475	0.396	0.331	0.277	0.232	0.194	0.164	0.138	0.116
20	0.820	0.673	0.554	0.456	0.377	0.312	0.258	0.215	0.178	0.149	0.124	0.104
25	0.780	0.610	0.478	0.375	0.295	0.233	0.184	0.146	0.116	0.092	0.074	0.059
30	0.742	0.552	0.412	0.308	0.231	0.174	0.131	0.099	0.075	0.057	0.044	0.033
40	0.672	0.453	0.307	0.208	0.142	0.097	0.067	0.046	0.032	0.022	0.015	0.011
50	0.608	0.372	0.228	0.141	0.087	0.054	0.034	0.021	0.013	0.009	0.005	0.003

Percent

Present value of $1

Percent

Period	13%	14%	15%	16%	17%	18%	19%	20%	25%	30%	35%	40%	50%
1	0.885	0.877	0.870	0.862	0.855	0.847	0.840	0.833	0.800	0.769	0.741	0.714	0.667
2	0.783	0.769	0.756	0.743	0.731	0.718	0.706	0.694	0.640	0.592	0.549	0.510	0.444
3	0.693	0.675	0.658	0.641	0.624	0.609	0.593	0.579	0.512	0.455	0.406	0.364	0.296
4	0.613	0.592	0.572	0.552	0.534	0.515	0.499	0.482	0.410	0.350	0.301	0.260	0.198
5	0.543	0.519	0.497	0.476	0.456	0.437	0.419	0.402	0.320	0.269	0.223	0.186	0.132
6	0.480	0.456	0.432	0.410	0.390	0.370	0.352	0.335	0.262	0.207	0.165	0.133	0.088
7	0.425	0.400	0.376	0.354	0.333	0.314	0.296	0.279	0.210	0.159	0.122	0.095	0.059
8	0.376	0.351	0.327	0.305	0.285	0.266	0.249	0.233	0.168	0.123	0.091	0.068	0.039
9	0.333	0.300	0.284	0.263	0.243	0.225	0.209	0.194	0.134	0.094	0.067	0.048	0.026
10	0.295	0.270	0.247	0.227	0.208	0.191	0.176	0.162	0.107	0.073	0.050	0.035	0.017
11	0.261	0.237	0.215	0.195	0.178	0.162	0.148	0.135	0.086	0.056	0.037	0.025	0.012
12	0.231	0.208	0.187	0.168	0.152	0.137	0.124	0.112	0.069	0.043	0.027	0.018	0.008
13	0.204	0.182	0.163	0.145	0.130	0.116	0.104	0.093	0.055	0.033	0.020	0.013	0.005
14	0.181	0.160	0.141	0.125	0.111	0.099	0.088	0.078	0.044	0.025	0.015	0.009	0.003
15	0.160	0.140	0.123	0.108	0.095	0.084	0.074	0.065	0.035	0.020	0.011	0.006	0.002
16	0.141	0.123	0.107	0.093	0.081	0.071	0.062	0.054	0.028	0.015	0.008	0.005	0.002
17	0.125	0.108	0.093	0.080	0.069	0.060	0.052	0.045	0.023	0.012	0.006	0.003	0.001
18	0.111	0.095	0.081	0.069	0.059	0.051	0.044	0.038	0.018	0.009	0.005	0.002	0.001
19	0.098	0.083	0.070	0.060	0.051	0.043	0.037	0.031	0.014	0.007	0.003	0.002	0
20	0.087	0.073	0.061	0.051	0.043	0.037	0.031	0.026	0.012	0.005	0.002	0.001	0
25	0.047	0.038	0.030	0.024	0.020	0.016	0.013	0.010	0.004	0.001	0.001	0	0
30	0.026	0.020	0.015	0.012	0.009	0.007	0.005	0.004	0.001	0	0	0	0
40	0.008	0.005	0.004	0.003	0.002	0.001	0.001	0.001	0	0	0	0	0
50	0.002	0.001	0.001	0.001	0	0	0	0	0	0	0	0	0

Present Value of an Annuity of $1

Present value of an annuity of $1

Period	Percent											
	1%	2%	3%	4%	5%	6%	7%	8%	9%	10%	11%	12%
1	0.990	0.980	0.971	0.962	0.952	0.943	0.935	0.926	0.917	0.909	0.901	0.893
2	1.970	1.942	1.913	1.886	1.859	1.833	1.808	1.783	1.759	1.736	1.713	1.690
3	2.941	2.884	2.829	2.775	2.723	2.673	2.624	2.577	2.531	2.487	2.444	2.402
4	3.902	3.808	3.717	3.630	3.546	3.465	3.387	3.312	3.240	3.170	3.102	3.037
5	4.853	4.713	4.580	4.452	4.329	4.212	4.100	3.993	3.890	3.791	3.696	3.605
6	5.795	5.601	5.417	5.242	5.076	4.917	4.767	4.623	4.486	4.355	4.231	4.111
7	6.728	6.472	6.230	6.002	5.786	5.582	5.389	5.206	5.033	4.868	4.712	4.564
8	7.652	7.325	7.020	6.733	6.463	6.210	5.971	5.747	5.535	5.335	5.146	4.968
9	8.566	8.162	7.786	7.435	7.108	6.802	6.515	6.247	5.995	5.759	5.537	5.328
10	9.471	8.983	8.530	8.111	7.722	7.360	7.024	6.710	6.418	6.145	5.889	5.650
11	10.368	9.787	9.253	8.760	8.306	7.887	7.499	7.139	6.805	6.495	6.207	5.938
12	11.255	10.575	9.954	9.385	8.863	8.384	7.943	7.536	7.161	6.814	6.492	6.194
13	12.134	11.348	10.635	9.986	9.394	8.853	8.358	7.904	7.487	7.103	6.750	6.424
14	13.004	12.106	11.296	10.563	9.899	9.295	8.745	8.244	7.786	7.367	6.982	6.628
15	13.865	12.849	11.939	11.118	10.380	9.712	9.108	8.559	8.061	7.606	7.191	6.811
16	14.718	13.578	12.561	11.652	10.838	10.106	9.447	8.851	8.313	7.824	7.379	6.974
17	15.562	14.292	13.166	12.166	11.274	10.477	9.763	9.122	8.544	8.022	7.549	7.102
18	16.398	14.992	13.754	12.659	11.690	10.828	10.059	9.372	8.756	8.201	7.702	7.250
19	17.226	15.678	14.324	13.134	12.085	11.158	10.336	9.604	8.950	8.365	7.839	7.366
20	18.046	16.351	14.877	13.590	12.462	11.470	10.594	9.818	9.129	8.514	7.963	7.469
25	22.023	19.523	17.413	15.622	14.094	12.783	11.654	10.675	9.823	9.077	8.422	7.843
30	25.808	22.396	19.600	17.292	15.372	13.765	12.409	11.258	10.274	9.427	8.694	8.055
40	32.835	27.355	23.115	19.793	17.160	15.046	13.332	11.925	10.757	9.779	8.951	8.244
50	39.196	31.424	25.730	21.482	18.256	15.762	13.801	12.233	10.962	9.915	9.042	8.304

Appendix D   Present Value of an Annuity of $1 *(concluded)*

Present value of an annuity of $1

Period	13%	14%	15%	16%	17%	18%	19%	20%	25%	30%	35%	40%	50%
1	0.885	0.877	0.870	0.862	0.855	0.847	0.840	0.833	0.800	0.769	0.741	0.714	0.667
2	1.668	1.647	1.626	1.605	1.585	1.566	1.547	1.528	1.440	1.361	1.289	1.224	1.111
3	2.361	2.322	2.283	2.246	2.210	2.174	2.140	2.106	1.952	1.816	1.696	1.589	1.407
4	2.974	2.914	2.855	2.798	2.743	2.690	2.639	2.589	2.362	2.166	1.997	1.849	1.605
5	3.517	3.433	3.352	3.274	3.199	3.127	3.058	2.991	2.689	2.436	2.220	2.035	1.737
6	3.998	3.889	3.784	3.685	3.589	3.498	3.410	3.326	2.951	2.643	2.385	2.168	1.824
7	4.423	4.288	4.160	4.039	3.922	3.812	3.706	3.605	3.161	2.802	2.508	2.263	1.883
8	4.799	4.639	4.487	4.344	4.207	4.078	3.954	3.837	3.329	2.925	2.598	2.331	1.922
9	5.132	4.946	4.772	4.607	4.451	4.303	4.163	4.031	3.463	3.019	2.665	2.379	1.948
10	5.426	5.216	5.019	4.833	4.659	4.494	4.339	4.192	3.571	3.092	2.715	2.414	1.965
11	5.687	5.453	5.234	5.029	4.836	4.656	4.486	4.327	3.656	3.147	2.752	2.438	1.977
12	5.918	5.660	5.421	5.197	4.988	4.793	4.611	4.439	3.725	3.190	2.779	2.456	1.985
13	6.122	5.842	5.583	5.342	5.118	4.910	4.715	4.533	3.780	3.223	2.799	2.469	1.990
14	6.302	6.002	5.724	5.468	5.229	5.008	4.802	4.611	3.824	3.249	2.814	2.478	1.993
15	6.462	6.142	5.847	5.575	5.324	5.092	4.876	4.675	3.859	3.268	2.825	2.484	1.995
16	6.604	6.265	5.954	5.668	5.405	5.162	4.938	4.730	3.887	3.283	2.834	2.489	1.997
17	6.729	6.373	6.047	5.749	5.475	5.222	4.988	4.775	3.910	3.295	2.840	2.492	1.998
18	6.840	6.467	6.128	5.818	5.534	5.273	5.033	4.812	3.928	3.304	2.844	2.494	1.999
19	6.938	6.550	6.198	5.877	5.584	5.316	5.070	4.843	3.942	3.311	2.848	2.496	1.999
20	7.025	6.623	6.259	5.929	5.628	5.353	5.101	4.870	3.954	3.316	2.850	2.497	1.999
25	7.330	6.873	6.464	6.097	5.766	5.467	5.195	4.948	3.985	3.329	2.856	2.499	2.000
30	7.496	7.003	6.566	6.177	5.829	5.517	5.235	4.979	3.995	3.332	2.857	2.500	2.000
40	7.634	7.105	6.642	6.233	5.871	5.548	5.258	4.997	3.999	3.333	2.857	2.500	2.000
50	7.675	7.133	6.661	6.246	5.880	5.554	5.262	4.999	4.000	3.333	2.857	2.500	2.000

Percent

Appendix E
Using Calculators for Financial Analysis

This appendix is designed to help you use either an algebraic calculator (Texas Instruments BA-35 Student Business Analyst) or the Hewlett-Packard 12C Financial Calculator. We realize that most calculators come with comprehensive instructions, and this appendix is only meant to provide basic instructions for commonly used financial calculations.

There are always two things to do before starting your calculations as indicated in the first table: clear the calculator and set the decimal point. If you do not want to lose data stored in memory, do not perform steps 2 and 3 in the first box below.

Each step is listed vertically as a number followed by a decimal point. After each step you will find either a number or a calculator function denoted by a box [   ]. Entering the number on your calculator is one step and entering the function is another. Notice that the HP 12C is color coded. When two boxes are found one after another, you may have an [f] or a [g] in the first box. An [f] is orange coded and refers to the orange functions above the keys. After typing the [f] function, you will automatically look for an orange coded key to punch. For example, after [f] in the first Hewlett-Packard box (right-hand panel), you will punch in the orange color coded [REG]. If the [f] function is not followed by another box, you merely type in [f] and the value indicated.

	Texas Instruments BA-35		Hewlett-Packard 12C	
First clear the calculator	1. [ON/C]	[ON/C]	1. [CLX]	Clears screen
	2. 0		2. [f]	
	3. [STO]	Clears Memory	3. [REG]	Clears Memory
Set the decimal point	1. [2nd]		1. [f]	
The TI BA-35 has two choices: 2 decimal points or variable decimal points. The screen will indicate Dec 2 or the decimal will be variable. The HP 12C allows you to choose the number of decimal points. If you are uncertain, just provide the indicated input exactly as shown on the right.	2. [STO]		2. 4 (# of decimals)	

The ⬚ g ⬚ is coded blue and refers to the functions on the bottom of the function keys. After the ⬚ g ⬚ function key, you will automatically look for blue coded keys. This first occurs on page 757 of the appendix.

Familiarize yourself with the keyboard before you start. In the more complicated calculations, keystrokes will be combined into one step.

In the first four calculations on pages 753 and 754 we simply instruct you on how to get the interest factors for Appendixes A, B, C, and D. We have chosen to use examples as our method of instruction.

	Texas Instruments BA-35	Hewlett-Packard 12C
A. Appendix A Compound Sum of \$1 $i = 9\%$ or .09; $n = 5$ years $S_{IF} = (1 + i)^n$ Sum = Present Value $\times S_{IF}$ $S = P \times S_{IF}$ Check the answer against the number in Appendix A. Numbers in the appendix are rounded. Try different rates and years.	To Find Interest Factor 1. 1 2. + 3. .09 (interest rate) 4. ⬚ = ⬚ 5. ⬚ y^x ⬚ 6. 5 (# of periods) 7. = answer 1.538624	To Find Interest Factor 1. 1 2. ⬚ enter ⬚ 3. .09 (interest rate) 4. + 5. 5 (# of periods) 6. ⬚ y^x ⬚ answer 1.5386
B. Appendix B Compound Sum of an Annuity of \$1 $i = 9\%$ or .09; $n = 5$ years $SA_{IF} = \dfrac{(1 + i)^n - 1}{i}$ Sum = Receipt $\times SA_{IF}$ $S = R \times SA_{IF}$ Check your answer with Appendix B. Repeat example using different numbers and check your results with the number in Appendix B. Numbers in appendix are rounded.	To Find Interest Factor Repeat steps 1 through 7 in part A of this section. Continue with step 8. 8. ⬚ − ⬚ 9. 1 10. ⬚ = ⬚ 11. ⬚ ÷ ⬚ 12. .09 13. ⬚ = ⬚ answer 5.9847106	To Find Interest Factor Repeat steps 1 through 6 in part A of this section. Continue with step 7. 7. 1 8. ⬚ − ⬚ 9. .09 10. ⬚ ÷ ⬚ answer 5.9847

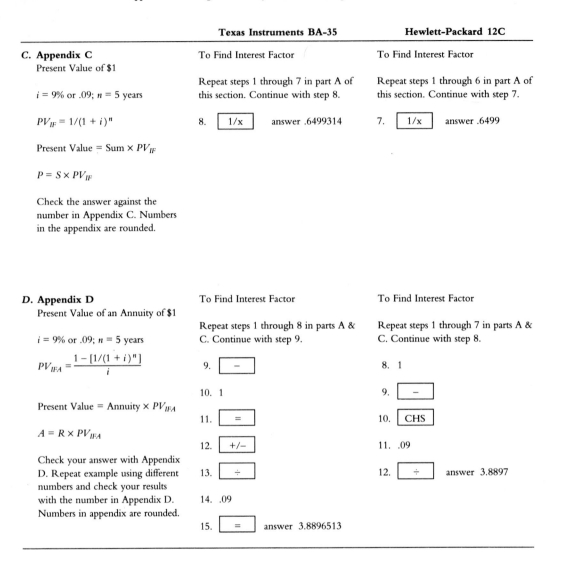

	Texas Instruments BA-35	**Hewlett-Packard 12C**
C. Appendix C	To Find Interest Factor	To Find Interest Factor
Present Value of $1		
	Repeat steps 1 through 7 in part A of	Repeat steps 1 through 6 in part A of
$i = 9\%$ or $.09$; $n = 5$ years	this section. Continue with step 8.	this section. Continue with step 7.
$PV_{IF} = 1/(1 + i)^n$	8. $\boxed{1/x}$ answer .6499314	7. $\boxed{1/x}$ answer .6499

Present Value = Sum $\times$ PV_{IF}

$P = S \times PV_{IF}$

Check the answer against the
number in Appendix C. Numbers
in the appendix are rounded.

D. Appendix D	To Find Interest Factor	To Find Interest Factor
Present Value of an Annuity of $1		
	Repeat steps 1 through 8 in parts A &	Repeat steps 1 through 7 in parts A &
$i = 9\%$ or $.09$; $n = 5$ years	C. Continue with step 9.	C. Continue with step 8.
$PV_{IFA} = \dfrac{1 - [1/(1 + i)^n]}{i}$	9. $\boxed{-}$	8. 1
	10. 1	9. $\boxed{-}$
Present Value = Annuity $\times$ PV_{IFA}	11. $\boxed{=}$	10. $\boxed{CHS}$
$A = R \times PV_{IFA}$	12. $\boxed{+/-}$	11. .09
Check your answer with Appendix	13. $\boxed{\div}$	12. $\boxed{\div}$ answer 3.8897
D. Repeat example using different	14. .09	
numbers and check your results		
with the number in Appendix D.	15. $\boxed{=}$ answer 3.8896513	
Numbers in appendix are rounded.		

On the following pages, you can determine bond valuation, yield to maturity, net present value of an annuity, net present value of an uneven cash flow, internal rate of return for an annuity, and internal rate of return for an uneven cash flow.

Bond Valuation Using Both the TI BA-35 and the HP 12C

Solve for V = Price of the Bond

Given:

C_t = $80 annual coupon payments or 8% coupon ($40 semiannually)

P_n = $1,000 principal (par value)

n = 10 years to maturity (20 periods semiannually)

i = 9.0% interest rate in the market (4.5% semiannually)

You may choose to refer to Chapter 12 for a complete discussion of bond valuation.

	Texas Instruments BA-35	Hewlett-Packard 12C
Bond Valuation	Set Finance Mode ⟨2nd⟩ ⟨FIN⟩	Clear memory ⟨f⟩ ⟨REG⟩
All steps begin with number 1. Numbers following each step are keystrokes followed by a box ☐ . Each box represents a keystroke and indicates which calculator function is performed.	Set decimal to 2 places Decimal ⟨2nd⟩ ⟨STO⟩ 1. 40 (semiannual coupon)	Set decimal to 3 places ⟨f⟩ 3 1. 9.0 (yield to maturity)
The Texas Instrument calculator requires that data be adjusted for semiannual compounding; otherwise it assumes annual compounding.	2. ⟨PMT⟩ 3. 4.5 (yield to maturity) semiannual basis	2. ⟨i⟩ 3. 8.0 (coupon in percent) 4. ⟨PMT⟩
The Hewlett-Packard 12C internally assumes that semiannual compounding is used and requires annual data to be entered. The HP 12C is more detailed in that it requires the actual day, month, and year. If you want an answer for a problem that requires a given number of years (e.g., 10 years), simply start on a date of your choice and end on the same date 10 years later, as in the example.	4. ⟨% i⟩ 5. 1000 principal 6. ⟨FV⟩ 7. 20 (semiannual periods to maturity) 8. ⟨N⟩ 9. ⟨CPT⟩ 10. ⟨PV⟩ answer 934.96 Answer is given in dollars, rather than % of par value.	5. 1.091992 (today's date month-day-year)★ 6. ⟨enter⟩ 7. 1.092002 (maturity date month-day-year)★ 8. ⟨f⟩ 9. ⟨Price⟩ Answer 93.496 Answer is given as % of par value and equals $934.96. If Error message occurs, clear memory and start over. ★See instructions in the third paragraph of the first column.

Yield to Maturity on Both the TI BA-35 and HP 12C

Solve for Y = yield to maturity

Given:

V = \$895.50 price of bond

C_t = \$80 annual coupon payments or 8% coupon (\$40 semiannually)

P_n = \$1,000 principal (par value)

n = 10 years to maturity (20 periods semiannually)

You may choose to refer to Chapters 12 and 13 for a complete discussion of yield to maturity.

	Texas Instruments BA-35	**Hewlett-Packard 12C**
Yield to Maturity	Set Finance Mode [2nd] [FIN]	Clear memory [f] [REG]
All steps are numbered. All numbers following each step are keystrokes followed by a box [ ]. Each box represents a keystroke and indicates which calculator function is performed.	Set decimal to 2 places	Set decimal [f] 2
	Decimal	1. 89.55 (bond price as a percent of par)
	[2nd] [STO]	2. [PV]
The Texas Instruments BA-35 does not internally compute a semiannual rate, so the data must be adjusted to reflect semiannual payments and periods. The answer received in step 10 is a semiannual rate, which must be multiplied by 2 to reflect an annual yield.	1. 20 (semiannual periods)	3. 8.0 (annual coupon in %)
	2. [N]	4. [PMT]
	3. 1000 (par value)	5. 1.091992 (today's date)★
	4. [FV]	6. [enter]
	5. 40 (semiannual coupon)	7. 1.092002 (maturity date)★
The Hewlett-Packard 12C internally assumes that semiannual payments are made and, therefore, the answer in step 9 is the annual yield to maturity based on semiannual coupons. If you want an answer on the HP for a given number of years (e.g., 10 years), simply start on a date of your choice and end on the same date 10 years later, as in the example.	6. [PMT]	8. [f]
	7. 895.50 (bond price)	9. [YTM] answer 9.65%
	8. [PV]	In case you receive an Error message, you have probably made a keystroke error. Clear the memory
	9. [CPT]	[f] [REG]
	10. [%i] answer 4.83%	and start over.
	11. [×]	★See instructions in the third paragraph of the first column.
	12. 2	
	13. [=] answer 9.65% (annual rate)	

Net Present Value of an Annuity on Both the TI BA-35 and the HP 12C

Solve for A = present value of annuity

n = 10 years (number of years cash flow will continue)

PMT = $5,000 per year (amount of the annuity)

i = 12% (cost of capital K_a)

Cost = $20,000

	Texas Instruments BA-35	**Hewlett-Packard 12C**
Net Present Value of an Annuity	Set Finance Mode [2nd] [FIN]	Set decimal to 2 places
All steps are numbered and some steps include several keystrokes. All numbers following each step are keystrokes followed by a box [ ]. Each box represents a keystroke and indicates which calculator function is performed on that number.	Set decimal to 2 places	[f] 2
	Decimal	[f] [REG] clears memory
	[2nd] [STO]	1. 20000 (cash outflow)
	1. 10 (years of cash flow)	2. [CHS] changes sign
	2. [N]	3. [g]
The calculation for the present value of an annuity on the TI BA-35 requires that the project cost be subtracted from the present value of the cash inflows.	3. 5000 (annual payments)	4. [CFo]
	4. [PMT]	5. 5000 (annual payments)
	5. 12 (cost of capital)	6. [g] [Cfj]
The HP 12C could solve the problem exactly with the same keystrokes as the TI. However, since the HP uses a similar method to solve uneven cash flows, we elected to use the method that requires more keystrokes but which includes a negative cash outflow for the cost of the capital budgeting project.	6. [%i]	7. 10 [g] [Nj] (years)
	7. [CPT]	8. 12 [i] (cost of capital)
	8. [PV]	9. [f] [NPV]
	9. [−]	answer $8,251.12
To conserve space, several keystrokes have been put into one step.	10. 20,000	If an Error message appears, start over by clearing the memory with
	11. [=] answer $8,251.12	[f] [REG] .

Net Present Value of an Uneven Cash Flow on Both the TI BA-35 and the HP 12C

Solve for NPV = net present value

n = 5 years (number of years cash flow will continue)

PMT = \$5,000 (yr. 1); 6,000 (yr. 2); 7,000 (yr. 3); 8,000 (yr. 4); 9,000 (yr. 5)

i = 12% (cost of capital K_a)

Cost = \$25,000

	Texas Instruments BA-35	**Hewlett-Packard 12C**

Net Present Value of an Uneven Cash Flow

All steps are numbered and some steps include several keystrokes. All numbers following each step are keystrokes followed by a box [   ]. Each box represents a keystroke and indicates which calculator function is performed on that number.

Because we are dealing with uneven cash flows, each number must be entered. The TI BA-35 requires that you make sure of the memory. In step 2, you enter the future cash inflow in year 1 and, in step 3, you determine its present value, which is stored in memory. After the first 1-year calculation, following year present values are calculated in the same way and added to the stored value using the [SUM] key. Finally, the recall key [RCL] is used to recall the present value of the total cash inflows.

The HP 12C requires each cash flow to be entered in order. The [CFo] key represents the cash flow in time period 0. The [CFj] key automatically counts the year of the cash flow in the order entered and so no years need be entered. Finally, the cost of capital of 12% is entered and the [f] key and [NPV] key are used to complete the problem.

Texas Instruments BA-35

Clear memory [ON/C] 0 [STO]

Set decimal 2 places

Decimal

[2nd]   [STO]

Set finance mode

[2nd]   [FIN]

1. 12 [%i]

2. 5000 [FV]

3. 1 [N][CPT][PV][SUM]

4. 6000 [FV]

5. 2 [N][CPT][PV][SUM]

6. 7000 [FV]

7. 3 [N][CPT][PV][SUM]

8. 8000 [FV]

9. 4 [N][CPT][PV][SUM]

10. 9000 [FV]

11. 5 [N][CPT][PV][SUM]

12. [RCL]   (answer 24420.90)

13. [−]

14. 25000 (cash outflow)

15. [=]   answer −\$579.10

Negative Net Present Value

Hewlett-Packard 12C

Set decimal to 2 places

[f] 2

[f]   [REG]   clears memory

1. 25000 (cash outflow)

2. [CHS]   changes sign

3. [g]   [CFo]

4. 5000 [g]   [CFj]

5. 6000 [g]   [CFj]

6. 7000 [g]   [CFj]

7. 8000 [g]   [CFj]

8. 9000 [g]   [CFj]

9. 12 [i]

10. [f]   [NPV]

answer −\$579.10
Negative Net Present Value

If you receive an Error message, you have probably made a keystroke error. Clear memory with

[f]   [REG]

and start over with step 1.

Internal Rate of Return for an Annuity on Both the TI BA-35 and the HP 12C

Solve for *IRR* = internal rate of return

n = 10 years (number of years cash flow will continue)

PMT = $10,000 per year (amount of the annuity)

Cost = $50,000 (this is the present value of the annuity)

	Texas Instruments BA-35	**Hewlett-Packard 12C**
Internal Rate of Return of an Annuity	Clear memory ON/C 0 STO	Set decimal to 2 places
	Set Finance Mode 2nd FIN	f 2
All steps are numbered and some steps include several keystrokes. All numbers following each step are keystrokes followed by a box ☐ . Each box represents a keystroke and indicates which calculator function is performed on that number.	Set decimal to 2 places Decimal 2nd STO 1. 10 (years of cash flow)	f REG clears memory 1. 50000 (cash outflow) 2. CHS changes sign 3. g
The calculation for the internal rate of return on an annuity on the TI BA-35 requires relatively few keystrokes.	2. N 3. 10000 (annual payments)	4. CFo 5. 10000 (annual payments)
The HP 12C requires more keystrokes than the TI BA-35, because it needs to use the function keys f and g to enter data into the internal programs. The HP method requires that the cash outflow be expressed as a negative, while the TI BA-35 uses a positive number for the cash outflow.	4. PMT 5. 50000 (present value) 6. PV 7. CPT 8. % i answer is 15.10%	6. g Cfj 7. 10 g Nj (years) 8. f IRR answer is 15.10% If an Error message appears, start over by clearing the memory with
To conserve space, several keystrokes have been put into one step.	At an internal rate of return of 15.10%, the present value of the $50,000 outflow is equal to the present value of $10,000 cash inflows over the next 10 years.	f REG .

Internal Rate of Return with an Uneven Cash Flow on Both the TI BA-35 and the HP 12C

Solve for *IRR* = internal rate of return (return which causes present value of outflows to equal present value of the inflows).

n = 5 years (number of years cash flow will continue)

PMT = $5,000 (yr. 1); 6,000 (yr. 2); 7,000 (yr. 3); 8,000 (yr. 4); 9,000 (yr. 5)

Cost = $25,000

	Texas Instruments BA-35	Hewlett-Packard 12C
Internal Rate of Return on Uneven Cash Flow	Clear memory $\boxed{\text{ON/C}}$ 0 $\boxed{\text{STO}}$	Set decimal to 2 places
	Set decimal 2 places	$\boxed{\text{f}}$ $\boxed{2}$
All steps are numbered and some steps include several keystrokes. All numbers following each step are keystrokes followed by a box $\boxed{}$. Each box represents a keystroke and indicates which calculator function is performed on that number.	Decimal $\boxed{\text{2nd}}$ $\boxed{\text{STO}}$	$\boxed{\text{f}}$ $\boxed{\text{REG}}$ clears memory
	Set finance mode	1. 25000 (cash outflow)
	$\boxed{\text{2nd}}$ $\boxed{\text{FIN}}$	2. $\boxed{\text{CHS}}$ changes sign
	1. 12 $\boxed{\%\text{i}}$ (your IRR est.)	
	2. 5000 $\boxed{\text{FV}}$	3. $\boxed{\text{g}}$ $\boxed{\text{CFo}}$
Because we are dealing with uneven cash flows, the mathematics of solving this problem with the TI BA-35 is not possible. A more advanced algebraic calculator would be required.	3. 1 $\boxed{\text{N}}$ $\boxed{\text{CPT}}$ $\boxed{\text{PV}}$ $\boxed{\text{STO}}$	4. 5000 $\boxed{\text{g}}$ $\boxed{\text{CFj}}$
	4. 6000 $\boxed{\text{FV}}$	5. 6000 $\boxed{\text{g}}$ $\boxed{\text{CFj}}$
	5. 2 $\boxed{\text{N}}$ $\boxed{\text{CPT}}$ $\boxed{\text{PV}}$ $\boxed{\text{SUM}}$	6. 7000 $\boxed{\text{g}}$ $\boxed{\text{CFj}}$
	6. 7000 $\boxed{\text{FV}}$	
However, for the student willing to use trial and error, the student can use the NPV method and try different discount rates until the NPV equals zero. Check Chapter 12 on methods for approximating the IRR. This will provide a start.	7. 3 $\boxed{\text{N}}$ $\boxed{\text{CPT}}$ $\boxed{\text{PV}}$ $\boxed{\text{SUM}}$	7. 8000 $\boxed{\text{g}}$ $\boxed{\text{CFj}}$
	8. 8000 $\boxed{\text{FV}}$	8. 9000 $\boxed{\text{g}}$ $\boxed{\text{CFj}}$
	9. 4 $\boxed{\text{N}}$ $\boxed{\text{CPT}}$ $\boxed{\text{PV}}$ $\boxed{\text{SUM}}$	
	10. 9000 $\boxed{\text{FV}}$	9. $\boxed{\text{f}}$ $\boxed{\text{IRR}}$
The HP 12C requires each cash flow to be entered in order. The $\boxed{\text{CFo}}$ key represents the cash in time period 0. The $\boxed{\text{CFj}}$ key automatically counts the year of the cash flow in the order entered and so no years need be entered. To find the internal rate of return, use the $\boxed{\text{f}}$ $\boxed{\text{IRR}}$ keys and complete the problem.	11. 5 $\boxed{\text{N}}$ $\boxed{\text{CPT}}$ $\boxed{\text{PV}}$ $\boxed{\text{SUM}}$	answer 11.15%
	12. $\boxed{\text{RCL}}$ (answer 24,420.90)	
	13. $\boxed{-}$	If you receive an Error message, you have probably made a keystroke error. Clear memory with
	14. 25000 (cash outflow)	
	15. $\boxed{=}$ Answer −$579.10 Negative NPV.	$\boxed{\text{f}}$ $\boxed{\text{REG}}$
	Start over with a lower discount rate (try 11.15). Answer is 24999.75. With a cash outflow of $25,000, the IRR would be 11.15%.	and start over with step 1.

Glossary

A

abnormal return Gains beyond what the market would normally provide after adjustment for risk.

adjustable rate mortgage A mortgage in which the interest rate is adjusted regularly to current market conditions. It is sometimes referred to as a variable rate mortgage.

advances Increases in the prices of various stocks as measured between two points in time. Significant advances in a large number of stocks indicate a particular degree of market strength. Also see *declines*.

after-acquired property clause The stipulation in a mortgage bond indenture requiring all real property subsequently obtained by the issuing firm to serve as additional bond security.

after-market performance The price experience of new issues in the market.

alpha The value representing the difference between the return on a portfolio and a return on the market line that corresponds to a beta equal to the portfolio. A portfolio manager who performs at positive alpha levels would generate returns better than those available along the market line.

American Depository Receipts (ADRs) These securities represent the ownership interest in a foreign company's common stock. The process is as follows: The shares of the foreign company are purchased and put in trust in a foreign branch of a New York bank. The bank, in turn, receives and can issue depository receipts to the American shareholders of the foreign firm. These ADRs (depository receipts) allow foreign shares to be traded in the United States much like any other security. Through ADRs, one can purchase the stock of Sony Corporation, Honda Motor Co., Ltd., and hundreds of other foreign corporations.

annuity Cash flows that are equally spaced in time and are constant dollar amounts.

anomalies Deviations from the basic proposition that the market is efficient.

anticipated realized yield The return received on a bond held for a period other than that ending on the call date or the maturity date. In computing the anticipated realized yield, the investor considers both coupon payments and expected capital gains.

arbitrage An arbitrage is instituted when a simultaneous trade (a buy and a sale) occurs in two different markets and a profit is locked in.

arbitrage pricing theory A theory for explaining stock prices and stock returns. While the capital asset pricing model bases return solely on one form of systematic risk (market risk), arbitrage pricing theory can utilize several sources of risk (GDP, unemployment, etc.). Under this theory, it is assumed the investor will not be allowed to earn a return greater than that dictated by the various sensitivity factors affecting returns. To the extent that he does, arbitrageurs will eliminate the extra returns by selling the security and buying other comparable securities—thus the term *arbitrage pricing theory*. Unlike the capital asset pricing model, there is no necessity to define K_M (the market rate of return).

asset-utilization ratios Ratios that indicate the number of times per year that assets are turned over. They show the activity in the various asset accounts.

automatic reinvestment plan A plan offered by a mutual fund in which the fund automatically reinvests all distributions to a shareholder account.

average differential return The alpha value that indicates the difference between the return on a portfolio or fund and a return on the market line that corresponds to a beta equal to the portfolio or fund.

B

balance sheet A financial statement that indicates, at a given point, what the firm owns and how these assets are financed in the form of liabilities and ownership interest.

balanced funds Mutual funds that combine investments in common stock, bonds, and preferred stock. Many balanced funds also invest in convertible securities as well. They try to provide income plus some capital appreciation.

banker's acceptance A short-term debt instrument usually issued in conjunction with a foreign trade transaction. The acceptance is a draft that is drawn on a bank for approval for future payment and is subsequently presented to the payer.

Barron's Confidence Index An indicator utilized by technical analysts who follow smart money rules. Movements in the index measure the expectations of bond investors whom some technical analysts see as astute enough to foresee economic trends before the stock market has time to react.

Barron's Group Stock Averages *Barron's* publishes stock averages covering 32 industry groups. These averages are especially useful to the analyst who is following the performance of a specific industry relative to the general market.

basis The difference between the futures price and the value of the underlying item. Thus, on a stock index futures contract, basis represents the difference between the stock index futures price and the value of the underlying index. The basis may be either positive or negative, with the former indicating optimism and the latter signifying pessimism.

basis point The unit of measure of change on interest bearing instruments. One basis point is equal to 0.01 percent.

best efforts The issuing firm, rather than the investment banker, assumes the risk for a distribution. The investment banker merely agrees to provide his best effort to sell the securities.

beta A measurement of the volatility of a security with the market in general. A greater beta coefficient than 1 indicates systematic risk greater than the market, while a beta of less than 1 indicates systematic risk less than the market.

beta-related hedge A stock index futures hedge in which the relative volatility of the portfolio to the market is considered in determining the number of contracts necessary to offset a given dollar level of exposure. If a portfolio has a beta greater than 1, then extra contracts may be necessary to compensate for high volatility.

beta stability The amount of consistency in beta values over time. Instability means prior beta values may not be reflective of future beta values.

Black-Scholes option pricing model A formal model used to determine the theoretical value of an option. Such factors as the riskless interest rate, the length of the option, and the volatility of the underlying security are considered. For a more complete discussion, see Appendix 15–A.

blind pool A form of limited partnership for real estate investments in which funds are provided to the general partner to select properties for investment.

bond indenture A lengthy, complicated legal document that spells out the borrowing firm's responsibilities to the individual lenders in a bond issue.

bond price sensitivity The sensitivity of a change in bond prices to a change in interest rates. Bond price sensitivity is influenced by the duration of the bond in that the longer the duration of a bond, the greater the price sensitivity. A less sophisticated but acceptable approach is to tie price sensitivity to the maturity of the bond rather than the duration.

bond swaps The selling of a given bond position and immediately buying into another one with similar attributes in an attempt to improve overall portfolio return or performance.

breadth of market indicators Overall market rules used by technical analysts in comparing broad market activity with trading activity in a few stocks. By comparing all advances and declines in NYSE-listed stocks, for example, with the Dow Jones Industrial Average, analysts attempt to judge when the market has changed directions.

bull spread An option strategy utilized when the expectation is that the stock price will rise. The opposite strategy is a bear spread.

business cycle Swings in economic activity encompassing expansionary and recessionary periods and, on average, occurring over four-year periods.

buying the spread A term indicating the cost from writing the call is more than the revenue of the short position. The opposite results in "selling the spread."

C

call option An option to buy 100 shares of common stock at a specified price for a given period.

call provision A mechanism for repaying funds advanced through a bond issue. A provision of the bond indenture allows the issuer to retire bonds before maturity by paying holders a premium above principal.

capital appreciation A growth in the value of a stock or other investments as opposed to income from dividends or interest.

capital asset pricing model A model by which assets are valued based on their risk characteristics. The required return for an asset is related to its beta.

capital gain or loss Occurs when an asset held for investment purposes is sold.

capital market line The graphic representation of the relationship of risks and returns with various portfolios of assets. The line is part of the capital asset pricing model.

cash settlement Closing out a futures or options contract for cash rather than calling for actual delivery of the underlying item specified in the contract—for example, pork bellies and T-bills. The stock index futures markets and stock index options markets are *purely* cash-settlement markets. There is never even the implied potential for future delivery of the S&P 500 Stock Index or other indexes.

CBOE Chicago Board Options Exchange, the first exchange for call options.

certificates of deposit Savings certificates that entitle the holder to the receipt of interest. These instruments are issued by commercial banks and savings and loans (or other thrift institutions).

certified financial planner (CFP) A financial planner who has been appropriately certified by the College for Financial Planning in Denver. He or she must demonstrate skills in risk management, tax planning, retirement and estate planning, and other similar areas.

chartered financial analyst (CFA) A security analyst or portfolio manager who has been appropriately certified through experience requirements and testing.

charting Use by technical analysts of charts and graphs to plot past stock price movements that are used to predict future prices.

circuit breakers The temporary suspension of trading of futures contracts when the market is falling rapidly. For example, the Chicago Mercantile Exchange has a rule that prevents market participants from trading Standard & Poor's Stock Index Futures at lower prices for 30 minutes after the S&P 500 Index has fallen 12 points.

closed-end fund A closed-end investment fund has a fixed number of shares, and purchasers and sellers of shares must deal directly with each other rather than with the fund. Closed-end funds trade on an exchange or over-the-counter.

closing purchase transactions A transaction in which an investor who is a writer of an option intends to terminate the obligation.

closing sale transaction A transaction in which an investor who is the holder of an outstanding security intends to liquidate a position as a holder.

coincident indicators Economic indicators that change direction at roughly the same time as the general economy.

combined earnings and dividend model A model combining earnings per share and an earnings multiplier with a finite dividend model. Value is derived from both the present value of dividends and the present value of the future price of the stock based on the earnings multiplier (P/E).

commercial paper A short-term credit instrument issued by large business corporations to the public. Commercial paper usually comes in minimum denominations of $25,000 and represents an unsecured promissory note.

commission broker An individual who represents a stock brokerage firm at an exchange and who executes sales and purchases stocks for the firm's clients across the nation.

commodities Such tangible items as livestock, farm produce, and precious metals. Users and producers of commodities hedge against future price fluctuations by transferring risks to speculators through futures contracts.

commodity futures A contract to buy or sell a commodity in the future at a given price.

compound sum The future value of an amount that is allowed to grow at a given interest rate over a period of time.

compound sum of an annuity Constant payments are made at equally spaced time periods and grow to a future value.

constant–dollar method Adjusting for inflation in the financial statements by using the consumer price index.

constant-growth model A dividend valuation model that assumes a constant growth rate for dividends.

construction and development trust A type of REIT that makes short-term loans to developers during their construction period.

consumer price index An index used to measure the changes in the general price level.

contrary opinion rules Guidelines, based on such factors as the odd-lot or the short sales position, used by technical analysts who predict stock market activity on the assumption that such groups as small traders or short sellers are often wrong. Also see *smart money rules*.

conversion premium The amount, expressed as a dollar value or as a percentage, by which the price of the convertible security exceeds the current market value of the common stock into which it may be converted.

conversion price The face value of a convertible security divided by the conversion ratio, gives the price of the underlying common stock at which the security is convertible. An investor would usually not convert the security into common stock unless the market price was greater than the conversion price.

conversion ratio The number of shares of common stock an investor receives in exchanging convertible bonds or shares of convertible preferred stock for shares of common stock.

conversion value The value of the underlying common stock represented by convertible bonds or convertible preferred stock. This dollar value is obtained by multiplying the conversion ratio by the per share market price of the common stock.

convertible security A corporate bond or a share of preferred stock that, at the option of the holder, can be converted into shares of common stock of the issuing corporation.

correlation coefficient The measurement of joint movement between two variables.

coupon rate The stated, fixed rate of interest paid on a bond.

covered options The process of writing (selling) options on stock that is already owned.

covered writer A writer of an option who owns the stock on which the option is written. If the stock is not owned, the writer is deemed naked.

creditor claims Claims represented by debt instruments offered by financial institutions, industrial corporations, or the government.

cross hedge A hedging position in which one form of security is used to hedge another form of security (often because differences in maturity dates or quality characteristics make a perfect hedge difficult to establish).

currency fluctuations Changes in the relative value of one currency to another. For example, the French franc may advance or decline in relation to the dollar. To the extent a foreign currency appreciates relative to the dollar, returns on foreign investments will increase in terms of dollars. The opposite would be true for declining foreign currencies.

currency futures Futures contracts for speculation or hedging in different nations' currencies.

current-cost method Adjusting for inflation in the financial statements by revaluing assets at their current cost.

current ratio Current assets divided by current liabilities.

current yield The annual dollar amount of interest paid on a bond divided by the price at which the bond is currently trading in the market.

cyclical indicators Factors that economists can observe to measure the progress of economic cycles. Leading indicators move in a particular direction in advance of the movement of general business conditions, while lagging indicators change direction after general conditions, and coincident indicators move in unison with the economy.

cyclical industry An industry, such as automobiles, whose financial health is closely tied to the condition of the general economy. Such industries tend to make the type of products whose purchase can be postponed until the economy improves.

D

data base A form of organized, stored data. It is usually fed into the computer for additional analysis.

debenture An unsecured corporate bond.

debt–utilization ratios Ratios that indicate how the firm is financed between debt (lenders) and equity (owners) and the firm's ability for meeting cash payments due on fixed obligations, such as interest, lease payments, licensing fees, or sinking-fund charges.

declines Decreases in the prices of various stocks as measured between two points in time. Significant declines in a large number of stocks indicate a particular degree of market weakness. Also see *advances*.

deep discount bond A bond that has a coupon rate far below rates currently available on investments and that consequently can be traded only at a significant discount from par value. It may offer an opportunity for capital appreciation.

derivative products Securities that derive their existence from other items. Stock index futures and options are sometimes thought of as derivatives because they derive their existence from actual market indexes but have no intrinsic characteristics of their own.

diagonal spread A combination of a vertical and horizontal spread.

dilution The reduction in earnings per share that occurs when earnings remain unchanged yet the number of shares outstanding increases, as in the conversion of convertible bonds or preferred stock into common stock.

direct equity claim Representation of ownership interests through common stock or other instruments to purchase common stock, such as warrants and options.

discount rate The interest rate at which future cash flows are discounted to a present value.

dispersion The distribution of values or outcomes around an expected value.

diversification Lack of concentration in any one item. A portfolio composed of many different securities is diversified.

diversification benefits Risk reduction through a diversification of investments. Investments that are negatively correlated or that have low positive correlation provide the best diversification benefits.

Such benefits may be particularly evident in an internationally diversified portfolio.

dividend payout ratio Annual dividends per share divided by annual earnings per share.

dividend valuation model Any one of a number of stock valuation models based on the premise that the value of stock lies in the present value of its future dividend stream.

dividend yield Annual dividends per share divided by market place.

dollar cost averaging The inventor buys a fixed dollar's worth of a given security at regular intervals regardless of the security's price or the current market outlook. This provides a certain degree of discipline and also means more shares will be purchased at low prices rather than high prices since the amount of the regular investment is fixed and only the number of shares purchased varies.

Dow Jones Industrial Average An index of stock market activity based on the price movements of 30 large corporations. The average is price-weighted, which means each stock is effectively weighted by the magnitude of its price.

Dow theory The theory, developed by Charles Dow in the late 1890s and still in use today, that the analysis of long-term (primary) stock market trends can yield accurate predictions for future price movements.

downside protection The protection that a convertible bond investor enjoys during a period of falling stock prices. While the underlying common stock and the convertible bond may both fall in value, the bond will fall only to a particular level because it has a fundamental, or pure, bond value based on its assured income stream.

downside risk The possibility that an asset, such as a security, may fall in value as a result of fundamental factors or external market forces. The limit of the downside risk for a convertible bond can be computed as the difference between the bond's market price and its pure bond value divided by the market price.

Du Pont analysis A system of analyzing return on assets through examining the profit margin and asset turnover. Also, the value of return on equity is analyzed through evaluating return on assets and the debt/total assets ratio.

duration The weighted average life of a bond. The weights are based on the present values of the individual cash flows relative to the present value of the total cash flows. Duration is a better measure than maturity when assessing the price sensitivity of bonds; that is, the impact of interest-rate changes on bond prices can be more directly correlated to duration than to maturity.

E

earnings per share The earnings available to holders of common stock divided by the number of common stock shares outstanding.

earnings valuation model Any one of a number of stock valuation models based on the premise that a stock's value is some appropriate multiple of earnings per share.

effective diversification The diversification of a portfolio to remove unsystematic risk.

efficient frontier A set of portfolios of investments in which the investor receives maximum return for a given level of risk or a minimum risk for a given level of return.

efficient hedge A hedge in which one side of the transaction effectively covers the exposed side in terms of movement.

efficient market The capacity of the market to react to new information, to avoid rapid price fluctuations, and to engage in increased or reduced trading volume without realizing significant price changes. In an efficient market environment, securities are assumed to be correctly priced at any point in time.

efficient market hypothesis The concept that there are many participants in the securities markets who are profit maximizing and alert to information so that there is almost instant adjustment to new information. The weak form of this hypothesis suggests there is no relationship between past and future prices. The semistrong form maintains that all forms of public information are already reflected in the price of a security, so fundamental analysis cannot determine under- or overvaluation. The strong form suggests that all information, insider as well as public, is impounded in the value of a security.

efficient portfolio A portfolio that combines assets so as to minimize the risk for a given level of return.

electronic book The data base system that covers all stocks listed on the New York Stock Exchange and keeps track of limit orders and market orders for the specialist.

emerging countries Foreign countries that have not fully developed their economic system and productive capacity. Examples might include Chile, Jordan, Korea, Thailand, and Zimbabwe. A number of these emerging countries may represent good risk-reduction potential for U.S. investors because the factors that influence their economic welfare may be quite different from critical factors in the United States. Investments in these countries, at times, may also provide high returns.

equal-weighted index Each stock, regardless of total market value or price, is weighted equally. It is as if there were $100 invested in every stock in the index. The Value Line Index is a prime example of an equal-weighted index.

equipment trust certificate A secured debt instrument used by firms in the transportation industry that provides for bond proceeds to purchase new equipment, which in turn is collateral for the bond issue.

equity participation The lender also participates in an ownership interest in the property.

equity risk premium An extra return that the stock market must provide over the rate on Treasury bills to compensate for market risk. It is defined as $(K_M - R_F)$ or the expected rate of return for common stocks in the market minus the risk-free rate.

equity trust A type of REIT that buys, operates, and sells real estate as an investment as opposed to construction and development trusts and mortgage trusts.

excess returns Returns in excess of the risk-free rate or in excess of a market measure such as the S&P 500 Stock Index.

exchange listing A firm lists its shares on an exchange (such as the American or New York Stock Exchange).

exchange privilege A feature offered by a mutual fund sponsor in which a shareholder is able to

move money between various funds under the management of the sponsor at a very minimal processing charge and without a commission.

exercise price (warrant) The price at which the stock can be bought using the warrant.

expectations hypothesis The hypothesis that explains the term structure of interest rates, stating that a long-term interest rate is the average of expected short-term interest rates over the applicable time period. If, for example, long-term rates are higher than short-term rates, then according to the expectations hypothesis, investors must expect that short-term rates will be increasing in coming periods.

expected value The sum of possible outcomes times their probability of occurrence.

extraordinary gains and losses Gains or losses from the sale of corporate fixed assets, lawsuits, or similar events that would not be expected to occur often, if ever again.

F

Fed The Federal Reserve serves as the central banking authority for the United States. The Fed enacts monetary policy, and it plays a major role in regulating commercial banking operations and controlling the money supply.

federal deficit A situation in which the federal government spends more money than it receives through taxes and other revenue sources.

federal surplus A situation in which taxes and other government revenues provide more money than is needed to cover government expenditures.

FIFO A method of inventory valuation in which it is assumed that inventory purchased first is sold first (first-in, first-out).

financial asset A financial claim on an asset (rather than physical possession of a tangible asset) usually documented by a legal instrument, such as a stock certificate.

financial-service companies Firms that provide a broad range of financial services to diversify their consumer base. Services may include brokerage activities, insurance, banking, and so forth.

fiscal policy Government spending and taxing practices designed to promote or inhibit various economic activities.

floating-rate notes The coupon rate on the note or bond is fixed for only a short time and then varies with a stipulated short-term rate such as the rate on U.S. Treasury bills.

floor broker An independent stockbroker who is a member of a stock exchange and who executes trades, for a fee, for commission brokers experiencing excessive volumes of trading.

floor value A value that an income-producing security will not fall below because of the fundamental value attributable to its assured income stream.

flow-of-funds analysis Analysis of the pattern of financial payments between business, government, and households.

foreign currency effects To the extent a foreign currency appreciates relative to the dollar, returns on foreign investments will increase in terms of dollars. The opposite would be true for declining foreign currencies.

foreign political risks The risks associated with investing in firms operating in foreign countries. There is the danger of nationalization of foreign firms or the blockage of capital flows to investors. There also may be the danger of violent overthrow of the political party in power, with all the associated implications. Punitive legislation against foreign firms or investors is another political risk.

fourth market The direct trading between large institutional investors in blocks of listed stocks. The participants avoid paying brokerage commissions.

fully diluted earnings per share The value of earnings per share that would be realized if all outstanding securities convertible into common stock were converted.

fundamental analysis The valuation of stocks based on fundamental factors, such as company earnings, growth prospects, and so forth.

funded pension plan Current income is charged with pension liabilities in advance of the actual payment, and funds are set aside.

futures contract An agreement that provides for sale or purchase of a specific amount of a commodity at a designated time in the future at a given price.

futures contract on a stock market index A futures contract based on a market index, such as the Standard & Poor's 500 Stock Index or the NYSE Composite Index.

G

general obligation bonds A municipal bond backed by the full faith, credit, and "taxing power" of the issuing unit rather than the revenue from a given project.

GNMA (Ginnie Mae) pass-through certificate Fixed-income securities that represent an undivided interest in a pool of federally insured mortgages. GNMA, the Government National Mortgage Association, buys a pool of securities from various lenders at a discount and then issues securities to the public against these mortgages.

going public Selling privately held shares to new investors in the over-the-counter market for the first time.

government securities Bonds issued by federal, state, or local governmental units or government agencies. Whereas corporate securities' returns are paid through company earnings, government securities are repaid through taxes or the revenues from projects financed by the bonds.

graduated-payment mortgage A type of mortgage in which payments start out on a relatively low basis and increase over the life of the loan.

greed index A contrary opinion index that measures how "greedy" investors are. Greed is thought to be synonymous with bullish sentiment, or optimism. Under the assumptions of the greed index, the more greedy or optimistic investors are, the more likely the market is to fall and vice versa.

gross domestic product (GDP) A measure of output from United States factories and related consumption in the United States. It does not include products made by U.S. companies in foreign markets.

growth company A company that exhibits rising returns on assets each year and sales that are growing at an increasing rate (growth phase of the life-cycle curve). Growth companies may not be as well known as growth stocks.

growth funds Mutual funds with the primary objective of capital appreciation.

growth stock The stock of a firm generally growing faster than the economy or market norm.

growth-with-income funds Mutual funds that combine a strategy of capital appreciation with income generation.

H

hedging A process for lessening or eliminating risk by taking a position in the market opposite to your original position. For example, someone who owns wheat can sell a futures contract to protect against future price declines.

hidden assets Assets that are not readily apparent to investors in a traditional sense, but add substantial value to the firm.

horizontal spread Buying and writing two options with the same strike price but maturing in different months.

I

Ibbotson and Sinquefield study A University of Chicago study examining comparative returns on stocks and fixed-income securities from the mid-1920s to the present.

immunization Immunizing or protecting a bond portfolio against the effects of changing interest rates on the ending value of the portfolio. The process is usually tied to a time horizon. In the process, if interest rates go up, there will be a decline in the value of the portfolio, but a higher reinvestment rate opportunity for inflows. Conversely, if interest rates go down, there will be capital appreciation for the portfolio, but a lower reinvestment rate opportunity. By tying all the investment decisions to a specified duration period, the portfolio manager can take advantage of these counter forces to ensure a necessary outcome.

income bond A corporate debt instrument on which interest is paid only if funds are available from current income.

income statement A financial statement that shows the profitability of a firm over a given period.

income-statement method A method of forecasting earnings per share based on a projected income statement.

index fund A fund investing in a portfolio of corporate stocks, the composition of which is determined by the Standard & Poor's 500 Index or some other index.

indifference curves These curves show the investor's trade-off between risk and return. The steeper the slope of the curve, the more risk-averse the investor is.

indirect equity claim An indirect claim on common stock such as that achieved by placing funds in investment companies.

individual retirement account (IRA) An IRA allows a qualifying taxpayer to deduct $2,000 from taxable income and invest the funds at a bank, savings and loan, brokerage house, mutual fund, or other financial institution. The funds are normally placed in interest-bearing instruments, or perhaps in other securities, such as common stock. The income on the funds is allowed to grow tax-free until withdrawn at retirement.

industry factors The unique attributes that must be considered in analyzing a given industry or group of industries. Examples include industry structure, supply/demand of labor and materials, and government regulation.

industry life cycle The movement of a firm or industry through stages of development, growth, expansion, and maturity.

inflation A general increase in the prices of goods and services.

inflation-adjusted accounting Restating financial statements to show the effect of inflation on the balance sheet and income statement. This is supplemental to the normal presentation based on historical data.

inflationary expectations A value representing future expectations about the rate of inflation. This value, combined with the real rate of return, provides the risk-free required return for the investor.

initial public offering (IPO) The process of bringing private companies to the public market for the first time.

insider trading Trading by those who had special access to unpublished information. If the information is used to illegally make a profit, there may be large fines and possible jail sentences.

institutional investor A type of investor (as opposed to individual investors) representing organizations responsible for bringing together large pools of capital for investment. Institutional investors include investment companies, pension funds, life insurance companies, bank trust departments, and endowments and foundations.

in the money A term that indicates when the market price of a stock is above the striking price of the call option. When the strike price is above the market price, the call option is out of the money.

interest-rate futures Futures contracts involving Treasury bills, Treasury bonds, Treasury notes, commercial paper, certificates of deposit, and GNMA certificates.

international tax problems Many foreign countries impose a 7.5 percent to 15 percent withholding tax against the dividends or interest paid to nonresident holders of equity or debt securities. However, it is often possible for tax-exempt U.S. investors to secure an exemption or rebate on part or all of the withholding tax. Also, taxable U.S. investors can normally claim a U.S. tax credit for taxes paid in foreign countries. The problem is more likely to be one of inconvenience and paper shuffling rather than loss of funds.

internationally oriented funds Mutual funds and closed-end investment companies that invest in worldwide securities. Some funds specialize in Asian holdings, others in South African, and so on.

intrinsic value Value of a warrant or option equal to market price minus the strike (exercise) price.

inverse pyramiding A process of leveraging to control commodities contracts in which the profits from one contract are used to purchase another contract on margin, and profits on this contract are applied to a third, and so on.

investment The commitment of current funds in anticipation of the receipt of an increased return of funds at some point.

investment banker One who is primarily involved in the distribution of securities from the issuing corporation to the public. An investment banker also advises corporate clients on their financial strategy and may help to arrange mergers and acquisitions.

investment banking The underwriting and distribution of a new security issue in the primary market. The investment banker advises the issuing

concern on price and other terms and normally guarantees sale while overseeing distribution of the securities through the selling brokerage houses.

investment companies A type of financial institution that takes proceeds of individual investors and reinvests them in securities according to their specific objectives. A popular type of investment company is the mutual fund.

J

Jensen measure of portfolio performance Jensen compares excess returns (total portfolio returns minus the risk-free rate) to what should be required in the market based on the portfolio beta. For example, if the portfolio beta is 1, the portfolio has a systematic risk equal to the market, and the expected portfolio excess returns should be equal to market excess returns (the market rate of return minus the risk-free rate). The question then becomes: Did the portfolio manager do better or worse than expected? The portfolio manager's excess returns can be compared to the market line of expected excess returns for any beta level.

junk bonds High-risk, low-grade bonds rated below BBB. They often perform like common stock and may provide interesting investment opportunities.

K

K_e The term representing anticipated rate of return equal to dividend yield plus expected growth in earnings and dividends. It is the discount rate applied to future dividends.

key indicators Various market observations used by technical analysts to predict the direction of future market trends. Examples include the contrary opinion and smart money rules.

L

lagging indicators Economic indicators that usually change directions after business conditions have turned around.

leading indicators Economic indicators that change direction in advance of general business conditions.

least squares trendline A statistically developed linear trendline that minimizes the distance of the individual observations from the line.

leveraged buyouts The management of the company or some other investor group borrows the needed cash to repurchase all the shares of an existing company. The balance sheet of the company serves as the collateral base to make the borrowing possible. After the leveraged buyout, the company may be taken private for a time in which unprofitable assets are sold and debt reduced. The intent is then to bring the company to the public market once again (or resell it to another company) at a large profit over the initial purchase price.

LIFO A method of inventory valuation in which it is assumed inventory purchased last is sold first (last-in, first-out).

limit order A condition placed on a transaction executed through a stockbroker to assure that securities will be sold only if a specified minimum price is received or purchased only if the price to be paid is no more than a given maximum.

limited partnership A business arrangement in which there is the limited liability protection of a corporation with the tax provisions of a regular partnership. All profits or losses are directly assigned to the partners for tax purposes. The general partner has unlimited liability.

Lipper Mutual Fund Investment Performance Averages Lipper publishes indexes for growth funds, growth-with-income funds, and balanced funds. Lipper also shows year-to-date and weekly performance for many other categories of funds.

liquidity The capacity of an investment to be retired for cash in a short period with a minimum capital loss.

liquidity preference theory A theory related to the term structure of interest rates. The theory states the term structure tends to be upward sloping more than any other pattern. This reflects a recognition of the fact that long maturity obligations are subject to greater price change movements than short maturity obligations when interest rates change. Because of increased risk of holding longer-term maturities, investors demand a higher return to hold such securities. Thus, they have a preference for short-term liquid obligations.

liquidity ratios Ratios that demonstrate the firm's ability to pay off short-term obligations as they come due.

long position A market transaction in which an investor purchases securities with the expectation of holding the securities for cash income or for resale at a higher price in the future. Also see *short position*.

long-term anticipation securities (LEAPS) Longer-term options with expiration dates of up to two years.

Lorie and Fisher study A University of Chicago study indicating comparative returns on financial assets over half a decade. It is similar to the Ibbotson and Sinquefield study in many respects.

M

margin account A trading account maintained with a brokerage firm on which the investor may borrow a percentage of the funds for the purchase of securities. The broker lends the funds at interest slightly above the prime rate.

margin maintenance requirement The amount of money that must be "deposited" to hold a margin position if losses reduce the initial margin that was put up.

margin requirements The amount of money that must be "deposited" to purchase a commodity contract or shares of stock on margin.

market A mechanism for facilitating the exchange of assets through buyer-seller communication. The communication, and not a central negotiating location, is the requisite condition for a market to exist, though some transactions (for example, trades at the various stock exchanges) do involve a direct meeting of buyers and sellers or their agents.

market capitalization The total market value of the firm. It is computed by multiplying shares outstanding times stock price.

market line On a graph, excess returns are shown on the vertical axis, the portfolio beta is shown on the horizontal axis, and the market line describes the relationship between the two.

market rate of interest The coupon rate of interest paid on bonds currently issued. Of course, a previously issued bond that is currently traded may

be sold at a discount or a premium so that the buyer in effect receives the market rate even if the coupon rate on this older bond is substantially higher or lower than market rates. The market rate is also known as the yield to maturity.

market-segmentation theory A theory related to the term structure of interest rates that focuses on the demand side of the market. There are several large institutional participants in the bond market, each with its own maturity preferences. Banks tend to prefer short-term liquid securities to match the nature of their deposits, whereas life insurance companies prefer long-term bonds to match their long-run obligations. The behavior of these two institutions and of savings and loans often creates pressure on short-term or long-term rates but very little on the intermediate market of five- to seven-year maturities. This theory helps to focus on the accumulation or liquidation of securities by institutions during the different phases of the business cycle and the resultant impact on the yield curve.

maturity date The date at which outstanding principal must be repaid to bondholders.

merger price premium The difference between the offering price per share and the market price per share of the merger candidate (before the impact of the offer).

monetarist An economic analyst who believes monetary policy tools, and not fiscal policy, can best provide a stable environment of sustained economic growth.

monetary policy Direct control of interest rates or the money supply undertaken by the Federal Reserve to achieve economic objectives. Used in some cases to augment or offset the use of fiscal policy.

money market account Accounts offered by financial institutions to compete with money market funds. The minimum deposit is $500 to $1,000, with a maximum of three checks drawn per month.

money market fund A type of mutual fund that invests in short-term government securities, commercial paper, and repurchase agreements. Most offer check-writing privileges.

money supply The level of funds available at a given time for conducting transactions in our econ-

omy. The Federal Reserve can influence the money supply through its monetary policy tools. There are many different definitions of the money supply. For example, M1 is currency in circulation plus private checking deposits, including those in interest-bearing NOW accounts. M2 adds in savings accounts and money market mutual funds, and so on.

mortgage trust A form of REIT in which long-term loans are made to real estate investors.

multinational corporations Firms that have operations in a number of countries. Multinationals are frequently found in such industries as oil, mainframe computers, and banking.

municipal bonds Tax-exempt debt securities issued by state and local governments (including special political subdivisions).

mutual fund A pooling of funds by investors for reinvestment. The funds are administered by professional managers. Technically, only an open-end (see definition) investment fund is considered to be a mutual fund.

mutual fund cash position An overall market rule that asserts that by examining the level of uncommitted funds held by large institutional investors, analysts can measure the potential demand for stocks and thereby anticipate market movements.

N

naked options The process of writing (selling) options on a stock that is not currently owned. It is highly speculative.

NASDAQ indexes Index measures for components of the over-the-counter market. The OTC Indexes are value-weighted.

National Association of Securities Dealers Automated Quotations System (NASDAQ) A computerized system that provides up-to-the-minute price quotations on about 5,000 of the more actively traded OTC stocks.

net asset value The net asset value (NAV) represents the current value of an investment fund. It is computed by taking the total value of the securities, subtracting out the liabilities, and dividing by the shares outstanding.

net debtor–creditor hypothesis Since inflation makes each dollar worth less, it is often argued that a person or firm that is a net debtor gains from inflation because payments of interest and return of principal are made with continually less-valuable dollars. Conversely, a net creditor loses real capital because the loans are repaid in less valuable dollars.

net working capital Current assets minus current liabilities.

New York Stock Exchange Index A market value-weighted measure of stock market changes for all stocks listed on the NYSE.

no-load mutual fund A mutual fund on which no sales commission must be paid. The fund's shares are sold, not through brokers, but rather through the mail or other direct channels.

nominal GNP Gross national product expressed in current, noninflation-adjusted dollars.

nominal return A return that has not been adjusted for inflation.

nonconstant growth model Dividend valuation model that does not assume a constant growth rate for dividends.

O

odd-lot dealer A member of a stock exchange who maintains an inventory of a particular firm's stock in order to sell odd lots (trades of less than 100 shares) to customers of the exchange.

odd-lot theory The contrary opinion rule stating that small traders (who generally buy or sell odd lots) often misjudge market trends, selling just before upturns and buying before downturns. The theory has not been useful in predicting trends observed in recent years.

open-end fund An open-end investment fund stands ready at all times to sell or redeem shares from stockholders. There is no limit to the number of shares. Technically, a mutual fund is considered to be an open-end investment fund. Also see *closed-end fund*.

open-market operations The Federal Reserve's action of buying or selling government securities to expand or contract the amount of money in the economy.

opening purchase transaction A transaction in which an investor intends to become the holder of an option.

opening sale transaction A transaction in which an investor intends to be a writer of an option.

operating margin Operating income divided by sales.

option The right acquired for a consideration to buy or sell something at a fixed price within a specified period.

option premium The intrinsic value plus a speculative premium.

option price The specified price at which the holder of a warrant may buy the shares to which the warrant entitles purchase.

Options Clearing Corporation Issues all options listed on the exchanges that trade in options.

options on industry indexes An option index contract tailored to a given industry. Thus, one who wishes to speculate on a given industry's performance or hedge against holdings in that industry can use industry index options (sub-indexes).

options to purchase stock index futures An option to purchase a stock index futures contract at a specified price over a given time. This security combines the options concept with the futures concept.

organized exchanges Institutions, such as the New York Stock Exchange, the American Stock Exchange, or any of the smaller regional exchanges, that provide a central location for the buying and selling of securities.

OTC National Market system A segment of the OTC stock market made up of stocks that have a diversified geographical stockholder base and relatively large activity in their securities. Stocks in the National Market system receive enhanced market activity reporting through the NASDAQ system.

over-the-counter market Not a specific location but rather a communications network through which trades of bonds, nonlisted stocks, and other securities take place. Trading activity is overseen by the National Association of Securities Dealers (NASD).

overall market rules Guidelines, such as breadth of market indicators or mutual fund cash positions, used by technical analysts who predict stock market activity based on past activity.

P

par bonds Bonds that are selling at their par or maturity values rather than at premium or discounted prices. Par value on a corporate bond is generally $1,000.

par value (bond) The face value of a bond, generally $1,000 for corporate issues, with higher denominations for many government issues.

partial hedge A hedge position in which only part of the risk is eliminated or lessened.

peak The point in an economic cycle at which expansion ends and a recession begins.

perpetual bond A bond with no maturity date.

personal savings/personal disposable income The rate at which people are saving their disposable income. This has implications for the generation of funds to modernize plant and equipment and increase productivity.

portfolio The term applied to a collection of securities or investments.

portfolio effect The effect obtained when assets are combined into a portfolio. The interaction of the assets can provide risk reduction such that the portfolio standard deviation may be less than the standard deviation of any one asset in it.

portfolio insurance Protecting a large portfolio against a decline. A common strategy is to sell stock index futures contracts in anticipation of a decline.

portfolio manager One responsible for managing large pools of funds. Portfolio managers may be employed by insurance companies, mutual funds, bank trust departments, pension funds, and other institutional investors.

preferred stock A hybrid security that generally provides fixed returns. Preferred stockholders are paid returns after bondholder claims are satisfied but before any returns are paid to common stockholders. Though preferred stock returns are fixed in amount, they are classified as dividends (not interest) and are not tax-deductible to the issuing firm.

present value The exact opposite of the compound sum. A future value is discounted to the present.

present value of an annuity The present value of an equal cash flow for several periods is determined.

price-earnings ratio The multiplier applied to earnings per share to determine current value. The P/E ratio is influenced by the earnings and sales growth of the firm, the risk or volatility of its performance, the debt-equity structure, and other factors.

price ratios Ratios that relate the internal performance of the firm to the external judgment of the marketplace in terms of value.

price-weighted average Each stock in the average is weighted by its price. The higher the price, the greater the relative weighting. The Dow Jones Industrial Average represents a price-weighted average.

primary earnings per share A firm's adjusted earnings after taxes divided by the number of shares of common stock outstanding plus common stock equivalents. Common stock equivalents include warrants and other options along with convertible securities that are paying low returns at the time of issue compared to other comparable securities.

primary market A market in which an investor purchases an asset (via an investment banker) from the issuer of that asset. The purchase of newly issued shares of corporate stock is an example of primary market activity. Subsequent transfers of the particular asset occur in the secondary market.

private placement The company sells its securities to private investors such as insurance companies, pension funds, and so on rather than through the public markets. Investment bankers may also aid in a private placement on a fee basis. Most private placements involve debt rather than common stock.

profitability ratios Ratios that allow the analyst to measure the ability of the firm to earn an adequate return on sales, total assets, and invested capital.

program trading Computer-based trigger points are established in which large volume trades are indicated. The technique is used by institutional investors.

prospectus A document that must accompany a new issue of securities. It contains the same information appearing in the registration statement, such as a list of directors and officers, financial reports certified by a CPA, the underwriters, the purpose and use for the funds, and other reasonable information that investors need to know.

public placement Public distribution of securities through the financial markets.

pure bond value The fundamental value of a bond that represents a floor price below which the bond's value should not fall. The pure bond value is computed as the present value of all future interest payments added to the present value of the bond principal.

pure pickup yield swap A bond swap where a bond owner thinks he or she can increase the yield to maturity by selling a bond and buying a different bond of equal risk. This implies market disequilibrium.

put An option to sell 100 shares of common stock at a specified price for a given period.

put provision This provision enables a bond investor to have an option to sell a long-term bond back to the corporation at par value after a relatively short period (such as three to five years). This privilege can be particularly valuable if interest rates have gone up and bond prices have gone down.

Q

quick ratio Current assets minus inventory (i.e., cash, marketable securities, and accounts receivables) divided by current liabilities.

R

R^2—the coefficient of determination It measures the degree of association between the independent variable(s) and the dependent variable. It may take on a value anywhere between 0 and 1.

real asset A tangible piece of property that may be seen, felt, held, or collected, such as real estate, gold, diamonds, and so on.

real estate investment trust (REIT) An organization similar to a mutual fund where investors pool funds that are invested in real estate or used to make construction or mortgage loans.

real GDP Gross domestic product expressed in dollars that have been adjusted for inflation.

real rate of return The return that investors require for allowing others to use their money for a given period. This is the value that investors demand for passing up immediate consumption and allowing others to use their savings until the funds are returned. Because the term *real* is employed,

this means it is a value determined *before* inflation is added.

registered trader A member of a stock exchange who trades for his or her own account rather than for the client of a brokerage firm.

reinvestment assumption with bonds The assumed rate of reinvestment for inflows from a bond investment. It is normally assumed that inflows can be reinvested at the yield to maturity of the bond. This, however, may not be valid. Interest rates may go up or down as inflows from coupon payments come in and need to be reinvested. A more valid approach is to assign appropriate reinvestment rates to inflows and then determine how much the total investment will be worth at the end of a given period. This process is known as terminal wealth analysis.

reported income versus adjusted earnings Reported income is generally based on historical cost accounting, whereas adjusted earnings have been modified for inflation (on inventory and plant and equipment).

repurchase A purchase by a firm of its own shares in the marketplace.

required rate of return The total return required on an investment. For common stock, it is composed of the risk-free rate plus an equity risk premium. Once determined, it becomes the discount rate applied to future cash flows.

reserve requirements Percentages of bank deposit balances stipulated by the Federal Reserve as unavailable for lending. By increasing or reducing reserve requirements, the Fed can contract or expand the money supply.

resistance level The technical analyst's view that as long as a given long-term trend continues, prices of a particular stock or of the market as a whole will not rise above the upper end of the normal trading range (the resistance level) because at that point, investors sell in an attempt to get even or take a profit.

retention ratio The percent of earnings retained in the firm for investment purposes.

return on equity Net income divided by stockholder's equity.

revenue bond A municipal bond supported by the revenue from a specific project, such as a toll, road, bridge, or municipal coliseum.

risk Uncertainty concerning the outcome of an investment or other situation. It is often defined as variability of returns from an investment. The greater the range of possible outcomes, the greater the risk.

risk-adjusted return The amount of return after adjustment for the level of risk incurred to achieve the return.

risk-free rate The required rate of return before risk is explicitly considered. It is composed of the real rate of return plus a rate equivalent to inflationary expectations. It is referred to as R_F.

risk premium A premium assumed to be paid to an investor for the risk inherent in an investment. It is added to the risk-free rate to get the overall required return on an investment.

S

secondary market A market in which an investor purchases an asset from another investor rather than the issuing corporation. The activity of secondary markets sets prices and provides liquidity. Also see *primary market*.

sector funds Mutual funds that specialize in a given segment of the economy such as energy, medical technology, computer technology, and so forth. While they may offer the potential for high returns, they are clearly less diversified and more risky than a typical mutual fund.

secured bond A bond that is collateralized by the pledging of assets.

Securities Act of 1933 Enacted by Congress to curtail abuses by securities issuers, the law requires full disclosure of pertinent investment information and provides for penalties to officers of firms that do not comply.

Securities Acts Amendments of 1975 Enacted to increase competition in the securities markets, this legislation prohibits fixed commissions on public offerings of securities and directs the Securities and Exchange Commission to develop a single, nationwide securities market.

Securities and Exchange Commission (SEC) The federal government agency created in 1934 to enforce securities laws. Issuers of securities must register detailed reports with the SEC, and the SEC polices such activities as insider trading, investor conspiracies, and the functionings of the securities exchanges.

Securities Exchange Act of 1934 Created the Securities and Exchange Commission to regulate the securities markets. The act further empowers the Board of Governors of the Federal Reserve System to control margin requirements.

Securities Investor Protection Corporation Created under the Securities Investor Protection Act of 1970, this agency oversees the liquidation of insolvent brokerage firms and provides insurance on investors' trading accounts.

security analyst One who studies various industries and companies and provides research reports and valuation studies.

security market line The graphic representation of risk (as measured by beta) and return for an individual security.

selling short against the box A short sale of securities with the objective of deferring the payment of taxes. This requires a short sale against shares already owned so that shares owned are delivered to cover the short position as the transaction is completed.

semistrong form of efficient market hypothesis The hypothesis states that all public information is already impounded into the value of a security, so fundamental analysis cannot determine under- or overvaluation.

serial payment A mechanism for repaying funds advanced through a bond issue. Regular payments systematically retire individual bonds with increasing maturities until, after many years, the entire series has been repaid.

settle price The term for the closing price on futures contracts.

shared-appreciation mortgage A type of mortgage in which the lender participates in any increase in value associated with the property being mortgaged.

Sharpe measure of portfolio performance Total portfolio return minus the risk-free rate divided by the portfolio standard deviation. It allows the portfolio manager to view excess returns in relation to total risk. Comparisons between various portfolios can be made based on this relative risk measure.

shelf registration Large companies file one comprehensive registration statement that outlines the firm's plans for future long-term financing. Then, when market conditions seem appropriate, the firm can issue the securities through an investment banker without further SEC approval. Future issues are said to be sitting on the shelf, waiting for the most advantageous time to appear. An issue may sit on the shelf for up to two years.

short position (short sale) A market transaction in which an investor sells borrowed securities in anticipation of a price decline. The investor's expectation is that the securities can be repurchased (to replace the borrowed shares) at a lower price in the future. Also see the definition for *long position*.

short sales position theory The contrary opinion rule stating that large volumes of short sales can signal an impending market upturn because short sales must be covered and thereby create their own demand. Also, the average short seller is often thought to be wrong.

sinking-fund provision A mechanism for repaying funds advanced through a bond issue. The issuer makes periodic payments to the trustee, who retires part of the issue by purchasing the bonds in the open market.

small-firm effect A market theory that suggests small firms produce superior returns compared to larger firms on both an absolute and risk-adjusted basis.

smart money rules Guidelines, such as *Barron's* Confidence Index, used by technical analysts who predict stock market activity based on the assumption that sophisticated investors will correctly predict market trends and that their lead should be followed. Also see *contrary opinion rules*.

specialist or dealer hedge A specialist on an exchange or dealer in the over-the-counter market buys and sells stocks for his own inventory for temporary holding (as a part of his market-making function). At times, he may assume a larger temporary holding than desired with all the risks associated with that exposure. Stock index futures or options can reduce the market, or systematic, risk, although they cannot reduce the specific risk associated with a security.

speculative premium The difference between an option or warrant's price and its intrinsic value. That an investor would pay something in excess of the intrinsic value indicates a speculative desire to hold the security in anticipation of future increases in the price of the underlying stock.

spot market The term applied to the cash price for immediate transfer of a commodity as opposed to the futures market where no physical transfer occurs immediately.

spreads A combination of options that consists of buying one option (going long) and writing an option (going short) on the same stock.

Standard & Poor's 100 Index An index composed of 100 blue-chip stocks on which the Chicago Board of Trade currently has individual option contracts.

Standard & Poor's 400 Industrial Index An index that measures price movements in the stocks of 400 large industrial corporations listed on the New York Stock Exchange.

Standard & Poor's 500 Stock Index An index of 500 major U.S. corporations. There are 400 industrial firms, 20 transportation firms, 40 utilities, and 40 financial firms. This index is value-weighted.

Standard & Poor's International Oil Index A value-weighted index of oil firms. Options on the index have been traded on the Chicago Board Options Exchange.

Standard & Poor's MidCap Index An index composed of 400 middle-size firms that have total market values between $300 million and $3 billion.

standard deviation A measure of dispersion that considers the spread of outcomes around the expected value.

statement of cash flows Formally established by the Financial Accounting Standards Board in 1987, the purpose of the statement of cash flows is to emphasize the critical nature of cash flows to the operations of the firm. The statement translates accrual-based net income into actual cash dollars.

stock dividend A dividend paid by issuing more stock, which results in retained earnings being capitalized.

stock index futures A futures contract on a specific stock index, such as the Standard & Poor's 500 Stock Index or the NYSE Composite Index.

stock index options An option contract to purchase (call) or sell (put) a stock index. Popular contracts include the S&P 100 Index, the American Exchange Major Market Index, and others. The purchaser of a stock index option pays an initial premium and then closes out the option at a given price in the future.

stock split The result of a firm dividing its shares into more shares with a corresponding decrease in par value.

stop order A mechanism for locking in gains or limiting losses on securities transactions. The investor is not assured of paying or receiving a particular price but rather agrees to accept the price prevailing when the broker is able to execute the order after prices have reached some predetermined figure.

straddle A combination of a put and call on the same stock with the same strike price and expiration date.

straight-line depreciation A method of depreciation in which the project cost is divided by the project life to calculate each year's depreciation amount.

strong form of the efficient market hypothesis A hypothesis that says all information, insider as well as public, is reflected in the price of a security.

Super Dot The computer system that allows New York Stock Exchange members to electronically transmit all market and limit orders directly to the specialist at the trading post or member trading booth.

support level Technical analyst's view that as long as a given long-term trend continues, prices of a particular stock or of the market as a whole will not fall below the lower end of a normal trading range (the support level) because at that point, low prices stimulate demand.

sustainable growth model A model that looks at how much growth a firm can generate by maintaining the same financial relationships as the year before. The interaction between return on equity and the retention of equity for reinvestment is considered.

swaps The procedure of selling out of a given bond position and immediately buying into another one with similar attributes in an attempt to improve overall portfolio return or performance.

syndicate A group of investment bankers that jointly shares the underwriting risk and distribution responsibilities in a large offering of new securities. Each participant is responsible for a predetermined sales volume. One or a few firms serve as the managing underwriters.

synergy A more-than-proportionate increase in performance from the combination of two or more parts.

systematic risk Risk inherent in an investment related to movements in the market that cannot be diversified away.

systematic withdrawal plan A plan offered by a mutual fund in which the investor receives regular monthly or quarterly payments from investment in the fund.

T

tax hedge An investor may have accumulated a large return on a diversified portfolio in a given year. To maintain the profitable position but defer the taxable gains until the next year, stock index futures or options contracts may be employed. For individual securities, individual stock options may be used when available.

tax swaps Selling of one bond position and buying into a similar one to take advantage of a tax situation. For example, one might sell a bond that has a short-term capital loss to take the deduction and replace it with a similar bond.

technical analysis An analysis of price and volume data as well as other related market indicators to determine past trends that are believed to be predictable into the future. Charts and graphs are often utilized.

term structure of interest rates This depicts the relationship between maturity and interest rates for up to 30 years.

terminal wealth table A table that indicates the ending or terminal wealth from a bond investment based on the reinvestment of the inflows at a specified rate (which may be different from the coupon rate). The initial investment can then be compared to the terminal wealth (compound interest plus principal) and an overall rate of return computed.

third market The trading between dealers and institutional investors, through the over-the-counter market, of NYSE-listed stocks. The third market accounts for an extremely small share of total trading activity.

trading range The high and low spread of prices that a stock normally sells within.

Treasury bill A short-term U.S. government obligation. A Treasury bill is purchased at a discount and is readily marketable.

Treasury bond A long-term U.S. government bond.

Treasury note An intermediate-term (one to seven years) U.S. government bond.

Treasury stock Stock issued but not outstanding by virtue of being held (after it is repurchased) by the firm.

trend analysis Comparable analysis of performance over time.

Treynor measure of portfolio performance Total portfolio return minus the risk-free rate divided by the portfolio beta. Unlike the Sharpe measure, which uses the portfolio standard deviation in the denominator, the risk measure here is the beta, or systematic risk. It enables the portfolio manager to view excess return in relation to nondiversifiable risk. The assumption is that all other types of risk have been diversified away. Once computed, the Treynor measure allows for comparisons between different portfolios.

trough The point in an economic cycle at which recession ends and expansion begins.

U

underpricing In selling formerly privately held shares to new investors in the over-the-counter market, the price might not fully reflect the value of the issue. Underpricing is used to attempt to ensure the success of the initial distribution.

underwriter hedge A hedge, based on stock index futures or options contracts, used to offset the risk exposure associated with the underwriting of new securities by an investment banker. If the market goes down, presumably the loss on the stock being underwritten will be compensated for by the gain on the stock index futures or options contract as a result of being able to repurchase it at a lower price. This, of course, is not a perfect hedge. The stock could go down while the market is going up, and losses on both the stock and stock index contract would occur (writing options directly against the stock may be more efficient, but in many cases such options are not available).

unfriendly takeover A merger or acquisition in which the firm acquired does not wish to be acquired.

unfunded pension plan Payments to retirees are made out of current income and not out of prior funding.

unit investment trusts (UITs) These are formed by investment companies with the intention of acquiring a portfolio of fixed income to be passively managed over a fixed period. The trust is then terminated.

unseasoned issue An issue that has not been formerly traded in the public markets.

unsystematic risk Risk of an investment that is random in nature. It is not related to general market movements. It may represent the temporary influence of a competitor's new product, changes in raw material prices, or unusual economic or government influences on a firm. It may generally be diversified away.

V

valuation The process of attributing a value to a security based on expectations of the future performance of the issuing concern, the relevant industry, and the economy as a whole.

valuation model A representation of the components that provide the value of an investment, such as a dividend valuation model used to determine the value of common stock.

Value Line Index The index represents 1,700 companies from the New York and American Stock Exchanges and the over-the-counter market. Many individual investors use the Value Line Index because it more closely corresponds to the variety of stocks the average investor may have in his or her portfolio. It is an equal-weighted index, which means each of the 1,700 stocks, regardless of market price or total market value, is weighted equally.

value-weighted index Each company in the index is weighted by its own total market value as a percentage of the total market value for all firms in the index. Most major indexes such as the S&P 500, S&P 400, and the NYSE Index, are value-weighted. With value-weighted indexes, large firms tend to be weighted more heavily than smaller firms.

variability The possible different outcomes of an event. As an example, an investment with many different levels of return would have great variability.

variable rate mortgage A mortgage in which the interest rate is adjusted regularly.

variable rate notes (See *floating rate notes*.)

vertical spread Buying and writing two contracts at different striking prices with the same month of expiration.

vesting A legal term meaning pension benefits or rights cannot be taken away.

W

warrant A right or option to buy a stated number of shares of stock at a specified price over a given period. It is usually of longer duration than a call option.

warrant break-even The price movement in the underlying stock necessary for the warrant purchaser to break even, that is, recover the initial purchase price of the warrant.

weak form of efficient market hypothesis A hypothesis suggesting there is no relationship between past and future prices of securities.

weighted average life The weighted average time period over which the coupon payments and maturity payment on a bond are recovered.

white knight A firm that "rescues" another firm from an unfriendly takeover by a third firm.

Wiesenberger Financial Services An advisory service that provides important information on mutual funds.

Wilshire 5,000 Equity Index A stock market measure comprising 5,000 equity securities. It includes all New York Stock Exchange and American Stock Exchange issues and the most active over-the-counter issues. The index represents the *total dollar value* of all 5,000 stocks. By measuring total dollar value, it is, in effect, a value-weighted measure.

World Index A value-weighted index of the performance in 19 major countries as compiled by Capital International, S.A., of Geneva, Switzerland.

Y

yield curve A curve that shows interest rates at a specific point for all securities having equal risk but different maturity dates. Usually, government securities are used to construct such curves. The yield curve is also referred to as the term structure of interest rates.

yield spread The difference between the yields received on two different types of bonds, or bonds with different ratings. It is important to investment strategy because during periods of economic uncertainty, spreads increase because investors demand larger premiums on risky issues to compensate for the greater chance of default.

yield to call The interest yield that will be realized on a callable bond if it is held from a given purchase date until the date when it can be called by the issuer. The yield to call reflects the fact that lower overall returns may be realized if the issuer avoids some later payments by retiring the bonds early.

yield to maturity The annualized rate of return an investor will receive if a bond is held until its maturity date. It is the market rate of return. The yield-to-maturity formula includes any capital gains or losses that arise because the par value is greater or less than the current market price.

Ying, Lewellen, Schlarbaum, and Lease study A research study that indicates there may be an opportunity for abnormal returns on a risk-adjusted basis in the many weeks between announcement of listing and actual listing of a security.

Z

zero-coupon bonds Bonds designed to pay no interest, in which the return to the investor is in the form of capital appreciation over the life of the issue.

INDEX